PUBLIC PAPERS OF THE PRESIDENTS

OF THE UNITED STATES

PUBLIC PAPERS OF THE PRESIDENTS

OF THE UNITED STATES

Lyndon B. Johnson

Containing the Public Messages, Speeches, and

Statements of the President

1968–69
(IN TWO BOOKS)

BOOK I—JANUARY 1 TO JUNE 30, 1968

UNITED STATES GOVERNMENT PRINTING OFFICE

WASHINGTON : 1970

PUBLISHED BY THE
OFFICE OF THE FEDERAL REGISTER
NATIONAL ARCHIVES AND RECORDS SERVICE
GENERAL SERVICES ADMINISTRATION

For sale by the Superintendent of Documents, U.S. Government Printing Office
Washington, D.C. 20402 - Price $10.50

FOREWORD

A PRESIDENT'S PAPERS, responding as they do to the public issues of his time, provide their own measure of a people's spirit. The pages in these volumes record the last 386 days of my administration. They reflect the problems and progress of a nation which in that brief span passed through many seasons.

The American people recoiled in anguish in 1968, as violence again struck down national leaders and lit flames in the skies above a dozen cities. We confronted the perils of inflation at home and the danger of the dollar's decline abroad. The agony of an odious war, forced upon us so cruelly for so long, cut deep divisions across our national life.

These, with all their shock and sorrow, are forever part of the fabric of that turbulent period.

But far more enduringly, 1968 was a time of resolution. Aroused by the ravage of violence, this Nation faced up, for the first time in its history, to the responsible need for gun controls. The far-reaching provisions of the Crime Control and Safe Streets Act provided the communities of America with tools which will strengthen their fight against crime for decades yet to come.

Challenged by the threat of an overheated economy, the Congress shouldered the painful necessity of a tax surcharge.

Impelled by the progress made in the four years preceding, the country persisted in the noble work of organizing a Great Society in which all its citizens could share. We launched a bold new program to put men who have always formed the hard-core unemployed behind the work benches of industry. We drew up a monumental housing blueprint which, in the course of a single decade, can provide decent shelter for every family. We made equality in housing the law of the land, furthering the pledge that every American shall receive the civil rights to which his humanity and his Constitution entitle him. We extended the protection of the consumer in the marketplace. We continued to preserve splendid areas of our continent for the enduring enjoyment of America's families.

And above all, on every field and in every forum, we pressed the search for peace.

For me, on a personal level, the year 1968 was a poignant time. For reasons that these pages reveal with all the candor a man can summon, I closed the door on a career of public service that stretched back over almost four decades.

As I write these words, gunfire still echoes and men still die in Vietnam. But the peace talks which began in Paris last year are still in session. It is too early, perhaps, to know for certain that we turned the corner to peace in 1968. But we will long remember that in 1968, for the first time, we felt the stirring of the winds of hope.

It is too early, perhaps, to know how successful was our five-year effort to broaden the concepts of justice and abundance and democracy. Down the road of our history, men will look back and make their judgment.

I hope—as I express it in the last pages of these volumes—that they will say we succeeded.

But I *know* they will say that we tried.

PREFACE

IN THIS VOLUME are gathered most of the public messages and statements of the 36th President of the United States that were released by the White House during the period January 1, 1968–January 20, 1969. Similar volumes are available covering the period November 22, 1963–December 31, 1967, and the administrations of Presidents Truman, Eisenhower, and Kennedy.

The series was begun in 1957 in response to a recommendation of the National Historical Publications Commission. An extensive compilation of the messages and papers of the Presidents, covering the period 1789 to 1897, was assembled by James D. Richardson and published under congressional authority between 1896 and 1899. Since that time various private compilations were issued, but there was no uniform, systematic publication comparable to the *Congressional Record* or the *United States Supreme Court Reports*. Many Presidential papers could be found only in mimeographed White House releases or as reported in the press. The National Historical Publications Commission therefore recommended the establishment of an official series in which Presidential writings and utterances of a public nature could be made promptly available.

The Commission's recommendation was incorporated in regulations of the Administrative Committee of the Federal Register issued under section 6 of the Federal Register Act (44 U.S.C. 306). The Committee's regulations, establishing the series and providing for the coverage of prior years, are reprinted at page 1403 as "Appendix D."

CONTENT AND ARRANGEMENT

The text of this book is based on Presidential materials issued during the period as White House releases and on transcripts of news conferences. Original source materials, where available, have been used to protect against errors in transcription. A list of White House releases from which final selections were made is published at page 1371 as "Appendix A."

Proclamations, Executive orders, and similar documents required by law to be published in the *Federal Register* and *Code of Federal Regulations* are not repeated. Instead, they are listed by number and subject under the heading "Appendix B" at page 1396.

The President is required by statute to transmit numerous reports to Congress. Those transmitted during the period covered by this volume are listed at page 1401 as "Appendix C."

The items published in this volume are presented in chronological order, rather than being grouped in classes. Most needs for a classified arrangement are met by the subject index. For example, a reader interested in veto messages sent to Congress during 1968 will find them listed in the index under the heading "veto messages."

The dates shown at the end of item headings are White House release dates. In instances where the date of the document differs from the release date that fact is shown in brackets immediately following the heading. Other editorial devices, such as text notes, footnotes, and cross references, have been supplied where needed for purposes of clarity.

Preface

Remarks or addresses were delivered in Washington, D.C., unless otherwise indicated. Similarly, statements, messages, and letters were issued from the White House in Washington unless otherwise indicated.

The planning and publication of this series is under the direction of David C. Eberhart of the Office of the Federal Register. The editor of the present volume was Warren R. Reid, assisted by Dorothy G. Chance. Dorothy P. Territo, Staff Assistant to the President, and William J. Hopkins, Executive Assistant to the President, provided aid and counsel in the selection and annotation of the materials. Frank H. Mortimer of the Government Printing Office developed the typography and design.

JAMES B. RHOADS
Archivist of the United States

ROBERT L. KUNZIG
Administrator of General Services
November 1969

CONTENTS

Book I

Book II

LIST OF ITEMS, Book I

LIST OF ITEMS, Book II

List of Items, Book II

Page

List of Items, Book II

Lyndon B. Johnson

January 1–June 30, 1968

1 The President's News Conference at the LBJ Ranch. *January* 1, 1968

THE PRESIDENT. Good morning, ladies and gentlemen.

I hope all of you had a good Christmas. I wish for each of you a Happy New Year.

[1.] I have asked you to come here today for a brief announcement, the details of which will be carried in a more lengthy statement which will be available to you later.[1]

The statement that I will make here concerns a firm and decisive step that the United States Government has taken today to improve our balance of payments situation.

I am taking a series of actions that are designed to reduce our balance of payments deficit by $3 billion as a target in the year ahead, 1968.

There are a good many details connected with each of these five specific actions. I counsel you to follow those details in the more formal statement.

But to roughly outline for you now those five decisive steps, I will say that the first is an Executive order [2] that I signed at 10:45 this morning that will give to the Secretary of Commerce, delegate to him, authority the President presently has to regulate foreign investment.

We anticipate that foreign investment abroad, which was in the neighborhood of some $5 billion this past year, as a result of the restraints effected by this mandatory program, contrasted to the voluntary program which we have just had—our target

is to improve our balance of payments situation by an additional $1 billion, as a result of tightening up on foreign investment abroad. The specific areas of the world which will be affected can come in the detailed statement.

Second, the Federal Reserve Board will exercise authority in connection with loans to be made abroad, some $9 billion last year.

We have, as a target to improve our balance of payments situation, as a result of the authority I delegate to the Federal Reserve Board, and the authority it already has—the regulation will follow that authority—to save an additional half billion dollars by tightening up on the loans made abroad. That will be $1½ billion.

I am directing the Secretary of State, the Secretary of Defense, and other appropriate members of my Cabinet to make a thorough, detailed study to effectuate every possible restraint we can in aid and in defense expenditures abroad, with a target goal of $500 million of improvement from our present defense, aid, and other expenditures abroad.

That would make $2 billion.

In addition, we now have a deficit of about $2 billion each year in our tourist account. We have appointed a committee headed by Mr. Robert McKinney, of Santa Fe, New Mexico, and I am asking him for a report on tourism in the next 90 days.[3]

In the meantime, the President is appealing to all American citizens to help their country in this situation by deferring any travel outside the Western Hemisphere that

---

[1] See Item 2.

[2] Executive Order 11387 "Governing Certain Capital Transfers Abroad" (4 Weekly Comp. Pres. Docs., p. 26; 33 F.R. 47; 3 CFR, 1968 Comp., p. 90).

[3] For the President's statement on February 19, 1968, upon receiving the report of the Industry-Government Special Task Force on Travel, see Item 83.

1

is possible to defer.

As I say, we have a net deficit of $2 billion in our travel-tourism account. We hope that our target of saving $500 million in tourism will be a realistic one. That will depend on the cooperation we get from the citizens themselves, and from the Congress, which will be asked to enact certain legislation in that field.

That makes $2.5 billion.

We have sent representatives of the President to various countries today to exchange views with our friends in the world about our trade situation, our imports into this country and our exports out of this country. We expect to formulate a program. Our target is to improve our trade balance by a minimum of $500 million to $750 million. The details of that program will be announced following these consultations.

If it is necessary, as a result of the nature and scope of the program we feel desirable, we will ask the Congress to act in that field.

In the last two fields—tourism and trade—we may and very likely will have a message later to the Congress in that connection.[4]

So, in summary, through this series of five direct actions, we are determined to improve our balance of payments situation in the neighborhood of $3 billion, and to bring it as closely into balance as is possible in the year 1968.

I will be glad to take some limited questions from you on this or on other matters.

I have staff here to give you a detailed backgrounding on all the problems relating to these five specific steps—Mr. Rostow, Mr. Califano, and Mr. Goldstein[5] from my

Washington office have come here this morning.

While I don't want to cut off questioning, I am very anxious for this very important story to go out, and I am very anxious for you to have all the information you need in connection with it. I'll be glad to take a limited number of questions.

If Mr. Rostow, Mr. Goldstein, and Mr. Califano will come up here now, I will take questions on this or any other subject for a period of a very few minutes, and then I'll yield to them.

QUESTIONS

PEACE IN VIETNAM

[2.] Q. Do you see any prospects for peace or the end of the Vietnam war this year, the new year?

THE PRESIDENT. We are very hopeful that we can make advances toward peace. We are pursuing every possible objective. We feel that the enemy knows that he can no longer win a military victory in South Vietnam. But when he will reach the point where he is willing to give us evidence that would justify my predicting peace this year—I am unable to do so—that is largely up to him.

FOREIGN TRAVEL

[3.] Q. Mr. President, can you tell us what type of legislation you are considering in the tourism field? For instance, cutting off customs exemptions, or what type of things?

THE PRESIDENT. I think we had better wait until we have that program completely formulated. I think that there are several items that are still under consideration. We believe that the most effective action that

---

[4] See Item 88.

[5] Walt W. Rostow, Joseph A. Califano, Jr., and E. Ernest Goldstein, Special Assistants to the President.

could be taken would be for the citizens themselves to realize that their traveling abroad and spending their dollars abroad is damaging their country. If they just have a trip in them that must be made, if they could make it in this hemisphere, or see their own country, it would be very helpful.

We are going to try to make that appeal to them. But we are going to support it to whatever extent is necessary to try to reach our target goal of $500 million improvement in the tourism situation.

GOLD COVER ON DOMESTIC CURRENCY

[4.] Q. Mr. President, do you plan to ask Congress to remove the gold cover on domestic currency?

THE PRESIDENT. We have made no recommendation on that in this message at all.

THE POSSIBILITY OF WAGE AND PRICE CONTROLS

[5.] Q. Mr. President, Secretary Wirtz said the other day that if you don't have a tax increase, then you will have to face up to the question of wage and price controls. How serious do you regard that prospect?

THE PRESIDENT. I think we are going to have a tax increase.[6] In this statement this morning, I ask both the employers and employees to exercise the utmost restraint in connection with their negotiations. Now, I do not hold to the view that wage or price controls are imminent at all. And I might say that statement was made without my knowledge. I don't know how accurately he is quoted. But the Government has not given

any consideration at this time to action of that type.

REPORTS OF POSSIBLE PAPAL PEACE MISSION

[6.] Q. Mr. President, when you were in Rome, did you and the Pope discuss his sending a peace mission to Hanoi?

THE PRESIDENT. The answer is no, although I don't want to get into the process of eliminating what we discussed and what we didn't discuss.

But we did not discuss specifically his sending any mission. We discussed a number of subjects where—if he decided, if His Holiness decided, he wanted to act in that area—that could call for such action. But we did not specifically discuss it.

Q. May I follow that up a bit? The Foreign Minister of North Vietnam, according to some reports——

THE PRESIDENT. We are familiar with those reports. As of now, they are just reports. We are evaluating them. They come from a newspaperman who has written in this field heretofore. We have found it advisable to carefully check the statements in the report. We are doing that now.

THE PRESIDENT'S CAMPAIGN PLANS

[7.] Q. Mr. President, it is 1968 and a presidential election year. Perhaps you would like to make an announcement of some kind on that subject. But if not, maybe you could go over with us your own thinking on the factors that will go into the decision for you as to whether you are going to run or not.

THE PRESIDENT. Thank you very much, Mr. Pierpoint,[7] for your invitation. I have no

---

[6] The Revenue and Expenditure Control Act of 1968 was approved by the President on June 28, 1968 (see Item 343).

[7] Robert C. Pierpoint of CBS News.

doubt but what I will do that, but if you can just restrain yourself for a little while, we will do it at a later date. This is balance of payments morning. I will have something to say in that field during the year 1968.

BALANCE OF PAYMENTS; THE NEED FOR MORE
STRINGENT MEASURES

[8.] Q. Mr. President, does your statement contain, and if not we would like to have it in your own words, just why——

THE PRESIDENT. My statement is my own words, Mr. Frankel.[8]

Q. No, that is not what I meant. If it does not say, could you tell us exactly what makes these more stringent measures necessary and why you think the voluntary program of restraints failed?

THE PRESIDENT. Well, generally speaking, our balance of payments has had a deficit for the last 17 out of the last 18 years. In 17 of the last 18 years we have had a deficit. The first three quarters of this year, that deficit was within bounds. In the last quarter, it goes much further than we would like to see it go. It makes it very evident to me that those who are determined to preserve the soundness of the dollar and our entire fiscal situation—that direct, additional actions are necessary in this field where we have, as I say, had a deficit in 17 of the last 18 years.

For that reason, we have promulgated this program and we are placing it into effect. We believe that these actions will result in a reasonable balance in the coming year.

PRINCE SIHANOUK'S REMARKS ON U.S.
MILITARY ACTION

[9.] Q. Mr. President, the Cambodian Prince Sihanouk is quoted as saying he

would like to meet with an envoy from the United States to discuss possible U.S. military action against the North Vietnamese seeking sanctuary in Cambodia. Can you tell us anything official regarding this newspaper report?

THE PRESIDENT. I can say that we have read with a great deal of interest—and I might say pleasure—the quoted statements by Prince Sihanouk. We are studying those statements very carefully, and confirming them.

When we have anything to announce on it, I will be in touch with you. I would say that we are quite encouraged by the reactions of Prince Sihanouk as reflected by the newspaper story. Any further announcement will be made after we have gone into it more thoroughly [9] and more definite statements can be made.

Mr. Davis? And then I believe Dan Rather [10] asked a question.

Dan, do you want yours, and then I will go to Mr. Davis?

MEETING WITH POPE PAUL

[10.] Q. Thank you very much.

Mr. President, Newsweek magazine has described, as I read it, your meeting with the Pope as somewhat less than cordial. Could you clear us up on that without getting into specifics of what you and the Pope discussed?

THE PRESIDENT. I tried to clear Newsweek up on it, but I couldn't do it. It is just made out of whole cloth. It just didn't happen. The people who participated in the confer-

---

[8] Max Frankel of the New York Times.

[9] On January 4 the White House announced the appointment of Chester Bowles, U.S. Ambassador to India, as the President's special emissary to meet in Phnom Penh with Prince Sihanouk (4 Weekly Comp. Pres. Docs., p. 35).

[10] Saville Davis of the Christian Science Monitor and Dan Rather of CBS News.

ence from our side were startled and shocked at their information. We told them it was just completely untrue. So that is our version. You can take Newsweek's or ours, whichever you want.

Mr. Davis?

EFFORTS TO CONTROL INFLATION

[11.] Q. Mr. President, since one of the leading factors in the foreign confidence in the dollar is the degree of the control of inflation in this country, do you anticipate that the tax increase and other measures of the sort will keep the rising of prices in this country sufficiently stable in the coming year?

THE PRESIDENT. We are very concerned with that, Mr. Davis. Prices have risen more than we would like to see them rise. We still have the best record of any industrial country in the world. But we are not happy with the record we have ourselves.

This statement, to some degree, deals with it. We have asked the Government officials responsible for supervision in this field to exert renewed efforts in an attempt to ask employers and employees to keep their negotiating agreements within the ball park so far as increased productivity is concerned, and not let the increases in one field go above increased productivity in the other. We are hopeful that that action will be successful.

BALANCE OF PAYMENTS DEFICIT FOR 1967

[12.] Q. Mr. President, you spoke about the balance of payments deficit in the last quarter. What is your estimate of that for the year as a whole?

THE PRESIDENT. I have that statement in the detailed statement, but I think it will be somewhere in the neighborhood of $3½ billion to $4 billion.

Q. That is for the year as a whole?

THE PRESIDENT. That is correct.

Now let's not prolong this thing if you want to get this story. There are a lot of details, just as I have repeated here, that these men are waiting to tell you. I want to answer any question you have that is really important to you; otherwise, let's go on with the purpose of the conference.

WAGE AND PRICE GUIDELINES

[13.] Q. Mr. President, you are urging employers and employees to keep within the ball park. Is there any specific figure, such as a guideline estimate, specifically?

THE PRESIDENT. I would refer you to my statement in the lengthy statement which you will see as soon as you get a chance to get to it. We want very much to try to emphasize the necessity of following guidelines. The guideline is the increased productivity. We feel that you can justify only the increased productivity.

IMPACT ON 1969 BUDGET DEFICIT

[14.] Q. Sir, I was just wondering if you have any idea now as to what the likely deficit in your fiscal 1969 budget might be since this could have an impact?

THE PRESIDENT. No. A lot of things could have impacts. But I think we have covered in this detailed statement about as much as we can. If you have any further questions after you get that and file your story, submit them to Mr. Christian [11] and we will try to work it out.

Thank you very much.

Merriman Smith, United Press International: Thank you, Mr. President.

_____

[11] George E. Christian, Special Assistant to the President.

5

FURTHER REMARKS BY THE PRESIDENT
FOLLOWING HIS NEWS CONFERENCE

[During a briefing subsequent to the President's news conference, the following exchanges between the President and reporters took place.]

LEGISLATION ON TRAVEL ABROAD

[15.] Q. You are asking people not to

THE PRESIDENT. We will have legislation toward that end?

THE PRESIDENT. We will have legislation in that direction. We would also like to have voluntary action upon the part of all of our citizens. We believe we can have both. We think that we can announce, number one, that it is important to the country that every citizen reassess his travel plans and not travel outside of this hemisphere except under the most important, urgent, and necessary conditions.

Second, we think that we can develop certain legislation that will insure and guarantee our reaching our goal of a half billion dollars to three-quarter billion dollars of the reduction from the $2 billion deficit we already have.

It must be obvious that our people are traveling a good deal when you consider all the travel that comes here and deduct it from what we travel abroad, and we still have a $2 billion deficit.

Now we have a target of reducing that by a half to three-quarters of a billion dollars. We don't mean to threaten anybody with anything. We do expect that it will be necessary to have certain adjustments made in our present travel policy, and we will ask the Congress to do it.

But we want to do that in concert with the Congress, after discussing it with them, and after reaching agreement with them.

Q. Mr. President, I am just curious as to whether the nature of this legislation will affect travel itself or the amount spent on travel?

THE PRESIDENT. I wonder if you can wait until we talk to the Congress about that. I think it will affect both. But let's don't tie it down and get hard on it, fixed, right here on January 1st, when Congress doesn't come back until January 15th. We would like to explore with them, give them our views of the most effective way of achieving this target, get their views, and try to get something that would be acceptable to both the executive and the legislative branches.

But we don't want to imply a threat to anyone on anything. We are too happy this New Year's, to get into that field.

Q. Thank you, Mr. President.

THE PRESIDENT. You can be sure, though, that we will ask Congress for legislation primarily to do with tourism and trade.

The other three, direct investment, bank loans, and reducing our own defense expenditures and aid expenditures abroad, the President can do, and he has done it. That is that.

One thing that is positive I would like to leave with all of you. This President, this administration, and we think the Congress, including Democrats and Republicans, are determined to achieve our goal of trying to bring our balance of payments in better equilibrium. We have outlined it here to the extent of some $3 billion.

It is pretty difficult to estimate a quarter of a billion here where we may fall short and a quarter of a billion we might exceed.

But we have a target and we are going to put all the muscle that this leadership, this Government has in the executive branch and the legislative branch behind the dollar, keeping our financial house in order.

MINIMIZING FOREIGN EXCHANGE COSTS

[At this point the President responded to a question relating to discussions to be held with NATO allies on minimizing foreign exchange costs.]

[16.] THE PRESIDENT. They have made arrangements to offset our expenditures to the extent that we could work them out with the British and the Germans as a result of the McCloy mission.[12] That is not included here.

These steps have been under consideration for some time. Before they are effectuated, we want to exchange views with all the leaders of the world. I have been in communication with them myself.

In addition, I will have representatives communicate with them in various parts of the world.

I have this balance of payments program announcement behind me now. We will be working in the days ahead on the budget. Mr. Schultze will be here tomorrow. He will be accompanied by Mr. Cater, Mr. Gardner,[13] and some other people. I will ask George to give you the announcement.

---

[12] John J. McCloy, Chairman, General Advisory Committee, United States Arms Control and Disarmament Agency, conducted negotiations early in 1967 with NATO countries relating to the costs of U.S. forces in Europe.

[13] Charles L. Schultze, Director, Bureau of the Budget, S. Douglass Cater, Jr., Special Assistant to the President, and John W. Gardner, Secretary of Health, Education, and Welfare.

In addition, we will be working all the time we are here on appointments, on budget reductions, and on the budget for next year.

As all of you know, because of the late adjournment date, we are behind on the reductions on which they resoluted in the last few days, as well as getting to work on the new budget.

NOMINATION OF GARDNER ACKLEY AS
AMBASSADOR TO ITALY

[17.] I am naming Mr. Gardner Ackley, the present Chairman of the President's Council of Economic Advisers, as the new Ambassador to Italy. We have received word from the Italian Government this morning clearing the agreement. When the Congress resumes its deliberations, his name will go forward to the Senate.

I consider Mr. Ackley one of my most trusted and closest friends and advisers. While he has been on the Economic Council now for several years, he agreed to stay on an extra year, which ends in January. I have asked him to take this post to Italy. Because of his interest in that field and his knowledge of the political and economic conditions in Italy, and his interest in that area, he has agreed to accept. The Senate willing, he will be going to that post as soon as he is confirmed.

Thank you very much.

Reporter: Thank you, Mr. President.

NOTE: President Johnson's one hundred and sixteenth news conference was held at the LBJ Ranch, Johnson City, Texas, at 11:07 a.m. on Monday, January 1, 1968.

2 Statement by the President Outlining a Program of Action To Deal With the Balance of Payments Problem. *January 1, 1968*

WHERE WE STAND TODAY

I want to discuss with the American people a subject of vital concern to the economic health and well-being of this Nation and the free world.

It is our international balance of payments position.

The strength of our dollar depends on the strength of that position.

The soundness of the free world monetary system, which rests largely on the dollar, also depends on the strength of that position.

To the average citizen, the balance of payments, and the strength of the dollar and of the international monetary system, are meaningless phrases. They seem to have little relevance to our daily lives. Yet their consequences touch us all—consumer and captain of industry, worker, farmer, and financier.

More than ever before, the economy of each nation is today deeply intertwined with that of every other. A vast network of world trade and financial transactions ties us all together. The prosperity of every economy rests on that of every other.

More than ever before, this is one world—in economic affairs as in every other way.

Your job, the prosperity of your farm or business, depends directly or indirectly on what happens in Europe, Asia, Latin America, or Africa.

The health of the international economic system rests on a sound international money in the same way as the health of our domestic economy rests on a sound domestic money. Today, our domestic money—the U.S. dollar—is also the money most used in international transactions. That money can be sound at home—as it surely is—yet can be in trouble abroad—as it now threatens to become.

In the final analysis its strength abroad depends on our earning abroad about as many dollars as we send abroad.

U.S. dollars flow from these shores for many reasons—to pay for imports and travel, to finance loans and investments, and to maintain our lines of defense around the world.

When that outflow is greater than our earnings and credits from foreign nations, a deficit results in our international accounts.

For 17 of the last 18 years we have had such deficits. For a time those deficits were needed to help the world recover from the ravages of World War II. They could be tolerated by the United States and welcomed by the rest of the world. They distributed more equitably the world's monetary gold reserves and supplemented them with dollars.

Once recovery was assured, however, large deficits were no longer needed and indeed began to threaten the strength of the dollar. Since 1961, your Government has worked to reduce that deficit.

By the middle of the decade, we could see signs of success. Our annual deficit had been reduced two-thirds—from $3.9 billion in 1960 to $1.3 billion in 1965.

In 1966, because of our increased responsibility to arm and supply our men in Southeast Asia, progress was interrupted, with the deficit remaining at the same level as 1965—about $1.3 billion.

In 1967, progress was reversed for a number of reasons:

—Our costs for Vietnam increased further.
—Private loans and investments abroad increased.
—Our trade surplus, although larger than 1966, did not rise as much as we had expected.
—Americans spent more on travel abroad.

Added to these factors was the uncertainty and unrest surrounding the devaluation of the British pound. This event strained the international monetary system. It sharply increased our balance of payments deficit and our gold sales in the last quarter of 1967.

THE PROBLEM

Preliminary reports indicated that these conditions may result in a 1967 balance of payments deficit in the area of $3.5 to $4 billion—the highest since 1960. Although some factors affecting our deficit will be more favorable in 1968, my advisers and I are convinced that we must act to bring about a decisive improvement.

We cannot tolerate a deficit that could threaten the stability of the international monetary system—of which the U.S. dollar is the bulwark.

We cannot tolerate a deficit that could endanger the strength of the entire free world economy, and thereby threaten our unprecedented prosperity at home.

A TIME FOR ACTION

The time has now come for decisive action designed to bring our balance of payments to—or close to—equilibrium in the year ahead.

The need for action is a national and international responsibility of the highest priority.

I am proposing a program which will meet this critical need, and at the same time satisfy four essential conditions:

—Sustain the growth, strength, and prosperity of our own economy.
—Allow us to continue to meet our international responsibilities in defense of freedom, in promoting world trade, and in encouraging economic growth in the developing countries.
—Engage the cooperation of other free nations, whose stake in a sound international monetary system is no less compelling than our own.
—Recognize the special obligation of those nations with balance of payments surpluses to bring their payments into equilibrium.

THE FIRST ORDER OF BUSINESS

The first line of defense of the dollar is the strength of the American economy.

No business before the returning Congress will be more urgent than this: to enact the anti-inflation tax which I have sought for almost a year. Coupled with our expenditure controls and appropriate monetary policy, this will help to stem the inflationary pressures which now threaten our economic prosperity and our trade surplus.

No challenge before business and labor is more urgent than this: to exercise the utmost responsibility in their wage-price decisions, which affect so directly our competitive position at home and in world markets.

I have directed the Secretaries of Commerce and Labor, and the Chairman of the Council of Economic Advisers to work with leaders of business and labor to make more effective our voluntary program of wage-price restraint.

I have also instructed the Secretaries of Commerce and Labor to work with unions

9

and companies to prevent our exports from being reduced or our imports increased by crippling work stoppages in the year ahead.

A sure way to instill confidence in our dollar—both here and abroad—is through these actions.

THE NEW PROGRAM

But we must go beyond this, and take additional action to deal with the balance of payments deficit.

Some of the elements in the program I propose will have a temporary but immediate effect. Others will be of longer range.

All are necessary to assure confidence in the American dollar.

TEMPORARY MEASURES

1. *Direct Investment*

Over the past 3 years, American business has cooperated with the Government in a voluntary program to moderate the flow of U.S. dollars into foreign investments. Business leaders who have participated so wholeheartedly deserve the appreciation of their country.

But the savings now required in foreign investment outlays are clearly beyond the reach of any voluntary program. This is the unanimous view of all my economic and financial advisers and the Chairman of the Federal Reserve Board.

To reduce our balance of payments deficit by at least $1 billion in 1968 from the estimated 1967 level, I am invoking my authority under the banking laws to establish a mandatory program that will restrain direct investment abroad.

This program will be effective immediately. It will insure success and guarantee fairness among American business firms with overseas investments.

The program will be administered by the Department of Commerce, and will operate as follows:

—As in the voluntary program, overall and individual company targets will be set. Authorizations to exceed these targets will be issued only in exceptional circumstances.

—New direct investment outflows to countries in continental Western Europe and other developed nations not heavily dependent on our capital will be stopped in 1968. Problems arising from work already in process or commitments under binding contracts will receive special consideration.

—New net investments in other developed countries will be limited to 65 percent of the 1965–66 average.

—New net investments in the developing countries will be limited to 110 percent of the 1965–66 average.

This program also requires businesses to continue to bring back foreign earnings to the United States in line with their own 1964–66 practices.

In addition, I have directed the Secretary of the Treasury to explore with the chairmen of the House Ways and Means Committee and the Senate Finance Committee legislative proposals to induce or encourage the repatriation of accumulated earnings by U.S.-owned foreign businesses.

2. *Lending by Financial Institutions*

To reduce the balance of payments deficit by at least another $500 million, I have requested and authorized the Federal Reserve Board to tighten its program restraining foreign lending by banks and other financial institutions.

Chairman Martin has assured me that

this reduction can be achieved:

—Without harming the financing of our exports;

—Primarily out of credits to developed countries without jeopardizing the availability of funds to the rest of the world.

Chairman Martin believes that this objective can be met through continued cooperation by the financial community. At the request of the Chairman, however, I have given the Federal Reserve Board standby authority to invoke mandatory controls, should such controls become desirable or necessary.

3. Travel Abroad

Our travel deficit this year will exceed $2 billion. To reduce this deficit by $500 million:

—*I am asking the American people to defer for the next 2 years all nonessential travel outside the Western Hemisphere.*

—*I am asking the Secretary of the Treasury to explore with the appropriate congressional committees legislation to help achieve this objective.*

4. Government Expenditures Overseas

We cannot forgo our essential commitments abroad, on which America's security and survival depend.

Nevertheless, we must take every step to reduce their impact on our balance of payments without endangering our security.

Recently, we have reached important agreements with some of our NATO partners to lessen the balance of payments cost of deploying American forces on the Continent—troops necessarily stationed there for the common defense of all.

Over the past 3 years, a stringent program has saved billions of dollars in foreign exchange.

I am convinced that much more can be done. *I believe we should set as our target avoiding a drain of another $500 million on our balance of payments.*

To this end, I am taking three steps.

First, I have directed the Secretary of State to initiate prompt negotiations with our NATO allies to minimize the foreign exchange costs of keeping our troops in Europe. Our allies can help in a number of ways, including:

—The purchase in the United States of more of their defense needs.

—Investments in long term United States securities.

I have also directed the Secretaries of State, Treasury, and Defense to find similar ways of dealing with this problem in other parts of the world.

Second, I have instructed the Director of the Budget to find ways of reducing the number of American civilians working overseas.

Third, I have instructed the Secretary of Defense to find ways to reduce further the foreign exchange impact of personal spending by U.S. forces and their dependents in Europe.

LONG TERM MEASURES

1. Export Increases

American exports provide an important source of earnings for our businessmen and jobs for our workers.

They are the cornerstone of our balance of payments position.

Last year we sold abroad $30 billion worth of American goods.

What we now need is a long-range systematic program to stimulate the flow of the products of our factories and farms into overseas markets.

We must begin now.

Some of the steps require legislation:

I shall ask the Congress to support an intensified 5 year, $200 million Commerce Department program to promote the sale of American goods overseas.

I shall also ask the Congress to earmark $500 million of the Export-Import Bank authorization to:

—*Provide better export insurance.*

—*Expand guarantees for export financing.*

—*Broaden the scope of government financing of our exports.*

Other measures require no legislation.

I have today directed the Secretary of Commerce to begin a joint export association program. Through these associations, we will provide direct financial support to American corporations joining together to sell abroad.

And finally, the Export-Import Bank—through a more liberal rediscount system—will encourage banks across the Nation to help firms increase their exports.

2. Nontariff Barriers

In the Kennedy Round, we climaxed three decades of intensive effort to achieve the greatest reduction in tariff barriers in all the history of trade negotiations. Trade liberalization remains the basic policy of the United States.

We must now look beyond the great success of the Kennedy Round to the problems of nontariff barriers that pose a continued threat to the growth of world trade and to our competitive position.

American commerce is at a disadvantage because of the tax systems of some of our trading partners. Some nations give across-the-board tax rebates on exports which leave their ports and impose special border tax charges on our goods entering their country.

International rules govern these special taxes under the General Agreement on Tariffs and Trade. These rules must be adjusted to expand international trade further.

In keeping with the principles of cooperation and consultation on common problems, I have initiated discussions at a high level with our friends abroad on these critical matters—particularly those nations with balance of payments surpluses.

These discussions will examine proposals for prompt cooperative action among all parties to minimize the disadvantages to our trade which arise from differences among national tax systems.

We are also preparing legislative measures in this area whose scope and nature will depend upon the outcome of these consultations.

Through these means we are determined to achieve a substantial improvement in our trade surplus over the coming years. In the year immediately ahead, we expect to realize an improvement of $500 million.

3. Foreign Investment and Travel in the United States

We can encourage the flow of foreign funds to our shores in two other ways:

—*First, by an intensified program to attract greater foreign investment in U.S. corporate securities, carrying out the principles of the Foreign Investors Tax Act of 1966.*

—*Second, by a program to attract more visitors to this land. A special task force, headed by Robert McKinney of Santa Fe, N. Mex., is already at work on meas-*

*ures to accomplish this. I have directed
the task force to report within 45 days
on the immediate measures that can be
taken, and to make its long term recommendations within 90 days.*

MEETING THE WORLD'S RESERVE NEEDS

Our movement toward balance will curb
the flow of dollars into international reserves.
It will therefore be vital to speed up plans
for the creation of new reserves—the Special
Drawing Rights—in the International Monetary Fund. These new reserves will be a
welcome companion to gold and dollars, and
will strengthen the gold exchange standard.
The dollar will remain convertible into gold
at $35 an ounce, and our full gold stock will
back that commitment.

A TIME FOR RESPONSIBILITY

The program I have outlined is a program
of action.

It is a program which will preserve confidence in the dollar, both at home and
abroad.

The U.S. dollar has wrought the greatest
economic miracles of modern times.

It stimulated the resurgence of a war-
ruined Europe.

It has helped to bring new strength and
life to the developing world.

It has underwritten unprecedented prosperity for the American people, who are now
in the 83d month of sustained economic
growth.

A strong dollar protects and preserves the
prosperity of businessman and banker,
worker and farmer—here and overseas.

The action program I have outlined in this
message will keep the dollar strong. It will
fulfill our responsibilities to the American
people and to the free world.

I appeal to all of our citizens to join me
in this very necessary and laudable effort to
preserve our country's financial strength.

NOTE: On the same day the President signed
Executive Order 11387 "Governing Certain Capital
Transfers Abroad" (4 Weekly Comp. Pres. Docs.,
p. 26; 33 F.R. 47; 3 CFR, 1968 Comp., p. 90).

For a statement by the President upon receiving
the report of the Industry-Government Special Task
Force on Travel, chaired by Robert McKinney, see
Item 83.

On January 15, 1968, Secretary of the Treasury
Fowler held a news briefing following a meeting
with the President on the balance of payments
situation. The text is printed in the Weekly Compilation of Presidential Documents (vol. 4, p. 68). For
the President's statement upon receiving the Secretary's report on the subject, see Item 449.

On March 30, 1968, the White House announced
the President's approval of a plan for an initial 12
percent reduction in overseas Government personnel
to be followed by further reductions later in the
year. The cutback plan, the announcement said, was
submitted by the Secretary of State and the Director of the Bureau of the Budget in response to the
President's instructions, and would immediately
affect American and foreign nationals presently
employed by 21 Federal agencies under the jurisdiction of the Ambassadors in every country except
Vietnam. It would result, the announcement added,
in yearly savings of $20 to $22 million in expenditures abroad. The full text of the announcement is
printed in the Weekly Compilation of Presidential
Documents (vol. 4, p. 618).

A bill amending the Export-Import Bank Act was
approved by the President on March 13, 1968 (see
Item 136. On July 7, 1968, the President approved a bill "to enable the Export-Import Bank
of the United States to approve extension of certain
loans, guarantees, and insurance in connection with
exports from the United States in order to improve
the balance of payments and foster the long-term
commercial interests of the United States" (see Item
377).

The President's statement was released at San
Antonio, Texas.

3　Statement by the President Upon Signing the Social Security Amendments and Upon Appointing a Commission To Study the Nation's Welfare Programs. *January* 2, 1968

SOCIAL SECURITY AMENDMENTS

This coming year will mark one-third of a century since social security became the law of the land.

Because of social security, tens of millions of Americans have been able to stand straighter and taller—unafraid of their future.

Social security has become so important to our lives, it is hard to remember that when it was first proposed it was bitterly attacked—much as Medicare was attacked and condemned before it came into being 2½ years ago.

Today, for the second time in 30 months, I am signing into law a measure that will further strengthen and broaden the social security system. Measured in dollars of insurance benefits, the bill enacted into law today is the greatest stride forward since social security was launched in 1935.

In March, 24 million Americans will receive increased benefits of at least 13 percent. In the years to come, as the 78 million American earners now covered by social security become eligible, they will gain even greater benefits.

　—For a retired couple, maximum benefits will rise from $207 to $234 and ultimately to $323 per month.
　—Minimum benefits for an individual will be increased from $44 to $55 a month.
　—Outside earnings can total $140 a month with no reduction in benefits.
　—65,000 disabled widows and 175,000 children will receive benefits for the first time.

　—Medicare benefits are expanded to include additional days of hospitalization.

Combined, the Social Security Amendments of 1965 and 1967 bring an average dollar increase of 23 percent. Medicare protection amounts on the average to an additional 12 percent. This makes total increases of 35 percent in the past 30 months.

When the benefit checks go out next March, 1 million more people will be lifted above the poverty line. This means that 9 million people will have risen above the poverty line since the beginning of 1964.

Social security benefits are not limited to the poor. They go to widows, orphans, and the disabled who without them would be reduced to poverty. They relieve an awful burden from the young who would otherwise have to divert income from the education of their children to take care of their parents.

Franklin Roosevelt's vision of social insurance has stood the test of the changing times. I wish I could say the same for our Nation's welfare system.

The welfare system today pleases no one. It is criticized by liberals and conservatives, by the poor and the wealthy, by social workers and politicians, by whites and by Negroes in every area of the Nation.

My recommendations to the Congress this year sought to make basic changes in the system.

Some of these recommendations were adopted. They include a work incentive program, incentives for earning, day care for children, child and maternal health services, and family planning services. I believe these changes will have a good effect.

Others of my recommendations were not adopted by the Congress. In their place, the Congress substituted certain severe restrictions.

I am directing Secretary Gardner to work with State governments so that compassionate safeguards are established to protect deserving mothers and needy children.

The welfare system in America is outmoded and in need of a major change.

COMMISSION ON INCOME MAINTENANCE PROGRAMS

I am announcing today the appointment of a Commission on Income Maintenance Programs to look into all aspects of existing welfare and related programs and to make just and equitable recommendations for constructive improvements, wherever needed and indicated. We must examine any and every plan, however unconventional, which could promise a constructive advance in meeting the income needs of all the American people.

That Commission of distinguished Americans will be chaired by Ben W. Heineman, chairman of the board, Chicago and Northwestern Railroads. Its membership will include Messrs. Thomas J. Watson, Jr., chairman of the board, IBM Corp.; Donald C. Burnham, president, Westinghouse Electric Corp.; James W. Aston, president, Republic National Bank, Dallas, Texas; Asa T. Spaulding, recently retired president, North Carolina Mutual Life Co., Durham, N.C.;

Henry S. Rowen, president, Rand Corp., Santa Monica, Calif.; George E. Reedy, Jr., president, Struthers Research and Development Corp., Washington, D.C.; Anna Rosenberg Hoffman, public and industrial relations consultant, New York City; Julian Samora, professor of sociology, University of Notre Dame; Robert M. Solow, professor of economics, MIT; Edmund G. "Pat" Brown, partner, law firm Bell, Hunt, Hart and Brown; and David Sullivan, general president, Building Service Employees International Union, New York.

Over the last third of a century in America we have proved that people who earn their living can make their lives better and more secure if they divert part of their incomes to protect themselves from the twists of fortune that face all men. Our challenge for the coming years is to see if we can extend that same human insurance and human dignity to persons who are not able to buy their own protection. Our challenge is to save children.

NOTE: As enacted, the Social Security Amendments of 1967 (H.R. 12080) is Public Law 90–248 (81 Stat. 821).

Major advances in social security and Medicare achieved by the 1965, 1966, and 1967 Social Security Amendments are summarized in a January 3 memorandum to the President from John W. Gardner, Secretary of Health, Education, and Welfare. The text of the memorandum is printed in the Weekly Compilation of Presidential Documents (vol. 4, p. 32).

The statement was released at San Antonio, Texas.

---

4 Statement by the President Upon Signing the Elementary and Secondary Education Amendments of 1967. *January 2*, 1968

NEARLY 3 years ago, at a little wooden schoolhouse a half mile down the road from

here, I signed the first Elementary and Secondary Education Act. I considered that moment one of the greatest victories of my life—because passing that law was one of the hardest battles of my life.

Federal aid to education has been argued for 20 years. It had divided some good friends into hostile, opposing factions.

But we got it passed. I felt then and I feel now that if the word "historic" has any meaning at all, this law deserved to be called historic.

Today we renew our investment in America's future by extending the Education Act.

This law has brought new help to all American schoolchildren—especially the poorest.

It has brought special educational and health services to 9 million of our poorest children.

It has created 3,600 new school libraries. Almost nine out of ten schoolchildren were helped by new teaching materials purchased during the first year of its library program.

It has launched, all over the Nation, more than 2,200 exciting new education projects outside the classroom. Nearly 17 million children are being made richer.

It has established 20 new regional laboratories for basic research in education: to explore the ways children learn and to improve the ways teachers teach.

This bill authorizes a new effort to prevent dropouts, new programs for handicapped children, new planning help for rural schools. It also contains a special provision establishing bilingual education programs for children whose first language is not English. Thousands of children of Latin descent, young Indians, and others will get a better start—a better chance—in school.

Today we celebrate not only the renewal and extension and improvement of this law—not only 3 years of progress in education; we also celebrate the fact that the great programs passed by the 89th Congress have

come of age. They have been tested in practice. They are working. They have begun to improve life for millions of Americans. And they have survived the trials and battles of Congress.

When the 90th Congress convened last year, there were some who predicted that the programs launched by the 89th Congress would be stopped in their tracks, turned back, and destroyed.

Some prophets feared that would happen—and others hoped it would happen!

Well, both of those views have been proven wrong. The 90th Congress was not as productive as I urged it to be. It left an agenda of unfinished business. But it did not turn back or halt or destroy the progress we have begun—not one single Great Society measure was repealed. The American people have spoken up on behalf of health and education and conservation and social progress. Their voices will not be ignored.

Medicare is a fact—and an unchallenged success.

The War on Poverty, the Model Cities Act, a whole range of consumer laws, dozens of measures which 3 years ago were only ideas; these programs live, and their promise lives.

The greatest of these is education—without which no other progress is possible.

We can cite educational statistics. We can publish reports and columns of numbers. But there is only one way, really, to measure the full scope and meaning of this law, and that is in the lives of children.

What this law means is that we are now giving every child in America a better chance to touch his outermost limits—to reach the farthest edge of his talents and his dreams. We have begun a campaign to unlock the full potential of every boy and girl—regardless of his race or his region or his father's income.

That is what we started 32 months ago

16

out in front of the Junction School and that is what we are going to continue, even though we will be somewhat restricted in the next year because of our international and fiscal problems.

So today, as I sign this bill, I repeat what I told those who were there that day: "No law I have signed or will ever sign means more to the future of America."

NOTE: As enacted, the Elementary and Secondary Education Amendments of 1967 (H.R. 7819) is Public Law 90–247 (81 Stat. 783).

Major provisions of the amendments are summarized in a White House release made public with the President's statement. The text of the release is printed in the Weekly Compilation of Presidential Documents (vol. 4, p. 30).

For the President's remarks upon signing the first Elementary and Secondary Education Act on April 11, 1965, at the former Junction Elementary School in Johnson City, Texas, see 1965 volume, this series, Book I, Item 181.

The statement was released at San Antonio, Texas.

---

5 Statement by the President Upon Signing Bills in Aid of Members of the Armed Forces. *January 2, 1968*

WHEN I visited our fighting men in Southeast Asia just a week ago, I carried one abiding message to them. I assured them the American people and their President honor and value their service in freedom's cause.

In foxhole and flightline, on carrier decks and jungle trails, those brave and committed men guard our security with their lives.

No words of ours—and no actions—can match or measure their sacrifice.

But in the ways that are open to us, this Nation can show its gratitude.

Recently, the Congress passed—and I signed into law—the fifth military pay act in 5 years. With those, basic military pay has been raised more than 40 percent.

Today I sign four other measures designed in modest ways to lighten the load of the soldier and his family. Three are especially tailored to the needs of men who serve in combat areas.

As a result of this new legislation:

—No fighting man will lose the annual leave time he earns in Vietnam. The current 60-day limit for accrued leave is now expanded to 90 days for those in battle areas.

—Our servicemen in combat zones can continue to enjoy their traditional privilege of mailing gifts costing up to $50 duty free.

—The families of men missing in action will have twice as much time—up to a year, or even more—to store their household goods at Government expense.

—A serviceman with a trailer home will receive a fair allowance for its commercial shipment—an increase from 51 cents to 74 cents per mile—when he is reassigned to a new station.

These are small measures. But they reflect a large concern for America's men-at-arms.

In another quiet way, they say: America does not forget.

NOTE: As enacted, the bills (H.R. 12961, 1141, 1341, and 3982) are Public Laws 90–236, 90–240, 90–245, and 90–246 (81 Stat. 764, 776, and 782).

For the President's remarks upon signing the military pay bill, see 1967 volume, this series, Book II, Item 546.

The statement was released at San Antonio, Texas.

6 Statement by the President on Federally Supported Vocational and Technical Education Programs. *January 5, 1968*

HELPING a man or woman learn the skills needed to secure a good job is one of our important tasks.

The vocational training partnership between Federal, State, and local governments prepares skilled workers to become self-supporting, to contribute many times over to the wealth of our Nation.

NOTE: The President's statement was made public as part of a White House release summarizing recent data relating to federally supported vocational and technical education programs. The release stated that Secretary of Health, Education, and Welfare John W. Gardner informed the President that 7.5 million Americans of all ages were presently being trained for skilled jobs through such programs. Of this number 3.7 million were in high school programs, 600,000 in post-secondary school programs, 200,000 in programs for school dropouts, and 3 million in adult education programs. The various programs would cost Federal, State, and local governments more than $1 billion per year. The text of the White House release is printed in the Weekly Compilation of Presidential Documents (vol. 4, p. 35).

The statement was released at San Antonio, Texas.

7 Remarks of Welcome in San Antonio to Prime Minister Eshkol of Israel. *January 7, 1968*

Mr. Prime Minister, Mrs. Eshkol, Mr. Secretary of State, my dear friends:

Shalom. The traditional greeting of Israel has very special meaning for all of us who have come here today.

We meet here in peace, and we will talk in peace.

And we will try to extend the peace that is in our hearts—extend it to all men who are willing to share our partnership of good faith and good purpose.

Mr. Prime Minister, we will be together for only 2 short days. But they will be long days full of friendship and full of happiness because you have come here to be with us.

These, too, will be hopeful days, because this land was born in that spirit—that spirit of promise and opportunity.

Here in this land our neighbors work hand in hand for the common good.

So, Mr. Prime Minister and Mrs. Eshkol, we extend to you this afternoon the hand of welcome to this land. We hope its spirit refreshes you after the long journey that you have taken.

I know that its hospitality will lift your heart.

Mr. Prime Minister, we hope that you find that peace which all Americans are proud to seek with you.

We are delighted to have you, sir.

[At this point Prime Minister Levi Eshkol responded briefly (see note). The President then resumed speaking.]

I know you people would want to meet Mrs. Eshkol and Mrs. Johnson.

Mr. Mayor, Congressman Gonzalez, Congressman Kazen, and other distinguished public officials, all you ladies and gentlemen, boys and girls:

It is a cold afternoon, but it is a warm welcome.

We are very proud of San Antonio and south Texas for the warmth of your welcome.

Thank all of you so much.

NOTE: The President spoke at 3:47 p.m. at Randolph Air Force Base, San Antonio, Texas, where Prime Minister Levi Eshkol was welcomed for his visit to the LBJ Ranch. Prime Minister Eshkol responded as follows:

Mr. President, Mrs. Johnson:

Mrs. Eshkol and I are very happy to be here as your guests.

Since 1964 we have with us fond memories of our first meeting. We come to you in friendship, and we know that friendship awaits us.

My central concern is peace—peace for my country and for the area of the world in which we live.

It was there in ancient days that men first expressed a striving for peace on earth.

I will not ever give up the hope that this will come to pass. We in our country are working towards this end.

And I know how much America is doing under your leadership, Mr. President, to help the cause of peace and justice in the world.

In the Biblical phrase, *Shalom larachok vele-karov*, which means peace be to him that is far, and to him that is near.

Mr. President, it is a great pleasure to be with you.

In his opening words the President also referred to Secretary of State Dean Rusk. At the close of his remarks he referred to Mayor W. W. McAllister of San Antonio and Representatives Henry B. Gonzalez and Abraham Kazen, Jr., of Texas.

On the same day the White House released a list of the members of the welcoming committee for the Prime Minister, an announcement by the Embassy of Israel of gifts to the President and his family from Prime Minister Eshkol, and a press report by George E. Christian, Special Assistant to the President, and Loyd Hackler, Associate Press Secretary, on the Prime Minister's visit to the LBJ Ranch.

8   Toasts of the President and Prime Minister Eshkol at a Dinner at the LBJ Ranch. *January 7, 1968*

Mr. Prime Minister, Mrs. Eshkol:

Welcome to our family table.

We are honored and happy to have you here in our home.

Here, we ask only that you enjoy the warm ties of friendship and partnership that mean so much to each of us, and both our peoples.

Our peoples, Mr. Prime Minister, share many qualities of mind and heart.

We both rise to challenge. We both admire the courage and the resourcefulness of the citizen-soldier. We each draw strength and purpose for today from our heroes of yesterday. We both know the thrill of bringing life from a hard but a rewarding land.

But all Americans—and all Israelis—also know that prosperity is not enough—that none of our restless generation can ever live by bread alone.

For we are equally nations in search of a dream. We share a vision and purpose far brighter than our abilities to make deserts bloom.

We have been born and raised to seek and find peace. In that common spirit of our hopes, I respect our hope that a just and lasting peace will prevail between Israel and her neighbors.

This past year has been a busy one for America's peacemakers—in the Middle East, in Cyprus, in Vietnam. Wherever conscience and faith have carried them, they have found a stubborn truth confirmed. Making peace is punishing work. It demands enormous courage, flexibility, and imagination. It is ill served by hasty slogans or half-solutions. I know you understand this, sir, better than most men. One of your ancestors said it for all men almost 2,000 years ago:

"Other precepts are performed when the occasion arises . . . but for peace it is written, 'pursue it.' "

That is our intention in the Middle East and throughout our world. To pursue peace. To find peace. To keep peace forever among men. If we are wise, if we are fortunate, if we work together—perhaps our Nation and all nations may know the joys of that promise God once made about the children of Israel: "I will make a covenant of peace with them . . . it shall be an everlasting covenant."

Let that be our toast to each other—our Governments and our peoples—as this new year begins. Its days are brighter, Mr. Prime Minister, because you lighten them with your presence here and the spirit you will leave behind.

To our friends, Prime Minister and Mrs. Eshkol, and to the people of Israel—*Shalom.*

NOTE: The President spoke at a private dinner in the dining room at the LBJ Ranch. As printed this item follows the text released by the White House Press Office.

Prime Minister Levi Eshkol responded as follows:

Mr. President, Mrs. Johnson:

For Mrs. Eshkol and myself this has been a wonderful experience to be here as your guests at your home in Texas. On our way here today we saw again the vastness and variety of America. But from the moment we met you we were made to feel once more the warmth of your friendship and the depth of your own view that in terms of rights and duties all peoples are equal: that they have equal right to be themselves and to be left in peace. I remember our first meeting in 1964. I have carried the memory of that with me. In the days of peril I thought often of your friendship.

This great land of Texas reminds me very much of parts of my own country though there is, of course, no comparison in size. I can see here the results of pioneering and dedication, the beauty men can create when they are free. The broadness of this place is matched by the breadth of your understanding and the depth of your friendship and the determination of America, which you symbolize, to buttress peace, to block its disruption by aggression, and to enlarge the horizons of man's opportunity.

On a personal note, Mr. President, in the nearly 4 years which have passed since I last had the pleasure of meeting you, threefold congratulations have been in order. Twice you have played the role of father of the bride, and now Mrs. Johnson and yourself have the joy of your first grandson.

In drinking to your health I wish for Mrs. Johnson and yourself all personal joy in the years ahead and for your country the realization of your dream of peace and human dignity.

Ladies and gentlemen: the President of the United States.

9   Joint Statement Following Discussions With Prime Minister Eshkol of Israel. *January 8, 1968*

PRESIDENT JOHNSON invited Prime Minister Eshkol to be his guest at the Texas White House on January 7 and 8, during the Prime Minister's visit to the United States.

The President and the Prime Minister held several meetings during which they discussed recent developments in the Middle East as well as a number of questions of mutual interest in the bilateral relations between their two countries.

The President and the Prime Minister considered the implications of the pace of rearmament in the Middle East and the ways and means of coping with this situation. The President agreed to keep Israel's military defense capability under active and sympathetic examination and review in the light of all relevant factors, including the shipment of military equipment by others to the area.

The President and the Prime Minister restated their dedication to the establishment of a just and lasting peace in the Middle East in accordance with the spirit of the Security Council resolution of November 22, 1967. They also noted that the principles set forth by President Johnson on June 19 constituted an equitable basis for such a settlement.

The President and the Prime Minister noted that under that Security Council resolution the Secretary General of the United

Nations has designated Ambassador Jarring as his Special Representative. They also noted with satisfaction that Ambassador Jarring is already engaged in discussions with the governments concerned and affirmed their full support of his mission.

The President and the Prime Minister reviewed with satisfaction developments in the relations between the United States and Israel since their last meeting in 1964 and expressed their firm intention to continue the traditionally close, friendly and cooperative ties which link the peoples of Israel and the United States.

Noting the mutual dedication of their governments and people to the value of

peace, resistance to aggression wherever it occurs, individual freedom, human dignity and the advancement of man through the elimination of poverty, ignorance, and disease, the President and the Prime Minister declared their firm determination to make every effort to increase the broad area of understanding which already exists between Israel and the United States and agreed that the Prime Minister's visit advanced this objective.

NOTE: The June 19, 1967, statement of principles is contained in the President's address to the Foreign Policy Conference for Educators at the Department of State. See 1967 volume, this series, Book I, Item 272.

The joint statement was released at San Antonio, Texas.

---

10 Statement by the President on the United States Savings Bond Program. *January 9, 1968*

I REGRET that circumstances prevent me from joining you tonight.

You are very much in my thoughts at this time.

Chairman Haughton and every member of your 1967 Payroll Savings Committee deserve the compliments and gratitude of your President and your Nation.

I congratulate you on your remarkable achievements in 1967—a payroll savings dollar volume of $3,500,000,000—and a total of 2,606,640 savings bonds buyers.

But for all that you have achieved in 1967, a greater and more urgent challenge awaits your Committee in 1968. The strength of the dollar has never been more essential to the stability of our world. The opportunity you have for maintaining that strength, for improving our international balance of payments, has seldom been larger or more imperative.

Today, the fate of nations and the fortunes

of peoples are intertwined as never before. A vast network of world trade and financial transactions binds millions in one community of opportunity. But their very interdependence also exposes men and governments to common dangers. Sickness in one economy can sap the strength of the world economy; a threat to one key currency endangers the economic health of all.

Today, the universal barometer of the world's economic climate is the strength of the American dollar.

Your own business fortunes rise and fall with the soundness of the dollar. The health of our own domestic economy depends on sound money. Its weakness or strength is equally critical to the health of the international economic system.

You know the present danger. When our dollar outflow is larger than our earnings and credits from foreign countries, a deficit unbalances our international accounts. We cannot let that deficit undermine the strength of the dollar and undercut the stability of the international monetary system. To do so would be to risk bankruptcy of our own prosperity and the fortunes of all nations whose growth is tied to our own.

On New Year's Day, I asked every American to recognize their personal responsibilities for protecting the unparalleled prosperity they now enjoy. I offered an action program for America to keep the dollar strong at home, and to keep men confident in its strength throughout the world.

Your experience and success in promoting savings bonds and Freedom Shares gives us special confidence in you. The savings you have encouraged are a deposit of great hope against the future. Their promise can be enlarged, and that future made brighter,

by how well you succeed in helping to restore a healthy balance to our international payments.

I welcome and encourage the man who will do most to sustain your leadership, your new Chairman, Bill Gwinn of United Aircraft. I am grateful to you all, old and new members of the Committee, for the example of your patriotism and the hopefulness you leave in our Nation's heart.

NOTE: The President's statement was read by Secretary of the Treasury Henry H. Fowler at a dinner-meeting of the U.S. Industrial Payroll Savings Committee in the Diplomatic Suite at the Department of State in Washington. In the statement the President referred to Daniel J. Haughton, chairman of the board of Lockheed Aircraft Corp., and William P. Gwinn, president of United Aircraft Corp., outgoing and incoming chairmen, respectively, of the U.S. Industrial Payroll Savings Committee.

The statement was released at San Antonio, Texas.

11 Memorandum Directing Reduction of AID Expenditures Overseas in Connection With the Balance of Payments Program. *January 11, 1968*

Memorandum for William S. Gaud, Administrator, Agency for International Development:

SUBJECT: Additional steps to reduce balance of payments costs

Your agency has made notable progress over the past few years in reducing expenditures made outside of the United States under the economic assistance program. Expenditures for goods and services purchased abroad declined from 27 percent of total AID expenditures in 1963 to 10 percent in 1967. At present, all development loans are used exclusively for procurement in the U.S. Eighty percent of grants for technical and supporting assistance and other expenses are used to pay for U.S. goods and services.

In the current situation, however, we can-

not rest on this record. I recently outlined a broad program to correct the balance of payments deficit. As a part of the Government actions under this program, we must take even more stringent steps to minimize the balance of payments costs of our AID programs. I therefore request that you take steps to reduce your expenditures overseas in calendar 1968 by a minimum of $100 million below what they were in 1967.

To achieve this reduction you should take steps to:

—reduce offshore expenditures for commodities, cash payments, technicians and other services to the bare minimum;

—increase the use of U.S.-owned local currencies that are excess or near excess to our needs;

—increase the contributions of AID receiving countries in the financing of our technicians and related costs;

—carefully review the requirements for personnel stationed abroad financed with U.S. funds.

In addition, I would like you to review and improve the effectiveness of our arrangements with individual countries to assure that AID-financed goods are additional to U.S. commercial exports.

I know that the additional measures called for will be difficult, coming on top of the very substantial efforts of the last few years. I am confident, however, that with ingenuity and resolve we can put into effect the arrangements necessary to carry on the economic aid program, which is vital to our interests and to the well-being of so many people in developing countries, with even less balance of payments impact.

LYNDON B. JOHNSON

NOTE: The memorandum was released at San Antonio, Texas.

12   Remarks Upon Presenting the U.S. Savings Bond Minuteman Award to the Tactical Air Command's 12th Air Force. *January 11, 1968*

General Clark, General Bond, ladies and gentlemen, mostly gentlemen:

I wanted so much to come here this morning in order to visit a good neighbor.

I wanted to come and salute the 12th Air Force, to thank you, to congratulate you, and to express my appreciation to all the people who support this mission.

The 12th Air Force has won many honors in your young lifetime. I have come here now to present you another one. And this is one that you must not recognize lightly.

This is the Minuteman Flag.

You know, as our Nation is challenged—and it is on many fronts, many times each year—we have to call upon all of our people to make their contribution in different ways. Some of them supply courage, brain, brawn, daring, and adventure.

Some of us support the men at the front in many ways—in attitudes, in helping their morale, in giving them good weapons, in paying taxes in order to see that they have the best equipment.

But this Minuteman Flag is what we call the patriot's emblem, because it declares that more than 90 percent of those of you who make up this command—nine out of every ten—have bought savings bonds in 1967.

So you not only supply the brain, the brawn, the horsepower, the will, and the courage to protect this country—you are supplying your part of the money.

I don't know how you feel, but I think I know how I would feel, and how I do feel, when I sit back here in another arena, on another platform, and see you carry all the responsibilities you carry. I want to help some.

I think all Americans ought to want to help some.

One of the things I am proudest of is the men who do the most fighting do the most financing, too.

The Defense Department has one of the best records for buying defense bonds, I guess because some of you sometime in your life have been told that your daddies bought thrift stamps and baby bonds to carry us through other critical periods.

It gives us all a lot of pride to see those of you who wear a uniform do what you are doing.

Today for the first time we are awarding these Minuteman Flags to battlefield units. In Vietnam today, 115 units fly this flag. And they are not alone.

In back of those men out there we have here at home tens of millions of bond buyers in the Defense Establishment, in the Federal Government, throughout all of our big production plants in this country.

These patriotic Americans today hold savings bonds and Freedom Shares that are valued at $52 billion. That is almost two-thirds of what our defense budget will be this year.

Because you have done that, we are stronger in our freedom and we are stronger in our finances.

I think one thing you men ought to know is that America's prosperity depends on the soundness of the American dollar. Every bond you buy strengthens the dollar you get in your paycheck.

The time is going to come when you are going to use these bonds, when you are going to need them. And your investment in freedom is going to pay off.

This is a very pleasant assignment for me. I am glad that General Clark and General Bond are here to salute the 12th Air Force.

I am glad that Congressman Pickle could come here and join us.

But most of all, I am proud of you men who, out of the pitiful earnings that you get, and the modicum pay that is in your envelope, still think enough of your country not only to give your life for it but to invest some of your dollars in it.

That is what is going to preserve freedom.

That is what is going to save this land.

Other people want what we have, and you are going to protect it .

We are proud of you.

Thank you.

NOTE: The President spoke at 11:52 a.m. at Bergstrom Air Force Base in Texas. In his opening words he referred to Lt. Gen. Albert P. Clark, Vice Commander, Tactical Air Command, and Gen. Charles R. Bond, Jr., Commander, 12th Air Force Tactical Command, Waco, Texas. During his remarks he also referred to Representative J. J. Pickle of Texas.

13   Message to President Saragat of Italy Following the Earthquakes in Sicily. *January 16, 1968*

Dear Mr. President:

I was deeply distressed to learn of the tragic loss of life caused by the earthquakes in Sicily. All Americans join me in offering our heartfelt sympathy to you and the people of Sicily. I am asking Ambassador Reinhardt to keep in close touch with the Italian authorities to determine in what way we can be of assistance in this sad moment.

Sincerely,

LYNDON B. JOHNSON

[President Giuseppe Saragat]

NOTE: The message was posted on the bulletin board in the press room at the White House on January 17. It was not made public in the form of a White House press release.

14   Annual Message to the Congress on the State of the Union. *January 17, 1968*

[Delivered in person before a joint session at 9:05 p.m.]

Mr. Speaker, Mr. President, Members of the Congress, and my fellow Americans:

I was thinking as I was walking down the aisle tonight of what Sam Rayburn told me many years ago: The Congress always extends a very warm welcome to the President—as he comes in.

Thank all of you very, very much.

I have come once again to this Chamber—the home of our democracy—to give you, as the Constitution requires, "Information of the State of the Union."

I report to you that our country is challenged, at home and abroad:

—that it is our will that is being tried, not our strength; our sense of purpose, not our ability to achieve a better America;

—that we have the strength to meet our every challenge; the physical strength to hold the course of decency and compassion at home; and the moral strength to support the cause of peace in the world.

And I report to you that I believe, with abiding conviction, that this people—nurtured by their deep faith, tutored by their hard lessons, moved by their high aspirations—have the will to meet the trials that these times impose.

Since I reported to you last January:

—Three elections have been held in Vietnam—in the midst of war and under the constant threat of violence.

—A President, a Vice President, a House and Senate, and village officials have been chosen by popular, contested ballot.

—The enemy has been defeated in battle after battle.

—The number of South Vietnamese living in areas under Government protection tonight has grown by more than a million since January of last year.

These are all marks of progress. Yet:

—The enemy continues to pour men and material across frontiers and into battle, despite his continuous heavy losses.

—He continues to hope that America's will to persevere can be broken. Well—he is wrong. America will persevere. Our patience and our perseverance will match our power. Aggression will never prevail.

But our goal is peace—and peace at the earliest possible moment.

Right now we are exploring the meaning of Hanoi's recent statement. There is no mystery about the questions which must be answered before the bombing is stopped.

We believe that any talks should follow the San Antonio formula that I stated last September, which said:

—The bombing would stop immediately if talks would take place promptly and with reasonable hopes that they would be productive.

—And the other side must not take advantage of our restraint as they have in the past. This Nation simply cannot accept anything less without jeopardizing the lives of our men and of our allies.

If a basis for peace talks can be established on the San Antonio foundations—and it is my hope and my prayer that they can—we would consult with our allies and with the other side to see if a complete cessation of hostilities—a really true cease-fire—could be made the first order of business. I will report at the earliest possible moment the results of these explorations to the American people.

I have just recently returned from a very fruitful visit and talks with His Holiness the Pope and I share his hope—as he expressed it earlier today—that both sides will extend themselves in an effort to bring an end to the war in Vietnam. I have today assured him that we and our allies will do our full part to bring this about.

Since I spoke to you last January, other events have occurred that have major consequences for world peace.

—The Kennedy Round achieved the greatest reduction in tariff barriers in all the history of trade negotiations.

—The nations of Latin America at Punta del Este resolved to move toward economic integration.

—In Asia, the nations from Korea and Japan to Indonesia and Singapore worked behind America's shield to strengthen their economies and to broaden their political cooperation.

—In Africa, from which the distinguished Vice President has just returned, he reports to me that there is a spirit of regional cooperation that is beginning to take hold in very practical ways.

These events we all welcomed. Yet since I last reported to you, we and the world have been confronted by a number of crises:

—During the Arab-Israeli war last June, the hot line between Washington and Moscow was used for the first time in our history. A cease-fire was achieved without a major power confrontation.

Now the nations of the Middle East have the opportunity to cooperate with Ambassador Jarring's U.N. mission and they have the responsibility to find the terms of living together in stable peace and dignity, and we shall do all in our power to help them

achieve that result.

—Not far from this scene of conflict, a crisis flared on Cyprus involving two peoples who are America's friends: Greece and Turkey. Our very able representative, Mr. Cyrus Vance, and others helped to ease this tension.

—Turmoil continues on the mainland of China after a year of violent disruption. The radical extremism of their Government has isolated the Chinese people behind their own borders. The United States, however, remains willing to permit the travel of journalists to both our countries; to undertake cultural and educational exchanges; and to talk about the exchange of basic food crop materials.

Since I spoke to you last, the United States and the Soviet Union have taken several important steps toward the goal of international cooperation.

As you will remember, I met with Chairman Kosygin at Glassboro and we achieved, if not accord, at least a clearer understanding of our respective positions after 2 days of meeting.

Because we believe the nuclear danger must be narrowed, we have worked with the Soviet Union and with other nations to reach an agreement that will halt the spread of nuclear weapons. On the basis of communications from Ambassador Fisher in Geneva this afternoon, I am encouraged to believe that a draft treaty can be laid before the conference in Geneva in the very near future. I hope to be able to present that treaty to the Senate this year for the Senate's approval.

We achieved, in 1967, a consular treaty with the Soviets, the first commercial air agreement between the two countries, and a treaty banning weapons in outer space. We shall sign, and submit to the Senate shortly, a new treaty with the Soviets and with others for the protection of astronauts.

Serious differences still remain between us, yet in these relations, we have made some progress since Vienna, the Berlin Wall, and the Cuban missile crisis.

But despite this progress, we must maintain a military force that is capable of deterring any threat to this Nation's security, whatever the mode of aggression. Our choices must not be confined to total war— or to total acquiescence.

We have such a military force today. We shall maintain it.

I wish—with all of my heart—that the expenditures that are necessary to build and to protect our power could all be devoted to the programs of peace. But until world conditions permit, and until peace is assured, America's might—and America's bravest sons who wear our Nation's uniform—must continue to stand guard for all of us—as they gallantly do tonight in Vietnam and other places in the world.

Yet neither great weapons nor individual courage can provide the conditions of peace.

For two decades America has committed itself against the tyranny of want and ignorance in the world that threatens the peace. We shall sustain that commitment.

This year I shall propose:

—That we launch, with other nations, an exploration of the ocean depths to tap its wealth, and its energy, and its abundance.

—That we contribute our fair share to a major expansion of the International Development Association, and to increase the resources of the Asian Development Bank.

—That we adopt a prudent aid program, rooted in the principle of self-help.

—That we renew and extend the food for freedom program.

Our food programs have already helped millions avoid the horrors of famine.

But unless the rapid growth of population in developing countries is slowed, the gap between rich and poor will widen steadily.

Governments in the developing countries must take such facts into consideration. We in the United States are prepared to help assist them in those efforts.

But we must also improve the lives of children already born in the villages and towns and cities on this earth. They can be taught by great teachers through space communications and the miracle of satellite television— and we are going to bring to bear every resource of mind and technology to help make this dream come true.

Let me speak now about some matters here at home.

Tonight our Nation is accomplishing more for its people than has ever been accomplished before. Americans are prosperous as men have never been in recorded history. Yet there is in the land a certain restlessness—a questioning.

The total of our Nation's annual production is now above $800 billion. For 83 months this Nation has been on a steady upward trend of growth.

All about them, most American families can see the evidence of growing abundance: higher paychecks, humming factories, new cars moving down new highways. More and more families own their own homes, equipped with more than 70 million television sets.

A new college is founded every week. Today more than half of the high school graduates go on to college.

There are hundreds of thousands of fathers and mothers who never completed grammar school—who will see their children graduate from college.

Why, then, this restlessness?

Because when a great ship cuts through the sea, the waters are always stirred and troubled.

And our ship is moving. It is moving through troubled and new waters; it is moving toward new and better shores.

We ask now, not how can we achieve abundance?—but how shall we use our abundance? Not, is there abundance enough for all?—but, how can all share in our abundance?

While we have accomplished much, much remains for us to meet and much remains for us to master.

—In some areas, the jobless rate is still three or four times the national average.

—Violence has shown its face in some of our cities.

—Crime increases on our streets.

—Income for farm workers remains far behind that for urban workers; and parity for our farmers who produce our food is still just a hope—not an achievement.

—New housing construction is far less than we need—to assure decent shelter for every family.

—Hospital and medical costs are high, and they are rising.

—Many rivers—and the air in many cities—remain badly polluted. And our citizens suffer from breathing that air.

We have lived with conditions like these for many, many years. But much that we once accepted as inevitable, we now find absolutely intolerable.

In our cities last summer, we saw how wide is the gulf for some Americans between the promise and the reality of our society.

We know that we cannot change all of this in a day. It represents the bitter consequences of more than three centuries.

But the issue is not whether we can change this; the issue is whether we will change this.

Well, I know we can. And I believe we will.

This then is the work we should do in the months that are ahead of us in this Congress.

The first essential is more jobs, useful jobs for tens of thousands who can become productive and can pay their own way.

Our economy has created 7½ million new jobs in the past 4 years. It is adding more than a million and a half new jobs this year.

Through programs passed by the Congress, job training is being given tonight to more than a million Americans in this country.

This year, the time has come when we must get to those who are last in line—the hard-core unemployed—the hardest to reach.

Employment officials estimate that 500,000 of these persons are now unemployed in the major cities of America. Our objective is to place these 500,000 in private industry jobs within the next 3 years.

To do this, I propose a $2.1 billion manpower program in the coming fiscal year—a 25 percent increase over the current year. Most of this increase will be used to start a new partnership between government and private industry to train and to hire the hard-core unemployed persons. I know of no task before us of more importance to us, to the country, or to our future.

Another essential is to rebuild our cities.

Last year the Congress authorized $662 million for the Model Cities program. I requested the full amount of that authorization to help meet the crisis in the cities of America. But the Congress appropriated only $312 million—less than half.

This year I urge the Congress to honor my request for model cities funds to rebuild the centers of American cities by granting us the full amount that you in the Congress authorized—$1 billion.

The next essential is more housing—and more housing now.

Surely a nation that can go to the moon can place a decent home within the reach of its families.

Therefore we must call together the resources of industry and labor, to start building 300,000 housing units for low- and middle-income families next year—that is three times more than this year. We must make it possible for thousands of families to become homeowners, not rent-payers.

I propose, for the consideration of this Congress, a 10-year campaign to build 6 million new housing units for low- and middle-income families. Six million units in the next 10 years. We have built 530,000 the last 10 years.

Better health for our children—all of our children—is essential if we are to have a better America.

Last year, Medicare, Medicaid, and other new programs that you passed in the Congress brought better health to more than 25 million Americans.

American medicine—with the very strong support and cooperation of public resources—has produced a phenomenal decline in the death rate from many of the dread diseases.

But it is a shocking fact that, in saving the lives of babies, America ranks 15th among the nations of the world. And among children, crippling defects are often discovered too late for any corrective action. This is a tragedy that Americans can, and Americans should, prevent.

I shall, therefore, propose to the Congress a child health program to provide, over the next 5 years, for families unable to afford it—access to health services from prenatal care of the mother through the child's first year.

When we do that you will find it is the best investment we ever made because we will get these diseases in their infancy and we will find a cure in a great many instances that we can never find by overcrowding our hospitals when they are grown.

Now when we act to advance the consumer's cause I think we help every American.

Last year, with very little fanfare the Congress and the executive branch moved in that field.

We enacted the Wholesome Meat Act, the Flammable Fabrics Act, the Product Safety Commission, and a law to improve clinical laboratories.

And now, I think, the time has come to complete our unfinished work. The Senate has already passed the truth-in-lending bill, the fire safety bill, and the pipeline safety laws.

Tonight I plead with the House to immediately act upon these measures and I hope take favorable action upon all of them. I call upon the Congress to enact, without delay, the remainder of the 12 vital consumer protection laws that I submitted to the Congress last year.

I also urge final action on a measure that is already passed by the House to guard against fraud and manipulation in the Nation's commodity exchange market.

These measures are a pledge to our people—to keep them safe in their homes and at work, and to give them a fair deal in the marketplace.

And I think we must do more. I propose:

—New powers for the Federal Trade Commission to stop those who defraud and who swindle our public.

—New safeguards to insure the quality

of fish and poultry, and the safety of our community water supplies.

—A major study of automobile insurance.

—Protection against hazardous radiation from television sets and other electronic equipment.

And to give the consumer a stronger voice, I plan to appoint a consumer counsel in the Justice Department—a lawyer for the American consumer—to work directly under the Attorney General, to serve the President's Special Assistant for Consumer Affairs, and to serve the consumers of this land.

This Congress—Democrats and Republicans—can earn the thanks of history. We can make this truly a new day for the American consumer, and by giving him this protection we can live in history as the consumer-conscious Congress.

So let us get on with the work. Let us act soon.

We, at every level of the government, State, local, Federal, know that the American people have had enough of rising crime and lawlessness in this country.

They recognize that law enforcement is first the duty of local police and local government.

They recognize that the frontline headquarters against crime is in the home, the church, the city hall and the county courthouse and the statehouse—not in the far-removed National Capital of Washington.

But the people also recognize that the National Government can and the National Government should help the cities and the States in their war on crime to the full extent of its resources and its constitutional authority. And this we shall do.

This does not mean a national police force. It does mean help and financial support:

—to develop State and local master plans to combat crime,

—to provide better training and better pay for police, and

—to bring the most advanced technology to the war on crime in every city and every county in America.

There is no more urgent business before this Congress than to pass the Safe Streets Act this year that I proposed last year. That law will provide these required funds. They are so critically needed that I have doubled my request under this act to $100 million in fiscal 1969.

And I urge the Congress to stop the trade in mail-order murder, to stop it this year by adopting a proper gun control law.

This year, I will propose a Drug Control Act to provide stricter penalties for those who traffic in LSD and other dangerous drugs with our people.

I will ask for more vigorous enforcement of all of our drug laws by increasing the number of Federal drug and narcotics control officials by more than 30 percent. The time has come to stop the sale of slavery to the young. I also request you to give us funds to add immediately 100 assistant United States attorneys throughout the land to help prosecute our criminal laws. We have increased our judiciary by 40 percent and we have increased our prosecutors by 16 percent. The dockets are full of cases because we don't have assistant district attorneys to go before the Federal judge and handle them. We start these young lawyers at $8,200 a year. And the docket is clogged because we don't have authority to hire more of them.

I ask the Congress for authority to hire 100 more. These young men will give special attention to this drug abuse, too.

Finally, I ask you to add 100 FBI agents

to strengthen law enforcement in the Nation and to protect the individual rights of every citizen.

A moment ago I spoke of despair and frustrated hopes in the cities where the fires of disorder burned last summer. We can—and in time we will—change that despair into confidence, and change those frustrations into achievements. But violence will never bring progress.

We can make progress only by attacking the causes of violence and only where there is civil order founded on justice.

Today we are helping local officials improve their capacity to deal promptly with disorders.

Those who preach disorder and those who preach violence must know that local authorities are able to resist them swiftly, to resist them sternly, and to resist them decisively.

I shall recommend other actions:

—To raise the farmers' income by establishing a security commodity reserve that will protect the market from price-depressing stocks and protect the consumer from food scarcity.

—I shall recommend programs to help farmers bargain more effectively for fair prices.

—I shall recommend programs for new air safety measures.

—Measures to stem the rising costs of medical care.

—Legislation to encourage our returning veterans to devote themselves to careers in community service such as teaching, and being firemen, and joining our police force, and our law enforcement officials.

—I shall recommend programs to strengthen and finance our anti-pollution efforts.

—Fully funding all of the $2.18 billion poverty program that you in the Congress had just authorized in order to bring opportunity to those who have been left far behind.

—I shall recommend an Educational Opportunity Act to speed up our drive to break down the financial barriers that are separating our young people from college.

I shall also urge the Congress to act on several other vital pending bills—especially the civil rights measures—fair jury trials, protection of Federal rights, enforcement of equal employment opportunity, and fair housing.

The unfinished work of the first session must be completed—the Higher Education Act, the Juvenile Delinquency Act, conservation measures to save the redwoods of California, and to preserve the wonders of our scenic rivers, the Highway Beautification Act—and all the other measures for a cleaner, and for a better, and for a more beautiful America.

Next month we'll begin our 8th year of uninterrupted prosperity. The economic outlook for this year is one of steady growth—if we are vigilant.

True, there are some clouds on the horizon. Prices are rising. Interest rates have passed the peak of 1966; and if there is continued inaction on the tax bill, they will climb even higher.

I warn the Congress and the Nation tonight that this failure to act on the tax bill will sweep us into an accelerating spiral of price increases, a slump in homebuilding, and a continuing erosion of the American dollar.

This would be a tragedy for every American family. And I predict that if this happens, they will all let us know about it.

31

We—those of us in the executive branch, in the Congress, and the leaders of labor and business—must do everything we can to prevent that kind of misfortune.

Under the new budget, the expenditures for 1969 will increase by $10.4 billion. Receipts will increase by $22.3 billion including the added tax revenues. Virtually all of this expenditure increase represents the mandatory cost of our defense efforts, $3 billion; increased interest, almost $1 billion; or mandatory payments under laws passed by Congress—such as those provided in the Social Security Act that you passed in 1967, and to Medicare and Medicaid beneficiaries, veterans, and farmers, of about $4½ billion; and the additional $1 billion 600 million next year for the pay increases that you passed in military and civilian pay. That makes up the $10 billion that is added to the budget. With few exceptions, very few, we are holding the fiscal 1969 budget to last year's level, outside of those mandatory and required increases.

A Presidential commission composed of distinguished congressional fiscal leaders and other prominent Americans recommended this year that we adopt a new budget approach. I am carrying out their recommendations in this year's budget. This budget, therefore, for the first time accurately covers all Federal expenditures and all Federal receipts, including for the first time in one budget $47 billion from the social security, Medicare, highway, and other trust funds.

The fiscal 1969 budget has expenditures of approximately $186 billion, with total estimated revenues, including the tax bill, of about $178 billion.

If the Congress enacts the tax increase, we will reduce the budget deficit by some $12 billion. The war in Vietnam is costing us about $25 billion and we are asking for about $12 billion in taxes—and if we get that $12 billion tax bill we will reduce the deficit from about $20 billion in 1968 to about $8 billion in 1969.

Now, this is a tight budget. It follows the reduction that I made in cooperation with the Congress—a reduction made after you had reviewed every appropriations bill and reduced the appropriations by some $5 or $6 billion and expenditures by $1.5 billion. We conferred together and I recommended to the Congress and you subsequently approved taking 2 percent from payrolls and 10 percent from controllable expenditures. We therefore reduced appropriations almost $10 billion last session and expenditures over $4 billion. Now, that was in the budget last year.

I ask the Congress to recognize that there are certain selected programs that meet the Nation's most urgent needs and they have increased. We have insisted that decreases in very desirable but less urgent programs be made before we would approve any increases.

So I ask the Congress tonight:
—to hold its appropriations to the budget requests, and
—to act responsibly early this year by enacting the tax surcharge which for the average American individual amounts to about a penny out of each dollar's income.

This tax increase would yield about half of the $23 billion per year that we returned to the people in the tax reduction bills of 1964 and 1965.

This must be a temporary measure, which expires in less than 2 years. Congress can repeal it sooner if the need has passed. But Congress can never repeal inflation.

The leaders of American business and the leaders of American labor—those who really have power over wages and prices—must act responsibly, and in their Nation's interest by keeping increases in line with productivity. If our recognized leaders do not do this, they and those for whom they speak and all of us are going to suffer very serious consequences.

On January 1st, I outlined a program to reduce our balance of payments deficit sharply this year. We will ask the Congress to help carry out those parts of the program which require legislation. We must restore equilibrium to our balance of payments.

We must also strengthen the international monetary system. We have assured the world that America's full gold stock stands behind our commitment to maintain the price of gold at $35 an ounce. We must back this commitment by legislating now to free our gold reserves.

Americans, traveling more than any other people in history, took $4 billion out of their country last year in travel costs. We must try to reduce the travel deficit that we have of more than $2 billion. We are hoping that we can reduce it by $500 million—without unduly penalizing the travel of teachers, students, business people who have essential and necessary travel, or people who have relatives abroad whom they want to see. Even with this reduction of $500 million, the American people will still be traveling more overseas than they did in 1967, 1966, or 1965 or any other year in their history.

If we act together as I hope we can, I believe we can continue our economic expansion which has already broken all past records. And I hope that we can continue that expansion in the days ahead.

Each of these questions I have discussed with you tonight is a question of policy for our people. Therefore, each of them should be—and doubtless will be—debated by candidates for public office this year.

I hope those debates will be marked by new proposals and by a seriousness that matches the gravity of the questions themselves.

These are not appropriate subjects for narrow partisan oratory. They go to the heart of what we Americans are all about—all of us, Democrats and Republicans.

Tonight I have spoken of some of the goals I should like to see America reach. Many of them can be achieved this year—others by the time we celebrate our Nation's 200th birthday—the bicentennial of our independence.

Several of these goals are going to be very hard to reach. But the State of our Union will be much stronger 8 years from now on our 200th birthday if we resolve to reach these goals now. They are more important—much more important—than the identity of the party or the President who will then be in office.

These goals are what the fighting and our alliances are really meant to protect.

Can we achieve these goals?

Of course we can—if we will.

If ever there was a people who sought more than mere abundance, it is our people.

If ever there was a nation that was capable of solving its problems, it is this Nation.

If ever there were a time to know the pride and the excitement and the hope of being an American—it is this time.

So this, my friends, is the State of our Union: seeking, building, tested many times in this past year—and always equal to the test.

Thank you and good night.

15 Memorandums Directing a Reduction of Personnel and Official Travel Overseas. *January 18, 1968*

Memorandum to the Heads of Executive Departments and Establishments:

SUBJECT: Reduction of overseas personnel and official travel.

Today I sent the attached memorandum to the Secretary of State and the Director of the Bureau of the Budget directing them to undertake a four-part program to reduce United States personnel overseas. I expect each Department and agency to cooperate fully in this endeavor.

In addition, I hereby direct the head of each Department and agency to take steps to reduce U.S. official travel overseas to the minimum consistent with the orderly conduct of the Government's business abroad. I have asked private U.S. citizens to curtail their own travel outside the Western Hemisphere in the interest of reducing our balance of payments deficit. Federal agencies should participate in this effort.

The policy applies particularly to travel to international conferences held overseas. Heads of Departments and agencies will take immediate measures to

—reduce the number of such conferences attended.

—hold our attendance to a minimum and use U.S. personnel located at or near conference site to the extent possible.

—schedule conferences where possible, in the U.S. or countries in which excess currencies can be used.

You should present your plans for travel to international conferences held overseas to the Secretary of State, who, with the Director of the Budget, will undertake a special review of this matter.

This directive shall not apply to

—travel necessary for permanent change-of-station for U.S. employees, for their home leave, and for medical and rest and recuperative leave.

—travel made necessary by measures to reduce U.S. employment overseas outlined in the attached memorandum.

—travel financed from available excess foreign currencies.

You are requested to submit to the Director of the Budget, not later than March 15, a statement on the actions you have taken to reduce all types of overseas travel, the results expected from such actions, and your recommendations as to any additional measures that might be taken.

LYNDON B. JOHNSON

Memorandum for the Secretary of State and Director, Bureau of the Budget:

SUBJECT: Reduction in U.S. employees and official travel overseas

As a part of my program for dealing with our balance of payments problem, announced on New Year's day, I would like you jointly to take the specific measures to reduce U.S. employment and curtail official travel abroad, as outlined herein. Within the Department of State, the Senior Interdepartmental Group, chaired by Under Secretary Katzenbach, shall serve as the focal point for carrying out this directive.

You should make these reductions in a way which maintains the effectiveness of our international programs. I would like you to give particular attention to personnel reductions which can be made through relocation and regrouping of functions, the elimination of overlapping and duplication, the discontinuance of outdated and marginal activities, and a general streamlining of operations.

I. *Reduction in U.S. personnel overseas*

This directive applies to all employees under the jurisdiction of U.S. diplomatic missions and includes the representatives of all U.S. civilian agencies which have programs or activities overseas. It also includes military attaches, Military Assistance Advisory Groups, and other military personnel serving under the Ambassadors. It does not apply to U.S. personnel in Vietnam.

The Secretary of Defense has already initiated measures to reduce staffing of the military assistance program. I am asking the Secretary to complete these studies in time to support the goals outlined below.

You are directed to take the following actions:

1. *As a first step, you should proceed, with appropriate participation by U.S. Ambassadors and agencies, to reduce the total number of American personnel overseas by 10 percent,* with reductions of at least this magnitude applied to all missions of over 100. Similar reductions should be made in employment of foreign nationals and contract personnel. Your decisions on this first phase, which shall be final, shall be completed by April 1.

2. *You should also initiate a special intensive review of our activities and staffing in 10 countries with very large U.S. missions.* Your objective, in this second step, should be to reduce U.S. employment by substantially more than the 10 percent immediate reduction

taken in the first step. Your final decisions should be made on this phase by August 1.

3. *As a third step, you should proceed to extend these intensive reviews of U.S. activities to other countries beyond the first 10 as rapidly as feasible.*

4. *Simultaneously, you should initiate special studies from Washington of functional areas* aimed at reducing instructions, assignments, and activities which unnecessarily create the need for maintaining or increasing overseas staff, e.g., reporting requirements, consular work, and administrative support.

Clearly, reductions of this magnitude will involve major changes in agency staffing and personnel plans. I am asking Chairman Macy of the Civil Service Commission to assist agencies in solving attendant personnel problems and in facilitating the reassignment of employees returning to the United States.

II. *Curtailment in official travel*

I am requesting all Department and agency heads to reduce official travel outside the U.S. to the minimum consistent with orderly conduct of the Government's business. I would like you to give special attention to measures to minimize travel to international conferences.

By April 1, I would like you to report on the actions taken in this regard and to recommend any additional steps required.

LYNDON B. JOHNSON

NOTE: An announcement of a plan for an initial reduction in overseas personnel in response to the President's memorandums is published in the Weekly Compilation of Presidential Documents (vol. 4, p. 618). A memorandum from the Director, Bureau of the Budget, reporting on reduction in overseas travel was made public on November 6, 1968 (vol. 4, p. 1579).

35

16 Statement by the President on the Nuclear Nonproliferation Treaty To Be Presented to the Eighteen-Nation Disarmament Committee. *January* 18, 1968

I AM most heartened to learn that the Soviet Union will join the United States as Cochairman of the Eighteen-Nation Disarmament Committee, to submit a complete text of a treaty to stop the spread of nuclear weapons and that this draft treaty will be submitted today to the Committee in Geneva. This revised text includes an agreed safeguards article and other revisions that will make the treaty widely acceptable.

We have worked long and hard in an effort to draft a text that reflects the views of other nations. I believe the draft presented today represents a major accomplishment in meeting these legitimate interests.

The text submitted today must now be considered further by all governments. Following its review by the conference in Geneva, it will be considered by the General Assembly in the spring. It is my fervent hope that I will be able to submit it to the Senate of the United States for its advice and consent this year.

The draft treaty text submitted today clearly demonstrates an important fact. In the face of the differences that exist in the world, the two nations which carry the heaviest responsibility for averting the catastrophe of nuclear war can, with sufficient patience and determination, move forward. They can move forward toward the goal which all men of good will seek—a reversal of the arms race and a more secure peace based on our many common interests on this one small planet.

I believe history will look on this treaty as a landmark in the effort of mankind to avoid nuclear disaster while ensuring that all will benefit from the peaceful uses of nuclear energy.

This treaty will be a testament of man's faith in the future. In that spirit I commend it to all.

NOTE: The text of the treaty is printed in the Department of State Bulletin (vol. 59, p. 9).

For the President's remarks at the signing of the treaty on July 1, 1968, see Item 349.

17 Remarks to Members of the Democratic National Committee's Advisory Committee on Youth Activities. *January* 19, 1968

YOUR VISIT reminds me of something a great American once said to the youth of his generation: "There is nothing so fine as to be 21 and an American. One is for a fleeting instant—and the other is forever."

Some of you look younger than 21. I hope you all make the most of every fleeting instant of your youth, by giving all your energy, your imagination, and your strength to America.

Never in our history have the young had so many opportunities to serve. I spoke in my State of the Union address of the restlessness that stirs our country today. I welcome that. It is healthy—it is valuable—it is the stream that fires our dream—so long as it is a constructive restlessness—so long as you and your peers are builders, and not destroyers—so long as you tackle our problems with reason, intelligence and the knowledge that they are your problems—the future belongs to you and it will be as good or as bad as you make it.

Whatever else America is today, whatever it will be tomorrow, you can be dead sure of one thing: America is and will always be the land of opportunity. And, for the young American seeking opportunity to grow—opportunity for excitement, and meaning in his life—the Democratic Party gives you the greatest opportunity and the largest reward.

I cannot exaggerate how much your party needs you. I am not like the football star who was being interviewed by a professional coach. "I'm pretty great, coach," he said. "I run the hundred in under 10 seconds—on a muddy field. I'm a ferocious blocker. I punt 70 yards. And I pass for 60 yards—against the wind."

The coach was very impressed. "That's wonderful," he said, "but every player has some weakness—what's yours?"

"Well," said the hero, "I have been known to exaggerate a little."

But there is no exaggerating the size of the role you can play in your party—or the good it can mean for America. We need your ideas—new ideas. We want your leadership—fresh leadership. We depend on you to recharge our purpose and put new life and muscle in our programs. Your advisory committee can be a keystone in that new effort. You can carry my message and the encouragement of the Democratic Party to every campus, community and home in our country. Tell them you found a big sign hanging on the White House gate. It says: "Jobs Open—Youth Wanted—Youth Welcome."

Young people don't have a monopoly on virtue—but they do have a monopoly on energy, and we'd all like to see that energy put to work creatively in the precincts and not destructively in the picket lines.

Sometimes I am disturbed, just as you are, by the righteous anger which some of our younger people show—anger which isn't based on information. The best cure for that, I think, is a brush with reality. And that is part of your job: to give young Americans a chance to touch not only the surface of the problems and challenges we face, but to learn the difficulty and complexity of those problems.

Your biggest opportunity, I think, is to destroy—once and for all—the old myth that politics is a profession for old men in baggy suits. You know it isn't true.

I know it isn't true. Now you have a great opportunity to introduce to America the young men and women who are helping to lead this country: people like—Sandy Trowbridge—Joe Califano—Ramsey Clark—Cliff Alexander. You have an opportunity to point out that the average age of the President's close personal staff is close to under 35.

They are young men like you. If you haven't heard the names, you and every American have felt their influence. If any of you have a good idea, or a problem, or something itching you that you think I should know about—call up one of your own kind. Call some of the young men who make the White House tick.

Call Tom Johnson, Larry Levinson, Matt Nimetz, Dick Moose, Ervin Duggan, Charles Maguire, Ed Hamilton, Fred Bohen, Matt Coffey, Bill Blackburn, Sherwin Markman, Peter Rosenblatt, Ben Wattenberg, Stan Ross, Larry Temple, Jim Jones.

You may not have heard of any of them. But you can bet that they have heard of you. You can be certain that they are with you—in all that you want to do for your party and your country.

I will always be with you. I want you to succeed—and to inspire others by your success. I want the youth of America to combine in the greatest work of America—the work of public service, the noble work of the political profession. I will always be proud to share that profession and that work with you.

Your job, really, goes more deeply into our national life than politics. For you will be offering hundreds of thousands of young Americans a chance to answer some serious questions about our Nation's purpose, our Nation's goals, our Nation's future. I suppose there is no more difficult job than dealing with those questions. But I know there is no challenge that is more satisfying or more rewarding.

It has always been so for the young American. Let me read you a page from our past:

"We must not let ourselves be engulfed in the passing waves which obscure the current of progress. The sinfulness and weakness of man are evident to anyone who lives in the active world. But men are also good and great, kind and wise. Honor begets honor; trust begets trust; faith begets faith; and hope is the mainspring of life. I have lived with the reality of war, and I have praised soldiers; but the hope of honorable faithful peace is a greater thing and I have lived with that, too. That a man must live with both together is inherent in the nature of our present stormy stage of human progress, but it has also many times been the nature of

progress in the past, and it is not reason for despair.

"Those who read this book will mostly be younger than I, men of the generations who must bear the active part in the work ahead. Let them learn from our adventures what they can. Let them charge us with our failures and do better in their turn. But let them not turn aside from what they have to do, nor think that criticism excuses inaction. Let them have hope, and virtue, and let them believe in mankind and its future, for there is good as well as evil, and the man who tries to work for the good, believing in its eventual victory, while he may suffer setback and even disaster, will never know defeat. The only deadly sin I know is cynicism."

NOTE: The President spoke at 12:28 p.m. in the Fish Room at the White House to members of the Democratic National Committee's Advisory Committee on Youth Activities. During his remarks the President referred to Alexander B. Trowbridge, Secretary of Commerce, Joseph A. Califano, Jr., Special Assistant to the President, Ramsey Clark, Attorney General, and Clifford L. Alexander, Chairman of the Equal Employment Opportunity Commission. He also referred to several members of the White House staff including Assistant Press Secretary W. Thomas Johnson, Jr., Deputy Special Counsel to the President Lawrence E. Levinson, Special Counsel Larry E. Temple, and Special Assistant to the President James R. Jones.

As printed above, this item follows the text released by the White House Press Office.

18 The President's News Conference of January 19, 1968

INTENTION TO NOMINATE CLARK M. CLIFFORD AS SECRETARY OF DEFENSE

THE PRESIDENT. I asked you to come here.

[1.] I had a rather extended visit with Secretary McNamara this morning. We reviewed a number of departmental matters,

budget matters, and other matters that concerned the Defense Department, including the progress he has made on the budget and the statements that accompanied it, which would be related to it, as well as his expected time of departure.

We agreed that Mr. McNamara would

leave sometime in February, not later than March 1st, depending on the progress he makes there.

I discussed with him again this morning, as I have several times before, his resignation and, since his resignation, his successor.

I considered four or five men that he suggested, as well as a number of other men suggested by myself and others.

I asked Mr. Clark Clifford to serve as Secretary of Defense this morning, and he has accepted. I intend to submit his name to the Senate at a very early date. The Senate being willing, he will be available to qualify when Mr. McNamara completes his present assignment.

Mr. McNamara has had a truly outstanding record of Government service. He has served as Secretary of Defense longer than any other man has ever served in that job. He has had 7 grueling years, but with a very highly satisfactory performance to two Presidents, and I think, generally, to the people of this country and to the people of other countries with whom he dealt.

I have never known a more competent public official, a more energetic or dedicated one.

It is with great regret to the President, everyone in the White House and in the Cabinet, that he will be assuming other duties. We are pleased that Washington is not losing him. He will not be far away to counsel with us when appropriate.

I think that is all I have to say. I will be glad to take any questions.

QUESTIONS

[2.] Q. What were the factors that pointed to Mr. Clifford?

THE PRESIDENT. Well, first he was very high on the recommendations of everyone who made recommendations to me, including Mr. McNamara.

Second, I have very intimately worked with him when he participated in the consolidation of the Army and the Navy and the Air Force, in the unification program, unifying the Department as an adviser of another President.

In 1949 I worked with him in connection with my duties with the Armed Services Committee on the amendments to the unification act after he had gotten the bill together that was passed earlier.

He was in Mr. Bundy's job, or what we might say Mr. Rostow now does,[1] with the Defense Department during the Truman administration.

He was liaison with the Defense Department Secretary, Secretary Forrestal and later Secretary Johnson.[2]

He came into the service as a lieutenant (jg) and he went out as a captain. He is familiar with all the services.

President Kennedy appointed him as a member of a task force to study the Defense Department, its administration and its organization and its management, in 1960.

Following the Bay of Pigs, when the President set up a Foreign Intelligence Advisory Board, one of the most important boards to be selected by the President, Mr. Killian[3] headed that Board, but Mr. Clifford was a member of it. When Dr. Killian got sick, I believe he recommended Mr. Clifford to be his successor. Mr. Clifford became Chairman of it. He was Chairman when I became Presi-

---

[1] Former Special Assistant to the President McGeorge Bundy and Special Assistant to the President Walt W. Rostow.

[2] James V. Forrestal and Louis A. Johnson, former Secretaries of Defense.

[3] Dr. James R. Killian served as Chairman of the President's Foreign Intelligence Advisory Board from May 5, 1961, to March 7, 1963.

dent. I continued him in that capacity, as I did most of the men serving with President Kennedy.

He has been a very wise and prudent counselor to many Presidents, and certainly to me, in the field of defense, and in the field of diplomacy.

As Chairman of that Board, he had to work very closely with the State Department. Secretary Rusk considered him eminently qualified and one of the finest men who could be available for the assignment. He has traveled throughout the world in his capacity as adviser to the President and Chairman of this Board. He has been in the Far East and South Vietnam I believe three times in the recent years. He was my counselor at Manila.

When we were planning the democratic developments in South Vietnam that led to the election of the Constituent Assembly, the President and the Vice President, and the Members of Congress, he was there.

He has been a counselor on most of the important decisions made in many of the international fields from defense to strength to weapons to actions.

I think he is universally regarded by those with whom I have talked as being a man that the Government ought to have if we could get him.

We have had such a high type of servant in the Secretary of Defense that I think Mr. Clifford did not feel in a position to turn me down just "period" when I asked him to do it.

I made the decision finally today, although I had him under consideration since his name was first mentioned last August, and again in November.

I saw some squib that some speculative reporter wrote that indicated he might be under consideration for this assignment. I commented to him at a social affair one eve-

ning, "I understand you are a candidate for the Secretary of Defense." He flushed a little bit and said he was not a candidate; he was not.

But if the Senate is willing, he is going to be Secretary of Defense.

Q. Mr. President, occasionally a Cabinet officer comes over with an understanding of serving for a year or some specified time. Is that the case here?

THE PRESIDENT. No. We have not discussed the term. I asked him if he would accept the appointment. He cleared his throat, and I said, "I expect to announce your appointment. If you would like to talk to me about it beforehand, I would be glad to see you."

He said all right, he would come over. He came over and he talked to me. He is aware that he is going to be announced, but he is not aware of how long he will serve, nor am I.

Q. Mr. President, was he given time to discuss it with his wife?

THE PRESIDENT. If she is not in the beauty parlor; if her whereabouts are not unknown.

Q. Did you just talk with him?

THE PRESIDENT. I talked to him here today.

Q. Will there be any other changes in the Defense Department?

THE PRESIDENT. I am sure there will be changes from time to time in all the departments, but I don't have any that I am aware of at this moment.

Merriman Smith, United Press International: Thank you, Mr. President.

NOTE: President Johnson's one hundred and seventeenth news conference was held in his office at the White House at 3:27 p.m. on Friday, January 19, 1968. As printed above, this item follows the text of the Official White House Transcript.

Later the same day Mr. Clifford met with reporters at the White House in the office of George E. Christian, Special Assistant to the President. The text of the news briefing is printed in the Weekly

Compilation of Presidential Documents (vol. 4, p. 86).

A biographical sketch of Mr. Clifford was also released by the White House on January 19 (4 Weekly Comp. Pres. Docs., p. 85).

19 Remarks to the Press on Announcing a Plan for a Pilot Health and Housing Project in Washington. *January* 20, 1968

DR. SWAN and the National Medical Association, Mayor Washington, and other leaders here have outlined to me this morning a plan that they are working on in cooperation with the Secretaries of HEW and HUD that will get at one of the problems that is troubling us all, namely, the care of our aged and the medical treatment of our aged and the housing of our aged.

They will review with you some of the details of what they have in mind. We are going to try to evolve a program here in the District of Columbia that will be a model and a sample for the rest of the country.

We are doing that in several fields. Mayor Washington can go into that. He has made remarkable progress since he took over a short time ago.

We don't want this to be just a conversation piece. We want results. We are planning an extended-care facility in the vicinity of Howard University. This will operate in close association with the resources of the Howard Medical School. It would be established for this purpose. We don't want to tie it down, but just to give you some vision of what we might be talking about, it would be in the neighborhood of a $3 million investment in comprehensive health service, including ultimately: (1) a medical building equipped for group medical practice, (2) a skilled nursing home, (3) social care institutions, (4) housing for the elderly, and (5) a neighborhood service center for our senior citizens.

So here in that complex you could have a place where your mother and father could go in their old age and be decently housed, and where a group of doctors could have facilities for treating people in that area, connected with the Howard University Medical School, where they have some several thousand students in undergraduate work in law and medicine.

There is nothing I know of that we need more of in this country than our health and housing care for the poor and for the elderly, unless it is housing care for the young. The old have trouble walking and the young don't know how. That is why we had infant care, jobs, housing, and health in our message the other day.

We are trying to set up a sample. We spent Saturday morning talking about it.

I also have been giving them a little of my philosophy about what we ought to do with the time allotted. They can go into any details they want.

Mayor, you might outline for this group, if they are interested, the five things on this list here.

The Secretaries of HEW and HUD can answer anything they want to. If any of you have any questions you want to ask me, I will answer. I don't want to have a press conference, but I will take some questions before I leave.

QUESTIONS

Q. Mr. President, this is the third or fourth grant that you have arranged for Mayor Washington of this kind since he took office. Could you expand on that a little? Is this something you are going to try to do as long as you can to make Washington a model by providing this kind of funds and assistance from your department?

THE PRESIDENT. Yes. We have the District of Columbia as one of the 14 cities that are designated to participate in the 14-city pilot program for comprehensive one-step neighborhood service centers. That is being funded.

There is a lot of gobbledygook there, but we want a neighborhood service center. We are trying it in 14 cities. If it functions there, we can extend it.

We want the Nation's Capital to be one of the first cities in a concentrated unemployment program. We talked about that the other night. We are going to try to get 500,-000 hard-core jobs.

We want the Nation's Capital to have a 335-acre new-town in-town project to provide low- and middle-income housing for 20,000 to 25,000 residents.

We want the Nation's Capital to be in the President's pilot five-city job program. That is the forerunner of the national program announced in the State of the Union the other night.

We want Washington to be a model city that will take all of these Federal services and give them special attention. It is one of the 63 model cities for which we are asking $1 billion in the budget this year.

I don't want to make a speech about it, but the one thing that I really want to do in the few months or few years I may be in the Presidency is get a good, inexpensive house where poor people can live under sanitary conditions. We have not done that yet.

We have a lot of FHA, public housing and high rises and all these fancy names, but we just don't have some concrete walls and concrete floors that do not fall down and sanitary wash basins and shower—where a real poor person can afford them.

We have to do that. I want to get a nursing home where your mothers and fathers, mother-in-law and father-in-law—when they get to a certain age and they will not live with you; they don't want their son-in-law or daughter-in-law taking care of them—where they can go and live out their life in decency.

It takes a lot of people working on a baby to keep a baby sanitary. I know, I have been babysitting.

My mother died of cancer. It took a lot of people to care for her. She protested up until the day she died that she did not want anyone looking after her. She was a proud woman.

There are a lot of them in the country. I want to see that they have a nursing home and medical facilities where they can go with their chins up and their chests out—and proud. That is what we are trying to work on here this morning.

Dr. Swan has a plan for a $3 million program. With the fine medical facilities of Howard University, we are going to put it in an area where these people can get it. We are going to try to provide economical housing with facilities and built in a way where they don't have to climb a lot of steps or climb a tree like the tomboys.

But it will be something planned for older people. That is what we are working on. It is a challenge to Bob Weaver and John Gardner and Dr. Swan. They are going to try to remind some of you young people that you do not spend enough time these days really carrying out the injunctions of "Honour thy father and thy mother."

Those of you who are fortunate enough

to be blessed—those of us who are here today—have to spend a little of our time thinking of those who are too weak to take care of themselves. It may be a baby who was born handicapped because his mother had German measles. We wiped that out last year. We have that behind us but there are so many other things we have to do.

That is what we have been talking about. Does that answer your question?

Q. Yes.

Q. Mr. President, have you a specific timetable for this project?

THE PRESIDENT. The quicker the better. Yesterday. It will take months. We will survey, explore, consider, collaborate, have criteria and all of these gobbledygooks, but if we just hammer enough, it will get done.

I have tried to break through as many ravines as I could this morning to get in down where you could understand what we are talking about. I hope we will be moving along. Dr. Weaver and Dr. Gardner can tell you, with Dr. Swan, how long it will take.

But I wish it had been yesterday. We are too late. This restlessness is justified in situations like this. Some of you were with me in San Antonio and you saw what could be done in that apartment we built there for old people.

We are trying to do something about it. I am trying to do something about it for the young, for the old, and I hope those of us in the middle can help on it while we can.

Q. On a national basis, aside from this timetable, if this works out, how long might it be before we see this kind of an operation nationally?

THE PRESIDENT. I think that depends on who is President, how much Congress votes, how successful we are on the pilot project.

I would hope that it would go like wildfire.

If we could ever get a "T" model nursing home that could be produced like the "T" model Ford was, I believe it would catch on and go over the country. Johnson City, Texas, needs a good one. Stonewall, Texas, needs a good one.

The bigger you are, the more it is needed. The question is how do we plan it, and how do we enlist the attention of the people of this country to help us get it built.

This is just the first step. The Federal Government can go in to 90 percent of the funds, underwriting them. This National Medical Association has gone out and has taken their resources.

They have several hundred thousand dollars in the bank, and they will put that up. They will provide the management and the direction. If it works, maybe other associations throughout the country will do it. If it fails, you fellows will have a field day.

NOTE: The President spoke at 12:30 p.m. in the Cabinet Room at the White House. In his opening words he referred to Dr. Lionel F. Swan, President of the National Medical Association, and Walter E. Washington, Commissioner of the District of Columbia. Following the President's remarks John W. Gardner, Secretary of Health, Education, and Welfare, Robert C. Weaver, Secretary of Housing and Urban Development, and Dr. Swan responded to further questions from the press (4 Weekly Comp. Pres. Docs., p. 97).

The plan was transmitted to the President with a letter from Secretaries Gardner and Weaver dated January 18 and released January 20. The letter stated that HEW, HUD, and the National Medical Association had agreed to join in a pilot undertaking to develop comprehensive health and housing facilities for the urban poor, particularly the elderly, in a number of cities throughout the Nation. The text of the letter and the plan is printed in the Weekly Compilation of Presidential Documents (vol. 4, p. 100).

As printed above, this item follows the text released by the White House Press Office.

20 Statement by the President on the Proposed Pilot Health and Housing Project in Washington. *January 20, 1968*

I BELIEVE this project can offer badly needed health and housing care for the elderly and the poor in Washington. I hope it will serve as an example for other cities which lack adequate health care in poverty areas.

The National Medical Association deserves great credit for taking the lead in sponsoring this project. It is an example of how concerned citizens in a voluntary association can work with government to solve urgent problems.

NOTE: The President's statement was made public as part of a White House release announcing the pilot health and housing project for the elderly and poor in Washington which the President covered in greater detail in his remarks to the press on the same day (see Item 19). The release is printed in the Weekly Compilation of Presidential Documents (vol. 4, p. 99).

21 Message to the Congress Transmitting Annual Reports on the Foreign Assistance Program for 1966 and 1967. *January 22, 1968*

To the Congress of the United States:

One of the clearest lessons of modern times is the destructive power of man's oldest enemies. Where hunger, disease and ignorance abound, the conditions of violence breed.

For two decades, this lesson has helped to shape a fundamental American purpose: to keep conflict from starting by helping to remove its causes and thus insure our own security in a peaceful world.

Four Presidents and ten Congresses have affirmed their faith in this national purpose with a program of foreign assistance.

The documents I transmit to the Congress today—the Annual Reports of our Foreign Assistance Program for fiscal 1966 and 1967—detail this program in action over a 24-month period. Their pages describe projects which range from the training of teachers in Bolivia to the fertilization of farmland in Vietnam—from the construction of a hydroelectric dam in Ethiopia to inoculation against measles in Nigeria. The reports tell of classrooms built and textbooks distributed, of milk and grain fortified with vitamins, of roads laid and wells dug, and doctors and nurses educated.

These are accomplishments largely unnoted in the swift rush of events. Their effect cannot be easily charted. But they are nonetheless real. In the barrios and the rice fields of the developing world they have helped to improve the conditions of life and expand the margin of hope for millions struggling to overcome centuries of poverty.

But the fundamental challenge still remains. The forces of human need still stalk this globe. Ten thousand people a day—most of them children—die from malnutrition. Diseases long conquered by science cut down life in villages still trapped in the past. In many vast areas, four out of every five persons cannot write their names.

These are tragedies which summon our compassion. More urgently, they threaten our security. They create the conditions of despair in which the fires of violence smoulder.

Our investment in foreign aid is small. In the period covered by these reports, it was only 5 percent of the amount we spent for our defense.

The dividends from that investment are lives saved and schools opened and hunger relieved. But they are more. The ultimate triumphs of foreign aid are victories of prevention. They are the shots that did not sound, the blood that did not spill, the treasure that did not have to be spent to stamp out spreading flames of violence.

These are victories not of war—but over wars that did not start.

I believe the American people—who know war's cost in lives and fortune—endorse the investment for peace they have made in their program of foreign aid.

LYNDON B. JOHNSON

The White House
January 22, 1968

NOTE: The reports are entitled "The Foreign Assistance Program, Annual Report to the Congress, Fiscal Year 1966" (Government Printing Office, 1967, 77 pp.) and "The Foreign Assistance Program, Annual Report to the Congress, Fiscal Year 1967" (Government Printing Office, 1967, 99 pp.).

22 Statement by the President on Senator Lister Hill's Decision To Retire From the Senate. *January 22, 1968*

LISTER HILL has been a giant in the Congress for nearly four and a half decades. He has built an enduring monument of good works, especially in the field of health. He will be sorely missed.

NOTE: Senator Lister Hill of Alabama served in the House of Representatives 1923–1938 and in the

Senate since 1938. The President's statement followed an announcement by Senator Hill that he planned to retire at the end of the 90th Congress in January 1969.

The statement was posted on the bulletin board in the Press Room at the White House. It was not made public in the form of a White House press release.

23 Message to the Congress Transmitting Third Annual Report on the International Coffee Agreement. *January 22, 1968*

To the Congress of the United States:

I am transmitting to you my Third Annual Report on the operation of the International Coffee Agreement as required by P.L. 89–23.

During the past year, the 65 member countries of the Agreement representing over 98 percent of the world trade in coffee continued to work together to stabilize coffee prices at levels equitable to both producers and consumers. Controls over export quotas were strengthened. Selective quota adjustments assured consumers of an adequate supply of various types of coffee at

reasonable price levels.

The present Agreement expires on September 30 of this year. Negotiations on an extended Agreement are underway with emphasis on production controls and a diversification and development fund. These measures are designed to hasten the day when production is brought into balance with demand and the controls being implemented under the Agreement can be placed on a standby basis.

The International Coffee Agreement continues to be of major benefit to both producers and consumers and merits the further support of the United States.

LYNDON B. JOHNSON

The White House
January 22, 1968

NOTE: The report, entitled "1967 Annual Report of the President to the Congress on the International Coffee Agreement" (18 pages, plus annexes), was published by the Department of State.

24 Special Message to the Congress—"To Earn a Living: The Right of Every American." *January 23, 1968*

To the Congress of the United States:

In this, my first message to the Congress following the State of the Union Address, I propose:

—A $2.1 billion manpower program, the largest in the Nation's history, to help Americans who want to work get a job.

—The Nation's first comprehensive Occupational Health and Safety Program, to protect the worker while he is on the job.

THE QUESTION FOR OUR DAY

Twenty years ago, after a cycle of depression, recovery and war, America faced an historic question: Could we launch what President Truman called "a positive attack upon the ever-recurring problems of mass unemployment and ruinous depression"?

That was the goal of the Employment Act of 1946. The answer was a long time in forming. But today there is no longer any doubt.

We can see the answer in the record of seven years of unbroken prosperity.

We can see it in this picture of America today:

75 million of our people are working—in jobs that are better paying and more secure than ever before.

Seven and a half million new jobs have been created in the last four years, more than 5,000 every day. This year will see that number increased by more than 1½ million.

In that same period, the unemployment rate has dropped from 5.7 percent to 3.8 percent—the lowest in more than a decade.

The question for our day is this: in an economy capable of sustaining high employment, how can we assure every American, who is willing to work, the right to earn a living?

We have always paid lip service to that right.

But there are many Americans for whom the right has never been real:

—The boy who becomes a man without developing the ability to earn a living.

—The citizen who is barred from a job because of other men's prejudices.

—The worker who loses his job to a machine, and is told he is too old for anything else.

—The boy or girl from the slums whose summers are empty because there is nothing to do.

—The man and the woman blocked from productive employment by barriers rooted in poverty: lack of health, lack of education, lack of training, lack of motivation.

Their idleness is a tragic waste both of the human spirit and of the economic resources of a great Nation.

It is a waste that an enlightened Nation should not tolerate.

It is a waste that a Nation concerned by

disorders in its city streets *cannot* tolerate.

This Nation has already begun to attack that waste.

In the years that we have been building our unprecedented prosperity, we have also begun to build a network of manpower programs designed to meet and match individual needs with individual opportunities.

OUR MANPOWER PROGRAM NETWORK

Until just a few years ago, our efforts consisted primarily of maintaining employment offices throughout the country and promoting apprenticeship training.

The Manpower Development Training Act, passed in 1962, was designed to equip the worker with new skills when his old skills were outdistanced by technology. That program was greatly strengthened and expanded in 1963, 1965 and again in 1966 to serve the disadvantaged as well. In fiscal 1969, it will help over 275,000 citizens.

Our manpower network grew as the Nation launched its historic effort to conquer poverty:

—*The Job Corps* gives young people from the poorest families education and training they need to prepare for lives as productive and self-supporting citizens. In fiscal 1969 the Job Corps will help almost 100,000 children of the poor.

—*The Neighborhood Youth Corps* enables other poor youngsters to serve their community and themselves at the same time. Last year the Congress expanded the program to include adults as well. In fiscal 1969, the Neighborhood Youth Corps will help over 560,000 citizens.

—Others, such as *Work Experience, New Careers, Operation Mainstream,* and the *Work Incentive Program,* are directed toward the employment problems of poor adults. In fiscal 1969, 150,-000 Americans will receive the benefits of training through these programs.

These are pioneering efforts. They all work in different ways. Some provide for training alone. Others combine training with work. Some are full-time. Others are part-time.

One way to measure the scope of these programs is to consider how many men and women have been helped:

—In fiscal 1963: 75,000.

—In fiscal 1967: more than 1 million.

But the real meaning of these figures is found in the quiet accounts of lives that have been changed:

—In Oregon, a seasonal farm worker was struggling to sustain his eight children on $46 a week. Then he received on-the-job training as a welder. Now he can support his family on an income three times as high.

—In Pennsylvania, a truck driver lost his job because of a physical disability and had to go on welfare. He learned a new skill. Now he is self-reliant again, working as a clerk with a city Police Department.

—In Kansas, a high school dropout was salvaged from what might have been an empty life. He learned a trade with the Job Corps. Now he has a decent job with an aircraft company.

Across America, examples such as these attest to the purpose and the success of our programs to give a new start to men and women who have the will to work for a better life.

These are good programs. They are contributing to the strength of America. And they must continue.

But they must reach even further.

47

I will ask the Congress to appropriate $2.1 billion for our manpower programs for fiscal 1969.

—This is the largest such program in the Nation's history.

—It is a 25 percent increase over fiscal 1968.

—It will add $442 million to our manpower efforts.

In a vigorous, flourishing economy, this is a program for justice as well as for jobs.

These funds will enable us to continue and strengthen existing programs, and to advance to new ground as well.

With this program, we can reach 1.3 million Americans, including those who have rarely if ever been reached before—the hard-core unemployed.

THE CONCENTRATED EMPLOYMENT PROGRAM

Our past efforts, vital as they are, have not yet effectively reached the hard-core unemployed.

These hard-core are America's forgotten men and women. Many of them have not worked for a long time. Some have never worked at all. Some have held only odd jobs. Many have been so discouraged by life that they have lost their sense of purpose.

In the Depression days of the 1930's, jobless men lined the streets of our cities seeking work. But today, the jobless are often hard to find. They are the invisible poor of our Nation.

Last year I directed the Secretary of Labor to bring together in one unified effort all the various manpower and related programs which could help these people in the worst areas of some of our major cities and in the countryside.

The Concentrated Employment Program was established for this purpose.

Its first task was to find the hard-core un-

employed, to determine who they are, and where and how they live.

Now we have much of that information.

500,000 men and women who have never had jobs—or who face serious employment problems—are living in the slums of our 50 largest cities.

The first detailed profile we have ever had of these unemployed Americans reveals that substantial numbers

—Lack adequate education and job training.

—Have other serious individual problems—such as physical handicaps—which impair their earning ability.

—Are Negroes, Mexican-Americans, Puerto Ricans, or Indians.

—Are teenagers, or men over 45.

As the unemployed were identified, the Concentrated Employment Program set up procedures for seeking them out, counseling them, providing them with health and education services, training them—all with the purpose of directing them into jobs or into the pipeline to employment.

As part of the new manpower budget, I am recommending expansion of the Concentrated Employment Program.

That program now serves 22 urban and rural areas. In a few months it will expand to 76. With the funds I am requesting, it can operate in 146.

JOB OPPORTUNITIES IN THE PRIVATE SECTOR

The ultimate challenge posed by the hard-core unemployed is to prepare rejected men and women for productive employment—for dignity, independence and self-sufficiency.

In our thriving economy, where jobs in a rapidly growing private sector are widely available and the unemployment rate is low, the "make-work" programs of the 1930's are not the answer to today's problem.

The answer, I believe, is to train the hard-core unemployed for work in private industry:

—The jobs are there: six out of every seven working Americans are employed in the private sector.

—Government-supported on-the-job training is the most effective gateway to meaningful employment: nine out of every ten of those who have received such training have gone on to good jobs.

—Industry knows how to train people for the jobs on which its profits depend.

That is why, late last year, we stepped up the effort to find jobs in private industry. With the help of American businessmen, we launched a $40 million test training program in five of our larger cities.

The program was built around three basic principles:

—To engage private industry fully in the problems of the hard-core unemployed.

—To pay with Government funds the *extra* costs of training the disadvantaged for steady employment.

—To simplify government paperwork and make all government services easily and readily available to the employer.

The Urgent Task

With that work, we prepared our blueprints. We have built the base for action.

Encouraged by our test program and by the progress that American industry has made in similar efforts, we should now move forward.

To press the attack on the problem of the jobless in our cities, I propose that we launch the Job Opportunities in Business Sector (JOBS) Program—a new partnership between government and private industry to train and hire the hard-core unemployed.

I propose that we devote $350 million to support this partnership—starting now with $106 million from funds available in our manpower programs for fiscal 1968, and increasing that amount to $244 million in fiscal 1969.

Our target is to put 100,000 men and women on the job by June 1969 and 500,000 by June 1971. To meet that target, we need prompt approval by the Congress of the request for funds for our manpower programs.

This is high priority business for America.

The future of our cities is deeply involved. And so is the strength of our Nation.

How This New Program Will Work

Our objective, in partnership with the business community, is to restore the jobless to useful lives through productive work.

There can be no rigid formulas in this program. For it breaks new ground.

The situation calls, above all, for flexibility and cooperation.

Essentially, the partnership will work this way:

The government will identify and locate the unemployed.

The company will train them, and offer them jobs.

The company will bear the normal cost of training, as it would for any of its new employees.

But with the hard-core unemployed there will be extra costs.

These men will be less qualified than those the employer would normally hire. So additional training will often be necessary.

But even more than this will be needed. Some of these men and women will need transportation services. Many will have to be taught to read and write. They will have health problems to be corrected. They will have to be counseled on matters ranging from personal care to proficiency in work.

These are the kinds of extra costs that will be involved.

Where the company undertakes to provide these services, it is appropriate that the Government pay the extra costs as part of the national manpower program.

The Concentrated Employment Program, in many areas, will provide manpower services to support the businessman's effort.

A National Alliance of Businessmen

This is a tall order for American business. But the history of American business is the history of triumph over challenge.

And the special talents of American business can make this program work.

To launch this program, I have called on American industry to establish a National Alliance of Businessmen.

The Alliance will be headed by Mr. Henry Ford II.

Fifteen of the Nation's top business leaders will serve on its Executive Board. Leading business executives from the Nation's 50 largest cities will spearhead the effort in their own communities.

The Alliance will be headed by Mr. Henry concerned not only with the policy but with the operation of the program.

It will:

—Help put 500,000 hard-core unemployed into productive business and industrial jobs in the next three years.

—Give advice to the Secretaries of Labor and Commerce on how this program can work most effectively, and how we can cut government "red tape."

The Alliance will also have another vital mission: to find productive jobs for 200,000 needy youth this summer—an experience that will lead them back to school in the fall, or on to other forms of education, training or permanent employment.

The Alliance will work closely in this venture with the Vice President. As Chairman of the President's Council on Youth Opportunity he will soon meet with the Alliance and with the Mayors of our 50 largest cities to advance this pressing work.

The Rewards of Action

The rewards of action await us at every level.

To the individual, a paycheck is a passport to self-respect and self-sufficiency.

To the worker's family, a paycheck offers the promise of a fuller and better life—in material advantages and in new educational opportunities.

Our society as a whole will benefit when welfare recipients become taxpayers, and new job holders increase the Nation's buying power.

These are dollars and cents advantages.

But there is no way to estimate the value of a decent job that replaces hostility and anger with hope and opportunity.

There is no way to estimate the respect of a boy or girl for his parent who has earned a place in our world.

There is no way to estimate the stirring of the American dream of learning, saving, and building a life of independence.

Finally, employment is one of the major weapons with which we will eventually conquer poverty in this country, and banish it forever from American life.

Our obligation is clear. We must intensify the work we have just begun. The new partnership I have proposed in this message will help reach that lost legion among us, and make them productive citizens.

It will not be easy.

But until the problem of joblessness is solved, these men and women will remain wasted Americans—each one a haunting reminder of our failure.

Each one of these waiting Americans represents a potential victory we have never been able to achieve in all the years of this Nation.

Until now.

A STRENGTHENED MANPOWER ADMINISTRATION

The programs I have discussed are the visible evidence of a Nation's commitment to provide a job for every citizen who wants it, and who will work for it.

Less visible is the machinery—the planning, the management and administration— which turns these programs into action and carries them to the people who need them.

I recently directed the Secretary of Labor to strengthen and streamline the Manpower Administration—the instrument within the Federal Government which manages almost 80 percent of our manpower programs.

That effort is now close to completion.

But we must have top administrators now—both here in Washington and in the eight regions across the country in which these manpower programs will operate.

As part of our new manpower budget, I am requesting the Congress to approve more than 600 new positions for the Manpower Administration. These will include 16 of the highest Civil Service grades.

The central fact about all our manpower programs is that they are local in nature. The jobs and opportunities exist in the cities and communities of this country. That is where the people who need them live. That is where the industries are—and the classrooms, the day care centers, and the health clinics.

What is required is a system to link Federal efforts with the resources at the State and local levels.

We already have the framework, the Cooperative Area Manpower Planning System (CAMPS) which we started last year.

Now I propose that we establish it for the long term.

CAMPS will operate at every level—Federal, regional, State and local. At each level, it will pull together all the manpower services which bear on jobs.

But its greatest impact will be at the local level, where it will:

—Help the communities develop their own manpower blueprints;

—Survey job needs;

—Assure that all federal programs to help the job seeker are available.

As part of our manpower budget, I am requesting $11 million to fund the Cooperative Area Manpower Planning System in fiscal 1969.

OCCUPATIONAL SAFETY AND HEALTH

The programs outlined so far in this message will train the man out of work for a job, and help him find one.

To give the American worker the complete protection he needs, we must also safeguard him against hazards on the job.

Today, adequate protection does not exist.

It is to the shame of a modern industrial Nation, which prides itself on the productivity of its workers, that each year:

—14,500 workers are killed on the job.

—2.2 million workers are injured.

—250 million man-days of productivity are wasted.

—$1.5 billion in wages are lost.

—The result: a loss of $5 billion to the economy.

This loss of life, limb and sight must end.

An attack must be launched at the source of the evil—against the conditions which cause hazards and invite accidents.

The reasons for these staggering losses are clear. Safety standards are narrow. Research lags behind. Enforcement programs are weak. Trained safety specialists fall far short of the need.

The Federal Government offers the worker today only a patchwork of obsolete and ineffective laws.

The major law—Walsh-Healey—was passed more than 3 decades ago. Its coverage is limited. It applies only to a worker performing a government contract. Last year about half of the work force was covered, and then only part of the time.

It is more honored in the breach than observed. Last year, investigations revealed a disturbing number of violations in the plants of government contractors.

Comprehensive protection under other Federal laws is restricted to about a million workers in specialized fields—longshoremen and miners, for example.

Only a few states have modern laws to protect the worker's health and safety. Most have no coverage or laws that are weak and deficient.

The gap in worker protection is wide and glaring—and it must be closed by a strong and forceful new law.

It must be our goal to protect every one of America's 75 million workers while they are on the job.

I am submitting to the Congress the Occupational Safety and Health Act of 1968.

Here, in broad outline, is what this measure will do.

For more than 50 million workers involved in interstate commerce it will:

—Strengthen the authority and resources of the Secretary of Health, Education, and Welfare to conduct an extensive program of research. This will provide the needed information on which new standards can be developed.

—Empower the Secretary of Labor to set and enforce those standards.

—Impose strong sanctions, civil and criminal, on those who endanger the health and safety of the American working man.

For American workers in intra-state commerce, it will provide, for the first time, federal help to the States to start and strengthen their own health and safety programs. These grants will assist the States to

—Develop plans to protect the worker.

—Collect information on occupational injuries and diseases.

—Set and enforce standards.

—Train inspectors and other needed experts.

Conclusion

When Walt Whitman heard America singing a century ago, he heard that sound in workers at their jobs.

Today that sound rings from thousands of factories and mills, work benches and assembly lines, stronger than ever before.

Jobs are the measure of how far we have come.

But it is right to measure a Nation's efforts not only by what it has done, but by what remains to be done.

In this message, I have outlined a series of proposals dealing with the task ahead— to give reality to the right to earn a living.

These proposals deal with jobs.

But their reach is far broader.

The demand for more jobs is central to the expression of all our concerns and our aspirations—about cities, poverty, civil rights, and the improvement of men's lives.

I urge the Congress to give prompt and

favorable consideration to the proposals in this message.

LYNDON B. JOHNSON

The White House
January 23, 1968

NOTE: For the President's statement upon signing the Health Manpower Act of 1968, see Item 447.

On October 11, 1968, the President approved a bill which contained a provision appropriating funds for the Manpower Administration, Department of Labor (Public Law 90–557, 82 Stat. 969).

A list of the officers and members of the National Alliance of Businessmen was made public by the President in his remarks to the press following the transmittal of the message (see Item 25). For the President's statement following a meeting with the officers in connection with the JOBS program, see Item 92.

25   Remarks to the Press on the Message "To Earn a Living: The Right of Every American." *January 23, 1968*

GEORGE CHRISTIAN asked that I make a brief statement similar to the one that I made with the members of the appropriate congressional committees earlier this morning about our JOBS program.

Six out of every seven jobs are in the private industry. Nine out of every ten jobs that we train people for are filled by private industry. When we train 10 people, we get nine of them jobs.

So we feel very deeply that since the greatest hope for jobs ultimately under our setup is in industry itself, and since the people that we have trained in the past have been successful in breaking into industry, we should now—with the cooperation of the businessmen of this country and the labor people in this country—try to get at the hardcore unemployed in this country and get them into training and shortly thereafter into jobs.

So we have revised our manpower program that was training only 75,000 a year in 1963 and is now training over 1 million a year.

Last year, we had a million and a half new jobs in this country. The last 4 years, we have had 7½ million new jobs in this country. We have to try to give additional training to fill more new jobs because we have people with new skills.

I have asked Mr. Henry Ford II to head up this National Alliance of Businessmen and employers. He will be Chairman of the new committee. He has accepted and will come to Washington this weekend to meet with me and with the other businessmen associated with him.

I have asked Mr. J. Paul Austin, the president of the Coca-Cola Company, to be Vice Chairman of this committee.

Mr. Leo C. Beebe, the vice president of the Ford Motor Company, is here now. He will be the Executive Vice Chairman in charge of this Alliance committee. Mr. Beebe is standing here by Secretary Wirtz and will participate in the briefing.

We have two or three additional names that we have not cleared but, before some of these that have been cleared leak, I think I had better just give them to you.

Mr. Roger P. Sonnabend, president of the Hotel Corporation of America, from Region I in Boston (Maine, New Hampshire, Connecticut, Rhode Island, Massachusetts, Vermont).

Region II (New York, New Jersey, Virgin Islands, Puerto Rico), Mr. Harold S. Geneen, chairman of the board of IT&T.

Region III (Washington, D.C., West Virginia, Maryland, Delaware, North Carolina, Pennsylvania, Virginia), John D. Harper,

53

president and chief executive officer of the Aluminum Company of America.

Region IV, Atlanta (Tennessee, Alabama, Mississippi, Georgia, South Carolina, Florida), Mr. J. Paul Austin, president of the Coca-Cola Company.

Region V, James Cook, president of the Illinois Bell Telephone Company (Illinois, Michigan, Ohio, Wisconsin, Indiana, Minnesota, and Kentucky).

Region VI, Kansas City, James C. McDonnell, Jr., who is the largest employer in the State. He is chairman of the board of McDonnell-Douglas Aircraft. This covers Missouri, Iowa, North Dakota, South Dakota, Kansas, Utah, Nebraska, Wyoming, Montana, Idaho, Colorado.

Region VII, Clyde Skeen, president of Ling-Temco-Vought (Texas, New Mexico, Oklahoma, Louisiana, Arkansas).

Region VIII, San Francisco, Walter A. Haas, Jr., president, Levi Straus and Company (Arizona, California, Washington, Oregon, Nevada, Alaska, Hawaii).

A. L. Nickerson, chairman of Mobil Oil, will be an at-large member.

There are also some additional names that will be coming shortly.

We plan to devote $350 million in putting 100,000 men and women on the job by June of 1969. The 3-year target is 500,000.

In addition to these 15 top business leaders—I have given you a partial list—we will have leading business executives from the 50 largest cities who will assume responsibility in their city and then name a committee. The regional man will help us work to get a city man; the city man will get a committee. We will try to get to the grass roots.

We are very pleased that the labor people are cooperative and helpful on this. They were thoroughly briefed on it. The NAM [National Association of Manufacturers], the Business Council, the Chamber of Commerce—we have gone to them for suggestions both for personnel and the program itself.

We know that in the past we have had high levels of unemployment. It has dropped from 7 million to 3.7 million, the lowest in 10 years. We want it to drop more.

In the past, it has been necessary for Government to go out and develop make-work projects. We find that in many of the large cities employers are asking for workers and workers are asking for employers—but they cannot take each other because the workers don't have the skill to do the job the industry needs.

Now industry is going to work with us to help them attain that skill. I hope that it won't be necessary for us to have any more public employment programs similar to what we had back in the thirties.

We think this is a better route. We are going to try it. It may not succeed. We don't want to predict defeat to begin with, but it is better to have tried and failed than not to have tried at all.

We are very heartened by the attitude of the labor people and very grateful and encouraged by the attitude of the business people.

Secretary Trowbridge of the Commerce Department, Secretary Wirtz of the Labor Department, and Mr. Califano will give you any details.

NOTE: The President spoke at 11:15 a.m. in the office of George E. Christian, Special Assistant to the President. During his remarks he referred to, among others, Alexander B. Trowbridge, Secretary of Commerce, W. Willard Wirtz, Secretary of Labor, and Joseph A. Califano, Jr., Special Assistant to the President.

As printed above, this item follows the text released by the White House Press Office.

26 Special Message to the Congress on Civil Rights. *January 24, 1968*

To the Congress of the United States:

In each of the past three years I have sent to the Congress a special message dealing with Civil Rights. This year I do so again, with feelings of both disappointment and pride:

—Disappointment, because in an ideal America we would not need to seek new laws guaranteeing the rights of citizens;

—Pride, because in America we can achieve and protect these rights through the political process.

The more we grapple with the civil rights problem—the most difficult domestic issue we have ever faced—the more we realize that the position of minorities in American society is defined not merely by law, but by social, educational, and economic conditions.

I can report to you steady progress in improving those conditions:

—More than 28 percent of nonwhite families now receive over $7,000 income a year—double the proportion of eight years ago in real terms.

—As of this month, 98 percent of America's hospitals have pledged themselves to nondiscrimination.

—The educational level of nonwhites has risen sharply: in 1966, 53 percent of the nonwhite young men had completed four years of high school, compared to 36 percent in 1960.

—The nonwhite unemployment rate has declined from 10.8 percent in 1963 to 7.4 percent in 1967.

—Great advances have been made in Negro voter registration—due to the enactment and enforcement of the Voting Rights Act of 1965, and the efforts of the people themselves. In the five Southern States where the Act has had its greatest impact, Negro voter registration has reached 1.5 million, more than double that in 1965.

—Negroes have been elected to public office with increasing frequency—in the North and in the South.

—Thousands of disadvantaged youths have received job training—and their first job opportunities—as a result of Federal programs.

—The proportion of Mexican-Americans enrolled in classes under the Manpower Development and Training Act, and as Neighborhood Youth Corpsmen, in the five Southwestern States is double their 12 percent ratio in the population.

—Twenty-one States, and more than 80 cities and counties, have enacted fair housing laws.

But I must also report that:

—One out of three nonwhite families still lives below the poverty level.

—The infant mortality rate for nonwhite children is nearly double that of whites. And it is nearly three times as high for children 28 days to one year of age.

—The percentage of nonwhites who have completed high school is still far below that of whites. And the quality of education in many predominantly Negro schools remains inferior.

—The nonwhite unemployment rate, while declining, is still twice as high as that for whites.

—A survey conducted in two Southwestern cities revealed that almost one out of two Mexican-American workers living in the slums faced severe employment problems.

—In too many areas of the Nation, election time remains a period of racial tension.

—Despite the growing number of States and local communities which have outlawed racial discrimination in housing, studies in some cities indicate that residential segregation is increasing.

—Despite the progress that many Negroes have achieved, living conditions in some of the most depressed slum areas have actually worsened in the past decade.

In the State of the Union message last week I spoke of a spirit of restlessness in our land. This feeling of disquiet is more pronounced in race relations than in any other area of domestic concern.

Most Americans remain true to our goal: the development of a national society in which the color of a man's skin is as irrelevant as the color of his eyes.

In the context of our history, this goal will not be easily achieved. But unless we act in our time to fulfill our first creed: that "all men are created equal"—it will not be achieved at all.

ONE NATION

Though the creed of equality has won acceptance among the great majority of our people, some continue to resist every constructive step to its achievement.

The air is filled with the voices of extremists on both sides:

—Those who use our very successes as an excuse to stop in our tracks, and who decry the awakening of new expectations in people who have found cause to hope.

—Those who catalogue only our failures, declare that our society is bankrupt and promote violence and force as an alternative to orderly change.

These extremes represent, I believe, forms of escapism by a small minority of our people. The vast majority of Americans—Negro and white—have not lent their hearts or efforts to either form of extremism. They have continued to work forcefully—and lawfully—for the common good.

America is a multiracial nation. Racism—under whatever guise and whatever sponsorship—cannot be reconciled with the American faith.

This is not to deny the vitality of our diversity. Our people are blessed with a variety of backgrounds. Pride in our national origins, in our religions, in our ethnic affiliations, has always been an American trait. It has given to all our people that sense of community, of belonging, without which life is empty and arid.

Our continuing challenge has been to preserve that diversity, without sacrificing our sense of national purpose; to encourage the development of individual excellence, without yielding in our pursuit of national excellence for all.

EDUCATION FOR ALL

We confront this challenge squarely in the area of education.

Our Nation is committed to the best possible education for all our children. We are also committed to the constitutional mandate that prohibits segregated school systems.

Some maintain that integration is essential for better education. Others insist that massive new investments in facilities and teachers alone can achieve the results we desire.

We continue to seek both goals: better supported—and unsegregated—schools.

Thus far, we can claim only a qualified success for our efforts:

—We still seek better methods to teach

disadvantaged youngsters—to awaken their curiosity, stimulate their interest, arouse their latent talent, and prepare them for the complexities of modern living.

—We still seek better methods to achieve meaningful integration in many of the various communities across our land—in urban ghettoes, in rural counties, in suburban districts.

But our lack of total success should spur our efforts, not discourage them.

In the last year many States, cities, communities, school boards and educators have experimented with new techniques of education, and new methods of achieving integration. We have learned much from these experiments. We shall learn much more.

We do know that progress in education cannot be designed in Washington, but must be generated by the energies of local school boards, teachers and parents. We know that there is no single or simple answer to the questions that perplex us. But our National goals are clear: desegregated schools and quality education. They must not be compromised.

The Task Ahead

We must continue the progress we have made toward achieving equal justice and opportunity:

—through the enforcement of existing laws;

—through legislation that will protect the rights and extend the opportunities of all Americans.

In the Executive Branch

The Department of Justice has just completed its most active year:

—Convictions were obtained in the im-

portant conspiracy case involving the deaths of three civil rights workers in Mississippi.

—A record number of civil rights suits were filed, involving school desegregation and discrimination in employment and public accommodations.

—The first Northern suit alleging voting discrimination was filed, and examiners were sent into 15 additional counties to assure fair registration and voting.

—The Community Relations Service has helped some 260 communities to resolve human relations problems.

Other Federal agencies have been equally active:

—The Secretary of Health, Education, and Welfare is now examining statistical reports from some 2,000 school districts throughout America—to insure compliance with Title VI of the 1964 Civil Rights Act, forbidding discrimination in such matters as the quality of school facilities and the establishment of school boundaries.

—The Office of Federal Contract Compliance of the Department of Labor stepped-up and broadened its enforcement of the Executive Order forbidding discrimination in employment by Federal contractors.

—The Secretary of Defense has moved to encourage the desegregation of housing facilities surrounding military bases, thus making available thousands of additional homes to members of the Armed Forces and their families regardless of their race.[1]

---

[1] A memorandum to the President from the Secretary of Defense marking the 20th anniversary of President Truman's 1948 desegregation order and citing progress since that time is printed in the Weekly Compilation of Presidential Documents (vol. 4, p. 1154).

57

—The Secretary of Housing and Urban Development has speeded the desegregation of public housing by establishing new site and tenant selection policies. He has initiated counseling services for low and moderate income families and has reorganized the Department's civil rights staff.

We will continue to expand our efforts. For wherever the Federal Government is involved, it must not be even a silent partner in perpetuating unequal treatment.

The Urgent Need for Legislative Action

The legacy of the American past is political democracy—and an economic system that has produced an abundance unknown in history.

Yet our forefathers also left their unsolved problems. The legacy of slavery—racial discrimination—is first among them.

We have come a long way since that August day in 1957, when the first civil rights bill in almost a century was passed by the Congress.

At our recommendation, the Congress passed major civil rights legislation—far stronger than the 1957 Act—in 1964 and 1965. The 89th Congress passed groundbreaking legislation of enormous importance to disadvantaged Americans among us—in education, in health, in manpower training, in the war against poverty. The First Session of the 90th Congress has continued these programs.

Yet critical work remains in creating a legal framework that will guarantee equality and opportunity for all. A start was made in the First Session of this Congress:

—The life of the Civil Rights Commission was extended for an additional five years.

—The House of Representatives approved legislation aimed at preventing violent interference with the exercise of civil rights. The Senate Judiciary Committee has reported a similar bill, which is now being debated on the floor of the Senate.

—The Senate passed a bill to reform the system of Federal jury selection.

—Hearings were held in the Senate on State jury legislation, on equal employment opportunity amendments, and on a Federal fair housing law.

In this session, *I appeal to the Congress to complete the task it has begun.*

—*To strengthen Federal criminal laws prohibiting violent interference with the exercise of civil rights.*

—*To give the Equal Employment Opportunity Commission the authority it needs to carry out its vital responsibilities.*

—*To assure that Federal and State juries are selected without discrimination.*

—*To make equal opportunity in housing a reality for all Americans.*

Protecting the Exercise of Civil Rights

A Negro parent is attacked because his child attends a desegregated public school. Can the Federal courts punish the assailant? The answer today is only "perhaps."

A Negro is beaten by private citizens after seeking service in a previously all-white restaurant. Can the Federal courts punish this act? Under existing law the answer is "no," unless that attack involved a conspiracy. Even there the answer is only "maybe."

Grown men force a group of Negro children from a public park. The question most Americans would ask is what punishment these hoodlums deserve. Instead, the question before the Federal court is whether it has jurisdiction.

The reach of century-old criminal civil rights laws is too restricted to assure equal justice to the persons they were designed to protect. Yet the right of Americans to be free of racial or religious discrimination—in voting, using public accommodations, attending schools—must be firmly secured by the law.

The existing criminal laws are inadequate:
—The conduct they prohibit is not set out in clear, precise terms. This ambiguity encourages drawn-out litigation and disrespect for the rule of law.
—These laws have only limited applicability to private persons not acting in concert with public officials. As a result, blatant acts of violence go unpunished.
—Maximum penalties are inadequate to suit the gravity of the crime when injury or death result.

The bill reported by the Senate Judiciary Committee remedies each of these deficiencies. It would prohibit the use of force to prevent the exercise by minorities of rights most of us take for granted:
—Voting, registering to vote, or campaigning for any office in Federal or State elections.
—Attending a public school or public college.
—Obtaining service at public accommodations.
—Serving or qualifying to serve on State or Federal juries.
—Obtaining a job, on the basis of ability, with any private or public employer.
—Using any Federal, State or local public facility.
—Participating in Federally-assisted programs or activities.
—Riding in a public carrier.

The bill would apply to any individual or group—public or private—that sought to prevent the exercise of these rights by violent means. And it would tailor the penalties to meet the seriousness of the offense.

We know that State and local authorities have often been slow, unwilling, or unable to act when lawful and peaceful attempts to exercise civil rights drew a violent response.

The Mississippi convictions of this year, and other recent cases, have given dramatic evidence that Federal laws can reach those who engage in conspiracies against law-abiding citizens. It is therefore imperative that these laws be clear and their penalties effective.

This bill will strengthen the hand of Federal law enforcement to protect our citizens wherever they encounter—because of their race, color or religion—violence or force in their attempt to enjoy established civil rights. Beyond this limited area, law enforcement is left where it belongs—in the hands of the States and local communities.

EMPLOYMENT

For most Americans, the Nation's continuing prosperity has meant increased abundance. Nevertheless, as I noted earlier, the unemployment rate for nonwhites has remained at least twice the rate for whites.

Part of the answer lies in job training to overcome educational deficiencies and to teach new skills. Yesterday I asked the Congress for a $2.1 billion manpower program to assist 1.3 million of our citizens. A special three-year effort will be made to reach 500,-000 hard-core unemployed of all races and backgrounds in our major cities.

But we must assure our citizens that once they are qualified, they will be judged fairly on the basis of their capacities.

Even where the Negro, the Puerto Rican, **and the Mexican-American** possess education and skills, they are too often treated as less than equal in the eyes of those who have the power to hire, promote and dismiss. The median income of college-trained nonwhites is only $6,000 a year. The median income of college-trained whites is over $9,000—more than 50 percent higher.

The law forbids discrimination in employment. And we have worked to enforce that law:

—More than 150 cases of employment discrimination are under investigation by the Department of Justice.

—Lawsuits have been filed to stop patterns and practices of discrimination by employers and unions in the North as well as the South.

But the Justice Department does not bear the major responsibility for enforcing equal employment opportunity. Congress created the Equal Employment Opportunity Commission in 1964 to receive and investigate individual complaints, and to attempt to eliminate unlawful employment practices by the informal methods of conference, conciliation, and persuasion.

This authority has yielded its fruits. Many employers and unions have complied through this process. We have gained valuable knowledge about discriminatory practices and employment patterns.

Since last September, the Equal Employment Opportunity Commission has, for the first time, processed more complaints than it has received, thereby reducing its backlog. In the last six months, the Commission increased its investigation rate more than 45 percent over the rate for 1966, and doubled the number of conciliations for the same period a year ago. Last month more complaints were investigated than in any month in EEOC history.

Yet even this stepped-up activity cannot reach those who will not agree voluntarily to end their discriminatory practices. As a result, only part of our economy is open to all workers on the basis of merit. Part remains closed because of bias.

The legislation that I submitted last year would empower the Equal Employment Opportunity Commission to issue, after an appropriate hearing, an order requiring an offending employer or union to cease its discriminatory practices and to take corrective action. If there is a refusal to comply with the order, the Government would be authorized to seek enforcement in the Federal courts.

I urge the Congress to give the Commission the power it needs to fulfill its purpose.

FEDERAL JURIES

The Magna Carta of 1215—the great English charter of liberties—established a fundamental principle of our system of criminal justice: trial by jury. Our Constitution guarantees this precious right and its principles require a composition of juries that fairly represents the community.

In some Federal judicial districts this goal has not been achieved, for methods of jury selection vary sharply:

—Some selection systems do not afford Negroes or members of other minorities an adequate opportunity to serve as jurors.

—Some obtain an excessively high proportion of their jurors from the more affluent members of the community, and thus discriminate against others.

In many cases these are unintentional deviations from the principle of a representative jury. But the Federal courts must be free from all unfairness—intentional or unintentional. They must be free, as well, from the appearance of unfairness.

In the first session of this Congress, I proposed, and the Judicial Conference supported, a Federal Jury bill. The Senate passed a bill that would require each judicial district to adopt a jury selection plan relying upon random selection, voter lists, and objective standards.

This bill guarantees a fairly chosen and representative jury in every Federal court, while retaining flexibility to allow for differing conditions in judicial districts.

I urge the House of Representatives to pass it early in this session.

STATE JURIES

Our system of justice requires fairly selected juries in State as well as Federal courts.

But under our Federal system, the States themselves have the primary duty to regulate their own judicial systems. The role of the Federal government is to ensure that every defendant in every court receives his Constitutional right to a fairly selected jury.

The Federal courts have acted to secure this right by overturning convictions when the defendant established that this jury was improperly selected. But this process—of conviction, appeal, reversal, and retrial—is burdensome on our courts, tardy in protecting the right of the defendant whose case is involved and ineffective in changing the underlying procedure for all defendants.

The legislation I have proposed would make it unlawful to discriminate on account of race, color, religion, sex, national origin or economic status in qualifying or selecting jurors in any State court.

It would empower the Attorney General to enjoin the operation of discriminatory selection systems—but only after he has notified the appropriate State officials of the alleged violation, and afforded them a reasonable opportunity to correct it.

The jury is one of the most cherished institutions of our Republic. Its selection should be no less fair in the State than in the Federal court system.

FAIR HOUSING

The National Housing Act of 1949 proclaimed a goal for the Nation: "A decent home and a suitable living environment for every American family."

We have not achieved this goal.

This year I shall send to the Congress a message dealing with our cities—calling for $1 billion for the Model Cities program—and calling upon the Congress, industry and labor to join with me in a ten-year campaign to build six million new decent housing units for low and middle-income families.

But construction of new homes is not enough—unless every family is free to purchase and rent them. Every American who wishes to buy a home, and can afford it, should be free to do so.

Segregation in housing compounds the Nation's social and economic problems. When those who have the means to move out of the central city are denied the chance to do so, the result is a compression of population in the center. In that crowded ghetto, human tragedies—and crime—increase and multiply. Unemployment and educational problems are compounded—because isolation in the central city prevents minority groups from reaching schools and available jobs in other areas.

The fair housing legislation I have recommended would prohibit discrimination in the sale or rental of all housing in the United States. It would take effect in three progressive stages:

—Immediately, to housing presently covered by the Executive Order on equal opportunity in housing.

61

—Then, to dwellings sold or rented by a nonoccupant, and to units for five or more families.

—And finally to all housing.

It would also:

—Outlaw discriminatory practices in the financing of housing, and in the services of real estate brokers.

—Bar the cynical practice of "block-busting," and prohibit intimidation of persons seeking to enjoy the rights it grants and protects.

—Give responsibility for enforcement to the Secretary of Housing and Urban Development and authorize the Attorney General to bring suits against patterns or practices of housing discrimination.

A fair housing law is not a cure-all for the Nation's urban problems. But ending discrimination in the sale or rental of housing is essential for social justice and social progress.

CONCLUSION

For many members of minority groups, the past decade has brought meaningful advances. But for most minorities—locked in urban ghettoes or in rural areas—economic and social progress has come slowly.

When we speak of overcoming discrimination we speak in terms of groups—Indians, Mexican-Americans, Negroes, Puerto Ricans and other minorities. We refer to statistics, percentages, and trends.

Now is the time to remind ourselves that these are problems of individual human beings—of individual Americans.

—Housing discrimination means the Negro veteran of Vietnam cannot live in an apartment which advertises vacancies.

—Employment statistics do not describe the feeling of a Puerto Rican father who cannot earn enough to feed his children.

—No essay on the problems of the slum can reveal the thoughts of a teenager who believes there is no opportunity for him as a law-abiding member of society.

Last summer our Nation suffered the tragedy of urban riots. Lives were lost; property was destroyed; fear and distrust divided many communities.

The prime victims of such lawlessness—as of ordinary crime—are the people of the ghettoes.

No people need or want protection—the effective, non-discriminatory exercise of the police power—more than the law-abiding majority of slum-dwellers. Like better schools, housing, and job opportunities, improved police protection is necessary for better conditions of life in the central city today. It is a vital part of our agenda for urban America.

Lawlessness must be punished—sternly and promptly.

But the criminal conduct of some must not weaken our resolve to deal with the real grievances of all those who suffer discrimination. Nothing can justify the continued denial of equal justice and opportunity to every American.

Each forward step in the battle against discrimination benefits all Americans.

I ask the Congress to take another forward step this year—by adopting this legislation fundamental to the human rights and dignity of every American.

LYNDON B. JOHNSON

The White House
January 24, 1968

NOTE: For statements or remarks upon signing related legislation, see Items 158, 195, 426.

27 Letter to the President of the Senate and to the Speaker of the House Urging Extension of the Arms Control and Disarmament Agency. *January 24, 1968*

Dear Mr. President: (Dear Mr. Speaker:)

In August 1965, I said: "President Eisenhower and President Kennedy sought, as I seek now, the pathway to a world in which serenity may one day endure. There is no sane description of a nuclear war. There is only the blinding light of man's failure to reason with his fellow man, and then silence."

Now as then arms control is the most urgent business of our time.

If men can join together with their neighbors to harness the power of nuclear energy for peaceful progress, they can transform the world. If not, they may well destroy the world.

This is the ultimate test of our century. On our response rests the very survival of this nation and the fate of every living creature on this planet.

The Arms Control and Disarmament Agency speaks for the United States in this critical area.

I urge the Congress to extend its life for three years and to authorize the necessary appropriations.

Just over five years ago the world looked over the brink of nuclear holocaust. The Cuban missile crisis brought home to every man and woman the unspeakable personal horror of nuclear war. It posed the problem, not in terms of megatons and megadeaths, but in terms of a man's home destroyed and his family wiped off the face of the earth.

One year later, the world took the first great step toward nuclear sanity—the Limited Test Ban Treaty.

From that treaty was born a common spirit and a common trust. National agendas were revised. Priorities were rearranged. Nations around the world joined in the quest for freedom from nuclear terror.

The United Nations passed a resolution against bombs in orbit. The United States and the Soviet Union installed a "hot line" between Washington and Moscow which has already been used to protect the peace. Last year a new treaty went into effect to preserve outer space for the works of peace.

The Arms Control and Disarmament Agency played a central role in all these important advances. Now the energy and perseverance of Director William Foster and his colleagues have brought us close to the next great step forward: a treaty banning the spread of nuclear weapons.

The United States and the Soviet Union have agreed to a complete draft Non-Proliferation Treaty and submitted it to the Eighteen-Nation Disarmament Committee in Geneva for consideration by other nations. This draft already reflects many of the interests and views of the nations which do not now have nuclear weapons. We believe such a treaty represents the most constructive way to avoid the terrible dangers and the criminal waste which all men recognize would flow from the further spread of nuclear weapons.

For at least twenty-five years, this treaty would:

—Prohibit any nuclear weapon state from transferring to any recipient, either directly or indirectly, any nuclear explosive device or the control of any such device;

—Prohibit any nuclear weapon state from helping non-nuclear weapon nations to

63

develop their own nuclear weapons;

—Prohibit any non-nuclear weapon state from receiving nuclear weapons and from manufacturing its own weapons;

—Provide for verification that no nuclear materials are diverted by non-nuclear weapon states to produce explosive devices;

—Encourage cooperation between nuclear and non-nuclear nations to insure that all will benefit from the peaceful uses of nuclear energy.

This treaty will not end tensions between nations nor will it eliminate the shadow of nuclear war which now menaces all mankind. But it will reduce the chances of nuclear disaster arising from local disputes.

It will avoid the tragic waste of resources on nuclear weapon technology by countries whose first and overriding concern must be economic growth and social progress.

And it will, we hope, bring world-wide acceptance of nuclear safeguards inspection as the basic protection which every nation must afford itself and its neighbors.

This treaty looks to the day when a final answer to the nuclear weapons problem will be possible. It does not limit the right or capacity of any present nuclear power to produce nuclear weapons. It does call for further negotiations to end the nuclear arms race and to move down the road to general and complete disarmament.

The lesson of the nuclear era is that this most sacred of human hopes will not be realized through intimidation of one nation by another nor by a single stroke of diplomacy. It will follow months and years of steady, patient effort. It will come step by step as men grow in wisdom and nations grow in responsibility.

The Non-Proliferation Treaty is not a creation of the United States. It is not a creation of the United States and the Soviet Union. It is the creation of all nations, large and small, who share the knowledge and the determination that man can and must and will control these cosmic forces he has unleashed.

When this Treaty comes into force, it will be for all the world the brightest light at the end of the tunnel since 1945.

Sincerely,

Lyndon B. Johnson

note: This is the text of identical letters addressed to the Honorable Hubert H. Humphrey, President of the Senate, and to the Honorable John W. McCormack, Speaker of the House of Representatives.

An act amending the Arms Control and Disarmament Act to extend the authorization for appropriations through fiscal year 1970 was approved by the President on May 23, 1968 (Public Law 90–314, 82 Stat. 129).

The quoted text at the beginning of the letter is from the President's statement on the draft treaty on nuclear weapons of August 17, 1965 (see 1965 volume, this series, Book II, Item 430).

See also Items 308, 349, 378.

28   Recorded Message to the Navajo People on the Occasion of Their Centennial Banquet. *January 24, 1968*

Chairman Nakai, distinguished guests, Navajo friends:

This is a proud moment for you. I speak for all Americans in saying how happy I am to share it with you.

Tonight you celebrate the centennial year of your people. It is a good time for men to gather in friendship, to look back over their shoulders at all their trials and their triumphs, to lift their eyes and hearts toward the future that is always fresh with new challenge and hope.

You knew this land thousands of years before our ancestors even knew it existed. You called a wild and beautiful country home for centuries before it was ever called America.

You helped to tame it and to shape it by your courage and your wisdom. And looking back with you tonight, looking ahead with you as the American people, the frontier people, our Nation is grateful for all that your experience and example has helped to build and will go on building.

You have much to teach us and to give us still.

We watched you last December when the terrible snows threatened you with disaster. A lesser people would have given in and perished—but instead, you gave all America a lesson in bravery and fortitude.

We have watched you bring the same unbreakable spirit to other problems in your daily lives and there are many of them.

But you do not fear them. You remember, as I do, the old Navajo legend that said that giants and demons first owned the earth and then they destroyed it.

You know, as I do, the real giants and the real demons that remain: giants of ignorance that can crush a man's hopes; demons of poverty and disease that can cripple a man's family and kill his children.

You know them as your ancient enemies but today you are going after them, you are fighting them and you are beating them as a new generation of Navajos—a modern generation of Americans. The wise men who lead you have kept the best of proud traditions.

They have joined it with the brightest of new enterprise and they have led the tribe across another frontier of endless promise.

You already run your own multi-million dollar sawmill. It gives you good jobs and better skills.

Your industrial development program is succeeding. Two large electronic manufacturers now rely on your energies and skills.

You have a strong community action program—the Office of Navajo Economic Opportunity—and it has brought you new hope by its job training and its home improvement and its legal services.

Just last week your people shared in a $675,000 cash bonus from the sale of uranium leases. That is the biggest moment of its kind in our history.

Your generation can be proud of all that you have achieved, but if you feel, as I do, you will be most proud of what you are doing for generations to come.

Today you have a wonderful community school at Rough Rock. It is your school. It is built of your spirit. It is rich with your heritage and culture. It is your tomorrow. It is America's future.

The children of Rough Rock must have the learning and the desire and the opportunity to enter other schools such as high schools and colleges and the great universities. They must have the chance to better themselves and to equip themselves for the building of a better life and for the building of a better America.

Your children will have that chance.

This year, 30 new kindergarten schools are going to rise up on your Navajo lands. They will be the first your children have ever known, but I promise you, they will not be the last. We have already begun this program. In a few weeks teachers will start training the staff for these kindergartens. They will be good teachers. They will be your kind of people, trained in your language and your culture, using special materials designed for your children's special needs. They will be followed, I hope, by other Americans who come to teach and who come to help and work with you, and learn with you and from you.

65

I am one who has lived close to a land that is much like yours. I have known people of your dignity and I have found strength in the quality of your life. It is the natural strength of the real America, spacious and unspoiled, a place of beauty and grandeur, where a man can find renewal and a nation can find its true purpose.

The Navajo have renewed themselves and you have new purpose and its promise is a nation's happiness.

We are thankful that you built new roads and bridges to open your land to your fellow citizens and to our foreign visitors. We hope that you and those who follow you will always keep open the bridge of culture and the road of trust.

They join us now as friends. They will always lead to a life of deeper understanding and greater fulfillment for the American family.

Thank you for giving me this chance to visit with you from a distance.

NOTE: The President recorded the message in the Cabinet Room at the White House. In his opening words he referred to Raymond Nakai, Chairman of the Navajo Tribe.

For remarks of the President upon signing two bills and a proclamation relating to the Navajo Indian Tribe, see Item 259.

29 Message to the Senate Submitting for Advice and Consent the International Grains Arrangement of 1967. *January 25, 1968*

To the Senate of the United States:

Today I submit to the Senate for its advice and consent the International Grains Arrangement of 1967.

This Arrangement is another step forward in our overall effort to strengthen and stabilize our farm economy, to improve our balance of payments, and to share our abundance with those in need.

The Arrangement is an outgrowth of the Kennedy Round of trade negotiations. It was agreed to last August at the International Wheat Conference in Rome. It has already been signed by most of the countries that are major exporters and importers of grain.

The Arrangement is in two parts:

—the Wheat Trade Convention, which will provide new insurance against falling prices in the wheat export trade,

—and the Food Aid Convention, which will bring wheat exporting and wheat importing nations into partnership in the War on Hunger.

THE WHEAT TRADE CONVENTION

The Wheat Trade Convention will help to stabilize prices in world commercial trade.

It sets minimum and maximum prices for wheat moving in international trade at levels substantially higher than those specified in the International Wheat Agreement of 1962. This will give our farmers additional protection against price cutting in world markets.

At the same time, the Arrangement includes provisions to insure that our wheat will be priced competitively in world markets; and that no exporting member country is placed at a disadvantage because of changes in market conditions.

Importing countries also receive protection and benefits under the Convention. In periods of shortage importing member countries will be able to purchase their normal commercial requirements at the established maximum price. After this requirement has been met, exporting member countries will be free to sell above the maximum price.

America's wheat farmers have supported the pricing provisions of previous wheat agreements. I am confident they will welcome the stronger price assurances of this Arrangement.

THE FOOD AID CONVENTION

The Food Aid Convention marks an important new international initiative in the assault on hunger throughout the world.

The countries participating in this Convention—both exporting and importing nations—undertake to establish a regular program of food aid over the next three years.

The program calls for 4.5 million tons of grain to be supplied each year; 4.2 million tons are already subscribed.

—The U.S. will supply 1.9 million tons in grains—under the authority of the Food for Freedom program.

—Other countries will supply 2.6 million tons—either in the form of grain or its cash equivalent.

This new program is a major joint effort to supply wheat and other food grains to needy nations on a continuing basis. It will help the developing nations of the world meet their food deficits while they work to expand their own food production. As these countries prosper and grow, many will become cash customers for agricultural products.

I enclose, for the information of the Senate, the report of the Secretary of State on the International Grains Arrangement.

I urge the Senate to give it early consideration.

LYNDON B. JOHNSON

The White House
    January 25, 1968

NOTE: The International Grains Arrangement was favorably considered by the Senate on June 13, 1968, and after ratification entered into force on July 1, 1968. It was proclaimed by the President on August 3, 1968.

The text of the Arrangement is printed in Treaties and Other International Acts Series (TIAS 6537) and in a publication of the Foreign Agricultural Service, Department of Agriculture (46 pp.).

30 Letter Accepting Resignation of John W. Gardner as Secretary of Health, Education, and Welfare. *January* 25, 1968

Dear John:

I accept your resignation with deep regret. You have served your Nation and your President well and faithfully. You have helped to build HEW during a critical period of its growth and to administer programs which touch the lives of all our citizens.

I have appreciated your willingness to stay in government beyond the term of your original commitment. I am pleased that you are going to undertake leadership in the area of pressing urban problems. You may count

on my continued strong support in any way I can be helpful.

    Sincerely,

LYNDON B. JOHNSON

[Honorable John W. Gardner, Secretary of Health, Education, and Welfare, Washington, D.C.]

NOTE: John W. Gardner served as Secretary of Health, Education, and Welfare from August 18, 1965, to March 1, 1968. His letter of resignation and a memorandum to the President summarizing recent developments in the fields served by the Department of Health, Education, and Welfare are printed in the Weekly Compilation of Presidential Documents (vol. 4, p. 125).

31 Remarks at the Swearing In of Jerre S. Williams as Chairman, Administrative Conference of the United States. *January 25, 1968*

Mr. and Mrs. Williams and family, Members of the Cabinet, Ambassador Goldberg, Members of Congress, Members of the Judiciary, ladies and gentlemen:

A poet once wrote, "Nothing is so hard but search will find it out." We think in Jerre Williams the Administrative Conference has found and will have as its Chairman one of our most distinguished scholars and professors of law. We are all glad that we were able to persuade him to leave his students and to serve two much larger constituencies, the Federal Government and the American public.

The Conference will need a man of his talents and of his energy.

In 1952 Mr. Justice Jackson observed that, "The rise of administrative bodies probably has been the most significant legal trend of the last century. . . . Perhaps more values today are affected by their decisions than by those of all the courts."

Even he couldn't have predicted how deeply the administrative process would penetrate the life of the American citizen in this year—1968.

Today it involves everything from the safety of public transportation to the wholesomeness of food; from communications and utilities to drugs and savings accounts.

We handle these vital programs well. But all of us know that we could handle them much better. It will be your job, Mr. Williams, to tell us how to do that.

The success of two temporary conferences—both chaired very ably by Judge Prettyman—convinced us that we needed a permanent agency for continuing review of the administrative process.

We needed a forum for the constant exchange of ideas between the agencies and the legal profession and the public.

We want the Administrative Conference to be the vehicle through which we can look at the administrative process and can see how it is working and how it could be improved and how it could best serve the public interest.

In a few days we will be naming the 10-member Council to work with Mr. Williams in picking the members of the Conference.

I want to ask all the agencies to cooperate fully with the Chairman and the Council. I have asked the agency heads to give Mr. Williams all the support they can to help get the Conference moving along.

Mr. Williams, we are very pleased to have you with us and I shall look forward with pleasure to seeing the Conference's first report.

NOTE: The President spoke at 1:06 p.m. in the East Room at the White House. In his opening words he also referred to Arthur J. Goldberg, U.S. Representative to the United Nations. During his remarks he referred to Robert H. Jackson, former Supreme Court Justice, and to E. Barrett Prettyman, Senior Circuit Judge of the U.S. Court of Appeals for the District of Columbia, who administered the oath of office.

For an announcement of the members of the Council of the Administrative Conference of the United States, see the Weekly Compilation of Presidential Documents (vol. 4, p. 251).

32   Toasts at a Dinner Honoring the Vice President, the Speaker of the House, and the Chief Justice. *January 25, 1968*

Mr. Vice President and Mrs. Humphrey, Speaker and Mrs. McCormack, Chief Justice and Mrs. Warren, members of the Supreme Court, members of the Cabinet, Governor and Mrs. Hughes, distinguished guests:

We have many dinners in this house during the course of a year. But none is quite as symbolic and meaningful as the one that we have in honor of the President of the Senate, the distinguished Speaker of the House, and the Chief Justice of the Supreme Court.

For this is the night when we pay formal tribute to a great American institution: the famous system of "checks and balances." That is not to be confused with balance of payments—which is something entirely different and considerably less reliable.

There have been times, in our history, when "check and balance" really meant "stop and freeze."

There have been times when the various branches of Government seemed fixed on different stars—when each seemed determined to bend the others to its will.

These occasions have always been quite interesting to the historians. They have also provided material for the commentators, and some little rhetoric for our political campaigns.

But they have never been very useful for the people of this country—whom each of us is sworn to serve.

This is not to say that strong opinions are out of place when great issues are debated. But after the strong opinions have been aired, the people want progress. They want a reasonable degree of cooperation between the branches in trying to meet the needs of the public. They want checks and balances—and then they want forward movement.

The great periods of progress in America have come when the leaders of each branch were more concerned with making progress than with establishing their predominance. When the good of the people was their single concern, their differences somehow paled into insignificance.

In their separate roles, bearing their diverse responsibilities, they contributed to the common good.

In our time, America has been blessed with three leaders who have always placed the interests of the people before institutional pride or personal power.

Hubert Humphrey is loyal to the Senate—John McCormack to the House—and Earl Warren to the Court. Yet they know that these great institutions exist only for a larger purpose—to serve the people. They have borne great responsibilities and all of them have helped to make great decisions. Yet somehow none of them has ever seemed to have forgotten the people. They have earned great honors, and they have occupied great offices. Yet they retain a simple integrity that communicates to every man and woman.

So tonight, here in the First House of the Land, we have come to celebrate these great institutions of our Government. And we mark, as well, the progress of our people and what they have known because men such as these three have served these institutions in our time—and through them, they have served the common good.

So I ask those of you who have come from throughout the land to join me tonight in a toast to the Vice President, the Speaker of the House, and the Chief Justice.

REMARKS OF THE VICE PRESIDENT

Mr. President, Mrs. Johnson, Mr. Speaker and Mrs. McCormack, Mr. Chief Justice and Mrs. Warren, and the honored guests of this evening:

Mr. President, you have greatly honored the Speaker and the Chief Justice and me this evening, and Mrs. Humphrey. You have not only opened this house to us, but more importantly, you have opened your heart to us.

We feel a fellowship and a friendship here tonight that goes far beyond the principles of constitutional law or even the heritage of government.

There is a fellowship and a friendship here which ties us and binds us together. I hope that somehow we can repay your kindness in the months ahead and to repay it with renewed efforts to lighten your awesome burdens.

We are all very conscious tonight of the tremendous demands upon you—the incredible burden that you bear—and the great responsibility that is yours.

For these are times of great decisions when, in the words of one of your predecessors, President Truman, "To be President of the United States is to be lonely—and very lonely."

In your State of the Union Address you spoke of our country as a mighty ship cutting through troubled waters. I like that analogy because it told us of the movement of this Nation and also of its strength. We know that this great ship, this America, cutting through stirred and troubled waters, can have but one hand on the helm.

Many of us, Mr. President, with you—advising you—counseling you—and hopefully, helping you—but only one hand at the helm. Yes, one hand must steer through the storms of the moment and at the same time, chart the course of the future.

We who work with you, well we know that the greatest victories can often go unnoticed and even unpraised. Crises that are averted are soon forgotten, although they may have menaced the security of all mankind.

We also know that historic legislation which has vastly enriched the life of every American is soon accepted as commonplace and taken for granted.

I guess, Mr. President, this is the price of leadership—leadership that is more than just a promise, but is in fact an achievement.

Meanwhile, this great ship, America, must move on towards what another President called its rendezvous with destiny.

Tonight in this room are men and women who are proud to be with you on this great adventure and this great fulfillment of the promise of America.

I am sure you know, Mr. President, how proud I am to be with you and the Speaker and the Chief Justice and the others.

So, Mrs. Johnson, Mr. Speaker and Mrs. McCormack, the Chief Justice and Mrs. Warren, Members of the Cabinet and the Congress and the honored guests who have gathered in this historic home—I ask you to join me tonight in a tribute to a man who is firm and resolute, who is strong and kind, and who governs with compassion and yet with understanding and strength.

To the President of the United States.

REMARKS OF THE SPEAKER OF THE HOUSE OF REPRESENTATIVES

Mr. President, Mrs. Johnson, Mr. Vice President, Mrs. Humphrey, Mr. Chief Justice and Mrs. Warren, my distinguished col-

leagues, distinguished members of the Cabinet, and other honored ladies and gentlemen present this evening:

I appreciate very much the kind words uttered by the President. We are gathered tonight in the President's Mansion, presently occupied by a family that is typical of American life—with high moral values that constitute an inspiration for all others to follow.

The Chief Executive of our country is a man of broad experience, unexcelled by any of his predecessors, of outstanding ability, a keen and penetrating and decisive mind, kind but firm, and possessing the moral and human courage to met the trying and challenging problems of this period of the world's history.

By word, deed, and action, he shows his love for mankind, with special compassion and consideration for the sick, the afflicted, the poor, the underprivileged, the persecuted, and the oppressed.

To such a man I offer a toast: Ladies and gentlemen, to the President of the United States.

REMARKS OF THE CHIEF JUSTICE

Mr. President, Mrs. Johnson, Mr. Vice President, Mrs. Humphrey, Mr. Speaker, Mrs. McCormack, my colleagues, members of the Cabinet, and distinguished ladies and gentlemen:

You do us great honor, Mr. President, in inviting us to your home on this occasion. I wish I could express in words the feelings that I am sure we all have, but I think I can do no more than to echo the words and the sentiments of the Vice President and the Speaker who have preceded me.

This is a great company that you have

brought together tonight—one that would inspire any American to be a part of. It represents exactly what you said a few moments ago, Mr. President, and what you emphasized in your State of the Union Message a few nights ago: The unity that our country needs and the unity that we have the strength to bring about if we have the will to bring it about.

To see the members of all branches of the Government here tonight in fellowship, in friendship, and with one spirit—the spirit to do for our country what needs to be done—any American who is in this company would be thrilled tonight, not only thrilled, but he would have his heart warmed by reason of the associations.

And it is my hope that this will be a great year for our country because of the fellowship that is manifested here tonight.

I am one who believes that although these are perilous times, that our country is strong enough, does have the unity when it is sufficiently hard pressed to do what is necessary for the benefit of all.

It is my hope that in this year which is a tremendously important year for you, Mr. President, that we will be able together to solve many of these great problems that you spoke of in your State of the Union Message last week.

So, in further answer of that hope, and that desire, ladies and gentlemen, may I ask you to join with me in a toast to the President of the United States and Mrs. Johnson.

NOTE: The President spoke at 10:10 p.m. in the State Dining Room at the White House. In his opening words he referred to Vice President and Mrs. Hubert H. Humphrey, Representative John W. McCormack of Massachusetts, Speaker of the House of Representatives, and Mrs. McCormack, Chief Justice of the United States and Mrs. Earl Warren, and Governor and Mrs. Richard J. Hughes of New Jersey.

33 Remarks to Student Delegates Attending the 1968 Senate Youth Program. *January 26, 1968*

Distinguished students, ladies and gentlemen:

I understand that you young people hold high elective positions in your schools. It is a great pleasure for me to welcome you here to the East Room in the White House as office holders.

If any of you have decided to run for re-election, I have a word of advice. The only thing that I know that is harder than holding an office is running for an office. So, be sure to preserve your strength—you may need it in the stretch.

I have been hearing so much about young people that I am ready to believe what a columnist had to observe recently: "One of the worst things that can happen to an American child nowadays is youth."

I have not asked you to come here this morning under any pretense that I am going to analyze you. I think enough people have you on the couch already—fussing about your morals and your manners, your hair length, and your hemlines.

But I want to talk instead in the few moments that you have given me, about a subject that intrigues you and disturbs me: How can young Americans influence the policies and events which determine so much of their own lives?

Well, the truth is they can—and they can't.

Mr. Clifford was not the only man who was considered for Secretary of Defense for a period of many months. But I must admit that none of his competition was under 25. There never will be a Senator under 30, or a President under 35—not without a constitutional amendment. Most heads of corporations and universities—most great generals, most scientists, professors, bankers, lawyers,

journalists—if you please, most of the so-called "power structure" are not going to be under 30. That is the way it is; and any who say otherwise are only flashing "fool's gold."

But I am not here this morning to discourage you. I recognize your restlessness. And I welcome what someone has written of you:

"Probably the most powerful head of steam ever created is that of young people trying to set on fire a world that they think is all wet."

But we must ask ourselves this question: How can this youthful head of steam become a constructive force in our national policy? How can your restlessness and your drive be satisfied—so that all America gains from your energies and from your ideals?

We have found many of the answers. But we must find more. Young people may have less power than they want. But let me tell you this: Many of you have a great deal more power than you think.

The longer I work in this house, the more I see how sensitive this Government is, how strongly it responds to the people's needs and desires. When the American people say something, when they really care about something—then the American system really works. It works not only for those over 30, but it works for those under 30 as well.

It works best not for those who "turn off" or those who "drop out"—but particularly for those who "butt in." And that is what I would remember—and recommend to those of you who want to change the world. I would suggest to you: "butt in", "butt in" to politics, "butt in" to politics hard, and loud, and clear; and then you have a chance to change the world from within.

You have something else going for you. Hard as it is for you to believe now, you are not going to be 17 or 18 forever.

But the basic power and the great advantage of youth is staying power. When these tense moments that we undergo today are just footnotes in our history, you young men and women are going to be running this Nation. It will be your turn then to cope with the tense moments that come your way. It will be you who confront them in government and business and science, and every field of human endeavor. I might add that your time of testing—the time when you will have the opportunity and responsibility to demonstrate your wisdom and to accept your responsibility—may be closer than you think. Look around this room and this house. Look at the faces of the people who labor here and those who turn off the switches after midnight every night. The men and women who make the White House go and really make it tick, who really keep this country moving, are generally your kind, mostly young, some of them not even 30, most of them under 40.

So, as you can see, youth always wins in the long run. And I think that is something that each of you will do well to remember.

Your Government's responsibility to you is to create the widest possible range of opportunities for your talents to exploit. Where those talents are threatened by disease, or by prejudice, or by poverty; wherever youth is wasted by circumstance—there is where a responsible government should and must intervene.

Not to write your ticket for you; but to set you free to write your ticket for yourselves.

That is what we are trying so hard to do. What I hope you will do is take advantage of these opportunities that you have—opportunities that are greater now for more of our people, for more of our youth, than they have ever been in the history of man.

That, really, is youth's real power. You have only to reach out and to seize it and thus to shape your own society. Let me ask you this question: How many young people in other countries can claim the power that you possess? What other generation has ever had your chance to speak up, to stand out, to make the world what you want to make it?

Make no mistake. When you young people speak up, people around here sit up. You won't see many people wearing hearing aids in the White House. You won't find anyone in this administration who wants to tune you out. We hear you. We want you. We need you considerably more, I think, than any of you may know.

I have spent 37 years of my life in government. If I have learned one thing in those 37 years it may be that the most important instrument of government is the ear.

I will go further than that. I use it about 20 hours a day. The test and the art of leadership and democracy is not the hand that rules, but the heart that hears.

I want to leave you with a promise. That promise is this: So long as I lead, you will be heard.

I have been listening to young voices all of my life, and other voices too.

This morning I am reminded of a voice that I heard more than 30 years ago when I was quite a young man. I was stirred, stirred by the eloquence of Franklin Roosevelt, who said: "The destiny of American youth is the destiny of America."

Some may ask today: What is our destiny? Well, I believe I know the answer.

I look at you young people—the smartest, the healthiest, the most prosperous, the best dressed, with more creature comforts and more advantages than your fathers or your grandfathers ever dreamed of, and yet you are the most straightforward and you are the most concerned generation that I have ever seen in all of my life. I draw a conclusion from that. I look at you and I know that America is going to make it—and America is going to make it big.

Thank you very much.

NOTE: The President spoke at 12:06 p.m. in the East Room at the White House. During his remarks he referred to Clark M. Clifford, who was sworn in as Secretary of Defense on March 1, 1968 (see Item 104).

The students, two from each State and from the District of Columbia, were in Washington in connection with the United States Senate Youth Program. The program, established in 1962 by Senate Resolution 324, provides selected officers of public and private school student bodies with a week's internship in the U.S. Senate and in the Federal Government generally. It operates under a grant approved each year by the trustees of the William Randolph Hearst Foundation.

34 Remarks Upon Presenting the Distinguished Service Medal to Gen. Wallace M. Greene, Jr., USMC. *January 26, 1968*

General and Mrs. Greene, Members of Congress, Members of the Cabinet, Members of the Joint Chiefs of Staff, and distinguished guests:

I know you will understand that on occasions Presidents are necessarily late, particularly when General Greene has you doing other things. He has brought some other matters to my attention the last few days.

Six weeks ago, I believe, the Marines established a beachhead here in the East Room.

Standing here on December 9, I gave a daughter in marriage to one Marine officer.

Today I extend the Nation's gratitude to another Marine officer.

A leader makes a mark on his time. General Wallace Greene has left his mark in a towering record of achievement. Over at Marine Corps Headquarters, they speak of a "management revolution"—of new techniques and innovations that have strengthened and have expanded the Corps in a time of great national trial and testing. And that has come about through the work of General Wallace Greene as Commandant.

But his mark is bigger and bolder than that.

The heroic performance of the Marines who fight to protect each of us in Vietnam—who are now resisting a massive attack from the North at this very hour—speaks more than I can ever say for the spirit and the courage of 76,000 separate men. But it also says something about the man who leads those men and the man who prepares those men for the call they must answer. His mark is on each one of them. His brand is there.

Those Marines in I Corps—which means Marine country in Vietnam—are also testing something that is new in warfare. Combined Action Platoons protect the population of about 80 villages. The Marine squads in those platoons train the villages' own Popular Forces—and then fight beside them when it's necessary.

But the Marines are not just stationed in those villages. They are not just stationed there. They live there as friends and neighbors:

—compassionate, understanding, helpful;

—working with the people;

—trying to assist them build schools, drill wells, and construct houses;

—showing them how to get more from their land;

—giving them medical treatment; looking after the lame and the sick and the halt and the young.

It is going to be a long time before the

final results of their work can be assessed. But the enemy has already made his judgment. Recently, the enemy, the Vietcong offered $1,750—dead or alive—for the Marine sergeant of one of those platoons.

That was more money than many of the villagers would ever see in an entire lifetime. But no one earned it—and no one really tried to earn it. When the sergeant's tour was up and he had to leave the village, all turned out for a farewell party for the man who had been a friend of each one of them.

That came about because of men like General Walt, General Cushman, and others who are leading them out there. But it also came about because of this tradition, this organization, this esprit de corps, this excellence, and this elite. It also came about because of this man who put his mark on each one of them in the organization he headed.

As a result, that village and other villages bear the mark of the Marines who have been there. They bear the mark of their Commandant's belief, that real victory is going to be won in the hearts of the people.

On General Greene's last visit to Vietnam—and he has made six in less than 4 years as Commandant—the men of one of his units presented him with a bullet. His name was engraved on it, along with this message: "Everything is gonna be alright." Now, if the President said it that way they would talk about his accent or his English.

I am sure that General Greene will keep that bullet among his proudest souvenirs. But that message in those words, with that accent, is a message for each one of us because this Nation has been blessed with great leaders—with leaders who have not always been recognized while they were here—sometimes have been abused—but men like Wallace Greene, who are brave

men, who are good men, just like the Marines he leads and the Marines he commands.

We are fortunate that his command has now passed to a fine officer on his team— General Chapman.

I am especially proud of the other men in top positions in the Marine Corps whom General Greene has brought to the top and has surrounded himself with and whom he leaves with us to carry on.

General Greene, we asked you to come here today with your wife—although I am not intimately acquainted with her contributions through the years, I am sure that she has had more to do with what you are today than you have had, because that is true of most of us.

My grandfather told me it always took two good women to make one good man— a good mother and a good wife.

So, I want to salute you, General Greene, in the Nation's name, for a job that has been honorably done, favorably done, and faithfully done—and I guess in your language "well done."

There are always pluses and minuses. And we've been talking about all the good things. Now I guess we ought to mention one bad thing. They tell me that the one thing that the Marines need and do not have is a belief in themselves as an organization.

I heard a story the other day that I think is apropos.

It said that the Redskins were interviewing a Texas boy for a place on the squad. He had just finished SMU. The coach said, "Tell us what you can do."

The boy said, "Well, I can do 100 yards in less than 10 seconds on a muddy field. My passing record last year was 64 yards average against the wind. I punt 71 yards on a fall day. I think that is about it."

"Well," the coach said, "those are the

good things. What are some of the minuses?"

He said, "Coach, I have been known to exaggerate."

Now, really, what makes it apropos, all these things the Marines claim they do and claim they stand for—even when they make all the claims—the good thing about it is they don't exaggerate.

[Secretary of the Navy Paul R. Ignatius read the citation, the text of which follows.]

The President of the United States takes pleasure in presenting a Gold Star in lieu of the second Distinguished Service Medal to

GENERAL WALLACE M. GREENE, JR.
UNITED STATES MARINE CORPS

for service as set forth in the following

CITATION:

For exceptionally meritorious service to the Government of the United States in a position of great responsibility while serving as Commandant of the Marine Corps from 1 January 1964 to 31 December 1967. Tireless, imaginative, far seeing, and fiercely dedicated to the enduring purposes of the Nation, General Greene consistently demonstrated preeminent leadership qualities as the Marine Corps met successfully its worldwide military commitments while concurrently implementing new and progressive management programs and techniques that have made it a model of military efficiency and economy. Under General Greene's inspiring guidance and dynamic leadership, the Marine Corps reached a level of unsurpassed combat readiness and managerial efficiency during a period of worldwide ten-

sions, conflicts and challenges to the national security of the United States. Under his supervision, the Marine Corps was substantially increased in size, and committed half of its combat forces to the defense of freedom in the Republic of Vietnam. Believing in the supreme worth of the individual, he consistently concerned himself with the individual well-being of not only the men and women for whom he was responsible, but also with the welfare and peace of mind of their dependents and parents. His advice on national security matters was invariably wise and respected. A rare mixture of compassion and strong determination, he earned the deep loyalty, profound respect and great admiration of all with whom he served—Marines, soldiers, sailors, airmen, statesmen, governmental leaders and civil servants alike. By his strong character and unimpeachable integrity, he has maintained the high standards of the Marine Corps and added new achievements to its illustrious history. General Greene's distinguished service to the United States during more than forty-one years of devoted duty reflects the highest credit upon himself, the Naval Service and his Country.

LYNDON B. JOHNSON

NOTE: The President spoke at 1:21 p.m. in the East Room at the White House. During his remarks he referred to his daughter Lynda Bird, who married Capt. Charles S. Robb on December 9, 1967, in the East Room, Lt. Gen. Lewis W. Walt, Assistant Commandant of the Marine Corps, who formerly served as Commanding General of the III Marine Amphibious Force in Vietnam, Lt. Gen. Robert E. Cushman, Jr., who succeeded General Walt, and Gen. Leonard F. Chapman, Jr., who succeeded General Greene as Commandant of the Marine Corps.

35 The President's Address to the Nation: The Situation With North Korea. *January 26, 1968*

My fellow Americans:

Over the past 15 months the North Koreans have pursued a stepped-up campaign of violence against South Korean and the American troops in the area of the Demilitarized Zone.

Armed raider teams in very large numbers have been sent into South Korea to engage in sabotage and assassination.

On January 19, a 31-man team of North Korean raiders invaded Seoul with the object of murdering the President of the Republic of Korea.

In many of these aggressive actions, Korean and American soldiers have been killed and wounded. The North Koreans are apparently attempting to intimidate the South Koreans and are trying to interrupt the growing spirit of confidence and progress in the Republic of Korea.

These attacks may also be an attempt by the Communists to divert South Korean and United States military resources which together are now successfully resisting aggression in Vietnam.

This week the North Koreans committed yet another wanton and aggressive act by seizing an American ship and its crew in international waters. Clearly, this cannot be accepted.

We are doing two things: First, we are very shortly today taking the question before the Security Council of the United Nations. The best result would be for the whole world community to persuade North Korea to return our ship and our men, and to stop the dangerous course of aggression against South Korea.

We have been making other diplomatic efforts as well. We shall continue to use every means available to find a prompt and a peaceful solution to the problem.

Second, we have taken and we are taking certain precautionary measures to make sure that our military forces are prepared for any contingency that might arise in this area.

These actions do not involve in any way a reduction of our forces in Vietnam.

I hope that the North Koreans will recognize the gravity of the situation which they have created. I am confident that the American people will exhibit in this crisis, as they have in other crises, the determination and unity which are necessary to see it through.

Thank you very much.

NOTE: The President spoke at 3:58 p.m. in the Fish Room at the White House. During his remarks he referred to the seizure by North Koreans of the intelligence ship U.S.S. *Pueblo* and its 83-man crew.

The President's remarks were broadcast nationally.

36 Statement by the President Upon Releasing Report of the President's National Advisory Panel on Insurance in Riot-Affected Areas. *January 27, 1968*

ONE OF THE most urgent needs in America's cities today is to assure that the property of businessmen and homeowners is adequately protected by insurance.

The events of last summer spotlighted this need. The rebuilding of our cities turns on its being met.

Last August, I appointed a Panel, chaired

by Governor Richard Hughes of New Jersey, to study the problem and recommend ways to answer it.

The Panel has just submitted a comprehensive report which recommends the course of action it believes will solve this problem. It calls upon the property insurance industry and State, local, and Federal Governments to contribute to a solution.

This Panel's work shows once again how the pubilc interest can be served when the Federal Government, business, and State and local officials come together responsibly to meet the pressing problems of our cities.

I have asked the Secretary of Housing and Urban Development to review the Panel's report and, working with the Secretaries of Commerce and the Treasury, the Attorney General, the Director of the Budget, and the Administrator of the Small Business Administration, to prepare whatever legislation is appropriate to carry out the Federal responsibilities.

The work of this Panel deserves the highest thanks of the Nation.

NOTE: The report is entitled "Meeting the Insurance Crisis of Our Cities" (Government Printing Office, 1968, 165 pp.). For a list of members on the Advisory Panel and a summary of the report, see the Weekly Compilation of Presidential Documents (vol. 4, p. 142).

37 Talking Points of the President at a Luncheon for the National Alliance of Businessmen. *January* 27, 1968

1. A Vital Task.

—Hard-core unemployment:
  • Destroys families;
  • Deprives children of a decent house, a decent meal, a decent life;
  • Is one of the major causes of civil disorders.

—Your task is to help find jobs for the 500,000 hard-core unemployed in the 50 largest cities.

2. Background.

—This program is an outgrowth of two things: (1) The recommendations made to me by a task force last summer. Two members of that task force are here today: Mr. Miller and Mr. Sonnabend. (2) The test program which we launched last October to find jobs in private industry for the hard-core in 5 large cities.

—From these two efforts we learned that:
  • Business is willing to help;
  • The job will not be easy, the hard-

core will be difficult to motivate, to train, to keep on the job;
  • The Government has a long way to go: to simplify its procedures, to cut red tape.

3. Why Private Industry?

—We turn to private industry for three reasons:
  • Six out of every 7 jobs are in private enterprise;
  • On the job training is the most effective program we have; 9 out of 10 people who go through those programs get jobs;
  • American industry can do the job: It knows how to train people for the jobs on which its profits depend.

—We also turn to private industry because the alternative, "make work" programs, will cost far more and do far less for the individual and his family.

—And the situation is not like the 30's when "make work" programs were necessary.

- In 1935, 42 million Americans were employed, 10.6 million were unemployed and no jobs were being created by the economy;
- Today, 75 million Americans are at work, less than 3 million are unemployed and the economy is creating more than a million and a half jobs each year. It has created 7½ million jobs in the last 4 years.

4. The Program.

—Our target is to put 100,000 men and women on the job by June 1969 and 500,00 by June 1971.

—For the first 18 months, we will devote $350 million to this program, $106 for the next 6 months, and $244 million for fiscal 1969.

5. How the Program Will Work.

—The Government will identify the unemployed.

—The company will train them and offer them jobs.

—The company will bear the normal cost of training as it would for any new employee.

—But the hard-core will need more. They will need additional training. Some will have to be taught to read and write, others will have health problems. They will need counseling.

—Where the private company agrees to provide these services, the Government will pay the extra costs. If the company does not wish to provide the services, the Government will.

6. Your Task: The Role of the National Alliance of Businessmen.

—Your job will be:
- To sell this program;
- To get private companies to agree to train and hire the hard-core;
- To advise me and the Secretaries of Labor and Commerce as to how this program can be improved, how we can cut Government red tape.

—The structure for the Alliance was outlined briefly in my message:
- You will serve as the executive committee, determining policy and developing guidelines for action;
- Eight of you will be regional representatives, responsible for the effective operation of the programs in each of the major cities in your regions;
- Fifty city representatives will be responsible for promoting the program in their cities. They will work through existing business councils or devise new mechanisms for involving the business sector in this urgent work.

—I want each of you who has agreed to be a regional representative to help in selecting the city representatives. They must be people whom you can work with and really get the job done.

—I want you to suggest some names to Henry Ford as soon as possible.

—I want each of you to designate a top official in your company who can work full-time on this program.

CONCLUSION

—I am deeply grateful for your willingness to accept this tremendous responsibility.

—I am deeply grateful that we have a man as able as Leo Beebe to work full-time on this program.

—I can assure you that you will receive the full support of this Government. The Departments of Labor and Commerce will give you all the help you need—including the people you will need to carry out this task.

—I know you are busy and that it will be hard for you to devote a great deal of time to this effort. But this is a working group and as I said in the State of the Union Message "I know of no task before us of more importance to us, to the country, or to our future."

NOTE: This is the text of the White House press release made public in connection with the luncheon

for the National Alliance of Businessmen, held in the Family Dining Room at the White House at 2 p.m. References in the text are to G. William Miller, president, Textron, Inc., Roger P. Sonnabend, president, Hotel Corporation of America, Henry Ford II, chairman of the board, Ford Motor Co., and chairman of the National Alliance of Businessmen, and Leo Beebe, vice president of the Ford Motor Co., and executive vice chairman of the National Alliance of Businessmen.

For the establishment of the National Alliance of Businessmen and its membership, see Items 24 and 25. The names of additional members are printed in the Weekly Compilation of Presidential Documents (vol. 4, p. 144).

38 Remarks at the Swearing In of Charles Zwick as Director, Bureau of the Budget. *January 29, 1968*

Thank you, Mr. Schultze, Mr. Zwick, members of the family, staff of the Bureau, ladies and gentlemen, members of the press:

I am told that in some circles of this Government the outgoing and the incoming Directors of the Budget have been referred to by some of their associates as Charles the First and Charles the Second.

From what they tell me of English history, Charles the First had a lot of tax trouble with the Parliament and ended by losing his head. Our Charles the First—Mr. Schultze—is only going to Brookings and the University of Maryland. And if there is an analogy, I would not want to be the one to suggest it.

Charles the Second was a somewhat different type—something of a high-liver, I believe. Mr. Schultze has assured me that that is not true of Charles Zwick. At least, it had better not be true.

I have, I think, as President, been blessed with the finest Directors of the Budget that any President has ever had. First Kermit Gordon, who served the Kennedy administration with distinction and who served me until he left in 1965 for the repository of Budget Directors, Brookings Institute; then

Charlie Schultze.

I am confident that Charlie Zwick is in the same class with those outstanding public servants, although I anticipate that in due time he will be available to Brookings. I issued a very fair warning to Brookings this morning—hands off at least for a while.

One of the first things you must do, Mr. Zwick, is to learn the basic vocabulary of the Budget Director. Your predecessors were masters at it. As they can tell you, the first word you have to learn to speak is like a child says "da da," a Budget Director has to say, "no, no."

And a Budget Director to serve his President and the American people, must learn not to say "no, no" to everything.

Today, we are sending up a budget for fiscal 1969.

We will read and we will hear a lot about this budget. I have been listening to it since 6 o'clock this morning. They tell me it is a record budget—all of them are. This is a record country. Each year we grow and as we grow our budgets grow. The newspapers will, no doubt, compare it to the telephone book, some to a mail-order catalogue, some will count its pages and weigh it and tell us just how many pounds it contains.

But no newspaper story or political rhetoric will tell the full story of the budget.

Behind these figures, hidden in these tables, lie the dreams and the hopes of the American people—200 million of them.

Just for example, take a line that says the "Teacher Corps," or the "Peace Corps," or "VISTA," and then think of all the gallant, eager young people whose dream of service to their country will be fulfilled by these cold numbers.

Think of the millions of people they serve. Think, if you will, of the millions of dollars that they save, the lives they redeem, and the doors of opportunity they open, and the freedom and liberty that they protect and advance.

The budget is a nation's strategy to solve the problems that confront the nation. It looks ahead—not until November or until July of 1969, but beyond—3 years many times and 5 years a great deal of the time. It looks as far as sensible men can see, and as far as the most expert in the Government can plan.

Their job is to measure the aspirations of Americans against the stern rule of how much these people are willing to pay to carry out their aspirations. We sometimes misestimate that for a few months.

Their job is to judge and to say: "This is worth the price; or this is not worth the price and should wait. This is a price America can afford. But this one, this is a price America cannot afford to pay now."

The budget provides a shape for some dreams, and limits for all—limits fixed by tough-minded men who worked, and argued, and compromised, and decided through months of tedious days and nights. And some who made proposals and were disappointed and came back and leaked

them to pressure groups to exercise that influence at the last moment.

All of it is a very difficult job.

But there are some tasks that we ask no man to do. We ask no man to put a price on freedom. We ask no man to skimp 1 dollar on the support of our fighting men or to withhold 1 penny that will help achieve the peace that we seek in Vietnam.

We never know just how much we spend there because we don't know how much we would spend if it ended tomorrow. Some say it costs us $25 billion; some say $23 billion. I asked the most expert man, I thought, the other day in that field and he said: "Well, we are spending about $50 billion. When you take the price increases and put that on, and you take our total budget this year and you subtract it, I would guess that we are in the neighborhood of about 10 percent of our total budget or 18 percent or 20 percent that we would save if we could get out of Vietnam tomorrow."

So, here at home these decisions are very difficult ones in that light, because some people think if we did not have Vietnam we would have money to solve all of our problems, because we do have plenty. We see the need for extra law enforcement efforts. We see the need for additional poverty efforts, better health, better housing, and more jobs, and better education.

Among the programs that are meant to answer those needs we must pick and choose—and we must say yes and no—and perhaps we must delay for another year a dam or an irrigation project or a public building or some kind of investment that we think is needed now.

Sometimes this budget says no, but not for all time. Our people want prudence in spending. They want strong hands controlling expenditures to the extent that they can be controlled. But they do not want to stand still. They know that the country is challenged here and abroad, and that the level of our taxing and spending should reflect our intention to meet those challenges.

The pace of our progress will be set, not by our abundance—for that is very great—but how much our people are willing to spend of it, and how much we are willing to tax ourselves to get the things that we think we need.

With this budget, I will renew my recommendation for a tax surcharge. As simply as I can, I want to speak of this budget in relation to the proposed tax measures.

First, virtually all of its additional spending—some $10.4 billion—virtually all of it is made mandatory by law or required for our national defense.

The social security and related items like Medicare, Medicaid, veterans, et cetera, runs about $4.7 billion. Defense is about $3.2 billion. That is roughly $8 billion.

Interest is $1 billion and that is mandatory. The pay bills are $1.6 billion and that is $10 billion-plus.

Now, there are the items. We cannot do much about the defense. We had requests for over $100 billion. We reduced them to under $80 billion.

We may have to put some of it back. We couldn't reduce it much more. We cannot reduce the interest at all or the pay, at all, or the Medicare or Medicaid or Social Security. They are all passed and we are collecting taxes to bring them in.

So that is where the $10 billion-plus will go in this new budget. We have some new items in the budget. But before we would give them to any Cabinet officer, we said, "Find an old one that you can postpone or eliminate."

Every major decision in building this budget was examined—most of it personally examined—and it was based on every bit of

information that I could lay my hands on.

That is the only way I know to make a budget that is fair to the people. We no doubt made some mistakes. We no doubt made some misjudgments. We no doubt put in some items that the Congress will want to share different judgment on. They will want to put in some things we didn't put in. They will want to take out some.

But that is the system of checks and balances.

I believe it is a sound budget and a realistic one. I believe it is the best budget that the judgment of dedicated men and women could devise. For this, I want to publicly acknowledge and thank Director Schultze and wish him and his family all the rewards of faithful service to our country; and to thank all the legion of loyal, most competent employees for their cooperation.

There is no agency in the Government that is closer to the President, more effective for the President, or that I have found more loyal or more competent, than the Budget Bureau, from the Director to the lowest-paid employee.

With that statement, I want to say goodby officially to Mr. Schultze, who unofficially I hope will be coming in and out from time to time to help me with the problems, and I want to welcome our new Director, Mr. Charlie Zwick, who I think knows full well already from his contacts here and there what he is in for.

NOTE: The President spoke at 11:38 a.m. in the Cabinet Room at the White House. In his opening words he also referred to Charles L. Schultze, outgoing Director of the Bureau of the Budget.

For Mr. Schultze's remarks which preceded the President's, see the Weekly Compilation of Presidential Documents (vol. 4, p. 146). The announcement of Mr. Schultze's resignation and the appointment of Charles J. Zwick is printed in the Weekly Compilation of Presidential Documents (vol. 4, p. 55).

For the Budget Message, see Item 39.

39   Annual Budget Message to the Congress, Fiscal Year 1969. *January 29, 1968*

To the Congress of the United States:

The budget I send you today reflects a series of difficult choices. They are choices we cannot avoid. How we make the choices will affect our future as a strong, responsible, and compassionate people.

We now possess the strongest military capability that any nation has ever had. Domestically, we have enjoyed an unparalleled period of economic advance. Nevertheless, we are confronted by a number of problems which demand our energies and determination.

Abroad we face the challenge of an obstinate foe, who is testing our resolve and the worth of our commitment. While we maintain our unremitting search for a just and reasonable peace, we must also continue a determined defense against aggression. This budget provides the funds needed for that defense, and for the maintenance and improvement of our total defense forces. The costs of that defense—even after a thorough review and screening—remain very large.

At home we face equally stubborn foes— poverty, slums and substandard housing, urban blight, polluted air and water, excessively high infant mortality, rising crime rates, and inferior education for too many of our citizens. In recent years, we have come to recognize that these are conquerable ills. We have used our ingenuity to develop means to attack them, and have devoted increasing resources to that effort. We would be derelict in our responsibilities as a great nation if we shrank from pressing forward toward solutions to these problems.

But faced with a costly war abroad and urgent requirements at home, we have had to set priorities. And "priority" is but another word for "choice." We cannot do everything we would wish to do. And so we must choose carefully among the many competing demands on our resources.

After carefully weighing priorities, I am proposing three kinds of actions:

- *First,* I have carefully examined the broad range of defense and civilian needs, and am proposing the *selective expansion* of existing programs or the inauguration of new programs only as necessary to meet those urgent requirements whose fulfillment we cannot delay.
- *Second,* I am proposing *delays and deferments* in existing programs, wherever this can be done without sacrificing vital national objectives.
- *Third,* I am proposing *basic changes, reforms, or reductions* designed to lower the budgetary cost of a number of Federal programs which, in their present form, no longer effectively meet the needs of today.

Federal programs bring important benefits to all segments of the Nation. This is why they were proposed and enacted in the first place. Setting priorities among them, proposing reductions in some places and fundamental reforms in others, is a difficult and a painful task. But it is also a duty. I ask the Congress and the American people to help me carry out that duty.

Even after a rigorous screening of priorities, however, the cost of meeting our most pressing defense and civilian requirements cannot be responsibly financed without a temporary tax increase. I requested such an increase a year ago. On the basis of changed fiscal conditions, I revised my request in a special message to the Congress last August. I am renewing that request now.

There is no question that as a nation we are strong enough, we are intelligent enough, we are productive enough to carry out our responsibilities and take advantage of our opportunities. Our *ability* to act as a great nation is not at issue. It is our *will* that is being tested.

Are we willing to tax our incomes an additional penny on the dollar to finance the cost of Vietnam responsibly? Are we willing to take the necessary steps to preserve a stable economy at home and the soundness of the dollar abroad?

One way or the other we will be taxed. We can choose to accept the arbitrary and capricious tax levied by inflation, and high interest rates, and the likelihood of a deteriorating balance of payments, and the threat of an economic bust at the end of the boom.

Or, we can choose the path of responsibility. We can adopt a reasoned and moderate approach to our fiscal needs. We can apportion the fiscal burden equitably and rationally through the tax measures I am proposing.

The question, in short, is whether we can match our will and determination to our responsibilities and our capacity.

BUDGET SUMMARY

I am presenting my 1969 budget under the new unified budget concept unanimously recommended by the bipartisan Commission on Budget Concepts I appointed last year. Among the many changes recommended by the Commission and incorporated in this year's budget presentation, two stand out:

• *First,* the total budget includes the receipts and expenditures of the *trust*

funds, which were excluded from the traditional "administrative budget" concept. Because some $47 billion of trust funds are included in the new budget concept, its *totals* are much larger than those in the old administrative budget.

• *Second,* when the Federal Government makes a repayable *loan,* the effect on the economy is very different than when it spends money for a missile, a dam, or a grant program. A loan is an exchange of financial assets. Unlike other outlays, it does not directly add to the income of the recipient. Consequently, the Commission on Budget Concepts recommended that the budget identify and distinguish "expenditures" from "lending," and, for purposes of evaluating economic impact, show a separate calculation of the surplus or deficit based on expenditure totals alone. My budget presentation follows this significant recommendation.

This budget carries a special section showing the relationship between the new and the old concepts.

The 1969 budget proposes outlays of $186.1 billion, of which:

• $182.8 billion is spending.
• $3.3 billion is net lending.

Including the effects of the tax increase I am proposing, revenues in fiscal year 1969 are estimated at $178.1 billion.

On the new budget basis, the overall deficit of $8.0 billion anticipated in 1969 compares with an estimated deficit of $19.8 billion in 1968. Thus, the reduction in the deficit is estimated to be $11.8 billion.

A better measure of the direct impact of the Federal budget on the Nation's income and output is given by the *expenditure account* (which excludes the lending programs of the Federal Government). The expendi-

SUMMARY OF THE BUDGET AND FINANCIAL PLAN

[Fiscal years. In billions]

Description	1967 actual	1968 estimate	1969 estimate
Budget authority (largely appropriations):			
Previously enacted...	$135.4	$125.1	....
Proposed for current action by Congress............................	....	3.3	$141.5
Becoming available without current action by Congress	58.7	69.9	73.1
Deductions for interfund and intragovernmental transactions and applicable receipts..	−11.5	−11.8	−12.9
Total, budget authority.....................................	182.6	186.5	201.7
Receipts, expenditures, and net lending:			
Expenditure account:			
Receipts..	149.6	155.8	178.1
Expenditures (excludes net lending)..............................	153.2	169.9	182.8
Expenditure deficit (−)...	−3.6	−14.0	−4.7
Loan account.			
Loan disbursements...	17.8	20.9	20.4
Loan repayments...	−12.6	−15.1	−17.1
Net lending...	5.2	5.8	3.3
Total budget:			
Receipts..	149.6	155.8	178.1
Outlays (expenditures and net lending).........................	158.4	175.6	186.1
Budget deficit (−)...	−8.8	−19.8	−8.0
Budget financing:			
Borrowing from the public.......................................	3.6	20.8	8.0
Reduction of cash balances, etc....................................	5.3	−1.0	*
Total, budget financing.......................................	8.8	19.8	8.0

	1966 actual			
Outstanding debt, end of year:				
Gross amount outstanding....................................$329.5		341.3	370.0	387.2
Held by the public.................................... 265.6		269.2	290.0	298.0

*Less than $50 million.

ture deficit in fiscal year 1969 is estimated at $4.7 billion, a reduction of $9.3 billion from 1968.

Between 1968 and 1969 the normal growth in revenues—associated with rising incomes and business activity—is expected to be $11.5 billion. This more than covers the rise in budget outlays between the two years—estimated at $10.4 billion. Consequently, all of the revenues from the proposed surcharge and the speedup in corporate tax payments will be applied towards reducing the budget deficit.

To carry forward the proposals in the

budget, I am requesting new budget authority of $201.7 billion for 1969, of which $141.5 billion will have to be provided through appropriation bills or similar action during the current session of Congress. The remainder will become available under existing law without current congressional action, including the social insurance trust funds and interest on the public debt.

FISCAL PROGRAM FOR 1969

ECONOMIC BACKGROUND.—The overall fiscal policy for 1969 has been designed to achieve four major goals:

- Continuation of sustained growth in jobs and real income for the American people.
- Lessening of inflationary pressures.
- Improvement in the U.S. balance of payments.
- Reduction in Federal borrowing, aimed at reducing the upward pressure on interest rates.

In March, the American economy will achieve a new milestone as it enters its eighth year of sustained expansion. No prior period in our history has been marked by an expansion of such long duration. Each month that we continue to move ahead creates its own new record. And this record translates into jobs, incomes, and rising living standards for the American people.

During the past 4 years, the continued expansion has resulted in:

- the creation of 7 and a half million new jobs;
- an increase of 21% in national output;
- a rise of 18.8% in per capita income after taxes and after adjustment for price change;
- a rise of 12% in output per man-hour in the private sector of the economy;
- a decline of 6½ million in the number

of people living in poverty; and

- a rate of unemployment which, for the past 2 years, has averaged less than 4% of the labor force and now stands at 3.7%.

Many factors contributed to this unparalleled achievement. But chief among them was the flexible use of fiscal policy—particularly the tax reductions and reforms of 1962, 1964, and 1965. A lagging economy was set in motion and sustained in expansion through these actions.

Between calendar years 1961 and 1965, economic growth was accompanied by a remarkable degree of price stability. Wholesale industrial prices rose by about one-half of 1% per year. The annual increase in consumer prices was about 1⅓%.

Since 1965, however, our economic achievements have been marred by an accelerated rate of price increases. Although these increases have not been as great as those in many other industrial countries, the consumer price index in the past 2 years has risen at an annual rate of 2.9%, and wholesale industrial prices at an annual rate of 1.8%.

Interest rates on loans and securities of all types have advanced sharply, first in 1966, and then after a short period of decline, again in 1967. Our balance of payments deficit—which had been reduced from $3.9 billion in 1960 to $1.4 billion in 1966—took a sharp turn for the worse in 1967.

The problems of rising prices and interest rates, and a worsening balance of payments, arise from many causes. And their correction will require a variety of measures. But central to any attack upon them is a fiscal policy which—through a combination of expenditure control and tax increase—sharply reduces the inappropriate stimulus of a large Federal budget deficit in today's vigorous economy.

BUDGET OUTLAYS AS A PERCENTAGE OF GROSS NATIONAL PRODUCT
[Fiscal years]

	Average 1958–1960 actual	1965 actual	1968 estimate	1969 estimate
Total outlays:				
Vietnam..	....	*	3.1%	3.0
Social insurance trust funds.........................	3.0%	3.4%	4.2	4.4
Other outlays......................................	16.0	14.6	14.2	13.9

*Less than 0.05%

We are now spending approximately $25 billion annually to support our efforts in Vietnam—in the 4 fiscal years, 1966 through 1969 combined, we will have spent more than $75 billion. Our annual expenditure for this purpose amounts to about 3% of gross national product. Other outlays, exclusive of social insurance trust funds, have been *declining* as a share of the Nation's income and output in recent years. It is not the rise in regular budget outlays which requires a tax increase, but the cost of Vietnam.

The tax increase I am requesting is in the same form as the one I recommended last year—a temporary 10% surcharge on individual and corporation income taxes. I again strongly urge its early approval by the Congress, with an effective date of January 1, 1968, for corporations and April 1, 1968, for individuals.

With enactment of the tax measures proposed in this budget—the surcharge, extension of excises, and the acceleration of corporate tax collections—the total budget deficit can be cut by more than half between 1968 and 1969. Without the tax measures, the deficit in 1969 would remain close to $20 billion for the second year in a row. In an economy already moving strongly upward, such a deficit in 1969 would clearly add sharply to inflationary pressures.

Inflation robs the purchasing power of those living on fixed incomes. It is a regressive tax which strikes hardest at those least able to afford it—the poor and the elderly.

By raising the price at which we must sell in foreign markets, inflation also causes our export industries to suffer and our imports to increase more rapidly. Perhaps even more importantly, failure to take decisive fiscal action to reduce our budget deficit would raise strong doubts throughout the world about America's willingness to keep its financial house in order.

Finally, unless we take action to reduce the budget deficit significantly, Federal borrowing is likely to be so large as to drive up interest rates and reduce the availability of credit, especially to home buyers, small businessmen, and State and local governments.

REVENUES.—The 178.1 billion in estimated revenues for fiscal year 1969 includes $12.9 billion from the tax measures I am proposing—the temporary income tax surcharge, the extension of present excise tax rates, and the speedup in corporation tax payments.

As I have repeatedly noted, the temporary surcharge represents a modest addition to our current tax bills. It would spread most equitably and fairly the cost of the commitments we must meet. It would exempt entirely from increased taxation about 17 million Americans whose low incomes place them within the first two tax brackets. It would not be haphazard and capricious like the tax of inflation. In terms of the income of individuals subject to the surcharge the tax increase

87

BUDGET RECEIPTS
[Fiscal years. In billions]

Source	1967 actual	1968 estimate	1969 estimate
Individual income taxes	$61.5	$67.7	$80.9
Corporation income taxes	34.0	31.3	34.3
Excise taxes	13.7	13.8	14.7
Employment taxes	27.8	29.7	34.2
All other receipts	12.6	13.3	14.1
Total	149.6	155.8	178.1
Under existing law	149.6	152.8	165.0
Under proposed legislation:			
Tax measures	....	3.0	12.9
User charges	....	....	.3

would average about one additional penny on the dollar. And, unlike inflation, it can be removed promptly if no longer warranted by our unusual outlays in Southeast Asia.

I am also proposing that the telephone excise tax of 10% and the automobile excise tax of 7% be extended at these rates beyond April 1, 1968, instead of dropping to 1% and 2%, respectively, as provided in present law. In addition, the Congress should enact the proposals made last year to modify the provisions for current payment of the corporate income tax so that they correspond to the current payment provisions applicable to individuals.

An estimated $4.4 billion of the increase in revenues in 1969 will come from employment taxes which finance social security and other trust fund programs. Under the recent amendments to the Social Security Act, the annual wages on which each employee's social security taxes are paid rose from $6,600 to $7,800 as of January 1, 1968, and the combined employer-employee payroll tax will increase from 8.8% to 9.6% on January 1, 1969.

I am also recommending a number of new and increased user charges for programs in which the services provided by the Federal Government yield direct benefits to specific individuals and businesses. These charges—notably in the field of transportation—will, and should, shift the burden of financing from the general taxpayer to those who benefit directly, and make the provision of these services dependent upon the willingness of the user to pay for them.

OUTLAYS.—The $186.1 billion in total budget outlays for 1969 represents an increase of $10.4 billion from the current fiscal year. Almost all of this increase is accounted for by rising outlays for defense and for relatively fixed charges under present laws.

Of the total $10.4 billion increase:

- $3.3 billion is for national defense;
- $4.2 billion is for the Federal Government's social insurance programs (chiefly social security and Medicare);
- $1.6 billion is for the second step of the civilian and military pay increase enacted last year; and
- $1.3 billion is for other relatively fixed charges (interest, public assistance, veterans pensions, etc.).

Outlays in relatively controllable civilian programs are estimated to rise by $0.5 billion from 1968 to 1969. This rise is more than accounted for by an increase of $1½ to $2 billion in payments on prior contracts and

CONTROLLABILITY OF BUDGET OUTLAYS

[Fiscal years. In billions]

Type of controllability	1967 actual	1968 estimate	1969 estimate	Change, 1968 to 1969
National defense..	$70.1	$76.5	$79.8	+$3.3
Relatively uncontrollable civilian programs:				
Open-ended programs and fixed costs:				
Social security, Medicare, and other social insurance trust funds..	30.3	34.3	38.5	+4.2
Interest...	12.5	13.5	14.4	+.9
Civilian and military pay increase......................	....	....	1.6	+1.6
Veterans pensions, compensation, and insurance...........	4.9	5.1	5.2	+.1
Public assistance grants...............................	4.2	5.2	5.7	+.5
Farm price supports (Commodity Credit Corporation).....	1.7	2.8	2.9	+.1
Postal operations.....................................	.8	.7	.3	−.4
Legislative and judiciary..............................	.3	.4	.4	*
Other..	2.4	2.7	2.8	+.1
Subtotal, relatively uncontrollable civilian programs.....	57.1	64.7	71.8	+7.1
Relatively controllable civilian programs, including outlays from prior year contracts and obligations.................	35.2	39.0	39.5	+.5
Undistributed intragovernmental payments (−).............	−4.0	−4.6	−5.0	−.5
Total budget outlays...............................	158.4	175.6	186.1	+10.4

*Less than $50 million.

obligations. On the other hand, budget outlays by the Federal National Mortgage Association trust fund are scheduled to decline. All other outlays in relatively controllable civilian programs will be essentially unchanged from 1968 to 1969.

Within this relatively stable total, however, there are a large number of individual increases and decreases. Tight budgeting does not mean an indiscriminate "hold-the-line" on all programs. Rather, it implies a rigorous application of priorities, providing increases where needs are urgent and returns high, slowing the growth of programs with less urgent priority, and reducing outlays where requirements have decreased or programs have become outmoded.

In the application of this priority system, my budget provides selective increases for a number of urgent domestic programs, particularly:

- manpower training;
- Model Cities;
- programs to control the rising crime rate;
- family planning and health care for mothers and infants;
- air and water pollution control; and
- research in better methods of education, and assistance in increasing the supply of qualified teachers.

These and the other selected programs for which I am recommending increases, respond to the most urgent needs of our Nation today—the basic problems of poverty, crime, and the quality of our environment. I urge the Congress to give them the most careful consideration. We can ignore these

89

BUDGET OUTLAYS

[Fiscal years. In billions]

Description	1967 actual	1968 estimate	1969 estimate	Change, 1968 to 1969
National defense	$70.1	$76.5	$79.8	+$3.3
Social security, Medicare, and other social insurance trust funds	30.3	34.3	38.5	+4.2
Other major social programs:				
Education	4.0	4.5	4.7	+.2
Health (excluding Medicare)	3.4	4.4	4.9	+.5
Labor and manpower	1.1	1.3	1.5	+.2
Economic opportunity programs	1.5	1.9	2.0	+.1
Welfare	3.9	4.6	4.9	+.3
Urban community development, and low and moderate income housing	1.1	2.0	2.3	+.4
Regional development	.2	.4	.5	+.1
Interest	12.5	13.5	14.4	+.9
Civilian and military pay increase	....	....	1.6	+1.6
All other	34.2	36.9	36.0	−.8
Undistributed intragovernmental payments (−)	−4.0	−4.6	−5.0	−.5
Total budget outlays	158.4	175.6	186.1	+10.4

problems only at grave risk of harm to the fabric of our society.

At the same time as I propose selected increases, I have taken other steps to hold budget totals to the minimum consistent with the national security and well-being. My budget provides for:

- *the cutback of controllable programs in 1968* which the Congress enacted upon my recommendation;
- *reductions, deferrals, and program reforms,* which would reduce program levels in a variety of Federal activities by $2.9 billion in 1969;
- a determined effort to *slow the pace of federally financed construction* programs as much as possible consistent with orderly government and sound practices;
- a *careful review of all budget requests* to insure that increases are recommended only in case of high priority programs.

BUDGET AUTHORITY.—Before Federal agencies can spend or lend funds, the Congress must enact authority for them to incur financial obligations and make the payments required to meet these obligations. Most of this authority is provided in the form of *appropriations.*

For fiscal year 1969, a total of $201.7 billion of such authority is proposed:

- New obligational authority of $197.1 billion for expenditure account programs, and
- Lending authority of $4.6 billion for loan account programs.

Not all of this authority will be fully obligated or spent in 1969; some of it is needed to provide the authority for major procurement, construction, loan contracts, and other large-scale activities in which obligations made in one year result in outlays over a period of years.

Of the total budget authority recommended for 1969, the Congress would have to act on $141.5 billion during the current session. The remaining authority will become available under existing law without further action by the Congress. Such authority consists chiefly of trust fund programs (under which the revenues of the special taxes and other specific receipts financing the programs are automatically appropriated) and interest on the public debt.

The authority for 1969 which the Congress is being asked to enact is $13.1 billion greater than the current estimate for 1968, but only $6.1 billion higher than the amount enacted 2 years ago. Current action by the Congress to provide budget authority varies widely from year to year because in several large programs—highways, TVA electric power construction, and the special assistance functions of the Department of Housing and Urban Development, for example— budget authority is provided in 1 year to cover a number of succeeding years. In fiscal

year 1968, there is a considerable decline in the amount of such multiyear authority.

Of the $15.2 billion increase in total budget authority in 1969, $6.2 billion is for the Department of Defense and military assistance program, $3.9 billion is available for trust funds, $0.9 billion is for interest on the public debt, and $1.6 billion for the military and civilian pay raises effective July 1, 1968.

The remaining increase in budget authority totals $2.6 billion.

Major increases in this remainder are:

- $586 million for public assistance and payments to the Medicare trust fund.
- $597 million for foreign economic assistance, to meet minimal development needs, primarily in Latin America and Asia, following the reductions in this program last year.
- $442 million for Federal manpower ac-

BUDGET AUTHORITY
[Fiscal years. In billions]

Description	1967 actual	1968 estimate	1969 estimate
Available through current action by the Congress:			
Previously enacted	$135.4	$125.1	....
Proposed in this budget	....	....	$138.4
To be requested separately:			
For supplemental requirements under present law	....	3.0	*
Upon enactment of proposed legislation	....	.2	.9
Allowances:			
Civilian and military pay increase	....	....	1.6
Contingencies	....	.2	.6
Subtotal, available through current action by the Congress	135.4	128.4	141.5
Available without current action by the Congress (permanent authorizations):			
Trust funds	41.7	50.1	54.0
Interest on the public debt	13.4	14.4	15.2
Other	3.6	5.4	3.9
Interfund and intragovernmental transactions (−)	−6.6	−7.4	−8.2
Applicable receipts from the public (−)	−4.9	−4.4	−4.6
Total budget authority	182.6	186.5	201.7

*Less than $50 million.

tivities of civilian agencies.

- $163 million for the Office of Economic Opportunity (apart from its manpower activities).
- $245 million for the Atomic Energy Commission, largely associated with the new Sentinel antiballistic missile system.
- $688 million for the Model Cities program.

Major decreases from 1968 to 1969 include:

- $401 million for construction grant programs of the Office of Education.
- $254 million for the Post Office, reflecting the postal rate increase enacted in 1967.
- $204 million for health construction grants.
- $218 million for the National Aeronautics and Space Administration, because requirements for the Apollo program are declining.
- $81 million for certain Corps of Engineers construction activities.

This budget includes for fiscal year 1968 $3.4 billion in supplemental appropriations recommended for enactment this year, along with the related outlays. Of this total, $1.1 billion represents the current year's cost of the pay raise for Federal personnel, over and above amounts the agencies have been able to absorb. The other major supplemental requirement is $1.6 billion for the Department of Health, Education, and Welfare, largely for welfare payments and medical assistance, and for the Government's payments to the health insurance trust fund.

BUDGET PROGRAM REDUCTIONS AND REFORMS

In this budget I am recommending two kinds of measures to reduce Federal outlays.

First, I am proposing certain reductions which primarily reflect the stringent nature of the 1969 budget. I am, for example, recommending a temporary reduction in certain construction programs, not because they have outlived their usefulness, but because a deferral of this construction is appropriate in a period when we must relieve inflationary pressures by reducing the deficit.

These reductions reflect a cut in existing program levels in terms of obligations, commitments, or contracts, which can be accomplished without substantially altering the character of the affected program. Such reductions are estimated to bring 1969 programs some $1.6 billion below 1968 appropriated levels.

Second, I am recommending long-run reforms and modifications to eliminate certain programs or make them more effective. As the economic and social profile of the Nation changes, Federal programs must also change—or run the risk of being inappropriate, ineffective, and irrelevant.

Under the reform proposals, the program level of older outmoded activities would be reduced, or, in certain cases, charges for benefits would be imposed or substantially increased. These proposed reforms are estimated to reduce the 1969 budgetary burden for these programs by $1.2 billion below the prior year's levels. The corresponding amount for 1970 is estimated at $1.4 billion.

Change will not be easy. Many revisions will require legislation, for which I seek congressional support and approval. Many of these programs have lived long lives and recipients have become accustomed to enjoying their benefits. Nevertheless, today's priorities demand change—no matter how difficult it may be.

The expenditure savings from these reductions and reforms will not all occur in 1969, but will be spread over several years. These

BUDGET PROGRAM REDUCTIONS AND REFORMS

[Fiscal years. In millions]

Agency and program

	Cuts below 1968 program level, as funded, 1969
BUDGET REDUCTIONS	
Agriculture:	
Farm operating loans..	−$50
Rural electrification loans...	−45
Forest roads and trails..	−29
Sewer and water loans..	−22
Water and sewer grants...	−3
Watershed protection program.......................................	−17
Flood prevention program...	−11
Agricultural research..	−15
Forest protection and utilization.....................................	−2
Great Plains conservation program...................................	−2
Other..	−1
Subtotal, Agriculture..	−197
Commerce:	
Ship construction...	−156
Research—Maritime Administration..................................	−7
Subtotal, Commerce...	−163
Health, Education, and Welfare:	
College facility grants...	−224
Books, equipment, guidance, and testing grants........................	−120
Health research facilities construction................................	−29
School aid to federally impacted areas................................	−17
Medical library construction grants..................................	−10
Subtotal, Health, Education, and Welfare.........................	−400
Housing and Urban Development:	
Grants for basic water and sewer facilities............................	−25
Public facility loans...	−10
Special assistance for market rate mortgages—Federal National Mortgage Association......	−27
Subtotal, Housing and Urban Development........................	−62
Interior:	
Reclamation program...	−27
Indian construction programs..	−22
Road programs...	−6
Sport fisheries construction..	−5
Commercial fisheries construction....................................	−1
Subtotal, Interior..	−61

93

BUDGET PROGRAM REDUCTIONS AND REFORMS—Continued

[Fiscal years. In millions]

Agency and program	Cuts below 1968 program level, as funded, 1969
BUDGET REDUCTIONS—Continued	
Justice: Elimination of new prison construction..	—$1
State: Educational exchange..	—1
Atomic Energy Commission:	
Production of special nuclear materials..	—12
Nuclear rocket program..	—10
Space electric power..	—8
Civilian application of nuclear explosives (Plowshare).................................	—6
Subtotal, Atomic Energy Commission...	—36
General Services Administration: Construction..	—143
National Aeronautics and Space Administration: Manned and unmanned exploration and other programs..	—447
National Science Foundation: Institutional science programs...............................	—31
Small Business Administration:	
Business loans..	—40
Economic opportunity loans..	—25
Investment company loans..	—25
Subtotal, Small Business Administration...	—90
Total, budget reductions.........	—1,632

PROGRAM REFORMS

Agency and program	1969	1970
Agriculture: Agricultural conservation program—limit to practices with long-term benefits..	—$120	—$120
Health, Education, and Welfare: School aid to federally impacted areas—tie payments more closely to Federal burden..	....	—100
Housing and Urban Development: Private housing—place greater reliance on the private market (requiring change in statutory interest rate ceilings)......................	—669	—669
Labor: Institute user charges to recover expenses under Longshoremen and Harbor Workers Compensation Act...	—3	—3

94

BUDGET PROGRAM REDUCTIONS AND REFORMS—Continued

[Fiscal years. In millions]

Agency and program	1969	1970
PROGRAM REFORMS—Continued		
Transportation:		
Airway services—increase taxes on users....................................	−$40	−$55
Waterways—impose tax on users...	−7	−14
Highway trucking—increase tax on diesel fuels and apply graduated use tax by weight...	−239	−250
Subtotal, Transportation...	−286	−319
Veterans Administration:		
Compensation—eliminate statutory payments for cases of arrested tuberculosis.....	−54	−54
Burial benefits—eliminate duplication with social security......................	−46	−46
Pensions—count railroad retirement benefits as part of income in setting amount of veterans pension..	−7	−7
Subtotal, Veterans Administration..	−107	−107
Small Business Administration: Disaster loans—employ more equitable and rigorous criteria...	−50	−50
Water Resources Projects of several agencies—raise the interest rate used for evaluating projects..	(1)	(1)
Total, program reforms...	−1,235	−1,368
Grand total, budget program reductions and reforms, 1969...................	−2,867	

[1] While no immediate savings are realized, the long-term effect could be substantial.

proposals, shown in the accompanying table, will touch nearly every major agency in the Federal Government.

There have been suggestions for a long-range study of Federal programs, evaluating their effectiveness and proposing reforms. Clearly, more study of potential program reforms is needed. My proposals this year represent a first step on which we can and should act now.

Throughout the years, it has been easier to discuss the need to restructure older Government programs, than actually to change them. I urge the Congress to take prompt and favorable action in support of these proposals to cull out lower priority programs.

FEDERAL DEBT

On the basis of all revenues and outlays included in the new unified budget, the Federal debt held by the public will increase to an estimated $298 billion on June 30, 1969, from $290 billion at the end of fiscal year 1968. A substantial amount of Federal debt is not held by the public but by Government agencies and trust funds. Federal gross debt—which is the sum of the amount held by the public and within the Government—is estimated at $387.2 billion at the end of fiscal year 1969.

During the past year the Congress substantially revised the permanent statutory

FEDERAL DEBT AND BUDGET FINANCING

[End of fiscal years. In billions]

Description	1967 actual	1968 estimate	1969 estimate
Federal debt held by the public....................................	$269.2	$290.0	$298.0
Plus: Debt held by Federal agencies and trust funds.....................	72.2	80.0	89.2
Equals: Gross Federal debt...	341.3	370.0	387.2
Of which:			
Treasury debt..	322.9	344.1	356.7
Other agency debt..	18.5	25.9	30.5
Budget financing:			
Borrowing from the public..	3.6	20.8	8.0
Reduction of cash balances, etc....................................	5.3	—1.0	*
Total budget financing...	8.8	19.8	8.0
Total budget deficit..	—8.8	—19.8	—8.0

*Less than $50 million.

debt limit, which applies to concepts used in previous budgets. It also provided for temporary further increases beginning with the fiscal year 1969, to take care of seasonal fluctuations. On the basis of the present fiscal outlook, and assuming enactment of the new tax measures which I have proposed, it should not be necessary to seek revision of the limit during this session of the Congress.

If and when it becomes necessary to revise the statutory limit, some modifications in the scope and nature of the limit may be appropriate, in line with the recommendations of the Commission on Budget Concepts.

Under the revised concepts presented in this budget, the Federal debt includes a wider range of Federal securities than the direct obligations of the Treasury Department, which have formerly been regarded as the public debt. Under the new concept, the debt includes:

• Direct obligations of the Treasury;
• Securities issued by other Federal agencies; and
• Certificates of participation in assets of

Federal agencies issued by the Export-Import Bank and by the Federal National Mortgage Association for itself and as trustee for several other agencies.

In total, agency obligations other than Treasury securities will amount to an estimated $25.9 billion on June 30, 1968, and will increase to $30.5 billion by June 30, 1969.

Increases in borrowing from the public represent the primary means of financing the budget deficit. Lesser amounts are available from time to time by drawing down the Treasury's cash balances or from a portion of the seigniorage on the Government's minting operations.

PROGRAM HIGHLIGHTS

The budget covers all the expenses which can be reasonably anticipated in the coming year. To assure that the total takes into account the inevitable uncertainties in estimating for a future period, $2.2 billion in new obligational authority and $2.0 billion in expenditures have been included as special allowances for 1969. These allowances provide for: (1) civilian and military pay increases required by law, and (2) unforeseen contingencies and the possible costs of new programs for which definite estimates cannot be made at the present time.

The Government's program and budget for 1969 are outlined briefly in the table and sections that follow.

NATIONAL DEFENSE.—In a world of shrinking distances, our own peace and security is bound up with the destiny of other nations. The defense budget for 1969 reflects our resolve to preserve the independence of Vietnam and to provide the forces essential for safeguarding our national security and international obligations.

Since 1961, excluding those forces added because of operations in Vietnam, we have increased our military capability in every

BUDGET OUTLAYS

[Fiscal years. In billions]

Function	1967 actual	1968 estimate	1969 estimate
Expenditures:			
National defense	$70.1	$76.5	$79.8
Excluding special Vietnam	(50.0)	(52.0)	(54.0)
International affairs and finance	4.1	4.3	4.5
Excluding special Vietnam	(3.7)	(3.9)	(4.0)
Space research and technology	5.4	4.8	4.6
Agriculture and agricultural resources	3.2	4.4	4.5
Natural resources	2.1	2.4	2.5
Commerce and transportation	7.3	7.7	8.0
Housing and community development	.6	.7	1.4
Health, labor, and welfare	39.5	46.4	51.9
Education	3.6	4.2	4.4
Veterans benefits and services	6.4	6.8	7.1
Interest	12.5	13.5	14.4
General government	2.5	2.6	2.8
Allowances:			
Civilian and military pay increase	....	....	1.6
Contingencies	....	.1	.4
Undistributed intragovernmental payments:			
Government contribution for employee retirement (−)	−1.7	−1.9	−2.0
Interest received by trust funds (−)	−2.3	−2.7	−3.0
Total expenditures	153.2	169.9	182.8
Total expenditures, excluding special Vietnam	(132.7)	(144.9)	(156.5)
Net Lending:			
International affairs and finance	.5	.7	.7
Agriculture and agricultural resources	1.2	.9	1.1
Housing and community development	1.7	3.3	1.4
All other	1.7	.9	.1
Total net lending	5.2	5.8	3.3
Total outlays	158.4	175.6	186.1
Total outlays, excluding special Vietnam	(137.9)	(150.6)	(159.8)

essential category. Our accomplishments include:

- A 45% increase in the number of combat-assigned Army divisions—from 11 to 16;
- A 62% increase in the funds for general ship construction and conversion to modernize the fleet;
- A 200% increase in the number of guided-missile surface ships;
- A 20% increase in the number of Air Force tactical fighter and attack aircraft, and a 100% increase in the total payload capability of all fighter and attack aircraft—Air Force, Navy, and Marine Corps;
- A 400% increase in our fixed-wing airlift capability—an increase which will reach 1,000% in the 1970's with the introduction of the mammoth C–5A transport; and
- A 185% increase in the number of nuclear weapons in the strategic alert forces.

While we stand ready to enter meaningful discussions with the Soviet Union on the limitation of strategic forces, it is necessary to assure that our defense capabilities remain equal to any challenge or threat. I am therefore recommending funds in this budget which will:

- Maintain our decisive strategic deterrent by: continuing to convert our strategic missile force to the more effective Minuteman III and Poseidon; equipping those missiles with multiple, independently targeted warheads and aids to help them penetrate enemy defenses; and modernizing our manned bomber force with additional FB–111 aircraft and improved short range attack missiles.
- Proceed with procurement of the Sentinel missile defense system to meet the threat posed by the emerging Chinese

nuclear capability. In addition, we will begin a revamping of our air defenses.

- Augment the firepower, mobility, and readiness of our general purpose forces by improving their air defenses, buying new fixed-wing aircraft and helicopters, and procuring other new weapon systems. We will also replenish munitions, supplies, and equipment consumed in Vietnam.
- Improve further our airlift-sealift capability by additional purchases of the giant C–5A aircraft and initial procurement of the fast deployment logistics ship.
- Continue the vigorous research and development effort which constitutes the Nation's investment in our future national security.

To accomplish these improvements, to meet all of our requirements in Vietnam, and to meet the full year's cost of the October 1967 civilian and military pay raise will require an increase of $3.3 billion in outlays for national defense in 1969.

We can and will meet all of our essential defense requirements. But we intend to insure that our defense dollars are spent as efficiently and effectively as possible. At my request, the Department of Defense will continue its searching review to reduce costs and to defer or stretch out all programs in which economies can be effected without reducing overall defense readiness.

INTERNATIONAL AFFAIRS AND FINANCE.— Through its international programs, the United States seeks to promote a peaceful world community in which all nations can devote their energies toward improving the lives of their citizens. We share with all governments, particularly those of the developed nations, responsibility for making progress toward these goals.

The task is long, hard, and often frustrating. But we must not shrink from the work of peace. We must continue because we are a Nation founded on the ideals of humanitarian justice and liberty for all men. We must continue because we do not wish our children to inherit a world in which two-thirds of the people are underfed, diseased, and poorly educated.

The $2.5 billion in new obligational authority requested for 1969 for the economic assistance program is essential to the success of our efforts. Most of our assistance is provided in concert with other industrialized nations, some of whom devote a larger proportion of their economic resources to this purpose than we do.

Our assistance, even when combined with the growing contribution of other industrial nations, cannot itself guarantee the economic growth of developing nations. But it can provide the crucial margin of difference between success and failure for those countries which are undertaking the arduous task of economic development. Since outside aid cannot substitute for effective self-help, we will continue to direct our economic assistance to those countries willing to help themselves.

The 1969 economic assistance program will continue the trend toward increasing concentration on improved agriculture, education, health, and family planning. The economic aid program I am proposing will:

- Accelerate growth in Latin America by modernizing agriculture and expanding education, and help lay the foundations for a Common Market, as agreed at Punta del Este last April.
- Support India's recovery from recession and drought, and assist Pakistan's drive toward self-sufficiency in food.
- Promote progress in the villages of Southeast Asia by helping them build schools, roads, and farms.

More than 90% of our AID expenditures in 1969 will be for purchases made in the United States, and I have directed intensified efforts to increase this percentage.

Upon completion of negotiations now in progress, I shall recommend legislation to authorize a U.S. contribution to a multilateral replenishment of the resources of the International Development Association, which is managed by the World Bank. I shall also request an increase in our subscription to the callable capital of the Inter-American Development Bank (IDB); this action will enlarge the borrowing and lending capacity of this vital Alliance for Progress institution without requiring expenditure of U.S. Government funds. These resources, together with our proposed contributions to the IDB's Fund for Special Operations and the Asian Development Bank, will permit us to provide effective support for sound development projects while we share the financial burden with other donors. Our contributions will include adequate balance of payments safeguards.

To assure sufficient food supplies for the developing countries, I am proposing extension of the Food for Freedom program beyond its expiration date of December 31, 1968.

The Export-Import Bank will continue to assist the growth of U.S. exports, so essential to our balance of payments. I will propose legislation to establish a new Export Expansion Program to guarantee, insure, and make direct loans for U.S. exports which do not qualify for Bank financing under existing criteria.

SPACE RESEARCH AND TECHNOLOGY.—This Nation's leadership in advanced technology was challenged 10 years ago by Sputnik and again 7 years ago by the first Soviet manned flight. We responded to these challenges with energy and imagination. We decided to create a national capability to operate in space. We established as a principal goal the development of launch vehicles and spacecraft large enough to transport men to the moon. We joined the strengths of our universities, industry, and government to accomplish this goal, to expand our knowledge of space, and to attain a leading position in aeronautics and space technology.

Our continuing stream of progress has been marked by many dramatic successes and by only a few tragic setbacks. The Mercury and Gemini programs have clearly demonstrated our progress in manned space flight. The recent, highly successful launch of the huge Saturn V rocket emphasizes the great strides we have made in creating a large launch vehicle capability. We will resume manned flight tests of the Apollo spacecraft this year, and proceed toward the manned lunar expedition.

To meet our most urgent national needs in some areas requires us to reduce spending in others. New obligational authority requested for the National Aeronautics and Space Administration in this budget is about $220 million below the 1968 amount. Expenditures will be $230 million below 1968, $850 million below 1967, and over $1.3 billion less than in 1966. This reduction reflects our progress beyond the costly research and development phases of the manned lunar mission, as well as the immediate need to postpone spending for new projects wherever possible.

Based on a careful examination of priorities, the 1969 budget provides increases in some areas to prepare for important advances in future years, while deferring other less urgent, new projects. The production of our large Saturn-class space boosters is continued but at a reduced rate. The development of a nuclear rocket engine to increase the capability of our Saturn V launch vehicle is also

continued, but at a smaller size and thrust than originally planned, to reduce development cost.

We will not abandon the field of planetary exploration. I am recommending development of a new spacecraft for launch in 1973 to orbit and land on Mars. This new Mars mission will cost much less than half the Voyager program included in last year's budget. Although the scientific result of this new mission will be less than that of the Voyager, it will still provide extremely valuable data and serve as a building block for planetary exploration systems of the future.

AGRICULTURE AND AGRICULTURAL RESOURCES.—In recent years, Federal agricultural commodity programs have succeeded in adjusting farm production to domestic and export needs. Wheat acreage was increased in 1967 to permit additional food aid for developing countries faced with low crop production. Cotton acreage will be increased in 1968 since surplus cotton stocks have been eliminated.

The commodity programs have helped raise incomes for many of our farmers. However, many poorer families living in rural areas benefit little from these programs. The combination of rapidly rising farm productivity and more slowly growing demand for farm products has left many rural people with low incomes. The result has been a massive migration to the cities, limited job opportunities for people remaining in rural areas, and widespread rural poverty.

Rising farm income plays a major role in improving economic conditions in rural areas. But other measures are needed:

- The Secretary of Agriculture is working with other Federal agencies and local groups to help more rural people participate in Federal programs that provide increased economic opportunities and improved living conditions.

- Legislation now before the Congress should be enacted to aid the establishment of multicounty area development districts. These districts would provide a broad base for planning and coordinating the development of public services and facilities in rural areas.
- Capital needs of Rural Electrification Administration borrowers to provide necessary electric power and telephone facilities in rural areas continue to expand. Legislation should be enacted to establish a cooperative bank for the telephone loan program and to permit the use of revolving funds for both the electric and telephone programs.

The Wholesome Meat Act of 1967 provides a new guarantee of safety for the American consumer. Under this act it will be possible to bring the same assurance of wholesomeness for meat sold in intrastate commerce as for meat now inspected under the Federal system.

NATURAL RESOURCES.—Federal programs to protect and develop our natural resources help strengthen our economic base and provide recreational opportunity for an expanding population.

The 1969 budget calls for deferral of some lower priority resource activities. But adequate provision has been made to:

- Protect our forests, conserve our fish and wildlife, and develop our mineral resources;
- Acquire new recreation areas;
- Clean up the Nation's water; and
- Continue water resource development.

Construction costs have been rising sharply in recent years—by 5% in 1966 and 6% in 1967. To reduce the impact of Federal construction activities on the economy, I am recommending that ongoing water resource projects be continued at minimum rates. In many cases this will require a delay in present construction schedules. New water resource development projects of the Corps of Engineers, the Bureau of Reclamation, and the Department of Agriculture, which had been recommended for starting in 1968 or had been added by the Congress, will be started over the 2-year period, 1968 and 1969. A small number of additional projects will be proposed for starting in 1969.

The Water Resources Council is developing a more appropriate interest rate to be applied in formulating and evaluating water projects. The revised rate will be related to the average estimated current cost to the Treasury of long-term borrowing. It will be higher than the rate now in use for project evaluation. The new rate will be applied to future projects in order to assure the most effective use of Federal funds in the development of the Nation's water resources.

Legislation to establish a National Water Commission is already before the Congress and is essential if we are to deal more effectively with the Nation's critical water problems.

We must also take steps to safeguard our scenic and historic areas and anticipate the resource needs of future generations. Legislation has been proposed and should be enacted promptly to authorize:

- The Redwoods National Park in northern California;
- The North Cascades National Park and National Recreation Area in the State of Washington;
- The Apostle Islands National Lakeshore in Wisconsin;
- A National Scenic Rivers System;
- A Nationwide System of Trails; and
- The Central Arizona Project.

I also recommend legislation to:

- Augment the revenues of the Land and Water Conservation Fund by use of part of the mineral leasing receipts from the

Outer Continental Shelf; and
• Establish a Federal-State system for regulation of surface mining operations.

COMMERCE AND TRANSPORTATION.—Many of the Nation's most urgent needs can be secured only with the dividends provided by continued economic growth. In addition to its overall fiscal policy, the Federal Government contributes to this growth in a variety of ways. For example, we:
• Provide aid to American businesses, and stimulate increased competition;
• Assist depressed areas of the Nation to share the fruits of prosperity; and
• Encourage safe and efficient systems of transportation and communication.

These are our long-standing goals, which require a slightly different emphasis each year to focus our efforts on the emerging needs of a rapidly changing society. The budget for 1969 is responsive to this need by:
• Encouraging private business to create job opportunities for those living in blighted urban areas;
• Enhancing the well-being of seriously depressed regions by helping selected communities take better advantage of existing Federal grant programs;
• Strengthening centers of potential economic growth within depressed regions to reduce excessive migration to larger urban centers where job opportunities often are not available;
• Improving our balance of payments, by increasing assistance to businesses to expand their exports and by attracting more tourists to the United States; and
• Providing improved statistics to aid business, labor, and government in sustaining economic growth.

Our economic growth and well-being rely heavily on fast, efficient movement of goods and people. The 1969 budget provides for continuing development of a prototype civil supersonic transport, for further tests of high-speed ground transportation, and for an expanded research program to stimulate innovation in our congested urban transportation systems.

I have directed the Secretary of Transportation to develop recommendaitons for providing and financing the facilities and services required to meet the long-term needs of the Nation's rapidly growing air transportation network.

I am also proposing a broad program of transportation user charges to apply the test of the marketplace to these activities, and to relieve the general taxpayer of some of the burden of financing special benefits for certain individuals and industries.

While we prepare for the future, we cannot overlook the urgent demands of the present. Safety will continue to receive high priority in the 1969 budget program. We must attack the tragic toll of traffic fatalities on the Nation's highways and equip our airways to handle increased air traffic safely and efficiently.

HOUSING AND COMMUNITY DEVELOPMENT.— Most Americans lead a comfortable life, in comfortable homes and comfortable surroundings. But millions of families are still crowded into housing unfit to live in, located in squalid surroundings, and burdened with wornout facilities and inadequate services. Without some assistance and the development of new techniques, our private economy cannot now provide good housing at costs these families can afford. Our cities cannot afford all the essential facilities and services. The Federal Government must continue and expand its assistance.

I propose to the Congress that we launch a program, in cooperation with private industry and labor, to build 6 million new housing units for low- and middle-income families over the next 10 years.

Under existing legislation and the new measures I will propose, we can begin this program in fiscal year 1969 with 300,000 housing units.

Federal aids for State and local services, especially those for education, health, manpower training, and basic income support are, to a large extent, directed at needy families. In addition, housing and community development programs are aimed more specifically at improving their surroundings. This budget provides:

- $1 billion for the 63 Model Cities now planning their programs to concentrate assistance to some 3.7 million people living in the most blighted areas of these cities, and for approximately 70 cities expected to start their planning in the late spring.
- $1.4 billion of advance funding for the urban renewal program for 1970, allowing the communities to start planning their action programs now.

To provide decent housing for all Americans, the housing industry must be able to compete on equal terms with other sectors for needed resources. However, in the past 2 years, housing has been at a disadvantage in competing for investment funds. The tax increase I have proposed will help solve this problem. In addition, specific steps to overcome the competitive disadvantage are being proposed to the Congress, including:

- Authority to lift the ceiling on interest rates for FHA and VA mortgages, which currently discourages savers from investing in mortgages.
- An orderly transfer of ownership of the Government's activities in the secondary mortgage market to private hands, so that private capital can be raised and mortgages purchased as required by market conditions.

Despite substantial progress, our urban problems remain complex. Their solutions will be difficult. Our understanding of the basic nature of the problems and of the correct solutions is deficient. To remedy this deficiency, the 1969 budget provides for a doubling of the general research funds available to the Department of Housing and Urban Development.

Detailed recommendations to augment our efforts to solve housing and urban problems will be presented in a separate message to the Congress.

HEALTH, LABOR, AND WELFARE.—Programs that help develop our most valuable resource—our people—are essential to the long-run growth and vitality of the Nation. No society can flourish unless its people have opportunities for jobs and the skills to perform them, receive adequate health care, and are free from the fear of basic economic insecurity. The 1969 budget will permit us to further these objectives.

Outlays for these programs are estimated at $51.4 billion, of which over 75% will be provided through trust funds which are largely self-financed.

Health.—Since 1963, Federal outlays for health have increased sixfold—from $1.7 billion to $10.7 billion. Medicare has provided insurance coverage against hospital and doctors' bills for nearly all older Americans. Under Medicaid, medical assistance has been extended to 8.5 million needy individuals. The number of medical and dental schools has been significantly increased, new mental retardation clinics and mental health centers, are providing services, and infant mortality has been reduced.

But our job is far from complete. This budget will reinforce our partnership with State and local governments in attacking health problems; speed research findings to victims of heart, cancer, stroke, and related diseases; intensify the attack on air pollution; expand health care for mothers and children; and increase voluntary family planning services.

To broaden and supplement these efforts, I will propose legislation to:

- Attack the problem of infant mortality by providing, for families which cannot afford it, access to health services from prenatal care for the mother through the child's first year.
- Increase the supply of health manpower.
- Establish more effective leadership and an improved personnel system for the health activities of the Department of Health, Education, and Welfare.

Labor and manpower.—The opportunity to work in a meaningful job is a fundamental right in our society. This opportunity is denied those who are ill-equipped through lack of education and job skills, and those who are handicapped by the effects of discrimination and a slum environment.

The 1969 budget provides for a wide range of manpower programs which will enable 1.3 million Americans to start on the road to economic self-sufficiency and individual dignity. Another 230,000 disabled Americans will be restored to productive employment through the vocational rehabilitation program.

The Concentrated Employment Program, which brings together a wide range of manpower and related services in selected geographic areas, will be expanded to an additional 70 areas—35 of them rural. This will bring to 146 the number of the Nation's most severe unemployment areas which will be served by this intensive effort.

Major increases are also planned in programs to enlist private employers in training and employing the hard-core unemployed. State and local manpower planning will be strengthened, and manpower activities in the Department of Labor have been restructured to improve delivery of manpower services.

Legislation will be proposed to:

- Update the unemployment insurance program by extending coverage, raising benefit levels for unemployed workers, increasing the length of benefits under certain circumstances, correcting abuses, and providing for services which would increase the workers' employability.
- Reduce threats to the health and safety of workers through a comprehensive Federal-State program and assure workmen's compensation benefits to uranium miners who contract lung cancer.

Economic opportunity programs.—Poverty in the midst of plenty casts an ugly shadow on our society. We have a commitment to remove that shadow.

We know that poverty cannot be eradicated overnight. But we must persist in our efforts to help those oppressed by poverty—whether they live in blighted urban areas or in impoverished rural counties. Work and training programs are being expanded and increasingly aimed at helping the poor. In addition, this budget will enable the Office of Economic Opportunity to provide:

- Improve planning capability of local Community Action Agencies.
- Services for a full academic year to 202,000 children through Head Start and a summer program for 450,000 children to remove basic disadvantages suffered by poor children on entering school.
- Head Start Follow Through to help 79,000 children retain the gains provided by the Head Start program.
- Assistance to make a college education possible for 31,000 deprived but talented youths through the Upward Bound program.
- Comprehensive family health services for the poor through nearly 50 neigh-

FEDERAL AID TO THE POOR [1]

[Fiscal years. In billions]

Category	1960 actual	1963 actual	1967 actual	1968 estimate	1969 estimate
Education	$0.1	$0.1	$2.0	$2.3	$2.5
Work and training	([2])	([2])	1.0	1.2	1.6
Health	.6	.9	3.2	4.1	4.7
Cash benefit payments	8.3	10.4	12.8	14.6	15.9
Other social welfare and economic services	.5	1.0	2.0	2.4	2.9
Total	9.5	12.5	21.1	24.6	27.7

[1] Figures represent new obligational authority for Federal funds and expenditures in the case of trust funds.
[2] Less than $50 million.

borhood health centers.

New approaches are being tested through cooperation among Federal agencies in multipurpose neighborhood center demonstration projects in 14 cities. These centers will develop service systems to render assistance more effectively to those in need.

Although the task is great and the problem complex, we have, in recent years, made substantial strides in reducing poverty. Between 1963 and 1967, the number of people living in poverty fell from over 35 million to less than 29 million, and from 19% of our population to under 15%. But 29 million poor people are still far too many.

In addition to programs of the Office of Economic Opportunity, various other Federal programs provide assistance to help reduce the number of those living in poverty.

Social security and public assistance.—The 1967 Social Security Amendments represent a major stride toward improving the incomes of 24 million of our people—the aged, the permanently disabled, and survivors or dependents. These beneficiaries are fortunate enough to have been covered by social insurance.

Other, less fortunate members of our society must depend on welfare. To assist those welfare recipients who cannot find work because of a lack of training and responsi-

bility for dependent children at home, this budget provides $100 million for training and $35 million for child care services.

The transition from welfare recipient to wage earner will also be eased by the recent amendments which provide an incentive to work by exempting a certain portion of earnings from consideration of continued eligibility for assistance.

Despite periodic revisions, much of the welfare system is outmoded and in need of change. Accordingly, I have appointed a commission to make a comprehensive review of existing welfare and related programs and to recommend whatever measures are necessary to provide a more equitable and effective system of assistance to needy people.

The budget includes funds under proposed legislation to expand the food stamp program of the Department of Agriculture. About three million low-income people will have better diets under this program by the end of fiscal year 1969.

EDUCATION.—As a nation we are committed to develop the skills and talents of all our citizens. The Federal Government is playing an increasingly important role in this effort.

The 90th Congress added the Education Professions Development Act of 1967 to the historic laws enacted in 1965 providing Federal aid to education—the Elementary and Secondary Education Act, the Higher Education Act, and the National Foundation on the Arts and Humanities Act. We now have basic legislation to improve education at all levels. Our task is to use these tools wisely and imaginatively, directing them to the areas of greatest need or potential.

For 1969, I propose that the Federal Government continue in its determination to help make high-quality education available to all of America's young people. The budget includes:

- $1.2 billion in grants for improving the elementary and secondary education of over 9 million children from low-income families;
- An expanded Teacher Corps;
- Increased grants for schooling of children with physical and mental handicaps which hinder learning for 1 child in 10;
- A new program to better the achievement of children whose native language is not English; and
- More than two million grants, loans, and part-time work opportunities for college students, including benefits under the GI bill.

America's children must be prepared for the challenges of the future. To help them meet these challenges, we must explore the ways students learn and improve the ways teachers teach through:

- Increases in education research, demonstrations, and curriculum development, including an experiment in model schools in the District of Columbia;
- A new $30 million program to prevent dropouts; and
- Innovations in training for the education profession through new patterns of operation and new ties among colleges and universities, States, and local schools.

In order to meet these urgent requirements within a stringent overall budget, several programs have been reduced or deferred, including grants for construction of academic facilities and purchase of school equipment.

I intend to propose legislation this year to:

- Improve Federal support to higher education by providing greater flexibility in administering student aid, providing counseling and tutoring for disadvantaged students, and encouraging schools to share libraries, computers, and other resources.
- Support innovative projects in vocational education, particularly to aid the disadvantaged.
- Provide advance financing for the newly authorized Corporation for Public Broadcasting.

VETERANS BENEFITS AND SERVICES.—Historically, this Nation has provided special benefits for the men and women who have served in the Armed Forces in times of national danger.

In 1969, special emphasis will be given to programs designed to help newly discharged veterans find satisfactory employment or to improve their career opportunities through vocational or academic training programs. For men and women still on active military duty, the budget provides for legislation to increase protection under the Servicemen's Group Life Insurance program and for expanded counseling and civilian job-training opportunities in the closing months of military service.

In addition to assistance in the development of veterans' career potential, this budget will also permit the continuation and improvement of the traditional programs of compensation, pensions, and medical care. Veterans hospitals will receive new medical services and improved nursing staffing. Applied medical research and medical education will be expanded.

Legislation should be enacted to relate veterans pension payments more closely to individual needs and provide better protection against loss of income. Studies are now underway to seek improvements in other veteran benefit programs.

GENERAL GOVERNMENT.—Rising crime rates are a major concern of the American people.

I am determined that the Federal Government do everything properly within its power to assist our States and localities in controlling crime. I have directed Federal agencies to intensify their efforts to destroy organized crime. The budget reflects expansions in both direct Federal action and Federal assistance to State and local governments.

Although the main responsibility for combating crime must rest with our State and local governments, the Federal Government can effectively aid this effort by:

- Encouraging modernization of law enforcement, corrections, and court systems;
- Assisting law enforcement agencies throughout the country to improve and expand the exchange of information; and
- Assisting in recruiting and training law enforcement personnel.

With the Law Enforcement Assistance Act of 1965, a start was made toward more effective Federal-State-local cooperation. Last year I proposed the "Safe Streets and Crime Control Act" to expand on this promising beginning. We will renew our efforts to secure the enactment of this legislation so that an expanded effort against crime can go forward.

The Federal Government's ability to take direct action has been strengthened by the Prisoner Rehabilitation Act of 1965, the Bail Reform Act of 1966, and the Narcotic Addict Rehabilitation Act of 1966. The budget supports these and other measures in an accelerated drive against crime.

Legislation is also needed to provide support for efforts to prevent, treat, and control juvenile delinquency. Such legislation is now pending before the Congress and should be enacted promptly.

The efforts of this Administration to bring home rule to the District of Columbia are well known. I am confident that the Mayor and the Council, by their actions and with community support, will prepare the way toward the goal of local self-government. Voting representation in the Congress is an additional necessity if District citizens are to participate fully in our democratic processes. I am again recommending that the authorized Federal payment to the District of Columbia be established equal to 25% of District revenues, so that the Federal Government will be contributing its fair share toward the needs of the Nation's capital.

NEW BUDGET CONCEPTS

In my budget message last year, I called for a thorough and objective review of budgetary concepts by a bipartisan group of informed individuals with a background in budgetary matters. I stated my hope that this group would recommend an approach to budgetary presentation which would assist both public and congressional understanding of this vital document.

In March of 1967, a Commission on Budget Concepts was established to make such a review and report its recommendations to me. The Commission consisted of 16 distinguished Americans, including the chairmen and ranking minority members of the Appropriations Committees of the Congress, as well as top Government financial officials and eminently qualified private citizens.

This budget puts into effect most of the major recommendations in the Commission's report, which was presented to me on October 10, 1967. These include:

- A single *unified budget statement* to replace the three concepts previously used.
- *Comprehensive coverage* in the budget of all programs of the Federal Government and its agencies, including some $47 billion of trust funds as well as Federal funds.
- *Division between an expenditure account and a loan account,* using the former as a measure of economic impact for fiscal policy purposes.
- *Offsetting against related expenditures those receipts of the Government* which are market-oriented in character, rather than based on the Government's sovereign power to tax and regulate.
- *Highlighting action required of the Congress* on the budget and relating that action more closely to outlays.
- *Treating sales of participation certificates,* which had previously been considered as an offset to Government expenditures as a means of financing the deficit.

Several other changes recommended by the Commission for adoption in future years are now under preparation for later application.

It is my hope that the far-reaching proposals made by the Commission, and their adoption for this budget, will serve the desired purposes of improving public understanding of the Federal budget and overcoming many of the inadequacies of the concepts formerly used.

PLANNING-PROGRAMING-BUDGETING SYSTEM

To improve the process by which Federal programs are planned and the Federal budget prepared, the Government is continuing to develop the Planning-Programing-Budgeting (PPB) system which has now completed its second year of operation. This system provides information and analysis to relate the programs we undertake to the ends they are to achieve, and to choose the most efficient ways of using our resources to reach our goals.

This year the program budgets developed under the system have been employed as the framework within which program costs and accomplishments were reviewed. As a result, the different programs now stand in a clearer relationship to each other and to their objectives.

The system is also providing comparisons of the cost and effectiveness of alternative ways to achieve our objectives. For example:

- The Department of Health, Education, and Welfare has analyzed the effectiveness of the cooperative Federal-State *vocational rehabilitation* program. This study indicated that the increase in lifetime incomes of participants is many times the rehabilitation cost, confirming previous judgments that this program merits high priority.
- In the area of non-service-connected *veterans pensions,* a series of studies was done to compare various benefit formulas from the point of view of their cost, the equity with which they treat beneficiaries, and the extent to which they protect beneficiaries against large loss of pensions from small increases in other income. These studies have shown the need for legislation, provided for in

this budget, that would relate pension payments more closely to the needs of the beneficiaries.

• Through the program evaluation system in the *Economic Development Administration* of the Department of Commerce, the number of jobs expected to result from proposed development projects in depressed areas has been estimated in relation to the extent of poverty and unemployment prevailing in the areas and to the costs of creating the jobs. This has assisted EDA in judging the most effective distribution of its resources among proposed projects.

We will extend the application of PPB during the next year, and strengthen it where it has already been introduced. In particular, we will continue to improve measures of the effectiveness of programs and to develop better alternatives.

IMPROVING GOVERNMENT MANAGEMENT

In recent years, the Federal Government has undertaken a number of vital new programs to improve America's urban and rural communities and enhance the way of life of all of our people.

To attain the full benefits of these programs, it is essential that they be made workable at the point of impact—whether it be the individual citizen, a State or local government, a university, or any of the other institutions involved in efforts to carry out our national goals. Effective and economical management is also essential to ensure that each tax dollar buys a full dollar's worth of essential services.

GOVERNMENT ORGANIZATION.—In the past 4 years, we have undertaken more fundamental reforms in managing the Government than, perhaps, at any other time in our history. We have witnessed such major

advances as the creation of two new cabinet agencies—the Departments of Transportation and of Housing and Urban Development. Significant reorganizations have taken place in other programs, among them the Public Health Service, the Community Relations Service, the Federal Water Pollution Control Administration, and the Bureau of Customs.

New strides were made last year by:

• Providing the District of Columbia with a modern governmental organization, replacing the obsolete three-member Board of Commissioners with a single chief executive and a nine-member council to exercise quasi-legislative functions.

• Creating the Social and Rehabilitation Service in the Department of Health, Education, and Welfare to unify the administration of related income support and social service and rehabilitation programs.

• Reorganizing the Bureau of the Budget to enhance its ability to help coordinate Federal programs and provide additional staff services for the solution of interagency and intergovernmental problems.

A key tool in improving Government organization is the President's authority to transmit reorganization plans to the Congress. That authority is scheduled to expire on December 31, 1968. Legislation is being proposed to extend the authority for an additional 4 years to help ensure the continued ability of the President to reshape programs and organizational structures to meet changing needs and circumstances.

The problems we face in the administration of new, comprehensive attacks on social problems often involve a number of agencies—as in the new Model Cities program. These problems cannot be solved simply by shifting functions between agencies. Heavy emphasis is therefore being given to improving both the formal and informal methods used to ensure that agencies work together effectively on related programs.

An example of the efforts being made in interagency cooperation is the program involving the Office of Economic Opportunity and the Departments of Labor, Housing and Urban Development, and Health, Education, and Welfare to aid 14 cities in the establishment of pilot neighborhood centers to provide comprehensive services to residents in low-income neighborhoods.

FEDERAL-STATE-LOCAL COOPERATION.—The need for cooperation and coordination between the partners in our federal system has also increased. The problems of managing many of our most important new programs are intensified by their intergovernmental character.

At the Federal level we must do what we can to assist our partners. We must assure that our programs are designed and administered in such a way as to mesh with State and local patterns of organization and operation to the maximum extent possible. We must ensure that Federal programs promote State and local initiative and action. To that end, we have taken a number of actions in the past year alone:

- Developed and put into operation a system through which State and local chief executives have the opportunity—often not previously available to them—to have a voice in developing Federal regulations and administrative procedures.
- Established procedures to improve Federal-State coordination in the designation of development planning districts.
- Provided an opportunity for areawide planning agencies to comment on proposed applications for specific grants that would affect the orderly development of their metropolitan areas.
- Taken initial steps to shorten processing time on applications under many vital grant programs by 50%.

Improvement is a continuous process, as it must be to meet the needs of a dynamic and rapidly changing society. We must prepare now to meet the public service needs of our people in the seventies. One of the prerequisites to satisfying the awesome demands of the future is a corps of competent, well-trained public servants. Enactment of the pending Intergovernmental Manpower Act will provide a significant stride forward in filling the gap of trained manpower at the State and local levels of Government.

Two additional measures are needed to improve the funding and management of intergovernmental programs significantly:

- *Joint Funding Simplification Act.*—This measure, which was sent to the Congress last year, will simplify and streamline the application, processing, and administration of a number of related grants by managing them as a single, unified project.
- *Funding improvements and consolidation efforts.*—To overcome the serious problems of planning education programs at the State and local level caused by grant delays, I am seeking early appropriations for elementary and secondary education. The amounts which will be available must be known in the spring, if local communities are to be able to use them most effectively in the ensuing school year. I am also proposing to consolidate related grants for college student aid and for vocational education. This consolidation, coupled with advance funding action similar to that mentioned above, will facilitate advance

planning by both the institutions and students.

Further action is underway to determine whether additional consolidations of grant programs are feasible. As proposals are developed, they will be promptly forwarded to the Congress.

Again, as last year, I must stress that State and local governments must help themselves too. Encouraging steps are being taken, but many serious problems of modernization of executive direction and financial systems remain which can only be remedied by those governments and their citizens.

Cost reduction.—I have continued to insist that the executive branch of the Federal Government be operated as economically and efficiently as possible.

Some examples of the actions agencies took in the past year to cut costs are:

• The Department of Defense achieved savings of over $339 million by value engineering. Under this program unnecessary equipment, facilities, procedures, and supplies are eliminated. A good example is the $2.1 million saved by the redesign of an aircraft camera. Performance was improved and unit costs were reduced by about 40%.

• The Manpower Administration of the Department of Labor, through improved work methods, achieved estimated savings of over $19 million.

• All Government agencies, by sharing automatic data processing resources through an exchange program, avoided costs of over $28 million. Redistribution of ADP equipment avoided new procurement of $80 million.

• The National Aeronautics and Space Administration, by utilizing idle, excess, and surplus Government property, avoided expenditures of over $22 million for new equipment or facilities. In ad-

dition, NASA saved over $16 million by improving procurement practices.

• A value analysis of the specifications for the computer display channel of the National Airspace System development enabled the Federal Aviation Administration to avoid costs of approximately $12 million.

• The Coast Guard reorganized its search and rescue mission function along the east and gulf coasts, leading to savings estimated at $14.6 million.

• The Post Office has improved its procurement of transportation to the extent that $107 million was saved in the period from 1965 through 1967.

Conclusion

This is a critical and challenging time in our history. It requires sacrifices and hard choices along with the enjoyment of the highest standard of living in the world. No nation has remained great by shedding its resolve or shirking its responsibilities. We have the capacity to meet those responsibilities. The question before us is whether or not our will and determination match that capacity.

In the past 4 years, this Nation has faced formidable challenges. We have confronted them with imagination, courage, and resolution. By acting boldly, we have forced a number of age-old concerns—ignorance, poverty, and disease—to yield stubborn ground.

The rollcall of accomplishments is long. But so is our agenda of unfinished business. Our heritage impels us to steadfast action on those problems of mankind which both gnaw at our conscience and challenge our imagination.

As your President, I have done all in my power to devise a program to meet our responsibilities compassionately and sensibly. The program is embodied in this budget for 1969. I urge active support for its principles and programs.

LYNDON B. JOHNSON

January 29, 1968

NOTE: As printed above, illustrative diagrams and references to the budget document have been deleted.

Letters from the President to the Speaker of the House of Representatives or the President of the Senate proposing changes in the 1969 budget are printed in the Weekly Compilation of Presidential Documents (vol. 4, pp. 829, 833, 1051, 1114, 1443, 1474).

40   Special Message to the Congress—"Our Pride and Our Strength: America's Servicemen and Veterans." *January 30, 1968*

To the Congress of the United States:

"TO CARE FOR HIM . . ."

Looking beyond the tragedy of war, Abraham Lincoln saw a nation's obligation "to care for him who shall have borne the battle and for his widow and his orphan."

His words are enshrined in the spirit of this country's concern for its veterans and servicemen.

America holds some of its greatest honors for the men who have stood in its defense, and kept alive its freedoms.

It shows its gratitude not only in memorials which grace city parks and courthouse squares across the land—but more meaningfully in the programs which "care for him . . . and for his widow and his orphan."

OUR ACCOMPLISHMENTS SO FAR

As the result of legislation over the past several years, today's veteran can continue his education through a new GI Bill of Rights, which right now is helping 400,000 men and women.

He can buy a home with a Veterans Administration-insured mortgage. Over 200,000 veterans have purchased houses because of this provision.

If he receives a pension, his increased pay-ments now can afford him a better standard of living.

If he is disabled, or needs special medical care, he is eligible for the same benefits his fellowmen of earlier conflicts received.

FY 1969 VETERANS BUDGET

In the Fiscal 1969 Budget, we will have budget outlays of $7.3 billion to provide services for America's 26 million veterans and their families, who make up 46 percent of the nation's population.

With these funds, we can continue the programs already in existence, and begin the new ones I will outline in this Message.

BASIC BENEFITS

Two programs to extend the basic benefits to America's veterans and servicemen are left on the unfinished agenda of the 90th Congress.

In my 1967 Message on America's Servicemen and Veterans, I proposed measures to:

—Increase Serviceman's Group Life Insurance from a maximum of $10,000 to a minimum of $12,000—with higher amounts scaled to the pay of the serviceman, up to a maximum of $30,000.

—Protect the veteran against disproportionate pension losses that could result from increases in other income such as Social Security.

I once again—once more—urge the Congress to enact these proposals.

Now, to continue and bring up-to-date our efforts to help the veteran and his family, I recommend two new legislative proposals.

First, I ask the Congress to increase the maximum guarantee on GI home loans from $7,500 to $10,000.

Home mortgage guarantees under the GI Bill normally cover about 35 percent of the value of a loan.

For eighteen years, that guarantee has remained at $7,500—adequate in 1950, but no longer so in today's housing market.

The increase I am recommending will help the veteran to purchase a decent home and get the financing protection which the law promises him.

Since World War II, with encouragement of the Government and supported by GI Bill guarantees, some $68 billion have been loaned by the private sector to home-buying veterans.

This suggests the beneficial impact the program has had on our economy.

But its meaning reaches deeper into the traditional values of American life. Almost 7 million veterans—many of them of modest means and some without even the money for a down payment—have experienced the satisfaction of home ownership through this program.

Second, I propose that the benefits of Vocational Rehabilitation be extended to service-disabled veterans being trained on a part-time as well as full-time basis.

Presently, a disabled veteran can take Vocational Rehabilitation and receive a training allowance only if he trains full-time. This restriction may present him with a hard choice: either leave his job for training, or forgo the training itself.

Clearly, that choice is unfair.

The disabled veteran should be able to keep his job while he prepares for a better one through vocational training, drawing the allowance it provides.

The Quality of Administration

The purpose of our veterans program is to serve those who have served us.

That purpose can be blunted unless the quality of program administration keeps pace with the growth of our veteran population. Last year, almost three quarters of a million servicemen and women returned to civilian life. This year, that number will increase to over 850,000.

The ultimate effectiveness of our programs turns on these conditions:

—The veteran must be aware of them.

—He must be able to choose among them.

—He must know that the help he needs will be there when he needs it.

We have tried to make certain that men leaving the service become familiar with the benefits that await them as veterans.

Last year, at my direction, the Veterans Administration took its services to the battlefield for the first time. VA teams counseled 220,000 fighting men in Vietnam, before they left their posts to return home.

I have asked the Administrator of Veterans Affairs to step up this program.

Late in 1966, the Veterans Administration began visiting sick and wounded servicemen at their bedsides in our military hospitals.

Since then, over 17,000 applications for special training and disability payments have been processed on the spot.

This program now operates in 110 military hospitals.

I have directed the Administrator of Veterans Affairs immediately to expand the program to the entire system of military hospitals.

Veterans Administration counseling is also now in operation at 150 military separation points.

I have directed the Administrator to extend this program to all 257 such centers.

Through these expanded services in hospitals and separation centers, the Veterans Administration can reach more than 70,000 servicemen each month.

The remaining task is to make certain all veterans are reached once they have returned to their communities.

Consider the man who comes home today. His Government has made a vast array of programs available to him. But what effect are the programs if he cannot find them? And in our major cities, where facilities are often scattered across widely-separated areas, this is a serious problem—particularly for those who need the programs the most.

The answer, I believe, lies in an effort we have never tried before for our veterans—the one-stop center. I believe we should locate in one place the offices where a veteran can receive personal attention and counsel on all the benefits the law provides him—from housing to health, from education to employment.

I have today ordered that U.S. Veterans Assistance Centers be opened in 10 major cities within the coming month. These cities are New York, Chicago, Los Angeles, Philadelphia, Detroit, Cleveland, Washington, D.C., San Francisco, Boston and Atlanta.

I propose to have one-stop centers in 10 other cities as soon as possible—Baltimore, Milwaukee, Houston, St. Louis, Pittsburgh, San Antonio, New Orleans, Indianapolis, Phoenix and Newark.

Based on the experience gained in these 20 pilot locations, we look forward to establishing one-stop centers in other cities.

We will seek and welcome participation in these centers by State and local officials, and by community organizations engaged in helping the veteran.[1]

JOBS AND TRAINING

Military Programs

A man who has fought for his country deserves gratitude. But gratitude can be no substitute for the job he wants—and needs.

Particularly is it necessary to assure job opportunities to the veteran who has received few other advantages from life. It is this man who must be the focus of our concern and our attention.

We are beginning.

We are helping him as he enters the Armed Forces—through Project 100,000—and as he prepares to muster out—in Project Transition.

Project 100,000 extends the responsibilities of citizenship and the benefits of military training to young men who would otherwise be rejected because of educational or physical limitations.

This program was launched at my direction by the Secretary of Defense in late 1966.

In the first year, almost 50,000 disadvantaged young Americans were prepared in Army classrooms and clinics to take their place in basic training.

The results of their special training speak in these statistics:

—96 percent graduated from basic training, almost the same rate for all trainees,

—Some have gone on to Non-Commissioned Officer schools.

---

[1] On July 11, 1968, William J. Driver, Administrator of Veterans Affairs, reported to the President that one-stop centers had been established in 21 major U.S. cities (4 Weekly Comp. Pres. Docs., p. 1095).

All have gained self-confidence and a sense of achievement which will serve them all the years of their lives.

I have asked the Secretary of Defense to enroll 100,000 men in this vital program during its second year.[2]

Project Transition gives a boost to disadvantaged men in the six months before they return to civilian life.

Men without civilian skills and without education receive a concentrated program of preparation. In classrooms and at work benches, through counseling and job placement services, they are prepared for the road home.

I have asked the Secretary of Defense to extend Project Transition—proven in practice at five bases last year—to all principal troop installations in the United States. Our target is to reach 500,000 servicemen in the year ahead and then follow their progress in civilian life.

Federal-State Employment Offices

Last year I was disturbed to learn that some veterans returning from service to their country had such difficulty finding jobs they had to rely on unemployment compensation.

This ought to be corrected.

To correct it, in August I directed the Secretary of Labor to give every returning veteran maximum assistance in obtaining useful and rewarding employment. Since that time, a system has been set up which operates in every State, through the network of more than 2,000 Federal-State Employment offices. That system has now made the names and addresses of 230,000 returning veterans available to Employment offices for personal contact.

The Secretary of Labor recently told me that early reports from the men, their parents, and Veterans Organizations show the program is achieving good results.

It is important that those results continue. It is in America's interest that this program succeed.

Civil Service

The Federal Government has long set an example for the rest of the nation as a good employer of veterans. Veteran's preference is deeply imbedded in our Civil Service system.

But I am convinced that the Federal Government can be even a better employer.

Last month I asked the Chairman of the Civil Service Commission to develop an action plan to accomplish this purpose.

That plan is now completed.

I will shortly sign an Executive Order putting the plan into effect.[3]

Its major impact will reach the veteran who needs experience, skill and education. He will be hired on a priority basis to fill jobs open in the first five levels of the Civil Service, without having to compete in the regular examination—provided he agrees to pursue a part-time educational program under the GI Bill.

This plan will also help veterans with technical or professional skills who want to work in the middle and upper Civil Service levels. Their applications will be given immediate attention.

Veterans In Industry

Most veterans, of course, will go into private industry—where six out of every seven

---

[2] In a memorandum of August 3, 1968, the Secretary of Defense reported to the President on the results of Project 100,000 (4 Weekly Comp. Pres. Docs., p. 1205).

[3] On February 9, 1968, the President signed Executive Order 11397 authorizing transitional appointments of veterans who had served during the Vietnam era (4 Weekly Comp. Pres. Docs., p. 270; 33 F.R. 2833; 3 CFR, 1968 Comp., p. 100).

Americans are employed.

Those returning to old jobs have rights protected under the law.

Those seeking new employment—or their first jobs—sometimes find the road difficult.

These young Americans, who have done so much for their country, merit the special consideration of the private employer.

That consideration cannot be imposed by Government decree—nor should it.

It is appropriate, however—particularly in these times when men are being called from their civilian pursuits to defend their country—for leaders of the Government to express their hope that right will be done to those who serve.

To help enlarge the opportunities for veterans' employment, I urge the enactment of a joint resolution expressing the sense of the Congress that private employers should give job priority to our returning servicemen.

Our objective is to make sure that every serviceman who returns to civilian life today and in the months ahead—no matter where he lives, what background he might have come from, what his hopes and ambitions are—will have the education he wants, the training he needs, and the opportunities for the job he is best suited for.

With the proposals I have outlined in this Message, I believe we can advance toward that day.

VETERANS IN PUBLIC SERVICE

If the veteran needs his country's help, the country needs his more.

The veteran of Valley Forge knew better than most the value of the nation he was building.

The veteran of Antietam knew better than most the value of the Union he helped to heal and save.

The veteran of the battles that rage across the mountains and lowlands of Vietnam today knows better than most the value of the freedom he preserves.

That man is an asset beyond measure to his nation.

Wherever we can, we should continue to enlist him—in service to his community, when military duty is over.

To do this, I propose the Veterans In the Public Service Act of 1968.

This measure will provide incentives to channel the talents of the veteran to the most urgent needs of rural and urban America today:

   —To teach the children of the poor;

   —To help man understrength police forces and fire departments;

   —To do meaningful work in local hospitals, where skills are short;

   —To fill the ranks of VISTA, to work in Youth Opportunity Centers and in the Concentrated Employment Program.

The pattern of benefits will vary, depending on the individual and the occupation pursued.

Here is an example of how the program will work for the veteran who wants to teach in a deprived area:

While he is getting the schooling that will qualify him for teaching, he will draw additional benefits of $50 a month for every month he agrees to teach—up to three years of such extra benefits.

While he is actually on the job teaching, he will draw a special training allowance, in addition to his regular salary—$80 a month for the first school year, $60 a month for the second.

Should he decide to pursue a graduate degree while he is still teaching, he could—

by continuing to teach beyond the second year—earn additional GI Bill educational benefits.

To launch this program, I have included $50 million in the Fiscal 1969 budget.

The Healing Work

The Veterans Administration operates the nation's largest medical complex—166 hospitals and their related clinics across the country.

Last year, these hospitals and clinics treated almost 800,000 bed patients. Nearly 7 million veterans received outpatient care.

Their treatment is of the best quality modern medicine can provide—and it is improving with greater advances in pre-hospital and post-hospital care.

But VA medicine not only serves the veteran. Its benefits extend to the entire nation.

In research, VA doctors have pioneered in such vital work as heart disease, cancer, mental illness, and organ transplant.

In 1955, no money was spent for VA medical research. Now that amount exceeds $45 million. Its gains make it one of the nation's best investments.

In medical manpower, the Veterans Administration helps to train nearly half of all the doctors who graduate from medical school today.

The number of all medical specialists trained in VA hospitals each year totals some 40,000—including nurses, dentists, and other disciplines ranging from audiologists to social workers, who take their skills to the communities of this country.

There is room in the VA system to train even more.

And there is a pressing need in the nation for more.

I have directed the Administrator of Veterans Affairs to step up the training of medical specialists.

To help overcome the medical manpower shortage in America, and at the same time improve care to America's veterans, our goal will be to train as many as 80,000 specialists a year in the VA system.

The U.S. Veterans Advisory Commission

Last year, I asked the Administrator of Veterans Affairs—in consultation with veterans' groups—to conduct a comprehensive study of the pension, compensation and benefits system for veterans, their families and their survivors.

I asked him to form an Advisory Commission which would evaluate these programs to assure that our tax dollars are being used most wisely, and that the Government is fully meeting its responsibilities.

That Commission, composed of 11 distinguished Americans, has now held hearings in cities all across the country.

We are looking forward to the recommendations of the Commission.

Every veteran who wants it—those who risked their lives at Belleau Wood, Iwo Jima and the DMZ—should have the right to burial in a National Cemetery situated reasonably close to his home. I have asked the Administrator of Veterans Affairs to make certain that the recommendations of the Commission include proposals to assure this right in a meaningful sense.

Conclusion

More than 20 years ago on the floor of the House of Representatives, I said that it is this nation's responsibility to see to it that "the veteran may return to his community as a free, upstanding and self-reliant citizen."

The times then, as complex as they seemed, were simple in perspective.

As President, I have seen—and acted on— the responsibilities unique to our own day.

The events of the past week have underscored their gravity.

Today, as in times past, it is on America's fighting men that this nation must depend.

Their service honors us all.

We look to that good day when they will return "as free, upstanding and self-reliant citizens."

It is in this spirit of concern for America's veterans that I submit this message to the Congress today.

LYNDON B. JOHNSON

The White House
January 30, 1968

NOTE: For statements or remarks upon signing related legislation, see Items 160, 229, 414. See also Item 419.

41 Message to the Congress Transmitting Report "U.S. Aeronautics and Space Activities, 1967." *January 30, 1968*

To the Congress of the United States:

This report details a year—and climaxes a decade—of American progress in space.

On January 31, 1958, a 31-pound EXPLORER I was fired from a JUPITER C rocket with 150,000 pounds of thrust. Ten years later, on November 9, 1967, a 280,000-pound APOLLO payload was launched into orbit by a SATURN V rocket with 7.5 million pounds of thrust.

In the time spanning those two events, the United States has placed 514 spacecrafts in earth orbit. Twenty-eight others have been sent on flights to the moon or distant planets.

The technology amassed through those expeditions has justified this nation's commitment to conquer the challenge of space. It has encouraged us to lift our eyes beyond our initial goals and plan for the decade ahead.

The fruits of that technology have not been limited to space exploration alone. The knowledge built through our space program has benefitted our earthbound lives. It has:

—revolutionized communications throughout the world;

—given us better weather information and more accurate navigational and geographic data;

—brought improved medical instruments and techniques, advanced education, and added to our store of scientific knowledge;

—spurred the development of more sophisticated aircraft and improved flight safety;

—strengthened both the security of this nation and our leadership in the search for a peaceful and secure world.

We can look with confidence to an expansion of these benefits as our space program moves into its second decade.

Our accomplishments thus far point to the path of progress ahead: fuller observations of the earth, increasingly productive manned flights, and planetary exploration.

The year 1967 itself began with a major tragedy. Three of our gallant astronauts died in a fire while testing the APOLLO capsule on the launching pad. Even as we saluted these men for the contributions they had made, we moved to improve the spacecraft as well as the safety procedures surrounding its use.

But though the year was shadowed by that disaster, its accomplishments significantly advanced our progress. The SATURN-APOLLO flight in November was the greatest launch triumph to date. As the result of our success in photographing lunar landing sites, we have for the first time a complete mapping of the moon.

It is most heartening to me that our space program moved forward in a spirit of international cooperation, giving new hope that the conquest of space can contribute to the establishment of peace. Eighty-four nations participated in cooperative space activities with us. The Outer Space Treaty went into effect, after Senate approval. The United Nations unanimously recommended a procedure for the emergency rescue and return of astronauts and space equipment. I shall shortly be sending that treaty to the Senate.

It is with pleasure that I transmit this record of achievement to the Members of Congress, whose judgment and support have been essential to our aerospace progress.

LYNDON B. JOHNSON

The White House
January 30, 1968

NOTE: The report, entitled "Report to the Congress From the President of the United States: United States Aeronautics and Space Activities, 1967," is printed in a publication of the National Aeronautics and Space Council (145 pp.) and in House Document 246 (90th Cong., 2d sess.).

For the President's message to Congress on the astronaut assistance and return agreement, see Item 387.

42 Statement by the President Upon Signing Order Establishing the President's Commission for the Observance of Human Rights Year 1968. *January 30, 1968*

IT IS seldom that any one man's life embodies both national leadership and a universal cause. It is rarer still when his spirit survives his death and endures as an inspiration for man's deepest hopes.

Such a man was born 86 years ago this day.

President Franklin Delano Roosevelt stands in life and death as a towering advocate of those timeless ideals that promise individual fulfillment to men and peace to the family of nations. His country pursues those ideals more than two decades after his death: social justice here at home and a community of mutually respecting nations throughout the world.

Today we take another and determined step toward those ideals. We mark the anniversary of President Franklin Roosevelt's birth in the most fitting and hopeful way—by building on his work.

I have today signed an Executive order establishing a Presidential Commission for the Observance of Human Rights Year.

The General Assembly of the United Nations has designated 1968 as International Year for Human Rights. It is the 20th Anniversary Year of the Universal Declaration of Human Rights. United Nations members are called up for appropriate national observances throughout this year.

Three months ago, in declaring 1968 Human Rights Year for the United States, I called upon "all Americans and upon all Government agencies—Federal, State and local—to use this occasion to deepen our commitment to the defense of human rights and to strengthen our efforts for their full and effective realization both among our own people and among all the peoples of the United Nations." The Commission I have appointed is composed of distinguished citizens and heads of executive agencies. They are charged with shaping the variety of our efforts into a major and purposeful national contribution.

The United States was founded on great and lasting principles of liberty and rights for the individual. Our Constitution and our laws preserve these rights. Our Government is devoted to enlarging them for all Americans.

But rights not perceived cannot be prized; rights not understood are rights not exercised, and soon weakened or destroyed. We have a great need and responsibility to educate our people in a fuller understanding of their rights.

We can lead by our example. Peace is the spur. If nations are not to rely forever on a fragile balance of fears, they must find confidence in making justice the guiding principle of their national and international affairs.

We seek justice as a safeguard against tyranny and catastrophe. Secretary of State George Marshall reminded us 20 years ago:

"Governments which systematically disregard the rights of their own people are not likely to respect the rights of other nations and other people, and are likely to seek their objectives by coercion and force."

Thus warned in 1948, America pledged her strength and hope with other signatories to the Universal Declaration of Human Rights. This great compact gave new power and coherence to man's often shapeless, and sometimes hopeless yearning for equality and freedom.

We reaffirm our allegiance to that Declaration today, and call upon all our citizens and institutions to advance its purposes to the extent of their abilities.

The Senate has signified that it will enlarge its own important role. It supported our participation in international agreements that further the protection of human rights by consenting to the Supplementary Convention on Slavery on November 2, 1967. In my proclamation designating Human Rights Year, I declared that ratification of the Human Rights Conventions was long overdue. It is my earnest hope that the Senate will complete the tasks before it by ratifying the remaining Human Rights Conventions.

America's domestic initiatives and successes in assuring our people the guarantees of our Constitution should be better understood by the international community.

The Commission I appoint today:

—can enlarge our people's understanding of the principles of human rights, as expressed in the Universal Declaration and the Constitution and in the laws of the United States;

—can provide a focus for governmental participation in Human Rights Year, enlisting the cooperation of organizations and individuals;

—and may conduct studies, issue publications, and undertake such other activities as it finds appropriate.

I have appointed the following distinguished citizens to serve on the Commission: W. Averell Harriman, Ambassador at Large; Anna Roosevelt Halsted of Washington, D.C.; A. Philip Randolph of New York; Tom Clark of Texas, former Associate Justice, U.S. Supreme Court; George Meany of Maryland, President of the AFL-CIO; Elinor L. Gordon of New York, President of the Citizens' Committee for Children; Robert Meyner, former Governor of

New Jersey; Dr. J. Willis Hurst of Atlanta, Ga.; Bruno Bitker of Wisconsin, Chairman of the Human Rights Panel at the White House Conference on International Cooperation in 1965.

I have asked Averell Harriman to serve as Chairman of the Commission. Anna Roosevelt Halsted has graciously agreed to act as Vice Chairman.

I have also today asked the following heads of executive agencies to serve on the Commission: the Secretary of State, the Attorney General, the Secretary of Labor, the Secretary of Health, Education, and Welfare, the Secretary of Housing and Urban Development, the Staff Director of the U.S. Commission on Civil Rights, and the Chair-

man of the Equal Employment Opportunity Commission.

I have selected these men and women with care and confidence, because I expect them to perform an outstanding service for every American, and for all who prize the rights that we possess and seek to make secure for others.

The Commission will have my strongest personal support.

NOTE: The President referred to Executive Order 11394 "Establishing the President's Commission for the Observance of Human Rights Year 1968" (4 Weekly Comp. Pres. Docs., p. 174; 33 F.R. 2429; 3 CFR, 1968 Comp., p. 97). The President also referred to Proclamation 3814 "Human Rights Week and Human Rights Year," signed October 11, 1967 (3 Weekly Comp. Pres. Docs., p. 1431; 32 F.R. 14193; 3 CFR, 1967 Comp., p. 88).

43   Remarks at the Presidential Prayer Breakfast. *February 1, 1968*

Distinguished head table guests, reverend clergy, gentlemen:

At this season of the calendar, the nights are long, the winds are chill, the light of day is often dull and gray. Our minds know that the chill will pass, that spring will come, that the days will be brighter once again.

What our minds know, our spirits often forget. We weary of the winter and despair of the coming of the spring. We are tempted to turn from the tasks of duty and to lay down the works that are ours to do.

At this season of the affairs of man, it is all much the same. The nights are very long. The winds are very chill. Our spirits grow weary and restive as the springtime of man seems farther and farther away.

It is for such seasons as this one that man was given by his Creator the saving strength of faith—the strength we summon to sustain us when we pray.

Once again, this is a season now when

America needs to draw upon the strength of our many faiths. In this great office of all the people, it is not my right or my privilege to tell citizens how or when or what they should worship. I can—and I do—tell you that in these long nights your President prays.

In the hours of this night just past, I found these lines of prayer that were repeated a quarter of a century ago by another President. It was in 1942—when we were challenged in both oceans—at a season when the winds of the world blew harsh and the dawn of a brighter day seemed very far away, Franklin Delano Roosevelt offered to this Nation these words and I repeat them in these times now:

"God of the free, we pledge our hearts and lives today to the cause of all free mankind. . . . Grant us a common faith that man shall know bread and peace, that he shall know justice and righteousness, freedom and security, and an equal chance to do his best, not only in our own lands, but throughout the world. And in that faith let us march toward the clean world our hands can make. Amen."

We cannot know what the morrow will bring. We can know that to meet its challenges and to withstand its assaults, America never stands taller than when her people go to their knees.

[The President spoke first to the gentlemen in the Shoreham Hotel's Regency Room and then to the ladies in the Blue Room.]

Distinguished head table guests, ladies:

Mrs. Johnson deeply regrets that conditions make it impossible for her to be here with you this morning. She always gets strength and pleasure from her associations with you. And she asked me to convey her regrets to you.

It is all too easy at a gathering like this to evoke our faith in a divine being without realizing the full implications of this invocation.

There are people here of many backgrounds and of different religious traditions. The bond that unites us cannot therefore be some special doctrine or theology. At the same time we do have a bond—this is not merely an empty ritual.

Basically we all share the conviction—which we explain in different ways, in different sacramental forms—that man is not just an atom, a random piece of matter living in a mechanical, purposeless universe.

We believe that there is in every one an inner compass, a spark of divinity, which sets him apart from the rest of creation.

We believe that this inner force gives mankind the capacity both for establishing ideals and for striving to bring these ideals to reality in a harsh and in an often hostile world.

And, at the same time, it makes him

responsible for his blunders and his betrayals. He cannot face God—or himself—and say "Don't blame me, I have no alternatives."

Belief in a divine providence is not—then—an escape or a tranquilizer. It is rather a compelling challenge to men to attain the ideals of liberty, justice, peace, and compassion.

It is often—as it is today in Vietnam—a call for very great sacrifice. For ideals unfortunately do not triumph simply because one believes in them or wishes for them. There are in the world today hundreds of millions of people who dream of a world free from war, oppression, and injustice—but until the power of idealism can match the brutal coercion of totalitarianism and aggression, their dreams will be empty.

What we pray for with all our hearts is an end to war and tyranny. We hope that in time the restless spirit of humanity will be freed in those parts of the world where it is now oppressed.

We are fighting now—as we fought 25 years ago—to prevent any further expansion of totalitarian coercion over the souls of men.

We do all of this with a very deep sense of humility—recognizing our own fallibilities and errors—but with an equally strong belief that the cause of humanity cannot be permitted to lose by default.

We can never be so arrogant as to claim God's special blessing for America, but we can express the hope that in His eyes we have at least tried to help make possible a new vitality of the human conscience—not only here in America, our beloved land, but we have tried it and are still trying it throughout all the world.

Thank you very much.

NOTE: The annual prayer breakfast of International Christian Leadership, Inc., a nondenominational group of laymen, was held at the Shoreham Hotel in Washington. The President spoke at 9:29 a.m.

44 Statement by the President Upon Signing Order Providing for Popular Election of the Chief Executive of the Ryukyu Islands. *February* 1, 1968

I HAVE signed an amendment to the basic Executive order that provides for the administration of Okinawa and other Ryukyu Islands.

The amendment I have signed provides that the Ryukyuan Chief Executive—who is now elected by the legislative body of the Government of the Ryukyu Islands—shall in the future be popularly elected by the Ryukyuan people.

This is another forward step in the continuing policy of the United States to afford the Ryukyuan people a voice in managing their own affairs—as great a voice as is compatible with the Ryukyus' role in maintaining the security of Japan and the Far East. The amendment will also further the identification of Ryukyuan institutions with those of Japan proper, where prefectural chief executives are directly elected. This is consistent with the agreement reached in my recent talks with Prime Minister Sato of Japan.

General Unger, our High Commissioner in the Ryukyus, announced this change today in a speech to the Ryukyuan Legislature.

It will insure that the Ryukyuan Chief Executive for the next term can be elected directly by the Ryukyuan people.

NOTE: The President referred to Executive Order 11395 "Further Amending Executive Order No. 10713, Providing for Administration of the Ryukyu Islands." The text is printed in the Weekly Compilation of Presidential Documents, the Federal Register, and Title 3 of the Code of Federal Regulations (3 Weekly Comp. Pres. Docs., p. 177; 33 F.R. 2561; 3 CFR, 1968 Comp., p. 99).

45 Message to the Congress Transmitting Annual Report of the National Endowment for the Humanities. *February* 1, 1968

To the Congress of the United States:

I am pleased to transmit to the Congress this second annual report of the National Endowment for the Humanities.

The Endowment and its advisory group, the National Council of the Humanities, represent the first major step ever taken by the Government to support this broad and significant range of human knowledge and achievement. Their creation by the National Foundation on the Arts and the Humanities Act of 1965 brought national concern and support to a field where such encouragement was long overdue.

This Report describes the Endowment's initial year of full activity. It shows that during fiscal year 1966, the Endowment developed programs seeking the broadest possible use of the funds available. In fiscal year 1967, it awarded approximately $4.5 million to a total of 412 institutions and individuals in 44 states and the District of Columbia.

The awards included:

—Eighteen grants designed to stimulate public understanding and use of the humanities. These grants promoted innovations in the field of instructional television, and encouraged historical societies and museums to make their resources more broadly available.

—Twenty-eight awards to revitalize the teaching of the humanities at all levels.

—Eighty-one grants in support of research and publication designed to expand the development of scholarly resources in all fields of the humanities. These funds now support the first sustained effort to produce definitive editions of the works of great nineteenth-century American authors, from Emerson to Whitman, and contribute to such diverse and important projects as the publication of the letters of Supreme Court Justice Louis Brandeis, the training of young American archaeologists, and the first publication of the complete works of John Dewey, one of America's greatest philosophers.

—Two hundred and eighty-five fellowship awards, providing funds for a year of independent research for established scholars, six to eight months of uninterrupted study for the scholar-teacher, and summer stipends for younger scholars.

Such projects and fellowships—representing only a small proportion of the many meritorious applications submitted—are proof that the Endowment has met enthusiastic acceptance by the scholarly community.

I commend this Report to the Congress, and urge early action to give the Endowment the resources we have requested to carry forward and expand its valuable work.

LYNDON B. JOHNSON

The White House
February 1, 1968

NOTE: The report is entitled "National Endowment for the Humanities, Second Annual Report, Fiscal Year 1967" (Government Printing Office, 46 pp.).

46   Remarks at the Signing Ceremony for the Economic Report. *February 1, 1968*

WE WANT to welcome the Governors who were kind enough to come to this little ceremony and we want to apologize to you for detaining you for a few moments.

We have come here this morning to sign this report and transmit it.

It tells of the achievement and abundance such as no other nation has ever known. But it also tells us a good deal more than that. It tells us of problems that prosperity can leave unsolved, or even that prosperity has created.

All the graphs in this report point upward. The figures climb and the superlatives abound. But here too there is a warning—a caution to all of our people and their elected representatives, and they cannot ignore it if our prosperity is to be protected and enlarged.

From the pages of this report history will write its own record of the American economic miracle.

—Never has our economy been so prosperous for so long.

—Never has employment been so high and affluence so widespread and poverty so limited.

This report sees no halt. In the year ahead, if we are fiscally responsible and act accordingly:

—Our gross national product will grow about $60 billion.

—96 percent of our labor force will remain employed.

But Whitman said, ". . . that from any fruition of success, no matter what, shall come forth something to make a greater struggle necessary."

So it is also true of the American economy. We have mastered the challenges of general unemployment and sluggish growth. But in doing this, successes have brought additional and new challenges: the need to check inflation and the need to reduce the persistent deficit in our international payments.

These challenges call for sacrifices. I do not think they are really great sacrifices considering what our people have gone through to achieve what we have today. But they do call for sacrifices, to be sure, but more than some seem willing to pay now.

In January 1967, in August 1967, in January 1968, and now again here in February, I plead with Congress to enact a tax of a single penny on the dollar of the average American's income. I am asking for one penny out of a dollar from the average American.

This tax would still leave income-tax rates for American families far below what it was when I became their President.

So I ask again today:

—not because any of us like taxes,
—not because I enjoy asking for higher taxes,
—not because a tax bill will solve all of our problems,
—not because our economy will explode this year without this tax.

But I ask the Congress to act promptly because I believe the tax bill is an essential part, a necessary ingredient to a balanced and considered program that will help us:

—to slow down price increases,
—to cut our balance of payments deficit,
—to maintain a smooth flow of credit, and finally
—to insure us against risks that I don't believe this Nation ought to take—because I don't believe we need to take them.

In short, I believe our Nation needs this tax bill to conduct, properly and prudently, the affairs of a great democracy.

Its passage would be an act of fiscal responsibility that would help the world maintain its faith in the dollar—the American dollar—and help the world maintain its faith in the responsibility of the American people.

The executive branch has its own responsibility. Recognizing this, I am establishing a Cabinet Committee on Price Stability. This Committee on Price Stability is to deal with the many aspects of price and wage problems, with its bottlenecks and with its inefficiencies.

Once again, I plead for the full cooperation of American leaders of business and labor. I ask that they devote themselves anew to resisting the false lure of higher prices and excessive wage increases—and the deadly spiral which saps the strength of our prosperity.

We are charged by history to invest billions to defend freedom abroad—and we are doing that today. Yet we cannot and must not stand still at home.

This Nation can afford to meet its responsibilities to the poor among us. Poverty is declining, but even today I am ashamed to say that one American out of every seven is still poor among us.

In the wealth of our abundance there is enough to continue our attack, I think, on poverty and the evils that attend it: poor housing, inadequate education and training, ill health and personal frustration and despair, and still defend our freedoms and protect and preserve our liberties.

We have the wealth. The question is, do we have the wisdom and do we have the will and do we have the determination to apply strength to remedy weakness, to give up a part of what we have as an investment in the future that I think will pay good returns?

As we meet here in the Cabinet Room this morning in this distinguished company, the world watches our every act. Some of the leading financial prognosticators expect us to return to the boom and bust patterns of the past. Some look for the surrender of America's economic leadership in the world and the diminishing of America's economic power in the world.

Those who await our decline and our demise, I hope, will find little encouragement. The Economic Report charts for us an entirely different course. It points the way to a balanced and to an enduring prosperity, it points the way to expanded job opportunities for all, it points the way to strong leadership in international economic affairs, and it points the way to the hope—the long-sought hope—that America will rid itself of poverty in this generation.

We have much to be thankful for. We have much to be grateful for. We have much to protect if we only realize how fortunate we are.

I have no doubt that we will do what is necessary to see that that good fortune is continued.

Thank you very much.

[At this point, the President signed the report. He then resumed speaking.]

This is the first pen I used to sign this Economic Report. This is the fifth Economic Report that I have signed.

This is my 37th year in government. Throughout all these years I have tried to look to leaders from whom I could learn much by both precept and example.

I am going to give this first pen to what I look upon as an ideal public servant of the greatest country in the world. He is the kind of man whom I wish every man in the Government was like. He is modest and able, firm, and strong, compassionate and determined and guided by only one rule—the greatest good for the greatest number.

His leaving here to take a post abroad will leave an empty spot and a certain amount of sadness for me because I have relied upon him as I have looked to my own family. But I have great satisfaction knowing that in this critical international period when we need to improve our relations and strengthen them with our friends in Italy and Germany and the other countries of that area, one of the ablest economic minds that this Nation has produced and one of its most dedicated servants will be the spokesman for the President and the United States of America.

Consoled only by this thought do I willingly bid him adieu.

NOTE: The President spoke at 11:03 a.m. in the Cabinet Room at the White House. In his opening words he referred to Governors Dewey Bartlett of Oklahoma, Lester Maddox of Georgia, Charles L. Terry, Jr., of Delaware, John A. Volpe of Massachusetts, John Bell Williams of Mississippi, William L. Guy of North Dakota, and Hulett C. Smith of West Virginia, who were in Washington to attend the Presidential Prayer Breakfast (see Item 43).

The tax bill to which the President referred was approved June 28 as the Revenue and Expenditure Control Act of 1968. For his statement upon signing the measure, see Item 343.

The Cabinet Committee on Price Stability was established by the President on February 23, 1968 (see Items 89, 90).

The first pen used by the President in signing the Economic Report was presented by him to Gardner Ackley, outgoing Chairman of the Council of Economic Advisers, who had been nominated as U.S. Ambassador to Italy.

47 Annual Message to the Congress: The Economic Report of the President. *February 1, 1968*

To the Congress of the United States:

Most Americans see the economy in terms of a particular job or farm or business. Yet the welfare of each of us depends significantly on the state of the economy as a whole.

It was never more necessary for all Americans to try to see the whole economy in perspective—to realize its achievements, to recognize its problems, to understand what must be done to develop its full potential for good. For, as a people, we face some important choices.

A Time for Decisions

Seldom can any single choice make or break an economy as strong and healthy as ours. But the series of interrelated decisions we face will affect our economy and that of the whole free world for years to come.

We face these hard decisions with a confidence born of success. Our economy has never been stronger and more vigorous than during the 1960's.

Our achievements demonstrate that we *can* manage our economic affairs wisely—that we *can* make sound choices.

If we now choose responsibly, we can look forward—at home—to more years of healthy prosperity, and of social and economic progress.

If we choose responsibly, and our friends abroad cooperate responsibly, we and they can look forward in confidence to the continuing smooth and rapid expansion of the mutually rewarding international exchange of goods and services.

But if we temporize—try to avoid the hard choices before us—we will soon discover that we have even more difficult choices to make. In six months or a year, we could find our prices and interest rates rising far too fast. In a few months we and our friends abroad could face new uncertainty and turbulence in international financial affairs.

If we wait for the problems to become acute and obvious, then everyone will be ready to act. By then, the tasks could well be much harder.

In the coming weeks and months we must choose

—whether we will conduct our fiscal affairs sensibly; or whether we will allow a clearly excessive budgetary deficit to go uncorrected by failing to raise taxes, and thereby risk a feverish boom that could generate an unacceptable acceleration of price increases, a possible financial crisis, and perhaps ultimately a recession;

—whether as businessmen and workers we will behave prudently in setting prices and wages; or whether we will risk an intensified wage-price spiral that would threaten our trade surplus and the stability of our economy for years to come;

—whether we will act firmly and wisely to control our balance-of-payments deficit; or whether we will risk a breakdown in the financial system that has underpinned world prosperity, a possible reversion toward economic isolationism, and a spiraling slowdown in world economic expansion;

—whether we will move constructively to deal with the urgent problems of our cities and compassionately to bring hope to our disadvantaged; or whether we are willing to risk irreversible urban deterioration and social explosion.

I know that Americans *can* face up to the tasks before us—that we *can* run our economic affairs responsibly. I am confident that we *will* take timely action to maintain the health and strength of our economy and our society in the months and years ahead.

The Record and Problems of Prosperity

The year 1967 was one of uncertainties and difficulties both in our external and our internal economic affairs. Yet there were reasons for confidence as well as concern, both internationally and domestically.

1967—A YEAR OF READJUSTMENT AT HOME

For the domestic economy, 1967 was a year of readjustment—after the strains of 1966.

Growth in the first half was at an annual rate of only a little over 1 percent, after correction for price increases. But vigorous growth resumed in the second half—at a yearly rate of around 4½ percent.

Last year had to be a year of readjustment because our economy began the year out of balance. Inventories were excessive, housing was in a slump, and business spending on new plant and equipment threatened to drop away from a level that seemed too high to be sustained.

Those imbalances no longer exist. That is why our economy is again advancing so strongly.

Because readjustments were necessary, the gains of 1967 were not as great as were those of 1966, nor as those anticipated for 1968. Yet it was a year of important economic progress on most fronts.

During 1967
—an additional 1¾ million persons found jobs;
—our unemployment rate, at 3.8 percent, matched that of 1966 and was lower than in any previous year since 1953;
—average earnings of factory workers rose by $4.80 a week;
—total employee compensation rose $33 billion;
—farm proprietors' net income dipped, but by yearend had returned to the level of a year earlier;
—total consumer income after taxes climbed $35½ billion;

—industrial production, after dropping almost 2½ percent, recovered by December to a new all-time peak; and
—the annual rate of housing starts rose a half million.

During 1967, prices also advanced—more than we would have wished. Even so, real purchasing power per capita available to consumers after taxes rose 3 percent.

1967—A YEAR OF EXTERNAL PROBLEMS AND PROMISE

The U.S. balance-of-payment deficit—a chronic problem since 1957—worsened in 1967 after several years of substantial improvement. In important measure this deterioration reflected the fears and uncertainties surrounding the devaluation of the British pound in November.

The same uncertainties also fed a massive wave of private speculation against gold late in the year. This subsided only after the United States and other countries in the "gold pool" demonstrated their determination—backed by the use of their monetary reserves—not to allow a change in the price of gold.

In the absence of strong new action by the United States—and by the surplus countries of Western Europe—there was danger that the deterioration of the U.S. payments balance and speculation against gold and currencies might feed upon and reinforce one another in a way that could touch off an international financial crisis in 1968.

Even if the dangers were remote, the grave consequences of such a crisis for the world economy demanded bold and immediate preventive action. It was taken on January 1. The substance of our measures, plans, and priorities is discussed later in this Report.

But 1967 saw progress as well as problems

on the international front. For it also brought the culmination of two giant forward steps in world international economic affairs, both long in gestation:

- In June, the Kennedy Round of negotiations produced agreement on the single most significant multilateral reduction in world trade barriers in history. It promises further to stimulate the expansion of international trade, already a major source of postwar economic growth throughout the world.

- In September, the member nations of the IMF reached agreement on plans to create by deliberate cooperative action a new form of world reserves, supplementing gold and the dollar. Once this plan comes into full operation, the vulnerability of the present system to speculation should gradually fade away, and so should any threat of a possible future strangulation of the growth of world trade and production.

SEVEN YEARS OF EXPANSION

If 1967 stood alone, it would have to be judged a satisfactory year, despite its problems.

But 1967 must not be seen in isolation—rather as the seventh year of the longest and strongest economic expansion in our history. The opening months of 1967 were merely a brief pause in the broad sweep of economic advance.

Over these seven years
—our total real output of goods and services has increased more than 40 percent;
—per capita income after taxes and valued in dollars of constant purchasing power has risen 29 percent;
—10 million more people are at work;

—more than 12 million Americans have moved above the poverty line.

Over just the past four years
—2¼ million more students are in college;
—5½ million new homes have been built;
—35 million new cars have been sold;
—use of electricity has risen one-third;
—5 million more families own stock, 23 million more have savings accounts, and the assets of private pension funds have grown by $40 billion; and
—35 percent more Negroes have found professional, technical, and managerial jobs.

Had the path of real output in 1961–67 followed the bumpy path of 1954–60
—the Nation's total real output over the past seven years would have been $340 billion lower (valued in today's prices) than it actually was—this cumulative difference is about equal, in real terms, to the Nation's total output in 1942.
—the annual rate of output today (valued in today's prices) would be $120 billion lower than in fact it is—this difference is equivalent to about $1,600 a year per person now employed.

Truly, the American people have enjoyed exceptional economic benefits over these seven years. But these striking benefits confer obligations.

- Over this period 8 million more families have achieved yearly incomes above $10,000. They—and the 6½ million who already enjoyed such incomes in 1960—have a special obligation to the more than 10 million households still in poverty.

- The seven-year *increase* of $820 in real per capita income (valued in today's prices) exceeds the current *total* average per capita income in nations with 70 percent of the world's population. This fact makes inescapable the obligation of the American people for helping to maintain security and for providing economic assistance to the developing world.

I believe that the American people—whose present affluence would have been beyond the belief of most of us only 20 years ago—accept these obligations. My policies, at home and abroad, continue to be founded on a vision of the opportunities and obligations for the wealthy to help the poor to help themselves.

THE ROLE OF POLICY

It is far more than coincidence that, during these seven years of achievement, fiscal and monetary policy have been actively and consciously employed to promote prosperity.

No longer does Federal economic policy rely primarily on the "automatic stabilizers" built into our system, or wait for a recession or serious inflation to occur before measures are taken.

Fiscal and monetary policies have not been perfectly executed nor perfectly coordinated in the past few years. But our policies have remained under continuous and coordinated review. And our actions have been consistently in the right direction, if not always perfectly timed nor in precisely the right degree.

THE PROBLEMS OF PROSPERITY

Healthy prosperity has brought exceptional gains in production, incomes, and jobs.

But prosperity has not solved all of our economic problems, and it has created some of its own. These are the priority problems facing us in 1968.

1. First and foremost, we must take the necessary steps to put our fiscal affairs in order. Unless we do we shall be unable to deal effectively with the other problems that confront us.

2. We must slow down the wage-price spiral. Although we cannot achieve stability all at once, we must make progress in 1968 toward our goal of reasonable price stability in a steadily growing, high-employment economy.

3. We must push forward vigorously to restore equilibrium in our international accounts. We shall do so in full awareness of our responsibilities to promote and sustain a strong and expanding world economy. And we will enlist the cooperation of all other nations who share those responsibilities.

4. We must deal more effectively with our urban problems. More and more of our people live in cities. Yet cities threaten to become less and less livable—unless we take decisive steps to correct: slum housing; inadequate public services; congestion, noise, and pollution; inadequate transportation; unplanned sprawl; segregation, discrimination, and deficient job opportunities; crime, delinquency, and alienation.

5. We must continue the struggle to expand the opportunities available to every citizen—especially our disadvantaged. They require education, training, and adequate health care to prepare them for useful careers, and freedom from discrimination in finding jobs and housing. Those unable to work need adequate income protection. The war on poverty must go forward.

FISCAL POLICY AND THE OUTLOOK FOR 1968

THE CURRENT ECONOMIC SITUATION

The month-to-month changes of our economic indicators were often puzzling in 1967. But, when seen in perspective, economic developments reveal.

—a slowdown—though not a decline—in the first half, as we predicted a year ago; and

—a strong and sustained recovery in the second half, as we predicted last January and again in August when I renewed my request for a tax increase.

• In the second half of last year, the annual rate of our gross national product advanced by $32½ billion. In only one earlier half-year—the second half of 1965—has it advanced by more.

• The unemployment rate in December was 3.7 percent. In only 2 months of the last 169 has it been lower.

• Factory orders and shipments of durable goods were at an all-time high.

• Personal income rose more than $12 billion in November and December.

• And, disturbingly, the rate of increase in industrial wholesale prices in the second half of 1967 has been exceeded in only 4 other half-year periods in the past 16 years.

Every prospect is for continued rapid increase of output in the months ahead. Most experienced observers agree that the pace now is—and in the months ahead will be—too fast for safety. The gain in gross national product in the current quarter is generally expected to be one of the largest in our history—a record we could gladly do without at this time.

THE CURRENT FISCAL SITUATION

Following the major tax cuts of 1964 and 1965—equivalent to about $23 billion in today's economy—the booming economy of 1965 and 1966 brought Federal revenues into balance with Federal spending. In both years there was a small Federal surplus on the comprehensive national income accounts basis.

The slowdown in economic growth that began in late 1966 dampened the growth of revenues. At the same time, the cost of our commitment to freedom in Southeast Asia was steadily rising.

As a result, the Federal sector account plunged into deficit—$12½ billion in calendar year 1967.

Sharply rising Federal spending was a strong expansionary force in the economy between mid-1965 and mid-1967. While housing was still recovering from the after-effects of tight money, and private demand was sluggish—during the first half of last year—the stimulus from Federal spending was welcome.

Federal spending has not been growing rapidly since mid-1967, nor will it increase rapidly in the next year and a half. But because of the already high level of defense outlays, total Federal expenditures are too large to be piled on top of *normal* private demand without overheating our economy. It is because private demand has now returned to normal after its temporary weakness that we now need new measures of fiscal restraint.

Without the proposed income tax surcharge and the maintenance of current excise tax rates, the Federal sector deficit on national income accounts would remain close to the level of 1967.

Unless action is quickly taken to expand Federal revenues, a deficit that large—in combination with a resurgent private economy—would have these consequences:

• It would speed up a wage-price spiral already turning far too rapidly.

• It would seriously impair our already difficult international economic position—by damaging confidence in the dollar, and by stimulating imports and putting exports at a competitive disadvantage.

• Financing such a deficit would increasingly strain financial markets, pushing interest rates further above present record highs, and threatening another financial squeeze and another slump in homebuilding.

THE ROLE OF FISCAL RESTRAINT

The extraordinary achievements of our economy during the past seven years were made possible by our willingness to use fiscal and monetary policies to stimulate adequate expansion of total demand.

Now, however, restraint is essential to our economic health. High interest rates and tight money can restrain the economy—and will do so if fiscal policy fails to do it. But the cost of monetary restraint is high and unfair, imposed primarily on a single industry—homebuilding.

We must demonstrate that we can use fiscal policies flexibly—that we can raise as well as lower taxes.

I therefore urgently renew my request that the Congress enact a temporary 10-percent surcharge on corporate and individual income taxes.

• For corporations, the surcharge would become effective January 1, 1968, and continue through June 30, 1969.

• For individuals the surcharge would become effective on April 1. The 10-percent increase in withholding tax would continue through June 30, 1969. Taxpayers in the lower income brackets would be exempted from any surcharge.

• The legislation should, as I recommended last year, put all corporations

on a fully current payments basis, and extend temporarily the telephone and automobile excise taxes otherwise scheduled to drop on April 1, 1968.

These measures would increase tax revenues in fiscal year 1968 by $3 billion, and in fiscal year 1969 by $13 billion.

If future circumstances should permit ending the surcharge before June 30, 1969, it can be promptly repealed.

The surcharge of 10 percent on individual income taxes would reduce individual incomes by about 1 percent on the average. With the low-income exemption, the surcharge would add nothing to the taxes of a family of four with an income of $5,000. It would increase the tax bill for a family of four making $25,000 by about 2 percent of income.

Effective Federal tax rates on individual income would still remain, on the average, about 10 percent lower than in 1963.

A tax increase in the form of a surcharge on present taxes has many advantages:

—it is simple, requiring no additional administrative expense or inconvenience to the taxpayer;

—it preserves the present progressiveness of the system as it applies to middle and upper incomes, and the present division between corporate and personal taxes;

—it is easy to identify and repeal when no longer needed.

THE ECONOMIC OUTLOOK WITH THE TAX INCREASE

The fiscal policies I am now proposing will

—accomplish a sharp reduction in the Federal deficit on national income accounts, and erase it early in 1969;

—encourage balanced economic expansion to continue at a rate appropriate to our rising productive potential;

—permit the unemployment rate to remain below 4 percent for the third straight year;

—allow credit to remain available, without soaring interest rates, to meet the needs of housing and other key areas;

—promote a gradual slowing down of price increases;

—in combination with the other measures we are taking, encourage an expansion of our foreign trade surplus.

Even with the surcharge, GNP should increase by some $60 billion, about 7¾ percent. With prices rising more than 3 percent, real output of goods and services in 1968 will be more than 4 percent above 1967.

• Consumer purchases and homebuilding activity will rise strongly.

• Expenditures to expand and modernize productive capacity will grow at the moderate pace consistent with business needs.

• While State and local governments will continue to increase spending at a fairly rapid rate, Federal purchases will grow by less than half as much as in 1967.

• There will be further large gains in private incomes, even after higher taxes and prices.

The economic outlook is thus favorable—assuming fiscal restraint is forthcoming. Damage has already been done to interest rates, to our trade surplus, and to the level of prices by the failure of Congress to act last fall. But it is still not too late to avoid far more serious problems if action is taken in the next few weeks.

I again urge the Congress to act promptly on my tax proposals.

PROBLEMS AND PROGRAMS IN OUR INTERNATIONAL ECONOMIC AFFAIRS

THE U.S. BALANCE-OF-PAYMENTS DEFICIT

On January 1, I announced the main elements of our new balance-of-payments program for 1968. That program deals decisively with the threat to the dollar that developed in 1967.

Nature of the Problem

It is important to be clear about the nature of our balance-of-payments problem. The United States has a sizable surplus of exports of goods and services over imports. Our past overseas investments bring in excellent and growing earnings, and our new overseas investments are running at a very high level. There is a small but growing reverse flow of foreign investment here.

We have heavy military expenditures overseas, which are not fully offset by our allies; and our aid program still accounts for a small outflow of dollars.

Our export sales, our investment return, and the inflow of investment from abroad are not large enough to finance our imports, our new investments abroad, and our net Government overseas expenditures.

The difference—the deficit—is financed partly by sales of gold and partly by increased foreign holdings of short-term dollar investments by foreign businesses, banks, individuals, and governments.

The position of the United States in its international economic affairs is thus much like that of a wealthy and prosperous businessman whose liquidity has come under strain.

His commercial operations remain highly successful, with the value of his sales well in excess of his costs.

His large long-term investments in other enterprises are yielding an excellent return, and he sees an abundance of further opportunities for profitable investments that will bring large future returns.

Both his income and his net worth are growing strongly every year. And he does not hesitate to spend freely on the good things of life, while also making large gifts to worthy causes.

But he has been borrowing extensively at short term to help finance his long-term investments. Each year, he adds more to his short-term debts than to his liquid assets. It is in this sense—but only this—that he has an annual deficit. It is a liquidity deficit. It is not a deficit in his profit and loss account, nor an overspending of his income.

Some of his short-term creditors—although not really doubting the strong excess of his assets over his liabilities—are nevertheless getting a bit concerned about continuing to expand—or even to renew—their short-term credits.

Should some of them refuse to renew their loans, his situation could become awkward. Other creditors might become nervous and would rush to present their claims. Financial pressures would extend to other, smaller businessmen with whom he had strong commercial ties, and whose basic positions were less sound.

That man—like the United States—needs to pull back for a while to strengthen his liquidity.

He will want to cut costs and increase sales in his commercial operations.

He will have to pass up for a while many of his attractive opportunities for profitable long-term investments.

He will need to review the terms of his spending and gifts—to ease their impact on his cash position.

Most of all, he wants no doubt to arise about his ability to meet his debts as they come due. He would easily survive a financial crisis with no major impairment of his income or net worth. But some other businessmen who bought from or sold to him could easily be dragged into bankruptcy.

Reducing the Deficit

Since 1961, the United States has been making a determined effort to reduce its liquidity deficit. Through 1965, steady progress had been made.

In 1966 the deficit held even, in spite of the rising overseas costs of Vietnam. But the deficit increased in 1967—particularly sharply in the fourth quarter—reversing that progress. The instability generated by devaluation of the British pound was responsible for a significant part of the deterioration, but not for all of it.

- Overseas defense costs rose despite tight controls on spending.
- The net balance of tourist expenditures shifted further against the United States.
- Private U.S. capital outflows rose, even though direct investment was held in check by the voluntary program; and foreign capital inflows decreased.
- Our trade balance failed to improve as much as we expected, mainly because of the economic slowdown in Europe.

Some of the steps we might consider to reduce our payments abroad—such as reverting to high tariffs or quotas—would reverse long-term policies and, by provoking retaliation, reduce our receipts by as much as or more than our payments. And many of the other things we could do would seriously and irresponsibly harm our domestic economy, friendly countries overseas, or the flow of world trade.

PROGRAM FOR 1968

We have a clear duty to act. And we are taking action—as constructively and responsibly as we can.

Domestic Economic Policies

The avoidance of excessive demand in our economy is crucial to the strength of the dollar as well as to our domestic prosperity.

If we place too much pressure on our resources, U.S. buyers will turn abroad for supplies and our imports will soar. And if our prices rise, we will weaken our export competitiveness and attract even more imports—not just immediately, but for years to come.

That is why the first order of business in defense of the dollar is to pass the tax bill.

We must also exert every effort to avoid the possible destructive effects on our trade surplus of strikes or the threat of strikes in key industries. I urge business and labor to cooperate with the Secretaries of Labor and Commerce in dealing with this danger to our export surplus.

Direct Balance-of-Payments Measures

In addition to assuring the health of our economy at home, we must act directly on the key international flows that contribute to our deficit. Our direct balance-of-payments measures are designed to move us strongly toward equilibrium—this year. Some measures are temporary and will be removed as soon as conditions permit. Others are designed for longer range needs. Several will require congressional action.

We have already put into effect

—a new mandatory program to restrain direct investment abroad, which will reduce outflows by at least $1 billion

from 1967.

—a tighter Federal Reserve program to restrain foreign lending by U.S. banks and other financial institutions, to achieve an inflow of at least $500 million.

We have begun action to save $500 million on Government expenditures overseas. Negotiations are already underway to minimize the foreign exchange costs of our essential security commitments abroad. Orders have already been issued to cut the number of civilian personnel abroad.

We are organizing major efforts to encourage foreign investment and travel in the United States.

I announced on January 1 that the Secretary of the Treasury would explore with the Congress legislative measures to help us achieve our objective of reducing our travel deficit abroad by $500 million this year. Those explorations are proceeding.

In the meantime, I again ask the American people to defer for the next two years all nonessential travel outside the Western Hemisphere.

I also announced on January 1

—that we were initiating discussions with our friends abroad on ways to minimize the disadvantages to our trade from various nontariff barriers and national tax systems abroad; and

—that we were preparing legislation in this area whose scope and nature would depend on the outcome of these consultations.

The consultations have been in progress since January 1. When they are completed, I will announce their outcome, and indicate what if any legislation we shall seek.

I am asking the Congress for the funds necessary to support long-term measures to stimulate exports, by

—intensifying promotion of American goods overseas; and

—expanding and strengthening the role of the Export-Import Bank.

Responsibilities of Surplus Countries

As we fulfill our responsibilities, other nations have an equal obligation to act. The balance-of-payments surpluses of our trading partners in continental Europe are essentially the mirror image of our deficit. Their constructive adjustments, as well as our own, can contribute to remedying our mutual imbalance.

For them, as for us, action at home heads the list. The nations of continental Europe should use their fiscal and monetary policies to pursue steady expansion of their domestic economies. Indeed, if they were to tighten credit and budgets in order to protect their surpluses, then we could not succeed in our efforts to come into equilibrium in a healthy world economy. Even worse, a competitive slowdown in world economic expansion could ensue, to the detriment of all peoples everywhere.

Surplus countries can also contribute to a smooth process of adjustment by reducing their barriers to trade, by increasing their economic assistance to developing countries, by expanding their capital markets to finance their own investment, by permitting wider access to these capital markets by other nations, and by meeting their full share of the foreign-exchange costs of our collective defense effort.

The world tried competitive beggar-my-neighbor policies in the 1930's and they ended in chaos. The surplus countries have the obligation to assure that this does not happen again.

THE DOLLAR AND THE INTERNATIONAL MONETARY SYSTEM

The interests of major nations are also linked together in the international monetary system. For us, there is a special responsibility, since the dollar is a world currency

—widely used by businesses abroad,

—held along with gold as a reserve asset by foreign central banks.

Our deficits in the past decade have sent more dollars abroad than businesses there needed to acquire, or than governments have wanted to hold as reserves. Many of these dollars were used to purchase gold from the United States.

Speculation generated by the strains on the international monetary system has caused further drains of gold from international reserves—much of it from our own.

As a result, U.S. gold reserves have declined to about $12 billion. This is still ample to cope with foreseeable demands on our gold stock. But persistent large U.S. deficits would threaten the entire international monetary system.

Our commitment to maintain dollar convertibility into gold at $35 an ounce is firm and clear. We will not be a party to raising its price. The dollar will continue to be kept as good as or better than gold.

Freeing Our Gold Reserves

I am therefore asking the Congress to take prompt action to free our gold reserves so that they can unequivocally fulfill their true purpose—to insure the international convertibility of the dollar into gold at $35 per ounce.

• The gold reserve requirement against Federal Reserve notes is not needed to tell us what prudent monetary policy should be—that myth was destroyed long ago.

- It is not needed to give value to the dollar—that value derives from our productive economy.
- The reserve requirement does make some foreigners question whether all of our gold is really available to guarantee our commitment to sell gold at the $35 price. Removing the requirement will prove to them that we mean what we say.

I ask speedy action from the Congress—because it will demonstrate to the world the determination of America to meet its international economic obligations.

Special Drawing Rights

Through U.S. deficits the dollar has been the major element of the recent growth of international reserves.

As we move into balance, the world can no longer look to the dollar for major future additions to reserves.

Neither can it depend on gold. Gold production has been leveling off in the face of rising industrial use and a steady drain into private hoards. What is needed is a reserve asset universally acceptable as a supplement to gold and dollars, that can be created in the amount needed to meet the desired expansion of world reserves.

The Special Drawing Rights plan agreed on in Rio de Janeiro last September provides such an asset. This plan will fundamentally strengthen—and ultimately transform—the international monetary system in the years ahead.

The agreement should be promptly ratified and swiftly activated on an adequate scale. I will call upon the Congress to approve U.S. participation.

TRADE

The Kennedy Round was completed on June 30, the most successful multilateral agreement on tariff reduction ever negotiated. Four years of hard negotiating were required—but the ultimate success was worth it. A fair bargain was struck. Our farmers and businessmen will get major benefits as new markets are opened to them.

We will continue to work with our trading partners—in the GATT and in other bodies—to find new approaches to the liberalization of world trade, with urgent consideration given to nontariff barriers.

Some would throw away the gains from three decades of liberal trade policy, retreating into shortsighted protectionism. Mandatory quotas on American imports would meet prompt retaliation abroad. All Americans would pay a high price for the benefit of a few.

Protectionism is no answer to our balance-of-payments problem. Its solution depends on expanding world trade.

The Government stands ready to help the few that may be hurt by rising imports—but in ways that expand trade, strengthen our economy, and improve our international relations.

Accordingly, I will shortly send to the Congress legislation which will

- —provide an extension of unused tariff-reducing authority;
- —liberalize the criteria for adjustment assistance to firms and workers; and
- —eliminate the American selling price system of customs valuation.

During the year ahead, opportunities may develop to expand peaceful trade with the countries of Eastern Europe and the Soviet Union. I again urge the Congress to provide the necessary authority for us to pursue such opportunities should they develop.

The United States has been discussing with other industrial countries a system of temporary generalized tariff preferences by all developed countries for all developing countries. Agreement was reached in the OECD on the general principles of such a system. It will be presented to the developing countries at the UNCTAD meeting in New Delhi.

We shall continue to consult with Members of Congress and representatives of American industry, agriculture, and labor as these discussions proceed.

AID TO DEVELOPING COUNTRIES

If economic progress were now to slow down in the developing countries that make up two-thirds of the free world—in the arc of Asia from Turkey to Korea, in Latin America, and in Africa—our hopes for a peaceful world would be menaced. In 1968 this means that we should

—approve a prudent AID program;
—quickly agree with other donor countries on a substantially increased replenishment of funds for the International Development Association;
—extend the Food for Freedom Act;
—authorize the United States to share with other donors in establishing the Special Funds of the Asian Development Bank.

Several less-developed countries have made great strides in the promotion of family planning. We must be prepared to assist their efforts if the grim race between food supplies and population is to be won decisively.

We can do these things—as in conscience we must—without detriment to our international payments. AID has already made great progress in reducing the impact of its program on the U.S. balance of payments. In 1968 that impact would be reduced by another $100 million, so that less than 8 percent of AID's dollar expenditures will be for non-U.S. goods and services.

THE RETURN TO PRICE STABILITY

Neither the United States nor any other free industrial nation has yet learned how to couple steady growth at high employment with reasonable stability of prices.

Our price record since 1960 has been superior to that of any other major industrial country. Even since mid-1965, we have done better than in past periods of hostilities—when direct controls were used.

But our recent record has clearly not been good enough. For one reason, firm discipline with respect to U.S. costs and prices is essential to a strong balance-of-payments position.

Rising prices are not just a last-year problem or a this- and next-year problem. They are a persistent, long-term problem for a high-employment economy—one that will not fade away by itself.

We must do what we can to minimize price increases in 1968. But we must also settle in for a long hard fight aimed toward 1969, 1970—and 1980.

One source of inflationary pressure is a rate of economic expansion that strains available productive resources. Too much demand will lift prices and wages all across the line.

Thus the readiness to apply fiscal and monetary restraint when demand threatens to become too strong must be the fundamental reliance in our battle to restore and then maintain stable prices.

RESPONSIBLE WAGE AND PRICE BEHAVIOR

But inflationary pressures also arise when labor and business each seek to expand their claims against the national product—through excessive wage settlements or unnecessary price hikes—at a faster rate than real national product is growing.

If labor seeks 80 percent of the total national pie and business 25 percent, the only result can be rising prices. This inflates the pie—but does not increase its substance.

Whatever the initial source which starts prices rising, the rise tends to perpetuate itself. Higher prices enlarge labor's wage demands. Faster wage increases raise costs, which makes prices rise some more. Once a wage-price spiral has begun, it is exceedingly difficult to slow it down.

In each of the last two years, our price level has risen by about 3 percent, and in the last six months by about 4 percent. With a somewhat stronger economy in 1968, and with labor unions building the expectation of further price rises into their wage demands, there is danger the spiral will accelerate. If it does, we face the prospect that the spiral will still be turning steadily in 1969 and into 1970. The longer it turns the harder it is to stop.

A highly restrictive fiscal and monetary policy could throttle the economy and create widespread unemployment and idle capacity in order to dampen upward pressures on wages and prices. But it would serve the objective of price stability only by sacrificing most of our other key economic objectives.

Dealing with inflation by creating a reces-

sion or persistent slack is succumbing to the disease—not curing it. The experience of 1957 and 1958—when the unemployment rate reached 7½ percent and consumer prices still rose 5 percent—is a clear reminder of the large costs of such a policy and of its limited effectiveness in halting a spiral in motion. This is a course which I reject—and which I am confident that the American people reject.

Therefore, in addition to urging prompt action by the Congress on my tax proposals, I must again urge—in the strongest terms I know—that unions and business firms exercise the most rigorous restraint in their wage and price determinations in 1968.

We must make a *decisive* turn back toward price stability this year. This will only be possible

—if the average gain in wages and fringe benefits incorporated in new labor agreements this year begins to move back toward parity with our gains in productivity; and

—if businesses absorb cost increases wherever possible, and avoid any price decision which would, on the average, increase their margins over labor and materials cost.

STRUCTURAL PRICE PROBLEMS

There are other sources of price increase we can begin to attack in 1968. We should not expect quick results. But, over the longer pull, an important contribution can be made.

There are a number of industries in which prices have climbed persistently because of supply bottlenecks in labor, materials, or capacity; because of backward technology; because of inefficient distribution systems or trade practices; or for other so-called "structural" reasons.

If we regard the battle against rising prices as a long-term task, it is time to begin to fight on every front where long-term results can be achieved.

Existing Government organization is not effectively suited to dealing with the full range and dimensions of the problem of prices.

CABINET COMMITTEE ON PRICE STABILITY

I am therefore establishing a Cabinet Committee on Price Stability, including the heads of the major relevant departments and offices of Government, coordinated by the Chairman of the Council of Economic Advisers and served by a small professional staff.

The Committee will focus the attention both of the private economy and of the Federal Government on the objective of price stability.

It will study and recommend—both for private and for public action—measures which can improve efficiency, remove bottlenecks, and improve technology in industries which are the source of persistent inflation. And it will give price stability a high priority in the formulation and administration of all Government programs.

The Committee will work closely with representatives of business, labor, and the public to seek ideas and initiatives to correct persistent structural problems that cause prices to rise and to inform them of the consequences of irresponsible wage and price behavior. It will not, however, become involved in specific current wage or price matters.

Through this new machinery, we seek to achieve a new and more effective cooperation among business, labor, and government in the pursuit of price stability in a free market economy.

CITIES AND HOUSING

The American city is in distress, plagued by poverty, unemployment, and slums; hobbled by inadequate public services, inefficient transportation, pollution, and congestion.

The city is also the source of an unprecedented affluence. Bitter poverty amidst spreading affluence spotlights the problems of the disadvantaged.

Yet that very affluence should be the source of great hope. For general affluence makes it possible to erase pockets of deprivation. We now have the means for a massive reconstruction of urban America.

The first step in an effective attack on urban problems came last year when 63 cities received the first round of Model Cities planning grants. By the end of this year, many of these cities will be ready to begin work. This first round will ultimately permit the transformation of 65 blighted areas, housing 3.7 million people, into decent places to live and work.

I will ask the Congress to fund fully the $1 billion authorization for the Model Cities program in fiscal year 1969.

Our next step will be to fulfill the commitment of the Housing Act of 1949—to provide every American family with decent housing. Our goal is to eliminate substandard housing in ten years. This task will require the full cooperation of labor, business, local government—and the residents of blighted areas.

Too long we have regarded the unemployed slum dweller as a national burden. The time has come to recognize him as a national resource, and to offer him a job rebuilding the slums in which he lives.

Our target for fiscal year 1969 is to begin 300,000 new and rehabilitated units—several times the current rate. Rent supplement and "turnkey" public housing programs will be modified and enlarged to engage private enterprise on a massive scale.

The expansion of federally assisted housing must not shrink the private housing market. During the next ten years we will need 20 million housing units in addition to those receiving Federal assistance.

Their production will balloon the need for mortgage money. I will therefore propose legislation to strengthen the mortgage market and the financial institutions that supply mortgage credit. I also propose that current interest rate ceilings on FHA and VA mortgages be lifted to allow them to compete on equal terms with other assets.

I also urge the Congress to complete action on legislation

—to strengthen regulation of savings and loan holding companies,

—to provide Federal charters for mutual savings institutions.

If we are to reconstruct the American city, we need knowledge and innovation as much as men and money. We lead the world in technology. Yet little of its power is directed to the problems of cities.

As a first step, I have named a panel to establish an Institute for Urban Development. This Institute will undertake the systematic analysis of fundamental urban problems for Government agencies.

The agonies of our cities will not yield easily or quickly—nor to simple solutions. Yet the breadth of our vision must be scaled to the magnitude of our problem—and our opportunity.

In the coming weeks, I shall send the Congress a message containing my detailed recommendations.

EXPANDING INDIVIDUAL OPPORTUNITY

America has historically taken pride in being the "land of opportunity." To a far greater extent than any earlier civilization, American society has provided opportunities for the majority of its citizens to achieve whatever their ambitions and abilities might permit.

Yet for a minority—steadily diminishing in every generation—opportunity has remained a myth.

The recent experience of prolonged prosperity and high employment has pried open the doors of opportunity for many who formerly were shut off from the main circle of abundance. Indeed, sustained prosperity is the single most important source of expanding opportunity.

But even prolonged and general prosperity leaves too many Americans untouched, unable to share in its rewards.

Despite our prosperity, there are still more than 10 million families whom we classify as poor. They include about one-seventh of our people. Many are Negro. But two-thirds are white. Many are old. But nearly half are children. Many live in urban areas. But about half live in small towns or in rural areas. Most were born poor.

Regardless of race, age, or where they live, they are not statistics, they are people. We cannot turn our backs on our fellow Americans who need help.

I regard it as a primary purpose of government to expand the opportunities for all citizens to share in our economic and social progress. For most, this means the opportunity for rewarding employment. For millions who are retired, disabled, or otherwise unable to seek active work, a share in prosperity requires wise and humane programs of income maintenance and social insurance.

For all, it means full access to education and to health care.

America has made great progress in recent years—in the creation of jobs, the provision of adequate incomes, and the improvement of health and education. The future holds promise of further advance.

EMPLOYMENT AND TRAINING

More Americans entered the labor force last year than in any year since World War II. And these job seekers were accommodated to a remarkable degree.

- The over-all unemployment rate averaged 3.8 percent as it did in 1966. Except for the years of World War II and the Korean war, this two-year average was the best in four decades.
- The unemployment rate for adult men—both white and Negro—was the lowest since World War II.

Yet there is no room for complacency in these achievements. The unemployment rate for Negroes, Mexican-Americans, and other minorities remains distressingly high, and far too many of our teenagers look for work and fail to find it.

We have already made impressive progress in improving job opportunities—through the Neighborhood Youth Corps, the Job Corps, our other manpower training and retraining programs, provision of day-care facilities for working mothers, and in many other ways.

Increasingly our efforts are concentrated on the disadvantaged who have been unable to share in our prosperity. In continuing partnership with State and local governments, we will expand our training and related manpower activities, with special emphasis on an enlarged Concentrated Employment program.

But this year the Federal Government is also seeking a new partnership with private industry to train and hire the disadvantaged. I believe this partnership can succeed—and must—in providing work opportunities for every American who wants a job and who will make reasonable efforts to prepare himself to hold it.

UNEMPLOYMENT INSURANCE

Even when there are enough jobs to go around and manpower is better matched to jobs, some will inevitably experience unemployment in our dynamic economy.

Our present unemployment compensation system was designed in the 1930's. The economy has greatly changed since then, but the unemployment compensation system has not.

In many cases, the man or woman unemployed today lost his job because his skills have become obsolete, not because his employer lost his market. That worker needs long-term benefits which can support him through a substantial period of retraining, guidance, and similar services—not merely cash benefits which run out at a critical moment. Further, the benefits provided under many State systems have proved inadequate to current needs.

I am therefore asking the Congress for new legislation to strengthen the Federal-State unemployment insurance system by increasing coverage, raising benefits, modifying eligibility conditions, increasing the Federal unemployment tax base and rate, providing federally financed extended benefits to be triggered by high unemployment; and to link extended benefits to the training and employment rehabilitation of the recipients.

EDUCATION

The Federal Government has done more to improve educational opportunities in the past three years than in all its previous history. In particular, attention has been focused on providing opportunities for children to throw off their legacy of poverty. Head Start, the Elementary and Secondary Education Act, and higher education legislation stand as landmarks of our progress.

One key program for 1968—based on the Education Professions Development Act of last year—gives special emphasis to the single most important element in the educational process—our teachers. We must attract more teachers to work with disadvantaged youth, and help such teachers develop the new skills and new sensitivities needed to teach the children from poor families.

I shall propose an Educational Opportunity Act—continuing our efforts to break down the financial barriers which keep young people from poor families from entering or remaining in college.

HEALTH

Victories in the progress of health care have recently been written in headlines. Soon a failing heart may no longer be an inevitable prelude to death. Less dramatic but equally important is that Medicare and Medicaid have brought the gains of medical research within the reach of millions.

But this is no time to pause. Our rising standards and our expanding powers to cure press against present limitations on our ability to supply medical care.

Much recent effort has centered on the health needs of our older citizens. This was right, for the elderly often combine high medical need with limited financial resources.

Now we must turn attention to our children. Millions of young Americans today receive inadequate medical attention—both a result and a cause of poverty. I therefore propose a five-year plan to bring complete health services to children of low-income families, beginning with prenatal care for mothers, and continuing through the first year of infancy.

The supply of qualified health personnel has lagged behind the expanding demand. I will shortly propose new measures to increase this supply.

Last year, medical care prices rose 7 percent, more than twice as fast as other prices. I shall propose new measures to slow down the spiraling cost of health care.

INCOME MAINTENANCE

I have recently appointed a Presidential Commission on Income Maintenance. This distinguished group of citizens, under the chairmanship of Mr. Ben Heineman, has a broad charter to examine every aspect of our present public welfare and income maintenance programs and to propose necessary reforms. The Commission will examine a number of major reforms proposed in recent years—including several varieties of minimum income guarantees. It will evaluate the costs and benefits of these proposals in terms of their effects both on the recipients and on the economy.

CONSUMER PROTECTION

The true test of the efficiency of any economic system is its ability to meet the needs of consumers. The American economy—with its free markets—has far surpassed all others in meeting this test.

But the market does not always give the consumer the protection he needs. There is a role, too, for Government action, especially as our wants and our products become more complex.

Last year the Congress enacted, and I approved, important new legislation to protect our consumers.

Important new measures are being proposed to the Congress for the protection of consumers. I hope that this Congress will go down in history as the consumer-conscious Congress.

OTHER ECONOMIC POLICIES

1. The Department of Transportation, now one year old, is moving vigorously toward rationalization and coordination of our transportation policies. I have asked its Secretary to develop new proposals to improve air safety and air service.

The number of air passengers has doubled in the past five years and will more than double again in the next ten. Airway and airport facilities must keep up with this growth. These facilities are costly and benefit primarily their users—who should pay the necessary costs.

2. Total holdings of our stockpile of strategic and critical materials now stand at $6.4 billion, of which $3.3 billion exceeds our stockpile requirements as presently determined. Continuing to carry these excess materials in the stockpile both imposes an unnecessary burden on our taxpayers and restricts their availability to our industries.

I renew my recommendation that I be given authority to dispose of many of these excesses, especially of nickel, platinum, beryl ore, magnesium, and castor oil, all currently in short supply in the commercial market.

3. Accurate, comprehensive, and timely statistics are essential to the development of sound economic policies by government, business, and labor.

Our economic statistics are the best and most comprehensive in the world. But they can be and need to be further improved. The costs will be exceedingly small relative to the benefits.

To this end, my 1969 budget provides for several new statistical efforts which can be rapidly and inexpensively translated into improved guides for public and private decisions.

CONCLUSION

A strong and sustained advance of production surely does not mean we have solved all economic problems—much less that the Nation is making satisfactory progress toward its broader and more fundamental goals.

Americans know how to create an expanding abundance. But we are still learning how to use it wisely and compassionately to further the self-development and happiness of men, women, and children.

Similarly, merely to achieve a balance in our international payments would not assure that our international economic relations amply serve the interests of this Nation and of world progress. We could bring our balance of payments into equilibrium by means which would weaken our domestic economy, forfeit our foreign policy objectives, or impair the vitality of world economic development.

This Administration will never forget that the purpose of our economy and of our economic policies is to serve the American people—not the reverse.

Yet this recognition would not justify policies which ignore the dangers of inflation, economic distortions, and ultimately recession. For these are equally enemies of our public purposes.

Nor will we forget that balance-of-payments policies should serve the Nation's basic goals abroad and at home—not the reverse.

Yet this recognition makes it no less necessary to deal firmly and decisively with our balance-of-payments problem. For a breakdown of the international financial system would bring incalculable harm not only to ourselves and free peoples around the world, but even to world peace and progress.

I am determined that our economic policies in 1968 will be prudent as well as creative; safe as well as ambitious; responsible as well as compassionate.

The American people are giving their sons and brothers to fight for freedom abroad. At home we must support their sacrifice by preserving a sound economy. I believe that the American people will accept the cost of doing that

—by paying an extra cent of each dollar of income in taxes,

—by accepting the cutback of lower-priority Federal programs, and

—by limiting the expansion of Federal spending to a few areas of the most vital priority.

Today the war in Vietnam is costing us 3 percent of our total production. That is a burden a wealthy people can bear. It represents less than one year's growth in our total output.

But one day peace will return. If we plan wisely—as the committee on post-Vietnam adjustment I announced in my Economic Report last year has been doing—and act boldly, we will have that 3 percent of output to add—over a year or two—to our normal 4 percent a year of economic growth.

If we preserve a healthy economy in the meantime, we will be prepared when our sons and brothers return to take full advantage of that bonus.

Our obligation to them demands that we do no less.

LYNDON B. JOHNSON

February 1, 1968

NOTE: The President's message together with the Annual Report of the Council of Economic Advisers is printed in "Economic Report of the President, Transmitted to the Congress February 1968" (Government Printing Office, 1968, 314 pp.).

48 Remarks Upon Presenting the Medal of Honor to Maj. Merlyn H. Dethlefsen, USAF. *February 1, 1968*

Major and Mrs. Dethlefsen and children, Secretary of the Air Force Brown, General McConnell, distinguished and honored Members of Congress, ladies and gentlemen:

This is an afternoon when it is good to stand beside a man in uniform. He is a brave man, who has come to claim the honor that his courage has earned. He is also a spokesman for the courage of thousands like him who are protecting you and serving us in Vietnam at this hour.

This is also a very special afternoon for all of them. They are not thinking of medals or ceremonies in the East Room, in face of a desperate enemy offensive. They are thinking of you and of us, and they will not fail us. They will not fail us even if it means dying before another morning comes.

That is as sure as this brave man is standing here. It is he who says the enemy will fail—again—and again—for as long as he threatens the freedom and the peace we Americans will never yield.

So as this Nation waits, let it take heart from the story of one who was there.

Major Dethlefsen had a most vital mission last March. His mission was to knock out a critical missile site in North Vietnam.

On the first pass, his flight leader was disabled and his own aircraft was badly damaged. Still, he made another pass, and pass after pass, at the site, under constant attack by enemy fighters, missiles, and antiaircraft fire combined.

He knocked out that site—he knocked it out maybe on a wing and a prayer—but he knocked it out and he did his job. He cleared the way for a bomber flight that was to follow without deadly fire from the enemy missiles.

This great courage demonstrated by this fearless man spared many American lives. He had plenty of time to think about the danger to himself, to figure the odds, and actually plenty of excuses to even turn away. But his courage was calculated. It came not from desperation, but it came from dedication. He answered a call that was far beyond duty, as others of his comrades are answering for you at this hour.

I stood before some of them at midnight at an air base in Thailand just a few weeks ago. I wanted so much that night to give medals to all of them. Instead, I gave them something just as meaningful—I gave them this Nation's pride in their unequaled bravery and their unexcelled record.

These are the men who have rewritten the rule book and the flight book of aerial warfare. These men are comparatively few in number, but each day they are pinning down from 500,000 to 700,000 North Vietnamese, and they number only a few hundred.

These same men are matching courage with a careful and with a very precise restraint.

We are using our greatest resources—of industry, of technology, of skilled and courageous men—to conduct a limited war at the lowest possible cost in human life.

Let those who would stop the bombing answer this question: "What would the North Vietnamese be doing if we stopped the bombing and let them alone?"

The answer, I think, is clear. The enemy force in the South would be larger. It would be better equipped. The war would be harder. The losses would be greater. The difficulties would be longer. And of one thing you can be sure: It would cost many more American lives.

The men who have met and who have matched the enemy on the ground these past few hours—in I Corps, in the II Corps, in the III Corps, in Saigon, the cities along the entire countryside—have a very special understanding and a very special appreciation, I assure you, of what air power really means. It cannot keep the enemy from ultimately moving into battle position. It cannot keep the sniper from climbing a roof. But it can and it does reduce their momentum. And it can keep many of the enemy's men off the backs of our men who are defending our lives.

Until we have some better signs than what we have had these last few days—that I hope any American can see and read loud and clear—that he will not step up his terrorism; and unless we have some sign that he will not accelerate his aggression if we halt bombing, then we shall continue to give our American men the protection America ought to give them, and that is the best America affords.

Major, as we honor you here in the East Room today, we think of so many who share your burden and who share our pride.

—The men on the ships like the *Pueblo,* who are not with us, but who perform the most perilous missions for their country's sake.

—The men who gave their lives to protect our Saigon Embassy yesterday, and to protect that staff from terrorism during a supposedly truce period.

—The men who will throw back the enemy in the hills of Khe Sanh.

They are the bravest and they are the best of the men that we can produce. And none, sir, will do better service to their courage or do better service to our cause, our cause of liberty, our cause of freedom, our cause of compassion and understanding—none will do better service to that cause than you, sir.

The distinguished Secretary of the Air Force, Harold Brown, will now read the citation.

[Text of citation read by Secretary Brown]

The President of the United States of America, authorized by Act of Congress, March 3, 1896, has awarded in the name of The Congress, the Medal of Honor to

MAJOR MERLYN H. DETHLEFSEN
UNITED STATES AIR FORCE

for conspicuous gallantry and intrepidity in action at the risk of his life above and beyond the call of duty:

On 10 March 1967, Major Dethlefsen (then Captain) was one of a flight of F–105 aircraft engaged in a fire suppression mission designed to destroy a key antiaircraft defensive complex containing surface-to-air missiles (SAM), an exceptionally heavy concentration of antiaircraft artillery, and other automatic weapons. The defensive network was situated to dominate the approach and provide protection to an important North Vietnam industrial center that was scheduled to be attacked by fighter bombers im-

mediately after the strike by Major Dethlefsen's flight. In the initial attack on the defensive complex the lead aircraft was crippled, and Major Dethlefsen's aircraft was extensively damaged by the intense enemy fire. Realizing that the success of the impending fighter bomber attack on the center now depended on his ability to effectively suppress the defensive fire, Major Dethlefsen ignored the enemy's overwhelming firepower and the damage to his aircraft and pressed his attack. Despite a continuing hail of antiaircraft fire, deadly surface-to-air missiles, and counterattacks by MIG interceptors, Major Dethlefsen flew repeated close range strikes to silence the enemy defensive positions with bombs and cannon fire. His action in rendering ineffective the defensive SAM and antiaircraft artillery sites enabled the ensuing fighter bombers to strike successfully the important industrial target without loss or damage to their aircraft, thereby appreciably reducing the enemy's ability to provide essential war material. Major Dethlefsen's conspicuous gallantry, consummate skill and selfless dedication to this significant mission were in keeping with the highest traditions of the United States Air Force and reflect great credit upon himself and the armed forces of his country.

LYNDON B. JOHNSON

[At this point the President resumed speaking.]

I know you are curious about what Mrs. Dethlefsen said to me. She is glad to have him back.

NOTE: The President spoke at 12:45 p.m. in the East Room at the White House. In his opening words he also referred to Secretary of the Air Force Harold Brown and to Gen. John P. McConnell, Air Force Chief of Staff.

49 Statement by the President Following Passage of the Truth-in-Lending Bill by the House of Representatives.
February 1, 1968

IN PASSING the truth-in-lending bill, the House of Representatives today brought every American consumer another step closer to knowing the cost of the money he borrows. I urge the House and Senate to resolve their differences promptly and to give the American consumer a strong truth-in-lending bill. I hope this will be the first of many measures that will mark this Congress as the consumers' Congress.

NOTE: The truth-in-lending bill was approved on May 29, 1968, as the Consumer Credit Protection Act (see Item 280).

50 Filmed Conversation of the President and George Meany, AFL–CIO President and Chairman of COPE.
February 2, 1968

MR. MEANY. Mr. President, this film we are making this morning will be shown to officers and members of our unions throughout the country, mostly the leaders of the American trade union movement at the local level.

I want to express our appreciation and the appreciation of the membership of the AFL–CIO for giving us this opportunity to talk to you about the many issues that we face, as well, perhaps, to talk a little bit about the issues we faced in the past, things that you are interested in and, of course, things that our members are very much interested in; for instance, the question of education, which I am sure you are greatly interested in.

THE PRESIDENT. Mr. Meany, I welcome this opportunity to talk with you and to the officers and members of your unions and specifically on this subject of education.

I was in Congress for 24 years. During that time we talked about education a great deal, and how important it was that we do something about it. But we did very little. We never had any overall comprehensive Federal aid to education during that period.

In 1964 and 1965, with the help of the AFL–CIO and the teachers of the country, and the mothers, we promulgated a program and finally passed through Congress a massive educational measure and supplemented it with more than 20 other bills.

The key bill is elementary and secondary education. So as a result, today, the Federal Government is doing more than three times as much in the field of education as it did 4 years ago when this administration began.

MR. MEANY. I think that's true. I think actually what happened in '64 and '65 was that for the first time in the history of this country the Federal Government assumed that there was a Federal responsibility for the education of the children of America at every level and what we, of course, have always held as a cherished goal of America's workers, that we would see the day when every boy and girl in this country would get all the education that he or she—that they could assimilate, that they had the aptitude for, and that they would get this irrespective of the economic circumstances from which they sprang.

THE PRESIDENT. That is the objective and the goal of this administration—to give every boy and girl in this country all the education that he or she can take. Through the Elementary and Secondary Education Act, through the Higher Education Act, we are taking care of the people between the first grade and the college graduates, even the graduate school graduates.

But we have responsibilities even beyond that which we are undertaking. In the Head Start program we are getting the youngster before he gets in the first grade. And in the adult education program, we are going back and taking people who are in their sixties, and some even in their seventies and giving them adult education programs and teachings.

The sad thing about the world in which we live is that four out of every ten people, Mr. Meany, cannot read and write. This illiteracy and this ignorance is a terrible handicap to peace in the world, because when people are uninformed and when people are ignorant, they cannot reason and make judgments that they do if they have had the benefits of education.

So not only here in our own country, but throughout the world, one of the number one problems of our time is education and how we can get it to the masses.

We have a massive program in this country. We are going to continue it. We are going to expand it.

MR. MEANY. Well, of course, that's true, of course, that we feel that education and lack of education—illiteracy—makes a contribution toward the development of a situation where peace is not possible.

So we have been in this fight for a long time. For instance, the fight on poverty, the fight for minimum wages—this is not new, this is not new to us, and not new to you. Now, the first of February this year the minimum wage in this country went to $1.60 an hour. The first of February last year there were about 8 million people added to that.

Now, what does this mean? This means in the final analysis that as far as those families are concerned, something concrete has been done in the war on poverty. The minimum wage law is part of the war on poverty. I am sure you can recall, because you were a Member of Congress back in 1938, I think it was, somewhere back there, when we passed the first minimum wage law, 25 cents an hour.

You remember that. I am sure you remember that because you voted for it. There were people who said then that this was going to bankrupt the country, this was going to be a terrible thing.

Now, in the final analysis, what it does, it brings more and more people into the mainstream of the American economy in the sense that they become purchasers and consumers in the marketplace.

THE PRESIDENT. I have been through several minimum wage fights—the 25 cents an hour one, the $1 an hour one when I was leader in the Eisenhower administration, when I was Majority Leader of the Senate, and finally the $1.60 that we have worked on the last few years.

I am glad it is going in effect. I think it is absolutely essential that we have some guarantees of some minimum for the people in this country. I remember when we passed the first act we had women, mothers of children, working for 6 and 7 cents an hour in pecan shelling plants in my State. People predicted havoc if we passed a 25-cent minimum wage, just as they do when we take any progressive step in this field.

But it wasn't havoc. It was a substantial improvement for the entire Nation. I am very happy that the Congresses of recent years have recognized the necessity for up-grading and keeping these minimums in effect.

MR. MEANY. All of these things are tied together—education, minimum wage, because, as you said before, people today want a better world. We want a better world, and I'm sure the common people all over the world want a better world. All these things help.

THE PRESIDENT. The thing you have done, though, Mr. Meany, that I think is a great monument to the labor movement in this country, to your leadership, and I think to the Government as well, is the health program that we have been able to enact into law in the last few years, Medicaid and Medicare, and the some 20-odd supplementary health measures, because it doesn't make any difference how smart a person is, it doesn't make any difference how skilled a person is, if he is in poor health he is not very productive.

So we must take precautionary measures in the health field. We are doing that. In the last few years, as a result of the leadership that labor and its individual members have given to the country and to the Congress, we have been able to pass the Medicare bill and the Medicaid bill, and supplementary health measures that result now in millions of people having a means to pay their doctors' bills, and millions of people who never had means to pay their hospital bill before. They now do not have to rely on their children to take care of them.

MR. MEANY. That's true.

THE PRESIDENT. And we're not going to be satisfied to stop there. We see that because we do not arrest the disease early enough, it brings on great complications and costs us much more.

MR. MEANY. You talk about health, and of course this leads you into another subject in which you are interested, and that is re-building the cities of America, because we have conditions in a number of our cities that are certainly, to say the least, unhealthy, and causing us a great many problems, and we, too, would like to see something done.

I hope that Congress is more cooperative in this coming session in going along with your program for helping the cities of America rebuild, because all of these things are tied together—the minimum wage, health, Medicare, urban renewal and all this sort of thing—and, of course, this brings us to a great big subject I am sure you must be interested in, and that is an overall housing program. Are we going to have an overall housing program this year? I hope we are.

THE PRESIDENT. We are. The greatest challenge that this Congress faces, really, in the domestic field, is the problem of the cities. I have a commission that has carefully gone into that and studied it. It is headed up by some of the ablest men in this country.

We know that the problems of the cities are many. First, we have some 500,000 hard-core unemployed people in those cities who are frustrated, that have no jobs, that have nothing to do. Our first problem is to try to find employment and training for that minimum, hard-core group that causes us problems in the cities.

The second thing is to get an overall housing program, certainly a program particularly for the poor, because we have had relatively a few thousand units built each year and there are more of them deteriorating and going out of date than new ones are replacing them. So we are having a minimum 10-year housing program where we hope that we can add not just a few thousand, but millions of homes for low-income people in this country.

We anticipate that this year we will have

a minimum of 300,000 new homes, instead of the 35,000 or 45,000 that we have had for poor and low-income groups.

We must, Mr. Meany, find some way in this country to find a decent, a sanitary, a structurally sound house at as low a cost as possible for our poor and low-income groups. Now, if we can go to the moon, and if we can perform all these other feats of science, we have got to find the answer to low-income housing, and we haven't done that in our cities.

This administration had a committee working under the direction of Mr. Edgar Kaiser. We are hoping that we can present to the Congress a program that the Congress will adopt that will launch us on a 10-year housing effort that will result in millions of new homes for the people who need them most.

MR. MEANY. Well, I am sure that you find that the AFL–CIO will be back of you in this effort. Mr. President, education, housing, poverty, minimum wages, all of these things are related. But they bring to mind another question, and that is this question of crime, crime in the streets that people are talking about today. This, too, is one of your problems.

THE PRESIDENT. Mr. Meany, that is one of the major problems facing this country. Now, what are we going to do about it?

First, if we are going to do something about crime, we are going to have to do something about what causes crime. Unemployment, ignorance, disease, filth, poor housing, congestion, discrimination—all of these things contribute to the great crime wave that is sweeping over this country. We are going to—through our poverty program, through our education program, through our conservation-recreation program—try to get at some of the causes of crime.

But in addition to that, the Federal Government cannot ever develop into a police state and have its base here in Washington. Our Founding Fathers protected against that when they wrote the Constitution. So this is a problem that begins first in the home with the parents.

Someone said to me when I was home during the holidays that it would be a good thing if all parents could say "Where are our children?" at 11 or 12 o'clock in the evening. What are they doing? Do the parents know?

So the problem begins at the home. And then if the laws are violated, the law enforcement is local law enforcement. The Federal Government cannot pick the chief of police in a given city. The Federal Government can't select the sheriff. The Federal Government doesn't select the local judges. And law enforcement is a local matter, with the local people, in a local community, and in the State.

Now, we are doing everything we can to give the maximum amount of assistance to the cities and to the States. But, as I say, it is a problem of the home, it is a problem of the local community, it is a problem of the State, and the Federal Government has many suggestions. It has recommended a gun control bill. It has recommended a safe streets bill. It has recommended to provide research assistance and counseling with the cities and with the States.

But no one wants a Federal police force and the Federal Government cannot, by itself, control crime. It can only supplement what the local authorities do, and that we are going to do.

MR. MEANY. Well, as I see it, it is a problem that has got to be approached in two ways: Number one, you have got to have law enforcement, because while we realize that it is the ghettos and the disease and the poverty that provide the atmosphere for this type of local crime, it is the people in the ghettos in most cases who are the victims.

THE PRESIDENT. They are the ones that suffer most.

MR. MEANY. They are the ones that suffer most from these riots, from these crimes, and there are people with criminal minds who take advantage of these conditions. So I think what we have got to do, we have got to eliminate the conditions to whatever extent we can, and as rapidly as we can, but at the same time we have got to have respect for law, because if we don't have respect for law, we won't even be able to eliminate these conditions.

THE PRESIDENT. I heartily agree with you, and I think that one of the most important bills that the Congress will have to face up to this coming year will be the safe streets bill that I recommended last year, and I hope the Congress will enact this year; the gun control bill; and the other measures that will get at the cause of crime and also provide a remedy.

MR. MEANY. Yes, because just strict law enforcement might help, but it will not solve the problem. We have got to have law enforcement, and we have got to have a program to eliminate the conditions that breed crime in our cities. I think we have a two-pronged approach in this thing.

THE PRESIDENT. If we attack the discrimination problem, if we attack the poverty problem, if we find jobs, if we can provide decent housing, if we can help rebuild our cities, we can get at some of these causes. But the local law enforcement has got to be done at the local level. This begins in the home. This begins in local conditions.

We can help them. We can supplement them, but we must not supplant them.

MR. MEANY. I agree with you completely. I would like to bring up one other subject

that I think is important. Don't you agree with us that we can do all these things and still keep our commitments to the other nations of the world, to the free people of the world? You see, we are always up against this argument that, well, we can't support the efforts of the people of South Vietnam to retain their freedom and independence which we are committed to do—we can't do that and at the same time do all these things on the home front.

We think America is big enough to do both.

THE PRESIDENT. America is big enough to do both. It can do both, Mr. Meany, and I believe that it will do both. This argument that is used—that because we are trying to protect freedom in some part of the world we can't protect our people at home—is a phony argument. It is an excuse.

Now, it is true that we do have to forgo some of the things. We can't do everything at once. We can't correct the neglect of centuries in a day. But we can try and we can make a start and we can get on our way. That we definitely are doing.

I am the father of two daughters. When I hear this argument that we can't protect freedom in Europe, in Asia, or in our own hemisphere and still meet our domestic problems, I think it is a phony argument. It is just like saying that I can't take care of Luci because I have Lynda Bird. We have to take care of both of them and we have to meet them head on.

Here is a nation with more people employed than ever in our history. Here is a nation with people working at better wages than ever in our history. Here is a time when our profits are higher than ever in our history. Here is a time when we have had 82 months of prosperity in this Nation. Here is a time when we have the greatest gross national product that we have ever had, and we are spending $25 billion in protecting freedom in Asia. To say out of the $800 billion we make, and the 25 billion we have to spend in Southeast Asia, that the other 775 shouldn't be used for the benefit of the people is just a very poor excuse.

We must educate our children. We can't neglect them. We must provide health for our people. We can't neglect it. We must provide conservation of our resources in this country. We cannot neglect that. We must find jobs for those who want jobs and who need jobs, and we are going to do it by encouraging private industry and the labor unions and the Government to work hand in hand in these matters, as we have been in the more recent years past.

There is no group that has been more helpful to bringing prosperity to this country and to launching a program for the benefit of all the people of this country than the AFL–CIO under your leadership.

I am happy to say that the businessmen generally have tried to listen and to be cooperative. I am hopeful in the days ahead that we can enact through the Congress a job program, a housing program, additional education measures, provide for additional steps that we ought to take in the health field, and at the same time protect freedom.

It is just a bunch of blarney that we can take care of one need we have and have to ignore all the others. It's just the same as saying you can take care of one child and you can't take care of the other.

MR. MEANY. I'm quite sure we have the same faith in America that you have; that America is big enough and strong enough to do this. Insofar as our commitments in Far East Asia are concerned, we in the trade union movement are very practical people. We know from experience what dictatorship means. We know it before anybody else knows it, because if anybody is going to

dictate any place in this world he must control the means of production. They can wait awhile about controlling the artists or the scientists or the writers, but they can't wait insofar as the worker is concerned. They have got to control him immediately. This is what Hitler did. This is what Mussolini did and this is what Stalin did and Lenin, when they came to power 50 years ago in the Soviet Union. They took control of the workers.

So we are more keenly aware of what dictatorship means. This is why we feel that you just can't stand by and see two or three million people go down the drain and hope that that's the end of it, because we are convinced that if we step aside, if we withdraw from Vietnam, that you are not going to satisfy the appetite of these people who believe in dictatorship. They will move down southeast, and the next thing you know they will be in the Philippines, and you know what that would mean to us.

So we are convinced that you are on the right track. The American trade union movement, as represented by the AFL–CIO, made it crystal clear at its last convention that we support the policy in Vietnam of fighting for the freedom of those people and that we also believe that we can do that and continue the Johnson program to make this a better nation for all of the American people.

THE PRESIDENT. Mr. Meany, our people are peace-loving people. We seek no war. We want peace in the world. But we have learned some things from participation in World War I and World War II and the Korean war and other disturbances in recent years, and that is you cannot successfully appease an aggressor. If you run and if you hide and if you let aggression spread, the time comes when you must face up to it sooner or later.

Now, we have the will for peace. We have

the machinery for peace. No one in the world wants peace more than I do. I live with war 24 hours a day. I read the casualty lists every morning. But I know that until the enemy, the Communist enemy, is willing to genuinely and sincerely sit down and talk about peace in good faith, that we shouldn't hold out all these illusions and all these hopes that can't be realized to our people.

So the best road to peace that I know of is to remain strong, and remain firm, and to stand on principle. We haven't had an appeaser President in my lifetime. Every President that has preceded me has stood on the principle that when we were called upon to resist aggression and to perform under the treaties that this country had entered into, that the word of the United States could be depended on. As long as I am President, we are going to keep our word.

We are not going to let any of our nations who are bound to us by treaties and alliances be gobbled up by any would-be conqueror, any would-be dictator, while we stand by under an umbrella. Now, if they want to talk peace and if they will agree to self-determination in South Vietnam, we are willing to meet them at the conference table tomorrow.

We said in San Antonio, we will stop our bombing now if you will come and have a prompt discussion and a productive discussion in good faith. You can make all the proposals you want to. We will make our proposals. We will exchange views.

But they have not accepted that proposal.

Now, I don't know how much further I can go. I don't think it would be in the interest of this Nation for us to stop our bombing, only to have them to continue theirs. A bomb dropped from a bicycle can kill as many people as a bomb dropped from a plane. It is rather ridiculous for some of our people to say "You ought to stop bombing," and then when I say, "Well, will we

have a prompt discussion?" they say, "We don't know."

We don't have that answer. Will they have a productive discussion? Well, we don't know. Will they talk about just North Vietnam? That's what's indicated. That problem is in South Vietnam.

So we must pursue and explore the meaning of these so-called offers so that we don't buy a pig in a poke and so we don't repeat the errors of Panmunjom and we don't let the Communists lead us down a road that we don't know where we are going.

MR. MEANY. I think in exploring, Mr. President, we should also take into consideration the fact that every bombing pause we have had has resulted in an immediate Communist buildup that has cost American lives. So those who want us to stop the bombing, and stop it without qualification, I would like to ask them how many American lives do we have to lose before we start bombing again in case the Communists don't come to the conference table.

This is the problem, and I know this is your problem.

THE PRESIDENT. It is, and we live with it every day. We have the professionals who have rendered great service in our foreign policy field for many years and they are taking every word that is said and exploring it in every place they can in an attempt to find a reasonable way to get to the peace table. But until the enemy is willing to go to the peace table, and is willing to say if you stop your bombing he will promptly come and talk, and that we can have productive discussions, and that he will not take advantage of our restraint to put extra pressure on during that period, then I think that we would be endangering the lives of our men, and some men don't have that responsibility. But as Commander in Chief I do have, and I must take that into consideration before I make these decisions. We are going to continue to search every day for peace, but a peace with honor.

MR. MEANY. I am sure that the American people are in agreement, Mr. President. They want peace, but they want peace with honor, and they don't want peace as a sacrifice of our good word and a sacrifice of our commitments that we have made.

On behalf of the American trade union movement, I can say to you we are with you in this effort. I want to thank you very much for giving us this time and letting us know what is on your mind, so our members can listen in and certainly get closer to you and your problems as a result. Thank you very much.

NOTE: The conversation was filmed at the White House on January 15, 1968, for showing first at New Orleans, Saturday, February 3, and thereafter at other regional COPE (Committee on Political Education) and union meetings.

As printed above, this item follows the text released by the White House Press Office.

51 The President's News Conference of *February 2, 1968*

THE PRESIDENT. [1.] Tom[1] will have copies made of this statement and distribute it to you later, so you don't need to take it verbatim. You may want to take notes as you go along. It is very brief. Then I will take any questions that may occur to you from it.

STATEMENT ON THE SITUATION IN VIETNAM

We have known for several months, now, that the Communists planned a massive winter-spring offensive. We have detailed information on Ho Chi Minh's order governing that offensive. Part of it is called a general uprising.

We know the object was to overthrow the constitutional government in Saigon and to create a situation in which we and the Vietnamese would be willing to accept the Communist-dominated coalition government.

Another part of that offensive was planned as a massive attack across the frontiers of South Vietnam by North Vietnamese units. We have already seen the general uprising.

General Westmoreland's headquarters re-

port the Communists appear to have lost over 10,000 men killed and some 2,300 detained. The United States has lost 249 men killed. The Vietnamese, who had to carry the brunt of the fighting in the cities, lost 553 killed as of my most recent report from the Westmoreland headquarters.

There were also a number of attacks on United States airfields throughout the country. We have confirmed the loss of 15 fixed-wing aircraft, and 23 helicopters were destroyed. A good many more were damaged but will be returned to service.

This is a small proportion of our aircraft and helicopters available in that area. Secretary McNamara, General Westmoreland, and the Joint Chiefs of Staff do not think that our military operations will be materially affected.

The biggest fact is that the stated purposes of the general uprising have failed. Communist leaders counted on popular support in the cities for their effort. They found little or none. On the other hand, there have been civilian casualties and disruption of public services. Just before I came into the room, I read a long cable from Ambassador Bunker which described the vigor with which the

---

[1] Wyatt Thomas Johnson, Jr., Assistant Press Secretary to the President.

Vietnamese Government and our own people are working together to deal with the problems of restoring civilian services and order in all of the cities.

In the meanwhile, we may at this very moment be on the eve of a major enemy offensive in the area of Khe Sanh and generally around the Demilitarized Zone.

We have known for some time that this offensive was planned by the enemy. Over recent weeks I have been in close touch with General Westmoreland, and over recent days in very close touch with all of our Joint Chiefs of Staff to make sure that every single thing that General Westmoreland believed that he needed at this time was available to him, and that our Joint Chiefs believe that his strategy was sound, his men were sure, and they were amply supplied.

I am confident in the light of the information given to me that our men and the South Vietnamese will be giving a good account of themselves.

As all of you know, the situation is a fluid one. We will keep the American people informed as these matters develop.

Now, I will be glad to take any questions.

QUESTIONS

NEGOTIATIONS WITH HANOI

[2.] Q. Mr. President, in your State of the Union Message, you said we were exploring certain so-called offers from Hanoi and as soon as you could you would report to the people on that.

Is there anything you can tell us today about the status of possible peace negotiations with them?

THE PRESIDENT. No. I would think that that statement is about as good as I could make on that general subject. That accurately describes what has been going on and what

is going on. But I do not have any success or results to report on it.

ASSESSMENT OF THE SITUATION IN
SOUTH VIETNAM

[3.] Q. Mr. President, does this present rampage in South Vietnam give you any reason to change any assessment that you have made previously about the situation in South Vietnam?

THE PRESIDENT. I am sure that we will make adjustments to what we are doing there.

So far as changing our basic strategy, the answer would be no. I think that there will be changes made here and there as a result of experience that comes from efforts such as they have made. Our best experts think that they had two purposes in mind.

First was a military success. That has been a complete failure. That is not to say that they have not disrupted services. It is just like when we have a riot in a town or when we have a very serious strike, or bridges go out, or lights—power failures and things. They have disrupted services. A few bandits can do that in any city in the land.

Obviously, they have in the Vietcong hundreds and thousands, so it is nothing unexpected to anticipate that they will try in cooperation with their friends from the North to coordinate their activities.

The ferocity and the violence, the deception and the lack of concern for the basic elements that appeal to human beings—they may have shocked a lot of people in that respect.

But the ability to do what they have done has been anticipated, prepared for, and met.

Now so much for the military movements. This is not just a civilian judgment. This is the judgment of the military men in the field for whatever that judgment is worth to us back here as experts—Monday morning quarterbacks.

That is the judgment of the best military advice I have here. I met with them yesterday at lunch at some length. I had General Ridgway [2] come down and spend some time with me and talked to him.

I have spent a good deal of time talking to General Taylor.[3] I had all of the Joint Chiefs of Staff in yesterday. We explored and discussed what had happened, what was happening, what might happen, and so forth.

I have talked to the Pentagon this morning, very early, and have been in touch with Secretary McNamara before his testimony.

Their general conclusion is that as a military movement it has been a failure.

Now, their second objective, obviously from the—what you can see from not only Vietnam but from other Communist capitals—even from some of our unknowing people here at home—is a psychological victory.

We have to realize that in moments of tenseness and trial—as we will have today and as we have had in the past days—that there will be a great effort to exploit that and let that substitute for military victory they have not achieved.

I do not believe when the American people know the facts, when the world knows the facts, and when the results are laid out for them to examine, I do not believe that they will achieve a psychological victory.

I do not want to be interpreted as unduly optimistic at all. I would rather wait and let the facts speak for themselves because there are many things that one far removed from the scene cannot anticipate.

In all of the battles, there are many disappointments for the commanders and even the commanders in chief.

So I think that at this very critical stage I would much prefer to be played low key than to give any false assurances. I can only say this: that based on the best military advice that I have, I feel confident that the men will give a good accounting of themselves.

Now, Sarah,[4] let's get yours, and we'll get through with that if you want.

THE "PUEBLO" AND ITS CREW

[4.] Q. Sir, I was going to shift from that question in view of what you just said to another question.

THE PRESIDENT. Go ahead.

Q. Have you any news on the crew of the *Pueblo*?

THE PRESIDENT. We understand from neutral nations and from reports from North Korea that the men are being treated well; that those who have suffered wounds are receiving treatment; that the body of the man who died is being held. We have received those reports and examined them. That is about the extent of the information we have on it.

Q. Did you say "men" or "man", sir, who died?

THE PRESIDENT. Man.

Q. Mr. President, are you confident that we can get back both the ship and the crew?

[2] Gen. Matthew B. Ridgway, USA (Ret.), former Supreme Allied Commander in the Pacific (1951) and in Europe (1953) and Army Chief of Staff (1953–55).

[3] Gen. Maxwell D. Taylor, USA (Ret.), Special Consultant to the President.

[4] Mrs. Sarah McClendon, representative of several Texas newspapers.

THE PRESIDENT. No, I am not. I don't want to hold out any hopes on information that I have that is not justified. All I can say is that these things take time.

The most comparable incident, I am told by the military people, to this one was the RB-47 that went down in 1960 and it took some 7 months of negotiations to get our pilots back. [5]

We are exploring every diplomatic means that is available to us. We have our best military men reviewing all that happened and, as I said in my statement to you and to the country some time ago, we are taking such precautionary steps as we may think the military situation justifies.

THE SAN ANTONIO FORMULA

[5.] Q. Clark Clifford's [6] testimony before the Armed Services Committee has raised some questions about the San Antonio formula.

THE PRESIDENT. Only in the press, not with anyone in the administration. Mr. Clifford said what I have said, what Mr. Rusk has said, what everybody has said, so far as the San Antonio formula is concerned. The country should know once and for all this morning that Mr. Clifford said just what I said at San Antonio.

POSSIBILITY OF NEED FOR ADDITIONAL
TROOPS

[6.] Q. Mr. President, is it possible that these developments in Vietnam that you

had outlined, plus the imminence of this major offensive, could lead to deployment of additional American combat troops in Vietnam?

THE PRESIDENT. I would not want to make predictions. Of course it is possible. The answer is yes. I wouldn't want your lead to say though, "Johnson predicts possibility of troops" because that is not anticipated. We see no evidence of that.

Yesterday I saw that George [7] said that of course we would consider calling up specialists or, of course we could consider some of these things. I must emphasize to you that lots of things would be considered, but so far as adding additional men, we have added the men that General Westmoreland has felt to be desirable and necessary.

There is nothing that has developed there that has caused him to change that estimate. We have something under 500,000. Our objective is 525,000. Most of the combat battalions already have been supplied. There is not anything in any of the developments that would justify the press in leaving the impression that any great new overall moves are going to be made that would involve substantial movements in that direction.

I would not want to foreclose any action in a matter like this. Anything can happen on a moment's notice. But we have constantly under advisement various things that we would want to anticipate. And after reviewing them now for several days, I have not seen the requirement or the necessity, nor have the Joint Chiefs, of making any additional requests to the Congress at this time involving additional authority.

It would be desirable, as it was last year, to have legislation a little more generous in one respect or two, or maybe more funds appropriated for military assistance that were

---

[5] See "Public Papers of the Presidents of the United States, Dwight D. Eisenhower, 1960–61," Item 231; and "Public Papers of the Presidents of the United States, John F. Kennedy, 1961," Item 8.

[6] Clark M. Clifford, former Naval Aide and Special Counsel to the President (1946–1950), who took office as Secretary of Defense on March 1, 1968 (see Item 104).

[7] George E. Christian, Special Assistant to the President.

reduced. We may have to get some adjustments in those fields, but there is nothing that is imminent at this moment.

THE "PUEBLO" INCIDENT AND VIETNAM

[7.] Q. Mr. President, how much, if any, definite information do you have on the connection between the *Pueblo* incident and what is happening now in Vietnam?

THE PRESIDENT. I do not have evidence that would say that they are definitely, positively one and the same here because I cannot prove that. Practically every expert I have talked to on Korea and North Vietnam and the Communist operation—all of them, I think without exception, believe there is a definite connection.

I would have you know, though, that that is based on their opinion and not on hard evidence that I could establish to CBS's satisfaction in a court of law.

NORTH VIETNAMESE PEACE FEELERS

[8.] Q. Mr. President, in light of what has happened in the last few days, or going back to the *Pueblo* incident, do you have any reason to believe that in the last 2 years there have been any genuine peace feelers put out by the North Vietnamese or other Vietnamese Communists, or have they been phony, except when they were winning in '64?

THE PRESIDENT. We have tried to explore every suggestion made by enemy and friend. I must say that in retrospect I do not think we have overlooked anything, and I do not think that we have found anything that would give an impartial judge reason to be encouraged.

VALIDITY OF BASIC ASSUMPTIONS

[9.] Q. Sir, do you see anything in the developments this week in these attacks in Vietnam that causes you to think you need to reevaluate some of the assumptions on which our policies, our strategy there has been based? I am thinking in terms of the security ratings, amount of population that is considered under Government control? Do you think the basic assumption is still valid?

THE PRESIDENT. We do that every week. I see nothing that would indicate that that shouldn't be done. We must do it all the time to try to keep up, and to be sure we have not made errors and mistakes. If you are saying, have we felt that what happened could not happen, the answer is no. As a matter of fact, Mr. Bailey,[8] if you have seen any of the intelligence reports, the information has been very clear that two things would happen:

One is that there would be a general uprising, as I stated.

Two, there would be a general invasion and attempt to secure military victory, and that the objective would be to get a military victory and a psychological victory.

That is one of the great problems the President has to deal with. He is sitting there reading these information reports while his own people, a good many of the best intentioned, are supplying him with military strategy, and the two do not fit in.

So you have to be tolerant and understand their best intentions while you are looking at the other fellow's hole card. That is what General Westmoreland has been doing while

[8] Charles W. Bailey 2d of the Minneapolis Star and Tribune.

all of these Monday morning quarterbacks are pointing out to him that this is the way he should move, or this is the way he should move.

This is a part of what happens when you look at history. It may be that General Westmoreland makes some serious mistakes or that I make some. We don't know. We are just acting in light of the information we have. We believe we have information about what they are trying to do there. We have taken every precaution we know of. But we don't want to give you assurance that it will all be satisfactory. We see nothing that would require any change of great consequence.

We will have to move men from this place to that one. We will have to replace helicopters. Probably we had 100-odd helicopters and planes seriously damaged and we will have to replace them.

Secretary McNamara told me he could have that done very shortly.

We will have to replace the 38 planes lost, but we have approximately 5,900 planes there. We anticipate that we will lose 25 or 30 every month just from normal crashes and so forth.

EVALUATION OF THE SITUATION

[10.] Q. Mr. President, do you believe, sir, their winter-spring offensive and their call for an uprising and their attempt to impose a coalition government is based on their belief that they are taking military punishment that they cannot sustain for a long time?

In short, sir, are we still winning the war?

THE PRESIDENT. Well, I see nothing in the developments that would indicate that the evaluation that I have had of this situation throughout the month should be changed.

I do think that the second phase is im-

minent. What we have expected is upon us. We have gone through the first phase of it. We will have to see what happens in the second phase. If it comes out as expected, I think I can give you a better answer to your question when it is over with.

I do not want to prophesy what is going to happen, although we feel reasonably sure of our strength.

VIETCONG MORALE

[11.] Q. Mr. President, one of the problems people seem to be having in making up their minds on the psychological importance of this goes back to our reports that the Vietcong were really way down in morale, that they were a shattered force.

Now people ask: Well, how, then, can they find the people who are so well-motivated to run these suicide attacks in so many places in such good coordination?

Some people say: Well, that proves they know they are licked and this is their dying gasp. And some people say: Well, it proves that we underestimated their morale. How do you feel, sir?

THE PRESIDENT. I haven't read those reports about underestimating all their morale, and their being out of it, and no more problems, and so forth. That hasn't been the information the Government has received.

We do think that we have made good progress there. We are for that. We don't want to overplay it or play it in high key. We just want to state it because we believe it is true.

But no one in authority has ever felt— that I know anything about—that you could not have an uprising of this kind, particularly when they have ordered it and predicted it and we have been expecting it.

As I view history, I think that you have things of this type replete throughout. You can expect it. I see it even in domestic problems. The fact that people's morale may be suffering and they may be having great difficulty doesn't keep them from breaking glass windows and shooting folks in a store or dashing into your home or trying to assassinate somebody. That goes with it. That is a part of the pattern.

Now whether they are doing this from a position of greater strength or greater weakness—I would say neither. I don't think that they are as weak as you picture them in your straw man that you place up there—that the Government has this feeling. I don't think we feel that way.

I think we know that a march on the Pentagon can disrupt traffic and tie up things and cause problems here. I think we can see what happened in Detroit. I think we can see what happened in Saigon.

I think there are times when a few highly energetic and courageous people could seize National Airport. But, could they hold it? Does it endure? Is it a victory? Do they pay more than it is worth and so on and so forth? Those are the things you have to evaluate.

Now, I am no great strategist and tactician. I know that you are not. But let us assume that the best figures we can have are from our responsible military commanders. They say 10,000 died and we lost 249 and the South Vietnamese lost 500. Now that doesn't look like a Communist victory. I can count. It looks like somebody has paid a very dear price for the temporary encouragement that some of our enemies had.

We have approximately 5,900 planes and have lost 38 completely destroyed. We lost 100-odd that were damaged and have to be repaired. Maybe Secretary McNamara will fly in 150 shortly.

Now, is that a great enemy victory?

In Peking today they say that we are in panic. You have to judge that for yourself. In other Communist capitals today they say that we have definitely exhibited a lack of power and that we do not have any military strength. You will have to judge that for yourself.

But General Westmoreland—evaluating this for us and the Joint Chiefs of Staff reviewing it for me—tell me that in their judgment it has not been a military success.

I am measuring my words. I don't want to overstate the thing. We do not believe that we should help them in making it a psychological success.

We are presenting these reports daily to the Armed Services Committee of the Senate where the Secretary of Defense is testifying and will be through a large part of next week.

There will be moments of encouragement and discouragement. And as things go on ahead, we can't estimate them, but they will be given to the committees who have jurisdiction.

Since the Armed Services Committees help draft our people and raise our armies and provide the equipment and so forth, the Secretary is appearing there morning and afternoon. He will be giving periodic reports that will be much more in detail and will supplement what I have said to you.

TALKS BETWEEN SOUTH VIETNAM AND NLF

[12.]   Q. Mr. President, do you still support talks between the South Vietnamese and the NLF? [9]

THE PRESIDENT. I have not changed the viewpoint that I expressed when I quoted

---

[9] National Liberation Front, political arm of the Vietcong.

the statement of President Thieu of South Vietnam in my interview with the correspondents.

RELATIONS WITH THE SOVIET UNION

[13.] Q. Mr. President, in your judgment, did the interview Premier Kosygin gave to Life's editors reflect any deterioration in our relations with Russia since the Glassboro talks?

THE PRESIDENT. I don't care to weigh and speculate on the developments in the Soviet Union. We just tabled last week a nonproliferation agreement with them. We have other plans for exchanges of thoughts on various subjects.

We would always like to improve our relations with the Soviet Union and with all nations where we can do that consistently.

PROPOSED CIVIL RIGHTS MARCH ON WASHINGTON

[14.] Q. Mr. President, some people interested in civil rights, including Martin Luther King, are planning a massive march on Washington this spring. There is some talk that they would like to stop the wheels of Government.

Are you planning to try to talk them out of this? Would you assess that for us?

THE PRESIDENT. I don't know what their plans are. I am not sure that they have developed them yet.

Of course, I would be hopeful that our energies, our talents, and our concerns could be directed in a more productive and a more effective manner.

I would hope that some of these people who are leaders of the causes could recognize that the Congress is having hearings every day on subjects of vital importance to their cause.

By coming there and following constitu-

tional methods, presenting their evidence to the Congress and persuading the Congress, it would be more helpful than just trying to stop the functioning of the Government who is also trying very much to help their cause to eliminate discrimination, get more jobs, and improve housing. Whatever time and attention the Government has to give to these things is taken away from things that they could be doing to help them.

So we will do all we can to work with all groups in this country to see that their views are heard, considered, and acted upon with promptness and understanding.

RELATIONS WITH SOUTH KOREA

[15.] Q. Mr. President, the *Pueblo* incident appears to have put a certain strain on relations between Washington and Seoul. Some political figures in South Korea are saying that the United States appears more interested in getting back the 83 men than in doing something about North Korean incursions into South Korea.

THE PRESIDENT. I don't know which political figures you refer to. I can't comment on that.

We are in very close touch with the President of that country. I think he understands how we feel.

I would be less than frank if I didn't tell you I was deeply concerned about 83 Americans, as I am sure the President of Korea is.

I am also deeply concerned about the situation in South Korea and the obligation we have there. We are going to be equal to that obligation. We are going to be true to our commitment.

We have some 50,000 men there. We are going to see that not only are they adequately informed and supplied, but that all of our plans take into consideration the recommendations of that Government that we have found to be not only a friendly Government but an effective one—and one of our best allies.

I have great respect for the President of South Korea and his judgments. They are being received, considered, and acted upon every day.

I see nothing in any of these developments to justify a concern on the part of South Korea or America that there is a strain in our relations. I think that is largely talk and speculation and so-called reports.

MEETINGS WITH NORTH KOREA

[16.]   Q. Are we now trying to arrange talks with North Korea at Panmunjom or has there been a meeting since yesterday there?

THE PRESIDENT. Yes, there has been a meeting between representatives of North Korea and the United States. We hope there will be additional meetings.

These meetings have not produced any satisfactory results as far as the United States is concerned.

I know of nothing that I should add to that statement. And I don't plan to.

Merriman Smith, United Press International: Thank you, Mr. President.

NOTE: President Johnson's one hundred and eighteenth news conference was held in the Cabinet Room at the White House at 12:05 p.m. on Friday, February 2, 1968.

52   Statement by the President Upon Appointing an Advisory Council To Evaluate Supplementary Educational Centers and Services. *February 3, 1968*

THE COUNCIL will help us to broaden the benefits of this program which has helped to enrich the educational experiences of 17 million children during the past 2 years.

This program helps us to bring the latest and the best in teaching facilities and methods to our children.

[Grants to the States] provide State education agencies with major new responsibilities and opportunities to assume leadership in the improvement of American education.

NOTE: The President's statement was made public as part of a White House release announcing the formation of the National Advisory Council on Supplementary Centers and Services. The Council was established under authority of provisions of the Elementary and Secondary Education Amendments of 1967 (81 Stat. 797) to ascertain the effectiveness of special educational programs set up under Title III of the Elementary and Secondary Education Act of 1965 (79 Stat. 39) and designed to supplement and strengthen elementary and secondary education. The release stated that the supplementary centers would provide facilities and resources which local school districts are unable to furnish, such as science laboratories for joint use by several schools, mobile remedial reading laboratories, visits by artists or lecturers to remote schools, and instruction in new methods of motivating and teaching handicapped children. The full text of the release, which lists the 11 members of the Council, is printed in the Weekly Compilation of Presidential Documents (vol. 4, p. 213).

53   Remarks at the Presentation of a Bust of Adlai E. Stevenson. *February 5, 1968*

Mr. Vice President, Mr. Secretary of State, members of the Stevenson family, Ambassador Goldberg, members of the Cabinet, distinguished Ambassadors and guests:

This day would have been Adlai Stevenson's 68th birthday.

Because the spirit of Adlai Stevenson's thought lives on, this ceremony is not an unhappy one—but rather it is an occasion for a very proud and grateful remembering.

I recall the time when President Kennedy appointed most of Adlai Stevenson's Chicago law firm to high Federal office. Ambassador Stevenson said, "I regret that I have but one law firm to give to my country." Considering the current situation with your law firm, Mr. Sharon—now that we have finally deprived you of Mr. Clifford—I hope that some of Mr. Stevenson's philosophy may rub off on you.

Of course, it is not only Adlai Stevenson's law partners and political associates who follow his lead today. A generation of Americans came to political maturity through his wit and his insight.

They know that Adlai Stevenson—twice defeated for the Presidency—did not finally lose the political battles to which he committed himself. They learned from Adlai Stevenson that tenderness and toughness are not opposites. They learned finally that compassion and understanding are the wellsprings of freedom—and that they must be guarded with an uncompromising tenacity. Adlai Stevenson was proof that an "egghead"—as he called himself—can be both soft-hearted and hard-boiled.

When one speaks of this gifted man, it is best always to speak in his own words.

Here is something of his wisdom.

"The contest with tyranny is not a hundred-yard dash—it is a test of endurance."

The month before he died he had this to say: "Retreat leads to retreat just as aggression leads to aggression in this still primitive international community."

In a letter written a few days before his death, he wrote: "Whatever criticisms may be made over the detail and emphasis of American foreign policy, its purpose and direction are sound."

It was Adlai Stevenson who said that "although America occasionally gags on a gnat, it has some talent for swallowing tigers whole."

And he said: "The costliest blunders have been made by dictators who did not quite understand the workings of real democracy, and mistook diversity for disunity."

But if Adlai Stevenson was tough, so too was he gentle; if he lived and served in the hard day-to-day world, so too did he have a vision of a better future for all mankind.

Twenty-three years ago in San Francisco, Adlai Stevenson helped to create the United Nations. He gave it the final 4 years of his remarkable life.

This sculpture, which I gratefully accept on behalf of the Government, will stand in the United States Mission to the United Nations.

On the day he died, I said: "He was an American. And he served America well. But what he saw, and what he spoke, and what he worked for is the shared desire of all humanity. He believed in us, perhaps more than we deserved. And so we came to believe in ourselves much more than we had."

Perhaps his belief in the United Nations was also more than its performance deserves—but I think not.

Franklin Roosevelt, and every President since, shared Adlai Stevenson's hopes for the United Nations. If we have sometimes been disappointed, we are not disheartened. In this institution—not yet 23 years of age—the world has fashioned an instrument that has—on many occasions—fulfilled the faith of its founders.

When it has failed, it has failed only at tasks where no other instrument of man has yet succeeded.

If it has not yet assured a lasting peace, disarmament, and the conquest of illiteracy and disease, it has helped to focus the world's concern on each of these.

No other organization has better represented the hope and the promise of mankind.

Pope Paul VI journeyed to the United Nations, just 3 months after Adlai Stevenson died. He said this: "One word more, gentlemen, one last word: this edifice you are building does not rest upon purely material and earthly foundations, for it would then be a house built on sand—above all, it rests on our consciences. . . ."

Adlai Stevenson would have appreciated that. No man of our time better understood that the call of conscience is the highest calling.

In his time he called upon the conscience of his generation by his passionate eloquence and by his personal example.

How much we miss him was best summed up on the floor of the United Nations General Assembly, after a session devoted to eulogizing his career. One delegate, after the eulogies had been made, turned aside and said very simply, "If only Stevenson could have spoken."

NOTE: The President spoke at 11:35 a.m. in the Cabinet Room at the White House. In his opening words he referred to Vice President Hubert H. Humphrey, Secretary of State Dean Rusk, and U.S. Representative to the United Nations Arthur J. Goldberg. Early in his remarks he referred to John H. Sharon, partner in the Washington law firm of Clifford and Miller, and to Clark M. Clifford, whose appointment as Secretary of Defense was announced January 19 (see Item 18).

The bust of Adlai Stevenson, by Pietro Lazzari, was commissioned by the family and friends of the late Ambassador and the presentation was made by Mr. Sharon.

---

54 Special Message to the Congress on Education: "The Fifth Freedom." *February 5, 1968*

To the Congress of the United States:

In two centuries, America has achieved—through great effort and struggle—one major educational advance after another: free public schooling; the Land Grant Colleges; the extension of the universities into the Nation's farms and homes; the unique venture that has placed a high school education within the reach of every young person.

I believe that our time—the mid-1960's—will be remembered as a time of unprecedented achievement in American education.

The past four years have been a time of unparalleled action:

—The Congress has approved more than 40 laws to support education from the preschool project to the postgraduate laboratory;

—The Federal Government has raised its investment in education to nearly $12 billion annually, almost triple the level four years ago.

The real significance of what we have done is reflected, not in statistics, but in the experiences of individual Americans, young and old, whose lives are being shaped by new educational programs.

Through Head Start, a four-year-old encounters a new world of learning.

Through Title I of the Elementary and Secondary Education Act, a disadvantaged youngster finds essential extra help—and school becomes a more rewarding place.

Through the Teacher Corps, a bright and eager college graduate is attracted to teaching and his talents are focused where the need is greatest.

These programs—all of them new—are

enriching life for millions of young Americans.

In our high schools, students find that once-empty library shelves are filled; the most up-to-date laboratory equipment is available; new courses, new methods of teaching and learning are being tested in the classroom.

A student who sets his sights on college is more likely than ever before to find help through Federal loans, scholarships and work-study grants.

Today's college student is more likely than ever to live and learn in new dormitories, new classrooms, new libraries and laboratories.

Today, thousands of parents who in their youth had no chance for higher education can say with certainty, "My child can go to college."

Above all, we can see a new spirit stirring in America, moving us to stress anew the central importance of education; to seek ways to make education more vital and more widely available.

That new spirit cannot be fully measured in dollars or enrollment figures. But it is there nonetheless. The achievements of the past four years have sustained and nourished it.

Yet for all our progress, we still face enormous problems in education: stubborn, lingering, unyielding problems.

The phrase, "equal educational opportunity," to the poor family in Appalachia and to the Negro family in the city, is a promise—not a reality.

Our schools are turning out too many young men and women whose years in the classroom have not equipped them for useful work.

Growing enrollments and rising expenses are straining the resources of our colleges—

and the strain is being felt by families across America.

Each of these problems will be difficult to solve. Their solution may take years—and almost certainly will bring new problems. But the challenge of our generation is to lead the way.

And in leading the way, we must carefully set our priorities. To meet our urgent needs within a stringent overall budget, several programs must be reduced or deferred. We can reduce expenditures on construction of facilities and the purchase of equipment. But, many of our urgent educational programs which directly affect the young people of America cannot be deferred. For the cost—the human cost—of delay is intolerable.

These principles underlie my 1969 budgetary recommendations and the proposals in this message. My recommendations are tailored to enable us to meet our most urgent needs, while deferring less important programs and expenditures.

ELEMENTARY AND SECONDARY EDUCATION

It took almost a century of effort and controversy and debate to pass the Elementary and Secondary Education Act.

The great question was this: Can there be a system of large-scale aid to education which does not diminish the independence of our local schools and which safeguards the rich diversity of American education?

In 1965 such a law was passed. Today it is at work in nearly 20,000 school districts: strengthening State and local school boards, local school officials and classroom teachers, and improving the quality of education for millions of children.

It may take a decade or more to measure the full benefits of the Elementary and Secondary Education Act. But already evidence is mounting to support my belief that this is the most significant education measure in our history.

Last year, Congress extended this law, the bedrock of all our efforts to help America's schools.

This year we have an opportunity to make that law a more efficient instrument of aid to education; to make it more responsive to the needs of the States and communities throughout the country.

I urge the Congress to fund Title I of the Elementary and Secondary Education Act well in advance of the school year, so that State and local school officials can make their plans with a clear idea of the resources that will be available.

Our resources are not unlimited—and never will be. So it is all the more important that in assigning priorities, we focus our aid where the need is greatest.

That firm principle underlies a six-point program which I am proposing to Congress under the Elementary and Secondary Education Act and other authorities:

1. Two innovative programs to help America's youngest and poorest children have been proven in practice. *I propose that funding for the Head Start and Head Start Follow Through programs be stepped-up from $340 million to $380 million.*

2. Last year, Congress authorized a special program to help Mexican-American, Puerto Rican and other children who are separated by a language barrier from good education. *I propose that we launch this bilingual education program with a $5 million appropriation.*

3. We are still doing less than we should do to prepare mentally retarded and physically handicapped children for useful lives. *I propose that our special programs for the handicapped be increased from $53 mil-*

lion to $85 million.

4. We must rescue troubled boys and girls before they drop out of school. *I propose full funding—$30 million—for a new Stay in School program, which will help schools tailor their own programs, from new and exciting methods of instruction to family counseling and special tutoring, to turn potential drop-outs into high school graduates.*

5. Upward Bound, a program for poor but talented students, has directed thousands of young Americans into college who might otherwise never have had a chance. *I propose that Congress increase funds for Upward Bound to serve 30,000 young Americans this year.*

6. Adult basic education classes last year gave about 300,000 men and women an opportunity to gain new earning power, new self-respect, a new sense of achievement. *I propose that Congress provide $50 million for this vital program.*

If we can invest vast sums for education, we must also be able to plan and evaluate our education programs; to undertake basic research in teaching and learning, and to apply that research to the classroom. For these efforts, *I propose appropriations of $177 million next year.*

New Strength for Vocational Education

Whatever else we expect of the local school, we demand that it prepare each student for a productive life. The high school graduate who does not enter college needs not only knowledge enough to be a responsible citizen, but skills enough to get and keep a good job.

One and a half million young men and women will leave high school and enter the labor force this year—in a time of high employment, when skills are at a premium.

Too many of them will find that they have no job skills—or only marginal skills, or skills which are not really needed in their communities.

A high school diploma should not be a ticket to frustration.

We must do more to improve vocational education programs. We must help high schools, vocational schools, technical institutes, and community colleges to modernize their programs, to experiment with new approaches to job training. Above all, we must build stronger links between the schools and their students, and local industries and employment services, so that education will have a direct relationship to the world the graduating student enters.

I recommend that Congress enact the Partnership for Learning and Earning Act of 1968.

This new program—streamlining and strengthening our vocational education laws—will:

—Give new flexibility to our system of matching grants, so the States can concentrate their funds where the need is greatest;

—Provide $15 million for special experimental programs to bridge the gap between education and work: for alliances between schools, employment services and private employers; for new summer training programs combining work and education;

—Totally revise and consolidate our existing vocational education laws, reducing paperwork for the States, the schools and other training centers;

—Encourage the States to plan a long-range strategy in vocational education.

TRAINED PROFESSIONALS FOR OUR SCHOOLS

The value of all these measures—and indeed, the effectiveness of our entire school system—depends on educators: teachers, teacher aides, administrators and many others.

It would profit us little to enact the most enlightened laws, to authorize great sums of money—unless we guarantee a continuing supply of trained, dedicated, enthusiastic men and women for the education professions.

To advance this essential purpose, I purpose

—*That Congress provide the funds needed to train nearly 45,000 teachers, administrators and other professionals under the Education Professions Development Act of 1967.*

—*That Congress authorize and appropriate the necessary funds so that 4,000 of our best and most dedicated young men and women can serve our neediest children in the Teacher Corps.*

HIGHER EDUCATION

The prosperity and well-being of the United States—and thus our national interest—are vitally affected by America's colleges and universities, junior colleges and technical institutes.

Their problems are not theirs alone, but the Nation's.

This is true today more than ever. For now we call upon higher education to play a new and more ambitious role in our social progress, our economic development, our efforts to help other countries.

We depend upon the universites—their

training, research and extension services—for the knowledge which undergirds agricultural and industrial production.

Increasingly, we look to higher education to provide the key to better employment opportunities and a more rewarding life for our citizens.

As never before, we look to the colleges and universities—to their faculties, laboratories, research institutes and study centers—for help with every problem in our society and with the efforts we are making toward peace in the world.

Student Aid

It is one of the triumphs of American democracy that college is no longer a privilege for the few. Last fall, more than 50 percent of our high school graduates went on to college. It is our goal by 1976 to increase that number to two-thirds.

In the past four years, we have significantly eased the financial burden which college imposes on so many families. Last year, more than one student in five attended college with the help of Federal loans, scholarships, grants and work-study programs.

But for millions of capable American students and their families, college is still out of reach. In a nation that honors individual achievement, financial obstacles to full educational opportunity must be overcome.

I propose the Educational Opportunity Act of 1968:
—To set a new and sweeping national goal: that in America there must be no economic or racial barrier to higher education; that every qualified young person must have all the education he wants and can absorb.
—To help a million and a half students attend college next year through the full range of our student aid programs, including guaranteed loans.
—To strengthen the Guaranteed Loan Program by meeting the administrative costs of the banks who make these loans. With a service fee of up to $35 for each loan, this program can aid an additional 200,000 students next year, bringing the total to 750,000.
—To provide $15 million for new programs of tutoring, counseling and special services so that the neediest students can succeed in college.
—To unify and simplify several student aid programs—College Work-Study, Educational Opportunity Grants and National Defense Education Act Loans—so that each college can devise a flexible plan of aid tailored to the needs of each student.

Aid to Institutions of Higher Learning

Today, higher education needs help.

American colleges and universities face growing enrollments, rising costs, and increasing demands for services of all kinds.

In 10 years, the number of young people attending college will increase more than 50 percent; graduate enrollments will probably double.

Our first order of business must be to continue existing Federal support for higher education.

I urge the Congress to extend and strengthen three vital laws which have served this nation well:

—*The National Defense Education Act of 1958,* which has helped nearly two million students go to college and graduate school.

—*The Higher Education Facilities Act of 1963,* which has helped nearly 1,400 colleges and universities meet growing enrollments with new classrooms, laboratories and dormitories.

—*The Higher Education Act of 1965,* which, in addition to its student aid programs, has strengthened college libraries, involved our universities in community service, and given new vitality to 450 developing colleges.

I also urge the Congress to fulfill the commitment it made two years ago, and appropriate funds needed for the International Education Act. This Act will strengthen our universities in their international programs—and ultimately strengthen the quality of the men and women who serve this country abroad.

We must apply more effectively the educational resources we have. We must encourage better cooperation between the Nation's colleges and universities; and we should move to increase each institution's efficiency by exploiting the most advanced technology.

To serve these purposes, *I recommend the Networks for Knowledge Act of 1968.*

This pilot program will provide new financial incentives to encourage colleges and universities to pool their resources by sharing faculties, facilities, equipment, library and educational television services. It will supplement the effort launched last year by the National Science Foundation to explore the potential of computers in education.

I also recommend three new measures to strengthen graduate education in America.

First, we should increase the Federal payment available to help graduate schools meet the cost of educating a student who has earned a Federal Fellowship. At present, Federal Fellowship programs are actually deepening the debt of the graduate schools because this payment is too low.

Second, we should launch a new program to stengthen those graduate schools with clear potential for higher quality. With enrollments growing, we must begin to enlarge the capacity of graduate schools. This program will underwrite efforts to strengthen faculties, improve courses and foster excellence in a wide range of fields.

Third, I urge the Congress to increase government sponsored research in our universities. The knowledge gained through this research truly is power—power to heal the sick, educate the young, defend the nation, and improve the quality of life for our citizens.

A Strategy for Higher Education

The programs I am presenting to the Congress today are aimed at solving some of the problems faced by our colleges and universities and their students in the years ahead. But accomplishing all these things will by no means solve the problems of higher education in America.

To do that, we must shape a long-term strategy of Federal aid to higher education: a comprehensive set of goals and a precise plan of action.

I am directing the Secretary of Health, Education, and Welfare to begin preparing a long-range plan for the support of higher education in America.

Our strategy must:

—Eliminate race and income as bars to higher learning.

—Guard the independence of private and public institutions.

—Ensure that State and private contributors will bear their fair share of support for higher education.

—Encourage the efficient and effective use of educational resources by our colleges and universities.

—Promote continuing improvement in the quality of American education.

—Effectively blend support to students with support for institutions.

Such a strategy will not be easy to devise. But we must begin now. For at stake is a decision of vital importance to all Americans.

EDUCATION AND THE QUALITY OF LIFE

Every educational program contributes vitally to the enrichment of life in America. But some have that enrichment as their first goal. They are designed not to serve special groups or institutions, but to serve all the American people.

We have tested in the past three years a new idea in government: The National Foundation on the Arts and Humanities.

That experiment has been an impressive success. It has proved that government can indeed enhance the Nation's cultural life and deepen the understanding of our people.

—With modest amounts of money, The Humanities Endowment has promoted scholarship in a wide range of fields and quickened public interest in the humanities.

—The Arts Endowment has brought new energy and life to music, drama, and the arts in communities all over America.

I believe the Foundation has earned a vote of confidence. *I urge that the National Foundation on the Arts and Humanities authorization be extended.*

We have acted also to launch an historic educational force in American life: public broadcasting—non-commercial radio and television service devoted first and foremost to excellence.

Last year the Congress authorized the Corporation for Public Broadcasting. This year we must give it life.

I recommend that the Congress appropriate the funds needed in fiscal 1968 and fiscal 1969 to support the initial activities of the Corporation for Public Broadcasting.

Last year I stressed the importance of a long-range financing plan which would ensure that public broadcasting would be vigorous, independent and free from political interference or control. The problem involved is complex. It concerns the use of the most powerful communications medium in the world today. It should not be resolved without the most thorough study and consultation.

I am asking the Secretary of Health, Education, and Welfare, the Secretary of the Treasury and the Director of the Bureau of the Budget—who have been studying this problem since the law was enacted—to work with the Board of Directors of the Corporation for Public Broadcasting and the appropriate Committees of the Congress to formulate a long-range financing plan that will promote and protect this vital new force in American life.

THE FIFTH FREEDOM

On January 6, 1941, President Franklin D. Roosevelt set forth to Congress and the people "four essential human freedoms" for which America stands.

In the years since then, those four freedoms—freedom of speech, freedom of worship, freedom from want, and freedom from fear—have stood as a summary of our aspirations for the American Republic and for the world.

And Americans have always stood ready

to pay the cost in energy and treasure which are needed to make those great goals a reality.

Today—wealthier, more powerful and more able than ever before in our history—our Nation can declare another essential human freedom.

The fifth freedom is freedom from ignorance.

It means that every man, everywhere, should be free to develop his talents to their full potential—unhampered by arbitrary barriers of race or birth or income.

We have already begun the work of guaranteeing that fifth freedom.

The job, of course, will never be finished. For a nation, as for an individual, education is a perpetually unfinished journey, a continuing process of discovery.

But the work we started when this Nation began, which has flourished for nearly two centuries, and which gained new momentum in the past two Congresses—is ours to continue—yours and mine.

LYNDON B. JOHNSON

The White House
February 5, 1968

NOTE: For statements or remarks upon signing related legislation, see Items 4, 503, 538, 554.

55 Memorandum Urging Support of the Red Cross by Federal Employees and Members of the Armed Forces. *February 5, 1968*

Memorandum for the Heads of Executive Departments and Agencies:
SUBJECT: Red Cross Month

The American Red Cross is an instrument of mercy for all of us. For more than 85 years its mission has been to serve the members of our Armed Forces and their families, to help our neighbors when natural disasters strike, and to aid all who are in need. The Red Cross Blood Program supplies nearly half of our peoples' need for blood. The safety and nursing programs of the Red Cross save countless lives.

This year the Red Cross must raise $121,-624,000, the largest annual goal since the end of World War II. It needs these funds to fulfill commitments for the relief of disaster victims, and to meet enlarged responsibilites to our men in uniform.

Within the Federal establishment, both here and overseas, the Red Cross participates in the Combined Federal Campaign. But nearly half of the 3,330 local chapters of the Red Cross rely for funds on independent campaigns conducted in March. This year, all Red Cross chapters will participate in a special SOS—Support Our Servicemen—campaign. There will be no additional on-the-job campaign among Federal employees.

To draw greater public attention to these efforts and to help recruit more Red Cross volunteers and blood donors, I will soon designate March 1968 as Red Cross Month. The American people have always increased their support of the Red Cross when they understood the need. And this year the need is very evident.

As President and as Honorary Chairman of the American Red Cross, I urge all employees of the Federal Government and all our men and women in uniform to give their best in support of the Red Cross. Its success must be our concern, because its mission of mercy is ours to share and treasure.

LYNDON B. JOHNSON

NOTE: On the same day the President signed Proclamation 3825 "Red Cross Month, 1968" (4 Weekly Comp. Pres. Docs., p. 222; 33 F.R. 2623; 3 CFR, 1968 Comp., p. 20).

56 Special Message to the Congress: "To Protect the Consumer Interest." *February 6, 1968*

To the Congress of the United States:

Speaking for every American, I present to the Congress my fourth Message on the American Consumer.

President Truman once observed that while some Americans have their interests protected in Washington by special lobbying groups, most of the people depend on the President of the United States to represent their interests.

In the case of consumer protection, however, the President—and the Congress—speak for every citizen.

A hundred years ago, consumer protection was largely unnecessary. We were a rural nation then: a nation of farms and small towns. Even in the growing cities, neighborhoods were closely knit.

Most products were locally produced and there was a personal relationship between the seller and the buyer. If the buyer had a complaint, he went straight to the miller, the blacksmith, the tailor, the corner grocer. Products were less complicated. It was easy to tell the excellent from the inferior.

Today all this is changed. A manufacturer may be thousands of miles away from his customer—and even further removed by distributors, wholesalers and retailers. His products may be so complicated that only an expert can pass judgment on their quality.

We are able to sustain this vast and impersonal system of commerce because of the ingenuity of our technology and the honesty of our businessmen.

But this same vast network of commerce, this same complexity, also presents opportunities for the unscrupulous and the negligent.

It is the government's role to protect the consumer—and the honest businessman alike—against fraud and indifference. Our goal must be to assure every American consumer a fair and honest exchange for his hard-earned dollar.

THE RECORD OF PROGRESS

Thanks to the work of the last two Congresses, we are now much closer to that goal than ever before. In three years, we have taken historic steps to protect the consumer against:

—Impure and unwholesome meat.
—Death and destruction on our highways.
—Misleading labels and packages.
—Clothing and blankets that are fire-prone, rather than fire-proof.
—Hazardous appliances and products around the house.
—Toys that endanger our children.
—Substandard clinical laboratories.
—Unsafe tires.

In addition to these, the first session of this Congress took important steps toward passage of other consumer proposals we recommended last year, including the Truth-in-Lending, Fire Safety and Pipeline Safety bills which passed the Senate, and the fraudulent land sales, mutual funds and electric power reliability measures.

This session of the Congress should complete action on these vitally needed proposals to protect the public. It has already begun to do so.

In passing the Truth-in-Lending Bill last week, the House of Representatives brought every American consumer another step closer to knowing the cost of money he borrows. I urge the House and Senate to resolve their differences promptly and to give the consumer a strong Truth-in-Lending law.

A NEW PROGRAM FOR 1968

But that record alone, as comprehensive as it is, will not complete our responsibility. The needs of the consumer change as our Society changes, and legislation must keep pace.

For 1968, I propose a new eight-point program to:
—Crack down on fraud and deception in sales.
—Launch a major study of automobile insurance.
—Protect Americans against hazardous radiation from television sets and other electronic equipment.
—Close the gaps in our system of poultry inspection.
—Guard the consumer's health against unwholesome fish.
—Move now to prevent death and accidents on our waterways.
—Add new meaning to warranties and guarantees, and seek ways to improve repair work and servicing.
—Appoint a government lawyer to represent the consumer.

SALES RACKETS

Every Spring, when families turn their thoughts to household improvements, the shady operator goes to work.

His office may be a telephone booth, a briefcase which he carries from door to door, or a car which he drives from state to state. His sales brochure may be a catchy newspaper advertisement.

With false and deceptive offers of attractive home repairs or items that are more promise than product, he preys most of all on those who are least able to protect themselves: the poor, the elderly, the ignorant.

Too often—and too late—the victim discovers that he has been swindled: that he has paid too much, that he has received inferior work, and that he has mortgaged himself into long-term debt. Some even lose their homes. A recent Report of the National Better Business Bureau estimates that deceptive practices in the home improvement field alone cost the consumer between $500 million and $1 billion yearly.

Sales rackets are not limited to home improvements. And sales rackets of all types are on the increase.

As the law now stands, there is no effective way to stop these unscrupulous practices when they are discovered. The legal machinery may drag on for two or three years before the violator can be ordered to cease and desist. In the meantime, countless more Americans are cheated.

In matters so flagrantly deceptive, the consumer and the honest businessman deserve greater—and speedier—protection.

I recommend that the Congress enact the Deceptive Sales Act of 1968 to give new powers to the Federal Trade Commission.

Under this Act, the FTC would be able to obtain Federal court orders to stop fraudulent and deceptive practices immediately while the case is before the Commission or the courts.

With this measure we can complete the cycle of protection for the consumer in fraud cases—by adding Federal court injunctions to the administrative and criminal processes which now exist.

Automobile Insurance

One area of major concern to the consumer is automobile insurance. Every motorist, every passenger, and every pedestrian is affected by it—yet the system is overburdened and unsatisfactory.

Premiums are rising—in some parts of the country they have increased by as much as 30 percent over the past six years.

Arbitrary coverage and policy cancellations are the cause of frequent complaint—particularly from the elderly, the young, the serviceman, and the Negro and Mexican-American.

A number of "high risk" insurance companies have gone into bankruptcy—leaving policyholders and accident victims unprotected and helpless.

Accident compensation is often unfair: Some victims get too much, some get too little, some get nothing at all.

Lawsuits have clogged our courts. The average claim takes about two and one-half years just to get to trial.

This is a national problem. It will become even more of a problem as we license more drivers, produce more automobiles and build more roads.

With more than 100 million drivers and 96 million motor vehicles in the United States, the insurance system is severely strained today.

While many proposals have been made to improve the system, many questions remain unanswered. The search for solutions must be pressed.

I propose legislation to authorize the Secretary of Transportation to conduct the first comprehensive study of the automobile insurance system. He will undertake this review with the full cooperation of the Federal Trade Commission and other appropriate agencies of the Executive Branch.

In recent months we have acted to make our cars and our highways safer. Now we must move to streamline the automobile insurance system—to make it fair, to make it simple, and to make it efficient.

Hazardous Radiation

It has been said that each civilization creates its own hazards. Ours is no exception. While modern technology has enriched our daily lives, it has sometimes yielded unexpected and unfortunate side effects.

Recently it was discovered that certain color television sets emit radiation which exceeds accepted safety limits.

We also know that poorly designed X-ray equipment is unnecessarily exposing some patients to the danger of radiation.

Such defects have introduced a new element into the problem of radiation hazards.

Intensive research has already probed this area. But those efforts have dealt primarily with radiation from medical equipment, isotopes, and nuclear devices.

We have long known that large doses of radiation can be fatal. But we have much more to learn about the harmful effects of lesser doses—effects which may not show up for many years.

Now modern science must be put to work on these hazards—particularly the hazards which confront the consumer.

I recommend enactment of the Hazardous Radiation Act of 1968. This measure will give the Secretary of Health, Education, and Welfare authority to

—Conduct intensive studies of the hazards and set and enforce standards to control them.

—Require manufacturers to recall defective equipment and devices.

The proposed legislation sets penalties for those who ignore the standards established by the Secretary of Health, Education, and Welfare.

WHOLESOME POULTRY

Last year, the Congress enacted the Wholesome Meat Act to insure the quality and safety of the food that American housewives put on their tables.

This year, the scope of that protection must be extended.

In 1967, Americans consumed over 12 billion pounds of poultry, most of it inspected under Federal law. But the 1.6 billion pounds which did not cross state lines received no Federal inspection. And State inspection is minimal at best. Thirty-one States have no poultry inspection laws. Of the remaining 19, only four have effective laws in operation.

The American consumer is paying for this neglect. He pays for it in poor quality, and in potential danger to his health.

In poultry processing plants that are Federally inspected, four percent—over 400 million pounds—of the poultry is rejected because it is diseased and contaminated. There is every reason to believe that the percentage of rejection would be even higher in uninspected plants.

There is no way of knowing how much unwholesome poultry is processed by these plants and passed on to the unsuspecting buyer. But we do know that:

—Conditions in many of these plants are poor and that quality control is far below Federal standards.

—Poultry can be seriously adulterated by impure water and unsanitary processing conditions.

—There is a practice among some poultry producers of sending to uninspected plants inferior poultry flocks which, under Federal inspection, would face rejection.

The housewife receives protection for the poultry that comes from a neighboring state. Why should she not receive the same protection when the poultry is processed and sold in the state where she lives?

I recommend the Wholesome Poultry Products Act of 1968.

This legislation follows the pattern of the Wholesome Meat Act. It will help the States develop their own programs and train inspectors.

At the end of two years, if the States do not have inspection programs at least equal to Federal standards, the Federal inspection requirements will prevail.

In the meantime, the Act will require those intrastate plants which pose a health hazard to clean up or close down.

WHOLESOME FISH

If poultry inspection is spotty today, fish inspection is virtually non-existent.

Each year, Americans consume about two billion pounds of fish—nearly 11 pounds per person. A common item in every family's diet, fish can also be an all-too common carrier of disease if improperly processed and shipped.

Last summer, the Senate Sub-committee on Consumer Affairs heard testimony which disclosed that a substantial amount of the fish sold in this country exposes the consumer to unknown and unnecessary dangers to his health.

It is impossible to show every link between contaminated fish and illness. Yet these links do exist: links to botulism, hepa-

176

titis, and other diseases. About 400 cases of food poisoning, reported on a single weekend in 1966, were traced to fish processed in dirty plants.

Despite these facts, the Nation has no adequate program for continuous fish inspection—either at the Federal or State level. Nor is there any systematic program for inspecting imported fish and fish products, which account for more than 50 percent of our annual consumption.

I propose the Wholesome Fish and Fishery Products Act of 1968.

The bill would authorize the Secretary of Health, Education, and Welfare to:

—Develop a comprehensive Federal program for consumer protection against the health hazards and mislabeling of fish, shellfish and seafood products.

—Set standards and develop continuous inspection and enforcement.

—Support research, training, and inspection programs.

—Help the states develop their own fish inspection programs.

—Assure that imported fish products are wholesome.

RECREATIONAL BOAT SAFETY

Until recently, boats were reserved for commerce, or were owned by the very wealthy. But in our changing pattern of leisure, more and more Americans are taking to the water.

Today, boating has become a major form of recreation, with more than eight million small boats now in operation. Everywhere we see them: on our shores, in our bays, in our lakes, and on our rivers.

In these waters, Americans find rest and relaxation. But some find unexpected tragedy as well.

Last year, boating accidents claimed more than 1,300 lives—about as many as were lost in aircraft accidents.

This problem, as tragic as it is, has not yet reached major national proportions. It has not yet reached the level of automobile accidents, which cost us 53,000 lives annually. But if the Nation had begun its highway safety campaign years ago, there is no way of knowing how many American lives could have been saved. That is all the more reason why we should start now.

I propose the Recreational Boat Safety Act of 1968:

—To help the states establish and improve their own boat safety programs. These programs could include the removal of hazardous debris from our lakes and rivers, boat operators education and licensing, safety patrols and inspections, testing of boats, and accident investigations.

—To authorize the Secretary of Transportation to set and enforce safety standards for boats and equipment.

This program would be directed by the Secretary of Transportation. But its ultimate success will depend on the cooperation of industry, State and local governments, and boat owners themselves.

REPAIRS, WARRANTIES AND GUARANTEES

"I wish I could buy an appliance that would last until I've finished paying for it."

That complaint, familiar to every American housewife, was recently passed on to my Special Assistant for Consumer Affairs. It is a complaint that cannot be ignored.

The products of American industry save us hours of work, and provide unmatched convenience and comfort.

But they can be a source of annoyance and

frustration.

Consumers have no way of knowing how long these products are built to last.

Guarantees and warranties are often meaningless—written in vague and complex language.

Repair work is sometimes excellent, sometimes shoddy, and always a gamble.

These are not problems that can be solved by legislation at this time. But they are problems that need attention now.

The Special Assistant to the President for Consumer Affairs, the Chairman of the Federal Trade Commission, the Secretary of Commerce and the Secretary of Labor will begin work immediately with the industry to:

—Encourage improvements in the quality of service and repairs.

—Assure that warranties and guarantees say what they mean and mean what they say.

—Let the consumer know how long he may expect a product to last if properly used.

—Determine whether federal legislation is needed.

A CONSUMER'S LAWYER

Less than two months after assuming office, I reaffirmed these basic rights of the American consumer:

—The right to safety.

—The right to be fully informed.

—The right to choose.

—The right to be heard.

To give added meaning to these rights, the first Special Presidential Assistant on Consumer Affairs and a Presidential Committee on Consumer Interests were appointed.

I said at the time that the voice of the consumer must be "loud, clear, uncompro-

mising, and effective" in the highest councils of Government.

Now it is time to move closer to that goal. It is time to appoint a lawyer for the consumers.

I plan to appoint a Consumer Counsel at the Justice Department to work directly under the Attorney General and to serve the Special Assistant to the President for Consumer Affairs.

But most important, he will act in the interest of every American consumer.

He will seek better representation for consumer interests before administrative agencies and courts. He will be concerned with the widest range of consumer matters—from quality standards to frauds.

TO PROTECT THE CONSUMER'S DOLLAR

One thing, above all, should be clear to us today. We *can* encourage safety and wholesomeness by law. We *can* curb abuses and fraud.

But all our actions will be in vain if we fail to protect the buying power of every American consumer.

The Nation is now in its 84th month of historic economic growth. More Americans are at work than ever before—earning more, and buying more.

But in the midst of prosperity there are signs of danger: clear and unmistakable signs. Prices are rising faster than they should. Interest rates are climbing—and indeed have passed their peaks of 1966.

A year ago, we asked the Congress for a modest but urgently needed tax increase to curb inflation. That request was repeated last August in a Special Message calling for an average tax of about a penny on a dollar of income.

This is a fair request. Your Government

is asking for only about half of what it returned to the taxpayer in the tax reduction of 1964. A penny on the dollar tax now will be much less painful than the far more burdensome tax of accelerating inflation in the months ahead.

And so today—as part of this consumer message—I again call for action on the tax request.

Business and labor leaders, consumers all, must respond to this Nation's call for restraint and responsibility in their wage-price decisions.

To Advance the Consumer Interest

For 1968, this message proposes eight new steps to advance the consumer interest.

This is not a partisan program or a business program or a labor program. It is a program for *all* of us—all 200 million Americans.

LYNDON B. JOHNSON

The White House
February 6, 1968

NOTE: For the President's remarks upon signing related legislation, see Items 264, 280, 418, 545.

57 Remarks Upon Signing Order Providing for the Coordination by the Attorney General of Federal Law Enforcement and Crime Prevention Programs. *February 7, 1968*

Good morning, ladies and gentlemen, Members of the Congress, Members of the Cabinet:

We have come here this morning to take an action that will result in this Nation really facing up to its major crime problem.

For decades now we have slighted our system of criminal justice. For decades now we have tolerated conditions that nourish crime. And we are paying the price and learning the results:

—Thousands of our young people are labeled with a criminal record while they are still just boys and girls.

—Property that is valued at literally billions of dollars is lost each and every year through crime.

—A dangerous new threat to the health and well-being of all of our young people has arisen right here among us in the form of drug addiction.

—Tens of thousands are killed or injured each year by criminal acts. I heard on the television early this morning that some 53,000 people died in highway accidents last year and a substantial part of those were because of people who were under the influence of alcohol, who should not have been driving at all. Thousands more of our people are afraid to even use our streets and almost everybody who lives in a metropolitan area—particularly our women—feel insecure in their homes.

—Our law enforcement agencies are terribly undermanned.

—Our court system—municipal, State, Federal—is clogged. Our correctional system is poorly equipped.

Now this year—this year—this Year of our Lord 1968, the forces of law and order must capture the initiative in the battle against crime.

We have appointed national commissions of experts who have researched the libraries, heard the testimony and explored the back alleys, but there is one thing that we all agree upon and that we all know—and which has been a fact since this Nation was founded. That is: that the frontline against crime is the statehouse, and is the city hall, and is the police precinct, and is the home.

Now a mayor can talk about what Washington ought to do. And a Governor can talk about States' rights in one speech and a national police force in the other. But all of us know that these laws are made in the States—and generally speaking, they are violated in the States. And in most instances, they must be enforced in the States.

Under our constitutional system, the prevention and the punishment of crime in the streets is committed to our State and to our local governments. There is where the task of securing public order is ultimately, finally, and actually going to be accomplished—if it is accomplished.

Now, this morning I want to repeat again what I have said again and again and again, over and over; that the full resources of the Federal Government are pledged to help in this task. We will supplement these efforts, but we will never supplant them. We are not going to hold out hope that any national police force will ever relieve the local police, the local sheriff, the local constable, the State police, the highway patrol, the local district attorney, or the local judge—because the Congress does not pass the laws on theft or murder or rape or robbery.

Now, I have urged the Congress to do what it could do to supplement the work of the local and State governments in this country. I am asking them to do this year what I hoped they would do last year on the plan we worked up the year before: that is to act—A-C-T—on legislation that we think is needed in this country.

The 90th Congress, I hope, will become— I think it must become—the Congress that gave the American people the security that they demand and the justice they deserve.

Very shortly there will arrive at the Congress a special message from the President on crime. It is not just another Presidential message. It contains the recommendations of experts from both parties and from various branches of Government.

I spent more than an hour last Saturday speaking to distinguished jurists from all over the land. I preceded that with talks with attorneys general from throughout the country. I met with committees from the Governors' Conference. This subject has been discussed and explored and studied and researched with all of them. Now the time has come to act.

This message contains a 22-point specific program of action. Some of it requires legislation. Some requires action by the Attorney General.

The first step is to coordinate the Federal Government's efforts so that each bureau is not running in different directions, like a chicken with its head cut off, and not knowing what they are doing.

Our law enforcement and our crime control efforts are spread throughout this vast system of government. We have some of it in the Treasury, some of it in HEW, some of it in Labor, and HUD, and certainly in poverty—OEO.

And, of course, finally we look to the Department of Justice because there we have the prosecution arm, the legal arm, and there is symbolized the most competent, able, and alert investigative arm that any country has ever produced, in the FBI built by J. Edgar Hoover.

Now, the total of all of these efforts, together with the new programs that we are asking for today, will result in our putting together $550 million—that is more than a half-billion dollars—for the next fiscal year. Now this is an increase of more than 25 percent over last year.

I am going to shortly sign this Executive order which gives the Attorney General, Ramsey Clark, the complete and final authority to coordinate and act in connection with the criminal law activities of all Federal departments, all Federal agencies. He is the "Mr. Big"—the last word on it. I want all of them to understand it and hear it loud and clear.

I want you to understand it, too, and I want him to understand it.

He has the power and the authority—and I believe the ability—to take all these Federal programs and put them together and to coordinate them; to supplement the actions of the State and those who talk about States rights; to supplement the local law enforcement agencies and to work with the crime prevention agencies.

You don't have to remember any name except Clark, Ramsey Clark. You can call him direct if you want any action.

He is setting up a very special office in the Justice Department to carry out this work. We hope this will mean that local law enforcement and all of their agencies will be able to contact a single office in Washington for information, for help, for counsel, for action concerning any supplementary programs that the Federal Government can supply that will help them to do the job that the Constitution placed upon them.

This is the first step in our crime program this year.

We have before us this morning men who have labored long and late in this field for years—Senator McClellan, whose name, like Mr. Hoover's, is known throughout this land as one who has put up a gallant fight against crime; Chairman Celler; the distinguished minority member, Mr. McCulloch here from the State of Ohio; Mr. Dawson; Mr. Holifield; all of these men have pioneered our legislative efforts. They are helping with our reorganization efforts, the Government reorganization.

The Federal Government is all on board, not only in the executive agency, but in the legislative agency. We have had numerous conferences with the Members of the House and with Senator McClellan in the Senate. The last one was last night.

Now this message today outlines the additional steps that the President and the executive branch of the Government think that we must take here and the Congress must take yonder and that must be taken out in our homes and must be taken in our shops and our buses and our subways and our streets.

Americans—of all races—want and deserve better law enforcement. And we intend to give it to them.

It may require some extra effort and it may require some extra money to get more police and better police, to use better methods. But whatever it takes, I am convinced that the average American father and mother will be willing to pay the price until we drive crime from our midst in these United States.

Thank you very much.

[At this point, the President signed the Executive order. He then resumed speaking.]

I just took a small number of these pens this morning because I am going to save most of them to sign that safe streets bill.

We met this week with some of our mayors. We are meeting later this month with all the Governors. They are coming here and the first topic on the agenda is going to be crime and how the States can appoint crime commissions and work with the cities. They can all study their laws, pass whatever new laws they need, and then be sure whatever they pass is enforced.

Then we want to do anything we can to work with them, support them and help them in that effort.

By the time the Governors get here, we hope we will have made substantial progress on our safe streets bill. That will be our primary action this year.

NOTE: The President spoke at 11:24 a.m. in the Cabinet Room at the White House upon signing Executive Order 11396 (4 Weekly Comp. Pres. Docs., p. 232; 33 F.R. 2689; 3 CFR, 1968 Comp., p.

99). During his remarks he referred to, among others, Senator John L. McClellan of Arkansas, and Representatives Emanuel Celler of New York, Chairman of the House Judiciary Committee, William M. McCulloch of Ohio, William L. Dawson of Illinois, and Chet Holifield of California.

For the President's special message to Congress on crime and law enforcement, and for his statement upon signing the Omnibus Crime Control and Safe Streets Act of 1968, see Items 59 and 320.

58   Remarks Upon Announcing Plans for the Rebuilding of the Silver Bridge, West Virginia–Ohio. *February 7, 1968*

Secretary Boyd, Governor Smith, Members of Congress, members of the task force:

I am pleased to announce a Federal-State program for the immediate reconstruction of the bridge between Gallipolis, Ohio, and Point Pleasant, West Virginia. This plan is a splendid example of constructive interaction between the National and State governments that is essential to modern America.

The tragic collapse of the Silver Bridge on December 15 has been a serious blow to this section of Appalachia:

—The bridge was part of a major traffic artery between Columbus and Charleston.

—It was an important economic asset to the whole region of southeast Ohio and northwest West Virginia.

—Its absence is impeding the area's economic development.

—The costs in lost time and extra mileage of detoured traffic amount to more than $1 million a month—all in addition to the direct losses to businesses in the area.

A Federal task force, headed by Secretary Boyd, working with the Governors of the two States, has carefully considered what the loss of this bridge means to the people who need it.

I have accepted their recommendation. We are going to roll up our sleeves and begin

work on a new bridge right away—and we will rush it to completion.

The Appalachian Regional Commission will allocate $2 million from their access road funds. These funds will be administered by the Department of Transportation in cooperation with the two States. The rest of the cost—about $4.5 million—will come from regular highway funds.

We plan an immediate start on both design and construction. New traffic approaches will be built simultaneously with the bridge. The use of modular sections will allow the deck of the new bridge to be built at the same time as the superstructure.

Our objective is to build this bridge in half the normal time. The extra costs of this crash program are justified and outweighed by the daily economic losses caused by the lack of this important traffic link.

This is good news. I am grateful to Secretary Boyd and the members of his task force: Governor Daniel, Secretary Resor, and Chairman Fleming, and to the Appalachian Regional Commission. I especially want to thank Governor Smith of West Virginia and Governor Rhodes of Ohio. I think you all can be proud of a real service to your people.

NOTE: The President spoke at 11:30 a.m. in his office at the White House. In his opening words he referred to Secretary of Transportation Alan S. Boyd and Governor Hulett C. Smith of West Virginia. At the close of his remarks he referred to Price Daniel, Director of the Office of Emergency Planning and former Governor of Texas, Stanley R. Resor, Secretary of the Army, Joe W. Fleming II, Federal Cochairman of the Appalachian Regional Commission, and James Rhodes, Governor of Ohio.

For the President's telegram to the Governors and to Representatives of West Virginia and Ohio following the Silver Bridge collapse, and for his statement upon establishing the task force to study the tragedy and conduct a nationwide bridge safety survey, see 1967 volume, this series, Book II, Items 552 and 558.

As printed above, this item follows the text released by the White House Press Office.

59   Special Message to the Congress on Crime and Law Enforcement: "To Insure the Public Safety." *February 7, 1968*

To the Congress of the United States:

To meet the challenge of crime to our society, I propose the following program of action for our Nation:

For our Governors and Mayors:

1. The Governors of our States and the Mayors of our Cities should examine their local situations—to make certain that they have the necessary laws in effect, that they are committing sufficient resources to their entire systems of criminal justice, and that they have efficient, well-trained and fully supported police departments and law enforcement agencies.

For the Congress and the Executive Branch of the Federal Government:

2. Prompt passage of the Safe Streets and Crime Control Act which I proposed last year.

3. A major Federal assistance program to provide educational opportunities and more training for the Nation's law enforcement personnel.

4. Appropriation of $100 million for the Safe Streets Act in fiscal 1969, double the amount I proposed last year.

5. Passage of the Juvenile Delinquency Prevention Act.

6. Enactment of an Alcoholism Rehabilitation Act, to help provide more effective treatment—rather than simple detention—of alcoholics.

7. Coordination of the Federal anti-crime effort under the Attorney General.

8. Establishment of a strong and unified United States Corrections Service within the Department of Justice.

9. In the fight against drug abuse,

—Legislation to make the illegal manufacture, sale and distribution of LSD and other dangerous drugs a felony, and possession a misdemeanor.

—A more than 30 percent increase in the number of agents enforcing our narcotics and dangerous drug laws.

—That the National Commission on Reform of Federal Criminal Laws undertake immediately a full-scale review of these laws.

—A step-up in our research, education, manpower training and rehabilitation efforts.

—Transfer to the Department of Justice the functions of the Bureau of Narcotics from the Treasury, and the Bureau of Drug Abuse Control from the Department of Health, Education, and Welfare.

10. A felony law aimed at those who cross state lines to incite and take part in riots.

11. In the fight against organized crime, top priority for the Justice Department's

Strike Forces in cities beset by racketeering.

12. New laws to enhance the Federal attack on big-time gambling.

13. Immunity legislation to compel the giving of testimony concerning activities linked with organized crime.

14. Legislation to permit the Government to appeal a pretrial court order granting a motion to suppress evidence.

15. Passage of effective gun control legislation.

16. Funds for 100 additional Assistant U.S. Attorneys in offices throughout the country, 100 additional FBI agents, and an increase in the number of lawyers in the Criminal Division of the Justice Department.

17. A program to develop better law enforcement communications.

18. An intensified effort to develop more modern weapons and equipment for police.

19. A Bank Protection Act.

20. An Auto Theft Prevention Act.

21. That a model crime prevention program be required in each Model Cities plan.

22. A Right of Privacy Act.

The Cost of the Federal Effort

Our total Federal anti-crime effort will require more than one-half billion dollars—some $557 million—in appropriations in the coming year. This is an increase of about 28% above this year's total of $435 million, and almost three times the amount appropriated in 1960.

The Cost of Crime

For decades our system of criminal justice has been neglected. As a result:

—Local law enforcement is undermanned and underpaid.

—Correctional systems are poorly equipped to rehabilitate prisoners.

—Courts at all levels are clogged; procedures are often archaic.

—Local juvenile offender systems—which must deal with increasing numbers of delinquents—are understaffed and largely ineffective.

For decades the conditions that nourish crime have been gathering force. As a result, every major city harbors an army of the alienated—people who acknowledge no stake in public order and no responsibility to others.

Thousands of Americans are killed or injured each year by criminal acts. Many thousands more are unable to use the streets of their cities without fear, or to feel secure in their homes or shops.

Far too many of our youth are saddled with a criminal record early in life, repeat their violations again and again, and find life-long difficulty in obtaining decent employment and social acceptance.

Property valued at almost $4 billion is lost through crime every year. Millions of dollars are taken from the productive economy by organized racketeers—money that should be in the pockets of the poor, or in the bank accounts of honest businessmen.

Drug abuse presents an insidious and growing threat to our nation's health, particularly the health of young people.

These conditions strike at all citizens, regardless of economic status. Neither affluence nor poverty affords protection against crime and violence.

Our Response

In the year just ended, the Federal Government—and some cities and States—made a significant new beginning toward coping with the intolerable costs of crime.

In 1965 I appointed a Commission of the

ablest lawyers, judges, and experts in law enforcement to study every aspect of crime in America. This Commission conducted the most comprehensive review and analysis of crime in our country that has ever been undertaken. We have made this report available to thousands of policemen, criminologists, and city and state officials to assist them in their work against crime. We are already beginning to see the healthy effects of the Commission's research and insights.

Today,

—The Federal organized crime drive is at an all-time high.

—The Department of Justice, through its Office of Law Enforcement Assistance, has helped fund hundreds of valuable projects, from police patrol helicopters to computerized criminal information networks.

—Other Federal agencies are contributing their share to this effort—in such fields as alcoholism control, juvenile delinquency, urban law enforcement planning, narcotics and drug control, prisoner rehabilitation programs and police-community relations.

—Half of our States have established State law enforcement planning commissions to help coordinate statewide efforts.

—Federal, State, and local agencies are sharing knowledge, pooling their resources and experimenting with new techniques and organizations.

—A Federal Judicial Center has been established to revitalize and modernize our Federal court system.

This year America must decisively capture the initiative in the battle against crime.

The major effort must be made by our cities and towns. State Governments must provide maximum support.

For our part, we must strengthen our Federal law enforcement effort to deal promptly, firmly and effectively with those who violate Federal criminal laws and we should assist states and cities in their local efforts.

I pledge my part.

I urge the Congress to do its part.

And most important, I urge the Governors and Mayors to do their part.

The Governors and the Mayors, as well as the Congress and the Executive Branch, must this year reaffirm for the American people the basic principle I stated last year: "Public order is the first business of government."

1. *The Responsibility for Local Law Enforcement.*

The Federal Government must never assume the role of the Nation's policeman. True the Federal Government has certain direct law enforcement responsibilities. But these are carefully limited to such matters as treason, espionage, counterfeiting, tax evasion and certain interstate crimes.

Crime is essentially a local matter. Police operations—if they are to be effective and responsible—must likewise remain basically local. This is the fundamental premise of our constitutional structure and of our heritage of liberty.

The existing pattern of law enforcement makes it clear that local governments must play the primary role in any effective program to combat crime:

—Of the 40,000 law enforcement agencies in the Nation, more than 39,750 are local, while some 200 are State, and the remaining few are Federal.

—Of the 371,000 full-time law enforcement officers in the Nation, 308,000 are local, while only 40,000 are State and 23,000 are Federal.

Under our Constitutional system, the prevention and punishment of crime in the streets is committed to State and local governments. It is essentially the task of mayors and local police, supported by their governors.

Today, I call upon every Mayor and every Governor of our Nation to:

—Examine the local ordinances and state criminal laws to see that they are fair, firm, effective and adapted to the criminal justice problems of the Twentieth Century.

—Review the adequacy of their correctional efforts: not just jails, but detention centers, half-way houses, social services, juvenile delinquency efforts, and well-trained probation and parole officers.

—Examine their judicial systems to make certain there is an adequate number of judges and prosecuting attorneys and that arraignments and trials are promptly held.

—Fully support their local police not only in public statements, but with the funds necessary for adequate salaries, first-rate training and the most modern equipment.

Two years ago—on March 9, 1966—I asked "the Attorney General to work with the Governors of the fifty States to establish statewide committees on law enforcement and criminal justice." Since then 25 States have taken advantage of Federal grants to help establish such statewide commissions: California, Connecticut, Delaware, Florida, Georgia, Illinois, Iowa, Kentucky, Maryland, Massachusetts, Michigan, Minnesota, Mississippi, Missouri, New Jersey, New Mexico, New York, North Dakota, Ohio, Pennsylvania, Rhode Island, Utah, Washington, West Virginia, Wisconsin.

I urge the remaining States to act this year. And I urge the Mayors of our cities to establish their own local crime commissions.

2. *The Safe Streets and Crime Control Act.*

While we reject Federal domination of law enforcement, we recognize that the Federal Government has an inescapable responsibility to help strengthen local law enforcement efforts.

Today, I renew my urgent request to the Congress for immediate passage of the Safe Streets and Crime Control Act which I proposed last year.

This Act is the cornerstone of the Federal anti-crime effort to assist local law enforcement.

It builds upon the fundamental tenets of the Crime Commission's report:

—That crime prevention is a major national priority.

—That better paid, better trained, better equipped police are urgently needed in almost every community.

—That correctional and other law enforcement agencies must have better information on the causes and control of crime.

—That we need substantially more—and more efficiently used—resources and personnel to provide faster action at all levels.

—That the entire system of criminal justice, at every level of government, must be modernized.

The bill I sent to Congress last year emphasizes flexibility and local responsibility. It provides:

—100% grants for research and demonstration projects.

—90% planning grants to State and local governments.

—60% action grants to implement new programs.

—50% construction grants for new facilities.

3. *Federal Assistance for education and training of law enforcement officials.*

Law enforcement means more than putting on a uniform. It means learning about the Constitution, about our laws, about weaponry, about people. It means keeping up to date as our knowledge grows and our techniques and equipment improve. Many local law enforcement agencies cannot now supply the advanced training our men need.

Because this training and education are so essential, I propose that the Safe Streets Bill as originally recommended be amended to:

—Authorize the Federal Bureau of Investigation to expand its training programs for State and local law enforcement personnel, both in the field and at the FBI National Academy at Quantico.

—Provide more substantial financial assistance to State and local law enforcement agencies to develop their own training programs.

—Establish a specific program of fellowships, student loans and tuition aid for State and local law enforcement officers.

—Create a National Institute of Law Enforcement and Criminal Justice to develop a major Federal research program for the application of the most advanced science and technology to law enforcement.

4. *As a measure of this program's urgency, I call on the Congress to appropriate $100 million for the Safe Streets Act in fiscal 1969—double the amount I proposed last year.*

5. *Youth and Delinquency.*

The great majority of our young people—members of the healthiest, the most intelligent and forthright generation this country has ever known—are devoting their energies and idealism to affirmative and useful endeavors. Millions are personally involved in bringing justice, strength and prosperity to America and to the world. In the Armed Forces, in the Peace Corps, in high schools and universities, in the poverty program and in other productive jobs, the youth of America are making a constructive record that is unequaled by any generation of Americans.

But for thousands of others, the years of youth are spoiled by crime:

—Youngsters under 18 accounted for one-fifth of all non-traffic arrests in 1965.

—Those under 24 accounted for half of all those arrested for major crimes of violence—homicide, rape, robbery and assault.

—Three out of four of those arrested for larceny, burglary, and auto theft were under 24.

This problem will not disappear by itself. It will not disappear simply as a consequence of the passage of criminal laws.

No child is born a criminal.

But, we know that children born into certain environments all too often view the policeman—and the civil order he protects—as an enemy, rather than as a protector. Many parents fail to impart to their children that respect for lawful and just authority on which a decent society depends. Thousands of these early, individual failures later become parts of a national tragedy.

In the past few years, we have devoted immense resources to education, job training, urban planning and rehabilitation and civil rights.

But these efforts are not enough. We need a more direct and immediate effort to deal with juvenile delinquency at the local level.

I urge the Congress to pass the Juvenile Delinquency Prevention Act that I proposed last year. This Act would:

—Authorize $25 million in assistance to State and local agencies in the first year to develop new plans, programs, and special facilities to deal with youthful offenders.

—Encourage the development of new community correctional programs which avoid the stigma and isolation that often follow prison experience.

—Help local authorities deal with delinquents effectively in terms of their individual needs, and avoid, whenever possible, separating young offenders from their families and from the society they will rejoin.

—Develop a greater range of alternatives to jail—for example, half-way houses, youth rehabilitation centers and family-type group homes.

Young Americans are our Nation's most valuable and valued resource. No loss is greater than when a youth—with the world before him—is cast into adulthood as a marked criminal. The health of our Nation requires a determined effort to master the problem of delinquency. But we must never forget that there is—as there should be—a limit to the extent to which public efforts can properly affect private lives. Neither the Executive nor the Congress— nor the policeman nor the youth worker— can substitute for parents. In their hands lie the ultimate responsibility.

6. *Alcoholism.*

Alcoholism is tragically high on the list of our Nation's health problems.

Five million Americans are alcoholics. They bring incalculable grief to millions of families. They cost their families, their employers and society billions of dollars.

While alcoholism is essentially a medical problem, it is also a problem of law enforcement. The local policeman—not the doctor— is usually the first point of contact between society and the public drunk, the intoxi-

cated driver or the down-and-out derelict.

Alcoholics and heavy drinkers overburden our law enforcement and judicial systems:

—There are currently about two million arrests each year for drunkenness— nearly one-third of all arrests.

—Excessive drinking plays a part in nearly half of all fatal traffic accidents.

—Local police and courts spend a disproportionate amount of time and effort on what is essentially a medical problem—time that should better be spent dealing with serious offenses.

—A large percentage of all inmates in short-term correctional institutions are there solely because of public intoxication and related minor offenses.

Yet these crowded institutions generally provide no services or programs to treat them. In virtually all our communities, alcoholics receive less adequate care than other sick people.

The Department of Health, Education, and Welfare is now engaged in a major program dealing with the causes and treatment of alcoholism. I recommend that the Congress strengthen this program with appropriations next year of $13.4 million in fiscal 1969.

To deal with the alcoholic whose behavior brings him into contact with the law, I propose the Alcoholic Rehabilitation Act of 1968. This Act would provide Federal leadership and assistance to States and localities in developing non-jail alternatives for the handling of alcoholics.

THE FEDERAL EFFORT

The Federal Government must have the tools it needs to become a more effective instrument in the war on crime: stronger laws, more personnel, and more resources.

7. Coordination.

The first step in an accelerated Federal anti-crime drive is better coordination. Our efforts must not be dissipated. Responsibility must not be fragmented.

At the present time, a large number of Federal agencies play a significant role both in front-line enforcement, and in programs to aid State and local agencies. The resources and experience of many different departments and agencies are needed in this effort. But, there must be a control room for Federal action.

Today I am acting in several ways to provide this coordination, and to mobilize the agencies of Government that participate in the work of fighting crime.

I signed this morning an Executive Order designating the Attorney General to:

—*Coordinate the criminal law enforcement activities of all Federal Departments and agencies,*

—*Coordinate all Federal programs that assist State and local law enforcement and crime prevention activities.*

The Attorney General will establish a special office in the Justice Department to carry out this critical work.

State and local law enforcement agencies will now have a single office in Washington to contact for information concerning all Federal programs which may affect them. These include projects as varied as:

—The Labor Department's training programs for sub-professionals in police and court work.

—Juvenile delinquency and alcoholism prevention efforts of the Department of Health, Education, and Welfare.

—The Department of Housing and Urban Development's planning and other assistance programs that affect law enforcement.

—The police-community relations programs in the Office of Economic Opportunity.

The Attorney General will not operate these programs. He will coordinate them and issue guidelines to ensure that they make the maximum impact in meeting the Nation's public safety needs.

8. Strengthened and Unified Corrections.

The apprehension and conviction of a criminal is doomed to ultimate futility if we do not deal effectively with him while he is in the hands of the law.

Our correctional system serves two primary functions. It protects the public through the detention or close supervision of convicted offenders. It also seeks to return them to a productive life through education, training, and other programs.

The number of released offenders who subsequently revert to a life of crime is disturbingly large. The Crime Commission estimated that about one-third of released criminals return to prison within five years.

The task of supervising hardened criminals, and of repairing and strengthening lives is difficult, and often unappreciated. This work requires highly trained personnel and carefully-supervised programs of parole and probation.

Today the Nation's correctional system is undermanned and underequipped. We must make it a strong arm in our total effort to protect the public from crime.

To achieve substantial improvements in this long-neglected area, I ask the Congress to increase the program funds available to the Bureau of Prisons by $3 million.

The Federal Government has developed a system of institutions and services—penitentiaries, reformatories, youth centers, parole and probation—to protect society and to lead violators to more worthwhile lives.

Yet our correctional system is fragmented. The courts supervise parole and probation, while the Executive Branch administers the prisons.

This division of responsibility impedes our efforts to build a strong and effective correctional system. We need a single, unified organization to coordinate the prison personnel who are responsible for the treatment of prisoners and the community personnel who supervise their parole.

I again ask the Congress to unify this system by establishing a United States Corrections Service within the Department of Justice.

9. *Narcotics and Drugs.*

In no area of law enforcement is there a greater need for a concentrated drive than in dealing with the growing problem of narcotics and dangerous drugs.

These powders and pills threaten our Nation's health, vitality, and self-respect.

Heroin addiction is largely an urban problem, focused in slum areas. But hallucinogens, such as marihuana and LSD (Lysergic Acid Diethylamide) have spread to suburban and rural regions, and are taken by far too many American youths. The improper use of dangerous drugs—barbiturates, pep pills, speed, other amphetamines—cuts across all segments of the population.

The present Federal laws dealing with these substances are a crazy quilt of inconsistent approaches and widely disparate criminal sanctions. Responsibility for their administration is found in no single Department of the Federal Government.

The Department of the Treasury, through the Bureau of Narcotics, is responsible for narcotics and marihuana enforcement—because historically jurisdiction in that area was based on the taxing power of the Federal Government. This Bureau has only about 300

agents for the United States and all its foreign operations.

The Department of Health, Education, and Welfare enforces the dangerous drug laws through its Bureau of Drug Abuse Control, which has only about 300 agents.

Penalties for improper use of these substances are inconsistent—and in the dangerous drug field, too weak.

The illegal sale of LSD, a powerful hallucinogen, is only a misdemeanor punishable by a maximum prison term of one year for the first offense. There is no penalty at present for possession of LSD for personal use.

Possession of marihuana, another hallucinogen, is punishable by a minimum term of two years and a maximum of ten for the first offense. Illegal sale is punishable by a minimum of five years.

These inconsistencies have seriously hampered law enforcement—for drug and narcotics peddlers do not observe bureaucratic niceties. More than 90% of seizures of LSD made by the Bureau of Drug Abuse Control have also turned up marihuana—but that Bureau is not authorized to make arrests for illegal trafficking in marihuana.

We can no longer deal with this major problem in a haphazard way. We must mobilize now to halt the growing trade in harmful narcotics and drugs.

I propose that the Congress immediately:

—Enact legislation to make the illegal manufacture, sale or distribution of LSD and other dangerous drugs a felony and the illegal possession of these drugs a misdemeanor.

—Provide funds to increase the number of Federal narcotics and dangerous drug agents by more than one-third.

In addition, I am requesting:

—The National Commission on Reform of the Federal Criminal Laws—an expert and distinguished Commission established by Congress last year—to give its immediate attention to a review of all our narcotics and drug abuse laws, and to recommend a balanced and consistent approach to this problem as soon as possible.

—The Secretary of Health, Education, and Welfare to increase the activities of his Department in the area of rehabilitation of drug addicts, and in alerting young people to the threat addiction poses to their lives.

Finally, and most important, I am today transmitting to the Congress a reorganization plan to transfer the functions of the Bureau of Narcotics and the Bureau of Drug Abuse Control to the Department of Justice.

There, in a new Bureau of Narcotics and Dangerous Drugs, these functions can work together with greater effectiveness and efficiency. This step implements the recommendation of the Hoover Commission of 1949, and of the 1963 Presidential Advisory Commission on Narcotics and Drug Abuse.

The new Bureau of Narcotics and Dangerous Drugs would be in a strong position to:

—Use the experienced manpower of the two existing Bureaus more efficiently by avoiding duplicating and overlapping investigations,

—Economize by consolidating regional offices,

—Provide a single channel of communications with State, local and foreign narcotic control authorities, and

—Improve liaison with the Organized Crime Section of the Department of Justice, and thus strike at an important aspect of organized crime—the illegal drug trade.

10. *Riot Control.*

Last summer many of our cities were shaken by disorders that cost scores of lives and millions of dollars in damage.

All Americans have thought about and discussed the causes of this national tragedy. We know the answers are complex. For this reason, I appointed, last August, a National Advisory Commission on Civil Disorders, and charged its members with three questions:

"What happened?"

"Why did it happen?"

"What can be done to prevent its happening again and again?"

We await their report and recommendations.

But there is no need to wait before protecting society against those who would tear it apart for whatever purpose.

I propose the Federal Anti-Riot Act of 1968.

This new law will make it a felony, punishable by up to 5 years in prison, for any person to incite or organize a riot after having traveled in interstate commerce with the intention to do so.

This is a narrow and carefully drawn bill. It does not impede free speech or peaceful assembly.

It is not a solution to our urban problems. But it does give the Federal Government the power to act against those who might move around the country, inciting and joining in the terror of riots.

This bill does not involve the Federal Government in dealing with disturbances that are locally incited and properly a matter for State and local authorities.

I urge those authorities—the Governors and Mayors of this Nation—to review carefully their State and local anti-riot laws to make certain they provide effective protec-

tion for their citizens.

This new law should be coupled with the Federal Firearms Bill. Both seek a common end—to reduce crime and disorder in our cities by restricting the interstate movement of two causes of death and destruction—the criminal agitator and the gun.

11. *Organized Crime.*

Organized crime is big business in America.

Its sinister effect pervades too many corners of America today—through gambling, loan sharking, corruption, extortion, and large movements of narcotics.

The Crime Commission reported:

"Organized crime is a society that seeks to operate outside the control of the American people and their governments. It involves thousands of criminals, working within structures as complex as those of any large corporation, subject to laws more rigidly enforced than those of legitimate governments. Its actions are not impulsive, but rather the result of intricate conspiracies, carried on over many years and aimed at gaining control over whole fields of activity in order to amass huge profits."

These conspiracies have taken over legitimate businesses. They have attempted to invade the councils of our cities.

It is clear that sporadic, isolated, uncoordinated attacks on this disciplined army of the underworld cannot obtain lasting results. Organized crime can be defeated only by organized law enforcement.

Under the direction of the Organized Crime and Racketeering Section of the Department of Justice, a "Strike Force" program has recently been initiated. Experienced investigators and attorneys from several Federal departments and agencies work together in a campaign concentrated on a single, organized criminal syndicate in a particular geographic area.

Strike Force Number One, centered in a large northern city, used skilled investigators from the Bureau of Narcotics, the Customs Bureau, the Secret Service, the Department of Labor, and Internal Revenue Service and the Federal Bureau of Investigation. This Strike Force, in cooperation with Canadian and local officials, was responsible last year for Federal indictments of 25 underworld figures.

Additional strike forces are now being formed. Within the next few months they will be moved, without public notice, into several parts of the Nation where organized crime now flourishes.

I have directed the Attorney General and this Government's law enforcement agencies to give this program the highest priority. Funds are included in my budget to support these additional Strike Forces.

STRONGER CRIMINAL LAWS

12. *Gambling Laws.*

Gambling provides the major source of revenue for organized crime. It is vital that the Government have statutory means to play a leading role in striking at illegal gambling activities.

The federal wagering tax produces needed revenue for the Federal Government from a source that is highly appropriate as long as illegal gambling flourishes. It is important that this tax, imposed by the Congress, be collected efficiently, and without infringing the constitutional rights of taxpayers.

I recommend that our gambling laws be strengthened this year.

First, we should broaden the law to make it a Federal crime to engage in gambling as a substantial business affecting interstate commerce.

Second, the Federal Wagering statute should be modified to preserve this valuable taxing authority in a form that does not raise constitutional problems.

These legislative proposals will be sent to the Congress shortly. *I urge their prompt consideration.*

13. *Immunity Legislation.*

Last year I requested immunity legislation to compel the giving of testimony concerning activities having strong links with organized crime. This kind of authority has proven its value in the past, but its current scope is limited. *I renew my proposal that immunity legislation be extended to the Racketeering Travel Act, to the Obstruction of Justice statute, to the criminal bankruptcy law, and to matters involving bribery, graft, and conflict of interest.*

14. *Effective Prosecution.*

Today, the prosecution in a Federal criminal case cannot appeal when a District Court grants a pre-trial motion to suppress evidence. In many cases, the suppression of that evidence may effectively terminate the prosecution.

The House of Representatives has enacted legislation authorizing the Government to appeal such orders when they believe an appeal is justified.

I ask the Senate to pass this legislation promptly.

15. *Gun Control.*

We cannot control crime without controlling the random and wanton distribution of guns.

There is little need to restate the arguments for taking this action. We must stop what amounts to mail order murder.

Newspapers and radios proclaim each day the tragic toll of death and injury caused by firearms. An estimated 750,000 Americans have died by this means since 1900—far more than have died at the hands of all our enemies in all the wars we have fought.

Once again I urge the Congress to enact the bill I proposed last year to:

—*Prohibit interstate mail order sales and shipments of firearms, except between Federal licensees.*

—*Prohibit over-the-counter sales of handguns to out-of-state purchasers.*

—*Regulate the sale of firearms to minors.*

—*Further regulate the importation of firearms into this country.*

As I said one year ago:

"This legislation will not curtail ownership of firearms used either for sport or self-protection. But it will place a valuable restraint on random trade in handguns—the use of which has more and more characterized burglaries and other crimes."

We know the facts. Failure to act upon them is irresponsible.

NEW STRENGTH FOR LAW ENFORCEMENT

16. *Additional Federal Anti-Crime Officials.*

Since 1960, the pending criminal caseload in the Federal system has increased by 90%. The total number of grand jury proceedings has grown by 31%. The total number of appeals has grown by 133%. During this period the number of District Court judges increased by 40%.

But the total number of Assistant United States Attorneys—the men throughout the country who bring the people's cases to court—increased by only 16%.

I am requesting the Congress to provide funds to enable us to add 100 additional Assistant U.S. Attorneys in offices around the country.

I am also requesting funds for more than 100 additional agents for the Federal Bureau of Investigation, and for a substantial increase in the number of lawyers for the Criminal Division of the Justice Department.

EFFECTIVE CRIME CONTROL IN AN AGE OF TECHNOLOGY

At its heart, the law enforcement problem has always been—and will remain—a human problem. Wretched living conditions produced high crime rates a century ago in immigrant neighborhoods. Today, slum conditions are producing equally serious crime problems among the new immigrants to our cities.

We have dedicated ourselves to change those conditions—and we shall.

But our responsibilities require us to find more immediate solutions to the rising crime rate, that will help us maintain order while we build better foundations for urban life.

17. *Improved law enforcement communications.*

The Crime Commission Report showed that the ability of the police to make an arrest often depends upon the time within which affected citizens contact them, the speed with which radio messages can be transmitted, and the response time of neighborhood police.

In spite of our advanced technological knowledge and capacities, it often takes many minutes for help to reach a citizen. Further, communications facilities for essential emergency services in many metropolitan areas are over-crowded and out of date.

To implement a four-point program to improve law enforcement communications:

— I am instructing the Attorney General to cooperate with the Federal Communications Commission, local law enforcement authorities, and the telephone companies to develop methods to make the ordinary telephone more effective for summoning police aid in times of emergency. Such a step, recommended by the Crime Commission, was recently endorsed by the largest telephone company in the Nation.

— I have requested the Federal Communications Commission to give the highest priority in the allocation of new radio channels to police and other emergency services in our largest cities.

— I am asking the Presidential Task Force on Communications Policy, established last August, to undertake a study to determine the total public safety radio-communications requirements and present capabilities in selected metropolitan areas.

— I am directing the Attorney General and the Secretary of Defense to develop a prototype, low-cost, light-weight personnel radio, which can be used by patrolmen throughout the Nation.

18. *Modern Weapons and Equipment.*

Revolvers and nightsticks are clearly inadequate for the many different crises faced by the police. New weapons and chemicals—effective but causing no permanent injury—have been and are being developed.

But too little is now known about their potential to preserve order while protecting lives. Too little is known about their limitations.

I am instructing the Director of the Office of Science and Technology, working with the Attorney General and law enforcement officials, to study these new weapons and chemicals and other new techniques in crime control. The results of this study will be made available to enforcement agencies throughout the country.

19. *Bank Protection.*

We must bring modern crime detection and protective equipment into our banks.

Robberies of financial institutions have

increased continuously in the past decade.

In 1955 there were 526 robberies committed against financial institutions protected by Federal law. In 1966 there were 1,871 such offenses—an increase of about 250%.

Silent alarms and camera systems now exist that can both deter these crimes and aid in investigation and prosecution. Yet many financial institutions have not yet installed them.

I urge the Congress to enact a Bank Protection Act of 1968, to direct those Federal agencies with responsibilities for banks and savings and loan institutions to issue regulations requiring the installation, maintenance, and operation of appropriate protective systems.

20. *Auto Theft Prevention.*

We must reduce the great number of automobiles that are stolen each year.

Auto theft is the third most frequent, and the second most costly crime in America.

It is a crime that involves the young. Over 60% of all auto thefts are committed by persons under the age of 18. This is often the first step in a life of crime—a first step that might be easily prevented.

A principal device in auto theft is the so-called "master key," which can be used to start a car's ignition. These keys are advertised. They can be ordered by mail.

I propose the Auto Theft Prevention Act of 1968, to prohibit the advertisement, mailing and shipment in interstate commerce of motor vehicle master keys and information and devices from which such keys can be made.

This Act, together with auto safety regulations proposed by the Secretary of Transportation—which would require anti-theft devices to be included in automobiles manufactured after December 31, 1969—should help counter the rising rate of auto thefts. Some of our automobile manufacturers have already announced plans to include such devices in future models.

21. *Model Precincts.*

We must take advantage of our Model Cities program—the most comprehensive urban development program this country has ever undertaken—to promote the goal of effective law enforcement.

The Model Cities program gives us an opportunity to plan ahead for law enforcement in a new environment. Many cities have begun to do so.

I am directing the Secretary of Housing and Urban Development, in cooperation with the Attorney General, to require each of the 63 cities now included within the Model Cities program, as well as any new grantees, to include within its total program a well-designed system for crime prevention and control. These could include such items as:

—Establishment of model precincts.

—Improvement of police-community relations.

—Creation of effective recruitment and training centers.

—New programs for youthful offenders.

The Model Cities program gives us an opportunity to create safe streets in safe neighborhoods through more effective crime prevention and law enforcement systems. We must seize that opportunity.

22. *Right to Privacy.*

We must protect the American people against a new threat to one of our oldest and most precious rights—the right of personal privacy.

The principle that a man's home is his castle is under new attack. For centuries the law of trespass protected a man's lands and his home. But in this age of advanced technology, thick walls and locked doors cannot guard our privacy or safeguard our personal freedom. Today we need a strong law—suited to modern conditions—to protect us from those who would trespass upon our conversations.

Last year I recommended to the Congress the Right of Privacy Act. *I urge the Congress to enact this legislation this year.*

CRIME CONTROL—A TASK FOR ALL AMERICANS

This 22-point program will, if adopted and put fully into practice, make the conditions of life for most law-abiding citizens safer, and thus freer and happier.

But in implementing it we must remain aware of its limitations, as well as its goals:

It is not a substitute for action by local law enforcement officials. The job of law enforcement—the basic responsibility—is for the local police, the local mayor, the city council, in short the people of our towns and cities.

It is not an answer to the frustrations of many young people. But it will help to steer thousands of young offenders to more productive lives.

It is not a solution to the illnesses of alcoholism and drug addiction. But it will enable us to deal with them more effectively.

It is not an answer to the blight of our cities and suburbs. But it will help to make our metropolitan areas more livable.

It does not establish a national police force, but it will help enable the Federal government to do its part well.

The Nation needs vigorous and substantial programs to meet the challenge of crime on all levels of Government—but most importantly at the local level where it affects us all most immediately and most directly.

There are some who view the crime problem in racial terms. The facts belie this. Crime affects all Americans. It is not a problem of rich against poor or white against Negro, because the hard facts show that crime victimizes most severely and most directly those in poverty and those in minority groups.

No people need or want effective and fair law enforcement more than those who live in our crowded inner cities.

For all Americans we must improve and strengthen our law enforcement system.

Speeches and strong words and good intentions will not solve our Nation's crime problem.

This message will not solve our Nation's crime problem.

Only action will be effective to control crime in the cities and states of our country: action at the local level, action at the state level and action by the Congress of the United States.

Today I pledge the resources of the Federal Government to support the governors and mayors of our Nation in an all-out war against crime.

I urge the Congress to join with me by passing the legislation I have recommended in this message.

LYNDON B. JOHNSON

The White House
February 7, 1968

NOTE: For statements or remarks upon signing related legislation, see Items 320, 424, 553, 561.

Other related legislation was approved by the President as follows: a bill to authorize the Bureau of Prisons to assist State and local governments in the improvement of their correctional systems, July 1, 1968 (Public Law 90-371, 82 Stat. 280); the District of Columbia Alcoholics Rehabilitation Act, August 3, 1968 (Public Law 90-452, 82 Stat. 618); an amendment to the Omnibus Crime Control and Safe Streets Act of 1968 relating to admissibility in evidence of confessions and eyewitness testimony, August 8, 1968 (Public Law 90-462, 82 Stat. 638).

The "Report of the National Advisory Commission on Civil Disorders" is dated March 1, 1968 (Government Printing Office, 425 pp.).

For remarks of the President upon signing Executive Order 11396 relating to coordination of Federal law enforcement and crime prevention programs by the Attorney General, see Item 57.

See also Item 60.

60 Special Message to the Congress Transmitting Reorganization Plan 1 of 1968 Relating to Narcotics and Drug Abuse Control. *February 7, 1968*

To the Congress of the United States:

In my first Reorganization Plan of 1968, I call for the creation of a new and powerful Bureau of Narcotics and Dangerous Drugs.

With this action, America will serve notice to the pusher and the peddler that their criminal acts must stop.

No matter how well organized they are, we will be better organized. No matter how well they have concealed their activities, we will root them out.

Today, Federal investigation and enforcement of our narcotics laws are fragmented. One major element—the Bureau of Narcotics—is in the Treasury Department and responsible for the control of marihuana and narcotics such as heroin. Another—the Bureau of Drug Abuse Control—is in the Department of Health, Education, and Welfare, and is responsible for the control of dangerous drugs including depressants, stimulants, and hallucinogens such as LSD.

Neither is located in the agency which is primarily concerned with Federal law enforcement—the Department of Justice.

This separation of responsibilities—despite the relentless and dedicated efforts of the agents of each Bureau—has complicated and hindered our response to a national menace.

For example, more than nine out of ten seizures of LSD made by the Bureau of Drug Abuse Control have also turned up marihuana—but that Bureau has no jurisdiction over marihuana.

In many instances, we are confronted by well organized, disciplined and resourceful criminals who reap huge profits at the expense of their unfortunate victims.

The response of the Federal Government must be unified. And it must be total.

Today, in my Message on Crime, I recommended strong new laws to control dangerous drugs. I also recommended an increase of more than thirty percent in the number of Federal agents enforcing the narcotic and dangerous drug laws.

I now propose that a single Bureau of Narcotics and Dangerous Drugs be established in the Department of Justice to administer those laws and to bring to the American people the most efficient and effective Federal enforcement machinery we can devise.

Under this Reorganization Plan the Attorney General will have full authority and responsibility for enforcing the Federal laws relating to narcotics and dangerous drugs. The new Bureau of Narcotics and Dangerous Drugs, to be headed by a Director appointed by the Attorney General, will:

—consolidate the authority and preserve the experience and manpower of the Bureau of Narcotics and the Bureau of Drug Abuse Control.

—work with states and local governments in their crackdown on illegal trade in drugs and narcotics, and help to train local agents and investigators.

—maintain worldwide operations, working closely with other nations, to suppress the trade in illicit narcotics and marihuana.

—conduct an extensive campaign of research and a nationwide public education program on drug abuse and its tragic effects.

The Plan I forward today moves in the direction recommended by two distinguished groups:

—the 1949 Hoover Commission.
—the 1963 Presidential Advisory Commission on Narcotic and Drug Abuse.

This Administration and this Congress have the will and the determination to stop the illicit traffic in drugs.

But we need more than the will and the determination. We need a modern and efficient instrument of Government to transform our plans into action. That is what this Reorganization Plan calls for.

The Plan has been prepared in accordance with chapter 9 of title 5 of the United States Code.

I have found, after investigation, that each reorganization included in the plan is necessary to accomplish one or more of the purposes set forth in section 901(a) of title 5 of the United States Code.

I have also found that, by reason of these reorganizations, it is necessary to include in the accompanying plan provisions for the appointment and compensation of the five new positions as specified in section 3 of the plan. The rates of compensation fixed for these new positions are those which I have found to prevail in respect of comparable positions in the Executive Branch of the Government.

Should the reorganization I propose take effect, they will make possible more effective and efficient administration of Federal law enforcement functions. It is not practicable at this time, however, to itemize the reduction in expenditures which may result.

I recommend that the Congress allow this urgently needed and important Reorganization Plan to become effective.

LYNDON B. JOHNSON

The White House
February 7, 1968

NOTE: Reorganization Plan 1 of 1968 is printed in the Weekly Compilation of Presidential Documents, the Federal Register, and Title 3 of the Code of Federal Regulations (4 Weekly Comp. Pres. Docs., p. 250; 33 F.R. 5611; 3 CFR, 1968 Comp., p. 149). It became effective on April 8, 1968.

---

61 Statement by the President on Appointing New Members of the National Council on the Humanities. *February 7, 1968*

IT IS gratifying to know that these distinguished Americans will serve the National Endowment for the Humanities in its effort to achieve educational and public goals of great importance to all our people. In the 2 short years of its existence, the Endowment has affected many diverse groups in the country. Children from inner-city schools are participating in summer enrichment programs. Men and women are receiving encouragement to further their interest in the history of their communities and States. Grants enable scholars to discover and interpret America's past, and permit young college teachers to pursue important research. Valuable programs such as these can only be identified and supported with the thoughtful guidance of the National Council on the Humanities. These new members will, I am confident, continue the excellent work of their predecessors.

NOTE: The President's statement was made public as part of a White House release listing nine newly appointed members of the National Council on the Humanities, which meets quarterly as an advisory board to the National Endowment for the Humanities. The two bodies were established on September 29, 1965, by the National Foundation on the Arts and the Humanities Act of 1965 (Public Law 89–209, 79 Stat. 845) in order to promote public understanding and appreciation of the humanities, and in that connection to award fellowships and grants to institutions and to support the publication of scholarly works on the humanities.

The text of the release, which lists outgoing and continuing as well as newly appointed members of the Council, is printed in the Weekly Compilation of Presidential Documents (vol. 4, p. 252).

62 Joint Statement Following Discussions With the President of the Commission of the European Communities. *February 7, 1968*

THE PRESIDENT and Mr. Jean Rey, President of the Commission of the European Communities, met at the White House on February 7. During his visit to Washington, Mr. Rey, accompanied by Vice President Hellwig and Commissioner Deniau, is also meeting with the Vice President, the Secretary of State, and other Cabinet and sub-Cabinet officials.

The President and Mr. Rey confirmed their belief in the need for continued progress toward the unity of Europe. The President reaffirmed the support of the United States for the progress of the European Communities. A strong and democratic Western Europe working as an equal partner with the United States would help to build a peaceful, prosperous and just world order. Both the United States and the European Communities recognize their responsibilities to the developing countries in expanding export earnings and development.

The President reviewed his balance of payments program with Mr. Rey and emphasized the firm intention of the United States to take the necessary action to restore equilib-

rium. The President and Mr. Rey recognized the need for both surplus and deficit countries to continue and intensify their individual and common efforts to achieve a better equilibrium in the international balance of payments.

The closest cooperation between the United States and the European Communities is necessary to ensure that international adjustment takes place under conditions of continued economic growth with financial stability. In particular, they agreed that the achievements of the Kennedy Round must be preserved, that protectionist measures should be avoided and that further progress should be made in the elimination of barriers to trade.

Mr. Rey told the President of his satisfaction with a meeting held on February 7 between his party and senior officials of the United States Government on matters of common concern pertaining to the economic interrelationship of Europe and the United States. The President and Mr. Rey agreed similar high level consultations would be useful in the future.

63 Special Message to the Congress on the Foreign Assistance Programs: "To Build the Peace." *February 8, 1968*

To the Congress of the United States:

Peace will never be secure so long as:

—Seven out of ten people on earth cannot read or write;

—Tens of millions of people each day— most of them children—are maimed and stunted by malnutrition.

—Diseases long conquered by science still

ravage cities and villages around the world.

If most men can look forward to nothing more than a lifetime of backbreaking toil which only preserves their misery, violence will always beckon, freedom will ever be under siege.

It is only when peace offers hope for a better life that it attracts the hundreds of millions around the world who live in the shadow of despair.

Twenty years ago America resolved to lead the world against the destructive power of man's oldest enemies. We declared war on the hunger, the ignorance, the disease, and the hopelessness which breed violence in human affairs.

We knew then that the job would take many years. We knew then that many trials and many disappointments would test our will.

But we also knew that, in the long run, a single ray of hope—a school, a road, a hybrid seed, a vaccination—can do more to build the peace and guard America from harm than guns and bombs.

This is the great truth upon which all our foreign aid programs are founded. It was valid in 1948 when we helped Greece and Turkey maintain their independence. It was valid in the early fifties when the Marshall Plan helped rebuild a ruined Western Europe into a showcase of freedom. It was valid in the sixties when we helped Taiwan and Iran and Israel take their places in the ranks of free nations able to defend their own independence and moving toward prosperity on their own.

The programs I propose today are as important and as essential to the security of this nation as our military defenses. Victory on the battlefield must be matched by victory in the peaceful struggles which shape men's minds.

In these fateful years, we must not falter. In these decisive times, we dare not fail.

No Retreat, No Waste

The foreign aid program for fiscal 1969 is designed to foster our fundamental American purpose: To help root out the causes of conflict and thus ensure our own security in a peaceful community of nations.

For Fiscal 1969, I propose:

—*An economic aid appropriation of $2.5 billion.*

—*A military grant aid appropriation of $420 million.*

—*New and separate legislation for foreign military sales.*

—*A five-year program to develop and manufacture low-cost protein additives from fish, to help avoid the tragic brain damage now inflicted on millions of children because of malnutrition in their early years.*

—*That the United States join with other nations to expand the International Development Association, the development-lending affiliate of the World Bank. For every two dollars the United States contributes, other nations will contribute three dollars.*

—*That the Congress authorize a contribution to new Special Funds of the Asian Development Bank.*

—*Prompt appropriation of the annual contribution to the Fund for Special Operations of the Inter-American Development Bank.*

—*A further authorization and appropriation of callable funds for the Inter-American Development Bank to stand behind the Bank's borrowing in private money markets.*

200

Common Effort for Common Good

I pledge to the Congress and to the people of America that these programs will be carried out with strict attention to the six basic principles of foreign aid administration we announced last year.

1. *Self-Help*

Self-help is the fundamental condition for all American aid. We will continue to insist on several dollars of local investment for every dollar of American investment. We will help those—and only those—who help themselves. We will not tolerate waste and mismanagement.

2. *Multilateralism*

This year, 90 percent of our AID loans will be made as part of international arrangements in which donors and recipients alike carry their fair shares of the common burden.

America now ranks fifth among donor countries in terms of the share of its national product devoted to official foreign aid. Japan increased her aid by nearly 50 percent last year. Germany has increased her aid budget despite fiscal restraints which have curtailed domestic welfare programs. Great Britain is maintaining aid levels despite severe financial problems. With the signing of the International Grains Agreement, other wealthy nations will for the first time be obligated to contribute food and money to the world-wide war on hunger.

This year we must take another important step to sustain those international institutions which build the peace.

The International Development Association, the World Bank's concessional lending affiliate is almost without funds. Discussions to provide the needed capital and balance of payments safeguards are now underway. We hope that these talks will soon result in agreements among the wealthy nations of the world to continue the critical work of the Association in the developing countries. The Administration will transmit specific legislation promptly upon completion of these discussions. I urge the Congress to give it full support.

3. *Regionalism*

Last year I joined with the Latin American Presidents to renew, reaffirm and redirect the Alliance for Progress.

The nations of free Asia began a general survey of their joint transportation and education needs, while work proceeded on projects to bring power, water and the other tools of progress to all.

The African Development Bank, financed entirely by Africans, opened its doors and made its first loan.

The coming year will present three major opportunities for the United States to add new momentum to these regional efforts:

A. *The Inter-American Development Bank.*

This Bank stands at the center of the Alliance for Progress. Last year, the Congress authorized three annual contributions of $300 million each to the Bank's Fund for Special Operations. The second of these contributions should be appropriated this year.

The Ordinary Capital of the Bank, which comes mainly from sales of its bonds in the private market, must now be expanded. Since 1960, we have appropriated $612 million which is kept in the U.S. Treasury to guarantee these bonds. Not *one* dollar of this money has ever been spent, but this guarantee has enabled the bank to raise $612 million from private sources for worthy projects. We must extend this proud record. *I urge the Congress to authorize $412 million in* *callable funds, of which $206 million will be needed this year.*

B. *The Asian Development Bank.*

This Bank has asked the United States, Japan, and other donors to help establish Special Funds for projects of regional significance—in agriculture, education, transportation and other fields. Last October I requested that the Congress authorize a United States contribution of up to $200 million. This would be paid over a four year period—only if it were a minority share of the total fund, and if it did not adversely affect our balance of payments. *I urge that the Congress take prompt and favorable action on this request.*

C. *The African Development Bank.*

This Bank has also asked for our help to establish a small Special Fund for projects which cannot or should not be financed through the Bank's Ordinary Capital. *We must stand ready to provide our fair share, with full safeguards for our balance of payments.*

4. *Priority for Agriculture and Population Planning*

Victory in the war on hunger is as important to every human being as any achievement in the history of mankind.

The report of 100 experts assembled last year by the President's Science Advisory Committee on the World Food Supply rings with grim clarity. Their message is clear: The world has entered a food-population crisis. Unless the rich and the poor nations join in a long-range, innovative effort unprecedented in human affairs, this crisis will reach disastrous proportions by the mid-1980's.

That Report also reminded us that more food production is not enough. People must have the money to buy food. They must have jobs and homes and schools and rising in-comes. Agricultural development must go hand-in-hand with general economic growth.

AID programs are designed *both* to stimulate general economic growth and to give first priority to agriculture. In India, for instance, about half of all AID-financed imports this year will consist of fertilizer and other agricultural supplies.

We have made a good start:

—India is harvesting the largest grain crop in her history. Fertilizer use has doubled in the past two years. Last year five million acres were planted with new high yield wheat seeds. By 1970 this will increase to 32 million acres.

—Brazil, with AID help, has developed a new grass which has already added 400,-000 acres of new pastureland and increased her annual output of beef by 20,000 metric tons.

—The Philippines is expecting a record rice crop this year which will eliminate the need to import rice.

In the year ahead, AID will increase its investment in agriculture to about $800 million—50 percent of its total development aid. In addition, I will shortly propose an extension of the Food for Freedom program to provide emergency food assistance to stave off disaster while hungry countries build their own food production.

We must also tap the vast storehouse of food in the oceans which cover three-fourths of the earth's surface. I have directed the Administrator of the Agency for International Development and the Secretary of the Interior to launch a five-year program to:

—Perfect low-cost commercial processes for the production of Fish Protein Concentrate.

—Develop new protein-rich products that will fit in a variety of local diets.

—Encourage private investment in Fish Protein Concentrate production and marketing, as well as better fishing methods.

—Use this new product in our Food for Freedom program to fortify the diets of children and nursing mothers.

But food is only one side of the equation. If populations continue to grow at the present rate, we are only postponing disaster not preventing it.

In 1961 only two developing countries had programs to reduce birth rates. In 1967 there were 26.

As late as 1963, this government was spending less than $2 million to help family planning efforts abroad. In 1968, we will commit $35 million and additional amounts of local currency will be committed. In 1969 we expect to do even more.

Family planning is a family matter. The United States will not undertake to tell any government or any parent how and to what extent population must be limited.

But neither we nor our friends in the developing world can ignore the stark fact that the success of development efforts depends upon the balance between population and food and other resources. No government can escape this truth. The United States stands ready to help those governments that recognize it and move to deal with it.

5. *Balance of Payments Protection*

Our ability to pursue our responsibilities at home and abroad rests on the strength of the dollar. Economic aid now helps—not hurts—our balance of payments position.

In 1963, the dollar outflow from foreign aid expenditures was over $600 million. Last year it was down to $270 million. I have already directed that even this figure be reduced in 1968 to less than $170 million. More than nine dollars of every ten dollars AID spends will buy American goods and services.

And the repayments of prior loans will more than offset the small outflow from new loans.

Moreover, our AID programs have a favorable long range impact on our balance of payments by building new markets for our exports.

6. *Efficient Administration*

Over the past few years AID has reduced by twenty percent the number of U.S. employees serving overseas in posts other than Vietnam. Last month I directed a ten percent reduction in the number of employees overseas in all civilian agencies. In addition, AID is further improving and streamlining its over-all operations.

A CREATIVE PARTNERSHIP WITH FREE ENTERPRISE

Foreign aid must be much more than government aid. Private enterprise has a critical role. Last year:

—All 50 states exported American products financed by AID.

—The International Executive Service Corps operated 300 projects in which experienced American businessmen counseled local executives.

—Nearly 3,000 American scientists and engineers shared their know-how with developing countries under the auspices of VITA Corporation, a private, U.S. non-profit organization.

—More than 120 American colleges and universities contributed to AID technical assistance programs.

—Thirty-three American states supported development work in 14 Latin American countries under AID's Partners of the Alliance program.

All of these efforts will be sustained and expanded in the coming year. We are committed to maximum encouragement of private investment in and assistance to the developing countries. We shall remain so.

A YEAR OF OPPORTUNITY, A YEAR OF RISK

LATIN AMERICA

I propose appropriations of $625 million for the Alliance for Progress.

The American Presidents met at Punta del Este last spring to reaffirm a partnership which has already produced six years of accomplishment:

—The nations of Latin America have invested more than $115 billion, compared with $7.7 billion in American aid.

—Their tax revenues have increased by 30 percent.

—Their gross national product has risen by 30 percent.

A new course was charted for that partnership in the years ahead. At Punta del Este, the American nations agreed to move toward economic integration. They set new targets for improvements in agriculture, in health, and in education. They moved to bring the blessings of modern technology to all the citizens of our Hemisphere.

Now we must do our part. Some nations, such as Venezuela, have progressed to the point where they no longer require AID loans. More than two-thirds of our aid will be concentrated in Brazil, Chile, Colombia and Central America. Each has done much to deserve our help:

—*Brazil* increased food production by 10% in 1967 and achieved an overall real economic growth of 5%. Inflation was cut from 40% in 1966 to 25% in 1967.

—*Chile,* under President Frei's Revolution in Freedom, has launched a strong program of agricultural and land reforms, while maintaining an overall growth rate of about 5%.

—*Colombia* has also averaged 5% growth while undertaking difficult financial and social reforms.

—*Central America* leads the way toward the economic integration so important to the future of Latin America. Trade among these countries has grown by 450% in the six years of the Alliance— from $30 million in 1961 to $172 million in 1967.

This peaceful Alliance holds the hopes of a Hemisphere. We have a clear responsibility to do our share. Our partners have an equally clear responsibility to do theirs. We must press forward together toward mutual security and economic development for all our people.

NEAR EAST AND SOUTH ASIA

I recommend $706 million for the Near East and South Asia.

Half the people we seek to help live in India, Pakistan and Turkey. The fate of freedom in the world rests heavily on the fortunes of these three countries.

Each is engaged in a powerful effort to fight poverty, to grow more and better food, and to control population. If they succeed, and in so doing prove the effectiveness of free institutions, the lesson will be heard and heeded around the world.

This is a year of special importance for all three countries.

India

India has survived two successive years of the worst drought of this century. Even as she fought to save her people from starvation, she prepared for the day when the monsoon rains would return to normal. That day has come. India is now harvesting the greatest grain crop in her history. With this crop, India can begin a dramatic recovery which could lay the groundwork for sustained growth.

India must have the foreign exchange to take advantage of this year of opportunity. A farmer cannot use the miracle seed which would double or triple his yield unless he can get twice as much fertilizer as he used for the old seeds. A fertilizer distributor cannot sell that much more fertilizer unless it can be imported. An importer cannot buy it unless he can get foreign exchange from the Government. India will not have that foreign exchange unless the wealthy countries of the world are willing to lend it in sufficient quantities at reasonable terms.

This is the crux of the matter. If we and other wealthy countries can provide the loans, we have much to look forward to. If we cannot, history will rightly label us penny-wise and pound-foolish.

Pakistan

Pakistan, though also plagued by drought, has continued its excellent progress of the past few years. Her development budget has been increased. Her military budget has been reduced. Agricultural production is growing faster than population. Private investment has exceeded expectations.

Now the Government of Pakistan has undertaken further steps to reform its economic policies—to free up its economy and give more play to the market. These reforms are acts of wisdom and courage, but they require foreign exchange to back them up. Pakistan deserves our help.

Turkey

Turkey's economic record is outstanding. Her gross national product has grown an average of six percent annually since 1962. Industrial output has grown nine percent per year. Food production is growing much faster than population growth.

Turkey's own savings now finance some

90 percent of her gross investment. Difficult problems remain, but we may now realistically look forward to the day—in the early 1970's—when Turkey will no longer require AID's help.

AFRICA

I recommend $179 million for Africa.

Just one year ago, I informed the Congress of a shift in emphasis in our aid policy for Africa. We moved promptly to put it into effect:

—There will be 21 U.S. bilateral programs in Africa in Fiscal 1969, compared to 35 last year.

—Most of our bilateral programs will be phased out in eleven more countries in the following year.

—Expanded regional and international projects will meet the development needs of the countries where bilateral aid is ended.

The past year has provided further evidence that this support for regional economic institutions and projects is a sensible approach to Africa's problems. It expands markets. It encourages economies of scale. It gives meaningful evidence of our concern and interest in African development.

This is not a policy of withdrawal from Africa. It is a policy of concentration and of maximum encouragement of regional cooperation. A continent of 250 million people has set out with determination on the long road to development. We intend to help them.

VIETNAM

I recommend a program of $480 million to carry forward our economic assistance effort in Vietnam. This effort will be intensified by the need to restore and reconstruct the cities and towns attacked in recent days.

Defense of Vietnam requires more than

success on the battlefield. The people of Vietnam are building the economic and social base to preserve the independence we are helping them to defend.

Since 1965, when galloping inflation loomed and continuity of government was repeatedly destroyed, the people of Vietnam have achieved two major civil victories which rank with any gallantry in combat:

—They have written a Constitution and established representative local and national governments through free elections, despite a concerted campaign of terror, assassination and intimidation.

—Runaway inflation has been averted, and the foundation laid for a thriving economy, despite the enormous stresses of war.

But still the innocent victims of war and terrorism must be cared for; persistent inflationary pressures must continue to be controlled; and the many problems faced by a new government under wartime conditions must be overcome. The framework for economic and social progress has been established. We must help the Vietnamese people to build the institutions needed to make it work.

In the coming year, we will:

—Improve our assistance to refugees and civilian casualties. The wages of aggression are always paid in the blood and misery of the innocent. Our determination to resist aggression must be matched by our compassion for its helpless victims.

—Intensify agricultural programs aimed at increasing rice production by 50 percent in the next four years.

—Concentrate our educational effort toward the Government's goal of virtually universal elementary education by 1971.

—Stress, in our import programs, the key commodities needed for agricultural and industrial growth.

The rapid program expansion of the past two years—in dollars, people and diversity of activities—is ended. The emphasis in the coming year will be on concentration of resources on the most important current programs.

We will pursue these constructive programs in Vietnam with the same energy and determination with which we resist aggression. They are just as vital to our ultimate success.

EAST ASIA

I recommend $277 million for East Asia.

For twenty years resistance to attack and subversion has been current and urgent business for the nations of East Asia. The United States has helped to make this resistance effective. We must continue to do so, particularly in Laos and Thailand.

But this year the larger portion of our aid to East Asian countries will be focused directly on the work of development. Asians know—as we do—that in the long run, economic, social and political development offer the best protection against subversion and attack. Despite communist pressure, they are getting on with the job. For example:

—For the last three years, the *Korean* economy has grown by a phenomenal 10 percent per year; domestic revenues have doubled since 1965; exports have grown tenfold in the last seven years. Population growth has fallen from 2.9 percent in 1962 to 2.5 percent today, and a strong national population program is contributing to further reductions. We are now able to plan for orderly reduction of U.S. economic aid as the capacity for self-support grows. Despite recent pressure from the North, the momentum and self-confidence of this gallant nation must be—and will be—maintained.

—*Indonesia* has stepped away from the brink of communist domination and economic chaos. She has undertaken the hard course of stabilization and rehabilitation and is moving toward development. She needs help from the U.S. and other donors, who are working together with the International Monetary Fund and the World Bank. It is overwhelmingly in our interest to provide it.

MILITARY ASSISTANCE PROGRAMS

I recommend $420 million for grant Military Assistance Programs under the Foreign Assistance Act.

More than three-quarters of our grant military assistance will support the military efforts of nations on the perimeter of the communist world and those nations where the U.S. maintains defense installations important to our own national security. These programs are a vital link in our own defense effort and an integral part of Free World collective security.

Elsewhere our programs focus on building the internal security necessary for lasting development progress.

Our aid—economic as well as military—must not reward nations which divert scarce resources to unnecessary military expenditures. More less-developed countries have resisted large expansion of military expenditures. Their military budgets have remained a small portion of national income. Their leaders have made politically difficult decisions to resist pressure to acquire large amounts of new and expensive weapons.

We must help them maintain this record and improve it. We will give great weight to efforts to keep military expenditures at minimum essential levels when considering a country's requests for economic aid.

In the coming year, we will work directly with the less-developed nations and examine our own programs, country-by-country, to deal more effectively with this problem. In addition, we will explore other approaches toward reducing the danger of arms races among less-developed countries.

Over the past several years, we have significantly reduced our grant military aid wherever possible. Where new equipment is essential, we have provided it more and more through cash and credit sales. I will submit separate legislation to authorize necessary military sales and provide for credit terms where justified.

Our military assistance programs will provide only what is needed for legitimate defense and internal security needs. We will do no more. We can afford to do no less.

Special Assistance to the Republic of Korea

The internal peace and order of this steadfast ally is once again threatened from the North.

These threats summon Korea to strengthen further her defenses and her capacity to deter aggression.

We must help.

I propose that Congress appropriate immediately an additional $100 million for military assistance to the Republic of Korea.

This can be accomplished within the authorizing legislation already enacted.

With this additional help, the Armed Forces of the Republic of Korea can gain new strength through the acquisition of aircraft and anti-aircraft equipment, naval radar, patrol craft, ammunition and other supplies.

AMERICA'S CHOICE

Foreign aid serves our national interest. It expresses our basic humanity. It may not always be popular, but it is right.

The peoples we seek to help are committed to change. This is an immutable fact of our time. The only questions are whether change will be peaceful or violent, whether it will liberate or enslave, whether it will build a community of free and prosperous nations or sentence the world to endless strife between rich and poor.

Foreign aid is the American answer to this question. It is a commitment to conscience as well as to country. It is a matter of national tradition as well as national security.

Last year some Americans forgot that tradition. My foreign aid request, already the smallest in history, was reduced by almost one-third.

The effects of that cut go much deeper than the fields which lie fallow, the factories not built, or the hospitals without modern equipment.

Our Ambassadors all over the developing world report the deep and searching questions they are being asked. Has America resigned her leadership of the cause of freedom? Has she abandoned to fate the weak and the striving who are depending on her help?

This Congress can give a resounding answer to these questions by enacting the full amount I have requested. I do not propose this as a partisan measure. I propose it as an extension of the humane statesmanship of both parties for more than twenty years.

I said in my State of the Union address that it is not America's resources that are being tested, but her will. This is nowhere more true than in the developing countries where our help is a crucial margin between peaceful change and violent disaster.

I urge the Congress to meet this test.

LYNDON B. JOHNSON

The White House
February 8, 1968

NOTE: For statements or remarks upon signing related legislation, see Items 290, 377, 417, 524.

64 Message to the Congress Transmitting Annual Report of the National Endowment for the Arts. *February 8, 1968*

To the Congress of the United States:

I am pleased to transmit the Annual Report of the National Endowment for the Arts for Fiscal Year 1967—the first full year of its existence.

The report offers abundant proof that the Endowment has made good use of its resources. With the advice and recommendations of the members of the National Council on the Arts, the Endowment has:

—Opened new opportunities for creative writers, art students, and visual and performing artists;

—Created three Laboratory Theatres—in Los Angeles, New Orleans, and Providence—for the presentation of professional theatre to secondary school students and the adult community;

—Assisted 17 resident professional theatres across the Nation;

—Initiated the first American Literary Anthology, representing the finest work appearing in literary magazines;

—Helped major museums expand their audiences and provide more services to their communities;

—Launched a program to enhance the environment of American cities with outstanding works of sculpture in outdoor public places;

—Created a new program to aid American composers and symphony orchestras;

—Stimulated the production and nation-wide distribution of programs on the arts for educational television;

—Rendered financial and technical assistance to agencies for the arts in 50 States, and District of Columbia, Guam, the Virgin Islands, and Puerto Rico enabling them to implement 295 new or expanded arts projects.

Throughout Fiscal Year 1967, the National Endowment for the Arts worked closely with private foundations, organizations and individuals, seeking to increase appreciation and support of the arts in the United States.

Since the Endowment was created, Federal grants totaling $10.5 million have been made. These Federal grants have been supplemented by nearly $16 million in contributions from States and cities, and from private agencies and individuals—dramatic evidence of the widespread support which now exists for those whose talent and genius enrich the life of our country.

The National Endowment for the Arts has made great progress toward realizing the mandate given it by the Congress to improve the quality of American life.

I transmit with pride this report of the Endowment's first full year of activities and urge the Congress to act promptly to extend the authorization for the National Endowment for the Arts.

LYNDON B. JOHNSON

The White House
February 8, 1968

NOTE: The report is entitled "National Endowment for the Arts and National Council on the Arts, Annual Report for the Fiscal Year Ended June 30, 1967" (Government Printing Office, 67 pp.).

65   Toasts of the President and Prime Minister Wilson of the United Kingdom.   *February 8, 1968*

Prime Minister and Mrs. Wilson, Vice President and Mrs. Humphrey, Members of the Cabinet, distinguished Members of the Congress, distinguished guests:

Let me thank you first of all for coming out on a winter's night to warm this house with friendship.

It could be said that we are gathered here to welcome a Prime Minister who has come in out of the cold.

I refer, of course, to the famous English winter—ending in July and reappearing in August.

But whatever the season, sir, there is always strength and comfort in standing beside you to field the challenges of the day. It is always a good day for any man or any nation when they can claim the British as comrades in adversity, or brothers in adventure, or as partners in advancement.

But I do not want tonight to wave either the Union Jack or the Stars and Stripes. We buried the need for that with Colonel Blimp, Yankee Doodle, and other caricatures of yesteryear. When Americans talk today of what Great Britain means to us—and means to the world in which we live—we are moved by a more meaningful English voice from the past. It was Robert Browning who spoke the truth for our time: "My sun sets to rise again."

Yes, these are difficult times for Great Britain—and they are very difficult times for the United States. Yes, we have our family differences still. And yes, Britain means as much to us as she ever meant.

—Our two nations are as close as ever.

—Our two peoples are as determined as

ever to master the trials of the moment and to move on to the triumphs of the future.

That is what the Prime Minister and I have spent the day talking about. We have ranged around the world, reviewing our large responsibilities, drawing on our experiences, exchanging insights, giving and getting much of value. But we always came back to one basic and unbreakable agreement.

—We want the same things for our people.

—They will not come easily or they will not come overnight, but our people shall have them if patience and perseverance can win them.

They are the simplest things to describe— but they are the hardest to achieve:

—A peace rooted in the good, firm earth of freedom;

—A world respectful of law, given to justice, hostile only to force;

—A life without the torment of hunger, ignorance, and disease;

—A higher standard of living and more opportunity for all.

It will come for us. If any man doubts it, let him look at how far the Americans and the British have come already in common purpose. Let him reflect on all that we have overcome already by sharing struggle and sacrifice.

And then let him look deeply into the well of our strength—the traditions and the character that shape us.

He will come quickly to the truth that sustains us: The American and British peoples are not short-distance crusaders. If we must tighten our belts for a time, it does not leave us breathless for the next battle. We are veteran campaigners, not amateurs and we never have been quitters. We have learned to pace ourselves—to accept temporary detours and steer around them.

I have enormous confidence, Mr. Prime Minister, in the character of my own people, in their ability to understand and master trial. I am very proud to place equal faith in your people, in their characteristic courage and fortitude. I say with them, and I say to them, using the slogan of the moment: The American people are backing Britain.

The greatness of nations, the size of their global role and influence—these laurels are not earned or held by the trappings of power alone.

Ultimately, nations can only lead and leave their mark if they have the power to attract and to instruct by example. The rank and worth of nations are decided, finally, by what pushes upward and outward from their roots—the character of citizens, the value of ideals, the quality of life, the purpose of a people.

What a magnificent opportunity for the people of Great Britain!

Character—ideals—culture—purpose. The world already knows them as unmistakably British qualities, as the benchmarks of civilized life, as standards of decency and development that surpass and survive the importance of any single epoch.

The new and struggling states of the world can gain much from these gifts of British example. The older nations can also learn from them, and can count on them for security and for progress. Britain itself will continue to build on them

—in British education, for example, where a revolution of learning and opportunity is already underway; and

—in British technology, where the native skills of an inventive and industrious people are establishing a new "workshop of the world."

Oh, there is so much, Mr. Prime Minister, that is waiting for our peoples on the road ahead.

The confidence and purpose that we show to the world will always be a reflection of our own relationship. I want it always to have the importance and to have the meaning that that great President of ours, Franklin D. Roosevelt, gave it more than a quarter of a century ago, when he welcomed King George VI to this house.

"I am persuaded," he said, "that the greatest single contribution our two countries have been enabled to make to civilization, and to the welfare of peoples throughout the world, is the example we have jointly set by our manner of conducting relations between our two nations."

It is a grand toast still. I renew its promise now, Mr. Prime Minister, by offering it as a tribute to you and to your people.

The thing our people want most tonight, Mr. Prime Minister, of course, is peace in the world. As you and I pursue it, I think we are entitled for a moment to have a little peace of mind—even a little music while we work.

The songs you will hear tonight have been challenged in some sections of the press today. When I heard that on my morning radio, I thought: "Well, there they go again, always wanting me to dance to their tune."

But I am a man who really, after all, loves harmony. I was ready to believe that Mr. Merrill and Miss Tyler were actually trying to maintain the balance of payments in their choice of songs tonight by paying you a compliment "On the Road to Mandalay," and paying me a compliment—"Oh, Bury Me not on the Lone Prairie."

I was ready to believe it until I had some Senator say to me this morning: "Well, what have they really got to sing about anyway?" I think that should settle the matter. If it doesn't, Mr. Prime Minister, I am prepared tonight to keep peace at any price. You sing "God Save the Queen," and I'll

sing "God Bless America."

Let us now drink to lasting harmony between the best of friends—the British and the American peoples.

Ladies and gentlemen, Her Majesty, The Queen.

NOTE: The President spoke at 10:27 p.m. in the State Dining Room at the White House. During his remarks he referred to Robert Merrill and Veronica Tyler, stars of the Metropolitan Opera. Prime Minister Harold Wilson responded as follows:

Mr. President, Mrs. Johnson, Mr. Vice President, Mrs. Humphrey, distinguished Cabinet officers, Your Excellencies, distinguished Senators, Congressmen, and friends:

It is my privilege, Mr. President, to rise and propose your health. On behalf of my colleagues, may I thank you for your kind hospitality to us this evening and for enabling us to meet this distinguished gathering of American citizens.

In particular, I should like to thank you for what you have said and the way in which you have said it.

It was one of the most moving speeches I think any of us has ever listened to.

You referred to the difficult times through which the United States, Britain, and the world are moving. You set out in words which all of us would endorse, your conception of the hopes and aspirations for our people—yours and, indeed, ours.

We welcomed everything you have said to us tonight. You referred to the days of Anglo-American relationships, the days of your great master and tutor, Franklin Delano Roosevelt. But I make bold to claim that relations between our two countries today, in 1968, in the years when you and I have been meeting, are no less close and no less intimate than they were in those perilous wartime days of the Anglo-American alliance.

I was particularly moved to hear you endorsing the slogan of backing Britain. Mr. President, the acoustics in this room are always a little dubious. Last year I dispensed with this machine and relied on my own voice. From this distance, I thought what you were saying was not backing Britain, but "buying British." I hope the acoustics will not blame me for it.

Mr. President, our talks this morning and this afternoon, as always, have been informal, friendly, and, above all, to the point. This meeting was arranged some time ago. We couldn't know the exact developments that we should be discussing in each part of the world where our talks today have led us.

What I particularly appreciate is that at this time we have been able to have such a thorough and wide discussion of the whole world scene. Inevitably, at this time—and I think this has been true of almost every discussion we have had together in the last 3 or 4 years—and true also of the contacts that we are able to maintain in between meetings—a great part of our discussion has related today to the situation of Vietnam.

I make no apology for the fact that on what should be a happy occasion, I want to devote most of my time this evening to referring to that situation, because the events of the last 10 days have brought home to millions of people far from the conflict, within our own countries, the indescribable horror and agony this war is bringing to a people for whom peace has been a stranger for a generation.

But the scenes of outrage that we have seen on our television screen can beget dangerous counsel. It can beget impatient and exasperated demands to hit back, to escalate in ways which would widen and not end that war.

The responsibility of power, Mr. President, as you know, means not only loneliness in a democracy, it means facing demands for punitive action whenever national "interests" are outraged. The hardest part of statesmanship is to show restraint in the face of that exasperation.

All those understandable demands for actions which are immediately satisfying could have incalculable effects, effects, indeed, on the whole world. That is why, Mr. President, your administration's attitude following the *Pueblo* incident is one which will earn tributes from reasoning men everywhere and, indeed, from history.

You referred just now, Mr. President, to the musical entertainment. When I read your press this morning, and I always believe everything I read in the American press, I said: "I hope they won't change the program for me. These are my favorite tunes."

"Mandalay"—I don't know why anyone thought that was embarrassing. We got out of Mandalay 20 years ago.

But if we are going to go back to Rudyard Kipling—and some of us are trying now to escape from him—I think one of the greatest phrases he used—which must have rung many times in your ears, Mr. President, when you talked about the hard and difficult times, and the misunderstandings of the things that statesmen have to do from time to time—was when Kipling, in his famous poem, said—and when things are really tough, one should either re-read that poem or read what Lincoln said when he was up against it—"If you can meet with Triumph and Disaster and treat those two impostors just the same."—once we can recognize that, it makes us a little more detached about some of the things we have to do.

Mr. President, the problem of Vietnam, as you have always recognized, can never be settled on a durable and just basis by an imposed military solution. Indeed, the events of these past days have underlined yet again that there can be no purely military solution to this problem; that there can be no solution before men meet around the conference table, determined to get peace.

I have said a hundred times that this problem will never be solved by a military solution, which I see as one of the lessons of the last few days—a determined resistance to see that a military solution is not imposed on the people of Vietnam.

I am frequently urged, as the means to peace, to dissociate the British Government from American action, and, in particular, to call for the unconditional ending of all the bombing.

Mr. President, I have said this a hundred times, too, in my own country, in Western Europe, in the Kremlin, that if I felt that by doing this I could ensure that this war ended one day earlier, or that it would ensure that peace, when achieved, was one degree more durable, one degree more just, I would do what I am urged and dissociate.

I have not done so, and I am going to say why. Over the past 3 years, Mr. President, as you know, as the Secretary knows, I have been in the position to know a good deal about the history of negotiations and consultations, and contacts and discussions, aimed at getting away from the battleground and getting around the conference table.

I recall our talks here in Washington at the time of your Baltimore speech, now nearly 3 years ago.

I recall the Commonwealth Prime Ministers Conference over 2½ years ago when 20 Commonwealth heads of government from Asia and Africa, from the Mediterranean, the Caribbean, Australia, Europe, and America, of widely differing views and widely differing loyalties over Vietnam, all of them, called for a cessation of the bombing, and, in return, a cessation of infiltration by the North Vietnamese Army into South Vietnam.

I recall a hundred proposals to our fellow Geneva cochairman to activate the Geneva Conference or any other forum to get the parties around the table.

I recall meetings and discussions in Washington, in London, in New York, in Moscow, and innumerable less formal consultations, with anyone and everyone who could help find the road to peace.

And all of these have failed—failed so far—to find a solution.

But it doesn't mean we were wrong—all of us here—to try and to go on trying.

I believe, and this is true even today against the differing background of all that is now happening on the battlefield, that the road to peace was fairly charted, not for the first time, but with greater and more meaningful clarity at San Antonio last September.

A fortnight ago I was in the Kremlin, and in many hours of discussion with the Soviet leaders I sought to spell out what San Antonio and what subsequent elucidations of San Antonio meant.

I believe the Soviet leaders now know, if they did not understand before, that what that formula means is that the United States would be prepared to stop the bombing given an assurance that prompt and productive discussions will start, and that this action will not be exploited to create a new situation of military advantage which would delay a political settlement.

It was, Mr. President, as you know, our purpose in Moscow to show that once the surrounding misunderstandings have been removed, this approach could be reconciled with the conditions laid down by the DRV [Democratic Republic of Vietnam] Foreign Minister, Mr. Trinh, on December 29th.

What I am saying now, interpreting, and I think you will agree I am interpreting correctly the San Antonio formula, really answers his latest speech this week which has been printed today.

There have been some, not only in Moscow, as I learned, who would believe that San Antonio meant that the United States were insisting, in advance, as a precondition, on a given outcome to the talks as a condition to stopping the bombing.

We believe that this reconciliation is possible once it is clear that all that is needed to start negotiations is assurance that the talks will begin promptly, and that they will be meaningful and directed in good faith to a peaceful settlement.

Given, therefore, good faith, we—all of us—America, the Soviet Union—we, ourselves, are to ask now whether the events of these past 10 days mean that there is not, that there cannot be, that good faith.

Whatever the discouragement of these past 10 days, all of us, Mr. President, feel for you in this conflict. I do not take that view, because, as I have said, this problem cannot be settled by a purely military solution. Negotiations for a political settlement will have to come. Every day that the start of those negotiations is delayed means more suffering.

This is not the time to attempt to set out what the provisions of such a settlement should be. But statesmen from many countries, differing deeply in their attitudes to the Vietnamese problem, have each in their own words stressed that the basic principle involved in that settlement is the right of the peoples of that area to determine their own future through democratic and constitutional processes—words, Mr. President, I am quoting from yourself.

Once willingness is shown to enter into prompt and productive discussions, we in Britain in our capacities as Geneva cochairman, or in any other appropriate way will play our full part in helping the parties to reach agreement. And with the political

settlement will come the enormous task of repairing the damage, of embarking on the great era, the great challenge, of economic and social reconstruction in that area.

Mr. President, the noises of battle, the noises of controversy, too, in all our countries, have perhaps caused many to forget your own proposals on the theme of economic reconstruction in Vietnam which I read in your speech at Baltimore now nearly 3 years ago. It may have been forgotten, but once again it will become, I hope soon, a reality.

I feel it right to add that within the resources we could make available we shall be ready to play our part.

It may be, Mr. President, that tonight in my speech of thanks and appreciation to you I have been striking—as indeed you, yourself, said—something of a somber note because of the circumstances in which we meet—somber but at the same time hopeful—hopeful because at the same time determined.

As you have said, when we have pursued a common aim, however dark the background against which we have been operating, that common aim, that hope and that determination have set an example to the world.

The problems with which so many of us here tonight are concerned, the problems we have dealt with in our wide-ranging talks earlier today, have not been confined even to the compelling and urgent problem brought about by the tragedy of Vietnam. We have discussed problems of Europe, of the Middle East, the problems of the developing world, problems of nuclear disarmament, the challenge of making a reality of the authority of the United Nations.

And all of these have proved again today, as in all of our continuing discussions and exchanges over these past years, to have their own urgencies and their own priorities.

But in a wider sense we are trying, together, to face challenges on a world scale, the challenge of a world increasingly dominated by the explosion of race and color.

Mr. President, whatever they say, neither you nor we have any need to apologize about our reaction to the challenge of race and difficulty; the challenge on a world scale of the population explosion; the challenge of the problems acute for advanced countries and for developing countries alike; the problem of freer movement of trade and freedom from the throes of outmoded international financial practices and international financial doctrines—may I add, and the worship of the Golden Calf.

It is therefore, Mr. President, in the confidence that together—we, the United States and Britain, our friends and partners in the Commonwealth, in Europe, in the United Nations—the years ahead will bring for us a new and fresh spirit to the attack on these problems—it is in that spirit and in that confidence that I have the pleasure now of proposing the health of the President of the United States of America.

66 Remarks to a Group of Benito Juárez Scholars. *February 9, 1968*

Secretary Oliver, distinguished students:

I welcome all of you to the White House, especially the young lady in the corner representing Panama among the 23 scholars.

It was nearly 2 years ago, in April 1966, that I spent a memorable day with President Diaz Ordaz in Mexico City.

One idea which emerged from our long conversations was a program for scholarships for students in our own hemisphere, the Abraham Lincoln Scholarships offered by Mexico to students from the United States and other Latin American countries, and the Benito Juárez Scholarships offered by the United States to students from Latin America.

A year later, in April 1967, we met with the Presidents of the Americas at the summit in Punta del Este. It was there that we pledged that we would give education a new priority in this hemisphere.

We said in our declaration at Punta del Este: "We will vigorously promote education for development. Education at all levels will be greatly expanded."

Our meeting here today, then, is part of that effort—a sign that the work we began in Mexico City and Punta del Este is beginning now to bear fruit.

Here in our own country, from fiscal year 1961 when we spent $19.3 billion for health, education, welfare, and social security, and from the fiscal year 1964 when I became President, when we spent $23 billion 200 million for these subjects, this year the budget contains $46 billion 700 million—more than twice what we were spending in 1964, and considerably more than twice what we were spending in 1961.

This is what we are doing here in this country.

We must carry on this work to the other countries in the hemisphere if we are to conquer the enemies of the hemisphere— ignorance, illiteracy, and disease.

While we may not be more than doubling our expenditures for health, education, welfare, and social security in the hemisphere as yet, you Benito Juárez Scholars are proof that we recognize the importance of education.

You are among the many who will study at universities here and then return home as teachers and as leaders to bring forth the effort in your country that we have brought forth in ours in the last 4 years.

Next week in Venezuela the Inter-American Cultural Council will meet to discuss the work that we began in Punta del Este.

A great educator and a great friend of Latin America will head the United States delegation to that meeting—Dr. Milton Eisenhower, former president of Johns Hopkins University.

The delegates to that meeting will discuss some urgent and difficult questions. Some of these questions will be:

—How can we stamp out illiteracy once and for all?

—How can we make our universities more efficient and more responsive to their societies?

—How can we enlist the blessings of science and technology, especially television and the satellites, in the cause of educating our people?

Those questions will occupy us for years to come. Statesmen and education ministers can meet and talk and begin to answer them. But the real answers are in the hands of you who will be teachers.

As Henry Adams wrote: "A teacher affects eternity; he can never tell where his influence stops."

The real hope of expanding democracy, of spreading knowledge, of achieving economic progress, is the hope that you bring to your hemisphere.

I wish all of you well in your studies and in your work back home. I pledge to you the enduring friendship, the encouragement and the support of the people of the United States. For we believe, as you believe, that men must have freedom to learn, and they must have learning to be free.

What we want for our own country we want for all of our friends in the Americas. We hope for it and we will work for it every place in the world. Good luck and God bless all of you.

[At this point, Mario Blacutt Mendoza of Bolivia spoke, thanking the President on behalf of the scholars. The President then resumed speaking.]

Just a few years ago I was teaching in a school a few miles from where Secretary Oliver lived. I started looking for him after I became President. I found he had moved out and had wound up here at the University of Pennsylvania. So today you are in a room with two former teachers. I hope the same thing doesn't happen to you that happened to us. [*Laughter*]

NOTE: The President spoke at 1:32 p.m. in the Cabinet Room at the White House. In his opening words he referred to Covey T. Oliver, Assistant Secretary of State for Inter-American Affairs, who accompanied the scholars.

67 Statement by the President Upon Signing Order Authorizing Transitional Civil Service Appointments to "Vietnam Era" Veterans. *February* 9, 1968

I HAVE signed an Executive order by which the Federal Government, the Nation's largest employer, will provide a special opportunity to Vietnam veterans to further their education while working in the public interest.

This Executive order—combining incentives for better jobs and better education—was discussed in my January 30 message on servicemen and veterans.

Under the order, Vietnam veterans who meet job requirements will be eligible to enter Federal employment—in "transitional appointments" at the five lowest civil service levels—without taking a competitive examination.

A qualifying veteran is one who served on active duty in our Armed Forces on or after August 5, 1964, who has completed less than 1 year of education beyond high school, and who meets all other civil service standards. He must agree to pursue an approved part-time or full-time educational program. His continued employment will depend on satisfactory job performance and educational progress.

The new program will not affect the budget and staff reductions I have ordered for Federal agencies. Vacancies in a wide range of skills and grades exist because of personnel turnover. And many of these skills are in short supply.

For those with the necessary initiative and

ability, this new program—together with the GI bill—offers a chance for both further education and better jobs.

I hope that the plan will be a model to private employers and to State and local governments. Chairman John Macy of the Civil Service Commission has assured me

that the transitional appointments program will receive high priority in the Federal Government. I hope that this, too, will set a precedent for employers throughout the country.

NOTE: The President referred to Executive Order 11397 (4 Weekly Comp. Pres. Docs., p. 270; 33 F.R. 2833; 3 CFR, 1968 Comp., p. 100).

68 Statement by the President Upon Signing Proclamation Marking the Anniversary of the League of United Latin American Citizens. *February* 10, 1968

I HAVE long been familiar with the high purposes and good work of the League of United Latin American Citizens.

LULAC is a household word in Texas. We know it to mean a group of patriotic, devoted Americans who, for 39 years, have taken an active concern in the well-being and the future of the 10.5 million Spanish-speaking Americans.

LULAC has always recognized that education is the key that will open the doors of opportunity. In the past 5 years this administration has made long strides toward our goal of giving every American all the education he wants and is capable of. This is LULAC's goal as well.

LULAC has councils in 19 States. An important part of its program is to teach English

to young Spanish-speaking Americans so they can make their full contribution to the society of which they are a part.

I know the dreams of these young Americans. In a little schoolhouse in Cotulla, Texas, I saw the hunger for learning in the eyes of children. I resolved then, as a young teacher, that I would do all in my power to satisfy their aspiration. In this effort of a lifetime, I have found LULAC at my side every step of the way.

It is therefore a special honor for me as President to proclaim the week beginning Sunday, February 11, as LULAC Week throughout the United States.

NOTE: The President referred to Proclamation 3827 (4 Weekly Comp. Pres. Docs., p. 280; 33 F.R. 2881; 3 CFR, 1968 Comp., p. 22).

69 Message to the Congress Transmitting Annual Report of the United States Arms Control and Disarmament Agency. *February* 12, 1968

To the Congress of the United States:

I am transmitting herewith the Seventh Annual Report of the Arms Control and Disarmament Agency.

Two weeks ago, on January 18, this agency

reported to me, and to the world, that agreement had at last been reached with the Soviet Union on a complete draft treaty to prevent the spread of nuclear weapons. The draft treaty, which has been submitted to the

Eighteen-Nation Disarmament Committee in Geneva for consideration by other nations, is the most significant achievement of the Agency since its establishment seven years ago.

On January 23, I forwarded to the Congress a request that the life of the Arms Control and Disarmament Agency be extended for an additional three years. At that time I noted the role of the Agency in bringing us close to the final conclusion of a non-proliferation treaty, and pointed out that the treaty "is not a creation of the United States. It is not a creation of the United States and the Soviet Union. It is the creation of all nations, large and small . . . ."

While the United States and the Soviet Union, as Co-Chairmen of the Geneva Conference, have had the responsibility for preparing the draft treaty, a reading of this Report will make plain the extent to which the draft has been responsive to interests and views of the nations which do not now have nuclear weapons.

In the course of a long and arduous negotiation, we have learned much of the concerns and desires of these nations. We have learned that it is not nuclear weapons they want, but security; not the destructiveness of the atom, but its benefits. We have been made aware of the depth of worldwide concern about the nuclear arms race.

The non-nuclear states have wanted their renunciation of nuclear weapons to be matched with a binding pledge by the nuclear powers to negotiate a halt in the arms race. They have not asked that the treaty require us to stop making nuclear weapons, or to divest ourselves of those now in our arsenals.

But they have asked us to pledge ourselves to move towards that ultimate goal. They feel the restraints they will voluntarily ac-

cept give them the right to such a pledge.

In drafting the non-proliferation treaty, the United States and the Soviet Union have acknowledged that right.

Under Article VI of the draft now before the Disarmament Committee, the nuclear nations will assume a solemn treaty obligation "to pursue negotiations in good faith on effective measures regarding cessation of the nuclear arms race and disarmament. . . ." It is an obligation the United States will undertake with the utmost seriousness—for it continues a policy begun in 1946, when this nation offered to place its nuclear weapons under international control. We reaffirmed that obligation at Geneva when the Disarmament Conference convened there six years ago.

A reading of this Report shows clearly that the United States is pursuing a broad program of research and negotiation in fulfillment of its commitment to disarmament. The non-proliferation treaty now under consideration is another step in that direction, as the hot line and the limited test ban treaty and the outer space agreement were before it.

No nation is more aware of the perils in the increasingly expert destructiveness of our time than the United States. I believe the Soviet Union shares this awareness.

This is why we have jointly pledged our nations to negotiate towards the cessation of the nuclear arms race.

This is why the United States urgently desires to begin discussions with the Soviet Union about the buildup of offensive and defensive missiles on both sides. Such discussions—and it is important to note that the Soviet Union has agreed to them, in principle at least—will aim at finding ways to avoid another costly and futile escalation of the arms race.

Our hopes that talks will soon begin reside

217

in our conviction that the same mutual interest reflected in earlier agreements is present here—a mutual interest in stopping the rapid accumulation and refinement of these munitions.

The obligations of the non-proliferation treaty will reinforce our will to bring an end to the nuclear arms race. The world will judge us by our performance.

The report I am forwarding today is testimony to the skill and determination with which the Arms Control and Disarmament Agency, under the leadership of Mr. William C. Foster, is supporting this nation's

effort to keep the somber and grim elements of the nuclear present from obliterating the promise of the future.

LYNDON B. JOHNSON

The White House
February 12, 1968

NOTE: The report is entitled "United States Arms Control and Disarmament Agency, Seventh Annual Report to Congress, January 1, 1967–December 31, 1967" (172 pp.).

For a statement by the President on January 18 on the Nuclear Nonproliferation Treaty and for his letter of January 23 requesting extension of the Agency, see Items 16, 27.

---

70 Remarks at a Ceremony Commemorating the 159th Birthday of Abraham Lincoln. *February 12, 1968*

General O'Malley, distinguished guests, ladies and gentlemen:

Carl Sandburg wrote of Abraham Lincoln: "None threw a longer shadow than he."

Across the world, whenever men have sought to breathe free and to stand tall— they have looked to Lincoln. On five continents, in shacks and huts and slums, and in drawing rooms as well—if men sought dignity, there was a picture of Abraham Lincoln tacked on the wall.

Those pictures in the places where men dream of freedom give us a true perspective of America's role in the world over the last 100 years.

When an American stands on these steps at this time—he knows that America stands for something, and that the values America stands for are perhaps the central issue of our time.

And if that is not always understood here in America, it is certainly known abroad.

To men around the world, the life of Lincoln told of the real America:

—a place where men could grow to a stature and a dignity previously undreamed of;

—a place where government of, by, and for the people could preserve and enhance that dignity.

As Lincoln once said, with his customary brevity: "I don't know who my grandfather was; I am much more concerned to know what his grandson will be."

Since Lincoln's time, that idea—that revolutionary American dream of human dignity and equality for all—has been spreading across the world.

And so, today when Americans are asked to help Lincoln's ideas flourish in places far from these steps we ask ourselves the hard and searching questions:

—Are these ideas still valid?

—Do they deserve a hearing elsewhere if free men so choose?

—Are we ourselves safer and stronger when they do get a hearing and when they flourish?

If we answer those questions affirmatively—and I believe that most Americans repudiate moral isolationism—we are sometimes forced by an adversary to back our beliefs with steel—just as Lincoln did.

And we must stick it out—just as Lincoln did. For we live in a time that Lincoln would have well understood.

—He heard the charges that the war was long and wrong;

—he saw Americans die—600,000 of them—and he brooded;

—he saw dissent, riot, and rebellion;

—he saw heavy taxes and inflation;

—he saw hunger and poverty.

Sad, but steady—always convinced of his cause—Lincoln stuck it out. Sad, but steady, so will we.

But perseverance by itself is a minor virtue, and Lincoln has more than that to tell us today.

He looked beyond a time of strife to a time of unity. Where others sought to open wounds and to rub them raw in their frustration and troubles, Lincoln sought to bind them up.

Lincoln knew that unity in America was not to be confused with the sleek face of conformity, and he never confused responsible dissent with disloyalty.

He knew that war in a democracy could defeat its own goals and he set a precedent by insisting on national elections in the midst of the war.

A journalist noted: "It is the first time that a people in possession of universal suffrage has been called to pronounce directly and finally for or against the continuation of a painful war."

But Lincoln saw the issue clearly: "If the rebellion could force us to forego, or postpone, a national election," he said, "it might fairly claim to have already conquered and ruined us."

And his opponent got over 40 percent of the votes.

These marble steps in recent years have borne eloquent witness to responsible dissent. A hundred years after the Emancipation Proclamation, a vast convocation of peoples have met here peacefully and dramatically to call upon all of us to honor our commitment to human rights for all of us. Today, we rededicate ourselves at this place to Lincoln's cause, the cause of full equality.

Lincoln once said: "Let every man remember that to violate the law is to trample on the blood of his father, and to tear the charter of his own and his children's liberty."

More than any man in our history, Lincoln sensed that our unity as a people would flow from diversity; that when the heat of passion subsided, the Northerner and the Southerner, the white and the Negro, the Republican and the Democrat—and those who would preach disunity and division and sow unrest in times of trouble, who would harass those who bear the burdens—finally they would all live together in this land and by their common efforts carve out its historical destiny.

And in Lincoln's spirit, we will achieve "a just and a lasting peace, among ourselves and with all nations."

NOTE: The President spoke at 12:40 p.m. from the steps of the Lincoln Memorial. In his opening words he referred to Maj. Gen. C. S. O'Malley, Jr., Commanding General, Military District of Washington, U.S. Army.

The ceremony commemorating Abraham Lincoln's birthday is sponsored annually by the Military Order of the Loyal Legion of the United States, District of Columbia Commandery.

71   Remarks Upon Presenting the 1967 National Medal of Science Awards.   *February 13, 1968*

Mr. Vice President, Mr. Speaker, Members of the Cabinet, Member of the Congress, Dr. Hornig, most distinguished guests:

Once again, America honors a dozen distinguished men of science.

Their achievements inspire us to consider not only what science has done for us, but to consider what remains for it to do.

We have asked much of our scientists. In return, we have provided considerable support to scientific endeavor.

In the current fiscal year, the Federal Government is spending $18 billion on scientific research and development, and assistance to science education.

For the coming year, we must make a Government-wide effort to reduce expenditures. So we have not been able to allot as much as we would like for fellowships for our basic research.

I begrudge every economy and every necessity of today that limits our support of science—even momentarily. Although our spending for science is vast in comparison with earlier days, I want it to be larger still. For science has a big job to do.

In 8 years, America will enter its third century. Science and technology enable us to look forward to an age that will further enlighten our lives, ease our labors, and exalt our civilization.

But there are other, grimmer forecasts. Wise men worry about a world that is unable to feed itself—about a society that is smothered in smog—about the coming of a "silent spring."

These flaws in our environment are not the fault of science alone. Their more immediate causes lie in the growth of technology, in industry, and, of course, urbanization.

But an aggrieved public does not draw the fine line between "good" science and "bad" technology. The passenger in the jet credits science with the miracle of flight. But when he is on the ground, he is just as quick to blame science—for the traffic jam at the airport, or for the noise of the jets overhead.

You and I know that Frankenstein was the doctor, not the monster. But it would be well to remember that the people of the village, angered by the monster, marched against the doctor.

In a democratic society, the public attitude toward science must always be a real concern of the scientific community. If that attitude is to be favorable, science must be prepared to play its part in correcting the flaws in our environment.

This is not a task for science alone, but for us all, for every citizen in the land and for every scientist as well.

There is a universe of problems to be mastered so our world can be made more livable for our children.

The stature of the scientists we honor today gives me great confidence that science will do its part.

We have come here to the East Room for this very pleasant occasion. And I am quite pleased to be a participant in bestowing the 1967 awards of the National Medal of Science.

Thank all of you for coming here and honoring us with your presence.

NOTE: The President spoke at 12:42 p.m. in the East Room at the White House. In his opening words he referred to Hubert H. Humphrey, Vice President of the United States, John W. McCormack of Massachusetts, Speaker of the House of Representatives, and Dr. Donald F. Hornig, Special Assistant to the President and Director of the Office of Science and Technology, who introduced the award winners and read the citations, which follow:

Jesse W. Beams, professor of physics, University of Virginia, "For sustained and ingenious contributions to the scientific development of high-speed centrifuges, a family of devices that are now widely applied in the physical and biological sciences, in medicine, and in engineering scale isotope-separation."

Francis Birch, professor of geological sciences, Harvard University, "For outstanding contributions to geophysics which have immeasurably increased our understanding of the composition and the processes of the interior of the earth."

Gregory Breit, professor of physics, Yale University, "For pioneering contributions to the theoretical understanding of nuclear structure and particle dynamics, for highly significant work in atomic and ionospheric physics and for the inspiration he has given to several generations of American physicists."

Paul J. Cohen, professor of mathematics, Stanford University, "For epoch-making results in mathematical logic which have enlivened and broadened investigations in the foundation of mathematics."

Kenneth S. Cole, senior research biophysicist, National Institutes of Health, and visiting professor of biophysics, University of California, Berkeley, "For highly original experimental and theoretical investigations of the electrical properties of biological membranes that have led to a deep understanding of the functioning of nerves."

Harry F. Harlow, professor of psychology, University of Wisconsin, "For original and ingenious contributions to comparative and experimental psychology, particularly in the controlled study of learning and motivations, the determinants of animal behavior, and development of affectional behavior."

Louis P. Hammett, retired professor of chemistry, Columbia University, "For his joining together physical and organic chemistry, creating new concepts, and replacing intuition by rigor in our growing understanding of chemical reactivity."

Michael Heidelberger, professor of immunochemistry, New York University, "For placing the science of immunology on a quantitative chemical basis, and for showing its power to reveal the structure of molecules found in the living organism."

George B. Kistiakowsky, professor of chemistry, Harvard University, "For contributions to physical chemistry, particularly to the understanding of reaction rates, and for statesmanship in the evolution of relationships between science and public affairs."

Edwin H. Land, president, Polaroid Corp., "For many discoveries and inventions in the field of polarized light, rapid photography, including quick processing of the final photograph, for the development of a unique theory of color vision, and for contributions to national defense."

Igor I. Sikorsky, retired engineering manager, Sikorsky Aircraft Division of United Aircraft Corp., "For pioneering in the development of multi-engined aircraft, both land and sea planes, and for developing the helicopter as a useful and important device of aerial transportation."

Alfred H. Sturtevant, professor of biology, emeritus, California Institute of Technology, "For a long and distinguished career in genetics during which he discovered and interpreted a number of important genetic phenomena in Drosophila and other organisms."

The National Medal of Science, the Federal Government's highest award for distinguished achievement in science, mathematics, and engineering, was established in 1959 by the 86th Congress.

The awards were made by the President on the basis of recommendations from the President's Committee on the National Medal of Science, chaired by Dr. Bryce L. Crawford of the University of Minnesota. A White House release of December 30, 1967, listing the recipients and giving further details of their scientific achievements, is printed in the Weekly Compilation of Presidential Documents (vol. 4, p. 11).

72 Remarks Upon Signing the Savings and Loan Holding Company Amendments of 1967. *February 14, 1968*

Members of Congress and distinguished guests:

The bill I will sign here today will strengthen and protect a cornerstone of American life—the savings and loan association.

We think of these institutions as a part of

hometown America. They are in every State; they are always close to where our people live. More than 40 million Americans put their savings there. These associations provide most of the mortgages that allow families to build or allow families to buy their homes.

One of the most encouraging aspects of

today's America is that nearly two-thirds of all the homes—37 million homes—are owned by the families who live in them.

It is good to know that two-thirds of my countrymen do not have a landlord to worry about. I have a nice house here, but I am always conscious that I am only a tenant.

My landlord is the people of the United States. Every morning—except Sunday and Monday—the landlord sends hundreds of delegates who tour through the downstairs part of the house—just to see if Mrs. Johnson and I are here and if we are keeping up the property well.

I could go on, but I don't want to get into that business about renewing the lease! I will have something to say about that at a later date.

This legislation that I am approving today gives additional protection to the tens of millions of people who invest in, and who borrow from, the savings and loan associations. For the first time it enables the Federal Home Loan Bank Board to regulate and supervise holding companies which own or control insured associations.

It is a well-devised safeguard against possible abuses. It is designed to enhance the soundness of the entire industry. It should encourage even greater public saving in these associations.

Public policy cannot be indifferent to the well-being of our savings and loan associations:

—They are much too important to their millions of shareholders.
—They are too necessary to a healthy mortgage market.

—They are too vital to America's growing economy.

The associations owned by holding companies are few. But if abuses in their operation should cause even one—even one—to become insolvent, public confidence in other savings and loan associations would be weakened. Thus, the problem of these associations under the control of holding companies is, I think, an important national problem.

It is a problem that this legislation seeks and is designed, we hope, to correct and to prevent.

I want to especially thank Senator Sparkman and Congressman Patman and all the members of their respective committees, Chairman Horne, and all the others who have worked so diligently to bring this day about.

I must frankly admit that I have been waiting for it some time. And I have been concerned every day during that waiting period lest something happen that this legislation is designed to prevent.

So it is with a great sense of satisfaction and some sense of accomplishment that we meet here in this room today where I will put my signature on a measure that I think is very much desired and needed.

NOTE: The President spoke at 1:41 p.m. in the Fish Room at the White House. During his remarks he referred to Senator John Sparkman of Alabama, Chairman of the Senate Committee on Banking and Currency, Representative Wright Patman of Texas, Chairman of the House Committee on Banking and Currency, and John E. Horne, Chairman of the Federal Home Loan Bank Board.

As enacted, the bill (S. 1542) is Public Law 90-255 (82 Stat. 5).

73 Statement by the President on the Treaty for the Prohibition of Nuclear Weapons in Latin America. *February 14, 1968*

ONE YEAR ago today, on February 14, 1967, the nations of Latin America gathered in Tlatelolco, Mexico, to sign a Treaty for the Prohibition of Nuclear Weapons in Latin America. Twenty-one nations of the region have now joined in this historic undertaking.

The United States considers this treaty to be a realistic and effective arms control measure of unique significance—not only to the peoples of Latin America, but to all the peoples of the world.

Today I am pleased to announce that the United States will sign Protocol II to this treaty which calls upon the powers possessing nuclear weapons to respect the status of denuclearization in Latin America and not to use or threaten to use nuclear weapons against the Latin American states party to the treaty. I have appointed Adrian S. Fisher, Deputy Director of the Arms Control and Disarmament Agency, as my emissary to sign the Protocol in Mexico with an appropriate statement.

Upon ratification by the Senate, the United States will assume the obligations to those countries within the region which undertake and meet the treaty's requirements. I am pleased to note that the drafters of this treaty have indicated that transit by the United States within the treaty zone will continue to be governed by the principles and rules of international law.

The Treaty of Tlatelolco has been closely related to the long effort to reach worldwide agreement to prevent the further spread of nuclear weapons. It will create a nuclear free zone in an area of 7½ million square miles, inhabited by nearly 200 million people. Like the Nonproliferation Treaty, this treaty, in addition to prohibiting the acquisition of nuclear weapons, also prohibits the acquisition of nuclear explosive devices for peaceful purposes. However, it has been drafted in such a way as to make it possible for Latin American parties to the treaty to obtain peaceful nuclear explosion services.

It is indeed fitting that this giant step forward should have had its genesis in Latin America, an area which has come to be identified with regional cooperation. I particularly wish to congratulate our distinguished friend, President Diaz Ordaz of Mexico, for the initiative and leadership which his Government has contributed to this treaty and thereby to the peace of this region and of the world.

In signing this Protocol, the United States once again affirms its special and historic relationship with the peoples of Latin America and its stake in their future. The United States gives this affirmation gladly, in the conviction that the denuclearization of this region enhances the development of its peaceful nuclear potential.

NOTE: On March 25 the White House announced the President's designation of Vice President Humphrey to sign Protocol II of the treaty on behalf of the United States at ceremonies to be held in Mexico City on April 1. Deputy Director Adrian S. Fisher of the Arms Control and Disarmament Agency was prevented by illness from attending the signing. The full text of the announcement is printed in the Weekly Compilation of Presidential Documents (vol. 4, p. 576).

The text of the treaty is printed in the "Seventh Annual Report to Congress of the Arms Control and Disarmament Agency, January 1, 1967 to January 18, 1968," pages 65–77 (Government Printing Office, 1968). The Vice President's remarks at the signing ceremony, together with the text of Protocol II, are printed in the Department of State Bulletin (vol. 58, p. 554).

74 Statement by the President on Secretary Gardner's Decision To Serve as Chairman of the Urban Coalition. *February* 14, 1968

I AM gratified that Secretary Gardner has agreed to serve as chairman of the Urban Coalition.

As Secretary of Health, Education, and Welfare, John Gardner has demonstrated that he understands the dimensions and the urgency of the problems facing our cities.

All of us know that the solution to the Nation's urban problems requires a new breadth of leadership in the cities themselves; not only leadership from Federal, State, and local governments, but bold leadership from the private sector.

The Urban Coalition offers such leadership. It promises to play a significant role in the effort to find solutions for the disturbing problems of the cities.

When Secretary Gardner told me about his interest in the chairmanship of the Urban Coalition, I encouraged and urged him to

accept it. I know he intends to work closely with the National Alliance of Businessmen and the Urban Institute, and I have assured him of my cooperation in the important efforts which he and the Urban Coalition are undertaking.

NOTE: The Urban Coalition grew out of a meeting of mayors and national leaders held in Washington on July 31, 1967. The group met to create a coordinating structure through which existing leadership and organizations could work together locally and nationally in a broad attack on the conditions that lead to violence in the cities. A convocation of 1,200 persons adopted on August 24, 1967, a statement of principles that became the charter of the Urban Coalition. In the spring of 1968 the Coalition was organized as a nonprofit corporation. A related nonprofit corporation, the Urban Coalition Action Council, was then formed to mobilize public support for the movement's legislative objectives. Each corporation is supported by contributions from a variety of interested individuals and groups including business firms and labor organizations. Local coalitions are being established in cities throughout the Nation.

75 Remarks at a Ceremony Inaugurating a Program of Community Service Projects for Older Americans. *February* 15, 1968

Secretary Wirtz, my distinguished friends:

One of our great poets had this to say about getting older: "The years between 50 and 70 are the hardest. You are always being asked to do things, and yet you aren't ancient enough to turn them down."

Well, today we are giving a great many older citizens a chance to do a great many things. And I'm willing to bet that we won't get turned down.

Today we are launching a program to provide work in community service projects for retired or unemployed citizens who are 55 and over.

The three contracts that were referred to by Secretary Wirtz that we will sign will create more than 3,000 job opportunities in the coming year. These jobs will be in schools, hospitals, in beautification projects, and other efforts that will improve life for all of us.

There are a good many of us in this room today who can remember seeing people grow old 20 or 30 years ago—seeing what old age did to them.

Too often, it meant being alone. Too often, it meant being dependent on someone else—their children or their sons-in-law. It meant that as the years mounted up, their savings dwindled down. And worst of all, it meant being sick and afraid because they just didn't seem to be able to afford to be sick.

Things have changed some since then, largely because of leadership that people like you have provided.

In March, more than 17 million older citizens will receive a social security increase of some 13 percent. When the benefit checks go out, another 1 million Americans will be lifted above the poverty line—a goal that we are working toward.

Medicare—that for many, many years was not seriously considered and after it was considered and passed, many said would not work at all—is now flourishing. More than 20 million senior citizens have its protection. Last year, 7½ million of these senior citizens received help in paying their medical bills. That is a fact—not a fantasy.

But beyond all of this, we all have another goal. That goal is to guarantee to every older American not only security, but the pride of being able to be active and being able to be productive.

Last year we took a major step toward that goal.

We passed a law forbidding age discrimination in employment.

We renewed and strengthened the Older Americans Act. It promised a new sense of involvement and usefulness to hundreds of thousands of our citizens.

And that is only a small part of the story. More than 4,000 Foster Grandparents in 38 States, nearly 300 older VISTA volunteers, 500 older Peace Corps volunteers, more than 3,000 members of SCORE—the Service Corps of Retired Executives—have already learned what it is to have a feeling of pride in serving others, regardless of one's age.

Now we meet here again this morning in another good cause. Soon, after the signing

of these three contracts, thousands of older citizens will know what it is to have a long life. They will know what it is to have a full life; to know what the wise Frenchman meant when he said: "Growing old is nothing more than a habit which a busy man has no time to form."

In this day of trouble and trial for our people, I want to salute those representatives, who are here in the Cabinet Room this morning, of the older Americans in our country, for your objectives, for your goals, for your persistence, and for the manner in which you have represented those for whom you speak.

You have spoken where it counts; you have been represented in the rooms where there is a payoff.

In December we signed a social security bill. It affected the lives of millions of people directly; it affected the lives of all of us— all 200 million—indirectly.

President Truman proposed Medicare. But you testified for it—and you worked for it— and you presented your opinion—and your concern—and your dissent—and your voice—and your logic—and your argument before the committees.

Those committees listened and they learned. And as a consequence, 7½ million of your fellow citizens have benefited.

There will be hearings in the days to come—hearings on poverty, hearings on education, hearings on health, hearings on security for older Americans.

While we have made great progress, we have just gone a few steps up a long road. I had three figures in my mind that were brought to me by the Budget Director this year when we signed the budget.

The first one was on manpower training that is very important to you. In 1960, our budget was $3 billion—$3 billion for manpower training.

225

By fiscal year 1964—just before I took office—that had increased to $4 billion plus.

From 1964 to 1968, largely through help that you and other concerned citizens have rendered in the Congress, in the precincts, and in the election, the Congress—by an overwhelming vote—increased that $3 billion in 1960 and that $4 billion in 1964 to $12 billion in this year's budget.

In poverty, which affects us all, but affects no one more than the older American—one million were removed from the poverty level by the last social security bill alone—that poverty group was receiving a little over $9 billion in the year 1960.

We had moved that $9 billion up to $12 billion by the fiscal year 1964. In 1964, we renewed our pledges that were made and our promises of 1960 when President Kennedy went from one end of this Nation to the other. We pleaded with the members of the appropriate committees to try to move forward with the New Frontier and the Great Society.

From 1964, when we had $12 billion, to '68, this year, we have $28 billion—more than double the amount of Federal funds spent for those below the level of $3,000.

Now, finally, if there is anything that is vital to every citizen of this land, it is health. It doesn't make any difference how many Ph.D.'s he has if he is bedridden and can't get out of his room and requires the care of other people.

Education is one of the reasons, I think, that America leads the world. I was reading a book last night; Europe was very concerned about our industrial management. They felt that we were taking the place that some of their citizens should be taking. But they said we have this great ingenuity and this great industrial management system

primarily because of the education of our people.

So health, education, and social security: In 1960 we were spending $19 billion in that field. Fiscal 1964—a little over 3 years later—we were spending $23 billion in that field.

We moved it up $4 billion. Since 1964, to 1968, we moved it not 1 billion, not 4 billion—but we have more than doubled it from $23 billion to $47 billion in the budget this year.

The social security bill, the poverty bill, the training bill—all of these items overlap. But the important thing is that we are moving along.

Now that is not nearly what we ought to do. That is not nearly as much as we want to do. But it is a sign when you can triple manpower and when you can more than double aid to poverty in one administration. When you can go in health, education, and social security from $23 billion to $47 billion, it is something that you are not justified in saying is being completely neglected.

So to those of you who have manned the ramparts—to those of you who have marched in the committee rooms—to those of you who have written the letters and talked to your Congressmen and your Senators of both parties, and the leaders of both parties, I salute, congratulate, and thank you for what you have done for your fellow man.

Thank you, very much.

NOTE: The President spoke at 12:20 p.m. in the Cabinet Room at the White House to a group of older Americans who were accompanied by Secretary of Labor W. Willard Wirtz.

Contracts running from 9 to 15 months and providing community service jobs for hard-core unemployed or retired men and women 55 years of age and older were awarded to the National Council on Aging, the National Council of Senior Citizens, and the National Farmers Union.

76   Remarks at the Swearing In of Merton J. Peck as a Member, Council of Economic Advisers, and Upon Designating Arthur M. Okun as Chairman. *February 15, 1968*

Dr. and Mrs. Peck and family, Mr. and Mrs. Okun and family, Secretary Wirtz, distinguished guests, ladies and gentlemen:

I want to welcome all of you to this ceremony this morning.

I stand here with one eye wet and one eye dry. Gardner Ackley's departure saddens me. I would hope that he feels the same way.

When Gardner took the CEA chairmanship more than 3 years ago, the economy was already setting peacetime records. He has kept the curve climbing, turning a youthful boom into a mature and solid 8-year expansion.

Of all the good advice Chairman Ackley has given to me throughout the years, I was happiest to accept one of his fine recommendations to appoint Art Okun as his successor.

Art brings many special talents to this new job. His forecasts are so amazingly accurate that one newspaper once called him the administration's secret weapon.

Far away from the limelight, he has been invaluable to international monetary policy—to the Treasury Department in developing the Rio Accord—to drafting the new system of Special Drawing Rights. And I am relying heavily on Chairman Okun and the Council to help us move this Nation and all nations towards swift acceptance of these new monetary arrangements.

To fill the Council vacancy, we have Merton Joseph Peck from Yale University.

I am delighted that he joins Jim Duesenberry and Art Okun at this particular time. One of our most urgent concerns in the Nation now is price stability. We have recently created a Cabinet committee to con-

centrate heavily on this problem. Dr. Peck is an expert on markets. He will bring special insights to price and wage problems arising from structural imperfections in labor markets, product markets, and markets for services.

Looking around us as we meet here this morning, we see more and more evidence of our economic strength. The January unemployment rate, we are pleased to say, was the lowest in more than 14 years. Corporate profits for the last quarter of 1967 were pointing upward again—to new records.

But we cannot rejoice without recognizing the dangers posed by price and cost increases. To preserve our recordbreaking prosperity, we must combine it with a return to price stability.

As we have long emphasized, the first order of business is the prompt enactment by the Congress of the penny on the dollar tax increase that we will need to pay for part of our extraordinary defense costs.

Second, we need full cooperation and restraint from business and labor in their price and wage decisions. Excessive wage and excessive price increases can weaken the dollar. They cannot win lasting gains for any group. The short-run sacrifices that we ask promise long-term benefits to all of us.

Third, we must work through the new Cabinet committee for structural improvements in every market—for greater efficiency, greater productivity, and greater incentives for cost-reduction and price competition.

I will continue to look to the Council of Economic Advisers for advice on guarding our prosperity against inflation.

I was talking to someone last night and

he was outlining for me the progress that our country has made throughout the years. He said, "Mr. President, there are two things that a leader must never take his mind off of in our political system. You will have many messages and many bills, but two simple rules, I suggest."

I said, "Tell me what they are"—because he was a man of wisdom and experience and nonpartisanship.

He said, "The first one is the buck—that dollar—it must be sound. It must be stable and people must have some of them. The next one is—you don't have to be told that one, but I want to remind you every day—the ballot. Because through the ballot people can gain the rewards they think they are entitled to. They can bring about the reforms that are essential. They can turn into motion the revolutions that are inside of all of us and they can bring them to reality and bring them to reality constitutionally and appropriately, and as we human beings should. We don't have to act like animals to get our revolutions and reforms translated into action. That comes through the ballot."

So, if my economic advisers are not trained counselors on the ballot, they are on the buck and that seems to be a major portion of a President's problem. I am going to continue to look to them to guard our prosperity against inflation. They will have the help of the President and I hope they will have the help of the Cabinet and the Congress and the business and labor communities.

The Council today enjoys a worldwide reputation, I think, a reputation of three wise men who have been responsible and are responsible in the future for guiding the American economic miracle.

We expect great things from you, Dr. Peck. I am happy to welcome you officially into the world's smallest, but the world's most vital fraternity.

Gardner, you are on sabbatical leave, but we will expect you to carry on your good work across the ocean.

NOTE: The President spoke at 1:15 p.m. in the Cabinet Room at the White House. In his opening words he also referred to Secretary of Labor W. Willard Wirtz. During his remarks he referred to James S. Duesenberry, member of the Council of Economic Advisers, and to Gardner Ackley, outgoing Chairman of the Council, whose nomination as Ambassador to Italy was announced by the President on January 1 (see Item 1).

Establishment of the Cabinet Committee on Price Stability was announced by the President in his message to the Congress transmitting the Economic Report (see Item 47). For his memorandums to the appointees and to department and agency heads directing their cooperation with the Council, see Items 89, 90.

The tax increase referred to by the President was enacted as the Revenue and Expenditure Control Act of 1968. For his statement upon signing the measure, see Item 343.

77 Message to the Inter-American Cultural Council, Meeting in Maracay, Venezuela. *February 15, 1968*

IF MAN is to achieve his fullest potential, he must have the freedom to learn—and he must have learning to be truly free.

You meet to put into action the purposes of the Punta del Este Declaration of Presidents. There is no more important work facing our hemisphere. Together, we must:

—assure basic education for all our people;

—make our secondary schools and universities centers of excellence; and

—harness science and technology in the work of education and development.

The largest share of what *must* be done, you *must* do. But I want you to know that we in the United States will help—with our resources, our technology, and the enthusiastic support of our people.

In preparing your programs you will use the tools that are at hand. But I hope your vision also will extend to the tools of tomorrow. I am particularly enthusiastic about the possibilities of combining advanced technology with advanced methods of teaching and research. Educational television already points the way. We are not far from the day when the satellite will help us

—leap across the barriers that today deny good education to millions of citizens, and

—unlock the doors to hidden natural resources on land and the surrounding seas.

With warm and vivid memories of my meetings with your Presidents last April, I send you greetings and best wishes for success in your deliberations.

NOTE: The President's message was delivered by Dr. Milton Eisenhower, chairman of the American delegation, as part of his plenary address to the meeting.

78 Remarks to the Washington Chapter of the National Conference of Christians and Jews. *February 15, 1968*

Cardinal O'Boyle, Chief Justice and Mrs. Warren, distinguished Ambassadors, head table guests, ladies and gentlemen:

Two weeks before the presidential election in 1928, Governor Alfred E. Smith spoke to a young friend in the strictest of confidence. "They aren't going to elect me President," he said. "They attacked me out there. They even tried to harm Mrs. Smith. I just didn't realize that the feeling against a Catholic went so deep."

And he was right. The feelings against Catholics did run deep in 1928 in this country. Across the Nation the Klan and the hate peddlers played on prejudice and fear. The symbol of the election of 1928 was neither donkey nor elephant, but the burning cross.

But following that election, four great men met in New York to found a new alliance against hatred—Charles Evans Hughes, Newton Baker, Roger Straus, and Carleton J. Hayes. They then and there established the National Conference of Christians and Jews.

You know I am a supporter of your work. Some of you will remember that around

Christmas and New Year's I met with His Holiness, the Pope, in Rome and I met with Prime Minister Eshkol at the LBJ Ranch. I told them then that I might even be here at this dinner tonight. I was gratified by their similar reactions.

His Holiness, the Pope, said to me: "Mr. President, you be sure to talk to Paddy O'Boyle and you tell him to be nice to Rabbi Segal." And then he said: "Mr. President, that will be good politics."

A few days later Prime Minister Eshkol said: "Mr. President, you be sure to talk to Rabbi Segal and you tell him to be nice to Cardinal O'Boyle. That will be good politics."

Well, you may not believe this, but Lady Bird said to me, "Lyndon, you be sure to be nice to Cardinal O'Boyle and Rabbi Segal because some day you may want to go back into politics."

The goal of the National Conference of Christians and Jews was to change the beliefs of a nation, nothing less. And those beliefs have been changed. The fires of religious hatred have been dampened.

Many organizations and many men deserve the credit and the gratitude for that. But few deserve it more than the great man whom I have come here to pay my respects to and whom you have come here tonight to honor.

Patrick Cardinal O'Boyle is one man who did not wait for a miracle. He worked with other good men and women to make it happen. He came to this city in 1948. In that year, 6 years, Mr. Chief Justice, before the Brown case, the Catholic schools of his archdiocese were integrated.

Fourteen years later at the Vatican Council inspired by Pope John XXIII, Patrick O'Boyle again waged his fight for conscience. The Council's declaration on non-Christian religions bears the imprint of this man's wisdom.

There is beauty and toughness to this man's life. If some Americans—worried by the strife in our cities—ask, "Oh, well, what's the use?"—Patrick Cardinal O'Boyle knows the ultimate and the only real answer. That lies in Americans being true to their ancient mission—to always advance and protect human dignity.

As we honor this great man tonight, we must also ask ourselves, "Do we still have the faith?" We must ask if we, like Cardinal O'Boyle, will be doers of the word, and not hearers only.

Do we really believe that men of different races and religions can live together in one land? Do we really believe that every American is entitled to a decent education, decent housing, decent job at a decent wage?

Do we believe that these things can come about peacefully?

I believe that we do. We have come, I know, a long way since 1928. Now, as then, there is hate and some fear among us. But now, as then, there are men who stand tall among us who raise the voice of conscience.

In the Book of Job we are told: "From out of the populous city, men groan: and the soul of the wounded cries for help." Thank God there are still good men such as this good man who respond always to that cry.

Thank you and good night.

NOTE: The President spoke at 9 p.m. in the International Ballroom at the Washington Hilton Hotel. In his opening words he referred to Patrick Cardinal O'Boyle, Archbishop of Washington, Earl Warren, Chief Justice of the United States, and Mrs. Warren. The President spoke following a dinner in honor of Cardinal O'Boyle who was presented with the Brotherhood Award of the National Conference of Christians and Jews.

79 The President's News Conference of *February 16, 1968*

THE PRESIDENT. [1.] George[1] tells me that he has given you something not to announce today. I want to give you something you can announce just as soon as you get out of here.

_____

[1] George E. Christian, Special Assistant to the President.

SECRETARY OF COMMERCE

We have accepted with very deep regret the resignation of Mr. Sandy Trowbridge— Mr. A. B. Trowbridge—the Secretary of Commerce. The resignation is effective March 1st.

We will send to the Senate the name of Mr. C. R. Smith, the former president of American Airlines, and the present chairman of the board of American Airlines.

Mr. Smith was born in Minerva, Texas, and for the last 30 years has been associated with American Airlines, residing in New York.

Mr. Smith is a member of the Business Council and has been for some 10 or 12 years. He is recommended very warmly and strongly by Secretary Trowbridge and other leaders, including Secretary Wirtz, with whom he will have to work closely.

Mr. Smith has agreed to move to Washington and join us effective March 1st.

CHAIRMAN OF THE CIVIL AERONAUTICS
BOARD

[2.] As you know, some time ago Mr. Charles Murphy informed us of his desire to leave the Civil Aeronautics Board. We are accepting his resignation from that Board. For the time being, he will be a consultant to the President, acting as a counsel for me here in the White House on a part-time basis.

He will be succeeded as Chairman of the Board, the Senate willing, by Mr. John H. Crooker. Mr. Crooker is a member of the law firm of Fulbright, Crooker, Freeman & Bates, in Houston, Texas.

I first knew him 38 years ago when he defeated my debating team in Houston High School. He was a star senior debater. I later took one of my men and Mr. Crooker and they defeated the State champions.

Since that time Mr. Crooker has graduated with honors from the Rice Institute, and with honors from the University of Texas Law School. He was on the Law Review there.

He is presently a resident of the District

of Columbia, representing his firm here. His nomination will go to the Senate very shortly.

He was born in 1914, and Mr. Smith was born in 1899. Mr. Smith is 68 years of age. Mr. Trowbridge is 37 years of age.

I think that is all I have. George will give you the biographies on these men.

QUESTIONS

MR. TROWBRIDGE'S RESIGNATION

[3.] Q. Is it health in Mr. Trowbridge's case?

THE PRESIDENT. The doctors had some question when he became Secretary of Commerce. He went through a very thorough examination. He had had a heart problem. He decided to accept the challenge. He did a very fine job.

He has been working long and hard, but he has suffered a little relapse. He has been out for a few weeks. After completing his examinations at Johns Hopkins with other doctors in the last few days, he gave me his letter yesterday resigning as Secretary of Commerce.

We are very hopeful that we can utilize his services to the extent his health will permit in some other capacity, but we have not even discussed that.

Q. Is he returning, Mr. President, to his private company?

THE PRESIDENT. I just answered that. As far as I know, he said to me that he would be available to us for anything he could do, so far as his health is concerned. But I do not think he has made any plans of any kind. I think he will have to speak for himself.

My judgment is he would wait for some time to see how his health comes along. Then if we could use him on something not so strenuous as a Cabinet job, we might be able to get him to do that. If not, he will make some private connection, I am sure.

Q. How long did he serve? From last June, Mr. President?

THE PRESIDENT. George will supply that information to you.

Q. Mr. President, are you concerned by what may seem to some as a considerable number of departures from your administration at high levels?

THE PRESIDENT. We always hate to see anyone depart, particularly men like Mr. Trowbridge. But in the light of the circumstances, I think I wouldn't want him to stay and I don't think you would, either.

MR. MURPHY'S DUTIES

[4.] Q. Mr. President, can you tell us anything more specific about what Mr. Murphy will be doing for you here?

THE PRESIDENT. He will be a counsel here at the White House, advising with the President, reporting directly to the President. His specific duties will be primarily legal. He was counsel to President Truman. He will be available, I think, for any assignment that the President desires to give him.

Q. I wondered, sir, if you might have any political assignments in mind for him?

THE PRESIDENT. None whatever.

A SECRETARY FOR HEW

[5.] Q. Do you foresee a new Health and Welfare Secretary soon?

THE PRESIDENT. I don't have any immediate timetable on that. We have a very outstanding man as Under Secretary.[2] I would anticipate that he would act for at least a few weeks.

---

[2] The nomination of Under Secretary Wilbur J. Cohen to succeed John W. Gardner as Secretary of Health, Education, and Welfare was announced by the President in his news conference of March 22, 1968 (see Item 153).

THE AID PROGRAM

[6.] Q. Mr. President, there have been some problems relative to the AID program lately. I wondered if you could give us your viewpoint as to what this amounts to, if you feel it jeopardizes your AID program this year, and what you are doing about it?

THE PRESIDENT. The AID program always has its problems with the Congress. The information I have about it is that the matter is now under consideration by the Justice Department. The Inspector General of the State Department has been very diligent in attempting to make a thorough study of the problems in the AID program. He is making his report available to the Attorney General and to the appropriate committees of the Congress.

GOVERNOR ROMNEY ON VIETNAM

[7.] Q. Mr. President, you may have noticed that Governor Romney now refers to our force in Vietnam as the Johnson-Nixon policy. Does that ring any bell?

THE PRESIDENT. No. I would think we shouldn't play politics with the war and try to associate it with name-calling.

I think most of the Americans at one time or another have agreed with the policy and there have been some departures from the ranks. But I am not going to say anything that I consciously believe will involve the war and the men who are fighting it in a political campaign.

STATUS OF GENERAL WESTMORELAND

[8.] Q. Mr. President, sir, there have been some rumors in the last couple of days from various Members of Congress that General Westmoreland might be transferred. Can you comment on that?

THE PRESIDENT. I think that has been thoroughly covered. I should think you could observe from the sources that they are not either my confidants or General Westmoreland's.

I don't want to attribute bad motives to anyone, but I would think it hardly likely that the Commander in Chief would get information about the future of General Westmoreland from a Republican Congressman from Wisconsin. I think that would be apparent to almost anyone.

I think that General Westmoreland is confronted with one of the great tests of his career, as we are in this country.

Just before he goes into battle there in South Vietnam—Khe Sanh, or whatever engagements may follow—I would not want to have him in doubt for a moment, or a single one of his men in doubt, about his standing with his Commander in Chief or with his superiors.

I am amazed that you would give the attention to him that you do in the light of my expression of admiration and respect for him so recently—in December, at Cam Ranh Bay, when I spoke very personally about him and gave him one of America's highest decorations.

I have observed this question being raised. I think it was first raised abroad. It continues to be raised here every day.

I don't know how to put a stop to it, except to say that I have never known a man with whom I have worked in the military for whom I had a higher regard or a greater respect.

I would hope that that statement could end the gossip and the rumors about General Westmoreland's future.

I think we all know that he has served there at my insistence and with the approval of the Joint Chiefs longer than one would ordinarily serve in an ordinary post.

But these are not ordinary times. They require each of us to help along and contribute whatever we can.

Just as General Taylor[3] said to me, "I have been away from my family now in three wars, but I am ready to go back again if you need me," General Westmoreland has said he would stay there as long as I want him to stay there.

While I don't want to be inconsiderate of him, I do think that it is in your interest and the Nation's interest, and the free world's interest, that this man, with his background, his experience, and his knowledge of conditions there be there at this critical stage.

I know the credibility problem. I cannot say to you that he will never leave.

I know he has been there over 4 years already. But I can tell you that I have no intention of seeing him leave, I have no plan for him to leave, and, if I did have, I don't think it would come to you the way it has.

I think all of you should give consideration to how these things come to you. Because if you flash around the world the doubt that someone has and then to remove that doubt he has to make a statement, when, in the normal routine of things it should be changed, then you say, "You misled us." So you get it either way—"Have you stopped beating your wife?"

I said to General Westmoreland, when I saw reports in the intelligence of what was being said about him, and I saw them picked up by certain overseas newspapers, and before they came into wide circulation here but appeared, I think, in one brief reference, that I wanted him to know very bluntly that I had never known a man in the military whom I had more confidence in. I don't know how to go any stronger than that.

---

[3] Gen. Maxwell D. Taylor, USA, Ret., Special Consultant to the President.

But there is a campaign on to get over the world that we have doubts in General Westmoreland. That campaign I don't believe is going to succeed. It is not going to succeed with me. I have no doubts about his ability, about his dedication.

If I had to select a man to lead me into battle in Vietnam, I would want General Westmoreland.

Does that make it clear to anybody and everybody, including all the foreign press that may want to pick it up?

You see, what irritates me is that I see these things about a week or two ahead of time. They originate, go around the world and then they get real hot here. There are reasons for doing these things. One of the reasons is to destroy people's confidence in the leadership.

With all the men we have at stake out there, with all the lives that are involved—it could be any of you or your boys—I just don't think that is the way to play it.

I see where General Westmoreland may be named a member of the Joint Chiefs of Staff. I have never discussed that with General Westmoreland for one second.

So far as I am concerned, if there is any way General Westmoreland could go, it would be up. Right now, he has the most important assignment I know of, and I am going to try to help him. I hope I am helping him by making it clear—repeat, clear—loud and clear—that every person that I know of who deals with General Westmoreland has great respect and confidence in him.[4]

---

[4] The President, in his news conference of March 22, 1968, announced his appointment of Gen. William C. Westmoreland, Commander, United States Military Assistance Command, Vietnam, to succeed Gen. Harold K. Johnson as Army Chief of Staff (see Item 153).

NUCLEAR WEAPONS AND VIETNAM

[9.] Q. Mr. President, could you address yourself, please, sir, to the gossip and rumors about nuclear weapons in Vietnam?

THE PRESIDENT. I think the Press Secretary covered that very well.

The President must make the decision to deploy nuclear weapons. It is one of the most awesome and grave decisions any President could be called upon to make.

It is reasonably apparent and known to all that it is very much against the national interest to carry on discussions about deployment of nuclear weapons; so much so that the act, itself, tries to guard against that.

I have been in the executive branch of the Government for 7 years. I think I have been aware of the recommendations made by the Joint Chiefs of Staff, by the Secretary of State, and by the Secretary of Defense during that period.

So far as I am aware, they have at no time ever considered or made a recommendation in any respect to the deployment of nuclear weapons. They are on our planes on training missions from time to time.

We do have problems. There are plans with our allies concerning what they do.

There is always a person available to me who has full information in connection with their deployment, as you newspapermen know. I think if any serious consideration were ever given, and God forbid there ever will be, I don't think you would get it by some anonymous caller to some committee of the Congress. I think most of you know that, or ought to know that.

No recommendation has been made to me. Beyond that, I think we ought to put an end to that discussion.

PROSPECTS FOR PEACE NEGOTIATIONS

[10.] Q. Mr. President, do you see any new, hopeful prospects for negotiating with Hanoi?

THE PRESIDENT. We look for them every day.

I would like to be able to say "Yes." In the last few days, preparatory to closing out the statement that Secretary Rusk issued yesterday, I believe, or the day before, we reviewed Hanoi's actions in response to more than 20-odd proposals made by well-intentioned and interested people.

We reviewed the many overtures that we had made, including the most recent one where we thought we went as far as honorable men could go—the San Antonio proposal.

As near as I am able to detect, Hanoi has not changed its course of conduct since the very first response it made.

Sometimes they will change "will" to "would", or "shall" to "should", or something of that kind. But the answer is all the same.

While we were prepared to go into the Tet truce, they were moving thousands of men from the North into the South for the subsequent attacks on that sacred holiday. I think that ought to be an answer that any elementary school boy or girl could understand.

If you want to go to the negotiating table, if you want to talk instead of fight, you don't move in thousands of people with hundreds of trucks through the night to try to catch people—innocent civilians—by surprise in the city, anticipating a general uprising.

We are familiar with all the approaches that have been made to them, and we have encouraged them all the time. But when it is all said and done, I don't want to leave the American people under any illusions, and I don't want to deceive them.

I don't think Hanoi is any more ready to negotiate today than it was a year ago, 2 years ago, or 3 years ago. I don't think it has been at any time during any of that period. Yes?

U THANT'S PEACE EFFORTS AND COMING
VISIT TO WASHINGTON

[11.] Q. Could I ask you whether your review included anything you may have had lately from the Secretary-General of the United Nations, or does that await your visit with him next week? [5]

THE PRESIDENT. The answer is yes, that does include such reports as we may have on conversations that have taken place in other capitals.

We have responded on occasions to other requests the Secretary-General has made of us. We applaud his efforts to try to bring about a just negotiation, and to get all sides to the peace table.

Ambassador Goldberg had a long meeting with the Secretary-General and got a full report on his recent trip, just as I got a full report on Prime Minister Wilson's recent trip.

I have received a good many reports from folks who have visited other capitals. We are always glad to hear those reports, although we are saddened, sometimes, that they don't bring us the hope we would like to have.

Ambassador Goldberg told me that the Secretary-General would like to see me. He had been to the Soviet capital and met with the leaders there. He had been to the British capital and met with the leaders there.

---

[5] The text of a White House statement following the President's February 21 meeting with United Nations Secretary General U Thant is printed in the Weekly Compilation of Presidential Documents (vol. 4, p. 323).

He has been to India. He has been to the French capital and met with the leaders there.

I told the Secretary-General that, of course, as long as I was in this place, I would always be glad to meet with him any time that he desired to. He suggested next Friday. I told Mr. Goldberg that I didn't know what plans you might have for Friday, but George tells me you always get a little restless, jittery, tired, worn, and snappish on Fridays. Washington's Birthday is Thursday. Maybe if we wanted to get the maximum out of this, we ought to be here where you could be with us on Wednesday. So we moved it up to Wednesday.

On Wednesday I expect to see the Secretary-General and thank him very much for another try, to hear his views and to give him mine.

Q. Will this be lunch or dinner that he is coming for?

THE PRESIDENT. That will be 11 o'clock.

GENERAL WESTMORELAND

[12.] Q. Mr. President, you mentioned a worldwide movement or scheme to undermine confidence in the American military leadership——

THE PRESIDENT. No, I don't think I said a worldwide scheme. I said we first heard reports in our intelligence reports that come to me every morning. At that time, the strategy was to discredit General Westmoreland's leadership. He had suffered great losses out there.

That was before it was determined that they didn't hold any of the cities they had attacked. But that followed with comments in other capitals, as it frequently does, namely, that there was great division in Washington, and that it was very probable that because of this great disaster General

Westmoreland had suffered, he would have to be recalled.

All I ask you to do is just imagine how you are going to feel if the rumor is around that the Chicago Tribune is getting ready to replace you and it gets into the papers, even when you haven't a battle on. Put yourself in General Westmoreland's position.

The very morning that we anticipated one of our most difficult attacks, this came through in reports.

I called in my secretary and I dictated a wire to General Westmoreland. I said, "I want to put it just as bluntly as I know how, that your Commander in Chief has never had more confidence in any military officer with whom, under whom, or above whom he served. Whatever you choose to do here will have my full support."

I made it just as strong as I know how to write it. Sometimes down in my country you can make things pretty strong. I didn't circularize it because I thought that would just give added encouragement to those who would like to feel there was a division.

I did, in response to a series of queries from a number of people, send him a wire. I told only one man and my secretary. I hadn't told Secretary McNamara and I hadn't told Secretary Rusk.

That afternoon I had three inquiries from newsmen about the wire saying, "We know you sent it to him. Give it to us."

I learned I couldn't even trust anyone on a matter like that except my secretary.

I haven't made the wire public, but I am telling you the contents of it.

That happened many days ago and I feel just as strongly about it now as I did then.

I want to emphasize that I don't want to leave the impression with any soldier in that command, with any parent of any man out there, that there is any justification whatever for all this rumor, gossip, talk, about General

Westmoreland's competence or about his standing with this President.

[13.] Q. Mr. President, how do you assess United States relations with South Korea in the wake of Mr. Vance's visit?

THE PRESIDENT. I think Mr. Vance's visit was a fruitful one. I think he had a very cordial and understanding discussion.

South Korea feels very distressed about the attempt that was made to assassinate their President and all the members of his family, as we certainly do.

We feel very deeply our problem connected with the *Pueblo*.

We have an understanding, a treaty, with them.

Mr. Vance had spent a good deal of time on matters of this kind in the 7 years he has been here.

He had lengthy talks with the Defense Minister, the Prime Minister, and the President.

He made that report to the Cabinet committee yesterday. We thought it was a very good report and his mission was a very helpful one.[6]

LEVEL OF ARMED FORCES IN VIETNAM

[14.] Q. Mr. President, are you giving any thought to increasing the level of our forces in Vietnam?

---

[6] On February 9 the White House announced that former Deputy Secretary of Defense Cyrus R. Vance would visit Seoul, Korea, as the President's personal representative for talks with President Chung Hee Park and other high Korean officials. Following his report to the President upon returning from that mission, Mr. Vance met with reporters at the White House. Texts of the announcement and news briefing are printed in the Weekly Compilation of Presidential Documents (vol. 4, pp. 280 and 293).

THE PRESIDENT. Yes, we give thought to that every day. We never know what forces will be required there. We have, tentatively, a goal. We would like to reach that goal as soon as we can. In light of the circumstances that existed when we set that goal, we hoped to reach it sometime this year.

In light of the developments and the subsequent substantial increases in the enemy force, General Westmoreland asked that he receive approximately half of the remaining numbers under that goal during February or early March.

Did you mean enemy forces or our forces?

Q. Our forces.

THE PRESIDENT. I said in light of substantial increases in the enemy force. You understood that, didn't you?

Q. Yes.

THE PRESIDENT. So General Westmoreland told us that.

We carefully reviewed his request in light of the information that had come in. We made certain adjustments and arrangements to comply with his request forthwith. That will be done.

When we reach our goal, we will be constantly reviewing the matter many times every day, at many levels. We will do whatever we think needs to be done to insure that our men have adequate forces to carry out their mission.

PRIME MINISTER WILSON'S STATEMENT ON
VIETNAM

[15.] Q. Mr. President, in light of your earlier comments on negotiations with North Vietnam, could you discuss with us the basis for Prime Minister Wilson's statement to the House of Commons, that there was only a narrow margin between the U.S. and Hanoi positions?

THE PRESIDENT. I have given you my

views. I assume you have means of getting any details of the Prime Minister's from him.

My views are very clear. I don't know anything I can add to them.

If I have confused you somewhat, I will be glad to help clear it up.

I have told you that I have never felt that

they have changed their position, modified it, or moderated it.

Douglas B. Cornell, Associated Press: Thank you, Mr. President.

NOTE: President Johnson's one hundred and nineteenth news conference was held in the Fish Room at the White House at 4:42 p.m. on Friday, February 16, 1968.

80   Letter Accepting Resignation of Alexander B. Trowbridge as Secretary of Commerce. *February 16, 1968*

Dear Sandy:

I cannot say that your letter of resignation came as a surprise. My concern for your health and knowledge of the physical stress that further duty would impose had prepared me for your decision.

Still, on the evidence of your fine performance as Secretary of Commerce and my own feelings of pride and gratitude, I can only accept it with genuine reluctance and sympathy.

You took office at an uncertain time in the history of the Department. You leave it surer of purpose, richer in assets, and stronger in resolve to match challenge with achievement.

These are your achievements, and they will last. The imprint of your devoted and dynamic leadership goes deep beyond the day. It will endure to invigorate the vital and expanding partnership of business and gov-

ernment upon which our people increasingly depend both for economic prosperity and social progress.

We who have advanced with you will miss you. All of your colleagues and friends are heartened by your intention to remain active in America's best interests. Lady Bird and I ask God's blessing on that. We want you and Nancy to go on in good health and all happiness to new rewards.

You will always be accompanied by our affection and admiration.

Sincerely,

LYNDON B. JOHNSON

[Honorable A. B. Trowbridge, Secretary of Commerce, Washington, D.C.]

NOTE: Mr. Trowbridge served as Secretary of Commerce from June 14, 1967, through March 1, 1968. His letter of resignation, dated February 15, 1968 and released with the President's reply, is printed in the Weekly Compilation of Presidential Documents (vol. 4, p. 300).

81   Remarks During a Weekend Tour of Military Installations. *February 17–18, 1968*

[1.]   Remarks at Fort Bragg, North Carolina. *February 17, 1968*

General Seitz, General Johnson, General Walt, troopers:

Wherever you are, wherever you go, each of you knows that you have with you always

the devotion, the concern, the prayers of all of those dear to you and to whom you are very dear.

As you depart once again to answer the

call from afar, I come here today as your President to tell you that on your journey the hearts of this Nation and the hopes of men in many nations fly with you and will follow with you until this duty is done.

It is never easy for men to leave. It is never easy to ask men to leave home and happiness for duty far, far away.

But the duties of freedom have never been easy. For your Nation, for all of its people, those duties may become more demanding, the trials may become more difficult, the tests more challenging, before we or the world shall know, again, that peace on this planet is once more secure.

In every capital where there was a prospect, in every forum where there was a promise, your Nation and its leadership has sought peace.

The answer of the enemy in Vietnam has been pillage. The enemy has launched a major counter offensive against the Government and the people of South Vietnam. He has marshaled his power around the cities of South Vietnam, in I Corps and elsewhere.

After 2½ years in which he has seen his grip on the people weaken, he has finally decided to try to win now—this year. His aim is to shake the Government of South Vietnam to its foundations, to shake the confidence of the South Vietnamese people, to destroy the will of your people—the American people—to see this struggle through.

In his first attempt 3 weeks ago, he failed. He did inflict terrible wounds on the people, and he took terrible losses himself. He did prove, again, what the world has long known—that terrorists can strike and can kill without warning before the forces of order can throw them back.

And now he has struck again. At this very hour, a second wave of terrorists is striking the cities. Our forces are ready. I know they will acquit themselves, as they always

have, however tough the battle becomes, and wherever it comes.

There has never been a finer fighting force wearing the American uniform than you and the one that you are going to join.

We long to see this bloodshed come to an end. Month after month we sought to find an honorable solution to the struggle that has torn Vietnam for 20 years. The enemy's answer was clear. It is written in the towns and the cities that he struck 3 weeks ago—in the homeless thousands who fled the scenes of battle—in the army that he has massed in the North near the DMZ.

And our answer—your answer—must be just as clear: unswerving resolution to resist these ruthless attacks, as we have resisted every other.

Now remember this: You, each of you, represent America's will—America's commitment—in a land where our own security, as well as South Vietnam's freedom, is now facing a deadly challenge. Men who have never been elected to anything are threatening an elected government and the painfully achieved institutions of democracy.

You—each of you—have a great role to play in this struggle. I believe—I know—that you will serve the cause of freedom just as your forefathers served it. You will serve it with bravery, you will serve it with skill, you will serve it with devotion.

We—all America—are proud of you. I came here to speak in behalf of all America, and to tell you that you are our finest because you are the Airborne.

[At this point the troops responded with "All the way, sir." The President then resumed speaking.]

God bless you and keep you.

NOTE: The President spoke at 5:05 p.m. In his opening words he referred to Maj. Gen. Richard J. Seitz, Commander of the 82d Airborne Division, Gen. Harold K. Johnson, Army Chief of Staff, and Lt. Gen. Lewis W. Walt, Assistant Commandant of the Marine Corps.

239

[2.]   Remarks at El Toro Marine Corps Air Station, California. *February 17, 1968*

General Walt, General Kyle, General Quilter, General Thrash, General Sawyer, troopers:

Tonight, I have come to bid you Godspeed as you leave—some of you for the second time—to defend your Nation's cause.

Your destination—I Corps in Vietnam—is torn and scarred tonight. More than any other stretch of territory, it is a place where the meaning of this war is clearly revealed.

The enemy, who set out 9 years ago to conquer South Vietnam by force, is showing precisely what he intends in I Corps. He makes no pretense of talking about land reform, or of improving the lives of the people. He wants, instead, his neighbor's land. He believes the way to get it is at the point of a gun.

He is undertaking what he calls his "Route 9 Offensive." He plans to strike along that route and to plant his flag on the free soil of the Republic of Vietnam. Defeated in every other part of the country, he has concentrated his major effort there, with regular forces of the North Vietnamese Army. At Quang Tri—at Hué—at Danang—at Khe Sanh—tonight United States Marines stand squarely in the path of his plan.

Freedom's defense could not be in better hands.

The Marines in Vietnam have not only shown how bravely they can fight. They have also pioneered in an effort that has no precedent whatever in warfare. They have shown the Vietnamese people, whose lives and homes they defend, how to hope. Side by side with their allies, they have planted seeds of freedom in hundreds of villages. They have inspired new courage, new confidence, in all the people. And the people will not forget.

And now the enemy has brought new heartbreak to the land he has invaded. He has marked his path with flame and terror—and the time of testing is still not over.

This is a decisive time in Vietnam. The eyes of the Nation and the eyes of the entire world—the eyes of all of history itself—are on that little, brave band of defenders who hold the pass at Khe Sanh and the area that is around it.

We do not doubt the outcome.

General Walt, who is here with me tonight, who has flown across the land with me today, tells me that he has walked every mile of I Corps. And General Walt believes it can be defended. And I read that same message in your eyes.

The enemy's tide will be broken. The villages—and the treasured city of Hué—will be rebuilt. Freedom will survive—because brave men like you are going there to preserve it.

You—and the men of the Airborne to whom I spoke earlier today at Fort Bragg—are the sons of America's best years, the best years any nation, any people, have ever known. Whatever the station from which you come, you—and your families—are living a life that no others have ever lived.

If there is goodness in our American life, it flows from the reality that we live in peace—without fear of our neighbors—without threat from aggressors—without hating or knowing that we are hated by ancient foes.

Peace has been, and peace is, the great American blessing. It is peace that we seek to help others find so that they may live as we in America are privileged to live.

When men cry, "Peace," do they not know that Americans cannot give peace to the world by ever abandoning it to aggressors? When men cry, "Peace," do they not understand that we cannot keep peace for ourselves by withdrawing from the challenges that the enemies of peace present?

But nations—like men—are never privileged to know and never able to choose the precise moment when their destiny is determined. We can only know—and we can only strive to answer—the call of duty when that call comes, and the call has come tonight.

The men at Khe Sanh, in I Corps, need help. They have asked for it. If you were there and they were here, they would come to help you.

I have asked you to go and help them. And I know you will do your duty and that you will get the job done. Our hearts and our hopes fly with you as you leave on this weekend.

May God keep you safely and someday bring you—and all with whom you stand—to live in a nation and to live in a world that is made peaceful by the duty that you now undertake.

May God bless and keep each of you. We are proud of you. Your Nation is proud of you. And we will be prouder when you come marching home after you have done the job.

Thank each of you, and good night.

NOTE: The President spoke at 8:42 p.m. In his opening words he referred to Lt. Gen. Lewis W. Walt, Assistant Commandant of the Marine Corps, Maj. Gen. Wood B. Kyle, Commander of the 3d Marine Division at Camp Pendleton, Calif., Maj. Gen. Charles B. Quilter, Commander of the 3d Marine Aircraft Wing, Maj. Gen. William G. Thrash, Commander of Marine Corps Air Bases West and Marine Corps Air Station, El Toro, and Brig. Gen. Webb D. Sawyer, Assistant Commander, 3d Marine Division.

[3.] Remarks on the Flight Deck of the U.S.S. *Constellation*. *February 18, 1968*

Admiral Roeder, Captain Flanagan, men of the "Constellation":

It is good to be here this morning with all of you who are here.

When you see them next, please convey the regards of the Commander in Chief to those men who were not contacted and had to spend Saturday night ashore.

As an old Navy man myself, from an earlier day, I know how deeply they all regret not being here with us this morning.

I am very privileged to be in your company.

Three times this ship stood on Yankee Station—this last time flying 10,000 sorties, 110 major strikes, against the heaviest concentrations of air defenses in the entire history of war. And I am very proud to say to you this morning, Captain, and to all the officers and all of the men of the *Constellation:* Well done.

I must depart shortly to the duties which always await. Having made this journey, I shall return with renewed gratitude and quickened pride for the men and women and the families of the services which keep my country secure.

It is a duty that no man should covet to decide that the sons of this Nation should be asked to go to the heart of danger. But when, from where the danger lies, there comes a call for support, it is a source of abiding gratification to know that the Nation can, and the Nation will, answer in full.

The call has come. I have seen your comrades of the Army, of the Marines, and of the Air Force—all working together as a team in harness to answer with a sureness and with a swiftness never known, never possible, before. Many men to whom I bade Godspeed only yesterday are giving the second measure, as many of you have already given, and are willing to give again. And to each of you givers, I salute you.

No money, no benefits, no privileges can compensate men for the duty which country asks and cause demands. In these times, as in all times past, the cause of freedom is a most demanding cause. It demands courage of those who must bear the battles. It demands constancy of those at home for whom the battles are borne.

Men may debate and men may dissent, men may disagree—and God forbid that a time should come when men of this land may not—but there does come a time when men must stand. And for America, that time has now come.

In Vietnam today, the foes of freedom are making ready to test America's will. Quite obviously, the enemy believes—he thinks—that our will is vulnerable. Quite clearly, the enemy hopes that he can break that will. And quite certainly, we know that the enemy is going to fail.

So we have taken our stand. We shall do all to stand—all that is asked—and all that may be required. The will of this generation of Americans will never be found wanting, abroad or at home.

You know—no men know better—that the tasks of war are tasks that all Americans abhor. But the tests of freedom are tests from which Americans will never turn.

Few of those tests are to be met by the tools or the tactics of war. The demanding cause that we champion never is more demanding than when it asks of us that we be a responsible nation—steadfast in our resolve, but no less steadfast in our restraint.

The past of nations, the past of powers, cannot guide or govern a nation whose power is greater than all the power of all nations past. Ours is such a power. We shall use it, as you have used it, with precision on the fronts of war, and with principle on the fronts of peace, praying always, as we prayed this morning, that our use will be wise and that the end will be just.

For you, for the Navy, Yankee Station is today. But the Navy that reaches out from there also has a mission for tomorrow. You are the picket ships in a line of freedom that stretches all the way around the world. All of you, the men who fly from these decks, the men who labor so faithfully and so competently and so unselfishly on those decks and below them, have a vigil to keep for peace.

I came here to spend the night with you, to look you in the eye and to tell you on behalf of all Americans that we are grateful to you and thankful for you. Our hearts will be with you when you leave your loved ones to return by summer to the duties that only you know so well.

But until freedom stands tall and strong in Asia, until this vast Pacific is a great community of peace, until the gun and the knife are sheathed, and until neighbors fear neighbors no more, Americans cannot rest, and Americans cannot sleep, and you Americans cannot be idle.

I am grateful that you are safely back home for the moment. And all the Nation is grateful for men like you.

As I prepare to leave you for the moment, as I greeted you yesterday, on behalf of all of your fellow countrymen, your Commander in Chief says God bless you and God keep you.

Each of you knows that there is a lot riding on you and that for you and your grandchildren, the kind of a world that they are going to live in is going to be determined by how well you do your job now and in the days ahead. The fact that you will do it well is not doubted by any.

Goodby and thank each of you.

Now I am going to run along to see a President of yesteryear—President Eisenhower.

As we look back on today in the years to come, when this moment is just a memory of times gone by, and people ask you the question, "Where were you in the time of testing and when your country was challenged?" each of you, with great pride, can answer, "I was with the *Constellation*."

Thank you.

NOTE: The President spoke at 10:14 p.m. In his opening words he referred to Vice Adm. Bernard F. Roeder, Commander of the First Fleet, and Capt. William R. Flanagan, Commander of the U.S.S. *Constellation*.

82   Letter to Senator Hart Expressing His Views on Pending Civil Rights Legislation. *February* 19, 1968

Dear Phil:

Again this week, the Senate of the United States is a crucial arena for human rights.

The issue is whether we will continue to move toward equality as a fact, as well as an ideal, in America.

We have made extraordinary progress in the past decade. Nevertheless equal justice is clearly not a reality for millions of Americans today. The civil rights legislation now pending before the Senate—about which you have asked my views—will not in itself achieve equality for every citizen; but it is a vital step along the way. Both conscience and reason insist that it be passed.

In one title of the pending legislation, we seek new and clear authority to punish those who would use violence and intimidation to prevent others from exercising the rights of American citizenship:

—the right to vote,

—to go to school,

—to obtain a job,

—to serve as a juror,

—and to use public facilities.

There should be no question about the exercise of these fundamental rights. There should be no doubt in anyone's mind that their exercise is protected by law against those who would use force to deny them.

Pending legislation before the Senate also seeks to ensure that every American has the opportunity to provide a decent home for his family. Segregation in housing—the product of long-standing discriminatory real estate practices—has compounded the Nation's urban problem. Minorities have been artificially compressed into ghettoes where unemployment and ignorance are rampant, where human tragedies and crime abound, and where city administrations are burdened with rising social costs and falling tax revenues. Fair housing practices—backed by meaningful Federal laws that apply to every section of the country—are essential if we are to relieve the crisis in our cities.

From every moral and practical standpoint, these measures are necessary. The wrongs they address are urgently in need of redress. Together with the other measures I have recommended to combat discrimination—particularly in the fields of employment and jury selection—they respond to the elemental demands of equal justice in America. They should be adopted without delay.

Sincerely,

LYNDON B. JOHNSON

[Honorable Philip A. Hart, United States Senate, Washington, D.C.]

NOTE: The Civil Rights Act of 1968 was approved by the President on April 11, 1968 (see Item 195).

83 Statement by the President Upon Receiving Report of the Industry-Government Special Task Force on Travel. *February 19, 1968*

THE STEPS recommended will help achieve our goal of reducing our travel deficit by $500 million this year. They will have a growing impact in future years.

But promoting travel to the United States will do more than ease our balance of payments problem. It will encourage international understanding. It will give Americans the chance to open their hearts and their homes to travelers from foreign lands.

[These recommendations] will receive prompt attention. The actions and recommendations to increase travel to the United States are an essential part of our program to reduce the Nation's travel deficit.

NOTE: The President's statement was made public as part of a White House release summarizing the report and its major recommendations. The release recalled that the task force was appointed by the President on November 16, 1967, under the chairmanship of Robert M. McKinney, former U.S. Ambassador to Switzerland, to recommend specific measures to increase foreign travel to the United States. The full text of the release is printed in the Weekly Compilation of Presidential Documents (vol. 4, p. 320).

The report is entitled "Report to the President of the United States From the Industry-Government Special Task Force on Travel" (Government Printing Office, 48 pp.).

84 Message to the Congress Transmitting Annual Report of the Civil Service Commission. *February 20, 1968*

To the Congress of the United States:

The Civil Service Commission Annual Report for fiscal 1967 reflects the importance of the most vital element in democratic government—the people who administer it, particularly those who quietly dedicate their lives to public service in the Executive Branch.

The 90th Congress has demonstrated its appreciation of our career public servants. Today's Government is more responsive because of your response.

The Civil Service Commission Report shows that our emphasis has been on recruiting, developing and fully using our civil servants to provide improved service to the public.

During fiscal year 1967—

• An Executive Assignment System was instituted to insure that, at the top career levels, the right man is found for the right job at the right time.

• The Federal recruiting and examining program—the foundation for good personnel management—was reorganized:
—to compete more effectively for the best available manpower and
—to provide improved service, information and job opportunities to every American.

• The training and education of Government employees was modernized and expanded.

• The Federal Government accelerated its drive for equal employment opportunities.

Last December the Congress responded fully to my proposals for equitable pay for Government workers. In moving to fulfill the earlier pay comparability promise, we have made Government jobs and public service careers substantially more attractive.

The record is one of significant progress.

At the same time, problems remain—some of which require legislative action.

As our society has grown more complex, so too has the administration of the public services which meet society's needs. Administrative weakness at any level of our Federal system—whether it be national, state or local—becomes a weakness at all levels. It deprives our citizens of adequate government machinery with which to meet their day-to-day and long-range needs. It cannot long be tolerated in a government of, by, and for the people.

We have become aware that state and local public agencies—too often inadequately staffed—are not always equipped to meet their expanding responsibilities to

—Rebuild our cities,

—Clean up our rivers and the air we breathe,

—Provide equal rights and equal opportunities for all our citizens,

—Plan and build better housing,

—Improve education and health services.

To do their share, state and local governments need help—primarily staffing and training assistance.

Last March 17, I submitted to the Congress two new legislative proposals to give them the help they need:

—*The Intergovernmental Manpower Act,* to assist state and local governments in meeting their critical manpower requirements. The Act would authorize the Federal Government to assist States and communities in recruiting, training, and developing a high quality corps of capable and responsive public employees. It would authorize the exchange of personnel between states and cities and the Federal Government. Through this exchange, all levels of government would understand each other's problems and work together more effectively to serve all the people.

—*The Education for Public Service Act,* to increase the number and quality of younger people preparing for careers in government. The Act would provide special fellowships for young men and women who will agree to embark on the great adventure of public service. It would assist colleges and universities in developing public service curricula to meet future governmental needs.

I urge prompt consideration and passage of this legislation to strengthen our Federal system and assure more efficient conduct of programs with shared administrative responsibilities.

Our mission—to meet the rapidly changing needs of our society—calls for our continued attention to excellence in the public service. I pledge you and the Nation mine.

LYNDON B. JOHNSON

The White House
February 20, 1968

NOTE: The 1967 annual report of the Civil Service Commission is printed in House Document 223 (90th Cong., 2d sess.).

85   Statement by the President Upon Signing the Commodity Exchange Act Amendments. *February 20, 1968*

IN MY State of the Union Message last month, I urged passage of a bill to protect further the integrity of the Nation's commodity exchanges and the funds of the thousands of Americans who deal in them. I am pleased to be able to sign that bill into law today.

It represents another significant step by a

Congress that has the opportunity to make its mark as the greatest consumer Congress in the history of our Nation.

Commodity exchanges are the national markets where agricultural products are bought and sold. Last year those markets handled approximately $75 billion in agricultural transactions.

Those simple facts make it quite clear that commodities are big business, and explain why the honesty and soundness of the commodity exchanges are important to all Americans.

Since 1922, the Commodity Exchange Act and other Federal legislation have encouraged cooperation between the Federal Government and the exchanges in preventing fraud and market manipulations. Under the Act, commodity market conditions have improved greatly. Nevertheless, additional safeguards have been needed for some time.

These amendments—the first of any substance in over 30 years—respond to that need.

The new legislation adds the active and growing market in livestock and livestock products to the commodities regulated under the act, and increases the criminal penalties for illegal trading abuses such as market manipulation and embezzlement. Although regulatory responsibility for commodity trading will remain primarily with the exchanges themselves, the new amendments will substantially strengthen the enforcement authority of the Secretary of Agriculture.

Consumer groups, food processors, farm organizations—and the commodity exchanges themselves—have joined the administration in supporting this legislation.

The Senate and House Committees on Agriculture and the Congress are to be commended for their prompt action on this milestone in commodity market regulation.

NOTE: As enacted, the bill (H.R. 13094) is Public Law 90–258 (82 Stat. 26), approved February 19, 1968.

86 Remarks to a Group of State Employment Service Directors. *February* 21, 1968

Secretary Wirtz, State Employment Directors, ladies and gentlemen:

I know you will understand if I am a little late. My morning was spent in a good cause. The time of yours that I spent was in pursuing a subject that all of us want to obtain more than anything else in the world—and that is peace.

I had a very pleasant visit with the Secretary General of the United Nations at some length. We ran over some.

I met with our own Security Council. That explains why I have asked your indulgence.

Part of the promise of America is that all of us should have a chance to earn a living.

We are happy to say that today more

Americans are working than have ever worked before—some 75 million of us.

Our economy has been moving forward, surging ahead. In the last 4 years, we have created more than 7½ million jobs. This year, God willing, if the economy continues as we hope, we will add another million and a half jobs.

I said the other day—and I repeat now—a very realistic person informed me the other evening that outside of peace in the world, there were two extremely important things for every man in public life to keep in mind. Since you are in public life—handling the Employment Service—I think I should remind you of this story.

One is the ballot. The remedy that we seek for almost anything that needs a remedy is the ballot. Everybody is equal on election day. You can pull that lever and you cast that vote.

The next thing he said is always vitally important—and that's the buck—the buck and the ballot, those two things. People are so much more rational when they have some money in their pocket. They are much more temperate and tolerant. There is just a better atmosphere—even here in the East Room—when all of us have jobs. And that is not an application for renewal.

But there are tens of thousands of people who are not here with us—scattered throughout the country—who do not have jobs. They have no real opportunity to work at all. There are reasons for this. They are unskilled and untrained and unschooled. There are many other reasons. Some of them are handicapped. Some of them are shut off because of discrimination. Some of them have incurred bad habits and have bad records or diseases that keep them from becoming employable.

All these people need our help.

I have found through my years in dealing with folks like this that there is no one who can really do more to help them than the State Employment Services.

Now, the plight of these folks is not their plight alone because you can see that it affects everyone in the Nation. When a person down the street shows up with smallpox, we all head for the basement and they put the quarantine on. When we have poverty in our cities, and the riots that have taken place in Detroit and Newark—the civil rights problems that we have—then I think America is going to have to answer that question.

I think America must.

How and where are we answering it?

Well, one way we are answering it is that I have recommended to the Congress a man-

power program this year that contains a budget that is the largest in the Nation's history. It is $2.1 billion.

We have initiated an historic effort to find jobs in private industry. We have a goal of 500,000 hard-core unemployed.

Mr. Henry Ford and a blue ribbon group of businessmen—employers, management people—have set up their own organization. They are going to come in this weekend and report to me what they are trying to do in the cities of the land, trying to reach the hard-core unemployed. That is a great step forward—and I hope it will be productive.

We have strengthened and streamlined the Manpower Administration.

Now we are beginning to launch the work incentive program. Its objective is very simple:

—Replace the dole with the payroll.

—Rescue thousands of Americans from the waste of welfare.

—Start them along the pathway to productive lives.

This program will begin in 6 weeks. Between April 1 and June 30, we plan to help 32,000 people now on relief rolls. In fiscal year 1969, we are going to help another 116,000.

The welfare check buys only food and clothing and a roof. But the paycheck does a good deal more. It brings hope and respect and dignity to its recipient. A paycheck is a man's passport to opportunity, for himself and his children.

As administrators of the State employment services, you are America's agents in this work. With the group of Employment Services I dealt with back in the dark days of the depression in 1935—we had an objective to work ourselves out of a job by getting everybody a job. We would go in there and see who you had registered and what their qualifications were, and try to get them jobs. We did and we went out of existence a short time later because we put boys in school and on highways and in parks and in CCC camps. We kept this country from undergoing a frightening, perilous situation.

So today I think you have that same chance and responsibility again. We don't have the unemployed walking the streets that we had then. But we have a more dangerous thing—these hard-core unemployed who are unskilled, and untrained, and unprepared.

We must do something about it.

You have that chance and that responsibility, I think, to help us fulfill this part of what we believe is America's dream. It is a dream that we all share. It is a dream of a much better world than we are living in now. It is a dream of a Nation and a world at peace. It is a dream of peace in the world and peace for themselves. It is a dream of an America with a sound currency and a sound economy. It is a dream of a happy Nation. It is a dream of a busy, bustling, thriving, "go-go" Nation. It is a dream of a Nation that is productive; it is turning things off the assembly line with every click of the stile.

We need you; we count on you.

We hope that you can put yourselves in the position for the moment of one of these hard-core fathers or mothers or sons or daughters.

As President Roosevelt used to say, "ill-fed, ill-clad, ill-housed, ill-prepared, ill-trained, and ill-skilled"; say to yourself, "There except for the grace of God would be I."

Keep that person constantly in front of you. Then you help us find him and take him by the arm and put him over here where he is no longer a taxeater, but a tax-producer and a taxpayer.

If you do that, we can preserve this land; we can move it forward to new heights.

If you can't do it, I don't know who can. That is the reason I took the time and I asked each of you to come here to meet with me.

I said to your dynamic and inspiring leader, Secretary Wirtz, that while you were here I wanted to personally try to give you this mission.

Go back home, find out who they are, where they are, what they can do, what they cannot do—and then help us find the answer to it.

If we don't, we will just smolder in our own flames. If we don't, we will be failures. If we don't, we won't be worthy of the appellation that we often give ourselves—"The leader of the world."

But I don't want to think about what will happen if we won't—because we are going to.

Thank you very much.

NOTE: The President spoke at 1:20 p.m. in the East Room at the White House at the conclusion of a 3-day meeting of State Employment Service Directors sponsored by the Department of Health, Education, and Welfare. In his opening words he referred to W. Willard Wirtz, Secretary of Labor.

87 Special Message to the Congress on Urban Problems: "The Crisis of the Cities." *February 22, 1968*

To the Congress of the United States:

The cities that sprang up along the seaports, the river banks and the prairie crossroads of America were built and grew with pride and hope—until the early 20th century.

For several decades, now, the tide has run against the growth, strength and vitality of our cities.

Today, America's cities are in crisis. This clear and urgent warning rises from the decay of decades—and is amplified by the harsh realities of the present.

The crisis has been long in forming. At the turn of the century, Lincoln Steffens told of "the shame of the cities." Jane Addams spoke of "the vast numbers of the city's disinherited."

Powerful forces swept the city after World War II, hastening its erosion.

People who could afford to began moving by the hundreds of thousands to new suburbs to escape urban crush and congestion. Other hundreds of thousands were trapped inside by a wall of prejudice, denial, and lack of opportunity.

They were joined by still thousands more from America's rural heartland—the unskilled and the unprepared, displaced by advances in technology. Their thirst was for opportunity, for jobs, and for a better life. They found instead a mirage: for stripped of its bright lights, the city for them was poverty, unemployment and human misery.

We see the results dramatically in the great urban centers where millions live amid decaying buildings—with streets clogged with traffic; with air and water polluted by the soot and waste of industry which finds it much less expensive to move outside the city than to modernize within it; with crime rates rising so rapidly each year that more and more miles of city streets become unsafe after dark; with increasingly inadequate public services and a smaller and smaller tax base from which to raise the funds to improve them.

But these problems exist in hundreds of smaller towns and cities across America— towns and cities whose growth is in numbers of people, but not in homes, or jobs, or public services, or schools or health facilities

to serve them. The result too often is that these cities grow with decay, human misery, lack of job opportunity and increasingly concentrated poverty.

If the promise of the American city is to be recaptured—if our cities are to be saved from the blight of obsolescence and despair— we must now firmly set the course that America will travel.

There is no time to lose.

THE PEOPLE OF THE CITY

The human problems of the city are staggering:

—Ghetto youth with little education, no skills and limited opportunity.

—Citizens afraid to walk their streets at night, and justifiably so.

—Negroes, Puerto Ricans and Mexican Americans barred by prejudice from full participation in the city's life.

Illiteracy and disease, a lack of jobs and even dignity itself—these are the problems of the city, just as its tenements, traffic jams and rats are problems.

The city will not be transformed until the lives of the least among its dwellers are changed as well. Until men whose days are empty and despairing can see better days ahead, until they can stand proud and know their children's lives will be better than their own—until that day comes, the city will not truly be rebuilt.

That is the momentous and inescapable truth we face in this hour of America's history.

No single statement or message can embrace the solutions to the city's problems. No single program can attack them.

No one can say how long it will take, or how much of our fortune will eventually be committed. For the problems we are dealing with are stubborn, entrenched and slow to yield.

But we are moving on them—now—through more than a hundred programs, long and short range, making financial commitments of more than $22 billion to the task.

THE WORK SO FAR

The last several years have witnessed a remarkable record of legislative achievement—and most of it has borne on the problems of the cities.

We struck down discrimination in job opportunities, public accommodations, and voting in the Civil Rights Acts of 1964 and 1965.

We provided job training for nearly two million disadvantaged men and women who now have the skills to support themselves and their families with dignity and self-respect.

We cut through a century of opposition and controversy to help the poor school child with the Elementary and Secondary Education Act of 1965.

We brought healing and health to the elderly and the poor through Medicare and Medicaid.

We moved to help combat the pollution that poisons a city's air and fouls its waters.

And, with the Economic Opportunity Act of 1964, we finally embarked on a concentrated effort to eliminate poverty in this nation. That landmark measure has helped to change the lives of 6 million Americans.

These programs have brought hope to people in every city and town in America. Children from the slums find a new chance to succeed through Head Start. Poor teenagers earn their first paychecks through a Neighborhood Youth Corps program and stay in school. Needy young men and women, whose talents might once have been

their life's frustration, go on to college through Upward Bound. Men find self-respect and good jobs through work training programs. Half a million volunteers are engaged in a mission of service to the destitute of their communities. More than 6 million Americans have been lifted out of poverty.

But almost 29 million citizens still remain in poverty.

If the problems of the city are to be solved, there can be no retreat in the War on Poverty. It must be pressed, with renewed emphasis on the most critical needs of the poor—job opportunities and education for the young, and the chance to join in cooperative self-help efforts to improve their own lives, as well as to participate in the broader community attack on poverty.

Last year the Congress extended the life of the poverty program for two years—but it appropriated only $1.77 billion, some $290 million less than we sought.

For Fiscal 1969, I recommend appropriations to the full level of Congressional authorization—$2.18 billion—for the antipoverty program.

All of these measures help the people who live in our cities.

They are new programs, and only now are they beginning to take hold in improving lives of men, women and children.

With other proposals I have made to Congress this year—for open housing, for safe streets, for gun control, for 500,000 new, private sector job opportunities for the hardcore unemployed, for better education—we can further protect and improve the lot and the life of the city dweller.

Today, however, I want to speak of programs designed especially for our cities—of shelter for its citizens and plans for its revitalization. This message, too, is for men and their families. For our lives are profoundly affected by the environment in which we live, the city in which we work and reside, the home in which we relax and renew our strength.

An Evolutionary Response

Five Presidents and fifteen Congresses have forged the Federal response to the problems of housing and urban development.

It began in 1937, when Franklin Roosevelt saw a third of the Nation ill-housed. He and the 75th Congress recognized that poor families could not, with their own resources, afford homes on the private market, and that some form of Government help was necessary if they were to have decent shelter. The result was the historic legislation that launched the Public Housing program.

Twelve years later, with the Housing Act of 1949, President Truman and the 81st Congress started urban renewal and pledged "as soon as feasible . . . a decent home and a suitable living environment for every American family."

In the 1954 Housing Act, President Eisenhower and the 83rd Congress expanded the program of urban renewal.

At the beginning of this decade, President Kennedy and the 87th Congress enlarged the Government's role to bring decent houses into the reach of families with moderate income.

In spite of these strides, when I became President:

—We had a loose collection of Federal housing agencies, each operating programs in isolation, not only of each other but also of the Federal assistance programs of other departments.

—Urban renewal was demolishing slum housing and dislocating people, but not enough new housing was being built for those forced to relocate.

—There was little interest in the private sector—by builders, architects and engineers—in providing decent shelter for poor families, and the public housing program was stagnated in numbers and in quality.

—Our concern with housing, health care, education, welfare and other social services was fragmented in the local neighborhoods where it counts.

Over the past four years, you in the Congress have approved our proposals to:

—Establish a Department of Housing and Urban Development to bring scattered housing and urban development programs together and give the American city the cabinet role it deserves.

—Begin a new program of Rent Supplements to increase the housing supply for needy families. Built and operated by private enterprise, the portion of rent paid by the Government declines as the tenant's income rises.

—Inaugurate the Model Cities Program, the first effort to attack blight on a massive scale and renovate entire neighborhoods, by providing special supplementary grants to those cities that concentrate the entire array of Federal, State and local programs, from health to housing, in the worst slum neighborhoods.

Even these achievements are not sufficient to deal with the crisis our cities face today. They do provide a base on which the proposals in this message build.

The Housing and Urban Development Act of 1968

I propose the Housing and Urban Development Act of 1968—a charter of renewed hope for the American city.

With this Act, the Nation will set a far-reaching goal to meet a massive national need: the construction of 26 million new homes and apartments over the next 10 years. Six million of these will finally replace the shameful substandard units of misery where more than 20 million Americans still live.

This Act will authorize the construction and rehabilitation of 2.35 million housing units with $2.34 billion of contracting authority for the first five years of the ten-year program.

Under this legislation, we will in the year ahead:

—Start 300,000 housing units for more than one million citizens who need Federal assistance to obtain decent housing. This is triple the rate of this year, and more than half the number built over the last decade.

—Continue to restore the core of our center cities—and with that, improve the lives of nearly 4 million Americans—through the Model Cities Program.

—Summon the talents and energies of private enterprise to the task of housing low-income families through the creation of a federally-chartered private, profit-making housing partnership.

—Make Urban Renewal a more effective instrument for reclaiming neighborhoods, through a new neighborhood development program.

—Add many thousands of construction job opportunities in the inner city.

—Stimulate the flow of private credit for home building in the city by providing flexible interest ceilings on FHA mortgages and transferring the secondary market operations of the Federal National Mortgage Association to private ownership.

—Help American cities develop modern and efficient mass transit systems and services.

—Offer the American family an alternative to crowded cities and sprawling suburbs, through a program to build new communities.

—Improve planning for the orderly development of public facilities for urban areas.

—Establish a base of research, analysis and knowledge of urban areas so we can make better informed decisions about the cities.

What Is Required

To achieve our housing goal, we must move from low to high production.

We can make that shift only if the challenge summons the commitment of

—*The capital and mortgage finance markets,* to supply the private funds which are the lifeblood of the construction industry. These funds must flow steadily and in increasing scale.

—*The home building industry,* to tap an expanded federally-assisted market for private low and moderate income sales and rental housing.

—*The genius of American business to bring to home building* its skill and resources and the methods of modern technology so that houses can be built faster, less expensively and more efficiently than ever before.

—*American labor,* which has pledged to provide the necessary skilled manpower without discrimination.

—*Government at all levels,* to improve the working relationships with each other, and with the builders, lenders, and low-income families who will be served by this program.

—*Most importantly, the Congress.*

First, the Congress must take steps now to insure strong, stable economic growth for the Nation as a whole and the home building industry in particular.

Once again I call upon the Congress to pass the anti-inflation tax which I recommended more than a year ago. Soaring interest rates will cripple the home building industry. The temporary surcharge tax legislation can help to keep that from happening.

Second, I urge the Congress to enact the fair housing legislation recommended repeatedly by this Administration.

Third, I urge the Congress to renew, fully fund and strengthen the basic housing and urban development legislation already on the books.

Homes for Americans

I urge the Congress to enact a program to provide 300,000 housing starts in fiscal 1969 for the poor, the elderly, the handicapped, the displaced, and families with moderate incomes.

This program would:

1. Enable 100,000 low-income families to buy or repair their own homes.

Home ownership is a cherished dream and achievement of most Americans.

But it has always been out of reach of the nation's low-income families.

Owning a home can increase responsibility and stake out a man's place in his community. The man who owns a home has something to be proud of and good reason to protect and preserve it.

With the exception of the pilot program I began last year, low-income families have been able to get Federal help in securing shelter only as tenants who pay rent.

Today I propose a program to extend the benefits of home ownership to the Nation's needy families.

Under this program, the broad outline of which has already been set forth in S. 2700,

low-income families will be able to buy modest homes financed and built by the private sector. These families will devote what they can reasonably afford—a specified percentage of their income—to mortgage payments, with the Government paying the difference in the form of an interest subsidy. Under this interest subsidy, the Federal Government would pay all but 1 percent of the interest on the mortgage, depending on the income of the homebuyer.

2. Start 75,000 public housing units, to provide homes for 300,000 Americans.

The job is to turn authorization to action—by accelerating the processing of applications, by moving quickly from commitment to construction, and by involving private industry fully under the new Turnkey concept.

Under Turnkey, a low-income project can be put up in less than half the time traditionally required for public housing.

Turnkey frees the builder from complicated and cumbersome procedures and stimulates his initiative to develop imaginative and well-designed buildings at lower cost.

We have already extended the Turnkey concept to enable private industry not only to build low-income housing developments, but also to manage them.

Some Public Housing projects built in the past—when the challenge was simply to get units in place—reflect a tasteless conformity, and an indifference to community amenities.

At my direction, the Secretary of the Department of Housing and Urban Development has been working with leading architects and planners to achieve higher design standards for public housing developments. We know new projects can be pleasant places to live, reflecting the needs of human beings, with attention to comfort and convenience.

Our concern must be not only with the quantity of new public housing, but with its quality as well.

I propose a $20 million program to promote improved tenant services in public housing developments.

With these funds, we can enable those who live in public housing to take better advantage of job, health and education opportunities.

We can help and encourage them to become involved, personally and responsibly, in the day-to-day problems of the projects where they live.

3. *Authorize 72,500 units under the Rent Supplement Program to provide shelter for almost 250,000 poor Americans.* In fiscal 1969, 35,000 dwelling units will be started under this program.

This program, which holds so much promise for the poor families of America, has been underfunded by the Congress. Last year, we sought $40 million in annual payment authority. The Congress granted only $10 million.

Rent Supplements is a free-enterprise program, strongly endorsed by the home building, real estate, and insurance industries which have responded enthusiastically to this new approach to low-income housing. It contains incentives for escape from poverty, while creating modest, but decent shelter for those in poverty.

If we are to match our concern for the cities with our commitments, this program must be adequately funded.

I recommend $65 million in authority for the Rent Supplement Program for Fiscal 1969.

4. *Begin to build 90,000 rental housing units for 360,000 members of moderate income families.*

A program to provide housing for families with incomes too high to qualify for public housing, but too low to afford standard housing began in 1961.

This is a below market interest rate program known as "221(d)(3)." It serves families earning between $4,000 and $8,000 a year.

After 5 years of testing, we are ready now to move this program into full production.

But first we must improve it.

I recommend legislation to strengthen the financial tools under which the moderate income rental housing program operates.

Under this legislation, capital financing would be shifted to the private sector, and the Government would increase its support by providing assistance to reduce rents to levels moderate income families can afford.

Now the Government provides financial support for loans at 3 percent interest. Under this new arrangement, the private sector would make loans at market rates. The Government would make up the difference between the market rate of interest and 1 percent. The loans would remain in private hands.

To Help the Non-Profit Sponsor

Many housing projects are sponsored by non-profit organizations—including church groups, and fraternal orders. In many instances these groups lack the technical and financial know-how which modern construction demands.

Their efforts are in the best interests of this Nation, and the Nation should help them.

I propose legislation to provide needed technical assistance and skills to the non-profit sponsors of our housing programs.

Through grants, loans, and technical assistance, this program will help small private non-profit organizations in our cities. These organizations will then be able to draw quickly upon architects, engineers and financial experts to speed the construction of low income housing.

THE BLIGHTED NEIGHBORHOOD

Model Cities

The slum is not solely a wasteland of brick and mortar. It is also a place where hope dies quickly, and human failure starts early and lingers long.

Just as the problem of the slum is many-faced, so must the effort to remove it be many-sided.

The Model Cities program gave us the tools to carry forward the Nation's first comprehensive concentrated attack on neighborhood decay.

It was developed by some of the country's foremost planners, industrialists and urban experts.

The program is simple in outline—to encourage the city to develop and carry out a total strategy to meet the human and physical problems left in the rubble of a neighborhood's decay.

That strategy, which Model Cities spurs through special grants, is to bring to a dying area health care services, as well as houses; better schools and education, as well as repaved streets and improved mass transit; opportunities for work, as well as open space for recreation.

This program is now in its early stages. Sixty-three cities are drawing their plans to reclaim the blighted neighborhoods where 4 million Americans live. By this summer, a second group of cities will begin their planning.

Last year, I requested full funding of the amount authorized for Model Cities—$662 million. But the Congress approved less than half that amount.

To the cities of this land, that cut came as a bitter disappointment.

In the cities' struggle for survival, we dare not disappoint them again. We must dem-

onstrate that they can rely on continued Federal support.

I recommend $2.5 billion for the Model Cities special grants over the next three years:

—$500 million for fiscal 1969.
—$1 billion each for fiscal 1970 and 1971.

In addition, for fiscal 1969 I recommend $500 million in appropriations for urban renewal solely related to the Model Cities program. This includes full funding for a $350 million increase in the authorization.

The total funds needed to move the Model Cities program forward in fiscal 1969 are $1 billion.

I urge the Congress to fund fully this vital request for the people who live in America's worst urban neighborhoods.

Urban Renewal

Urban Renewal is the weapon that deals primarily with the physical side of removing blight. An essential component of the Model Cities Program, it is a major instrument of reform in its own right.

Last year, nearly 900 American communities were reclaiming inner city land under urban renewal.

Last year, the Congress appropriated $750 million for Urban Renewal in Fiscal 1969.

To give communities sufficient lead time for planning, I recommend that the Congress appropriate now $1.4 billion for fiscal 1970.

Even at these higher appropriation levels, under existing law Urban Renewal will not operate at sufficient speed to overtake the decay of our cities.

The lag between a community's decision to rebuild a neighborhood and the breaking of ground is far too long. Urgent neighborhood needs go unmet, awaiting the development and approval of a total plan for an entire area.

We must begin now to make urban renewal more immediately responsive to urban needs.

To apply our resources more quickly, I recommend that Congress authorize a new Neighborhood Development Program under Urban Renewal.

This legislation would permit detailed planning and execution to proceed segment by segment in an urban renewal area. Under existing law, neither demolition nor rehabilitation can begin on any portion of the area to be renewed until it is ready to begin throughout the entire area.

With this Neighborhood Program, cities can start work quickly on the most pressing problems that are to be renewed, with the emphasis on the construction of new and rehabilitated housing.

MEETING THE INSURANCE CRISIS OF OUR CITIES

Insurance protection is a basic necessity for the property owner. But for the resident of the city's inner core and the local businessman who serves him, protection has long been difficult to obtain.

The problem has been heightened by civil disorder or its threat.

Last August I established a Special Panel to seek the solutions to this problem. The Panel, headed by Governor Richard Hughes of New Jersey, offered a clear example of how the States, industry and the Federal Government can join in a constructive effort.

The Panel looked deeply into the property owner's dilemma, and reported:

"Society cannot erase the suffering of the innocent victims of fire, windstorm, theft, or riot. But it can at least provide the opportunity to obtain insurance to safeguard their capital, and thereby prevent a disastrous occurrence from becoming a permanent tragedy."

The Panel recommended a comprehensive program of mutually supporting actions by the insurance industry, the States, and the Federal Government.

My advisers and I have reviewed the Panel's proposals carefully. We believe they are sound.

Accordingly, I call upon the insurance industry to take the lead in establishing plans in all States to assure all property owners fair access to insurance. These plans will end the practice of "red-lining" neighborhoods and eliminate other restrictive activities. They will encourage property improvement and loss prevention by responsible owners.

I call upon the States to cooperate with the industry and, where necessary, to organize insurance pools and take other steps to cover urban core properties. These measures will assure that all responsible property owners can obtain insurance, and provide a method of spreading equitably throughout the insurance industry risks that no single insurer would otherwise accept.

I recommend that the Congress establish a cooperative Federal-State-Industry program by chartering a National Insurance Development Corporation within the Department of Housing and Urban Development.

This Corporation will bring together all those vitally interested in the inner city insurance problem—members of the public, State insurance regulators and other State officials, insurance industry representatives, and interested Federal agencies.

The Corporation will perform a number of vital functions in support of the actions of private industry and the States to assure adequate property insurance in all areas of our Nation's cities.

Through the sale of reinsurance against

the risk of civil disorders, the Corporation will marshal the resources of the insurance industry and add to this the backing of the States and the Federal Government. Without this reinsurance, many insurers and State insurance regulators do not believe the industry can move forward to provide adequate property insurance in urban areas.

This program will assist the insurance industry and the States to offer adequate property insurance for the inner cities. Through reinsurance, the program can help the States provide for the contingency of any large emergency losses.

For those companies who participate in this program, *I recommend tax deferral measures, proposed by the Panel, to increase the industry's capacity to insure homes and businesses in the center city.*

This program will encourage insurance companies to increase their reserves to cover unusual losses. Any deferred taxes will be invested in appropriate Government securities, so that no Federal revenues will be lost by the tax deferral unless unusual losses do occur.

Insurance is vital to rebuilding our cities. It is a cornerstone of credit. It can provide a powerful incentive for homeowners and businessmen to rehabilitate their own property and thereby improve the community.

THE PRIVATE SECTOR

The Federal role—a quarter of a century in the making—is designed to assure that every citizen will be decently housed.

The Government's concern is to stimulate private energy and local action—to provide capital where needed, to guarantee financing, to offer assistance that encourages planning and construction.

The real job belongs to local government and the private sector—the homebuilder, the mortgage banker, the contractor, the non-profit sponsor, the industrialist who now sees in the challenge of the cities a new opportunity for American business.

All of the programs I have outlined in this message are directed toward the deeper involvement of the private sector. That involvement must match the massive dimension of the urban problem.

What is needed is a new partnership between business and Government. The first outlines of that partnership are already visible.

We see it in:

—The recent undertaking of the American Bar Association to improve the landlord-tenant laws—now more medieval than modern—and to attack other legal problems in our urban centers.

—The commitment of 318 of the Nation's life insurance companies to invest $1 billion of their capital in low-income housing.

Within the next several days, the Savings and Loan Associations and the Mutual Savings Banks of this Nation will announce their plans to intensify the investment of their capital for similar purposes.

NATIONAL HOUSING PARTNERSHIPS

How can the productive power of America—which has mastered space and created unmatched abundance in the marketplace—be harnessed to meet the most pressing unfilled need of our society: rebuilding the urban slum?

Last June, I asked a selected Commission of leading industrialists, bankers and labor leaders to study this question. That Commission, headed by Edgar F. Kaiser, has now given me an interim report with many valuable recommendations.

Acting on the Commission's recommendation, *I propose that the Congress authorize the formation of privately-funded partnerships that will join private capital with business skills to help close the low-income housing gap.*

The Kaiser Commission identified three principal reasons why American industry has not yet been attracted to the field of low- and moderate-income housing. The problems and the steps proposed to meet them are:

1. *Concentration of Risk*

The profitability of individual housing projects varies widely and the risk of loss on any one project is high. The proposed national partnerships would permit industrial and financial firms to pool their investments and spread their risks over a large number of projects.

2. *Rate of Return*

Substantial operating losses are usually incurred in the first 10 years of a housing project's life to cover operating expenses, interest and depreciation.

By employing the partnership form of organization, which some building owners now use, under existing tax law these operating losses can be "passed through" to each investor, and offset against the investor's other taxable income. This reduces the investor's current income taxes otherwise payable, and makes possible an annual cash return on investment comparable to the average earnings of American business in other manufacturing enterprises.

3. *Management*

The management personnel of major corporations are inexperienced in the field of low-income housing. They cannot afford to devote substantial time to occasional housing ventures.

The proposed national partnerships would be strongly financed organizations, fully committed to long term activity in the single field of housing for the poor. As such, the proposed partnerships should be able to attract top flight management and technical experts on a competitive career basis.

The objective of these partnerships will be to attract capital from American industry and put that capital to work. Their exclusive purpose will be to generate a substantial additional volume of low- and moderate-income housing. They will use the best private management talent, planning techniques and advanced methods of construction. They will probe for the savings inherent in the latest technology and in economies of scale.

They will:

—Participate in joint ventures throughout the country in partnership with local builders, developers and investors.

—Join with American labor to open new job opportunities for the very people their projects will house.

—Participate in our existing and proposed Federal programs for assisting low- and moderate-income housing projects on the same basis as other project sponsors.

This new undertaking will begin with one national partnership. We expect that others will follow as the approach proves itself.

A New Era in Home Financing

The supply of credit is not unlimited. The Nation's banks, insurance companies, pension funds and other financial sources have an obligation to their depositors and shareholders to seek a fair and competitive return for their investments.

To insure that home financing remains competitive with alternative long-term investment opportunities, I recommend that the Congress:

—authorize the Secretary of Housing and Urban Development to adjust the FHA interest rate ceilings.

—authorize Federal insurance of bond obligations issued by private mortgage companies or trusts holding sizable pools of FHA-insured and VA-guaranteed home mortgages.

—transfer the secondary market operations of the Federal National Mortgage Association to completely private ownership.

FHA Interest Rates

Mortgages insured by the Federal Housing Administration and the Veterans Administration can by law carry no more than a 6 percent interest rate. In today's market this is no longer competitive. In practical terms, the result is the sale of mortgages at substantial discounts.

Discounts require hard cash beyond the normal downpayment. They erode the hard-earned equity of a home-owner and the profit margin of the builder of new housing. For when the rate of return on federally-insured mortgages is less than lending institutions can obtain from other investments, they require property-sellers to absorb discounts. To sell their homes, therefore, sellers realize less than they originally anticipated. And when builders of large projects—with 90% mortgages of $1 or $2 million, or more— must find additional hard cash to pay deep discounts, they will defer construction until the cash requirements are reduced.

As a result, many a house goes unsold and many apartment projects go unbuilt in a deep credit squeeze.

To assure a steady flow of funds into homebuilding, *I recommend that the Congress authorize the Secretary of Housing and Urban Development to adjust the FHA interest rate ceilings to reflect the economic realities of the financial markets. I have already recommended a similar adjustment on the interest rates for home loans to veterans.*

Federally-Insured Mortgage Bonds

Some private institutional and individual investors have shunned investments in home mortgages because they could realize nearly comparable rates of return in other investments, and avoid the bookkeeping and paper work associated with hundreds of individual mortgages.

These pools of savings—in large institutional pension funds, private trusts, and occasionally in individual estates—can be attracted to residential finance. It will take a new, marketable financial investment, with competitive yields and security. Such a bond-type obligation can be created to cover federally-insured mortgages held by private mortgage bankers or trusts.

To enhance the attractiveness of such an obligation to investors, and thus attract additional funds to the housing market, *I recommend that the Congress authorize the Department of Housing and Urban Development to insure mortgage bonds that are secured by pools of FHA-insured and VA-guaranteed mortgages.*

Federal National Mortgage Association

Through the Federal National Mortgage Association, the Federal Government has helped keep mortgage funds flowing by buying mortgages when credit was tight and selling them when money was plentiful.

Today, FNMA is a hybrid, owned in part by private shareholders, in part by the Government, but managed by Government officials.

This secondary market operation is largely a private function, which ought to be performed by the private sector—as the Congress has always intended.

I propose legislation to transfer the secondary market operation of the Federal National Mortgage Association on an orderly basis to completely private ownership.

This new FNMA, concerned exclusively with providing an increasing and continuous flow of funds into residential financing will close an important gap in the existing network of financial institutions.

This change will not affect the Government's special assistance to selected types of mortgages which are not yet readily accepted in the private market.

URBAN TRANSPORTATION

In the modern city the arteries of transportation are worn and blocked. The traffic jam has become the symbol of the curse of congestion.

It was only a few years ago, however, that we recognized this as a national problem. In signing the Urban Mass Transportation Act in 1964, I said:

"This is a many sided challenge. We cannot and we do not rely upon massive spending programs as cure-alls. We must instead look to closer cooperation among all levels of government and between both public and private sectors to achieve the prudent progress that Americans deserve and that they expect."

Under this Act, we are

—Aiding cities to draw the blueprints to modernize, expand and reorganize their transportation systems.

—Helping to train specialists in the urban transportation field.

—Advancing research to improve the system and the service.

—Assisting communities to buy the capital equipment and to build terminals

for their transit systems.

We must step up this effort.

In the year ahead, we expect to increase our grants to cities from $140 million to $190 million.

I recommend that the Congress provide $230 million for fiscal 1970 so cities can begin now to plan the improvement of their mass transit systems and service to the people.

Urban transportation is the concern of our two newest Departments—Housing and Urban Development, and Transportation.

The Department of Housing and Urban Development is responsible for the development of the metropolitan community—and transportation is an essential part of that effort.

The Department of Transportation is responsible for the coordination of different—but closely related—modes of transportation. Moreover, research facilities bearing on transportation—out of which will come the transportation technology of tomorrow—are concentrated in this Department.

When the Department of Transportation was established in 1966, the Congress required both Secretaries of Housing and Urban Development and Transportation to study this problem and recommend the arrangement which would best assure the Government's ability to meet the transportation needs of America's urban citizens.

On the basis of their intensive study, and their recommendations, *I will shortly submit a reorganization plan*

—Transferring to the Department of Transportation the major urban transit grant, loan, and related research functions now in the Department of Housing and Urban Development.

—Maintaining in the Department of Housing and Urban Development the

leadership in comprehensive planning at the local level, that includes transportation planning and relates it to broader urban development objectives.

RESEARCH AND TECHNOLOGY FOR THE CITIES

Federally-sponsored research has helped us guard the peace, cure disease, and send men into space.

Yet, we have neglected to target its power on the urban condition. Although 70 percent of our people live in urban areas, less than one-tenth of one percent of the Government's research budget has been devoted to housing and city problems.

We must:

—Learn how to apply modern technology to the construction of new low-income homes and the rehabilitation of old ones.

—Test these ideas in practice, and make them available to builders and sponsors.

—Look deep into the fiscal structure of the cities—their housing and building codes, zoning, and tax policies.

—Learn how best the Federal Government can work with State and local governments—and how States and local governments can improve their own operations.

—Evaluate our city programs, so we can assess our priorities.

Last year, I sought the first major appropriations for urban research: $20 million. Congess appropriated only half that amount.

I once again propose a $20 million appropriation for urban technology and research. This will assist the universities and private institutions of America to carry out the studies so crucially needed.

These funds, along with those from other Government agencies, will also help launch the new Urban Institute, which I recently recommended. This is a private non-profit research corporation formed to create a bank of talent to analyze the entire range of city problems.

PLANNING FOR THE FUTURE

A passenger on an airline flying from Miami to Boston is rarely out of sight of city lights below.

As our urban areas expand, the citizen's sense of community broadens. He may live in one locality, work in another and seek leisure in still another.

The face of the landscape is changing with our growth.

The question is: *How* shall our communities grow?

Unless we decide now for order and purpose, the result will be surrender to chaos, confusion, ugliness and unnecessary and exorbitant cost.

The key to orderly growth is planning—planning on an area-wide basis.

Planning, both immediate and long-range, is the function and the responsibility of the State and community. But the Federal Government has long recognized the need for its support.

That need grows as the problem grows.

I urge the Congress to provide $55 million in Fiscal 1969 to assist planning for the orderly growth of our urban areas, a 22 percent increase over last year.

So essential is orderly development to the future of our urban centers that we must provide incentives to encourage it. In 1966 the Congress authorized—but did not fund—such a program of incentive grants.

I ask Congress to authorize $10 million for a program of area-wide Incentive Grants in Fiscal 1969.

The Federal share of a project will increase by up to 20 percent of the costs of projects of areawide significance—if they are part of a comprehensive area plan.

The far-sighted community which responds to this incentive program will find its burdens lighter in providing hospitals, roads, sewage systems, schools and libraries.

NEW COMMUNITIES

Over the next decade, 40 million more Americans will live in cities.

Where and how will they all live? By crowding further into our dense cities? In new layers of sprawling suburbia? In jerry-built strip cities along new highways?

Revitalizing our city cores and improving our expanding metropolitan areas will go far toward sheltering that new generation. But there is another way as well, which we should encourage and support. It is the new community, freshly planned and built.

These can truly be the communities of tomorrow—constructed either at the edge of the city or farther out. We have already seen their birth. Here in the Nation's capital, on surplus land once owned by the Government, a new community within the city is springing up.

In other areas, other communities are being built on farm and meadow land. The concept of the new community is that of a balanced and beautiful community—not only a place to live, but a place to work as well. It will be largely self-contained, with light industry, shops, schools, hospitals, homes, apartments and open spaces.

New communities should not be built in any set pattern. They should vary with the needs of the people they serve and the landscapes of which they are a part.

Challenge and hard work await the founders of America's new communities:

—Careful plans must be laid.
—Large parcels of land must be acquired.
—Large investments in site preparation, roads and services must be made before a single home can be built and sold.
—The development period is long, and return on investment is slow.
—But there is also a great opportunity for, as well as a challenge to, private enterprise.

The job is one for the private developer. But he will need the help of his Government at every level.

In America—where the question is not so much the standard of living, but the quality of life—these new communities are worth the help the Government can give.

I propose the New Communities Act of 1968.

For the lender and developer, this Act will provide a major new financing method.

A federally-guaranteed "cash flow" debenture will protect the investment of private backers of new communities at competitive rates of return. At the same time, it will free the developer from the necessity to make large payments on his debts, until cash returns flow from the sale of developed land for housing, shops and industrial sites.

For the local and State government, the Act will offer incentives to channel jointly-financed programs for public facilities into the creation of new communities. The incentives will take the form of an increased Federal share in these programs.

A SENSE OF PLACE AND PURPOSE

"A city," Vachel Lindsay wrote, "is not builded in a day."

Nor—we know well—will its problems be conquered in a day. For the city's tides have been ebbing for several decades. We are the inheritors of those tragic results of the city's decline.

But we are the ones who must act. For us that obligation is inescapable.

Our concern must be as broad as the problems of men—work and health, education for children and care for the sick. These are the problems of men who live in cities. And the very base of man's condition is his home: he must find promise and peace there.

The cry of the city, reduced to its essentials, is the cry of a man for his sense of place and purpose.

Violence will not bring this. But neither should fear forestall it.

The challenge of changing the face of the city and the men who live there summons us all—the President and the Congress, Governors and Mayors. The challenge reaches as well into every corporate board room, university, and union headquarters in America. It extends to church and community groups, and to the family itself. The problem is so vast that the answer can only be forged by responsible leadership from every sector, public and private.

We dare not fail to answer—loud and clear.

To us, in our day, falls the last clear chance to assure that America's cities will once again "gleam, undimmed by human tears."

No one can doubt that the hour is late.

No one can understate the magnitude of the work that should be done.

No one can doubt the costs of talk and little action.

As we respond to the cities' problems—to the problems caused by the accumulated debris of economic stagnation, physical decay and discrimination—let us recall and reaffirm the reasons for our national strength: unity, growth and individual opportunity.

And recalling these truths, let us go forward, as one nation in common purpose joined, to change the face of our cities and to end the fear of those—rich and poor alike—who call them home.

LYNDON B. JOHNSON

The White House
February 22, 1968

NOTE: For statements or remarks upon signing related legislation, see Items 195, 229, 343, 426.

88   Letter to the President of the Senate and to the Speaker of the House Proposing a Bill To Simplify the Entry of Foreign Visitors. *February 23, 1968*

Dear Mr. President: (Dear Mr. Speaker:)

I ask the Congress to eliminate unnecessary and cumbersome barriers which inhibit foreign visitors and businessmen from traveling to the United States.

Over a half century ago we began to require each foreign visitor to obtain a visa from an American Consul abroad.

This process of pre-screening obliges every visitor—other than a national of Canada or Mexico—to establish to the satisfaction of the Consul:

—that he is not ineligible for a visa under some 25 specified grounds of eligibility;

—that he has a residence abroad to which he intends to return;

—that he will not accept employment while in the United States.

Those requirements have been rendered obsolete by a major increase in tourism from

263

abroad, by a revolutionary reduction in travel time, and by the fact that 35 other nations require no visas from American tourists.

This system clearly must be reformed.

Last Monday, I received a report from my special Industry-Government Commission on Travel. The report outlined a broad program to increase tourism to the United States, improving our balance of payments and promoting international understanding.

With regard to these entry requirements, the Commission stated:

"Present entry procedures for vacation and business visitors to the United States are outmoded. They serve only to project an adverse image of this nation's willingness to receive foreign guests."

By imposing time-consuming entry requirements, we discourage tourism to the United States at a time when we are acutely concerned with our balance of payments.

By imposing stringent requirements, we appear to a foreign visitor to be greeting him grudgingly rather than graciously.

By imposing complicated requirements, we add an unnecessary and increasingly expensive workload to our consulate staffs abroad.

I believe the time has come to stop imposing these unnecessary requirements on our visitors. To accomplish this, I propose the Non-immigrant Visa Act of 1968.

This Act would authorize the Secretary of State and the Attorney General to issue regulations exempting visitors to the United States for 90 days or less from the visa requirement and from all but the most serious grounds of ineligibility.

Under the Act:

—The Secretary of State would designate the countries whose citizens would be entitled to this privilege. Initially, this would be done on the basis of reciprocity.

—Foreign nationals who have been convicted of serious crimes, or narcotics traffickers, will still be barred.

—Entering aliens will continue to be examined by immigration and naturalization service officers at points of entry. This will afford full protection to our internal security.

—Persons entering under these conditions will be required to have a valid passport, and a non-refundable round-trip ticket. They will not be allowed to alter their status as a visitor while they are in this country.

This new Act will improve our foreign relations and promote a better understanding of America throughout the world.

It will improve our balance of payments and strengthen the dollar.

It will allow us to treat travelers from abroad more efficiently and more hospitably.

With the cooperation of private industry, the government is seeking new ways to attract more visitors to our shores in 1968. This new Act can be a vital part of that effort.

The Secretary of State will shortly send to the Congress further recommendations to improve our non-immigrant visa laws.

I consider the proposals in this letter to be of urgent concern. I ask the Congress to give them prompt and favorable consideration.

Sincerely,

LYNDON B. JOHNSON

NOTE: This is the text of identical letters addressed to the Honorable Hubert H. Humphrey, President of the Senate, and to the Honorable John W. McCormack, Speaker of the House of Representatives.

The proposed legislation was not enacted by the 90th Congress.

For a statement by the President upon receiving the report of the Industry-Government Special Task Force on Travel, see Item 83.

The letter was released at Austin, Texas.

89   Memorandum Establishing the Cabinet Committee on Price Stability.   *February 23, 1968*

Memorandum for the Secretary of the Treasury, the Secretary of Commerce, the Secretary of Labor, the Director of the Bureau of the Budget, the Chairman of the Council of Economic Advisers:

In accord with the announcement in my Economic Report transmitted to the Congress on February 1, 1968, I appoint you to serve on a Cabinet Committee on Price Stability.

This Cabinet Committee reflects our deep concern for a more effective Government effort in dealing with the long-run problems of inflation. This step will fortify our fiscal and monetary policies which are the first line of defense against inflation. As I said in my Economic Report, "Existing Government organization is not effectively suited to deal with the full range and dimensions of the problem of prices." We must develop a strong and imaginative program for 1968 and subsequent years through the work of this Committee. This program is intended to strengthen free market institutions.

The Chairman of the Council of Economic Advisers will coordinate the work of the Committee, which I expect will meet on a regular schedule and in addition hold special meetings to deal with any urgent problems that may arise.

The Chairman of the Council of Economic Advisers will recruit and supervise the professional staff necessary to carry out the work of the Committee and will provide administrative services to the Committee.

I assign the highest priority to the work of this Cabinet Committee which must take effective steps this year in the pursuit of price stability. I expect each of you to contribute to the maximum extent possible to the work of this Committee. I am also sending a memorandum to other relevant Government departments and agencies to enlist their full support for your work, and you should call upon them to the maximum extent to which they can be helpful.

As recommended in the Council's report, I anticipate that the Committee will:

1. Prepare and publish from time to time studies in depth of economic conditions in those industries which are a persistent source of inflationary pressure.

2. Study intensively and make constructive recommendations concerning all aspects of Government policy that affect prices in particular sectors.

3. Work with representatives of business, labor, and the public to enlist cooperation toward responsible wage and price behavior and structural improvements that promote the achievement of overall price stability.

4. Hold a series of conferences both with representatives of business, labor, and the public interest at large, and with representatives of particular industries or particular segments of labor:

—to attempt to reach some consensus on appropriate general standards to guide private price and wage decisions;

—to identify remediable problems that inhibit price stability in particular areas, and attempt to design cooperative programs for private and governmental action to deal with these problems.

5. Recommend suitable legislation which would advance the objective of price stability in a free market economy.

At the outset, I ask the Committee to consider pending proposals for legislative and administrative change in order that any actions taken be focused as sharply as possible on contributing to price and cost stability.

I expect the Committee to begin its work promptly.

LYNDON B. JOHNSON

P.S. This will be a small committee but its work is vital. Each of you should not undertake this responsibility unless you can give it your fullest attention and your highest priority.

NOTE: The memorandum was released at Austin, Texas.

90 Memorandum Directing Agency Cooperation With the Cabinet Committee on Price Stability. *February 23, 1968*

Memorandum for All Departments and Agencies:

In accord with the announcement in my Economic Report transmitted to the Congress on February 1, 1968, I have established a Cabinet Committee on Price Stability, consisting of the Secretaries of Treasury, Commerce, and Labor, the Director of the Budget, and the Chairman of the Council of Economic Advisers.

This Cabinet Committee reflects our deep concern for a more effective Government effort in dealing with the long-run problems of inflation. This step will fortify our fiscal and monetary policies which are the first line of defense against inflation. As I said in my Economic Report, "Existing Government organization is not effectively suited to deal with the full range and dimensions of the problem of prices." We must develop

a strong and imaginative program for 1968 and subsequent years through the work of this Committee. This program is intended to strengthen free market institutions.

I assign the highest priority to the work of this Cabinet Committee which must take effective steps this year in the pursuit of price and cost stability. I request each of you to cooperate to the maximum extent possible with the work of this Cabinet Committee. The Chairman of the Council of Economic Advisers, who is coordinating the work of the Cabinet Committee, will keep you informed of the activities of the Committee and will contact you as necessary about the possibilities for your contribution to this vital work.

LYNDON B. JOHNSON

NOTE: The memorandum was released at Austin, Texas.

91 Statement by the President Summarizing Actions on the Recommendations of the Inter-Agency Committee on Mexican American Affairs. *February 23, 1968*

LAST OCTOBER, in El Paso, I attended a conference of high purpose. There, with the Vice President and members of the Cabinet, I met with 1,200 Spanish-speaking Americans.

This was the first time that the Mexican-

American community had an opportunity to discuss matters of direct concern—ranging from education to economic opportunity, housing to health—with the highest officials of Government.

The aim of the 3-day conference was to

assure that America's second largest minority was receiving its fair and just share of Federal programs in these areas.

Out of that conference, ideas and suggestions flowed to a Cabinet-level committee on Mexican-American affairs, which I appointed last June.

Based on the recommendations of the committee—many of which stemmed from the El Paso conference—I have taken the following actions:

In education:

—I have signed into law the first Federal bilingual education program. It will help Spanish-speaking children overcome the barriers of language which have prevented them from receiving the fullest benefits of education.

—I have asked Congress to provide funds to expand and improve adult and vocational education programs aimed particularly at those Americans who have no high school diplomas. About 20 percent of these are Spanish-speaking.

I have instructed the Secretary of Health, Education, and Welfare to:

—Accelerate the training of specially-trained teachers to work with Mexican-American schoolchildren and migrant workers.

—Insure compliance with title VI of the 1964 Civil Rights Act. This forbids discrimination in school-district boundaries and in quality of education, wherever the schools receive Federal financial assistance.

In health and welfare:

I have requested the Secretary of Health, Education, and Welfare to:

—Simplify application and claim procedures in Medicare, social security, and other programs serving the Mexican-American communities.

—Gather and analyze data on the health

of Spanish-speaking Americans.

I have asked the Congress to increase its support of special medical programs for migrant farmworkers, most of whom are Mexican-Americans and Puerto Ricans.

I have appointed a distinguished Mexican-American scholar, Dr. Julian Samora, to a Presidential commission evaluating the Nation's welfare system.

In housing:

The Department of Housing and Urban Development has selected a number of cities to begin planning under the Model Cities program. Among them are San Antonio, Eagle Pass, and Waco, Texas; Denver and Trinidad, Colorado; Albuquerque, New Mexico; New York City; and San Juan, Puerto Rico—all with large Spanish-speaking populations.

—I have directed the Secretary of HUD to work with Laredo, Texas, and its sister city in Mexico, Nuevo Laredo, in an international cooperative effort to help develop a Model Cities program that will improve the condition of life in this border area.

—I have requested, in the 1969 budget, $1 billion for the Model Cities program to revitalize and rebuild entire slum neighborhoods and barrios. In my special message on the cities, I asked the Congress, industry, and labor to begin a 10-year program to construct 6 million new housing units for low- and moderate-income families, many of whom are Spanish-speaking.

—I have urged the Congress—once more—to pass a fair housing law, insuring that all Americans can have the opportunity to live in a place of their own choosing.

In Federal employment:

I have instructed all Federal agencies:

—To work together to increase employment opportunities for Spanish-speaking Americans.

—To require employees to know Spanish where they serve large groups of Spanish-speaking people.

—To reexamine their hiring and recruiting methods to assure that potentially good workers are not refused jobs because a language barrier works against them in written examinations.

In private employment:

—I have asked Congress for funds to extend a test training program to relocate workers from areas of high unemployment to those where work is available.

—I have moved to assure that Federal manpower training programs provide English language training for Spanish-speaking people who need it.

—I have proposed the Job Opportunities in Business Sector (JOBS) program— a new partnership between government and private industry—to train and hire those who have the greatest difficulty finding work.

—I have directed the Secretary of Labor to bring together in one unified effort all manpower programs for an attack on hard-core rural and urban unemployment. As a result, the concentrated employment program is underway in several of the largest cities of the Southwest. I have recommended expansion of this program in the 1969 budget.

—I have urged Congress again, as I did last year, to give the Equal Employment Opportunity Commission the power to order a halt to employment discrimination.

In rural matters:

—I have asked the Congress to authorize a major project to improve Forest Service grazing land in the Southwest, to serve the small rancher.

—I have instructed the Secretary of Agriculture to expand the activities of the County Extension Service to meet more fully the needs of the small Mexican-American farmer.

—I am directing the Secretaries of Agriculture and Labor to hold hearings so that they can set realistic minimum wages for certain farmworkers.

Last June, when I established the Inter-Agency Committee on Mexican American Affairs, I said, "We today affirm this truth: that what we do for any minority, we do as well for the majority. After all, we do all of this for America."

These convictions remain firm and resolute.

With this report of progress and action, we have begun the journey toward full opportunity for the Mexican-Americans, Puerto Ricians, and other Spanish-speaking people of our land.

NOTE: For a statement by the President on the first annual report of the Inter-Agency Committee on Mexican American Affairs, see Item 437.

The statement printed above was released at Austin, Texas.

92 Statement by the President Following a Meeting With Officers of the National Alliance of Businessmen. *February* 24, 1968

A MONTH ago, I called on American business to join in a new and unprecedented venture—to place 500,000 citizens, the hard-core unemployed, in private industry jobs.

This morning I met with Mr. Henry Ford II, Mr. Paul Austin, and Mr. Leo Beebe, the leaders of the National Alliance of Businessmen, whose mission it is to guide this program to success.

I can report to the Nation that:

—Over 60 of America's top business executives have agreed to participate in the Alliance. They will spearhead its drive in our 50 largest cities.

—Detailed plans have been laid. A strategy has been shaped. A tight schedule has been worked out.

Now the test is to turn these plans into action—into good private industry jobs for the thousands of men and women in this country who want to work. These are the people who need special help and training to overcome the poverty of opportunity that has dimmed their hope and their courage.

In this task—as in other crucial efforts to rebuild our cities, to lift men from poverty, to clean our air and water—business has responded to the Nation's call. When indus-

try joins America's most urgent work, it strengthens the Nation in which it grows and prospers.

So today, we are heartened as the JOBS program gets underway. We look to it with the highest hopes for success.

America is well served by Henry Ford, Paul Austin, Leo Beebe, and all the other business leaders who are engaged in this vital work.

NOTE: The National Alliance of Businessmen was proposed by the President in his January 23 message to the Congress on manpower and occupational health and safety programs (see Item 24). Following the meeting, two announcements were issued by the White House. The first summarized the discussions and listed the executive board members and metropolitan chairmen of the Alliance, and the second gave the text of a concluding statement by Alliance Chairman Henry Ford II. Both announcements are printed in the Weekly Compilation of Presidential Documents (vol. 4, pp. 358–360).

The statement was released at Austin, Texas.

93   Special Message to the Congress Transmitting Reorganization Plan 2 of 1968, Urban Mass Transportation. *February 26, 1968*

To the Congress of the United States:

As long as he has lived in cities, man has struggled with the problem of urban transportation. But:

—Never before have these problems affected so many of our citizens.

—Never before has transportation been so important to the development of our urban centers.

—Never before have residents of urban areas faced a clearer choice concerning urban transportation—shall it dominate and restrict enjoyment of all the values of urban living, or shall it be shaped to bring convenience and efficiency to our citizens in urban areas.

How America and its cities solve the trans-

portation problem depends largely on our two newest Federal Departments—the Department of Transportation and the Department of Housing and Urban Development:

—The Department of Housing and Urban Development is responsible for the character of all urban development.

—The Department of Transportation is concerned specifically with all the modes of transportation and their efficient interrelationship.

At present, responsibility for program assistance for urban highways and urban airports, and urban mass transportation is divided between the Department of Transportation and the Department of Housing and Urban Development. As a result:

—Federal coordination of transportation systems assistance is more difficult than it need be.

—Communities which have measured their own needs and developed comprehensive transportation proposals must deal with at least two federal agencies to carry out their programs.

To combine efficiently the facilities and services necessary for our urban centers and to improve transportation within our cities, State and local government agencies should be able to look to a single federal agency for program assistance and support. The large future cost of transportation facilities and services to the Federal Government, to State and local governments, and to the transportation industry makes wise investments and efficient transportation systems essential.

An urban transportation system must:

—combine a basic system of efficient, responsive mass transit with all other forms and systems of urban, regional, and inter-city transportation;

—conform to and support balanced urban development.

In this, my second reorganization plan of 1968, I ask the Congress to transfer urban mass transportation programs to the Secretary of Transportation and to establish an Urban Mass Transportation Administration within the Department of Transportation to strengthen the organizational capacity of the Federal Government to achieve these objectives.

The plan transfers to and unifies in a new Urban Mass Transportation Administration in the Department of Transportation those functions which involve urban mass transportation project assistance and related research and development activities. Because urban research and planning and transportation research and planning are closely related, however, the plan provides that the Department of Housing and Urban Development perform an important role in connection with transportation research and planning insofar as they have significant impact on urban development.

We expect the Department of Transportation to provide leadership in transportation policy and assistance. The Department of Housing and Urban Development will provide leadership in comprehensive planning at the local level that includes transportation planning and relates it to broader urban development objectives.

The transfer of urban mass transportation programs will not diminish the overall responsibilities of the Department of Housing and Urban Development with respect to our cities. Rather, adequate authority is reserved to that Department to enable it to join with the Department of Transportation to assure that urban transportation develops as an integral component of the broader development of growing urban areas.

The new Urban Mass Transportation Administration in the Department of Transportation, working with other elements of the Department, will consolidate and focus our efforts to develop and employ the most modern transportation technology in the solution of the transportation problems of our cities.

The reorganization plan provides for an Administrator at the head of the Administration who would be appointed by the President, by and with the advice and consent of the Senate. The Administrator would report directly to the Secretary of Transportation and take his place in the Department with the heads of the Federal Aviation Administration, Federal Highway Administration, Federal Railroad Administration and the Coast Guard.

I have found, after investigation, that each reorganization included in the reorganization plan transmitted herewith is necessary to accomplish one or more of the purposes set forth in section 901(a) of title 5 of the United States Code.

I have also found that it is necessary to include in the accompanying plan, by reason of these reorganizations, provisions for the appointment and compensation of the new officer specified in section 3(b) of the plan. The rate of compensation fixed for this officer is comparable to those fixed for officers in the Executive Branch of the Government having similar responsibilities.

The reorganizations included in this plan will provide more effective management of transportation programs. It is not feasible to itemize the reduction in expenditures which the plan will achieve, but I have no doubt that this reorganization will preserve and strengthen overall comprehensive planning for developing urban areas while simultaneously insuring more efficient transportation systems for our cities than would otherwise have occurred.

I strongly urge that the Congress allow the reorganization plan to become effective.

LYNDON B. JOHNSON

The White House
February 26, 1968

NOTE: Reorganization Plan 2 of 1968 is printed in the Weekly Compilation of Presidential Documents, the Federal Register, and Title 3 of the Code of Federal Regulations (4 Weekly Comp. Pres. Docs., p. 363; 33 F.R. 6965; 3 CFR, 1968 Comp., p. 150). It became effective on June 30, 1968, as provided by section 6 of the plan.

94   Special Message to the Congress: "Prosperity and Progress for the Farmer and Rural America." *February 27, 1968*

To the Congress of the United States:

The farm was here before the factory.

It was the promise of productive land that pushed our people westward, and America was built on a foundation of farms and ranches supplying the food and fiber for a bountiful and restless Nation.

It was the farmer's qualities—his hard work and perseverance, his independence and initiative—which gave strength to a Nation's character.

Agriculture, our first industry, remains our greatest. It is the vital center of our economy—fueling our industry and commerce, feeding our people and the hungry of the world.

—Almost 18 million Americans work at growing our crops, processing them and shipping them to market, and supplying our farmers.

—Americans spend $125 billion yearly for the products of our agriculture— which brings the family the most nourishing food in the world, at a modest share of its income.

—The harvest of one out of every four acres moves into foreign markets. Last year American farm exports set a new record—$6.8 billion.

—Millions of people in other lands live today because of food grown and shipped from American farms.

—Agricultural technology, combined with modern machinery, seeds, and fertilizers, has revolutionized production. Each farmer today grows enough food for 40 persons, compared to only 10 thirty years ago.

But the American farmer, who helped to build America's prosperity, still does not fully—or fairly—share in it.

While retail food prices have risen in

recent years, the prices the farmer receives have actually declined 9 percent in the past two decades.

Too many rural communities have been by-passed in the climb to abundance, the poverty of its people standing in stark contrast to the wealth of the land.

THE RECORD TO DATE

Farm-led and farm-fed, the depression of the 1930's plunged American agriculture into its darkest hour. The plight of the farmer was intolerable—five cent cotton and 20 cent corn, failure and foreclosure.

Out of those grim days, as the Nation regained strength, the basic principles of a national farm policy evolved, guiding the farmer's recovery. Through conservation and credit, price stabilization and research, a partnership with government grew. It was a new concept, but it rested on an honored American tradition—that the Nation's strength lies in independent, land-owning farmers and ranchers.

When Franklin Roosevelt signed the Agriculture Adjustment Act of 1938—30 years ago this month—he could tell America: "By experience we have learned what must be done to assure agriculture a fair share of an increasing national income, to provide consumers with abundant supplies of food and fiber, to stop waste of soil, and to reduce the gap between huge surpluses and disastrous shortages."

The farmer rose to the challenge of the time as he fed and clothed America's victorious armies of World War II—and, in its aftermath, fed a war-ravaged world.

But in the middle fifties the farmer fell victim to his own progress and to government indifference. Production increased while Federal programs faltered. As a result:

—Farm income from 1952 to 1960 dropped by almost 20%. Farmers netted $2¼ billion less per year than in 1952.
—Farm surpluses swelled. By 1960, the Commodity Credit Corporation had accumulated over $8 billion in stocks.
—Exports, a major source of farm income, failed to keep pace with rising production.

While farm programs cost the taxpayer more, farmers received less and less.

These were bitter disappointments—and from them we learned much. They led to the constructive programs of the sixties which have already shown these signs of progress:

—Today, net income per farm is 55% higher than at the beginning of the decade.
—1966 set an all time record for gross farm income and net income per farm.
—1967 produced the second highest per farm income in two decades, even after a disappointing price drop.
—Exports soared to a record $6.8 billion last year, up 51% from 1960.
—Price-depressing surpluses in most commodities have been eliminated. Commodity Credit Corporation investments are down $4.5 billion from 1960. Inventories are below $1 billion for the first time since 1953.

THE PROBLEM TODAY

But as significant as these achievements are, their importance to the farmer is diminished by the realities he faces:

—His income lags. It is less than two-thirds the per capita income of the city dweller.
—His production costs are rising, and he is trapped in a vicious price-cost squeeze.
—For most commodities, he has no practical means of tailoring his output to total demand. Now he grows his crop or

raises his livestock—and hopes for a
good market. If that market does not
come, he will not receive a fair price for
the fruits of his toil.

What Is Required

Much will be required to assure the
farmer his fair and full share of America's
abundance.

First, we must reinforce the partnership
between the farmer and his Government.

Like any sound businessman, the agricultural producer seeks a fair return for his
efforts and his risks. Yet, because of the
individual nature of his operation he does
not have the means to assure this return. It
is here that he needs the helping hand of
his Government.

That partnership works to the benefit of
all. For the prosperity of the farmer is of
concern to all—from the factory worker who
makes the tools and machines the farmer
buys, to the family who buys the food and
fiber the farmer grows, and to the whole
economy which is strengthened by a steady
flow of farm income.

Second, we must seek out new ways to
solve an old problem—overproduction, the
consequence of the American farmer's enormous capacity to produce far more food than
we are able to consume. For more than
thirty years we have tried to balance supply
and demand, to shatter the income-depress-
ing cycle of glut and scarcity.

We have not yet succeeded in reaching
that difficult goal—but in recent years we
have made great strides. The foundation for
progress is now in place with the Food and
Agriculture Act of 1965. That Act gives us
the machinery to tailor production to demand, to produce the right kind of food—
at the right time—in the right amounts.

We are learning to operate that new ma-

chinery more skillfully now in cooperation
with farmers and their organizations.

Still, more is needed to reach the farmer's
just goal of parity of income—a fair return
for his labor, management and investment.

I believe 1968 can be the year in which we
move closer than ever before to that elusive
goal. It can be a year of decision for the
American farmer.

*I propose a 7-point plan to bring new pros-
perity to rural America.*

1. Permanent extension of the farmer's
   basic charter—the Food and Agriculture Act of 1965.
2. Continuation of the Food for Freedom
   Program through 1971.
3. Creation of a National Food Bank—a
   security reserve of wheat, feed grains
   and soybeans to protect the consumer
   against food scarcity and the farmer
   against falling prices.
4. New bargaining authority for the
   farmer, to give him a stronger voice in
   setting terms and conditions for the sale
   of his products.
5. Stronger regulatory programs to guard
   the farmer against fraud in the market
   place.
6. Aid and hope for the small farmer.
7. Continued revitalization of America's
   rural heartland by improving men's
   lives through decent housing, better
   jobs, and more rapid community development.

Taken together, these measures can hasten
the day when the men and women who
grow our food can share more fully in the
abundance they help to create.

The Food and Agriculture Act

The Food and Agriculture Act of 1965
is the backbone of our support for the farmer.

—For the first time, it recognized that

stabilizing the market supply of our basic commodities—wheat, feed grains, and cotton—is a continuing, not a temporary, problem.

—It established price supports at near-world levels for these major commodities—with payments to stabilize incomes and acreage allotment programs to prevent surpluses from piling up.

—It provided the flexibility to adjust the farmer's production to meet domestic needs, export demand and projected shipments under the Food for Freedom Program.

Two years after its passage, the Act faced a severe test. Larger wheat and feed grain allotments for 1967 crops set under the Act were followed by a series of unforeseen events: world-wide bumper crops, smaller total demand—and lower prices for the farmer. These are the uncertainties to which every estimate—involving millions of acres, millions of tons of food and the variability of weather—is subject.

Those events of 1967 once more spurred the old cry: 'get the government out of agriculture."

But the 1965 Act did not fail the farmer.

Direct payments under the Act provided the margin between profit and loss for many producers: an additional 48 cents for each bushel of wheat, 15 cents for each pound of cotton, 20 cents for each bushel of corn.

To terminate the 1965 Act would bring catastrophe and ruin to many farmers.

Cash prices to the farmer would fall—and there would be no government payments to cushion the impact. Farm income could drop by as much as one-third—back to 1959 levels.

—Wheat prices would drop to about $1.10 a bushel—compared with the 1967 blend price of $1.89, including the wheat certificate.

—Corn prices would drop to about 75 cents a bushel, compared with a blend price of $1.30 in 1967.

—Cotton would sell for 18 cents a pound, compared with 42 cents in 1967 with price support payments.

—With lower grain prices, livestock supplies would soon overburden the market so that livestock prices would decline by at least 10%.

Certainly the Act can be improved. Suggestions to strengthen it should be carefully reviewed. But it must be continued.

This should be permanent legislative authority. The need for price protection will not end in one—or two—or even the four years provided in the 1965 Act.

While the Congress may choose to modify these programs in future years, the farmer should not run the risk of sudden termination of this vital protection. Only permanent authority will assure that he is never the innocent victim of a program lapse.

Although the Act does not expire until 1969, it should be extended this year. Before this Congress adjourns, the 1969 wheat program must be announced. And before Congress meets in 1969, final year programs for all the other commodities under the current Act must be announced.

The agricultural producer, like all prudent businessmen, should be in a position to make his plans well in advance.

To postpone consideration of this vital legislation until next year would create grave risks for the American farmer.

I recommend that the Congress begin hearings at the earliest possible date to extend the Food and Agriculture Act of 1965.

FOOD FOR FREEDOM

The clock continues to tick in the developing nations—as the shadow of hunger threatens to turn into a nightmare of famine.

274

That awesome problem has long summoned America's attention. Since World War II, we have helped meet world food needs with contributions from the storehouse of our agricultural abundance.

In 1966, I proposed that the United States lead the world in a war against hunger. At that time, I asked the Congress to join in a new and concerted food aid program—Food for Freedom. Two years of achievement show that the program was wise as well as compassionate:

—The bounty from America's farmlands and granaries has rescued millions of people from the brink of starvation.

—Developing nations are helping themselves through national policies centering on agricultural development.

—Sales are now shifting from foreign currencies to dollars. This repayment trend will improve our own balance of payments.

—Food shipments are creating future overseas markets for the products of our farms and our industry, as the economies of developing nations grow stronger.

This lifeline of hope to the needy of the world cannot be withdrawn. The Food for Freedom Program expires at the end of this year.

I recommend that the Congress continue the Food for Freedom Program for three more years—to December 31, 1971.

As before, our efforts must be rooted in self-help. Aid that does not encourage the maximum effort of each nation to feed its own people is illusory—and a deception to those who receive it.

Our efforts must also continue to be grounded in world cooperation, because hunger is a world problem which must be met by many nations.

The Kennedy Round turned that principle to action as other nations joined the United States in the International Grains Agreement.

I recently asked the Senate to approve that Agreement. It calls for a three-year program of food aid. Participating nations have agreed to supply 4.5 million tons of grain annually. The U.S. share—1.9 million tons—will be met as part of the Food for Freedom Program.

The Grains Agreement is good news for the American farmer. It provides new insurance against falling wheat prices. And it builds new cash customers for his products.

I again urge the Senate to ratify the International Grains Agreement at the earliest possible time.

Security Commodity Reserve—A National Food Bank

When the talk is of farm surpluses, the term "food scarcity" has an unrealistic ring. Yet even America is not completely immune from a natural disaster or some other emergency that could imperil our food supply.

America's food stocks are also affected by another factor—our humane response to the hardship and hunger that may strike other nations.

In the light of these contingencies, *we must develop a national food strategy* to assure that:

—Production is sufficient to meet domestic needs.

—Additional production is scaled to meet requirements for exports and food aid shipments.

—A security reserve is on hand to protect against unforeseen emergencies or variations between production estimates and actual need.

The Food and Agriculture Act of 1965 and the Food for Freedom Program provide a solid basis for this national strategy. Acreage allotments established under the 1965 Act are based on anticipated domestic consumption and foreign demand. Food for Freedom shipments furnished an important part of that total demand.

But, as we have learned, no system of estimates can be precise. Searing winds, drought and flood can deplete production quickly and cause scarcity. And as we have also learned, surplus stocks—even when temporary—can depress the farmer's income.

What America needs is a National Food Bank—where deposits can be made in time of plenty, and withdrawals in time of shortage.

Last year, legislation was introduced to create such a Bank—a Security Reserve of wheat, feed grains, and soybeans. Hearings have been held in both Houses.

I urge the Congress to complete consideration of this important legislation at the earliest possible date. This Administration will continue its strong support of a measure which includes these principles:

—The establishment of a reserve owned by farmers through strengthened reseal provisions in the price support program. The farmer would control sales from a part of this reserve, but some of these stocks would be held under long-term arrangements for emergency use.

—Authority for the Secretary of Agriculture to purchase an additional reserve at market prices. It should not be necessary for prices to drop to the support levels to add to the reserve stocks held by the government.

—Insulation of this food bank from the commercial market. The Secretary of Agriculture should not sell reserve stocks at less than parity adjusted for government payments.

A National Food Bank can provide important protection for *all* Americans.

—The *farmer* will not have to bear the burden of depressed prices when production exceeds current needs.

—The *consumer* will be protected from unanticipated food scarcity.

—The *government* will have a reserve stock "cushion" in making acreage allotment decisions, and in responding to international emergencies.

FARMER BARGAINING POWER

Government programs for wheat, feed grains, cotton, or other basic commodities strengthen the bargaining power of participating farmers. Under the loan program with its recently expanded reseal privileges, the farmer can hold his crop for a better market.

But items which provide 60 percent of gross farm income—including livestock, poultry, fruits and vegetables—are not covered by Government price support and payment programs.

The producer sells these commodities for what the market will bear.

This is fair enough—if the farmer has the power to bargain effectively with those to whom he sells. But he does not.

—There are millions of farmers and their power is diffused and fragmented. In contrast, the distributors and processors who buy the farmer's products are relatively few and well organized.

—Farmers do not have the means to tailor carefully their production to market demands. If they produce too much, they have little hope for a decent price at market time.

—Most businessmen can set a price for their goods. Most farmers must sell their products for "what they can get."

In some ways, government action helps the farmer to bargain for better terms in the market place. Government purchases under Section 32, Food Stamp, School Lunch, Milk, and commodity distribution programs create additional demand—and even out over supplies which could depress prices.

Still, the Government is—and can be—a customer for only a fraction of the total market.

The fact remains that the farmer does not have the bargaining power he needs—he still does not have the ability to price his products for a fair profit.

Some farmers—in cooperatives and marketing associations—have found that their collective voice is far stronger than individual efforts. They have utilized marketing orders and marketing contracts to achieve higher prices and better terms of sale.

They are the pioneers.

Now thousands of other farmers are beginning to think about farmer bargaining.

They seek an end to the frustration caused by their lack of bargaining power.

They see the opportunities for lower costs and better prices through market organization and coordination of supply.

They know the value of transforming haphazard farm production into steady flows of products of uniform quality—fitted to the needs of our modern food industry.

Several months ago, I directed the Secretary of Agriculture to study the various bargaining and marketing tools available to agricultural producers.

I asked agricultural economists and other experts from outside the government to participate in this effort. The farm organizations have taken leading roles in advancing bargaining techniques.

It is now time for the Congress to join this effort.

I urge the House and Senate Committees on Agriculture to hold hearings this session on the various means of strengthening farm- *er bargaining power in the market place.*

Among the issues the hearings should consider are these:

—Will bargaining efforts be equally effective for all commodities?

—What kind of bargaining unit should farmers establish?

—For what should farmers bargain? Better price? Uniform quality? Other terms of sale?

—Should the bargaining unit be able to limit marketing or production to meet bargaining objectives? If so, how should these limitations be administered or enforced?

One matter is clear. The government may act as an advisor, or it may serve as an umpire. But the plan must be designed for farmers to use if they choose. It cannot be forced upon them. Under any proposal, farmers must make their own decisions and control their own destinies.

Upon completion of these studies and the Congressional hearings, we will make specific recommendations for action.

FRAUDULENT PRACTICES

Fraudulent and deceptive practices sap the vitality of our economy. In the case of the farmer, they impose special hazards and handicaps. Wherever these practices are found, they must be rooted out.

Last week, I was proud to sign a measure guarding against fraud and manipulation in the Nation's commodity exchanges.

But there is still unfinished farmer protection business before Congress.

I urge the Congress to modernize the Packers and Stockyards Act.

This Act is intended to safeguard livestock and poultry producers against cases of deceit, fraud and unfair competition. The present law has failed to keep pace with developments in the livestock and poultry industries since the Act was first adopted almost half a century ago.

LIFE IN RURAL AMERICA

The proposals I have discussed to this point are designed to place American commercial agriculture on a sounder and stronger footing.

But this is only half the battle.

For there are thousands of men and women in rural America who need a different kind of help.

The statistics tell the grim story:

—Farm employment has fallen by 46% between 1950 and 1967.

—Nearly 1.5 million small farmers earn less than $5,000 per year. Their resources are meager and they have little to sell. Their existence may hang on a thin thread: a few acres of tobacco and cotton, an old-age pension, and the Food Stamp Program.

—The rate of unemployment and underemployment in rural America far exceeds the national average.

—10 million people in rural America— one in every five falls under the poverty line, and millions of families live in housing that shames a modern nation.

What promise is there for the sharecropper who has been replaced by a machine? What new job will open up to the 50-year-old farmer who has spent his entire life working the soil? What future can a young farm boy aspire to, when only one out of ten can expect to earn a living as a full-time farmer?

Unprepared and untrained—with nowhere else to go—they have left the land they know and streamed into the teeming slums of American cities.

The problem they pose touches us all. It is a problem of urban America no less than rural America.

We have long spoken of parity of opportunity for rural Americans. I speak now of making that promise a reality.

It will require action—both long and short range. The foundation of that effort has been built.

—The war on poverty is quietly transforming the lives of thousands of men and women in rural America.

—"Operation Outreach," launched last year, brings 90 Federal programs, from health to housing, from education to economic development, to the countryside. Under the coordination of the Secretary of Agriculture, Technical Action Panels organized at the regional, state, district and county level are assuring that these programs turn into effective action for the people.

Food Stamps

But some people still go hungry in rural America.

The Food Stamp Program has been an effective instrument to supplement the purchasing power of low-income families. When I signed the Food Stamp Act of 1964, the program was being tested in 43 areas. Today, it is operating in over 850 counties. By early summer, it will extend to 1200, providing the basic essential of life to over two million needy men, women and children.

I recommend that the 1969 appropriation authorization for the Food Stamp Program be increased from $225 million to $245 million.

The Small Farmer

Many of our poorest farmers cannot leave the farm for other work. They are untrained.

And they have passed the age when job opportunities can open up a new life. They are boxed in.

They cannot "go into something else," for there is no place else to go. But they can be aided more effectively—and economically—on the farm.

I have directed the Secretary of Agriculture to focus the full range of the programs under his jurisdiction to help the small farmer.

I am also proposing legislation that will:

—Increase funds available to small farmers to begin new farm and non-farm enterprises; and to provide credit to help the farmer to convert his land into income producing recreation areas.

—Improve the loan program for grazing associations.

—Establish a credit program for rural cooperatives now ineligible for assistance from the Banks for Cooperatives or the poverty program.

I am also asking the Congress to appropriate additional funds to help low-income ranchers, who depend on National Forest lands for much of their livestock grazing, and to increase technical assistance to cooperatives owned by small farmers.

Rural Electrification

Thirty years ago, the lights went on across the farmlands of America. Rural electrification liberated the farmer and his family from the tyranny of darkness. Lights, appliances, radios—all the conveniences of modern living—replaced the kerosene lamp and the flickering candle. Electricity eased the farmer's burden, and brought industry and jobs to rural America.

Rural electrification is a great American success story.

We must advance that success and bring it up to date by assuring the growth of the nation's rural electrification systems in the areas they have been called upon to serve. Those systems must have access, under fair and reasonable rates, to bulk power supplies. In this way, they can continue to provide a reliable, uninterrupted, and inexpensive flow of electricity into America's farm communities on a par with more populous communities.

Rural Housing

There are places in the hollows and small country towns that look as if America had never moved forward from the grim days of depression.

Over three million families outside our metropolitan areas live in ramshackle and dilapidated dwellings.

More than half of the Nation's 6 million substandard housing units are outside our metropolitan areas.

But our federal housing programs have not been able to reach effectively enough into those dusty roads of a by-passed America.

I propose that we move now to correct this situation.

First, I have already recommended legislation to launch a new program, in cooperation with industry and labor, to add 6 million new housing units over the next 10 years for families with low and moderate incomes.

I am directing the Secretary of Agriculture to work with the Secretary of Housing and Urban Development in bringing this new program to our rural areas.

Much of the necessary assistance can be rendered by the Farmers Home Administration. For more than three decades, it has helped provide home financing for rural citizens.

I want to make certain that the residents of rural America participate fully in this important housing program.

Second, I have recommended legislation which will:

—Authorize the Secretary of Agriculture to reduce the interest rates for low and moderate income families so they can borrow under existing rural housing loan programs.

—Broaden the eligibility for credit under the rural housing loan program.

—Make low-income non-rural residents who have jobs in rural areas eligible for housing loans.

Third, I have directed the Secretary of Housing and Urban Development to insure that the rent supplement program has maximum impact in rural as well as urban areas.

Jobs and Rural Development

The rural American displaced by technology has a proud heritage of hard work. He does not want welfare. He wants a job.

If the jobs are in the cities, men will move there.

Eighteen months ago, in Dallastown, Pennsylvania, I said:

"History records a long, hard struggle to establish man's right to go where he pleases and to live where he chooses. . . . We lose that freedom when our children are obliged to live someplace else if they want a job or if they want a decent education. Not just sentiment demands that we do more to help our farms and rural communities. I think the welfare of this Nation demands it. And . . . I think the future of the cities of America demands it, too."

Today 70 percent of our people live on 1 percent of our land. By the turn of the century—if present trends continue—there will be 240 million Americans living in urban areas occupying only 4 percent of this great and spacious nation.

I think we can change this trend by setting a goal of full parity of opportunity for Rural America. Industry, technology and transportation can bring jobs to the countryside rather than people to the cities. And government must help.

In our growing economy, private enterprise—today—is creating thousands of new jobs in the small towns of America. We can do more to develop job opportunities and to provide assistance to those who want work.

With legislation now on the books, we can move to reduce rural underemployment and unemployment by the end of 1968. I have directed:

—The Secretaries of Commerce and Agriculture to develop an expanded credit program for firms seeking to locate new plants in rural areas.

—The Secretary of Commerce and the Administrator of the Small Business Administration to give top priority to loans for the construction of industrial buildings in rural areas.

—The Secretary of Labor to extend work training and job counseling programs. With the Census Bureau, he will undertake regular surveys of labor market conditions in rural areas.

—The Secretaries of Agriculture, Labor, and Health, Education, and Welfare and the Director of the Office of Economic Opportunity to coordinate expanded area-wide manpower planning, and concerted education and training services.

—The Secretary of Housing and Urban Development and the Director of the Office of Economic Opportunity to help finance the creation of additional community centers where the rural resident can have access to all the programs designed to help him and his family.

—The Secretary of Labor to extend the Concentrated Employment Program, which brings together a wide range of manpower and related services in selected geographical areas, to an additional 70 areas—35 of them rural.

In addition, I have recommended legislation which would provide training facilities—and temporary housing during training—to enable low-income rural residents prepare for improved employment opportunities.

But jobs alone are not enough to make the countryside more livable and more convenient for rural Americans. What is needed is a restoration of rural-urban balance—a balance that assures rural America its full, fair share of educational, economic, social and cultural opportunity.

To help accomplish this, I recommend that the Congress:

—Increase Federal programs to assist rural communities in building modern water and sewer systems.

—Extend the period of eligibility for grants for comprehensive water and sewer projects.

—Authorize recreation projects in Resource Conservation and Development areas.

—Appropriate funds for ten new multi-county, multi-purpose Resource Conservation and Development areas during Fiscal 1969. This will give the Nation fifty-one such areas, encompassing 100 million areas.

In addition, I urge the Congress to take action on two important measures pending before it:

—To finance comprehensive planning for groups of rural counties. Such planning can help rural communities attract business and industry and make better use of Federal programs. It can help neighboring communities pool their resources—health, education, training— to meet the common needs of their people.

—To provide additional sources of financing for rural telephone systems. We must continue to build and upgrade our telephone systems to speed economic development and community growth.

THE SPECIAL NEED

Our earliest destiny was shaped by those who, in Jefferson's words, "labor in the earth."

The hand that worked the plow—that led the team—that husked the corn—was the hand that guided America to its greatness.

The stability and endurance of the farmer are a priceless part of our nation's heritage. His love of the land expresses the American dream—that a man should be able to shape his own destiny with his own hands.

The American farmer today stands in the proud tradition of generations of his fathers.

But he is faced, as no generation before him, with the problems of an accelerating technology. It is bringing fundamental and forceful change to the farmer and the rural community.

The farmer and the rural community need government's help, and government must respond.

Since I have been President, I have been proud to sign 184 measures designed to assist farmers and the rural community. Each of these has filled a special need.

The proposals I have outlined in this message continue that vital work.

This is a total program—one for the years ahead as well as for today—through which the American farmer can claim his place and privilege in the life of his Nation.

LYNDON B. JOHNSON

The White House
February 27, 1968

NOTE: For statements or remarks upon signing related legislation, see Items 363, 386, 417, 450, 451, 519, 534.

Other related legislation was approved by the President as follows: an amendment to the Packers and Stockyards Act, approved July 31, 1968 (Public Law 90–446, 82 Stat. 474); the Department of Agriculture and Related Agencies Appropriation Act of 1969, approved August 8, 1968 (Public Law 90–463, 82 Stat. 639); a bill to increase Federal programs to assist rural communities in building modern water and sewage systems, approved August 15, 1968 (Public Law 90–488, 82 Stat. 770).

The International Grains Arrangement was transmitted to the Senate on January 25, 1968 (see Item 29).

95 Annual Message to the Congress Transmitting the Budget for the District of Columbia, Fiscal Year 1969. *February 27, 1968*

To the Congress of the United States:

I am transmitting the budget of the District of Columbia for the fiscal year beginning July 1, 1968.

The budget proposes fiscal 1969 appropriations of $609 million. Revenues from existing sources will total $371.6 million. New taxes will raise an additional $18.9 million. The proposed Federal payment is $83.5 million. The remainder of the budget—$135.8 million—represents Federal loans for public facilities and commitments required today for construction costs in subsequent years.

This budget requests the minimum funds necessary to meet the needs of the citizens of the Capital of the United States.

Preparation of the budget was begun by the outgoing three-commissioner government. Mayor Walter Washington and his Deputy have reviewed it intensively, and made modifications in the relatively brief time available for this purpose. This budget has been considered and amended by the District Council after public hearings. Most significantly, for the first time in nearly 100 years, the citizens of the District have had the opportunity to voice their views on budgetary proposals before a city council.

Through careful and thoughtful development of this budget, the reorganized District Government has shown that it can conduct the public's business efficiently and judiciously with active public participation. This augurs well for prompt achievement of the city's goal of self-government.

The District budget for 1969 requests funds to combat the urgent and complex problems being experienced by all the major cities of our Nation. These problems include an increase in the crime rate, growing public health needs, traffic congestion, educational demands, housing shortages, expanding welfare requirements, spiraling demands for job training and employment assistance, and air and water pollution. To attack these problems, the budget calls for funds to:

• Strengthen the police, courts, and corrections systems, including an increase in police manpower and modernization of police communications and data processing equipment.

• Improve the public school system and higher education in the District of Columbia, including improved incentives to attract and retain first-rate teachers, school construction and modernization and establishment of two new public colleges.

• Improve public health and human relations services, including the new community health center program.

• Establish a comprehensive neighborhood service center by bringing a wide range of health, recreation, and other social services together for residents in their own neighborhood.

- Build recreation centers and provide for the vital Summer Enrichment Program.
- Begin construction of the rapid rail transport system and continue construction of interstate highways.
- Expand programs to combat air and water pollution and step up the District's rat control efforts.

These improvements represent the first installment of the new District Government's promissory note to its citizens. Their needs and their expectations are great. Their budg-

et—set forth in the transmittal letter of the Mayor—is sound and realistic and requests urgently needed funds. I recommend that the Congress approve the District budget and revenue measures for fiscal 1969.

LYNDON B. JOHNSON

February 27, 1968

NOTE: The text of the budget and annexes, together with Commissioner Walter E. Washington's letter of transmittal to the President, is entitled "District of Columbia: the Budget of the United States Government, Fiscal Year 1969" (Government Printing Office, 58 pp.).

For statements or remarks upon signing related legislation, see Items 203, 272, 420, 436, 542.

96   Remarks at the National Rural Electric Cooperative Association Convention in Dallas. *February 27, 1968*

Mr. Hunter, Mr. Ellis, ladies and gentlemen, members of the National Rural Electric Cooperative Association:

It is good to be here with you. I have been spending a few days at a ranch on the Pedernales Co-op line, and I just felt that I didn't want to go back to big city life without stopping by and visiting with you.

Whenever I see so many country people in a big city like this, I think of that old definition of a farmer: "A person who occasionally visits the city to see where his sons and his profits went."

I think all of you know there is a good deal of truth in that.

The REA was founded a third of a century ago to try to halt the drain of life and wealth from the countryside. Men and women rallied to the REA banner from all over America, and they did it for the same reason: to try to make life better in the rural areas.

You have struggled for years to win that better life. And many of your dreams have come true. Many more will come true for your children. Not long ago, it was only 5 percent of America's farms that had electricity; today, only 5 percent of them don't have it.

I share your great pride in that progress, and I thank you for it—because all along your struggles have been my struggles. Clyde Ellis knows so well how much of my early life and heart went into building that Pedernales Rural Electric Cooperative in Johnson City, along with dozens of other cooperatives in this State.

I know the thrill, I think, as you know it, that every man and woman feels when he or she walks out into their front yard on a cold night to see what his house looks like, all lit up for the first time.

We had some very tough battles over the years—in the thirties, the forties, the fifties— and, yes, we lost some of them—temporarily.

But in 1961, the REA went back into high gear under that great President, John Fitzgerald Kennedy. And, in the last 4 years we have been proud to shove the throttle forward into even higher gear. In just a few years we won a 50 percent increase in kilowatt hours—nearly as much as in all the years of the REA combined.

But we are not going to settle for that. It isn't enough to say that the lights will never go out again in the countryside. It isn't time to stand pat and be satisfied with the status quo—not when your battles are America's battles—not when your struggles for a better rural life can also mean better cities, better suburbs, a better future for every American.

And so long as I am your President, I will do all in my power to work with you, to help you, to encourage you.

I will support the right of your systems to territorial integrity—to continue serving the areas where you pioneered.

I will support your right of access to additional power, so that the growing needs of your areas can be met with full and always dependable power. This means, to me, guaranteed access to bulk quantities—and a larger participation in the regional pools and other giant power complexes that will meet the power needs that we are going to have in the 1970's.

As long as I am your President, and even when I am a private citizen, I will support the principle of parity so that you can give rural people the rates and the services that are enjoyed by city people.

Most of all, I will support your most critical struggle—to gain, and win, fresh sources of capital to finance adequately your future growth.

I was disappointed, but not disheartened, last year when the Congress failed to approve the Rural Electrification Bank.

The REA Bank bill made good sense. It would have opened the way for stronger cooperatives to obtain needed capital from the great private money market. But all the people who have been fighting and slugging

REA for 30 years and more came out of hiding and put their brands on it—and they cut the life out of it. They butchered it so badly that even the friends of REA couldn't support the remains that were left.

I know that your need for expanded financing has not died. And nothing can kill my determination, either, to see that you get that expanded financing. Your long-range study committee is working right now to try to find a successful formula. This administration will continue to work right along beside you to help you.

These are only some of the few initiatives that we must take right now to try to win our battle for a better America. I sent other strong recommendations to the Congress today in my special message on the farmer and rural America. I am going to send a copy of that message to every member of this organization, because you are interested in more than just the power needs of the farmer.

You are interested in the farmers' need for power and the farmers' need for prices, and the farmers' need for the same things that the city man needs—education for his children, clothes for them to wear, adequate purchasing power, a roof over their heads, a chance for them to live normal, healthy lives like all children in this country live.

This farm message proposes to put the farmer on the same basis with the other citizens of this land. We need your help to get him there.

The farm recommendations that I sent to the Congress today are companion recommendations to the ones I sent to Congress last week in my special message on the cities.

This is a turning point in our history. You recognize it, I think, with your convention theme—Target: Rural-Urban Balance.

That balance could make the life or death

difference for this land that we love, this America of ours. It can mean the growth or the decay of our countryside and our cities. It can decide whether we live and work in harmony across this spacious continent—or cram together in rising hostility in a few concrete beehives.

Your vision has tipped the balance before, when the REA rescued the countryside from depression and darkness. Rural America 1968 shines with the blessings that you started to bring to it 30 years ago.

But your target is not the past 30 years. Your target must be the next 30 years. The question you and I want answered, therefore, is this: What will rural America be like in the year 2000? Will country life be far better or far worse in the third century?

So I came here this morning on rather short notice, at your invitation, to call on you now—here and now—as President Franklin D. Roosevelt called upon you 30 years ago, to give us new answers for a new day.

You have the know-how to do it. Your experience gives you the edge—and I want it to be the cutting edge that clears the way to the future.

You can answer the farmers and ranchers who want a stronger voice in shaping their own economic destiny.

You can answer their needs to organize, to learn the techniques of cooperative effort, and to learn how to bargain better and more collectively.

You can answer the needs of rural people for modern business skills—the knowledge to price their products, the knowledge to market their goods fairly and justly, and to manage their affairs in order to get a maximum profit.

You can answer the desires of small communities to plan efficiently for vital public services—better schools, better streets, better

hospitals, and, yes, better water and sewer systems that will serve the small towns and the countryside, too—the facilities that bring towns and people together.

You can answer the hunger for rural jobs by going out and being the business-getters—the community builders who invite and who attract the big companies to the small towns—the new payrolls and new capital that mean new opportunity and new fulfillment for the people you serve.

And you can help answer another great and another human need. That is the need for pride—to be proud of ourselves—pride in a home, pride in our family, pride in our farm, our shop, our store, our main street, or even our farm-to-market road—pride that makes a fellow want to get up and paint his barn if he can finance it, or mend his fence, or thresh his wheat—that makes a town fix up, spruce up, and lift up its head.

A beautiful America can be a proud America. Your local leadership, through your board of directors, through your managers, through your employees, through your transportation system and communications system, can help us to preserve and nurture the beauty that gives a man joy and gives a community spirit.

These opportunities can be your targets. They are what we mean when we talk about a rural-urban balance, and use those high-sounding city words. We mean by that, that the problems of the cities, the suburbs, and the country are a single national problem. We can only solve that problem as national thinkers, and get away from our narrow, parochial leanings. We can only solve it as one single-minded people that pool their common experience and their common strength in one determined purpose, for one determined people, for one great and determined nation.

We mean that every American should have the right to live where he wants to live—city or country—without losing any right to a happy, a full, and, yes, a prosperous life.

We mean that rural America must offer these rights to every American: good jobs for men and women, good schools for children, good hospitals for the sick, good homes for the families—all the good and all the necessary things to enlarge and to enrich the quality of life.

So let this be our declaration of domestic partnership, of domestic interdependence. Let us vow here and now to work side by side throughout the length and breadth of this good land, so that all of our people may have a fuller share of the better life that is their right.

That was the purpose of what I called the Great Society. Make no mistake about it—it is taking root, it is thrusting up, it is reaching out to banish need and to bring new hope into millions upon millions of lives.

We see it in Medicare. We see it in elementary education. We see it in antipoverty—attempts to try to improve the lot of all the poor people in our land. We see it in the biggest social security increase ever passed. We see it in more people working today than have ever worked before in the history of this land. We see it in health, in education, in conservation from one end of this Nation to the other.

If it is the work of 1 year, or 10, or if it is the work of the remainder of this entire century, or the third century as well—I am thankful for the chance to have launched it. I am thankful and grateful to you of the Rural Electrification Administration in this country for helping to advance my hopes for a great America. I predict and I pledge you—and strong, countless other Americans like you—that the Great Society that is designed to help people is here to stay.

This can be a nation of greatness for all, if we only work together; if we have the common will to rise above trial; if we have the matching strength to carry our responsibilities at home and our responsibilities abroad; if we have the unity, the good judgment, and the sound commonsense to persevere in the greatest purpose of all—the work of peace on earth.

Persevere in Vietnam we must and we will. There, too, today we stand at a turning point. The enemy of freedom has chosen to make this year the decisive one. He is striking out in a desperate and a vicious effort to try to shape the final outcome to his purposes.

So far we think he has failed in his major objectives. He has failed—at a terrible cost to himself and a tragic cost to his civilian victims.

I saw General Westmoreland's report this morning and he shows, since the Tet period, 43,000 of the enemy have been killed and 7,000 have been captured. He has lost 50,000 men since that holiday period began—because thousands of our courageous sons and millions of brave South Vietnamese have answered aggression's onslaught, and they have answered it with one strong and one united voice.

"No retreat," they have said. Free men will never bow to force and abandon their future to tyranny.

That must be our answer, too, here at home. Our answer here at home, in every home, must be: "No retreat from the responsibilities of the hour and the day."

We are living in a dangerous world and we must understand it. We must be prepared to stand up when we need to.

There must be no failing of our fighting sons.

There must be no betrayal of those who

fight beside us.

There must be no breaking of America's given word or America's commitments. When we give our word it must mean just what it says. America's word is America's bond. Isn't that the way you feel about it?

There must be no weakening of the will that would encourage the enemy or would prolong the bloody conflict.

Peace will come of that response, of our unshakable and our untiring resolve, and only of that. The peace of Asia and the peace of America will turn on it. I do not believe that we will ever buckle. I believe that every American will answer now for his future and the future of his children.

I believe he will say: "I did not retreat when the going got rough. I did not fall back when the enemy advanced and things got tough, when the terrorists attacked, when the cities were stormed, the villages assaulted, and the people massacred."

I think every American would want to say: "Where was I? I stood up to be counted. I stood fast beside my brothers and my sons who went away to fight for me. I stood firm with my Government to fight to preserve the way of life that we hold so precious and so dear."

I believe in the wisdom and the fortitude of the American people. I believe in the good sense and the stout hearts of people like you. I believe with all my faith in the American future that you have worked so long and so well to shape.

It will be a future of limitless promise where every citizen, regardless of race or region, can grow to his fullest measure. It will be a shining land where rural poverty and urban slums have gone the way of the kerosene lamp—if we only have the vision, the determination, the stick-to-it-iveness, and do not allow the dividers among us to succeed.

I had a letter last night from a great historian whom most of you have followed through the years—Mr. Allan Nevins. And he said: "My friend, Mr. President, don't be discouraged by the croakers. We have had the croakers since the days of our first revolution, and they are always present but rarely successful."

Yes, this land will be a shining and peaceful land, where rural poverty has been conquered. It will be a nation not only of rural beauty and urban energy, but of rural energy and urban beauty, too. And the men and women in this room today should pledge themselves to make it so. And I pledge myself, here and now, to you that I will go the last mile with you.

I want to thank the leaders of agriculture in the 50 States, the leaders of the REA and this great organization which has done so much to preserve the unity of all co-op REA movements; the great agricultural leaders in the Congress: Chairman Poage, Chairman Ellender—and Chairman Whitten, who honors us with his presence, who heads up all agricultural appropriations.

The journey we make will remake America, and I think that every American looks ahead with my eagerness and my excitement to that. This Nation shares my pride and my happiness in moving on with you.

We have a long road ahead. There will be much blood, sweat, and tears shed en route. The weak will drop from the line. Their feet will get sore and their voice will get loud. But in the spirit of the pioneers, there are new problems to be solved—there are new areas to be worked.

I hope that you will leave this great convention inspired and stimulated, to be not only a part of a great rural movement in this country that remade America, but as a part of a continuing movement to better humanity. That is about the only reason, after all, that

we are here. That is about the only justification for our presence.

What can we do to better the life of human
beings—brown, black, and white—people in
our own land, people throughout the world?
There is not much difference between a crying baby's voice wherever he lives, whatever
his parents. They all want the same thing.

The average family everywhere in the
world has the same needs: food to sustain
their bodies, clothes to cover their nakedness,
a roof over their heads to protect them as
shelter from the rain and the sun, a school
where their children can listen and learn, a
church where they can worship according to
the dictates of their own conscience.

People don't ask for much. That is precious

little. But America is leading the way in the
world for better health, for better education,
for better conservation, and for a better rural
and city life.

You are leading the way for America.

Thank you and goodby.

NOTE: The President spoke at 11:23 a.m. in the Dallas
Memorial Auditorium. In his opening words he re-
ferred to T. W. Hunter, President, and Clyde T.
Ellis, Executive Manager of the National Rural Elec-
tric Cooperative Association. Later he referred to,
among others, Representative W. R. Poage of Texas,
Chairman of the House Agriculture Committee, Sen-
ator Allen J. Ellender of Louisiana, Chairman of the
Senate Agriculture and Forestry Committee, and
Representative Jamie L. Whitten of Mississippi,
Chairman of the House Appropriations Committee.

On the same day the White House also released
the text of remarks to the convention by the President's daughter, Luci Johnson Nugent.

97   Remarks at a Birthday Dinner in Austin for Governor John B. Connally of Texas. *February 27, 1968*

*Governor and Mrs. Connally, Chairman
Erwin, Congressman Pickle, Mr. Strauss,
distinguished guests:*

I want to thank all of you for the very special welcoming committee outside. As I
came in rather hurriedly I was looking at all
those well-dressed demonstrators and I knew
I was at the right place. I knew it was a
gathering either for John Connally or Lyndon Johnson.

But since this is your birthday, John, I will
just assume that these signs said, "Happy
Birthday, Governor."

My father always said there were three
places where a man didn't make a speech—
at least a very long speech: at rodeos, country
dances, and cocktail parties. He could have
added a fourth occasion: at a dinner given
by friends of John Connally.

No one here tonight needs me to make a
speech about John. That would only add, I

guess, to your surplus problems—being
about as useful as another entry in the Governor's race.

So I came by just to offer a few personal
thoughts to match all of your warm memories of friendship with a very good man
whom I consider a very great American.

On my way down to the ranch today I
jotted down five of them—one for each
decade in the Governor's very remarkable
life and very brilliant career.

I thought first, John, of how happy I am
to share in your birthday—and of how many
Americans have great cause to celebrate with
us. You pass the half-century mark today.
I think it is safe to predict that the influence
of your wise leadership on this State and
this Nation will be felt for the next half-
century, and many generations after.

Secondly, I thought of how this particular birthday also marks a very happy coin-

288

cidence. Today you are 51, John. That is the magic number that every man of politics prays for—a simple majority. Throughout the years we have worked long and hard—and I might say late—trying to maintain it, too. I take this as a very good omen for your future and for America's future. We who know you best know that there are very few men who are more experienced in political life—few men who are more devoted to making politics the shining instrument of the people's welfare—few men who are more capable of attracting the finest of our young men and women into the noble work of government—and more valued for all these reasons as a man whose greatest gifts to democratic government are, I think, yet to come.

You have given much already, John. It is fitting now that your friends and your people return the favors of your mind and your heart. That is my third thought—how perfect it is to come here tonight to honor the man and to perpetuate his purpose with the John B. Connally Professorship in Law.

I personally thank each of you. This is much more than an academic endowment. It is a national investment. As a fount of learning in this great university, it will help assure the continued greatness of our country and of our country's cause. From it will come the knowledge so necessary to nourish freedom; the truths so necessary to uplift our lives; and, I pray, the understanding of each other that men always need so desperately if they are ever to know the final wisdom of living as brothers, in a hectic world, in search for peace.

I would like to make my fourth point, John, by saying that you have almost been a brother to me for more than 30 years. In all of that time I have tried very hard never to embarrass you and I am not going to be-

gin now by getting sentimental. Only, let me recall, please, sir, that I gave you your first job. That may be where that phrase "LBJ's Boy John" came from. That was in the old NYA days here in Texas. Just looking at Nellie's gown tonight is proof of how far, John, you have come from $12 a month.

We have come together all along that road, from the NYA days until tonight, you and I. There is no price tag that is equal to the value of the closeness, the experiences, the hardships, the heartaches, the happiness, and the loyalty that we have shared. There is no need of that between us or between our families. We actually need nothing but the comfort of knowing that we are going to go on together, giving and getting strength from each other, in good times and in hard times—and there will be both. They will always be the best of times when I can say, as I have so often said, and always thankfully: "There is no man on this earth that I would rather have by my side all the time than John Connally."

That leaves me with one final thought, John, thought number five. It is a little thought that often is trampled in the big rush of busy men. But it has brought us here together and we will all be better men for taking it away from here tonight.

That thought is simply this: The best of one's life is always one's friends.

So, thank you, John and darling Nellie, for reminding all of us of that. And God bless both of you always for the lesson of your lives. It is wonderful to be here with you.

Thank you very much.

NOTE: The President spoke at 9:54 p.m. in Gregory Gymnasium at the University of Texas in Austin. In his opening words he also referred to Frank Erwin, Chairman of the University Board of Regents, Representative J. J. Pickle of Texas, and T. H. Strauss, Chairman of the Texas Fine Arts Commission.

98 Message to the Congress Transmitting Report on Federal Disaster Relief Activities in 1967. *February 28, 1968*

To the Congress of the United States:

I am transmitting to the Congress the report of activities in 1967 under the Federal Disaster Relief Act.

During 1967, eleven "major disasters" were declared under the authority of P.L. 81–875. More than $25 million were allocated to meet these disasters.

Through quick and effective action at the Federal, State and local levels, countless lives were saved, public facilities restored, and property losses kept to a minimum.

The floods in Alaska in August caused an estimated $90 million in damage. Quick Federal, State and local action helped complete all priority restoration before the winter freeze set in.

When hurricane Beulah struck in Texas last September, Federal forces immediately joined in evacuation, rescue, and relief operations. As a result, death, injury and loss were kept to a minimum during one of the worst storms in our history.

In addition, four allocations—totalling more than $13 million—were authorized for disasters that took place in previous years. The process of rebuilding after an earthquake or a hurricane is long and hard, and our commitment to the people of a ravaged area must often extend over several years.

A perfect year for this program would consist of no expenditures—no disasters. Until that time comes, I am confident that we will continue to respond quickly to help State and local governments alleviate the suffering and repair the damage wrought by natural disasters.

I commend this report to your attention.

LYNDON B. JOHNSON

The White House
February 28, 1968

NOTE: The report is printed in the Weekly Compilation of Presidential Documents (vol. 4, p. 384).

99 Remarks Upon Presenting the Medal of Freedom to Robert S. McNamara. *February 28, 1968*

Secretary and Mrs. McNamara and family, Members of the Cabinet, Members of Congress, Mr. Chief Justice, distinguished guests:

Thomas Jefferson said: "When a man assumes a public trust, he should consider himself as public property."

The man we honor here today has lived that philosophy for more than 7 long years.

The General Services Administration does not list him among our official assets, but he is one of America's most valuable public properties.

Bob McNamara may not have accomplished the impossible. But he has achieved the unlikely: managing and directing the huge complexity that is the Defense Establishment of the United States of America.

Those of us who served in Government during the Second World War came out of that conflict very proud of our Armed Forces—but all of us were deeply concerned for our future.

President Truman, that great leader of our country, at that time said:

"One of the strongest convictions which I brought to the Office of the Presidency was that the antiquated defense setup of the United States had to be reorganized quickly as a step toward insuring our future safety and preserving world peace. From the beginning of my administration I began to push hard for unification of the Military Establishment into a single department. . . ."

As a Congressman I spent hours and days listening to the testimony for and against unification. Most of the arguments came down to one common denominator: It just can't be done. It is impossible.

No one heard that refrain more often than the man who is about to become our new Secretary of Defense. Clark Clifford was here in the White House trying to help President Truman. He has told me this:

"I know so clearly what President Truman had in mind all during that time. And all through the years he kept hoping that we could and we would someday reach that point. Under Bob McNamara we finally did."

So, Bob McNamara has really served faithfully three Presidents: as a member of the Cabinet under President Kennedy and myself, and—after 20 years—as the man who made our Defense Department what Harry Truman wanted it to be.

Now, another distinguished American assumes the leadership of the establishment that he helped to create—and that Bob Mc-Namara helped to perfect.

The task, I think, and I think Bob Mc-Namara thinks, could not have passed to abler and wiser hands.

In Bob McNamara, the World Bank is gaining an executive of vision and a thinker who is also preeminently—with apologies to Mrs. Johnson—a doer.

Daily we read the reports that the developing nations are hopelessly far behind. The gap between the "haves and the have-nots" is said to be so wide and so growing that it is a great threat to world peace and that it will never be narrowed.

I do not generally make predictions on such matters and certainly my record does not compare with certain noted columnists, but I am going to make a prediction here in the East Room this morning.

I predict that 20 years from now another President will stand here someday and say: "A revolution of achievement in the developing nations began with the appointment of Robert S. McNamara to the World Bank in 1968."

For many long and quite demanding years Bob McNamara has guided our Defense Establishment. He has helped to give America the strongest, most efficient military power in history.

Now he is going to try, try to build the kind of world that alone can justify that strength.

We are asking him to attack the root causes of violence and turmoil—poverty, disease, ignorance, and hopelessness.

Those are the ancient enemies of the human race, which have never been defeated before. But our generation has the strength and the power and the resources, I hope, to eliminate them from the face of the earth.

What now is needed is intelligence—and organization and the will.

In this intensely loyal, brilliant, and good man, America is giving to the world and— if I may be personal—I am giving the world the very best that we have to win the most important war of all.

America is grateful for what he has done— and I speak for all of America this morning—and more important, for what he is about to do.

Mr. Secretary, on behalf of your fellow Americans, all of them, your country salutes you.

I will now read the citation of the highest medal that the President can award to a civil servant.

[Text of citation read by the President]

PRESIDENTIAL MEDAL OF FREEDOM CITATION
ROBERT S. MC NAMARA

For seven years, you have administered our complex Defense establishment—unifying our strength so that we might respond effectively wherever the security of our free world was challenged.

A brilliant analyst and modern administrator, you have brought a new dimension to defense planning and decision-making.

You have grasped the urgent social crisis of our time—the awakening of hope among the world's poor.

You have understood that while freedom depends on strength, strength itself depends on the determination of free people.

Your seven long years of unshakeable loyalty to the Republic, to the President, and to all who served beside and under you in the services, is an example for the public servant and an inspiration for your countrymen.

May your selfless service—spent in defending freedom—bring even greater rewards in the larger work you now undertake to promote freedom throughout the world.

LYNDON B. JOHNSON

The White House
February 28, 1968

NOTE: The President spoke at 1:20 p.m. in the East Room at the White House. In his opening words he also referred to Earl Warren, Chief Justice of the United States.

---

100   Remarks Opening the Midyear Conference of Governors of the States and Territories. *February 29, 1968*

I AM delighted to welcome you once again to this house.

This morning I want to talk about the primary business of government: public order.

To many people, that phrase means one thing: crime control. That is—to be sure—a major concern and responsibility of every public official. A people blessed by affluence and opportunity—but nevertheless beset by crime and civil disorder—is a troubled people. You and I—together with the Congress, the mayors, and the police departments—have work to do in meeting the challenge of lawlessness in America.

I shall talk more specifically about some of this work a little later. But first, I want to broaden the scope of that term—public order—and give it the larger meaning I believe it entails.

In our democracy, public order does not finally rest on force. It rests on the consent of our people. It rests on their belief that public order is the climate in which they may attain their goals:

—a good job,
—a decent home,
—an education for their children that will truly prepare them for life,
—physical well-being for their families,
—freedom from discrimination,
—safety in their homes and on the streets,
—a sense of purpose and participation in their community.

When individuals or groups attack the public order—for whatever reason—they must be stopped. No society can tolerate attacks upon itself.

But it is just as important that the public order be truly public—not the private preserve of a favored few. It is important that every citizen have a personal stake in the preservation of order. People must believe, and believe mightily, that there is always an avenue of opportunity for them—and for their children—in the cities of America.

The responsibility of government is inescapable here, just as in the control of crime. It is a responsibility not just to the poor and disadvantaged—but to every citizen who wants to live in peace, without fear and without hatred.

The National Government—responding to the people's will—has begun to meet that responsibility.

Eight years ago, the Federal budget included $9½ billion in aid to the poor. This year's budget proposes over $27 billion for the same purpose—three times the figure of 1960. This has been, in every sense, a revolution of responsibility—and each of us who helped to bring it about can be proud of it.

But even this vast effort cannot achieve the conditions of public order—unless it engages the determination of a healthy and responsible private industry—and Governors, mayors, State and city governments who recognize and carry out their responsibilities.

Let me give you some examples.

A month ago, I called upon the leaders of American industry to spearhead an unprecedented venture:

—placing 500,000 of America's hard-core unemployed in private industry jobs, and finding work for 200,000 poor youngsters this summer.

They responded—vigorously. Sixty-five of the Nation's top business executives—under the leadership of Mr. Henry Ford—have formed a National Alliance of Businessmen, to lead the drive in our 50 largest cities. They put together a topflight, full-time staff, drawn from industry and Government. They have developed detailed plans and a tight schedule—reflecting the urgency of their mission.

They will move in our 50 largest cities 2 weeks from now.

My question is, whether we in government—State, Federal, and local—will keep up with them.

Can your State employment service—which will implement this program at the local level—find the hard-core unemployed to fill the jobs and help negotiate $350 million worth of contracts in the next 16 months?

Industry is moving to meet its responsibilities. Will we meet ours?

The availability of health care—and the means to obtain it—is another element in maintaining a decent public order.

The cost of our Medicaid program—as no one knows better than you and I—is extremely high. We must find means of improving it, of reducing its costs and estimating them more precisely. We cannot return to the time when to be poor was inevitably to be sick—without medical attention. But we must make the program fair to the taxpayer, as it is responsive to those who need it.

The other day I sent to the Congress a supplemental estimate of $568 million for Medicaid, a 50 percent increase in the original 1968 budget estimate of $1.2 billion.

There are many reasons why that supplemental was necessary. Nevertheless, I think you will all agree that it represents a pretty wide error in budget estimating. It is true that medical costs have risen sharply. But we in the Federal Government have inadequate information on which to predict what the States will do:

—how many persons will be covered,
—what kind of services they will receive, and
—what are the cost implications?

Let us try to arrive at a solution to this together. I propose that we establish a joint Federal-State task force, where a select group of State budget directors and health and welfare officials can work with HEW and our Budget Bureau to bring about improvements in reporting and estimating the cost of Medicaid.

I am asking Acting Secretary Wilbur Cohen to get this effort underway immediately.

I know that many of you have discussed the amendments in the welfare system Congress adopted last fall. We have had enough experience with the various welfare programs to know that they have many shortcomings. The remedies that have been proposed are many and various. Because welfare involves so many factors—fiscal, economic, social, and moral—I have asked a distinguished group of Americans, including three present and former Governors, to examine alternative income maintenance programs, and to report their findings to me. Their commission is headed by Mr. Ben Heineman, chairman of the Chicago Northwestern Railroad.

By 1975, State and local government employment will grow to 11 million.

Each year, every year, you will have to recruit a quarter of a million new administrators, technicians, and professional employees just to keep your programs going. And this does not include the teachers.

Last year, I asked the Congress to help avert this manpower crisis.

I proposed the Public Service Education Act aimed at increasing the number of good students who choose careers in government.

I proposed the Intergovernmental Manpower Act—to help you train specialists and administrators, and to let us exchange some

of our best people—on a temporary basis—so that they might learn to work more effectively together.

These are vital and important proposals—but they are still just proposals, pending before the Congress.

I hope you will urge the Congress to make these measures a reality so we can get on with the job.

Each year billions of dollars pass to the States in the form of Federal grants-in-aid. In fiscal 1969, over $20 billion will be channeled in this way.

We are working with you to assure that these funds flow swiftly and surely, unhindered by redtape.

We are doing this by:
—consulting with your auditors and accountants;
—cutting back on paperwork and forms; and
—trying, wherever we can, to combine separate grants into single packages for maximum action.

There is much more room for improvement.

Last year, I asked the Congress—in legislation called the Joint Funding Simplification Act—to ease your work and ours.

That proposal is also before the Congress. I ask your help in urging the Congress to act quickly upon it.

Even if all the actions I have described this morning are taken, much that we will have done will be in vain if lawlessness dominates our cities.

No more important domestic challenge faces the American people than to preserve civil peace and to restore respect for the law.

As elected officials of your States, this is your concern. Law enforcement, as much as any responsibility of government, is primarily a local responsibility.

Wise tradition—which comes from our Founding Fathers—dictates that the work of law enforcement must be local. The war on crime cannot and should not be directed from the Nation's Capital. Yet the fact of crime—and the fear of crime—are national problems because they concern every American.

The sordid symptoms of crime mock our democratic society. They depress the daily lives of our people. Crime is an intolerable extra burden on the poor. It is an agent of suffering in millions of lives—rich and poor.

While it may never be cured completely, I am determined that it will be better controlled.

As President, I will do my part.

I have asked Congress and the Nation to move now—this year—on a 22-point action program I have submitted.

Today, I urge you to exercise the same leadership in a crusade for law enforcement in your State, that I am determined to exercise at the national level. This effort must be nationwide. Every Governor must commit the influence and power of his office to the fight.

Two years ago I asked the Attorney General to work with the Governors to establish statewide commissions on law enforcement and criminal justice. Since then, only half of the States have taken advantage of Federal assistance to set up these commissions.

I urge the remaining 25 States to act now—this year. I ask you to join me in urging the mayors of our large cities to establish their own local crime commissions.

There are pressing and obvious needs in the fight against lawlessness: better trained, better paid, and more effective police forces; fairer and more efficient systems of criminal justice; and—tragically—better means of responding when public order breaks down under the impact of riots. The measures I have sent to Congress will help you meet many of those needs.

I have asked the Attorney General to discuss them with you today.

If you—as the highest elected officials in your States—will add your support, I predict that this year Congress will strengthen the alliance of the Federal Government, States, and local governments in the fight against lawlessness by enacting the proposals that are now before it.

I hope this meeting will help forge the strongest and most effective Federal-State campaign for public order—in every sense of the phrase—that our country has ever witnessed.

If we act as we must, we shall strengthen and extend that order in every American community. That is our duty—and our opportunity.

NOTE: The President spoke at 9 a.m. in the White House Theater. An agenda for the conference was released by the White House on February 25. The Governors, the release said, would attend three panels: on law enforcement, to be led by the Attorney General; on the state of the economy, to be led jointly by the Secretary of the Treasury, the Under Secretary of Commerce, and the Chairman of the Council of Economic Advisers; and on Vietnam, to be led jointly by the Secretary of State and the Chairman of the Joint Chiefs of Staff. These topics, the release stated, were the most frequently requested as subjects for discussion by the Governors in response to a questionnaire sent them by Price Daniel, Director of the Office of Emergency Planning and Presidential liaison officer to the Governors. The full text of the release is printed in the Weekly Compilation of Presidential Documents (vol. 4, p. 361).

For the President's message to Congress on crime, containing the 22-point action program referred to above, see Item 59.

As printed above, this item follows the text released by the White House Press Office.

101   Remarks at a Farewell Ceremony at the Pentagon Honoring Secretary McNamara. *February 29, 1968*

Secretary McNamara, Secretary Nitze, General Wheeler, members of the Joint Chiefs of Staff and armed services, ladies and gentlemen:

I don't have a speech to make here today. I just thought that I would come over and join with all of you and with all of Bob McNamara's fellow workers in saying goodby to him.

I have heard this place here at the Pentagon referred to as the "Puzzle Palace." Bob McNamara may be the only man who ever found the solution to the puzzle and he is taking it with him. But whatever it is called, it is one of the most important buildings on this earth.

I am sorry that this is so, but until men and nations are content to leave one another in peace it will be so.

That makes you people very important people. A great deal depends on the quality of your performance, on your character, on your intelligence, on your patriotism, on your pride in your own service, and on your ability to rise above narrow service rivalries.

Bob McNamara's career is just about the textbook example of the modern public servant. But I suspect there are many others out there before me now in uniform and in civilian clothes, high ranking and not so high ranking, who also qualify as modern public servants.

I want to say to each of you that your country is grateful to you for the quality of the work that you do on behalf of all of us, as your country is grateful to this good man, Bob McNamara, to whom we have come here today to say goodby and farewell.

NOTE: The President spoke at 12:26 p.m. at the Pentagon. In his opening words he referred to Robert S. McNamara, outgoing Secretary of Defense, Paul H. Nitze, Deputy Secretary of Defense, and Gen. Earle G. Wheeler, Chairman of the Joint Chiefs of Staff.

A press pool report by Raymond L. Scherer of NBC News and George R. Packard of Newsweek magazine, concerning the incident in which the President, Secretary McNamara, and 11 other men were trapped for 12 minutes in a stalled Pentagon elevator prior to the ceremony, is printed in the Weekly Compilation of Presidential Documents (vol. 4, p. 391). See also the President's remarks concerning the incident, in the following item.

102   Toasts of the President and Governor John A. Volpe of Massachusetts at a Dinner Honoring the Governors. *February 29, 1968*

Distinguished Governors, charming ladies, friends—and favorite sons:

I am delighted to welcome you to the White House—temporarily. Today will certainly have proved one thing to you. Washington is an exciting town. Even a little elevator ride can be a big event.

Let me give you a confidential briefing on

what really happened in the Pentagon today.[1]

—First of all, the elevator was Number 13.

—And there were 13 of us in there.

—And today is Leap Year.

I felt sorry for that poor elevator operator. A voice came over the intercom and asked:

---

[1] See note to Item 101.

"Do you have a full load there?"

I was interested in his reply.

The operator looked at the Secretary of Defense—and swallowed once. He looked at me—and swallowed twice.

Then he snapped: "A load? Affirmative, buddy!"

I turned to Bob McNamara. "What's wrong with this thing?" I said—in my softest voice. "Don't ask me," he replied. "I don't work here any more."

I looked at him sadly, and thought: "That's real efficiency for you—he's not even out of the building and the computers have broken down."

The Secretary must have read my thoughts. He clicked his fingers and exclaimed: "I've got it, Mr. President. This is February 29th and we didn't program the computer for Leap Year!"

As we walked away, I saw Bob McNamara whip out his famous little black book. I peeked over his shoulder and read the notation: "Check elevator budget at the World Bank."

Driving back to the White House, I made a note of my own—for our Republican guests tonight. The other party has been so kind to me lately—approving just about everything that I do—that I just wanted to give their most vocal supporters an inside tip.

Standing stuck inside that elevator today, I thought of my Republican friends. I hoped they would realize that it can take a long time to get to the top in this town.

Years ago our predecessors were pretty independent of one another—the Chief Executive of the Nation and the Chief Executive of the State. But the 20th century has imposed a partnership on the two of us. Like all partnerships, sometimes we grow restless in that arrangement, as partners frequently do.

But there is one thing in the last analysis we all know, whether it is a partnership in our home or in our business or in the Government that runs our country, we have got to make it work.

Now that is what I am trying so hard to do. I am trying to make it work. We now have more than 450 Federal grant-in-aid programs in the United States. They amount to more than $17 billion of the taxpayers' money that is spent every year.

They involve almost every major function of this Government in this society.

They touch the lives, I think, of every single American. We, the leaders, the Chief Executives of America, have a responsibility to all America.

It is just disgraceful for us to spend any of our time and our talent chewing on each other. You have problems that need to be solved that I don't know much about, but if I can help I want to help because if you are a better Chief Executive, your State is a better State.

I have problems and God knows they are legion. I don't know the answers to all of them. And I need help. If we solve them you have a better nation. You have a slice of this Nation and your children have a slice of this Nation.

So we must never lose sight of the fact that some folks would like to take a little temporary advantage with great injury to the longtime national good. But I hope and I believe they are not in this room tonight.

I want to pay public tribute to the tireless efforts of three good men who largely have inaugurated and brought this relationship to what it is today, between the Chief Executive of the Nation and the Chief Executives of the States. First, Governor Buford Ellington of Tennessee who left his home and came here and valiantly served me until I told him that he could probably do me more good as the Governor of Tennessee.

Then, that dynamic and very able leader,

297

Farris Bryant from the State of Florida. Governor Bryant served his term here with great distinction and great appreciation from all of us who worked with him.

Now, Governor Price Daniel. Thanks to your cooperation and your understanding, all of us together have made these programs, I think, somewhat more effective than they would have been otherwise.

Your own distinguished chairman, Governor Volpe, has said that this is the best working relationship that the Federal Government and the States have had together. I know of no one who tries harder to make it so than Governor Volpe, and I want to thank you, Governor.

I have often spoken of Buford Ellington and Farris Bryant—but this is the first opportunity I have had to say anything about Price Daniel.

He has served in practically every important post there is in government: State legislator, speaker, attorney general, Governor, and United States Senator. Now he sits in the Security Council with us. He was your colleague as Governor for many years; he was my colleague as a Senator for many years. He knows government, I think, at both ends—the local, State, and Federal level. I know Price Daniel as the soul of honor.

All of us have to have a little partisanship in us to enjoy life, but these three men who work with you, I think, have a minimum amount of it: Buford Ellington and Price Daniel and Governor Bryant.

I doubt that there is a man in this room from any State in the Union who can do more with the President—and with the Cabinet—than Price Daniel. I tell you that only so you will know that you have a good lawyer retained here in Washington for you. He is your advocate.

I am glad and gratified that Governor Daniel and his lovely wife have come here to try to bring us closer together and to serve our common interests.

Last year, we made a very determined effort to put our partnership on a face-to-face basis. Cabinet officers and other high officials, at my instruction, got away from the smog of Washington and went into 44 State capitals at the request and with the approval of the Chief Executives of these States.

Many other States sent their officials here to meet with us. In all, there have been more than 2,500 State and Federal officials meeting to try to better the ways to serve the people who pay all of us and entrust all of us with the responsibilities.

Their agenda was 20th century America. In these meetings we explored the challenges of housing, pollution, transportation, law enforcement, New Haven railroads, education, health, job opportunities.

These challenges, we know, leapfrog State boundaries. They confront us all as Americans. Because there is one thing we should never lose sight of:

—when a child in one area gets a better education than a child in another;

—when a baby in one neighborhood has a higher chance of survival than a baby in another neighborhood;

—when the smoke of one city poisons the air of another city;

—when the crowded highways in one State slow the commerce in another State.

All of these start as local issues but in a very short time they stretch into national problems.

The Federal Government must face up to national problems and we try to. We think we are doing better every day. But there are no final answers here along the Potomac. The answers really are out there where you are, in the hinterland and hometowns of America.

So, America's problems must be met first and discovered and understood and evaluated. Then they must be mastered. Where? In the final analysis out there where Mr. and Mrs. America live, in your hometowns and in your home State.

We must never assume that States and cities are barren of ideas. Many of today's greatest social innovations have their roots in local government.

There is no substitute that we can find for that. Local government is the living heart of the greatest idea—the American idea. It is up to us to keep it vibrant, to give it new vigor and new strength each day, to give our people new confidence. It is up to us to nourish and reawaken the pride in communities and the pride in country that made this Nation great.

This can be the richest dividend of our partnership.

I want to tell this story and then I will not ask your indulgence further. Sunday a week ago I spent the most delightful day, I think, that I have had since I became President. I got up at 7 o'clock in the morning and had breakfast with 26 enlisted men of the *Constellation* aircraft carrier that just came back from Vietnam. Then I visited with some officers and they reviewed their targets—the powerplants and the bridges and the supply routes.

Then I went to church services with them. I stood on top of that carrier under a beautiful sunny sky off the coast of California.

Then I called President Eisenhower and asked him if I could go by and talk with him because I needed his counsel and I needed the strength that comes from it. I went by and I spent the entire day with him. I enjoyed it because I was learning and listening and profiting from this wise man who had the unparalleled experience in guiding the affairs of men, of soldiers, and government servants.

He enjoyed it, I think, because he was beating me every hole.

[The President spoke off the record for a period of time.]

I came away from that meeting hoping that by precept and example we could extend that attitude and that love of country and that element of putting national interest first, not only to this house, but to every statehouse in this land.

So, to you Governors and your charming ladies, we have tried our best today to understand your problems—and to work with you on them. We are glad you came and hope you will be back next year. If I am here to entertain you, we will make it an even better year.

If you would join me now in a toast to the Union, to the States, and to the people.

NOTE: The President spoke at 10:25 p.m. in the State Dining Room at the White House. During his remarks he referred to former Governors Buford Ellington of Tennessee, Farris Bryant of Florida, and Price Daniel of Texas, who served successively as Directors of the Office of Emergency Planning and Presidential liaison officers to the Governors. As printed, this item follows the text released by the White House Press Office.

Governor Volpe responded as follows:

Mr. President, Mrs. Johnson, Mr. Vice President, members of the Cabinet, my colleagues, the first ladies of the States, and friends:

Mr. President, I feel something peculiar around here. Could it be a draft?

I am sure you all enjoyed those violins this evening. Mr. President, we had the Boston Symphony Orchestra give a concert in Boston a couple of weeks ago at which Jack Benny—I was going to say the principal performer—was the principal, but he wasn't the principal performer. But we had a wonderful occasion that evening.

After the concert, we all went over to the Somerset Hotel for a buffet and reception to Jack Benny. At that party, the orchestra wasn't there, but Jack Benny was there with his violin. He was joined by an accompanist that had not played the guitar for a long time.

It happened to be the Governor of Massachusetts. I would have loved to have had my guitar here to accompany the violins.

On behalf of my colleagues—and as Chairman of the National Governors' Conference—we certainly want to say how much we have enjoyed your friendship, your hospitality, which you have always shown to us—and particularly do we thank you for the wonderful briefings that we had today and this very enjoyable evening here at the White House tonight.

I have worked with three Presidents. I am pleased to say that I know of no President who has worked any harder to develop and promote better Federal-State relations than you have, Mr. President.

I am sure that we can all say today that the communication between the Federal establishment and our respective States is certainly fine and we have a chance—as we did today—to get in on the takeoffs on much of the legislation being proposed

instead of waiting until we have landed. For your great cooperation, we are very happy.

I have also had the privilege of working with—both as colleagues and in their present positions—Governor Ellington, Governor Bryant, and my good friend, Governor Daniel.

I want to say that every one of them has done you a great service—and their country a great service—and has been cooperative and helpful. I didn't notice too much partisanship at all, Mr. President.

Mr. President, we know the great tribulations that you face. In these days, I personally want to say that I offer up a prayer for you every day that the dear Lord will help you and guide you in the difficult decisions in the difficult days that lie ahead.

So ladies and gentlemen, will you toast with me as I am privileged to offer a toast to the President of the United States.

103   Message to the Congress Transmitting the Sixth Annual Report of the Peace Corps.   *March 1, 1968*

To the Congress of the United States:

I transmit to the Congress the Sixth Annual Report of the Peace Corps—an idea come of age, no longer a novelty but now a part of American life.

The Peace Corps is one of President Kennedy's most enduring achievements. It is now larger than ever. Today, the Peace Corps is a leading employer of new college graduates. Last year 21,000 college seniors formally applied for membership in the Peace Corps—3.5 percent of the graduating classes. In one college, 25 percent applied, in another 20 percent and in a third 17 percent.

More than 12,000 Peace Corpsmen are doing America's work in 57 countries. They are in:

—Micronesia, on lonely islands across the Pacific, working in many fields—from teaching to drafting legislative proposals.
—Peru, helping villagers develop schools and social clubs.
—Colombia, helping expand and improve

the educational television network.
—Malawi, conducting a successful program of tuberculosis control.

In the long run, perhaps the Peace Corps' most significant contribution will be made at home. Last year, for the first time, the number of returned Volunteers surpassed those in the field. By 1980, the Agency estimates 200,000 of them will be involved in every level of our society.

Many Volunteers return and continue their studies; others enter the business world. What most returned Volunteers seek is a career serving others. Thus, they teach in ghettos, work in anti-poverty projects, and join the government on the local or national level.

This, then, is the Peace Corps: seven years old and still growing. The idea of service to humanity is much older, but few institutions have embraced the concept as fervently and capably as has the Peace Corps. As this report indicates, our journey has begun and the future is promising.

If you would confirm your faith in the American future—take a look at the Peace Corps.

LYNDON B. JOHNSON

The White House
March 1, 1968

NOTE: The 53-page report is entitled "Peace Corps 6th Annual Report."

104 Remarks at the Swearing In of Clark Clifford as Secretary of Defense. *March 1, 1968*

Mr. and Mrs. Clifford and members of the Clifford family, Chief Justice Warren and Mrs. Warren, distinguished Governors, Members of the Cabinet, Members of the Congress, ladies and gentlemen:

I appreciate your indulgence. I hope all of you understand that the tardiness was prompted not by my usual delays, but the fact that we were unsuccessful in getting the Senate to stop talking.

We tried. We even had a cloture vote that failed. But it is over now and all the Members but four are here. We will go ahead and begin.

This is a great day for us here in the White House. We were finally successful in persuading Clark Clifford—prevailing upon him—to move from the "kitchen cabinet" to the East Room.

Some people have compared this appointment to a wedding. After a very long and sometimes secret courtship, we are finally making an honest man out of him.

I have never mentioned this before, but I had some serious reservations about naming Clark to any particular Cabinet job—I think he had some reservations, too—because there is really one serious flaw that he has. He owns or is paying on a summer house on Nantucket Island.

I have worked with such people before. If I try to reach them, the White House operator usually says, "I am sorry, Mr. President, but the fog is in."

But then I heard about Clark's devotion, and I observed it. Twenty years ago he was up there when President Truman called him back to Washington. The fog was in. It took 48 hours to get Clark back to the Capital. But he finally made it. And ever since then he has suffered Washington summers rather than make himself unavailable to his President.

So, I figured that if we can get that kind of loyalty when he is a private citizen, what can we expect when we are paying him $35,000 a year?

Clark Clifford has served his country and three different Presidents for more than 25 years—in time of peace and in time of war.

He served as President Truman's Special Counsel in the difficult days when America was trying to forge a durable peace from the fires of a world war.

A farsighted man might have predicted even then that Mr. Clifford would become the Secretary of Defense, for he had a very important hand in creating this modern Defense Department.

The legislation that he prepared, that he drafted, and which he struggled on for months for a unified military system, to bring it under strong civilian control, finally became a fact.

He was the architect of the very smooth and efficient transition between the administrations of President Eisenhower and President Kennedy.

At the request of President Kennedy, he became Chairman of the President's Foreign Intelligence Advisory Board following the Bay of Pigs situation. At my request, he has continued in that position through the years.

In looking through some of the statements of yesteryear, I observed that on November 23, 1963, I received a very short note from Mr. Clifford. It said, "Mr. President, let me know if there is anything I can do to be helpful."

Well, he has been helpful in a thousand different ways since that day—to me, to the First Lady, to the members of our family, the Cabinet, and others who needed his wise and sage counsel.

Mr. Clifford did more than draft the legislation, though, that created this Department of Defense. He helped shape the character of that whole Department. That character is grounded in a principle that is as old as America itself. And we want to reiterate it upon every appropriate occasion.

That is that control of the military will reside firmly and forever in the hands of men who are directly responsible to the people of the United States.

It was Thomas Jefferson who wrote that he knew of "no safe depository of the ultimate powers of the society but the people themselves. . . ."

That principle is the core of the National Security Act of 1947, and its amendments in 1949.

It has been strengthened by Secretary McNamara in his brilliant service of 7 years in the Cabinet.

It will be upheld by Secretary Clifford. He, like Secretary McNamara, will always have the support of the President in doing so.

Mr. Clifford is wise in the ways of strength. He knows that might alone cannot bring peace. Military strength cannot correct the conditions which breed violence, the awakening of hope, and the frustration of accomplishment among the world's poor.

The danger comes not from those who have something to lose, but from those who feel that they have nothing to lose.

So I believe, and I think Clark Clifford believes, in a certain formula for the future.

Each time a nation develops enough to give the people of that nation a life worth living, then the world moves one step back from chaos.

Yesterday, with sadness, most of you in this room said farewell to a good and great Secretary of Defense. This morning we gain a worthy and a wise successor in Clark Clifford. He has the confidence of the President and of the President's Cabinet. He has worked with them just as if he were a member.

He has the confidence of the Congress which confirmed him in record time. And he has the confidence of the press.

I can assure all of you that is no small achievement.

So, Mr. Secretary, on behalf of your new and really biggest client, the American people welcome you aboard.

The Chief Justice honors us by his willingness to be present this morning to administer the oath.

NOTE: The President spoke at 12 noon in the East Room at the White House. In his opening words he referred to, among others, Chief Justice Earl Warren, who administered the oath of office, and Mrs. Warren. Following the administration of the oath of office, Mr. Clifford spoke briefly. The text of his remarks is printed in the Weekly Compilation of Presidential Documents (vol. 4, p. 396).

105   Remarks Upon Signing the Fire Research and Safety Act of 1968.   *March 1, 1968*

Secretary Trowbridge, distinguished Members of the Senate and the House, ladies and gentlemen:

First of all, I want to welcome to the East Room this afternoon 200 business leaders and State officials from throughout the Nation.

Their mission here is to spearhead the new JOBS program in 50 of our largest cities. These people are the doers and the movers of the National Alliance of Businessmen. They are going to roll up their sleeves and find the answer to one of America's most urgent needs—decent jobs for 500,000 men and women who are the hard-core unemployed—the people who want to work but who need that special help and training to put them on the road to productivity.

As Mr. Clifford said when he was sworn in a few moments ago as Secretary of Defense, he was thankful for the opportunity, after living in this land for 61 years, to have a chance to pay the debt to the country that he owed the country.

I am thankful that we have businessmen, the creatures and the product of our free enterprise system and our peculiar system of government, who in their affluence, and in a period of prosperity, the like of which they have not known before, are willing to leave their companies and spend their time and talents to help those who are less fortunate, those who haven't done so well, but who could pull down our whole system if our system can't be made to work for them, too.

To you businessmen who are undertaking this new venture under the leadership of that dynamic business executive, Henry Ford II, I salute you. And I thank you. I have great hopes for the work ahead.

The measure we have come here today to sign deals with another very important national problem.

It is a terrible thing when tragedy strikes so often that it no longer even shocks us.

Just the other week, Mrs. Johnson and I were shocked by a terrible story that we saw in the newspaper: 10 children were burned to death in one awful night. A complete family was wiped out, was destroyed, was no more.

There were other fires that night; hundreds of other Americans died that night. Hundreds more were scarred and crippled.

The most shocking thing about all of these tragedies is that they are repeating tragedies. They happen night after night. They go on day after day.

Fire, as I think most of you know, is our third largest cause of accidental death in America.

In 1966 alone, more than 12,000 of our fellow human beings died in fires. That is more than we lost in Vietnam all year from the enemy's bullets.

Almost $2 billion in homes and businesses went up in flames.

Man invented fire for his own safety and security, but man has really never learned how to control it. We all live with the threat of an accidental fire.

Our little baby with a match, the bursting gas stove, the leaking pipe, the careless smoker in the bed, the exploding pipeline—all of these are shocking accidents, but the most shocking truth of all is terribly clear. That is this:

This great Nation of which we are all so proud and dedicated leads the entire world in technology, but it falls so far behind the other nations in protecting its own people. Our per capita death rate is twice that of

Canada. It is four times that of the United Kingdom. It is six and one-half times that of Japan.

This is a shameful waste. This is something that we should stop, we must stop, and we are going to stop.

But we cannot stop it when many of our firefighting techniques date back to the Chicago fire of 1871. Many of our firefighters are as ill-trained and ill-equipped.

So, the bill we sign today is a Fire Research and Safety Act for all Americans. It will help us put out many of these fires before they ever start.

It authorizes, for the first time in our history, a fire research and safety program, so that now we can launch new studies into the causes of fires and into new methods of fire prevention and control. We can educate the public on how to avoid fire hazards. We can set up new training programs to improve our firefighting techniques and to strengthen the local fire departments.

This important measure is a tribute to the work of a great American leader, the work of the distinguished Secretary of Commerce, Sandy Trowbridge, who leaves us today. He fought for this bill and many other good bills of a like nature, and he succeeded. He did it because it is needed, because it is right, and because it is going to protect all of us.

This is the first consumer bill passed at this session of Congress. It is one of the 12 consumer bills that we recommended last year. We batted 33⅓ percent. We got four of them at the first session.

We sent up six new consumer proposals this year. I wish we had a subcommittee on each one of them, working morning, afternoon, and night now, so that we could get them reported before we get in a rush to get out of here in July. I appeal to the Mem-

bers of Congress to get them assigned for hearings. I will furnish the witnesses immediately.

We need legislation of this type. It costs us little. The hazards are great. The clock is ticking. Time is wasting. So, we should be moving ahead. And I am glad we are moving ahead with this proposal.

I hope we can come back into this room again soon to sign these other dozen or so measures that are now pending.

All Americans should know, should remember, should be restless and dissatisfied until we actually get the signature on a truth-in-lending act.

An explosion in a major city tomorrow would get us a pipeline safety bill quickly, but we shouldn't have to wait until people die to get it. It is there, and I hope it is enacted.

We need a strong poultry bill. We need a fish inspection bill.

The list is long, but so are the needs of this public that we represent. Consumer legislation deserves a high priority. It concerns every American.

Sometimes I think it concerns one American more than it does any of the others. I want to salute Miss Betty Furness this morning for the great leadership she has given to this field. I want to challenge her to try to wake up the women of America, and the men, too, for that matter, to get behind these consumer measures that we have recommended, that we have submitted, and that we hope will pass.

We say on what has come to us this morning, well done.

Thank you very much.

NOTE: The President spoke at 1:25 p.m. in the East Room at the White House. In his opening words he referred to Alexander B. Trowbridge, Secretary of Commerce. During his remarks he referred to Betty Furness, Special Assistant to the President for

Consumer Affairs.

As enacted, the bill (S. 1124) is Public Law 90–259 (82 Stat. 34).

For statements or remarks by the President upon signing other consumer legislation, see Items 229, 264, 280, 418, 441, 451, 545.

106   Telegram Requesting the Parties in the Copper Strike To Resume Negotiations at the White House.   *March 1, 1968*

THE COPPER STRIKE is now in its 231st day. The parties remain divided on major issues. There is no foreseeable prospect that the parties, if left to themselves, will resolve this dispute in the near future.

The shortage of copper resulting from the strike is having a substantial impact upon the economy of the nation and the balance of payments, and it has grave implications for our defense effort. It is also having a devastating effect upon the participants in the dispute and the several states directly involved. Therefore, the public has a vital interest in the immediate resolution of this dispute.

Because of that public interest, on January 24, 1968, the Secretaries of Commerce and Labor appointed a mediation panel of the most eminent impartial labor relations experts, consisting of Professor George Taylor, Chairman, Monsignor George Higgins, and Mr. George Reedy. That panel held several days of hearings, public and private, and on February 17, 1968, issued suggested guidelines to the parties on procedural issues in the dispute. Regrettably, these have not been put into effect by the parties.

In my judgment, the national interest requires further and immediate governmental effort to resolve the copper strike. To that end, I am requesting that you meet with me together with representatives of all major copper companies and union representatives of the striking employees at the White House on Monday, March 4, at 4:00 p.m. I am requesting you to resume collective bargaining negotiations on an around the clock basis with the assistance of the Secretaries of Defense, Labor, and Commerce and the members of the mediation panel. The well considered guidelines proposed by the panel should be of material help in the intensified negotiations to bring about an immediate settlement of the strike. The national interest requires that the parties, with the assistance I am providing, agree to contract terms which will end the strike. I am confident that in light of the urgency of the situation, all concerned will respond to my request in the interest of our nation.

LYNDON B. JOHNSON

NOTE: This is the text of identical telegrams sent to the following persons: I. W. Abel, United Steelworkers of America; P. L. Siemiller, International Association of Machinists and Aerospace Workers; Paul Jennings, International Union of Electrical, Radio and Machine Workers; Walter P. Reuther, International Union, United Automobile Workers; R. D. Bradford, American Smelting and Mining Company; C. Jay Parkinson, Anaconda Company; Frank R. Milliken, Kennecott Copper Corporation; Robert Page, Phelps Dodge Corporation; and Gordon M. Freeman, International Brotherhood of Electrical Workers.

For remarks of the President on March 4 to company and union representatives, see Item 112.

The text of the telegram was released at Houston, Texas.

107 Remarks at the NASA Manned Spacecraft Center, Houston, Texas.   *March 1, 1968*

Mr. Webb, Dr. Gilruth, distinguished officials of the Manned Spacecraft Center, Dr. Seitz, the President of the National Academy of Sciences, who honors us today with his presence, Dr. Charles Draper, the Director of Instrumentation at the Laboratory at MIT, ladies and gentlemen:

This is my first visit here to this Center in several months. I want to assure all of you, though, that Jim Webb keeps me fully informed about your progress and about your problems and about your needs. And I might say he is never bashful about mentioning money.

I have great faith in Jim Webb and Dr. Gilruth and their associates, and you. I believe what they tell me. But every now and then I just like to come down here and see for myself. That is one reason that I shall spend 2 hours here this afternoon.

Since we arrived, we have been excited at seeing the lunar sample receiving laboratory, the centrifuge trainer, the docking simulator trainer, and now we have a chance to see all of you. That is what is most important, because you are what makes this go.

We want you to know that we in Washington who are trying to lead this country in this great effort really care about you and about what you are doing.

I have spent almost 38 years in the Nation's Capital. In all of that period of time, I have voted for thousands of bills and I have written a few. But the one legislative enactment that I suppose I am proudest of is the bill that I wrote and introduced that made possible NASA, that brought into existence this great facility and others in the program throughout this Nation.

Your inventiveness and your own high standards are raising American industry to ever higher levels of technological perfection. Our store of knowledge has grown richer with the success of our Ranger and our Surveyor and our Orbiter spacecraft.

I rode down here this afternoon with two distinguished scientists—Dr. Seitz, the President of the National Academy of Sciences, and Dr. Draper of MIT. We talked about some of the things that you can expect the world to give all of us in just a few years.

Today, I want to review for you some of those things we talked about coming down here this afternoon.

I predict that 10 years from now some other President will come here someday, and stand where I am, and congratulate the people of this Center—some of you may still be around—for your amazing achievements.

He will see them at work in a giant station in space. He will see them at work assessing the exact status and the value of wheat and rice as they are growing all over this earth.

He will see them predicting with phenomenal accuracy the amount of water that is available to each farmer for growing next year's crops.

He will see them controlling thousands of peaceful air and space vehicles that are at work for mankind in all the regions of the earth.

He will see them developing a worldwide overview of all of our great cities, an overview that can be used by scientists and engineers to guide new economic and political institutions in every region of this earth.

Political scientists and social scientists—as well as physical scientists, engineers, and administrators—will then know, because of the work at this Center, more than our generation can ever know about the causes of pollution, about the use of recreational areas, about all the knowledge that mankind needs if we are to continue our steady advance toward a great destiny.

Messages and pictures coming into this Center will show the President standing here 10 years from today what the astronomers are observing from the back side of the moon. It will show him what machines are doing for mankind on our sister planets of Venus and Mars. It will show him what massive energy from an eruption on the sun is starting on its journey to affect human beings all over this planet Earth.

Isn't that exciting? Isn't that worthwhile? Aren't you proud to be a part of a great effort that is going to produce this in order to better all humanity?

We have invested billions of dollars during the past 10 years in our efforts in space, in order to bring about in the next 10 years the dream that I have just told you about. But the true value to our Nation of this investment and of all the work that we are doing here today is really beyond calculation. I am certain that as future generations look back on our incredible decade, they will be unanimous in their belief that the treasure that we have dedicated to sending man to explore the stars was the most significant and important investment ever made by any people.

You will have to go through some heartbreaks and some headaches. And there will be little men with poison pens, without vision, who will seek to scrub your great efforts. But they will not prevail. We may have to reduce some of the plans that we have, but we will not forget you. We will not stop our work. We will proceed.

Two months ago, when I visited your colleagues in New Orleans, I said this:

"We are all the descendants of those voyagers who found and settled the New World.

"Today we stand here at the gateway to another and a more glorious New World.

"We will not surrender our station. We will not abandon our dream. We will never evacuate the frontiers of space to any other nation."

I repeat that pledge and I repeat that purpose to you and to the Nation here today.

We are very close to a landing on the moon. Our space programs for the decade of the sixties are drawing to a close. Yet a mighty intellectual and technological effort, such as you are engaged in here, cannot just be turned on and off. We all must pull up our belts and be determined to stay the entire course. We must continue to build new strength by using the strength we have. We must continue to cross over new frontiers. This will certainly be our course in the next 10 years.

As a further step toward joining hands with the world's scientific community, I came here today to make an important announcement to you, the people of this country, and to the scientific world. I want to announce that we will build facilities here in this great space capital of Houston to help the world's scientists work closer together, more effectively on the problems of space. We are going to establish here in Houston a new Lunar Science Institute alongside of this great Center that you have. It will be initially operated by the National Academy of Sciences and Rice Institute.

I am so pleased that Dr. Croneis could be here with us today.

We hope and we expect that other great universities from all parts of the Nation will join with Rice in this endeavor.

This new institute is a center of research that is designed specifically for the age of space. Here will come the scientists—and their students—from all corners of the world.

Here we will welcome them—who are interested in the sciences of space. We will strengthen the cooperation between NASA and our great educational institutions, the outstanding universities of this land. And we will set new patterns of scientific cooperation which will have, I think, profound effects on man's knowledge of his universe.

This new Houston Lunar Science Institute will provide new means of communication and research for the world's entire scientific community. It will help unite the nations for the great challenge of space.

Let this new institute stand as a symbol. Let it show the world that we do not build rockets and spacecraft to fly our flag in space, or to plant our banner on the surface of the moon.

Instead, we work and we build and we create to give all mankind its last great heritage. We are truly reaching for the stars.

You are the pioneers in that adventure. You can be proud of it. We are proud of you.

I congratulate all of you for what you are doing and are about to do in this great human adventure.

And I hope you haven't gotten too cold listening to us.

Thank you very much.

NOTE: The President spoke at 5:10 p.m. at the Manned Spacecraft Center in Houston. In his opening words he referred to James E. Webb, National Aeronautics and Space Administrator, Dr. Robert R. Gilruth, Director of the Manned Spacecraft Center, Dr. Frederick Seitz, President of the National Academy of Sciences, and Dr. Charles Draper of the Massachusetts Institute of Technology. Later he referred to Dr. Carey Croneis, Chancellor of Rice University in Houston.

The President referred to remarks made during a visit to New Orleans on December 12, 1967 (see 1967 volume, this series, Book II, Item 533, pages 1123 and 1124).

108 Remarks at the Schlesinger Old Folks Home, Beaumont, Texas, Upon Signing Proclamation "Senior Citizens Month, 1968." March 1, 1968

Congressman Brooks, Congressman Pickle, Mr. Phillips, Mr. Schlesinger, ladies and gentlemen, and my very dear friends:

Several months ago, at Stanford University in California, a scientific miracle took place: The researchers there demonstrated their ability to create life in a laboratory. Shortly after the Stanford experiments, a South African heart surgeon transplanted a human heart for the first time.

These were great achievements. One day they may change and improve the lives of millions of our people, just as medical research has improved our lives over the past decades from a life expectancy of 54 years in 1920 to a life expectancy of more than 70 years today. Medical science is going to continue slowly and painstakingly to make all

of our lives better lives.

Yet, as all of this medical activity is going on, I couldn't help but think that it is not only scientists and medical researchers who make life better for men and women all over the world.

Men in public life can also make life better—and when they are doing their job right, they do make life better for other people.

So I think it is quite important for us to constantly engage in a little introspection and ask ourselves, what are we doing to try to better the lives of others?

When he was 87 years old, a great man in public life, Senator Theodore Francis Green, had this to say about being what is now called a "senior citizen": "Most people say that as you get old you have to give up things. I think you get old because you give up things."

The social miracle that has been happening in our country has allowed tens of millions of older people not to give up things, and not to be afraid of their future. We call that miracle something you never heard of 30 years ago or 50 years ago—we call it "social security."

Medicare is a case in point. It is hard to believe that only 2½ years ago, millions of elderly Americans lived in fear of a sudden medical emergency that could wipe out their savings after a lifetime of hard work.

That was what we called "social insecurity." The enactment of the Medicare bill that we got passed in 1965 eliminated that insecurity and eliminated that fear for more than 19 million proud, elderly Americans—nearly 10 percent of the total population of America. Action by public men, by politicians—an amendment to the law—completely changed life in America, and made it better just as surely as the new scientific advances are going to make life better.

Medicare, like the rest of the social security system, affected the young as well as the old. A man of 40 years of age benefits from Medicare if his dear old father or mother who is 70 years old is covered. Otherwise he might have to pay his father's or mother's hospital bills. Medicare to him may mean that he can afford to send his 18-year-old daughter to college. So, again, life has been changed for the better for all of them.

But perhaps the most important change was the change in attitude between father and son and grandson. Medicare meant the end of a great deal of family friction over dollars. The end of that friction has been a blessing in millions of homes in America.

More dollars—more dignity—will be the result of the new social security amendments that I signed into law in January of this year.

I am here tonight because tomorrow morning, just a few hours from now—all over this great land we love, in all the 50 States of the Union—those dollars will reach home for the first time.

This new law provides the largest, single dollar increase in benefits since social security first started. That means an increase in benefits at an average of 16 percent for 24 million of our elder citizens. It goes up to a new maximum of $234 per month for a retired couple.

Counting the increases of 1965 and including the dollar value of Medicare, that adds up to a 35 percent increase over what it was 30 months ago. Now, that's not enough as far as I am concerned. I asked the Congress and I recommended to the Congress and I urged the Congress to give us an increase averaging 20 percent. And I intend to keep on fighting for that.

Now, let us think, for a moment, what our lives might be like if we didn't have social insurance.

Not long ago, for many Americans, old age was a real calamity. A man might work until he died—or he could work until he became dependent upon his children.

Today, when an elderly man or woman lives with his son or daughter, it is probably because he wants to live there and not because he has to live there. His social security check now is his personal declaration of independence and belongs to him alone.

For a younger man, social security gives protection against long illness or disability. It gives his wife and children protection in the event he dies when he is young. Today, there are 5½ million widows and orphans in this country getting insurance checks—

up to a new monthly maximum under this new law that runs as high as $395 per month. A man earning $8,000 today—with three children aged 2, 4, and 6—knows that if he should die his family would receive some measure of security—about $90,000 in payments over the course of the years to come.

When I discovered America up in my hills almost 60 years ago, we never heard of anything like that. We never dreamed of anything like that. We couldn't envision anything like that. But it is here.

And finally, a young man today knows that he is building up insurance toward his own retirement. A young, able worker, starting out today, knows that he and his wife can get a monthly income of at least $323 a month when he retires.

That is what this new law provides. That is what the young men know they can work toward. That is what the older people know is in store.

Social security was first started, after I had gone to Washington, by a great American—a man who said, "The only thing we have to fear is fear itself." That man's name was Franklin Delano Roosevelt.

As we meet here tonight, we see, a third of a century after Franklin Roosevelt started it—33 years ago—that what social security really buys is freedom from fear—not just for older Americans, but for younger Americans, too.

This is a proud day for me. It has been a long trip to get here—one that began 33 years ago under Franklin Delano Roosevelt. And we are not through yet.

We are continuing to move forward.

The one thing that I want to see as much as I want to see anything else in the world, except peace among all men, is to see in this land that I lead during the time allotted me the most modern miracles that we can

produce placed into a good home for elder citizens.

I want it to have the best floors and the best roof. I want it to have the most attractive walls and the best windows. I want it to be the place that can be kept clean—where the water is always hot when you want it and always cold if you need it.

I want it where an elder person can get in his bath without fear of slipping or can get out of his bed without fear of breaking his hip. I want it where his food can be good, and he can have a good bed to sleep on, a good room to eat in, and a good place to spend his last days.

I am trying so hard to have a group produce a model home.

Now, I have looked at what you have here. I am proud of what you have here. It is so much better than the old flophouses or the old places that we had in my day.

There is not a person in this room who was born into a place like this. All of you came from an age when we didn't have the modern conveniences. We read by kerosene lamps. We didn't have the benefits of electricity. We didn't have the tile on the floor. We didn't have the modern plumbing facilities that you have here.

But we don't have near enough—not even here. I am going to continue to work until the day comes when we can put in every community in this land a place where we can enjoy the twilight of our careers. Not just our mothers and fathers now, but my grandsons and my granddaughters can know that they don't have to pay attention to any son-in-law or any brother-in-law; that they have earned it on their own. They will get their own social security check and they can go to a home that is clean and decent, and get a good bed and get good food and get good care.

Their country can do that for them if it

does care. And this country, under my leadership, does care or else I wouldn't be here tonight.

I am issuing a proclamation here tonight. This is the first Presidential proclamation that is issued in a home like this. But it says: "Senior Citizens Month, 1968." And [*reading excerpts from the proclamation*] the respect that we show for older Americans is not an act of charity. It comes from the recognition that this generation owes all it possesses to those who have borne responsibility in years past.

We have not always recognized the debt that we owe them.

It was three decades ago that we first passed social security. But we are honoring our fathers and mothers whose days will be long on this earth.

But perhaps the greatest need of age is the need to know that one's contributions are valued. In a society where youth is so highly prized, older men and women need to know that their wisdom and their experience and the example that they have set in their lives are still important to us and to all their fellow citizens. Their contributions are one of our Nation's most valuable assets—a resource that should be celebrated by every generation.

Therefore, I, Lyndon B. Johnson, President of the United States of America, do hereby designate the entire month of May 1968, as Senior Citizens Month in honor of them.

I call upon every Federal, State, and local government in partnership with private and voluntary organizations to join in community efforts to give meaning to the theme of this special month—meeting the challenge of the later years.

Let special emphasis this year be placed on making known the contributions that older Americans have made to our welfare.

Let us demonstrate the greatness of our society by bringing new meaning and new vigor to the lives of our elders who built the framework of our present prosperity and our greatness.

So I invite all the Governors of the States, the Governor of the Commonwealth of Puerto Rico, the Commissioner of the District of Columbia, and appropriate officials in other areas subject to the jurisdiction of the United States, to join in the observation of Senior Citizens Month.

In witness whereof, I have hereunto set my hand this, the first day of March, at Beaumont, Texas, in the year of our Lord, 1968, and of the Independence of the United States of America, the 192d year.

So that proclamation is now in force and the month of May will be set aside to honor our elder citizens and our fathers and our mothers.

I have now the first checks of the millions that will go out under this new law. It is not all we wanted. It is the best, though, I could get and it is more than what we had. I am thankful for that.

The first one goes to Miss Helen Hayes McFarland who was born in Fannin, Texas, on July 26, 1883. She is 84 years young.

The next is Mr. Luther Napoleon Smith.

Mr. Romaldo Perez Torrez was born in Guadalajara, Mexico, February 7, 1887, age 82.

Muchas gracias, amigos, Adios.

Now, I am going to run along. I have enjoyed being with you so much. I hope everything goes well for you.

I thank you and the people of Beaumont in Jefferson County for all of the good work you do—particularly sending me a good Congressman like Jack Brooks who works for the people.

NOTE: The President spoke at 7:14 p.m. to a group of senior citizens at the Schlesinger Old Folks Home in Beaumont, Texas, upon signing Proclamation

3833 "Senior Citizens Month, 1968" (4 Weekly Comp. Pres. Docs., p. 414; 33 F.R. 4167; 3 CFR, 1968 Comp., p. 27). In his opening words he referred to Representatives Jack Brooks and J. J. Pickle, both of Texas, William W. Phillips, Jr., treasurer, and A. W. Schlesinger, founder and honorary chairman of the board of trustees of the home.

During his remarks the President referred to Theodore Francis Green, Senator from Rhode Island 1937–1961, and Dr. Christiaan Barnard who performed the first human heart transplant operation on December 3, 1967, at Groote Schuur Hospital in Capetown, South Africa.

109   Remarks at a Testimonial Dinner in Beaumont, Texas, for Representative Jack Brooks. *March 1, 1968*

My good friend, Congressman Jack Brooks, Mrs. Brooks, Congressman and Mrs. Jake Pickle, Mr. and Mrs. Wilson, Judge Fisher, my very dear friends of Jefferson County and this entire district:

This has been a very delightful and very productive day for me. I can think of no way that I would enjoy concluding it more than doing just what I am doing here tonight.

I have come here to pay a tribute to a good friend and a great Congressman, the husband of Charlotte Brooks.

I have always thought that an appropriate time for me to announce any major political decision that I had in mind would be at a dinner in honor of a good friend, in your home State, among the people you love. I have never forgotten that Jefferson County made the difference in one of my landslide races.

Therefore, I am announcing tonight that there will be an investigation of the elevator industry and why they get stuck and I am going to be the first witness.[1]

I must say it is a great pleasure for me to see so many smiling, friendly faces in one large room. In fact, this audience looks so friendly that I had a somewhat difficult time believing that you were all Democrats.

And after I saw all of these tuxedoes, I knew you weren't all Democrats. But it is almost enough to make a man believe in consensus again.

People sometimes ask me if some of the party bickering that we have from time to time doesn't bother me a great deal. I have to say in all candor—all candor—that I have been a politician long enough to prize party harmony above just about anything— and I have been a Democrat long enough never to really expect it.

As one of our great humorists once said, "I am not a member of any organized political party. I am a Democrat."

But I have learned something else over the years. I have learned that Democrats do their fighting before they have chosen the candidate—but once the candidate is named, we then have time to put aside our differences and to unite for victory.

I have read enough history to know that, after all, I have had it pretty easy and I shouldn't feel very sorry for myself compared to other Democratic Presidents.

Thomas Jefferson got along so miserably with his own Vice President, Aaron Burr, that Burr used to vote against him on all the major bills in the United States Senate. Burr finally joined up with the Federalists to defeat Jefferson in the next election.

Andrew Jackson had it even worse. As soon as he was elected, his party split right down the square middle. His Vice President, John C. Calhoun, caused so much trouble that Jackson finally had to dissolve his entire Cabinet to get rid of the Calhoun supporters in his own Cabinet.

[1] See note to Item 101.

Franklin D. Roosevelt was called every name in the book and some of them that never had gotten in the book. Then they made up some new names when he decided he would break precedent and run for a third term.

In 1940, with most of Europe in flames, four Democratic Senators, opposing mobilization—and remember we passed the draft act by a vote of 203 to 202 in August before Pearl Harbor in December—said that President Roosevelt could negotiate a just peace—that is with Hitler—if he would only make an effort.

Sounds kind of familiar, doesn't it?

I suppose some of you are young enough to remember Harry Truman's plight. They tried to deprive President Truman of the nomination in 1948. They kept him sitting out in the anteroom until way after the midnight hours. And when he had the courage to fight naked aggression in South Korea, his poll of something over 60 dropped to something over 20—the lowest point in modern times—because he stood and fought for what he believed was right.

So you see, actually when you take everything else into consideration, I am leading a rather tranquil and somewhat united party, by comparison.

I am on very excellent terms—at least I was this afternoon—with my Vice President. I enjoy the cooperation most all the time of my congressional leaders. I don't have two splinter groups with their own political ambitions chawing at me from either side as President Truman did—at least I don't have them yet, anyway.

So I am not too concerned really about party conflicts. Next summer when the national convention chooses the nominee—whoever it may be—then I believe all the strays will come back to the fold.

And we are going to welcome them with open arms.

In the meantime, I stopped off here in Beaumont tonight to tell you how very proud I am that you have produced men like Jack Brooks and sent him to the Congress—men who aren't afraid to stand up and be counted and represent all the people all the time.

Now, you have heard a lot about credibility and credibility gaps. And I thought, as I was driving over here, before I said all that was in my heart to say about Jack, I ought to tell you a story about Darrell Royal [2] sending one of his all-Americans up to play on the Washington Redskins team—trying to at least get an assignment there.

He was a proud Texan. He was being interviewed by Otto Graham. [3] And Graham said, "Tell me about yourself, young man. I know you made all-American. I know you are from the University of Texas and I know you are a triple-threat man, but just give me some specifics."

And the youngster summoned up all of his Texas courage and said, "Well, Mr. Graham, I can run the 100 yards in a little less than 10 seconds on a muddy field. I was the principal passer on our championship team. We have a lot of wind in football season down our way. My average pass was 64 yards against the wind last year."

And Graham said, "Well, what about your punting?"

He said, "71 yards, sir, average for the season."

"Well," Graham said, "that is very good. All of us have our pluses and our minuses. There are some good things and some bad, and you have a remarkable record of good things. Now, tell me some of the bad things about yourself."

"Well," he said, "Coach, I guess I do ex-

---

[2] Football coach at University of Teaxs.
[3] Coach of the Washington Redskins Football Team, 1968.

aggerate a little."

So if I do appear to be generous with Jack, I hope you will not charge it to my credibility, but to my generosity and to, maybe, my Texas exaggeration.

Jack Brooks is a man of unusual courage and great conviction and always possessed with great compassion.

He and I just left the old folks' home where the brightest thing in their life was a $10 or $12 increase in their social security check.

Every person who bought a ticket here tonight could have given them that increase for one full year.

Jack Brooks is a steadfast man who doesn't panic by the harsh headlines of the hour.

Jack Brooks is a pretty good carpenter. And I have seen the results of his efforts right here in Southeast Texas and I have been on the receiving end of some of his pleas. I have seen it from Beaumont to Galveston. I have seen it in new roads, new channels, new dams, new seawalls, new ports, new bridges, and what have you.

Most of all, I have seen it in new and growing industries.

Jack is a fellow that believes in the greatest good for the greatest number. He is a progressive man without being radical. He is a prudent man without being reactionary. And what do you expect to get out of your Congressman, if you have got all that?

The thing that I like to see that has flowed from his efforts and the efforts of others like him and those of you who support him is the faces of the working people of this district—earning good wages, living in good houses. I have looked at your bank deposits. I have looked at your corporation profits. I have looked at the prosperity that we enjoy in this Nation and particularly in this district.

Jack Brooks made a speech not long ago

when he said, "What we seek is not security from the cradle to the grave, but what we seek is opportunity from the cradle to the grave—for every citizen."

He took advantage of his opportunity. He got tired of selling newspapers. He became a reporter and got in the Texas Legislature. He moved on up the ladder to one of our senior Congressmen.

While he is still young in years, he is old in experience and seniority. And he has just begun to move. You haven't heard the last of him yet.

This very day, today, is a birthday for your country. Today, this Nation is celebrating that birthday. It marks the seventh long year of the longest period of uninterrupted prosperity that America has ever known.

And that has been brought about by Republican managers and Democratic workers, or vice versa.

That has been brought about by private enterprise and public enterprise. That has been brought about by Catholics, Jews, Protestants, and men of all races and all religions and all regions.

But in these 7 years, our total production has grown by more than $300 billion. It has grown more in these 7 years than our total production 18 years ago. Our total production when I went to Washington—and I don't think I am too old a man—it is just 15 times more than it was when I went to Washington.

Purchasing power since 1960 per person, has risen 29 percent—oh, you say, the price has gone up, but that is after the price increases—up 29 percent.

Corporate profits since 1960—after taxes—have risen by 93 percent.

This prosperity has given us more than luxury and a great deal more than leisure. It has given us the opportunity for the first time, really, in our history, to try to attack the ancient enemies of mankind. And what are these real enemies of mankind? They are the sickness that I saw where you have diseased bodies, advanced age, and crippled bones. Illiteracy—boys and girls that never learned to read or write or never got through grade school. Human misery—broken homes, acquired bad habits, LSD, marijuana. Poverty—between 20 and 30 percent of our people are still at the bottom of the ladder.

Some of us get so high up that we can't see down. But that doesn't mean that those down there are not still there and that we don't have to live with them and live by them.

This administration is trying to do something about those things.

When President Eisenhower left the Presidency, he was spending $3 billion a year on manpower training—equipping people to become skilled people to work.

President Kennedy raised that training program to $4 billion.

Men like Jack Brooks in the last 4 years have moved it from $4 billion to $12 billion, which means just about three times the efforts made to train people to hold jobs—and that is why more people are working tonight than have ever worked in this country before and unemployment is at its lowest level.

President Eisenhower did the very best he could for the poor people of this country. His Federal budget contained $9½ billion for the poor.

President Kennedy was a champion of the poor—and the poor had a lot to do with electing him to the Presidency. He moved that $9½ billion up to $12 billion in his 3 years in office.

This year the budget contains not $9 billion, not $12 billion, but $28 billion for the poor.

Health—we have passed 24 health bills in the last 3 years—more than have been passed by all 35 Presidents who preceded us.

Who can be against doing something about health? They did fight Medicare from Truman's day until my day. But there hasn't been one bill introduced to repeal it. They dare not.

Education—we have passed 18 education bills—more than have been passed in all the 35 Presidential administrations before.

Conservation—except for the administration of Theodore Roosevelt, we have probably brought more land into the public domain than any other administration. For the first time we have brought more in than we took out.

The social security bill this year is the largest single increase in the history of the Nation—$5 billion. That is more than the whole Federal budget when I went to Washington—just the increase this year in social security, the bill I just signed in December, that gave them an average increase of 16 percent.

In health, education, welfare, and security—when President Eisenhower left that office in 1960, we were spending $19 billion for the health of our citizens, for the education of our children, for the welfare of our people, and for the security in old age.

President Kennedy moved that $19 billion up to $24 billion. The budget this year has $48 billion for health, education, and welfare.

Some people think that we are neglecting the homefront while we defend freedom wherever it is attacked in the world.

Jack Brooks' voting record reflects a concern for every citizen in this district—from the oldest that we just left to the youngest that we just saw in the lobby. From the richest—some of whom are in this room—to the poorest—who are on the other side of the tracks.

I don't want to pin a label on him because he defies labels.

But I will just say this: He is an able, he is a dedicated, and he is a good public servant.

I don't know much more that I can say except to say that a man who has served you long and well as he has, a man who wore the uniform when our Nation was challenged, a man who supports the men in uniform tonight, is certainly worthy of what you good people have done by according him this honor.

And you have accorded me a great honor in asking me to come by here tonight and giving me this warm welcome.

I am leaving here real early in the morning to go up to Marietta, Georgia. There, the workmen of this country, the industrial genius and management of this land, the technology of the 20th century will roll off of the production lines the first Lockheed C–5A, which is a new jet transport aircraft.

It will be a first in moving great numbers of men great distances.

I spent a weekend a couple of weeks ago telling members of the 82d Airborne that I was sending back to Vietnam—most of them had been there once—and telling members of the Marine Corps that I was sending back to Vietnam—practically all of them had been there several times—and telling the crew of the *Constellation* carrier that was in port getting refurnished to go back again how much they had done for their country, and how much we in their country wanted some day to do for them.

I stood there on the steps of one of our C–130's as these husky men of the 82d Airborne, with that patch that they wear with such pride, with sad faces told their wives and their mothers goodby, and with a quick step marched onto that plane knowing that

in 24 hours they would be landed in the I Corps area of Vietnam where the fighting is the hottest.

There was a time when a man was sent overseas when he had 24 days to get there. There is not much consolation knowing that when you tell your wife goodby that they are going to be shooting at you in 24 hours. But this wasn't a time for consolation.

I shook their hands and felt the strong response as they got on that plane.

Then I went on to California—this was in North Carolina at the headquarters at Fort Bragg. I went on to California to El Toro. And I told the Marines goodby.

It is Jack's old outfit. Once a Marine, always a Marine.

And I will give you a rule, if you need any advice—don't ever take on the Marines, here or abroad.

President Truman took them on here one time, much to his sorrow.

But some of these men are not only so well prepared to serve their country, so dedicated to what we stand for, but so determined to do it that I want to tell you this story, because it pulled my heartstrings out. It touched me to the core.

I asked most of them—I would stop every second or third man, and say, "Where are you from?" And he would say, "Iowa, sir," or "Illinois, sir," or "New York, sir," or "Texas, sir." We had a goodly number of them from Texas. One of them was from Lampasas, Texas, right near my backyard.

This young Negro man stood straight and at attention. And I said, "What is your State?" He said, "Ohio, sir." And I said, "Have you been to Vietnam before?" "Four times, sir." That kind of brought me down—cut me down to size.

And I said, "Do you have a family?" He said, "Yes, sir." I said, "Well, how many are there in your family?" "One boy, sir."

316

I said, "How old?" And it just looked like I was asking for it every time. He said, "Born yesterday morning."

Now, when you love your country enough to go and expose yourself to death four times in 5 years, and to leave your baby boy that was born yesterday morning, you have a right to be proud of your citizenship.

We have a right to be proud of those 500,000 men who are out there defending us because if they weren't defending us there, in my judgment, many more hundreds of thousands would have to be defending us nearer home.

They are giving a good account of themselves. When I explained to them why I had to ask them to go back the second time— the 82d Airborne, the Marines to go back— some of them the third and fourth time, I tried to make it as simple as I could.

I said, "There is no human in the world that wants peace any more than your President."

Nearly every man and woman in the United States wants peace, just like I think nearly every man and woman would like to be worth a million dollars—but wanting it and getting it are two different things.

On more than 30 occasions, neutral nations, or mediators or would-be negotiators, have made proposals that the United States has accepted and in each and every instance the other side has turned down.

We have said to the enemy that we seek nothing in Vietnam except for the people of South Vietnam to have the right to determine their government by self-determination and not have it imposed upon them from the outside.

Mr. Ho Chi Minh is determined to impose it upon them from the outside. The South Vietnamese have an elected President, an elected Vice President, an elected Senate, and an elected House—in a constitutional election.

But Mr. Ho Chi Minh, who has never been elected to anything in his life, has determined that his might will make right and that he will take that little country.

We are pledged to them. It is not a commitment that I made, but a commitment that the United States made. That is a pretty big commitment—the United States promise in 1954 that "in the face of common danger" we will respond to your need.

So we are responding. And until he is willing to leave his neighbor alone, we are going to be there defending that neighbor.

Now, there are some people who think there are better courses. There are some people who think that you can have peace. Well, I am ready and in the market for their proposals tomorrow morning.

I examine every suggestion that comes to me. The best trained minds of this Nation do the same thing.

I asked the Secretary of State and the Secretary of Defense only yesterday to take Senator X's speech, and take Senator Y's television appearance, and take Senator Z's statement, and take General So-and-so and analyze them all and see if there is any alternative plan they have that we could profit from.

The President of the United States—not because it is me—any President has the best trained men whom West Point and other academies can turn out to lead our armies. They are not Johnson City boys. They are the best that our military academies can turn out.

Mr. Rayburn said one time about George Marshall—he said General Marshall wanted him to go look at the atomic bomb project. He wanted $2 billion and he couldn't tell him what he wanted it for. Now, he said: "If we can beat the Germans to it, we will win the war, and if we don't, we will lose it. I want you to appropriate $2 billion. I can't tell you what it is for. I can't put it in writing."

Mr. Rayburn said, "Well, I am going to give you the $2 billion. If the Germans beat us to it, why, I will have to resign because I will be defeated. But if you tell me you need it and you have got to have it, I am going to give it to you because if you don't know more about this war than I do, we have wasted a hell of a lot of money on West Point all of these years."

We have the most competent generals and we have the most skilled diplomats—and the general doesn't like to die or doesn't like to fight any more than you do. He is just as afraid of death as you are.

Secretary Rusk wants peace more than anybody, even maybe a little bit more than I do, because he has been working for it all through the Korean episode. He is a Georgia boy who is a Rhodes Scholar, who was head of the Rockefeller Foundation, who gave up dozens of thousands of dollars a year to come down and take the brutal treatment that always comes to any public servant who serves as Secretary of State.

But he is there tonight and working all day Sunday trying to find some way to do it. Now, if there is a way, we are going to find it.

But in the meantime, we are going to support those men out there. We are going to try to find peace with honor. We are not going to be quislings, and we are not going to be appeasers, and we are not going to cut and run.

At the same time we are going to do all we can to avoid a wider war. We are not going to fight the war that Asians ought to fight for themselves. The South Vietnamese are drafting this month all their 19-year-olds. In June, they will get their 18-year-olds although our average draftee is 20.4 years old.

If we had drafted as many men according to our population as they have drafted, instead of our having a little over 3 million in our service, we would have 9 million.

If we had lost as many men according to our population as the South Vietnamese have lost—you hear all of these ugly things about it—it wouldn't be 19,000—it would be hundreds of thousands.

The South Vietnamese have much to be desired. I don't think you can compare the American people to any other people and certainly not to the people of Southeast Asia. They die at 35 or 40 years of age. Their annual per capita income is less than $100 a year.

You cannot expect and you cannot get as much from them as you can get from that Marine whose baby boy was born yesterday morning. They have their weaknesses. Certainly, they have corruption just like we have in Boston, in New York, in Washington, and in Johnson City.

There is somebody stealing something in Beaumont right now.

Of course, they have their inefficiencies. You change officers every now and then because you think the one you had is not efficient. We are doing our best to get them to be as free from corruption as is possible.

We are doing our best to get as much efficiency in that government as we can get, just like I try to improve on my wife's ways of life. She is constantly working on me. But I don't think that it behooves either of us to come out here and say to the world that "Lady Bird is no good" and for her to say that her husband is no good, and that he is corrupt, inefficient, and incompetent.

We cannot win a war that way and we cannot win an election that way.

When you hear these people going over all those things, you just have to ask yourself, "What good is going to come from that kind of talk?" They are our allies. We want to improve them. Now, is that talk really improving them?

I said to Ambassador Bunker and General Westmoreland when I talked to them one time several months ago to see if they couldn't stretch just a little bit to meet some of this criticism in this country by improving the situation there—and both of them said to me: "We are just going to push it just for all we can, but remember this, Mr. President, and never lose sight of it: There is a great danger that if we push it to the breaking point, we will wind up with worse than we have."

So during these perilous times, I think that you all should know that we are not seeking aggrandizement. We do not covet anybody's territory. We do believe that if Hitler starts marching across the face of Europe that we ought not wait until the last minute to let him know that might doesn't make right.

And if Communist nations in Southeast Asia start invading their neighbors that we have a treaty with and a solemn obligation and a contract with, we have got to let them know that might doesn't make right. And we are doing that.

So I just ask you to try to remember that your leaders are just as concerned with the frustrations, the tribulations, and the problems today as you are. They are just trying to do as much as they know how about it.

I hope that any help you can give us, you will give us, any strength you can lend us, you will lend us, and any prayers that you can extend to us will be extended because I believe that in the end right will prevail. And I know we are right.

Thank you, and good night.

NOTE: The President spoke at 8:53 p.m. at the Ridgewood Motor Hotel in Beaumont, Texas. In his opening words he also referred to Representative J. J. Pickle of Texas, Mrs. Pickle, Bassel Wilson, former mayor of Cameron, Texas, and stepfather of Representative Brooks, Mrs. Wilson, and Joseph Jefferson Fisher, U.S. District Judge for the Eastern District of Texas.

110 Remarks at the Rollout Ceremony for the C–5A Cargo Plane, Marietta, Georgia. *March 2, 1968*

Thank you very much, Mr. Haughton. Governor Maddox, Secretary Brown, General McConnell, my dear, beloved former Chairman, Carl Vinson, Chairman Rivers, Senator Talmadge, Senator Monroney, all distinguished Members of Congress, ladies and gentlemen:

I think that perhaps most of you have heard the story of the man who built a big boat in his basement—and then couldn't get it out. That didn't happen in Georgia.

I believe someone has measured those doors. This may sound strange, and ordinarily I wouldn't take your time to make such an observation. I wouldn't be worrying about it, but after I went over to that building—that Carl Vinson, Mendel Rivers, and Dick Russell planned—Friday to tell Secretary McNamara goodby and spent 13 minutes in an elevator—and really never did get to the top—I want to be sure that the logistics have been worked out.

It was about 23 years ago this very month, less than 100 miles from where we are standing today, an American President wrote the last words of his life—for a speech that he never got to deliver. His words carried counsel for his country and it was just emerging from world war and surveying its new obligations.

Franklin Roosevelt's final paper—written at Warm Springs, Georgia—contains this great message that we could all well afford to remember: ". . . great power," he said, "involves great responsibility."

In the troubled time since those days, America has learned much about strength and a great deal about responsibility.

We have come here this morning for the rollout of a new era in our Nation's strength.

The exciting adventure which produced this plane began just a few years ago.

America was then developing its capacity to meet any danger that threatened it. One critical element was very much missing. Our country just could not move a fighting force quickly over long distances.

Now, with this plane, this crucial need is met.

The C-5A *Galaxy* can only be described in most extraordinary terms:

—It is the biggest aircraft in all the world. Its cargo floor alone is longer than the first flight that was made by the Wright Brothers.

—Its jet engine is twice as powerful as any that is now in existence.

—It can do three times the work of the biggest cargo plane that the United States now has. It cuts operating expenses almost in half.

—It can span the Pacific, from California to Japan, in one single jump.

But most important of all: For the first time, our fighting men will be able to travel with their equipment to any spot on the globe where we might be forced to stand—and they will travel rapidly and efficiently. Today it would take 88 cargo planes to move an infantry brigade from Hawaii to Vietnam. Their heaviest equipment would have to go by water.

Now, that entire operation that would formerly take 88 cargo planes and the equipment going by water can be handled by just 20 of these new aircraft.

So it is much more than a rollout of a great aircraft that you are seeing here today. We are observing a long leap forward in the effective military might of America.

And on such an occasion it is well to look back over the development of our awesome strength and the responsibility that that strength has placed upon all of us.

The guns of World War II had hardly silenced when this country made the historic commitment that binds us today.

In the wake of war, we were the only real effective force left in the free world. The road that we set out to travel was without precedent or parallel in all our history. Before then, military strength had always cleared a path to empire.

We pledged our strength to work with others to deter aggression and to help build the institutions of peace.

Our strength became a shield behind which men could find their way back to stability—and some could begin the long work of freedom and justice for their people.

The road has not been an easy one for America.

The exercise of strength has brought anguish to the Nation when her sons have had to fight in distant places, as many are fighting today.

And no sons of any State in the Union give a finer account of themselves than the sons of Georgia, wherever they are stationed.

But looking back over the long road that we have come, we can ask: What other road could America have traveled? How would history judge us if we sat by and let freedom die because we feared to use our strength in freedom's defense?

Since Franklin D. Roosevelt, four Presidents have kept America's course firm. All of those four Presidents have been supported every step of the way by two of the great sons of Georgia—Dick Russell and Carl Vinson.

Senator Talmadge and the other members of the Georgia delegation, Chairman Rivers and the other members of the Armed Services Committee, Senator Monroney and the other Members of the Senate, have all contributed valiantly and generously to our achievements.

But the lead horses—the ones that we all saluted, the ones we all listened to, the ones we all asked for permission to speak—there sits one of them and the other one is thinking of us today.

I would have you good folks of Georgia know that there are a lot of Marietta, Georgias, scattered throughout our 50 States. There are a lot of good people in a good many places.

There are a lot of good workmen that are led by Mr. Siemiller and some of our finest technicians. All of them would like to have the pride that comes from this production.

The people of Johnson City would even be very happy to have this payroll.

But all of them don't have the Georgia delegation. And none of them had Carl Vinson and Dick Russell.

An entire generation of Americans have supported them in the decision to walk the path of responsibility, in partnership with our friends and our allies.

Since we have never used our might for empire, we never measure our effectiveness in conquests.

—We see its success in the fact that a third world war—so freely predicted just 10 years ago—has not enflamed the globe—at least as yet.

—We see its success in a Europe that was once in shambles, that is now vital, progressive, and growing strong.

—We see it in a Latin America which once faced the threat of complete Communist takeover—they actually still have Cuba. It now has an opportunity—the other nations in this hemisphere—to grow in freedom.

—Violence has flamed in new states in Africa, but many of them today are moving towards stability.

—In Asia, the agony of battle in the Vietnam nation where so many of our people are standing now, clouds the fact of progress in that area. In Vietnam itself, a people under savage attack from outside aggression have held three elections, have adopted a constitution, have elected a president, a vice president, a senate and a house, and are slowly—if with great difficulty—building a nation despite the enormous destruction that is being imposed by an outside aggressor.

These are the rewards of the responsible use of strength for more than 20 years by responsible men.

Today, we are no longer alone in strength among our friends. But United States strength is still essential to the preservation of peace and freedom and order in this world. And without United States strength, the forces of aggression would triumph and the security of the United States would be imperiled—as surely as it was when we faced the danger just a few years ago across a ravaged Europe.

Then our responsibility was new and it was uncertain. Today, we know its cost. But we also know the much larger cost that we would pay if we cut and ran, or if we turned our back, or if we sought the easy way out of appeasement.

This aircraft that we roll out here today is a signal, it is a signal that responsible men shall never abandon the road of responsibility. We shall march it proudly—as we have marched it since that day when Franklin Delano Roosevelt, under a Georgia sky at Warm Springs wrote his last words: "Great power involves great responsibility."

Under the leadership of the men that this great State produces, responsibility will always be recognized and that responsibility will always be met.

Thank you.

I have something else I want to thank Georgia for and that is my Associate Press Secretary, Tom Johnson—one of the finest, ablest, young sons in America from Georgia.

We are very, very proud in this Nation of

Lockheed and the men who built this job on time. Thank you.

NOTE: The President spoke at 12:02 p.m. at the Lockheed-Georgia plant at Marietta, Ga. In his opening words he referred to Daniel J. Haughton, Chairman of the Board of Lockheed Aircraft Corp., Lester Maddox, Governor of Georgia, Harold Brown, Secretary of the Air Force, Gen. John P. McConnell, Air Force Chief of Staff, Carl Vinson, former Representative from Georgia and former Chairman of the House Armed Services Committee, L. Mendel Rivers, Representative from South Carolina and present Chairman of the Committee, Herman E. Talmadge, Senator from Georgia, and A. S. Mike Monroney, Senator from Oklahoma. Later he referred to Richard B. Russell, Senator from Georgia, and P. L. Siemiller, President of the International Association of Machinists and Aerospace Workers.

111 Special Message to the Congress: "Health in America." *March 4, 1968*

To the Congress of the United States:

My health recommendations to the Congress this year include five major new goals:

First, to reduce sharply the inexcusably high rate of infant mortality in the United States.

Second, to meet the urgent need for more doctors, nurses, and other health workers.

Third, to deal with the soaring cost of medical care and to assure the most efficient use of our health resources.

Fourth, to lower the shocking toll of deaths caused by accidents in America.

Fifth, to launch a nation-wide volunteer effort to improve the health of all Americans.

Each of these goals—and others which I will discuss in this message—will require an unprecedented national commitment. Each will take years to achieve. But every one of them must be reached if we are to guarantee to every citizen a full measure of safety, health and good medical care.

The first generation of Americans built their dream of a new nation on the conviction that life, liberty and the pursuit of happi-

ness are the inalienable rights of every man.

For nearly two centuries, our Nation has sought to make those rights a reality for more and more of our people.

It has fallen to this generation to assure that those rights have real meaning for every citizen. And this generation of Americans has made an historic commitment to open new opportunities—for economic advance, for educational fulfillment, for equality—for every citizen:

—Through unprecedented economic growth during the last 83 months and the war against poverty, nearly 12 million Americans have been lifted out of the depths of want and despair.

—Through more than 18 landmark education measures in the last four years, a tripling of the Federal investment in education, and a doubling of all public and private expenditures on education in the last six years, the Nation is moving rapidly to give every American child a real chance for full growth and development.

—Through the landmark Civil Rights Acts of 1964 and 1965, we have moved closer to the day when equal justice and opportunity will become a reality for all Americans.

We have sought also to make these basic rights meaningful to the older person stricken with arthritis, to the poor child with rheumatic fever, to the infant who in an earlier day might have suffered the ravages of polio.

In the last three years, the Federal Government enacted nearly 30 new health measures. We have increased its investment from $6 billion to nearly $14 billion annually to assure that the benefits of modern medicine are available to all our people:

—To make medical care available to those who need it most, the elderly and the poor, expenditures have risen from $1 billion to nearly $8 billion. Another $2.5 billion is spent each year to bring the finest health care to our servicemen and veterans.

—To build new laboratories, hospitals and health clinics, and to train the men and women to work in them, expenditures have risen from $2 billion to nearly $3 billion annually.

—To prevent and control disease, expenditures have risen from $450 million to nearly $700 million.

The real meaning of these statistics is found in the lives of people who have been helped:

—19.5 million Americans, 65 and over, are now able to receive the medical care they need without suffering crushing economic burdens.

—20 million children who have been vaccinated against measles, and 323,000 fewer children suffer from measles each year.

—30 million have been protected against diphtheria, polio, tetanus and whooping cough, reducing by more than 50 percent the number of children who suffer from these diseases.

—43,000 retarded children can now look forward to more productive lives because of the 150 special clinics built to serve them.

—47 million Americans live in communities served by new mental health centers.

—The life expectancy of Americans continues to increase, promising millions a longer and fuller life. In 1920, it was 54.1 years; today it is over 70.

And the discoveries of modern science promise a better life for all citizens: the prevention of German measles, the advances in treating leukemia, the progress in understanding life's processes.

We must continue to build upon those proud achievements.

THE BIRTHRIGHT OF SOUND HEALTH

The American child is born into a land richer with promise than any nation in the history of the world.

But to share in that promise, he must survive the perils of birth and infancy. For too many American children, the hazards of survival are steep.

This great, wealthy, resourceful Nation—which should lead the world in saving its young—instead ranked 15th in infant mortality in 1965.

In that year, nearly 25 infants out of every 1,000 born in this country died before the age of one. Thousands more were handicapped for life because of inadequate health care in their first year.

The infant mortality rate among poor families was nearly double the national average. In certain city ghettos and pockets of rural poverty the rate was 7 times that in surrounding suburban areas.

Those figures shamed this enlightened Nation. And we acted to meet the problem.

Through the Maternal and Child Health program:

—300,000 women are now receiving family planning services.

—390,000 receive maternity care.

—680,000 infants are getting the attention so crucial to their later development.

Through the Crippled Children's program, 460,000 children will be treated for handicapping conditions each year.

Through Medicaid, thousands of needy mothers and their infants are receiving the care vital to their health and well being.

The infant mortality rate in this country dropped from 25.2 deaths per thousand in 1963, to 22.1 per thousand in 1967—a 12% decline in four years.

The success of these programs in two cities demonstrates that the tragic rate of infant mortality can be reduced even faster. Last year, because of modern medicine and a concentrated effort, the rate in Washington, D.C. fell 8.5%; the rate in Chicago in the first 10 months of the year dropped 15%.

In 1963, 100,000 infants died. In 1967, that figure was reduced to 80,000. But this progress is not enough. For thousands more did not receive the medical care so vital to their future growth and development.

THE CHILD HEALTH IMPROVEMENT AND PROTECTION ACT OF 1968

This Nation must accelerate its efforts. The cost of future care rises every time a child's disease or handicap is left unattended. A man's potential is diminished every time an affliction that could be cured in childhood causes permanent damage. Most important of all, America's conscience is scarred and her future dimmed every time a child dies

needlessly.

We must now attack the problem of infant mortality on a nationwide basis by providing essential medical care to the 700,000 needy mothers who give birth each year and to their infants.

To launch this effort, *I recommend a $58 million increase in appropriations for the maternal and child health care programs in fiscal 1969.* $25 million of this increase will provide for the expansion of maternity and infant care centers and clinics.

Our goal is to assure every needy American family:

—Adequate prenatal and postnatal care for the mother.

—A safe delivery by trained health professionals.

—Competent examination of the child at birth, and expert treatment when needed.

—The best of modern medical care for the infant during his first year to prevent disease, cure illness, and correct handicaps.

—An opportunity, on a voluntary basis, to plan the number and spacing of children.

To fulfill this objective, *I propose the Child Health Act of 1968.*

With this authority, the Nation will be able to provide comprehensive medical care for every needy mother and her infant.

FOR AMERICA'S YOUNG

As we launch a major new effort to improve health care for the very young, we must not lose sight of our responsibility for all of America's children. We are encouraged by the gains made under our pioneering efforts:

—Head Start and other preschool programs which have brought education and health care to more than 2 million children.

—Medicaid which will provide health care to more than 3 million children this year.

—137 new mental retardation clinics have been built to serve over 40,000 retarded children.

Nevertheless, the dimensions of what remains to be done are seen in these grim statistics:

—436,000 children are victims of cerebral palsy.

—424,000 have epilepsy.

—12.3 million have eye defects.

—2.5 million have hearing impairments.

—3.2 million have speech defects.

—2.3 million have orthopedic handicaps.

—4.8 million are emotionally disturbed.

To continue our efforts to meet the needs of America's children, *I recommend that the Congress provide $1.4 billion in fiscal 1969—an increase of $215 million—for child health services under Medicaid and other Federal health programs.* These funds will provide:

—3.5 million poor children with health services under Medicaid.

—More than 1 million children with comprehensive health services at 56 Children and Youth Centers.

—500,000 Head Start children with medical examinations and follow-up treatment.

—460,000 children with treatment for handicapping conditions.

—200,000 children with family services at Neighborhood Health Centers.

The Benefits of Research

The history of our times is not solely a study in crisis. It is also one of hope: when

polio was conquered; when other infectious diseases that had plagued man for centuries fell one after another; when breakthroughs in genetics brought a better understanding of the process of life.

These are the quiet successes achieved in countless laboratories, leaving their mark forever on the future of man.

1967 was a breakthrough year which brought many rich dividends:

1. Measles can now be completely prevented.

2. The creation of life in a California test tube startled the world.

3. The Minnesota-trained doctor's first heart transplant was an historic milestone.

But none of these achievements were the result of a single year's research. They came from the careful work of many years. They were made possible by the Federal Government's continuing support to scientists who seek to expand our store of fundamental knowledge. That support has grown from $1 billion in 1963, to nearly $1.5 billion today, and comprises 65 percent of the Nation's total expenditures for biomedical research.

Yet we have only begun to unlock the secrets of better health and a richer life.

Our understanding of disease and human development is woefully incomplete. We can control some types of cancer, but do not yet know their exact causes.

We are still groping to understand the causes and the cures of mental illness. We have only begun to discover the reasons for mental retardation.

The relentless search for knowledge must go on. To assure the breakthroughs of next year, and the years after, *I recommend that the Congress provide $1.5 billion for health research in fiscal 1969.*

POPULATION AND HUMAN REPRODUCTION

Two vital fields long neglected by research are population and human reproduction. Thousands of parents want help in determining how to plan their families. Thousands of others are unable to have the children they desire.

Our lack of knowledge impedes our effort to provide the help they need.

—Far too little is known about the physiology of reproduction and its effect on all aspects of human life.

—Searching studies are needed to determine the complex emotional, sociological, physiological and economic factors involved.

A wide range of scientists must bring to these problems their specialized disciplines—biologists, behavioral scientists, biochemists, pharmacologists, demographers, experts in population dynamics.

To launch this effort, *I have directed the Secretary of Health, Education, and Welfare to establish a Center for Population Studies and Human Reproduction in the National Institute of Child Health and Human Development.* The Center will serve to give new energy and direction to the research activities of all Federal Departments and Agencies in these fields.

I am asking the Congress to appropriate $12 million to support the research activities of the Center during its first year of operation.

As we move to expand our knowledge of population and human reproduction, we must make that knowledge available to those who want it. Last year, the Federal Government helped to bring information and counseling on a voluntary basis to more than 500,000 women. But there are millions more who want help.

I recommend that the Congress provide *for an increase in funds from $25 million in fiscal 1968 to $61 million in fiscal 1969 so that three million women can have access to family planning help if they so desire.*

HEALTH MANPOWER

Several years ago, this Nation set out to encourage the training of more doctors, nurses and medical technicians.

As the result of the imaginative programs recommended by the Administration and approved by the Congress over the last five years,

—An additional 100,000 doctors, nurses, dentists, laboratory technicians, and other health workers are being trained this year to meet the health needs of our growing population.

—More than 850 medical, dental and nursing schools have enlarged their capacity or improved their instruction.

This rate of progress is encouraging. But our increasing population and the demand for more and better health care swell the need for doctors, health professionals and other medical workers.

Yet we lack the capacity to train today those who must serve us tomorrow.

To train more health workers and to train them better and faster, *I propose the Health Manpower Act of 1968.*

This Act will extend and strengthen five vital measures which are due to expire in June 1969:

(1) *The Health Educational Act of 1963* will be reinforced to:

—Provide new classrooms, laboratories and libraries needed to train more doctors and other health professionals.

—Authorize new operating and project grants which will encourage the schools to expand their enrollment, improve their curricula, and reduce the length of their training.

—Extend financial aid to thousands of students each year.

—Simplify procedures so that schools can obtain funds for joint research-teaching-library projects through one application.

(2) *The Nurse Training Act of 1964* will be improved to:

—Strengthen the loan, scholarship, and traineeship program so that nearly 50,000 nursing students can be helped through school in the first year of the program.

—Encourage nursing schools to expand enrollment and overcome high attrition rates by revamping their curricula and tailoring their courses to the needs of the students.

(3) *The Health Personnel Training Act of 1966* will be continued to speed the training of paramedical personnel and other health workers by

—Constructing new classrooms.

—Improving the quality of instruction.

—Developing new curricula and methods of training.

(4) *The Health Research Act of 1965* will be amended to permit greater emphasis on the development of research facilities meeting critical regional or national needs.

(5) *The Graduate Health Training Act of 1964* will be extended to increase the number of skilled administrators and public health workers.

I urge the Congress to appropriate $290 million in fiscal 1969 to carry forward our vital health manpower programs.

This effort will be bolstered by the Veterans in Public Service Act, which I recently proposed to the Congress. Under that Act, the talents of the veteran will be enlisted for service to his community. For those who return to meet critical health manpower

shortages, there will be special benefits while they are in training and on the job.

I urge the Congress to launch this program promptly so that we can bring the skills and experience of the veteran to bear on our pressing health needs.

PARTNERSHIP FOR HEALTH

In 1966 we launched the Partnership for Health. Its purpose was to support State and local efforts to:

—Identify the health needs of each State and city.

—Mobilize the resources of the State to meet those needs.

—Determine what additional resources, facilities, equipment and manpower, are required.

In the brief period since its enactment, this great Partnership has pioneered in the expansion of State and local responsibility for the health of our citizens.

Every State and many communities have now created health planning agencies which are at work developing and implementing bold new health strategies. This planning, tailored to the special needs of each State, will forge Federal, State and local efforts into an effective instrument to bring better health care to the people.

This important work must continue— and it must be expanded.

I recommend that the Congress appropriate $195 million for the Partnership For Health in fiscal 1969, an increase of $35 million over fiscal 1968—an increase of 22 percent.

THE REGIONAL MEDICAL PROGRAM

In 1966, we began the Regional Medical Program to reduce the toll of death and disability from heart disease, cancer, stroke and related illnesses. Its purpose is to translate research into action, so all the people of our Nation can benefit as rapidly as possible from the achievements of modern medicine.

Fifty-four regions, spanning the nation, have begun planning. Eight regions have already begun action programs. Most of the others will start by the end of the year.

These programs are concentrating regional resources and developing more effective ways to attack the three chief killers in this country. Thousands of Americans stricken by heart disease, cancer or stroke are already receiving better care.

But these threats to our health and vitality remain stubborn and unyielding.

I recommend that the Congress extend the Regional Medical Program and increase—by almost 100 percent—to $100 million the funds available for the program in fiscal 1969.

CONTROLLING COSTS OF HEALTH CARE

Virtually every family feels the burden of rising costs of medical care.

Thousands of Americans today are not getting urgently needed medical care because they cannot afford it.

Others pay for it only by giving up necessities, postponing a long-held dream, or mortgaging their futures.

The outlook is sobering. It has been estimated that between 1965 and 1975, the cost of living will increase by more than 20 percent. But the cost of health care will increase by nearly 140 percent by 1975:

—Average payments per person will nearly double, from about $200 a year to some $400 a year.
—Drug payments will rise by 65 percent.
—Dental bills will increase 100 percent.
—Doctors bills will climb 160 percent.
—Payments for general hospital services

will jump 250 percent.

Part of these increases will be for expanded and improved health services. But a large part of the increase will be unnecessary—a rise which can be prevented.

Last year I appointed a Commission of distinguished citizens—physicians, hospital officials, teachers, business executives, and other leaders—to make a comprehensive study of health manpower and medical care.

The Commission, which reported in November, cited three major deficiencies in present practices which contribute to unacceptable increases in medical costs:

—Most health insurance plans encourage doctors and patients to choose hospitalization even when other, less costly, forms of care would be equally effective.
—Health professions are generally paid in proportion to the amount of service they render. There are no strong economic incentives to encourage them to avoid providing care that is unnecessary.
—Hospitals charge on a cost basis, which places no penalty on inefficient operations. Moreover, present systems of hospital management make it very difficult to maintain effective control over hospital costs.

The Commission concluded:

"If the needs for health care are to be met, the health care system must be organized to employ its resources with more wisdom and effectiveness. The two areas which appear to offer the greatest potential for improvement are (1) reducing unnecessary (or unnecessarily expensive) medical care and (2) increasing efficiency in the provision of hospital care."

It will not be easy to carry out this recommendation.

But unless we do—unless we act now—health care will not improve as fast as it should.

Congress has recognized this problem of rising medical costs. Late last year it authorized the Secretary of Health, Education, and Welfare to test different types of payment systems under Medicare, Medicaid, and the Maternal and Child Health programs.

I have directed the Secretary of Health, Education, and Welfare to begin immediately extensive tests of incentives designed to reduce the cost of medical care.

First, we must explore ways to prevent unnecessary hospitalization. Our experience in Medicare can serve as a guideline. Under that plan, hospital stays are limited to periods which are clearly necessary, and payments are provided for other less expensive types of care which serve the patient equally well: outpatient clinic service, home treatment, nursing home care. We can also draw on the experience of new private prepaid comprehensive plans featuring incentives designed to reduce unnecessary hospitalization.

Second, we must test incentives designed to control the cost of hospital care itself. The Health Manpower Commission reported that costs among some of the Nation's best hospitals vary by as much as 100%, without significant differences in quality or scope of services. This shows that savings in hospital costs can be achieved. We must find ways to encourage efficiency and penalize waste.

These tests will call for the cooperation of doctors, hospitals and insurance companies.

They will be the pioneer efforts. If they are successful—and if they can be applied on a broad basis—they will hold much promise for the American people.

I recommend that the Congress authorize the Secretary of Health, Education, and Welfare, under Medicare, Medicaid, and the

Maternal and Child Health programs, to employ new methods of payment as they prove effective in providing high quality medical care more efficiently and at lower cost.

It is appropriate that the Government—which pays more than 20% of the Nation's medical bill—take the lead in stemming soaring medical care costs.

But this can be only part of the effort. Ultimate success will depend on the ingenuity of our health profession and institutions, and the insurance systems allied with them.

The rewards of success—and the penalties of inaction—demand a dedicated effort by all. Unless the cost spiral is stopped, the Nation's health bill could reach a staggering $100 billion by 1975. The cost of providing adequate medical care to a family could double.

The Cost of Drugs

Beyond this, we must make certain that the American taxpayer does not pay needlessly high and exorbitant prices for prescription drugs used in Federally-supported programs.

Recent surveys have shown, for instance, that 12 drugs of the same type range in retail price from $1.25 to $11 for 30 tablets. The taxpayer should not be forced to pay $11 if the $1.25 drug is equally effective. To do this would permit robbery of private citizens with public approval.

I recommend that the Congress authorize the Secretary of Health, Education, and Welfare to establish a reasonable cost range to govern reimbursement for drugs now provided under Medicare, Medicaid and the Maternal and Child Health programs.

This payment method will apply in all parts of these programs, except in those cases where hospitals and other health care institutions have established effective and reliable systems for cost and quality control.

The physician will be free to select more expensive drugs of the same quality and effectiveness, if he chooses, but reimbursement will be limited to the payment range established by the Secretary.

To Protect the American Patient

The wide array of medication available to the American patient is a tribute to modern science.

But the very abundance of drugs creates problems.

In our society, we normally demand that the consumer be given sufficient information to make a choice between products. But when the consumer is a patient, he must rely exclusively on his doctor's choice of the drug that can best treat his condition.

Yet the doctor is not always in a position to make a fully informed judgment. He has no complete, readily available source of information about the thousands of drugs now available.

He must nonetheless make a decision affecting the health, and perhaps the life, of his patient.

To make sure that doctors have accurate, reliable and complete information on the drugs which are available, *I recommend that the Congress authorize this year publication of a United States Compendium of Drugs.*

This Compendium would be prepared by the Secretary of Health, Education, and Welfare, in cooperation with pharmaceutical manufacturers, who would bear the cost of its publication, and with physicians and pharmacists.

It will give every doctor, pharmacy, hospital, and other health care institution complete and accurate information about prescription drugs—use and dosage, warnings, manufacturer, generic and brand names, and facts about their safety and effectiveness.

The Tragedy of Accidents

More than 630,000 Americans died in accidents in the last six years.

This is a tragedy heightened by the fact that much of it is senseless and unnecessary.

Thousands of deaths will be prevented under the Highway and Traffic Safety laws passed by the Congress in 1966. Thousands more can be prevented by prompt medical attention.

The needed medical services are often available. But because of an inadequate rescue system, the victim dies before he reaches the hospital.

The compelling need is for modern, effective rescue systems to give immediate attention to accident victims—on the spot and while they are being speeded to the hospitals.

We have proven excellent rescue systems in action, saving fighting men injured in battle. First in Korea, and now in Vietnam, the military has shown the speed and effectiveness of helicopter crews, paramedical personnel and communications experts mobilized to save the lives of wounded men.

Few States and communities have drawn upon that experience. In many areas, ambulance crewmen are not even trained in first aid. Ambulances themselves are rarely well-equipped. Communications systems are inadequate, if they exist at all.

I have directed the Secretaries of Transportation, Health, Education, and Welfare, and Defense to devise a test program to help our States and communities develop effective rescue systems to fit their own needs.

In a previous message to the Congress this year, I proposed the Occupational Safety and

Health Act of 1968, to safeguard 75 million American workers on the job.

Through this Act we can attack the conditions which cause nearly 15,000 deaths and 2.2 million injuries each year.

With these measures, we can move far toward reducing the tragic toll of accidental death and injury in America.

PHYSICAL FITNESS

For more than a decade the Federal government has taken a direct interest in improving the physical fitness of Americans.

President Eisenhower, President Kennedy and I have taken steps to encourage our citizens—particularly the young—to pursue the active life.

Through these efforts, boys and girls across America have discovered the joys of exercise and sports competition.

But here—as in our health programs—we must look not only at the progress that has been made, but at the problems that remain.

—In tests of physical strength and stamina, American children still score substantially lower than children in other countries.

—32 million children get less than the recommended physical fitness program in school; seven million get none at all.

—Only 50 percent of all college students meet accepted physical fitness standards.

Physical fitness activities and sports contribute to more than health. They teach self-discipline and teamwork. They offer excitement and a wholesome alternative to idleness. They combat delinquency. They permanently enrich the individual and his society by developing qualities of leadership and fair play.

To expand opportunities to engage in exercise, active recreation, and sports, I am

establishing the President's Council on Physical Fitness and Sports, to be chaired by the Vice President.[1]

The Council will be a Cabinet-level group, with an Advisory Committee of distinguished citizens, to develop national goals and programs to promote sports and fitness in America.

As a first step, the Council will call a national conference to explore the long-term requirements of physical fitness and sports in the nation.

LEADERSHIP AND EFFICIENT MANAGEMENT

Health expenditures in the United States are now nearly $50 billion a year. The Federal Government pays $14 billion of that amount, up from $5 billion four years ago to $16 billion in fiscal 1969.

The expanding Federal programs must be managed efficiently, with the most careful attention to the most urgent needs of the American people. *To that end, I am today directing the Secretary of Health, Education, and Welfare to submit to me a modern plan of organization to achieve the most efficient and economical operation of the health programs of the Federal Government.*[2]

But better organization and leadership will be wasted if we cannot find and hold the quality of people essential for these great tasks.

I recommend the Health Personnel Act of 1968 to modernize the health personnel sys-

---

[1] The President's Council on Physical Fitness and Sports was established by Executive Order 11398 of March 4, 1968 (4 Weekly Comp. Pres. Docs., p. 435; 33 F.R. 4169; 3 CFR, 1968 Comp., p. 102).

[2] On June 15, 1968, Secretary of Health, Education, and Welfare Wilbur J. Cohen submitted a report to the President recommending changes in organization and coordination of Federal health programs (4 Weekly Comp. Pres. Docs., p. 972).

tem within the Department of Health, Education, and Welfare. This act will provide:

—Pay increases and a flexible personnel to attract and retain professionals of the highest caliber.

—A new promotion system based upon quality of performance.

MOBILIZATION FOR HEALTH

In our drive toward a healthier America, Federal programs and Federal dollars have an important role to play. But they cannot do the job alone.

An even larger role belongs to State and local government, and to the private enterprise system of our Nation. The medical and hospital associations, the health care institutions, the health insurance industry, the communication media, voluntary civic associations, employers and labor unions, charities and church groups must join this effort. I call upon them to join in a 12-point volunteer effort to build a healthier America:

(1) To examine every child under the age of five to identify potentially crippling ailments and provide early and effective treatment.

(2) To use the public airways for public profit by offering regular health programs on television and radio to help every American preserve his cherished birthright of good health.

(3) To give prominent magazine and newspaper coverage to good health practices for our children and older Americans.

(4) To identify and reward new approaches by medical societies, group practice organizations and hospitals for delivering better health care at lower cost.

(5) To expand voluntary health insurance to those not now covered and

include services not now included.

(6) To establish local systems of new incentives to recruit, train, retrain, license and effectively use nurses and medical corpsmen leaving the Armed Services, and other vital members of the health team.

(7) To make home health care part of the education of every young girl in all the schools of America.

(8) To encourage the opening of health centers to provide complete care in every community.

(9) To make physical fitness programs and recreational facilities available to people of all ages and in all walks of life.

(10) To alert teenagers and their parents to the danger of drug abuse.

(11) To develop better programs for health services for the one-third of the working poor who suffer from chronic illness.

(12) To mobilize a new spirit of public concern and private action to meet and master our health problems.

Great changes have taken place in the financing of medical care in this country. The Federal Government will invest some $16 billion in the health field in fiscal 1969. We should now expect our Nation's great private resources, through volunteer and cooperative action, to step up their efforts to bring better health to all our citizens.

HEALTH CARE FOR ALL AMERICANS

In the medical research laboratories of the world, a quiet revolution is changing the condition of man. Enemies which have held man in hostage throughout history are conquered each year. Hope turns daily to promise, and promise to practical achievement.

But progress cannot be measured in the

laboratory alone. Triumph in a test tube is not triumph enough—if it remains there.

Success in a laboratory, however brilliant, is not complete if barriers of poverty, ignorance or prejudice block it from reaching the man who needs it, or the child who wastes away without it.

With the program I have outlined in this message, I believe we can move closer to our goal of decent health care for every American.

This is a program to assure that American medicine will continue to build on its great record, and that its benefits will enrich and improve the life of every citizen.

I urge the Congress to act promptly on this program.

LYNDON B. JOHNSON

The White House
March 4, 1968

NOTE: For statements or remarks upon signing related legislation, see Items 446, 447, 536, 545.

---

112 Talking Points of the President Before Union and Company Negotiators in the Copper Strike. *March 4, 1968*

I APPRECIATE your prompt response to my invitation to come to Washington today to discuss the copper dispute.

I asked you here because of our deep concern over the continuation of the strike and the effect it is having on our domestic economy, on our international balance of payments, and on our defense mission in Southeast Asia.

IMPACT OF STRIKE

The strike is now in its 234th day. It involves all of our major copper producers, their shareholders and 60,000 workers in the copper industry. Ninety percent of the Nation's copper mining capacity and 80 percent of its refining capacity has been closed down.

At first—because of inventory buildup and the availability of imported copper—the impact of the strike was limited to the parties. Now, this is *no longer so*.

BALANCE OF PAYMENTS

First, our balance of payments position is being seriously threatened. The strike is weakening our dollar.

—Our trade deficit in copper—because of the strike—reached about $50 million monthly in late 1967. In January it jumped to a huge $95 million.

—If this trend continues, the trade deficit from copper alone will run over $1 billion yearly. This is one-quarter of last year's entire, intolerable deficit.

DEFENSE DELIVERIES

The copper shortage is causing some civilian production to close down. Many of these plants also produce materials and supplies vital to our defense efforts.

When civilian production lines close, defense production lines in the same plant may also be forced to shut down.

If the present situation continues, we may feel a tight pinch.

—It may cause delays and it may hinder our ability to gear up production to meet any increased threats abroad. Our fighting men in Vietnam must have all the equipment they need for their missions, and indeed their lives—without any interruption.

333

—There is virtually no item in our defense arsenal that does not depend on copper to some extent—from ammunition to complex electronic gear on our ships and planes.

—We are now operating under a tight margin of safety—so much so that all producers have been told that they cannot ship U.S. refined copper except under defense-rated orders.

IMPACT ON THE NATION'S ECONOMY

The strike is now threatening domestic prosperity.

—Reductions in production and employment in copper-using industries have already begun, and will increase rapidly.

—Among the industries that will be hit hardest are electrical machinery, electronics, automobiles and trucks, heating and air conditioning.

—Prices are up from a prestrike level of around 40 cents a pound to over 80 cents.

—Civilian copper consumption is now down to 65 percent of the prestrike level.

—The precarious nature of the copper supply situation was dramatized by last week's dock tieups.

—In five States—Arizona, Utah, Montana, Nevada, New Mexico, all of whose Governors and Congressmen I met with last week—40,000 copper workers have been out since last July. Local businesses are failing. State and local tax revenues have dropped sharply. Welfare payments have jumped.

IMPACT ON COMPANIES AND WORKERS

To the workers the strike has meant a quarter of a billion dollars in lost wages, with the rate running at $7 million weekly.

To the companies, the strike has meant a drop of $123 million (from 1966) in 1967 after tax profits.

To the industry generally, a long tieup will speed the search for substitute metals and thus mean the permanent loss of profits and jobs.

BARGAINING HISTORY

Free collective bargaining is the keystone of our industrial democracy. This is the way labor disputes should be settled.

The Government has offered to help the parties break the deadlock through the collective bargaining process.

—Throughout the dispute, the Mediation Service has assigned a special team to assist the parties.

—Last September, Secretaries Wirtz and Trowbridge requested the parties to meet with them in Washington.

—In January, Secretaries Wirtz and Trowbridge appointed a mediation panel of three outstanding labor experts: Dr. George Taylor, Mr. George Reedy, and Monsignor George Higgins.

—Last month, that panel developed a framework to help guide the parties toward settlement.

A TIME FOR RESPONSIBLE ACTION

I recognize that issues of deep principle separate the parties. Yet, there comes a time when these differences must be resolved in the larger interests of our Nation, of the continued strength of our economy, and for the men who fight for all of us half a world away in Vietnam.

There comes a time when our dollar must be defended, our armies equipped, and our domestic economy kept on a steady and healthy course.

I have always believed that the answers to a labor dispute must be found in free collective bargaining.

I urge the parties to get on with their bargaining on an urgent, intensive around-the-clock basis.

I ask the parties to consider very carefully the proposals of the Taylor panel as a framework for constructive bargaining.

I have asked Secretaries Wirtz, Clifford, and Smith and the Taylor mediation panel to assist you in any way they can in finding just and fair answers to this dispute.

So now, as you begin your negotiations across the street, I urge you to take the Nation's interest into your hearts and into your minds as you speed the search for a fair and just settlement.

I have asked the Secretaries to keep in touch with me on the progress of the bargaining.

Before you begin your bargaining, I think it would help you realize how deeply the Nation's interest is involved as you hear from Secretary Clifford and Secretary Fowler.

NOTE: This is the text of the White House press release made public in connection with the meeting held in the White House at 4 p.m. The President commented on the terms of a proposed settlement in his news conference of March 30, 1968 (see Item 169[21]). The strike was settled in early April 1968.

---

113 Special Message to the Congress on the Problems of the American Indian: "The Forgotten American." *March 6, 1968*

To the Congress of the United States:

Mississippi and Utah—the Potomac and the Chattahoochee—Appalachia and Shenandoah . . . The words of the Indian have become our words—the names of our states and streams and landmarks.

His myths and his heroes enrich our literature.

His lore colors our art and our language.

For two centuries, the American Indian has been a symbol of the drama and excitement of the earliest America.

But for two centuries, he has been an alien in his own land.

Relations between the United States Government and the tribes were originally in the hands of the War Department. Until 1871, the United States treated the Indian tribes as foreign nations.

It has been only 44 years since the United States affirmed the Indian's citizenship: the full political equality essential for human dignity in a democratic society.

It has been only 22 years since Congress enacted the Indian Claims Act, to acknowledge the Nation's debt to the first Americans for their land.

But political equality and compensation for ancestral lands are not enough. The American Indian deserves a chance to develop his talents and share fully in the future of our Nation.

There are about 600,000 Indians in America today. Some 400,000 live on or near reservations in 25 States. The remaining 200,000 have moved to our cities and towns. The most striking fact about the American Indians today is their tragic plight:

—Fifty thousand Indian families live in unsanitary, dilapidated dwellings: many in huts, shanties, even abandoned automobiles.

—The unemployment rate among Indians is nearly 40 percent—more than ten times the national average.

—Fifty percent of Indian schoolchildren—

335

double the national average—drop out
before completing high school.
—Indian literacy rates are among the lowest in the Nation; the rates of sickness
and poverty are among the highest.
—Thousands of Indians who have mi-
grated into the cities find themselves
untrained for jobs and unprepared for
urban life.
—The average age of death of an American Indian today is 44 years; for all
other Americans, it is 65.

The American Indian, once proud and
free, is torn now between white and tribal
values; between the politics and language
of the white man and his own historic culture. His problems, sharpened by years of
defeat and exploitation, neglect and inadequate effort, will take many years to
overcome.

But recent landmark laws—the Economic
Opportunity Act, the Elementary and Secondary Education Act, the Manpower Development and Training Act—have given us
an opportunity to deal with the persistent
problems of the American Indian. The time
has come to focus our efforts on the plight
of the American Indian through these and
the other laws passed in the last few years.

No enlightened Nation, no responsible
government, no progressive people can sit
idly by and permit this shocking situation
to continue.

I propose a new goal for our Indian programs: A goal that ends the old debate about
"termination" of Indian programs and
stresses self-determination; a goal that erases
old attitudes of paternalism and promotes
partnership self-help.

Our goal must be:
—*A standard of living for the Indians
equal to that of the country as a whole.*
—*Freedom of Choice: An opportunity to
remain in their homelands, if they*
*choose, without surrendering their dig-
nity; an opportunity to move to the
towns and cities of America, if they
choose, equipped with the skills to live
in equality and dignity.*
—*Full participation in the life of modern
America, with a full share of economic
opportunity and social justice.*

I propose, in short, a policy of maximum
choice for the American Indian: a policy
expressed in programs of self-help, self-development, self-determination.

To start toward our goal in Fiscal 1969,
I recommend that the Congress appropriate
one-half a billion dollars for programs targeted at the American Indian—about 10
percent more than Fiscal 1968.

STRENGTHENED FEDERAL LEADERSHIP

In the past four years, with the advent of
major new programs, several agencies have
undertaken independent efforts to help the
American Indian. Too often, there has been
too little coordination between agencies; and
no clear, unified policy which applied to all.

*To launch an undivided, Government-
wide effort in this area, I am today issuing
an Executive Order to establish a National
Council on Indian Opportunity.*[1]

The Chairman of the Council will be the
Vice President who will bring the problems
of the Indians to the highest levels of Government. The Council will include a cross
section of Indian leaders, and high government officials who have programs in this
field:
—The Secretary of the Interior, who has
primary responsibility for Indian

---

[1] Executive Order 11399 "Establishing the National Council on Indian Opportunity" is printed
in the Weekly Compilation of Presidential Documents, the Federal Register, and the Code of Federal
Regulations (4 Weekly Comp. Pres. Docs., p. 448;
33 F.R. 4245; 3 CFR, 1968 Comp., p. 105).

Affairs.

—The Secretary of Agriculture, whose programs affect thousands of Indians.

—The Secretary of Commerce, who can help promote economic development of Indian lands.

—The Secretary of Labor, whose manpower programs can train more Indians for more useful employment.

—The Secretary of Health, Education, and Welfare, who can help Indian communities with two of their most pressing needs—health and education.

—The Secretary of Housing and Urban Development, who can bring better housing to Indian lands.

—The Director of the Office of Economic Opportunity, whose programs are already operating in several Indian communities.

The Council will review Federal programs for Indians, make broad policy recommendations, and ensure that programs reflect the needs and desires of the Indian people. Most important, I have asked the Vice President, as Chairman of the Council, to make certain that the American Indian shares fully in all our federal programs.

SELF-HELP AND SELF-DETERMINATION

The greatest hope for Indian progress lies in the emergence of Indian leadership and initiative in solving Indian problems. Indians must have a voice in making the plans and decisions in programs which are important to their daily life.

Within the last few months we have seen a new concept of community development—a concept based on self-help—work successfully among Indians. Many tribes have begun to administer activities which Federal agencies had long performed in their behalf:

—On the Crow Creek, Lower Brule, and

Fort Berthold reservations in the Dakotas and on reservations in several other states, imaginative new work-experience programs, operated by Indians themselves, provide jobs for Indians once totally dependent on welfare.

—The Warm Springs Tribes of Oregon ran an extensive program to repair flood damage on their reservation.

—The Oglala Sioux of South Dakota and the Zunis of New Mexico are now contracting to provide law enforcement services for their communities.

—The Navajos—who this year celebrate the 100th anniversary of their peace treaty with the United States—furnish many community services normally provided by the Federal government, either through contract or with funds from their own Treasury.

Passive acceptance of Federal service is giving way to Indian involvement. More than ever before, Indian needs are being identified from the Indian viewpoint—as they should be.

This principle is the key to progress for Indians—just as it has been for other Americans. If we base our programs upon it, the day will come when the relationship between Indians and the Government will be one of full partnership—not dependency.

EDUCATION

The problems of Indian education are legion:

—Ten percent of American Indians over age 14 have had no schooling at all.

—Nearly 60 percent have less than an eighth grade education.

—Half of our Indian children do not finish high school today.

—Even those Indians attending school are plagued by language barriers, by isolation in remote areas, by lack of a tradition of academic achievement.

Standard schooling and vocational training will not be enough to overcome the educational difficulties of the Indians. More intensive and imaginative approaches are needed.

The legislation enacted in the past four years gives us the means to make the special effort now needed in Indian education: The Elementary and Secondary Education Act, the Education Professions Development Act, the Vocational Education Act, and the Higher Education Act.

The challenge is to use this legislation creatively.

I have directed the Secretary of the Interior and the Secretary of Health, Education, and Welfare:

—*To work together to make these programs responsive to the needs of Indians.*

—*To develop a concentrated effort in Indian education with State and local agencies.* This is critical if the two-thirds of Indian schoolchildren in non-Indian public schools are to get the special help they sorely need.

Pre-School Programs

In the past few years we as a Nation have come to recognize the irreplaceable importance of the earliest years in a child's life. Pre-school education and care—valuable for all children—are urgently needed for Indian children.

We must set a goal to enroll every four and five-year-old Indian child in a pre-school program by 1971.

For 1969, I am requesting funds to:

—*Make the Head Start Program available to 10,000 Indian children.*

—*Establish, for the first time, kindergartens for 4,500 Indian youngsters next*

September.

To encourage Indian involvement in this educational process, I am asking the Secretary of the Interior to assure that each of these kindergartens employ local Indian teacher aides as well as trained teachers.

Federal Indian Schools

Since 1961, we have undertaken a substantial program to improve the 245 Federal Indian schools, which are attended by over 50,000 children. That effort is now half completed. It will continue.

But good facilities are not enough.

I am asking the Secretary of the Interior, in cooperation with the Secretary of Health, Education, and Welfare, to establish a model community school system for Indians. These schools will:

—Have the finest teachers, familiar with Indian history, culture and language.

—Feature an enriched curriculum, special guidance and counseling programs, modern instruction materials, and a sound program to teach English as a second language.

—Serve the local Indian population as a community center for activities ranging from adult education classes to social gatherings.

To reach this goal, I propose that the Congress appropriate $5.5 million to attract and hold talented and dedicated teachers at Indian schools and to provide 200 additional teachers and other professionals to enrich instruction, counseling and other programs.

To help make the Indian school a vital part of the Indian community, I am directing the Secretary of the Interior to establish Indian school boards for Federal Indian Schools. School board members—selected by their communities—will receive whatever training is necessary to enable them to carry out their responsibilities.

Higher Education

Indian youth must be given more opportunities to develop their talents fully and to pursue their ambitions free of arbitrary barriers to learning and employment. They must have a chance to become professionals: doctors, nurses, engineers, managers and teachers.

For the young Indian of today will eventually become the bridge between two cultures, two languages, and two ways of life.

Therefore, we must open wide the doors of career training and higher education to all Indian students who qualify.

To reach this goal:

—*I am requesting $3 million in Fiscal 1969 for college scholarship grants, to include for the first time living allowances for Indian students and their families to help capable young Indians meet the costs of higher education.*

—*I am asking the Secretary of Health, Education, and Welfare to make a special and sustained effort to assure that our regular scholarship and loan programs are available to Indian high school graduates.*

—*I am asking the Director of the Office of Economic Opportunity to establish a special Upward Bound program for Indian high school students.*

HEALTH AND MEDICAL CARE

The health level of the American Indian is the lowest of any major population group in the United States:

—The infant mortality rate among Indians is 34.5 per 1,000 births—12 points above the National average.

—The incidence of tuberculosis among Indians and Alaska natives is about five times the National average.

—More than half of the Indians obtain water from contaminated or potentially dangerous sources, and use waste disposal facilities that are grossly inadequate.

—Viral infections, pneumonia, and malnutrition—all of which contribute to chronic ill health and mental retardation—are common among Indian children.

We have made progress. Since 1963:

—The infant death rate has declined 21 percent.

—Deaths from tuberculosis are down 29 percent.

—The number of outpatient visits to clinics and health centers rose 16 percent.

But much more remains to be done.

I propose that the Congress increase health programs for Indians by about ten percent, to $112 million in Fiscal 1969, with special emphasis on child health programs.

But if we are to solve Indian health problems, the Indian people themselves must improve their public health and family health practices. This will require a new effort to involve Indian families in a crusade for better health.

Recent experience demonstrates that Indians have been successful in working side by side with health professionals:

—They have organized tribal health committees to review Indian health problems and design programs for solving them.

—They have launched new programs in sanitation, mental health, alcoholism, and accident control.

—A cooperative Indian-government project to provide safe water and disposal systems for 44,000 Indians and Alaska native families has proved successful. For every Federal dollar spent, Indian Americans have contributed another 40 cents in labor, materials and actual funds.

I am directing the Secretary of Health, Education, and Welfare to build a "community participation" component into every Federal health program for Indians which lends itself to this approach.

Essential to this effort will be a large, well-trained corps of community health aides drawn from the Indian population: nursing assistants, health record clerks, medical-social aides and nutrition workers. These community health aides can greatly assist professional health workers in bringing health services to Indian communities.

I recommend that the Congress appropriate funds to train and employ more than 600 new community Indian health aides in the Public Health Service.

These aides will serve nearly 200,000 Indians and Alaska natives in their home communities, teaching sound health practices to the Indian people in several critical fields: pre-natal health, child care, home sanitation and personal hygiene.

Our goal is first to narrow, then to close the wide breach between the health standards of Indians and other Americans. But before large investments in Federally-sponsored health services can pay lasting dividends, we must build a solid base of Indian community action for better health.

Jobs and Economic Development

The plight of the Indians gives grim testimony to the devastating effects of unemployment on the individual, the family, and the community:

—Nearly 40 percent of the labor force on Indian lands is chronically unemployed, compared with a national unemployment rate of 3.5 percent.

—Of the Indians who do work, a third are underemployed in temporary or seasonal jobs.

—Fifty percent of Indian families have cash incomes below $2,000 a year; 75 percent have incomes below $3,000.

With rare exception, Indian communities are so underdeveloped that there is little, if any, opportunity for significant social or economic progress.

Two percent of all the land in the United States is Indian land. Indian lands are about the size of all the New England States and a small slice of New York. But many of their resources—oil, gas, coal, uranium, timber, water—await development.

The economic ills of Indian areas can have a major impact upon neighboring regions as well. It is not only in the best interests of the Indians, but of the entire Nation, to expand Indian economic opportunity.

Jobs

Special employment programs have been established to help meet the needs of Indians. In 1967 alone, more than 10,000 men and women received training and other help to get jobs under the Indian Bureau's programs—double the number served four years ago. These programs:

—Provide all-expenses-paid training and placement for Indian adults.

—Develop projects in cooperation with private industry, in which families prepare together for the transition from welfare dependency to useful, productive work.

To meet the increasing demand, I propose that the Indian Vocational Training Program be expanded to the full authorization of $25 million in Fiscal 1969—nearly double the funds appropriated last year.

In the State of the Union message, I proposed a 25 percent increase—to $2.1 billion—in our manpower training programs for Fiscal 1969.

As a part of this effort, I have asked the Secretary of Labor to expand the Concentrated Employment Program to include Indian reservations.

Area Development

The economic development of potentially productive Indian areas suffers from a lack of base capital to permit Indians to take advantage of sound investment opportunities and to attract private capital.

The Indian Resources Development Act, now pending before Congress, contains provisions to spark this kind of investment.

The central feature of this Act is an authorization of $500 million for an Indian loan guaranty and insurance fund and for a direct loan revolving fund.

These funds would:

—Provide the foundation for the economic development of Indian lands.

—Encourage light industry to locate on or near Indian reservations.

—Permit better development of natural resources.

—Encourage development of the tourist potential on many reservations.

The Indian Resources Development Act would also permit the issuance of Federal corporate charters to Indian tribes or groups of Indians. This charter gives them the means to compete with other communities in attracting outside investment.

I urge the Congress to enact this program for the economic development of Indian resources.

Roads for Economic Development

Without an adequate system of roads to link Indian areas with the rest of our Na-

tion, community and economic development, Indian self-help programs, and even education cannot go forward as rapidly as they should.

Large areas inhabited by Indians are virtually inaccessible. For example, on the vast Navajo-Hopi area there are only 30 percent as many miles of surfaced roads per 1,000 square miles as in rural areas of Arizona and New Mexico.

The woefully inadequate road systems in Indian areas must be improved. Good roads are desperately needed for economic development. And good roads may someday enable the Indian people to keep their young children at home, instead of having to send them to far-away boarding schools.

I propose an amendment to the Federal Highway Act increasing the authorization for Indian road construction to $30 million annually beginning in Fiscal 1970.

Essential Community Services

Housing

Most Indian housing is far worse than the housing in many slums of our large cities.

To begin our attack on the backlog of substandard housing:

—I have asked the Secretary of Housing and Urban Development to increase Indian home construction by an additional 1,000 units this coming year, for a total of 2,500 annually.

—I propose that the Congress double the Fiscal 1968 appropriations—to $6 million in 1969—for a broad home improvement program.

These steps are a strong start toward improving living conditions among Indians, while we deal with the underlying causes of inadequate housing. But the present housing law is too rigid to meet the special needs

341

and conditions of our Indian population.

I am therefore submitting legislation to open the door for more Indians to receive low-cost housing aid, and to extend the loan programs of the Farmers Home Administration to tribal lands.

In addition:

—The Secretary of Housing and Urban Development will review construction standards for Indian homes to ensure flexibility in design and construction of Indian housing.

—The Secretaries of the Interior and Housing and Urban Development will explore new low-cost techniques of construction suitable to a stepped-up Indian housing program.

Community Action

Programs under the Economic Opportunity Act have improved morale in Indian communities. They have given tribes new opportunities to plan and carry out social and economic projects. Community action programs, particularly Head Start, deserve strong support.

I am asking the Congress to provide $22.7 million in Fiscal 1969 for these important efforts.

Water and Sewer Projects

Shorter life expectancy and higher infant mortality among Indians are caused in large part by unsanitary water supplies and contamination from unsafe waste disposal.

The Federal Government has authority to join with individual Indians to construct these facilities on Indian lands. The government contributes the capital. The Indian contributes the labor.

To step up this program, I recommend that the Congress increase appropriations for safe water and sanitary waste disposal facili-

ties by 30 percent—from $10 million in Fiscal 1968 to $13 million in Fiscal 1969.

CIVIL RIGHTS

A Bill of Rights for Indians

In 1934, Congress passed the Indian Reorganization Act, which laid the groundwork for democratic self-government on Indian reservations. This Act was the forerunner of the tribal constitutions—the charters of democratic practice among the Indians.

Yet few tribal constitutions include a bill of rights for individual Indians. The basic individual rights which most Americans enjoy in relation to their government—enshrined in the Bill of Rights of the Constitution of the United States—are not safeguarded for Indians in relation to their tribes.

A new Indian Rights Bill is pending in the Congress. It would protect the individual rights of Indians in such matters as freedom of speech and religion, unreasonable search and seizure, a speedy and fair trial, and the right to habeas corpus. The Senate passed an Indian Bill of Rights last year. *I urge the Congress to complete action on that Bill of Rights in the current session.*

In addition to providing new protection for members of tribes, this bill would remedy another matter of grave concern to the American Indian.

Fifteen years ago, the Congress gave to the States authority to extend their criminal and civil jurisdictions to include Indian reservations—where jurisdiction previously was in the hands of the Indians themselves.

Fairness and basic democratic principles require that Indians on the affected lands have a voice in deciding whether a State will assume legal jurisdiction on their land.

I urge the Congress to enact legislation that would provide for tribal consent before such extensions of jurisdiction take place.

OFF-RESERVATION INDIANS

Most of us think of Indians as living in their own communities—geographically, socially and psychologically remote from the main current of American life.

Until World War II, this was an accurate picture of most Indian people. Since that time, however, the number of Indians living in towns and urban centers has increased to 200,000.

Indians in the towns and cities of our country have urgent needs for education, health, welfare, and rehabilitation services, which are far greater than that of the general population.

These needs can be met through Federal, State and local programs. *I am asking the new Council on Indian Opportunity to study this problem and report to me promptly on actions to meet the needs of Indians in our cities and towns.*

ALASKAN NATIVE CLAIMS

The land rights of the native people of Alaska—the Aleuts, Eskimos and Indians—have never been fully or fairly defined.

Eighty-four years ago, Congress protected the Alaska natives in the use and occupancy of their lands. But then, and again when Alaska was given statehood, Congress reserved to itself the power of final decision on ultimate title.

It remains our unfinished task to state in law the terms and conditions of settlement, so that uncertainty can be ended for the native people of Alaska.

Legislation is now pending to resolve this issue. I recommend prompt action on legislation to:

—Give the native people of Alaska title to the lands they occupy and need to sustain their villages.

—Give them rights to use additional lands and water for hunting, trapping and fishing to maintain their traditional way of life, if they so choose.

—Award them compensation commensurate with the value of any lands taken from them.

THE FIRST AMERICANS

The program I propose seeks to promote Indian development by improving health and education, encouraging long-term economic growth, and strengthening community institutions.

Underlying this program is the assumption that the Federal government can best be a responsible partner in Indian progress by treating the Indian himself as a full citizen, responsible for the pace and direction of his development.

But there can be no question that the government and the people of the United States have a responsibility to the Indians.

In our efforts to meet that responsibility, we must pledge to respect fully the dignity and the uniqueness of the Indian citizen.

That means partnership—not paternalism.

We must affirm the right of the first Americans to remain Indians while exercising their rights as Americans.

We must affirm their right to freedom of choice and self-determination.

We must seek new ways to provide Federal assistance to Indians—with new emphasis on Indian self-help and with respect for Indian culture.

And we must assure the Indian people that it is our desire and intention that the special relationship between the Indian and

343

his government grow and flourish.

For, the first among us must not be last.

I urge the Congress to affirm this policy and to enact this program.

LYNDON B. JOHNSON

The White House
March 6, 1968

NOTE: For remarks of the President upon signing related legislation, see Items 195, 259.

On August 23, 1968, the President signed the Federal Aid Highway Act of 1968 amending the act of 1956 by authorizing appropriation of additional sums for Indian road construction (Public Law 90–495, 82 Stat. 815).

114 Remarks to the Members of the Joint Savings Bank-Savings and Loan Committee on Urban Problems. *March 6, 1968*

I WELCOME YOU here to the Cabinet Room today.

As leaders of America's great savings bank and savings and loan industries, you have provided the bulk of the capital that has built the homes, built the great suburbs and the residential areas which are the pride of the entire world.

America has served you well, and I understand that you are here this morning to serve the Nation by helping meet one of its most urgent problems—the rebuilding of the inner city.

To be effective will require commitment and ingenuity. The problems and needs are large indeed.

We have just ourselves completed—with the assistance of Secretary Weaver, Secretary Wood, Mr. Haar, and others in their Department, Mr. Brownstein and others—the cities message. We undertook everything that we could conceive of that we had the resources to undertake—and may have undertaken more than the Congress will really give us to undertake. But we dealt with it in some detail.

I think 20 years from now you will look at that message and see that we were not unaware of the problems.

I selected the most able city officials, private officials, chiefs of police, Governors, Congressmen, and Senators in the civil disorders study—they spent an unprecedented amount of money—millions of dollars in the period of several months—and I think made one of the most thorough and exhaustive studies ever made. It outlined not only what the situation was, but why it was, and what could be done about it.

Now, every Cabinet official and every independent agency is taking that study—and I recommend it to you—and they are evaluating and trying to see first, what we already have done that is pointed up—put that in this basket; see what we have not done and what they recommend to be done, what remains to be done—and put that in this basket. Then try to get it done.

There is no group in America that can try to do more to help us improve the cities and improve the quality of men's lives and offer them hope when they have only despair than you folks who have the financial horsepower to do something about it.

We need not only your words but your actions and we need your performance. You have shown that you can act or you would not be here. You have shown that you can perform or you would not have this program outlined.

The Government has been attacking the problems of the cities as best we can with our resources. I think you ought to know that right now we have, under the direction of Mr. Henry Ford and Mr. Paul Austin, president of the Coca Cola Company, a group that will number probably 750 by the end of this week. They are top executives, presidents and leaders of big corporations in America who are out to find jobs for hardcore unemployed in these cities.

That is a massive effort, the like of which has never been made before. To me, that shows a real awakening of the American business conscience in this country and the desire to do something about it.

I had lunch with the original group. I have met with some 50 others—and now we are spreading it to 150—the day before yesterday. Now it is moving to 750. That is the private group.

In housing, renewal, poverty, health, and education when I became President, the Federal budget had $9 billion for all the programs assisting the cities.

I want you to remember this, which is why I want to try to emphasize it. Don't expect this to be printed because they always print that we don't do enough. They don't print what we do. The Republicans say that we do too much.

But that effort has moved from $9 billion in these fields—this is the Federal budget, not a State or county or private or savings and loan budget—but the Federal budget has moved from $9 billion in 1964 to $22 billion in 1969.

Any of you who have more than doubled your appropriation in any field know what that means. How much more we can get the Congress to go, I don't know. But we have moved from $9 to $22 billion and one thing is definitely clear, that if you expect to go farther you have to acknowledge what you have done and recognize it as inadequate and try to do more. We do that. We have gone from $9 billion to $22 billion and we want to go just as much as the traffic will

bear—as much as the Congress and the budget can permit.

Now, we can only finance these things by two means: by taxing them and I have been trying to get a tax bill for a year and a half, or by borrowing it. I have been having difficulty with both.

We have been having difficulty getting the tax measure and difficulty borrowing with the interest rate going up. You know what is going on there because you pay interest on all your deposits.

So, we want to welcome you here as partners of ours in this great venture of trying to do something to rebuild our cities and find employment for our people and to help us with our Model Cities program, with our supplemental programs, our FHA programs and our expanded manpower and private industry programs and better jobs and better wages.

We also welcome your pledge to provide more counseling and advice to neighborhood groups and individuals. Many people in the ghetto whom you will reach wouldn't come in off the streets and talk about a loan. Many of them have never been in a bank. Many have been the victims of unjust financial arrangements themselves. So, you have to go out and talk to them. We hope that you can do that. We think that is worthy of your energy.

We have seen what frustration among people and what decay in the cities can do. We saw it in Newark. We saw it in Watts. We saw it in Detroit.

We want to do everything we can to avoid a recurrence of that. We cannot correct all the errors of centuries in 4 years or 40 years, but we can do our best and all that we are capable of doing.

I am trying to do that. Every Cabinet officer is trying to do it. I hope that most of the Members of the House and Senate will help us. I particularly welcome the savings and loan people and the business group and their cooperation.

I think when the history of the period is written they will say that labor has had a social consciousness and has tried to fight for better social conditions for the working people of this country.

I am proud to say that during the period that I have been President the businessmen have answered every call that I have made upon them.

If you had told me 4 years ago that you could expect the industrial giants of this country, the head of Coca Cola, the head of Ford, heads of the big insurance companies, and heads of the banking industry to be out here finding jobs for hard-core unemployed and developing plans for every city in the country I would have told you that it is going to be tough to get it done.

But they are doing it and you are doing it, too. We welcome you as a partner in this venture. I hope all of you will have a chance to read the cities message. I don't want to cram it down anyone's throat. I don't want to comment on it. It is there and anyone can see it. You don't have to be led up to it.

I hope all of you will have a chance to read the Civil Disorders Commission report. It is a very distinguished group and a lot of talent went into that report after hearing witness after witness.

Then you will see what our problems are and what the recommended remedies are.

I won't ask you to embrace every recommendation they make, but I hope you can help us all that you can in good conscience.

I would note one thing: It is easier to build than it is to destroy. If we don't get on with our building we are not going to prevent destruction that ought to be prevented.

Mr. Rayburn used to have a favorite saying in the House of Representatives when I was a Member. He said, "Any donkey can kick a barn down, but it takes a good carpenter to build one."

I want to appeal to you to be good carpenters. We have enough folks who can kick and find things wrong and be out of humor with their country and their Government. They will trample just anything.

But what we need is some cheerful people with optimism and a vision who want to help their fellow man and who will do it.

We have so much to be thankful for. We should not be feeling sorry for ourselves too much in this country. There is no other citizen of any other country who is as blessed as our citizens with the fruits of its products.

We ought to put a little bit of that back as seed corn and I know you will.

I thank you for coming.

[At this point Secretary Weaver and several members of the Committee addressed the group. The President then resumed speaking.]

We have had the insurance industry in with private meetings with the President and others in connection with the rent supplements and model cities and other legislation very important to the cities.

We have had the leaders of the labor groups in. We have had this very important group here today. In the months ahead I will be having a series of meetings asking them to study the cities message and the Civil Disorders Commission recommendations and any private suggestions that the insurance companies may make, the banking industry may make, or the savings and loan institutions may make—we want to explore them all. We want to try to get the Congress to go along with the recommendations we have made that you have just endorsed in connection with VA, FHA, Model Cities, and rent supplements, and so on.

346

We hope someday that we can look back on the meetings I have been having every day now where we are just talking, but we can see that this talk has resulted in some action.

You have a definite program that you are committed to here that will be a great breakthrough if we can carry it out together—and I think we can.

If there is any encouragement at all that comes to me it is the reawakening on the part of Americans to their social responsibilities.

We talked about the health care for people in their sixties for 20 years and did absolutely nothing about it but talk. But there are literally millions in hospitals at this moment because we finally took some action and did something about it.

We are talking about poverty now and every President has talked about it. But we got $1.77 billion up there last year and we have raised that this year to $2.2 billion, approximately.

We are doing something about it. It is not as much as we would like to do. If we had $200 billion we could not cover it all, but we are taking some of our resources at a very critical time and going into it. We have to do it here.

I think for the first time the American business community is realizing that there is a part that it needs to play and it is playing.

I sat in this room 2 years ago when people were talking about and criticizing the regulations that had been issued back in President Kennedy's administration on financing a house. I asked for open housing and I said: "How can I ask a man to come back from Vietnam—and he has the money he has saved and his wife has held together the family, and he wants to get a roof over his head, and how can I tell him no because he happens to be brown or black and he has

to go someplace else? We have to have the congressional commitment. Let's ask them for open housing."

People went wild. I didn't think there was anybody in the room for it. And there wasn't.

Within 2 years we have come where we passed it through the House and we actually got cloture. We didn't have a vote to spare, not a single one.

But if we go on with it now, there are going to be a lot of houses to be built for the people who will have new opportunities and you will be surprised how people are going to adjust to it. People will look back and say, "Did we oppose that? Did we oppose that man—the fellow who lost an arm or leg to protect us?" If a man can buy it and pay for it, they are willing to do it.

So, we are moving ahead, but nobody is moving ahead more than the American businessmen. I am proud of them. I am proud of you bankers.

You can't exist unless you can get your money back with a little profit to pay for your work. I don't expect you to be unsound. I expect you to be prudent because if you are not, why, we are all in trouble.

But I am glad that you have enough adventure left in you, enough patriotism left in you, and interest in your fellow man because after you are gone from here they are not going to remember much about your financial statement. Your neighbors are not going to say how much you had in real estate, how much you had in interest, stocks, and so on. They don't remember that about my daddy or granddaddy—there wasn't much to remember—they didn't have much.

It is what you are doing to help your fellow human beings that will be remembered.

You are doing a lot by saying that you are going to help undertake the problem in the cities.

Thank you very much.

NOTE: The President spoke at 11:35 a.m. in the Cabinet Room at the White House. During his remarks he referred to Robert C. Weaver, Secretary of Housing and Urban Development, Robert C. Wood, Under Secretary, Charles M. Haar, Assistant Secretary for Metropolitan Development, Philip N. Brownstein, Assistant Secretary for Mortgage Credit and Federal Housing Commissioner, Henry Ford II, Chairman of the National Alliance of Businessmen, Paul Austin, President of Coca Cola Company and Vice Chairman of the Alliance, and the late Sam Rayburn of Texas, former Speaker of the House of Representatives.

A White House announcement listing the members of the Joint Savings Bank-Savings and Loan Committee on Urban Problems is printed in the Weekly Compilation of Presidential Documents (vol. 4, p. 451).

As printed above, this item follows the text released by the White House Press Office.

115   Remarks at the Swearing In of Cyrus R. Smith as Secretary of Commerce.   *March 6, 1968*

Mr. Smith and family, Justice Fortas, Members of the Cabinet, distinguished Members of the Congress, ladies and gentlemen:

This ceremony could well be the opening scene in a replay of one of my favorite late show dramas, "Mr. Smith Goes to Washington."

As I recall, the hero of that movie caused quite a stir when he hit the Nation's Capital.

Now, Mr. C. R. Smith, you have come back to Washington again. We all recall pleasantly your last starring role—when you were stationed here during World War II. You were decorated then as an organizer of wartime air transport—and for solving the problem of flying The Hump.

The script, C. R., really hasn't changed very much. You will find—as Dean Rusk and I already know—that there are still plenty of humps to get over. Some of them are over here. But, since you were here the last time, we have added a few gaps.

We all know, though, that you are well equipped. And we hope that American Airlines has let you bring along one of your most valuable assets—that battered old Oliver typewriter that has long sat by your desk, a machine on which you hunt and peck out the personal directives that you need when you want fast action.

You are going to need that typewriter, C. R. Your new employers—the people of the United States—are going to be asking for action, and some of them want it fast. The businessman, the workingman, the family man—all of these are your new board of directors. Your new business is the most urgent business of America—Congress will be reminding you of that from time to time—and that is the people's welfare.

You might begin, Mr. Smith, by putting that typewriter to work on a letter to Mr. Henry Ford and your friend, Mr. Paul Austin of Coca Cola Company, and the other 750 national leaders—the many members of the National Alliance of Businessmen. You can thank them for rolling up their sleeves, leaving their business—as you have left yours—and taking on leadership responsibilities in helping us to tackle one of the toughest problems that America faces—the crisis in our cities, the unemployment in our ghettos, the hard core who have no jobs, the training and hiring of these people whom we find that our system has been unable to fit into it.

These men are some of our best American businessmen, and they care about tomorrow. They are taking the very unusual step, I think, of investing their skill and their faith to earn the ultimate profit—not something that will show on their balance sheets this year, but will be a rich and full dividend for all of American life.

If you would move America forward, I think you must first move its private citizens forward—and chief among them is the American businessman.

Never—except possibly during World War II—have I seen such an effective exercise of business responsibility as I see in the making now. The promise for America is immense.

Mr. Ford, Mr. Austin, and others came across the land to see me last week and told me of their plans, and of the fact that various companies are assigning their best people to go out into the ghettos and the cities of America and demonstrate the social consciousness of the leaders of the free enterprise system.

In these last few months, these giant corporations, banks, insurance companies, hundreds of businesses—the economic muscle of America—are indicating that they are going to try to help.

I met with the bankers a few weeks ago; I met with the insurance industry a few weeks ago. I met with the savings and loan institutions from throughout the country this morning. All of them are developing programs to help us try to remake and re-build these deteriorated areas of our land.

This remaking is going to demand the best of all of us—and the best of business and Government. I think you are going to be the connecting link in that partnership.

It is a historic venture. The American people will be the beneficiaries. So, they are going to look to you, C. R.—as a leader who pioneered again in the adventure of flight.

I think most of America—I know the Cabinet, certainly, the leaders in Congress who honor you with their presence here this morning—share my confidence that you are going to lead us forward in the greater adventure of reaching for the dream and finding the destiny of America.

We welcome you. We hope your stay here will be pleasant. Happy landing.

[At this point Justice Fortas administered the oath to Mr. Smith, who responded with brief remarks. The President then resumed speaking.]

I want to say on behalf of the Cabinet, and such Members of Congress as I may be able to speak for, that we join you, C. R., in your hope and your wish that we, too, can end even, at least.

NOTE: The President spoke at 1:13 p.m. in the East Room at the White House. In his opening words he also referred to Associate Justice Abe Fortas of the U.S. Supreme Court, who administered the oath of office. During his remarks he referred to Dean Rusk, Secretary of State, Henry Ford II, Chairman of the National Alliance of Businessmen, and Paul Austin, Vice Chairman.

116 Statement by the President Upon Designating Ambassador Robert M. McKinney To Head the President's Foreign Visitor Program. *March 6, 1968*

I HAVE asked Ambassador Robert M. McKinney to coordinate the efforts of private industry and Government necessary to implement the recommendations of the commission on travel. He will be in charge of the President's foreign visitor program.

I have asked Ambassador McKinney to report to me on the results of his efforts by

May 31, 1968. I have also asked him to consider and recommend long term measures which will ensure for the future the continued and increased forward momentum of the program.

The commission's recommendations aim to improve our international travel account by positive expansionary measures. They are designed to make the United States the world's preeminent tourist bargain.

Several steps have already been taken by the travel industry and the Government:

—On February 23, 1968, I asked the Congress to liberalize our visa regulations making it easier for bona fide foreign tourists to visit the United States.

—Members of the American travel and hotel industry are offering attractive discounts to foreign tourists, and they are significantly increasing their promotional activities abroad.

—The Civil Aeronautics Board has sanctioned proposals to grant discounts to foreign tourists on domestic airlines; similar proposals are pending before other U.S. regulatory agencies.

—The members of the International Air Transport Association are considering a proposal to reduce fares for tourists flying to the United States.

I have asked Ambassador McKinney to work closely with the interested agencies of Government and the appropriate congressional committees to speed passage of the visa bill and to coordinate early implementation of other measures designed to facilitate the entry of foreign tourists.

We will shortly be issuing the first tourist hospitality card. These cards will identify the foreign tourists as eligible for discounts from participating firms and government-operated facilities. I urge American travel, hotel, motel, restaurant, and other tourist related firms which have not yet joined in this program, to consider its advantages to them and to their country.

I have asked Ambassador McKinney to keep in close touch with industry to ensure that all interested American businessmen are aware of the discount program and its benefits, to answer their questions regarding the program, and to consider their suggestions for its improvement.

Many State and local governments are already actively encouraging foreign travel. We had an opportunity to discuss these efforts with the Governors only last week. Ambassador McKinney will work with Governor Price Daniel, Director of the Office of Emergency Planning, in asking State and local governments to intensify their efforts to attract foreign travelers.

All departments and agencies of the Federal Government are expected to cooperate fully with Ambassador McKinney in implementing the President's foreign visitor program.

America's greatest tourist attraction is its people. We Americans have always prided ourselves on our hospitality. I ask all Americans, individually and through our fine community organizations, to make a special effort to make foreign visitors truly welcome in the finest tradition of American hospitality.

NOTE: The Industry-Government Special Task Force on Travel submitted a report to the President on February 19, 1968 (see Item 83).

117   Remarks at the Eastern Regional Meeting of the National
      Council on Aging.   *March 6, 1968*

*Mr. Meyer, Mr. Shelley, Mrs. Mathiasen,
Mr. Secretary, Mr. Commissioner, my good
friends:*

Something very remarkable happened all
over America this last weekend that you
have had a lot to do with. Before you left for
home and your meeting broke up, I had
hoped that I could get under the wire and
get some of the engagements of the White
House behind me and come over to talk to
you about what happened—and express my
appreciation to you, and through you, to the
other good people in this country who helped
us.

On every street in this Nation—on Main
Street, on Elm Street, on Fifth Avenue—the
day-to-day life of tens of millions of Americans was changing because it was on Saturday that 24 million social security checks
went into the mail boxes. The dollar amount
of those checks was on an average of 16
percent higher than it had been just 1 month
before.

You know, and I know, that that was the
greatest single increase in the entire history
of social security in America since our great
President first brought it to the American
people, Franklin Delano Roosevelt.

In a single stroke, more than 1 million
Americans were lifted above the poverty
line. Of course, the great majority of the
people who benefited were elderly people.
A retired couple receiving maximum benefits now gets $234 each month instead of
the former amount, $207—$234, up from
$207.

A typical couple on benefits now gets $169
a month, up from $139—$139 to $169.

Now, all the 200 million people do not
know that. They should know it—but all
the people don't know how some of the peo-

ple actually live. That is one of the big
problems that we have in this country. But
these 24 million know it—and those are the
numbers.

Now, what those numbers mean in terms
of day-to-day experience for millions of
Americans is heartening. Our studies show
that much of the dollar increase, actually all
of it, goes for necessities—for food, shelter,
and clothing.

But the studies also show that the money
is used for the amenities of life—for the
things that make the difference between living and just existing.

—Enough money, for example, so that
occasionally a grandparent can travel to
see his grandchild.
—Enough money to buy a gift for a grandchild instead of going there without any
little present at all.
—Enough money for a man and his wife
to take an adult education course, or to
plant a new flowerbed, or to improve
a new driveway, or to put some flowers
in the backyard instead of the front
yard.

In all, in the last 2½ years, social security
insurance benefits have gone up in this
country by 35 percent. The aged have more
than a third more to live on today than they
did in 1965. Now, these are the men and
women who, in their working years, made
this country. They made it what it is. They
made it great. They made it prosperous.
They made it the envy of all the world.

You wouldn't think it should be when you
read about what terrible shape we are in
according to some people today. But there
are not many anywhere who would not
want to trade with us.

No one is more deserving of a share of

that praise than these people. The Bible tells us, "Honor thy father and thy mother."

That is the goal of our activity for the aged in this administration.

An elderly parent has the right to dignity and independence. He has earned that right.

We live in a society that we think is prosperous enough so that no old person must feel that he is a burden on a son or a daughter—to say nothing of a son-in-law.

We have been working toward that, and I believe we are succeeding.

In 1960, the Federal Government spent $13 billion for all of its programs for all of its pensions for the aged. By 1963, when I came into office, that amount had moved from $13 billion to $17 billion.

This year's budget asks for not $17 billion, but $33 billion—almost twice as much as in 1963. Now, that is not because of the Vietnam war; that is in spite of the Vietnam war.

The social security increases that went into effect on Saturday were substantial. But I came across the river today for this 5-minute appearance to tell you that they are not substantial enough in my judgment.

I recommended to the Congress. I pleaded with the Congress. I urged the Congress to pass a 20 percent increase with a $70—$70 minimum for individuals.

We didn't get a 20 percent increase. We got only a 16 percent increase. We didn't get a $70 minimum. We got a $55 minimum. And I got a little heck en route.

Well, I don't think $55 and 16 percent is enough. It is not enough. It is not enough for the people to live on. I thought so last year and I think so this year.

If all goes well we are going to get that additional increase or keep on fighting for it.

There is a reason for all of us to be here. Some of us have different views. Some of us look at things differently. Some of us are tall and some of us are short. Some are slender and some are fat. It takes all kinds of people to make up a world. But the best justification for any of us being here is what we are ready and willing to do and what we are able to do to better humankind.

People with financial statements are not long remembered because of that statement. There are a few who have perpetuated their memory, but they are not remembered very long. But what you do for your fellow man is never forgotten.

So, in the limited time allotted each of you here in the richest nation in all the world, there is nothing that can occupy that time to a better advantage than to try to bring peace in the world and peace and good will at home.

The best way to have peace in the world and peace and good will at home is to make it possible for every human being to have at least the bare necessities of life:

—a roof over their head,

—clothes to cover their body,

—food to sustain themselves,

—a modicum of recreation now and then.

The American people don't ask much—school for their children and a place to worship God according to the dictates of their own conscience.

But Franklin Roosevelt said in his time, "One-third of our people are ill-clad, ill-housed, and ill-fed."

We have moved things along considerably since that time. But we still have people who are ill-clad, ill-fed, and ill-housed. And we should not be satisfied with ourselves for one minute until poverty is banished from this land, until our ill-clad are clothed, until our ill-fed are fed, and until our ill-housed have a roof over their head.

Now that is what good people like you work for. You work for it in the group that needs it the most.

est priority.

For Fiscal 1969, I propose a program to complete this vital agenda for action.

First, I recommend that we assure the people that their water supplies will be pure and plentiful now and in the years ahead by:

—Prosecuting the war on water pollution with conviction, combining Federal, State and local efforts to finance the construction this year of $1.5 to $2 billion in community waste treatment plants.

—Creating a National Water Commission to plot the course of water resource management for the next century.

—Helping to assure the quality of community water supplies through the Safe Drinking Water Act of 1968.

—Meeting the water needs of one of America's fastest growing regions by authorizing the Central Arizona Project.

Second, I recommend that we guard the landscape against the waste products of modern life by:

—Protecting rivers, beaches and coastal areas against the devastation of oil spillage and other hazardous substances through strong legislation to control them.

—Preventing the future despoilment of thousands of acres of mining land through the Surface Mining Reclamation Act of 1968.

—Discovering efficient methods to dispose of the millions of tons of refuse and trash that threaten to engulf city and countryside, through an extension of the Solid Waste Disposal Act, and to accelerate the development of economical systems which will convert waste into useful by-products.

—Transforming our highways into corridors of beauty through prompt action to continue the Highway Beautification Program, and building new roadside parks for the traveling family.

Third, I recommend that we advance in the battle for clean air over America's cities by:

—Fully exploiting our vast technology to find new and effective pollution abatement methods.

—Investing $128 million as the Federal share in pollution control and research, more than has ever been committed in a single year before.

—Organizing for action, through the designation of Air Quality Control Regions under the landmark Air Quality Act of 1967.

Fourth, I recommend that we bring a sense of fulfillment, outdoor recreation and serenity to all Americans by:

—Bringing new national parks closer to the people who live crowded city lives by development of the redwood groves of California, the Northern Cascades of Washington and the historic Potomac River.

—Adding thousands of new acres of unspoiled and primitive lands to the wilderness system.

—Completing action on the nationwide networks of scenic rivers and trails.

—Focusing now on the problem of noise and its impact on our daily lives.

Fifth, I recommend that we explore the peaceful promise of the ocean's depths by:

—Beginning to plan now with other nations to launch an International Decade of Ocean Exploration.

—Putting our most advanced marine technology to work in the development of improved buoys for better prediction of weather and ocean conditions.

WATER POLLUTION CONTROL

America's rivers, lakes and coastal waters have nourished her growth: irrigated the farms, powered the dynamos, and provided transport for commerce.

But we have not used our waters well.

Our major rivers are defiled by noxious debris. Pollutants from cities and industries kill the fish in our streams. Many waterways are covered with oil slicks and contain growths of algae that destroy productive life and make the water unfit for recreation. "Polluted Water—No Swimming" has become a familiar sign on too many beaches and rivers. A lake that has served many generations of men now can be destroyed by man in less than one generation.

Only recently have we begun to reverse this trend—to undertake a program to preserve waters that are still clean, and purify those that have become infested with pollution.

The conditions have worsened through decades of neglect and indifference. They affect entire industries. They involve thousands of miles of waterways and thousands of communities that border them.

We have discovered not only that the problems of pollution are formidable, but that their solutions must be interlocking.

—Water quality standards must be set for entire bodies of water, varying from place to place depending on the water's use.

—Standards must be enforceable and they must apply to both municipalities and industries.

—Waste treatment plants must be constructed and other methods developed to prevent pollutants from reaching the water.

—New methods of cooperation and enforcement must be established at all levels, for waters bearing poisons do not stop at city, county or State boundaries. Clearing one part of a stream is no answer. Water bodies must be cleaned in their entirety.

America took strong action to combat the problem in 1965 with the Water Quality Act, and took another major step a year later with the Clean Water Restoration Act. Under those measures, the long and difficult task of cleaning the waters of our land has begun.

Water Quality Standards

Now, for the first time in our history, all the States have taken inventory of their water resources, considered their future needs, and developed quality standards.

As the law requires, these standards, and the plans to carry them out, have been submitted to the Secretary of the Interior for approval.

Many of the plans have already been approved. This is welcome news for communities and businessmen alike. Now they can take action because they know the standards they must all meet.

I have asked the Secretary of the Interior to speed the review of the remaining standards and plans so the Federal Government can more effectively help the States and communities turn their blueprints into action.

The Construction of Treatment Plants

The heart of a water pollution control program is the community waste treatment plant which prevents refuse, debris and filth from reaching the waters. To meet the Nation's critical needs calls for both the construction of new plants and the improvement of existing facilities.

Through the Clean Water Restoration Act, the Federal Government can provide financial help—from 30 to 55 percent of the cost—for the construction of municipal waste treatment works. Already, under that Act and earlier authority, 8,000 grants, totalling more than $1 billion, have been made. They have helped local communities build more than $4.5 billion worth of plants, to control the pollution in 67,000 miles of water on which almost 66 million Americans depend.

More is required, however. The problem is pressing and the backlog of needed plants is great.

With accelerated Federal help, we can stimulate the construction of $1.5 billion to $2 billion in waste treatment plants under the $700 million authorization approved by the Congress for Fiscal 1969.

This will be done in two ways.

First, I recommend an appropriation of $225 million for grants under the Clean Water Restoration Act. This should generate about $500 to $600 million of plant construction.

Second, I recommend legislation to allow the Secretary of the Interior to make annual installment payments in addition to the lump sum grants as is presently the practice. This would permit the Federal Government to make construction commitments up to a total of $475 million in Fiscal 1969.

Under this new financing method, the $475 million would generate a total of about $1 to $1.4 billion of construction. Communities would be able to build many of their urgently-needed plants without delay and get them into the fight against pollution now.

User Charges

Capital and operating costs of treatment plants are expensive, and it is right that those costs be borne by those who receive the plant's benefits. Accordingly, the new financing program will require, as one criterion

for assistance, that municipalities impose a system of user charges on those who use the plants.

A system of user charges would not only provide an equitable way of sharing costs, but would accomplish other desirable purposes, as well. Such charges would:

—Provide an incentive for industries to curb pollution through improved manufacturing techniques.

—Relieve the pressure on the overloaded tax bases of local governments.

SAFE COMMUNITY WATER SUPPLIES

As America's cities grew and developed their own water supply systems, cholera and typhoid posed a grim threat to health and safety.

That threat was countered long ago.

Now, we in America drink tap water without a thought as to its safety. And yet— that water is not always as safe as it should be.

We do not have enough information on the long-term health effects of substances in drinking water.

New hazards—chemical and industrial wastes, and other materials—are creating new problems.

The Nation's Public Health Service cannot respond fully to this danger. Its authority is limited by a law passed almost half a century ago.

A recent study has indicated that about 30 percent of the Nation's public drinking water systems may fall below Federal standards.

To help the cities and communities of America assure citizens that the water they drink is safe, I propose the Safe Drinking Water Act of 1968.

This measure will strengthen the authority of the Secretary of Health, Education, and

359

Welfare to:

—Develop, adopt and enforce improved standards relating to chemical contaminants in drinking water.

—Conduct a comprehensive study of the safety of public drinking water supplies in the United States.

—Determine whether any additional steps are necessary in this area.

The new law will help move us toward this goal: That every glass of drinking water drawn from America's public water supply systems will meet proper health standards.

WATER MANAGEMENT AND PLANNING

National Water Commission

We will not have served the water needs of Americans if we meet only the requirements of today's population. A prudent nation must look ahead and plan for tomorrow.

First, we must continue our sound programs of water management, research, and advance planning to solve supply problems and to prepare for the future needs of farms and factories, and growing city populations.

Second, we must establish a board to develop long-range policy for water resources.

Last year I asked the Congress to establish a National Water Commission to:

—Work with Federal, State and private agencies in a survey of our long-term water needs.

—Explore the effect of water development projects on regional growth.

—Identify alternative policies and programs to meet national and regional water resource objectives.

Both the Senate and the House of Representatives have passed legislation to establish this Commission. The measure is now in conference.

I urge the Congress to complete its action

and authorize this much-needed Commission.[1]

Central Arizona Project

A vast area of the Western United States is arid. Thousands of acres are in danger of becoming a barren wasteland as underground sources of water are used up or depleted.

We have the techniques and know-how to overcome this problem.

Now legislation is required to authorize a program to bring water from the Colorado River to meet the urgent needs of the people of Arizona.

Proposals affecting the canyons and the gorges of this mighty and historic river have been the subject of searching national debate. Out of this discussion, a plan has evolved that will require no dams on the Colorado River, preserve its scenic values, and at the same time permit the immediate construction of essential water supply facilities.

I ask the Congress to authorize the Central Arizona Project this year.

OIL POLLUTION ABATEMENT

Last year, when the *Torrey Canyon* sank off the coast of Cornwall, the 30 million gallons of oil it was carrrying spread destruction throughout the coastal waters, killing fish and birds, and then the refuse of this devastation swept onto the beaches.

Only this week, at home, tragedy struck again. The tanker *Ocean Eagle* broke in half at the mouth of San Juan Bay, spewing some 1½ million gallons of oil over some of

---

[1] The Commission was established on September 26, 1968, by the National Water Commission Act (Public Law 90–515, 82 Stat. 868). The membership of the Commission was announced on October 9, 1968 (4 Weekly Comp. Pres. Docs., p. 1465).

the finest beaches in the Western Hemisphere.

Major disasters rarely occur. But minor oil spills are frequent—and their combined effect, although less dramatic, can also be harmful.

Last year, I asked the Secretary of the Interior and the Secretary of Transportation to study the problem of oil pollution in American waters. Their report warns us that we must protect the beaches, places of recreation, coastal and inland waters, and our fisheries from spillage not only of oil, but of other hazardous substances as well.

We need a comprehensive system to control oil pollution and to provide for prompt clean-up.

We also must be able to cope with the spillage of large quantities of such susbtances as chlorine.

Last year the Senate passed S. 2760 to deal with the problem of oil pollution.

I propose we build upon and strengthen that bill through the Oil Pollution and Hazardous Substances Control Act of 1968.

This act, together with the earlier Senate legislation, would:

—As a general rule, make the discharge of oil unlawful if it occurs from a shore facility or a ship operating within 12 miles from shore. The 3-mile territorial and 9-mile contiguous zones are thus both covered. This greatly expands the previous standard of liability, which was limited to "gross or willful negligence" and to the 3-mile limit.

—Impose upon the oil pollutor responsibility for cleaning the beaches and waters.

—Empower the Federal Government to clean up oil spills whenever the owner or operator fails to act, but require the pollutor to reimburse the Government for the clean-up costs. Prior law limited

the owner's liability to the salvage value of the ship. The proposal will make them liable for the full costs of clean-up.

—Authorize the Government to establish regulations for shipboard and related marine operations to reduce the possibility of oil leakage at the source.

—Provide protection against large and dangerous discharges of pollutants other than oil by requiring those responsible to take whatever clean-up or other action the Government considers necessary. If the pollutor fails to act, the Government will take the necessary steps, and hold the pollutor liable for the costs.

AIR POLLUTION

"Metals corrode, fabrics weaken and fade, leather weakens and becomes brittle, rubber cracks and loses its elasticity, paint discolors, concrete and building stone discolor and erode, glass is etched and paper becomes brittle."

This is not a description of the effects of a new weapon.

It is a sobering report on the results of pollution in the air we breathe.

And that air is not divisible into convenient shares. Polluted air affects the lungs of all—rich and poor, manager and worker, farmer and urban dweller.

Of all the problems of conservation, none is more urgent than the polluted air which endangers the American people. We have been fortunate so far. But we have seen that when winds fail to blow, the concentrations of poisonous clouds over our cities can become perilous.

Air pollution is a threat to health, especially of older persons. It contributes significantly to the rising rates of chronic respiratory ailments.

It stains our cities and towns with ugliness, soiling and corroding whatever it touches. Its damage extends to our forests and farm-lands as well.

The economic toll for our neglect amounts to billions of dollars each year.

The Clean Air Act of 1963 gave the Federal Government authority to help States and local communities plan effective programs to combat pollution.

In 1965, at my request, the Congress strengthened that Act by empowering the Secretary of Health, Education, and Welfare to set standards controlling automobile exhaust pollution—a major and mobile source of air contaminants.

Last year we took a giant step with the Air Quality Act of 1967. That Act:

—Will help our States abate pollution in the only practical way—on a regional basis. For air knows no man-made boundary.

—Gives the Government standby power to impose Federal standards or enforce State standards, if the States do not act.

—Gives the Secretary of Health, Education, and Welfare new power to stop serious cases of pollution that present a clear hazard to the public's health.

—Through accelerated research and testing, will help provide the technological answers to this baffling problem: How can we most economically and effectively prevent pollution at its source—in the fuels, while those fuels are being burned, or before the fumes reach the air?

To carry out our efforts to fight air pollution, I am seeking some $128 million for Fiscal 1969—more than we have committed in any past year.

I have directed the Secretary of Health, Education, and Welfare to designate the Nation's principal Air Quality Control Regions within the next few months, and to publish Air Quality criteria and related information on control techniques. This information will give States, local governments and industry the cost and control data they need to carry out their responsibilities.

One day we will have clean air over America—but only if all-levels of Government and industry work closely and conscientiously. The legislation now on the books provides the framework for a partnership without precedent, matching the dimension of the need. The problem deeply affects us all, and all of us share the responsibility for solving it.

I am confident that those responsibilities will be carried out—and that we can return to the American people a fundamental right of their national heritage: the right to breathe clean air.

Assistance in Hardship Cases

We have looked carefully into the question whether water and air pollution control will have a serious economic impact on American industry.

According to recent studies, the cost should be small for most firms.

In some cases, however, pollution control costs may present undue financial hardships to both a business and a community. *I have asked the Secretary of Commerce and the Administrator of the Small Business Administration to give priority attention to providing assistance in these hardship situations.*

Air and Water Pollution From Federal Installations

In the field of pollution, it is not enough for an enlightened Federal government to stimulate the work of the States, localities and private industry. It must also set a good example for the Nation.

Across America, federal installations are adopting the latest air and water pollution control methods. During the coming year, that effort will be intensified.

We expect to devote $53 million to the task, for thirteen separate federal agencies and 360 air and water pollution abatement projects.

NOISE CONTROL

What was once lyrically described as "the busy hum of traffic" has now turned into an unbearable din for many city dwellers.

The crescendo of noise—whether it comes from truck or jackhammer, siren or airplane—is more than an irritating nuisance. It intrudes on privacy, shatters serenity and can inflict pain.

We dare not be complacent about this ever-mounting volume of noise. In the years ahead, it can bring even more discomfort— and worse—to the lives of people.

I am directing all departments of Government to take account of noise factors in choosing the location and design of buildings, highways and other facilities whose construction is assisted by Federal funds.

I also urge the Congress to take prompt action on legislation to strengthen the authority of the Secretary of Transportation to deal with aircraft noise. We need greater capacity to deal with the rapidly growing noise problem created by our expanding air transportation system.

SURFACE MINING

An air traveler over some of the richest country in America can look down upon deep scars gouging the earth, acres of ravaged soil stretching out on either side.

Advances in mining technology have al-

lowed us to extract the earth's minerals economically and swiftly.

But too often these new techniques have been used unwisely and stripping machines have torn coal and other minerals from the surface of the land, leaving 2 million acres of this Nation sterile and destroyed. The unsightly scars of strip mining blight the beauty of entire areas, and erosion of the damaged land pours silt and acid into our streams.

Under present practices, only one-third of the land being mined is also being reclaimed. This start has been made by responsible individuals, by mining companies, and by the States that have already enacted laws to regulate surface mining.

America needs a nationwide system to assure that all lands disturbed by surface mining in the future will be reclaimed. This can best be achieved through cooperative efforts between the States and the Federal Government.

I propose the Surface Mining Reclamation Act of 1968. Under this Act:

—Criteria will be established which the States will use in developing their own regulatory plans.

—The States, assisted by Federal grants, will develop their own plans within two years and submit them to the Secretary of the Interior for review and approval.

—The Secretary will impose Federal standards if the State plans are inadequate or if they are not submitted.

Surface mining also occurs on Federal lands. To enable Government to take the lead in this important conservation effort, I have directed that:

—Federal Agencies assure that their regulations require the reclamation of Federal lands leased for surface mining.

—From now on, Federal contracts for the purchase of coal and other surface-mined minerals contain effective reclamation clauses.

SOLID WASTE DISPOSAL

In 1965, I recommended and the Congress approved a national planning, research and development program to find ways to dispose of the annual discard of solid wastes—millions of tons of garbage and rubbish, old automobile hulks, abandoned refrigerators, slaughterhouse refuse. This waste—enough to fill the Panama Canal four times over—mars the landscapes in cities, suburbia and countryside alike. It breeds disease-carrying insects and rodents, and much of it finds its way into the air and water.

The problem is not only to learn how to get rid of these substances—but also how to convert waste economically into useful materials. Millions of dollars of useful by-products may go up in smoke, or be buried under the earth.

Already scientists working under the 1965 Act have learned much about how soils absorb and assimilate wastes. States and local communities have drawn up their plans for solid waste disposal.

That Act expires in June, 1969.

To continue our efforts, I recommend a one-year extension of the Solid Waste Disposal Act.

In addition, *I am directing the Director of the Office of Science and Technology working with the appropriate Cabinet officers to undertake a comprehensive review of current solid waste disposal technology.* We want to find the solutions to two key problems:

—How to bring down the present high costs of solid waste disposal.

—How to improve and strengthen government-wide research and development in this field.

AGRICULTURAL WASTES

The new agricultural and land management techniques that increase the productivity of our farms have also brought new problems:

—Soil and other substances polluting our streams are the result of the erosion of farmlands and other areas. This cause of pollution has never been fully controlled and rapidly expanding suburban development has aggravated it.

—Added amounts of animal wastes are generated from the efficient concentration of cattle, hogs and sheep in feed lots.

We must not permit harmful effects on fish, other wildlife and on drinking water supplies of chemicals from fertilizer and pesticides—whatever their source.

Many of these problems can be dealt with through existing programs. But some will require new research and new approaches.

I am instructing the Secretary of Agriculture to conduct a government-wide review of these problems.

THE SPLENDOR OF A CONTINENT

Before anything else, Americans had the splendor of a continent. Behind the facade of our cities, beyond the concrete ribbons that connect them, much of that splendor remains.

It is there because men of vision and foresight—men like Gifford Pinchot, Theodore Roosevelt and Franklin Roosevelt—determined that the people's oldest legacy, the inheritance of a spacious land, must be preserved.

It is for each generation to carry on that work.

In our time, the task has become more difficult—but ever more urgent. Our numbers grow, our cities become more crowded, the pace of our lives quickens—but man's need to raise his spirits and expand his vision still endures.

A clear stream, a long horizon, a forest wilderness and open sky—these are man's most ancient possessions. In a modern society, they are his most priceless.

National Parks and Recreation Areas

In the past several years, we have authorized the addition of more than 2.2 million acres to the Nation's Park System.

We are actually preserving more lands— over 1.7 million acres in 1967—for conservation and the recreational enjoyment of America's families than the bulldozer and power shovel are taking over.

A park, however splendid, has little appeal to a family that cannot reach it.

The magnificent areas preserved in the early days of conservation were remote from the cities—and many Americans had to travel half a continent to visit them.

The new conservation is built on a new promise—to bring parks closer to the people. The man who works hard all week—the laborer, the shopkeeper, the subway rider— deserves a chance to escape the city's crush and congestion. He should have the opportunity to give his children a weekend of recreation and beauty and fresh air.

To provide this chance is the purpose of our program.

In the last several years, 32 of the 35 areas set aside by the new conservation—seashores, lakeshores, and parks—were located near large urban centers—North, West, East, and South. They are within easy driving distance of 120 million of our people. For example:

—The resident of New York City can within an hour or so reach the beaches and waters of the Fire Island National Seashore, established in 1965.

—A family living in the Washington, D.C. area has—since 1965—been able to enjoy the advantages and scenic wonders of Assateague Island National Seashore, only three hours away by car.

—Citizens of Chicago will soon be able to visit the conveniently located Indiana Dunes National Lakeshore, whose development began last year.

—A father in Kentucky can take his son hunting and camping in the new "Land Between the Lakes" recreation area, which will serve millions of Americans in the Southeast.

—Boy Scout troops in the Southwest can explore and hike through the Guadalupe National Park in Texas.

—People in North Carolina will have easy access to the Cape Lookout National Seashore, now underway.

In 1967, almost 140 million visits were made to National Park areas. These visits are increasing steadily—a tribute to the quality and importance of our parks. It is also a signal that more parks are needed.

Paramount among our last-chance conservation opportunities is the creation of a Redwood National Park in Northern California to preserve the tallest, most ancient sentinels of nature on the American continent. A park in this region would benefit millions of Americans living on the West Coast who could reach the park within an afternoon's drive.

I urge the House to seize this opportunity and complete action on a Redwood bill this year.

I also recommend that the House complete action on two other major additions to the Park System that we sought and the Senate approved last year:

—*North Cascades National Park* in Washington State, the American Alps, an unsurpassed spectacle of mountain beauty in the great Northwest.

—*Apostle Islands National Lakeshore,* along Wisconsin's most scenic water areas.

We can achieve a new concept in conservation—greater than a park, more than the preservation of a river—by beginning this year to make the Potomac a living part of our national life.

That great river, coursing through Maryland, Virginia and West Virginia, cradles much of our early history. Five million people live within 50 miles of its shores, and its legend beckons millions more from every part of the Nation. For the Potomac is truly the American River.

I urge the Congress to authorize the development of a uniquely historic area—the Potomac National River. Failure to act now will make us the shame of generations to come.

Scenic Trails, Rivers and Wilderness Areas

The urgent work of conservation leads us into three other areas.

A citizen should be able to leave his car behind and explore a scenic trail on foot, by bicycle or horse. He can do that if we establish a nationwide network of scenic trails, many near our large cities and through historic areas. *Once again, I urge the Congress—as I did last year—to authorize a network of scenic trails.*

"The time has come," I said in 1965, "to identify and preserve free-flowing stretches of our great scenic rivers before growth and development make the beauty of the unspoiled waterway a memory."

Let this be the session of Congress that grasps the opportunity.

Last year the Senate passed a bill to save seven wild rivers and five scenic rivers. *I urge the Congress to complete action this year on legislation which would establish a scenic rivers system.*

One of the greatest delights for an American is to visit a primitive area of his land in its natural splendor.

In 1964, the Congress passed the Wilderness Act—a milestone in conservation policy. It permits the Government to set aside, at little cost to the taxpayer, some of the truly unspoiled areas of our continent.

Last year I asked the Congress to add the first four wilderness areas to the system: San Rafael in California, Mount Jefferson in Oregon, San Gabriel in California, and Washakie in Wyoming.

I urge the Congress to complete action on these wilderness areas.

I am today recommending the addition of seven new areas to the wilderness system, embracing more than 400,000 acres of mountain and forest and lake. These new wilderness areas are:

—Mt. Baldy in Arizona's Apache National Forest.

—The Desolation Wilderness in California's Eldorado National Forest.

—The Flat Tops, in Colorado's Routt and White River National Forests.

—Pine Mountain in Arizona's Prescott and Tonto National Forests.

—The Spanish Peaks, in Montana's Gallatin National Forest.

—The Ventana Wilderness in California's Los Padres National Forest.

—Sycamore Canyon in Arizona's Coconino, Kaibab, and Prescott National Forests.

We are now surveying unspoiled and

primitive areas in Arkansas, Oklahoma, Georgia, and Florida as further possible additions to the Wilderness system.

The Land and Water Conservation Fund

The machinery to finance the acquisition of Federal recreation lands and to help the States plan, acquire and develop their own parks and forests is provided by the Land and Water Conservation Fund.

That Fund draws upon revenues from motorboat fuel taxes, Federal recreation area admission charges, and proceeds from the sale of surplus Federal lands.

For Fiscal 1969, I recommended new obligational authority of $130 million for the Land and Water Conservation Fund—an increase of $11 million over 1968.

But this alone may not be enough. The need for more recreation acreage to serve our growing population—along with rising land costs—requires that the Land and Water Conservation Fund be enlarged.

The longer we wait to acquire land for recreational purposes, the more those lands will cost.

A suitable addition to those sources of revenues now authorized can be found in the receipts from our mineral leases in the Outer Continental Shelf. That Shelf belongs to the people, and it is only right that revenues from it be used for the people's benefit. *I recommend that the Congress authorize the use of part of these revenues to augment the Land and Water Conservation Fund to raise it up to a level of $200 million a year for the next five years.*

THE NATION'S HIGHWAYS

More than any other mark we make upon the land, the signature of mid-20th Century America is found in the more than 3 million miles of highways that cross and link a continent.

It is not enough that those highways be roads of utility. They must also be safe and pleasant to travel.

We have embarked on a major campaign to make them safe, in the Highway and Traffic Safety Acts of 1966.

In 1965—in the Highway Beautification Act—we set out to make them attractive. In partnership with the States, we determined to remove and control the eyesores that mar the landscape—auto graveyards, unsightly billboards, junk heaps.

Early last year I asked the Congress to extend that Act—which expired on June 30, 1967—for two additional years. The Senate passed a one-year extension. It is still awaiting House action. The Highway Beautification Act represents an important item of unfinished business before the Congress. *I urge the Congress to complete action on the bill so that we can get on with the job of making America a more beautiful place to live.*

Our highways must be in harmony with the communities and countrysides of which they are part. Too often in the past, this need has received little more than lip service.

A distinguished Citizens' Advisory Committee on Recreation and Natural Beauty, under the Chairmanship of Mr. Laurance Rockefeller, has reported: "Highways have effects that reach far beyond those who drive on them; yet our present devices for choosing locations are still based mostly on requirements of the highway user rather than the community at large."

Under the new authority in the Department of Transportation Act, we are moving now to assure that natural beauty and recreational factors are woven into the highway and freeway planning process, along with traditional engineering and cost considerations.

—The Secretary of Transportation is requiring States to give full consideration to the views of local groups—and private citizens in preparing their route selections for Federally-supported highways.

—The Secretaries of Transportation, Housing and Urban Development, Interior, and Agriculture will review exceptional cases which raise questions concerning a proposed highway route's impact on scenic and historic values.

Roadside Parks

A highway should not be an unending ribbon of concrete from point to point.

American families traveling on their roads should be able to stop, to stretch their legs, to open a picnic lunch and relax before going on their way.

A park along the roadside—with landscaped grounds, an outdoor stove and tables, a path to explore—should be part of every travel experience. These way stations are not expensive. But they can add immeasurably to the comfort and enjoyment of a family on a trip.

I have directed the Secretary of Transportation to work with the Governors and Highway Commissioners of each State on a priority program to increase substantially the number and quality of rest and scenic areas along the Federal-aid Highway System.

VOLUNTEERS FOR CONSERVATION

All across America, men and women, boys and girls are making their cities and communities better places to live. In garden clubs and civic leagues, in Scout troops, 4–H clubs, and Junior Chambers of Commerce, they are planting and painting, cleaning and building, growing and repairing.

This is the army of conservation volunteers, and they number in the millions.

I propose this action program for volunteers to make America a place of beauty, enriching its communities and raising the spirits of their people, volunteers to:

—Increase local conservation efforts in every community, through the full participation of all citizens.

—Extend the National Paint-Up, Clean-Up, Fix-Up Week, now an annual event, to a seasonal event, four times a year.

—Encourage every city to beautify its approaches, through the planting of trees, shrubs and flowers native to the area.

—Impress upon every citizen the contribution he can make simply by observing the "No Litter" signs as he drives along the highway and walks along the street. Clean-up is costly. For example, it takes $2,000 of the taxpayers' money each year to keep each mile of highway leading into the Nation's capital free of refuse.

—Call upon the news media to encourage the conservation work of local groups. Television and radio stations, which are granted the public airways, have a special obligation to highlight these worthy public events.

The volunteer work for conservation deserves recognition and honor. It deserves help in mobilizing for greater efforts in the years ahead.

Accordingly, I am asking the President's Council on Recreation and Natural Beauty and the Secretary of the Interior in cooperation with the Governors and Mayors to join with private organizations in sponsoring a series of regional workshops to focus atten-

tion on those areas where greater private conservation efforts would be particularly
productive.

THE OCEANS

The seas are the world's oldest frontiers.
As Longfellow observed, they not only separate—but unite—mankind.

Even in the Age of Space, the sea remains our greatest mystery. But we know
that in its sunless depths, a richness is still
locked which holds vast promise for the
improvement of men's lives—in all nations.

Those ocean roads, which so often have
been the path of conquest, can now be turned
to the search for enduring peace.

The task of exploring the ocean's depth
for its potential wealth—food, minerals, resources—is as vast as the seas themselves. No
one nation can undertake that task alone.
As we have learned from prior ventures in
ocean exploration, cooperation is the only
answer.

*I have instructed the Secretary of State to
consult with other nations on the steps that
could be taken to launch an historic and
unprecedented adventure—an International
Decade of Ocean Exploration for the 1970's.*

Together the countries which border the
seas can survey the ocean's resources, reaching where man has never probed before.

We hope that those nations will join in
this exciting and important work.

Already our marine technology gives us
the ability to use the ocean as a new and
promising source of information on weather
and climate. We can now build and moor
electronic buoys in deep water. Unattended,
these scientific outposts can transmit to shore
data for accurate long-range forecasts.

The benefits will be incalculable—to farmers, to businessmen, to all travelers.

*This year we can begin development of
improved ocean buoys. I urge the Congress*
*to approve my request for $5 million in the
Fiscal 1969 Coast Guard budget for this
program.*

As we turn more and more of our attention to the exploration and the promise of the
seas, America must train more ocean scientists and engineers.

In 1966, I signed the National Sea Grant
College and Program Act. This new partnership between the Federal Government and
the Nation's universities will prepare men
and women for careers in the Marine
Sciences.

*I recommend that the Congress appro-
priate $6 million in Fiscal 1969 to advance
this program.*

THE CRISIS OF CHOICE

Three years ago, I said to the Congress:
". . . beauty must not be just a holiday
treat, but a part of our daily life."

I return to that theme in this message,
which concerns the air we breathe, the water
we drink and use, the oceans that surround
us, the land on which we live.

These are the elements of beauty. They are
the forces that shape the lives of all of us—
housewife and farmer, worker and executive, whatever our income and wherever we
are. They are the substance of The New
Conservation.

Today, the crisis of conservation is no
longer quiet. Relentless and insistent, it has
surged into a crisis of choice.

Man—who has lived so long in harmony
with nature—is now struggling to preserve
its bounty.

Man—who developed technology to serve
him—is now racing to prevent its wastes
from endangering his very existence.

Our environment can sustain our growth
and nourish our future. Or it can overwhelm
us.

369

History will say that in the 1960's the Nation began to take action so long delayed.

But beginning is not enough. The America of the future will reflect not the wisdom with which we saw the problem, but the determination with which we saw it through.

If we fail now to complete the work so nobly begun, our children will have to pay more than the price of our inaction. They will have to bear the tragedy of our irresponsibility.

The new conservation is work not for some Americans—but for all Americans. All will share in its blessings—and all will suffer if the work is neglected. That work begins with the family. It extends to all civic and community groups. It involves city hall and State capitol. And finally it must engage the concern of the Federal Government.

I urge the Congress to give prompt and favorable consideration to the proposals in this Message.

LYNDON B. JOHNSON

The White House
March 8, 1968

NOTE: For statements or remarks upon signing related legislation, see Items 150, 386, 420, 458, 501, 502, 505, 510, 547.

123 Statement by the President on the Conservation Message. *March 8, 1968*

THERE ARE many things that Americans take for granted—a park, a tree, a field, a river.

Now the beauty of America is in danger.

But today we are moving to lift that danger—to renew, to restore, to reclaim, and to refresh the spirit of our land and of our people.

This is the work of the new conservation. It can be the new strength of America.

I sent Congress today an action program:

—An action program that will fight pollution that fouls the air we all breathe and blights our rivers and our streams.

—An action program to continue the great work which now enables 120 million

Americans to reach a national park or lakeshore or camping area in just an afternoon's drive from the crowded city.

—An action program to make every community a place of pride for its people.

Now the question is for each of us: What kind of America do we really want to live in—and what kind of America do we want to leave to our children?

So I call upon all Americans—every mother and father, every businessman and worker, every Governor and every mayor— to join us in this urgent task of conserving America the beautiful.

NOTE: The President also recorded the statement for radio and television broadcast.

124 Message to the Congress Transmitting Second Annual Report on Marine Resources and Engineering Development. *March 11, 1968*

To the Congress of the United States:

Science and technology are making the oceans of the world an expanding frontier.

In preparing for the coming decades, we must turn our attention seaward in the quest for fuels, minerals, and food—and for the natural beauty of the seashore to refresh the spirit.

Yet the sea will yield its bounty only in proportion to our vision, our boldness, our determination, and our knowledge.

During the past year we have taken new steps to strengthen the Nation's scientific and technological base for understanding and using the oceans. We have made good progress but much remains to be done in the years ahead.

The National Council on Marine Resources and Engineering Development, chaired by the Vice President, has made significant progress in mobilizing the resources of the Federal Government to meet these challenges. I am pleased to transmit to the Congress the Council's recommendations and annual report.

The Fiscal Year 1969 Budget, which is now before the Congress, includes $516 million for marine science and technology programs. Increased funding is proposed for:

—Broadening education and research in marine sciences, particularly in the Sea Grant and other university programs.

—Speeding up our research for an economical technology for extracting fish protein concentrate for use in the War on Hunger.

—Development of improved ocean buoys to collect accurate and timely data for better prediction of weather and ocean conditions.

—Expanding the Navy's advanced technology needed for work in the deep oceans, and for rescue, search and salvage.

—Constructing a new high-strength cutter for the Ice Patrol and oceanographic research in Arctic and sub-polar areas.

—Preventing and alleviating pollution from spillage of oil and other hazardous ship cargoes.

—Continued mapping of the continental shelf to assist in resource development and other industrial, scientific, and national security purposes.

—Increased research and planning to improve our coastal zone and to promote development of the Great Lakes and of our ports and harbors.

—Application of spacecraft technology in oceanography, and improved observation and prediction of the ocean environment.

Other nations are also seeking to exploit the promise of the sea. We invite and encourage their interest, for the oceans that cover three-fourths of our globe affect the destiny of all mankind. For our part, we will:

—Work to strengthen international law to reaffirm the traditional freedom of the seas.

—Encourage mutual restraint among nations so that the oceans do not become the basis for military conflict.

—Seek international arrangements to insure that ocean resources are harvested in an equitable manner, and in a way that will assure their continued abundance.

Lack of knowledge about the extent and distribution of the living and mineral resources of the sea limits their use by all nations and inhibits sound decisions as to rights of exploitation. I have therefore asked the Secretary of State to explore with other nations their interest in joining together in long-term ocean exploration.

Such activities could:

—Expand cooperative efforts by scientists from many nations to penetrate the mysteries of the sea that still lie before us;

—Increase our knowledge of food resources, so that we may use food from

371

the sea more fully to assist in meeting world-wide threats of malnutrition and disease;

—Bring closer the day when the peoples of the world can exploit new sources of minerals and fossil fuels.

While we strive to improve Government programs, we must also recognize the importance of private investment, industrial innovation, and academic talent. We must strengthen cooperation between the public and private sectors.

I am pleased and proud to report that we have made substantial progress during the first full year of our marine science program, dedicated to more effective use of the sea.

We shall build on these achievements.

LYNDON B. JOHNSON

The White House
March 11, 1968

NOTE: The report is entitled "Marine Science Affairs—A Year of Plans and Progress; The Second Report of the President to the Congress on Marine Resources and Engineering Development" (Government Printing Office, 228 pp.).

A White House announcement and summary of the report is printed in the Weekly Compilation of Presidential Documents (vol. 4, p. 490).

125   Remarks at the Swearing In of John H. Crooker, Jr., as Chairman, Civil Aeronautics Board.   *March 11, 1968*

Mr. and Mrs. Crooker; my dearly beloved friend, Judge Crooker; Chairman and Mrs. Murphy; Members of the Congress; Judge Skelton; Members of the Cabinet; ladies and gentlemen:

Now that springtime is upon us and spring training seems to have begun around Washington, I am going to employ the language of baseball this morning to say that the lineup changes that we are here in the East Room to formalize—John H. Crooker to the Civil Aeronautics Board and Charles Murphy to the White House—are good for both teams.

I know them both as good Americans and as old and valued friends. John brings to the CAB his wide experience in the law, his very rare intellectual capacity, and a most perceptive and discerning judgment. I think he is, in every way, a most excellent successor to Charles Murphy.

As for you, Charley, you have been around somewhat longer. You are no stranger here today. We welcome you back to the White House. I am not forgetting our understand-ing that you will be here on more or less a part-time arrangement. Charley and other members of his family emphasized that to me as we discussed this matter. But I think, Charley, that you should know now that "part-time" is a rather relative term. And I believe anyone who has been in the White House and as close to it as long as you have should realize that.

The other day, one of my assistants was asked what were the working hours here at the White House. He had been here some time with me, so the answer came back—because he knew it—quickly. He said, "It varies somewhat, but generally, the hours are from nine to five—twice a day."

The Civil Aeronautics Board is 30 years old. In 1938, the unfolding wonder of aviation had taken hold of this country and had taken hold of the imagination of the American people. There was a new set of folk heroes that year. Among them were Howard Hughes, who flew around the world in less than 4 days, and another young man who, a week later, made his name a part of the language. It was "Wrongway" Corrigan who, flying alone, left New York for Los Angeles and wound up in Dublin.

Americans looked to the skies and saw their new highways. A new industry—air transportation—was coming of age.

Congress, that year, passed the Civil Aeronautics Act. We are delighted to see the distinguished leaders of aviation in the Congress, Senator Monroney and Chairman Staggers, and many others in our midst this morning, as well as Governor Rampton from Utah and Chairman Moss, and others.

That act was to assist the development of this fledgling industry, and to assure our people that these airways would serve their needs and would serve the people's convenience.

In 1938, our young airlines carried about a million and a half passengers. Last year, Americans flew—not a million and a half passengers—they flew on more than 120 million trips.

In 1938, the remarkable DC-3 was the workhorse of the air transport industry. Early this month—the other day, in Marietta, Georgia—Senator Monroney, Secretary Boyd, and others of us inspected the huge military transport. Its immense cargo area can carry a weight that is equivalent to more than 10 DC-3's.

The CAB will work with our airlines to see that aviation technology will be employed for the full benefit of all our people. I hope that they can work closely with our Congress and our trusted leaders who supervise the activities.

The CAB is looking ahead to the further development of vertical and short takeoff aircraft. And these may very well revolutionize travel between our major cities and could ease much of the congestion that plagues our major airports today.

We have come a long, long way since 1938, but the challenge of aviation is certainly not behind us.

I hope that Chairman Crooker and all the members of his Commission, majority and minority party members, will constantly counsel with and work with the Congress in a cooperative effort to fully take advantage of our potential.

I sometimes think that we have the power and the capacity and the strength to deal with any foe anywhere in the world except within our own boundaries. A great deal of our weaknesses are caused by pitting our strength against each other and chewing on ourselves.

So I hope that the members of the Commission, with the wise and sage advice of Chairman Crooker, can continue a partnership with the Members of the House and the Senate, the transportation industry in this country, and the Transportation Department in this country, to realize the full potential that is ours.

We really, in this country, have nothing— as President Roosevelt said one time—to fear except fear itself.

We have the strength. We have the resources. We have the ability. We have the imagination. We have the greatest system of government ever known to man, if we can only guard our vanities and suppress our ambitions and exercise patience and tolerance with our fellow man.

I knew Johnny Crooker as a boy in short trousers when he was defeating my debating teams and reflecting on my talents back in the Houston public schools.

I have observed him come from young manhood to a maturity and a position that any youngster would want to emulate. I have never known a person with more intellectual capacity, with a higher dedication and patriotism to his country, and a greater potential and capability to make a success of this job.

My prayers and my support will be with him every step of the way.

NOTE: The President spoke at 1:15 p.m. in the East Room at the White House. In his opening words he referred to John H. Crooker, Sr., senior partner in the law firm of Fulbright, Crooker, Freeman, Bates, and Jaworski of Houston, Texas, Charles S. Murphy, outgoing Chairman of the Civil Aeronautics Board who was appointed as a counselor to the President, Mrs. Murphy, and Byron G. Skelton, Associate Judge of the United States Court of Claims, who administered the oath of office.

During his remarks the President referred to, among others, Senator A. S. Mike Monroney of Oklahoma, Representative Harley O. Staggers of West Virginia, Chairman of the House Interstate and Foreign Commerce Committee, Governor Calvin L. Rampton of Utah, Senator Frank E. Moss of Utah, and Secretary of Transportation Alan S. Boyd.

126 Statement by the President on the Senate's Action in Passing the Civil Rights Bill. *March* 11, 1968

EVERY AMERICAN can be proud of the Senate's action today.

By an overwhelming vote, the Senate has once again affirmed our Nation's commitment to human rights under law.

Bringing this debate to a close required more than perseverance. It required a dedication to America's fundamental ideals—and a determination to serve those ideals through law. In an hour of contention and stress, those who work within the law to enlarge the liberties of all men are the true peacemakers—and they deserve the thanks of their countrymen.

Now the House becomes the arena where these great issues will be tested.

I believe that the Members of the House—having once said that every family has the right to the kind of shelter it desires and can afford, having once said that Americans should be protected in the exercise of their basic rights, and having often expressed their will to curb violence in our cities—will reaffirm their support for the policies contained in this measure.

I hope this bill will soon be before me for signing into law. I salute those who this day acted to bring that time—and a more perfect Union—closer to hand.

NOTE: The Civil Rights Act of 1968 was approved by the President on April 11, 1968 (see Item 195).

127 Memorandum Approving the Adoption by the Federal Government of a Standard Code for Information Interchange. *March* 11, 1968

Memorandum for the Heads of Departments and Agencies:

I have today approved a recommendation by the Secretary of Commerce, submitted under provisions of Public Law 89-306, that the United States of America Standard Code for Information Interchange be adopted as a Federal standard.

In my memorandum to you of June 28, 1966, I stressed the need for achieving, with industry cooperation, greater compatibility among computers. The earlier adoption of the Standard Code for Information Interchange as a voluntary standard by the United States of America Standards Institute reflects a national concern with this need.

The adoption of this code as a Federal standard is a major step toward minimizing costly incompatibility among our vast Federal computer and telecommunications data systems.

I have also approved recommendations of the Secretary of Commerce regarding standards for recording the Standard Code for Information Interchange on magnetic tapes and paper tapes when they are used in computer operations.

All computers and related equipment configurations brought into the Federal Government inventory on and after July 1, 1969, must have the capability to use the Standard Code for Information Interchange and the formats prescribed by the magnetic tape and paper tape standards when these media are used.

The standard code will be used as the basic code in those networks of the National Communications System whose primary function is either the transmission of record communications or the transmission of data related to information processing. The standard will be implemented on a time-phased basis that is to be specified in National Communications System long-range plans.

The heads of departments and agencies are authorized to waive the use of these standards only under compelling circumstances of particular applications. Such waiver is to be coordinated with the Department of Commerce (National Bureau of Standards) before it is exercised so that the Department may effectively accomplish the goals of the Federal computer equipment standards program conducted under Public Law 89–306.

The Department of Commerce will provide you with the details of these standards and their application.

LYNDON B. JOHNSON

NOTE: For the President's memorandum of June 28, 1966, on the use and management of computers by Federal agencies, see 1966 volume, this series, Book I, Item 296.

128   Remarks Upon Signing the National Visitor Center Facilities Act of 1968. *March 12, 1968*

Secretary Udall, Senator Randolph, Congressman Gray, Members of the Congress, interested citizens, ladies and gentlemen:

Each year more than 10 million people visit this Nation's Capital and some 2 million come here to the White House.

They arrive in a strange city. They have to make their way through very unfamiliar streets. If they can find a lot to park their car in, they then must cope with the public transportation system that has confused many a world traveler.

There is no central clearinghouse where a visitor can gather information about our many monuments, museums, and Government buildings. He must needlessly waste hours deciding what to see and determining when he can see it.

The tourist and the student are invited to Washington. Then they are told to go and fend for themselves.

It is as if we asked someone to come to our house to visit with us and then we told him to find the kitchen and fix his own dinner.

The bill that I am signing here will assure that in the future our visitors to Washington will at least be given a proper welcome.

Under the National Visitor Center Facilities Act of 1968:

—A visitor center will be created in what is now known as Union Station. A new railway passenger terminal will be built nearby.

—A parking lot to hold 4,000 cars will be built adjacent to the Union Station.

—Low-cost public transportation will be available to take our visitors from the center to points along the Mall and the Capitol grounds.

—There will be a Capitol Visitor Center, right in the Capitol Building, where you can find out where to go, what time events take place, the points of history about the building and about our Congress. You will also be able to get books and pictures about the Capitol.

—An advisory commission, chaired by the distinguished Secretary of the Interior, will conduct a continuing review of the visitor's problems and the visitor's needs, so that we can keep our facilities up to date.

We are making a very special effort this year to try to attract foreign visitors to our country.

We hope that the visa requirements for foreign tourists can be eased. Hospitality cards will be issued which will entitle foreigners to very special discounts at hotels and Government-operated facilities. I hope many restaurants and other firms will join in this program.

Naturally, many of these foreign visitors are going to come here to our Capital—come to Washington.

And I think it is all the more important now, when all Americans will be opening their hearts and their homes to visitors from other lands, that the Nation's Capital should provide a very special welcome.

For Americans and foreigners alike, we want Washington to symbolize the best of our country—a city of beauty and warmth and hospitality.

For the fact that the Congress has brought me this legislation and for their presence here this morning, I express my appreciation.

NOTE: The President spoke at 10:36 a.m. in the Cabinet Room at the White House. In his opening words he referred to Secretary of the Interior Stewart L. Udall, Senator Jennings Randolph of West Virginia, and Representative Kenneth J. Gray of Illinois.

As enacted, the bill (H.R. 12603) is Public Law 90-264 (82 Stat. 43).

129 Remarks Upon Presenting the Medal of Honor to Maj. Robert J. Modrzejewski and 2d Lt. John J. McGinty III, USMC. *March 12, 1968*

Major and Mrs. Modrzejewski and family; Lieutenant and Mrs. McGinty and family; Secretary Ignatius; General Chapman, Commandant of the Marine Corps; distinguished Members of the Congress; ladies and gentlemen:

We have just heard an extraordinary tribute to the courage of two men. They are Marines. They are comrades. They are heroes. But they are first and last—Americans.

In the story of their triumph, the voice of a people's character and a nation's greatness is brought before us. We should all understand that that is a voice with steel in it.

Last night I remembered another voice from another troubled and decisive time. I turned to the pages of a book where another President spoke to this Nation in time of a war. He told of the stories of courage and heroism on far battlefields. He called for the same strength of character and staunchness of spirit in every American home here and in every American heart.

Said President Franklin D. Roosevelt in the early months of another Pacific war: "As we here at home contemplate our own duties and our own responsibilities, let us think, and let us think hard, of the example which is being set for us by our fighting men. Our soldiers and our sailors are members of well-disciplined units. But they are still and forever individuals—free individuals. They are farmers and workers, businessmen, professional men, artists, and clerks. They are the United States of America. That is why they fight. We, too, are the United States of America."

Americans loathed war in that day, too. Forced to fight a war, Americans were impatient and frustrated by setbacks.

President Roosevelt also spoke to that anxiety when he said, 5 months after Pearl Harbor, "We have had no illusions about the fact that this is a tough job—and a long one."

And this Nation has no illusions now.

This is an anxious time for America. It calls for every fiber of our courage, every resource of our intelligence, every capacity for sound judgment that the American people can summon—and that the American people possess.

I think if we are steady, if we are patient, if we do not become the willing victims of our own despair, if we do not abandon what we know is right when it comes under mounting challenge—we shall never fail.

Responsibility never comes easy. Neither does freedom come free.

These brave men whom we have asked to come here to the East Room today and whom we honor now, know that better than

we, perhaps. They know in the most immediate way that men can ever know it. They know it in the face of an aggressor's fire.

Major Modrzejewski and Lieutenant McGinty stand in the long unbroken rank of heroes who have been this Nation's pride and have been this Nation's strength from the beginning when America itself as Lafayette once said "was a dream that every man carried in his heart."

Men like these Marines have seen America all through our troubled periods. They have fought with valor, in the early months, the enemy's expanded war, when the regular units of the North Vietnamese Army were beginning to cross the border as aggressors in significant size.

Today, the enemy force waging destruction south of the DMZ is made up of many, many regular units who have already invaded their neighbor nation from the north. International aggression is open now and it is undisguised.

The early pretense of attempting to fool some of the people some of the time that this was only a civil war has now had the cloak pulled from around it and even they have abandoned it, as have their spokesmen.

So let us have no illusions about that, either. And let no one ever suffer any illusions about the will and about the faith of free men, the American fighting man, the family of citizens who stand by him here and who stand by him out there.

Yes, we all loathe war. Yes, we argue about war. But we are one people and we have learned the hard lesson of history.

President Franklin Roosevelt had to say it and he said it with a heavy heart. I must repeat it now and my heart is heavy, too.

"The price for civilization must be paid in hard work and must be paid in sorrow and in blood—and the price is not too high."

377

But my heart this morning is proud and it is confident, too. I look at these two gallant Marines and I see America. I see in their countenance the answer to aggression. I see in their face the certainty of freedom and I see in their presence the hope and the promise of peace.

Secretary Ignatius will now read the citations.

[Text of citations read by Secretary Ignatius]

The President of the United States in the name of The Congress takes pleasure in presenting the Medal of Honor to

MAJOR ROBERT J. MODRZEJEWSKI
UNITED STATES MARINE CORPS

for service as set forth in the following

CITATION:

For conspicuous gallantry and intrepidity at the risk of his life above and beyond the call of duty while serving as Commanding Officer, Company K, Third Battalion, Fourth Marines, Third Marine Division, in the Republic of Vietnam from 15 to 18 July 1966. On 15 July, during Operation HASTINGS, Company K was landed in an enemy infested jungle area to establish a blocking position at a major enemy trail network. Shortly after landing, the company encountered a reinforced enemy platoon in a well organized, defensive position. Major (then Captain) Modrzejewski led his men in the successful seizure of the enemy redoubt, which contained large quantities of ammunition and supplies. That evening a numerically superior enemy force counterattacked in an effort to retake the vital supply area, thus setting the pattern of activity for the next two and one-half days. In the first series of attacks, the enemy assaulted repeatedly in overwhelming numbers but each time was repulsed by the gallant Marines. The second night the enemy struck in battalion strength, and Major Modrzejewski was wounded in this intensive action which was fought at close quarters. Although exposed to enemy fire, and despite his painful wounds, he crawled 200 meters to provide critically needed ammunition to an exposed element of his command and was constantly present wherever the fighting was heaviest. Despite numerous casualties, a dwindling supply of ammunition and the knowledge that they were surrounded, he skillfully directed artillery fire to within a few meters of his position and courageously inspired the efforts of his company in repelling the aggressive enemy attack. On 18 July, Company K was attacked by a regimental size enemy force. Although his unit was vastly outnumbered and weakened by the previous fighting, Major Modrzejewski reorganized his men and calmly moved among them to encourage and direct their efforts to heroic limits as they fought to overcome the vicious enemy onslaught. Again he called in air and artillery strikes at close range with devastating effect on the enemy, which together with the bold and determined fighting of the men of Company K, repulsed the fanatical attack of the larger North Vietnamese force. His unparalleled personal heroism and indomitable leadership inspired his men to a significant victory over the enemy force and reflected great credit upon himself, the Marine Corps and the United States Naval Service.

LYNDON B. JOHNSON

The President of the United States in the name of the Congress takes pleasure in presenting the Medal of Honor to

SECOND LIEUTENANT JOHN J. MC GINTY III
UNITED STATES MARINE CORPS

for service as set forth in the following

CITATION:

For conspicuous gallantry and intrepidity at the risk of his life above and beyond the call of duty as Acting Platoon Leader, First Platoon, Company K, Third Battalion, Fourth Marines, Third Marine Division, in the Republic of Vietnam on 18 July 1966. Second Lieutenant (then Staff Sergeant) McGinty's platoon, which was providing rear security to protect the withdrawal of the battalion from a position which had been under attack for three days, came under heavy small arms, automatic weapons and mortar fire from an estimated enemy regiment. With each successive human wave which assaulted his thirty-two-man platoon during the four-hour battle, Second Lieutenant McGinty rallied his men to beat off the enemy. In one bitter assault, two of the squads became separated from the remainder of the platoon. With complete disregard for his safety, Second Lieutenant McGinty charged through intense automatic weapons and mortar fire to their position. Finding twenty men wounded and the medical corps-

man killed, he quickly reloaded ammunition magazines and weapons for the wounded men and directed their fire upon the enemy. Although he was painfully wounded as he moved to care for the disabled men, he continued to shout encouragement to his troops and to direct their fire so effectively that the attacking hordes were beaten off. When the enemy tried to out-flank his position, he killed five of them at point-blank range with his pistol. When they again seemed on the verge of overrunning the small force, he skillfully adjusted artillery and air strikes within fifty yards of his position. This destructive fire power routed the enemy, who left an estimated 500 bodies on the battlefield. Second Lieutenant McGinty's personal heroism, indomitable leadership, selfless devotion to duty, and bold fighting spirit inspired his men to resist the repeated attacks by a fanatical enemy, reflected great credit upon himself, and upheld the highest traditions of the Marine Corps and the United States Naval Service.

LYNDON B. JOHNSON

NOTE: The President spoke at 12:45 p.m. in the East Room at the White House. In his opening words he also referred to Secretary of the Navy Paul R. Ignatius and Gen. Leonard F. Chapman, Jr., Commandant of the Marine Corps.

A White House announcement of the ceremony is printed in the Weekly Compilation of Presidential Documents (vol. 4, p. 492).

130   Special Message to the Congress Transmitting HUD–DOT Joint Report on Urban Transportation Organization. *March* 12, 1968

To the Congress of the United States:

In accordance with the requirement of Section 4(g) of the Department of Transportation Act, I am forwarding for the information of the Congress a joint report and

recommendations by the Secretaries of the Department of Transportation and Housing and Urban Development on the logical and efficient location of urban mass transportation functions in the Executive Branch.

This report contains a valuable summary of studies and deliberations conducted by the two Secretaries over the past year. Reorganization Plan 2, which I transmitted to the Congress on February 26, 1968, will carry into effect those recommendations requiring action by the Congress.

LYNDON B. JOHNSON

The White House
March 12, 1968

NOTE: The report, entitled "Report to the President on Urban Transportation Organization, Prepared Jointly by the Department of Housing and Urban Development and the Department of Transportation," is printed as House Document 281 (90th Cong., 1st sess.).

131 Letter to the Speaker of the House Urging Prompt Action on the Civil Rights Bill. *March* 12, 1968

[Released March 12, 1968. Dated March 11, 1968]

Dear Mr. Speaker:

Today—by a vote of 71 to 20—the Senate took an historic step toward strengthening human rights in America.

Two years ago the House by a 259 to 157 vote on final passage sent to the Senate a civil rights measure which contained a fair housing provision.

Several provisions of the Senate bill will be familiar to the Members of the House—particularly the fair housing section, the title that gives new protection to persons exercising their individual rights, and provisions affecting those who contribute to civil disorder.

The fate of this bill now rests with the House of Representatives.

I deeply believe, Mr. Speaker, that passage of this legislation is more important today than ever before.

Prompt action by the House on this bill will be a signal

—to minority group Americans, that the path to peaceful progress is open and available to all who choose to walk it;

—to all Americans, that our national purpose is being served, and the requirements of our national conscience met, through lawful democratic processes;

—and to the world, that America is determined to achieve racial harmony and social justice for all her people.

To one man—the Negro veteran of Vietnam—the fair housing provision will have a special meaning. I do not need to tell you what he has done for our country. It is up to us—to all of us—to assure him the elemental rights in his own country for which he risked his life overseas. That man—and his race—are entitled to the justice this bill provides.

Mr. Speaker, I urge the Members of both parties in the House of Representatives to complete this work—vigorously and promptly. It will be nonpartisan recognition of justice and equality for all American citizens.

Sincerely,

LYNDON B. JOHNSON

[Honorable John W. McCormack, Speaker of the House of Representatives, Washington, D.C.]

NOTE: The Civil Rights Act of 1968 was approved by the President on April 11, 1968 (see Item 195).

132   Remarks at a Dinner of the Veterans of Foreign Wars. March 12, 1968

Commander Scerra, Senator Russell, distinguished Members of Congress, members of the Veterans of Foreign Wars, ladies and gentlemen:

I came here to join you briefly this evening because it gave me a chance to share in the high honor that your great organization is paying to a champion of the American fighting man, a great friend of the American veteran, a leader for decades of all the people of this country, and I am very proud to say my longtime and good friend, Richard Russell of Georgia.

I would also like to take a moment now to pay tribute to another splendid Georgian—a great American—Dean Rusk. I do not believe ever in our history has this office been filled by a more dedicated or by a more sincere American. I have never heard United States policy and our commitments so eloquently stated—and under such very trying circumstances—than was done by Secretary Rusk in the last 2 days before the Senate Foreign Relations Committee.

If this Nation is secure—and if it is kept secure—all Americans will owe a great debt to these two great Georgians, Dick Russell and Dean Rusk.

I have always heard that the Veterans of Foreign Wars dinner attracts more Members of Congress than any other social event. As I look around this room tonight, I can well believe that. I see many of my oldtime friends from Capitol Hill here. I do still have some friends left up there.

Of course, many of my political friends are home tonight, watching TV. I am told that there is a special on tonight—from New Hampshire.

You know the New Hampshire primaries are unique in politics. They are the only

races where anybody can run—and everybody can win.

I think New Hampshire is the only place where candidates can claim 20 percent is a landslide, and 40 percent is a mandate, and 60 percent is unanimous.

I had an early report from New Hampshire this morning on these unbiased television networks. They had counted 25 votes there—the first 25, and the vote for LBJ was zero. I said to Mrs. Johnson, "What do you think about that?" She answered, "I think the day is bound to get better, Lyndon."

Well, it has been a long day. And I have not been home to dinner yet. But I am proud to come here and to bring to this great organization my message of gratitude. I want to thank your commander and every member of this organization for all that you have done—for all that you are doing—for the security and well-being of the United States of America.

I want to thank you for the support that you gave our surtax proposal which would make fiscal responsibility possible and would give confidence to the rest of the world.

I want to thank you for your support when the debt ceiling had to be raised.

I want to thank you for joining me and helping me settle the railroad strike.

I want to thank you for endorsing the extension of the draft so we would not have to send our Army home.

I told Tiger Teague,[1] my dear friend, Chairman of the Veterans Committee, coming in tonight: I want to thank all of you for backing every piece of legislation to aid our men in Vietnam when they come home

---

[1] Olin E. Teague, Representative from Texas.

and when they join you as Veterans of Foreign Wars.

I want all of those who hear me or read me to know that I believe that you are great spokesmen for the American veteran—for the man who has laid his life on the line for his country.

But you have also been a voice for responsibility in all world affairs. You have understood that duty always travels with strength, that the greatness of a nation is measured by its willingness to fulfill its moral obligations to its own people, as well as to mankind.

The United States, at the end of the Second World War, did not go out in search of new obligations. Our strength, and our commitment to man's freedom, brought those obligations right here to our door. Four Presidents now have recognized those obligations. Ten Congresses have verified them.

They have been costly—in blood and in treasure. The only higher cost would have come from our ignoring them or from our failure to assume them. The price of isolationism—whether it is the old-fashioned kind of isolationism that is rooted in ignorance, or the new-fashioned kind that grows from weariness and impatience—whatever its kind, isolationism exacts the highest price of all and, ultimately, as we have learned, it is unpayable.

Our goal, my friends, is not the unlimited extension of American responsibilities anywhere. It is clearly not the conquest of a single foot of territory anywhere in the world. It is not the imposition of any form of government or economy on any other people on this earth.

Our goal is peace—the blessed condition that allows each nation to pursue its own purposes:

—free of marching invaders and aggressors;

—free of terror in the night;

—free of hunger, and ignorance, and crippling disease.

If we take up arms, we take them up only to guard against those enemies. It is to help the nation builders. It is to try to shield the weak so that time can make them strong. It is to bar aggression. It is to build the lasting peace. That is your country's single purpose today.

We send our young men abroad because peace is threatened—in other lands tonight, and ultimately in our own.

We take our stand to give stability to a world where stability is needed desperately.

We rattle no sabers. We seek to intimidate no man.

But neither shall we be intimidated. And from American responsibilities, God willing, we shall never retreat. There is no safety in such a course. Neither reason nor honor nor good faith commends such a course.

You of the VFW have been the strong right arm of many Commanders in Chief, of many Presidents. You have been a voice of conscience and responsibility for many years for many millions of Americans. I ask only that you hold straight to that course. You will help to lead your Nation and you will help to lead your world beyond danger to the peaceful day when free men know not fear, but when free men know fulfillment.

I will leave you now in that confident expectation.

But before I go, just let me close as I began, with a word about our great honored guest who strives daily to make this Nation more secure, and also a word about a resident of his State in his early manhood—our great Secretary of State.

There is something I would like to say about Dean Rusk. He is a good and a wise man. He has known the heat of the kitchen—as well as the television lights. The dignity that comes from the clay soil from which he sprang—he has known it long enough to know that good humor and great patience also play their part in history, too.

So, I will return home now to watch another television replay—I am going home to look at the "Dean Rusk Show."

That's the show, you know, that was 2 years in production. We had a great cast— but no plot.

We also had trouble picking the title. "Gunsmoke" had already been taken. We finally decided on "Shoot-Out at Capitol Hill."

Then we couldn't find a sponsor. They all said, "Sorry, quiz shows are dead."

I saw Secretary Rusk tonight before I came over here. He looked different. I said, "Where have you been?" And you know— for the first time in 2 complete days the Secretary of State did not have an answer.

But you men of the Veterans of Foreign Wars, who, in order to qualify for your membership, have had the answer.

You have Dick Russell's appreciation and Dean Rusk's gratitude and my thankfulness.

Thank you so much.

NOTE: The President spoke at 9:16 p.m. at the Sheraton Park Hotel in Washington. In his opening words he referred to Joseph A. Scerra, National Commander of the Veterans of Foreign Wars, and to Senator Richard B. Russell of Georgia, who received the VFW's fifth annual Congressional Award presented to an outstanding Member of Congress.

133 Special Message to the Congress on the District of Columbia: "The Nation's First City." *March* 13, 1968

To the Congress of the United States:

A British Ambassador, serving here in the early part of the century, glimpsed the great hope of the American people for their capital city. He wrote:

"What you want is to have a city which everyone who comes from Maine, Texas, Florida, Arkansas or Oregon can admire as being something finer and more beautiful than he had ever dreamed of before; something which makes him even more proud to be an American."

Washington—the city of noble monuments, quiet splendor and the close touch of history—is truly the Nation's pride.

But Washington is also another city— a community of families with their needs, their wants and their expectations.

For too long, America saw only the historic city and ignored the city of people. At the seat of democracy, democracy's work went undone, and the other Washington be-

came a place to be endured rather than enjoyed.

Last year, Washington came into its own. After a century of waiting we gave it the machinery of modern government.

Now that government is going about its quiet—but exciting—mission.

A Mayor is in city hall, in touch with the people, his leadership infusing confidence. A City Council is in action, providing meaningful representation for the citizens of the community.

These are the breakthroughs. Now we must consider the followthroughs.

That is the concern of this Message. It presents my proposals to:

—Redouble the attack against crime
—Revive the hopes of the people with: jobs for those who need them, education for the children who must prepare for the future, decent homes for the families so long without them

—Renew the historic city for the enjoyment of all the American people

—Reinforce the new strength of municipal government through further reorganization, and long-overdue salary increases for the public servants of the nation's Federal city.

To Drive Crime From Our Midst

The long shadow of crime falls over the streets of the nation's capital, mocking its proud institutions.

Each time a storekeeper is threatened at gunpoint—each time a woman is terrorized on her way home from work—each time a burglar breaks into a home at night—the liberty of every citizen is diminished.

Crime today is the first problem in the nation's first city. It is on the rise. The *rate* of increase in January was the lowest in 19 months—but that fact would provide little comfort for the victims of these crimes:

—24 murders and rapes
—758 automobile thefts
—786 robberies and aggravated assaults
—1864 burglaries and major larcenies.

As we know, crime feeds on society's oldest imperfections—poverty, ignorance, blocked opportunities, the lack of a job and the dimming of hope.

In the District as in the nation these are the urgent matters on our agenda for action. But the clear fact remains that progress can only be achieved in a climate of public order.

And so long as there are those who flout the law and tyrannize their neighbors, public order depends on an effective police force.

The District's Police

Our goals for the District's police force are these: that it have the full confidence of the community, operate at full strength, be fully effective, fully equipped and fully paid for the risks of protecting our lives and property.

Strength and Efficiency

The uniformed strength of the Police Department is now fixed at 3,100.

It has always been a problem to recruit and retain enough qualified men to reach full strength.

Within the last year, the numbers of vacancies have been sharply reduced. A pioneering program by Mayor Washington to recruit returning servicemen at their separation points has added to the Department's strength.

In the coming months, the Mayor will be stepping up all of his recruiting programs, with particular emphasis on reaching eligible young men who live in the District.

I have asked the Mayor to conduct a searching survey of the needs of the city, to determine whether the authorized strength of the Department should be further increased.

Freeing a trained policeman from routine tasks and clerical work—and moving him from precinct house to patrol car—will help to enhance the public safety.

I propose that we do this in three ways.

First, I recommend that the Congress add 127 new civilian employees to the Department for work in precinct houses.

Second, I recommend that the Congress expand the Police Cadet Corps from 100 to 150 recruits. These young men can take over many of the routine police functions while they are training.

Third, I recommend legislation authorizing the Mayor to organize, train and equip a force of 700 reserve police officers.

This reserve force would release regular policemen for needed law enforcement assignments. It would also widen and strengthen citizen participation in crime control in their neighborhoods, thereby strengthening police-community relations.

The reservists would serve without pay. They would receive free uniforms, be carefully trained, and operate under the close supervision of the police department.

Training and Equipment for the Police Force

Last week the District of Columbia achieved a long-sought and much-needed objective. Every patrolman is now equipped with radio communications, to be in instant contact with his headquarters.

Throughout the Department, the most advanced communications networks and computers are being installed.

Modern equipment, from patrol cars to motor scooters, are also being added.

I urge the Congress to approve the budget request of $3.4 million for these and other essential crime-fighting tools.

I also urge the Congress—once again—to enact promptly the Safe Streets and Crime Control Act, which will strengthen the local police forces of all the cities of this land, including the nation's capital.

Each day's delay in enacting this vital anti-crime legislation carries a heavy cost. It can be counted in the murders, rapes and robberies that could be prevented, but are not—in the fear that could be forestalled, but is not.

Police Salaries

Many a young man who might be attracted to police work is deterred by the prospect of salaries too low to raise a family in decency and comfort. It is an imprudent city which rewards the protectors of its safety and property by forcing them to live on the margin.

Salaries paid District policemen are now not competitive with those in other major cities—Washington ranks 11th in a comparison of 20 similar areas.

The Nation's Capital City police force should serve as a model for all the cities of America.

Initially the Mayor recommended a 7 percent pay increase for District policemen. That would have raised the minimum starting salary of a police private to $7,500 a year and move Washington from 11th to 5th place among the Nation's cities. That amount is now programmed in the D.C. Budget.

Recently, the House endorsed legislation which would provide for a 10.1 percent increase, with an $8,000 starting salary. That measure is now pending before the Senate. The Mayor and I endorse the salary increases provided in the House bill.

If the Congress approves these higher pay levels, additional revenue will be required. The Mayor will shortly prepare and submit formally to the Congress a supplemental revenue bill to finance these long-overdue and well-deserved pay increases for the city's police force.

GUN CONTROL

If the District is to wage a successful battle against crime, it must have a strong gun control law.

Last year, almost 2,500 major crimes were committed in the Nation's Capital at gunpoint—murders, assaults and robberies.

Laxity in gun control legislation is an open invitation to tragedy. A pistol in dangerous hands is like a ticking time bomb. And today, in the District of Columbia, alcoholics, juveniles and mental incompetents are free to own deadly weapons.

The proposal I have recommended—the D.C. Gun Control Act—would help bring safety to the District's streets, homes and stores. It would:

—Require individuals to obtain a permit to possess or carry a pistol and limit the sale of pistols to those with valid permits.

—Prohibit possession of pistols by persons under 21, drug users, alcoholics, or mental incompetents, as well as drug addicts, felons, and other criminals.

—Add ten years imprisonment to the regular penalty when a firearm is used in a robbery or an attempted robbery.

—Require all rifles or shotguns to be unloaded and encased while being **carried**.

—Require stricter licensing of persons who manufacture, sell or repair firearms, and require records and reports to be made concerning sales and repairs.

This legislation is designed to safeguard the public order and to stop tragedy.

It would not, however, prevent any law-abiding citizen from owning firearms if he can show the need for such weapons to protect himself or his property.

I again recommend that the Congress promptly enact a strict gun control law for the Nation's Capital city.

CRIMINAL CASE BACKLOG

When criminal justice works slowly, it no longer serves as a deterrent. Quick action must be taken to remove the staggering backlog of criminal cases in the District of Columbia Court of General Sessions.

To accomplish this, I urge the Congress to act on pending legislation to increase the number of judges on the court from 21 to 26.

I also endorse the legislation's provision to increase the compensation of the Chief Judge of the Court from $24,000 a year to $28,000 and that of each Associate Judge from $23,500 a year to $27,500.

UNIFIED LOCAL COURT SYSTEM

To assure effective judicial machinery responsive to the needs of its people, a unified local court system for the District is needed. Several proposals pending before the Congress seek to achieve some measure of reform. But they do not go far enough.

After long study, the Judicial Council's Committee on the Administration of Justice has recommended that the following improvements be made:

—Transfer the Juvenile Court to the Court of General Sessions as a division of that Court.

—Place the administration of the Juvenile Court under the Chief Judge of the Court of General Sessions.

—Make the present judges of the Juvenile Court associate judges of the Court of General Sessions.

—Establish a unified social services unit of the Court of General Sessions.

—Transfer the criminal non-support and paternity jurisdiction of the Juvenile Court to the Domestic Relations Branch of the Court of General Sessions.

I am asking the Mayor to study these proposals and, in consultation with the Courts and the Attorney General, to develop legislation which will create a unified local court system of the highest excellence for the nation's capital.

EDUCATION

Quality Education for All Children

Education is the great adventure that leads to equality of opportunity. Every child should have the benefit of an educational program shaped to his capabilities, and designed to develop his full potential.

Only the teacher in the classroom can give him this.

Teachers are in short supply, and the competition for them is intense. A good teacher finds little attraction to join or stay in a school system which demeans him with inadequate pay.

Today, among 20 comparable big city areas, the District ranks 15th in salaries for beginning teachers. This sharply reduces the District's chances of recruiting qualified teachers. And it hampers the education of Washington's 150,000 schoolchildren.

I recommend that the Congress lift the minimum starting salary for teachers in the District of Columbia to $7,000, and provide comparable increases for experienced teachers. The Mayor joins me in this recommendation.

This legislation is needed. It is essential. It will move the District from 15th to second place among the largest cities in the Nation. It will help the Nation's first city build a school system of first rank. The Mayor's supplemental program will include new revenue proposals to finance this vital community service.

The District Schools and the Community— A Model for the Nation

How can the schools of our central cities serve their pupils better? How can they become portals to success for more of their children? How can they reduce the number of failures and dropouts? How can they overcome the handicaps accumulated through years of neglect? How can they serve and involve the citizens of the community?

These are the critically important questions faced in the District of Columbia, as in every major city of America.

The Passow Report [1] provides Washington

with a blueprint for the total revival of its schools. It is a framework which will enable the people of the Nation's capital to build a vital and responsible school system.

I propose a major model school experiment in the District, embracing a significant area of the city. This program will:

—Revive the interest of citizens in their schools.

—Help teachers improve the skills of their profession through retraining opportunities.

—Bring to students the best in teaching methods and materials.

—Revise the curriculum to make it serve the young people of our city.

—Equip high school graduates with marketable skills.

—Seek alliances between employers and the schools.

—Give children the chance to learn at their own pace, reducing both dropouts and failures.

—Serve a section of the city where the needs of students and schools are greatest.

To support this program I have included $10 million in my 1969 budget for the Office of Education to supplement the funds providing regular support for the D.C. schools.

With these additional resources, we can launch an exciting new venture in education—to continue for the next five years— as we seek new levels of quality and service in the schools of the nation's capital. That effort can become a beacon to the school systems in the other cities of the Nation.

I expect that this effort will result in:

—New programs for preschool children.

—Special attention to individual needs in the early years when children are learn-

---

[1] Survey on Washington, D.C. educational system by 180 educators headed by Dr. A. Harry Passow and made public in September 1967. The study urged special education for disadvantaged children to promote equal opportunity among the poor.

ing to read.

—Opportunities for high school youngsters to work and attend school at the same time.

—Improved counseling and health services for children.

—A system for teacher retraining on a regular basis.

—New levels of cooperation among the schools and other agencies serving the people of the District.

Schools and the Community

But schools will not serve children well unless they also serve the entire community. We need to develop a new concept—the Community School. It can be a place:

—for both learning and recreation.

—for adults, as well as children, serving the interests of people of all ages.

—for activities during summers and weekends and evenings.

—for reaching the family to reinforce the values the school seeks to impart.

With a small grant from the Mott Foundation of Flint, Michigan, the D.C. schools have already begun to pioneer in developing community schools.

To enlarge this effort, I am directing the Commissioner of Education to work with the D.C. school system and the community service agencies of the District to start, as part of the new model program, a large-scale community school experiment.

An Elected D.C. School Board

Community education policies cannot be developed in a vacuum. They cannot serve the people unless the people have a voice in their formulation.

As I said last summer when I proposed an elected school board for the District of Columbia:

"Washington's 150,000 schoolchildren and their parents—who now for the first time will be able to know the benefits of modern government—must also be able to exercise one of their most fundamental rights. They must have a voice which can be heard in the operation of their school system."

Both the Senate and the House have already passed bills to provide for an elected school board.

I urge final Congressional action on a bill which would:

—*have the school elections correspond with the general elections.*

—*provide for close coordination between the Board of Education and the District Government to achieve the goal of schools as true centers of community life.*

HOUSING

High on the list of the District's critical needs is decent housing.

The new housing program I have proposed to the Congress—to provide 6 million homes for low and moderate income families during the next ten years—will have a strong effect on Washington.

Already the District has been the scene of major pioneering successes:

The first "Turnkey" Project in the nation, fully engaging the private sector in the construction of low income housing, was built here.

The Nation's capital was among the 63 cities selected to plan and develop a Model Cities program. This will rebuild an entire slum neighborhood physically and bring new opportunities to its residents—health, jobs, education, recreation. Planning for this historic project is now rapidly proceeding.

The first conversion of Federal surplus land into a new community—undertaken last year at my direction—is off to a good start at the 335-acre site of the National Training

School for Boys, known as Fort Lincoln:

—A team of outstanding city planners and architects has been selected.

—The community is being planned with the help of the residents of the neighborhood, to assure that the new area fills the highest aspirations of the people of Washington.

—The community will embody the latest advances in housing construction and education, as well as planning.

This work can truly serve as a model for the Nation.

Mayor Washington has informed me that ground can be broken at the Fort Lincoln site by the summer.

During these planning months for the new community—before it actually takes shape—it can be put to constructive use. Its hills and ridges, its gymnasiums, classrooms, playfields and picnic groves should be available for the enjoyment of families from all the neighborhoods in the city.

I am asking the Mayor and the Federal agencies concerned to develop an action program to promote the maximum interim use of the site for the benefit of the citizens of Washington.

"Seed Money" for Low Income Housing Sponsors

Many unions, church groups and other non-profit organizations want to sponsor low and moderate income housing for the people of the District.

They are unable, however, to obtain the funds they need—"seed money"—for the early stages of development.

I recommend legislation to establish a program under which the District government may advance loans to non-profit sponsors of low income housing.

I also recommend legislation to establish a revolving fund for that program which will *be financed by unclaimed property in the District.*

Retaliatory Evictions

One of the most abhorrent injustices committed by some landlords in the District is to evict—or threaten to evict—tenants who report building code violations to the Department of Licenses and Inspections.

This is intimidation, pure and simple. It is an affront to the dignity of the tenant. It often makes the man who lives in a cold and leaking tenement afraid to report those conditions.

Certainly the tenant deserves the protection of the law when he lodges a good faith complaint.

I recommend legislation to prevent retaliatory evictions by landlords in the District.

JOBS

As in every other city of America, there are men and women in Washington out of work—not because they prefer to be idle, but because years of opportunity denied have left them without skills, and often without ambition.

I have proposed to the Congress a major program to tackle the problem of the hardcore unemployed.

The spearhead of this effort is the National Alliance of Businessmen, which has selected Washington as one of the 50 cities where its job training and hiring program for the hard-core unemployed will proceed.

Improvement of outmoded laws in the District will help women and youngsters find meaningful work.

I recommend legislation to:

—*Do away with the archaic requirements which must be met by youngsters under 16 before they can take after school jobs or work during the summer. Many*

389

needy children are deterred from earning a paycheck because the procedures for getting a work permit are overly stringent and detailed.

—*Amend the "Female 8-Hour Law" whose provisions relating to certain business establishments in the District no longer accord with modern working conditions. This change will permit women to volunteer for overtime work and pay.*

The District as the Nation's Capital

Pennsylvania Avenue Commission

A Commission I appointed three years ago has made significant progress in its task of revitalizing the Pennsylvania Avenue area between the White House and the Capitol. Work has begun on the new FBI building. A great reflecting pool will grace the front of the Capitol.

The Commission is successfully linking the efforts of the Federal Government with private enterprise in developing this historic thoroughfare. It estimates that for every $1 spent by the Government $10 of private capital will be invested in the development of Pennsylvania Avenue.

But the Commission—so important to the District's future—still operates under a temporary charter. And the development of Pennsylvania Avenue is long-range work.

I again strongly recommend that the Congress enact legislation to give permanent status to the Commission on Pennsylvania Avenue.

Woodrow Wilson Memorial

A year ago I called attention to the proposal by the Woodrow Wilson Memorial Commission to establish in the Nation's Capital an International Center for Scholars as a living memorial to the 28th President

of the United States.

I then directed that the Temporary Commission on Pennsylvania Avenue develop a more detailed proposal for such a Center.

That Commission has now recommended that the Center be built on the north side of the area designated as Market Square in the Pennsylvania Avenue Plan. Through an imaginative combination of public and private leadership and financing this Center could serve as "an institution of learning that the 22nd Century will regard as having influenced the 21st."

The dream of a great scholarly center in our Nation's Capital is as old as the Republic itself. There could be no more fitting monument to the memory of Woodrow Wilson than an institution devoted to the highest ideals of scholarship and international understanding.

I recommend legislation authorizing the establishment of a Center to be operated by an independent board of trustees within the framework of the Smithsonian Institution. Trustees for the Center in collaboration with the Government of the District of Columbia and the Pennsylvania Avenue Commission and with the approval of the National Capital Planning Commission will work out detailed plans for the Center and for the development of Market Square.

International Center

Last year, I recommended that the Congress authorize an International Center, a large site at which foreign chanceries and the offices of international organizations could be located. After study, it now seems clear that acquisition of the site proposed at that time is not possible.

I am, therefore, recommending new legislation to authorize the use of 34 acres of the old National Bureau of Standards terrain for these worthy purposes. The new site has the support of the Secretary of State, all other interested Federal Agencies including the National Capital Planning Commission, and the Mayor of the District of Columbia. I hope for early Congressional review and approval of this legislative proposal, important alike to the Federal Government, to the District, and to the international community located in Washington.

National Visitor Center

Washington, D.C., attracts millions of visitors each year.

For all of its many years, the Nation's Capital lacked a center where the tourist and student could learn about the workings of his Government and find information about the city's monuments and museums.

The visitor of the future will have such a place to go, and will be able to enjoy more fully his stay in Washington.

Earlier this week I signed legislation authorizing the establishment of a National Visitor Center at Union Station.

Last year I asked the National Capital Planning Commission to conduct a thorough study of a transportation center in the vicinity of Union Station—one that would provide a hub to the airports, buslines and railroads that serve the Nation's Capital. *I am requesting the Commission to speed the completion of the study of a Transportation Center so that its recommendations can be fully integrated into the detailed planning of the Visitor Center.*

Addition to the National Gallery of Art

I urge Congressional approval of legislation to authorize the Trustees of the National Gallery of Art to construct an addition to the National Gallery of Art on Pennsylvania Avenue immediately east of the Gallery.

The construction will be paid for with private funds generously donated. The new building will provide additional exhibition space and room for a center for advanced studies in the history of art. It will also permit the expansion of the Gallery's extension services to the schoolchildren of the Nation.

Strong Municipal Leadership

Those at the top levels of the city's government—the Mayor, the Deputy Mayor, and members of the Council—should be adequately compensated.

They are in positions of great responsibility. They preside over a city which is not only the Nation's capital but the center of the fastest-growing metropolitan area in the United States.

I recommend legislation to raise the salary of the Mayor from $29,500 to $35,000 and the salary of the Deputy Mayor from $28,000 to $30,000.

The proposed increase would give the District's chief executives compensation comparable to that received by their counterparts of other major cities.

The members of the District Council who serve on a part-time basis also merit an increase in salary.

I recommend legislation to raise the salary of the Council Chairman from $10,000 a year to $15,000; the salary of the Council Vice Chairman from $9,000 a year to $12,500, and the salary of other Council members from $7,500 a year to $10,000.

If the Council is to be broadly representative of the District, it must call upon the services of residents from all walks of life. Many who live in the District are also employees of the Federal Government. But the civic minded Government employee can serve on the Council only at a penalty. He is encumbered by the "dual compensation" law, whose effect is to bar him from receiving the supplementary salary for Council work—even though that work is extensive, involving long hours, nights and weekends.

This restriction does not apply to Council members who are privately employed.

There is no justification for this artificial discrimination. It should be ended.

I recommend legislation to exempt Council members from the "dual compensation" law.

Supergrades

The city's administration can only be as effective as the men and women who operate the machinery of government—the trained managers, technicians, planners and experts in all the phases of the city's life.

The need to attract capable executives is of the highest importance for the new government of the Nation's first city.

I urge the Congress to take prompt action on pending legislation which will give the Mayor authority to classify and make appointments to 50 positions at the top levels of the Civil Service—Grades GS–16, 17, and 18.

The legislation would also authorize the Mayor, with the approval of the President, to place six additional positions at levels IV and V of the Executive Schedule.

Removing Hatch Act Restrictions

The freedom to engage in the political life of the community which District Commissioners have always enjoyed should now be given to their successors—the Mayor and members of the Council.

This would not be inconsistent with the requirement for a nonpartisan Council. That forbids the Council from taking actions, or organizing itself, along partisan political lines. But it should not prevent members from participating in the political life of the city and the party of their choice if they wish

to do so.

I endorse legislation recently introduced in the Congress to exempt the Mayor and the Council members from provisions of the Hatch Act prohibiting Federal and District employees from participating in political activity.

I also recommend that the Federal conflict-of-interest restrictions on Council members be adjusted to reflect a proper relationship with their part-time duties.

Financing the District Government

Federal Payment Formula

The Congress has always recognized the fair share of the funds to operate the government of the Nation's capital city must come from the United States Treasury.

I again propose a realistic formula for the Federal payment to the District. I recommend legislation to establish the annual payment authorization at a level equal to 25 percent of District general fund revenues.

This formula would provide a continually updated and equitable Federal payment. It would enable the District to compute the Federal share when it is planning its budget, so that priorities could be established among its most urgent needs.

This proposal does not involve the automatic payment of Federal funds for District purposes. The District government would not be able to spend either local revenues or the Federal payment authorization until funds have been appropriated by Congress. The District budget would continue to be acted upon each year by the Appropriations Committees of the House and Senate.

Local Revenue Proposals

The District has developed new local revenue proposals for Fiscal 1969 that are prudent, equitable, and realistic.

These requests, presented in the District Budget for Fiscal 1969, reflect the unanimous view of the Council and the Mayor. They represent a responsible approach to balancing expenditures with income.

I recommend early approval of the legislative proposals in the District's revenue package. I also urge the Congress to support the Mayor's supplemental tax package developed to pay for the higher salaries for policemen, firemen, and teachers endorsed in this message. As important as they are, these increases should not come at the expense of the urgent construction and community service programs already incorporated in the D.C. Budget for FY '69.

STRENGTHENING THE MACHINERY OF GOVERNMENT

Last year, I told the Congress that once a Mayor and Council were appointed "it will be possible to effect further improvements, both in the structure of the District Government and in its relationships to other agencies serving the Nation's Capital."

Now it is time for those improvements.

Now it is time to strengthen the machinery of government in the District, to make it even more responsive to the needs of the people it serves.

We can do this by taking several steps:

I have signed today an Executive Order placing the National Capital Housing Authority under the direct supervision of the Mayor.[1] This will provide greater scope and direction in the District's drive to build homes for the citizens of Washington.

[1] Executive Order 11401 "Modifying Executive Order No. 6868 of October 9, 1934, as amended, designating the authority to carry out the provisions of the District of Columbia Alley Dwelling Act" (4 Weekly Comp. Pres. Docs., p. 510; 33 F.R. 4559; 3 CFR, 1968 Comp., p. 106).

I am also today submitting two reorganization plans to the Congress.[2]

First, to vest the functions of the D.C. Recreation Board in the Mayor. The Recreation Board is an autonomous agency, but it controls policy, operations and facilities affecting the youth of the city—swimming pools, playgrounds, and recreation centers. It is essential that these recreational programs be fully coordinated with the District's Youth, Summer and Poverty programs. The reorganization I propose will help to accomplish that vital purpose.

Second, to enable the Mayor to appoint the five-member Board of the Redevelopment Land Agency. Today he can only appoint three members. The reorganization would also place the Board under the Mayor's effective control. The Redevelopment Land Agency is primarily responsible for carrying out urban renewal projects within the District. Giving the Mayor appointive authority will strengthen the city's attack on urban decay.

REPRESENTATION IN CONGRESS

The citizens of the District have too long been denied a basic American right of representative government.

They have been denied a community voice where in a democracy that voice counts most—in the halls of the Congress.

The needs of the District cannot be adequately represented in the Congress by proxy, any more than could the needs of one of the 50 States.

I again endorse legislation to give the citizens of the District representation in Congress. I urge early action by the Congress on the proposals which it has under active consideration.

[2] See Items 134, 135.

THE UNFULFILLED PLEDGE

With the proposals in this Message we can carry forward the important work we began last year.

I ask the Congress to give them prompt and favorable consideration.

Even as I urge this, I look to the future, when the promise of the past will be achieved.

The oldest pledge of this Nation is self government for the people. That pledge remains unfilled for the 800,000 citizens of America's first city—160 years after James Madison wrote in the Federalist Papers that the citizens of the city which served as the Nation's capital would have: "A voice in the election of the government which is to exercise authority over them."

Last year's reorganization has rekindled the promise of democracy in Washington. But the promise of democracy can never substitute for democracy itself.

I endorse home rule for the citizens of the Nation's capital. For the 37 years I have been a resident of this city I have looked to the day when the promise of home rule would be realized and the District of Columbia could enter into full membership in the American Union. As long as I am President I will work to hasten that day's arrival.

LYNDON B. JOHNSON

The White House
   March 13, 1968

NOTE: For statements or remarks upon signing related legislation, see Items 128, 203, 272, 320, 420, 436, 523, 542.

---

134 Special Message to the Congress Transmitting Reorganization Plan 3 of 1968, District of Columbia Recreation Functions. *March 13, 1968*

To the Congress of the United States:

In the past few years Congress and the President have pledged to make the Nation's Capital a model of excellence for America: in government, in housing, in city planning, in law enforcement, in transportation.

But the quality of any city is not just a matter of efficiency and public order. If it is to be truly great, the city must be lively and inviting—a place of beauty and pleasure.

The city's life is lived not only in its buildings, but in its pools, playgrounds and recreation centers, in the places where the young gather to find excitement and delight, where the old come to find relaxation, fresh air, companionship.

In Washington, recreation is a vital element of the city's school enrichment activities, its model city project and its summer programs.

But the D.C. Recreation Department is not an integral part of the District Government. With its six-member independent board, the autonomy of the Department prevents the D.C. Commissioner from providing policy supervision to the city's recreation activities and from relating them to other community service programs—in health, education, child care, and conservation.

There is no reason to distinguish between recreation and other community service programs now vested in the Commissioner.

Accordingly, I am today submitting to the Congress Reorganization Plan No. 3 of 1968. This plan brings recreation programs under the authority of the D.C. Commissioner. It enables the new City Government to make recreation an integral part of its strategy to bring more and better community services to the people who live in the city.

The Plan achieves these objectives by abolishing the present Recreation Board and the Office of the Superintendent of Recreation. It transfers their functions to the D.C. Commissioner.

The accompanying reorganization plan has been prepared in accordance with chapter 9 of title 5 of the United States Code. I have found, after investigation, that each reorganization included in the plan is necessary to accomplish one or more of the purposes set forth in section 901(a) of title 5 of the United States Code.

Closer coordination of recreation with other municipal improvement programs of the District Government and the improved efficiency of recreation management will produce a higher return on the taxpayer's investment in recreation programs, though the amount of savings cannot be estimated at this time.

I urge the Congress to permit this reorganization plan to take effect.

LYNDON B. JOHNSON

The White House
March 13, 1968

NOTE: Reorganization Plan 3 of 1968 is printed in the Weekly Compilation of Presidential Documents, the Federal Register, and Title 3 of the Code of Federal Regulations (4 Weekly Comp. Pres. Docs., p. 511; 33 F.R. 7747; 3 CFR, 1968 Comp., p. 152). It became effective at the close of June 30, 1968, under the provisions of section 6 of the plan.

135 Special Message to the Congress Transmitting Reorganization Plan 4 of 1968, District of Columbia Redevelopment Land Agency. *March 13, 1968*

To the Congress of the United States:

Urban Renewal is a vital weapon in the Nation's attack on urban blight and physical decay. In the firm hands of a local executive determined to improve the face of his city, it is a powerful tool of reform.

In the District of Columbia, urban renewal is managed by a Federal Agency, the D.C. Redevelopment Land Agency, headed by an independent five-man Board of Directors. Although the District Government pays the entire local share of the costs of urban renewal and although the Commissioner of the District of Columbia appoints three of the five members of the RLA Board, the Agency need not follow the Commissioner's leadership or administrative direction.

To strengthen the D.C. Commissioner's authority to initiate and guide the administration of urban renewal, I am today transmitting to the Congress Reorganization Plan No. 4 of 1968. This plan:

—gives the D.C. Commissioner the authority to appoint all five members of the RLA Board, by transferring to him the appointment function now vested in the President;

—transfers to him the authority to prescribe the rules and regulations governing the conduct of business by RLA. This function is now vested in the Board of Directors.

Urban Renewal involves slum clearance, demolition, the relocation of families, the provision of new housing, the stimulation of rehabilitation and new employment. Throughout the Nation, it is clear that authority and leadership by the local chief executive is essential to weld together the full range of municipal functions and community service programs to change conditions in city slums.

In our Capital City the hopes for a balanced New Town and new housing development on the Fort Lincoln site in Northeast Washington, the rebuilding of the Shaw neighborhood, and a successful Model Cities program hinge on the leadership of the D.C. Commissioner. Members of the Congress have repeatedly stressed the need to establish the Commissioner's effective control of all functions essential to local redevelopment. The attached plan takes a major step toward that objective.

The plan does not alter the corporate status of the Redevelopment Land Agency or any of the authorities now vested by law in the Agency.

The accompanying reorganization plan has been prepared in accordance with chapter 9 of title 5 of the United States Code. I have found, after investigation, that each reorganization included in the plan is necessary to accomplish one or more of the purposes set forth in section 901(a) of title 5 of the United States Code.

There are no direct savings deriving from this plan. However, it will improve the management of programs aimed at reviving the deteriorated social, economic, and physical structure of this city, our National Capital. The benefits and savings from a more successful attack on these problems cannot be estimated in advance, but their reality cannot be denied.

To achieve our goal of a model Capital, I therefore urge the Congress to permit this reorganization plan to take effect.

LYNDON B. JOHNSON

The White House
March 13, 1968

NOTE: Reorganization Plan 4 of 1968 is printed in the Weekly Compilation of Presidential Documents, the Federal Register, and Title 3 of the Code of Federal Regulations (4 Weekly Comp. Pres. Docs., p. 512; 33 F.R. 7749; 3 CFR, 1968 Comp., p. 153). It became effective on May 23, 1968.

136   Remarks Upon Signing Bill Amending the Export-Import Bank Act of 1945. *March 13, 1968*

Chairman Linder, Members of Congress, ladies and gentlemen:

Like a girl getting married, the Export-Import Bank is legally changing its name this morning. It used to be known as the Export-Import Bank of Washington. From now on it becomes the Export-Import Bank of the United States of America.

The change of the Bank's name is both symbolic and real. It will play a larger role in a cause of national importance that touches every citizen and will help increase the flow of exports and improve our balance of payments position, I hope.

The strength of our dollar, the soundness of the free world monetary system, really depend on the strength of that position.

Last year our balance of payments deficit reached $3 billion 600 million, the highest since 1960. To correct this requires an urgent and a concerted effort by all of us. Each of us can be blamed for it. But to correct it, all of us must make proper efforts—the business community, the leaders of labor, the leaders of the executive branch of the Government, the Congress of the United States, and finally, the public.

Unless we act now—and unless we act soon—we run a very grave and very unnecessary risk.

We have the responsibility today for world economic leadership. But we must exercise that responsibility. I think it is very essential to the national interest that we pass a tax bill now—that we move forward on the rest of the balance of payments program that we have recommended.

If we have not recommended all of the things that you would like to see considered, I would be glad to have recommendations from anyone else. But they need attention.

The law that I will shortly sign is a part of our total balance of payments program as we see it. This measure will enable a great institution—under a great Chairman—that has already done much for our country, to do even more, I think. I hope it does more.

So today we have come here to the Fish Room to give the Export-Import Bank some of the financial horsepower that it very desperately needs in order to carry out that important job.

I am going to ask every official in this Government—the Secretary of Commerce, the Secretary of the Treasury, the Secretary of Agriculture, and all the other leaders—to concentrate their efforts on trying to stimulate our exports and to work in close cooperation with this bank and the authority that the Congress has wisely entrusted to it.

The Bank is now 34 years old—perhaps a little old for a girl to be changing her name. But sometimes they do—even at that age. It is better late than never.

I wish for her a very long, very happy, and very productive life.

NOTE: The President spoke at 11:51 a.m. in the Fish Room at the White House. In his opening words he referred to Harold F. Linder, President and Chairman, Export-Import Bank of the United States.

As enacted, the bill (S. 1155) is Public Law 90-267 (82 Stat. 47).

137   Remarks of Welcome at the White House to Prime Minister Egal of the Somali Republic. *March 14, 1968*

Prime Minister and Mrs. Egal, Mr. Foreign Minister, Secretary and Mrs. Rusk, distinguished guests, ladies and gentlemen:

Mr. Prime Minister, it is a very special pleasure this morning to welcome you and Mrs. Egal to our Nation's Capital.

Vice President Humphrey has told me of the warm reception that he received on his visit to your country. He speaks often of the friendliness of your people and the warm hospitality he received from you and your President.

The people of America, Mr. Prime Minister, are delighted to have this opportunity to return your friendship.

We have watched with interest and admiration the development of the Somali Republic in the last 8 years. We know that you have succeeded in building one of the most effective democratic governments in all of Africa. We are aware of your noble efforts to bury ancient antagonisms and to get on with the work of peace.

I understand, Mr. Prime Minister, that this is your first visit to the United States. You will find many differences between our countries. But you will also find much that is the same.

Like you, we value the dignity and the freedom of the individual.

Like you, we are striving to perfect our democratic institutions, to provide better homes, better medical care, and better schools for all of our people.

Like you, we are working with all of our hearts and our minds to secure a just peace.

We are deeply proud that we have been able to offer a measure of help to your people in your own efforts to achieve these common goals.

I had hoped that we might welcome you this morning in the warm glow of a Washington spring. But Mother Nature has seen fit to give us instead just a parting taste of winter. But I know that you will find that our friendship for you and for your people flourishes in every season.

Mr. Prime Minister, we bid you and your lovely lady the warmest of our welcomes.

NOTE: The President spoke at 11:35 a.m. on the South Lawn at the White House, where Prime Minister Mohamed Ibrahim Egal was given a formal welcome with full military honors. In his opening words the President also referred to Haji Farah Ali Omar, Minister for Foreign Affairs of the Somali Republic, Dean Rusk, Secretary of State, and Mrs. Rusk.

Prime Minister Egal responded as follows:

Mr. President, Mrs. Johnson, Mr. Secretary of State, Mrs. Rusk, distinguished friends, ladies and gentlemen:

On behalf of the Somali delegation, my wife, and myself, I would like to thank you very much for your very kind words of welcome.

Both my Government and my people were greatly honored by the kind invitation you have extended to me to visit the United States.

Even though my people are geographically remote from the shores of the United States, yet they know and feel that they share with the people of this great country the irresistible bonds of similar institutions of government, mutual belief in democratic rule, and a commitment to preserve the dignity of man and his supremacy over all institutions of government.

Our country, Mr. President, is as large as your State of Texas, as big as Portugal and Spain together. Even though remote in distance by the standards of a bygone age, it has been brought closer to your nation by the modern advancement of technological development.

We are close to others, also, in the family of nations, because geographically we are a crossroads of Africa, Asia, and the Middle East. Our coastline on the Indian Ocean, as well as in the Gulf of Aden, is as long as yours in the Pacific.

We thus overlook the sealine to more than half the world.

During my visit, Mr. President, I shall try to learn from your great country examples of democratic rule to take back with me to enrich and further develop our own institutions.

At the same time, I feel that I shall have ample opportunity for making comparisons between our own institutions and yours because, Mr. President, even while Europe was being ruled by the arbitrary decree of the elects of God, we in Somalia were practicing a very advanced pastoral democracy.

After independence, we naturally had to adapt the structure of our institutions to serve a modern, independent sovereign state. But the essence of democracy, the belief in the principle, and most important of all, the will to work the institutions of democracy, were all there, all along, since time immemorial and since the beginning of our nation.

I feel, Mr. President, that in this form of government and with its preoccupation with the liberties of the individual, it has within itself the seeds for the ultimate success of the human race.

For that, we are proud to acknowledge with you, Mr. President, and with all those who practice it, a bond of brotherhood and a common goal for our endeavors.

Mr. President, I should once again like to thank you for your kind invitation and for your kind words of welcome.

I hope that my short stay in the United States will contribute to a closer cooperation between our people and our countries.

Thank you.

---

138 Remarks at the Federal Woman's Award Ceremony. *March 14, 1968*

Mrs. Louchheim, distinguished award winners, ladies and gentlemen:

I yield to no President in my esteem for women. After all, I married one—and I have helped to raise two. The press has noticed that I like to quote from previous Presidents; they observe that fact on occasion.

Today, I thought that it would be appropriate to let you hear from some of my predecessors and what they thought about women, what they had to say about women, and about how the Presidency finally came to grips with what Garfield called "the woman question." We do have other questions, as you can see, but we are going to talk about just this one now.

Here are a few examples of what Presidents have thought. I want to admit in the beginning that they have been shortened somewhat and they are completely out of context.

George Washington said, "I never did, nor do I believe I ever shall, give advice to a woman."

James Madison thought that he detected "in the female mind the capacity for studies."

Lincoln wasn't so sure. "A woman," he said, "is the only thing that I am afraid of that I know will not hurt me."

James Garfield sensed something was happening. He said, "Put that aside as a jest if we will, still the woman question is rising on our horizon."

William Howard Taft took a stand. "I am not in favor of suffrage for women."

Warren Harding faced the inevitable. "Let us not share the apprehension of many as to the danger of this momentous extension of franchise."

But Calvin Coolidge finally found a use for the ladies in national life. He said, "I want every woman to vote." I need not add that he spoke in an election year.

Fortunately, for the women of America and for our country itself, we have come far since those days. But even today, women still have a cruel discrimination in jobs. But we are—I think—making some progress.

I am proud today that more and more women occupy what I believe to be most important positions in this Government.

I wish I could find more, for the women of America remain one of the largest untapped resources for the great tasks of this Nation.

One of the ladies on my staff advised me that I should not speak to you women of your charm, or your grace, or your beauty. "They don't want to hear that," she said.

I paused and then said, "Well, that has not been my experience."

She said that I should compliment you instead on your great influence in the high councils of your Government and that is good advice. In your cases, that is very easy for me to follow.

You, as winners of the Federal Woman's Award, represent extraordinary achievement in several vital fields. Each of you can be proud of your contribution to the quality of the Federal service and to the capacity of this Government of yours.

You have helped to shape and to administer programs for our people. You have proven your personal capacities for judgment and for leadership and fidelity and dedication and integrity.

For all of these things, for being where you are today, for doing what you are doing today to serve our country, to serve our people, to serve our common employer—the people of the United States—I have asked you to come here to the Cabinet Room so that on behalf of the people of the United States I could express my thanks to each of you, and offer my congratulations to all of you and to the great number of fine, dedicated women that you speak for and that you symbolize.

NOTE: The President spoke at 1:10 p.m. in the Cabinet Room at the White House. In his opening words he referred to Mrs. Katie Louchheim, Chairman, Board of Trustees of the Federal Woman's Award and Deputy Assistant Secretary of State for Educational and Cultural Affairs.

The recipients of the Federal Woman's Award were

—Dr. Ruth Rogan Benerito, Research Chemist and Investigations Leader, Southern Utilization Research and Development Division, New Orleans, La., Department of Agriculture, cited "for her exceptional achievements in basic scientific research and the successful application of her findings as a source of immense benefit to the public";

—Dr. Mabel Kunce Gibby, Clinical Psychologist and Coordinator of Counseling Psychology, VA Hospital, Coral Gables, Fla., Veterans Administration, cited "for her remarkable creativity and leadership, ceaseless dedication, and unique success in restoring handicapped persons to meaningful and productive lives";

—Frances M. James, Statistician, Council of Economic Advisers, Executive Office of the President, cited "for her outstanding competence and impressive achievements in economic statistics, and her extraordinary loyalty and devotion to duty";

—Mrs. Ruby Grant Martin, Director, Operations Division, Office for Civil Rights, Office of the Secretary, Department of Health, Education, and Welfare, cited "for her courageous and effective administration of the civil rights compliance program and her exceptional contribution to racial justice in the field of education";

—Dr. Lucille Farrier Stickel, Wildlife Research Biologist, Patuxent Wildlife Research Center, Laurel, Md., Bureau of Sport Fisheries and Wildlife, Department of the Interior, cited "for her pioneering personal research and original research techniques and applications in evaluating the significance of pesticide residues in wild animals";

—Rogene L. Thompson, Supervisory Air Traffic Control Specialist and Crew Chief, Federal Aviation Administration, Anchorage, Alaska, Department of Transportation, cited "for her extraordinary abilities and unique accomplishments in analyzing and solving tremendously complex problems of air traffic control";

—Dr. Nina Bencich Woodside, Chief, Bureau of Chronic Disease Control, D.C. Department of Public Health, Government of the District of Columbia, cited "for her superior leadership, initiative, and professional and administrative competence in developing a new range of public health services in adult health and geriatrics."

The Federal Woman's Award was founded in 1960 to give public recognition to outstanding Government career women. The award winners are chosen by a board of trustees consisting of 12 persons prominently identified with Federal personnel administration, both in and out of Government.

139   Remarks at a Reception Honoring Secretary Trowbridge. *March* 14, 1968

Secretary and Mrs. Trowbridge, Secretary Smith, Secretary Samuels, ladies and gentlemen:

I was a little hesitant about coming over here tonight. The last time I went to a going-away party for a Cabinet member, I got stuck in an elevator.

Just because I got here on time, you probably thought the trip over was uneventful. What you don't know is that I left the White House at noon to get over here. On the way out, I ran into Senator Fulbright, who said he just wanted to ask me a question or two. But he got bronchitis and went home and went to bed—and I came over here to Sandy's party.

Sandy Trowbridge is a young man of considerable foresight.

Still I doubt very much if he ever imagined—on that day several years ago when he was asked to become an Assistant Secretary of Commerce—that things would really turn out quite as they did.

It was always predictable that he would do a first-rate job. It was even possible that somebody might recognize that performance here in Washington.

But not many people would have supposed that he would become one of the youngest Cabinet secretaries in the history of this country—and also one of the youngest retirees.

I don't know what the immediate future holds for this splendid young man. I hope there is a little rest, to begin with.

I spoke to Sandy about a week ago, and I asked him what he was going to do.

He said, "I don't really know, Mr. President, but I can promise you one thing: I'm not going to run for President." Of course, I guess I ought to point out—that was a week ago. [*Laughter*]

But the long term prediction is much easier. Sandy Trowbridge will be one of this country's leaders—leaders in government service or private life—for decades to come.

About the time he took his chair at the Cabinet table, we were thinking about joining his department and Bill Wirtz's department into one. There may be some folks around town still who remember that proposal. It did not, I may say, become one of my better known legislative achievements.

His beginning, then, was not exactly auspicious. But to a Marine, that is no cause for alarm. Sandy took on his duties with great vigor and with high spirits. He became known as one of the most brilliant, intelligent, cooperative, and determined men in public life. He was a great asset to his Government. He was a great comfort to his President—and he was a model public servant.

I can assure you that I have never enjoyed a working relationship with anyone, anywhere, any time, more than the one that I had with Sandy Trowbridge. And I look forward to a different, but no less satisfactory relationship in the years to come.

To him and to his charming wife and family, I express publicly my deep debt of gratitude for our association and for the constructiveness of his every action.

I want to thank all of you who came over here tonight to wish Sandy well. I must say that I was wondering why so many of you looked so thoughtful out there this evening. Then it occurred to me that perhaps you are all reassessing the possibility of running for President yourself. So I don't want to interrupt you in that. [*Laughter*] I will just say this: Sandy, thank you very much. God bless you and your lovely family.

Please let me know when and where I can serve you.

NOTE: The President spoke at 7:38 p.m. at the Department of State. In his opening words he referred to outgoing Secretary of Commerce Alexander B. Trowbridge, who was retiring for health reasons, Mrs. Trowbridge, the new Secretary of Commerce C. R. Smith, and Under Secretary of Commerce Howard J. Samuels. Later he referred to Senator J. W. Fulbright of Arkansas and Secretary of Labor W. Willard Wirtz.

Early in his remarks the President referred to difficulties with an elevator at the Pentagon on the day of the farewell ceremony for Secretary of Defense Robert S. McNamara (see Item 101).

---

140 Toasts of the President and Prime Minister Egal of the Somali Republic. *March* 14, 1968

Mr. Prime Minister and Mrs. Egal, Mr. Vice President and Mrs. Humphrey, Mr. Chief Justice and Mrs. Warren, Secretary Rusk and Mrs. Rusk, Your Excellencies, distinguished guests, ladies and gentlemen:

Webster defines "egalitarian" as one who believes in equal opportunity for all men.

It is not usually the function of the President to expand on Webster.

But I think we can add to Mr. Webster's definition.

We are all egalitarians tonight, not only in our belief in the equality of man, but in our admiration of a man for whom that philosophy might have been named. No statesman is struggling harder today to realize the dream of democracy for his own people than the man that we honor tonight, Prime Minister Egal.

After our talk this afternoon, Mr. Prime Minister, a friend told me of an old Muslim saying that I am sure you know. It says: "There are four things which can never be retrieved—the spoken word, the sped arrow, times past, and the neglected opportunity."

Mr. Prime Minister, you have practiced the wisdom of that proverb.

Your words have always served the cause of peace. You have stayed the arrows of conflict which threatened to bring bloodshed to the Horn of Africa. And you have lost no time, and you have neglected no opportunity, in the search for true progress for all of your people.

You come to us, Mr. Prime Minister, from a new Africa where change is as certain as the sunrise. You are one of those who have determined that change shall always mean promise for your people.

You have helped to found a true democracy, where each man has a voice in his nation's future. You have done much to lessen the tensions that threatened East Africa with the waste of war. And you have begun the long, hard job of economic development to bring your people the food and shelter and education that all men seek and that all men deserve.

Mr. Prime Minister, we here in the United States are inspired by your courage. We admire your perseverance. And most of all we are delighted by your presence here this evening.

Ladies and gentlemen, I invite you to join me now in a toast to a wise leader and his people.

To the President and to the people of the Somali Republic—and to the Prime Minister and his charming lady, Mrs. Egal.

NOTE: The President spoke at 10:54 p.m. in the State Dining Room at the White House at a dinner honoring Prime Minister Mohamed Ibrahim Egal. In his opening words he also referred to Vice President and Mrs. Hubert H. Humphrey, Chief Justice and Mrs. Earl Warren, and Secretary of State and Mrs. Dean Rusk.

Prime Minister Egal responded as follows:

Mr. President, Lady Johnson, Mr. Humphrey, Mrs. Humphrey, Mr. Secretary of State, Mrs. Dean Rusk, distinguished friends, ladies and gentlemen:

When I came to the United States, naturally, as the Prime Minister, I came to talk to the Government of the United States as a man. I came to take a closer look at the man who holds the final decision on so many things and, in fact, on so many things that affect our lives wherever we are in this globe of ours that is getting smaller and smaller.

Having seen your President, Mr. Johnson, I feel I am going back with a comfortable feeling and I will feel happy and can sleep nights in the comfort and knowledge that that power is in the right hands.

Mr. President, I feel humbled by the glowing tribute you have paid to me and my colleagues for the little we have done for the Horn of Africa.

We have indeed tried our best to bring about peace between our people—our people in Somalia, our people in Kenya, our people in Ethiopia—in the concept of the OAU and the ideals of pan-Africanism. We feel that they are all our people. We owe a duty to them all and it is our duty to look after the prosperity of all.

I do not feel, Mr. President, that what we have done is at all worthy of so much praise. In fact, your praise and the tribute you have paid to us will only inspire us more—to do more service to those people who, God knows, need more help.

Mr. President, the greatest problems of Africa today are not politics. It is as though it is not the objective of Africa to fight each other but have intelligent attitudes of confrontation.

We have greater frontiers, better frontiers, frontiers of economic development, to fight against poverty, against ignorance, and against the evils which we wish to leave behind.

These, Mr. President, are targets which have to be met by ourselves. These are targets for which we need the assistance of friends like the United States.

We are going to leave wars, confrontations, bickering and rivalry, and jealousy behind. Your tribute and your example and your want for others will be a constant inspiration for us along that road.

Mr. President, ladies and gentlemen, will you rise with me to drink to the health of the President of the United States and the friendship between Somalia and the United States of America.

141 Remarks at a Meeting of the National Alliance of Businessmen. *March 16, 1968*

Mr. Ford, Mr. Austin, distinguished Mayors, Mr. Meany, Mr. Young, Mr. Smith, members of the Alliance, distinguished guests:

I wanted to come by here and principally do just one thing: to tell each of you—and through you your families that you have left this weekend—how proud your President is of the business community and of your recognition of the problems that this country faces, and also tell you how much confidence I have in your ability and your leadership to help me do something about these problems that I can't do by myself or I can't do with the other things that are available to me.

In all of my public life, I have never had anything that made me so appreciative as to know that men of Mr. Ford's, Mr. Austin's, and the other business leaders' background, stature, standing, accomplishments, and financial statements, if you please, would have enough concern for their fellow man to give their time, their money, their talent, and their heart to try and do something about it.

So that is why I am here. And I am especially happy to be with you when I think of the alternatives I have. I don't know, but you may have observed that there are several things going on in Washington this morning.

We have the negotiators on the copper strike who are here. There are bankers from all over the world down at the Federal Reserve trying to do something about the gold drain. And then there is the group at the Bobby Kennedy press conference.

But, Henry, I will take the businessman's luncheon every time.

Of course, always in this life that we all live, you have to take your chances. It seems everybody speculates these days. Some people speculate in gold—a primary metal. And some people just go around speculating in primaries.

The press asked for my reaction to the recent activities of the Senator from New York. I don't want to tell you all of my reactions this morning.

But when I read in the paper that he had pushed Henry Ford out of the "Meet the Press" program Sunday, I thought he was going too far too early.

If there is anyone anywhere who doubts the future of America, who has any concern about where we are going, I think it would do him good to come here and look into your faces to see where you have been. Then he could understand what our potential is.

You men come here this morning from cities across this Nation.

You have come here not to complain of a crisis, you have come here to meet it.

You have come not to just croak about trouble, but you have come here to tackle it.

You are really pioneers. Today, you are starting off on a journey of very high purpose.

You are launching the most massive and the most urgent job program in the history of this Nation—a job to provide hundreds of thousands of hard-core unemployed jobs in America's largest cities.

The Government is going to undertake to find these men and women and make them available to you.

Your mission is to train them, to hire them, and to try to get from them useful and productive employment.

In short, we want to take people who are destined to be continued taxeaters and through your processing, with some help from us, make out of those taxeaters fellow taxpayers.

Each time you place a jobless man on a payroll, you reduce his drain on you and on the Treasury and on your company. This will help to strengthen the Nation.

So yours is a challenging assignment. But American business has always been equal to its challenges.

There may be more than 500,000 who need your help. If there are, I expect you to meet your goal and then do what the doughboy did in World War I and what your sons

403

are doing now in Vietnam—and what our men did in other wars, who were engaged in World War II and Korea.

So the spirit that brings you here, I think, is the spirit that makes America tick and go.

It is the strength that has guided this country in every crisis and every trial we have ever had.

I think it will again.

Earlier this week in the East Room of the White House, I awarded the Medal of Honor to two of our bravest fighting Marines. As I stood there before them, and I heard once again the words "above and beyond the call of duty," I reflected on this. I recognized that not every man is called upon to give above and beyond the call of duty.

Not every man is called upon to give even his full measure of devotion. Not every man is called upon to serve his country, or to exercise his talents and his responsibilities.

But those who carry the burdens of public office must do their duty as they see it. They must do the right thing "as God gives us to see the right."

As your President, I want to say this to you today: We must meet our commitments in the world and in Vietnam. We shall and we are going to win.

To meet the needs of these fighting men, we shall do whatever is required.

We and our allies seek only a just and an honorable peace. We work for that every day—to find some way to settle this matter with the head instead of the hand. We seek nothing else.

The Communists have made it clear that up to now, thus far, they are unwilling to negotiate or to work out a settlement except on the battlefield. If that is what they choose, then we shall win a settlement on the battlefield.

If their position changes—as we fervently hope it will—then we in the United States and our allies are prepared to immediately meet them anywhere, any time, in a spirit of flexibility and understanding and generosity.

But make no mistake about it—I don't want a man in here to go back home thinking otherwise—we are going to win.

At the same time, we have other commitments, other international commitments, and we have very urgent commitments here at home.

All of these commitments ultimately wind up, as you executives know, representing a drain on the Treasury.

To do what must be done means that we must proceed with utmost prudence.

We must tighten our belts.

We must adopt an austere program.

We must adopt a program of fiscal soundness.

This week we passed a law removing the useless and burdensome gold cover.

This week the Federal Reserve Board has increased the rediscount rate in an attempt to bring some restraints.

We are meeting at this moment with the members of the Central Banks in the world as well as with the leaders of the Congress. We are talking to the congressional leaders about adjustments and reductions that can be made in our national budget.

Hard choices are going to have to be made in the next few days. Some desirable programs of lesser priority and urgency are going to have to be deferred.

That is why we hope that the free enterprise system—the private employers of America—can help the Government take some of this responsibility. Because every one of these men whom you can employ, help train, and prepare, means one less that the Government has to deal with.

But the key to fiscal responsibility is still unturned according to all the fiscal experts.

404

The key is the penny-on-the-dollar tax bill that is now pending. This tax increase will yield less than half of the $23 billion per year that we returned to the taxpayer in the tax reductions of 1964 and 1965.

We are paying lower tax rates than we have paid any time since World War II. We are in the middle of a war in Vietnam and we have all of these problems here at home.

If we could just go back to the tax rate that was on the books when I became President—before two reductions—we would take in $23 billion more this year. So I appealed to the Congress last week—and I will again next week—and I call upon the Congress now to meet the urgency of the hour with the responsibility that it requires.

Now, with all of these measures taken, our fiscal position is going to be strengthened. We will be able to supply what is needed to win a just and a lasting peace in Vietnam—hopefully at the negotiating table, but on the battlefield if we must.

We will fulfill our commitments abroad and here at home to try to move forward with a program of better health, education, and training for all of our people—more security and better houses for all of our families.

If our economy is strong, we can take care of most of these essential needs—not as quickly as we would like—but soundly, efficiently, and, I hope, adequately.

None of this is going to be easy or pleasant. But I believe that Americans will resolutely bear their share of the burden in helping to meet their needs at home—rather than push us into fiscal chaos or rather than fail to give our fighting sons the help and the support that they need.

As a young man, I grew up hearing a lot of namecalling. Some of it was applied to the economic royalists and the business community and the free enterprise system. I am glad that has gone out of fashion in this country. I have not heard it in several years.

I am glad that Henry Ford, and the mayor of Cleveland, and George Meany can sit here at this table side by side, because they all represent something special to this country—as you do.

Now is the time for us to exercise the patriotism that we have by trying to unite together to support the worthy causes of our country and to try to solve the dangerous problems that our country faces. You are doing that.

This will be a memorable meeting. I hope that they get a picture from the front because I think that every person in this meeting will someday want to point to his children—and if he is fortunate enough, his grandchildren—and say to them: "I was there when this all began, when there was a real awakening on the part of the social consciousness of the business power structure in this country who gave their talents and their money and their time to try to help those who needed help and who could not help themselves."

I am grateful to each of you personally, regardless of what party you belong to, what church you attend, or what section you live in.

You are serving this Nation just as patriotically and as needfully as your sons are serving it who wear the uniform.

Thank you very much.

NOTE: The President spoke at 10:05 a.m. at the Sheraton Park Hotel in Washington. In his opening words he referred to Henry Ford II and J. Paul Austin, chairman and vice chairman, respectively, of the National Alliance of Businessmen, George Meany, president, AFL–CIO, Whitney M. Young, Jr., executive director of the National Urban League, and C. R. Smith, Secretary of Commerce. During his remarks he also referred to Senator Robert F. Kennedy of New York and Mayor Carl B. Stokes of Cleveland, Ohio.

142   Remarks to Delegates to the National Farmers Union
Convention in Minneapolis.   *March 18, 1968*

*Mr. Vice President, Mr. Dechant, Senator
Mondale, Chairman Robert Poage, ladies and
gentlemen:*

I thank you very much for this warm
reception. It does a man good after the
weather that we have had in Washington. I
presume some of you have read that we have
had a cool spell come through there lately.
And along about the latter part of last week
it got considerably colder.

But I wasn't at all surprised. "The Farmers Almanac" for a long, long time has been
indicating some atmospheric disturbances
might be moving in from the Senate.

So I flew down to the Southwest to spend
Sunday with my grandson. We had a family
gathering at the ranch. I was glad to learn
that we had had good rains, things had
warmed up a good deal, and we could stop
our winter feeding. That does make a good
deal of difference, when you can stop buying
cottonseed cake.

I am very proud to be a part of your convention, and to be invited by Tony to come
here today. I don't intend, by dropping by, to
steal any honor away from your distinguished
guest, one of the finest young men who has
ever come to the Senate—Walter Mondale—
who works for the farmer every day that he
is there, and for all the people.

Minnesota has a way of picking good
public servants. I have never known you
to pick a better one than this young Senator.

I like both of your Senators. I like the
way they vote, and I like the way they
talk—except in election year sometimes.

One of the public servants that I am
proudest of—I have worked with Gene
McCarthy, Walter Mondale, and all of your
House delegation for years—is your present

Vice President, who was once my leader
in the Senate until I asked him to try to help
us lead the Nation. I have never had any
doubts about Hubert Humphrey, and I have
no doubts this morning about Hubert's farm
credentials.

I called him a little after 5 o'clock, before
daylight down in our country. His Secret
Service agent came back and said, "The Vice
President cannot be reached." And I said to
Jimmy Jones there at my bed, who had been
reached about an hour earlier by me and
told to come on up and let's get going,
"Jimmy, it is bad when the President of the
United States can't reach the Vice President."

He said, "Well, I know it, but he lives
out of Minneapolis, out in rural Minnesota."
He said, "He is probably up doing his
chores before he goes in to greet us." He said,
"Just quit fussing about the Vice President,
because he is all right."

Then about that time the operator came
on the line very pleased and said, "Mr.
President, I have found the Vice President.
He is in a downtown Minneapolis hotel
suite."

I said, "Well, wake him up and put him
on the line. I want to talk to him. I may
come up there to see him today."

And while they were getting Hubert
awakened—the Secret Service agent—Jimmy
Jones explained, "I'll bet you what he has
been doing, Mr. President, is milking the
lines from his St. Patrick's Day speech last
night in Pennsylvania."

You don't know how happy I am that we
could meet together this morning. I don't
believe anyone can claim that I am a new
recruit to the farmer's cause.

You and I wear many of the same campaign ribbons. Some of them represent victories; a good many of them represent hopes that have been dashed, disillusionments and defeats. Mine go back to the thirties. Yours go back 66 years—during which the Farmers Union has been providing leadership for the farmers of this country.

You have produced many great leaders from your organization. I have known and liked and worked closely with Jim Patton, Tony Dechant, and your fine State presidents for many years. Much of the legislation that has helped the American farmer to a better day originated in the Farmers Union meeting, was lobbied through the Congress by Farmers Union leaders, and was signed because the Presidents thought that they were for the best interests of the farmers.

I think, I hope, I believe I know what the farmer wants—and I want the farmer to have it.

I think that all of you want a fair price for your products—and if I have the power, you will have it.

I think that all of you want assurance that rising costs will not wipe out a lifetime investment—and I pledge you that if I can help you, every resource of mine you will have, including assurances that we will do everything that we can to control rising costs.

You want parity—you want a fair deal— you want an even chance to share in the rich and good life of this Nation—and I want you to have it.

You want the justice, the decency, and the opportunity that every American has the right to claim as his native right—and you will have them.

And so long as I am your President, you will always have my understanding, my admiration, and my wholehearted support in fighting with you to try to reach these goals. And we know that it will be a fight.

Your great Secretary, Orville Freeman, a Minnesota product, spent some of this weekend preparing papers telling me just how tough the fight was going to be. I came here this morning to ask you to join us in this fight to try to reach these goals.

There are some people in this country who have forgotten that without farms there would be no factories. There are some people who must know that without our people, there would be no cities.

There are those who no longer believe, it seems, in the partnership between the farmer and the Government—who tell us, on the airwaves from time to time, that we should "Get the Government out of agriculture."

There are those who fail to realize that many of the problems of urban America are a reflection of the failures in rural America. And when you get the Government out of agriculture, you sometimes get the farmer off the farm.

You know—as I know—that the farmer's problems are the problems of all America, and not any one group. And you know that the solutions to those problems are going to require the sympathy, the understanding, and the help of each good American in this country.

So I did my spring planting a little early this year. Three weeks ago, the President sent to the Congress a message on the farmer and rural America.

Just as I asked the mayors and the businessmen and other good Americans to read the report made by the national disorder commission on the problems in the cities, I ask each of you and all of you to get a copy of that message, and read the farm program outlined in that message. Try to help us preserve this freedom for the farmer and a reasonable amount of prosperity for his family.

Now, when you read that message, or when you see that message, much of it is going to sound familiar to the Farmers Union, because you and your leaders designed much of it, recommended much of it, and supported all of it.

Since I am a drop-in and not a dropout, and since your time is limited and they are waiting for me at the Capital now, I am just going to point out briefly some of the things that I asked for in that message, and that I need your help on.

I asked Congress to extend the supply management programs of the Food and Agriculture Act of 1965, and I asked them to extend it this year.

Chairman Poage tells me that his committee will give consideration to these recommendations shortly. We hope that with his assistance, and with Walter Mondale's assistance, with the help of all the Minnesota delegation, we can get permanent authority.

The farmer should not be asked to grow more than the market can take at a fair price.

I have asked the Congress to continue the direct payment programs of the 1965 act—they are the difference between profit and loss for many farmers each year.

I have asked the Congress to extend the Food for Freedom Act for an additional 3 years—because it is right for this Nation, whose sons came from many nations, to try to help hungry people eat when we have an abundance—and because I think it is good business for our farmers to help build new markets for our products in other lands around the world.

I have asked the Congress to authorize a National Food Bank—a security reserve for wheat, feed grains, soybeans—which would give the farmer higher prices, protect the

consumer from food scarcities and shortages, and provide the Government with an emergency food "cushion" in reaching supply-management decisions so we would not get caught short when we had a bad estimate.

I have asked the Congress to find the ways to give the farmer more bargaining power in the marketplace. Our working people and our good laboring friends in this country have not met all their needs or their desires. They still have many objectives and goals that we want to help them reach.

But the reason the farmer's income does not compare favorably with a laboring man's income is one reason, primarily, in my judgment: Labor has bargaining power; the farmer has none.

If you are to continue to pay the prices that industry charges and sets, if you are to continue to pay the wages that American workers are entitled to get, you are going to have to be put on an equal basis with industry and labor in bargaining power.

As you have so many times in the past, the Farmers Union has joined with us to help us to work, strive, and fight in order to get bargaining power for the American farmer.

Finally, I have asked the Congress for the programs to bring parity of opportunity to the rural children in America; to give them better elementary education; to give them better library facilities; to give them better transportation; to give us better farm credit; to give us more rural jobs; to give us decent housing; to give us adequate diets, with adequate consumer protection for the housewives; to give us the chance to lead a full and productive life.

The average farm family doesn't ask for much: the right to earn enough to clothe the bodies of their children, and to fill the stomachs of their hungry; to provide a roof over their house where they live; to have a school that their children can attend and a church where they can worship according to the dictates of their own conscience; and occasional recreation—to ride a boat, to see a movie, or some little something once in a while.

That is not asking much. It is not too much. But until we get it, we are not going to be satisfied—and we are going to fight together—until we reach those goals, until we reach those objectives.

During the months to come, you are going to hear these programs cussed—you may hear something cussed besides programs, too—and you are going to hear them discussed. I tell you now, it is not going to be easy to pass them. It is going to be harder this session than it would be in a normal session, because some of you may remember that there is something coming up down the road in November.

Some voices today express doubt that the American farm and the American farmer can survive. They say that we must sacrifice that priceless heritage—that American dream—on the altar of progress.

I say that they are just as wrong as they can possibly be.

If the farmers of America will only wake up and speak up courageously and forcefully in their own behalf—if we and you together have the patience and the determination, and the good, common horsesense to preserve, improve, and build upon the progress we have made in our agricultural programs— if we trust our hopes instead of relying on our fears and the demagogues who would mislead us, American agriculture can grow and prosper as it has never grown before.

I believe—and I have been in most of the 50 States of this Union, and I am just a few hours away from rural America at this moment—that rural America stands for the very best in all America.

Now, there is another area in which all Americans—mothers and fathers, farmers and city dwellers—must demonstrate that same courage, that same patience, that same determination.

For many years we have been engaged in a struggle in Southeast Asia to stop the on-rushing tide of Communist aggression.

We faced it when the Greek Communists were a few miles out of Athens a few years ago. We faced it when we had to fly zero weather into Berlin to feed the people when that city was beleaguered and cut off. We faced it on the Pusan Peninsula when our men were fighting for the hills of Korea and everybody said, "They are not worth it."

We fight Communist aggression the same today in Southeast Asia. This tide threatens to engulf that part of the world, and to affect the safety of every American home. It threatens our own security and it threatens the security of every nation allied with us. The blood of our young men this hour is being shed on that soil.

They know why they are there. I read 100 letters from them every week. They do not have the doubts that some at home preach. They have seen the enemy's determination. They have felt his thrust trying to conquer those who want to be left alone to determine their government for themselves, but whom the aggressor has marched over to try to envelop. Our fighting men know, from the evidence in their eyes, that we face a ruthless enemy. You make a serious mistake if you underestimate that enemy, his cause, and the effect of his conquest. They know from the carnage of the enemy's treacherous assaults that he has no feelings about deliberate murder of innocent women and children in the villages and the cities of South Vietnam.

They are not misled by propaganda or by the effort to gloss over the actions of an enemy who, I remind each of you, has broken every truce, and who makes no secret whatever of his intention and his determination to conquer by force and by aggression his neighbors to the south.

At the same time, during these past 4 years, we have made remarkable strides here at home.

We have opened the doors of freedom, full citizenship, and opportunity, to 30 million minority people, and we have sustained the highest level of prosperity for the longest period of time ever known.

But the time has come this morning when your President has come here to ask you people, and all the other people of this Nation, to join us in a total national effort to win the war, to win the peace, and to complete the job that must be done here at home.

I ask all of you to join in a program of national austerity to insure that our economy will prosper and that our fiscal position will be sound.

The Congress has been asked by the President—January, a year ago—to enact a tax bill which will impose upon the average citizen an additional one cent for each dollar in taxes. I ask you to bear this burden in the interest of a stronger Nation.

I am consulting with the Congress now on proposals for savings in our national budget—in nondefense, non-Vietnam, in other items all across the board.

If I can get the help of the Congress—and it is their will—we shall make reductions in that budget. They will postpone many needed actions that all of us would like to see taken in another time.

All travel outside the Western Hemisphere by Government officials and by all private citizens which is not absolutely essential to you should, in the interest of your country, be postponed.

I have already called for savings and cuts in expenditures and investments abroad by private corporations. We are going to intensify this program.

We have spent the weekend in an attempt to deal with the very troublesome gold problem. We have said that we are no longer going to be a party to encouraging the gold gambler or the gold speculator.

Most of all, I ask your help, and I come here to plead for your patriotic support, for our men, our sons, who are bearing the terrible burden of battle in Vietnam.

We seek not the victory of conquest, but we do seek the triumph of justice—the right of neighbors to be left alone; the right to determine for themselves what kind of a government to have. We seek that right and we will—make no mistake about it—win.

I am deeply aware of the yearning throughout this country, in every home of this land and throughout the Western world, for peace in the world. I believe all peoples want peace. I know that our peoples want peace, because we are a peace-loving nation. There is none among you who desires peace more than your own President and your own Vice President.

We hope to achieve an honorable peace and a just peace at the negotiating table.

But wanting peace, praying for peace, and desiring peace, as Chamberlain found out, doesn't always give you peace.

If the enemy continues to insist, as he does now—when he refuses to sit down and accept the fair proposition we made, that we would stop our bombing if he would sit down and talk promptly and productively—if he continues to insist, as he does now, that the outcome must be determined on the battlefield, then we will win peace on the battlefield by supporting our men who are doing that job there now.

We have a constitutional system. A majority of Americans have the right to select the leaders of their own choosing.

That is all we are asking for in South Vietnam.

You have provided your President with 100-odd ambassadors, the most trained men in every diplomatic outpost throughout the world.

Through West Point and Annapolis, you have provided your President with the best trained, best educated, most experienced and best led group of men that has ever formulated the strategy or the tactics for any nation.

Your President welcomes suggestions from committees, from commissions, from Congress, from private individuals, from clubs, from anyone who has a plan or program that can stand inspection and can offer us any hope of successfully reaching our goal, which is peace in the world.

We consider them all, long and late. We work every day of every week trying to find the answer.

But when aggressors in the world are on the march, as they were in World War I and II, as they were in Korea, as they were in Berlin, and as they were in other places in our national history, then we must unite until we convince them that they know they cannot win the battle in South Vietnam from our boys, as they are trying to win the battle from our leaders here in Washington in this country.

That is very dangerous for them, to think for a moment that they can attack the moral fiber of our own country to the point where our people will not support the policy of their own Government, of their own men whom they have committed to battle.

You may not have a boy in that battle that is going on now—or you may. But whether you do or you don't, our policy ought to be the same. We ought not let them win something in Washington that they can't win in Hué, in the I Corps, or in Khe Sanh. And we are not going to.

Now, this one final word: We ask every Senator, every Congressman, every farmer, and every businessman to join with us in our program of trying to unite this Nation, and trying to support our commitments and our own security.

We thought in the early years of World War I, before the *Lusitania* was sunk, that we had no concern with what happened across the waters. But we soon found out that we couldn't stand on that position.

We thought in World War II that we had no concern with what Hitler was doing in other parts of the world, and he wasn't very dangerous anyway, and we could sit this one out.

But we soon found that we lived in a very small world.

Even though we hadn't gone beyond our shores, they sank our fleet at Pearl Harbor.

We soon learned that we must never permit an aggressor's appetite to go uncontrolled because the person he eats up today may make him more hungry for you tomorrow.

We want peace and we are ready to meet now, this minute.

But you may want peace with your neighbor, too, and you may be willing to go across the road and into his yard to try to talk him into it. But if he keeps his door barred and every time you call him the call goes unanswered, and he refuses to meet you halfway, your wanting peace with him won't get it for you.

So as long as he feels that he can win something by propaganda in the country—that he can undermine the leadership—that he can bring down the government—that he can get something in the capital that he can't get from our men out there—he is going to keep on trying.

But I point out to you the time has come when we ought to unite, when we ought to stand up and be counted, when we ought to support our leaders, our Government, our men, and our allies until aggression is stopped, wherever it has occurred.

There are good, sincere, genuine people who believe that there are plans that could bring us to peace soon.

Some think that we ought to get it over with, with a much wider war.

We have looked at those plans, and looked at them carefully.

We have looked at the possible danger of involving another million men.

We have tried to evaluate how you could get it over with, with less cost than we are now paying.

We do not seek a wider war. We do not think that is a wise course.

There is another extreme that thinks that you can just have peace by talking for it, by wishing for it, by saying you want it, and all you need to do is to pull back to the cities.

We had that plan tested in the Tet offensive. They killed thousands and thousands in the cities.

Those of you who think that you can save lives by moving the battlefield in from the mountains to the cities where the people live have another think coming.

If you think you can stop aggression by getting out of its way and letting them take over, roll over you, you have another think coming, too.

Most of these people don't say, "Cut and run." They don't say, "Pull out." They don't want a wider war. They don't want to do more than we are doing. They say that they want to do less than we are doing.

But we are not doing enough to win it the

way we are doing it now, and we are constantly trying to find additional things that it is reasonable, and prudent, and safe to do.

So you have one extreme that says, "Let's go in with flags flying and get it over with quickly, regardless of the dangers involved."

You have another group that says, "We are doing too much. Let's pull out. Let's be quiet. We want peace."

Then you have a third group that says, "We don't want to conquer you. We don't want to destroy your nation. We don't want to divide you. We just want to say to you that we have an obligation. We have signed 42 alliances with people of the world. We have said that when an aggressor comes across this line to try to dominate other people, and they call on us to help, we are going to come and help, until you decide to leave your neighbors alone."

We think that we are making progress on getting them to decide. They think they are making progress on getting us to decide to give up and pull out.

But I think they will find out in the days ahead that we are reasonable people, that we are fair people, that we are not folks who want to conquer the world.

We don't seek one acre of anybody else's soil.

We love nothing more than peace, but we hate nothing more than surrender and cowardice.

We don't ask anybody else to surrender. We just ask them to sit down and talk, meet at a family table and try to work out our differences. But we don't plan to surrender, either; we don't plan to pull out, either; we don't plan to let people influence us, pressure us, and force us to divide our Nation in a time of national peril.

The hour is here.

This Government has the best diplomats. This Government has the best generals. This

Government has the best admirals. This Government has the best resources in every corner of the globe.

Although I have had more Secretaries of State than any President in modern times, or more would-be Secretaries of State, I still think this Government has one of the most able and patriotic men I have ever known sitting in that chair, and I think his policy is sound.

So as we go back to our homes, let's go back dedicated to achieving peace in the world, trying to get a fair balance here at home, trying to make things easier and better for our children than we had them,

but, above all, trying to preserve this American system, which is first in the world today.

I want it to stay first, but it cannot be first if we pull out and tuck our tail and violate our commitments.

Thank you very much.

NOTE: The President spoke at 10:41 a.m. at the Leamington Hotel in Minneapolis, Minn. In his opening words he referred to Vice President Hubert H. Humphrey, Tony T. Dechant, President of the National Farmers Union, Senator Walter F. Mondale of Minnesota, and Representative W. R. Poage of Texas. During his remarks he referred to Senator Eugene J. McCarthy of Minnesota, James R. Jones, Special Assistant to the President, James G. Patton, former President of the National Farmers Union, and Orville L. Freeman, Secretary of Agriculture.

143 Remarks at the Conference on Foreign Policy for Leaders of National Nongovernmental Organizations. *March* 19, 1968

Secretary Rusk, distinguished guests:

Secretary Rusk and I are very pleased to welcome you here today. Your presence, I think, proves a very basic truth about our American democracy—that is that foreign policy is the people's business. It is not restricted to any favored few. It is the proper concern of every American who is interested in his Nation's destiny.

The primary business of our foreign policy is to build a world in which we and our children and our neighbors throughout the world may live in freedom and may live in dignity.

The heritage of 5,000 years of human civilization then hangs on our success.

I have said many times that these are years of testing. I have said that what is being tested is the will of America—not the capacity of America. We have the will; we have the strength; we have the power. But the test is—do we have the will; do we have the spirit to succeed?

History has elected to probe the depth

of our commitment to freedom. How strongly are we really devoted to resist the tide of aggression? How ready are we to make good on our solemn pledges to other nations?

Since the end of World War II, Americans—regardless of political party—have answered, not with words, but with deeds, with billions through the Marshall Plan, to give new life to a shattered Europe; with leadership in creating the United Nations and all the collective security arrangements that meant to insure that no aggressor ever again would doubt the resolve of free men to stand up and to defend freedom.

We demonstrated with a tireless quest for rules to keep the nuclear beast in his cage and with foreign aid programs to help lift the less developed countries—containing two of every three citizens of the free world—to help them to true independence.

Now, these are the basic themes of what American foreign policy is all about. They have been essentially the same for more than

20 years now, under all administrations—Republican and Democratic.

They are the same themes that are being challenged at this moment and defended by our men in Vietnam. There in South Vietnam, aggression fights not only on the battlefield of village and hill and jungle and city—the enemy has reached out to fight in the hearts and minds of the American people.

He has mounted a heavy and a calculated attack on our character as a people, on our confidence and our will as a nation, on the continuity of policy and principle that has so long and so proudly marked America as the real champion of man's freedom.

Let no single American mistake the enemy's major offensive now. That offensive is aimed squarely at the citizens of America. It is an assault that is designed to crack America's will. It is designed to make some men want to surrender; it is designed to make other men want to withdraw; it is designed to trouble and worry and confuse others.

But it is, in effect, an assault that is designed to crack your country's will.

We are the aggressor's real target because of what we represent.

When we are gone, I ask you, what other nation in the world is going to stand up and protect the little man's freedom anywhere in the world?

Yes, the enemy seeks more than the conquest of South Vietnam. He seeks more than the collapse of all of Southeast Asia. He seeks more than the destruction of the Pacific dream where a new and a prospering Asia sees its hopeful future.

Aggression at this moment is striking in Vietnam at the very root of life—at the very idea of freedom—at the right of any man or any nation to live with its neighbors without fear, to find its own free destiny, and to determine it for itself.

We cannot fail these anxious and these expectant millions. We just must not fail ourselves.

We must not break our commitment for freedom and for the future of the world. We have set our course. We will pursue it just as long as aggression threatens it.

And make no mistake about it—America will prevail.

This afternoon I am reminded of another day many years ago—the year was 1937 and I had just returned to Washington as a young Congressman in my twenties. That, too, was a time of grave challenge. But it was also a time of great hope and great promise.

You may recall that there were great popular movements in those days against any violence in international affairs. Well-meaning, sincere, good people around this entire country were pledging themselves never to bear arms. They were castigating our Government for any involvement beyond our own shores. They were even refusing to spend $5 million to fortify Guam.

President Roosevelt went to Chicago one night in 1937. He delivered a speech which still holds much for all of us today. Franklin D. Roosevelt warned the world that night that the shadow of aggression threatened not only the nations that were immediately in the aggressor's path, but it threatened the future of all free men and women.

On that night in Chicago he asked the nations of the world to "quarantine the aggressors."

For liberty and independence can be secure only if free men resolve to draw a line, to stand on it, and to hold it.

President Roosevelt called for "a concerted effort in opposition to those violations of treaties and those ignorings of humane instincts which today are creating a state of international anarchy and instability from which there is no escape through mere isolation. . . ."

Well, that was 1937. It took some time and it took a world catastrophe to wake men up and for them to finally hear that message when we were attacked.

So, let this generation of ours learn from the mistakes of the past. Let us recognize that there is no resigning from world responsibility. There is no cheap or no easy way to find the road to freedom and the road to order. But danger and sacrifice built this land and today we are the number one nation. And we are going to stay the number one nation.

Our forefathers asked no quarter of the beast and the plague and the hunger that they found when they came to the new world.

In the words of a great President, Abraham Lincoln, "with firmness in the right, as God gives us to see the right, let us strive on to finish the work we are in."

I ask your help in finishing that work. Thank you and good night.

NOTE: The President spoke at 6 p.m. at the Department of State, which sponsored the conference. In his opening words he referred to Dean Rusk, Secretary of State.

144 Presidential Unit Citation Awarded the 6234th Tactical Fighter Wing, 7th/13th Air Force (Southeast Asia), Pacific Air Forces. *March* 20, 1968

CITATION TO ACCOMPANY THE AWARD OF

THE PRESIDENTIAL UNIT CITATION

TO THE

6234TH TACTICAL FIGHTER WING

The 6234th Tactical Fighter Wing, Pacific Air Forces, distinguished itself by extraordinary heroism in connection with military operations against hostile armed forces in Southeast Asia, from 8 April 1965 to 8 April 1966. Throughout this period, the gallantry, professionalism, determination, and esprit de corps consistently demonstrated by the personnel of the 6234th Tactical Fighter Wing were instrumental factors in the successful completion of their assigned mission under extremely difficult and hazardous conditions. During this period, personnel of the Wing flew 10,797 sorties, totaling 26,165 hours, in the face of fire from modern, sophisticated enemy air defense weaponry, to include surface-to-air missiles. The pilots of the 6234th Tactical Fighter Wing were responsible for the destruction or damage of important military targets in North Vietnam, including airfields, petroleum storage areas, railroads, and missile sites. As a result of the Wing's operation against the infiltration routes used by the North Vietnamese, the support of the hostile forces in South Vietnam was made more difficult and costly. During this period of sustained combat operations, the Wing developed and implemented a new training program and perfected techniques for use in the F4C (Phantom) night operations, which proved exceptionally effective in assuring target destruction and providing security for aircrews. The extraordinary heroism and outstanding performance demonstrated by this unit in the pursuit of its mission are in keeping with the highest standards of performance and traditions of the United States military service and reflect great credit upon the unit and the United States Air Force.

LYNDON B. JOHNSON

145 Message to the Congress Transmitting Annual Report of the National Science Foundation. *March* 20, 1968

To the Congress of the United States:

I am pleased to submit to the Congress the Seventeenth Annual Report of the National Science Foundation for fiscal year 1967.

This Report highlights a year of advance in exploring the frontiers of science and in educating the scientists of tomorrow. During fiscal year 1967, the Foundation has:

—Provided $220 million to support scientific research projects in every State of the Union. Some 5,500 scientists carried out this work in colleges and universities.

—Invested $123 million to improve science education at every level from elementary school through the university. These funds provided training for about 38,000 high school teachers, 5,000 elementary school teachers, and 5,000 college instructors.

The Foundation's programs have helped to unearth new information of both scientific and practical importance. For example, we have now:

—Learned more about how genes pass on hereditary characteristics. This knowledge may some day lead to control of diseases and the prevention of inherited defects.

—Neared completion at Cornell University of the world's most powerful circular electron accelerator, an atom smasher that will enable us to advance our understanding of the atom.

—Begun sea grant programs to develop knowledge and to train manpower for developing our marine resources.

—Increased support for the national weather modification program to speed the day when we can reduce losses caused by drought, hail, and violent storms.

—Supported research on a new plastic for possible use as heat shields for re-entry of space vehicles.

The National Science Foundation also continues to increase its support of social science research. A Special Commission on the Social Sciences was established by the National Science Board to provide guidance in this important area.

In my 1967 message to Congress on Health and Education, I directed the National Science Foundation, working with the Office of Education of the Department of Health, Education, and Welfare, to establish an experimental program for developing the educational potential of computers. This has been done through a newly established Office of Computing Activities. The day is not far when these exciting new machines will be contributing to the education of our people.

The Annual Report of the National Science Foundation deserves the attention of the Congress and the American people. It is proof that we are penetrating the unknown, educating new generations of scientists, and making our scientific research yield maximum value.

LYNDON B. JOHNSON

The White House
March 20, 1968

NOTE: The report, transmitted to the President on January 15, 1968, is entitled "National Science Foundation: Seventeenth Annual Report for the Fiscal Year Ended June 30, 1967" (Government Printing Office, 219 pp.).

146 Letter to the President of the Senate and to the Speaker of the House Urging Actions To Increase American Exports. *March* 20, 1968

Dear Mr. President: (*Dear Mr. Speaker:*)

In this letter I ask the Congress to take further steps to improve America's balance of payments position. That position is the hinge of the dollar's strength abroad and the soundness of the Free World monetary system.

Both actions I recommend today will help to increase America's exports—a vital element in the balance of payments equation.

I urge the Congress to:

—Allocate $500 million of the Export-Import Bank's existing authority as a special fund to finance a broadened program to sell American goods in foreign markets.

—Approve promptly the $2.4 million supplemental appropriation which I submitted on March 11. This will enable the Commerce Department to launch a 5-year program to promote American exports.

Last year, the United States exported some $30 billion worth of products—the highest in our history. The trade surplus resulting from that commerce was about $3.5 billion—large but far from large enough.

Our concern now must be to improve that record as part of a long-term program to keep the dollar strong and to remove the temporary restraints on the flow of capital abroad.

For more than three decades, the Export-Import Bank has effectively encouraged the sale of American goods abroad. Through loans, guarantees and insurance, it has financed billions of dollars in U.S. exports—the products of our farms and factories. But new competitive conditions in world trade demand added scope and flexibility in the Bank's operations.

The $500 million allocation I am requesting will finance export transactions not covered under the Bank's present program. It will:

—Support the determined efforts of the entire business community to expand exports.

—Assist American firms who now sell only within the United States to expand their markets and send their goods abroad.

—Make available to American firms export financing more competitive with that provided by other major trading nations and especially suited to developing new markets.

To achieve the greatest benefit from this new export financing plan, I will establish an Export Expansion Advisory Committee.

chaired by the Secretary of Commerce, to provide guidance to the Board of Directors of the Export-Import Bank.

The Kennedy Round has added a new and exciting dimension to the expansion of trade opportunities for American business. We must be prepared to take full advantage of these and other opportunities now unfolding in foreign commerce. I believe that a long-range and sustained promotional program can go far to stimulate the flow of American exports.

In my Fiscal 1969 Budget, I requested a $25.7 million appropriation to launch such a program. In order to get an immediate start, I asked the Congress last week for a $2.4 million supplemental appropriation for Fiscal 1968. With these funds, we can participate in more trade fairs, establish Joint Export Associations for various industries, conduct marketing studies, and take other steps to stimulate the growth of sales abroad.

The new authority for the Export-Import Bank and the supplemental appropriation for export promotion will reinforce our trade position. These measures will help business firms penetrate and secure new foreign markets and provide the follow-on services to expand their position in these markets.

I urge the Congress to take prompt action on these requests.

The threat posed by our balance of payments deficit is immediate and serious and requires concerted action.

We have been moving in a number of ways to counter that threat and to carry out the program I announced on January 1, 1968.[1]

The proposals in this letter to increase our exports are part of a national balance of payments strategy.

We have already acted to:

—Restrain the flow of direct investment funds abroad, and foreign lending by banks and other financial institutions.
—Reduce the number of government personnel in overseas posts, curtail government travel abroad, and negotiate new arrangements to lessen the impact of military expenditures overseas.
—Initiate discussions with other countries on actions to improve our trade position.
—Launch a new program, in cooperation with private industry, to attract more foreign visitors to these shores. As part of this program, I have asked for a supplemental appropriation of $1.7 million to strengthen the U.S. Travel Service.
—Remove the outmoded and unnecessary gold cover, in legislation which I signed yesterday.[2]
—Reach an agreement with our six active gold pool partners to halt speculative attacks on gold reserves.

Further measures await Congressional action.

One is the elimination of obsolete and burdensome visa requirements which now discourage foreign travelers from visiting our land.

Another is legislation to reduce the expenditures of Americans traveling abroad.

Finally, there is the anti-inflation tax—the most critical measure of all. This tax—one penny on every dollar earned—is the best investment Americans can make for fiscal responsibility at home and for a strong economic position abroad.

The nations of the world look to us now for economic leadership. The fabric of international cooperation upon which the world's postwar prosperity has been built is now threatened. If that fabric is torn apart,

---

[1] See Item 2.

[2] Public Law 90–269, 82 Stat. 50.

the consequences will not be confined to foreign countries—but will touch every American. We must not let this happen. Prompt enactment of the tax bill will be clear and convincing proof of our leadership and an exercise of our responsibility.

The hour is late. The need is urgent.

I call upon the Congress to act—now.

Sincerely,

LYNDON B. JOHNSON

NOTE: This is the text of identical letters addressed to the Honorable Hubert H. Humphrey, President of the Senate, and to the Honorable John W. Mc-Cormack, Speaker of the House of Representatives.

A bill broadening the authority of the Export-Import Bank was approved by the President on July 7, 1968 (see Item 377).

The Export Expansion Advisory Committee was established on July 31, 1968 (see Item 422).

On March 27, 1968, the President signed Proclamation 3837 "World Trade Week, 1968" (4 Weekly Comp. Pres. Docs., p. 583; 33 F.R. 5079; 3 CFR, 1968 Comp., p. 32).

147   Remarks of Welcome at the White House to President Stroessner of Paraguay.   *March* 20, 1968

Mr. President:

In the language of diplomacy, our meeting this morning is called an "official visit." But if the weather that you brought with you continues, I think we should call it an "official picnic."

It was about this time last year that it was my pleasure to visit Uruguay for the historic Punta del Este conference.

It was there that the leaders of Latin America and the United States reaffirmed the historic pledge of the Alliance for Progress: "to bring our people accelerated economic progress and broader social justice within the framework of personal dignity and political liberty."

You and I, Mr. President, together with our fellow Presidents, resolved "to achieve to the fullest measure the free, just, and democratic social order demanded by the peoples of this hemisphere."

It is very clear that there has been progress in Latin America toward the goals of social justice during the 1960's. Insofar as these goals have been approached in many nations, those who love freedom take new heart from their example. Insofar as they have not yet been achieved, those who fear for

freedom have even greater cause to spur their efforts.

It is also clear that there has been progress in Latin America toward the goals of economic prosperity—but I think we all know, not near enough progress. The vast resources of a great continent are just now beginning to really be tapped.

Your country, Mr. President, has made an impressive beginning toward regional growth—with the great hydroelectric plant, whose energies you will share with Argentina and Brazil, with the Trans-Chaco Highway which will help join the peoples of several nations in new communications and new prosperity.

The Alliance for Progress is helping to bring social and economic hope to millions in Paraguay and to the other countries of the hemisphere. We are proud to be partners in this effort that is being made in this hemisphere for these peoples.

You are welcome among us, Mr. President, and I look forward to our discussions together.

The first day of spring gives us a wonderful excuse to meet. If anyone from the press should ask us what we discussed we can always answer, "Well, first, we talked about the weather."

NOTE: The President spoke at 11:35 a.m. on the South Lawn at the White House where President Alfredo Stroessner was given a formal welcome with full military honors. President Stroessner responded in Spanish. A translation of his remarks follows:

Mr. President and Mrs. Johnson:

It is an honor for me to be in the United States of America as a special guest of the Government of this powerful, noble, and hospitable country. My presence here comes at an exceptional time for the free world, to which by its own right my country belongs. I bring, Mr. President, the homage of the Paraguayan people to the great people of the United States of America, together with the testimony of a sincere friendship, never contradicted by our deeds.

I wish to express my admiration for the creative capability of this great Nation, at the forefront of Christian civilization, whose principles you have defended, are defending, and will surely continue to defend in the future, with faith in what is right and with the blood of its sons in the crucial moments of world history.

You have had the kindness of remembering on this solemn occasion the time at which President Rutherford B. Hayes acted as arbiter in our boundary problem. The results of this arbitration gave Paraguay title to the disputed lands, a decision that the Americas acknowledged as an expression of justice on the part of the country of George Washington.

I feel certain that my visit to the United States of America will help to increase even more the traditional ties of friendship between our two peoples and that cooperation, solidarity, and mutual assistance will be the legitimate instruments of an active and constructive pan-Americanism.

Surely these instruments will redound to the benefit and happiness of millions of human beings in our hemisphere who await the determination of a formula which will accelerate their development and integration within a framework of peace, democracy, and liberty.

My country is proud to have lived up to its duties as an American nation, and in its name I reaffirm

to you its willingness to go on upholding the standard of a glorious civilization, of which the United States is the unquestioned leader.

Assuming with all seriousness its international and internal responsibilites, Paraguay will always honor its word, founded in the confidence given it by its historical background, full of glowing deeds whose significance commits us before posterity.

I am persuaded that if our peoples contribute every day to the forging of a better understanding between themselves we shall be in a better condition to face problems related to development, self-determination, and democracy.

The spiritual heritage of the American directs us to the achievement of progress. Paraguay lives up to the ideal of making full use of its own economic resources, in order to earn the respect and appreciation of others.

Thus, we hope to stimulate the building of more schools, more university facilities, more houses, more roads, better health assistance for the people, more material and spiritual accomplishments which will be the foundation of structural changes and social reforms without which the Americas will be unable to wage their memorable struggle for democracy and liberty.

My country has faith and confidence in its future. The institutions established by mutual accord to improve the well-being of all Americans deserve all of our support. The Alliance for Progress is a vast plan and a great effort to overcome problems caused by underdevelopment, and on its stage the role played by the United States of America is of vital importance.

The same should be said in relation to the project of the Latin American Common Market, to which my country gives its warm support with the same sincerity with which it has collaborated in all the other credit programs designed to strengthen our economy.

Mr. President, I feel a fervent desire to once again shake your friendly hand, here in your own noble country. Please receive the sincere affection of my people, whom I have the honor to serve with all the energies of my spirit.

Please accept, Mr. President, the testimony of my friendship, in the assurance that God will always bless the United States of America in its struggle for freedom, justice, and welfare for all people.

148 Toasts of the President and President Stroessner of Paraguay. *March 20, 1968*

President Stroessner, Vice President and Mrs. Humphrey, Justice and Mrs. Brennan, *distinguished guests, ladies and gentlemen:*

Mrs. Johnson and I were very happy to

be able to welcome two visitors this morning—very important visitors: President Stroessner and the first day of spring.

I think it is appropriate, though, Mr. President, for me to put in a word here and warn you and caution you about our Washington climate. The political winds blow very strong around here. I have observed in the last few days that it can turn very chilly, very suddenly. A little reassessment will change the entire course of these things.

One famous American humorist, Mark Twain, must have been thinking of Washington when he once said: "In the spring, I have counted 136 different kinds of weather inside of 24 hours."

Mr. President, that is particularly true of Washington in election years.

Just last week, we had a new weather front move in very suddenly. This one came from up on the Hill of the United States Senate and caught some people just standing out in the cold. They had to start running just to keep warm.

But we, Mr. President, are very glad that we can offer you our warm hospitality here in this first house of the land tonight. I know you will agree with me that all of us can learn much from the family of Latin American nations. They are a family of nations that have learned to live together and to live in peace together.

There has been no fighting of any real significance among them for more than a quarter of a century now. Mr. President, this is the trend that should unite all of the continents in a common cause. This thing we call peace is a thing that we want most. It can be the contagious spirit that excites all mankind to the miracles that men can work if only men can learn to work together in trust—and in friendship—and in peace.

Mr. President, your administration's motto is "Peace and progress and work." I share your very deep conviction that there can be no lasting peace without genuine progress.

All men of all faiths want peace. But there are different kinds of peace; men have different judgments about the better ways to obtain peace.

The great Prime Minister of Great Britain thought of one way to get peace—Mr. Chamberlain—but he was disillusioned.

Another Prime Minister, Mr. Churchill, thought of another way to get peace. As a consequence, many men had to pledge their lives, their blood, and their treasure.

But now it has been more than two decades. I think it has been confirmed in the eyes of history that a quick peace, an easy peace, is not necessarily a just peace—and a peace with honor that will last.

Frequently you can lose more lives with a phony peace than you can with a just one.

So, Mr. President, I know that you agree that there can be no genuine progress without peace in the world and without a fair reward for hard work. That statement will stand emphasis in this country—and in other countries in the world today. There can be no assurance of a fair reward unless people can share fully in all the aspects of their national life.

Mr. President, I have been thinking of your visit since we were together in Punta del Este and since the unity and peaceful nature of the nations of the Western Hemisphere was brought together there and we resolved to unite.

The United States tonight stands eager and ready to encourage such developments as are contained in your administration's motto throughout Latin America.

Mr. President, we take great pleasure, Mrs. Johnson and I, in welcoming you to this house as a leader who is trying his best to speed the growth of his nation and who, I have observed, is making contributions to the progress of this hemisphere.

As your representative of your country sits on the Security Council of the United Nations and works in his own way every day to try to better humanity, the American people take this opportunity to express to you, and through you to him and your people, our gratitude for his conscientious approach and his dedicated effort.

Ladies and gentlemen, I should like to ask all of you to join me in a toast to President Alfredo Stroessner and particularly to the good people of Paraguay.

[Following the toast the President continued speaking, as follows:]

Mr. President, when I was a young man in grade school one of my first declamations that I had to memorize contained the phrase that "The most beautiful vision these eyes ever beheld was the flag of my country in a foreign land."

One of the greatest honors that any citizen of the United States can have is the privilege of wearing a uniform of his country. The greatest honor that the President can bestow upon any man who wears that uniform on behalf of this Nation is the Medal of Honor. They come few and far between. They are given only to the most gallant and the most courageous and the most dedicated who have demonstrated in battle their love for freedom and liberty.

Tonight, Mrs. Johnson and I are privileged to have among us the parents of a young man who wore that uniform and wore it with pride and distinction and who never had a chance to see that Medal of Honor because he gave his life in order that we might live— just as this man [*indicating portrait of Lincoln*] gave his life in order to preserve the Union.

I think it would be quite appropriate and I would ask that each of you join me in standing and paying silent tribute to 2d Lt. Robert J. Hibbs of 316 West 18th Street, Cedar Falls, Iowa, whose father and mother, Mr. and Mrs. Walter E. Hibbs, are our guests here this evening.

Lieutenant Hibbs was awarded the highest decoration this Nation can give posthumously on January 26, 1967, for service above and beyond the call of duty for us.

Mr. Hibbs, will you and Mrs. Hibbs stand, please.

NOTE: The President spoke at 10:18 p.m. in the State Dining Room at the White House at a dinner honoring President Alfredo Stroessner. In his opening words he also referred to Vice President Hubert H. Humphrey, Mrs. Humphrey, Associate Justice William J. Brennan, Jr., of the U.S. Supreme Court, and Mrs. Brennan.

President Stroessner responded in Spanish, a translation of which follows:

Mr. President and Mrs. Johnson, ladies and gentlemen:

I feel a vivid emotion, as President of my country, to be at the White House beside the illustrious Chief Executive of the United States of America, who has elected to honor Paraguay in my person.

The White House is the symbol of the history of a great people and the official residence of eminent statesmen who have ruled from here the destiny of a noble and great federation of States, continuing with the thought the glorious George Washington initiated in this part of the world which first brought forth a government of, for, and by the people.

I am the bearer of a message of sincere friendship on the part of the Paraguayan people for the people of the United States of America. In this centennial of our great national ordeal as a nation, that still resounds and which we celebrate in this moment, is to be found the root of our will to be free, to be sovereign, and independent of all foreign power.

These are the causes that the forefathers of our country waved as a banner for human redemption, as an emblem of fraternity towards America and the world.

As a Paraguayan and as an American, I am honored to be seated at this table where President Johnson, in his high post as head of this Government, remembers the glorious past of my country and my people.

Today, President Johnson and I are renewing the fruitful and profitable personal conversations initiated on the occasion of the meeting of the American Presidents in Punta del Este. We have agreed that we should face together the many problems that confront our peoples' governments, using first of all our own spiritual and material resources—and then seeking the cooperation, solidarity, and mutual assistance of the other countries of the hemisphere which foster the noble ideal of an active, positive, and constructive pan-Americanism.

I consider it one of the great privileges of my life to again visit Washington after 15 years and to be able to establish a constructive dialogue with the eminent leader of this country, who, from his office, is defending with intelligence, patience, and valor the sacred principles of democracy and freedom in the world.

It is not an easy task to have the immense responsibility of conducting a country like yours, Mr. President.

You are serving your country, upholding its principles, and renewing its hopes and ideals in the march toward the formation of a better world—a world of peace, work, and happiness.

It is necessary, Mr. President, to possess—as you do—a high level of physical and moral energy in order to stay at the helm of a country which is at the forefront of the modern world. Your country is a glowing expression of the spiritual force of the new world, that weighs in the balance of justice, directing it to the final triumph of the common good.

I wish to express my deep gratitude for your splendid courtesy and friendship in recalling the glorious past of my people, always ready to defend its freedom. The people of the United States of America know that my country is ready to honor that past, firm in its determination to fight any menace to democracy and liberty.

This was clearly demonstrated not long ago when we were at the side of those who courageously assured the people of the Dominican Republic the privilege of governing themselves, by their sovereign will as expressed at the polling booths.

My visit to the hospitable land of liberty takes place shortly after I have once again received a clear-cut mandate from my people, freely expressed at the polls in a civic example seldom seen in my country.

This election was held with the participation of four political parties which reflect the various political beliefs in our country, and resulted in their participation in the three powers of the state. I have again accepted the honor of this responsibility as I have always maintained that, in a democracy, every citizen should serve the people to the extent of his ability, without expecting to be entitled to any personal gain.

My country is working in peace. I feel proud of the stability of its currency, of its republican institutions, and of its continued progress. Its potential wealth is fairly distributed throughout its territory, and only awaits our continued effort to incorporate it into the mainstream of the economy.

This economy is prospering from productive work and is fortified by the incorporation of foreign capital, which finds in our country the climate of respect, peace, and security that we have achieved, under ideal conditions for a profitable investment under protection of the law.

All of my efforts since assuming office would have been in vain if it were not for the heroic spirit of the Paraguayan people, which is legendary in this hemisphere.

The greatest homage we can render to the memory of our dead is to work ceaselessly to improve the nation which they defended with their supreme sacrifice.

My Government is dedicated to the acceleration of progress throughout our fertile land, which until now has not suffered from the population explosion which characterizes other regions of this planet.

Economic and social development is a common task of all the free countries of Latin America, and in this spirit, my country is ready to support continuously all the projects which work toward this great objective in order to achieve the goals of the Alliance for Progress.

These projects include the hydroelectric plant at Acaray, development of a great international highway system, and the improvement of a river communications complex serving our neighboring countries, as well as ourselves.

Mr. President, I have been moved with sincere emotion in Arlington Cemetery at the Tomb of the Unknowns who died in the battle for freedom and democracy, and at the grave of the great President, John F. Kennedy, passed away.

Please accept, in the name of my party and me, our profound thanks for the magnificent demonstrations of friendship which we are receiving from your people and your Government, ever since we have been guests of this great and gracious country.

On returning to my country, I shall take with me the assurance of a friendship strengthened even further by the personal contact which we are maintaining in the best American spirit.

I raise a toast to the generous people of the United States of America, gallant exponents of a great cause and a great principle for which we shall fight side-by-side, shoulder-to-shoulder—for the personal good fortune of the distinguished Mrs. Johnson and for the illustrious President, Lyndon B. Johnson, who honors us with his moving and noble tributes, which I accept in the name of my people—for the happiness of all ladies and gentlemen who are here with us at this table of friendship, and for that of all the free peoples of the universe.

149 Remarks to the First Graduating Class at the Foreign Service Institute's Vietnam Training Center. *March* 21, 1968

Ambassador Allen, most distinguished graduates, ladies and gentlemen:

Today those of you who have gathered here at the White House set out as warriors for peace. I asked you to come here because I want all the people of America to know of your particular mission.

You must expect that your efforts will go largely unreported. Your progress is going to be harder to see and harder to measure.

But the victories you win are the ones on which peace will be built in Vietnam.

Let no one misread our purpose: Peace is our goal.

Let no one mistake our resolve: Peace will be won.

It will be peace with honor. It will be a peace in which the people of South Vietnam will be free to live the lives they choose to live.

Peace will come because brave men—and free men—are preventing aggressors from taking a neighbor's land by force.

Peace will come because men like you are willing to help the people of South Vietnam forge a free nation. It will come because those beleaguered people themselves—after a century of colonialism and a generation of war—have not broken before the enemy's terror.

There is a deep and a quiet courage among millions of simple people in Vietnam. It goes largely unreported—the stories of the farmers, the stories of the teachers in the schools, the stories of the students and the mothers and the fathers and the families who sacrifice and struggle go unnoticed in the anguish of war.

But when the enemy unleashed his savage attack over the Tet holidays, he thought that he would crack the will of the Vietnamese people.

But he was wrong.

He did not crack the will of the students in the high school in Quang Nam. Instead, they turned out in a body to volunteer for the emergency work of reconstruction.

He did not crack the will of the citizens of the Hang Xang District in Saigon, who fought the Vietcong with sticks, or the nurses near Baria, who hid a Korean medical team while the enemy occupied their hospital for more than 30 hours.

Stories like these were repeated up and down this ravaged land. We did not read about them. The enemy attack is what got the headlines.

But in Vietnam there were heroes by the hundreds that dark week—who were unseen and unsung. And their actions spoke for a free people who are determined to find their own way into their own future.

Their will did not, as expected, break under the fire.

Neither shall ours break under frustration.

Peace will come to Vietnam. The terror of an invading enemy will be turned back. The work of reconstruction will go on. And a nation will rise, strong and free.

I think that each of you standing here on the White House steps today will be proud to say that you were there—that you were a part of helping a struggling people come into their own, participate in self-determination, and become a part of liberty and freedom in the world.

I think you will be proud to say that you were there because you will be the builders of the peace.

I am honored to greet you this morning.

Thank you very much.

NOTE: The President spoke at 11:42 a.m. in the Rose Garden at the White House to a graduating class of 16 young men from the State Department, the United States Information Agency, and the Agency for International Development, who had completed the one-year course prior to assignment in Vietnam. In his opening words the President referred to former Ambassador George V. Allen, Director of the Foreign Service Institute.

150   Remarks Upon Signing Bill To Designate the San Rafael Wilderness, California. *March 21, 1968*

Secretary Udall, Congressman Aspinall, distinguished Members of the Congress, ladies and gentlemen:

We have come here to the Cabinet Room this morning to preserve another part of America's richest legacy—the land itself.

We assure that more of our beautiful country is going to remain forever wild, remain just as the first American saw it, just as God made it.

The bill that we will sign this morning will cost the taxpayer nothing, yet we think that it will enrich America forever.

The Wilderness Act that I signed in 1964 was a milestone in conservation. It represented the thoughts and the dreams of leading conservationists—like Secretary Udall and others, who had worked with him. They finally were able to bring to me a bill that incorporated into law their vision. It set aside 9 million unspoiled acres.

As we meet here, we are participants today in adding to that another 143,000 acres—the San Rafael Wilderness.

San Rafael is rocky, rugged, wooded, and lonely.

It is lonely, but it is also near enough to be only an hour's drive from the homes of millions of Americans.

San Rafael is part of the new conservation, the enlightened land policy that puts parks where people can get to them.

In the last few years—with the help of a conservation-minded Congress and leaders of public thought in this country and public life and private life—we have been able to put 32 seashores, lakeshores, and parks near our large metropolitan centers. That has made them within easy drive of 120 million people.

A growing America will absorb about one million acres a year. But this year we are going to turn a million and a half acres into parks and seashores, forests, and wilderness for the people.

We will be putting back into the public domain more land than we are taking out, for a change.

I want so much to protect and extend the legacy of our land. I want so much to take the pieces of our birthright that we should never have lost—and I want to reclaim them, restore them, and return them to the American people.

San Rafael is part of that work. I have asked the Congress to approve three other wilderness areas. Soon I am going to ask them to approve some more.

Wilderness parks should be a part of the America of tomorrow—the kind of America that we think we are building today.

I am very proud to sign this bill. I believe

that it will enrich the spirit of America.

We can be sure that, when the terrible trials of this generation are only ancient memories, what we do today will still endure.

I am so glad that we still have in our country dedicated men who make it their first concern to conserve our resources, to make it possible for our children to enjoy some of the things that are our blessings.

To Secretary Udall, who has been in the forefront of all of these conservation movements, to Mr. Laurance Rockefeller, and to all the other conservation organizations and societies and groups, on behalf of the American people, I say to them—along with the Members of Congress who have helped them, who have supported them, and who have put their own necks on the line in passing measures of this kind—well done, and thank you.

NOTE: The President spoke at 12:35 p.m. in the Cabinet Room at the White House. In his opening words he referred to Stewart L. Udall, Secretary of the Interior, and Representative Wayne N. Aspinall of Colorado. During his remarks he referred to Laurance S. Rockefeller, Chairman of the Citizens Advisory Committee on Recreation and Natural Beauty.

As enacted, the bill (S. 889) is Public Law 90–271 (82 Stat. 51).

For the President's remarks upon signing the Wilderness Act on September 3, 1964, see 1963–64 volume, this series, Book II, Item 554.

151   Toasts of the President and Former Chancellor Ludwig Erhard of Germany.   *March 21, 1968*

Professor Erhard, Mr. Vice President, Mr. Secretary of State, Members of the Cabinet and the Congress, distinguished guests:

My appointment calendar describes this occasion as what we call a "working luncheon."

I suspect that our guest today might be thinking to himself, "Is there ever any other kind of luncheon?"

It has been a great privilege to me to have, as a working partner, Professor Erhard. We have been friends for a very long time, and he has always been a very strong and a very wise friend of this country.

So I am very happy today to speak for all of our people in bidding the Professor welcome once more to this Nation and to this house.

We know that you have just returned from an extended visit to Latin America. I was delighted to have the benefit of your observations on the development and progress in that part of the world. We always value any impressions that you can share with us. Your Latin American travels are heartening evidence of Europe's commitment to helping the developing countries and providing leadership and strength to those who need it, who value it, and who, I hope, will profit from it. We in this country welcome that role and we want to work with you to enlarge it.

To my guests here today, I know that you know and the world knows that Professor Erhard had a large hand in creating the economic miracles that brought new life to Europe. It was the spirit of Atlantic cooperation that made so much of that prosperity that came possible. And it is the same staunch spirit—of common trust and common hopes—that unites the Atlantic peoples now, as they search for new miracles and for a greater prosperity for tomorrow.

The value and the vitality of that cooperation, as Professor Heller just observed a few moments ago, was demonstrated here in

Washington only this last weekend at the meeting of the gold pool countries. We are going on now to build upon that partnership, build a stronger and a more efficient international monetary system.

There are still many difficulties and hurdles in the way. We have overcome many obstacles in making the progress that we made last weekend; we have others yet to overcome.

I know that our distinguished guest will approve and support our common efforts. We are, in fact, building on the strong foundations of cooperation that he, himself, set in place as a statesman and as a visionary in the postwar years.

It gives me a great deal of pride to be privileged to acknowledge the debt that the entire Atlantic community owes to this wise man. We are always happier for the pleasure of his company, richer for the experiences that he shares with us and wiser for his counsel, and surer for his steadfastness. In all of the conversations that I have had with leaders of other nations, I have never been surer of any than I was of those with Chancellor Erhard.

This luncheon today is but a very small mark of the high regard and the very warm affection that we in this country hold for this good man and this grand servant of our world, Professor Erhard.

So to this special group of outstanding representatives of various parts of our American life, I would like to ask you to share with me and join with me in toasting a friend and comrade in bright hope—Professor Erhard; in a toast to the President of the Federal Republic of Germany; and in a toast to our friends, the people of Germany.

NOTE: The President spoke at 2:09 p.m. in the Family Dining Room at the White House. In his opening words he also referred to Vice President Hubert H. Humphrey and Secretary of State Dean Rusk. Later

he referred to Walter W. Heller, professor of economics at the University of Minnesota and former Chairman of the Council of Economic Advisers.

Mr. Erhard responded as follows:

Mr. President, Mr. Vice President, gentlemen:

It is a great privilege and a great pleasure for me to be here. It is almost 5 years now that have gone by since I met for the first time with you, Mr. President. During all this time we have had a close understanding. Our attitudes spiritually, morally, and politically have been very close to each other indeed.

We have always acted from the responsibility—not only for your people and for my people—but with the knowledge that whatever we do has a bearing on the entire free world.

I know that your country today faces many problems and has many worries. You can be convinced that I am observing these, watching these, and sharing these with you just as much as I am concerned about the problems in my own country.

Not only in my official capacity in the past, but also personally, it has been proven again and again how close our views and our attitudes have been.

The political views that you hold and that I am holding have a bearing on many aspects of what happens in the free world. That is the reason why, although now that I am no longer in my office, I will do anything that I can in order to speak out and to do whatever I can for maintaining the solidarity of the Atlantic community.

I think that looking at Europe from the viewpoint of the United States, there is a certain lack of clarity to be found in the picture. Too much is made of what is observed and it troubles many people to a point that I believe they could draw the wrong conclusions.

I already told your distinguished Secretary—with whom I had a few words before coming here to this luncheon—that this picture is not indeed so; that the position in Europe in general and the feeling of the European people in general is much closer to the United States, and is much more pro-American than you would believe from certain obscure demonstrations and other manifestations.

It has become fashionable and it is so cheap to go out and say, "I am against the war in Vietnam"— as if all the other people were violently for war and for carrying on any warfare.

I believe this is a very wrong view and very wrong attitude indeed.

This is not what is transpiring in Vietnam. It is not a question of just what is going on today; it is not just a question of this moment. But it has a very deep, important bearing on the future of the world in general.

As you know, I have just returned from a trip to Latin America. I would like to communicate to you the feeling that I had in all the five countries that I visited, namely, that the government in those countries and the leading circles feel a great gratitude for the United States.

I am keenly aware of what the United States has done for this area. As far as I am concerned, I feel that I should do everything possible to urge my own country to become more active in this region and to increase their participation in helping Latin America.

It is important, not only with regard to the improvement of the well-being of the living standard in this area, but it may very well be that one day the decisive battle between a system of freedom and a free order and totalitarianism might be fought in the arena of South America.

I know how some people feel and I know how easy it is to be critical toward those who have helped you. It seems human nature that debtors just don't love their creditors.

But I can assure you from my experience during this trip that the feeling was very much one of gratitude for the United States.

As regards my own country, I am not ashamed to say and I don't want to restrain myself, that I feel a very great sense of gratitude for what the United States has done to help Germany.

I believe that the standards that seem to apply in civilian life and that are accepted in our Western civilization, a standard of honesty and decency, should just as well apply to all the dealings of the governments with each other.

Our problems in Europe are great also, but I do not want to address myself to these. All I want to say is that I will always fight to the best of my ability for the maintenance of the Atlantic community and for unity in the Atlantic community.

I am afraid that if the Atlantic community should collapse this might lead eventually to disaster for the entire free world and it might, in the shorter range, lead to the coming up of isolationism—not only in the United States, but also in Europe—and neither of us can afford such a development.

I would like to say that in good days, as much as in bad days, you have stood by our side. I believe that today, where the situation for some of us seems to be on the bad side, it is all the more necessary that we stand together in trust and in cooperation.

I would like to close by proposing a toast to your health in the spirit of the very close friendship that has always united us. In proposing this toast to your health and well-being, I am automatically toasting the health and well-being of the entire American Nation. I wish you the best in the future and I hope that you will be successful in completing your historic mission.

152 Message to the Congress Transmitting Annual Report of the National Capital Housing Authority. *March 22, 1968*

To the Congress of the United States:

I am pleased to transmit the 1967 Annual Report of the National Capital Housing Authority.

The functions of the District Government are now under the direction of a single executive, Mayor Washington. If the National Capital Housing Authority is to continue to carry out its mission in an effective manner, its operations must be closely meshed with other District activities relating to housing. Last week, to assure this coordination, I signed an Executive Order abolishing the existing 6-member Board of the Authority, and designating Mayor Washington to carry out the functions of the Authority.

This change will provide unified direction of the Authority's activities and insure the best use of our resources in providing more and better housing for eligible families.

The provision of safe, decent, economical housing is one of the major objectives of the Mayor and the City Council. Work is progressing rapidly, for example, on planning for a model community at Fort Lincoln.

In the wide range of housing to be developed for this community, public housing will be included in a balance with other low-income, moderate, and higher income units.

During the past fiscal year, the Authority has moved forward in a number of areas to expand the supply of available housing:

—Through a variety of means, privately-owned dwellings were acquired and rehabilitated.

—Construction was begun on 3 projects totaling 446 dwelling units.

—The first "Turnkey" project in the Nation, Claridge Towers, containing 343 units was acquired and opened for occupancy.

—The first major low-rent housing development in Washington with all units designed for large families was fully occupied during the fiscal year.

Nothing can do more to instill hope and lessen despair for many of our citizens than good housing. The Authority now maintains over 9,000 units of housing, but this is not adequate to meet the urgent needs of the District. Far more must be accomplished and in the least possible time.

I fully expect the National Capital Housing Authority, under the leadership of Mayor Washington, to play a leading role in making our Capital City one to which all America can look with pride.

LYNDON B. JOHNSON

The White House
   March 22, 1968

NOTE: The report, submitted to the President on January 15, 1968, is entitled "33d Annual Report of 1967, National Capital Housing Authority" (Government Printing Office, 24 pp.).

The President referred to Executive Order 11401 "Modifying Executive Order 6868 of October 9, 1934, as amended, designating the authority to carry out the provisions of the District of Columbia Alley Dwelling Act" (4 Weekly Comp. Pres. Docs., p. 510; 33 F.R. 4559; 3 CFR, 1968 Comp., p. 106).

153 The President's News Conference of *March* 22, 1968

THE PRESIDENT. I have a few appointments that I thought you would be interested in and would give you something to do over the weekend. I want to keep all of you occupied. There are no trips in the offing.

AMBASSADOR TO FRANCE

[1.] I am naming Sargent Shriver as Ambassador to France. Secretary Rusk talked to him today in Europe. He understands that the French Government has cleared him. The nomination will go to the Senate and when acted upon by the Foreign Relations Committee and the Senate, he will go through a period of briefings here, and then go to the Paris post at a reasonably early date.

SECRETARY OF HEALTH, EDUCATION, AND WELFARE

[2.] I am asking Mr. Wilbur Cohen to be my new Secretary of Health, Education, and Welfare. He is the present Under Secretary. His successor has not been chosen.

We have tentatively reviewed some names together and we will meet again and talk about the Department, his functions, and the specific types of people we would like to carefully consider for Under Secretary. It will take some time, but we will make that announcement as soon as a decision is reached.

OFFICE OF ECONOMIC OPPORTUNITY

[3.] I am asking Mr. Bert Harding, the Deputy to Mr. Shriver, to take over the duties of the poverty program during the time Mr. Shriver is away, and while he is going through the Senate confirmation hearings. When I make a permanent decision on the Poverty Director, you will be informed.

JOINT CHIEFS OF STAFF

[4.] I have had under consideration for some time the filling of the expiring terms of certain members of the Joint Chiefs of Staff. On January the 19th, Mr. McNamara [1] gave me several alternatives here with his recommendations. I have had Mr. Clifford [2] review those alternatives and those recommendations.

We have not completed action on all of them, but I have secured the consent of General Wheeler [3] to an extension of one year in his term that would expire normally July 2, 1968.

Secretary McNamara, in this longhand note, was hopeful these could be announced in early February. General Wheeler has had a physical and taken the necessary steps, and he is available. If Congress is willing, his term will be extended for 1 year. The resolution will be submitted. It will be necessary to get congressional action.

I have conferred with Senator Russell, the Chairman of the Armed Services Com-

mittee, and Congressman Rivers. [4] They both enthusiastically support this decision.

General Johnson's [5] term expires as Chief of Staff of the Army in July 1968. He plans to retire. He has notified us of his desire to retire. He will be succeeded by General Westmoreland, [6] who will assume the duties, assuming the Senate acts on the confirmation at that time, on July 2, 1968.

We have not selected a successor to General Westmoreland.

COMMANDER IN CHIEF, PACIFIC

[5.] Admiral Sharp's [7] term ends May 1st. We are going to ask Admiral Sharp if it is possible for him to continue through a July date so that we can have this transition smooth and simultaneous. If that is possible, we will ask him to continue to July 2d.

His successor will be named from nominations from the services. The Air Force will nominate a man, the Navy will nominate one, and perhaps the Army, the Chairman of the Joint Chiefs, and the Secretary will make that recommendation.

I believe that is all that I have now.

I would say that the resolution on General Wheeler will go up very shortly. The nomination on Mr. Cohen will go up today if the Senate is still in session. If not, it will go up when the Senate is in session. The same thing will be true of Mr. Shriver.

I would be glad to take any questions that any of you may have. If I am not talking

---

[4] Senator Richard B. Russell of Georgia, Chairman of the Senate Armed Services Committee, and Representative L. Mendel Rivers of South Carolina, Chairman of the House Armed Services Committee.

[5] Gen. Harold K. Johnson, Chief of Staff, United States Army.

[6] Gen. William C. Westmoreland, Commander, United States Military Assistance Command, Vietnam.

[7] Adm. U. S. Grant Sharp, Jr., Commander in Chief of U.S. Forces in the Pacific.

---

[1] Robert S. McNamara, former Secretary of Defense.

[2] Clark M. Clifford, Secretary of Defense.

[3] Gen. Earle G. Wheeler, Chairman, Joint Chiefs of Staff.

loudly enough, I will sit down and you can hear through the microphone.

QUESTIONS

GENERAL WESTMORELAND

[6.] Q. Mr. President, when would you anticipate General Westmoreland coming back to this country?

THE PRESIDENT. July 2, 1968, is when I would anticipate his taking over the duties of Chief of Staff. I don't know what the pleasure of the Senate committee would be. But, they very likely would want him present to act upon him.

When they do want to act upon him, if they want him personally present, I would imagine that would be when he would return, Smitty,[8] but I am not sure.

GENERAL WESTMORELAND'S SUCCESSOR

[7.] Q. Mr. President, when would you think would be the latest that you would have to name a successor to him in Vietnam?

THE PRESIDENT. July 2. That successor post specifically doesn't require Senate confirmation. General Westmoreland would be relieved of his duty effective that day. I would think a successor would be named much earlier. But your question, as I understand it, was the latest I would announce a successor.

PROSPECTS FOR PEACE

[8.] Q. Mr. President, are we any closer to peace?

THE PRESIDENT. I cannot answer that question. Peace is a very elusive thing. We cannot pinpoint a time or a date that may be in other people's minds. We are trying constantly each day to think and plan in every way we can for a solution that would bring a resolution to what is happening in South Vietnam.

But what may be in the enemy's mind I am not able to speak with any real authority. I would not want to try to be prophetic about what their decisions might be. We are living, I think, in a very dangerous time. It is taxing the ingenuity, the determination, and the strength of the leaders of the Nation, as well as our fighting men.

I have no doubt about what the resolution will be. But as to the moment or the exact timing of it, I cannot speak for it.

THE PRESIDENT. Mr. Frankel.[9]

FUTURE STRATEGY IN VIETNAM

[9.] Q. Thank you. To help us meet the invariable discussion that will greet some of these appointments, could I ask two questions?

One, does the replacement of General Westmoreland imply any change of search and destroy strategy with which his name has been associated or any other tactical adjustment in Vietnam?

THE PRESIDENT. The strategy and the tactical operations have nothing to do with the appointments as such. I do not know at this time who the commanding general of our troops there will be.

Therefore, I cannot speak for his plans or for his program. I feel that General Westmoreland is a very talented and very able officer. He was considered for the Honolulu assignment and for the Chief of Staff assignment that has been held by many of the greatest men in our military history—such as General Pershing, General Eisenhower,

---

[8] Merriman Smith of United Press International.

[9] Max Frankel of The New York Times.

and General Wheeler.

After thorough consideration for many months and upon the recommendation of both the outgoing Secretary and the incoming Secretary who evaluated every general in the Army, to be Chief of Staff of the Army, General Westmoreland was selected.

Now, what contributions he will make to the Joint Chiefs of Staff will be a matter for him to decide and what the recommendations his successor will make will be for him to decide.

I don't think it would be fair or correct or possible today to announce the program of the unannounced, unknown successor.

SARGENT SHRIVER

[10.] Q. The second part, Mr. President, goes to Mr. Shriver. Did he ask to be relieved of his OEO duties, or is this just a good time?

THE PRESIDENT. No, I would not say that he asked to be relieved. He told me many months ago that he had been in the poverty job and in the Peace Corps job in Washington for many years—some 7 years—that he had looked forward to the possibility of some foreign service, that the opportunity that he had for relations with other nations in the Peace Corps was a very satisfying experience for him. He said if there were anything that would be available where he could serve his country abroad, he would be glad to be considered for it.

I told him there were two places that he could be considered for. He gave me his preference. He had discussed this with the Secretary of State before he discussed it with me.

After our conversation, I sent him back to the Secretary of State. They exchanged views. And the Secretary recommended to me that his name be submitted to the French Gov-

ernment. That was done some time ago.

In accordance with the custom, we attempted to respect their wishes on the matter and made no announcement until they had been given the courtesy of considering his name and acting upon it.

They did that, I believe, yesterday.

The Secretary talked to Mr. Shriver today and informed him that the French Government had acted upon it and that he was prepared to submit to the President his recommendation if Mr. Shriver felt that he wanted that done in light of the action of the French Government.

Mr. Shriver stated that he did. Secretary Rusk submitted it to me this afternoon following the luncheon I had with him.

Does that answer both of your questions?

Q. Yes, sir; very well.

ADDITIONAL TROOPS FOR VIETNAM

[11.] Q. Mr. President, have you reached a decision on the question of additional combat troops for Vietnam?

THE PRESIDENT. I have not. I have no specific recommendations at this point. The people in the field and the people in the Department are giving this matter very thorough consideration—replacements, extra needs, developments that are taking place there, the enemy's actions, and so forth.

When I have any recommendations that I am able to act upon and do make a decision, I will announce it to the extent that I can without involving our security.

I don't want to speculate on it because, first, I don't have a recommendation or facts enough to know. If I don't know, I don't know who does know, because the decision really has to be made here.

Figures from 1,000 to 1,000,000 you will be reading, hearing, and reporting. But that is a matter of somebody else's credibility. I want to try to watch mine.

SUPPLEMENTAL APPROPRIATION FOR DEFENSE

[12.] Q. Mr. President, do you know yet whether you will have to have a supplemental appropriation for Defense?

THE PRESIDENT. No. We have not made a decision on that. We do know that there are going to be some step-ups in filling inventory needs. The new Secretary has talked and consulted frequently with the Chairmen of the two Armed Services Committees about certain of those needs.

I don't want to get into specifics, but they involve everything from types of spare parts to ammunition, to guns, to certain types of equipment, both for us and for our allies, for extra troop commitments that our allies are making and for extra equipment commitments that we are making, such as to Korea.

So, when those things are decided upon and costed out, the Congress will be informed.

THE PRESIDENTIAL ELECTION CAMPAIGN

[13.] Q. Mr. President, rightly or wrongly, speculation grows that the coming presidential election campaign is going to be one of the most bruising, if not one of the most brutal, in memory, partly because of the devisive and emotional issues of Vietnam and race in this country.

Do you have any comment on that and, as a footnote, do you have any reaction to Governor Rockefeller's action yesterday? [10]

THE PRESIDENT. First, reaction—I don't know whether it is hope or speculation, but

both, maybe. My reaction is that I would hope that is not true. I would hope that the American people and their candidates for public office can discuss the issues with those people factually in an atmosphere where people can deliberate and make a decision based on what is best for their country. I hope and I believe that can be done.

I would not want to accept the anonymous speculators' judgment that it is going to be a bloody and bruising campaign, or whatever other adjectives you used.

So far as Governor Rockefeller is concerned, I am not in the practice of selecting or speculating on the candidates of the other party. I do not want to interfere in their business. My relationship with most of the Governors is very good.

I don't believe there has ever been a period when any President had more cooperation or better relationships with the States than the Federal Government and this President have with the Governors and the States at this time.

Right at the top of this list is Governor Rockefeller. He has been very cooperative, very helpful, very wise and constructive in all of his suggestions. We communicate with each other frequently in connection with the problems of the cities, the problems of the ghettos, the problems of the defense of the Nation, foreign relations, and other matters. I have always found him, while not always in agreement, always constructive.

SENATOR KENNEDY'S CANDIDACY

[14.] Q. Mr. President, within your own party, sir, Mr. Weisl, [11] the Democratic National Committeeman in New York today said that Senator Kennedy of New York [12] has a lust for power to become President.

---

[10] Governor Nelson A. Rockefeller of New York had announced his decision not to be an active candidate for the Republican presidential nomination.

[11] Edwin L. Weisl, Sr.

[12] Senator Robert F. Kennedy.

How do you evaluate or what is your reaction to Senator Kennedy's entrance into the presidential race?

THE PRESIDENT. I would have no comment on Senator Kennedy's entrance other than to say I was not surprised. And I could have made this statement to you this time last year.

THE PRESIDENT'S CANDIDACY

[15.] Q. When are you going to announce your own entrance into the race, sir?

THE PRESIDENT. When I get to that bridge, I will cross it. I am not there yet.

REPORT ON CIVIL DISORDERS

[16.] Q. Mr. President, there have been some people in public life who expressed disappointment that you did not react the way they felt you should to the report of the Commission you appointed on civil disorders.[13] I wonder if you could tell us how you feel about some of this criticism and about the report?

THE PRESIDENT. I don't know much about the criticism. I spent a good deal of time selecting the Commission. I tried to select men of ability and dedication and competence in this field. I thought I picked a very good Commission.

I did not, in any way, make suggestions to them after I appointed them and explained to them the kind of study I hoped could be made. We selected an outstanding staff director. We provided several hundreds of thousands of dollars to the staff—I believe something over $1 million. We provided a

good many Government people. We co-operated at the White House in every way we could.

We thought the report was a very thorough one, very comprehensive, and made many good recommendations. We did not agree with all of the recommendations, as certain statements have indicated.

When the report was received, we asked that copies of it be widely distributed to the Cabinet, to the Congress, to the Governors, to the Mayors, to the housing people and the Attorney General in connection with matters under his jurisdiction. He was asked to give special attention to the problems that they dealt with.

We felt that overall the Commission wanted to be and was constructive and helpful.

A good many of the things they recommended we had already made decisions on. Those are in one basket.

A good many more recommendations we had incorporated into our cities message [14] that had gone up and was pending. There was a difference in amounts, perhaps, although they did not cost out theirs. I am not sure how much difference, but we could recognize differences.

Housing, for instance. We recommended all that we thought that we could get the Congress to act upon—6 million over this period of time—and it represented a great acceleration. The Commission felt that it should be more.

I would not oppose more if we could get more and if we could get more funded. But we recommended what we thought we could build, realistically, and what we could get funded.

---

[13] The "Report of the National Advisory Commission on Civil Disorders" is dated March 1, 1968 (Government Printing Office, 425 pp.).

[14] For the President's message to Congress "The Crisis of the Cities," see Item 87.

I asked the Budget Director the day after the report was prepared:

One: To have each Cabinet officer analyze it and to divide it into three phases: What we were doing that they had recommended, see how we could improve on it in line with their suggestions.

Two: To see what they had recommended that we had already requested authorization on and appropriations for: jobs, employment, housing, civil rights matters, and to try to accelerate those and get them passed.

Three: To put in this basket the things that we recommended that we had not taken action on and then to call upon the Cabinet officers to submit to me their recommendations on the things that had not been acted upon.

The Budget Director did that. We have heard from those Cabinet officers and have taken some action on them. From time to time I am sure that we will not only be acting upon other things in the report, but some things not covered by it.

We don't agree with everything in the report and they don't agree with everything we are doing. But there is a general "simpatico" of views, I think, between the Cabinet officers who handle these programs and the recommendations of the Commission. In some cases there is a different sum in amounts and emphasis.

We think it was a good report made by good men of good will that will have a good influence. We hope that every person in the country can read it and try to take such action as they can to implement it.

I talked to the Assistant Secretary of HEW. I talked to Secretary Gardner himself. I talked to Mr. Whitney Young and Mr. Wilkins and a good many of the leaders who

are interested in housing, particularly Mr. Weaver.[15]

Some of our people, I think, talked to the leaders in the Senate and the House.

We want to take action on every recommendation that we can embrace that they think would be helpful.

I have detailed comments from the various Cabinet officers on parts of it, but I do not think you want me to go into this. But I will read one department's brief comments:

"The Department of Commerce concurs with the Commission that the Federal strategy of the cities is needed, but devoted its comments to economic development and employment, the suggestion that in addition to the budget, the Economic Development Administration and the Department of the Army are well along in their planning for civil disturbance control.

"My staff has prepared a thorough analysis of the agencies using initial reports from the agencies and the data they will provide.

"This, in effect, will provide information on main points.

"Funds are now being devoted to areas in which they have made recommendations; additional action to carry out the recommendations within existing funds; action to carry out very high priority Commission recommendations by modest budget add-ons; which recommendations cannot be implemented now; actions through Federal leadership consultations; State, local and private

---

[15] Whitney M. Young, Jr., Executive Director, National Urban League, and Robert C. Weaver, Secretary of Housing and Urban Development. The President may also have referred to Roy Wilkins, Secretary of the National Association for the Advancement of Colored People, or his nephew Roger W. Wilkins, Director, Community Relations Service, Department of Justice.

agencies to promote adoption and acceptance of the Commission's recommendations."

This budget report came back to me in the middle of March. It already has been reviewed by all the departments and has been communicated to most of the appropriate chairmen of the various committees.

Merriman Smith: Thank you, Mr. President.

THE PRESIDENT. Any of you all want to wait and visit with my grandson, I will be glad to have you.

NOTE: President Johnson's one hundred and twentieth news conference was held in his office at the White House at 5:30 p.m. on Friday, March 22, 1968.

154 Remarks to Delegates to the Conference of the Building and Construction Trades Department, AFL–CIO.   *March 25, 1968*

President Haggerty, President Meany, presidents of the internationals—I met so many presidents out here this morning:

When I awoke, I heard some sounds of hammering in my ears this morning. I turned over and said to Mrs. Johnson, "Is that another campaign headquarters going up across the street?"

She said, "No, dear, this is a good Monday. Your friends from the building trades have come to town."

It gives me a great deal of pleasure and pride to come here and stand with the builders of America.

We share the same pride in our country's past. We hold the same great faith in our Nation's future.

That future depends on the sons of labor—workingmen like you—who roll up their sleeves and do the job.

We are at work in this Nation—building a bigger, a better, and a more prosperous America.

If anyone doubts this, you—the warriors of progress—know the answer, because you have been there with me every step of the way.

Over the last several years:

—12 million Americans have risen from poverty—and that's progress.

—16 million schoolchildren face a better future because of educational breakthroughs—and that's progress.

—20 million older Americans—your mothers and your fathers—no longer fear the crushing burden of medical bills in their old age—and that's progress.

—41 million American workers are protected by a higher minimum wage—and that's progress.

—75 million Americans are today working in better jobs at better wages, at higher pay, than they have ever worked before in all American history—and that's progress.

These are the mighty foundations that we put in place. We are not going to sit by and let them be torn down in a partisan political election year.

We are going to build on them—we are going to help shape a better future for the working people of this country and for their families.

We are pledged to bring safety to the workbench and to bring safety to the jobsite to protect our fellow human beings.

It is a shocking and, I think, a shameful fact that:

—Every year, 15,000 American workers die in job accidents—15,000 tragedies,

15,000 heartbreaks.

—Every year, 2 million workers are injured on the job. How can we ever replace a lost eye? How can we ever substitute for a severed hand?

—Every year, a billion dollars are lost in wages. More than 200 million mandays are wasted because of accidents.

This year, I asked the Congress for a worker's safety bill to protect you. And I ask you this morning to give me your help and join with me to help us make this the law of the land this year.

We are pledged to make your hard-earned dollar more secure when you buy an automobile or a refrigerator on credit.

We are going to do away with the hidden interest charges.

With your help, we will—at long last—put truth into lending and pass the truth-in-lending bill this year to protect American workers.

We are pledged to make sure that every one of your sons and daughters who wants a college education has an opportunity to get one.

The day is passing in this America when only the children of the rich can go to college.

So I ask you to work with us as we strive to pass the Economic and Education Opportunity Act of this year and to pass it through the Congress before we go home for the election.

These are some of the measures that will benefit the working people of America. They not only benefit the working people, but their neighbors as well.

Our fight—yours and mine—is to make life better in this country not just for some, not just for most—but to make life better for all the people.

I see the great milestones of our progress only as a starting point.

Every day—in a hundred ways—we are reaching out to those Americans who are still lost in the dark corners of American society.

Let there be no cruel delusion that this job is an easy one. Let there be no false hope that the solutions are going to be quick. For we are cutting through a century of neglect.

But we are cutting through, we are moving on, and we are not going to be stopped.

And when you look back over the history of our glorious past and you see the record of achievement, instead of the record of promises, you men of the AFL–CIO and you men of the building trades are going to be proud to say to yourselves and say to your children that during the decade of the sixties—from 1964 to 1968—that we wrote upon the statute books of this Nation 24 far-reaching health bills to protect our minds and our bodies, that we wrote 18 education bills to protect our children—from Head Start at 4 years old until adult education at 72—that we did move forward, that we did make progress, and that we did adopt a program of social justice for all Americans that had never been written into law by any administration at any time in all the history of America.

So I came here to say thank you and I came here to tell you that you are the Nation's strong right arm as we tackle the work ahead.

We are going to break new ground in a massive housing program for the poor. We have submitted to the Congress blueprints for 6 million new homes over the next 10 years.

This will wipe away—we hope once and forever—the shameful backlog of crumbling tenements and the shacks where families now live.

Next year we have a goal of starting 300,-

437

ooo new homes. That is a pretty big order for this first year. In all the last 10 years put together, we have only built 500,000 new homes.

And you are the men who must lead the way, not only to pass this legislation, but to build these houses.

We are setting out now to try to find work for hundreds of thousands of men and women who have never before in their lives earned a steady paycheck.

You know—better than anyone else—the dignity of a decent job.

And I know what you are doing to help open new opportunities within your own ranks.

I thank you. And I tell you that I will appreciate your doing everything you can to help us meet this vital problem that not only confronts me as your agent, as your President, and as a manager of this great Nation, but that confronts all the people of this Nation—because smallpox down the street works its way up to your block, too, and poverty, homelessness, hunger, disease, and crime cannot be quarantined. It will get to your block, too.

So the hour is here. Now is the time. You are the people to help us get this job done.

We have a program to build that better America in a climate of law and order. And we are going to build it even as we meet our commitments in a world where freedom is under attack.

This is not any new experience for us. We have had our will tested before. We had it tested across the waters in World War I— and many of you wear the badges of honor, of service of that day.

We had it tested in World War II when we had enemies in both oceans that were trying to bring democracy, freedom, and liberty to its knees.

We saw it tested when the Greek guerrillas

were 7 miles out of Athens and President Truman brought into force the Truman Doctrine.

We saw it tested in Korea when we were there on that little Pusan Peninsula and most of the folks were talking about "What did Korea and all of those mountains mean to us?"

We have seen it tested over the skies of Berlin when the people of that desolate city were hungry and we had to feed them with our courage, with our planes, and with our cargoes landing, many times, in zero-zero weather.

But every time we were tested, we were not found wanting—and we are not going to be found wanting now.

Now, the America that we are building would be a threatened nation, if we let freedom and liberty die in Vietnam. We will do what must be done—we will do it both at home and we will do it wherever our brave men are called upon to stand.

This is the America that we have faith in—this is a nation that is building. This is a wonderful country that is growing.

I hope you men are determined to help us meet these problems. I hope you men are determined to see us help get justice, not just for ourselves, but for all the people of this Nation and for all the people of the world.

I sometimes wonder why we Americans enjoy punishing ourselves so much with our own criticism.

This is a pretty good land. I am not saying you never had it so good. But that is a fact, isn't it?

So I say that the average American does not ask for much. He is entitled to equal opportunity and equal justice. His ancestors have come here from all the lands of the world seeking liberty and freedom. They are not only here to protect it, but they are here to preserve it.

The average fellow, about all that he insists on having—and he must have a lot of drive and desire to get that—is a roof over his head; he would like to have title to it. He wants clothes to cover his naked body and the bodies of his family, food to give him strength and sustain him as he produces a better country, a decent school for his children to attend so they can prepare themselves to be good citizens, a church to worship in where he can go and worship according to the dictates of his own conscience, and maybe a little recreation now and then—maybe taking Molly and the babies in the car for a ride on Sunday afternoon, or to a movie once in a while, or to watch a television program if the politicians are not monopolizing it.

That is about all he asks—not much, a roof over his head, clothes on his body, food in his stomach—and that is what you builders are helping us get.

I want to say that there has never been a period in American history when the statehouse and the White House, when the Congress and the Capital, had more and better and more cooperative support from the workingmen of America than they have had the last 4 years.

We wouldn't have had the Education Act. We wouldn't have had the College Higher Education Act. We wouldn't have had Medicare where your fathers and your mothers no longer have to worry about what their sons-in-law and their daughters are going to do—they can go and show their card and be taken care of.

We have all of these things because George Meany, President Haggerty, Andy Biemiller, Lane Kirkland, and you men back home supported us in those efforts.

They laughed at you when you said "All the way," but we have gone all the way and we are still going.

Thank you very much.

NOTE: The President spoke at 11:18 a.m. at the Washington Hilton Hotel. In his opening words he referred to C. J. Haggerty, president of the Building and Construction Trades Department, AFL–CIO, and George Meany, president of the AFL–CIO. Later he referred to Andrew Biemiller, legislative representative of the AFL–CIO, and Lane Kirkland, assistant to the president of the AFL–CIO.

155   Remarks to Delegates to the Second Annual Conference on Farm Policy and Rural Life.   *March 25, 1968*

Secretary Freeman, my fellow citizens:

This is such a lovely evening that I thought I would leave my corral long enough to come over here and visit with you briefly. That seems to be getting harder to do every day that goes by.

Every day there seem to be more and more people who are running around the country trying to figure out a way to keep me down on the farm.

It is always a great pleasure for me to meet with my fellow farmers, especially as talented a group as this. America has produced great dairy farmers, great cattlemen, and the best wheat growers on earth, but very few of them can equal you here today. For I want you to know and the world to know that you have mastered the hardest skill of all: You know how to make hay in Washington.

Secretary Rusk is having a meeting with some wise men in the next room. He met me at the elevator as I came in. And he said, "Mr. President, I am turning over the State Department to a group of farmers tonight."

I said, "Well, I just hope they are not all from Arkansas, Dean."

Daniel Webster used to say that he admired farmers because they were the founders of human civilization. Without the man who tills the soil, nothing else is really possible because he feeds us, he clothes us, and upon occasions he even gives us good advice.

It has been my experience as a rancher that this advice is not always heeded. And you would be amazed how little it helps sometimes to be President of the United States. They just still don't listen.

I hope that someone was listening a few weeks ago when we sent to Congress our message on the farmer and on rural America.

So many times when I have read these reports on our cities—and I have seen the wreckage on the television film at night of our towns burning—I have just wondered if we could have just spent a small proportion of the money that we are going to have to spend now in those cities, in helping to keep the people living on the farm, how much better it would be.

We offered some advice in that message to the Congress that was designed to give the American farmer the kind of parity that really counts: parity of the pocketbook.

We advised extending the supply management programs of the Food and Agriculture Act of 1965 with permanent authority because the farmer just should not be asked to grow more than the market can possibly take at a fair price.

We advised continuing the direct payment programs which are the difference between the profit and loss for many farmers every year.

We advised extending the Food for Freedom Act for an additional 3 years because it is right and because it is good business for our farmers to build new markets in new lands.

We advised creating a national food bank, a security reserve of wheat, feed grains, and soybeans, which would give the farmer higher prices, which we think would protect the consumer from food scarcity and which would provide our great country with a cushion of emergency food at all times.

We advised Congress to help us find ways to give the farmer more bargaining power in the marketplace. Everyone has power in the marketplace except the farmer.

We advised a whole range of programs to bring parity of opportunity to rural America—rural jobs, better credit, decent housing, adequate diets, and above all, the chance to lead a full, productive, and free life.

I don't know how much of that advice is going to be taken or how much is going to be heeded, if any.

But I do believe, and I do promise you tonight that we have given that advice and we do intend to stand here as long as we can stand here and fight for what we think is right—and that is right.

You just might want, perhaps, to add a few comments of your own.

I have a feeling that the Congress would welcome you with open ears if you should observe to them that the time is near when Americans should try to spend some time preparing for themselves, trying to make life better for their own people—although we are very interested in all parts of the world—and maybe adjust our differences, bend a little bit, and accommodate ourselves to our neighbor's view some.

We just don't always enjoy the luxury of finding out all of the things that are wrong with us and talking about them all the time because pretty soon an average observer looking at our country wouldn't conclude what we know. From what he reads and from what he hears, he would think it is a pretty bad place.

I may have been in Washington too long. I may have had too much faith. But somehow or other, I really think that this is the best land in all the world, with the best system in all the world, where the people are the best fed, the best housed, the best clothed, and the best educated and have the most freedom of any citizen that lives under any other flag.

Now, that is not enough. We are going to make it better. We are going to continue to move from here. We are going to continue to improve on what we have.

But we are not going to spend much time talking about what is wrong. We are going to talk about what is right and why we have got to have it.

With your help and with God's help, we will get somebody to listen to this advice. And we will have a program that we hope— we hope—will keep them down on the farm.

Thank you very much.

NOTE: The President spoke at 7:47 p.m. in the Diplomatic Reception Room at the Department of State. In his opening words he referred to Orville L. Freeman, Secretary of Agriculture. The Conference was sponsored by the United States Department of Agriculture, the Office of Economic Opportunity, and the Department of Health, Education, and Welfare.

156   Remarks to the Christian Citizenship Seminar of Southern Baptist Leaders.   *March 26, 1968*

Dr. Valentine and registrants at the Christian Citizenship Seminar:

It is good to have you here this afternoon. Our last meeting, I seem to remember, was held on the same day of the year, and almost here on the identical spot. I guess you might say that one sign of spring is when the Baptists come to the Rose Garden. I am sorry we could not have been here earlier when more spring was here and the sun was out.

I am not fortunate enough to be a Baptist.

I am a member of the Disciples of Christ, but I have always felt very close to your denomination. Everybody else in my household that I grew up in was Baptist. My part of the country is Baptist. My mother was a Baptist. My grandfather and great-grandfather were Baptists. George Washington Baines was an early Baptist preacher who became the second president of Baylor University during the Civil War.

He came to Texas in a buckboard to be a circuit-riding preacher. He came the way that most of the Baptists came to the frontier: very early, by the cheapest form of transportation. He was determined to do one thing—and that was save souls.

The Methodists waited until times were somewhat more prosperous; then they came by horse and buggy.

The Presbyterians came later—but by that time we had trains.

Finally, they say, when Pullman cars were added to the trains, the Episcopalians arrived.

But the Baptists—as all of you are prone to point out—came "firstest with the mostest!"

My good friend, Brooks Hays, told me once about a victory for my church, the Disciples of Christ—the Campbellites.

He said the Disciples converted a whole full church of Baptists down in the hill country. Right away, the new converts passed a resolution. The resolution read something like this, "Be it herewith resolved that we are no longer Baptists. Henceforth, we will be Christians."

Those pioneers left us not only a heritage of courage and rugged individualism. They left us a legacy based on steady faith and earnest good works.

For them, religion was concerned not only with the hereafter, but religion was concerned with the here and the now. There was no faith without works.

For them in a less complex time, caring for the sick and helping their poor and standing by their neighbors were acts of very simple morality. They were rooted in faith. They could be trusted. They were loyal to their fellow man.

Now, things are not so simple. The man who is sick, or the man who is poor, or the victim of discrimination, the man who urgently needs our help may live across the city or could be living across the entire country.

But for us, as for our forebears, there can be only one answer to that old question, "Who is my neighbor?"

That man—even though he lives far away—we should trust him. He is our neighbor. We should be loyal to him. He is our responsibility. And we must not pass by on the other side.

This is not just a religious truth. I think it is a very urgent social fact. So, for all that you are doing to support compassion and for all that you have done to bring about better understanding, I want to say that your President is grateful and your country is the beneficiary. I think your countrymen are thankful, too.

I am glad that you have chosen to study your responsibilities in the face of change and upheaval and disorder.

This is a subject that is very much on the minds of all Americans who care these days.

We believe—in fact we think we know—that the past few years have been a time of considerable progress that history will take due note of. The actions of the Congress, we think, show it. The statistics, we believe, show it—in health, income, education, housing, race relations, and in a dozen other fields.

But we know also that times of progress and change can be times of restlessness and discontent and great tensions. Now we are living through such a time—when men who once accepted poverty and once lived with discrimination as their lot in life simply do not accept it any more. So we know that there must be even more work and even more rapid progress in the days ahead.

Those who have studied this problem most deeply have suggested to us a wide range of solutions for us to consider. The Congress will be considering those solutions. They are now. We will be debating them in the months to come.

Those solutions suggest that crime and violence and despair arise from one cause—from a cause of ignorance and poverty and joblessness. And I think there is very good evidence to that effect. They suggest that the cure for joblessness is a job. They suggest that the cure for ignorance is some training and some education. They suggest that the cure for bad rat-infested slum housing is better housing. And the ultimate cure for crime is to give every citizen a sense of pride and a chance to participate in the development of his community—a sense of his stake in law and order.

I think all of you will agree with that.

So, therefore, we are working—we are working just as hard as we know how—to try to evolve a program to meet all these distressing conditions. We are—this afternoon, and yesterday, and tomorrow—asking for as much, as often as we believe the Congress and the people can and will accept.

But those who have pondered the problem see a deeper solution.

The only sure and lasting solution to frustration and discontent and disorder, they say, lies far beyond these government programs. The only lasting solution won't cost a cent—but it is going to be, really, the hardest to achieve.

It will require, actually, a great change— a change in men's hearts—in the way that men treat their neighbors. It will require a change in men's eyes—in the way men see their neighbors.

There, my dear friends, is where each of you can come in. You are teachers. You are preachers. You are religious leaders of a great congregation in a great section of this country, the American South.

As I have said many times before, when it comes to the rights and it comes to the well-being of American citizens, when it comes to the relationship between a man and his neighbor, there is—and there must be— no Southern problem. There is no—and there must be no—Northern problem. There is—and there must be—only an American problem.

But because much of that American prob- lem began in the region which you and I call home, I would like the solutions to begin there, too. So I am glad that each of you has shown your concern about it. I am looking to you for action and for leadership and for inspiration.

We have our debates from time to time. Some of us are advocates of sprinkling and others insist on total immersion. But I think that all of us can agree on one very essential fact: All of us believe—as George Washing- ton believed—that the roots of public policy must lie in private morality.

So all of us, whether we are political lead- ers or religious leaders, have a very urgent stake in answering that old Biblical question, "Who is my neighbor?"

I might add in parting that I would hope very much that each of you and all of you could always "Love thy neighbor as thyself."

Thank you very much.

NOTE: The President spoke at 5:34 p.m. in the Rose Garden at the White House. In his opening words he referred to Dr. Foy Valentine, executive secre- tary-treasurer of the Christian Life Commission of the Southern Baptist Church. Later he referred to Brooks Hays, Representative from Arkansas 1943– 1959, and Special Assistant to the President 1961– 1963.

157   Remarks of Welcome at the White House to President Tubman of Liberia.   *March 27, 1968*

Mr. President, Mrs. Tubman, Secretary and Mrs. Rusk, distinguished guests:

There are two flags flying here, each of them with a star and stripe in red, white, and blue. They speak more powerfully than any words of all that binds the two nations that meet here in friendship today.

The flag of the Republic of Liberia is fashioned after our own flag. That nation's Constitution and legal system are also drawn from an American example. We are proud to recognize this evidence of an extraordi- nary and a very enduring friendship.

It began in 1816 with a blow for freedom. The Congress of the United States struck the chains from 88 American slaves, freeing them to return to Africa. President Monroe and the American people gave funds and diplomatic aid to help establish a new and an independent nation.

Liberia's first hundred years are called the "century of survival." Big powers and hungry neighbors tried to swallow up that little state. But this was also a century of kinship between the Liberian people and the American people. In crises, the two nations joined to uphold their common and their treasured birthright:

—the idea of self-determination;

—the right of every nation to live free of interference and intimidation by another nation;

—the duty of all nations to make common cause in defending the indivisible freedom and the inseparable peace of mankind.

There are men today who still scorn those ideas; there are men who still assault those rights. There are still small and helpless nations in this world that come under vicious attack.

But there are also men who have known the fight for survival—who have learned the necessity for free men to unite against aggression—and who today accept the duty of sharing in the struggle for peace in the world.

In all the years of our long partnership, Liberia and America have given many such men to each other, and have given them to the world. One man has stood out among them for a quarter of a century now. I am proud to welcome America's staunch friend—one of Africa's most senior and most respected statesmen—President Tubman of Liberia.

He is no stranger to this house or to our hearts. This is his fourth visit to our land and I can just recall his first visit some 25 years ago to meet with our great President, Franklin D. Roosevelt.

President Tubman has seen the world transformed since that first visit. His leadership has helped to charge a most electrifying and eventful period of change. President Roosevelt saw its promise and he also saw its peril when he looked ahead just before his death. "The only limit to our realization of tomorrow," he said, "will be our doubts of today. Let us move forward with strong and active faith."

You moved your nation and your continent forward, Mr. President.

Twenty-five years ago, you stood almost alone as an independent nation in a largely colonial Africa. As we meet here today, more than 30 African states now stand with you as masters of their own destiny.

That, I think, is a reflection—a reflection of your own deep faith in freedom, your own belief that the nations of Africa must join as equals and must advance in unity. We admire your vital contribution to the creation of the Organization for African Unity. We encourage your efforts to enlarge regional cooperation, and we hope that your forthcoming West African summit conference in Monrovia will add to your success.

You have stabilized and you have enlarged the life of your own people with a unification policy extending the franchise and the representation throughout your land.

You have made vast improvements in the physical, educational, and administrative structure of your own country.

Your open door policy has drawn foreign capital to greatly speed your own economic development.

We have stood together, Mr. President, through all the trials as well as through all the triumphs of this past quarter of a century. We have followed President Roosevelt's very good advice, moving forward with "strong and active faith."

So let us continue in that spirit, allowing no doubts of today to limit the promise of what we can achieve tomorrow. Let the flags of our two nations fly together, as they do here today, marking a place of honor and a place of hope where free men can rally in peaceful and always progressive purpose.

Mrs. Johnson and I are most happy and very honored to welcome you and Mrs. Tubman back to this land that is made up of your good friends—and always of your very firm partners.

NOTE: The President spoke at 11:45 a.m. on the South Lawn at the White House, where President William V. S. Tubman was given a formal welcome with full military honors. In his opening words President Johnson also referred to Secretary of State Dean Rusk and Mrs. Rusk.

President Tubman responded as follows:

Mr. President:

It is a moment of pleasure for me and Mrs. Tubman to be received by you at this time. This is true not only in times of unbroken peace and serene prosperity, but even when times are troubled and testing—as they are today.

The close ties between our two nations have existed for more than a century—and happily, show no sign of slackening.

Nevertheless, the reaffirmation on occasions as this serve to remind us of the vitality of the bonds of our relations and to demonstrate once more that rich dividends can flow from our traditional association.

The fact that that friendship has remained solid and secure over the years is not explained by the material advantages we have derived from it, but rather by its having grown out of our sincere devotion and dedication to the principles and ideals of constitutional democracy.

It is my conviction, Mr. President, that the principles asserted in your Declaration of Independence and enshrined in ours, which have unfailingly sustained us in the past, will continue to be the bedrock of our policies and broad highway along which our two peoples will always travel.

As we meet today, I am sure, Mr. President, that the hopes of the Liberian people are high and that they are listening with interest for the results of our meeting. This, I believe, applies as well to other parts of Africa.

They have heard of your many pronouncements and have been moved by your personal interest in the future of Africa. They believe that in your heart you are looking at all times for the right answers to some of the problems facing them.

In particular, your program for education, health, and general welfare as a concerted effort in the world has deeply excited them.

As you and your great people have in the past faced and overcome numerous challenges, we know that America is ready to help Africa face and overcome the challenges of our times.

I believe that from our meeting I will be able to return home and tell my people how deeply you and your great people are committed to bring about a new day—not only for Africa, but for mankind.

For the warm welcome which you and the American people have accorded us, I thank you—and with my thanks go the thanks and good will of the Liberian people. They wish me to express their continued deep regard for and sense of friendship with you and the people of the United States.

158   Remarks Upon Signing the Jury Selection and Service Act of 1968.   *March 27, 1968*

Distinguished Members of Congress, ladies and gentlemen:

We have come here today to infuse some new strength into our democratic system of government.

Trial by jury is one of the oldest democratic rights enshrined in the American system. For all the years of our Republic, that fundamental right has supported a government based on the rule of law.

One of my earliest experiences was coaching debating teams back in high school and college. The subject was "Resolved: The Jury System Should be Abolished." Every time we took the affirmative of that position we had difficulty.

That is true because the sacred principles of our Constitution demand that juries should fairly represent the peoples of the communities that those juries serve.

But the principle has not always been observed in this country and has not always been practiced among our people.

Too often the jury lists have tended to exclude citizens who were poor or who were not "in" or who may have lacked charisma or may have been members of a minority group.

Now, this discrimination—sometimes we call it "highhat"—was not always intentional. But sometimes it was intentional. And more often it was certainly a result of a very haphazard selection system.

Each departure from the ideal—whether it was deliberate or not, and we won't spend a lot of time debating whether it was deliberate—left a great scar on the thing we take so much pride in, that we call American justice.

So, the bill that I will sign shortly, takes a principle and makes it into a statute. From now on, all of our Federal juries in this country will be, in the language of the law, "selected at random from a fair cross section of the community."

This measure reinforces the precious legal rights of all of our citizens. And it does more than that alone. It advances the civil rights of those who still reach for their full, and what we believe their proper, place in our society.

Every move that we can make in this country toward the goal of complete equality for all of our people, I think, is a very good step on a very proud journey.

We are drawing closer, I think, ever closer to the fulfillment of a promise that this Nation made to ourselves and to the world many, many years ago. More than 100 years ago Lincoln signed the Emancipation Proclamation. But emancipation was a proclamation; it wasn't a fact.

As I sign this bill today, I look ahead to another bill, to another day after the parliamentary technicians get through playing around with it and after the reluctant search their consciences.

I am hopeful that the Civil Rights Act—which we have passed through a body that has been very difficult, in my experience, to pass civil rights bills through, in past years—can pass the House of Representatives; and we will finally put the law on the side of the man who seeks a home for his family.

I am shocked to even think that the boys I put on the plane at the 82d Airborne—most of whom were Negro boys going back to Vietnam the second time to protect that flag and to preserve our freedom—that they can't live near the base where they have to train in this country; they must drive 15, 20, or 30 miles sometimes to get to their homes.

To those of you who have joined in the years of fighting that have been going on, I want to say to each of you: You have my deep gratitude and you have my personal thanks.

I think the conscience of America calls on the Congress to quit fiddling and piddling and take action on this civil rights bill. The time for excuses has ended. The time for action is here. We must protect every citizen of this land in the exercise of his civil rights.

I am honored that you could join me this morning on this historic occasion.

NOTE: The President spoke at 1 p.m. in the Fish Room at the White House. As enacted, the bill (S. 989) is Public Law 90–274 (82 Stat. 53).

The Civil Rights Act of 1968 was approved by the President on April 11, 1968 (see Item 195).

159   Toasts of the President and President Tubman of Liberia.
March 27, 1968

President and Mrs. Tubman, Vice President and Mrs. Humphrey, Secretary and Mrs. Rusk, ladies and gentlemen:

While I was doing my homework for President Tubman's visit, I came across a Liberian proverb that will serve as my text tonight. "A man who is asked to talk an inch and speaks a yard should be given a foot."

I very much appreciate the warning, Mr. President. In the present circumstances, I think it would be rather extravagant for me to encourage any man to give me the foot.

It would also be an extravagance for me to talk at length about our most distinguished guest tonight. He is one of the truly legendary leaders of our time. Americans have known him and admired him for more than a quarter of a century now:

—as the symbol of the first and oldest free republic in Africa;

—as the architect of Liberian unity and the builder of Liberia's modern growth;

—as a farsighted statesman whose influence today is a very powerful force for African unity in the world;

—as the staunch and dependable foe of aggression, as well as a stalwart guardian of peace;

—as a faithful friend who visits us often, and never fails to leave us with the gifts of his wisdom and his strength.

We are also aware that President Tubman has just been elected to his sixth term in office. This Nation is very happy to share the confidence of your people and to wish all of you good fortune, sir.

I was quite pleased to ask Vice President Humphrey to go as my special envoy to your inauguration. Upon that occasion he was supposed to deliver a very personal message to you, and I hope that he got it straight. When I approached the Vice President, he said, "This will make President Tubman's 24th year in office."

Then he said to me, "What shall I offer him, Mr. President—your congratulations or your condolences?"

Mr. President, I do want to offer you my congratulations this evening—congratulations on your shrewd political sense. Today your party is known as the True Whig Party. You were very wise, I think, in scrapping the old title—the Grand Old Party.

That party seems to be enjoying some increasing popularity in this country—certainly here at this table tonight.

Though the emphasis of your life, Mr. President, has always been on deeds, I would like to conclude now by recalling some of your words for those who have come here from across the land tonight.

You have challenged your own people and the peoples of Africa to avoid the pitfalls of the past and to seize the brightest promise of the future. Speaking to the Conference of Independent African States, you had this to say:

"We can avoid the fatal luxury of racial bigotry, class hatred, and disregard for the natural rights of all men to be free and independent. Our liberty and our resources should not be used for the political or economic enslavement of other peoples, but for their advancement and improvement; and thereby lay for ourselves and our posterity an enduring foundation upon which our entire future may rest."

That is a challenge that Americans can understand. Mr. President, we accept it in our own land and in every land where the promise of liberty has yet to be fulfilled for every human being.

We accept your leadership and your partnership, Mr. President, in the faith that has joined our two nations for more than a century and a half. We are grateful and we are proud to reach forward with you into the next century, and even beyond.

So my friends, I will ask you now to toast that journey and to toast that kinship that will brighten our way. Ladies and gentlemen, please join me in a toast to our faithful friends, the people of Liberia, President Tubman, and his gracious lady, who honors us with her presence.

NOTE: The President spoke at 10:05 p.m. in the State Dining Room at the White House at a dinner honoring President William V. S. Tubman of Liberia. In his opening words he also referred to Vice President and Mrs. Hubert H. Humphrey and Secretary of State and Mrs. Dean Rusk.

President Tubman responded as follows:

Your Excellency, President Johnson; Mrs. Johnson; Excellencies; distinguished ladies and gentlemen:

Mrs. Tubman and the members of my party join me in extending to you, Mr. President, Mrs. Johnson, and to the American people, sincere thanks for the very warm and cordial reception we have received everywhere since our arrival in your historic and great country.

We are most grateful to you, Mr. President, for the high compliment you have paid us and for your kind references to the traditional relationship which binds our two nations and people together.

We are aware that even the most durable friendship can benefit from intermittent periods of renewal. This is especially important when friends share mutually cherished ideals and aspirations; when they can exchange ideas on issues of immediate and urgent concerns, not only to themselves, but to mankind everywhere, and when they can together chart the course along which they may choose to travel. Thus have we come in this time of tension and unrest to renew the bonds of our friendship, to exchange ideas, to rest, reset our compass and give new dimensions and new perspectives for our century-old relationship.

Much is at stake. Our own destiny is involved in the events now unfolding on the world scene. In some parts of this world, including our own continent of Africa, millions of people are still grappling with the problems of wasting disease, abject poverty, illiteracy, hunger, and underdevelopment.

These peoples possess the natural resources. They have the will and the desire to work and develop those resources. But unfortunately, they lack the capital and the technical know-how so essential to their future progress.

They must, therefore, look to the developed nations for assistance in developing these resources.

We express the hope that working with such friends as you, Mr. President, and your great Government, the United Nations and its specialized agencies—as well as other global organizations—a new beam of sunshine will radiate itself on the international spectrum, dispersing the dark clouds of despair and save mankind from the awful consequences of a world conflagration.

Your great Nation, Mr. President, is—and must always remain—the bastion of freedom, the depository of democracy, and the citadel of hope for millions of people around the earth.

Mainly upon your shoulders, Mr. President, have been thrust the weighty and awesome responsibilities of defending liberty, of upholding justice, and of assisting in securing the peace.

It would appear to me that the statement made by your late President, Franklin Delano Roosevelt, in his day applies—when he said, "This generation of Americans has a rendezvous with destiny."

So it seems to continue in your day, Mr. President.

We have not brought you, Mr. President, nor your Government, any magic formula for winning the peace. But we have brought with us the greatest gift of our people—the reassurance of our firm and steadfast support, our good will, and our sincere wishes for the continuing progress and success of Your Excellency and the people of the great United States of America.

Ladies and gentlemen, please join Mrs. Tubman and me in toasting warmly to the health of President Johnson, Mrs. Johnson, the Government and people of the great United States of America.

160 Remarks Upon Signing a Bill To Liberalize Provisions Relating to Veterans Pensions. *March 28, 1968*

Mr. Driver, Chairman Teague, Senator Randolph, Senator Anderson, and other distinguished Members of the House of Representatives, ladies and gentlemen:

I am glad you could come here this morning. I think we all appreciate the fact that every month these days more than 70,000 of our best young men take off their uniforms and go back into civilian life.

These new veterans—like their brothers and their fathers—have served their time and made their contribution to freedom and to liberty and to the things that we hold dear.

They are heroes come home—men who were ready to do all they could, including laying their life on the line in the terrible test that we are going through in Vietnam and other places.

I hope that America will never forget these men—just as she has never forgotten others in other wars who have made other contributions.

I think that we ought to observe that since World War II, about 11½ million veterans have received educational training and been given educational benefits by the taxpayers of this country under the programs very wisely conceived in the Congress—what we call the various GI bills. Almost a half million—some 390,000 veterans are at this moment in school or in training somewhere in this country.

So the bill that we are going to sign shortly is another instance of the Nation's enlightened and compassionate tradition of trying to care for those who have carried out their obligations in an earlier day.

This bill, they tell me, will benefit approximately 1 million human beings who are Americans and veterans—mostly it happens to be the older veterans of other wars—and either their dependents or their survivors. It also protects these Americans against a very sharp reduction in benefits which would have occurred because of increases in other income, such as social security payments.

This bill is one of the several measures to aid veterans that are pending in the Congress and I hope we may be able to get passed this year with the help of the Congress. Among these bills we have proposed to Congress is the Veterans in the Public Service Act.

That bill is designed to put the best of America to work on the worst of our problems here at home. We think the veterans are among our best and we know that we have a very great need for good personnel on the worst problems we have.

So we would provide incentives to veterans to serve in the city slums as teachers, in the hospitals of the country to care for the sick, to aid us in our urban areas as policemen or as firemen—very necessary public duties that we are having difficulty finding people trained, equipped, and ready to perform.

We also have a good many of the rural hollows of the country where we need leadership. The training these men have received gives them a particular leadership that is very much in need.

Since Korea, we have discharged about 5 million, and sent them back into private life. But we have not emphasized to them or

449

helped them prepare to fill our greatest needs.

They have just gone wherever they could go. Only about 100,000 of them—of the 5 million—got into teaching. So we want very much to encourage more of these young heroes to come back and set an example in the classroom, on the street, in the recreation areas, in the slums, and in the hollows to inspire our youngsters and to provide leadership for them. And this veterans in the public service bill we think will do that.

I want to pay tribute to the Members in the House and the Senate who handle our veterans legislation—Chairman Teague, Senator Randolph, the members of the Finance Committee and the Labor and Public Welfare in the Senate, Veterans Committee in the House. They resist terrible pressures every day in an attempt to do what is fair by the Government and the taxpayer and do what is right by the serviceman. They have, over the years, been models, I think, for prudence and—at the same time—justice.

So all you members of both parties who are here this morning, I thank you for your help. You have been among the least of my problems. You could have been among the greatest. I am very aware of it.

In addition, I want to pay public tribute to a career man whom I did not know when I named him to one of the most important posts in Government. There is not a Cabinet officer who handles much more money—other than perhaps HEW and Defense. There is not a more efficient administrator in Government and not a finer public servant. I do not know what party he belongs to. I don't even know what State he comes from. All I know is that he does a great job for our country.

Mr. Driver—to him and to his associates who are career public servants, their President, on behalf of all the country, says "Thank you," too.

NOTE: The President spoke at 11:43 a.m. in the Cabinet Room at the White House. In his opening words he referred to W. J. Driver, Administrator of Veterans Affairs, Representative Olin E. Teague of Texas, Chairman of the House Committee on Veterans' Affairs, Senator Jennings Randolph of West Virginia, and Senator Clinton P. Anderson of New Mexico.

As enacted, the bill (S. 12555) is Public Law 90–275 (82 Stat. 64).

161 Statement by the President on the Death of Yuri Gagarin. *March 28, 1968*

YURI GAGARIN'S courageous and pioneering flight into space opened new horizons and set a brilliant example for the spacemen of our two countries. I extend the deep sympathy of the American people to his family and to relatives of Colonel Engineer Vladimir Seryogin.

NOTE: Soviet cosmonaut Yuri Gagarin and his co-pilot, Vladimir Seryogin, were killed on March 27 when their jet plane crashed northeast of Moscow during a routine training flight.

The statement was read to members of the press by George E. Christian, Special Assistant to the President, in his office at the White House at 12:32 p.m. on Thursday, March 28, 1968. It was not made public in the form of a White House press release. A similar message was sent to the Soviet Government.

162   Remarks to Editors and Publishers of the Foreign Language Press.   *March 28, 1968*

Ladies and gentlemen:

I am very pleased to welcome the ethnic press of this Nation to the East Room of the White House this afternoon.

Of course, it is difficult for me to read some of your newspapers because of the language gap. But I hope you don't feel too bad about that.

These days, it is difficult for me to read some of the English newspapers as well.

An observer of America 30 years ago wrote that America was fighting wars with itself. This was 1938. The wars were:

—the rich versus the poor,

—isolationists versus internationalists,

—Catholic versus Protestant,

—gentile versus Jew,

—white versus Negro,

—old-stock Americans versus immigrants, and

—immigrants against one another.

I don't think anyone in 1938 could imagine how much headway we would make in America in 30 years—at least on some of these issues. The frictions between religions and between nationalities, the discrimination against ethnic groups—these have been eased somewhat. In some instances, they have been eased almost to the vanishing point.

But some of the issues are still very much with us.

So we in government today address ourselves to the problems that remain with us. As we do, we ask the help of those who have known for at least these 30 years those problems firsthand.

The problem of poverty among us still exists. Many of those who were poor in 1938—perhaps some of the 5 million readers of your newspapers—are now among the privileged and so are their children. But for some of your readers, poverty is as real as where next month's rent is going to come from—just as poverty is real for the Americans in Appalachia, and for the Americans in the ghettos, just as poverty or the threat of poverty is real for the aged Americans who need more social securiy and Americans on fixed income who must be protected against inflation.

I am pleased to say today that we are adding one Federal poverty project that will help us fight poverty. It is a Department of Labor grant of almost $200,000 that will enable ethnic fraternal organizations in Pittsburgh to begin training household workers for industry. The women who are now earning $8 to $10 a day will soon begin to earn $18 to $20 a day—and we expect that this will be only the first of many programs in this direction.

The race problem—that is still with us, too. In 1938 it was noted that "The dice are loaded against the colored people." Today we are trying to unload those dice. And we ask for help and we ask for your understanding and we ask Americans to ask themselves, who once faced the loaded dice of discrimination and prejudice, to try to unite and help us with this problem.

The split concerning America's role in the world—the split that they referred to in 1938 as isolationism versus internationalism—still exists in this country. In 1968—as in 1938—

some Americans are asking, "Why does it matter to us whether some faraway little nation retains its right to self-determination?"

Once again, I think many of your readers have had personal experiences that may help them—and may help us—to answer that kind of question that is being asked in the homes of America this afternoon. They have seen the nations enslaved and they have seen nations tyrannized; and they have seen that tyranny is a contagious disease. They can see that it reaches epidemic proportions if it is not stopped and if it is not halted.

So your President asks for your help. We have seen over 30 years that America can resolve the wars that it fights with itself. We can live with each other if we try and we can build greatness here as we have in the last 30 years.

You have helped us to build this greatness in America through your newspapers, through your community services, and through your interest in building a better and a stronger America. You have done it, and we have done it—and with your help we will all continue to work toward a still greater and a still fairer America.

I have no doubt that when historians record this period of time that they will say that we in 1968 were as enlightened and were as aware of the dangers that confronted us and were as responsible in facing up to those dangers as were our citizens of 1938.

So have faith, be men of steady purpose, and I have no doubt but what America will not only protect its own great heritage and traditions, but will also make its due and proper contribution to helping those who want to help themselves.

Thank you very much.

NOTE: The President spoke at 5:40 p.m. in the East Room at the White House.

163 Remarks to Representatives of the Police Athletic League of Philadelphia. *March* 29, 1968

General Wilson, Mr. Klieman, distinguished students, and guests:

I am told that this pledge that you have just heard has been signed by thousands of young people. I think it is a good pledge. It is one that I am delighted and very proud to accept here on the White House steps this morning on behalf of all the people of America.

I think there is nothing more important that you could do for your country during this period than, as you say, "learn and practice the rules of fair play, respect the rights of others, and obey the laws of our city, our State, and our country."

I would like to quote something which another President, President Lincoln, said

to another group of young people about 130 years ago. President Lincoln had not yet become President, but he was deeply concerned about the situation in this land. He said:

"I hope I am over wary; but if I am not, there is even now something of ill omen amongst us. I mean the increasing disregard for law which pervades the country—the growing disposition to substitute the wild and furious passions in lieu of the sober judgment of courts, and the worse than savage mobs for the executive ministers of justice . . . . Accounts of outrages committed by mobs form the everyday news of the times."

So, as you can see, there have been rioters

and there have been mobs in other days, too. Their victims then were runaway slaves and gamblers, and sometimes just simply unhappy, unfortunate citizens who happened to walk down a street where passion had been aroused. But, as Lincoln realized, whatever the objectives of these people, whoever their victim, the real danger was to our own Constitution and to the freedom of our own country.

If our country is to survive, Lincoln said, we must all realize that "there is no grievance that is a fit object of redress by mob law."

Now, this is as true in 1968 as it was in 1838. And there is no more hopeful sign for this Nation's future than the proof that you have brought today that the overwhelming majority of young people in your great city are aware of this truth.

So, I am very happy and honored and proud that you have come here under the auspices of the Police Athletic League. This is a great organization, not only in Philadelphia, but it is a good organization throughout the country. Unfortunately, it is all too often true that our policeman's lot is not a very happy lot. But this is a most happy occasion for all of us here today and I hope that we can have many more like it.

I am glad to meet you and to greet you. I hope the other young people of this land will see in you an example that they want to emulate.

Thank you very much.

NOTE: The President spoke at 11:29 a.m. in the Rose Garden at the White House to 114 boys and girls representing the Police Athletic League of Philadelphia. The group had come to present the President with a pledge signed by approximately 125,000 Philadelphia students affirming their dedication to law and authority. In his opening words the President referred to Brig. Gen. George B. Wilson, Marine Corps Reserve, (Ret.), president of the Police Athletic League, and Paul Klieman, chairman of the League's 1968 campaign.

164   Remarks at a Luncheon Meeting of the AFL–CIO Committee on Political Education.   *March 29, 1968*

Mr. Meany and ladies and gentlemen:

I am delighted that you invited me to be present with you at lunch here today. I wanted to come by because I had heard by the grapevine that there were some political educators in town.

That was surprising to me. It was good news to me because I thought they were all out in Indiana and Wisconsin and Nebraska.

But this is, as I understand it, the "Graduate School of Politics." George Meany tells me that most of you have already earned your advanced degrees.

Well, we know one thing: You are led by a great political teacher and philosopher, Dean Meany. He tells me his courses are short and brief, and to the point: the three R's of politics—Republicans, reaction, and runaways.

I want to talk to you very seriously for a few minutes about the state of your Nation today, about the kind of a country that you live in. This America is the most progressive society that history has ever known. It is the richest; it is the freest; it is the strongest; it is the most productive. We ought to be proud of some of these things instead of crying about most of these things.

I want to say, without any fear of contradiction, that America right now is reaping the harvest of social ideas that have fired the hearts of our people for generations. Our campaigners, our politicians, and our orators have been talking about them for decades—but we are doing something about them today.

Our people have hungered for this for a long, long time—hungered for when every child could look forward to the promise of all the education he could master, regardless of the economic status of his father or mother, when the aged had the hope of some genuine security in their old age, when workers knew something about the dignity of a decent wage with a minimum floor under it, when health care was available to all the people of this country, and when full legal equality for all citizens is at long last near our grasp.

For 30 years, the great leaders—like Franklin Roosevelt and Harry Truman and Adlai Stevenson and John Kennedy—stirred the Nation's deepest hopes by giving eloquent voice to these dreams.

They began the long work of turning hope to reality; you helped them every step of the way.

But now in your day and in our time, America has woven these great visions into the fabric of its national life.

Twelve million Americans today have already been freed from the chains of poverty. Medicare has today—not tomorrow, today—become a reality, after Harry Truman proposed it more than 20 years ago, and we talked about it all that time.

Today—right now—20 million of our mothers and our fathers—20 big million of them—are no longer oppressed by heavy, big medical expenses.

We broke through years of deadlock to get help for our schools. It was not easy getting the Catholics and the Jews and the Baptists—and all the others—together on an elementary education bill.

But today, the deprived youngsters by the millions are being better educated for a brighter future because we have written into the law of the land—the last 4 years—18 broad national education acts for the benefit of these youngsters.

We took the first major civil rights bills in a century—and we quit talking about them. We enacted them into the law of the land.

This year, hundreds of thousands of our fellow citizens who never visited a voting booth, who were never allowed to mark a ballot, will vote for the first time because of these measures.

We achieved a higher minimum wage law for 42,800,000 people who work. At this hour, as I speak, America's labor force is 75 million strong. They are at work, at better jobs, at better wages than at any time in your entire life.

I came here to tell you we have just begun.

This year—with your help—we are going to bring safety to the worker at his jobsite. This year we are going to protect his hard-earned dollar by putting truth into lending with a special law we have recommended to the Congress that has been passed through both Houses.

We are going to put through an education bill that will put a college education within reach of every worker's son and daughter who wants to go to college.

We are going to continue to press all of the unfinished work of this Nation.

We know that great problems still beset us. Other nations have them, too. The restlessness that is abundant in the United States is in every corner of the globe; you just have to look at the television or the front pages of the newspapers to see about it.

We have tough and we have well-entrenched problems in the world.

At home, none of these problems is more urgent than the problem of our cities. It has been forming now for more than 100 years—

but America has mobilized its force to meet it. We have a cities message, with our recommendations, pending before the Congress.

People who want to do something about the cities can go up there and vote for that message—or get somebody else to vote for it.

We have put together a program that will rebuild the American city. It is the most ambitious housing program that ever was recommended to any Congress. We have proposed to the Congress that we construct 6 million new homes for the poor people of this country over the next 10 years. That is enough homes to replace every crumbling hovel that is now standing.

We intend to start 300,000 of these units this year. That is more than half as many as were built in the last 10 years. The next 10 years we are going to build 6 million. The last 10 years, we built 500,000. We are going to do 12 times as much the next 10 years as we did the last 10 years. And I say, that is not to be sneered at.

Thousands of our men and women who have never held steady work are trapped inside of the ghettos. They are unskilled; they are unschooled; they have little hope. They are the hard-core unemployed.

Well, we are setting out to restore some hope. You, your leaders, the men sitting at this table, the leaders of business, the leaders of your Government who are speaking to you are united in undertaking a massive campaign—a campaign of understanding, a campaign of compassion, a campaign of selflessness. Love they neighbor as thyself. We are trying to do something to help them.

We are going to find jobs for many of those who have been bypassed. We are going to train them. We are going to awaken their hope—and we hope we can give them a decent chance to know the self-respect that goes with employment and with a good job.

We will not let violence and lawlessness

take over this country. We will not let it block our efforts.

I believe—and I think you believe—that America believes that the crime that haunts the streets of our cities today is a national disgrace.

Our major governmental programs will strike at the roots of crime. But crime is an immediate problem that demands immediate action. Law enforcement is a local responsibility. It can be no other way in the America that our forefathers founded.

But we are determined to achieve a safer nation. We will cooperate with all the local law enforcement officers to do that.

We have put before the Congress a crime-fighting program that will strengthen the police forces all across this Nation and give them strength that is much needed at this very hour.

We have drawn the line against crime in our streets—and that includes rioting; that includes looting; and that includes arson, motivated for whatever reason.

I want to again assure you that the resources of your Government stand behind local law enforcement agencies to the full extent of our constitutional authority. Mindless violence—destroying what we have all worked so hard to build—will never be tolerated in America.

We are going to finish the work that we have started—the work of building a better, a more prosperous, and a more peaceful country. That will not be two Americas; that will be one America.

I was looking at the history of 1938 yesterday, and some of the speeches that were made then sounded like some of the things we are going through in 1968. But we went through them—and we pulled out of them—and we had a safe and happy and peaceful landing.

We are going to be a united people. We

are going to do what we must do at home—and we will, while we are doing that, fulfill every responsibility that America has in the world in which we live.

Thank you very much.

NOTE: The President spoke at 1:30 p.m. at the Washington Hilton Hotel. In his opening words he referred to George Meany, president of the AFL-CIO.

165 Remarks to a Group of Young Democrats.
March 29, 1968

I AM SORRY I don't have my television cameras with me. This is one of the most pleasant visions that these eyes have ever beheld, to see the young leaders of our country come to the capital of the world to learn something about what is happening in the world and then to do something about it.

I just came from another meeting. I was in the hotel visiting with another generation: Dean George Meany and his postgraduate workers from the Committee on Political Education.

I also thought I ought to take advantage of this chance away from the White House to talk to some of the undergraduates; that is why I dropped by with you.

I have never seen a school where you could learn as much from the teachers as you could from the students. That is why I came here to learn.

I taught in a schoolroom for a long time. I know this is sound. Any teacher can learn more from his students than he can from his teachers, if he wants to do it.

I am glad to see so many of you young people who have decided that you would come here to Washington in the spring instead of the hot sands of Fort Lauderdale. Instead of that, I guess you will get on the hot pavement of politics while you're here. We need you.

I saw another young activist who was a little under the weather this morning before I left the White House. He is not feeling very well. He is teething. We think little

Lyn is cutting his eighth tooth because he has a fever of 104. It may be that the campaign is just heating up and it is getting contagious.

I understand you have had several panel discussions here today. Someone told me you had a special one set up for me. It was called "What's My Line?" So, here I am, as your "mystery guest" to tell you how proud I am of this Nation, of what we are doing, of what we are going to do, of the progress that we have made, of the work that is yet undone.

In all the decades that I have been around, I have seen the croakers and the doubters who worry and are worried about what shape the world is in. But I have also known what our young people are going to do about it.

I have seen them in two World Wars, Korea, and Vietnam, go far away from home to protect that flag and their liberty and our freedom. I have seen them come back without the blush of shame on their cheek and without a spot on them.

I believe that this generation loves this country as much as my generation loves this country. I think you are going to be able to do more about it. You are going to make it go farther faster. You are going to make it better, more prosperous, and more peaceful because of what you are doing.

When I was a young man struggling to get through high school and later trying to get out of college, my mother would frequently try to strengthen me and encourage me by saying, "Son, remember that these hardships you are going through and these sacrifices you are making only serve to develop character."

That was pretty hard for me to believe because I would just as soon have had some character without them. But I do realize that you don't get full employment without dreaming of it and without planning for it; without working for it and without fighting for it.

I do realize that you cannot rebuild our cities without plans, without work, and without the will to do something about it.

I do know that you can't have peace in the world just because you wish for it. I do know that some men have tried to get peace by avoiding war, only to bring on wider war.

I do know that drive and desire are very important for all people, particularly for young people. But drive and desire don't necessarily give you the answer to all of our problems.

In my time I have seen the Greek Communists 7 miles from Athens.

I have seen the American planes over Berlin feeding a hungry nation. In zero-zero weather those planes kept landing.

I have seen our men hemmed in, in a little area of space in Korea with a lot of people advocating "Come home."

I have seen the dark days when a conqueror would have dominated the entire scene of Europe and some of our own great leaders were advocating that Britain move to Canada for safety's sake.

Yet I have seen an American will that drove unemployment from our midst and that faced up to the ancient enemies of this country: ignorance, illiteracy, and poverty, and started programs to combat all of them, instead of just sitting around talking about it all day.

I know, as you know, that none of those roads were easy roads; just as none of those hours that a half a million young men are spending now protecting us are easy for them. Not a single one of them wouldn't like to trade places with us, but they wouldn't trade what we have in this country for what any other country has to offer.

I remember the croakers and the doubters who roamed our legislative halls when they refused to fortify Guam with $5 million that President Roosevelt had thought was necessary, when they almost sent the Army home by a vote of 203 to 202 in August before Pearl Harbor in December.

Yes, I have seen all these things in my day. I saw the prophets who said, "These beardless kids could never fly the bombers over Berlin and never bring Hitler to his knees."

But they came through, just like our young people are coming through now, at home and abroad. And he who underestimates them or lacks faith in them is making a tragic error of judgment.

I am proud of every one of the more than 3 million people who wear the uniform and I am proud of every one of you who are willing to courageously stand up here and support them.

There will be many dark moments. There will be many long nights.

In the words of a great eloquent trustee and protector of ours of another day, "There will be blood and there will be sweat and there will be tears," but the principles that brought this Nation into existence, the traditions which have guided us, the things in which we believe, the strength that we have, are going to be used to protect the weak and to lift up the helpless and to see that might does not make right in this world.

With your help and with God's guidance, we are going to build here a safer, a better, a freer, a more prosperous America for our children than was built for us—and that is saying a lot.

Thank you and goodby.

NOTE: The President spoke at 1:55 p.m. at the Washington Hilton Hotel. During his remarks he referred to George Meany, president of the AFL–CIO, and to his grandson, Patrick Lyndon Nugent.

166 Statement by the President on the Disorders in Memphis. *March 29, 1968*

THE TRAGIC events in Memphis yesterday remind us of the grave peril rioting poses. This Nation must seek change within the rule of law in an environment of social order. Rioting, violence, and repression can only divide our people. Everyone loses when a riot occurs.

I call upon all Americans of every race and creed, the rich and the poor, the young and old, our governments, businesses, unions, and churches to strive to prevent violence, to obey the law, and to preserve conditions of social stability which are essential to progress.

I urge local law enforcement to deal firmly, but always fairly and without fear, with every infraction of law, to work unceasingly to prevent riots, and to train diligently to control them should they occur.

I urge State law enforcement to prepare full support for local law enforcement whenever aid is needed to maintain order. Order must be preserved.

If Federal assistance is needed, it is available, but our system of government and our security depend on capable local law enforcement.

NOTE: Racial disorders had occurred in Memphis, Tenn., on March 28 in support of a strike by city garbage collectors.

167 Remarks at a Reception for the Members of the Citizens' Advisory Committee on Recreation and Natural Beauty. *March 29, 1968*

Mrs. Johnson, Mr. Vice President, Mrs. Humphrey, Mr. and Mrs. Rockefeller, Members of the Cabinet, Members of the Congress, members of the Citizens' Committee, and my fellow Americans:

This is really a day to remember. This happening may turn out to be one of the more impressive demonstrations of "flower power" and architectural power, too, for that matter, and urban planning power, too, and political and business power, too—power which, used with vision, power which, used with imagination, can and will shape a newer and a better country.

Many years ago, John Burroughs wrote these words, "I am in love with this world. It has been my home. It has been my point of outlook into the universe. I have never bruised myself against it nor tried to use it ignobly."

Since the death of that great American naturalist, there have been many of us who also were in love with this world. But like too many suitors, we have been somewhat careless lovers. We have many times just taken our world for granted.

Sometimes we have done this in the name of progress. Often we have done it through sheer neglect. We have used our world ignobly.

Now, the time has come when we cannot be so careless. Unless we do better, we may suffer through a stark emergency of the environment. We may create a hostile world:

—a world to bruise ourselves against;

—a world of sprawling cities, unplanned or badly planned;

—a world whose water is full of sludge, whose winds are full of soot;

—a world whose landscape has been totally neglected, stripped, marred, and wasted.

All of this need not happen if we choose well, and particularly if we plan well and if we act well.

We have not been inactive these last 4 years. We have saved more. We have built more. We have preserved more than ever before in our history.

More than 2,200,000 acres of new park lands have been set aside for the American people. We have passed many major laws to save our rivers and our coasts and our lakes from water pollution. We have acted decisively to prevent the pollution of 67,000 miles of our American waterways. We have acted to try to clean the air of our congested cities.

There are some, I know, who see beautification as a frill, as an extra, or as something that is luxurious enough to postpone.

Well, they make me impatient because I am convinced that beauty and order in our environment are not frills. I am convinced that they are urgent necessities because they will determine whether our grandchildren can live in a decent land or whether they will be surrounded by glittering junkheaps.

When Mrs. Johnson and Mrs. Lasker and their many other hard-working colleagues put some playground equipment in the schoolyards, when they improve some neigh-

borhood park, when they plant an avenue of flowering trees, then I think their shovels dig deep into the future of this land because those shovels, while digging deep, are really changing the lives of our children.

When Stewart Udall saves a redwood forest, when his voice and his leadership help us put another national park within easy reach of every citizen, when he convinces the Congress that they should join us in trying to dot the areas near the big cities with some recreational spots, when more park land comes into the public domain than ever before, then the lives of our people are being changed and we are grateful for these gifts of vision and devotion.

When Laurance Rockefeller, that quiet and patient and persistent servant of the people who just spoke to you, reclaims a wilderness or sponsors another new conservation project, he enriches not only the landscape, but the lives of the people.

When Nat Owings designs a grand avenue for our Capital, he builds a monument to our Nation's vision.

When the planners and businessmen and architects work to try to save and improve our cities, I think that they are literally saving our lives.

These efforts are what history is going to remember us by.

I remember the leader in the Senate when I first came there in this field. He is present with us today, Senator Paul Douglas. I want to acknowledge his influence on my thinking and I think it has been influential on the thinking of all other Americans.

So I hope that when the history of our time is written, that that history will write of us: "Their cities were places for people, and not just places for freeways. Their highways were designed not only by engineers, but by conservationists and by urban planners. Their business and their civic leaders joined hands to try to overcome the blight and the decay and the pollution—and they won. They lived satisfying lives in a setting worthy of free men. Theirs was truly an age of beauty."

My friends, that is no pipedream. It is a blueprint for action.

Today, here in the East Room, we can celebrate some progress, some action. I am sending to the Congress a message that will call for 26 new wilderness areas—all the way from Maine to California.

I ask these forward-looking, progressive members of the Senate Interior Committee who are here with us, and the members of the House Committee, and all of those interested in conservation and in our children to recognize that we are taking a major step in an attempt to save another precious and another neglected resource. And that is the score of islands which lie off of our coasts and our lakes.

We have, in the 1960's, begun a great program to save the Nation's seashores. We now have a necklace of national seashores on all three of our coasts—the Atlantic, the Gulf, and the Pacific.

Today I am directing the Secretary of the Interior, Mr. Udall, to prepare a major program to save the wild islands. They represent some of the most magnificent, unspoiled beauty spots that are left in our continent. We must get an island conservation and recreation program going soon. We must get it going before it is too late.

Now, we have come to the point where we meet to sign an order designating our beloved and distinguished Vice President as Chairman of the Council on Recreation and Natural Beauty. He will give it vitality; he will give it vision. He will give it leadership, as he gives everything that he touches.

Mr. Vice President, this order doesn't spell out a role for Mrs. Johnson, but I rather suspect, if my experience is worth anything to you—I said to one of the Senators yesterday, "It is a shame I don't have a relationship with you like I do with Mrs. Johnson; when we have our differences, we talk them over with each other and then we go on our way, but when we have differences with the Senate, we use the processes of the Associated and United Press"—so Mr. Vice President, I suspect that you are going to be getting some advice from Mrs. Johnson from time to time, just as I do.

I am not competing with Drew Pearson, but I expect you will take it—just as I do.

In any event, to those of you who have spent your time and your talent and your resources in trying to help clean up this country—trying to give us better air and better water and better land and beauty spots and places where we can rest and where our children can play—I want to personally, on behalf of all of my countrymen, say to each of you leaders: We thank you.

We are very proud that you are interested in things like this. We are very grateful that you have inspired us and given us leadership and—yes—strength, and even sometimes, a little comfort.

Thank you very much.

NOTE: The President spoke at 5:24 p.m. in the East Room at the White House. In his opening words he referred to Mrs. Lyndon B. Johnson, Vice President and Mrs. Hubert H. Humphrey, Laurance S. Rockefeller, Chairman, Citizens' Advisory Committee on Recreation and Natural Beauty, and Mrs. Rockefeller. Later he also referred to Mrs. Albert D. Lasker, philanthropist and trustee of the John F. Kennedy Center for the Performing Arts, Stewart L. Udall, Secretary of the Interior, Nathaniel Owings, Chairman, Temporary Commission on Pennsylvania Avenue, Paul H. Douglas, Chairman of the National Commission on Urban Problems and Senator from Illinois 1949–1967, and Drew Pearson, syndicated columnist.

On the same day the President signed Executive

Order 11402 "Making the Vice President of the United States the Chairman of the President's Council on Recreation and Natural Beauty" (4 Weekly Comp. Pres. Docs., p. 598; 33 F.R. 5253; 3 CFR, 1968 Comp., p. 107). Vice President Humphrey submitted the Council's report to the President on October 28, 1968 (4 Weekly Comp. Pres. Docs., p.

1551).

The Citizens' Advisory Committee on Recreation and Natural Beauty and the President's Council on Recreation and Natural Beauty were established by Executive Order 11278 of May 4, 1966 (2 Weekly Comp. Pres. Docs., p. 607; 31 F.R. 6681; 3 CFR, 1966 Comp., p. 107).

168 Letter to the President of the Senate and to the Speaker of the House Urging the Addition of New Areas to the Nation's Wilderness System. *March* 29, 1968

Dear Mr. President: (Dear Mr. Speaker:)

Inevitably, our work as public leaders affects not only us but our posterity. It may be that our most important constituents are not our contemporaries, but the men and women who will inherit America from us in twenty years or fifty years.

Our grandchildren and our great-grandchildren will live in a different America from the one we know; but it will be an America we have helped to build. They will work in buildings and factories we erect; travel on highways we lay out; live in cities and suburbs we construct; seek solace and recreation in parks and wilderness areas we preserve.

So we must build well now.

Unless we do, much of the wild and beautiful America that we know and our grandfathers knew will be lost forever—buried in the debris of our hurrying civilization.

Last year, I recommended that Congress incorporate four areas into the National Wilderness Preservation System.

Last week, it was my pleasure to sign into law an act setting aside the first of the preserves: the San Rafael Wilderness Area.

Now I am urging that Congress consider making 26 additions to the Nation's wilderness system—additions totaling 977,081 acres. They come from our national forests, from the National Wildlife Refuges and from the National Parks and Monuments System.

The proposed new wilderness areas are:
—The Mt. Baldy Wilderness in Arizona.
—The Pine Mountain Wilderness in Arizona.
—The Petrified Forest Wilderness in Arizona.
—The Sycamore Canyon Wilderness in Arizona.
—The Desolation Wilderness in California.
—The Lassen Volcanic Wilderness in California.
—The Lava Beds Wilderness in California.
—The Pinnacles Wilderness in California.
—The Ventana Wilderness in California.
—The Flat Tops Wilderness in Colorado.
—The Cedar Keys Wilderness in Florida.
—The Island Bay Wilderness in Florida.
—The Passage Key Wilderness in Florida.
—The Pelican Island Wilderness in Florida.
—The Okefenokee Wilderness in Georgia.
—The Craters of the Moon Wilderness in Idaho.
—The Edmunds Wilderness in Maine.
—The Birch Islands Wilderness in Maine.
—The Monomoy Island Wilderness in

Massachusetts.

—The Huron Islands Wilderness in Michigan.

—The Michigan Islands Wilderness in Michigan.

—The Seney Wilderness in Michigan.

—The Spanish Peaks Wilderness in Montana.

—The Great Swamp Wilderness in New Jersey.

—The Wichita Mountains Wilderness in Oklahoma.

—The Wisconsin Islands Wilderness in Wisconsin.

In support of each recommendation, I am transmitting a letter and a report from the Secretary of Interior or the Secretary of Agriculture.

There was a day when "conservation" was regarded as an activity far removed from the workaday world of most Americans or work for forest rangers and game wardens. No longer. Many of these areas, as you will note, are close to the centers of American population. They can and will be enjoyed by millions of our people seeking the solitude and splendor of the land as God made it. So they are a trust and a responsibility for all of us.

I urge Congress to give prompt and favorable consideration to these proposals.

Respectfully,

LYNDON B. JOHNSON

NOTE: This is the text of identical letters addressed to the Honorable Hubert H. Humphrey, President of the Senate, and to the Honorable John W. Mc-Cormack, Speaker of the House of Representatives.

For statements or remarks upon signing related legislation, see Items 502, 505, 510, 547.

The San Rafael Wilderness was approved by the President on March 21, 1968 (see Item 150).

The San Gabriel Wilderness was approved on May 24, 1968 (Public Law 90–318, 82 Stat. 131).

169 The President's News Conference of March 30, 1968

THE PRESIDENT. [1.] We have some nice spring weather, I see.

Mr. Zwick, the Director of the Budget, is here. We will have a release [1] that you are somewhat familiar with involving reduction in foreign personnel abroad in various Government departments. It runs from $12 million to $15 million for the transitional year, and to $20 million to $25 million for the coming fiscal year.

Mr. Zwick will be glad to answer any specific questions you have on that at the conclusion of the meeting.

I would be glad to take any questions you want to ask.

---

[1] See Weekly Compilation of Presidential Documents (vol. 4, p. 618).

QUESTIONS

WISCONSIN DEMOCRATIC PRIMARY

[2.] Q. Do you know who is going to win the Democratic primary in Wisconsin?

THE PRESIDENT. No, I don't.

ADDRESS TO THE NATION

[3.] Q. Mr. President, there has been talk about another bombing pause. Can you tell us what your thinking on that possibility is?

THE PRESIDENT. I don't think that a military strategy that is under review from time to time, or troop deployments, or matters of that kind, ought to be speculated on until the President has made a decision. There is not anything to announce at this time.

I do think that as a result of the intensive review that the President and the diplomatic and military and congressional officials have given Vietnam in recent weeks, particularly since the Tet offensive, that it would be well if the President would speak on that subject rather fully.

Therefore, I plan to speak from my office tomorrow evening to the country at 9 o'clock.[2] I will at that time discuss troop speculations that have taken place, what our plans are, and what information we have that we are able to talk about now. I will also talk about other questions of some importance.

It will be more or less a report on the reviews which have taken place, together with an announcement of some actions that we are taking.

REQUEST FOR A TAX INCREASE

[4.] Q. Mr. President, Representative George Mahon[3] said yesterday it would be meaningful, that you really should ask the people for a greater tax increase than the 10 percent surcharge. I wonder if you are prepared to do that?

THE PRESIDENT. We can't do much about it between now and Sunday evening. I will cover that in my statement Sunday evening—my views on the entire fiscal policy. These remarks are being prepared now.

POOR PEOPLE'S MARCH ON WASHINGTON

[5.] Q. Mr. President, how do you feel about the proposed Poor People's March on Washington next month in light of the

events in Memphis this week, sir?[4]

THE PRESIDENT. I recognize that there are many serious problems, some anticipated and some that frequently are not anticipated, that flow from situations of this kind.

In this season of the year, we are very concerned about dealing properly and adequately and appropriately with the various protests and marches that may take place.

The Attorney General has met with the Governors and with the mayors and has been in touch with them from time to time. Generally, he tries to plan and anticipate problems to the extent he can with the mayors and with the Governors, whose primary responsibility it is to maintain order.

In the case of Washington, the Attorney General and Mayor Washington[5] and others have given a good deal of their time to it. I would hope if there is a march that it will be in keeping with the law, that the law will be obeyed, that the individual rights of all will be respected, and that no violence will flow from it.

Q. Mr. President, on that point, there has been a suggestion in the Senate that there be an injunction to stop the march, or some type of restriction. What is your personal viewpoint on that?

THE PRESIDENT. I am not familiar with the suggestions. I have given my viewpoints generally. We believe that these marches should be kept within the law. We know of no way to prohibit people who comply with the law from exercising their rights.

DECISION ON VIETNAM AND THE PRESIDENT'S
ADDRESS

[6.] Q. Mr. President, does your speech tomorrow indicate that you have come to

---

[2] See Item 170.
[3] Representative George H. Mahon of Texas, Chairman of the House Appropriations Committee.

[4] See Item 166.
[5] Mayor Walter E. Washington of the District of Columbia.

the end of your A to Z evaluation? Does the speech tomorrow on Vietnam mean that you have arrived at a decision?

THE PRESIDENT. No, Helen.[6] We are constantly reviewing this problem every day—we will never fully complete our work until we have peace in that area of the world.

We haven't even completed our work in Europe. We are reviewing it every day.

My statement tomorrow night will deal with evaluating the problems as I see them, giving the Nation my views on those problems, and announcing certain actions that I propose to take.

That is not to say that we have completely closed the door and nothing else will be considered. I will have conferences next week. They are rather important ones in connection with the actions that I will announce tomorrow night. But I think you will get from the speech pretty generally the Government's position and the course that we intend to take.

Q. Sir, will it be painful?

THE PRESIDENT. Well, you call me and tell me after you hear it.

Q. It will be on television, though, won't it?

THE PRESIDENT. We are going to make it available, if they choose to carry it.

EXCHANGE OF PRISONERS

[7.] Q. Mr. President, have the talks that resulted in our releasing the three North Vietnamese sailors been encouraging to you as far as our making progress on the *Pueblo* [7] and in having dialogue with the North Vietnamese generally?

THE PRESIDENT. We are always glad to

be able to get the release of our prisoners and to be able to reciprocate the actions they take.

I don't know just how to describe those releases in your terms. You will have to draw your own conclusions there. We are pleased that those exchanges have worked out to the extent they have. We would like to see more of them.

STATUS OF U.S. DEFENSE SYSTEM

[8.] Q. Mr. President, this last week Senator Stennis said something about the Defense Department being down to kind of a barebones position and there has been a request for some $3 billion or $4 billion in addition. Are you satisfied with the status of the preparedness or do you have any special concern at the present time?

THE PRESIDENT. We are constantly trying to strengthen the weaknesses that develop in the defense system of the Nation—the shortages that appear. Sometimes it is helicopters. Sometimes it is helicopter parts. Sometimes it is M–16 rifles. Sometimes it is ammunition. Some days it may be various fuels of certain kinds at certain spots.

Overall, I think generally there has never been a war fought as far away as this one has been fought that has been as well supplied and has had as few necessities in short supply.

But that is not to say that we don't make errors. That is not to say that we don't goof at times. We are constantly trying to find those goofs and correct them.

There will be some increases in certain items like helicopters, parts, guns, ammunition, and other things that flow from the needs that we found that appeared after the Tet offensive. The cost of those items is being worked on now. They are substantial, but there is not anything like the amounts that

---

[6] Helen Thomas of United Press International.

[7] United States intelligence ship seized by North Korea on January 23, 1968. The crew was released on December 22, 1968 (see Item 641).

have been speculated on. I will try to give you some more accurate estimate of them tomorrow evening.

I would say they will involve a few billion dollars, but not anything like the $10 billion to $20 billion that I have seen and heard people use. It will not be anything like the hundreds of thousands of callups and deployments that I have heard speculated upon.

HANOI'S RESPONSE TO THE SAN ANTONIO FORMULA

[9.] Q. Mr. President, has there been any change in the San Antonio formula, and has there been any reaction from Hanoi to it in a positive way?

THE PRESIDENT. We extended the offer at San Antonio. And that offer still stands. They have commented on that offer. As far as I am aware, they have not indicated to anyone that it was acceptable to them.

We constantly explore leads that we think might offer some hope. But I am not able to point specifically to any action that they have taken in response to the San Antonio formula that makes me believe that it is acceptable, totally acceptable, to them now.

THE MISSING F-III AIRCRAFT

[10.] Q. Mr. President, do you have a report on the F-111 that disappeared in Southeast Asia, whether it was shot down or just crashed?

THE PRESIDENT. Do you want to be a little more specific?

Q. This week an F-111 flying over North Vietnam or in the vicinity disappeared.

THE PRESIDENT. The only information that I know that is available is that it did not return; that it is missing. That is the last information I have.

THE PRESIDENT'S CAMPAIGN PLANS

[11.] Q. Mr. President, do you have any plans tomorrow to discuss your future role in this campaign, or candidacy?

THE PRESIDENT. No.

Q. Mr. President, there was a story a week ago saying—on what authority it wasn't indicated——

THE PRESIDENT. What story? I don't want to chase these vacuums.

Q. It was a dope story. The authority wasn't indicated, but it said you won't announce your plans as far as 1968 are concerned until the August convention in Chicago. Is that possible?

THE PRESIDENT. I won't comment on any of those stories. I will cross that bridge when I get to it. The fact that it is a dope story is the best evidence of its total unreliability. Usually those stories are the thoughts of people who are not making the decisions, although we haven't made any decision on the matter yet.

MEETINGS ON ACTIONS TO BE TAKEN

[12.] Q. You mentioned that you were going to have a series of important meetings next week related to your speech tomorrow.

THE PRESIDENT. I said we will be meeting through next week on all of these matters, trying to implement them and carry them out, review them.

Q. I was wondering if those meetings were going to be here in Washington or whether you are considering another specific meeting?

THE PRESIDENT. I will be here in Washington at least some of next week. If there are any meetings out of Washington, I will make an announcement when they are definitely determined.

PREMIER KOSYGIN

[13.] Q. Mr. President, do you have any plans to meet again with Premier Kosygin this year?

THE PRESIDENT. No. We have no plans.

PLANS TO ATTEND HEMISFAIR OPENING

[14.] Q. Do you plan to go to the Hemis-Fair opening next weekend, Mr. President, and meet with President Diaz?[8]

THE PRESIDENT. It is difficult for me to talk this far ahead, Helen. Of course, we would like to. Mrs. Johnson has plans to be there. If I can, I would like to. But there may be other items that would not make it possible for me to go there.

CAMPAIGN MANAGER

[15.] Q. Sir, I realize the fact that you are not yet a candidate for reelection, but would you please tell us who you consider to be your main leader in your organization, the manager of your organization?

THE PRESIDENT. No. I just hope that all of you are as helpful as you can be.

DR. MARTIN LUTHER KING, JR.

[16.] Q. Mr. President, as regards the Memphis turbulence, have you talked to Dr. Martin Luther King,[9] or do you plan to, sir?

THE PRESIDENT. No, I have not talked to Dr. Martin Luther King.

FRENCH POSITION ON THE GOLD PROPOSALS

[17.] Q. Mr. President, there are indications out of Stockholm that the French are declining to go along with our latest proposals on gold. Are you disappointed in that?

THE PRESIDENT. Yes, I think I would say I am disappointed, but it is not unexpected. Is that clear?

You don't think I ought to advertise the wire services? What is this? Is this Reuters?

The Agence France-Presse says a spokesman for the French delegation declared— I just saw this before I came out, and I thought this would be helpful to you—"We decline to associate ourselves with the final communiqué of the Conference of Ten." French Minister of Finance and Economy Michel Debré will distribute a statement and answer correspondents' questions as soon as possible.

Mr. Ed Fried of my staff is there with Secretary Fowler and Mr. Martin.[10] He has reported to me from time to time. His first reports said that the first day was spent in staking out positions, with no great surprises; that Mr. Debré carried on discussions extensively, and they seemed to be isolated on most issues; that he spoke on each issue.

The outcome has not yet been determined. So I would hope that this conference will be successful. We will have to read the communiqué that is in the process of being prepared.[11]

It is obvious that the French have not agreed with our position. We have tried to be tolerant and flexible. We are very proud of our representation there—Secretary Fowler, Mr. Martin, and others—and we are very pleased generally with the cooperation that comes from the other members.

Now, just what will come out finally, I

---

[8] Gustavo Diaz Ordaz, President of Mexico.

[9] Dr. Martin Luther King, Jr., president of the Southern Christian Leadership Conference.

[10] William McC. Martin, Jr., Chairman, Board of Governors of the Federal Reserve System.

[11] On March 17, 1968, the White House released the text of a communiqué by governors of the central banks of gold pool member nations following their meeting in Washington (4 Weekly Comp. Pres. Docs., p. 536).

don't want to say at this time, although I hope that it will be successful.

THE F–III–B AIRCRAFT

[18.] Q. Mr. President, on the F–111, the F–111–B was shot down also by the Armed Services Committee on a 11 to 2 vote this week after an expenditure of I think somewhere in the neighborhood of $1 billion.

I wonder what your view is on that and the plans to go into some other new plane?

THE PRESIDENT. I think you specialists in that field could better deal with that. The Navy and Mr. Clifford have some first-hand information on what has taken place on that.

I don't think I could add anything to what you already know or change your opinion in any way.

NEW COMMANDER IN VIETNAM

[19.] Q. Mr. President, do you expect to name a new Vietnam commander tomorrow?

THE PRESIDENT. No.

SITUATION IN THE MIDDLE EAST

[20.] Q. Mr. President, we have had a renewal of hostilities in the Middle East in the past few days. Have you had any personal involvement in trying to cool things off there outside of what we are doing at the U.N.?

THE PRESIDENT. We keep in very close touch through our diplomats in that part of the world. They are reporting to me all the information that they have together with any suggestions they may have.

That is under the general jurisdiction of the Assistant Secretary in charge of the Mid-

dle East, Mr. Battle.[12] I have had a number of meetings with the Secretary of State and the Assistant Secretary, Mr. Battle, as well as with Ambassador Goldberg. I have had a number of conversations with Ambassador Goldberg at the U.N.

We are trying to exercise all of the strength we can in the direction of avoiding hostilities and maintaining peace consistent with the five points that I announced back last June. That is our general position.

That is what we think should be considered and carried out. We are trying to help with the Jarring [13] mission wherever we can.

Ambassador Goldberg and Mr. Battle are working on the general problem every day. We deplore and regret violence wherever it originates on both sides.

We think fighting is a very poor substitute for reasoning and meeting with each other. We would hope that all sides to the controversy would be more amenable to talking it out rather than fighting it out.

But I cannot say to you that we have their agreement to that kind of a program as yet.

COPPER STRIKE SETTLEMENT AND THE ECONOMY

[21.] Q. Mr. President, could you discuss with us your view of the effects of the copper developments, the settlement, that seems to be emerging and the price increases that seem to be emerging?

THE PRESIDENT. We are very happy that we are able to resume production and to get

---

[12] Lucius D. Battle, Assistant Secretary for Near Eastern and South Asian Affairs.

[13] Gunnar Jarring, Swedish Ambassador to the Soviet Union and United Nations mediator in the Middle East dispute.

the strike settled. We regret very much the inflationary aspects attached to that settlement.

We did everything we could to try to keep the increases in wages and prices lower.

In a free enterprise system where you have collective bargaining, unless you have mandatory controls which we do not have, all you can do is to lay down your views and express them and appeal to the individuals concerned to bear them in mind in their collective bargaining decisions.

Chairman Okun of the Council of Economic Advisers spoke very emphatically about the effect of these decisions. He spoke and I think released his statement to the press.

I would hope that all the copper producers would not follow the example that had been set of accelerating a general round of price increases.

We are very concerned about the inflation picture. We have been appealing to the country to give us support and to the Congress to give us support that we think would help to avoid inflation.

Early in 1966, we felt that the time had come when we ought to consider restoring some of the tax revenues that we had repealed in 1964 and 1965.

We counseled with labor and business and the congressional leadership. It was evident that it would be impossible to get a tax increase in 1966.

In 1967, we were more hopeful. Both business and labor agreed to support us. But as you know, the Congress did not agree with us for various reasons.

Some thought the economy was sluggish and didn't need it. Some thought that there ought to be reductions in the budget and a variety of reasons.

The economy, I think, demonstrated that

it could take a tax increase and that it would be desirable. Most of the bankers, insurance companies, and economists testified to that effect as well as the labor leaders.

But the demand was made that we reduce expenditures. We could not act on that until Congress had their chance to do it. When they did, they reduced appropriations by several billion dollars and expenditures by somewhere between $1 and $2 billion.

The leadership thought that was not enough and asked us to reduce them even further. We agreed and recommended a formula to Congress that was known as the 2–10 formula that made additional reductions which ran about $8 billion or $10 billion in appropriations and about $4 billion in expenditures last year.

In light of this, we were hopeful that we would get a tax bill to deal with the constant increase in prices, the constant challenges to the dollar, the fear that we had of the increase in interest rates, and the effect that would have on employment, on housing, and all of the other matters.

Congress has not seen fit to favorably act upon the tax bill. Although I do believe that if the country would indicate its willingness to face up to this very necessary situation, I believe Congress might act favorably.[14]

I think the country ought to know that it is very dangerous not to act. We are carrying on quite a gamble. Unless we have a tax bill with the increased expenses that we have in our defense setups in supporting our fighting men, as well as what we are trying to do in our domestic programs, then the price that we are going to have to pay is going to be much higher than the price we would pay by acting prudently and passing a tax bill.

So I think that that would be the best

---

[14] The Revenue and Expenditure Control Act of 1968 was approved by the President on June 28, 1968 (see Item 343).

action we could take to help the price situation. In the meantime, we are going to try to encourage labor and encourage business to exercise restraint in their bargaining decisions.

We cannot force them. We do not have the power to restrain them and keep them from reaching these decisions.

We encourage collective bargaining in this country. But we do think that in this instance the increases are excessive.

Helen Thomas, United Press International: Thank you, Mr. President.

NOTE: President Johnson's one hundred and twenty-first news conference was held in the Rose Garden at the White House at 12:15 p.m. on Saturday, March 30, 1968.

170   The President's Address to the Nation Announcing Steps To Limit the War in Vietnam and Reporting His Decision Not To Seek Reelection.   *March 31, 1968*

Good evening, my fellow Americans:

Tonight I want to speak to you of peace in Vietnam and Southeast Asia.

No other question so preoccupies our people. No other dream so absorbs the 250 million human beings who live in that part of the world. No other goal motivates American policy in Southeast Asia.

For years, representatives of our Government and others have traveled the world—seeking to find a basis for peace talks.

Since last September, they have carried the offer that I made public at San Antonio.

That offer was this:

That the United States would stop its bombardment of North Vietnam when that would lead promptly to productive discussions—and that we would assume that North Vietnam would not take military advantage of our restraint.

Hanoi denounced this offer, both privately and publicly. Even while the search for peace was going on, North Vietnam rushed their preparations for a savage assault on the people, the government, and the allies of South Vietnam.

Their attack—during the Tet holidays—failed to achieve its principal objectives.

It did not collapse the elected government of South Vietnam or shatter its army—as the Communists had hoped.

It did not produce a "general uprising" among the people of the cities as they had predicted.

The Communists were unable to maintain control of any of the more than 30 cities that they attacked. And they took very heavy casualties.

But they did compel the South Vietnamese and their allies to move certain forces from the countryside into the cities.

They caused widespread disruption and suffering. Their attacks, and the battles that followed, made refugees of half a million human beings.

The Communists may renew their attack any day.

They are, it appears, trying to make 1968 the year of decision in South Vietnam—the year that brings, if not final victory or defeat, at least a turning point in the struggle.

This much is clear:

If they do mount another round of heavy attacks, they will not succeed in destroying the fighting power of South Vietnam and its allies.

But tragically, this is also clear: Many men—on both sides of the struggle—will be lost. A nation that has already suffered 20 years of warfare will suffer once again. Armies on both sides will take new casualties. And the war will go on.

There is no need for this to be so.

There is no need to delay the talks that could bring an end to this long and this bloody war.

Tonight, I renew the offer I made last August—to stop the bombardment of North Vietnam. We ask that talks begin promptly, that they be serious talks on the substance of peace. We assume that during those talks Hanoi will not take advantage of our restraint.

We are prepared to move immediately toward peace through negotiations.

So, tonight, in the hope that this action will lead to early talks, I am taking the first step to deescalate the conflict. We are reducing—substantially reducing—the present level of hostilities.

And we are doing so unilaterally, and at once.

Tonight, I have ordered our aircraft and our naval vessels to make no attacks on North Vietnam, except in the area north of the demilitarized zone where the continuing enemy buildup directly threatens allied forward positions and where the movements of their troops and supplies are clearly related to that threat.

The area in which we are stopping our attacks includes almost 90 percent of North Vietnam's population, and most of its territory. Thus there will be no attacks around the principal populated areas, or in the food-producing areas of North Vietnam.

Even this very limited bombing of the North could come to an early end—if our restraint is matched by restraint in Hanoi. But I cannot in good conscience stop all bombing so long as to do so would immediately and directly endanger the lives of our men and our allies. Whether a complete bombing halt becomes possible in the future will be determined by events.

Our purpose in this action is to bring about a reduction in the level of violence that now exists.

It is to save the lives of brave men—and to save the lives of innocent women and children. It is to permit the contending forces to move closer to a political settlement.

And tonight, I call upon the United Kingdom and I call upon the Soviet Union—as cochairmen of the Geneva Conferences, and as permanent members of the United Nations Security Council—to do all they can to move from the unilateral act of deescalation that I have just announced toward genuine peace in Southeast Asia.

Now, as in the past, the United States is ready to send its representatives to any forum, at any time, to discuss the means of bringing this ugly war to an end.

I am designating one of our most distinguished Americans, Ambassador Averell Harriman, as my personal representative for such talks. In addition, I have asked Ambassador Llewellyn Thompson, who returned from Moscow for consultation, to be available to join Ambassador Harriman at Geneva or any other suitable place—just as soon as Hanoi agrees to a conference.

I call upon President Ho Chi Minh to respond positively, and favorably, to this new step toward peace.

But if peace does not come now through negotiations, it will come when Hanoi understands that our common resolve is unshakable, and our common strength is invincible.

Tonight, we and the other allied nations are contributing 600,000 fighting men to assist 700,000 South Vietnamese troops in defending their little country.

Our presence there has always rested

on this basic belief: The main burden of preserving their freedom must be carried out by them—by the South Vietnamese themselves.

We and our allies can only help to provide a shield behind which the people of South Vietnam can survive and can grow and develop. On their efforts—on their determination and resourcefulness—the outcome will ultimately depend.

That small, beleaguered nation has suffered terrible punishment for more than 20 years.

I pay tribute once again tonight to the great courage and endurance of its people. South Vietnam supports armed forces tonight of almost 700,000 men—and I call your attention to the fact that this is the equivalent of more than 10 million in our own population. Its people maintain their firm determination to be free of domination by the North.

There has been substantial progress, I think, in building a durable government during these last 3 years. The South Vietnam of 1965 could not have survived the enemy's Tet offensive of 1968. The elected government of South Vietnam survived that attack—and is rapidly repairing the devastation that it wrought.

The South Vietnamese know that further efforts are going to be required:

—to expand their own armed forces,

—to move back into the countryside as quickly as possible,

—to increase their taxes,

—to select the very best men that they have for civil and military responsibility,

—to achieve a new unity within their constitutional government, and

—to include in the national effort all those groups who wish to preserve South Vietnam's control over its own destiny.

Last week President Thieu ordered the mobilization of 135,000 additional South Vietnamese. He plans to reach—as soon as possible—a total military strength of more than 800,000 men.

To achieve this, the Government of South Vietnam started the drafting of 19-year-olds on March 1st. On May 1st, the Government will begin the drafting of 18-year-olds.

Last month, 10,000 men volunteered for military service—that was two and a half times the number of volunteers during the same month last year. Since the middle of January, more than 48,000 South Vietnamese have joined the armed forces—and nearly half of them volunteered to do so.

All men in the South Vietnamese armed forces have had their tours of duty extended for the duration of the war, and reserves are now being called up for immediate active duty.

President Thieu told his people last week: "We must make greater efforts and accept more sacrifices because, as I have said many times, this is our country. The existence of our nation is at stake, and this is mainly a Vietnamese responsibility."

He warned his people that a major national effort is required to root out corruption and incompetence at all levels of government.

We applaud this evidence of determination on the part of South Vietnam. Our first priority will be to support their effort.

We shall accelerate the reequipment of South Vietnam's armed forces—in order to meet the enemy's increased firepower. This will enable them progressively to undertake a larger share of combat operations against the Communist invaders.

On many occasions I have told the American people that we would send to Vietnam those forces that are required to accomplish our mission there. So, with that as our guide, we have previously authorized a force level of approximately 525,000.

Some weeks ago—to help meet the enemy's new offensive—we sent to Vietnam about 11,000 additional Marine and airborne troops. They were deployed by air in 48 hours, on an emergency basis. But the artillery, tank, aircraft, medical, and other units that were needed to work with and to support these infantry troops in combat could not then accompany them by air on that short notice.

In order that these forces may reach maximum combat effectiveness, the Joint Chiefs of Staff have recommended to me that we should prepare to send—during the next 5 months—support troops totaling approximately 13,500 men.

A portion of these men will be made available from our active forces. The balance will come from reserve component units which will be called up for service.

The actions that we have taken since the beginning of the year

—to reequip the South Vietnamese forces,

—to meet our responsibilities in Korea, as well as our responsibilities in Vietnam,

—to meet price increases and the cost of activating and deploying reserve forces,

—to replace helicopters and provide the other military supplies we need,

all of these actions are going to require additional expenditures.

The tentative estimate of those additional expenditures is $2.5 billion in this fiscal year, and $2.6 billion in the next fiscal year.

These projected increases in expenditures for our national security will bring into sharper focus the Nation's need for immediate action: action to protect the prosperity of the American people and to protect the strength and the stability of our American dollar.

On many occasions I have pointed out that,

without a tax bill or decreased expenditures, next year's deficit would again be around $20 billion. I have emphasized the need to set strict priorities in our spending. I have stressed that failure to act and to act promptly and decisively would raise very strong doubts throughout the world about America's willingness to keep its financial house in order.

Yet Congress has not acted. And tonight we face the sharpest financial threat in the postwar era—a threat to the dollar's role as the keystone of international trade and finance in the world.

Last week, at the monetary conference in Stockholm, the major industrial countries decided to take a big step toward creating a new international monetary asset that will strengthen the international monetary system. I am very proud of the very able work done by Secretary Fowler and Chairman Martin of the Federal Reserve Board.

But to make this system work the United States just must bring its balance of payments to—or very close to—equilibrium. We must have a responsible fiscal policy in this country. The passage of a tax bill now, together with expenditure control that the Congress may desire and dictate, is absolutely necessary to protect this Nation's security, to continue our prosperity, and to meet the needs of our people.

What is at stake is 7 years of unparalleled prosperity. In those 7 years, the real income of the average American, after taxes, rose by almost 30 percent—a gain as large as that of the entire preceding 19 years.

So the steps that we must take to convince the world are exactly the steps we must take to sustain our own economic strength here at home. In the past 8 months, prices and interest rates have risen because of our inaction.

We must, therefore, now do everything we can to move from debate to action—from talking to voting. There is, I believe—I hope there is—in both Houses of the Congress—a growing sense of urgency that this situation just must be acted upon and must be corrected.

My budget in January was, we thought, a tight one. It fully reflected our evaluation of most of the demanding needs of this Nation.

But in these budgetary matters, the President does not decide alone. The Congress has the power and the duty to determine appropriations and taxes.

The Congress is now considering our proposals and they are considering reductions in the budget that we submitted.

As part of a program of fiscal restraint that includes the tax surcharge, I shall approve appropriate reductions in the January budget when and if Congress so decides that that should be done.

One thing is unmistakably clear, however: Our deficit just must be reduced. Failure to act could bring on conditions that would strike hardest at those people that all of us are trying so hard to help.

These times call for prudence in this land of plenty. I believe that we have the character to provide it, and tonight I plead with the Congress and with the people to act promptly to serve the national interest, and thereby serve all of our people.

Now let me give you my estimate of the chances for peace:

—the peace that will one day stop the bloodshed in South Vietnam,

—that will permit all the Vietnamese people to rebuild and develop their land,

—that will permit us to turn more fully to our own tasks here at home.

I cannot promise that the initiative that I have announced tonight will be completely successful in achieving peace any more than the 30 others that we have undertaken and agreed to in recent years.

But it is our fervent hope that North Vietnam, after years of fighting that have left the issue unresolved, will now cease its efforts to achieve a military victory and will join with us in moving toward the peace table.

And there may come a time when South Vietnamese—on both sides—are able to work out a way to settle their own differences by free political choice rather than by war.

As Hanoi considers its course, it should be in no doubt of our intentions. It must not miscalculate the pressures within our democracy in this election year.

We have no intention of widening this war.

But the United States will never accept a fake solution to this long and arduous struggle and call it peace.

No one can foretell the precise terms of an eventual settlement.

Our objective in South Vietnam has never been the annihilation of the enemy. It has been to bring about a recognition in Hanoi that its objective—taking over the South by force—could not be achieved.

We think that peace can be based on the Geneva Accords of 1954—under political conditions that permit the South Vietnamese—all the South Vietnamese—to chart their course free of any outside domination or interference, from us or from anyone else.

So tonight I reaffirm the pledge that we made at Manila—that we are prepared to withdraw our forces from South Vietnam as the other side withdraws its forces to the north, stops the infiltration, and the level of violence thus subsides.

Our goal of peace and self-determination in Vietnam is directly related to the future of all of Southeast Asia—where much has happened to inspire confidence during the past 10 years. We have done all that we knew how to do to contribute and to help build that confidence.

A number of its nations have shown what can be accomplished under conditions of security. Since 1966, Indonesia, the fifth largest nation in all the world, with a population of more than 100 million people, has had a government that is dedicated to peace with its neighbors and improved conditions for its own people. Political and economic cooperation between nations has grown rapidly.

I think every American can take a great deal of pride in the role that we have played in bringing this about in Southeast Asia. We can rightly judge—as responsible Southeast Asians themselves do—that the progress of the past 3 years would have been far less likely—if not completely impossible—if America's sons and others had not made their stand in Vietnam.

At Johns Hopkins University, about 3 years ago, I announced that the United States would take part in the great work of developing Southeast Asia, including the Mekong Valley, for all the people of that region. Our determination to help build a better land—a better land for men on both sides of the present conflict—has not diminished in the least. Indeed, the ravages of war, I think, have made it more urgent than ever.

So, I repeat on behalf of the United States again tonight what I said at Johns Hopkins—that North Vietnam could take its place in this common effort just as soon as peace comes.

Over time, a wider framework of peace and security in Southeast Asia may become possible. The new cooperation of the nations of the area could be a foundation-stone. Certainly friendship with the nations of such a Southeast Asia is what the United States seeks—and that is all that the United States seeks.

One day, my fellow citizens, there will be peace in Southeast Asia.

It will come because the people of Southeast Asia want it—those whose armies are at war tonight, and those who, though threatened, have thus far been spared.

Peace will come because Asians were willing to work for it—and to sacrifice for it—and to die by the thousands for it.

But let it never be forgotten: Peace will come also because America sent her sons to help secure it.

It has not been easy—far from it. During the past 4½ years, it has been my fate and my responsibility to be Commander in Chief. I have lived—daily and nightly—with the cost of this war. I know the pain that it has inflicted. I know, perhaps better than anyone, the misgivings that it has aroused.

Throughout this entire, long period, I have been sustained by a single principle: that what we are doing now, in Vietnam, is vital not only to the security of Southeast Asia, but it is vital to the security of every American.

Surely we have treaties which we must respect. Surely we have commitments that we are going to keep. Resolutions of the Congress testify to the need to resist aggression in the world and in Southeast Asia.

But the heart of our involvement in South Vietnam—under three different Presidents, three separate administrations—has always been America's own security.

And the larger purpose of our involvement has always been to help the nations of Southeast Asia become independent and stand alone, self-sustaining, as members of a great world community—at peace with themselves, and at peace with all others.

With such an Asia, our country—and the

world—will be far more secure than it is tonight.

I believe that a peaceful Asia is far nearer to reality because of what America has done in Vietnam. I believe that the men who endure the dangers of battle—fighting there for us tonight—are helping the entire world avoid far greater conflicts, far wider wars, far more destruction, than this one.

The peace that will bring them home someday will come. Tonight I have offered the first in what I hope will be a series of mutual moves toward peace.

I pray that it will not be rejected by the leaders of North Vietnam. I pray that they will accept it as a means by which the sacrifices of their own people may be ended. And I ask your help and your support, my fellow citizens, for this effort to reach across the battlefield toward an early peace.

Finally, my fellow Americans, let me say this:

Of those to whom much is given, much is asked. I cannot say and no man could say that no more will be asked of us.

Yet, I believe that now, no less than when the decade began, this generation of Americans is willing to "pay any price, bear any burden, meet any hardship, support any friend, oppose any foe to assure the survival and the success of liberty."

Since those words were spoken by John F. Kennedy, the people of America have kept that compact with mankind's noblest cause.

And we shall continue to keep it.

Yet, I believe that we must always be mindful of this one thing, whatever the trials and the tests ahead. The ultimate strength of our country and our cause will lie not in powerful weapons or infinite resources or boundless wealth, but will lie in the unity of our people.

This I believe very deeply.

Throughout my entire public career I have followed the personal philosophy that I am a free man, an American, a public servant, and a member of my party, in that order always and only.

For 37 years in the service of our Nation, first as a Congressman, as a Senator, and as Vice President, and now as your President, I have put the unity of the people first. I have put it ahead of any divisive partisanship.

And in these times as in times before, it is true that a house divided against itself by the spirit of faction, of party, of region, of religion, of race, is a house that cannot stand.

There is division in the American house now. There is divisiveness among us all tonight. And holding the trust that is mine, as President of all the people, I cannot disregard the peril to the progress of the American people and the hope and the prospect of peace for all peoples.

So, I would ask all Americans, whatever their personal interests or concern, to guard against divisiveness and all its ugly consequences.

Fifty-two months and 10 days ago, in a moment of tragedy and trauma, the duties of this office fell upon me. I asked then for your help and God's, that we might continue America on its course, binding up our wounds, healing our history, moving forward in new unity, to clear the American agenda and to keep the American commitment for all of our people.

United we have kept that commitment. United we have enlarged that commitment.

Through all time to come, I think America will be a stronger nation, a more just society, and a land of greater opportunity and fulfillment because of what we have all done together in these years of unparalleled achievement.

Our reward will come in the life of freedom, peace, and hope that our children will enjoy through ages ahead.

What we won when all of our people united just must not now be lost in suspicion, distrust, selfishness, and politics among any of our people.

Believing this as I do, I have concluded that I should not permit the Presidency to become involved in the partisan divisions that are developing in this political year.

With America's sons in the fields far away, with America's future under challenge right here at home, with our hopes and the world's hopes for peace in the balance every day, I do not believe that I should devote an hour or a day of my time to any personal partisan causes or to any duties other than the awesome duties of this office—the Presidency of your country.

Accordingly, I shall not seek, and I will not accept, the nomination of my party for another term as your President.

But let men everywhere know, however, that a strong, a confident, and a vigilant America stands ready tonight to seek an honorable peace—and stands ready tonight to defend an honored cause—whatever the price, whatever the burden, whatever the sacrifice that duty may require.

Thank you for listening.

Good night and God bless all of you.

NOTE: The President spoke at 9 p.m. in his office at the White House. The address was broadcast nationally.

171   The President's News Conference of *March 31, 1968*

[The news conference was held immediately following the President's announcement of his decision not to seek reelection.]

Q. How irrevocable is your decision?

THE PRESIDENT. It is just as irrevocable as the statement says—completely irrevocable. You just take the statement and read it. There were no shalls, no woulds, no buts; I just made it "will."

Q. Can you describe the processes that led you to this decision; how long ago it started, what the factors were?

THE PRESIDENT. I don't have any calendar on it. I spent some time considering it. I guess perhaps the turning point was probably last November when General Westmoreland [1]

_____
[1] Gen. William C. Westmoreland, Commander, United States Military Assistance Command, Vietnam.

was back here. But it wasn't anything definite or firm at that point.

Q. Why was it when Westmoreland was back here?

THE PRESIDENT. That just happened to be the time.

Q. Mr. President, now that you have made this announcement, how do you feel?

THE PRESIDENT. I feel as good as a fellow could feel who has gone through what I have gone through today. I think I feel pretty good.

Q. Do you have a candidate for the Democratic nomination?

THE PRESIDENT. No. I made that clear, how I felt about that. You all get the speech and read it; all these questions will be answered for you.

Q. Mr. President, how about the why— why was it last year you began thinking in these terms? I am sure there are some personal considerations in here. I remember your saying as much as 2 years ago, I think you told Ray Scherer [2] not to regard you as such an automatic man, that the life back at the ranch and the university appealed to you. Was this part of what went into your decision?

THE PRESIDENT. No. I tried to explain that in about 590 words tonight.

Q. I wondered about other considerations, other than the campaign.

THE PRESIDENT. Well, I wouldn't say that I pointed to every consideration, but I think that basically it is just as I stated it.

Q. Mr. President, was there anything other than General Westmoreland's visit last November that goes into this decision?

THE PRESIDENT. No. His visit didn't bring it about at all. I just said that was the point that I remember identifying when I really turned that corner. I talked to him about it and that is why I remembered the date.

Q. Did you tell the Vice President this morning about the decision?

THE PRESIDENT. Yes. I didn't tell him that I was going to state this tonight, but I discussed it with him—and have discussed it with him a number of times.

Q. Mr. President, what do you think will be the situation of the Democratic Party now that you have made this announcement?

THE PRESIDENT. I don't know.

Q. Did Senator Kennedy's [3] entry into the race have anything to do with the timing of your announcement?

THE PRESIDENT. Well, it added to the general situation I talked about that existed in the country.

Q. Mr. President, will you support any nominee of the Democratic Party?

THE PRESIDENT. I am not going to spend much of my time on partisan politics between now and then. When the time comes to take an active part, I will make my announcement. But I don't want to get into that now.

I tried to make it clear that I don't want to mix up the Presidency and party politics when we have a half million men out there who are willing to give their lives in order to protect us back here. I want to try to get all the people in this country to support us to the extent I can.

Therefore, as I said tonight, I am not going to spend an hour on it or a day on it.

However, I will vote like every good American ought to vote. If there is anything that I think I should say concerning my own personal affairs, I will be glad to say it at the proper time—but I will have to select that time.

Q. Mr. President, is it your hope that removing the personal and political factor from this situation would put you in a better position to bring about a peaceful settlement?

THE PRESIDENT. I would hope that by what I did tonight that we can concentrate more of our energies and efforts on trying to bring about peace in the world and we will have a better chance to do it.

Q. Mr. President, are you now ready still to go anytime, anyplace, anywhere for peace?

THE PRESIDENT. We said that tonight.

Q. Have you had any kind of response yet, Mr. President, from any foreign capitals?

THE PRESIDENT. Yes.

Q. Where?

Q. Good response?

THE PRESIDENT. Yes.

Q. What response?

THE PRESIDENT. Well, I am not going to get into that.

Q. Mr. President, you have done more

[2] Raymond L. Scherer of NBC News.
[3] Senator Robert F. Kennedy of New York.

for our country than a number of people—whether it is education, housing, et cetera; more than any other President.

THE PRESIDENT. I have not done near enough. That is one of the reasons for the announcement tonight. I want to do a lot more these next 9 months.

Q. Why don't you stay on, since you have not done as much——

THE PRESIDENT. I have 9 months to do what I am going to try to do. I hope, by the end of that time, I will have contributed my part and done my duty. But I have several months yet to do it. And I am going to spend all the time I can trying to get the big job done.

Q. With these fundraising dinners that are coming up, does that mean, sir, that you will not participate—like the one in Washington Thursday night?

THE PRESIDENT. I don't know what my schedule will be Thursday. I want to do anything that I can to see that first things come first. I feel that the most important thing for us right now, that I have this week, is some of the efforts I launched tonight.

I just don't know what I will be doing on these dates.

Q. Mr. President, there are many men around the country, like Governor Hughes [4] and Mayor Daley, [5] who supported your candidacy for reelection. Did you convey your thoughts to them of this decision then, before you made it on television tonight? Or did they learn about it as everybody else did?

THE PRESIDENT. No. I had not talked to them. I talked to some folks after the speech tonight. I have not personally talked to them.

Q. Mr. President, could you say whether the way was prepared for this step of de-escalation that you have taken, by diplomacy?

THE PRESIDENT. I am not sure I understand what you are saying.

Q. Well, you said you had no assurance that Hanoi would accept your suggestions of tonight. I was wondering if you could say whether or not the way had been prepared, however, perhaps by third parties or by other forms of negotiation for presentation at this time?

THE PRESIDENT. No, I would not have anything to say about that.

Q. You would not want to say, for example, whether you have discussed——

THE PRESIDENT. I said I wouldn't have anything to say about that.

Q. Mr. President, you said your decision is irrevocable. If this peacemaking initiative is successful, do you foresee a situation where you could be under great pressure to run again?

THE PRESIDENT. No, I cannot. My statement speaks for itself and is very clear. I don't see any reason why we ought to have these high school discussions about it. I am genuinely sincere in what I said. There wasn't any reason that caused me to say it except I felt that it was the thing that I ought to do in the interest of my country and in the interest of the people who had so much at stake.

I don't feel very good about asking half a million men to stand out there and defend us, and offer their lives and die for us, and for me not to do everything I can to put myself in a position to do a job as successfully as they do theirs.

I think that if I do not have the aura of a political campaign around me and I am not out trying to win a primary or a State convention or please some party leader, that my efforts might be a little more fruitful.

I have never been a deep partisan, some

[4] Governor Richard J. Hughes of New Jersey.
[5] Mayor Richard J. Daley of Chicago.

of you have referred to some of my actions as consensus. I do think now is the time—if it is at all possible to do so—to try to remove yourself from any selfish actions and try to turn in as good a result as the men out there are turning in.

So, as I have told you before—we have priorities and this is the top priority.

Q. Sir, then you are sacrificing yourself.

THE PRESIDENT. No, no, I am not sacrificing anything. I am just doing what I think is right, what I think is best calculated to permit me to render the maximum service possible, in the limited time that I have left.

Q. Can you amplify on these rather important meetings you hope to have this week?

THE PRESIDENT. This gentleman standing up there with the blue tie on will be involved in some of them—and you can just guess what will be the general subject matter.

Q. Who is he?

THE PRESIDENT. The Secretary of Defense. That question was from Miss Thomas.[6] [*Laughter*]

Q. Sir, maybe somebody asked you this before I got here. But Senator Jackson[7] raised tonight the question of continuity here. You will stay in office until January?

THE PRESIDENT. That is my plan, God willing.

Q. And you do not feel under these circumstances you will provide the country——

Is Mr. Humphrey coming back to the country right away?

THE PRESIDENT. I am not sure. I would think tomorrow.

Q. Mr. President, Mr. Christian[8] said earlier that Horace Busby[9] and then, during these months of decision-making, that Mr. Clifford knew when he was appointed Secretary of Defense that you might be leaving.

THE PRESIDENT. Yes.

Q. He did?

THE PRESIDENT. He did not know that I would not be a candidate, but he did not know that I would be.

Q. What role did Mrs. Johnson play in your decision?

THE PRESIDENT. The same role she plays in every decision I make—a very important one.

Q. Did Governor Connally[10] know?

THE PRESIDENT. Yes.

Q. Has he known it for a good while?

THE PRESIDENT. No, he did not know until tonight that I was going to say what I said tonight—but he knew before he announced that he was not going to run for Governor that there was a strong possibility that I would not run for President. He told me that he would like to consider that in his decision; if I thought that I was going to run and it was important that he run, he would like to consider it.

I told him no, that I felt that I was not sure what my plans were and if he felt like he did not want to run, that would be all right with me.

So, I think that he understood. I talked to very few people about this. I discussed it with Mr. Clifford. I discussed it with Mr. McNamara before he left—in fact, I guess, last August—about the possibility.

I discussed it with Secretary Rusk, Governor Connally, and I have talked with Mr. Busby about it and some of the staff members—Mr. Christian.

But generally speaking, I have asked the people whom I have great confidence in—both in their judgment and in their ability—

---

[6] Helen Thomas of United Press International.

[7] Senator Henry M. Jackson of Washington.

[8] George E. Christian, Special Assistant to the President.

[9] Horace Busby, management consultant, Washington, D.C.

---

[10] Governor John B. Connally of Texas.

to counsel with me in private, and several members of my family and my very close official family.

Q. Mr. President, you may have answered this before I got here—but, is your health all right?

THE PRESIDENT. Perfect. Never better.

Q. Sir, there is a very delicate question that comes up here, and I don't have anyone to ask it of but you, and you are the only one who has the answer, and Mr. Clifford.

THE PRESIDENT. You ought to be in the habit of asking delicate questions; go ahead.

Q. But sir, what affect do you think this will have on the troops in the field tonight?

THE PRESIDENT. I think they will understand what I have done and the reasons for it. I would hope they will appreciate the value— if any—that flows from it. I think they will. I discussed that with General Westmoreland and asked him what effect he thought it would have when he was here in November.

Q. Mr. President, do you care to discuss what your plans might be after January?

THE PRESIDENT. No. I have no immediate plans.

Q. Do you intend, for instance, to return to Texas?

THE PRESIDENT. I said I don't have any immediate plans.

Q. Sir, what effect will this have on the dollar, do you think?

THE PRESIDENT. Well, I hope that what I said tonight will strengthen it.

Q. Mr. President, will you ask your Cabinet aides and others also not to spend any particular amount of time on the campaign?

THE PRESIDENT. No. I have not asked them to spend or not to spend any time. The Secretary of State and the Secretary of Defense, who are the principal Cabinet officers involved in Vietnam, do not engage in partisan political activities, although that is just a matter of their choice. They are perfectly free to do so because individuals, like institutions, have the right of dissent. They have the right to answer and defend and advocate and so forth in this country.

But it has been generally the practice of the Secretary of State and the Secretary of Defense, under my administration, to try to avoid being involved in deep partisan matters. I think they have been reasonably successful in that. That is not to say that they would not attend a public meeting and speak on Vietnam. I don't want them to ever be intimidated because somebody might say that a Cabinet officer is traveling out of town at Government expense and $48 is paid by the Government—and try to hush him up that way.

Just as we invite people to express their views, who may differ with us, we reserve that same privilege for our own people.

Q. Mr. President, do you plan to go to the Democratic Convention?

THE PRESIDENT. I have no plans at this time one way or the other.

Q. Would you like to be a member of the Texas delegation to the convention?

THE PRESIDENT. No.

Q. Mr. President, perhaps one other question that we could ask you: The historical record shows that when people are known to be leaving seats of power, they sometimes suffer a diminution of influence. Do you anticipate any difficulty along that line and had you put this into your calculation of the timing of your announcement?

THE PRESIDENT. Yes. It was, I guess, 16 years ago this week that President Truman made a similar announcement, March 29, 1952. This is March 31. But you were not at my meeting March 29, so I had to wait because I didn't want you to be scooped. I had a press meeting yesterday or the day before, but I thought it would be better to wait until all of you could be here.

Q. Mr. President, by any chance, did you discuss this before tonight with President Truman?

THE PRESIDENT. I think the answer would be no to this particular event tonight. I have discussed with him the problems of the Presidency and the service of the Presidency and things of that nature, but if you asked me, did I talk to him about announcing that I would not be a candidate, and I would not accept the nomination—the answer is no.

Q. Mr. President, can you tell us anything about the reaction within your family?

THE PRESIDENT. Oh, I think that it is a mixed reaction. I can't really speak for them. You are running pretty dangerous when you speak for women, but I think they all go along with the decision I made. Lynda has not been here and she wasn't sure that it was as imminent as it was, but she came in at about 6:30 or 7 o'clock this morning. Her mother and I met her. We wanted to be at the door when she came back.

So, we discussed it back and forth a good deal of the day. She had ridden all night and she slept part of the day.

I took time out with Luci to go to church with her while Lynda slept.

Q. Mr. President, is it fair to interpret what you said tonight and in fact everything that you are doing as really a plea to all the candidates and all parties to just leave this war out of their campaign?

THE PRESIDENT. No. You just take my script, that is the safest thing for you to follow. I just gave my own views, briefly and succinctly as I knew how. I hope it was all right and I would hope that you thought it was the best thing to do; at least, I did.

Q. Mr. President, did you get any calls asking you to reconsider?

THE PRESIDENT. Yes. We have had a good many calls. I won't go into the content of them.

Q. Sir, does this mean that in the months ahead——

THE PRESIDENT. I don't want to hold an individual press conference now with you, Sarah.[11] You have had your share of questions. Get one more and let's go on.

Q. Does this mean in the months ahead that you are going to devote the main part of your time on getting peace and does it mean that you will also be still working to bolster your domestic programs or not?

THE PRESIDENT. It means I am going to work on all of the problems of the country. High on that list of problems, of course, and a thing that concerns most of us, is an early peace, if it could be found. There are many other problems, though, that require attention every day. We hope we will not neglect any of them.

I think maybe we will go out and take a trip tomorrow, but I am not positive, so I can't announce it tonight. If any of you want to go with me, you might want to check in early in the morning. If we make a decision to go I won't know until I have a meeting a little later in the evening.

Mr. Christian or Tom [12] will notify you. The best thing for you to do is go home and get some sleep and get comfortable and be ready early in the morning in case we go, if you want to go. If you don't, why we can get by without you.

Q. Why don't you go get some sleep, too?

---

[11] Mrs. Sarah McClendon, representative of Texas newspapers.

[12] Wyatt Thomas Johnson, Jr., Assistant Press Secretary to the President.

Merriman Smith, United Press International: Mr. President, thank you very much.

NOTE: President Johnson's one hundred and twenty-second news conference was held in the Oval Room at the White House at 11 p.m. on Sunday, March 31, 1968.

172 Remarks in Chicago Before the National Association of Broadcasters. *April 1, 1968*

Mayor Daley, Mr. Wasilewski, ladies and gentlemen:

Some of you might have thought from what I said last night that I had been taking elocution lessons from Lowell Thomas. One of my aides said this morning, "Things are really getting confused around Washington, Mr. President."

I said, "How is that?"

He said, "It looks to me like you are going to the wrong convention in Chicago."

I said, "Well, what you overlooked was that it is April Fool."

Once again we are entering the period of national festivity which Henry Adams called "the dance of democracy." At its best, that can be a time of debate and enlightenment. At its worst, it can be a period of frenzy. But always it is a time when emotion threatens to substitute for reason. Yet the basic hope of a democracy is that somehow—amid all the frenzy and all the emotion—in the end, reason will prevail. Reason just must prevail—if democracy itself is to survive.

As I said last evening, there are very deep and very emotional divisions in this land that we love today—domestic divisions, divisions over the war in Vietnam. With all of my heart, I just wish this were not so. My entire career in public life—some 37 years of it—has been devoted to the art of finding an area of agreement because generally speaking, I have observed that there are so many more things to unite us Americans than there are to divide us.

But somehow or other, we have a facility sometimes of emphasizing the divisions and the things that divide us instead of discussing the things that unite us. Sometimes I have been called a seeker of "consensus"—more often that has been criticism of my actions instead of praise of them. But I have never denied it. Because to heal and to build support, to hold people together, is something I think is worthy and I believe it is a noble task. It is certainly a challenge for all of us in this land and this world where there is restlessness and uncertainty and danger. In my region of the country where I have spent my life, where brother was once divided against brother, my heritage has burned this lesson and it has burned it deep in my memory.

Yet along the way I learned somewhere that no leader can pursue public tranquillity as his first and only goal. For a President to buy public popularity at the sacrifice of his better judgment is too dear a price to pay. This Nation cannot afford such a price, and this Nation cannot long afford such a leader.

So, the things that divide our country this morning will be discussed throughout the land. I am certain that the very great majority of informed Americans will act, as they have always acted, to do what is best for their country and what serves the national interest.

But the real problem of informing the people is still with us. I think I can speak with some authority about the problem of communication. I understand, far better than some of my severe and perhaps intolerant critics would admit, my own shortcomings as a communicator.

How does a public leader find just the right word or the right way to say no more or no less than he means to say—bearing in mind that anything he says may topple governments and may involve the lives of innocent men?

How does that leader speak the right phrase, in the right way, under the right conditions, to suit the accuracies and contingencies of the moment when he is discussing questions of policy, so that he does not stir a thousand misinterpretations and leave the wrong connotation or impression?

How does he reach the immediate audience and how does he communicate with the millions of others who are out there listening from afar?

The President, who must call his people and summon them to meet their responsibilities as citizens in a hard and an enduring war, often ponders these questions and searches for the right course.

You men and women who are masters of the broadcast media surely must know what I am talking about. It was a long time ago when a President once said, "The printing press is the most powerful weapon with which man has ever armed himself." In our age, the electronic media have added immeasurably to man's power. You have within your hands the means to make our Nation as intimate and as informed as a New England town meeting.

Yet the use of broadcasting has not cleared away all of the problems that we still have of communications. In some ways, I think, sometimes it has complicated them, because it tends to put the leader in a time capsule. It requires him often to abbreviate what he has to say. Too often, it may catch a random phrase from his rather lengthy discourse and project it as the whole story.

How many men, I wonder, Mayor Daley, in public life have watched themselves on a TV newscast and then been tempted to exclaim, "Can that really be me?"

Well, there is no denying it: You of the broadcast industry have enormous power in your hands. You have the power to clarify and you have the power to confuse. Men in public life cannot remotely rival your opportunity—day after day, night after night, hour after hour on the hour—and the half hour, sometimes—you shape the Nation's dialogue.

The words that you choose, hopefully always accurate, and hopefully always just, are the words that are carried out for all of the people to hear.

The commentary that you provide can give the real meaning to the issues of the day or it can distort them beyond all meaning. By your standards of what is news, you can cultivate wisdom—or you can nurture misguided passion.

Your commentary carries an added element of uncertainty. Unlike the printed media, television writes on the wind. There is no accumulated record which the historian can examine later with a 20–20 vision of hindsight, asking these questions: "How fair was he tonight? How impartial was he today? How honest was he all along?"

Well, I hope the National Association of Broadcasters, with whom I have had a pleasant association for many years, will point the way to all of us in developing this kind of a record because history is going to be asking very hard questions about our times and the period through which we are passing.

I think that we all owe it to history to complete the record.

But I did not come here this morning to sermonize. In matters of fairness and judgment, no law or no set of regulations and no words of mine can improve you or dictate your daily responsibility.

All I mean to do, and what I am trying to do, is to remind you where there is great power, there must also be great responsibility. This is true for broadcasters just as it is true for Presidents—and seekers for the Presidency.

What we say and what we do now will shape the kind of a world that we pass along to our children and our grandchildren. I keep this thought constantly in my mind during the long days and the somewhat longer nights when crisis comes at home and abroad.

I took a little of your prime time last night. I would not have done that except for a very prime purpose.

I reported on the prospects for peace in Vietnam. I announced that the United States is taking a very important unilateral act of deescalation which could—and I fervently pray will—lead to mutual moves to reduce the level of violence and to deescalate the war.

As I sat in my office last evening, waiting to speak, I thought of the many times each week when television brings the war into the American home.

No one can say exactly what effect those vivid scenes have on American opinion. Historians must only guess at the effect that television would have had during earlier conflicts on the future of this Nation:

—during the Korean war, for example, at that time when our forces were pushed back there to Pusan;

—or World War II, the Battle of the Bulge, or when our men were slugging it out in Europe or when most of our Air Force was shot down that day in June 1942 off Australia.

But last night television was being used to carry a different message. It was a message of peace. It occurred to me that the medium may be somewhat better suited to conveying the actions of conflict than to dramatizing the words that the leaders use in trying and hoping to end the conflict.

Certainly, it is more "dramatic" to show policemen and rioters locked in combat than to show men trying to cooperate with one another.

The face of hatred and of bigotry comes through much more clearly—no matter what its color. The face of tolerance, I seem to find, is rarely "newsworthy."

Progress—whether it is a man being trained for a job or millions being trained or whether it is a child in Head Start learning to read or an older person of 72 in adult education or being cared for in Medicare—rarely makes the news, although more than 20 million of them are affected by it.

Perhaps this is because tolerance and progress are not dynamic events—such as riots and conflicts are events.

Peace, in the news sense, is a "condition." War is an "event."

Part of your responsibility is simply to understand the consequences of that fact—the consequences of your own acts, and part of that responsibility, I think, is to try—as very best we all can—to draw the attention of our people to the real business of society in our system—finding and securing peace in the world—at home and abroad. For all that you have done and that you are doing and that you will do to this end, I thank you and I commend you.

I pray that the message of peace that I tried so hard to convey last night will be accepted in good faith by the leaders of North Vietnam.

I pray that one time soon, the evening news show will have, not another battle in the scarred hills of Vietnam, but will show men entering a room to talk about peace.

That is the event that I think the American people are yearning and longing to see.

President Thieu of Vietnam and his Government are now engaged in very urgent political and economic tasks which I referred to last night—and which we regard as very constructive and hopeful. We hope the Government of South Vietnam makes great progress in the days ahead.

But some time in the weeks ahead—immediately, I hope—President Thieu will be in a position to accept my invitation to visit the United States so he can come here and see our people too, and together we can strengthen and improve our plans to advance the day of peace.

I pray that you and that every American will take to heart my plea that we guard against divisiveness. We have won too much, we have come too far, and we have opened too many doors of opportunity, for these things now to be lost in a divided country where brother is separated from brother. For the time that is allotted me, I shall do everything in one man's power to hasten the day when the world is at peace and Americans of all races—and all creeds—of all convictions—can live together—without fear or without suspicion or without distrust—in unity, and in common purpose.

United we are strong; divided we are in great danger.

In speaking as I did to the Nation last night, I was moved by the very deep convictions that I entertain about the nature of the office that it is my present privilege to hold. The Office of the Presidency is the only office in this land of all the people. Whatever may be the personal wishes or preferences of any man who holds it, a President of all

the people can afford no thought of self.

At no time and in no way and for no reason can a President allow the integrity or the responsibility or the freedom of the office ever to be compromised or diluted or destroyed because when you destroy it, you destroy yourselves.

I hope and I pray that by not allowing the Presidency to be involved in divisions and deep partisanship, I shall be able to pass on to my successor a stronger office—strong enough to guard and defend all the people against all the storms that the future may bring us.

You men and women who have come here to this great progressive city of Chicago, led by this dynamic and great public servant, Dick Daley, are yourselves charged with a peculiar responsibility. You are yourselves trustees, legally accepted trustees and legally selected trustees of a great institution on which the freedom of our land utterly depends.

The security, the success of our country, what happens to us tomorrow—rests squarely upon the media which disseminate the truth on which the decisions of democracy are made.

An informed mind—and we get a great deal of our information from you—is the guardian genius of democracy.

So, you are the keepers of a trust. You must be just. You must guard and you must defend your media against the spirit of faction, against the works of divisiveness and bigotry, against the corrupting evils of partisanship in any guise.

For America's press, as for the American Presidency, the integrity and the responsibility and the freedom—the freedom to know the truth and let the truth make us free—must never be compromised or diluted or destroyed.

The defense of our media is your responsibility. Government cannot and must not and never will—as long as I have anything to do about it—intervene in that role.

But I do want to leave this thought with you as I leave you this morning: I hope that you will give this trust your closest care, acting as I know you can, to guard not only against the obvious, but to watch for the hidden—the sometimes unintentional, the often petty intrusions upon the integrity of the information by which Americans decide.

Men and women of the airways fully—as much as men and women of public service—have a public trust and if liberty is to survive and to succeed, that solemn trust must be faithfully kept. I do not want—and I don't think you want—to wake up some morning and find America changed because we slept when we should have been awake,

because we remained silent when we should have spoken up, because we went along with what was popular and fashionable and "in" rather than what was necessary and what was right.

Being faithful to our trust ought to be the prime test of any public trustee in office or on the airways.

In any society, all you students of history know that a time of division is a time of danger. And in these times now we must never forget that "eternal vigilance is the price of liberty."

Thank you for wanting me to come. I've enjoyed it.

NOTE: The President spoke at 11 a.m. at the Conrad Hilton Hotel in Chicago at the 46th annual convention of the National Association of Broadcasters. In his opening words he referred to Richard J. Daley, Mayor of Chicago, and Vincent T. Wasilewski, President of the National Association of Broadcasters. The remarks were broadcast nationally.

173   Message to the Congress Transmitting Second Annual Report of the Appalachian Regional Commission. *April* 2, 1968

To the Congress of the United States:

I am pleased to transmit to the Congress the Second Annual Report of the Appalachian Regional Commission, for fiscal year 1967.

This report marks the end of the second year of the Federal-State effort to lift the 18 million people in Appalachia up to economic parity with the rest of America.

The Congress has already expressed its confidence in the program by revising and extending it for another two years. More than $300 million have been obligated for programs which will help the people of Appalachia on their way to self-sufficiency.

The framework of the program is commendable in itself. Federal, State, and local authorities have been working together, rec-

ognizing that need does not respect State lines, and poverty does not stop at the boundaries which separate communities.

This report shows proof, I believe, that such a partnership—seeking common solutions to common problems—can work to rebuild a segment of America, to provide its citizens with a chance to share in America's plenty.

Our ultimate goal is to assist Appalachia to attract and hold public and private investments—the cornerstones on which economic well-being is built.

We have not yet achieved that goal, but in two years we have made a strong beginning.

One of our first aims was to unify Appalachia internally—and to make it accessible to the affluent nation outside. Had it remained an enclave of poverty, it would have withered and died.

As the report testifies, we made substantial progress in Fiscal 1967 on the Appalachian Development Highway System.

Highways that today are lines on the planner's map will tomorrow be asphalt bonds to the rest of America. We are providing access to opportunity.

For a region to survive, its people must be healthy, its children educated, and its land productive.

Among the programs approved for construction in Fiscal 1967 were:

—100 facilities for vocational and higher education

—75 for health care

—27 libraries

—37 facilities to combat water pollution

—And 20 projects to restore ravaged mine areas.

On December 28, I signed an executive order which will increase the strength and efficiency of our partnership for regional economic development.

Under this order, the Secretary of Commerce will provide effective liaison between the Federal Government and our six regional commissions.

He will also become the chairman of a Federal Advisory Council on Regional Economic Development. This council will help him coordinate the activities of the Federal Government in the six regions.

By placing this authority in the hands of the Secretary of Commerce, I intend to encourage the private and business resources of our country to take a hand in these regional ventures.

Our work has just begun. I am confident that future reports will justify the faith we have placed in this program.

LYNDON B. JOHNSON

The White House
April 2, 1968

NOTE: The report, transmitted to the President on December 20, 1967, is entitled "The Appalachian Regional Commission, Annual Report, 1967" (92 pp.).

The Commission was established by the Appalachian Regional Development Act of 1965, approved on March 9, 1965 (Public Law 89–4, 79 Stat. 5).

The President referred to Executive Order 11386 of December 28, 1967, "Prescribing Arrangements for Coordination of the Activities of Regional Commissions and Activities of the Federal Government Relating to Regional Economic Development, and Establishing the Federal Advisory Council for Regional Economic Development" (3 Weekly Comp. Pres. Docs., p. 1778; 33 F.R. 5; 3 CFR, 1968 Comp., p. 85).

174 Remarks at a Cost Reduction Awards Ceremony at the Department of Agriculture. *April 2, 1968*

Secretary Freeman, award winners, members of the Department of Agriculture:

I am pleased that a few days ago you asked me to come over here and be with you on this occasion.

I am pleased for several reasons.

I am especially pleased now that I am going to have more time to spend on the farm, that I could have a little closer contact with the people who do so much to try to make life better for our farmers.

This Department is one of my favorite departments in the Government. It is manned by the most dedicated people. For 37 years I have been coming here, talking to you about the problems of forgotten people. In the hurly-burly of the 20th century, I sometimes think that the people who need our help the most really get the least. Those are the farmers of this country.

Things are so unjust for them in many ways—weather, insects, labor, price, inconveniences, remoteness, roads, communications—that most of them are leaving and coming into the cities and creating problems for us. That is also a problem for every Secretary of Agriculture we have. That is a problem for all the people who work here.

I expect, generally speaking, the Secretary of Agriculture has been the most unpopular man in the Cabinet, among the people that he tries to do the most for. That is to be expected sometimes. You will remember Senator Barkley's old story, "What have you done for me lately?"

A lot of people who have had injustice visited upon them—if you haven't done something good lately—they think you are to blame for it.

So the Secretary and the Department—they call them bureaucrats—are to blame for it.

But I believe that this Department is manned by the most patriotic, most selfless, most dedicated people I know in Government. I have watched it very closely.

I know it is headed by one of the greatest public servants I have ever known.

When I came into the Government as President, I was told by some of my accounting and economic experts that there were three outstanding, great administrators in Government who could head any big corporation in this country. They listed those three. I was shocked that Orville Freeman was one of the three. They said he was one of the best administrators in Government.

The other two they named—there was no reflection on anyone else—were Mr. Webb, who had been Director of the Budget and who was running a pretty big operation, and

Mr. McNamara, who was Secretary of Defense.

So I watched their budgets, their employees, their efficiencies, and their programs. I came to believe that from what I learned from them myself. I thought it was accurate.

My budget experts through the years have maintained that position.

That is not possible without your help. Secretary Freeman couldn't do these things and couldn't have that reputation. This Department couldn't—that is, except for the people from the highest to the lowest who are working every day for efficiency, for cost effectiveness.

I am pleased to look at the charts over there and see that, since 1965, you have withheld from expenditure over $1 billion that you have saved for the taxpayers of this country. That is a good record. That is one I am very proud of. I hope that each of you are proud of it.

Another thing that I think you know is close to my heart is trying to finance this Government and support our men at the fighting front.

I have, on occasions, asked the people in the Government to try to think over their little budget—it is very small—but see if they couldn't put in it somewhere a savings bond where they could help the Government pay the bills of the war and some of the other expenses we have.

During the other wars, we had thrift stamps, baby bonds, and things of that kind.

In this one, we haven't really twisted many arms or appealed to people too strongly. But this Department has had an outstanding record.

I don't know whether you know it or not, but you have practically doubled a good record by doubling the amount of savings bonds you are already buying. More than sixty-odd thousand employees buy them every month. They take from their check and buy a bond to try to help those boys out there.

I appreciate that because that shows you are on the team and that you want to help.

I know there are a lot of Republicans in the Department of Agriculture. I know that from experience—from talking to them.

I hope there are more Democrats because we always want to stay a little in the majority, if we can.

But the thing I have observed most is: Regardless of your party affiliation, your dedication is to your country and to the industry that you serve. Your genuineness, your faithfulness, your dedication in coming here on time every morning and burning the lights at night to try to help the poor and the people who produce our food and feed the world and take less percentage of our dollar today than any time in our history, is not only a tribute to our Government and to our Secretary, but it is an indication of the kind of people you are.

I am a Hereford breeder. I sell registered calves. I am going to have a lot of time to work on it pretty soon.

But we look at bloodlines. We can look at the bloodline and pretty well tell the kind of calf we are going to get. When I look at the people who serve here, year in and year out, I pretty well know what kind of product we are going to have, and whether it is down at the home demonstration level,

the girls showing us how to bottle our cucumbers, or can our peaches, or whether it is the county agent or the soil conservation man helping us with our terraces, or whether it is the county committee where we go to talk about our allotments—in every one of those places you will find good, honest, dedicated people, whatever church they belong to, whatever party.

That is something everybody in this Department can be proud of.

There is one thing I have left out, though I have talked longer than I intended to. I have noticed a good many of you I have come in contact with, have your families in your job, too. I want to thank them for being on the team and helping the American farmer.

We haven't done as good a job as we ought to. If we had, the farmers wouldn't be moving out and going to the cities. We have to find some way to help move them back.

I am going to try to set a good example. I am going back myself.

Thank you very much.

NOTE: The President spoke at 10:34 a.m. at the Department of Agriculture auditorium at a ceremony honoring 66 employees of the Department who were credited with ideas saving $22 million a year. In his opening words he referred to Orville L. Freeman, Secretary of Agriculture. During his remarks the President referred to Alben W. Barkley, former Representative and Senator from Kentucky and Vice President of the United States 1949–1953, James E. Webb, National Aeronautics and Space Administrator and former Director of the Bureau of the Budget, and Robert S. McNamara, President of the International Bank for Reconstruction and Development and former Secretary of Defense.

---

175 Message to the Congress Transmitting Annual Report on Communications Satellite Activities. *April 2, 1968*

To the Congress of the United States:

The Communications Satellite Act of 1962 requires that the President transmit to the

Congress an annual report on the activities and accomplishments of the past year.

This is the fifth annual report under this

landmark legislation. It reflects, as did the others, steady progress toward the ultimate goal of providing mankind with new capabilities for worldwide communication.

In the brief span of five years, satellite technology has grown dynamically. The possibilities envisioned in 1962 have been greatly exceeded.

Indeed, the rapid tempo of progress in telecommunications has created challenging problems in the proper use and orderly expansion of this vital national resource. Last August 14, in a report to the Congress on our communications policies, I announced the creation of a task force to examine the course we should follow in the future.

We know that we must provide the environment in which telecommunication can play its increasingly crucial role in the affairs of our nation, and provide bridges of understanding among all nations.

The role of communications is not limited to commercial use. It must also provide a "network for knowledge" so that all peoples can share the scientific, educational, and cul-

tural advances of this planet.

Failure to reach these goals can only contribute to apathy, ignorance, poverty and despair in a very large part of the world. Success in our telecommunications policies can be a critical link in our search for the understanding and tolerance from which peace springs.

Communication by satellite is a tool—one of the most promising which mankind has had thus far—to attain this end.

We must use it wisely and well.

LYNDON B. JOHNSON

The White House
April 2, 1968

NOTE: The 11-page report is entitled "Annual Report on Activities and Accomplishments Under the Communications Satellite Act of 1962, January 1–December 31, 1967."

The Communications Satellite Corporation made public its "Report to the President and the Congress for the Calendar Year 1967" (47 pages) to coincide with the release of the President's report.

For the President's special message to Congress of August 14, 1967, on communications policy, see 1967 volume, this series, Book II, Item 346.

176   Message to the Congress Transmitting Annual Report on the Food for Freedom Program.   *April 3, 1968*

To the Congress of the United States:

I am pleased to transmit to the Congress the 1967 report on the Food for Freedom program.

The bounty of America's farms have long given hope to the human family.

For the pioneers, who first plowed our fertile fields, their harvest brought liberation from the age-old bondage of hunger and want.

For the victims of two world wars, our food nourished the strength to rebuild with purpose and dignity.

For millions in the developing nations,

our food continues to rescue the lives of the starving and revive the spirit of the hopeless.

We share our bounty because it is right. But we know too that the hungry child and the desperate parent are easy prey to tyranny. We know that a grain of wheat is a potent weapon in the arsenal of freedom.

Compassion and wisdom thus guided the Congress when it enacted Public Law 480 in 1954. Since then, the productivity of the American farmer and the generosity of the American people have combined to write an epic chapter in the annals of man's humanity to man.

In 1966, I recommended that Congress alter Public Law 480 to reflect new conditions both at home and abroad. The Congress accepted my major recommendations, and added provisions of its own to strengthen the Act. I am proud to report that in 1967 we successfully fulfilled the letter and spirit of these new provisions.

Congress directed that the Food for Freedom program should encourage international trade.

—In 1967 world trade in agricultural products reached an all-time high of $33.9 billion, nearly 20 percent higher than in 1966.

Congress directed that the Food for Freedom program should encourage an expansion of export markets for our own agricultural commodities.

—In the past two years, this nation has enjoyed unparalleled prosperity in agricultural exports. Since 1960 our agricultural exports have grown from $3.2 billion to $5.2 billion—a gain of 62 percent.

Congress directed that we should continue to use our abundance to wage an unrelenting war on hunger and malnutrition.

—During 1967 we dispatched more than 15 million metric tons of food to wage the war on hunger—the equivalent of 10 pounds of food for every member of the human race.

Congress determined that our Food for Freedom program should encourage general economic progress in the developing countries.

—Our food aid has helped Israel, Taiwan, the Philippines, and Korea build a solid record of economic achievement. With our help, these nations have now moved into the commercial market, just as Japan, Italy, Spain and others before them.

Congress determined that our food aid should help first and foremost those countries that help themselves.

—Every one of our 39 food aid agreements in 1967 committed the receiving country to a far-reaching program of agricultural self-help. Many of these programs are already bringing record results.

Congress directed that we should move as rapidly as possible from sales for foreign currency to sales for dollars.

—Of the 22 countries participating in the Food for Freedom program in 1967, only four had no dollar payment provision. Last year, six countries moved to payments in dollars or convertible local currencies.

Congress directed that we should use Food for Freedom to promote the foreign policy of the United States.

Statistics alone cannot measure how Food for Freedom has furthered America's goals in the world. Its real victories lie in the minds of millions who now know that America cares. Hope is alive. Food for Freedom gives men an alternative to despair.

Last year was a record year in world farm output. With reasonable weather, 1968 can be even better. New agricultural technology is spreading rapidly in the developed countries. New cereal varieties are bringing unexpectedly high yields in the developing lands. An agricultural revolution is in the making.

This report shows clearly how much we have contributed to that revolution in the past year. But the breakthrough is only beginning. The pride in accomplishments today will seem small beside the progress we can make tomorrow.

LYNDON B. JOHNSON

The White House
April 3, 1968

NOTE: The report is entitled "The Annual Report on Activities Carried Out Under Public Law 480, 83d Congress, as Amended, During the Period January 1 Through December 31, 1967" (processed, 114 pp. with appendices and tables).

177 Excerpts of Remarks to a Group of Foreign Editors on a Statement by the Government of North Vietnam. *April 3, 1968*

I AM GOING to a meeting at lunch. I am a little late. . . . I am going to review the Hanoi statement this morning that indicated that there might be some movement.

The other night we looked long and hard. We had consulted lots of governments and a great many experts. We tried to take one positive step that could lead to peace and if it were recognized by the other side, it could lead to another positive step and another one until maybe we could find some way to end this terrible war . . . .

So, we are now trying to study the [Hanoi] statement and we will make a comment on it. We are very interested in it and if it says what some people think it says, it is something that we are very interested in . . . .

NOTE: The editors were at the White House for a tour, movie, and reception prior to accompanying Mrs. Johnson on a Discover America tour of Texas beginning April 5. The President came into the White House Theater as they were viewing the movie, "The President's Country," and spoke briefly with them.

For a related statement by the President see Item 178.

As printed above, this item follows the text released by the White House Press Office.

178 Statement by the President Following Hanoi's Declaration of Readiness To Begin Discussions. *April 3, 1968*

TODAY the Government of North Vietnam made a statement which included the following paragraph, and I quote:

"However, for its part, the Government of the Democratic Republic of Vietnam declares its readiness to appoint its representatives to contact the United States representative with a view to determining with the American side the unconditional cessation of the United States bombing raids and all other acts of war against the Democratic Republic of Vietnam so that talks may start."

Last Sunday night I expressed the position of the United States with respect to peace in Vietnam and Southeast Asia as follows:

"Now, as in the past, the United States is ready to send its representatives to any forum, at any time, to discuss the means of bringing this war to an end."

Accordingly, we will establish contact with the representatives of North Vietnam. Consultations with the Government of South Vietnam and our other allies are now taking place.

So that you may have as much notice as I am able to give you on another matter, I will be leaving tomorrow evening, late, for Honolulu. I will meet with certain of our representatives, American representatives from South Vietnam, for a series of meetings over the weekend in Hawaii.

Thank you very much.

NOTE: The President read the statement at 5:05 p.m. in front of the West Lobby at the White House for broadcast by radio and television.

The President's plans for the trip to Honolulu were later changed. Arrangements were made for Gen. William C. Westmoreland, Commander, United States Military Assistance Command, Vietnam, to fly to Washington to meet with the President at the White House on April 6.

On April 6 George E. Christian, Special Assistant to the President, issued a statement concerning further U.S. efforts to arrange talks with the North Vietnamese Government (4 Weekly Comp. Pres. Docs., p. 658).

179 Statement by the President on the Assassination of Dr. Martin Luther King, Jr. *April 4, 1968*

AMERICA is shocked and saddened by the brutal slaying tonight of Dr. Martin Luther King.

I ask every citizen to reject the blind violence that has struck Dr. King, who lived by nonviolence.

I pray that his family can find comfort in the memory of all he tried to do for the land he loved so well.

I have just conveyed the sympathy of Mrs. Johnson and myself to his widow, Mrs. King.

I know that every American of good will joins me in mourning the death of this outstanding leader and in praying for peace and understanding throughout this land.

We can achieve nothing by lawlessness and divisiveness among the American people. It is only by joining together and only by working together that we can continue to move toward equality and fulfillment for all of our people.

I hope that all Americans tonight will search their hearts as they ponder this most tragic incident.

I have canceled my plans for the evening. I am postponing my trip to Hawaii until tomorrow.

Thank you.

NOTE: The President read the statement at 9:07 p.m. outside the entrance to the West Lobby at the White House for broadcast by radio and television.

Dr. King, president of the Southern Christian Leadership Conference and a leader in the civil rights movement, was assassinated on April 4 in Memphis, Tenn.

See also Item 180.

180 Address to the Nation Upon Proclaiming a Day of Mourning Following the Death of Dr. King. *April 5, 1968*

Mr. Vice President, Mr. Speaker, Mr. Chief Justice, my fellow Americans:

Once again, the heart of America is heavy—the spirit of America weeps—for a tragedy that denies the very meaning of our land.

The life of a man who symbolized the freedom and faith of America has been taken. But it is the fiber and the fabric of the Republic that is being tested.

If we are to have the America that we mean to have, all men—of all races, all regions, all religions—must stand their ground to deny violence its victory in this sorrowful time and in all times to come.

Last evening, after receiving the terrible news of Dr. King's death, my heart went out to his family and to his people—especially to the young Americans who, I know, must sometimes wonder if they are to be denied a fullness of life because of the color of their skin. I called the leaders of the Negro community and the white communities, the judiciary, the legislative and the executive branches of our National Government, and the leaders of our city halls throughout the Nation, throughout the night, and asked them to come here to the White House and meet with me this morning.

We have been meeting together this morning.

No words of ours—and no words of mine—can fill the void of the eloquent voice that has been stilled.

But this I do believe deeply:

The dream of Dr. Martin Luther King, Jr., has not died with him. Men who are white—men who are black—must and will now join together as never in the past to let all the forces of divisiveness know that America shall not be ruled by the bullet, but only by the ballot of free and of just men.

In these years, we have moved toward opening the way of hope and opportunity and justice in this country.

We have rolled away some of the stones of inaction, of indifference, and of injustice.

Our work is not yet done. But we have begun.

We must move with urgency, with resolve, and with new energy in the Congress, in the courts, in the White House, the state-houses and the city halls of the Nation, wherever there is leadership—political leadership, leadership in the churches, in the homes, in the schools, in the institutions of higher learning—until we do overcome.

I have asked the Speaker of the House of Representatives, the leadership of the Congress, and the Congress to receive me at the earliest possible moment. They are in adjournment over the weekend. But I would hope that could be no later than Monday evening, in the area of 9 o'clock, for the purpose of hearing the President's recommendations and the President's suggestions for action—constructive action instead of destructive action—in this hour of national need.[1]

I did not understate the case last Sunday evening when I talked of the divisiveness that was tearing this Nation apart. But together, a nation united, a nation caring, a nation concerned, and a nation that thinks more of the Nation's interests than we do of any individual self-interest or political interest—that nation can and shall and will overcome.

I have issued a proclamation to the people of the United States which I shall read.

[Text of Proclamation 3839 "Death of Martin Luther King, Jr."]

By the President of the United States of America, a Proclamation

To the People of the United States:

The heart of America grieves today. A leader of his people—a teacher of all people—has fallen.

Martin Luther King, Jr., has been struck down by the violence against which he preached and worked.

Yet the cause for which he struggled has not fallen. The voice that called for justice and brotherhood has been stilled—but the quest for freedom, to which he gave eloquent expression, continues.

Men of all races, all religions, all regions must join together in this hour to deny violence its victory—and to fulfill the vision of brotherhood that gave purpose to Martin Luther King's life and works.

Now, THEREFORE, I, LYNDON B. JOHNSON, President of the United States, do call upon all Americans to observe Sunday next, the seventh day of April, as a day of national mourning throughout the United States. In our churches, in our homes, and in our

---

[1] The address was later canceled.

private hearts, let us resolve before God to stand against divisiveness in our country and all its consequences.

I direct that until interment the flag of the United States shall be flown at half-staff on all buildings, grounds and naval vessels of the Federal Government in the District of Columbia and throughout the United States and its Territories and possessions.

I also direct that the flag shall be flown at half-staff for the same length of time at all United States embassies, legations, consular offices, and other facilities abroad, including all military facilities and naval vessels and stations.

IN WITNESS WHEREOF, I have hereunto set my hand this fifth day of April, in the year of our Lord nineteen hundred and sixty-eight and of the Independence of the United States of America the one hundred and ninety-second.

LYNDON B. JOHNSON

That concludes the proclamation. Thank you, my fellow Americans.

NOTE: The President spoke at 1:22 p.m. in the Fish Room at the White House after attending a memorial service for Dr. King at Washington Cathedral. In his opening words he referred to Vice President Hubert H. Humphrey, Representative John W. McCormack of Massachusetts, Speaker of the House of Representatives, and Earl Warren, Chief Justice of the United States. The address was broadcast nationally.

On the same day the White House Press Office released a list of civil rights leaders and Government officials who met with the President following the death of Dr. King (4 Weekly Comp. Pres. Docs., p. 641).

From April 4–11, 1968, racial violence spread through many cities of the United States, including the District of Columbia. On April 5 the White House released a statement on the civil disorders by Wyatt Thomas Johnson, Jr., Assistant Press Secretary to the President (4 Weekly Comp. Pres. Docs., p. 658). On the same day the President signed Proclamation 3840 "Law and Order in the Washington Metropolitan Area" (4 Weekly Comp. Pres. Docs., p. 641; 33 F.R. 5495; 3 CFR, 1968 Comp., p. 35); and Executive Order 11403 "Providing for the Restoration of Law and Order in the Washington Metropolitan Area" (4 Weekly Comp. Pres. Docs., p. 642; 33 F.R. 5501; 3 CFR, 1968 Comp., p. 107).

See also Items 179, 180, 183, 184.

181 Joint Statement Following Discussions With President Tubman of Liberia. *April 5, 1968*

PRESIDENT William V. S. Tubman has concluded an official visit to the United States at the invitation of President Johnson. He was accompanied by Mrs. Tubman, several members of his cabinet and other government officials. While in Washington, President Tubman met with President Johnson and with Secretary Rusk for conversations on matters of mutual interest and concern.

During their meetings, the two Presidents reaffirmed the importance they place on the close and historic ties between the governments and peoples of Liberia and the United States. President Johnson expressed his appreciation for the spirit of cooperation which is the bedrock of these relations and assured President Tubman of the importance which he places on a strong relationship with Liberia.

In expressing Liberia's appreciation of the contribution which A.I.D. and the Peace Corps are making to Liberia's development, President Tubman outlined to President Johnson the economic problems and opportunities which lie ahead. He emphasized in particular the determination of the Liberian Government to become self-sufficient in food production and thus to make a contribution to world food needs. This will require assistance in production techniques and an extension of Liberia's road system to facilitate marketing and distribution. President Tubman stressed the importance which his Government attaches to the development of the Southeast region of the country through the establishment of transport facilities with special reference to the construction of a modern port at Harper. He expressed the strong hope that the United States would consider participating in this development to a substantial degree.

President Tubman also expressed his deep concern over the instability of primary commodity prices on world markets and in this connection made specific reference to the serious fall in the prices of Liberia's major export commodities. President Tubman expressed the hope that the United States Government would take a sympathetic attitude toward proposals for the stabilization of primary commodity prices.

President Johnson affirmed the deep and abiding interest of the United States in the economic and social progress of Liberia. He appreciated in this connection the problem for Liberia presented by the fall in commodity prices. He pledged United States support for the Liberian Government's effort to advance the country's growth, and a thorough and sympathetic review of the projects being proposed. The United States, responding to Liberia's agricultural needs, will assist in increasing rice production and in extending the road system. The United States and possibly interested third parties

will study thoroughly the proposal for the Southeast region and the port at Harper. The United States also will pursue a vigorous program of support for general education in Liberia and will help to staff and train Liberians in the new medical center at Monrovia.

President Tubman and President Johnson found a wide range of agreement on many international issues and reaffirmed their adherence to the worldwide applicability of the principles of national independence and self-determination. President Tubman, speaking of Africa, outlined the progress the continent was making in building strong and independent states. He emphasized the spirit of cooperation evolving through the Organization of African Unity and other emerging regional organizations. In this connection, he made particular reference to the importance he attaches to the forthcoming conference in Monrovia of West African Chiefs of State to discuss regional economic questions.

President Johnson congratulated President Tubman for his outstanding statesmanship in the institutional development of Africa and his leadership in convening the Monrovia conference. He expressed the deep and sympathetic interest of the United States in such African initiatives and asked President Tubman to convey to the African leaders at Monrovia his best wishes for the success of their conference.

NOTE: See also Items 157, 159.

182   Letter to the Speaker of the House Urging Enactment of the Fair Housing Bill. *April 5, 1968*

Dear Mr. Speaker:

Two years ago I asked the Congress to guarantee a basic American right—the right of a man to secure a home for his family

regardless of the color of his skin.

The House of Representatives passed such a law, but it died in the Senate.

Last year, I again submitted Fair Housing

legislation. This legislation languished in Committee.

This year, I once again appealed to the Congress to confirm this fundamental of human dignity. The signs, at long last, were hopeful. The Senate passed a Fair Housing law last month. On March 11, I wrote to you urging you to pass the Senate bill. But since then, this urgent legislation has been blocked in the House.

Last night America was shocked by a senseless act of violence. A man who devoted his life to the nonviolent achievement of rights that most Americans take for granted was killed by an assassin's bullet.

This tragedy has caused all good men to look deeply into their hearts. When the Nation so urgently needs the healing balm of unity, a brutal wound on our conscience forces upon us all this question: What more can I do to achieve brotherhood and equality among all Americans?

There are many actions the Congress can take, on its part. The most immediate is to enact legislation so long delayed and so close to fulfillment.

We should pass the Fair Housing law when the Congress convenes next week.

Mr. Speaker, I urge the members of the House of Representatives to rise to this challenge. In your hands lies the power to renew for all Americans the great promise of opportunity and justice under law.

I ask you to bring this bill to a vote in the House of Representatives at the earliest possible moment.

The time for action is now.

Sincerely,

LYNDON B. JOHNSON

[Honorable John W. McCormack, Speaker of the House of Representatives, Washington, D.C.]

NOTE: The fair housing bill was enacted as Title VIII of the Civil Rights Act of 1968 (82 Stat. 81). For the President's remarks upon signing that measure see Item 195.

The text of the letter was given to newsmen by the White House Press Office but was not made public in the form of a press release.

---

183 Telegram to the Acting Governor of Illinois in Response to His Request for Federal Troops in Chicago. *April 6, 1968*

IN RESPONSE to your official request made pursuant to your discussion with Mayor Daley that federal troops be sent to assist local and state police and the Illinois National Guardsmen under your command and on your representation that "under existing circumstances, the law enforcement resources of the state are unable to suppress the serious domestic violence in or near the city of Chicago, State of Illinois," I have directed the troops you requested to proceed to O'Hare Field and to Glenview Naval Air Station. They will be available on arrival for immediate deployment as required to support and assist police and the Illinois National Guard forces.

LYNDON B. JOHNSON

[Honorable Samuel H. Shapiro, Acting Governor, State of Illinois, Springfield, Illinois]

NOTE: The President's telegram was in response to Acting Governor Shapiro's telegram of the same date requesting the assistance of Federal troops to quell civil disturbances in Illinois (4 Weekly Comp. Pres. Docs., p. 659).

On April 7 the President signed Proclamation 3841 "Law and Order in the State of Illinois" and Executive Order 11404 "Providing for the Restoration of Law and Order in the State of Illinois" (4 Weekly Comp. Pres. Docs., p. 659; 33 F.R. 5497, 5503; 3 CFR, 1968 Comp., pp. 36, 108).

See also Items 179, 180, 184.

184   Telegram to the Governor of Maryland in Response to His Request for Federal Troops in Baltimore. *April 7, 1968*

IN RESPONSE to your official request that federal troops be sent to assist local and state police and the Maryland National Guardsmen under your command and on your representation that "under existing circumstances, the law enforcement resources of the state are unable to suppress the serious domestic violence in or near the city of Baltimore, State of Maryland," I have already directed the troops you requested to proceed at once to Druid Hill Park, Baltimore. They will be available on arrival for immediate deployment as required to support and assist police and the Maryland National Guard forces.

LYNDON B. JOHNSON

[Honorable Spiro T. Agnew, Governor, State of Maryland, Annapolis, Maryland]

NOTE: The President's telegram was in response to Governor Agnew's telegram of the same date requesting Federal troops to aid in suppressing domestic violence in Baltimore (4 Weekly Comp. Pres. Docs., p. 660).

Also on April 7 the President signed Proclamation 3842 "Law and Order in the State of Maryland" and Executive Order 11405 "Providing for the Restoration of Law and Order in the State of Maryland" (4 Weekly Comp. Pres. Docs., pp. 660, 661; 33 F.R. 5499, 5505; 3 CFR, 1968 Comp., pp. 36, 109).

See also Items 179, 180, 183.

185   Remarks to the Press With General Westmoreland Following the General's Report on the Situation in Vietnam. *April 7, 1968*

FOR THE past two days, General Westmoreland has been here in Washington conferring with me and my senior advisers, briefing us on the military situation in South Vietnam and exploring personnel and other matters that we desired to take up with him.

He has spent the lunch hour and this afternoon with Secretary Rusk, since the Secretary returned from a visit to the Pacific area.

General Westmoreland is leaving shortly to return to South Vietnam and will stop over, at my request, in California to brief General Eisenhower on the matters that we discussed here.

General Westmoreland will have a brief statement to make to you before he goes to the plane. Along with Secretary Clifford, I expect to go to the plane with General Westmoreland and continue our talks until his departure.

[At this point General Westmoreland spoke briefly. The President then resumed speaking.]

Ladies and gentlemen, General Westmoreland is due to arrive back in Saigon on Tuesday. After his arrival Ambassador Bunker will come to Washington for conferences during the latter part of the week with the President and with his senior advisers, the Secretary of State and the Secretary of Defense.

Thank you very much.

NOTE: The President spoke at 4:10 p.m. in front of the entrance to the West Lobby at the White House. General Westmoreland's remarks follow:

Yesterday and today I conferred with the President, the Secretary of State, Secretary of Defense, the Chairman of the Joint Chiefs of Staff, and other officials of the Government. I discussed the military situation in South Vietnam, the status of enemy forces, the performance of the Vietnamese military, mobilization and modernization of the Vietnamese Armed Forces, and current and future military operations and plans.

I told the Commander in Chief that:

—Despite the initial psychological impact of the enemy's Tet offensive, the enemy failed to achieve a public uprising by the people of South Vietnam, to bring about the defeat of the Armed Forces of Vietnam, or to achieve his military objectives.

—The Vietnamese Government is proceeding rapidly to increase the strength of its Armed Forces by 135,000 men.

—An assessment of the performance of the Vietnamese Armed Forces during the past several months reveals that, in general, they fought bravely and well.

—The spirit of the offensive is now prevalent throughout Vietnam, with the advantage being taken of the enemy's weakened military position in Vietnam.

—Our troops of all services have continued to perform in magnificent fashion and their conduct since the first of the year has been enhanced and my admiration for them has likewise been increased.

—Militarily, we have never been in a better relative position in South Vietnam.

—The enemy's siege of Khe Sanh has been relieved by ground action. Following news from my command, I have sent a message to General Cushman, congratulating him and the troops under his operational control for their success in relieving the Khe Sanh base and wresting the initiative from the enemy. A copy of my message will be distributed to you.

Ladies and gentlemen, in view of the sensitive nature of the present situation, I have nothing further to say.

186   Message to U.S. Armed Forces in Southeast Asia on the Lifting of the Siege of Khe Sanh. *April 8, 1968*

THE RELIEF of the forces which have held the base at Khe Sanh is an occasion for me to express the pride and confidence I feel in those who are carrying forward the Nation's struggle against aggression in Southeast Asia.

Side by side with your South Vietnamese comrades—and our other fighting allies—you have taken the full initial weight of the enemy's winter-spring offensive; and you have now seized the initiative.

The enemy intended to destroy the constitutional government of South Vietnam and its armed forces. In this he failed.

The enemy intended to overrun the base at Khe Sanh. For this purpose he emplaced around that base at least two divisions of North Vietnamese regulars. Less than 6,000 U.S. Marines and South Vietnamese Rangers—backed by our tremendous air capacity—pinned them down, kept them away from the populated areas at the peak of the winter-spring offensive, and imposed heavy casualties.

Now the siege of Khe Sanh is lifted.

But clearly the fighting in South Vietnam is not yet at an end.

The enemy may throw new forces into the battle.

You, I know, intend to continue to move forward.

But by your gallant and skillful support for the brave people and armed forces of South Vietnam, you have brought nearer the time of peace in that suffering land and in all of Southeast Asia.

As we seek now to find through negotiations an honorable peace in Vietnam, I wish you to know that we are grateful for what you have already accomplished and will be counting on you more than ever, until the blessed day when the guns fall silent.

187 Remarks to the Press Announcing Receipt of a Message From Hanoi. *April 8, 1968*

TONIGHT I will be going to Camp David, at the conclusion of the day, with certain staff members.

Tomorrow morning, I will have breakfast there with Ambassador Bunker, Secretary Rusk, and Secretary Clifford.

Ambassador Bunker will arrive at Andrews in the early morning, somewhere around 7 o'clock. He will pick up the two Secretaries and come on to Camp David for a meeting there tomorrow.

I have a message from Hanoi replying to our message of April 3d. We have taken steps to notify our allies.

We shall be trying to work out promptly a time and place for talks.

Any other announcements will have to come from Mr. Christian, if there is anything else to announce.

NOTE: The President spoke at 1:36 p.m. in the Cabinet Room at the White House. During his remarks he referred to Ellsworth Bunker, U.S. Ambassador to the Republic of Vietnam, Secretary of State Dean Rusk, Secretary of Defense Clark M. Clifford, and George E. Christian, Special Assistant to the President.

188 Remarks to the Press on Meetings With Ambassador Bunker at Camp David and on Continuing Contacts With Hanoi. *April 9, 1968*

AMBASSADOR BUNKER arrived here a little before 8 o'clock from South Vietnam. He flew from Tokyo nonstop. We had breakfast together, those of us here at the table. Ambassador Bunker has given us a rather complete review of the developments in South Vietnam since his last personal visit here, with emphasis on the period since the Tet offensive.

We will be meeting here throughout the day and will be joined for a 1 o'clock lunch by Ambassador Harriman and Secretary Bundy.

Later today or tomorrow, either here or in Washington, I will meet with Admiral Sharp, Commander in Chief of the Pacific area.

Ambassador Bunker will be returning to South Vietnam when our meetings here are concluded.

Since I saw you yesterday in the Cabinet Room, we have consulted with our allies about the message that I referred to yesterday and alternative sites. We are back in touch with Hanoi and discussing a number of alternative locations which could be convenient to both sides. We are in agreement with our allies and are prepared for ambassadorial contacts just as soon as arrangements can be completed.

I will ask Mr. Christian to keep in touch with you and if there are any other announcements during our stay here, he will relay them to you as well as keep you informed of any other developments.

NOTE: The President spoke at 10:38 a.m. at Camp David near Thurmont, Md. During his remarks he referred to Ellsworth Bunker, U.S. Ambassador to the Republic of Vietnam, W. Averell Harriman, U.S. Ambassador-at-Large, William P. Bundy, Assistant Secretary of State for East Asian and Pacific Affairs, and George E. Christian, Special Assistant to the President.

A statement by Mr. Christian on possible sites for discussions with representatives of North Viet-

nam is printed in the Weekly Compilation of Presidential Documents (vol. 4, p. 673).

See also Item 189.

189   Remarks to the Press at Camp David With Ambassador Bunker Following the Ambassador's Report on the Situation in Vietnam.   *April 9, 1968*

ADMIRAL SHARP will be coming at 5:30 or 5:45.

These gentlemen are returning to Washington tonight. Ambassador Bunker will be my guest while he is there, at the White House. I will be seeing him tomorrow. He will probably be returning Thursday.

We spent the afternoon hearing from Ambassador Bunker and going over a series of questions that we raised with him largely relating to the relationship between our Government and the South Vietnamese Government. We talked to him about what progress had been made since he had been there and what his general observations were.

His review was on the political front, diplomatic and economic front, very similar to what General Abrams and General Westmoreland and Admiral Sharp will go over with us on the military matters.

I don't know if this is the place for any extravaganza press conference, but I asked the Ambassador if he would point out some of the high points and give you his judgments for such consideration as you may care to give them or pass on to the American people on the situation there from a political and economic standpoint.

I think I need not recall to you that Ambassador Bunker is one of our most experienced and trusted and most highly regarded Ambassadors in the entire service. He has

held a number of the most critical assignments that any Ambassador has ever undertaken.

His most recent assignment was the Dominican Republic, where he went and spent many months seeing a new government born and helping it through its early stages.

I thought I knew most of what was happening in Vietnam and felt very encouraged about the relationship between our Government and their Government and their people; but Ambassador Bunker's report today uncovered a lot of things that I had not realized or recognized or appreciated.

So maybe he will want to touch on some of those things for your general edification.

Ambassador Bunker.

AMBASSADOR BUNKER. As the President said, I have come to report on the situation, as I see it, after Tet. If Tet was a psychological and a political success abroad, it certainly was a resounding military defeat for them in Vietnam.

I am beginning to think it was also a psychological and political defeat as well. It did create, obviously, many thousands of refugees and much economic damage. But there are other elements of strength which have developed and become evident there since the Tet offensive.

Although the Vietnamese forces, for example, many of them, were only at half strength, nevertheless with our assistance, they did smash the attacks. They inflicted very heavy casualties and drove the Communists from every city in the country.

The Government did not collapse, but turned to—with great will and determination—its recovery program. The ARVN forces did not defect. The people, after the initial shock, emerged strengthened in their anger and their hatred for Communists and their determination to resist.

The rate of volunteers for the forces rose dramatically. The Government is drafting 18- and 19-year-olds and has more than doubled the number of men it is going to take into the Armed Forces this year. Students are flocking to the training centers—certainly in a very surprising turn-around of attitude.

There is a new sense of danger, of urgency and patriotism taking hold in the country. The legislature is behaving in a responsible way. The President is going about improving the governmental administration and machinery, attacking corruption, and has replaced some 14 provincial chiefs since Tet.

Finally, I may say that Khe Sanh has not turned into another Dienbienphu. The news, as you know, has come in that the siege has been lifted. This will certainly have a very dramatic and favorable impact throughout South Vietnam.

So, I think the Government is much more self-confident than before Tet and there is much greater unity in the country today, I think, than we have ever seen before—a turning-to with the will. And I think it has made very substantial progress since this Tet offensive.

As you know, also, our forces now are on the offensive—our forces and the Vietnamese, throughout the country.

President Thieu is in the process of reorganizing the Government and making many improvements so that I am very much encouraged with what has happened there and look to the future with a good deal of confidence.

Q. May we ask some questions?

AMBASSADOR BUNKER. Yes.

Q. Mr. Ambassador, what impact psychologically has the possibility of talks looking toward negotiations had on the people and the Government? Are they disturbed by this or are they favorably impressed by it?

AMBASSADOR BUNKER. No, I don't think they are disturbed by it. Their position on talks, on negotiations, as you know, has been similar to ours.

Q. Mr. President, has anything new come in on what you told us about earlier today?

THE PRESIDENT. No.

Reporter: Thank you very much.

NOTE: The President spoke at 4:17 p.m. at Camp David at a press briefing held with Ellsworth Bunker, U.S. Ambassador to the Republic of Vietnam.

During his remarks he referred to Adm. U. S. Grant Sharp, Jr., Commander in Chief of U.S. Forces in the Pacific, Gen. William C. Westmoreland, Commander, United States Military Assistance Command, Vietnam, and Gen. Creighton W. Abrams, Deputy Commander.

On the same day the White House released the text of two press pool reports on the Camp David meetings. The reports were given at 11:20 a.m. and 4:52 p.m. at the American Legion Hall in Thurmont, Md.

190   Remarks of Welcome at the White House to Chancellor
       Josef Klaus of Austria. *April 10, 1968*

Mr. Chancellor and Mrs. Klaus, Under Secretary Katzenbach, distinguished guests, ladies and gentlemen:

We welcome you to the beautiful Washington spring, Mr. Chancellor, at a time of turbulence and hope in our Nation.

As it is for us here in America, so it is around the world.

There is turbulence today in America— and in Eastern Europe—and in Southeast Asia—and there is hope, as well, in all of those places.

So our aim at this season is to sift the hope from the turbulence, so that hope may grow unfettered. As we go about that business, our hopes ride upon compassion, upon our sense of national purpose, and upon our feeling of responsibility in the time of challenge, and upon what an earlier era called "self-discipline." These times demand too:

—self-discipline between the races;

—self-discipline to persevere in the healing tasks of our Nation;

—self-discipline in the long and hard work of finding and seeking and bringing about a just and lasting peace.

In any society, men of good will and moderation are in the majority. The cynics— and there are always some of them—are in the minority. Those in the majority are the proportions that God set out when He made us all. It is the task and the test of democracy to assure that the moderate and good-willed majority prevails and has its way.

Mr. Chancellor, the experience of your nation tells us that it can. Austria was formed upon that democratic impulse for peace and for stability. A new society was forged from a four-power occupation force, in what was then the most turbulent area of the entire world.

You give us additional cause to believe that hope can coexist with turbulence and that freedom and order will, in time, prevail. We expect, this spring day in Washington, that this will happen in our country, in America, and that it will happen in Southeast Asia, and it will happen wherever men of good will earnestly seek and pursue peace and equity and justice for all. Mr. Chancellor, we are so glad that you could come here and honor us by your visit. We welcome you as a friend, sir, and we look forward with pleasurable anticipation to our exchanges together.

Thank you very much.

NOTE: The President spoke at 11:43 a.m. on the South Lawn at the White House where Chancellor Klaus was given a formal welcome with full military honors. In his opening words the President also referred to Nicholas deB. Katzenbach, Under Secretary of State. Chancellor Klaus responded as follows:

Mr. President:

May I thank you also on behalf of Mrs. Klaus, most sincerely for having invited me officially to meet you and to visit your great country.

I highly appreciate the fact that I can meet you in spite of the difficult time when you are confronted with grave problems and difficult decisions which are of a particular bearing, not only for the future of the United States, but of the whole world.

I am glad to be here and to have the opportunity to renew the ties of friendship which so happily exist between our two countries.

The Austrian people will never forget the help of the United States which was decisive for the overcoming of the postwar difficulties. It has been especially since then that my country is particularly attached to your generous people.

I am looking forward with great pleasure to my talks with you, Mr. President, and with the distinguished members of your Government and the United States Congress.

I am pleased that my schedule provides for an

extensive tour across your country.

Again, may sincerest thanks for having invited Mrs. Klaus and me to the United States.

191 The President's News Conference of April 10, 1968

THE PRESIDENT. I have a few announcements to make that I think will be of interest to you.

CIVIL RIGHTS BILL

[1.] First of all, as you know, the civil rights bill that we submitted to the Congress some time ago will shortly become law, having been acted upon in the House of Representatives this afternoon.

Senator Mansfield[1] has talked to me within the hour, informing me that they have completed action. It is now up to the House to send it to the President. We will have a signing ceremony at a very early date.[2]

We have passed many civil rights pieces of legislation, but none more important than this. When we first met to consider the subject of open housing, there were only two or three in the room representing government, housing groups, civil rights groups, and others, who felt that we could approach this subject in any way other than by a regulation that had doubtful legality and certainly whose coverage would be quite limited.

I took the position at that original meeting that if we really believed in open housing, equal housing, and fair treatment to all of our citizens, we should have a congressional declaration to that effect and a statute that would give us that protection.

It has been a long, tortuous, and difficult road.

There have been days of sunshine and sorrow.

But it is now a finality. I congratulate first the Members of the Senate who had the courage and the wisdom to pass the bill, and invoke cloture; and then to the Members of the House of Representatives of both parties who supported that measure.

I have a brief statement that George[3] will give you as soon as it is off the typewriter. It says:

STATEMENT BY THE PRESIDENT

"Today the Nation's Congress passed the Civil Rights Act of 1968. This is a victory for every American. The only true path of progress for a free people is the one that we will take when this legislation is made the law of the land.

"Through the process of law, we shall strike for all time the shackles of an old injustice.

"I call upon the Congress now to complete its work of hope for millions of Americans who now look to it for action."

APPOINTMENTS

POSTMASTER GENERAL

[2.] I have received and accepted the resignation of Mr. Larry O'Brien as Postmaster General.

---

[1] Senator Mike Mansfield of Montana, Majority Leader of the Senate.

[2] See Item 195.

[3] George E. Christian, Special Assistant to the President.

Larry asked to see me this morning when I returned to town. He came in and talked to me about his resignation and told me he would like to resign. I told him what I told the other members of the Cabinet the other day, that since I was not going to be a candidate for reelection, I realized the Cabinet had made many sacrifices in order to serve me and serve the country, and that now was the time for any of them to make decisions concerning their families and their future.

So Larry told me that he would present his resignation.

He has. It is accepted.

I have sent to the Senate the name of W. Marvin Watson as his successor. He is the Appointments Secretary who has served me ably—as Larry has—for a good deal of the time I have been President.

A biographical sketch will be given to you by the Press Office.

I have never been served by a more competent, more efficient, nor more likable or effective employee than Larry O'Brien. We shall miss him, but we are very happy to cooperate with him in his desire to enter private life after having given fully of himself to his country for 7-plus years.

PRESIDENTIAL ASSISTANTS

[3.] To replace Marvin Watson, we will have Mr. Jim Jones, of Oklahoma, and Mr. Larry Temple. They both are good men. It will take at least two good men to replace what Marvin has been doing here.

Mr. Larry Temple is from Texas; former Appointments Secretary and assistant to Governor Connally. Mr. Jones is from Oklahoma and has been with us, as you know, as deputy to Mr. Watson.

COMMANDER IN CHIEF, PACIFIC

[4.] I have named Admiral John McCain to succeed Admiral Sharp, as Commander in Chief of the Pacific. I did this on the recommendation of Admiral Sharp, the Joint Chiefs, and Secretary Clifford.

COMMANDER OF U.S. FORCES, VIETNAM

[5.] I have named General Abrams to succeed General Westmoreland.

Biographical sketches on all of these will be given to you when you retire.

As you know, General Abrams is the present deputy to General Westmoreland, and we think the man most competent to assume this very heavy responsibility.

DEPUTY COMMANDER IN VIETNAM

[6.] To succeed General Abrams, we are naming General Andrew Goodpaster, who was with the Security Council during the Eisenhower period and is a lieutenant general. He is now head of the War College. He has been a very trusted adviser to me during the period of my Presidency.

He has also been the person I have selected to brief General Eisenhower from time to time, if that will help you in identification. He will be deputy to General Abrams.

We have discussed this with General Eisenhower. We will have General Wheeler, who has assumed this responsibility on occasions, and General Westmoreland will be our contact. Whenever General Eisenhower desires to receive a briefing, they will perform the functions previously performed by General Goodpaster, who will be out of the country.

General Abrams, General Goodpaster, and Admiral McCain have been recommended by the Joint Chiefs of the services, by Secretary Clifford, and in the case of Admiral McCain, by Admiral Sharp and the Navy service; in the case of General Goodpaster, by General Westmoreland and General Abrams, under whom he will work, as well as President Eisenhower.

We discussed this with General Eisenhower. I would not say he recommended it, but he showed pleasure in the appointment. But, I don't want to leave the impression that he was dictating it or pushing this matter. Of course, all of these nominations are based upon the recommendation of the Secretaries involved, and the advice of the Joint Chiefs of Staff.

I think that is all the announcements I have for you.

QUESTIONS

ADMIRAL MC CAIN

[7.] Q. Where is Admiral McCain now, Mr. President?

THE PRESIDENT. Naval Forces in Europe. He is 57 years old and has served as Commander in Chief of the Naval Forces in Europe. He is a military adviser and representative of various mutual defense alliances.

EXCHANGE WITH HANOI

[8.] Q. Can you take us any further along the road on the exchange with Hanoi?

THE PRESIDENT. No.

PRESIDENT'S COMMISSION ON CIVIL DISORDERS

[9.] Q. Mr. President, Mayor Lindsay [4] has said that your Civil Disorders Commis-

sion is being reconvened. Can you give us your thoughts on that?

THE PRESIDENT. I am not aware of it. I don't know.

MR. O'BRIEN'S RESIGNATION

[10.] Q. Did Mr. O'Brien tell you why he wanted to resign at this time?

THE PRESIDENT. No. He said he wanted to enter private life. He told me about some of his plans, but I don't think he has them definitely fixed yet. He is not exactly sure of where he is going.

ADDRESS TO JOINT SESSION OF CONGRESS

[11.] Q. Mr. President, do you still plan to address a joint session of Congress?

THE PRESIDENT. I have nothing to add to what I have already told you. That has been postponed for the time being.

THE VICE PRESIDENT'S POSSIBLE CANDIDACY

[12.] Q. Mr. President, there is some indication that the Vice President might declare for the Presidency. I was wondering if you felt you would have to maintain——

THE PRESIDENT. I would not get into that at all.

CIVIL RIGHTS BILL

[13.] Q. Mr. President, on the signing of the civil rights bill, you said "early date." Could that be as early as tomorrow, or somewhere down the road?

THE PRESIDENT. Let me tell you when I know. I can't speculate because I can't tell when I will receive it.

Helen Thomas, United Press Interna-

---

[4] Mayor John V. Lindsay of New York City.

tional: Thank you, Mr. President.

NOTE: President Johnson's one hundred and twenty-third news conference was held in his office at the

White House at 4:43 p.m. on Wednesday, April 10, 1968. As printed above, this item follows the text of the Official White House Transcript.

192 Broadcast Statement by the President Following the Passage of the Civil Rights Act. *April 10, 1968*

TODAY, the Nation's Congress passed the Civil Rights Act of 1968.

This is a victory for every American because the only true path to progress for a free people is the one we will take when this legislation is made the law of the land.

Through the process of law, we shall strike for all time the shackles of an old injustice.

A few years ago when we met here in the White House and discussed open housing and how to handle it by regulation or statute, there were very few who thought that in our time we could bring this justice to all Americans. But the Congress today has shown that if we have the will, there is a way.

Therefore, I call upon the Congress again now to complete its work of hope for millions of Americans by passing the measures recommended in more than 20 messages I have sent to the Congress and in some 15 appropriations bills in order that we can move forward with our program of social justice and progress.

Now we look to the Congress for action—not just on this civil rights bill—but on the many other measures pending before it.

NOTE: The President spoke at 5:15 p.m. in the Fish Room at the White House.

As printed above, this item follows the text released by the White House Press Office.

See also Item 195.

193 Toasts of the President and Chancellor Klaus of Austria. *April 10, 1968*

Chancellor and Mrs. Klaus, Mr. Vice President and Mrs. Humphrey, distinguished guests, ladies and gentlemen:

In the dark days before World War II, the writer Stefan Zweig said of the disappearance of Austria from the map of Europe, "Nobody saw that Austria was the cornerstone of the wall and that Europe must break down when it was torn out."

Tonight, ladies and gentlemen, we celebrate what the Austrian people and their leaders have done to put that cornerstone back into the wall—so solidly that all of Europe is much stronger.

A native Austrian—Justice Felix Frankfurter—who became one of America's wisest

men of law, liked to say that "there is no inevitability in history—except as men make it."

Perhaps never in the recorded ages of man has that been truer than in the era that we now live in. And perhaps that is both the greatness as well as the trial of our age.

We have seen in our era that men can make their own destiny.

We have seen men shape their destiny in countries that were once only colonies.

We see today the young people everywhere restlessly seeking to have a voice in their own future.

We have seen, on every continent, the unquenchable thirst for self-determination.

Nowhere has this appeared more clearly than in Austria—where a free and a proud people willed themselves a new nation out of the ruins of war.

Our guest this evening has played a leading part in showing that history is not inevitable, but rather responsive to the highest goals of the human spirit. He is a seeker of peace and harmony throughout Europe and around the world.

Mr. Chancellor, I can assure you that your efforts have not gone unappreciated in this city.

Ladies and gentlemen, I ask you to join me this evening in a toast to the people of Austria, the President of the Republic of Austria, and to our most distinguished guest and his lady, Chancellor Josef Klaus.

NOTE: The President proposed the toast at 10:21 p.m. at a dinner in the State Dining Room at the White House. Chancellor Klaus responded as follows:

Mr. President, Mrs. Johnson, ladies and gentlemen:

Thank you very much, Mr. President, for your kind words. We have been all the more delighted to accept your invitation to pay a visit to the United States since we knew that this is indeed a visit to friends. Between the United States and Austria, there are, happily, no unsolved political problems.

Already one of my predecessors, the late Chancellor Raab, emphasized during a visit to the White House, our gratitude to the American people for the help which was given to us in difficult times. In the extremely difficult postwar years when we were suffering from the consequences of the war, it was the unselfish help of the American people which enabled us to preserve our freedom and reconstruct our country.

We understand, Mr. President, America's problems. We know how heavy the responsibilities are that you have to bear.

Despite our neutrality, we are well aware that we are not living in an isolated island and that international conflicts do affect our country, also.

We are, therefore, always prepared to participate actively in all efforts for maintaining peace in the world. We are always ready to offer our good offices wherever they are needed.

I have had the opportunity to inform you, Mr. President, of our countless little problems; the general slowdown of economic activity in Europe has not spared us, although results have perhaps not been so strong as in some other countries. But its effects were nevertheless reinforced by a strong movement of protectionism in many parts of the world.

May I take the opportunity to thank you, Mr. President, and your administration, for having shown so much understanding for our problems and may I thank you for your efforts to promote world trade.

Your statement, Mr. President, of this morning, was encouraging indeed, to pursue in the future a policy of easing the tensions and a policy of promoting the cooperation among all nations.

I don't have to say how much I appreciate your kindness, Mr. President, in asking me to come to Washington in a time when you are confronted with most important decisions, not only for your country, but for the whole world.

May I assure you that the people of Austria follow very closely the events in East Asia as well as in the United States. The Austrian people welcome your most recent decisions as an essential step toward peace in Vietnam.

I would like to ask you to toast with me to the health of the President of the United States, to Mrs. Johnson, and to the people of the United States.

To the President.

---

194   Joint Statement Following Discussions With the Chancellor of Austria. *April 11, 1968*

PRESIDENT JOHNSON and Austrian Chancellor Klaus conferred at the White House on April 10.

The President and the Chancellor had a broad exchange of views on the international situation. Developments in Southeast Asia were reviewed and hope was expressed that an equitable solution to the present conflict would be reached. The Middle East question was also discussed. The Chancellor reviewed the situation in Europe with emphasis on Austria's relationship with her neighbors and with the members of the European Communities. The President and the Chancellor stressed the essential role of the United Nations in the maintenance of peace. They also agreed that the proposed Nonproliferation Treaty would greatly strengthen the foundations of peace and would be a significant step toward halting the arms race and the achievement of general and complete disarmament.

The President and the Chancellor underlined the common desire of their countries to create an atmosphere of cooperation and to bring about relaxation of tensions all over the world. The importance of strengthening the international monetary system and of promoting international trade was also dis-cussed. To this end it was agreed that international cooperation will continue to be necessary. They also noted the helpfulness of expanded East-West trade in peaceful goods as a means of improving international relations—a development in which Austria has played a significant role.

The President and the Chancellor expressed great satisfaction over the excellent relations between the United States and Austria. They agreed that high-level consultations greatly contribute to further strengthening the existing friendship between the two countries.

195 Remarks Upon Signing the Civil Rights Act. *April* 11, 1968

Members of the Congress, Members of the Cabinet, distinguished Americans, and guests:

On an April afternoon in the year 1966, I asked a distinguished group of citizens who were interested in human rights to meet me in the Cabinet Room in the White House. In their presence that afternoon, I signed a message to the Congress. That message called for the enactment of "the first effective federal law against discrimination in the sale and the rental of housing" in the United States of America.

Few in the Nation—and the record will show that very few in that room that afternoon—believed that fair housing would—in our time—become the unchallenged law of this land.

And indeed, this bill has had a long and stormy trip.

We did not get it in 1966.

We pleaded for it again in 1967. But the Congress took no action that year.

We asked for it again this year.

And now—at long last this afternoon—its day has come.

I do not exaggerate when I say that the proudest moments of my Presidency have been times such as this when I have signed into law the promises of a century.

I shall never forget that it was more than 100 years ago when Abraham Lincoln issued the Emancipation Proclamation—but it was a proclamation; it was not a fact.

In the Civil Rights Act of 1964, we affirmed through law that men equal under God are also equal when they seek a job, when they go to get a meal in a restaurant, or when they seek lodging for the night in any State in the Union.

Now the Negro families no longer suffer the humiliation of being turned away because of their race.

In the Civil Rights Act of 1965, we affirmed through law for every citizen in this land the most basic right of democracy—the right of a citizen to vote in an election in his country. In the five States where the

Act had its greater impact, Negro voter registration has already more than doubled.

Now, with this bill, the voice of justice speaks again.

It proclaims that fair housing for all—all human beings who live in this country—is now a part of the American way of life.

We all know that the roots of injustice run deep. But violence cannot redress a solitary wrong, or remedy a single unfairness.

Of course, all America is outraged at the assassination of an outstanding Negro leader who was at that meeting that afternoon in the White House in 1966. And America is also outraged at the looting and the burning that defiles our democracy.

We just must put our shoulders together and put a stop to both. The time is here. Action must be now.

So, I would appeal to my fellow Americans by saying, the only real road to progress for free people is through the process of law and that is the road that America will travel.

I urge the Congress to enact the measures for social justice that I have recommended in some twenty messages. These messages went to the Congress in January and February

of this year. They broke a precedent by being completed and delivered and read and printed. These measures provide more than $78 billion that I have urged the Congress to enact for major domestic programs for all Americans in the fiscal 1969 budget.

This afternoon, as we gather here in this historic room in the White House, I think we can all take some heart that democracy's work is being done. In the Civil Rights Act of 1968 America does move forward and the bell of freedom rings out a little louder.

We have come some of the way, not near all of it. There is much yet to do. If the Congress sees fit to act upon these twenty messages and some fifteen appropriations bills, I assure you that what remains to be done will be recommended in ample time for you to do it after you have completed what is already before you.

Thank you very much.

NOTE: The President spoke at 5 p.m. in the East Room at the White House. During his remarks he referred to Dr. Martin Luther King, Jr., civil rights leader who was assassinated on April 4, 1968 (see Items 179, 180).

As enacted, the bill (H.R. 2516) is Public Law 90–284 (82 Stat. 73).

196 Statement by the President on the Need for Federal, State, and Local Cooperation in Civil Defense and Emergency Preparedness. *April 13, 1968*

WHILE we are working for peace, and hope that there never will be an attack upon this country, it has been the long-established policy of our Nation to maintain both military and nonmilitary preparedness.

The national security requires an effective partnership between the Federal and State and local governments. The Advisory Council and the Federal Government cannot do this job alone. Chief executives of all governmental units should continue to discharge

their clear and compelling responsibility for leadership in civil defense and emergency preparedness.

Much progress has been made, but this is a continuing task. Additional fallout protection for our citizens and complementary preparedness programs will continue to strengthen our strategic defense posture. These preparations will also increase the effectiveness of State and local governments in coping with natural disasters. In time of emergency, what matters most is advance preparations.

I look forward to receiving the recommendations of the Council.

NOTE: The President's statement was made public as part of a White House release announcing the reappointment for 3-year terms of four members of the National Civil Defense Advisory Council established by the Federal Civil Defense Act of 1950 (64 Stat. 1247). The full text of the release, which lists the Council members, is printed in the Weekly Compilation of Presidential Documents (vol. 4, p. 680).

The Council's recommendations adopted at its meeting on May 28, 1968, were not made public but were embodied in a resolution transmitted to the President on June 11, 1968.

197   Remarks Upon Arriving at the Honolulu International Airport. *April* 15, 1968

Governor Burns, Admiral Sharp, Senator Inouye, Senator Fong, Mrs. Mink, ladies, and gentlemen:

I am very grateful for your coming out to welcome us to this wonderful State. During the past few weeks I have been meeting with our senior military and diplomatic officers from Vietnam—Ambassador Bunker, General Westmoreland, and his successor, General Abrams.

I have come to Hawaii this time principally to meet with President Park, the leader of our brave ally, South Korea. I came a few days early so that I might review the situation in Vietnam with Admiral Sharp and his advisers and with his successor as Commander in Chief of the Pacific, Admiral McCain.

I hope that the next President of our country will be able to come to Hawaii during his term of office solely in order to discuss the peaceful development of Asia and the Pacific.

In the coming months, I am going to do everything within my power to try to bring that about and to make that possible. Today part of our search for peace lies through the processes of diplomacy. Another lies in the ability of our allied forces to meet every challenge that may confront them on the battlefield.

Here in Honolulu we shall be discussing both aspects of this search for peace during the next several days when we are here among you.

My friends, I thank you very much for offering us once again the hospitality that is so much a part of the Hawaiian tradition. I always enjoy coming here.

Thank you very much.

NOTE: The President spoke at 1:15 p.m. at Honolulu International Airport. In his opening words he referred to John A. Burns, Governor of Hawaii, Adm. U.S. Grant Sharp, Jr., Commander in Chief of U.S. Forces in the Pacific, Daniel K. Inouye and Hiram L. Fong, Senators from Hawaii, and Patsy T. Mink, Representative from Hawaii.

198   Remarks at the Iolani Palace in Honolulu. *April* 15, 1968

Governor Burns, Senator Inouye, Senator Fong, Mrs. Mink, distinguished public officials, ladies and gentlemen:

With a greeting such as this from people such as you I am almost inclined to reassess my decision to go home on next Thursday. I have been tempted many times to come here to Hawaii and to stay. There are few places in our country that can match the natural beauty of Hawaii, the cordiality of its people, the harmony of its many races, its great economic potential, and by no means least, the quality of its Governor, its congressional delegation, and its public officials.

My friends, I have come back to Hawaii to meet with a leader of one of America's bravest allies—President Park of South Korea. I have come to review the military situation in South Vietnam with Admiral Sharp and with his successor, Admiral McCain.

During the next few days we shall be discussing our goal of peace in Asia. And we shall be discussing the twin paths we are taking to reach that goal, the path of diplomacy and the path of military preparedness.

We shall be discussing our diplomatic initiative in seeking talks with North Vietnam. We shall be discussing the readiness of our allied forces to meet every challenge on the battlefield of South Vietnam.

Both of these paths are essential to our quest for an honorable and secure peace in South Vietnam.

I know how concerned you are—as I am—that this time, after years of fruitless pauses and proposals, the two sides may get down to serious talks about ending this brutal war.

I announced 2 weeks ago that we would sharply limit our bombing of North Vietnam and that we were willing to meet at any suitable place to begin talks. Very promptly we proposed four neutral sites—Vientiane, Rangoon, Djakarta, and New Delhi—where both sides have representatives and adequate communications.

All of these are readily accessible to Hanoi. All of these are located in the region which has the most direct and vital interest in the achievement of a stable peace.

Hanoi has given us two messages and has suggested two locations. We have responded by pointing out certain obvious reasons why each of the two sites was not suitable. As of now we have had no response or comment from Hanoi, other than radio statements, about any one of the locations that we have suggested.

For us, this is not a propaganda exercise. We have sent serious and considered messages aimed at bringing about the earliest possible contact. Ambassador Harriman and Ambassador Vance are ready. What is needed today is an equally serious reply, reacting to our proposals for neutral sites or offering additional suggestions of neutral capitals where both of us have representatives and communications.

It is now 2 long weeks since I restricted our bombing and urged North Vietnam to come to the conference table.

We are eager to get on with the task of peacemaking. Precious time is being lost. Asians and Americans alike are ready to let diplomacy go to work—now—without any further delay.

There will come a time—and I am sure of it—when the guns will be silent in Vietnam, when Asians will know not only peace, but freedom to manage their own affairs—when the reality of Asia's prosperity matches the richness of Asia's potential.

We have contributed much to bringing that day nearer and we and the world will gain from it the only prize worth gaining—security for ourselves and our children, the chance to be free, the chance to live in peace.

I know that many sons of these Islands have paid the price of freedom in this conflict—as in others before it. If we are steady now in our quest for an honorable settlement, we shall redeem their sacrifice in a great Pacific at peace with itself and with all others.

Thank you, my dear friends in Hawaii, for your warmth, for your hospitality, and for your contribution to a great Nation.

NOTE: The President spoke at 1:50 p.m. at the Iolani Palace in Honolulu. In his opening words he referred to Governor John A. Burns, Senators Daniel K. Inouye and Hiram L. Fong, and Representative Patsy T. Mink, all of Hawaii. Later he referred to Adm. U. S. Grant Sharp, Jr., outgoing Commander in Chief of U.S. Forces in the Pacific, his successor, Adm. John S. McCain, Jr., and W. Averell Harriman and Cyrus R. Vance, Ambassadors at Large, appointed as U.S. negotiators at proposed peace talks with North Vietnam.

199   Remarks at the Governor's Mansion in Honolulu at a Reception for Members of the Mexico-United States Interparliamentary Conference. *April* 15, 1968

Governor Burns and distinguished members of the delegation from Mexico and the United States, my friends of Hawaii:

Thank you so much for thinking of me and asking me to come by and visit with you and enjoy some of this very colorful atmosphere and this exchange between friends.

Since the first meeting of this group in Mexico City, you have met alternately in Mexico and the United States. This parliamentary group, I am informed, does not make binding decisions or even pass resolutions. But you do promote understanding, communication, and friendship between the people of the United States and the people of our beloved sister republic, Mexico.

I have met five times since I have been President with your President of Mexico:

—first at my home in Texas,

—then at our Nation's home in Washington,

—at President Diaz Ordaz's home in Mexico,

—in the Chamizal and at Amistad, and

—with all of our colleagues in this hemisphere, at Punta del Este.

We have always talked about how we could build together, how we could help each other, how we could help other nations achieve the cooperation and the great mutual respect that we have known between ourselves, Mexico and the United States.

We have built much together. In the years ahead, there is even much more remaining to be done. We must work along our border to improve beautification on public works, on jobs, on schools, on health, on the way that we treat our neighbor—whether he lives on one side of the border or the other side.

We must strengthen our trade ties and try to remove the remaining frictions that exist between us. We must look increasingly at our national economic problems to see how we can reinforce and how we can help each other.

So, I think meetings like this are very good because we can resolve here to press forward to move ahead and to move ahead together.

We are fortunate to share a continent and a common boundary. We share a common hope for our people and a common future.

I want to meet with your President later this year. At that time, we will do more than exchange pleasantries; we will review the progress that we have made together. I hope that we can see together what is happening along our border; not just the monuments of steel and cement such as Falcon and Amistad Dams but the monuments of friendship in the hearts of both of our peoples.

There is a new dimension of friendship that is born of the common trial in the floods of the lower Rio Grande Valley, and of hope, as your President and I raised our flags at Chamizal last October.

I appreciate so much getting a wire from you yesterday asking me to come by briefly to say a word to you. I hope your meeting here is fruitful in this great State of Hawaii, because Hawaii has much to teach all of us—and all the world—about the different races living together and living together in prosperity and in harmony.

The one big problem that faces all humankind, all three billion of us, is how can we learn to live together in prosperity and in

harmony, without friction and without war.

I say to my friends from across the border—and to my friends of Hawaii—we do so much appreciate all of you being here together and it has been a delightful chance for me to bring you my best wishes and to join with you in the prayer that is in the hearts of both of our countrymen, and for that matter, I think, people everywhere in the world.

Peace on earth, good will to men.

NOTE: The President spoke at 6:40 p.m. at Washington House in Honolulu, the official residence of Governor John A. Burns of Hawaii.

On the same day the White House released the text of a press pool report covering the reception. The report listed the 14 members of the United States delegation to the Interparliamentary Conference, chaired by Senator John Sparkman of Alabama.

200   Remarks at the Korean Consulate in Honolulu. *April 17, 1968*

Mr. Consul General Kim, President Park, ladies and gentlemen:

I am delighted to be able to join President Park on this occasion, not only because I share his pleasure in this meeting, but because this occasion tells us so much of our past and our future. Today we had a most pleasant and productive discussion.

When I say us, I mean all the peoples of the Pacific who are determined to live as independent nations and free human beings.

You Americans here tonight of Korean descent know that this State has demonstrated to the rest of our Union—and to the entire world, for that matter—that America's concern for human dignity reaches out across the Pacific as well as across the Altantic.

Our ties across the Pacific go back a long way—at least a century and a quarter—to the time when we became involved in China and then a little later in Japan. But it is only

in the past 27 years that we have learned that the destiny of the United States is—once and for all—bound up with the fate of the peoples of Asia and the Pacific.

Until the end of the Second World War, we in America gave little thought to the history and the problems of our neighbors in Korea.

Then, suddenly, we found ourselves caught up—as we have with many other peoples—in Korea's emergence from colonialism to independence.

Through no fault of their own, the people of Korea have had to bear more suffering and challenge than any other nation emerging from colonialism—with the possible exception of the people of Vietnam.

Together we have seen through a terrible war and a period of uncertainty and confusion. Together we have had the privilege of sharing in the adventure of a new nation moving forward in a miracle of progress.

These ties—these memories—are important. They are as much a part of our history as they are of Korea's.

But, equally important is the fact that this new nation and this free South Korea of whom President Park is the spokesman—and a very able one—is now helping to build a new structure of cooperation in Asia.

As we face now in Vietnam—hopefully—a movement from war to peace, I wish to tell all of you, my fellow citizens—and you, my dear friend, President Park—what I deeply believe.

I deeply believe that this Nation will continue to play its part in helping to protect and to develop the New Asia.

I deeply believe that my successor—whoever he may be—will act in ways that will reflect America's abiding interest in Asia's freedom and in Asia's security.

The commitments of America in Europe and Asia—all made by Congresses and Presidents before my administration—are color-blind. They run with the security of the Nation and with our basic human values. They will remain firm in the years ahead.

Because we know that peace among our neighbors of Asia is just as important to America as peace among our neighbors in Europe. Dignity, independence, and freedom are universal aspirations of men—east and west, north and south.

The days are long gone when Americans could say that Asians are not our kind of people. People who love peace and freedom—whatever their color or their religion or their national origin—are our kind of people. The fight against racism and bigotry knows no international dateline.

We wish to see Asia—like Europe—take an increasing responsibility for shaping its own destiny. And we intend and we mean to help it do so.

We look—eagerly, even impatiently—to the day when the real battle of Asia can be joined with all of our resources:

—the struggle against poverty and hunger, illiteracy and disease;

—to increase the supply of food and to assist those who are trying to plan the size of families;

—to exploit to the hilt the fantastic possibilities for developing the Mekong Valley, and all the other great conservation works of this continent.

In these works of peace the United States of America will take its fair share along with the other responsible nations of the industrial world.

And in their benefits and in their development all the nations of Southeast Asia should participate—not just our present allies—but North Vietnam and all human beings in that great region who long for freedom and dignity and liberty.

America will remain the friend and the ally and the partner of Europe.

But America will also remain the friend and the ally and the partner of free men in Asia.

This is my faith. This is my belief. This is my judgment.

I came here tonight to salute that great and gallant leader of the Korean people whose friends of Korean descent have gathered here, to say that we applaud your leadership, we admire your progress, and we in America feel that we are not only an Atlantic nation, but we are equally a Pacific nation.

In this part of the world, almost two-thirds of all humanity live. If that is what we are interested in—and that is all that really justifies our survival, a desire to better humanity—if that is what we are interested in, then it is going to take at least more than half of our efforts, and we pledge to you sincerely tonight those efforts.

Good night and God bless you.

NOTE: The President spoke at 7:30 p.m. at the Korean Consulate in Honolulu. In his opening words he referred to Consul General Se Won Kim and President Chung Hee Park of the Republic of Korea.

201   Joint Statement Following Discussions With President Park of Korea. *April 17, 1968*

AT THE INVITATION of President Lyndon B. Johnson of the United States, President Chung Hee Park of the Republic of Korea visited Honolulu on April 17 and 18 to exchange views on the current international situation and matters of common interest and mutual concern.

KOREAN SITUATION

The two Presidents reviewed in detail the serious threat to the security of the Republic of Korea and to peace in East Asia resulting from the increasingly belligerent and aggressive actions of the north Korean communists during the past eighteen months, including the attack directed at the official residence of the President of the Republic of Korea and the seizure of USS PUEBLO in international waters in January. They reviewed the plans of their two governments for dealing with the grave situation created by these north Korean acts of aggression. President Park expressed his deep sympathy for the families and relatives of the crew of the USS PUEBLO and sincerely hoped that they will soon regain their freedom from the hands of the north Korean communists.

The two Presidents agreed that further aggressive actions by the north Korean communists would constitute a most grave threat to peace. In that event, their two governments would immediately determine the action to be taken to meet this threat under the Mutual Defense Treaty between the United States and the Republic of Korea. In accordance with this Treaty President Johnson reaffirmed the readiness and determination of the United States to render prompt and effective assistance to repel armed attacks against the Republic of Korea.

President Johnson reaffirmed the adherence of his government to the Joint Policy Declaration which was signed on July 27, 1953 by the sixteen nations which supported the Republic of Korea during the Korean War.

The two Presidents reviewed the extraordinary measures which have been taken to strengthen Korean and American forces in the Republic of Korea. They agreed that these efforts should be continued in order that the Armed Forces of their countries would be able to deal effectively and swiftly with all contingencies in Korea.

The two Presidents recognized the need for strengthening security of the Republic of Korea as important not only for Korea but for the security of the general area. President Johnson recognized the need for continuing modernization of the armed forces of the Republic of Korea and the two Presidents reviewed the contribution which U.S. military assistance would make to such modernization and to the strengthening of the effective counter-infiltration programs which have already been developed by the Republic of Korea. They agreed that the first meeting between their respective Defense Ministries at ministerial level should be held in Washington in May to discuss and deliberate these matters further.

President Park outlined and discussed the various measures being taken by his government to ensure public safety and to thwart north Korean attempts at infiltration and sabotage. President Johnson expressed his satisfaction with and support for those measures, including the organization of the Homeland Reserve Force, which he felt were wise and farseeing.

President Johnson expressed his admiration for the rapid economic progress of the Republic of Korea, which has continued without pause despite the attempts of the north Korean regime to disrupt public order and confidence in the South. The two Presidents agreed that continued private investment from the United States and other friendly countries was desirable, and should be encouraged.

VIETNAM

The two Presidents reviewed in detail the situation in South Vietnam where Korean and American forces are fighting shoulder-to-shoulder to assist the Republic of Vietnam to defend against aggression and to assure the right of the South Vietnamese people to determine their own future without external interference or terrorist pressure.

The two Presidents noted the vigorous actions taken by the South Vietnamese Government to strengthen and increase its armed forces and to improve government effectiveness.

The two Presidents agreed that the common goal of an honorable and secure peace required the earnest pursuit of a diplomatic solution coupled with continued resolution and military firmness. They expressed the policy of their governments to sustain their efforts to meet the requirements of the struggle in all respects until peace is attained.

President Johnson reviewed the developments in the past two weeks, initiated by his decision—in consultation with the Republic of Vietnam and with the nations contributing military forces to its support—to reduce the area of bombing in North Vietnam. President Park expressed his satisfaction with these developments.

President Johnson explained in detail the current status of efforts to set a time and place for early contacts between American and North Vietnamese representatives. He reviewed with President Park the position that American representatives would take in contacts, reaffirming that the United States Government would continue to consult fully with the Republic of Korea and other allies concerning negotiating developments and positions to be taken on the allied side at each stage.

Looking forward to their common hope that serious talks on the substance of peace could begin in the near future, the two Presidents reaffirmed that the allied position would continue to be based on the Manila Communique of 1966.

The two Presidents also reaffirmed the position stated in the Seven-Nation Foreign Ministers Meeting of April 1967—that a settlement in Vietnam, to be enduring, must respect the wishes and aspirations of the Vietnamese people; that the Republic of Vietnam should be a full participant in any negotiations designed to bring about a settlement of the conflict; and that the allied nations which have helped to defend the Republic of Vietnam should participate in any settlement of the conflict.

ASIA AND THE PACIFIC

President Park highly commended the great role and persistent efforts of the United States to bring about freedom, peace and prosperity in Asia and the Pacific. He expressed his conviction that a continued United States presence in this region is essential to a just and lasting peace.

President Johnson expressed determination that the United States should continue its efforts for stability and security in the region, in accordance with the desires and aspirations of Asian peoples themselves.

In this regard, the two Presidents reaffirmed their commitment to the "Declaration on Peace and Progress in Asia and the Pacific" issued at the Summit Conference in Manila in October, 1966.

CONCLUSION

President Park expressed his deep appreciation to President Johnson and to the Governor and citizens of Hawaii for the warmth of their reception and for the many courtesies extended to him during the visit.

NOTE: The joint statement was released at Honolulu, Hawaii.

202 Statement by the President Upon Signing Bill Relating to Indemnity Payments for Law Enforcement Officers. *April 20, 1968*

TO HELP ENFORCE the laws of the United States, the Federal Government depends heavily upon 350,000 State and local police officers.

When these men pit their lives against the bank robber, the counterfeiter, or the kidnaper, they are enforcing Federal law. Sometimes, duty well-done and justice well-served results in their injury or death.

The sacrifices of these brave men are no less than those of Federal law enforcement officers, and it is only right that they and their families should have equal protection if tragedy should strike.

This bill gives that protection.

Should a local policeman be killed or injured while enforcing Federal law, it assures that he and his family will receive benefits at least equal to those the Federal Government provides for its own law enforcement officers.

Justice and progress demand that our Nation be safe for all our citizens.

Every community in America owes a daily debt to the policemen who safeguard our lives and property. I hope this enlightened and compassionate action of the Congress will stimulate State and local governments to review and increase their own indemnity payments, many of which are clearly inadequate.

This is an act of simple justice for policemen who offer their lives for the cause of American justice. I am proud that it will bear my signature.

NOTE: As enacted, the bill (H.R. 11816), approved April 19, 1968, is Public Law 90–291 (82 Stat. 98). The statement was released at Austin, Texas.

203 Remarks Upon Signing the District of Columbia Elected Board of Education Act. *April 22, 1968*

School Board members, City Council members, Members of the Congress, ladies and gentlemen:

Today, democracy comes a bit closer to reality here in our Nation's Capital.

Today, we meet here to give the citizens of the District of Columbia the right to elect their own school board.

In the process, we will put nine good men and women out of work. They have done a splendid job. But—as they know better than anyone—selection by Federal court is no substitute for election by the people.

Education in this city has long been the direct concern of the people. Now it becomes the people's direct responsibility.

This has been a momentous year for the District of Columbia.

We have installed a mayor and a city council in city hall. The new government is responding to the needs and the hopes of the people—in day-to-day operations, and in crisis as well.

With this legislation, we will restore another basic right of popular government— the right of people to help shape the education of their children.

But this right will be hollow unless it is given strength and substance by better education.

We want to make our Capital City a showcase for the entire Nation.

We want to make the schools in the District of Columbia not just places where our children are kept, but where they can fully prepare for life and for full citizenship in this country.

We want the schools to serve all the citizens of the community, young and old alike, and serve them all year round.

We want to make the schools of the National Capital models for all the rest of America to follow.

The bill I sign today will bring us part of the way.

Now we must sustain the momentum of that progress. So I ask the Congress to give the people of the District of Columbia:

—the $155 million in the District budget to run better schools, to pay teachers better salaries, to build more and better classrooms; and

—the special $10 million appropriation to begin a new program of model community schools.

Washington should become—in every sense—a model city. It must be a place where democracy is enshrined not only in monuments, but in the lives of its people.

The people must be given the right to elect their own representatives in the Congress of the United States.

The people must be given the most basic right of all—home rule.

For almost four decades, as a resident of this First City, I have looked to the day when these rights would become reality.

Someday they will be. Of that I am sure. I am glad today we are meeting here in the Fish Room to take another step toward making them so.

Thank you very much for coming.

NOTE: The President spoke at 5:32 p.m. in the Fish Room at the White House. As enacted, the bill (H.R. 13042) is Public Law 90–292 (82 Stat. 101).

204   Message to the Congress Transmitting Fifth Annual Report on Special International Exhibitions.   *April 23, 1968*

To the Congress of the United States:

I am pleased to transmit the Fifth Annual Report on Special International Exhibitions conducted during Fiscal Year 1967 under the Mutual Educational and Cultural Exchange Act of 1961.

These exhibitions help tell the story of America.

They enable America's economic, social and cultural achievements to be exhibited at leading international fairs and in other priority locations. They help build bridges of understanding between the United States and other countries.

Each exhibition shows how American accomplishments relate to the interests and capabilities of the host countries. Because these National Pavilions feature equipment and products of American industries, they also contribute to mutually profitable trade relationships.

Nearly 110 million people—primarily in Eastern Europe and the developing countries—have visited more than 190 of these exhibitions since this program began in 1954.

The following exhibitions were presented during the fiscal year 1967 period:

Trade Fair Exhibitions in Bulgaria, France, Ghana, Hungary, Poland, Thailand, the USSR, Yugoslavia and West Berlin covered a wide range of subjects in the fields of agriculture, industry, science, education, and space exploration.

"Expo 67", in Montreal, highlighted the United States Pavilion with its theme "Creative America." Daily attendance from opening day on April 28, 1967, until June 30, 1967 averaged 55,000 visitors.

Special "East-West" Exhibitions on "Hand Tools-USA" and "Industrial Design-USA" were shown in Moscow and five other cities of the USSR to an audience of more than one and a half million people.

Labor Missions and Exhibits, presented by the Department of Labor at trade fairs in Hungary, Poland, Thailand and Yugoslavia portrayed aspects of the American labor scene to priority audiences.

Trade Missions were organized by the Department of Commerce in twelve countries of Africa, Europe, Latin America and the Middle East.

As in previous years, hundreds of private American firms contributed machines, products, company executives and technicians to assist in carrying out this program.

All Americans are indebted to them for their help in conveying a better understanding of America to peoples of other nations.

LYNDON B. JOHNSON

The White House
April 23, 1968

NOTE: The report is entitled "Special International Exhibitions, Fifth Annual Report, July 1, 1966–June 30, 1967: Report of the United States Information Agency" (37 pp.).

205   Remarks at the Ratification of the Protocol of Amendments
      to the Charter of the Organization of American States.
      April 23, 1968

*Secretary Rusk, Secretary General Mora, Dr.
Sanz, distinguished Ambassadors, distinguished Members of the Congress, ladies and
gentlemen:*

Twenty years ago, our American Republics met in Bogotá to charter the Organization of American States. Our goal was to consolidate peace and solidarity among our nations in the Western Hemisphere.

Eight years ago, we broadened and deepened our commitment. With the Act of Bogotá and the Alliance for Progress, we joined forces to create a social and economic revolution on these continents.

It was 1 year ago that our countries went back to Punta del Este to review our progress—and to declare a new decade of urgency. For we found that, while we had achieved much in the 20 years and in the 8 years, the basic human problems still demanded many new commitments.

The program that we approved a year ago rested on three main pillars: more food, better education, and closer economic integration.

I asked you to come here this morning so I could tell you that we are encouraged by these beginnings:

—Last year Latin American farms produced food at twice the rate of new mouths to feed.
—Since Punta del Este, funds for education in Latin America have increased by more than 6 percent, to $2 billion.
—The Inter-American Development Bank has loaned $81 million in Latin America just to build new roads and industries and to increase electric power across national boundaries.

—Throughout Latin America manufacturing production has increased by about 7 percent.
—The Andean Development Corporation has joined together six nations—Bolivia, Chile, Colombia, Ecuador, Peru, and Venezuela—in a new step toward building a common market for all of Latin America.

Today, we take another step toward perfecting the OAS. The Charter amendments we ratify will streamline the political, economic, and cultural machinery of our organization. They will enable the OAS to meet its greatly increased responsibilities—and to meet them far more promptly and more efficiently.

Despite all that we have accomplished over these past two decades, no one knows better than those in this room how far we have yet to go.

As I said only a year ago at Punta del Este:

"The pace of change is not fast enough. It will remain too slow—unless you join your energies, your skills and commitments in a mighty effort that extends into the farthest reaches of this hemisphere.

"The time is now. The responsibility is ours."

I believe that we are moving forward in this hemisphere. The dimensions of poverty, ignorance, and disease to be overcome in our Americas are quite sobering—but they are not crushing. Our confidence in what the Alliance can and will do should spring from what has been done.

At Punta del Este my fellow Presidents and I called for a bold plan to overcome the physical barriers to Latin American unity. The Latin American countries have too long been isolated from each other. They have looked across the seas to Europe and the United States. They have neglected the sinews of transportation and communications which can bind together a continent—as happened here in the United States.

For example:

—The man in Lima, Peru, who wishes to talk to a man in Rio de Janeiro must do so through the telephone exchange in Miami or New York.

—The traveler from southern Brazil to Buenos Aires—roughly the same distance, I think, as from Boston to Washington—may take as much as 2 to 3 days for that route.

—Most of all, the nations throughout the continent have great natural resources which their neighbors cannot or do not use. Locked behind the high mountain ranges, deep rain forests, forbidding deserts that divide South America, we find fertile lands and many unknown resources.

Central America has already demonstrated what can be accomplished when such resources are made freely available by an interlocking system of roads and communications. Without these systems, the achievements of the Central American Common Market would have never been made possible.

The new frontiers of the South American heartland beckon to the daring and the determined. A start has already been made. I should like to cite three examples: A satellite for Latin America will be launched this fall, capable of bringing fast communications for the first time to the entire hemisphere. Chile, Panama, and Mexico will be the first to join the satellite network. Next year Argentina,

Brazil, Peru, and Venezuela will join the system.

The marginal highway on the eastern slopes of the Andes is opening a vast new frontier that is offering work and opportunities for hundreds who are living in crowded seaboard cities.

A large dam and powerplant is rising on the Acaray River between Paraguay and Brazil. It will bring electricity into thousands of homes and factories in three countries.

Now, these are just some of the illustrations of what can be done and what is being done. I believe the time is here and the time is now for us to prepare a plan, a specific blueprint for carrying forward this gigantic enterprise—an enterprise that is capable of uniting the continents with roads and river systems, with power grids and pipelines, and with transport and telephone communications.

In order to do this, I would suggest to my fellow Presidents and to those who direct our Alliance for Progress, that they establish a high-level task force, the finest collection of planners that we can bring together, under the leadership of a distinguished Latin American, to prepare a 5-year plan for speeding up the physical integration of our own hemisphere. I assure you that the United States will lend its full cooperation and support.

I am reminded of some famous words of Simón Bolívar to the leaders of his own day when he said:

"Do not forget that you are about to lay the foundations of a new people, which may some day rise to the heights that Nature has marked out for it, provided you make those foundations . . . ."

After almost a century and a half, we are still building the foundations of progress for all of the Americas. But I hope and I believe and I want us to be building them together.

This morning I would observe, let us continue in the spirit of Bolívar who dreamed of an America "sitting on the throne of liberty . . . showing the old world the majesty of the new."

Thank you very much.

NOTE: The President spoke at 11:30 a.m. in the East Room at the White House. In his opening words he referred to Dean Rusk, Secretary of State, José A. Mora, Secretary General of the Organization of American States, and Dr. Carlos Sanz de Santamaría, Chairman of the Inter-American Committee on the Alliance for Progress.

For the President's remarks of April 1967 at Punta del Este, see 1967 volume, this series, Book I, Item 176.

The text of the Protocol of Amendments to the Charter of the Organization of American States is printed in Senate Executive L (90th Cong., 1st sess.). On April 23, 1968, the White House Press Office released background information on the Protocol as follows:

BACKGROUND TO THE PROTOCOL OF AMENDMENTS TO CHARTER OF ORGANIZATION OF AMERICAN STATES

The Charter Amendments (which are the first to be adopted since the Charter was signed in 1948) provide needed streamlining of the Organization of American States. The Amendments modernize the machinery of the OAS. They grant certain fuller responsibilities, as in the field of peaceful settlement. They also incorporate the principles of the Alliance for Progress in the Charter.

Among the more significant changes called for by the Amendments are:

1. Replacement of the Inter-American Confer-

ence, which meets every 5 years, by a General Assembly, which will meet annually.

2. Redesignation of the OAS Council as the Permanent Council, and the granting of additional responsibilities to the Inter-American Economic and Social Council and the Inter-American Council for Education, Science, and Culture. The Economic and Cultural Councils become directly responsible to the General Assembly, as is the Permanent Council. These changes are designed to augment the importance given in the OAS structure to economic, social, educational, and scientific activities.

3. Elimination of the Inter-American Council of Jurists and the upgrading of the Inter-American Juridical Committee.

4. Assignment to the Permanent Council and its subsidiary body (the Inter-American Committee on Peaceful Settlement) a role in assisting member states in resolving disputes between them.

5. Incorporation of the Inter-American Commission on Human Rights in the OAS Charter.

6. Inclusion of a procedure for the admission of new members.

7. Election of the OAS Secretary General and Assistant Secretary General by the General Assembly for 5-year terms, rather than by the Council for 10-year terms, as presently provided.

8. Incorporation in the Charter of the principles of the Alliance for Progress in the form of expanded economic and social standards covering self help efforts and goals, cooperation and assistance in economic development, improvement of trade conditions for basic Latin American exports, economic integration, and principles of social justice and equal opportunity.

The Protocol of Amendments to the OAS Charter was signed at the Third Special Inter-American Conference in Buenos Aires on February 27, 1967. The Amendments will enter into force among the ratifying states when the Protocol has been ratified by two-thirds of the members. To date, Argentina, Guatemala, Mexico, and Paraguay have deposited their instruments of ratification.

206 Remarks Introducing Ambassador Edward Clark Following the OAS Charter Ceremony. *April 23, 1968*

I WANT to take advantage of this occasion to introduce all of you to a distinguished American who is with us this morning who will be playing, in the days ahead, a key role in our relations with Latin America.

The man whom I have reference to has just completed a tour of duty as our Ambas-

sador to Australia. As Ambassador to Australia, I believe that he learned and understood and knew more about the geography of that country, the resources of that country, and the people of that country and had more interest in them than, generally speaking, most ambassadors are able to display or to accumulate in that brief period.

He did such an outstanding job that when I gave thought to the selection of someone as United States Executive Director on the Inter-American Development Bank, someone whom I wanted to know the geography of Latin America, someone whom I wanted to know the resources of Latin America, someone whom I wanted to know the people of Latin America and to bring all three of these together in the way that the Inter-American Development Bank could play its major role and the United States of America could give its major contribution, I asked Ambassador Clark to take this assignment.

The Bank, as you know, is the financial cornerstone of our Alliance for Progress. In the first 7 years of its operation, it has authorized more than 450 loans totaling close to $2.5 billion. These loans have gone for water systems, schools, health stations, and huge dams and highways, satellite communi-cations, and many other activities.

That is why the Bank has earned the title of the Bank of the Alliance in integration.

While Ambassador Clark will be only one of many individuals who make up the personnel of that great institution, I feel sure that he will be an interested one and a very active one.

Last Friday the Senate confirmed Ambassador Clark's appointment to this Bank. It gives me a great deal of pleasure this morning to wish him well in this new assignment and to say to our friends in Latin America that I don't know of an individual in this country who, in my judgment, could or would or can or will display more interest in your problems or do more about helping you solve them.

Thank you very much.

NOTE: The President spoke at 11:52 a.m. in the East Room at the White House.

207   Message to the Senate on the International Coffee Agreement.   *April 23, 1968*

To the Senate of the United States:

A year ago this month, I met with the leaders of the American states in Punta del Este, Uruguay. In that historic meeting we reinforced the bonds of friendship that link this Nation with our 230 million neighbors to the South. We pledged to continue and extend hemisphere cooperation.

Today I recommend that the Senate renew and strengthen one of the most important economic agreements of our time—the International Coffee Agreement, which expires in September 1968.

The Coffee Agreement was born in 1962 as a first fulfillment of the Alliance for Progress. More than 60 nations joined together in that Agreement. President John F. Kennedy hailed it as "a heartening example of international cooperation to resolve a vitally important economic problem."

That problem, in its broad dimension, was to stabilize world coffee prices to benefit both the coffee producer and coffee consumer. For years, wide price swings had wasted the resources and hindered the growth of developing nations who depend so heavily on coffee exports.

Coffee is the economic lifeblood of more

than 40 developing nations—from plantations to small cooperatives, spanning Latin America, Africa and Asia. Second only to petroleum as a source of foreign exchange for developing countries, coffee exports yielded over $2.3 billion in 1966. These exports have helped to build schools, hospitals, factories and roads—the pillars of peace and progress. And they have provided the funds for the growing nations to buy the products of America's farms and industries.

America is a nation of coffee drinkers. We consume about half the supply of traded coffee. Our coffee industry is the world's largest. We must assure the American consumer all the coffee he wants at fair and reasonable prices.

The 1962 agreement—which the Senate ratified in 1963—has done the job of promoting price stability for coffee consumers and producers alike:

—Coffee import prices have been fair. They are almost 25 percent lower than the average price between 1953 and 1962, and 10 percent higher than during the world coffee slump of 1962.

—The sharp price fluctuations that plagued the world coffee market in past years have been avoided.

—Coffee consumers and roasters have been assured steady supplies at predictable and stable prices.

The 1968 agreement I propose will extend this record of success. It builds on the experience we have gained over the last several years by:

—Assuring that different types of coffee will be available at fair prices to meet changes in consumer tastes and preferences.

—Providing fair treatment in trade for all forms of coffee.

—Attacking the problem of coffee surpluses by production control and by creating a Diversification Fund to encourage shifts to other crops.

Woodrow Wilson once said that "the highest and best form of efficiency is the spontaneous cooperation of a free people." Nothing so embodies that philosophy as the International Coffee Agreement. It shows that large industrial nations and small developing nations—guided by the principles of self-help and harmony—can work together for the benefit of all.

That good work has been carried on for the past five years. Through the International Coffee Agreement the machinery of economic cooperation is now in place—tested over the years and now improved.

Without that machinery, we could return to the days of ruinous coffee price swings, disrupting the economies of many friendly nations, impairing world coffee trade, and endangering the continued flow of coffee at reasonable prices to the tables of American families.

I urge the Senate to give this instrument of international cooperation its early and favorable consideration.

The Secretary of State will shortly submit legislation to implement the agreement.

LYNDON B. JOHNSON

The White House
April 23, 1968

NOTE: The Agreement was favorably considered by the Senate on June 28, 1968, and after ratification entered into force provisionally on October 1, 1968. It was proclaimed by the President on November 18, 1968. The text is printed in Treaties and Other International Acts Series (TIAS 6584).

208 Statement by the President on the Administrative Conference of the United States. *April 24, 1968*

I AM DELIGHTED that the Administrative Conference is now fully organized and will hold its first plenary session next month. It is heartening that so many eminent private citizens will contribute their time and talent to this important endeavor. Through this Conference major improvements will be achieved in the processes of Government that vitally affect our citizens every day.

NOTE: The President's statement was made public as part of a White House release announcing the executive departments and independent agencies designated by the President for membership in the Administrative Conference of the United States.

The release stated that the Conference is the "new permanent forum established by Congress through which the Government agencies will work with representatives of the public to improve the processes by which they administer programs affecting private rights and interests." The release listed the 32 public members of the Administrative Conference as well as the 10 members of the Council of the Conference appointed by the President on February 7, 1968. The full text is printed in the Weekly Compilation of Presidential Documents (vol. 4, p. 703).

209 Remarks to a Group of United States Attorneys. *April 24, 1968*

Mr. Attorney General, Mr. Deputy Attorney General, Assistant Attorneys General, District Attorneys, ladies and gentlemen:

When we met together here a year ago, I appealed to you to make a very special effort. I have come back today to personally thank you for the credit you have brought to your Nation, the diligence you have brought to your job, and the great satisfaction that you have given your President.

I asked you to do everything that you could within the limitations of your office and your personnel to reduce your case loads. I am very grateful for your response.

I know that it is through long hours and hard work that you have reduced that load and chipped away substantially at that backlog.

I know that you feel as I do that we must not rest on our past performance because the problem of controlling crime and the problem of achieving justice is about as important a problem as we have in our Republic. We have a big job to do in the months ahead

and with your help, we are going to do it.

So, this afternoon, I wanted to ask you to make an even greater effort for your country, for your Attorney General, and for your President to try to clear your dockets this year. I ask this even though I am fully aware that your workload increases as the cause of justice is advanced.

I have asked the Congress, upon the urgent recommendation of your Attorney General, to extend to you more help. We have requested a 14 percent increase in the number of Assistant United States Attorneys.

This is the biggest increase that has ever been sought in any 1 year from the Congress. But never before in our 178-year history has the office of the United States Attorney been so burdened with such great responsibilities.

Only a few years ago, a United States Attorney would not be concerned with protection to the consumer or with the many aspects of civil rights, or with the major disorders in the streets.

But today, this Government has taken a stand and it has taken that stand against the sale of dangerous fabrics. It has taken a stand against the sale of unwholesome meat to our citizens.

It has dozens of laws on behalf of the consumer that have been passed that must be enforced and executed and dozens more that are now being considered.

The Government has said that no longer can a man be denied work because of the color of his skin, nor can he be denied his vote, either.

We have set our face against lawlessness, and with all of these commitments, it just means one thing—your workdays are longer and you are away from home a good deal more.

When riots flared in our cities recently, I know that some of you worked around the clock to keep yourselves, your Attorney General, and your President here in Washington fully informed.

I don't know whether you realize it or not, but I doubt that there are any individuals more responsible for the rather remarkable record, with thousands upon thousands upset and restless in the streets of the Nation—the big metropolitan areas—with dozens of thousands of troops there attempting to stop the burning and the looting and things of that nature. There was not one fatality as a result of a Federal gun.

I think a large part of that was due to the cool judgment, the wise counsel, the sober and able leadership of the Justice Department from the top to the bottom. And I am grateful for that.

Lives were spared. Lives were saved. We can rebuild property. We can replace the loss of money. But a life taken can never be restored.

In your districts, I think that you are the outstanding representatives of the Federal Government. As a representative, you have a very important function to perform for this majestic Government because you are the living symbols of the United States Government's dedication to what we like to refer to as justice in this country.

You are the living symbol of order under the law. So many people look to you, not only for advice and for counsel, but they emulate you and they learn from you—both by precept and example.

There will be some things in this administration that will not be remembered long. But if there is one thing that our children learn from our service here, I hope it is this: that I don't think there was ever a period when there were more dedicated people, more diligently discharging their duties, earnestly and genuinely seeking to do the greatest good for the greatest number.

For whatever progress we may have made, whatever semblance of justice that we may have brought about, we are deeply in the debt of those of you who have come here this afternoon.

I did not ask you to come here to try to stimulate you or try to inspire you. I just asked you to come here to let you know that we cared about you.

I see one or two of you out there whom I have been able to recognize and in a measure reward for your outstanding service by elevating you to one of the most precious honors that can come to a citizen—to become a member of the judiciary of this country.

The only thing that I regret is that I just don't have a judgeship for each of you because you deserve it.

You have been faithful to your trust and you have reflected credit on your President.

That is a good way of saying that you have served your country well.

Thank you so much.

NOTE: The President spoke at 5:10 p.m. in the East Room at the White House. In his opening words he referred to Attorney General Ramsey Clark and Deputy Attorney General Warren Christopher.

210 Remarks at a Democratic Party Dinner in Chicago. *April 24, 1968*

Mr. Chairman, Governor Kerner, Mr. Mayor, Dick Daley, Governor Shapiro, General Clark, Colonel Arvey, members of the delegation of Chicago—one of the finest delegations in all the Congress—my fellow Democrats, ladies and gentlemen:

First, on behalf of Mrs. Johnson and myself, I want to thank each and every one of you for this wonderful welcome. I never really realized that withdrawal pains could be so pleasant. For a minute, while you were standing there, I closed my eyes and I thought that I had leaped ahead of time to that other hall over by the stockyards. But then I remembered who I was—the President—not the Vice President, nor one of the Members of the Senate.

As we came in down here tonight, I saw four of your men out there shouting, with their placards. They were yelling "thief, scoundrel, and murderer" and some other ugly names that I cannot repeat to this audience.

My Secret Service detail, Mr. Mayor, and your Colonel Reilly both seemed to be slightly alarmed and I had to tell them that it was only—as nearly as I could judge—four out-of-town Democratic leaders working to unite the Party. Colonel Reilly readily assured all of us that they could not have been Chicago Democrats.

Mayor Daley, we are so glad that you asked us to come. All of you have honored us by asking us here tonight. I am so proud and so happy to share your honors and the great pride that you people of Chicago feel with your great mayor and my true and loyal friend for many years.

I not only want to thank Dick and Mrs. Daley and their wonderful family from the bottom of my heart, but Mrs. Johnson and I will always be grateful for the strength that their loyalty and their cooperation and their steadfastness have given us every step of the way—all these years, all along that lonely road.

Governor Kerner and Governor Shapiro, General Clark, I want to thank you, too. I want to explain that I came out here tonight to repay part of my debt. Mayor Daley extended this invitation to me last year. John Bailey, my beloved Chairman of the National Committee, renewed it several times. I promised to attend. When I make a promise, I try to keep it.

Now some Chicago newspapers have been wondering if there is any very special significance to my visit here tonight. But, as I told the mayor as we came up the steps, the answer to that is quite simple. Dick, I just do enjoy coming to party dinners because I used to be in politics myself.

I am here tonight to speak, not as a fellow Democrat, but to speak to you as a fellow American. I have come to talk to you about the tests of our times—and the trust of our parties.

For more than 100 years, both of our parties—Democratic and Republican—have drawn enduring strength from leaders who have known the shores of these lakes and who have walked the grass of these Middle

Western plains.

In a time of danger and division for America, it was from the prairies of Illinois that the Nation heard the counsel of unity and compassion from the strong Republican voice of Abraham Lincoln.

In our times—when danger confronted us and confronted all mankind—it was from these same prairies that we and the world were inspired by the counsel of sanity and good sense—from the brave and eloquent and wise Democratic heart of Adlai Stevenson.

In this vital year, as we approach our national decisions together, I believe that the example of such men from the heart of America must be the example that governs America's head.

When this Republic was born, Thomas Jefferson looked about at the energy and the creativity that stirred among the people in the first years of our freedom. He was excited and he was inspired at what he saw. He wrote to a friend. He said, "It is like a new time."

He could have been writing about our own day.

No man could serve where I have served now for more than 4 years and 5 long months—in this great office of all the people—without sensing that we are once again in "a new time."

Yes, there are fears and doubts and suspicions and questions.

There are young men and women wondering if there is a place for them in a world that they did not make—in a world that they deeply yearn to make far better than they think it is.

There are mothers and fathers in every land and I am one of those fathers and she is one of those mothers—who despise war as their children despise it.

I will devote all of my days and all of my powers and all of my energies to winning the peace that is the prayer of every single American family.

There are men and women, boys and girls, whose souls rage each day against the bare walls and the bleak windows of their lives—where the sunlight of hope seldom ever shines.

But the story of our land—America, the beautiful—the story of our times—the United States of America—is not a dismal story of wrongs without end. Here—here in America, as nowhere else since time began, we are striving eagerly to let the sunlight shine upon all of our people. Because that is what America is all about.

Step by step, year by year, we are moving out of the darkness and out of the shadows, out into a new day of light and justice for all of our people.

True, our society does still bear burdens and scars from times long before any of us were born. We cannot correct the injustice of centuries in a matter of hours or days or months. But we are on our way and we have acted to relieve those burdens and to heal those wounds. Nowhere else—in no other society on this earth—are so many so devoted to leaving this earth better than they found it.

I ask you, is there anyone in the room tonight who would trade where you are for where you were when you discovered this land? [Audience: No.]

It is this purpose that is throbbing through our Republic tonight. It must be served. With God's help, it will be served.

The progress of America is the achievement of a nation that is unified: not a nation in lockstep, not a nation where all men must think alike or act alike or vote alike—but a nation in which the labors and the talents of the people make common cause toward common goals.

Our parties and our politics must ever

serve this purpose. They must never be permitted to divide or to divert us from the goal of one America.

In saying this to you, my friends, tonight, I am only repeating the wisdom and the warnings of great Americans throughout all of our history. From the first days of the Republic to our times, the leaders who have loved America have warned continuously against the divisive spirit of faction and special interests. Every generation of Americans has had to heed that warning.

However strong we may be, however prosperous we are, however just its purposes or however noble its causes, no nation can long endure when citizen is turned against citizen—when class is turned against class—when cause is turned against cause—and race against race—and section against section—and generation against generation—by the mean and the selfish spirit of partisanship.

The decisions that we must make this year are among the most vitally important decisions that Americans have ever been called upon to make. Perhaps more than at any time in all of our past, we shall be choosing our future—and we shall be choosing the future of our children.

The trial of our course and our wisdom will continue far beyond the terrible ordeal of Vietnam.

The test of our compassion will continue long after the ordeal of our great cities.

Through all the ten thousand tomorrows of this century, the generations of Americans who are living now—and those who will live later—will awake each morning into a new world. In that new world, each day may bring challenge—and I hope each hour will bring promise.

If the challenges are to be met—if the promises are to be realized—then America's political parties must become the guardians of all the people.

America will not be served by parties which only serve—or refuse to serve—those in business, or those in labor, or those in agriculture, or those in a specific minority, or those in the cities, or those of one race, or one heritage, or one faith. We can and we must move on the broad highway toward greatness as a nation only if the parties themselves are broad and open, receptive to all, and always responsive to all of the people.

Our politics today is changed—and it is changing. Our issues are new. Our alignments are new. Our styles are new. Our slogans are new. And all of this is good—for it reflects and it serves the changes that are being wrought by America's own advances in the world. But the purpose of our politics is not changed, and it must not change—for that purpose is to serve the unity of all of our people all of the time.

In this time—and at this place—here in this great city of Chicago—with the presence of these devoted leaders, it is fitting to recall the words of one of our great American leaders, Abraham Lincoln, when he spoke 110 years ago in a small Illinois town. He was then referring to the authors of our Declaration of Independence. Abraham Lincoln had this to say:

"Wise statesmen as they were, they knew the tendency of prosperity to breed tyrants, and so they established these great self-evident truths, that when in the distant future some man, some faction, some interest, should set up the doctrine that none but rich men, or none but white men, were entitled to life, liberty and the pursuit of happiness, their posterity might look up again to the Declaration of Independence and take courage to renew the battle which their fathers began. . . ."

So, not as partisans, not as Democrats, and not as Republicans, but only and always as Americans let us look to the good that has been wrought. Let us look to the victories that have been won for all of our people. Let us look at how far we have come and how far we must go. Let us look at the progress that our grandfathers and our fathers have made since they came to these shores. Let us look to the advances that we have made together in unity and in understanding and let us, too, take courage—to renew, and to sustain, that battle which our fathers began.

When I talked to the mayor late this afternoon and he asked me again to reconsider, I told him that I had been engaged the last several days in a complete reassessment of my own personal situation. I have come to the conclusion that I stood today just where I stood last year when he first invited me. I told him I would be here.

NOTE: The President spoke at 9:14 p.m. at the Conrad Hilton Hotel in Chicago. In his opening words he referred to John M. Bailey, Chairman of the Democratic National Committee, Otto Kerner, Governor of Illinois, Richard J. Daley, Mayor of Chicago, Samuel H. Shapiro, Lieutenant Governor of Illinois, William G. Clark, Attorney General of Illinois, and Col. Jacob M. Arvey, Democratic National Committeeman from Illinois. Later he referred to Col. John Reilly, Director of Public Events for the city of Chicago.

211   Remarks of Welcome at the White House to King Olav V of Norway. *April 25, 1968*

His Majesty, Secretary Rusk, distinguished guests, ladies and gentlemen:

It has been said that America is the half-brother of the world.

And certainly that is true, Your Majesty, of Norway and Norwegians. There are almost as many Norwegian Americans as there are Norwegians in your own country.

Here in our country, Americans of Norwegian descent number more than 3 million. They include many of our most distinguished Americans, our very able Vice President among them.

Your Majesty, it was just 21 years ago that President Truman spelled out America's family relationship with Europe.

1947 was the year of the Truman Doctrine and the Marshall Plan. It was also the year that postwar isolationism in the United States was finally buried. President Truman understood the implications of America's involvement in European affairs. He said:

"This is a serious course upon which we embark.

"I would not recommend it except that the alternative is much more serious."

Today there is no doubt that Europe is once again a very vital and prospering center of the world. There should also be no doubt that the United States remains as closely bound to our North Atlantic partners— closely joined in common history, culture, ideals, and endeavors.

The real question today is not whether America and Europe are still partners. Of course we are partners. But the real question is, what will we be partners for?

President Truman said back there in 1947, ". . . we must assist free peoples to work out their own destinies in their own ways."

If there is evidence anywhere in the world today that a small, free nation can become a great and creative and independent nation, that example is surely to be found in your country—Norway.

I believe that Americans and Europeans must rededicate themselves to the purposes of partnership that united us and has united us for 21 years.

The original concepts of the Truman

Doctrine and the Marshall Plan are valid today, as we stand here. They are valid all over the world.

So, working together, I think there is nothing that we cannot do together. We can make every continent of this world a better and safer place for the children and the grandchildren of our world. We can better humanity wherever humanity exists.

It will not be easy. It will take us decades. It will require energy and talent and resources and treasure.

But as President Truman so wisely and courageously observed, the alternative is harder to accept.

Your Majesty, we celebrate the joint efforts of our past. We look forward to future cooperation for human dignity. I welcome you to America as an old friend of this country.

I thank you again on behalf of Mrs. Johnson and myself for the cordiality with which your people received us and for the warm exchanges we had in your country in our most pleasant visits with you.

We are so happy to have you in our country. The sunshine now is coming out to welcome you.

NOTE: The President spoke at 10:36 a.m. on the South Lawn at the White House where His Majesty was given a formal welcome with full military honors. In his opening words the President also referred to Secretary of State Dean Rusk. King Olav responded as follows:

Mr. President, Mrs. Johnson, ladies and gentlemen:

I would like to thank you for the very warm and friendly words which you have just directed to my country and to myself. I accept these kind words as a token of the exceptionally close relationship and strong sense of community which have for so many years existed between our two nations.

Let me in my turn tell you how happy I am to be here and to bring greetings from Norway to you, Mr. President, and to the people of America.

The strong friendship and admiration which we Norwegians feel towards the American people is indeed deep rooted. These sentiments go all the way back to the great American Revolution when Norwegians, themselves a dependent nation at that time, came to regard this new union of the 13 States on the other side of the Atlantic as an inspiring example and as a bold people's exercise of self-determination in the ideals of freedom and of human rights.

To the initial feeling of admiration was added the new sense of kinship and community based on the thousands of family bonds when, during the 19th century, more than half a million Norwegians came to this country to build a new future and make their contribution to the growth of the American Nation and to the development of the United States.

Needless to say, I am today looking forward with expectation and pride to meet again a great number of their descendants during my trip across this vast continent.

During the Second World War, when our two countries became allies, a new fundamental dimension was added to Norwegian-American relations. The rise of the United States of America to what it represents today has indeed been a great and breathtaking adventure.

But hardly in any period of this great Nation's history has there been so many dramatic events and such an unparalleled progress and affluence as the three decades which have lapsed since I, as Crown Prince of Norway, toured this country for more than 2 months.

I am, therefore, deeply grateful, Mr. President, for your kind invitation to revisit the United States, to renew my acquaintances with you personally and with other distinguished leaders of this great Nation and to take stock of the tremendous developments in all fields of human endeavor which have taken place here since my first visit.

Thank you, Mr. President.

212   Remarks to Members of the Organization of Administrative Assistants to Democratic Members of Congress. *April 25, 1968*

Mr. Chairman, Mr. Speaker, Mr. Leader, Members of the Congress, and members of the Burro Club:

In a very real sense, it is good to be back home again—even if only for a brief visit. As your Chairman has told you, in this room some 35 years ago, I won my first political victory on Capitol Hill. I was elected Speaker of the "Little Congress"—an organization very similar to yours. And it was an upset.

On the way up here, I read an article that Gould Lincoln wrote in the Washington Star, on April 28, 1933. It is headed "Progressives Put Over New Slate in Election Drive, 'Little Congress' Upset." I guess they have been upset ever since.

But it was a combination of Democrats and farm labor members. We have had some combinations like that since.

We pledged ourselves to be always mindful of the forgotten man. We said, "The election will mark a New Deal for all 'Little Congresses' that everyone—regardless of party affiliation—will receive fair, equal treatment from the Chair; committees will be named on an equitable basis of membership and seniority."

So even then, we were not deep partisans, although we were rather visionary progressives—I must admit.

The Chicago Tribune did not claim that my opponents had won before the votes were counted. But it was—I must admit—a surprise to most members of the club, including myself, when we came out on top.

We have a far more crucial election coming up this November. As you know, I have announced that I will not seek or accept our Party's nomination, but that does not mean that I am just going to be an uninterested or passive bystander.

I have a philosophy which I want to discuss with you very briefly. I picked from some of the citations—the honorary degrees that have come to men in public life—a citation from a New England university, a great university—Brown University in Rhode Island.

When they awarded me a doctor's degree back some 10 years ago in 1959—when I was

connected with the legislative branch of the Government and we had a Republican President—the president of that New England university and that faculty prepared this citation. I have always prized it very highly, coming from where it did, the section it did, the people it did, and the quality of the school.

It said: "When the Executive and the Legislature are divided, anything or nothing can happen. As Majority Leader of the Senate, you have used your political strength in the national interest to make it possible for the moderates of both Parties to join with you to do the possible and to seek the best. Your skill as a politician has been notable, but you have subordinated politics to national interest, the service for which you will best be remembered."

I would hope certainly that that is true. But this year I think that I could not be uninterested—not when the record that you and I have helped to make is going to be put before the country.

I believe that you know, and that our children will know, and all history will know, that that is an unparalleled record. I can't go over the hundreds of measures that we have been talking about for generations that we have been doing something about the last 4 years, but I do want to hit some of the highlights.

In 1964, I had reviewed the campaign speeches of all of our Presidents and the documents in our offices of the President's messages. All of our Presidents had been concerned with the poor—but it was your Congress that did something about it and passed the War on Poverty Act, the first time that poverty had been recognized as a legislative enactment by itself.

The broadest civil rights laws of the century were passed. Abraham Lincoln, 100 years ago, issued the Emancipation Proclamation—but it was a proclamation, not a fact. And we have made them facts—in voting; there are a million more people voting who never voted before because of our Voting Rights Act. Because of our Accommodations Act, all people can sit at tables in public dining rooms and can have rooms and public accommodations in hotels.

And now the most difficult of them all—the equal housing—which we have just signed.

President Truman pledged to the people of this country that he would recognize "Honor thy father and thy mother and their days would be long on the earth" by passing Medicare.

We talked about it in campaign speeches for more than 20 long years—but you voted it.

And you members of the Burro Club had to stand up and persuade some of your own members to quit shimmying.

I remember one of the most difficult jobs I ever did when I was a secretary was to get a certain Congressman to vote for the Social Security Act. He really thought that it was socialism. And so many people thought that way—as they did about Medicare.

I remember walking down the streets of my town as a Member of Congress after President Truman had made the suggestion. There wasn't a doctor in the whole area who would hardly speak to me; we were socially ostracized. But anyone who is against Medicare today would be ostracized. I can't find anyone who doesn't approve of Medicare.

We had a pioneer program of Federal aid to education. Federal aid and Federal control were very ugly words for years. They were ugly when I came in to be President.

The B'nai B'rith invited me to be their principal speaker. They gave me a big award; it glorified my achievements. I was proud and I came home and talked to Lady Bird and my daughters about what a generous thing it was to do.

But I picked up the paper the next afternoon and they had passed a resolution on my Federal aid to education bill.

I do know that centuries from now, people will point to what this Congress did when it passed 18 major educational measures in the past 4 years—and 26 major health measures that are enduring; more than have been passed in all the Congresses combined.

I know you are proud of that record—model cities, auto safety. The first minimum wage I voted on was 25 cents an hour; we passed one for $1.60—some little difference.

We have new protection for consumers. We have meat inspection and product safety and flammable fabrics.

And over the years, we have the greatest achievements in conservation—even since the Teddy Roosevelt-Gifford Pinchot days—with more parks and more seashores open to more people than ever before in our history.

During this period, we have actually put more land back in the public domain than we have taken out, and including the interstate highway system and the freeways, that is saying something.

You members of the Burro Club helped write that record. You did it just as surely as you cast the votes that passed the bills or if you had signed the law as the President did.

Anyone who has spent any time on Capitol Hill knows the vital role that an assistant plays in the legislative process. When I came here they told me no Congressman was any better than his secretary. That was before we called them administrative assistants and special assistants.

This record I just talked to you about is a Democratic record. But it was not achieved at all by bitter partisanship. It wasn't written by men who cared more for party label than they did for public interest. The secret of our success, I think, as a party, lies in our belief that serving the people and meeting their needs without concern for any narrow ideology or any special interest is really the only criteria and the only standard of good government.

Now, that has been my personal philosophy. Many years ago, when I served as Majority Leader, I remember saying that our political philosophies are the sum of our life experiences. They cannot be squeezed into any one- or two-word label that you hang around your neck. They should not sacrifice the life and blood of individuality by any sterile dogma or any canned definition.

Ten years ago I was writing an article on my philosophy when I was a Member of the Senate. That article was published in the Texas Quarterly, a magazine of the University of Texas, where I hope to teach and lecture some before long. Some of you here in this room may remember that article. The rest of you may find something of value in it for your own public lives.

I want to repeat part of it today because it has been my basic faith throughout the years. I said in that article what I said the other night in my March 31st speech. "I am a free man first; an American second; a United States Senator third; and a Democrat fourth—in that order."

I described the roots of my personal faith, the first principles of my public philosophy. Here is the way I described them: "First, every American has something to say and under our system he has a right to an audience." And plenty of them had it under my administration—I can assure you.

"Second, there is always a national answer to each national problem.

"Third, achievement of the full potential of our resources, physical, human and otherwise, is the highest purpose of government policies—next to the protection of those rights

that we regard as inalienable.

"Fourth, that waste is the continuing enemy of our society and the prevention of waste—waste of resources, waste of lives, waste of opportunity—is the most dynamic of the responsibilities of our government."

Now, these were very simple personal beliefs. They were expressed 10 years ago. But they are my beliefs and they were not adopted from some textbook and they were not adopted from some other man. They have grown with me and they have stayed with me during the years I was a member of the "Little Congress" and its Speaker. They have been with me for almost 60 years now. I can tell you that these beliefs have strengthened me and they have sustained me. And they have led me to one fundamental conviction and I put that down in that article. This is what it said:

"The Congress reaches a very dubious decision when its choices are made solely by head counts of a partisan division. I do not believe that we have arrived at any answer until we have truly found the national answer—the answer that all reasonable men can agree upon.

"Our work is not done until that answer is found, even if the process requires years of our lives."

I remember a great Speaker of that body whom Speaker McCormack and I worked closely with for years. He said to me one time that the thing he was so proud of our Party for was that we do not hate their Presidents. Just because they are not members of our Party, we don't go around hating their Presidents.

Last night I spoke to a gathering in Chicago. I took along with me an excerpt from a statement that I made back in 1953 when our Party was rather disorganized and we had just had a great war hero elected to office and we had been turned out of power.

As a very young man I had become a leader of the Senate Democrats because I think no one else over there who had been around long enough would want the job.

It was the afternoon of January 2, given to the Democratic Conference of the Senate. I said: "My colleagues, we are now in the minority. I have never agreed with the statement that it is the business of the opposition to oppose." That was a very famous statement attributed to a very famous American who was then the Majority Leader whose name was Robert Taft. He said: "It is the business of the opposition to oppose."

I said I did not agree with that statement. "I do not believe the American people have sent us here merely to obstruct. I believe we are here to fight for a positive program, a program geared not to opposing the majority, but to serving America. I think that is the real desire of every good Democrat, even though he may disagree as to methods.

"So, working together, I think we can do more than preserve the gains of the past 20 years that we have legislated. I think we can go forward today, even though we are in the minority, with a positive program—a program that is pro-American and not anti-Republican. If we go forward as positive Americans and not negative oppositionists I am convinced that the time is not too far distant when the Democratic Party will again be in the majority."

Two years later, we were in the majority in the Congress. And we kept that majority for 6 years of that 8-year Republican administration because of that philosophy. We have elected two Democratic Presidents since that philosophy was expressed.

If we continue to act on those beliefs—if we will continue to act in that atmosphere—elections will take care of themselves, the Democratic Party will remain in the majority, our national challenges will be faced, our

national answers will be found, and the American people will prosper and the world will share in the new blessings that we could achieve by unity.

You and I and the Democratic candidate will be taking that faith to the country again this year. I made my announcement and one of the most motivating reasons for that announcement was that no one in the world—no one who sought our treasure or tried to stall freedom—could have any doubt that any person in this country—candidate or non-candidate—could effectively pressure this President and his actions for at least the next 9 months; that we were going to be above and beyond any petty, mean, personal, selfish, partisan action or any cowardly action, because I honestly believe that there are those in the world who would not hesitate to take advantage of any weakness in our system that they could detect or any differences that they could exploit.

So, I would hope that I could remove myself from the nose cone of a volcano, where I could act independently and with complete liberty, with only one criteria—the greatest good for the greatest number and providing a national answer to a national problem and an international answer to an international condition. And that is what we propose to do.

I would hope that you would not be personally critical or that you would not be vituperative or you would not hate or you would not descend to the level of narrowness or selfishness or trying to carry out a burning personal ambition for ambition's sake only.

I hope that we can unite around the standards that I have expressed today and I would hope that we can hold them high, because I genuinely believe that if we do, the voters will respond to them as they have in seven out of the last nine Presidential elections since 1932 and in 16 out of the 18 congressional elections in the same period.

With that record, and with that faith, I have not the slightest doubt—not the slightest doubt—that any would be divisive force will ever make any serious inroads in this country.

I would conclude only by saying this: That the longer you live, the more you learn. But what I am saying now, I knew when I came here—that there are no more dedicated people in the rice paddies of Vietnam or patrolling the DMZ in Korea, or protecting freedom in Germany at this hour than the men and women who serve this Government, particularly those who serve this Congress. Your Speaker and your Majority Leader are examples of highest patriotism, greatest intellect, absolute complete integrity and confidence.

But most of all, their every act—their every test—has been the greatest good for the greatest number of people.

That is why we are all here, actually. The Good Lord put us here to better humanity. Otherwise there is no excuse for us. I hope that the Democratic Party—not as Democrats, not as sectionalists, not as regionalists, not as members of any church or any race—but as human beings, will never forget that they are free men first; that they are Americans second; that they are agents of the public—public servants third; and Democrats fourth—but always in that order.

If we do what is best for America, don't you ever have the slightest doubt that America will do what is best for you.

Thank you.

THE CHAIRMAN. Mr. President, we have those clippings you mentioned in your speech that were made 35 years ago when you were elected Speaker of the "Little Congress" in a frame.

We deeply appreciate your coming to visit with us. We think you are a great American. We are proud of you—and most of us wish you were running.

THE PRESIDENT. Apropos to what the chairman has just said, I want to repeat what I said in Chicago last night. I said one of the men in the White House Press Corps said, "Mr. President, why are you going to a Party dinner in Chicago?"

I said, "Because I like to go to Party dinners, and I used to be in politics myself."

NOTE: The President spoke at 1:40 p.m. at a luncheon meeting of the Burro Club, whose members serve as administrative assistants to Democratic Members of Congress. The luncheon was held in the Cannon House Office Building on Capitol Hill. In his opening words the President referred to J. Richard Sewell, President of the Club, Representative John W. McCormack of Massachusetts, Speaker of the House of Representatives, and Representative Carl Albert of Oklahoma, House Majority Leader.

The occasion marked the 35th anniversary of the President's election as Speaker of the "Little Congress" when he was secretary to Representative Richard M. Kleberg of Texas in 1933.

As printed above, this item follows the text released by the White House Press Office.

213   The President's News Conference of *April 25, 1968*

UNITED STATES REPRESENTATIVE TO THE UNITED NATIONS

THE PRESIDENT. [1.] I have today accepted with regret the resignation of Arthur Goldberg as U.S. Representative to the United Nations. Ambassador Goldberg has expressed to me his desire to leave this position for personal reasons. He will continue at the United Nations, probably until around the early part of June, while certain matters that he now has underway are being handled and disposed of.

Ambassador Goldberg has, in conversations over the last several months, assured me that he would be available to the Government to consult and help out with any problems that we might feel he was equipped to help us handle.

To replace Ambassador Goldberg, I am appointing the Honorable George Ball. He is a distinguished public servant who has held many important positions—including Under Secretary of State—and who serves me unofficially in many advisory capacities at the present time.

Mr. Ball will be available to take over when Mr. Goldberg leaves. We anticipate a smooth transition.

I will answer questions if you have any.

QUESTIONS

COMMUNICATION WITH HANOI

[2.] Q. What do you hear from Hanoi?

THE PRESIDENT. I have no comment. I have nothing new really to add to what you have been told in the official briefing.

AMBASSADOR GOLDBERG'S PLANS

[3.] Q. Mr. President, has Ambassador Goldberg informed you as to what his future plans are? Is he going into private law practice?

THE PRESIDENT. Ambassador Goldberg will have a statement, I think, later in the day. That is a matter for him to handle.

TAX INCREASE

[4.] Q. Are prospects for a tax increase improving?[1] How do you see that, Mr. President?

THE PRESIDENT. I am unable to evaluate them. If I remember, you had a tip or two from up there before. You may get that information there better than we can.

Our position is the same; there has been no change in it. We would like very much to see the Congress act upon the recommendation we have made. The tax proposal is still in the committee.

I would say the members of the committee are better able to tell you about what action they might take or whether they will take any than I am.

THE PRESIDENT'S PLANS

[5.] Q. Mr. President, the reports on the Hill are that you told them at lunch today what you are going to do next year. Can you tell us?

THE PRESIDENT. The meeting today was off the record. I told Tom [2] to check with them and if they have no objection, I don't have any objection to releasing portions of that statement that might be of interest to you. I didn't tell them anything that you haven't already known for a long, long time—so don't feel sorry for yourselves.

Q. Did you tell them you were going back to Texas to teach at the university?

---

[1] The Revenue and Expenditure Control Act of 1968 was approved by the President on June 28, 1968 (see Item 343).

[2] Wyatt Thomas Johnson, Jr., Assistant Press Secretary to the President.

THE PRESIDENT. I will give you the transcript.[3]

ARTHUR KRIM

[6.] Q. What are your plans for Arthur Krim?[4]

THE PRESIDENT. I will make that announcement in due time.

MILITARY SITUATION IN VIETNAM

[7.] Q. Sir, can you give us any new advice on the military situation in Vietnam? There have been conflicting reports out of the Embassy in Saigon about what is happening. Can you give us something more authoritative?

THE PRESIDENT. I don't think so. You have reporters out there. The information I have available to me is not much different from what you have. I don't know what conflicts you are talking about.

Q. Stories about an impending attack and then reports to the contrary.

THE PRESIDENT. We do have reports like that.

SECRETARY OF STATE RUSK

[8.] Q. You have seen the Secretary of State more often than you usually do in the past 36 or 48 hours. Would you tell us what has been the subject of these conversations?

THE PRESIDENT. First, I would deny that that is true. Secondly, we had our regular Tuesday meeting and we talked then, as we do at most of our meetings, about world conditions and matters that relate to his Department and to my duties here.

We had a Security Council meeting yesterday. I see and talk to the Secretary of State practically every day, so I would not agree with your premise.

Q. I was thinking especially about the 5:30 meeting yesterday. That was not unusual?

THE PRESIDENT. No, not at all, nor is 4:30 in the evening or 8:30. There is nothing different about that; I often see him several times a day.

Q. Was Ambassador Goldberg in that meeting yesterday afternoon with the Secretary?

THE PRESIDENT. I don't ever discuss off-the-record meetings. I have a long-standing rule that I keep a man's confidence. If a meeting is set up as off the record, I keep it that way. I cannot be responsible for what other people may say. You won't find me discussing any off-the-record appointments I have.

ACTION IN CIVIL DISORDERS

[9.] Q. In view of the efforts your administration has made during the winter to avoid personal injury and death in civil disorders that might occur in the cities, could you give us your view on whether or not city police ought to shoot at looters?

THE PRESIDENT. I have made a statement that expresses my view. It is in writing and has been distributed to you. I suggest that you read it.[5]

Richard McGowan, New York Daily News: Thank you.

NOTE: President Johnson's one hundred and twenty-fourth news conference was held in his office at the White House at 4:15 p.m. on Thursday, April 25, 1968. As printed above, this item follows the text of the Official White House Transcript.

---

[3] See Item 212.
[4] Arthur B. Krim, former treasurer of the Democratic National Committee.

[5] See Item 209.

214   Toasts of the President and King Olav V of Norway. *April 25, 1968*

Your Majesty, Vice President and Mrs. Humphrey, distinguished guests, ladies and gentlemen:

Neither the man nor the nation nor the traditions that we salute this evening, are strangers to America. The man and his family have been here before. The nation is one of the great nations that helped make America. The traditions have influenced our own.

Still, this is the first time that a reigning Norwegian monarch has visited here. This gives us a very special occasion to express the gratitude, as well as the admiration, that has been in all of our hearts so long.

Last night I went to dinner in Chicago with 7,800 politicians and partisans. Tonight I dine with a King. There, Your Majesty, is democracy—with a little "d." It is really a wonderful system when the President of our country, in an election year, can attend two consecutive dinners on two consecutive nights and deliver two nonpolitical speeches.

You don't know how grateful I am because I do need the practice.

I think I must also say that I very much envy our distinguished guest. He is that rarest of all visitors to this house—a man who is nonpolitical by law. I think some of you might suspect the very special pleasure that we had in meeting today, how much of common interest that we had to talk about—just the two of us nonpoliticians.

Sitting there in the White House listening to His Majesty, I began thinking of the life of kings. Then I got some ideas about my own retirement plans. I have not forgotten that the kind people of a small South Pacific island once upon a time offered me their throne. But perhaps I might just as well for-get it now because someone might say that I was thinking of establishing the 51st State and planning to crown everything with the "comeback."

Your Majesty, our admiration for Norway has never been more substantial than it is now. As you may know, sir, I come from a section of our country known for its modest restraint in describing its own merit. I know you will observe that when you visit us in the days ahead.

But I must admit that even I am in total awe of your modesty and your restraint. I know that if I could speak for Norway following the Winter Olympics, I don't think that I could ever stop talking about it. However, what transpired during the Winter Olympics was really not out of character for Norwegians. The world has always admired the courage and the ability and the hearty endurance of the people of Norway. Their courage during the dark days of World War II is legendary. Their ability as artists and statesmen is no less so.

Let us remember that Norway was the home of Ibsen, Grieg, and more recently of Trygve Lie.

The sons of Norway endured in the bitter winds of the open prairie to find a new prosperity in our own land and to give new strength to our own society.

One of the sons of Norway in America, Hubert Humphrey, has shown all of these qualities. They have already led him to the second highest office in this land.

Your Majesty, Americans know that Norway is a friend of dignity all around the world. We know that Norwegians have built a fine life at home that is based on freedom and based on equality.

We celebrate the fact that Norway and the

United States are allied in the causes of peace and the causes of progress. We work together in the United Nations, at Geneva, at the OECD in Paris, and in many other major international forums. In the Atlantic Alliance, Norway stands courageously on NATO's northern flank.

Your Majesty, you mentioned to me this morning that we share a sense of community—and that is so. I know that you will feel at home as you visit throughout our country in the weeks ahead. And we are so pleased that you could come here and spend some time with us.

I believe that your presence will further intensify that sense of community of which you spoke.

Ladies and gentlemen, I would like to ask you to join me in a toast to His Majesty, the King of Norway, to the people of Norway, and always to the Norwegian-American enduring friendship.

NOTE: The President spoke at 10:09 p.m. in the State Dining Room at the White House. In his opening words he referred to Vice President and Mrs. Hubert H. Humphrey. During his remarks he referred to, among others, Trygve Lie, first Secretary General of the United Nations. King Olav responded as follows:

Mr. President, Mrs. Johnson, ladies and gentlemen:

I thank you, Mr. President, for the kind words you have just spoken to me and for the cordial welcome I have received in the United States.

As you are aware, Mr. President, I know your country from a number of previous visits. The first time I came to the United States was in 1939. On that occasion, the Crown Princess and I stayed here for over 2 months and visited many of the individual States.

I returned seven times during the Second World War, when my wife and my children had the good fortune to enjoy the hospitality of America, and there have been later occasions in which I revisited your great country.

The common feature of all these visits, Mr. President, is the great understanding and hospitality which the American people have shown and which I have appreciated most deeply.

Over the years, strong ties have been knit between our two countries. Since the latter half of the last century a large number of Norwegians have settled in the United States. It is highly gratifying to us to see how the descendants of our immigrants still cherish their connection with the land of their forefathers. Many of these people keep in touch with and seek out their relatives in Norway and we are happy to know that the valuable bonds of kinship are consequently kept intact.

Our two countries are also firmly united by our respective constitutions and by the common view of freedom and democracy which they express. We Norwegians are proud of our Constitution—as the American people are of theirs. It is well known that when the Constitution of Norway was drafted in 1814 the American Declaration of Independence and the American Constitution were a great inspiration to us at that time.

Norway and the United States were joined by even closer ties during the Second World War. I welcome this opportunity to convey to the American people the warm gratitude that all Norwegians feel for the exertions made by the United States to help us, as well as other nations, to regain our liberty.

We know what sacrifices were demanded of you. I and my countrymen will always honor the memory of those brave sons of America who gave their lives that we might live as free men in a free Norway.

Allow me, too, to tell the American people how grateful we are for the financial help we received after the Second World War. The war had devastated large areas of Europe. The economic systems had collapsed and the various countries lacked the stability and the international cooperation which were needed to get reconstruction going.

To Norway—as to other countries—the Marshall aid was of immeasurable importance in helping us to overcome the ravages of war and in paving the way for further progress.

In the effort to build a better world after the war, our two lands have worked side-by-side within the United Nations. The United States and Norway have attached decisive importance to the United Nations as a preserver of peace and an organization for the furthering of economic and social progress and international understanding.

There is now much more contact between nations of the world than ever before. The need for an active participation in international affairs is constantly increasing.

We consider it a very important part of our foreign policy to see to it that the principles of the United Nations always remain the guiding light in international relations. It is our hope that active and earnest cooperation within the United Nations will help to put mankind on the road to a better and more confident future.

The recently drafted nonproliferation agreement concerning nuclear weapons is a conspicuous example of the usefulness of getting together to secure peace. The Norwegian people warmly welcome this agreement which the United States has so greatly helped to bring about.

In international and economic relations, Norway considers the results of the Kennedy Round—initiated, Mr. President, by your predecessor—as an important step toward the liberalization of world trade.

In accordance with our principles in these matters, we think it particularly important to extend and develop the initiative provided by these negotiations and to safeguard the results that were achieved.

Since time immemorial, the sea has been vital to our existence, and a highway between my country and other nations. Norway has no great fertile land and has little national wealth. But in the ocean, we have developed a specialty which has proved important to the free world, both in peace and in war.

At an early date, Norwegian shipping was able to offer its services based on open competition to most other countries. Our merchant navy at present ranks with the largest and most highly modernized fleets in the world. And I am glad to know that Norwegian ships are frequent callers in most American ports.

So, Mr. President, the Atlantic Ocean is no barrier between us, but serves, on the contrary, to unite us. I hope Norwegian shipping will always be able to continue this valuable intercourse.

A large number of young Norwegians come to the United States to study at American institutions of learning. Many Norwegian students benefit from American scholarships and thus become acquainted with your great society and the American system of education.

In this way, additional contacts are made between our two countries.

On behalf of all these, my countrymen, I here extend my cordial thanks to the United States and the American people.

I do not wish to conclude, Mr. President, without emphasizing relief and pleasure which we, too, experienced in my country at the news of the initial negotiations for peace in Vietnam. I know that I speak for all my countrymen when I express my fervent hope that these negotiations may be attended with success and lead to a peaceful settlement.

I also express to you, Mr. President, my deep sympathy in connection with the tragic death of Dr. Martin Luther King. The people of Norway share the grief of America at his passing away.

I thank you again, Mr. President, for the friendly reception I have been accorded in your country and your Capital.

I propose a toast to the President of the United States and Mrs. Johnson, to the United States and to the American people.

215 Remarks at a Meeting With the Board of Trustees of the Urban Institute. *April 26, 1968*

I AM HAPPY to welcome you to the Cabinet Room.

This is an exciting day for the Nation and for me.

You have launched something America has needed and wanted for a long time. It is a new Urban Institute. It will promise to give us the power through knowledge to help solve the problem that weighs heavily on the hearts and minds of all of us—the problem of the American city and its people.

You will not lay a single brick or build a single house. But the work the Institute will do—the studies and the evaluations and the free and searching inquiries—will build the strongest foundation upon which we can renew our cities and transform the lives of people.

We know today only how much we do not know about the cities:

—Data to inform our decisions is weak or missing.

—Urban research is splintered and fragmented.

—Relationships between jobs and housing and income and education are unclear.

The Urban Institute is an important response to this "knowledge gap." It will fill a real need by:

—Bridging the gulf between the lonely scholar in search of truth and the decision-maker in search of progress through effective programs.

—Bringing together all the disciplines

542

needed—not only scientists and administrators, but economists, planners, and architects. And it will get them to work together—in cities, and on the problems of cities.

—Taking a comprehensive view of urban life and seeking to understand the forces that produce decay as well as growth.

You know better than most that there are no overnight remedies to the problems that formed and hardened decades ago.

But we are moving—and you will help dispel the darkness that remains. Some day the light will shine. Of that I am sure. The work of this Institute can help speed the coming of that day.

As you begin your venture, let me offer these suggestions:

—Your research must be of the highest quality but also of the greatest practicality.

—Your staff must not only think hard about the city, but work amidst the pressure and conflicting forces of life in the city.

—Your work must be to distinguish the long range from the temporary, the real from the illusory.

—Above all, the Institute must operate in a climate of intellectual freedom and organizational independence. The search for truth must be uncompromising, unhindered by partisan coloration or blocked by conventional wisdom.

I wish this Institute had been established a decade ago so that we could now be reaping its results. But now you have begun it, and it will serve us in the years ahead. It is a sound investment in the future of our land.

The Institute was shaped and molded by good men like Kermit Gordon, McGeorge Bundy, Irwin Miller, Arjay Miller, Richard Neustadt, Cyrus Vance, and Robert McNamara. They worked not as Democrats or Republicans—but as Americans.

I know the Institute will get off to a fast start because you have made a wise and excellent choice for its first President. Your selection of William Gorham, one of the ablest young men in public service during the last 8 years, pleases me.

The Institute is now launched and christened, and I wish you good luck and Godspeed in your journey ahead.

NOTE: The President spoke shortly before noon in the Cabinet Room at the White House. As printed above, this item follows the text released by the White House Press Office, which also made public a prospectus for the Institute. The full text of the prospectus, which lists the 15 members of the Institute's Board of Trustees, is printed in the Weekly Compilation of Presidential Documents (vol. 4, p. 719).

216   Remarks at the Swearing In of W. Marvin Watson as Postmaster General.   *April 26, 1968*

Marvin Watson and family, Justice Fortas, distinguished members of the Cabinet, leaders of the Congress, distinguished guests, ladies and gentlemen:

The Postal Service is one office of the Government that touches the lives of all Americans every day. This year, I am told, the Post Office Department will handle 83 billion pieces of mail. The Post Office Department today has employed in it more than 700,000 people. Nine States have smaller populations than does the Post Office Department.

Its annual budget is equal to the budgets of Michigan, New Jersey, Massachusetts, and Florida—all combined. A job that is this big needs a good manager and a good leader, and I think the best man whom I could find for that job has been selected.

I have indicated on occasions in the past something about the respect that I have for Marvin Watson and I don't think that he needs any assurances of how I feel about him—and I don't need any about how he feels about me. I think both of us know how you feel or you would not be here.

I just want to observe, though, that he has served here in the White House for more than 3 years. I think he knows the weight of responsibility in Government. I think he knows the pressure for decision and the necessity for action. I have found him always cool in crisis, and we have had enough of them for me to test him. He has been constant in his service and his devotion and he has always been wise and frank in his counsel.

I believe he is a man to match the demands of his new duty.

A year ago I appointed a special commission of outstanding private citizens to undertake a major analysis of the organization and the operation of the Postal Service. At that time, Larry O'Brien had suggested that the Postal Service and his job be abolished and turned over to a Government corporation. Marvin seemed to think that we ought to give consideration to that idea then—at that time. Now, I gather that he is not so sure.

In any event, I have asked this commission to consider not only the feasibility of a Government postal corporation, but every proposal that could result in better mail service for our people.

I will be looking forward to their recommendations and I know the new Postmaster General will give them his closest attention without delay.

We have already begun a far-reaching program to try to modernize the Postal Service. This work is expensive. But I think we must not permit the Postal Service to deteriorate. The price of a poor Postal Service is far greater than the cost of remodeling the Service into the smooth-running system it must be.

I hope the new Postmaster General can lead this modernization program with the approval of the Congress and the cooperation of the Congress and make sure that the American taxpayer gets 100 cents worth of value for every dollar we spend.

Now, from what I have observed of Marvin Watson, I believe that we can count on him to do that. Marvin's frugality is a legend around here. One of his many duties has been to keep a very close eye—keep two close eyes on the White House operation and the White House expenditures.

I think that every American citizen should be glad to know that Marvin spends the people's tax money just like his own.

Marvin, we will all miss you. We believe that our loss here will be the Post Office Department's gain. The presence of these people here is a sufficient testimony to your fairness and to your service and to the high esteem in which you are held in the Government—particularly the executive and congressional branches.

NOTE: The President spoke at 1 p.m. in the Rose Garden at the White House. In his opening words he also referred to Associate Supreme Court Justice Abe Fortas, who administered the oath of office. Later he referred to Lawrence F. O'Brien, who preceded Mr. Watson as Postmaster General.

Following the administration of the oath of office, Mr. Watson spoke briefly. His remarks are printed in the Weekly Compilation of Presidential Documents (vol. 4, p. 721).

For a statement by the President upon receiving the report of the Commission on Postal Organization, see Item 391.

217 Remarks Upon Accepting an Award From the International Narcotics Enforcement Officers Association. *April* 29, 1968

IT IS a pleasure to welcome you here today—and it is a privilege to accept your award.

I enlisted in your cause long ago.

You are the frontline fighters against a menace that is no longer just a national problem. It has become a national scandal.

There is no greater tragedy than the young boy or girl who forfeits a future to the enslavement of dangerous drugs and narcotics.

There is no greater evil than the sale of that slavery to the young.

With your help, we are going to put a stop to it.

This year we in the Federal Government are taking new and long overdue measures to crack down on the pusher and peddler:

—We have set up a new Bureau of Narcotics in the Justice Department to strengthen the Federal machinery. The Congress approved this reorganization 2 weeks ago.

—We have asked for a 30 percent increase in the number of Federal agents to enforce our narcotics laws.

—We are seeking new legislation to make it a felony to manufacture and sell LSD and other dangerous drugs illegally.

—We have undertaken an intensive review of all Federal narcotics laws, to bring them up to date.

But you and I know that enforcement is only part of the answer.

We have to make certain that every young man and woman in America is fully alerted to the ruinous danger of drug addiction.

We have to try to find new ways to salvage the lost life of the addict and bring him back into the community as a productive and healthy citizen.

This is the job that confronts all of us— every Governor and mayor, every lawmaker and law enforcer, every teacher and every parent.

It is a big job. But there is none more important. It is a job to assure the future strength and vitality of our Nation.

Thank you.

NOTE: The President spoke shortly after noon in the Cabinet Room at the White House, where he was presented with an award in recognition of his efforts to combat narcotics abuse.

On October 24, 1968, the President approved a bill relating to traffic in and possession of drugs (see Item 561).

As printed above, this item follows the text released by the White House Press Office.

218 Special Message to the Congress: "Strengthening the International Monetary System." *April* 30, 1968

To the Congress of the United States:

Twenty-four years ago, President Franklin D. Roosevelt asked the 78th Congress to approve a monetary plan which he called the "cornerstone for international economic cooperation."

The Bretton Woods Agreement—and the International Monetary Fund which it cre-

ated—helped map the recovery of a war-ravaged world.

Today I ask the Congress to take another historic step. I seek approval of an amendment to the International Monetary Fund Agreement, to adapt it to changing world conditions. This change—the first since the Agreement was ratified in 1945—is both timely and necessary. It will prepare us for the era of expanding world trade and economic opportunity that unfolds before us.

RECOVERY AND EXPANSION

The financial statesmen who shaped the Bretton Woods Agreement in 1944 looked beyond the holocaust of war to a time of peace. They remembered the harsh lessons of a depression which had led the world into war.

They knew what had to be avoided—restrictive monetary policies that strangled progress, competitive depreciation of currencies that led to instability, and the breakdown of international cooperation that impeded trade.

They knew what had to be built—a cooperative monetary system to foster world economic expansion in a climate of mutual trust and assistance.

The machinery established at Bretton Woods—through the International Monetary Fund—brought stability to the exchange rates among the currencies of different nations. It brought order to international financial markets and transactions. It created a carefully designed system of cooperation in dealing with international financial problems.

The machinery as it operated in the quarter-century since World War II produced a record of unparallel economic progress. The economies of war-ruined nations were rebuilt and have grown on an unprecedented scale. World imports surged from $59 billion in 1948 to $202 billion in 1967.

But when Franklin Roosevelt urged approval of the Bretton Woods Agreements, he foresaw that "the experience of future years will show us how they can be improved."

That experience is now part of our history.

The very success of the system in stimulating trade has put new pressures on the Bretton Woods machinery and shows us how that machinery must now be changed.

The rapid growth in world trade and in the flow of capital is outpacing the growth in monetary reserves. The world must take action to provide sufficient reserves for this growth. If it does not, strains and uncertainties in the international monetary system—and the limitations they create—could turn the clock backward to the dark days of restrictive economic policies, narrow interests, empty ports and idle men.

Today I propose that the United States lead the way in the action that is needed.

I recommend that the Congress approve changes in the International Monetary Fund Agreement to create a new form of international reserve—the Special Drawing Right.

BACKGROUND TO ACCEPTANCE

The request I make today is not a hasty solution to a newly-discovered problem. It represents the careful work of five years.

The first part of that period was devoted to intensive study by the outstanding economists and financial specialists of many nations.

This laid the base for action. In July 1965—with bi-partisan support and suggestions from the Congress—I directed the Secretary of the Treasury to initiate negotiations. The past three years have been marked by steady progress through patient negotiations—in The Hague, in London, in Rio and in Stockholm.

From the studies and the negotiations has emerged the concept of Special Drawing Rights as a new system for the deliberate and orderly addition to international reserves. They are the refined product of thoughtful and considered agreement among leading experts from the treasuries and central banks of the Free World and the International Monetary Fund.

Throughout the negotiations leading to the development of the Special Drawing Rights plan, the Secretary of the Treasury had the benefit of advice from the Advisory Committee on International Monetary Arrangements. This panel, chaired by former Secretary of the Treasury Douglas Dillon, consisted of some of the nation's leading bankers, economists and businessmen with outstanding experience in the field of international finance.

THE NEED FOR INTERNATIONAL RESERVES

International reserves are to world trade what working capital is to a growing business. As trade expands—just as when business grows—more reserves are needed.

Nations use international reserves to settle their accounts with each other. And these reserves are an important factor in maintaining stable exchange rates among currencies. They are essential to provide time for countries to restore equilibrium in their balance of payments through an orderly process of adjustment.

Reserves must be unimpeachable in quality. They must be acceptable to other nations, as well as to the nation that holds them. Traditionally, international reserves have consisted mainly of gold, dollars and sterling.

But today the world's supply of international reserves cannot meet the requirements posed by growing world trade and capital flows.

In 1948, total world reserves were $48 billion. Of this, gold accounted for $33 billion, or almost 70 percent. The remaining 30 percent was divided among dollars—6 percent—and other foreign exchange plus reserve claims on the International Mone-

tary Fund.

Today, reflecting the vast increase in world trade, total reserves have grown to $73 billion. Of this, gold accounts for $39 billion, a decrease to 54 percent of the total. Dollars, on the other hand, have risen to 25 percent—or $18 billion. The remainder is divided between other foreign exchange and reserve claims on the International Monetary Fund.

Gold became less and less dependable as the source of regular addition to world monetary reserves. Because the U.S. was running a balance of payments deficit, the dollar took up the slack left by gold and provided the largest share of the new reserve growth over the past two decades. Thus, the growth of world reserves has been linked mainly to deficits in America's balance of payments.

With gold unable to meet reserve needs, and with the prospect of reduced dollar supplies for international reserves as the U.S. moves toward balance of payments equilibrium, one fact clearly emerges: the world needs some new form of acceptable international reserve to supplement existing reserves.

It is the purpose of Special Drawing Rights to fill that need.

THE SIGNIFICANCE OF SPECIAL DRAWING RIGHTS

International agreement on the Special Drawing Rights proposal comes at a time when the world monetary system has been subjected to uncertainty and speculation following the devaluation of the pound sterling last November.

To all nations of the free world, this agreement will bring new strength.

To the United States, it can provide an opportunity to rebuild gradually the reserves

547

which we have lost over the past years. But in a broader sense, the Special Drawing Rights are of value to the United States because of the strength they will bring to the world monetary system.

As the world's largest trading and investing nation, we prosper where other nations have adequate resources to assure their expansion of production, employment and trade.

These Special Drawing Rights are a landmark in the long evolution of international monetary affairs. For the first time a reserve asset will be deliberately created by the joint decision of many nations. These nations will back that asset with their faith and resources—the strongest support that any asset has ever had. Special Drawing Rights will assure the world economy of an adequate and orderly growth of international reserves, regardless of unpredictable fluctuations in the production of gold or in its private use.

How the Special Drawing Rights Will Work

Special Drawing Rights—to be issued only to governments, and exchanged only among governments—will be a special kind of international legal tender. They will perform the same basic function in the international monetary system as gold, dollars, or other reserve currencies. They will carry a gold value guarantee and will bear a moderate rate of interest.

Special Drawing Rights will be created after careful consultation and broad agreement. Participating countries with 85 percent of the weighted votes must decide that a need for additional reserves exists.

This process will assure wide participation in the use of the new asset and confidence in its acceptability.

These new reserve assets will be distributed in accordance with each member's quota in the International Monetary Fund. Under this arrangement, for example, the United States—whose quota is about 25 percent of the International Monetary Fund's resources—would receive about $250 million out of each $1 billion of Special Drawing Rights issued. The share of the Common Market countries as a group would be about $180 million; the United Kingdom, $115 million; Canada and Japan, about $35 million each; other developed countries, $105 million; and the developing countries as a group, $280 million.

A participating country will benefit from the program, but it will have responsibilities as well. It is committed to accept Special Drawing Rights from other countries when it is in a strong balance of payments and reserve position. The amount it is required to accept is limited to three times the value of Special Drawing Rights distributed to it by the International Monetary Fund. This limitation is sufficiently broad to assure effective use of the new asset.

The commitment to accept Special Drawing Rights from other countries insures their high quality and liquidity, and gives them the status of a true international reserve asset.

The machinery to create Special Drawing Rights will be put into place when 65 International Monetary Fund member-nations accounting for 80 percent of the weighted votes accept the plan.

As one of the leaders in the formulation of this proposal, and as the member with the greatest percentage of the votes—about

22%—it is fitting that the United States be one of the first nations to accept the Special Drawing Rights plan.

OUR HOPE FOR TOMORROW

International finance—the subject of this Message—is complex and intricate.

But its effects extend far beyond monetary institutions. They reach out to farmland and production line, sales office and show room.

For the heart of this message is a plan to sustain a prosperous and growing world economy through an orderly expansion of trade. As that occurs, we all benefit—the worker with a better paycheck, the businessman with a new order, the farmer with another market, the family with a wider choice of products.

As the world's economy grows, a promise grows with it. Franklin Roosevelt defined it almost a quarter of a century ago in his first message on the Bretton Woods Agreement—as a hope

"for a secure and fruitful world, a world in which plain people in all countries can work at tasks which they do well, exchange in peace the products of their labor, and work out their several destinies in security and peace; a world in which governments, as their major contribution to the common welfare are highly and effectively resolved to work together in practical affairs . . ."

That was the hope of America then. It is the hope of America now.

The Congress can move far toward making this hope a reality by its contribution to a sound world monetary system.

I urge the Congress to cast a vote for a stronger world economy by approving the historic Special Drawing Rights legislation I submit today.

The key role of the dollar also gives America another special responsibility. A strong dollar is essential to the stability of the international financial structure. We must fulfill our responsibilities by dealing swiftly with our own budgetary and balance-of-payments deficits. Let me remind the Congress once again of the clear and critical need to pass the tax bill—the best investment America can make to keep the dollar strong.

LYNDON B. JOHNSON

The White House
April 30, 1968

NOTE: The Special Drawing Rights Act was approved by the President on June 19, 1968 (see Item 317); the Revenue and Expenditure Control Act of 1968 was approved by the President on June 28, 1968 (see Item 343).

---

219   Remarks Upon Presenting the National Teacher of the Year Award to David E. Graf. *April* 30, 1968

Commissioner Howe, Senator Percy, Congresswoman Reid, Doctor Fuller, friends and families of David Graf:

I am glad that you could come here and be with us today at the White House.

I am sorry that we are running a little late.

But we have had some reports this morning that delayed us and delayed the press.

It does give me an opportunity to honor a very dedicated man, as well as a very dedicated profession. I have been participating in these presentations now for some years.

It gives me an opportunity to study, as well, at close hand the Teacher of the Year. That interests me, because teachers exercise a great influence for good throughout the world and particularly in democratic societies.

The man whom we honor today is not only an outstanding teacher, but he is a very outstanding citizen.

In World War II, he earned an array of decorations—including the Purple Heart and the Bronze Star.

He founded a sheltered workshop for the mentally retarded, with this hopeful name: The Open Door.

He is a gifted amateur architect; and like most architects, he combines dreams with hard, practical common sense.

His career is building a future for young Americans—and he is going to do this by teaching them job skills and by introducing them to the world of work.

Mr. Graf is the 18th Teacher of the Year—and he is the first teacher of vocational education to earn this honor.

I think that it is fitting and timely—for this is a time of progress and change in vocational education.

For too many years, vocational education was the stepchild in our educational system. It was last in line for our funds; it was last in line for our attention—and the vocational classroom was far too removed from the actual world of commerce and industry.

I remember taking a course in vocational education in my college days. I remember on the final examination I got an F. The question was: "What does the Constitution say about education?"

I wrote about six or eight pages. When I got my theme back telling them what the Constitution said about education, the professor gave me an F and wrote on it, "nothing."

So if any of you think that the Constitution charters you to do a lot in the field of education, you will have to read between the lines instead of the lines.

But since that time we have made a great deal of progress in all of our adventures into education in behalf of the Federal Government and particularly in the field of vocational education.

We are trying very hard to breathe new life and new funds into this particular field, particularly our vocational education field.

When I became President in 1964, the States, communities, and the Federal Government all together were spending about $300 million a year for vocational education. In all of our States—$300 million a year. One dollar out of six of that was a Federal dollar.

So we were spending about $50 million a year.

Today, the Nation as a whole is spending three times as much—nearly $1 billion a year—on these programs. The Federal share has grown to not one out of every six but one out of every four. The number of students enrolled in these courses has grown to more than 7 million—a 50 percent increase since 1964.

That is a bigger increase than we have had even in our cost of living.

But real achievement depends on something besides just a lot of enrollment figures and how many dollars you are spending on something. It depends on the men—and we have met here in the Cabinet Room to pay honor to one of these dedicated men, David Graf, for his originality and his persistence.

Mr. Graf, you do us great honor by coming here. This plaque and this gold clasp symbolizing this honor we do not intend at all as gifts to you. Rather, they are recognition of your gift to the Nation and to those of us who want to see the teaching profession occupy the high place to which it is entitled.

If you will come forward now, I would like to present this to you.

NOTE: The President spoke at 1:10 p.m. in the Cabinet Room at the White House. In his opening words he also referred to Harold Howe II, Commissioner of Education, Charles H. Percy, Senator from Illinois, Charlotte T. Reid, Representative from Illinois, and Dr. Edgar Fuller, Executive Secretary of the Council of Chief State School Officers.

Mr. Graf, a vocational education and industrial arts teacher in Sandwich, Ill., was selected for his "skill in hand-crafting future careers for his teen-age students and for his superior ability to impart knowledge and inspire students with a love of learning."

The "Teacher of the Year" is chosen from a group of finalists selected by a screening committee of national educational leaders. The award is sponsored by Look magazine in cooperation with the Council of Chief State School Officers, an organization of State superintendents and commissioners of education.

220 Message to the Congress Transmitting the Annual Manpower Report of the President. *May 1, 1968*

To the Congress of the United States:

It is a traditional event for the President to submit to Congress an annual report on the progress of our manpower programs.

Although the custom is long-established, there is nothing routine about this report or its subject: jobs for our citizens: more useful, more satisfying jobs to give Americans a sense of full participation in their society.

Four months ago I told Congress that jobs are "the first essential."

In my first special legislative message this year, I proposed that Congress launch a new $2.1 billion manpower program—the most sweeping in our history.

At the same time I called on the leaders of American commerce and industry to form a National Alliance of Businessmen to provide jobs for hundreds of thousands of the hard-core unemployed.

On April 25, the Alliance reported to me on its progress so far:

—More than 500 executives, whose talents command more than $15 million in salaries alone, have volunteered to work full time in fifty of our largest cities. They are assisted by 7,000 other volunteers.

—By mid-April, the Alliance had received pledges of 111,000 jobs—66,000 perma-

nent jobs for the hard-core unemployed, and 45,000 summer jobs for poor young people.

—Labor unions, the Urban Coalition, Chambers of Commerce, churches, schools and many civic groups have joined this crusade to give the words "full employment" a new meaning in America.

Meanwhile, the Government's new Concentrated Employment Program has been active in more than 50 cities meshing its efforts with the National Alliance of Businessmen. And the administration of our job programs has been given new energy through reorganization and strong leadership.

These are hopeful beginnings. But certainly they are no grounds for complacency.

In every city, there are men who wake up each morning and have no place to go; men who want work—but cannot break the confining welfare chain or overcome the barriers of life-long discrimination, or make up for the lack of schooling and training.

When we talk about unemployment, we are talking about these citizens, who want and need personal dignity and a stake in America's progress.

When we talk about manpower programs, we are talking about hope for these

Americans.

And every time we tabulate new statistics of success in these programs, we are recording a small personal triumph somewhere: a man trained; a youth given a sense of his value; a family freed at last from welfare.

That hope is what makes this great task so exciting—and so vital.

To every member of the Congress, upon whom our manpower programs depend, I commend this report.

I urge the Congress to support these programs by approving the $2.1 billion man-power budget request I recommended in January.

LYNDON B. JOHNSON

The White House
    May 1, 1968

NOTE: The President's sixth report under the Manpower Development and Training Act of 1962 is printed in "Manpower Report of the President, Including a Report on Manpower Requirements, Resources, Utilization, and Training by the United States Department of Labor" (Government Printing Office, 323 pp.).

The funds requested by the President for the manpower program are included in the Departments of Labor, and Health, Education, and Welfare Appropriation Act, 1969 (Public Law 90–557, 82 Stat. 969).

221 Remarks Upon Presenting the Medal of Honor to Capt. Robert F. Foley and Sgt. John F. Baker, Jr., USA. *May 1, 1968*

Captain Foley, Sergeant Baker, Secretary Ball, Secretary Resor, General Johnson, Members of the Congress, ladies and gentlemen:

The battlefield is the scarred and the lonely landscape of man's greatest failure.

But it is a place where heroes walk.

Today we come here to the East Room of the White House to honor two soldiers, two soldiers who—in the same battle and at the same time—met the surpassing tests of their lives with acts of courage far beyond the call of duty.

Those who were there will not forget that day.

Captain Foley and Sergeant Baker fought in the same company. Now, together, they join the noblest company of them all.

They fought because their Nation believed that only by honoring its commitments, and only by denying aggression its conquest, could the conditions of peace be created in Southeast Asia and the world.

Now we are pursuing—with all the resources at our command—the hope of peace through negotiations.

But until honorable peace is a reality, we must continue to rely and to depend on the qualities of courage and endurance which men like this have demonstrated and which men like this possess. Men like this have seen our country through every crisis that has ever confronted our Nation.

There will come a day when the last American soldier will have stacked arms in Vietnam. The last sortie will have been flown. The last ship will have sailed out.

No American bases will remain. No American flags will mark the presence of American strength.

But that distant land will always now be part of the legend of our own. Quan Dau Tieng and a hundred other places which once were battlefields will echo to an ancient rollcall—the roster of brave men like these, who stood and who fought when freedom asked it.

I was talking only this week to young Members of Congress who have traveled up and down the battlefields of Vietnam— former graduates of West Point like Congressman Murphy of New York who went there to see, to hear, and to observe, Congressman Irwin of Connecticut, and others. Without exception, those men who know and those men who have seen, come back and tell me that never in all of our glorious history have the American people ever had more reason to be proud of their men—their morale, their competency, and their cause— than we do now.

So I want to say to Captain Foley, to Sergeant Baker, and to their loved ones, because of what they did, freedom has survived where freedom could have been crushed so easily.

Let us not forget that as we continue to press forward vigorously toward the peace for which every person hungers. No, let us not forget them. And we will not forget them.

Thank you.

[Secretary of the Army Stanley R. Resor read the two citations, the text of which follows.]

The President of the United States of America, authorized by Act of Congress, March 3, 1863, has awarded in the name of The Congress the Medal of Honor to

CAPTAIN ROBERT F. FOLEY, INFANTRY
UNITED STATES ARMY

for conspicuous gallantry and intrepidity in action at the risk of his life above and beyond the call of duty:

On 5 November 1966, while serving as Commander, Company A, 2nd Battalion, 27th Infantry, near Quan Dau Tieng, Republic of Vietnam, Captain Foley's company was ordered to extricate another company of the Battalion. Moving through the dense jungle to aid the besieged unit, Company A encountered a strong enemy force occupying well concealed, defensive positions, and the company's leading element quickly sustained several casualties. Captain Foley immediately ran forward to the scene of most intense action to direct the company's efforts. Deploying one platoon on the flank, he led the other two platoons in an attack on the enemy in the face of intense fire. During this action both radio operators accompanying him were wounded. At grave risk to himself he defied the enemy's murderous fire, and helped the wounded operators to a position where they could receive medical care. As he moved forward again one of his machine gun crews was wounded. Seizing the weapon, he charged forward firing the machine gun, shouting orders and rallying his men thus maintaining the momentum of the attack. Under increasingly heavy enemy fire he ordered his assistant to take cover and, alone, Captain Foley continued to advance firing the machine gun until the wounded had been evacuated and the attack in this area could be resumed. When movement on the other flank was halted by the enemy's fanatical defense, Captain Foley moved to personally direct this critical phase of the battle. Leading the renewed effort he was blown off his feet and wounded by an enemy grenade. Despite his painful wounds he refused medical aid and persevered in the forefront of the attack on the enemy redoubt. He led the assault on several enemy gun emplacements and, singlehandedly, destroyed three such positions. His outstanding personal leadership, under intense enemy fire during the fierce battle which lasted for several hours, inspired his men to heroic efforts and was instrumental in the ultimate success of the operation. Captain Foley's magnificent courage, selfless concern for his men and professional skill reflect the utmost credit upon himself and the United States Army.

LYNDON B. JOHNSON

The President of the United States of America, authorized by Act of Congress, March 3, 1863, has awarded in the name of The Congress the Medal of Honor, to

SERGEANT JOHN F. BAKER, JR.

UNITED STATES ARMY

for conspicuous gallantry and intrepidity in action at the risk of his life above and beyond the call of duty:

Sergeant John F. Baker, Jr. (then Private First Class), greatly distinguished himself on 5 November 1966 while serving with Company A, 2d Battalion, 27th Infantry, on a combat operation in the Republic of Vietnam. Enroute to assist another unit that was engaged with the enemy, Company A came under intense enemy fire and the lead man was killed instantly. Sergeant Baker immediately moved to the head of the column and together with another soldier knocked out two enemy bunkers. When his comrade was mortally wounded, Sergeant Baker, spotting four Viet Cong snipers, killed all of them, evacuated the fallen soldier and returned to lead repeated assaults against the enemy positions, killing several more Viet Cong. Moving to attack two ad-

ditional enemy bunkers, he and another soldier drew intense enemy fire and Sergeant Baker was blown from his feet by an enemy grenade. He quickly recovered and single-handedly destroyed one bunker before the other soldier was wounded. Seizing his fallen comrade's machine gun, Sergeant Baker charged through the deadly fusillade to silence the other bunker. He evacuated his comrade, replenished his ammunition and returned to the forefront to brave the enemy fire and continue the fight. When the forward element was ordered to withdraw, he carried one wounded man to the rear. As he returned to evacuate another soldier, he was taken under fire by snipers, but raced beyond the friendly troops to attack and kill the snipers. After evacuating the wounded man, he returned to cover the deployment of the unit. His ammunition now exhausted, he dragged two more of his fallen comrades to the rear. Sergeant Baker's selfless heroism, indomitable fighting spirit, and extraordinary gallantry were directly responsible for saving the lives of several of his comrades, and inflicting serious damage on the enemy. His acts were in keeping with the highest traditions of the United States Army and reflect great credit upon himself and the Armed Forces of his country.

LYNDON B. JOHNSON

NOTE: The President spoke at 11:40 a.m. in the East Room at the White House. In his opening words he also referred to Under Secretary of State George W. Ball, Secretary of the Army Stanley R. Resor, and Gen. Harold K. Johnson, Army Chief of Staff.

222 Presidential Unit Citation Awarded the 2d Battalion, 31st Regiment, 21st Infantry Division, Army of the Republic of Vietnam. *May 2, 1968*

BY VIRTUE of the authority vested in me as President of the United States and as Commander-in-Chief of the Armed Forces of the United States, I have today awarded

THE PRESIDENTIAL UNIT CITATION (ARMY)

FOR EXTRAORDINARY HEROISM

TO

2D BATTALION, 31ST REGIMENT

21ST INFANTRY DIVISION

ARMY OF THE REPUBLIC OF VIETNAM

The 2d Battalion, 31st Regiment, 21st Infantry Division, Army of the Republic of Vietnam, distinguished itself by gallantry in action while engaged in military operations in Chuong Thien Province, Republic of Vietnam on 4 September 1966. Employed as a heliborne reaction force during operation Dan Chi, the 2d Battalion inflicted a serious defeat on the enemy. Another ARVN infantry battalion was pinned down in an open rice paddy in a savage fight against a main force Viet Cong battalion reinforced with a local guerrilla company. The total estimated enemy strength was over one thousand men. The enemy was fighting from well-prepared log and mud entrenchments with mutually supporting fields of fire across open rice paddies. The 2d Battalion was ordered to move into the operational area to reinforce the sister battalion and attack along the friendly forces' left flank into the left sector of the objective.

The enemy attempted to ward off this attack on their flank by placing additional troops into position directly to the front of the 2d Battalion. Due to the increased intensity of enemy fire, the total deployment of the 2d Battalion required one hour and fifteen minutes. Upon completion of this deployment, rapid reorganization permitted the unit to attack almost immediately. Without the assistance of artillery, air strikes or armed helicopter support, the 2d Battalion assaulted across 600 meters of open rice paddies. Advancing upon heavily fortified positions, the 2d Battalion was engaged by six enemy machine guns. All organic support weapons were employed in the destruction of these positions. Now within 100 meters of the woodline, the 2d Battalion closed with the enemy in ferocious hand to hand combat. The pride, courage and determination of these brave soldiers, coupled with outstanding leadership at all echelons, routed the enemy from his positions, resulting in 105 enemy killed in action. The dedication and unit professionalism which characterized the performance of the Battalion was instrumental in the fierce and rapid destruction of the Viet Cong insurgents. The actions of the 2d Battalion, 31st Regiment, were in the highest traditions of all fighting men and have reflected great credit upon the unit and the Army of the Republic of Vietnam.

LYNDON B. JOHNSON

223 The President's News Conference of May 3, 1968

FORTHCOMING CONVERSATIONS WITH HANOI IN PARIS

THE PRESIDENT. Good morning, ladies and gentlemen.

[1.] I was informed about 1 o'clock this morning that Hanoi was prepared to meet in Paris on May 10th, or several days thereafter.

As all of you know, we have sought a place for these conversations in which all of the parties would receive fair and impartial treatment. France is a country where all parties should expect such treatment.

After conferring with the Secretaries of State and Defense, Ambassadors Goldberg and Ball, Mr. Harriman, and Mr. Vance,[1] I have sent a message informing Hanoi that the date of May 10th and the site of Paris are acceptable to the United States.

We will continue in close consultation at all stages with our allies, all of whom I would remind you now have representation in the French capital.

We hope this agreement on initial contact will prove a step forward and can represent a mutual and a serious movement by all parties toward peace in Southeast Asia.

I must, however, sound a cautionary note. This is only the very first step. There are many, many hazards and difficulties ahead. I assume that each side will present its viewpoint in these contacts.

My point of view was presented in my television statement to the American people on March 31st.

I have never felt it was useful for public officials to confuse delicate negotiations by detailing personal views or suggestions or elaborating positions in advance. I know that all of you, therefore, will understand that I shall not discuss this question further at this conference.

MEETING OF U.S.-MEXICO COMMISSION FOR BORDER DEVELOPMENT AND FRIENDSHIP

[2.] I am delighted to have with us this morning the Chairmen of the Mexican-United States Border Commission between our two countries, which is meeting here in Washington. I especially welcome Señor Vivanco and Mr. Telles, the American Chairman.[2]

I am glad that discussions have been fruitful here.

I will be glad to take any questions that you may have.

QUESTIONS

NORTH VIETNAM'S ACTIONS SINCE MARCH 31

[3.] Q. Mr. President, without trying to contravene your desire not to discuss this further, I would like to refer to your March 31st statement, when you expressed the hope that after we cut back our bombing, you hoped that this would also lead to additional restraints on both sides.

---

[1] Secretary of State Dean Rusk, Secretary of Defense Clark M. Clifford, Arthur J. Goldberg, former U.S. Representative to the United Nations, his successor, George W. Ball, Ambassador at Large W. Averell Harriman, and former Deputy Secretary of Defense Cyrus R. Vance, private adviser to the President.

[2] José Vivanco, Chairman of the Mexican Section, and Ambassador Raymond Telles, Chairman of the United States Section, United States-Mexico Commission for Border Development and Friendship. A White House announcement and summary of their February 3 report to the President is printed in the Weekly Compilation of Presidential Documents (vol. 4, p. 212).

Since March 31st, has there been any detectable military restraint on the part of the North?

THE PRESIDENT. We have been quite concerned with the developments since my March 31st statement, and we have been following them very closely. You may be sure that we are aware and will at all times protect the American interests.

ROLE OF SOUTH VIETNAMESE GOVERNMENT AND ARMY

[4.] Q. Mr. President, you have had some talks with your diplomatic and military leaders from Vietnam recently, both here and in Honolulu. Can you comment on the state of affairs in Vietnam and whether or not the South Vietnamese Government and army are prepared to take over more of the burden of the war?

THE PRESIDENT. We think that they are working to that end. We think that they are making progress. We have detected increased efforts there and among our other allies, and certainly in this country, to expedite our equipment so that they may be able to effectively carry a larger share of the burden.

As you know, they have taken certain actions in connection with their own draft, drafting 19-year-olds and drafting 18-year-olds. They have substantially increased their callup of forces.

I think they are doing about all that we could expect them to do under the circumstances.

THE 1968 CAMPAIGN

[5.] Q. Mr. President, will this new move by Hanoi toward the peace table in any way affect the other part of your announcement of March 31st against running for another term?

THE PRESIDENT. No.

Q. Mr. President, to go on, perhaps could you clarify the second part of your March 31st statement for us to this extent:

Could you tell us whether you plan to campaign on behalf of the Democratic candidate, no matter who he may be?

THE PRESIDENT. I would not want to go into that matter at this time. I will be glad to visit with you about it after the convention, when we see what the situation is.

PUBLIC DISCUSSION DURING NEGOTIATIONS

[6.] Q. Mr. President, referring to your statement here, you spoke of the delicate nature of these negotiations that are going to take place in Paris. Would you go far enough to say that perhaps it would be a good idea to declare a moratorium in our political campaign and public discussion of these negotiations while they are taking place?

THE PRESIDENT. No, I would not urge that. I think my viewpoint was presented about as effectively as I knew how in my March 31st statement.

I do not think we do justice to our country and keep faith with our people when we spend our time pursuing personal ambitions that result in dividing our people.

I think we must be very careful not to do that. That does not mean that we must put a stop to expressing individual viewpoints.

In my own judgment, we still have too much division in this country and too many people thinking of self and too few people thinking of country.

I would remind everybody of President Kennedy's statement in his inaugural address with regard to that. I don't think we have put an end to all the division since March 31st, although I do think that some of the personal criticism has been more restrained and has abated.

I do think that our country has benefited from it. I think it will continue to benefit by individuals recognizing what their individual duties are and permitting the Executive, the Secretary of State, and the Secretary of Defense to discharge their proper constitutional duties.

We frequently confuse the world in our democratic system, which has been a part of our history, by a clamor of voices, individuals assuming to speak for the United States, or at least other nations assume they do speak for the United States, when it does not represent the official Government position.

So I would not say that we should stop discussing these very important problems, but I do say that everyone should measure what he has to say, and the public generally should size up the man who is free to comment on any given occasion, on any given subject, most of which he may not have all the details on, or may perhaps not have enough information to justify the decisions or judgments he reaches.

We in the White House, in the State Department, and in the Defense Department, try to constantly develop this information with our Ambassadors from throughout the world, with our Ambassadors to the United Nations, Ambassador Goldberg and Ambassador Ball, who met with us this morning—Ambassador Goldberg, whom I talked to at length—and try to take a careful reading and evaluate all the conflicting reports.

Now, there are just no other people who have that information available to them. While we always are anxious and welcome suggestions from any source—private, editorial, congressional, judicial, or whatnot—we do think that our Nation's best interests are served sometimes if those suggestions are made privately, even though they don't

make a headline, to the Secretary of State or the Secretary of Defense or to the President.

VISIT OF PRESIDENT THIEU AND OTHER ALLIES

[7.] Q. You have invited President Thieu of South Vietnam to the United States. Can you say anything today about the imminence of that visit?

THE PRESIDENT. Yes. We expect it to be in the next few weeks. We expect to have visits with various of our allies—the Prime Minister of Australia, representatives from Thailand, representatives of South Vietnam. We expect them to come here.

We just finished a very successful, productive meeting with the very able President of South Korea. We will be meeting with representatives from these countries in the days ahead.

MEETING WITH PRESIDENT TRUMAN

[8.] I plan to leave here after the press conference this morning to go to Kansas City to meet with President Truman later in the day. We talked about this before the announcement early this morning, so we plan to carry out that program. After you have a chance to file your statements, we will proceed to Kansas City.

THE POOR PEOPLE'S MARCH ON WASHINGTON

[9.] Q. Mr. President, sir, the Reverend Dr. Abernathy,[3] who is leading the Poor

---

[3] Dr. Ralph D. Abernathy, president of the Southern Christian Leadership Conference and leader of the Poor People's March which converged on Washington from all parts of the country during the first weeks of May 1968, and occupied a campsite in West Potomac Park known as Resurrection City, U.S.A. The purpose of the march was to bring to the attention of Congress and the administration the need for intensified action on behalf of some 29 million economically disadvantaged Americans.

People's March on Washington, was quoted yesterday as saying that the "shantytown" they are going to build here will remain here until something is done.

I wonder, sir, if you could give us your view as to whether Congress might respond affirmatively to this kind of pressure or whether you think it would be wiser for them to work for the kind of Congress that will pass the programs they want from their home bases?

THE PRESIDENT. The Congress now has under consideration some $80 billion worth of recommendations that the President has submitted in connection with social matters, welfare, the poor, security payments, additional food allotments, and so forth.

We are hopeful, and we expect, that the Congress will give due consideration to all of these matters and act in the best interests of the country.

We recognize that there are a good many different viewpoints as to the adequacy of what the Federal Government is doing for the poor and what we are doing in connection with the urban crisis that we face in this country.

We all think more should be done. We all want more to be done.

Reverend Abernathy and the people represented in his march have presented their viewpoint respectfully to the many members of the Cabinet who have listened with interest and concern. We are now attempting to do everything that we think can properly be done to meet the needs of the country.

The people of this country must always have a right, and we hope the opportunity, to present to their Government their viewpoints, as long as that is done lawfully and properly.

We do expect that the poor will be better served if, after that viewpoint is presented, the Congress and the appropriate adminis-

trative agencies can have the time to try to act upon it and execute it.

We hope that the presentation made will be nonviolent, although we are well aware that no single individual can give any assurances that they can control a situation like this. It contains many inherent dangers. We are concerned with them. We have made extensive preparations.

Every person participating and every person in the Capital should be aware of the possibilities of serious consequences flowing from the assemblage of large numbers over any protracted period of time in the seat of Government where there is much work to be done and very little time to do it.

So we expect the leaders to present their viewpoints. We expect to seriously consider them. We believe the Congress will do likewise. Then we expect to get on with running the Government as it should be run.

CABINET MEMBERS AND OTHER PRESIDENTIAL
APPOINTEES AND THE POLITICAL CAMPAIGN

[10.] Q. Mr. President, sir, it has been traditional for the Secretaries of State and Defense to keep out of politics in an election year. I wonder if you could tell us why you have extended this rule to all members of your Cabinet?

THE PRESIDENT. I told you that in some detail on March 31st.

I felt that perhaps the Communist leaders of the world were getting a false impression of this country because of the great divisiveness that existed and the personal statements that were being made, the acrimony that existed.

I felt that I could better serve my Nation by trying to withdraw from that personal campaign, and try to unite the country. I felt that if I did that, perhaps I could get the help and the cooperation of the various candidates of both parties in trying to heal the wounds, unite the Nation, and present a united front to the world instead of a divided one.

Now, I think it would be very difficult to do if the President took that position, and his Secretary of State or his Secretary of Defense, or any of the other Cabinet members, or the Presidential appointees ran around the country campaigning for one candidate or the other.

Every person has the right to state who he is going to vote for and to campaign for whomsoever he pleases. But I don't think he should do it as an appointee of the President while he is paid to perform a public service.

I think he has plenty to occupy him. He ought to stay on the job and do that job well. Of course, he can vote for whomsoever he pleases, but if he desires to run up and down the country campaigning for any individual, I hope he will give me an opportunity to have someone else take over his job here in Washington.

I made that abundantly clear—I thought I made it clear—in my March 31st statement. But I have tried to clarify it some since.

THE NEED FOR ACTION ON THE TAX BILL

[11.] Q. Mr. President, what, in your opinion, are the prospects for Congress enacting your recommended tax increase this session?

THE PRESIDENT. I think we have a long and difficult road ahead. My own views were expressed by Secretary Fowler to the Appropriations Committee this week.

If I were making up the budget for the next fiscal year in May, as I made it up last fall, I would perhaps add some to it instead of taking from it.

We have additional needs from our men in uniform, additional equipment in the form of helicopters, armaments, ammunition, and things that we couldn't foresee at that time.

We have very serious problems in the cities that should be met; very serious problems with the poor that need more attention.

So it is my personal view, the President's view, that the $186 billion expenditure is a very lean budget.

However, the President cannot handle these tax matters alone under our Constitution. Since 1966 I have felt that it was very important for many reasons—to avoid large deficits, to try to help the inflation picture, to get the confidence of the financial leaders of the world, and to best serve our own people—that we have a tax increase.

I got little, if any, support for it in 1966. In 1967 that support increased some and the business leaders and the labor leaders agreed to try to help me.

The Congress has not been that cooperative. They talk about increasing taxes, but they haven't taken any action in that direction except for the action the Senate took.

They tied to that certain restrictions that I do not believe would serve the national interest. I do not think we could live with them. I think they would really bring chaos to the Government.

We have informed the leadership of our views on that, but we must receive their views and consider them.

The Appropriations Committee, responding to suggestions from Mr. Mills of the Ways and Means Committee,[4] and others, met this week, and by a very close vote determined that they expected to prune the President's requests and try to reduce expenditures by $4 billion, and obligational authority or appropriations by $10 billion, and the

---

[4] Representative Wilbur D. Mills of Arkansas, Chairman of the House Ways and Means Committee.

President would be called upon to rescind about $8 billion.

We did not agree with that viewpoint. We do not think it is the wisest course for the Nation.

We had pointed that out a number of times, but we said that if that is the only way that we can get the Ways and Means Committee to take action, if that is the only way that we can get Mr. Mills to report out a tax bill and try to pass a tax bill, after more than 2 years of urging, if the Congress in its wisdom, decides that it wants to do this and submits this kind of a program to the President, the President, while he will not recommend it and does not urge it, and does not submit it, would reluctantly approve it.

That may have just whetted the appetite, because as it appeared that the tax bill might be possible, other views began to be expressed which, in my judgment, will serve the purpose of killing a tax bill if they are insisted upon, because in my judgment the Congress is not going to cut more than $10 billion in appropriations, and more than $8 billion in rescission, and more than $4 billion in expenditures.

If it did so, it would injure the national interest instead of serving it.

Actually, in my judgment, if Congress is left alone, it probably will not reduce appropriations the $10 billion planned, will not rescind the $8 billion, and will not reduce expenditures more than $1½ or $2 billion. That is all it did last year, until the President stepped in and asked them to take additional action.

I am informed by the Appropriations Committees this year that they would not anticipate more, normally, than a $1½ billion cut. So it is easy to demand figures that cannot be reached.

The Senate has voted increases to the budget, not decreases, in the supplemental appropriation bill it passed. But it does serve as an excuse to people who don't want a tax bill at all to say, "Well, unless you cut expenditures deeper, you can't get a tax bill."

We would hope that the Congress, in their wisdom, would conclude that the action taken by the House Appropriations Committee—namely, to reduce appropriations $10 billion, to have that as their goal, rescissions $8 billion, and $4 billion expenditures—would be acceptable.

We will have to await the pleasure of the Congress. This is an independent decision for them to make.

You asked for our view. I have tried to give it. I have been giving it for 2 or 3 years.

I want to make it perfectly clear to the American people that I think we are courting danger by this continued procrastination, this continued delay.

The President can propose, but the Congress must dispose. I proposed a budget. If they don't like that budget, then stand up like men and answer the roll call and cut what they think ought to be cut. Then the President will exercise his responsibility of approving it or rejecting it and vetoing it.

In my judgment, they will not send me appropriation bills that cut more than $4 billion. If they do, it will be some phony paper cut. I have seen no inclination there to do this. But there are individuals who think that can be done.

I don't want to charge any partisanship, but I would hope that men of both parties would try to go as far to meet us in the executive department as we have gone to meet their view. If they do that, I think we can have a tax bill.

I do think that we can absorb some reductions that Congress would normally make anyway, without wrecking our urban program, killing off all of our Corps of Engineers' public works projects, or stopping

561

our highway building or taking needed items from the men who fight to defend us.

But I think the time has come for all of the Members of Congress to be responsible and, even in an election year, to bite the bullet and stand up and do what ought to be done for their country.

The thing that I know that needs to be done more for their country than anything else, except the step we have taken this morning to try to find a peace solution, is to pass a tax bill without any "ands," "buts," or "ors." If they want to effect reductions, then as each appropriation bill comes up, they can offer their amendments like men out on the floor, and call the roll. But don't hold up a tax bill until you can blackmail someone into getting your own personal viewpoint over on reductions.

THE "PUEBLO" SITUATION

[12.] Q. Mr. President, could you give us your present assessment of the *Pueblo*[5] situation? Have you evaluated these confessions, sir, that have been coming from North Korea?

THE PRESIDENT. We have nothing to report that is new. Secretary Katzenbach,[6] the day before yesterday, and Secretary Rusk, yesterday, reported all of the information we have in connection with the *Pueblo* situation.

We have made it clear to the North Korean authorities that we think these people should not be held; that they should be released; that we will carefully examine all of the evidence following their release.

If there is any indication that we have

---

[5] The U.S.S. *Pueblo,* an intelligence ship seized by North Korea on January 23, 1968. One crew member died in captivity; the remaining 82 men were released on December 22, 1968 (see Item 641).

[6] Under Secretary of State Nicholas deB. Katzenbach.

acted improperly, or have violated their boundaries, we will take appropriate action.

That is where the matter stands. We think the next step is up to them.

We hope that upon careful reflection, they will release the men. Then the United States will fairly and impartially look at all the facts available and take a position in keeping with those facts.

THE NEXT PRESIDENT

[13.] Q. Mr. President, without indulging in politics or partisanship, what particular qualities do you look for in your successor to the Presidency?

THE PRESIDENT. Let's leave that to another day. I am going to devote a good deal of my attention in the months ahead to the Presidency, while I am in office, and as soon as I get out of office, on how we can improve the office, how we can improve its administration.

I don't think the question is nearly so much a matter of the individual's personality as it is his background, his training, and his philosophy.

Between now and November, the American people will have adequate opportunity—more opportunity, perhaps, than they want—to judge each person.

Who am I, after almost 40 years in political life, in public office by virtue of the votes of the people—who am I to question their good judgment?

MILITARY DEPENDENTS, TROOP LEVELS, AND THE BALANCE OF PAYMENTS

[14.] Q. Mr. President, in 1960 President Eisenhower directed that no more dependents accompany U.S. military personnel to Europe because of the balance of payments problem. The balance of payments problem, of course, is much more serious now.

I wonder whether you have given any thought to either sending the dependents home and shortening the tours of the troops there, or even reducing the troop level a little more than you have.

THE PRESIDENT. I can assure you that we have given all the thought of which we are capable to the balance of payments situation and all of its ramifications. We are taking every prudent step that we feel we can take to improve our balance of payments situation.

That does involve the rotation of troops. That does involve efforts on the part of the Government to reserve our expenditures, not only dependents, but in all other fields.

We know of few questions that are as important to us as the improvement of our balance of payments situation.

Merriman Smith, United Press International: Thank you, Mr. President.

NOTE: President Johnson's one hundred and twenty-fifth news conference was held in the East Room at the White House at 10:02 a.m. on Friday, May 3, 1968. The news conference was broadcast live on radio and television.

224 Remarks Following a Visit With President and Mrs. Truman at Their Home in Independence, Missouri. *May 3, 1968*

MRS. JOHNSON and I always renew our strength and our faith by visiting with the President and Mrs. Truman.

They have walked the same path that we are now walking. They have rendered a great service to their country in many capacities for many years. I think it is especially appropriate that we could be here at this period of the year because next week is President Truman's 84th birthday.

We are all so grateful and so thankful that we have had the benefit of his wisdom and patriotism with us all of these years.

One of the first men to call me when I undertook the awesome responsibilities of the Presidency was this great leader and this friend of mine of many years.

He has been with me all the way, all the time. And he has given us strength and comfort.

Today, I talked to him about his experiences in the Pacific, his leadership in the dark days of the Korean conflict as well as the latter days of the European struggle and the Pacific struggle.

I reported to him on the developments in

NATO, in Europe, in our trade negotiations and the developments that are taking place in the new Asia.

I talked to him about my conversations with the leader of the Republic of South Korea, the nation who enjoys its freedom and its independence today because of the courage of Harry Truman and the wisdom of Harry Truman supported by America's fighting men.

I talked to the President about the oncoming peace talks in Paris and the problems that we would encounter there.

I asked for his suggestions, his advice, and as always he gave them to me frankly and with the bark off.

I am leaving refreshed and reinvigorated and happy at what I have seen and what I have heard, and eternally thankful that Mrs. Johnson and I have been privileged to know greatness and to witness it again here today in this typically American home with these typical American people.

One of my great friends, Eric Hoffer, had breakfast at my bedside a couple of mornings ago. He was telling me of his great admiration for President Truman. He said, "The reason I think so much of him is because the whole United States is full of Trumans. He is so much like all of us."

That is why I enjoy President Truman so much. As I told one of his old friends yesterday, Smitty of the United Press, "The country is made up of Harry Trumans. He is so much like all of us."

Thank you, Mr. Truman, for letting us come in here. Thank you, Mrs. Truman. We hope we can come back often.

NOTE: The President spoke at 2:50 p.m. on the front porch of the Truman home in Independence, Mo. Near the close of his remarks he referred to Merriman Smith of United Press International.

225 Remarks at the Dedication of the Smithsonian Institution's National Collection of Fine Arts. *May 3, 1968*

Distinguished Regents of the Smithsonian, Secretary Ripley, Dr. Scott, ladies and gentlemen:

This is a proud moment. I wanted to say that dedicating the new home of this National Collection makes me feel like a proud father, but on the plane this evening coming back from Kansas City, Mrs. Johnson said that would sound boastful.

So then I thought I might say that I felt like a proud grandfather. But some people, she told me, think I already talk too much about my grandson.

So tonight, my friends, I am authorized to tell all of you that I do feel very much like a proud uncle of the National Collection.

I think you know how an uncle is. He doesn't visit very often, but he likes his relations to do well and it is good to see that the National Collection is doing well.

If I will never be remembered as a patron of the arts, I should be delighted to be known as an uncle of the arts.

Truly, this is a historic night for all of us. Until now, the United States was the only great country which had no national museum devoted to its own art.

The American collection was shunted about our Capital like a cultural stepchild. It was always in search of a home. Tonight it has a home, a great, historic home whose

sandstone came from quarries that were first operated by George Washington, and whose halls welcomed Abraham Lincoln on the night of his Inaugural Ball.

So tonight, thanks to the tireless dedication of many, many Americans, we see laid out before us the creative history of our great Nation.

From the beginning, America was known as a very vigorous and a very dynamic nation. It grew quickly in size, in population, and in wealth. From the beginning, America was a wonder of the world, and also a hope for the world.

And it would have been most unusual, I think, if all of this energy had not been accompanied by great artistic outpouring. As we can see here this evening, it was and it is.

Through art, it is said, the soul of a nation is revealed. This new museum is a great resource for America, and for all the world, for that matter.

I am proud that I can be here with you to open this museum. I am very proud of the patrons who have made it possible. I am proud to wish it a long, a happy, and a prosperous life.

Let me add another word. This is a day that we shall remember for another reason. It was 1 o'clock this morning that I was awakened and informed that Hanoi was prepared to meet us in Paris, to talk about peace.

We often think about peace as an absence of war. But, in fact, peace is a struggle, an achievement, an endless effort to convert hositility into negotiation, bloody violence into politics, and hate into reconciliation.

I have sought this moment for more days and nights than you will ever credit, and in enough places for all the historians to judge that we were fully credible when we said "any time, anywhere."

Now we shall begin. The days, the weeks, and the months ahead are going to be very hard and hazardous and trying, and exact the best from all of us. But with every fiber of my being, I shall try to move us from fighting to peace, from enmity to brotherhood, and from destruction to common efforts on behalf of the men and women and children of all of Southeast Asia.

In all of this, I ask all of you for your prayers.

Thank you, and good night.

NOTE: The President spoke at 10:09 p.m. at the Old Patent Office Building at 7th and F Streets in Washington. The building was completely renovated under the auspices of the Smithsonian Institution to serve as a modern museum for the National Collection of Fine Arts and, later, for the National Portrait Gallery which opened in October 1968. In his opening words the President referred to S. Dillon Ripley, Secretary of the Smithsonian Institution, and David W. Scott, Director of the National Collection of Fine Arts.

226   Letter to the Speaker of the House Urging Immediate Action on the Tax Surcharge.   *May 5, 1968*

[Released May 5, 1968. Dated May 4, 1968]

Dear Mr. Speaker:

Time is fast running out on one of the most crucial legislative measures of the decade—the tax surcharge. Further delay is a ticket to disaster.

I have repeatedly urged passage of this vital revenue measure. It is modest—about a penny on the dollar earned. It is an American imperative, essential in its importance to the national interest:

—To help ward off inflation that will rob the pockets of the poor and elderly and the millions of families living on fixed incomes.

—To support responsibly the needs of our sons and brothers in Vietnam who fight to defend us all.

—To safeguard our dollar, the guardian of our prosperity at home and the bulwark of the free world monetary system.

The $186 billion budget I submitted in January was tight. It was tailored to finance responsibly the urgent work we must pursue in our cities, to help the poor and to protect our national security.

The budget which was made up last year and the year before contemplated tax increases which the Congress has not enacted. But the President can only propose in matters of taxes and appropriations. Under the Constitution he cannot dispose. That is the duty and power and responsibility of the Congress.

Now the Congress is indicating that reductions in the January budget will be necessary to secure passage of the tax bill. I do not recommend or urge such reductions—for the budget is already lean.

But so crucial is the tax surcharge to the national interest that I would reluctantly accept some reductions if they are realistic and reasonable.

565

The House Appropriations Committee late last week approved a formula which included a $4 billion reduction in expenditures for fiscal 1969.

To accept reductions any deeper than this in an already lean budget—designed to meet the urgent needs of our people at home and abroad—is unwise.

As Secretary Fowler stated, the reduction formula voted out by the House Appropriations Committee will be approved by me, although I know it will require great sacrifices. I think it would be a serious mistake to go beyond that formula. But above all, it is essential that the Congress act and act at once.

I know that you will, as you have always done throughout your career, place the interest of the Nation first and do all in your power to secure passage of the necessary tax legislation. I cannot too strongly urge immediate favorable action by the Congress on the vitally needed tax increase.

Sincerely,

LYNDON B. JOHNSON

[Honorable John W. McCormack, Speaker of the House of Representatives, Washington, D.C.]

NOTE: The Revenue and Expenditure Control Act of 1968 was approved by the President on June 28, 1968 (see Item 343).

227 Remarks at a Reception for the White House Fellows. *May 6, 1968*

I PERHAPS should have waited until you at least had time to participate in the refreshments, but I know it will be refreshing when I have gone.

Since I must go to the Senate, I think I will just start now and interrupt your meeting.

First, I want to welcome the members of the Cabinet and the President's Commission on White House Fellows, the new Fellows and the old Fellows, and all my friends.

I am happy to have this second chance to meet with the White House Fellows and their ladies. You were kind enough to invite me to come last Saturday. I was sorry I could not be there.

My own disappointment was considerable. Your invitation was most attractive to a man in my position—a short timer in Washington. It could have been my last chance to make the scene at Dupont Circle on a Saturday night.

I had another very personal reason for wanting to join you. As a man considering a new career, I think it is wise to keep up my contacts, especially with important people.

At least I think you are important people.

You have been handpicked for very high honors, and I think for very high office. You are very privileged young people.

You found room at the top for 3 years. Today another year begins for you.

Nineteen new White House Fellows are here as the fourth class of important and privileged young Americans.

So I am very proud and happy that I can join with Mrs. Johnson to ask you to come here, to congratulate you, and to welcome you to Washington.

There are 68 of you now. That is one for each year of this century.

I would like to think that there is some special significance to that coincidence.

I want to believe that you are the men and women who will complete the great unfinished agenda of America for this century, so that we may launch the third century of our continuing American adventure with even higher goals and I hope with an even greater purpose.

The next century is crowding in on us in this room right now.

It is pressing us with a rush of change—the new challenges that are flung by science and technology; by population increases; by 40 percent of the people in the world who can't spell "dog"; 40 percent of the people in the world who can't write "cat"; by the unexplored oceans and untamed weather; by poverty and injustice in our own land; by giant cities that need rebuilding; by our schools, our farms, our hospitals, and our corporations that need to change to keep up with that challenge; by all the unexpecteds and the unknowns, including the greatest of all—how to understand other people and how to learn to live together in this world without war.

So that is your agenda, and that is your life. It will be your job and your privilege to work on that agenda while you are here in Washington.

I hope all of you take it as your job—your particular responsibility to repay that privilege when you leave Washington by continuing to work as private citizens on your public agenda, working in your law firms, in your executive suites, on your campuses, on your city governments, and in your hometowns.

I am going to try, as one of my last orders, to see that you do that.

I am going to ask a committee of the 68 White House Fellows, whom I will take great care in selecting, to work with me and some of the members of my Cabinet, with some of those who have worked in my administration, in the Kennedy administration, in the Truman administration, and the Roosevelt administration, to make a study of the Presidency, to see how we can improve it, how we can strengthen it.

It won't be exactly another Hoover Com-

mission on the entire Government, but it will be on the Presidency, itself, which is a rather important office.

In the years to come we need to improve it, strengthen it, and do whatever we can to make it stronger.

In addition to that, I am going to amend the Executive order that created the selection committee, of which the most distinguished and honored Mr. Douglas Dillon is Chairman, to provide for an increase in membership.

In President Roosevelt's day that would have been known as packing the court.

But I hope I can make that change without being charged with any ulterior motives.

I would like for some of you 68 Fellows who have come, who have seen, and who have not forgotten, to sit around with some of these old timers who really constitute this generation gap.

I would like for you to sit with them—the Johnny Oakes's of the New York Times, the John Macy's of the Civil Service Commission, Judge Hastie.

I would like for you to talk with them as members of the board, as their equals on the board, and as fellow members. Then I would like for you to go throughout the country and work with these panels so that the next group selected can even be an improvement on the group that you make up.

I look upon you as the future. You can make it or you can break it by committing yourself, or by copping out: by going home after 1 year at the top, or by sliding back into the comfortable routine of a cynical private life, by being too busy, or too timid, or too awed to apply what you have learned here by staying involved, or by remaining committed.

I think you are going to learn a great deal in this town.

But it is a part of your privilege that you

will come to know a basic truth. That truth is how much government can do and how much government cannot do.

If you grasp this, if you keep your eyes open and your wits sharp, you will learn the magnificent promise and the exciting truth of your own lives.

You will learn how very much you can do for your own future, and particularly for the future of your country; how very much we need you, your commitment, and your involvement.

And we need it now, because the future is now.

In the last century, a great English statesman looked ahead and declared, "You cannot fight against the future. Time is on our side."

Well, was Gladstone really right? Some people wonder.

Is time really on our side today, or is our century already so different, and are we already so beset and so divided by all of our problems that even time is working against us?

There are some, I think, who might answer yes, by their criticism or their cynicism.

There are others who agree by their obstruction or their silence.

There are a few who surrender reason to passion and hope to frustration, who fear that they have no place in the future; or that the future, itself, is overwhelmed by the vast complexity and variety of modern life.

I understand that some of you in the White House Fellows Association have been asking yourself some of these questions.

You want to know if time is on our side, if you really have a relevant role to play; if, in fact, our problems might not have made your Association and your purposes obsolete even before you get organized and get going.

Well, I am pleased that you are concerned. That is the first evidence that we are making progress. That is the first step to commitment and, I think, to success.

I would like to try and take you just one step further in the few moments I have with you by suggesting some answers and also by suggesting some actions for you as individuals, and to your Association.

Let me first make clear my own commitment.

This Nation is not going to retreat before the future. This administration has acted for 4 long years now to meet the challenges of the day and to set the stage for new triumphs of tomorrow.

We have believed that time is on our side, and we have tried to work every minute to make the most of our time at the top.

I promise you here and now this afternoon, that in the time left to us we will put every last ounce of energy and strength, every last second of the day, to strong, to timely, and, I pray, to wise and to enduring purpose.

That is my personal commitment. That is my responsibility as your President.

It is the only legacy that I am concerned to leave to my successor—a Nation that has grown in achievement, a people that are richer in fulfillment, an America that is united and strong in unfearing pursuit of the greater achievement and fulfillment that the future offers us.

Now let me ask you a question: What is your responsibility? What legacy do you want to leave to your children?

I hope that you will not tell them that you gave up on your world because you couldn't roll up your sleeves, as Rex Tugwell once said, and remake it overnight.

I hope you will be able to tell them, and I hope you will be able to show them, that you found the road of life was hard; you observed that it was steep and slow, but that you made it to the mountaintop. And as you went along, you took your country with you.

You are standing on one peak of life's experience right this minute. You are young and you are privileged Americans. You are bright. Most of you are healthy, happy, and I hope, well off.

Now, how do you think you got that way? How did that happen? Some of you had to fight for the privileged position tnat you have this afternoon.

But all through your years, all through the life of this Nation, other Americans were fighting to raise you up. They were fighting to try to protect you. They were fighting to try to better your life; to improve your system of government; to give you new advantages and better educational opportunities; to make you what you are, because they refused to retreat before the future that has now come true for you, for those of you who are very gifted and young, and, I think by being both, you are quite fortunate.

One of the men who fought for you, and who was fighting for you when I was a young man and first came to this town, was a close and dear friend. His name was Henry Stimson. He was a wise man with a warm place in his heart for young people.

He left a legacy for the future: "Let them learn," he said, "from our adventures. Let them charge us with our failures. And let them do better in their turn. But let them not turn aside from what they have to do, nor think that criticism ever excuses or substitutes for inaction. Let them have hope and virtue and let them believe in mankind and its future, for there is good as well as evil. And the man who tries to work for the good, believing in its eventual victory, while he may suffer setback and sometimes even disaster, will never know defeat. The only deadly sin that I know—the only deadly sin that I know—is cynicism."

Isn't that the truth for your time, too? Isn't that the answer that you are looking for?

It is not very difficult to "poor mouth." It is so comfortable and convenient sometimes to knock your own system.

It is hard to remember, sometimes, that this is really a great and a going concern, that our Nation is the envy of the world, and that there are citizens all over the world who would just give anything to trade places for it.

We can remember that without ever being satisfied with what we have or what we are.

It is difficult to put things in perspective. It is difficult to remember the giant strides that have been brought to us, despite our many problems—to the miracles of life that we have taken so much for granted, despite our plagues and our persecutions, despite our wars, despite the many calamities that we have envisioned from time to time—and I have endured and lived through a goodly number of them—man has persevered.

In the face of natural disasters, great tumults, setbacks and sins, generation after generation of Americans and our fellows on this planet have been blessed with fortune after fortune.

Through all the years, all the errors and all the dangers, reform and improvement have been the password to man's increasingly better and brighter future.

Man has been many things through all the centuries of his existence, but he has been wonderfully and mainly distinguished by one characteristic of his human nature: Man has always been, and I hope always will be, the great experimenter.

That is what you are. You are, after all, one of my first experiments.

The White House Fellows and the White

House Fellows Association are really an experiment in democracy. You have succeeded beyond many of our original hopes.

So, I ask you now, as individuals and as an association, to commit yourself, to dedicate yourself, to organize yourself, for the greater successes that you can bring to this Nation.

You are relevant. No one can make your experiment irrelevant but yourselves.

No one can make democracy obsolete but the citizens of democracy who don't care.

Ever since we began our great experiment originally in democratic government, there have been those who wondered—sometimes in curiosity and a great many times in despair—whether this experiment would ever work.

A century ago there were many who thought we had reached a dead end. Abraham Lincoln had to remind those cynics and those skeptics that the American experiment, for all its failings, was plainly still the last best hope on earth.

Thirty-five years ago the doubters thought that we were up a blind alley. President Franklin D. Roosevelt had to rally a people. He had to prove the vitality of a system by urging our people not to be paralyzed by their doubts.

One of the most stirring speeches I have ever heard in this town was when he stood there on that bleak, windy March day and took the oath of office.

He said, "The only thing we have to fear is fear itself." And how true that is this moment. Just a few years ago, some of these people were saying that we had reached a deadlock of democracy, but we moved on, we moved away, and, I am proud to say, we moved up.

Again and again in the American experience, it is the pessimists who have proven to be the false prophets. It is the optimists whose courage and faith have carried us on.

That is your inheritance. That is why you are here in the White House this afternoon.

So it is your turn, now, to pick up and carry on. For every complaint about our society and about our progress, you and I can point to a new program. We can point to a new landmark act of the Congress. We can point to a new public or new private initiative; or a new partnership of business and government, of church and community, of university and corporation, of American with American.

That is your America.

It is a growing and going concern. It is not slack and it is not soft. But it is creative and it is challenging both to the muscle and to the mind.

It is a land of limitless opportunity and great promise for all young people. There is no more promise anywhere on this earth.

For every lament about the alienation of our young, you and I can point to millions of active, committed, and involved young men and women who really deeply believe in the American experiment, who are willing to work for its improvement, who want to broaden and deepen its successes, so that every American—every single one of us— may know the full blessings of democracy.

Well, it is a big job. It is a most difficult and hard job. But there are enough of you now in the fourth year of this program to roll up your sleeves and do something about it.

Your association is new, but you can begin small. Plant an acre, put down a seed. You live and you work for all of America. You can see yourselves as the Johnny Appleseeds of a new America.

When you leave Washington, you can be the ones to go out and plant the ideas and plow the furrows that point to the future; that can awaken and unite our Americans in a new community of splendor with high, noble purposes.

You are relevant. We do care about you. You are needed.

You are a national association, and I am convinced that you have a national role to play in helping to master the human problems that concern you and concern me.

Let me suggest something to you: You might want to organize by regional committees. Our new Alliance of Businessmen has done just that, to solve a great and urgent problem, under the leadership of Mr. Henry Ford of Ford Motor Company, and Mr. Paul Austin of Coca Cola. They are out, going down the streets and the highways, finding jobs for people who can't find jobs for themselves—the hard-core unemployed.

In just a few weeks now, the businessmen have demonstrated that they are winning that battle. In less than 3 months since they first met here in the White House they have secured pledges for 111,000 new jobs for hard-core unemployed and disadvantaged youth.

That is quite different from what it was when I came into this town, when they had the midget on Mr. Morgan's knee, and when the President was talking to businessmen in terms of economic royalists.

Some of you are business executives. Some of you have the power and the opportunity to work as partners with this National Alliance of Businessmen, to help those who can't help themselves.

You will find many other partners who are ready and eager to cooperate with your Association on a great variety of social problems—churches, law firms, universities, unions, farmers, the people of America who are working harder than ever to try to solve the problems of America.

Your regional committees could divide this Nation into four quarters. You could set a target list of problems and opportunities for each region.

The first target that I had when I came to this town as a young man was to participate with a group of brain trusters, of which I did not include myself. We wrote the report on economic conditions in the South. It was in the early 1930's. That report spread all across the land and people started working on the recommendations.

We haven't completed all of them yet.

One of the first ones to come out of it was the minimum wage of 25 cents an hour. Women were working in our section for 6 cents an hour.

I remember—well, I remember a lot of things about that report.

You could, I think, set a time limit for results. I think you could set that time limit with that target here today. It could be your next meeting a year from now.

Then you could come back here with a new scorecard. You could come back to the President and tell the President that you have worked with the National Alliance of Businessmen, that you have worked with Mr. Gardner in his Urban Coalition, that you have worked on the campuses and the city halls, in the churches, and you have many other partners.

You could come back here prepared to hold up your scorecard and say: "Mr. President, like the National Alliance of Businessmen, we have helped x number of unemployed find a job. We have helped x number of businessmen to involve themselves in the problems of the cities. We have helped x number of young Negroes, Puerto Ricans, Mexican-Americans, American Indians, or underprivileged, get into a classroom for the first time. We have gone out ourselves into x number of slums and we have worked with x number of mayors and local officials to try to get rid of those slums. We have tried to build new homes instead of burn old ones. We have used our management and our talents to help *x* number of small businessmen improve their lot and get ahead. We have served as a bridge between *x* number of city halls and universities, between *x* numbers of universities and community leaders, between the campus and the street corner, between the executive suite and the ghetto store, and between the police station and the church, the factory, the supermarket, the farm, the tenement, and the apartment house."

A year from now, I hope that a committee from your Association will be able to come to this house, to this room, and say to your President, "Mr. President, it was a privilege to work 12 months for my country at the top."

A tour of duty in Vietnam is just 13 months, as you know.

"We have tried to repay our country. We have remained committed and dedicated. We have done our best, singly and together, to bring all of our people closer in the work of building—building one united, one progressive—yes, one peaceful America."

You should not need any greater challenge than that. I hope you don't need any more encouragement than that.

But if you do, I am sure you will find that encouragement in association with your other White House Fellows. Some of them are so good that I have never let them leave the White House. Some of them are so good that I am taking them to Texas with me.

I am sure that if you do need some more encouragement, you too can find it in the leadership of the distinguished American who has agreed to serve as Mr. Dillon's replacement.

I want to pay a word of tribute to Mr. Dillon. I first knew him as a lieutenant in the Navy in this town. I don't know what

he did before he put on that Navy uniform several decades ago, but I know what he has done since.

He has served every day, doing the greatest good for the greatest number of people, trying to better humanity. I think this final job he has done as Chairman of the White House Fellows is not one of the minor undertakings he has had, and it is not one of the smaller contributions of the many that he and his wife have made to this country.

I want to salute and to thank Mr. Dillon for his understanding.

He is more fortunate than some of us in his health, his brains, and his pocketbook, but he has been willing to spend them all on trying to make this a better nation.

The man who succeeds him I know will have a lot to shoot at, but he will do his best. He is the Chairman of the President's Commission.

I am proud and happy to announce that Judge William Hastie of the Third U.S. District Court of Appeals will carry on for our former and our very able Chairman.

Mrs. Johnson and I, finally, are very pleased to congratulate all of you, and to wish you good fortune, and to tell you that it has been our good fortune to know those who have come before. We hope we will have a chance to meet those of you as you come afterwards.

NOTE: The President spoke at 4:43 p.m. in the State Dining Room at the White House. During his remarks he referred to, among others, John Oakes, editorial page editor of the New York Times, and John W. Macy, Chairman of the Civil Service Commission, both initial members of the Commission on White House Fellows, Rexford G. Tugwell, Under Secretary of Agriculture from 1934 to 1937 and Governor of Puerto Rico from 1941 to 1946, Henry L. Stimson, Secretary of State from 1929 to 1933 and Secretary of War from 1940 to 1945, C. Douglas Dillon, former Secretary of the Treasury and outgoing Chairman of the President's Commission on White House Fellows, and John W. Gardner, former Secretary of Health, Education, and Welfare.

Announcements of the selection of the 1968–1969 White House Fellows and of the designation of Judge William H. Hastie as the new Chairman of the President's Commission on White House Fellows, made on May 6, 1968, are printed in the Weekly Compilation of Presidential Documents (vol. 4, pp. 757, 758). On the same day the President signed Executive Order 11410 "Amending Executive Order No. 11183, establishing the President's

Commission on White House Fellowships," which related to the designation of future chairmen (4 Weekly Comp. Pres. Docs., p. 758; 33 F.R. 6911; 3 CFR, 1968 Comp., p. 113).

The program, designed to give outstanding young Americans top-level experience with the workings of the Federal Government, was established on October 3, 1964 (see 1963–64 volume, this series, Book II, Item 622).

228 Remarks at a Reception for Senator Hayden Following the Senator's Announcement of His Decision To Retire. *May 6, 1968*

Senator Hayden and Members of the Senate and their staffs:

I came here with mixed emotions this afternoon. On the one hand I am tempted to take Carl Hayden at his word, and believe the unbelievable, that this Congress is finally to lose the strength and the wisdom and the inspiration of Carl Hayden's leadership.

But then I remember what strange times we are living in. It is very hard to believe any announcement of political intentions these days.

One day the politicians who have declared out are back in. The next day the politicians who have declared in have backed out.

It may well be that Carl Hayden has rendered another great service to the Nation by his announcement today, and I came here to help him.

Looking at us two noncandidates, both models of long-term credibility, no American in his right mind could any longer doubt the veracity of any politician.

Carl Hayden and I both are on the brink of new careers. We are looking back to our old professions. I know there is still a need for teachers, and I am going back to where I began. But I wonder if Carl has recently cased the market for frontier sheriffs.

We are both young men, both Democrats, both from the Southwest, both have served

many years in Congress, and I believe that he is the only man who is now in the United States Senate who was in the United States Senate when I came to Washington.

Now it seems we both have reached retirement age together. In fact, I understand the same man [1] who was after my job last election, Carl, is now after your job.

Some men have had long and very distinguished careers here in the Senate because of their oratory, some by becoming the champions of some particular cause, some by the glamour of their personalities, some by their ability to work harder, longer, and better.

Carl Hayden is not famous as an orator. His glamour is the old-fashioned kind that we associate with a handsome sheriff in the Arizona Territory. But the people of Arizona sent him here, and they sent him back again, again, and again, simply because he worked harder for their interests, more intelligently for their interests, for the benefit of all the people, than anyone else they could ever find in 56 years who lived in the State of Arizona.

He has told generations of freshmen here in the Senate, and I was one of them, that when he first came here he asked a man

---

[1] Former Senator Barry Goldwater opposed President Johnson for the Presidency in 1964 and declared his candidacy for Senator Hayden's seat in 1968.

how to get reelected, and he said, "Well, you know, Carl, there are two kinds of horses, show horses and work horses."

Without disparaging the show horses a bit this afternoon, he made the case by his example of being a work horse.

His work was the arduous kind that is done in the committee rooms. It was long; it was painstaking; it was nighttime sessions. It was poring over testimony and figures of a thousand appropriation bills involving billions of dollars, trying to bridge the gap between public needs and public resources, always trying to serve his main client: the people, the people of the United States—serve them with integrity, with imagination, and always with great care.

Whatever his intentions, he became a kind of show horse as well as a work horse. He became the Senator whom his colleagues would always point out to their constituents and say, "There is the Senator's Senator. There is Mr. Integrity from the State of Arizona."

I might say that all that nonpolitical hard work turned out to be the best politics that anyone around here ever saw. And if I am not mistaken, there never was a glamorous public figure, there never has been a silver-tongued orator in the Senate, who served as long as 56 years in the Congress of the United States.

His monuments are everywhere in the State of Arizona. But he was never a one-State Senator. He was the third Senator in every State.

His understanding, his generosity of spirit, knew no boundaries, and no man will ever leave this Hill—and I say this as sure of anything as I am sure my name is Lyndon Johnson—no man will ever leave service on this Hill with more friends than Carl Hayden has.

And no man will ever leave here with a prouder record of accomplishment.

The name Carl Hayden will stand for serving the public interest as long as there is a Congress.

My friend, it is an understatement to say that we shall miss you.

America is stronger for what you have done in these 56 years, and it is going to be poorer when you have left these halls.

I came here from the other end of the Avenue today to speak on behalf of all the people, to tell you that you fought a good fight.

You haven't finished the course, but you have kept the faith. Everybody that knows you respects you and—I am speaking for the ladies, too—loves you.

NOTE: The President spoke at 5:18 p.m. in the New Senate Office Building.

Carl Hayden served in the House of Representatives from February 19, 1912, to March 3, 1927, and in the Senate from March 4, 1927, to January 3, 1969.

229 Remarks Upon Signing Bill To Permit Increases in Interest Rates on Insured Home Loans. *May 7, 1968*

Secretary Weaver, Members of Congress, Mr. Clarke, Mr. Rogg, my friends the Home Builders:

I have not been too closely in touch with homebuilding recently, but I can tell you about a nice house where there is going to be a vacancy in January.

It is a good location. You have a 4-year lease, with an option to renew at the pleasure of the landlord.

It is very close to where you work. We have a playroom for dogs, children, and grandchildren—and, Helen, for godmothers.

Open occupancy, too.

I am particularly glad that you home-builders timed your meeting to come to Washington at this period. As you know, I am getting ready to move from my present residence, and I thought that some of you might want to give me some tips on how to remodel a home on the range for one of the unemployed, or maybe how to purchase a home on the Avenue for Presidents at Palm Springs.

I have come here to sign a measure that I think is of vital importance to all the people who want to build or who want to buy homes.

It empowers our distinguished Secretary, Mr. Weaver, and the Administrator of Veterans Affairs to adjust interest rates on FHA and GI home loans to changing market conditions for the next 17 months. Those market conditions are changing and they are going to change more if we don't get a tax bill soon.

Thanks to this particular act, the veteran who has come home from Vietnam, the young wage earner who is on the way up in life, or the family that is seeking escape from the ghetto will find it easier to buy a home.

I think you homebuilders should know that I am very proud of America's home loan programs. They have helped to fulfill the dream of home ownership for 16 million American families, but unrealistic and arbitrary interest ceilings can cripple these programs.

The bill we will sign today which Congressman Dorn and Senator Randolph, and others, have helped to pass and brought here, will prevent that.

This bill, important as it is, though, cannot guarantee the prosperity of the homebuilding industry because homebuilding, like every other industry, flourishes best in a well-balanced and an expanding economy.

The past 7 years of unprecedented prosperity have shown what a free economy can do. We have created 10 million new jobs. We have added nearly $250 billion to our real output per year.

This increase alone is more than the United States was able to produce in any year up to 1939.

Now, that is very significant, and I hope all of us understand it. We are not saying you never had it so good. We are just saying that the increase in your gross national product has been more than the entire gross national product was in the year 1939.

So that is one of the things that your industry has contributed toward and the economics of this country have contributed toward. It is something we really don't want to lose.

We had a situation like that in 1929, and we did lose it very shortly. We can lose it here if we are not careful.

The real income of the average American has risen 31 percent. That is a bigger gain than in the previous 19 years combined.

For the past 5 years of our period of prosperity, homebuilding was one of the leaders in the advance. It contributed to our prosperity and it also benefited from our prosperity. We were building at least a million and a half homes a year, and we showed that the housing industry need not suffer the sharp ups and downs.

But in 1966 the performance took a sharp turn for the worse. Homebuilding sagged to the lowest level in 20 years.

Thousands of builders were deprived of their livelihood and their profits were wiped out. Hundreds of thousands of Americans lost their opportunity to buy or to build better homes.

The need for homes has always been there and the income was there. But the mortgage credit, which is the lifeblood of homebuilding, was nowhere to be found. We just couldn't get credit to build the homes that we needed and that we had the income to pay for.

We could have avoided this if we could have passed a tax increase. I knew it and the homebuilders knew it.

I called together the leadership of the Congress and they told me we couldn't get four votes in the entire committee of 25 for the tax bill.

I called together the business group of this country, some 300 businessmen. There wasn't a one of them who would raise his hand for a tax increase.

I called together the labor people and they did not favor a tax increase.

In 1967, though, we went ahead and urged the Congress publicly to pass it.

In August 1967 we repeated the recommendation.

In January 1968 and again in March of 1968 we have done the same thing.

The sad lesson of history is that it has this meaning: It is time to show that America has learned its lesson.

While we have let this tax bill languish, we have seen mortgage interest rates go from 5½ percent to 7 percent and even 8 percent. Three years ago, no one would have believed that an 8 percent mortgage rate was possible in the United States. But today interest rates are nearing the highest point in 50 years and I think this is something that should disturb every American. If we do not act now, an even worse shock is in store for you. I want to warn you about it.

If we do not act, 10 percent mortgage rates are not outside the realm of possibility, according to the best economists who can see into the future. Tight money is the price that we pay for excess deficits and our refusal to act on a tax bill in wartime. We have never had a war during which we wouldn't pass a

tax bill. But now, for 3 years, we have said first, we didn't need it; second, that we couldn't afford it; third, it would hurt the economy; and fourth, we ought to take care of spending first. One excuse after the other.

Only responsible fiscal policy can check inflation and prevent another disastrous credit crunch. Yesterday's long-awaited action by the House Ways and Means Committee gives us some hope that we can soon have a realistic tax bill.

I congratulate the Congress and the committee on that action. I asked the leadership this morning to please ask each conferee to stand up and do what is best for his country.

If we must cut $4 billion in expenditures to get $10 billion in taxes, we will do it. But if you cut more than $4 billion, you involve great dangers. If the Congress will go along and take the action on the 10–8–4 formula, if some individual can find another $2 billion that he can cut, he can always offer that in an amendment the rest of the year and let the Congress vote on it.

I think that we just must act now to chart a course of fiscal prudence. We are willing to accept the 10–8–4 formula that the Appropriations Committee of the House voted and that the Ways and Means Committee voted yesterday.

We think we must do that if America is to fulfill her promise to her people, and most of all, her responsibility to the world.

Today our economic future is being decided up here on Capitol Hill. We have come to a crossroads. One road leads to stable economic expansion.

We have had 87 months of the greatest prosperity any nation has ever known, and the only time in all of our history we have gone this long. Why must we just sit idly by and reverse that and go back downward?

The other road leads to a feverish boom. One road leads to stable prices; the other road leads to a stepup in inflation.

One road leads to easier credit; the other leads to soaring interest rates.

We have already paid more in extra interest rates and extra costs and extra high prices than we would get out of the whole tax bill.

With these choices before us, I believe this Nation will travel the road of reason, the road of restraint, the road of prudence, and the road of responsible fiscal policy.

I hope America will travel the right road, because America must. I am doing everything I know how to give the Congress and the country the kind of leadership they need in this trying hour.

I have never thought that tax bills were popular. I have never relied on polls for them. You can ask anybody, "Do you favor a tax increase?" and the answer will be "No."

But if you ask them, "Do you favor a tax increase, or do you favor increased inflation, increased prices, and increased fiscal ruin?" that is a different matter.

I think the average person in this country is a prudent person and a fair person. We cannot fight a war in our cities, we cannot fight a war on poverty, we cannot fight a war on ignorance and illiteracy and disease, we cannot fight aggressors in Vietnam and reduce taxes at the same time.

Yet I want to show you what we have done. [*From this point on, the President referred to a series of charts to illustrate his points.*]

These are the individual income tax rates. Now, when I became President, the person who made $1,000 a year was paying a 20 percent rate. We reduced that to 14. The person who earned from $2,000 to $4,000 was paying a 20 percent rate. We reduced that to 17. The person who made $8,000 to $12,000 was paying 26 percent. We reduced that to 22 percent.

The person who earned $44,000 to $52,000

was paying 59 percent. We reduced that to 50 percent. The person who was earning over $400,000 was paying 91 percent. We reduced that to 70 percent.

If we had the same tax rates that we had when I became President, before we got into the difficulties that we have, the extra expenditures, we would take in $24 billion more this year.

Now, I am not asking you to go back to the rates that we had here under the Kennedy administration and the Eisenhower administration. I am asking you to just go back enough to get not $24 billion, but $10 billion of the $24 billion. That is all.

Here is the corporate tax rate. This is your corporate tax rate. I reviewed these this morning with the leadership.

The corporation that had earnings of $25,000, we charged them 30 percent. We reduced that when we came in to 22 percent. A corporation here was paying 52 percent. We reduced that to 48 percent. Now we are just asking for a part of it.

Here is your personal income. Let me show you what we were doing.

Here is where we were when we came in. That is the income in America. I hope every one of you will see that. When you really "poor mouth" and you feel sorry for yourself, think about your mother and your father and what they did in '29 to '31.

Here is what you have done. You have gone from $466 right here to over $700. That is during these 4 years. You have almost doubled your personal income. Congressmen have not doubled theirs, but the country as a whole has doubled it. Maybe the reporters have not doubled it. But the facts are here: from $466 to a little over $700. That is personal income.[1]

Here is your corporate profits. Let's see

---

[1] The President was speaking in billions of dollars.

about your income to your corporations. They were a little under $60 billion; here they are over $90 billion. Up 33 percent in 3½ to 4 years.

Here is your personal income and your tax receipts. Here it was $466. Then it moves up to $498. Then $538, $584, $626, and that is '67; '68, you remember, goes up to $700.

Here are the tax receipts. All the time the income was going up, even though we reduced taxes, tax receipts went up.

This is the last one, the corporate profits before taxes and income tax receipts. Here is the corporate profit. This is what they made after taxes. You see, when we came in here in '63 how much they had to make? They made $60 billion and we took only $20 billion. Here they got $66 billion and we took $24 billion. Here they got $76 billion and we took $26 billion. Here they made $83 billion and we took $31 billion. Here they made $80 billion and we took $33 billion. Look at this line here, the blue line.

So those are not going down. Now, if you want to keep them going up, every businessman I know, every labor man I know, every economist I know who is a student of this situation, they tell us that if you have a gross

national product running over $800 billion, with the expenditures that we have to make in the cities, in Vietnam, and our poverty program, if you would avoid inflation, if you would avoid runaway prices, if you would avoid high interest rates, if you would avoid a slump in the homebuilding industry, then you must have a moderate tax bill.

We have had it in every war we have been in. We must have it now.

I don't know what is going to happen, but I am going to do my best. I hope that all of you will do yours.

NOTE: The President spoke at 10:40 a.m. in the Cabinet Room at the White House. In his opening words he referred to Robert C. Weaver, Secretary of Housing and Urban Development, Lloyd E. Clarke, President of the National Association of Home Builders, and Nathaniel H. Rogg, Executive Vice President of the Association. Early in his remarks he referred to Helen Thomas, the reporter who covered the marriages of the Johnson daughters Luci Baines and Lynda Bird and the births of their children. Later he referred to Representative W. J. Bryan Dorn of South Carolina and Senator Jennings Randolph of West Virginia.

As enacted, the bill (H.R. 10477) is Public Law 90–301 (82 Stat. 113).

For the President's statement upon signing the Revenue and Expenditure Control Act of 1968, which enacted his proposed tax increase, see Item 343.

230   Remarks Upon Presenting the 1968 Scholastic Achievement Awards to Blind College Students. *May 7, 1968*

Miss Peterson, Mr. Baker, Mr. DuBoff:

I am very glad to welcome you here to the Cabinet Room of the White House today.

We have the very distinct pleasure of presenting awards to three outstanding young people—people who each in their own way

represent a triumph of the spirit.

They are blind.

Sherrill Peterson has been blind since birth.

Larry Baker and Leonard DuBoff became blind as young men.

They have more in common than their

handicap: They share a determination, a self-respect, and a faith in their own ability.

Each one is graduating in the top few percentage points of his or her class. If they had been lesser human beings, they could have taken a different path. They could have wallowed in self-pity, depending on charity and living very empty lives. They could have let their blindness become more than just a physical affliction.

But they knew, as we do, that the time has passed when the handicapped are shunted off in the backwaters of society, and the time has passed when our only attitudes toward the blind are pity and rejection.

So they chose to stand on their own, asking to be treated not with sympathy, but to be treated with respect.

They want the burdens of responsibility, as well as the rewards.

They know the value of many things that some of us take for granted.

None of us is completely safe from the terrible accidents which could take our sight. We are making progress in the fight against the many causes of blindness.

Yet, we still have in America 400,000 people who are legally blind, a million more whose eyes are so bad that they can't read a newspaper, and 3½ million who have only partial vision.

What Sherrill, Larry, and Leonard have proven is that none of these people need be lost as wage earners or active family members, or contributors to our communities.

One of the great pleasures I had early in my days in the White House was to take a distinguished lawyer who was blind and put him on the Tax Court. And the fine

things I have heard about his performance have really made me pleased that I took that action.

Now, it is true that none of us would envy your handicap, but all of us would do well to envy your character.

I remember once overhearing an argument between two men. One was blind. The other man was chewing the blind man up one side and down the other for a business decision he had made.

When the argument was over, someone went up to the sighted fellow and said, "You should not have done that. Didn't you know he was blind?"

The man was a little surprised. "What does that have to do with anything?" he said. "That man has a better mind than you and I put together, and he made a stupid mistake. He would never have forgiven me if I hadn't bawled him out."

So I say to all of you that I would never have forgiven myself if I had not come here to meet with you and to recognize you, to try to gain strength from you, and to learn from you.

Thank you very much.

NOTE: The President spoke at 12:08 p.m. in the Cabinet Room at the White House. In his opening words he referred to the three award winners, Sherrill Rae Peterson of the University of Illinois, Larry Dale Baker of Indiana University, and Leonard David DuBoff of Hofstra University. They were assisted, as are some 1,500 blind college students yearly, by recorded textbooks supplied by Recording for the Blind, a national nonprofit organization, which sponsors the annual scholastic achievement awards to blind students.

At the ceremony a version of "Abraham Lincoln" by Carl Sandburg, recorded by volunteer readers, was presented to the President.

231 Presidential Unit Citation Awarded the 20th Tactical Reconnaissance Squadron, Pacific Air Forces. *May 7, 1968*

CITATION TO ACCOMPANY .THE AWARD OF
THE PRESIDENTIAL UNIT CITATION
TO THE
20TH TACTICAL RECONNAISSANCE SQUADRON

The 20th Tactical Reconnaissance Squadron distinguished itself by displaying extraordinary gallantry in connection with military operations against an opposing armed force in Southeast Asia from 1 April 1966 to 31 December 1966. During this period the 20th Tactical Reconnaissance Squadron provided the majority of all United States Air Force daylight photographic intelligence taken over North Vietnam. Flying its combat missions in the face of some of the most effective and sophisticated air defense systems yet experienced by Air Force tactical aircraft, the Squadron contributed materially to the success of the tactical reconnaissance program in Southeast Asia. Through outstanding performance, extraordinary heroism, complete dedication and total teamwork, the Squadron accomplished its mission and maintained a high sortie rate despite extensive combat damage, aircraft losses, and extremely bad weather conditions over targets and recovery airfields. The courage, dedication, high professionalism and superb airmanship displayed by members of this unit are in keeping with the highest standards of performance and reflect great credit upon themselves, the unit and the United States Air Force.

LYNDON B. JOHNSON

232 Remarks of Welcome at the White House to Prime Minister Thanom Kittikachorn of Thailand. *May 8, 1968*

Your Excellency, Lady Chongkol, Secretary and Mrs. Rusk, General and Mrs. Chapman, distinguished guests, ladies and gentlemen:
Welcome to the United States.

It has been many months since we began planning this visit. Yet, because of the events of the last few days, your arrival today is especially timely.

There is a fresh breeze of hope circulating around the world. It concerns both of our Nations, as well as many other nations.

Thus, it is a good time for men to meet and to reflect. It is a time to set our long term aims and our aspirations for the days ahead.

Mr. Prime Minister, America's aims are simple and straightforward.

We believe that freedom and peace in America can only be secured if America remains involved in, and concerned with, the future of human freedom throughout the world.

We believe that the cause of freedom and progress can be worked for both economically and politically.

The experience of Thailand over recent years shows that great economic progress is possible when a motivated people seek it, and work toward it, in freedom. The Thai economic growth rate over the last 7 years has surpassed 7 percent per year—one of the highest rates in all the world.

We believe that human freedom thrives

best when men have the right to determine their own political destiny.

That has been our aim in Vietnam: to help a nation in its struggle to determine its own destiny. As that simple—but very difficult—objective becomes secure, the American role in Vietnam will diminish and disappear. I stated that in Manila in 1966; it was stated by General Westmoreland again in late 1967; it has been stated by our Secretary of State; and Secretary Clifford restated it just a few weeks ago.

In Bangkok in 1966, at your beautiful university there, I said to the leaders in Hanoi, "Let us lay aside our arms and sit down . . . at the table of reason. . . . Enough of this sorrow. Let us begin the work of healing. . . ."

There is hope now, finally, some hope that that offer will bear fruit and that an honorable peace could come.

The world knows that the brave Thai people have been in the front rank of those who fought the good fight for freedom in Southeast Asia. Thailand was the first nation—the first nation—to join with America in the successful U.N. effort in Korea in 1950. Thailand was the first member to ratify the SEATO Treaty. Thai troops today stand and fight shoulder to shoulder with us in South Vietnam.

Mr. Prime Minister, it is good to have such a staunch ally by one's side as we begin this time of hope and recommitment to our principles.

Welcome again. We look forward with great pleasure to the time that you can spend here with us and to the profitable exchanges that we sincerely believe will take place.

NOTE: The President spoke at 11:40 a.m. on the South Lawn at the White House where Prime Minister Thanom Kittikachorn was given a formal welcome with full military honors. In his opening words the President also referred to Lady Thanpuying Chongkol, wife of the Prime Minister, Secretary of State and Mrs. Dean Rusk, Gen. Leonard F. Chapman, Commandant of the Marine Corps, and Mrs. Chapman.

The ceremony was to be telecast by satellite to Thailand to inaugurate the new Sri Racha earth station there.

For the President's remarks at Chulalongkorn University in Bangkok, see 1966 volume, this series, Book II, Item 557.

The Prime Minister responded as follows:

Mr. President, Mrs. Johnson, ladies and gentlemen:

May I express my heartfelt appreciation, Mr. President, for your generous words of greeting.

My wife and I have been happy to accept your kind invitation to visit the United States and to bring with us for you, Mr. President, and for Mrs. Johnson and the American Nation, the greetings and good wishes of Their Majesties the King and Queen, as well as those of the Thai people.

We also vividly remember your visit to our country, the first official visit ever paid by a President of the United States to Thailand. The Thai people greatly rejoiced in welcoming you as the Chief of State of a country we, in Thailand, hold to be our great friend and ally.

Mr. President, while some people may not be clear in their thinking, as their minds are beclouded by doubts, we in Thailand fully realize and appreciate how much the United States and its gallant soldiers have done and are still doing to help defend small nations against aggression and, thus, to preserve the delicate peace in the world.

We know the extent of sacrifices such a decision involves, but the lesson of the recent past tells us that they are smaller than those which would have to be borne if the aggressors were allowed to strengthen themselves with the spoils of their victims.

The Thai Nation and, indeed, the free nations of Asia, will always remember you, Mr. President, as the courageous defender of freedom in Asia and as the man who has spared the United States and the world from another holocaust.

Thailand, on its part, has accepted to shoulder its share of sacrifices and responsibility. At the same time, the Thai Nation and people are with you and those enlightened Americans in your incessant quest for a lasting and meaningful peace—a genuine peace which is not a facade covering a surrender—but a peace which guarantees freedom and the right for small nations to exist with dignity and independence.

With this purpose in mind, we have come to Washington to join with you, Mr. President, in our unrelenting search for a peaceful and progressive future in Southeast Asia.

Thank you.

233 Toasts of the President and Prime Minister Thanom Kittikachorn. *May 8, 1968*

Your Excellency, Lady Chongkol, Mr. Vice President, Mr. Secretary of State, distinguished guests, ladies and gentlemen:

Mr. Prime Minister, your visit today is historic and very pleasing in more ways than one. Right after we finish this dinner, you and I will go upstairs to the Treaty Room in the White House. We will place a telephone call to Bangkok. Together, we will talk to your Acting Prime Minister and, thus, we will inaugurate a new and a direct telephone service between our two Nations that are so many thousands of miles apart.

I have already assured the Prime Minister that I will not abuse the privileges of this new Thai line. His personal phone number will continue to remain unlisted.

As we meet here tonight, our Nations are linked closer together in another way. Your arrival at the White House this morning, Mr. Prime Minister, is being telecast to Thailand. This is the first direct telecast from the United States across the Pacific to the new Asian mainland. Your Government, sir, has helped to make this miracle possible. You have had the vision, the imagination, and the courage to go ahead and build the ground station that is now receiving signals from an American satellite which is orbiting far out over the Pacific.

This telecast is evidence of a tremendous and recent leap in man's ability to communicate with man—to see, to speak, and to learn about the world in which he lives—to better understand all the peoples of the earth, and all the truths that can join us as one human family on one peaceful planet.

It is our space technology that has given us the miracles of satellites and these worldwide telecasts. Most of us never recognize

that at all. It is the millions of dollars and the many millions of man-hours that are invested in our space program that give America and Thailand a new link tonight— just as this technology draws all men closer in understanding and the partnership that can come from it.

That, I think, is the real message that should go out over the airwaves tonight. I hope that it will be heard—and, Mr. Boggs, I hope it will be heeded in the Congress— when the critics of the space program sit down to do their budget calculations.

Personally, I am delighted that we have already slipped under this wire.

Speaking of telecasts, I am tempted to ask the Prime Minister for equal time tonight, because I understand that he made a very special side trip on his recent visit to Florida. He requested—and I think was granted—a special tour of the hall where the Republican Party will evolve its plans to defeat us and where it will hold its convention a little later this year.

Mr. Prime Minister, should you choose to visit Chicago, I think there are some people who would be delighted to serve as your guide. The Vice President has a very crowded schedule these days but he has never failed me in any request I have made. I am sure if you put Chicago on your itinerary and you desire to go and take a look at the convention hall, we could call upon the Vice President to go and show you through it.

I have some doubt, Mr. Prime Minister, as to who is going to be the star of the telecast that you will see. As you and I were making some very solemn speeches this morning, according to the press, out here on the South Lawn, Mrs. Johnson noticed that the cameras kept looking away from us. She told me later that they missed what we had to say because they were focused on a very happy little boy in the White House doorway. He had a Thai flag in one hand and an American flag in the other hand, and every time he saw a camera, your grandson looked directly into the eye of it and waved both flags so the camera could see them.

I learned to admire your little grandson this morning, Mr. Prime Minister. He is a fast learner, and I predict he has a great public future. I believe he is only 2 years old. He seems to have done something that I have been unable to do in 60 years—he has mastered the very difficult art of charming the American press.

Luckily, I did not bring my own grandson along this morning. If I had, Mr. Prime Minister, I don't think that either of us would have been in any pictures at all.

Mrs. Johnson and I know that this visit is your first opportunity to see two of your grandchildren. We know from personal experience how delightful that must be for you and your wife. We are very pleased to share with all of you that joy.

Our families mean much to both of us. We both know in very personal terms what it means to have members of our immediate family away from home fighting in Vietnam—you, through your own son, and me through both of my sons-in-law. The hope that sustains us, and the things which make our burdens easier, is the conviction that our sons have seen their duty—and they are going to succeed in it.

These young men—and the many hundreds of thousands like them—are our guardians tonight. I believe in all faith and in great pride that these young men are also the builders of a greater and a better world.

They are the builders of a more secure and a prospering new Asia, a peaceful and progressive partnership among men.

All of us know and value the contributions that the Royal Thai Government, under your own wise and strong leadership, is making daily to that dream.

Your role in SEATO is fundamental to the collective security and growth of Southeast Asia. You stand steadfast with us and our allies, holding up the shield behind which a new Asia is building tonight. By helping to mediate old and outworn quarrels, you are inspiring your neighbors to come and reason together and to work in new and creative enterprises.

By working through the United Nations, you are helping to harness the mighty Mekong River for the benefit of literally millions of your own people and millions of your neighbors. By creating and encouraging a host of new cooperative institutions, you are laying the foundations of a system where Asians can work out their own destiny in their own way.

These are the goals—and these are the stakes—of our common commitment in Southeast Asia. These are the reasons why I take those commitments so seriously, why we are pledged to honor them scrupulously. We seek nothing more than an honorable settlement of conflict and difficulty. But, Mr. Prime Minister, we are determined to accept nothing less.

We will negotiate in good faith, but we will never—we will never—abandon our commitments nor will we ever compromise the future of Asia at the negotiating table. We will sit down in Paris as cordial, fairminded, and openhanded men. However hard or however long the labor, we will not tire in keeping our public trust.

I hope that our own people, all of them, and our adversaries as well, will realize that increased infiltration, sending new MIGs to new airfields south of the 20th parallel, will not go unnoticed, even when we have summoned all of our patience and our fairness in an attempt to peacefully sit down at the table and be fair with our fellow men.

Mr. Prime Minister, it is as I described it the other evening. We want to move from enmity to brotherhood, from destruction to common efforts on behalf of the men, women, and children of Southeast Asia.

In this we ask the prayers of all of our fellow men tonight throughout the world, because this is the eve of our delegation's departure for what I hope with all of my heart will be the table of peace.

Let us toast their going. Let us toast their success and to the precious gift that they may bring us on their return.

But let us never enjoy the illusion for a moment that the road is not going to be long, hard, and difficult; that it will try men's patience and men's souls.

Let us remember and toast tonight others whose mission is peace, to the gallant and the magnificent soldiers of Thailand whose courage and whose sacrifices give their South Vietnamese and American comrades so much heart. These brave men and their families give us all so much confidence that the day of reconciliation must come someday, and we hope it will come soon.

Ladies and gentlemen, those of you who have come from throughout the breadth of this land, from most of the 50 States, I should like to ask you to toast now to all that we share with the people of Thailand and all of our warm regards for Their Majesties, the King and the Queen of Thailand.

NOTE: The President proposed the toast at 10:13 p.m. at a dinner in the State Dining Room at the White House. In his opening words he also referred to Lady Thanpuying Chongkol, wife of the Prime Minister, Vice President Hubert H. Humphrey, and Secretary of State Dean Rusk. During his remarks

he referred to Representative Hale Boggs of Louisiana, member of the Ways and Means Committee of the House of Representatives. The Prime Minister responded as follows:

Mr. President, Mrs. Johnson, Mr. Vice President, distinguished guests, and friends:

May I thank you, Mr. President, most sincerely for your generous words of welcome and for your gracious hospitality extended to all of us. I am indeed grateful to you, Mr. President, for your heartening expression of friendship toward Thailand and its people.

We highly value the opportunity given by this visit to meet and exchange views with you, Mr. President, and with other distinguished leaders of your Government on many matters of mutual interest and concern.

I feel highly gratified that on the vital question of peace and stability of Southeast Asia, with particular relation to Vietnam, the United States and Thailand share the same views that aggression must not be allowed to succeed and that smaller nations must not be subjected against their will to alien domination by the sheer use of force, terror, and subversion. For if such conquest were allowed to take place, the seeds of wider conflict would be sown with dire consequences for our Nations and the rest of mankind.

With keen realization of this great danger, you have taken, Mr. President, a courageous stand to forestall the dreadful event and prevent grievous sacrifices which otherwise would befall your great Nation and the rest of the world.

For this wise and farsighted decision, the Thai people and the free nations of Asia are forever grateful to you and will always keep in their memory the name of Lyndon Baines Johnson as a benefactor who has gallantly upheld the cause of their freedom and independence.

They fully realize how difficult and painful it must have been for you, Mr. President, as a man of peace, to reach such a momentous decision which would involve the well-being and the lives of many brave, young men, especially your sons-in-law.

If any vindication were to be needed, it will be by history that, in accepting the present heavy and grievous burden, many more lives will have been spared for this great Nation and the rest of the world.

Already the course that the United States and its allies have taken is proven to be a correct one as our firm resolve has convinced the aggressors that they cannot overcome free nations by violence and conquest.

A grave and important task, however, remains to be accomplished, namely, that of preventing the enemy of freedom from reaping at the conference table the victory they could not achieve on the battlefield, for otherwise, the costly sacrifices of our gallant soldiers would have been in vain.

You, Mr. President, and the American Nation, may rest assured that Thailand and its people, who have braved the risk of war and destruction, stand with you and the United States in forging a firm and meaningful peace which will insure that free peoples will always remain free.

Conscious of its duty, the Thai Government and people have not remained idle. As fighting goes on, they have, by themselves, and in conjunction with some of their neighbors, laid the foundations for peace and future progress of Southeast Asia.

We shall need you, as perhaps you will need us, to join together in constructive endeavors in building a better and more harmonious world in which free men can engage without fear of death and destruction in the pursuit of their happiness.

It will always be our fond hope, Mr. President, that the great American Nation and the small Thai Nation will always join hands in such a practical and mutually beneficial partnership for peace, for freedom and progress.

I should like now to propose a toast to the President of the United States and to the everlasting friendship between the American Nation and the Thai Nation.

234   Statement by the President Following House Action on Appropriations for Urban Programs. *May 8, 1968*

THE HOUSE has just passed the fiscal 1969 appropriation for the Department of Housing and Urban Development.

This measure is a step forward—but it does not go far enough.

The sums voted for our city programs are higher than the amounts approved by Congress last year. But they fall far short of the request the President made in the January budget for the important model cities and rent supplement programs so essential to ease the crisis in our cities.

I hope the Senate will fully restore the amounts to the minimum levels I recommended so that we can move forward with the urgent task of rebuilding the American city.

NOTE: The proposed legislation was approved on October 4, 1968, as the Independent Offices and Department of Housing and Urban Development Appropriation Act of 1969 (Public Law 90–550, 82 Stat. 937).

235   Letter to the Majority Leader of the Senate on the Crime Control and Safe Streets Bill. *May 9, 1968*

[Released May 9, 1968. Dated May 8, 1968]

Dear Mike:

The Senate is approaching a moment of decision for America, as debate proceeds on the Crime Control and Safe Streets Act of 1968.

I would hope that three facts—three crucial facts—can illuminate that debate.

First, a harsh reality faces the most affluent Nation on earth. Crimes of violence threaten to turn us into a land of fearful strangers. The triple-lock door and the street that empties quickly at nightfall are unhappy symbols in modern America. The rapist and the mugger, the racketeer and the robber leave heavy scars on our society.

Second, the key to effective crime control is effective law enforcement—at the local level. As I have repeatedly stressed, crime is a local problem. It must be defeated in the community it corrodes.

Third, the machinery of local law enforcement all across the Nation must be strengthened before it can carry out its mission effectively. Far too many local police forces are ill-paid, ill-equipped, and ill-trained.

Fifteen months ago, based on a study I had conducted by the President's Crime Commission, which was composed of the most carefully selected and outstanding experts in the field—the most authoritative study of crime in America ever conducted—I then urged the Congress to immediately launch a massive effort to revitalize local law enforcement—from crime prevention to the apprehension of criminals to the system of corrections.

That proposal—the Safe Streets program—is now embodied in Title I of the bill before the Senate.

Through federal *grants* to *local* communities and states, it will put new strength into the entire network of crime control and criminal justice. It will give the policeman on the beat—who risks his life to protect our homes and families—better training and equipment for his job. It will reward him with better pay for his service. It will put the resources of modern science behind his efforts.

I urge the Senate to pass Title I. It is long overdue and urgently needed. Delay will be a victory for the criminal—from the petty thief to the kings of organized crime. The losers will be the American people.

The pending bill also addresses itself to another urgent national concern—the need for gun control legislation.

I have sought a proper and strong gun control bill for as long as I have been President.

Title IV takes a long step toward public safety, by helping to keep pistols and other hand guns away from the dangerous and the deranged.

But it does not go far enough.

It fails to provide the same protection against weapons which are just as deadly in criminal hands—the rifle and other long guns.

Now, it is time to stand up and show we are not a Government by lobby but a Government of law.

Has not the high powered mail order rifle brought tragedy enough to America? What in the name of conscience will it take to pass a truly effective gun control law?

The issue of immediate importance is to bring safety to our streets.

We can best do this by:

—Strengthening the Gun Control Law.

—Writing the provisions of Title I (the Safe Streets Program) into the statute book without delay.

—Not encumbering the legislation with provisions raising grave constitutional questions and which might jeopardize the prompt passage of Title I.

In the clear and compelling interest of 200 million Americans, I urge the Senate to enact Title I—now.

The mugger and the murderer will not wait.

Neither must we.

Sincerely,

LYNDON B. JOHNSON

[Honorable Mike Mansfield, United States Senate, Washington, D.C.]

NOTE: The Omnibus Crime Control and Safe Streets Act of 1968 was approved by the President on June 19, 1968 (see Item 320). The act was amended on August 8, 1968 (Public Law 90–462, 82 Stat. 638).

The Gun Control Act of 1968 was approved by the President on October 22, 1968 (see Item 553).

236 Remarks Upon Presenting the Young American Medals for Bravery and Service. *May 9, 1968*

Attorney General Clark, Director Hoover, Dean Griswold, distinguished Members of Congress, ladies and gentlemen:

This morning we have come here to the Cabinet Room because it gives us an opportunity to honor courage—not, as often in these times, the courage of the battlefield, but the quieter courage that is exhibited by our finer citizens in their everyday life.

I am doubly pleased because these awards pay tribute to the idealism and the commitment of our American youth.

There is a great deal of ferment among many of our young people today. Some of it is foolish and some of it is self-destructive. But most of it represents power—power for good, power for constructive change. I think most of it is brave and most of it is selfless.

William Glynn is receiving the Young American Medal for Bravery. He was just 15 years old when he saved a drowning man off Long Island. For more than 2 hours, he battled 14-foot waves to keep the exhausted and the unconscious man from slipping away to a certain death.

Carmalita Capilla and Mary Lynne Donohue are receiving medals for service.

Carmalita devoted almost all of her free time to helping the less fortunate mentally ill at Hawaii State Hospital. One hospital official said, "You could follow Carmalita by the trail of smiles she left with the patients."

Mary Lynne was president of the Sheboygan Association of Youth. She directed more than 1,000 young people in fundraising for the March of Dimes and the USO.

She was a member of the Steering Committee of the Sheboygan Human Rights As-sociation. Somehow, she still managed to finish in the top 5 percent of her high school class.

There were 70 other nominees—from 23 States, Guam, and Puerto Rico—who did not win medals. But we value them nonetheless.

In this period of our history, when we so often see on our screens and so often read in our newspapers the mistakes that have been made and the errors that have been committed, it is refreshing and stimulating to hear and to see some of the things that make our Nation the great nation that it is.

They—and you—are a credit to your generation. You are an inspiration to your President and to your country.

Thank you very much.

NOTE: The President spoke at 11:43 a.m. in the Cabinet Room at the White House. In his opening words he referred to Attorney General Ramsey Clark, J. Edgar Hoover, Director of the Federal Bureau of Investigation, and Solicitor General Erwin N. Griswold, formerly Dean of Harvard Law School.

The President presented the gold Young American Medals to the following:

—William G. Glynn III, 16, of Westbury, Long Island, N.Y., who at the age of 15, while surfing off Fire Island, rescued a man who had fallen from a jetty and was being swept out to sea;

—Carmalita Capilla, 19, of Kailua, Oahu, Hawaii, who devoted her school holidays and vacations in 1966 to a wide range of volunteer services to mental patients at the Hawaii State Hospital and organized "Teens Against Mental Illness," a volunteer group of hospital workers; and

—Mary Lynne Donohue, 19, of Sheboygan, Wis., who as president of the Sheboygan Association of Youth directed more than 1,000 young people in fundraising projects for the USO, March of Dimes, muscular dystrophy, and other endeavors, and organized a Christmas party for 60 children in the Head Start program. Mary Lynne also served on the steering committee of the Sheboygan Human Rights Association, which sponsored lectures by human rights leaders and recruited volunteers for Head Start.

Winners were selected by the Young American Medals Committee, composed of Mr. Hoover, Solic-itor General Griswold, and Clifton F. Sessions, Director of Public Information, Department of Justice. The awards, for the year 1966, make a total of 29 awarded for bravery and 14 for service since 1950 when Congress established the program under the Justice Department (Public Law 638, 64 Stat. 397).

237   Joint Statement Following Discussions With the Prime Minister of Thailand.   *May 9, 1968*

AT THE INVITATION of President Lyndon B. Johnson of the United States, Prime Minister Thanom Kittikachorn of the Kingdom of Thailand paid an official visit to Washington on May 8 and 9. This visit afforded the President and the Prime Minister and several of his senior Cabinet colleagues an opportunity to exchange views on current developments in Thailand and on the situation in Southeast Asia.

THAILAND

The Prime Minister described the dynamic economic expansion currently taking place in Thailand. He mentioned the major role played by private initiative and emphasized Thai interest in promoting foreign investment in his country. He also referred to the forthcoming promulgation of a new Constitution by His Majesty the King.

The President and the Prime Minister discussed the externally-supported, Communist-directed subversion and insurgency in Thailand, especially in the northern and northeastern regions. In this connection, the Prime Minister described his Government's programs for providing security to the rural population and improving their social and economic conditions. He also noted that while welcoming foreign assistance in the form of training, equipment and advice, the Royal Thai Government regarded defeating the insurgency as a Thai responsibility to be carried out by its own forces. The President made clear the intention of the United States to continue its assistance to Thailand to help provide the Royal Thai Government with the means of meeting illegal Communist activities. He stressed American support in the field of accelerated rural development, especially with regard to roads and water resources.

The President re-emphasized the determination of the United States to stand by its treaty commitments to Thailand and its other allies in Asia. He recalled with pleasure the three visits he has made to Thailand. He noted the pledge that he had given at the time of his visit to Bangkok in 1966 that the commitment of the United States was not of a particular political party or administration, but of the people of the United States, and that "America keeps its commitments."

VIETNAM

The President and the Prime Minister reviewed in detail the situation in South Vietnam. They reaffirmed their determination to assist the Republic of Vietnam in defending itself against aggression in order to assure its people the right to determine their own future free from external interference and terrorism. They also stressed the importance of this defense to the security of other nations in the region.

The President and the Prime Minister reviewed the military situation including the recent initiatives of the Government of South Vietnam and actions by the United States and its allies to increase their forces there.

The Prime Minister noted that additional Thai forces, the first increments of a Thai division, will deploy to South Vietnam shortly to join Thai troops already fighting with South Vietnamese, American, and other allied units. The President paid tribute to the contribution Thailand is making to our common defense interests by making base facilities available for use by the United States. He also praised the hospitality extended American servicemen by the Thai people.

The President and the Prime Minister agreed that the attainment of a just and durable peace required both a strong military posture and the pursuit of a diplomatic solution. They agreed to continue their efforts on both these fronts until such a peace is secured.

The President reviewed in detail the developments that had followed his initiative of March 31 to halt bombing in the major part of North Vietnam and to invite talks. The President and the Prime Minister expressed satisfaction that Paris had now been agreed as the site for talks, and the President reviewed the position that American representatives would take in the opening stages of these talks. The President reaffirmed that at each stage the U.S. Government would continue its full consultations with the Royal Thai Government and its other allies concerning negotiating positions and developments. The President and the Prime Minister also reaffirmed the position stated in the Seven-Nation Foreign Ministers Meeting of April 1967—that a settlement in Vietnam, to be enduring, must respect the wishes and aspirations of the Vietnamese people; that the

Republic of Vietnam should be a full participant in any negotiations designed to bring about a settlement of the conflict; and that the allied nations which have helped to defend the Republic of Vietnam should participate in any settlement of the conflict. Expressing the hope that the Paris conversations would result in serious discussions on the substance of peace in Vietnam, the President and the Prime Minister reaffirmed that the Manila Communique of 1966 would form the basis of the allied position. The two leaders emphasized their determination that the South Vietnamese people shall not be conquered by aggression and shall enjoy their inherent right to decide their own way of life and form of government. The President and the Prime Minister also noted the importance of ensuring full compliance with the provisions of the 1962 Geneva Accords on Laos.

In discussing the situation which would follow a cessation of hostilities in Vietnam, the President and the Prime Minister agreed that close and continuous consultation on economic and security questions would be required to assure a smooth transition from war to peace.

REGIONAL COOPERATION

The President and the Prime Minister further reviewed the favorable trends in regional cooperation in Southeast Asia and Thailand's leading role in furthering these developments. Particular note was taken of the accomplishments in the United Nations Economic Commission for Asia and the Far East (ECAFE) and the Mekong Committee, to whose studies and projects they attach considerable importance, and of the evolution of several new Southeast Asian organizations which raise hope for a new era of constructive common endeavor for a lasting peace and sustained progress of the area. Referring to his speech at Johns Hopkins in April 1965, the President cited our support for Southeast Asian regional development as clear evidence of the United States continuing concern for and commitment to the nations of this region.

In particular, the Prime Minister reported to the President discussions held in New York with a US team headed by Mr. Eugene R. Black concerning the favorable outlook for the Pa Mong dam on the mainstream of the Mekong River. The President and the Prime Minister agreed on the importance of this project and the desirability of accelerating present project feasibility studies under the Mekong Committee.

In conclusion, Prime Minister Thanom Kittikachorn expressed his grateful appreciation for the gracious hospitality extended to him and Thanpuying Chongkol as well as the members of their party by the President of the United States and for the warm and friendly welcome accorded them by the Government and the people of the United States.

238 Remarks to a Group of Young People Representing the Vocational Industrial Clubs of America. *May 10, 1968*

I AM very proud of what we have been able to do in the vocational education field.

I have observed nothing in my contacts with young people—and I have two or three groups a day, in the hope that I can learn something from them and keep contact with them, and maybe they can learn something from coming here—that pleased me more than your presentation. I don't think I have heard a better one.

The fact that you were aware that you were in the presence of Jackson, Lincoln, and Roosevelt, and tied it into the remarks you had to make, and where the wood came from, is just another indication that our school system is doing a pretty good job in this day and time.

All we hear sometimes are challenges to our future. A lot of people wonder about what our young people are doing, then we see a demonstration like you put on here this morning. It makes me think that every dollar we have invested in our schools has been returned with interest.

Yes, I served with Mr. Doughton of North Carolina for a long time. He was a great leader of the Ways and Means Committee. I have had a rather intimate association with the Members of Congress from your State. My grandfather came from your State.

I am so proud we are producing 18-year-olds in this Nation who can come in the presence of the President in the Cabinet Room and probably make a better presentation than either the President or the members of the Cabinet. I hope the people you represent are as proud of you as I am. I hope you will tell your family what an excellent job the President thought you did.

We are very, very strong for vocational education. We are very proud of the landmark legislation we passed. Under 35 Presidents, the primary legislative matters in the educational field were in the field of vocational education, the George-Deen Act, the Smith-Hughes Act, and creating the Office of Education itself, in Andrew Johnson's time.

But when you added all of those educational matters together, you had less than you could count on your fingers in 35 previous administrations. Because the emphasis has been on learning and moving forward in the 21st century, and the need to know, driving ignorance from our midst, we have passed three times as many bills in the last 4 years in the educational field as we did in all the other 35 administrations put together. We see that it is paying off in all of you.

Thank you.

NOTE: The President spoke at 11:50 a.m. in the Cabinet Room at the White House. During his remarks he referred to the late Robert Lee Doughton, Representative from North Carolina from 1911 to 1953.

Prior to the President's remarks he was presented with a gavel in appreciation of his efforts in making opportunities for vocational training in industry and technology more available to young Americans. The presentation was made by 18-year-old Lynn Register of Columbus, Ga., president of the Vocational Industrial Clubs of America. The gavel is the work of VICA member Terry Lovelace, 16, a carpentry and cabinetmaking student at Alleghany High School, Sparta, N.C. Its handle is of white hickory from The Hermitage, home of Andrew Jackson in Nashville, Tenn.; its mallet of oak from the Old State House in Springfield, Ill., where Abraham Lincoln delivered his "House Divided" speech; and its sounding block of wood from the Hyde Park estate of Franklin D. Roosevelt. The gavel and sounding block are mounted on a base of wood grown on the farm of the late Representative Doughton. On a plate affixed to the base are engraved the words: "To Lyndon B. Johnson, America's Great Education President."

The Vocational Industrial Clubs of America, organized in 1965, is a national youth organization providing leadership, citizenship, and character development programs and activities for secondary and college students in the technical, industrial, and health occupation fields. VICA clubs in 35 States, Puerto Rico, and Guam number some 71,000 members.

As printed above, this item follows the text released by the White House Press Office.

239   Remarks at a Luncheon Honoring Dr. José Mora and William Sanders on Their Retirement as Officials of the Organization of American States.   *May 10, 1968*

Dr. Mora, Mr. Sanders, distinguished Ambassadors, Members of Congress, distinguished friends, ladies and gentlemen:

We have come here to the White House today to honor two of the outstanding public servants of this hemisphere.

José Mora and William Sanders have guided our Organization of American States through the most challenging decade in its history. Their stewardship has seen the launching of the Alliance for Progress and the Inter-American Development Bank.

They have witnessed and shared in the great movement toward economic integration that was reflected in the Central American Common Market and the Latin American Free Trade Association.

They stood in the frontlines defending our hemisphere during the times of great peril, and they stood beside us as we adopted a new charter of promise and hope in the Americas in the Presidents' action program of Punta del Este.

For almost half of this decade, I have worked shoulder to shoulder with these two distinguished men. We have strengthened the security of our hemisphere beyond doubt. We have waged a successful battle for economic opportunity and social justice in Latin America.

In these years, just to cite a few facts, the average per capita growth in Latin America has more than doubled over the first 3 years of the Alliance, from nine-tenths of 1 percent in 1961 through 1963, to $2\frac{2}{10}$ percent from 1964 through 1967.

The United States has put $7 billion 700 million at the service of the Alliance for

Progress. That is 35 percent higher per annum in the last 4 years than we did in the first 3 years.

The enrollment in our primary schools has increased by almost 7 million students, and in secondary schools by close to 2 million students. The number of cooperatives has increased by over 35 percent. A quarter of a million land titles have already been distributed, and tax collections, which rose $489 million in the 1961 through 1963 period, increased from $489 million to nearly $3 billion during the 1964 to 1967 period.

Our inter-American system has always been a trail blazer in the quest for a better world. We have pioneered procedures for the peaceful settlement of disputes. There has been no armed conflict between the members of our community now for more than 30 years.

We have championed the principle of self-determination of peoples. We have acted to preserve it—collectively—when it was threatened in our hemisphere.

We have developed the modern concept of collective security. We are pursuing the goal of representative democracy. Elections held throughout the hemisphere during the last 2 years show that we are making great progress.

We are demonstrating that through the Alliance for Progress, by all of us working together, nations in a region can build economic democracy and Latin America recently gave the world a model for preventing the spread of nuclear weapons.

All of this could not have been achieved without the dedication of wise men—men who saw that in laboring for cooperation between all the nations of America, they would serve the interests of each nation and its people.

Mr. Sanders, we are very proud of your dedicated service to the inter-American cause.

Dr. Mora, I am reminded of Emerson's words: "An institution is the lengthened shadow of one man." You leave your high office knowing that the OAS will carry the mark of your achievements throughout history. You leave with the deep gratitude of this Nation—of this Nation's President and of this Nation's people—for making the new world a better and a safer place for free men to pursue their destiny.

There is so much that is undone. There is still so much to be done. But it can and it will be done. If those who follow you in this institution cast the same shadow of solidarity and progress for our hemisphere, then we have many good years to look forward to.

I ask you to rise and join me in a toast to Dr. Mora and Mr. Sanders.

[Following the toast Dr. Mora spoke briefly. The President then resumed speaking.]

Dr. Mora, it gives me a great deal of pleasure to present you, for your services, this little box that has an inscription on it. We are very grateful for all you have done. This represents the feeling of all the people here.

I said something about divisiveness in my speech of March 31st. It doesn't mean that anyone here feels that way. It doesn't apply to this group. For instance, we have seated at this very table the Rockefellers and the Meanys. We come from the great open spaces of the cactus country of Southwest Texas, from one of the largest ranches in our country, to Mr. Hewitt over here from the Black Lands of Illinois.

We have the leaders of industry, the leaders of the press, the leading ambassadors from this continent. They are all here today.

We all join in this tribute to an outstanding man who has done a very constructive service for all of us.

This is a token of our appreciation.

NOTE: The President spoke at 2:13 p.m. in the State Dining Room at the White House. In his opening words he referred to Dr. José A. Mora, Secretary General of the Organization of American States, and William Sanders, Assistant Secretary General.

During his remarks he referred to William A. Hewitt, Chairman, Deere and Co., Moline, Ill.

Dr. Mora's remarks are printed in the Weekly Compilation of Presidential Documents (vol. 4, p. 778).

240 Message on the Occasion of the National Day of the Kingdom of Laos. *May 10, 1968*

Your Majesty:

I extend to you and to the people of Laos the sincere good wishes of the people of the United States of America on the National Day of the Kingdom of Laos.

On this occasion we wish to reaffirm our support of the staunch efforts of the Lao people to achieve peace and tranquility. It is our earnest hope that the neutrality of the Kingdom of Laos will be respected and honored by all nations.

I assure you that the principles embodied in the 1962 Geneva Agreements guide our relations with your country, and we continue to support full implementation of the provisions of those Agreements as the best means of assuring an enduring peace for your country.

With personal regards.

LYNDON B. JOHNSON

[His Majesty Sri Savang Vatthana, King of Laos]

NOTE: The National Day of the Kingdom of Laos falls on May 11.

241 Remarks to Members of the Business Council Meeting in Hot Springs, Virginia. *May 11, 1968*

Mr. Nickerson and members of the Council:

I have come here today for basically two reasons.

First, I want to say to you—and, through you, to all the American business community—"Thank you."

Over the past 4½ years, our Nation has moved as it has seldom moved before.

Here at home, we have sustained and carried forward the longest period in history of uninterrupted expansion of this economy for which you have such a direct responsibility.

In the world, we have sustained the strength of the free world alliances against aggression everywhere. We have stood our watch on the walls of freedom, and we have—like those who preceded us—guarded the flame of man's hopes for peace on this earth.

The two parties met this morning in Paris for more than 2 hours and agreed on procedures for official conversations between the United States and the Democratic Republic of Vietnam. These official conversations will begin at 10:30 a.m., Monday, May 13.

As no other generation before has done— or has been able to do—this generation of Americans has gone out to meet the future. We have not been content that our times should be prosperous while future times would be impoverished by our neglect. In these few years, we have grasped the nettle firmly. We have undertaken to respond to the thorny challenges, the trying challenges, and the toughest challenges our society presents.

Some would call what we have done, "liberal." Others—although perhaps none present here—might call it, "conservative." For myself, I would call this response of the American people over the last 4 years, and this performance of the American system, "responsible."

That is why I came here today, on your invitation and mine, to say again to each of you—and, through you, to the business community that you symbolize—"Thank you from the bottom of my heart."

I am everlastingly grateful to the leadership of American management for the strength and the complete support you have given me—all along the way. The commitment of the energy, the initiative, and the intelligence of the modern business community has been a most decisive factor in the social progress we have begun in this decade.

I hope it may always be.

The day is long past in American affairs when any worthy group or any worthwhile interest can be served by setting class against class. I came into politics when that was a favorite pastime. I am glad I am going out when you never hear of it any more. A new day, a new time has come when political leadership must be tested not by its talents for division, but rather by its capacity for responsibility and for unity.

For I say this to you with great earnestness: If America is to keep her commitment abroad or at home, if we are to eliminate the causes of poverty, if we are to open the doors of opportunity and self-respect for all, if we are to have—as we should have—a just society where law and order prevails, if we are to leave our children an environment of decency and a vision of hope, then all sectors of this society must be brought together—closer together—to fulfill together the American

promise.

For the leadership and responsibility you have offered during my years as your President, I most sincerely thank you.

On December 4, 1963—when I had been in office just a matter of hours and days—I first spoke to the Business Council as President. I then asked you for your help on the Nation's tax policies. For nearly 1 year, a needed tax reduction had been stalled in the Congress—and Secretary Dillon and Secretary Fowler had worked feverishly and untiringly to move that bill. But with your strong and very able support and help, the tax cut soon became the law of the land.

You know the great good that flowed from that wise move. Our position today has both similarities and contrasts to the situation of 4½ years ago. Once again, I need your help to pass a tax bill which has been in the Congress for more than a year now. Once again, tax action is the most essential and most urgent step to preserve the health of our prosperity.

Unfortunately, this time it is a tax increase that we need rather than a tax cut. Our special defense costs in Southeast Asia have added almost $30 billion to our budget. By the most stringent management, we have been able to hold the needed tax increase down to only $10 billion, a third of the cost of the war and less than half of the tax cuts that we enacted in earlier years.

The principles of good fiscal management are the same in 1968 as they were in 1963. Then the budget was a drag on the economy. Today, the deficit is clearly the most dangerous stimulus in the economy, threatening the stability of the dollar at home and aboard. We can eliminate that key danger just as soon as we can enact a tax surcharge.

To achieve a broad nonpartisan compromise on an adequate fiscal program, I agreed to accept a major cutback of $4 billion in spending for fiscal 1969 and $18 billion in reductions in present legislative authority for Government spending programs. That is, I believe, as far as the Congress is likely to vote and will safely go, and I believe it is much farther than Congress would normally go in the regular appropriation process that they will follow if this measure now is voted down.

Last year they voted about a billion and a half reductions in expenditures. This year the clerks of both committees tell us that of the bills that have passed thus far, the indication is that the reductions will be less than $2 billion.

You know—I think, I know, and I believe all Americans know that we do have urgent needs at home and abroad.

I doubt there is a man in this room who wants to bring to a halt this Government's programs that are essential to the pursuit of justice and harmony in our American cities, as I understand was discussed with you this morning by that very able Mr. Beebe and Mr. Kaiser, who have worked so long and so hard to be helpful.

I am sure there is no thinking American—in any walk of life—who wants to sow more seeds of despair and frustration by eliminating the programs that are so vital to human well-being throughout the land. I am confident there are none among us who want the Nation to turn its back upon the future and fail the commitment we have made to the young Americans who come after us.

We have needed action on taxes now for more than 2½ years. And the record is clear on what that delay has cost us:

—Our rate of price increase has accelerated from less than 2 percent to 4 percent.
—Our international trade position has eroded to the poorest quarterly performance since 1959.

—Our interest rates have jumped 1½ or 2 percentage points to the highest levels in nearly 50 years.
—The millions of Americans who have no defense against inflation are losing through price increases, alone, three or four times what the surcharge would cost them.
—Millions of home buyers, homebuilders, consumers, and small business borrowers have paid five and ten times the cost of the tax surcharge through higher interest rates.

Keeping the Government's fiscal house in order is an absolutely essential first step to meet the problems that endanger our prosperity. I am proud that the business community is generally united behind the tax bill; it recognizes that higher taxes are insurance for the greater goal of sustaining prosperity and fiscal stability. But your voices must be heard throughout the land if we are to help make fiscal responsibility a reality.

A proper fiscal program will give us the opportunity to get back on the road toward price stability, balance-of-payments equilibrium, and healthy credit markets. But even at best, the journey is going to be a difficult one and a long one.

Beyond the first step, that journey is in your hands much more than in mine, or even my successor's. The strength of the dollar at home and abroad will depend on millions of decisions that are made by American labor and American business. These will determine how rapidly our productivity grows, how well our costs are held down, and how forcefully and competitively we can sell our products in world markets.

Let me mention some of the key decisions—just a few—that you will be making in the months ahead.

Those of you in the steel industry will participate in decisions this summer that will determine whether we avoid the dual dangers that face us: on the one hand, a costly strike, and on the other, a severely inflationary wage and price adjustment. The relative stability of steel prices has been one of the key favorable factors in our recent price record and it must be preserved.

Those of you in the automobile industry will determine whether we meet and whether we beat the foreign competition for the small-car market or whether the import share of the American auto market will keep growing.

All of you employers will help determine through your hiring and your training programs how much and how fast we can melt the stubborn hard core of unemployment—that is giving us so much trouble—through private initiative.

All of you who export or who can export will determine whether we undertake the imaginative efforts needed to develop new directions and new markets for our goods. Today, less than one-third of our trade is with the vast regions of Asia, Africa, and Latin America, which make up the less developed world.

Your actions will continue to determine whether we can get balance-of-payments savings that we urgently need from our emergency foreign investment program. With its typical initiative, American business has turned to the capital markets of Europe to raise needed funds. In the first 4 months of 1968, borrowing by American firms in the Eurobond market exceeded $700 million, more than five times the amount borrowed just a year earlier.

I am confident of your intelligent response to these challenges. All of my relations with business and all of my economic policies as

President have been based on a very deep faith and belief and a confidence in private enterprise, in free markets, and in profits as a reward for productive contribution.

I maintain that faith and confidence. As your President, I do not advocate any system of mandatory direct controls on wages and prices. For more than 4 years now, in all the Vietnam crisis, we have been able some way, somehow, to successfully avoid taking the steps that we had not been able to avoid in other similar crises. We must not stifle the market system; we must try to perfect it.

Perfection requires a coordinated battle by Government, business, and labor against the virus of inflation. We cannot tolerate the rapid price increases that we are suffering today. But neither can we weaken our economy with heavy unemployment, slack and sluggish growth, in order to defend against inflation.

I proposed an alternative a few months ago: If increases in wage settlements and profit margins in 1968 could be held to the 1967 rate, we could make decisive progress toward our goal, once the tax bill was enacted. But so far, we have failed. The wage settlements have moved the other way. They have moved upwards, towards 6 percent, and profit margins seem to have also widened.

If business and labor do not accept these suggestions or these answers, then I would like to hear your answers—because this is a national problem, not a partisan problem. It is a problem that confronts all Americans. Noninflationary prosperity is not a goal merely for business or for labor, nor for Democrats or Republicans. It is a challenge to the entire Nation. I have asked for the privilege, as I did only a few months ago, of speaking to the AFL–CIO council of labor leaders in exactly the same terms that I speak to you. And I plan to do that next Tuesday afternoon. Indeed, I think this is a challenge to every industrial nation of the world, and it has not been solved, so far as I can see, anywhere. But America is the nation that can solve the problem, and 1968 is the year that we should begin.

When I became your President, I determined then that—after a long and satisfying career of service to the Nation—I had no personal partisan cause to serve.

I have no such cause or interest to serve now.

Back in the days when I was in politics— [*laughter*]—some used to say that I wasn't much of a politician anyway—and as I look back on it, maybe they were right. Maybe it is bad politics to be for increasing taxes in an election year. But in retrospect, as I reflect, I have won a few elections and I have had great respect for the intelligence of the American people. I think that they are wise enough and they are patriotic enough and they are farsighted enough to know that what is best for their country is best for them—whether they are politicians or just individuals.

I have respect for the ability of the American people to recognize that what is bad for their future and for the prosperity of the people is the very worst kind of politics. And I think that further delay on taking the actions that we must take, including actions on the tax measure, is very clearly bad for the future and the prosperity of all the American people.

So I come here to thank you; to ask for your continued leadership; to say to you that there has never been a time in the history of the business community when more en-

lightened, unselfish leadership has been given to your country than now, as you must have observed from some of these people who have appeared here with you; and to say to you again, the country needs you and needs you badly now.

It needs your support. It needs your curiosity and your interest in what's happening in this country and the world—whether it is the college campuses here or in Paris, whether it is in the peace talks in Paris or other capitals. It needs your untiring labors to help find for us peace in the world; to help keep America moving forward; above all, to try to bring an end to the bitterness and the hatred and the divisiveness that can and is, in places, occurring in this country.

Therefore, all that you can do to bring about a united, cooperative, and responsible America will pay rich dividends in the future.

Thank you for listening.

NOTE: The President spoke at 10:30 a.m. at the Homestead Hotel in Hot Springs, Va. His opening words referred to Albert L. Nickerson, Chairman of the Business Council. Later he referred to C. Douglas Dillon, Secretary of the Treasury 1961–1965, his successor Henry H. Fowler, Leo C. Beebe, Executive Vice President of the National Alliance of Businessmen, and Edgar F. Kaiser, Chairman of the President's Committee on Urban Housing.

The Revenue and Expenditure Control Act of 1968, which enacted the President's recommended tax increase, was approved on June 28, 1968 (see Item 343).

For the President's remarks to members of the Business Council on December 14, 1963, see 1963–64 volume, this series, Book I, Item 23.

The Business Council was originally formed on June 26, 1933, by Secretary of Commerce Daniel C. Roper under the name of Business Advisory Council for the Department of Commerce. On July 10, 1961, the group's advisory functions were broadened to serve all areas of Government, and its name was changed to the Business Council. Its members include over 100 financial and industrial executives.

242 Remarks at the Annual Dinner of the White House Correspondents Association.   *May 11, 1968*

Mr. Vice President, Mr. Cormier, Mr. Kilpatrick, ladies and gentlemen:

A very funny thing happened to me tonight when I was on my way out of the White House—[*laughter*]—I mean tonight. When I joined George Christian to come over here, he said, "Mr. President, I think you forgot something." [*The President indicated his White House identification pass.*] So that is how I came to be wearing this. You may not like to wear your pass, but what do you think about me? I finally had to start using it after my announcement on March 31st.

One day, as I was walking over to my nap, a guard stopped me in the hall and looked at me very carefully and said, "Excuse me, buddy, but do you work here?"

So, Frank and Carroll, I am so glad you all remembered me tonight.

You do remember me, don't you, Hubert?

THE VICE PRESIDENT. And how!

THE PRESIDENT. Last year when I was with you, I gave some advice to your new president. And this year I have some more.

Carroll, the most important thing is unity. You've got to end divisiveness among the reporters in the West Lobby. You've got to end partisanship between wires and weeklies, between the reels and the stills, between the black and the white and the color.

And there is only one way to really do it, Carroll—neither seek nor accept it.

And you'll find out that once you step aside, things start happening:

—Mary McGrory may even call you a statesman.

—Walter Lippmann may think so, but can't quite bring himself to say so.

—College students do their "thing" some-

where else, or against another president, and a different "Dean."

Well, this may be my valedictory address to the press. So tonight I can be even more frank with you than I have customarily been in the past—if that is humanly possible.

As some of you may have heard, I have had my troubles with the press. But that's not at all unusual. There has always been some friction between the press and us in the academic community. Why this friction? We intellectuals agree that it is not so much a matter of substance—we just plain don't like your style—much too earthy.

As you know, the relationship between Presidents and the press has always been a very intriguing one—sort of a lovers' quarrel.

I think all of us will remember what Thomas Jefferson said in 1787, that if he had to choose between "a government without newspapers, or newspapers without a government," he would gladly choose the newspapers. And I think it's of some interest to note that Jefferson said that before he actually became President.

But eventually, of course, he became President Jefferson, and then he expressed his opinion this way, "Nothing can now be believed which is seen in a newspaper. Truth itself becomes suspicious by being put into that polluted vehicle."

And here is one more opinion about the press, "The only security of all is in a free press." And if that last one sounds to you like a platitude that's uttered by an elder statesman, then you are right. It too was spoken by Thomas Jefferson, in 1823, and that was long after he had retired to his little place in Virginia—the "TBJ Ranch."

But we must get on—it is all summed up best, I think, in these lines that were penned by a famous Texas statesman and poet, "The pen is mightier than the sword, if it's your ox that's being gored."

Despite all the friction, however, I do admire and I do envy the press. I have always hankered to be a reporter since I was a college editor.

I have always wanted to come up with one of those hard news leads like, "The mood at the White House this evening—[*laughter*]—is one of cautious optimism." Or one like this, "The President fired the opening gun of his reelection campaign last night." I seem to recall reading that last one June 3d, and then October 12th, and again on November 9th, and would you really believe it—March 30th. And this has been really an especially good year for the press!

You've had some real surprises to report. Who would have ever thought that Scotty Reston would have left Washington before Lyndon Johnson? But you know how it is in this town—journalists come and journalists go.

And I am told that my March 31 decision not to run surprised some people. But if you think that was a surprise, you just wait till you hear Lady Bird's announcement!

You know somewhere, people just never do seem to quite understand me. On March 31st, I clearly said in very measured words, "I will not seek and I shall not accept the nomination of *my* party." I repeat—*my* party! And ever since that night, I have been waiting for Everett Dirksen to drop by.

As I was reminded earlier, 12 months ago we did share another evening like this together. Some of you may remember that I concluded my remarks that evening with a reference to our struggle, all of our struggle, for peace.

That struggle goes on as we gather here again tonight. We cannot yet celebrate the seizing of any tantalizing prizes. We reach out still for the elusive happiness of peace, but we have not yet failed.

Much has happened in a year to give us heart, some things to lift our hopes.

This morning Ambassador Harriman and Cy Vance completed the technical arrangements to open the talks in Paris for which we have waited and worked and longed so long.

This week in Jordan, in Israel, and in Egypt, other men are working to try to find a way to peace in the Middle East.

In Cyprus and in Nigeria, men are trying to pull away from the old habits and the memories of violence to once again set their feet on new paths to peace.

In the cities and the communities across our country, this is our work, too. We know that the frustrations and the fears that go hand in hand with the problems of poverty and race can pull this Nation to disaster.

But we know something better and truer in our hearts: We have in ourselves, in our institutions, the real power to show the world that we are still Americans, the place on earth which promised in the 18th century that reason and justice would triumph, that all men were born to stand equal before God and the law, the place on earth where every single child would grow with an equal chance to fulfill the talents that his Creator had given him.

And no man sitting as President in the spring of 1968 could help feeling and knowing in his heart that humanity had really reached one of those rare and eventful moments when history turns, placing mankind on the edge of a very great decision.

Looking about him, at his Nation and his world, a President could see the making of catastrophe all around him. He could see

599

the raw elements of hatred and prejudice, of division and demagoguery and disorder all over the place, to carry a blind race of men over the brink into a nuclear age.

But a President could also look about him and find promise that would balance the peril. He could see and he could feel a stirring and a movement that is often submerged or hidden in the clamor—the quiet joining of many hands, men trying to pull together the strands of decency and common sense, compassion, and moderation.

Every day of my Presidency, I put my hand to this work. It has gone long into every night.

I did what I did on March the 31st to put the full weight of the Presidency and of the President on the hopeful side of the balance. Now, 6 weeks later, the scales have not yet settled. It is too soon to cast up the accounts.

But I do want to tell you what I really feel in my heart tonight.

I make no predictions. I pretend neither to be a pessimist nor an optimist, but I know what we have in the scales tonight: all of our good faith and all the skill we can summon, all the reason and resolve that we can place in the service of peace. And from all that, from all that which I have seen in the years as President, from all that I have learned in my entire public life, I think this may be enough to tip the balance.

In the final reckoning, each of us is going to be accountable. This is our year of decision. And our decisions now will bind the destinies of men for the long years to come throughout the lives of our grandchildren.

We can take history at its turn. Together, we can move this Nation and our world, and we can move them away from conflict and toward conciliation. We can move them away from violence and toward orderly change; away from frustration and toward fulfillment; away from the fears and the hatreds and the torments that tear people apart, toward the respect, the friendship, and the tolerance that bring people together and that can allow the world of men to finally live at peace.

History does not turn by itself. It is turning tonight because we have tried—tried so hard for so long. And, yes, whatever we may have said or done or thought, we have tried to do what we thought was right.

If we are to seize the full promise of this moment, if we are to continue turning the tides of time and fortune in man's favor, it will take a strong and a unified America to do it. It will ask all of our old faith and wisdom and courage.

We are called once again to show the strength of our character and the greatness of our American spirit.

You have been the reporters of my hopes and the recorders of my convictions throughout these many days of my Presidency. There have been days and nights when you told the people that I had asked for their help and for their prayers as I tried to lead them and as I worked for peace in the world. So, tonight as I leave you, I ask again for yours.

Thank you and good night.

NOTE: The President spoke at 10:51 p.m. at the Washington Hilton Hotel. In his opening words he referred to Hubert H. Humphrey, Vice President of the United States, Frank Cormier of the Associated Press, outgoing president of the White House Correspondents Association, and Carroll Kilpatrick of the Washington Post, the new president. During his remarks he referred to George E. Christian, Special Assistant to the President, Mary McGrory of the Washington Star, Walter Lippmann, syndicated columnist, James B. Reston of the New York Times, Mrs. Lyndon B. (Lady Bird) Johnson, Senator Everett McKinley Dirksen of Illinois, Minority Leader of the Senate, and Ambassador at Large W. Averell Harriman and Cyrus R. Vance, U.S. negotiators at the Paris peace talks with North Vietnam.

243 Message to the Congress Transmitting First Annual Report on Highway Safety Programs. *May 13, 1968*

To the Congress of the United States:

I am pleased to transmit the first annual report on the administration of the Highway Safety Act of 1966.

Each year, more than 50,000 Americans die on our highways. Millions more are injured. Billions of dollars are lost by death, disability, and protracted stays in hospitals.

This report, which covers the period from September 9, 1966, to December 31, 1967, shows that we have begun to take effective action to stem this terrible tide.

During this period

—We established a National Highway Safety Bureau.

—We issued highway safety standards.

—All 50 States received Federal grants-in-aid to help them and local communities to improve their highway safety programs.

—A broad research program has begun, which will provide sound guidelines for future safety standards.

The fight to stop the slaughter on our highways will be long and hard. I hope the Congress will be encouraged by this report to continue its strong support of these vital programs.

LYNDON B. JOHNSON

The White House

May 13, 1968

NOTE: The report of the Department of Transportation, dated March 1, 1968, is entitled "First Annual Report to Congress: September 9, 1966 to December 31, 1967, on the Administration of the Highway Safety Act of 1966" (95 pp. plus appendices). The act was approved by the President on September 9, 1966 (Public Law 89–564, 80 Stat. 731).

244 Message to the Congress Transmitting First Annual Report on Traffic and Motor Vehicle Safety Programs. *May 13, 1968*

To the Congress of the United States:

This year, we can expect 53,000 Americans to die on our Nation's highways.

We can expect almost 4 million Americans to be injured in automobile accidents—nearly 10,000 people hurt every day.

We can expect automobile fatalities to be the largest cause of death in the 15 to 35 age group.

Year after year, those expectations become gruesome reality.

In 1966, we took our first major step to combat this shameful waste. And now I am pleased to transmit to the Congress the first annual report of the National Traffic and Motor Vehicle Safety Act of 1966.

This report covers the period between

September 9, 1966, and December 31, 1967, and I believe it shows a promising beginning.

During this period

—Two hundred safety-related recall campaigns were conducted by the motor vehicle industry.

—The first Federal motor vehicle standards in history were issued and are already in application on all cars manufactured after January 1 of this year.

—Additional standards were issued for vehicles manufactured after January 1, 1969.

—A sound research program has been begun, to provide a firm basis for future safety standards for vehicles and for State safety programs.

Our efforts are beginning to tell: the rate of increase of traffic deaths has slowed somewhat. Still, the destruction wrought by Americans on themselves, their fellow citizens, and their property is of tragic proportions.

I hope that this report will encourage the Congress to continue its support for these programs, and I commend it to your attention.

LYNDON B. JOHNSON

The White House
May 13, 1968

NOTE: The report of the Department of Transportation, dated March 1, 1968, is entitled "First Annual Report to Congress: September 9, 1966 to December 31, 1967, on the Administration of the National Traffic and Motor Vehicle Safety Act of 1966" (86 pp. plus appendices). The act was approved by the President on September 9, 1966 (Public Law 89-563, 80 Stat. 718).

245 Proclamation 3850, Prayer for Peace, Memorial Day, 1968. *May 13, 1968*

By the President of the United States of America a Proclamation

On Memorial Day, we remember our debt to those who have died so that we might live in freedom.

We remember also those Americans who today, at home and in the lands of our allies, stand guard against all who threaten our freedom.

On this Memorial Day, we who remain free by the sacrifice of the dead and the service of the living will requite our debt to both with thoughts and acts of gratitude and love.

And we will gain renewed inspiration from their sacrifice—to push forward with the task of trying to bring about a just and enduring peace by every reasonable means.

The Congress, by joint resolution of May 11, 1950 (64 Stat. 158), has requested the President to issue a proclamation calling upon the people of the United States to observe each Memorial Day as a day of prayer for permanent peace and designating a period during such day when the people of the United States might unite in such supplication.

Now, THEREFORE, I, LYNDON B. JOHNSON, President of the United States of America,

do hereby designate Memorial Day, Thursday, May 30, 1968, as a day of prayer for permanent peace, and I designate the hour beginning in each locality at eleven o'clock in the morning of that day as a time to unite in such prayer.

I urge the press, radio, television, and all other information media to cooperate in this observance.

And I urge all Americans, wherever they may be on this designated day, to join their prayers to the Almighty to bestow upon this Nation the blessing of peace restored and lasting among all the nations of the world.

On this Memorial Day—as a special mark of respect to the memory of the gallant Americans who have sacrificed their lives in Vietnam, so that this Nation might live to be for all people everywhere a symbol of peace and justice and freedom—I direct that the flag of the United States be flown at half-staff during the entire day, instead of during the customary forenoon period, on all buildings, grounds, and naval vessels of the Federal Government throughout the United States and all areas under its jurisdiction and control.

I also request the Governors of the States

and of the Commonwealth of Puerto Rico and the appropriate officials of all local units of government to direct that the flag be flown at half-staff on all public buildings during that entire day, and request the people of the United States to display the flag at half-staff from their homes for the same period.

In Witness Whereof, I have hereunto set my hand this thirteenth day of May, in the year of our Lord nineteen hundred and sixty-eight, and of the Independence of the United States of America the one hundred and ninety-second.

Lyndon B. Johnson

NOTE: Proclamation 3850 was released at Austin, Texas.

246 Remarks Upon Dedicating the Hall of Heroes and Presenting the Medal of Honor to a Member of Each of the Nation's Military Services. *May 14, 1968*

Secretary Clifford, Members of Congress, Secretaries of the Services, members of the Joint Chiefs of Staff, members of the Joint Chiefs of Staff from some of our neighboring nations, distinguished guests, ladies and gentlemen:

It was in August of 1776, the month after the Continental Congress announced the American people's Declaration of Independence, that George Washington's troops were struggling to make their independence a reality—with their rifles.

Fired by the glory of his cause, but aware always of its terrible costs, Washington voiced the words that have whispered in the mind of every leader since that time—every leader who has had to commit men to the agony of battle: "Good God, what brave men must I lose this day."

In the mind and in the heart of this President, those words have echoed without stop throughout the hours of many days and many long nights.

Thirty-three times I have awarded the Medal of Honor to America's fighting men. On 19 of those occasions, I have been able to make the presentation myself.

Each ceremony has been—for me—one of emotions in deep conflict.

First of all, there is pride. Any man is exalted who stands in the presence of bravery.

But there is always, too, a haunting and a humbling awareness that it is the battlefield which illuminates the courage that we honor.

Today we confer the Medal of Honor on four more gallant Americans. This is the first time that four men—from each of the military services—have been so honored together.

As we meet here, other men—in Paris— are beginning the very hard negotiations that we hope will one day silence the guns in a free Vietnam.

Diplomacy's painful work now is to forge, from the fires of hostility, the way in which men can live without conflict and in mutual accord.

The world prays that the way to peace will be found at that distant table—the peace with honor for which these men, and their comrades, have fought so long and so nobly.

When it comes, that peace will be the monument of many men. Among them are Charles C. Hagemeister, Richard A. Pittman, James E. Williams, and Gerald O. Young. They will place their names now in a new Hall of Heroes, created here in the

Pentagon as a memorial to all who have earned their country's highest award for courage in combat.

In that Hall, which we open here today, a noble muster rings out, calling: "Valor—in the service of our country."

And—from every hour of America's need, from every crisis of America's history—the answering call comes back: "Here, sir . . . here, sir."

In this Hall of Heroes, 3,210 men—who have served above and beyond the call of duty—stand guard on a Nation's pride, and on the freedom that those men have bought so dearly.

Thank you.

[The texts of the four citations follow.]

The President of the United States of America, authorized by Act of Congress, March 3, 1863, has awarded in the name of The Congress the Medal of Honor to

SPECIALIST FIVE CHARLES C. HAGEMEISTER,
UNITED STATES ARMY

for conspicuous gallantry and intrepidity in action at the risk of his life above and beyond the call of duty:

Specialist Five (then Specialist Four) Charles C. Hagemeister, distinguished himself at the risk of his life above and beyond the call of duty on 20 March 1967 while serving as a Medical Aidman, Company A, 1st Battalion, 5th Cavalry. While conducting combat operations against a hostile force in Binh Dinh Province, Republic of Vietnam, Specialist Hagemeister's platoon suddenly came under heavy attack from three sides by an enemy force occupying well concealed, fortified positions and supported by machine guns and mortars. Seeing two of his comrades seriously wounded in the initial action, Specialist Hagemeister unhesitatingly and

with total disregard for his own safety, raced through the deadly hail of enemy fire to provide them medical aid. Upon learning that the platoon leader and several other soldiers also had been wounded, Specialist Hagemeister continued to brave the withering enemy fire and crawled forward to render lifesaving treatment and to offer words of encouragement. Attempting to evacuate the seriously wounded soldiers, Specialist Hagemeister was taken under fire at close range by an enemy sniper. Realizing that the lives of his fellow soldiers depended on his actions, Specialist Hagemeister seized a rifle from a fallen comrade, killed the sniper, three other enemy soldiers who were attempting to encircle his position and silenced an enemy machine gun that covered the area with deadly fire. Unable to remove the wounded to a less exposed location and aware of the enemy's efforts to isolate his unit, he dashed through the fusillade of fire to secure help from a nearby platoon. Returning with help, he placed men in positions to cover his advance as he moved to evacuate the wounded forward of his location. These efforts successfully completed, he then moved to the other flank and evacuated additional wounded men despite the fact that his every move drew fire from the enemy. Specialist Hagemeister's repeated heroic and selfless actions at the risk of his own life saved the lives of many of his comrades and inspired their actions in repelling the enemy assault. Specialist Hagemeister's conspicuous gallantry and indomitable courage are in the highest traditions of the United States Armed Forces and reflect great credit upon himself.

LYNDON B. JOHNSON

———————

The President of the United States in the name of The Congress takes pleasure in presenting the Medal of Honor to

SERGEANT RICHARD A. PITTMAN
UNITED STATES MARINE CORPS

for service as set forth in the following

CITATION:

For conspicuous gallantry and intrepidity at the risk of his life above and beyond the call of duty as a member of First Platoon, Company I, Third Battalion, Fifth Marines during combat operations near the Demilitarized Zone, Republic of Vietnam. On 24 July 1966, while Company I was conducting an operation along the axis of a narrow jungle trail, the leading company elements suffered numerous casualties when they suddenly came under heavy fire from a well concealed and numerically superior enemy force. Hearing the engaged Marines' calls for more firepower, Sergeant (then Lance Corporal) Pittman quickly exchanged his rifle for a machine gun and several belts of ammunition, left the relative safety of his platoon, and unhesitatingly rushed forward to aid his comrades. Taken under intense enemy small-arms fire at point blank range during his advance, he returned the fire, silencing the enemy positions. As Sergeant Pittman continued to forge forward to aid members of the leading platoon, he again came under heavy fire from two automatic weapons which he promptly destroyed. Learning that there were additional wounded Marines fifty yards further along the trail, he braved a withering hail of enemy mortar and small-arms fire to continue onward. As he reached the position where the leading Marines had fallen, he was suddenly confronted with a bold frontal attack by 30 to 40 enemy. Totally disregarding his own safety, he calmly established a position in the middle of the trail and raked the advancing enemy with devastating machine-gun fire. His weapon rendered ineffec-

tive, he picked up an enemy submachine gun and, together with a pistol seized from a fallen comrade, continued his lethal fire until the enemy force had withdrawn. Having exhausted his ammunition except for a grenade which he hurled at the enemy, he then rejoined his own platoon. Sergeant Pittman's daring initiative, bold fighting spirit and selfless devotion to duty inflicted many enemy casualties, disrupted the enemy attack and saved the lives of many of his wounded comrades. His personal valor at grave risk to himself reflects the highest credit upon himself, the Marine Corps and the United States Naval Service.

LYNDON B. JOHNSON

The President of the United States in the name of The Congress takes pleasure in presenting the Medal of Honor to

BOATSWAIN'S MATE FIRST CLASS JAMES E.
WILLIAMS, UNITED STATES NAVY

for service as set forth in the following

CITATION:

For conspicuous gallantry and intrepidity at the risk of his life above and beyond the call of duty as a member of River Section 531 during combat operations on the Mekong River in the Republic of Vietnam. On 31 October 1966, Petty Officer Williams was serving as Boat Captain and Patrol Officer aboard River Patrol Boat (PBR) 105 accompanied by another patrol boat when the patrol was suddenly taken under fire by two enemy sampans. Petty Officer Williams immediately ordered the fire returned, killing the crew of one enemy boat and causing the other sampan to take refuge in a nearby river inlet. Pursuing the fleeing sampan, the U.S. patrol encountered a heavy volume of small arms fire from enemy forces, at close range, occupying well-concealed positions along the river bank. Maneuvering through this fire, the patrol confronted a numerically superior enemy force aboard two enemy junks and eight sampans augmented by heavy automatic weapons fire from ashore. In the savage battle that ensued, Petty Officer Williams, with utter disregard for his own safety, exposed himself to the withering hail of enemy fire to direct counter-fire and inspire the actions of his patrol. Recognizing the overwhelming strength of the enemy force, Petty Officer Williams deployed his patrol to await the arrival of armed helicopters. In the course of this movement he discovered an even larger concentration of enemy boats. Not waiting for the arrival of the armed helicopters, he displayed great initiative and boldly led the patrol through the intense enemy fire and damaged or destroyed fifty enemy sampans and seven junks. This phase of the action completed, and with the arrival of the armed helicopters, Petty Officer Williams directed the attack on the remaining enemy force. Now virtually dark, and although Petty Officer Williams was aware that his boats would become even better targets, he ordered the patrol boats' search lights turned on to better illuminate the area and moved the patrol perilously close to shore to press the attack. Despite a waning supply of ammunition the patrol successfully engaged the enemy ashore and completed the rout of the enemy force. Under the leadership of Petty Officer Williams, who demonstrated unusual professional skill and indomitable courage throughout the three hour battle, the patrol accounted for the destruction or loss of sixty-five enemy boats and inflicted numerous casualties on the enemy personnel. His extraordinary heroism and exemplary fighting spirit in the face of

grave risks inspired the efforts of his men to defeat a larger enemy force, and are in keeping with the finest traditions of the United States Naval Service.

Lyndon B. Johnson

The President of the United States of America, authorized by Act of Congress, March 3, 1896,[1] has awarded in the name of The Congress, the Medal of Honor to

CAPTAIN GERALD O. YOUNG, UNITED STATES AIR FORCE

for conspicuous gallantry and intrepidity in action at the risk of his life above and beyond the call of duty:

Captain Young distinguished himself on 9 November 1967 while serving as a Helicopter Rescue Crew Commander in Southeast Asia. Captain Young was flying escort for another Helicopter attempting the night rescue of an Army ground reconnaissance team in imminent danger of death or capture. Previous attempts had resulted in the loss of two helicopters to hostile ground fire. The endangered team was positioned on the side of a steep slope which required unusual airmanship on the part of Captain Young to effect pickup. Heavy automatic weapons fire from the surrounding enemy severely damaged one rescue helicopter, but it was able to extract three of the team. The commander of this aircraft recommended to Captain Young that further rescue attempts be abandoned because it was not possible to suppress the concentrated fire from enemy automatic weapons. With full knowledge of the danger involved, and the fact that supporting helicopter gunships were low on fuel and ordnance, Captain Young hovered under

---

[1] This date was incorrectly stated in the citation. It should be March 3, 1863.

intense fire until the remaining survivors were aboard. As he maneuvered the aircraft for take-off, the enemy appeared at point-blank range and raked the aircraft with automatic weapons fire. The aircraft crashed, inverted, and burst into flames. Captain Young escaped through a window of the burning aircraft. Disregarding serious burns, Captain Young aided one of the wounded men and then attempted to lead the hostile forces away from his position. Later, despite intense pain from his burns, he declined to accept rescue because he had observed hostile forces setting up automatic weapons positions to entrap any rescue aircraft. For more than 17 hours he evaded the enemy until rescue aircraft could be brought into the area. Through his extraordinary heroism, aggres-

siveness, and concern for his fellowman, Captain Young reflected the highest credit upon himself, the United States Air Force, and the armed forces of his country.

LYNDON B. JOHNSON

NOTE: The President spoke at 11:33 a.m. in the inner court at the Pentagon upon presenting the Medal of Honor to Sp 5c Charles C. Hagemeister of Lincoln, Nebr., Sgt. Richard A. Pittman of Stockton, Calif., Boatswain's Mate 1st Class James E. Williams of Darlington, S.C., and Capt. Gerald O. Young of Anacortes, Wash. In his opening words the President referred to Clark M. Clifford, Secretary of Defense.

Following the presentations the President dedicated the Hall of Heroes established to honor recipients of the Medal of Honor. The Hall is located in the A Ring on the second floor of the Pentagon. Its walls are lined with plaques bearing the names of over 3,000 Medal of Honor winners representing all the armed services.

247　Message to the Congress Transmitting Annual Report of the Commodity Credit Corporation.　*May 15, 1968*

To the Congress of the United States:

I am pleased to transmit to the Congress the Annual Report of the Commodity Credit Corporation for fiscal year 1967.

The Report shows that the Corporation has continued to reduce agricultural surpluses. This success is directly related to the substantial gains in the level of farm income since 1960—amounting to 24 percent in total realized net income, and 50 percent in net income per farm.

Despite this progress, per capita income for farmers still falls short of the level for urban workers.

Parity of income for farmers remains an unachieved goal. We began moving closer to its achievement with the passage of the Food and Agriculture Act of 1965. This legislation gives us the flexibility needed to adjust wheat, feed grain and cotton production levels. Supply management programs

are vital if we are to improve returns to the Nation's farmers.

In my 1968 Message on the Farmer and Rural America, I have recommended the permanent extension of the 1965 Act to insure that authority for basic commodity programs will not be terminated. The farmer could ill-afford such a lapse.

With surpluses gone, the market operates more freely today than in many years. But the absence of surpluses also means that we must carefully maintain planned security reserves—a National Food Bank. I have recommended the new legislation which will be required to establish such a Bank. We must be able to hold reserve stocks of commodities in readiness for emergency use. At the same time our farmers must be protected against the price-depressing effects of such reserve stocks, particularly during their build-up.

Even though burdensome surpluses are no longer overhanging farm markets, farmers still need and use price-support loans to protect their prices from the depressing effects of temporarily large supplies, particularly at harvest time. In fiscal year 1967, farmers took out loans of nearly $1.4 billion on 1966 crops, and at the end of the year, price-support loans outstanding on these and previous crops totaled $1.5 billion. In addition, price-support purchases, primarily of dairy products, amounted to $327 million.

Commodity inventories owned by CCC at fiscal year end had a value of $1.9 billion. This was more than $1.2 billion less than a year earlier and more than $2 billion less than two years ago. The inventories have dropped further since the end of last fiscal year. The smaller inventory level is bringing substantial reductions in CCC's storage, handling and transportation costs. In fiscal year 1967, these costs were down to $310.7 million, compared to $472.9 million in fiscal year 1966 and $513.6 million in fiscal year 1965.

The CCC, in financing P.L. 480 sales for foreign currency and under long-term credit, helps to provide added outlets for U.S. farm production and to supplement the supply of agricultural commodities for people in the less developed countries. During fiscal year 1967, the total costs of this financing amounted to nearly $1.3 billion.

The fiscal 1967 Report demonstrates that the broad authority of the Commodity Credit Corporation is being used to benefit both the U.S. farmer and those in great need abroad. No longer the caretaker of large and costly surpluses, the CCC is returning to its original objective of helping farmers to hold commodities off markets for better prices. And farmers are moving into a new era of balance between supply and demand, while continuing to help free the world from the danger of hunger.

LYNDON B. JOHNSON

The White House

May 15, 1968

NOTE: The 40-page report entitled "Report of the President of the Commodity Credit Corporation, 1967" was published by the Commodity Credit Corporation, Department of Agriculture.

For the President's message of February 27, 1968, on the farmer and rural America, see Item 94.

A bill extending the Food and Agriculture Act of 1965 was approved by the President on October 11, 1968 (see Item 534).

248 Message to the Congress Transmitting Reports on Incentive Awards to Members of the Armed Forces. *May 15, 1968*

To the Congress of the United States:

I am happy to transmit to the Congress reports of the Secretary of Defense and the Secretary of Transportation on cash awards to members of our Armed Forces for noteworthy suggestions, inventions, or scientific achievements.

The cash awards program, first authorized by Congress in September 1965, has proved an excellent incentive for reducing costs and increasing efficiency in the Armed Forces.

The largest percentage of awards—89 percent—continues to be in the $50 and under range. Of the 34,527 awards, however, 1,094 awards were over $250. The total amount paid in awards for suggestions in 1967 was $1,307,832.

In the Department of Defense, over $63,000,000 in first-year benefits have resulted from suggestions submitted by military personnel during 1967. In the Coast Guard, since the inception of the program, benefits have amounted to over $391,000. This raises the total amount of tangible benefits received during the relatively short life of the program to over $119,000,000. Many additional benefits not measurable in dollar amounts have resulted from suggestions concerning safety and other matters.

Few investments of public funds have ever returned such prompt results in economy and efficiency. Few forms of recognition have so widely benefitted the morale or encouraged the initiative of our men and women in uniform.

I urge every Member to examine the truly remarkable and encouraging achievements described in these reports of the Secretary of Defense and the Secretary of Transportation.

LYNDON B. JOHNSON

The White House
May 15, 1968

NOTE: The reports are entitled "Report of the Secretary of Defense on Cash Awards Made Pursuant to 10 U.S.C. 1124" (3 pp., processed) and "Summary of Coast Guard Military Incentive Awards Program for Period 1 July 1966 to 31 December 1967" (2 pp., processed).

249   Remarks of Welcome at the White House to President Bourguiba of Tunisia.   *May 15, 1968*

Your Excellency, distinguished guests, ladies and gentlemen:

This morning America welcomes a friend:

—a patriot who has brought his country into independence,

—a leader who has given North Africa and the Mediterranean a vivid example of what modern men can achieve in an ancient land,

—a statesman who has worked for just peace throughout his region and in the world at large.

You have come, Mr. President, to a land that deeply admires what you and your people have accomplished in 12 years of nationhood.

America's friendship with Tunisia demonstrates that a nation of great size and power can play a role in the development of a smaller nation—without in any way detracting from its liberty of choice or its independence of action.

The United States neither has nor desires political dominion in North Africa and the Middle East. What we seek is what the war-weary people of the Middle East most desire

themselves, that is, the hope of a better life and justice and peace.

Last June I reconfirmed our commitment to these goals in the Middle East. I committed us to pursue a peace based on five principles:

—first, the recognized right of national life;

—second, justice for the refugees;

—third, innocent maritime passage;

—fourth, limits on the wasteful and destructive arms race; and

—fifth, political independence and territorial integrity for all.

I restate these principles today. Many debates and many discussions have taken place since last June 19th. The United Nations Security Council passed its important resolution on November 22d. Our commitment to those principles—and to that resolution—has not changed. It will not change.

America respects and supports the aspirations of people who are new to independence, who work to preserve and to strengthen their freedom. It is a particular pleasure to welcome the great leader of such a nation as this, this morning.

Mr. President, we are pleased and proud to have you in America.

NOTE: The President spoke at 11:37 a.m. on the South Lawn at the White House, where President Habib Bourguiba was given a formal welcome with full military honors. The Tunisian President responded as follows:

Excellencies, distinguished guests, ladies and gentlemen:

Mr. President, we have been very deeply moved by the very kind words which you have just said, the feelings which you have expressed, and that significantly cordial welcome which has been given to us by yourself, Mr. President, as well as by the Government and the people of the United States.

Those words and that welcome bear witness to the fact of the consideration and the esteem that you have toward Tunisia and its people.

It is very sincerely that I am expressing to you my gratitude for all those manifestations of friendship.

The visit which I am making today to the United States is a very glad occasion. It is a true pleasure for me to be again in this hospitable land and to convey to you as well as to the great American people the feelings of friendship and of appreciation of the Tunisian people.

This mutual esteem and trust which is characteristic of the relationships between our countries are based on our common dedication to the same ideal of dignity, of progress, and that of peace and justice. They also reflect our respect for moral values, as well as our firm determination to continue working for the safeguarding of peace in the world and for a greater understanding among men.

Without recalling the beginnings of our diplomatic relations which date back, as you know, to 1789, I want to say that the United States for us is, first of all, the country which gave to our cause a precious measure of support during the dark days of our struggle by recognizing in our national movement the true and authentic expression of the aspirations of the Tunisian people.

We do not forget that the United States was the first nation to recognize our independence and the first to help us to preserve it and to strengthen it.

Today, 12 years after its succession to sovereignty, which is synonymous with responsibility, the Tunisian people will look back with pride on the road that it has traveled.

The Tunisian people have been untiringly active with a view to assure to the greatest extent possible the well-being of each and every one and also a full measure of dignity.

The Tunisian people have built a modern state and have undertaken a true social revolution based on the enhancement of men and women, on the renovation of structures, and with the cooperation of all those countries which respect our sovereignty.

In this endeavor, we have always been guided by the same principles which we had laid down more than 30 years ago. We have been unswerving with regard to the objectives to be attained. But we have been first and foremost concerned with the most efficient means to reach such goals.

We have gone forward without diminishing ideals, without prejudice, and without bearing grudges of any kind. We have refused to lead our people into dreamlike ventures inspired by demagoguery or the seeking of prestige.

On the contrary, we have always worked along the more realistic methods which are much more difficult because they require as much dynamism, courage, and as much clear thinking and as much integrity.

In that phase of our struggle for development and well-being, your country, Mr. President, has given us assistance with no strings attached and thus it helped us to face in better conditions the problems that go hand in hand with economic and social development in a country which was not richly endowed by nature.

Mr. President, I have mentioned to what extent Tunisia is indebted to the United States, but the truth must be said that all the nations that cherish security, democracy, and well-being also have been and are indebted toward your country. The world shall never forget the decisive role played by the United States during and after World War II so that liberty and moral values might emerge triumphant. Nor has the world forgotten the important contribution made by your great Nation in the struggle against hunger and underdevelopment in general.

The position of superpower which is yours today in the world has imposed very heavy responsibilities which you have assumed with great courage and fortitude. I know that those responsibilities may be a source of gratification, but at the same time they are a hard burden.

Regardless of that, you have accepted them so as to preserve the balance of powers and forces in the world and to safeguard peace throughout the world.

In a manner similar to that of other countries, Tunisia has always been concerned with maintaining friendly relations with the United States on the basis of mutual esteem and a fruitful cooperation, while always preserving its freedom and its independence.

Tunisia today can congratulate herself on having been fully successful in that manner, in that way which is the dialogue among the peoples.

In this century of technological advances, we

must all join our efforts so as to make sure that men shall be triumphant over technique. The important thing is to have a sincere and loyal cooperation among all the countries. That might be the way to avoid a catastrophe that would doom the whole of mankind.

As far as we are concerned, we are convinced that it is possible to bring together all the peoples in a peaceful competition so as to build a better world, a more human world, and a more brotherly world.

In conclusion, Mr. President, I would like to renew the expression of my thanks and to take advantage of this opportunity to bring to the Nation of the United States the friendly greeting of the Tunisian people.

250   Toasts of the President and President Bourguiba. *May 15, 1968*

Your Excellency, Mr. Vice President, distinguished guests, ladies and gentlemen:

We honor tonight a courageous patriot— the founder of modern Tunisia.

President Bourguiba, who knows something of fighting, lives with the benefits of peace. In the new schoolhouses, hospitals, highways, and the fertile fields that mark his ancient country, he sees what peace has brought to his people and what he believes it can bring the developing world.

He is a revolutionist, yes, but he is a builder, too. He led his nation to independence, and building on a freedom that is newly won. President Bourguiba knows that a nation may be politically independent, but not truly free, unless its people, living in peace, are free to pursue the better life to which all men aspire.

A just peace can be achieved all around the Mediterranean:

—if men will turn their thoughts and their energies and their resources to its achievement;

—if men will acknowledge that compromise can show strength, that wisdom may travel with forbearance, that honor lies in statesmanship.

It is they—the people of the Middle East— who must take up the work of a just peace. Others cannot do it for them. But America will always try to help them in that work as I explained to the President earlier today— without concern for our own gain.

Tonight I reaffirm that the United States stands ready to assist all these troubled nations in their peaceful development. We have dedicated ourselves, within the United Nations and outside, to achieve a durable peace. We have pledged our help to resolve the age-old problems that obstruct the path toward comity between nations.

Tonight, with a friend who has given the world hope by his example, we again renew that pledge.

President Bourguiba, I understand that in your country you are affectionately called "the Supreme Combatant." In our country we would call you the "Grand Champion."

Ladies and gentlemen, let us now raise our glasses in salute to a champion of peace, freedom, and justice—to President Bourguiba of Tunisia.

NOTE: The President proposed the toast at 10:17 p.m. at a dinner in the State Dining Room at the White House. In his opening words he also referred to Vice President Hubert H. Humphrey. President Habib Bourguiba responded as follows:

Mr. President, ladies and gentlemen:

According to certain so-called realists, a statesman, in order to be successful, should be hard as rock, cold as the calculating machine; he should have a dry heart and do away with those weaknesses such as friendship, faithfulness, and enthusiasm.

If that were to be true, I must be a very poor statesman because I confess that I am a man of feeling and I am very honored to cherish certain friendships such as yours, Mr. President, and that of your great country in particular.

It is my intention to remain faithful to those friendships regardless of circumstances.

Before knowing you, Mr. President, I had heard that it was said that you had the same defects as I have just described. Ever since I have been your guest, I have noticed that those accusations were well-founded and that reassures me a great deal because if you and I have been statesmen for the last 37 years, if we have been able to serve our respective countries for such a long span of time and carry out today the responsibilities that go to the leadership of a nation, that means that maybe the so-called realists are not quite right.

Furthermore, those realists have never been able to explain to us how come you cannot raise anything on rock, neither wheat nor cotton nor anything of value.

Mr. President, my friendship towards your country dates back to the period when the United States had not yet achieved the status of a great power which it enjoys today. It predates the cold war and the assistance given to development. Therefore, my friendship is not based on political or economic considerations, but rather on a firm realization of the lasting qualities of the American people, on its contribution to modern civilizaton, and the part that it is playing in this century.

A few weeks ago, exactly on March 20, in a letter which I sent to my friend, Ho Chi Minh, I wrote as follows:

"I also know of the United States of America. I know the men that govern that country. I know their psychology and the imperatives of their domestic and foreign policy. I have not forgotten the American Revolution nor the generous ideas of emancipation and universality which the United States defended in the aftermath of the First World War, nor have I forgotten the prominent part they played in the last world war when the essential human values which are at the very basis of our life seemed to be at the point of submersion and the pitiless barbarity of the Nazis and the Japanese militants. Nor can I forget that even more recently the United States has played a decisive role in their influence next to their allies and to favor the decolonization of a great number of peoples in Africa and Asia."

That is the very essence of my thinking. Having said this, Mr. President, I fully know that your country is now undergoing an unprecedented period of frustration at the same time that you are faced with tremendous problems, both at home and abroad.

I know that your people, who represent from 5 to 6 percent of the world's population, nevertheless produce each year 50 percent of the world's wealth.

You are concerned at the present in better distributing this wealth within the boundaries of your Nation where the colored minority has not yet reached the level of well-being and dignity which is necessary for national unity and for the good name of the United States.

I also know that you are concerned at the same time, in spite of your deficit, with the balance of payments, with helping the underdeveloped countries to come as full partners into the 20th century.

In both of these areas what has been done so far still is not sufficient. You know it better than anyone else and you have told it to me. And I have told you, Mr. President, and this I want to repeat before our friends who are gathered here tonight, that this time where your country is concerned with electoral campaigns, I did not come here to ask you to help us, I came here to thank you and to thank the American people and the Congress of the United States for the work you have been able to do so far for my country.

I also came here to express to you our feelings on a certain number of problems of foreign policy which are of concern to the United States, to Tunisia, and to most other countries.

The first of those problems, obviously, is that of Vietnam. I rejoice as you do when I note that the war is no longer the only political path and that from one side and from the other some headway has begun leading to deescalation.

That is the way that I have always recommended because I believe that it will lead to an honorable compromise, perhaps difficult to work out, but which is the only solution, since military victory is unattainable. Here again, being consistent with another shortcoming that I have, or defect, which is frankness, I will tell you that I said to President Ho Chi Minh in that same letter of March 20:

"Today the main thing is to assure for a foreseeable future, the security of North Vietnam, the independence of the South and the possibility that those two countries may one day become re-united through peaceful means.

"It is also important, I believe, to act in such a way that no great power can have hegemony over the North or the South, and thus upset the world balance. The important thing is that the countries that neighbor Vietnam should not be submitted to pressures that would cause upheavals in the situation as it exists in the area.

"Now, it seems to me that these objectives, these goals, are reasonable ones, and that they can be accepted by yourself, by all the Vietnamese, both from the North and South, who are mainly concerned with the independence of their country and that they can also be accepted by the United States of America.

"All that I know about yourself, about the statements made by your Government and the statements made by the leaders of the National Liberation Front and all that I know about the leaders of the United States and their declarations, all of this authorizes me to think that today on those bases we have present the conditions for fruitful negotiations.

"It is obvious that the United States and other great powers have hoped to control North and South Vietnam so as to prevent those nations from coming under the control or the influence of other great powers. Today I think we can hope that an independent Vietnam, free from any foreign occupation, would be for all those powers an acceptable solution because it does not upset the balance to which they attach such great importance.

"I feel that through the continuation of war no other objectives could be reached. It is therefore necessary, without wasting one day, to start on the work toward negotiations and the matters of procedure become only secondary even though they may present certain important moral aspects."

Mr. President, the other problem which is of concern to us is that of the Middle East and that strikes even closer to home, if such a thing is possible. The United States is not directly involved in those problems, but still, the United States has the obligation, as well as the means, to help in finding a solution, and this, through an understanding with the other great powers, and also taking into consideration the interests of the countries concerned.

This tragedy that we are witnessing in the Middle East presents three aspects which should cause deep concern to any straight-thinking man and also should make such straight-thinking men try to act.

The first aspect of that is something that, as far as I know, is without precedent in history. As a matter of fact, ever since the Balfour Declaration of 1917 we have been witnessing an action which consisted, on the part of a government, that of Great Britain, to offer to the persecuted people, namely the Jewish people, the land belonging to another people, the Palestinian people.

The second aspect is something that has lasted since 1948 and has become worse in 1967, that is, the spectacle of a million men and women who were thrown out of their country, of their homes, of their lands and are living in camps and are fed and clothed and housed by international charity.

The third aspect, finally, is the occupation by Israel, first in 1956, and then in 1967, of new Arab territory through the force of arms as well as the fact that they tend to maintain to keep themselves in these territories or to appropriate certain of them.

When we think about the situation and when we go beyond the rather superficial analysis which dawns from day to day, we realize that there are other elements in this problem which make it ex-

tremely complex and of a rather difficult solution.

The Balfour Declaration to which I made reference awhile ago, and through which the British Government committed itself to give a part of Palestine to the leaders of the Zionist movement, so as to found a homeland for the Jews is something, when we think of it, rather along the lines of the Congress of Berlin and the other conferences through which the European powers have cut up in pieces and divided among themselves the countries of Africa and Asia.

But in the case of the Balfour Declaration, it was not a matter of giving a country to a nation which would send its nationals, regardless of their denomination; it was rather a matter of putting into Palestine people from a single denomination regardless of their nationality. But that is not the most important thing.

What seems to me very important and basic is the fact that this decision made by the British, which is unfair for the Arabs of Palestine, which is unjustifiable from the point of view of the rights of people, this decision has nevertheless become legitimate as a result of the action of the international community on two occasions.

The first time, right after the First World War at the San Remo Conference, and the second time it was made legitimate in 1947 by the United Nations.

Myself, as a man of principle, I deeply regret that the League of Nations in so doing has ignored the 14 points of President Wilson, and I also regret that the organization of the United Nations, with an overwhelming majority, including the five great powers, has taken a decision which was not in conformity with its own charter, a charter based on the right of people to self-determination.

As a statesman, while I feel very deeply the tremendous injustice which strikes at this small people, while I understand that we should protest against the consequences of this injustice, I still have been recommending year after year, in the Arab conferences, in all my statements and all my writings, that we take into full account all those different factors, particularly the fact that the community of nations as a whole has approved the creation of Israel, and has, beyond any doubt, given to it an international stamp of legality.

Now, starting from the premise that the Arabs do not have on their side either military force or international law, I have pleaded that the Arabs should accept the frontiers that were established by the United Nations in 1947, frontiers which should have been guaranteed by the great powers.

Within those frontiers, with borders established by the United Nations, Israel would have attained the peace and security that it is trying to reach. As for the Arabs, they would have bowed before an accomplished fact, though it may have been unjust, but at the same time, accepting the legality given by the United Nations, the Arabs would no longer have been alone, as they have always been, as a matter of fact, since 1948.

They could have saved a good portion of Palestine. They would not have to make so many military expenses that were excessive as well as useless. And they would have avoided the humiliating defeat of 1967.

In other words, the Arabs, having abandoned the idea of rejecting the other party beyond the sea, could have arrived at the containment and would have thus regained the support of world opinion.

Unfortunately, I was not heard by the Arab leaders of the Middle East because they did not want to listen to me, even though the people themselves seemed to have some understanding for the points of view and the reasoning that I used.

The war of June 1967, was not avoided. This war brought a new element into the situation, and now I want to say that this element has a decided influence on the evolution of this country, that is in the years to come, and therefore, it also affects the solution of the conflict.

The new fact that we are witnessing in this part of the world, is the appearance on this stage of the Palestinians themselves since last June. This fact is something that I have been wishing for for several years. It is something which is emerging stronger and stronger from day to day.

I pleaded to the responsible heads of state and the responsible statesmen to take into account this fact, unless they want to continue to reason on the basis of premises that are no longer valid, because the fact is that today it is the Palestinian people themselves which is going to take, day by day, an ever greater measure of responsibility in the struggle to regain its rights on its land and responsibility for the type of compromise that may put an end to that struggle.

The outcome of this political-military struggle, which the other Arab countries are no longer qualified to lead, but which they have to support, will depend on the willingness of the Palestinian people to make sacrifices, to organize itself, and particularly to display a high degree of maturity.

I don't think that I could be accused of being an extremist, but I want to say that we in Tunisia are going to give our support to that struggle because it is a just struggle and because we have a firm conviction that it will lead to a durable solution which can only be a compromise between the aspirations and the likes of one side and the other, all of this based on the will to resist and the will to survive shown by each of the two communities.

What there is today between Palestinians and Israelis is fear and particularly a mutual contempt. From this struggle will emerge the esteem of the one for the other, and therefore, the assertion by each of the parties of the right of the other party to live, the right to security and the right to development. Then, there will be a valid solution because it has been accepted and not imposed.

Therefore, there will be peace and then there will be cooperation. Such is, Mr. President, my opinion about the problem of the Middle East. This is something which I have explained to the politicians themselves, in Jericho in 1965, when I told them, "That is what I would have done if I had been in your place."

I want to add that the last word will belong to those who are directly concerned with this matter, that is, the Palestinians themselves.

Now, I would not like to conclude my remarks without repeating again the expression of the great joy that I have felt in visiting you here, Mr. President, in making this visit which, for reasons beyond our control, could not have been done at the date that had been originally established.

Allow me, particularly, to express my gratitude for the very kind gesture that you had at the time when you sent directly to my bedside the eminent cardiologist, Dr. Mattingly. I can assure you that the Tunisian people, deeply moved by your very spontaneous act, saw that it was the hallmark of a friendship which has remained steadfast for more than 20 years.

Now, I just want to thank you once more for your kind hospitality and to wish to you, Mr. President, and to the American people that you may be able to solve, in the spirit of peace and understanding, the overwhelming problems which your own society is facing at the present time.

I have no doubt that the United States, in spite of her formidable power, will remain faithful to the image which I carry in my mind, and the image which I mentioned a moment ago, that is, the country of freedom, the generous ideas, ideas of emancipation and universality which you have been depending on ever since the dawn of your Republic.

In conclusion, I want to make the wish that the negotiations now undertaken to bring peace to Vietnam be fully successful so that you may dedicate all your energies to building the great American society as well as to contribute in a decisive manner to peace and progress in the world.

251 Presidential Unit Citation Awarded the 355th Tactical Fighter Wing, Pacific Air Forces. *May 16, 1968*

CITATION TO ACCOMPANY THE AWARD OF
THE PRESIDENTIAL UNIT CITATION
TO THE
355TH TACTICAL FIGHTER WING

The 355th Tactical Fighter Wing, Pacific Air Forces, distinguished itself by extraordinary heroism and outstanding professionalism while participating in combat operations in Southeast Asia from 1 January 1966 to 10 October 1966. During this period aircrew members and support personnel demonstrated exceptional valor and outstanding devotion to duty in the face of extremely difficult circumstances. Flying over 11,000 sorties, many against the most heavily defended targets in North Vietnam, the Wing expended 36,091 tons of bombs, 22,224 rockets, 101 missiles and 1,160,000 rounds of 20 mm ammunition to inflict severe damage to a major military complex, an enemy arsenal, key transportation facilities, surface-to-air missile sites and major fuel storage areas. These sorties destroyed large quantities of war materiel and made the enemy's movement of equipment, personnel and supplies into South Vietnam more costly and difficult. In addition, two enemy aircraft were destroyed and eight were damaged in aerial combat. Support personnel of the Wing not only were able to maintain the high sortie rate despite the severe weather conditions and battle damage to the aircraft but also made major improvements in the base to greatly increase its efficiency and to increase its capacity three-fold. The extraordinary heroism, superb airmanship, aggressiveness and dedication to mission accomplishment displayed by members of the 355th Tactical Fighter Wing have reflected the highest credit upon themselves and are in keeping with the highest traditions of the United States Air Force.

LYNDON B. JOHNSON

252 Message to the Congress Transmitting Annual Report of the St. Lawrence Seaway Development Corporation. *May 16, 1968*

To the Congress of the United States:

It is my pleasure to submit to Congress the 1967 Annual Report of the Saint Lawrence Seaway Development Corporation.

The Seaway had its second best year in nine years of operations—registering a total of 44 million tons of cargo. The record season for Seaway tonnage was 1966 when 49.2 million tons were moved through the Montreal-Lake Ontario waterway. We hoped that the Seaway would reach the 50-million ton mark in 1967, but a strike plus some slackening in demand for grain, resulted in reduced traffic.

While overall tonnage was somewhat disappointing, there are many bright spots in the report. General cargo, for example, increased to six million tons from 5.5 million. Iron ore shipments also were higher with 16.4 million tons moving through the Seaway locks to the steel mills of the Midwest. These increases indicate the growing appreciation of the waterway's advantages as a means of reducing transportation costs.

The Seaway has truly placed Midwest

ports on the sealanes of the world. More than 600 salt-water vessels made 1,284 trips into the Lakes in 1967.

However, reduced traffic, along with an adjustment in the division of toll revenue between Canada and the United States caused income to fall from $7.1 million to $6.1 million.

Despite this loss, $4 million was returned to the U.S. Treasury. This makes a total repayment of $28.9 million since the Seaway opened in 1959.

A major concern of the Corporation is the need to repair Eisenhower Lock. The Cor-

poration retained the Corps of Engineers to direct the work which will continue until 1971. Fortunately, it will not interfere with the navigation seasons. In my budget for fiscal year 1969, I requested that funds be made available to cover the cost of repair.

I commend this report to your attention.

LYNDON B. JOHNSON

The White House
    May 16, 1968

NOTE: The 28-page report, submitted to the President on March 1, 1968, is entitled "Saint Lawrence Seaway Development Corporation Annual Report, for the year ended December 31, 1967."

253 Remarks at the Swearing In of Wilbur J. Cohen as Secretary of Health, Education, and Welfare. *May 16, 1968*

Secretary Cohen and family, Mr. Vice President, Members of the Cabinet, ladies and gentlemen, distinguished Members of Congress:

One thing I have always noticed about Wilbur Cohen is that he never does anything without a reason. Usually I can figure out what he is up to. But for the life of me, I just can't understand why he chose the man he did to administer the oath of office this morning.

In any discussion of our social history, two landmark laws deserve very special mention, social security and medical care. Each was passed after very long and searching debate in the Congress. Each looked at one time or another like it was a very lost cause.

Each is a monument to the compassion and the enlightenment of the American Nation and each bears the indelible mark of one man—Wilbur Cohen.

If there is any man in America whose record and whose devotion to public service qualify him for high office, it is Wilbur Cohen. I am glad that I had a chance to

participate in that decision that brought him to the highest office in his field.

He has been a planner, he has been an architect, he has been a builder, and he has been a repairman on every major piece of social legislation in the last 35 years.

He hasn't minded being a private in the rear ranks and now he is a general in the front ranks. But he will be doing the same things.

During the early years of the long battle for health insurance Wilbur wasn't always the best loved leader in the land, at least in the medical society meetings.

After one earnest speech before a medical society, I am told a doctor came up and offered to provide Wilbur personally with free medical care. In fact he volunteered to make a no-cost incision—from here all the way over to here [*indicating the neck*]. He said he could economize by not using anesthetics.

But Wilbur kept on working and as we meet here today, more than 19½ million Americans are getting the benefits of Medicare and the benefits of his long hours, his patience, and his understanding and his devotion to his country.

Today the reformers would do well, I think, if they would just take Wilbur Cohen's life and study it. In a time when we are hearing so much about power, black power, white power, green power, and student power, perhaps someone should do an analysis of another kind of power—"Wilbur power."

You might define it as "Will power" with something added. Certainly it is the power of optimism over pessimism. Certainly it is the power of involvement over indifference. It is the power of reason over rhetoric. It is the power of the patient, persistent reformer over the noisy zealot. I have found that it is power that gets the job done.

Wilbur Cohen knows that you cannot move a nation from an ivory tower. But he has also learned that you can't move a nation with a bulldozer.

It took more than 20 years to achieve Medicare, and this man's determination and his skill in the agonizing art of turning dreams into law worked the miracle when lesser men could only stamp their feet in frustration.

A friend once said that Wilbur feels every person in the country who is at home alone, who is sick, is his personal responsibility.

But we did not come here for this ceremony simply to praise Wilbur's past record, great as that is. Wilbur Cohen is taking the oath of office today because I believe that he knows the needs of our country.

He knows the need to raise the national spirit. He knows the need to win new victories in new ways against disease and ignorance and poverty. He knows how urgent it is to erase the old indignities and to do it now, to end the old inequalities and to do it now, and to replace neglect with opportunity and to do it now.

Our future is filled with unfinished business, but it is rich with hope and with a great deal of opportunity, too.

So, Wilbur, we welcome you, knowing that any man who marries a redhead from Texas is a man who really loves challenges.

NOTE: The President spoke at 1:06 p.m. in the East Room at the White House. Following his remarks Vice President Hubert H. Humphrey administered the oath of office to Secretary Cohen. The Secretary's remarks in response are printed in the Weekly Compilation of Presidential Documents (vol. 4, p. 805).

---

254 Presidential Unit Citation Awarded the 23d Tactical Air Support Squadron, Pacific Air Forces. *May 16, 1968*

CITATION TO ACCOMPANY THE AWARD OF
THE PRESIDENTIAL UNIT CITATION
TO THE
23D TACTICAL AIR SUPPORT SQUADRON

The 23d Tactical Air Support Squadron distinguished itself by extraordinary gallantry during combat operations in Southeast Asia from 15 April 1966 to 20 September 1966. The Squadron played a major role in the development of a new supply route interdiction technique which increased the effectiveness of our efforts and made it more costly and difficult for the enemy to supply his forces. Flying slow, highly vulnerable light aircraft often under extremely bad weather conditions the forward air controllers of the Squadron provided thorough surveillance over enemy supply routes deep in enemy territory and accurately directed highly effective fighter strikes against an important part of the heavily defended enemy supply route. By their courage and selfless dedication, the forward air controllers served as an inspiration to other members and evoked devotion and pride throughout the Squadron. The extraordinary professionalism and heroism displayed by members of this unit in the development and pursuit of its mission are in keeping with the highest standards of performance in the United States Air Force and reflect great credit upon themselves and the Armed Forces of their country.

LYNDON B. JOHNSON

255 Joint Statement Following Discussions With the President of Tunisia. *May 16, 1968*

ON May 15, 1968, President Johnson welcomed President Bourguiba of Tunisia as his guest for a State Visit to the United States. The two Presidents had a mutually valuable exchange of views on Tunisian-United States relations and on African, regional and world developments.

President Bourguiba described the successful efforts Tunisia is making to consolidate its independence, develop its economy and achieve new social goals for all its people, men and women, young and old. He expressed Tunisia's appreciation for American assistance, which has contributed significantly to Tunisian economic development. President Johnson recalled the longstanding interest of the United States in Tunisia's efforts to achieve in peace and security its goals of economic development and social progress.

President Bourguiba expressed his understanding of America's aim in supporting the principle of national independence and self-determination in Southeast Asia and commended President Johnson for seeking talks on the Viet Nam problem. The two Presidents shared the hope that a general easing of world tensions would be brought about by patient and persistent efforts to achieve a just settlement in Viet Nam.

President Bourguiba stressed the urgency of a just settlement of the Middle East problem. President Johnson expressed his agreement, and in that connection reiterated his firm belief that justice for all was to be found in the five principles he had enunciated on June 19, 1967. The two Presidents reaffirmed their strong support for the Security Council Resolution of November 22, 1967, as offering the surest road to peace, and called on all Governments to cooperate fully with the Jarring Mission toward this end.

President Johnson noted with great satisfaction the priority given by Tunisia to building up sound and fruitful relations with its Maghrebian neighbors, as well as with other regions of Africa. He explained the United States Government's belief that regional economic cooperation offered an effective means of hastening the process of development and contributing to the lessening of world tensions.

The two Presidents consider that this State Visit, with the many demonstrations of American friendship for Tunisia which it evokes, is a symbol of the common political philosophy, the belief in freedom, the respect for the dignity of the individual, and the profound disposition toward peace, which are shared by the Tunisian and the American peoples.

256 Message to the Congress Transmitting Annual Report on the Operation of the Automotive Products Agreement With Canada. *May 17, 1968*

To the Congress of the United States:

I am pleased to transmit to the Congress the second annual report on the operation of the Automotive Products Trade Act of 1965. By this Act Congress authorized implementation of the United States-Canada Automotive Products Agreement.

The Agreement was designed to create a broader U.S.-Canadian market for automotive products to obtain for both countries and both industries the benefits of specialization and large-scale production. We have moved far toward this goal.

Automotive trade between the United States and Canada was $730 million in 1964, the year before the Agreement went into force. Trade in 1967 was over $3.3 billion. The Agreement has also stimulated increased trade in allied products.

Industry, labor and consumers in both countries continue to benefit from this growth in commerce and from the increased efficiency made possible by the Agreement. It is dramatic proof of what can be accomplished when friends and neighbors choose the path of cooperation.

LYNDON B. JOHNSON

The White House
May 17, 1968

NOTE: The report was made public as a committee print, Senate Committee on Finance, 90th Congress, 2d session (Government Printing Office, 81 pp., May 21, 1968).

257 Remarks at the First-Day-of-Issue Ceremony for the Law and Order Postage Stamp. *May 17, 1968*

Mr. Attorney General Clark, Postmaster General Watson, Senator Byrd, Senator Dirksen, Members of Congress, ladies and gentlemen:

This stamp is a symbol of our country's commitment to law and order.

It may seem as easy for a public man to come out in favor of law and order as it is to be in favor of Mom's blueberry pie. But there is no legislation pending on Mom's blueberry pie. So everyone can be for it without fear of repercussion.

But there is legislation before the Congress that deals with law and order. Passing that legislation, passing a fair and effective crime control law, requires action. It demands judgment, determination, and courage.

The prime case in point is the gun bill.

I cannot tell you this morning exactly how many Americans have been killed or maimed because there has been no effective national gun control law in America. But I do think I can tell you this, and I believe common sense will tell it to you also:

That some of the 6,500 murders, some of the 60,000 robberies, some of the 43,000 aggravated assaults that occur each year in this land of ours might have been prevented by passage of an effective gun control law.

Yesterday, the Senate approved a halfway version of the gun bill. I do not think it is adequate. It doesn't cover long guns and rifles. It would still, I believe, permit murder by mail order.

Gun bills have been debated. They have

been debated long. I believe they have been debated long enough.

When 70 percent of the American people have said that they favor a strong gun control law, then we should not impose a weak control law on the public.

I believe that we need to go all the way to safety now, not just part of the way.

On the face of this stamp there is a picture of a policeman with a little boy. For almost a year and a half we have been trying to help that policeman with our safe streets and our crime control program.

This followed a study by the most eminent authorities in the Nation, appointed by the President, which spent months and months studying this whole question. They were called the President's Crime Commission.

This safe streets and this crime control program are our biggest weapons in the fight against the random criminal and against the organized racketeer.

But there are efforts underway, I am fearful, to water down this bill and to weaken it.

Law and order in this year of 1968 is not just a platitude, it is an action program.

Part I is a gun bill. Part II is the safe streets bill.

The American people, I believe, want both, not speeches, not halfway measures.

I believe the American people will judge us by what we do and not what we say.

I believe the American people want the full protection of forceful and effective law in dealing with these criminals.

Thank you very much.

NOTE: The President spoke at 11:46 a.m. in the Fish Room at the White House. In his opening words he referred to Attorney General Ramsey Clark, Postmaster General W. Marvin Watson, Senator Harry Flood Byrd, Jr., of Virginia, and Senator Everett McKinley Dirksen of Illinois.

The Omnibus Crime Control and Safe Streets Act of 1968 and the Gun Control Act of 1968 were approved on June 19 and October 22, 1968, respectively (see Items 320 and 553).

258 Remarks With Senator Mansfield on the Floor of the Senate Following a Luncheon in Honor of the President. *May 17, 1968*

Mr. President and Members of the Senate:

I appreciate very much your asking me to come here today. I always enjoyed my association with the Senate. I served here as a Senator, a whip, a Minority Leader, a Majority Leader, and later as Vice President.

I always profit from what I learn from the Members of this great body, and I appreciate all that you have done to ease my burden to help us better govern this Nation.

I hope that through the years to come, I shall have the privilege of seeing all of you from time to time and that together we can

continue to build and develop this Nation and continue to make it the best country in all the world.

NOTE: The President spoke at 1:57 p.m. at the invitation of Senator Mike Mansfield of Montana, Majority Leader of the Senate, and Senator Everett McKinley Dirksen of Illinois, Minority Leader. His remarks followed a luncheon given in his honor in the Senate Conference Room at the Capitol. Preceding the President's remarks, Senator Mansfield spoke as follows:

Mr. President, I was discussing with the distinguished Minority Leader the question of which seat the President of the United States should occupy if he had his choice, either that of the Presiding Officer or that of the Majority Leader of this body, where he served so effectively and efficiently in those positions for so many years.

We decided that for the time being at least he should not be half a member of the establishment, but a full-fledged Member of the Senate.

I would like at this time, with the concurrence and approval of my colleagues, to break tradition, in a certain sense, and call upon the President of the United States for a few remarks as the Majority Leader of the Senate.

As printed above, this item follows the text released by the White House Press Office.

259 Remarks Upon Signing Two Bills and a Proclamation Relating to the Navajo Indian Tribe. *May 17, 1968*

Secretary Udall, Senator Mansfield, Members of Congress, Commissioner Bennett, distinguished guests, ladies and gentlemen:

About 8 weeks ago I sent to the Congress a special message entitled "The Forgotten American."

It gives me a great deal of pride that this was the first special legislative message on the American Indian ever sent by a President to the Congress.

We are determined that the American Indian—the forgotten American—will be forgotten no more.

This afternoon we have met in the Cabinet Room to pay tribute to the Nation's largest Indian tribe, living in the largest Indian community: the Navajo Indian Tribe of Arizona, New Mexico, and Utah.

The first items I sign this afternoon will be a law and a proclamation designating 1968 as the centennial year of this great tribe.

The President of the Senate and the Speaker of the House will very shortly appoint a Navajo Centennial Commission. I hope that this centennial will be a lively and pleasant and successful celebration. I can think of no better way for our citizens to join in the observance than to visit the American Southwest, the home of the Navajo people, to see firsthand their colorful history and culture.

Finally, I am signing a bill which frees $5,500,000 for spending by the State of Utah on health, education, and general welfare for the Navajo people there. Until now these funds could be spent only on roads and school tuition.

This moment is a good one for the Navajo people. I hope there will be more of them. I hope that in the days to come, I will be signing many laws to benefit all of America's Indian citizens—the first citizens among us.

Thank you.

NOTE: The President spoke at 5:50 p.m. in the Cabinet Room at the White House. In his opening words he referred to Stewart L. Udall, Secretary of the Interior, Senator Mike Mansfield of Montana, Majority Leader of the Senate, and Robert L. Bennett, Commissioner of Indian Affairs.

As enacted, the two bills (S. 391 and S. 2745) are Public Laws 90–306 and 90–309 (82 Stat. 121, 123).

The President also signed Proclamation 3851 "Centennial of the Signing of the 1868 Treaty of Peace Between the Navajo Indian Tribe and the United States" (4 Weekly Comp. Pres. Docs., p. 818; 33 F.R. 7483; 3 CFR, 1968 Comp., p. 46).

On July 24, 1968, Bertrand M. Harding, Acting Director of the Office of Economic Opportunity, reported to the President that a $454,150 grant had been approved to establish the Navajo Community College, the first college for Indians in the United States. The report stated that the college, located on the Navajo reservation in Arizona, New Mexico, and Utah, was expected to open in January 1969 with an enrollment of 400 students (4 Weekly Comp. Pres. Docs., p. 1151).

For the President's message to Congress "The Forgotten American," see Item 113.

On January 24, 1968, the President recorded a message for the Navajo people on the occasion of their centennial banquet (see Item 28).

260 Remarks to Members of the Association of American Editorial Cartoonists. *May 18, 1968*

Mr. Poinier, ladies and gentlemen, my friends and fellow crusaders:

To be perfectly frank and honest with you, I am very surprised to see you here on Saturday afternoon. I think it is a wonderful day, though, for America when the press demonstrates such a very high sense of responsibility—by choosing to watch the President instead of the Preakness.

This has been an extraordinary day for me. I woke up with my favorite New York morning paper—The New York Times—and saw my wife below the Statue of Liberty, sandwiched in between a Republican Governor that's a candidate for my job and a Republican mayor who's a candidate for somebody's job. There she was pinned by two Republicans.

I am deeply touched that you should come here and pay this extraordinary tribute to me—a man who on March 31st declared himself an early scratch.

I hope you lovely ladies will let me share some of this credit with your husbands who could have been at the racetrack. I may have saved all of you some housekeeping money. Who knows? I also hope that my reassessment has not caused any commotion in your own households. I understand that some of you gentlemen may be thinking of changing your occupations, too. You will have to turn in your drawing pads—because you are going to miss me that much—all of me—my button nose—my cute ears—my big, ten-gallon hat—my big, blacksnake whip.

I have always envied you your freedom of expression. You are living proof of the wonders of democracy—where one man's artistic license is another man's credibility gap. So I am going to miss you, too, although it will be nice to bite into my morning Texas grapefruit without you biting back in your morning newspaper.

But we will not be too far apart. I think some of you may know that a collection of your work, spanning all the years of my public life, will be on display in the Johnson Library at the University of Texas. It has been assembled by an impartial panel of experts: Marvin Watson, Jack Valenti, Governor John Connally, my cousin Oriole, Patrick Lyndon Nugent, and Yuki as the tiebreaker. The family had no trouble finding a title for this historic volume. It will be called "In Cold Blood."

I suppose, though, I could have had it worse. After all, I could have been up against a columnist with all of your talent. Thank goodness Walter Lippmann never learned to draw.

Some of you may remember what Boss Tweed said when Thomas Nast was crusading against him. He said, "I don't care what they print about me. Most of my constituents can't read anyhow. But them damn pictures!"

Well, most of my constituents can read. A modern President gets both barrels from the press. And I have learned something from you cartoonists. You have taught me that there are some virtues to being a Republican. It must be wonderful to belong to a party that offers you the natural protection of an elephant hide.

Yes, you are teachers—and your talents and traditions are unique. You are quite in the American tradition. The best of your art is innovation, a creative and constant search for the truth to lead us on.

I like your imagination and your humor,

even if I don't like the characters that you select for it sometimes. The greatest of your skills are those that you sharpen against the whetstone of argument and controversy—those that serve as the cutting edge of democratic dialogue and the destiny of free men.

There are some who say you are at your best when you are most angry or, I think, sometimes just downright cruel. I disagree. Your talent and your tradition are much too precious to be spent in just negative and destructive purpose.

I believe you will continue to make constructive use of your gifts. The best memories you have given me for all my life are those that I hope your profession will continue to give this Nation all of its life: humor, understanding, courage, compassion, faith, and the best of all your wit and wisdom.

Mrs. Johnson is sorry that she cannot be here this afternoon. She has, I think, this week broken a record that Mrs. Roosevelt established after some four terms in the White House. Mrs. Johnson has had the help of a jet instead of an iron horse.

There is something about this house that causes some women not to like to stay in it all the time, I have observed.

We are glad though that some of you women who are here for the first time can spend a part of your weekend with us. We hope you have enjoyed your trip. We have enjoyed seeing you. And I will have a chance to say hello to some of you in the next room.

Thank you very much.

[At this point President Johnson was presented a collection of cartoons which were drawn on the day he withdrew from the 1968 presidential campaign. He then resumed speaking.]

Is Mrs. Willie Day Taylor here? Willie Day is one of the best things that has happened to us in our life. I mean all of the Johnsons. She has raised both of my daughters. She has stood by watching me with my wife and she has nursed me all through the years.

Thank goodness, with your help, she has collected, I think, the most unusual collection of cartoons of any person in public life. I want to thank her, again, for her dedication through the years.

I want to thank all of you for not just your talents, but your generosity and the trouble you have gone to, to help her help me.

Thank you.

NOTE: The President spoke at 4:35 p.m. in the East Room at the White House. His opening words referred to Arthur B. Poinier, president of the Association of American Editorial Cartoonists. During his remarks he referred to, among others, Nelson A. Rockefeller, Governor of New York, John V. Lindsay, Mayor of New York City, W. Marvin Watson, Postmaster General, Jack Valenti, president of the Motion Picture Association of America and former Special Assistant to the President, John B. Connally, Governor of Texas, Patrick Lyndon Nugent, the President's grandson, his dog Yuki, and Mrs. Willie Day Taylor, Staff Assistant and a close personnel friend of the Johnsons.

261 Message to the Senate Asking Its Advice and Consent to U.S. Accession to Convention Establishing the Customs Cooperation Council. *May 20, 1968*

To the Senate of the United States:

Today I ask the Senate to give its advice and consent to accession by the United States to the Convention Establishing a Customs Cooperation Council.

The Council is the major international organization for improving and simplifying customs procedures. It started out as largely a European organization. Now 53 countries are members. Almost all our major trading partners participate in its work.

The objectives of the Convention are to assist international trade by working for:

—uniformity and simplicity in the customs systems of its members;

—solutions to customs administration problems;

—cooperation among governments in these matters.

The Council's recommendations are not binding but they are widely accepted by most of our major trading partners. They have an increasing importance for United States trade.

The United States sends observers to meetings of the Council and its Committees. I believe that accession to the Convention would be of clear advantage to the United States. We would have increased oppor-

tunities to participate in the Council's recommendations and to benefit from its work.

As the world's largest trading nation, we would be better able to do our part in helping to improve customs procedures so as to expand international trade.

I recommend that the Senate give favorable consideration to United States accession to this Convention.

LYNDON B. JOHNSON

The White House
May 20, 1968

NOTE: The convention was favorably considered, with reservation, by the Senate on October 4, 1968. On October 18 the President signed the instrument of accession incorporating the Senate reservation. The convention will enter into force for the United States upon appropriation of implementation funds, on which action was not completed in the 90th Congress. The text of the convention is printed in the United Nations Treaty Series (vol. 157, p. 129) and in Senate Executive G (90th Cong., 2d sess.).

---

262   Remarks at a Dinner Honoring Floyd B. Odlum, Founder and Chairman of the Arthritis Foundation.   *May 20, 1968*

Mr. Odlum, Miss Cochran, Dr. Clark, my dear friend, Ed Weisl, ladies and gentlemen:

Nothing could give me greater pleasure than to come here with Mrs. Johnson tonight to join you in paying honor to Floyd Odlum.

We are glad to be here. I say that for some very personal reasons. This dinner is a wonderful opportunity for a man in my position today. I like to spend a night out once in a while. I think most of you would be surprised how hard it is this time of the year to find a simple old-fashioned, nonpolitical dinner. Finding one in New York is almost like finding a parking place in New York. I hope they don't tow us away before we are through tonight.

Ever since March 31, that Sunday night when I said that I did not want to spend

a single hour of a single day on politics, I have had to screen the Presidential invitations most carefully. The dinner tonight was no exception. One of my assistants brought me your invitation and he said, "Mr. President, I think you would want to join in honoring your dear old friend of many years, Floyd Odlum."

"Absolutely," I said. "But is Floyd running for anything?"

The answer was "No."

"Well," I said, "will there be any candidates there?"

The reply was, "No"—eight times.

"You are sure it is nonpolitical," I said, "no partisan speeches, no fundraising?"

All the answers were "No."

So, here I am.

Personally, as you may observe, I feel very relaxed tonight. It is a wonderful feeling being able to count the days instead of the votes.

Floyd Odlum's life, his career, and his civic concerns reflect not only a great deal about the man, but a great deal about his country.

He has built a legendary record of personal and financial successes.

But we who know Floyd are much more impressed by the riches that he has given than by the riches that he has received.

His unselfish spirit tells us something about the America that we love. It reflects the truth, I believe, about a land and about a people who, for all of our faults—of which we are constantly reminded—remain, after all, the most compassionate people on the entire earth.

Tonight we honor Floyd Odlum's contributions to a noble and vital cause: arthritis and the Arthritis Foundation.

For a long time—and especially in the past 4½ years—I have made health and education a very special interest of mine, for at least two reasons:

First of all, it puzzled and it troubled me that these two vital fields were so often, and for so many years, the stepchildren of our public policy.

Second, everything in all my background and my career has led me to the earnest conviction that we can find no solutions for our problems unless we can overcome physical incapacity and ignorance—wherever they exist.

During my administration I have tried to show just how much government can do in these fields.

But I have known all along how little government can really do—without the active and the vocal support of private citizens and private organizations. You are such citizens—and the Arthritis Foundation is such an organization.

Surely no more vexing health problem can be named than the one that you battle: arthritis.

It is the Nation's number one crippler.

It robs the Nation's economy of nearly $4 billion a year in lost time, in medical expenses, in diminished strength and productivity, to say nothing of the pain and anguish that flows from it. Worst of all, it ruins lives.

Like so many problems that we face in this Nation of ours, this one is deep-seated and pervasive and mysterious, and still, as yet, unyielding. Like many other problems, it is buried beneath the layers of ignorance and the years of indifference. Like many other problems, this one is a long, long way from final solution. But like most of our problems, it is within our power to solve it. If we have the will, we will find the way.

A very famous commentator on the social scene once said, "It was the best of times, it was the worst of times, it was the age of wisdom, it was the age of foolishness . . . it was the season of Light, it was the season of Darkness, it was the spring of hope, it was the winter of despair; we had everything before us, we had nothing before us, we were all going direct to Heaven, we were all going direct the other way. . . ."

That was Charles Dickens, one of the earlier warriors against poverty and ignorance and illness and injustice. He was describing a period nearly 200 years ago. And he saw many similarities in his own period a little over a century ago.

I think most of you, if you review that language, would find many similarities tonight.

As a people, we Americans have never been as prosperous. Our gross national product has risen to over $830 billion—and the median family income in our America is over $8,000 per year.

In the past 7 years the growth alone of our Nation's wealth—the growth alone—has been greater than our entire gross national product was just 30 years ago, when I came to Washington.

Yet, we have never been more conscious of—or more troubled about—the poverty in our midst.

More Americans than ever before are in school today. One-third of all the Nation's population is in school. More people are going to college. More people are going to adult education classes. We start them in Head Start at 4 years old and a good many in adult education at 74 years old. We have more people in job training and all the other forms of education, from the postcradle to the postgraduate.

Yet never have we been more restless about the shortcomings of public education; never have we been more eager to extend the opportunity for learning to those whom we have neglected so long.

Our Nation's health standards tonight are at an alltime high, measured by any index that you can devise: life expectancy way up, infant mortality, incidence of disease, delivery of health services.

Yet never have we as a people been more anxious and more eager to extend the quality and the reach of our health care.

There are some despairing critics who look at this gap between achievement and expectation and claim there is a sickness in our society.

To me, the fact that we recognize a gap—a gap between achievement and expectation—represents a symptom of health, a sign of renewal, a sign that this great, prosperous, thriving, growing Nation has not yet succumbed to complacency or to self-indulgence.

I suppose there will be many who call me a Pollyanna for saying that, and, as I recall, I have been called worse. But I am no Pollyanna.

I simply refuse to accept the diagnosis of fatal sickness in our society.

I refuse to follow those who say that. I refuse to accept the diagnosis of indifference in our society—and I say "Shame on you who point that out"—because I see and I am thankful that I see millions of Americans and billions of dollars working tonight to conquer poverty and disease and ignorance.

I see an unprecedented outpouring of imagination and concern and money to cure the handicap of poverty.

I refuse to accept a diagnosis of deep racism in our society—because I see a people who are struggling as they have never struggled before to overcome injustice; and I cannot and I will not ignore the progress that we have made in this decade to write equality in our books of law.

I was reading an introduction to a book by MacGregor Burns the other night. We were talking about the progress that we had made in extending equality to our fellow citizens and the progress that I had made.

This distinguished Negro author said, "Mr. President, you are going to have to recognize that you must resign yourself to the fact that we have passed five national laws in recent years to insure equality among men. You are going to have to be satisfied in history with the knowledge that you were instrumental in passing all five of them."

That is one way of saying that in the last few years, the last decade, since the first one was passed in 1957—the one before that was 85 years ago—we cannot correct the neglect and the injustices of a century in a year or even in 4 years—but we are working at it.

Now let's look at these simple facts. In 30 years of struggle—from 1935 to 1964—we increased the Federal share of our gross national product that went into health and medical care from .2 percent to .7 percent—in 30 years from .2 percent to .7 percent. Then, in the last 4 years we more than doubled it—from .7 percent to 1.7 percent.

The same thing is true in the field of education. From 1935 to 1964, the Federal share of our gross national product for education moved from .1 percent to .7 percent. But in the last 4 years we doubled that, too—in 4 years from .7 percent to 1.4 percent.

Now, these, I think, are some true measures of the progress that you and we, as a people, are making, of how much of our Nation's wealth that we allocate to these two areas of great public concern—the education of our mind and the health of our bodies.

In the past 5 years, the Federal Government has enacted over 30 major health measures—more than were enacted all put together in the preceding 35 Presidential administrations.

Don't tell me that we are not conscious of progress in this country. It has more than doubled, in the last 4 years, annual spending on health, from $6 billion to almost $14 billion per year.

We are beginning to see the results. The death rate in the United States is now as low as it has ever been in all this Nation's history, notwithstanding all of our 20th century adventures and our gadgets. It is 3 percent lower today, our death rate, than it was in 1963 when I came into office, at an annual saving of 54,000 American lives.

We saved 54,000 American lives here. Although we have lost 7,000 in Vietnam, we have saved 54,000 here.

Infant deaths have declined 13 percent since 1963. That is what you have done. That is what your dollars have done. That is what men like Floyd Odlum and the Arthritis Foundation have done.

The infant deaths today are the lowest rate in our Nation's history, although we are still 15th among the nations of the world in infant mortality. I can't be proud of that and I am doing something about that, too. We are going to have "Kiddie Care" some of these days just like we have Medicare.

Medicare today brings the guarantee of adequate health services to almost 20 million senior citizens in this country.

No, now is no time to retreat from this progress.

This Nation has not yet solved its problems. We must frankly face it. Poverty, racism, ignorance, and illiteracy still plague us from coast to coast. No section has a complete mortgage on it.

But we are on the move and we are making progress. We ought to acknowledge it. The age-old ills which agitate our communities can be solved.

They will not be solved if we give way to hysteria or to crippling despair or to bad-mouthing our country all day long, all week long.

They will not be solved if we delude ourselves with labels and slogans which are substitutes for ideas.

They will be solved by realism, by determination, by nonpartisanship, by commitment, and by hope and vision and self-discipline and the generosity—in the heart of all of us—that exists in the heart of Floyd Odlum.

They will be solved by the impatience of the American people—but not by the pessimism and the bad-mouthing of the American people.

They will be solved by the concern of individuals—like the man we honor tonight, and those of his friends who show by their presence where their heart is and where their interest is and where their pocketbook is—organizations like the Arthritis Foundation.

That is why I came here, because I want

to thank all of you on behalf of all Americans.

Who among us knows whether tomorrow we might be one of these unfortunate victims of this crippler?

Yes, we must face the future with the spirit that was attributed to Winston Churchill in a story which may or may not be true. There have been credibility gaps in other periods in our history. I am told that the Prime Minister was visited by a delegation of temperance ladies who came to complain about Mr. Churchill's consumption of brandy.

One little old lady addressed Mr. Churchill and declared, "Why, Mr. Prime Minister, if all the brandy that you drank in a year was poured into this room, it would come up to here."

Mr. Churchill, the Prime Minister, looked solemnly at the floor, and then at the ceiling, and then at the little lady's hand somewhere near the midway mark. Then he muttered, "So little done; so much yet to do!"

So I want to leave with that thought—so little that we have done, so much that we have yet to do.

Thank you.

NOTE: The President spoke at 9:15 p.m. in the Grand Ballroom of the Waldorf Astoria Hotel in New York City. In his opening words he also referred to Jacqueline Cochran, the aviatrix, who is Mrs. Odlum in private life, Dr. William S. Clark, president of the Arthritis Foundation, and Edwin L. Weisl, Sr., Democratic National Committeeman from New York.

---

263 Remarks to the Board of Governors of the American Bar Association and to Its Standing Committee on the Federal Judiciary. *May 21, 1968*

Board of Governors, Mr. Attorney General, members of the Standing Committee on the Federal Judiciary, ladies and gentlemen:

We are very glad that you could come back to the White House again. I extend to you a warm welcome this morning.

I want, first of all, to thank you for what you are doing for your country and to also suggest a few additional ways that you can help us some more.

You know that I can't let you get by with just thanks because there is so much for all of us to do.

Our association has been a very rewarding one for me—and I hope for you. I have tried to give the closest attention, and most serious consideration to your suggestions and your judgments on potential nominees to the Federal Bench.

It is very clear to all of us here that you have taken your responsibilities with the serious concern that they deserve, striving to be fair, striving to serve the law and the country and the President.

Your reward and mine will come in the constantly improving administration of justice here in America.

You have also made your voice heard on a number of social and constitutional issues. I am very happy to say that I believe it has been a voice of progress.

You have been indispensable allies in supporting the legal services program, one of the real success stories of our War on Poverty.

Your help on the new disability amendment to the Constitution was essential to its passage. You have made a very profound contribution to the electoral reform question.

You have been making your opinions clear to the Congress about the Safe Streets and the Crime Control Act. You have argued for Federal grants to the cities and States, for an effective gun control law, and against some of the very unwise and unfortunate amendments that have been proposed as Title II of that bill.

In short, you have been acting in such a way that the President might just express his gratitude and retire, if our times were what used to be called "normal times."

But, as you know, each of you knows these are not "normal times." They are very extraordinary times. They are full of danger and yet they are full of promise for our society.

Our old institutions today are under serious challenge. There is tension between the generations, between the "haves" and the "have-nots," between the schooled and the unschooled.

Attitudes are changing swiftly. Relationships between people are changing. The line between freedom and license has become unclear to many people. Threats and counterthreats fill the air every day. There is a degree of intolerance and almost totalitarian vehemence that says, "Either see it my way or you will be sorry." That is not the way of a democracy. Those are not the attitudes that have made us a great Nation and a free people.

We have always been a confident people, sure that we could accomplish whatever tasks there were to do. As a people we have been like a powerful worker whose muscles were freedom and whose bones were law. That interaction between law and freedom has always given us strength and elasticity and the will to endure, and the sense to change.

If the law is to remain strong and vital, then those who love it and those who live by it must make it an instrument of progress and not a weapon to defend every element of the status quo.

If freedom is to be the property of all, not just those who assert it at the expense of others, it must be governed and informed by law. It must rest on the sustained respect for the rights of others.

I hope the bar will carry the message of freedom under law into every community. As the old term has it—"You follow the law."

I hope you will also help to guide your fellow citizens through a time when the values on which our law depends have come under widespread challenge.

My association with you and our relationship with you has been a source of a pleasant operation with me. I have drawn from you both strength and comfort. Your counsel has been wise and your attitude has been cooperative.

I want to pay you all the tribute that I know how to pay you this morning, and say again, thank you very much for what you have done. Thank you more for what I hope you may be able to help us all do in facing the challenges that we see all around us.

Thank you very much.

NOTE: The President spoke at 12:05 p.m. in the Fish Room at the White House. In his opening words he referred to Attorney General Ramsey Clark.

264   Remarks Upon Signing Joint Resolution Authorizing a Study of Motor Vehicle Insurance.   *May 22, 1968*

Secretary Boyd, Chairman Magnuson, Chairman Staggers, distinguished Members of Congress, Miss Furness, ladies and gentlemen:

The automobile has changed the face and changed the character of our country. It has brought farms and factories and beaches and mountains closer to the cities. It has given jobs and new convenience to millions of our people. For far too many of our citizens each year, however, it is the instrument of a great deal of suffering and loss to them.

Less than 2 years ago, we acted to try to make cars and highways safer. We passed what were called the traffic safety and highway safety acts of 1966.

We take another forward step today, with the automobile insurance study resolution. It is the first effort of the Federal Government to work for the consumer in this matter of daily concern to every American.

Auto insurance is important, not only to the 100 million Americans who drive autos, but to every passenger and to every pedestrian.

In my State of the Union and consumer messages to Congress, I have called for the first comprehensive study of the automobile insurance system. The resolution authorizing this study is before us here today.

Now, we are going to find out:

—why insurance premiums have jumped so suddenly; they are up 44 percent in the last 10 years;

—why thousands of policy holders are left helpless when insurance companies fail, as at least 80 have done since 1961;

—why the courtrooms are jammed with auto liability suits, with delays in some places of almost 5 years before they can come to trial;

—why equal access to auto insurance is not available to all Americans; and

—why compensation of accident victims is often unequal and unfair.

These are difficult questions. There is little of the dramatic in them. Their answers will not come easily or quickly. But the step we are taking today is a beginning and we are moving forward.

Some day, history and every American will thank the farsighted and compassionate Members of Congress, like Senator Magnuson, and Congressman Staggers, and Congressman Moss, and many others who have launched this newest advance in protection for the American consumer.

Of course, I think history will long remember and treat kindly Miss Furness for coming here and assuming the leadership in the executive department for what we are doing.

NOTE: The President spoke at 11:46 a.m. in the Fish Room at the White House. In his opening words he referred to Alan S. Boyd, Secretary of Transportation, Senator Warren G. Magnuson of Washington, Chairman of the Senate Commerce Committee, Representative Harley O. Staggers of West Virginia, Chairman of the House Interstate and Foreign Commerce Committee, and Betty Furness, Special Assistant to the President for Consumer Affairs. At the close of his remarks he referred to Representative John E. Moss of California, member of the House Interstate and Foreign Commerce Committee.

As enacted, the joint resolution (S.J. Res. 129) is Public Law 90–313 (82 Stat. 126).

265 Presidential Unit Citation Awarded the Delta River Patrol Group (Task Group 116.1), U.S. Naval Forces, Vietnam. *May 22, 1968*

THE PRESIDENT of the United States takes pleasure in presenting the Presidential Unit Citation to

DELTA RIVER PATROL GROUP

(TASK GROUP 116.1)

for service as set forth in the following

CITATION:

For exceptionally meritorious and heroic service from 9 May 1966 to 30 June 1967 while serving with friendly foreign forces engaged in armed conflict with communist insurgent (Viet Cong) forces in the Mekong Delta region of the Republic of Vietnam. Charged with patrolling the major waterways of the Mekong Delta, Delta River Patrol Group has encountered the enemy daily in an ever-continuing, ever-intensifying struggle for control of this vital area. From the outset of its unprecedented operations, Delta River Patrol Group has met with determined enemy resistance, and has undergone repeated attacks, at point-blank range, from various weapons in the Viet Cong arsenal. Among the battles waged by the Patrol Group are the fiercest engagements ever fought in the Mekong Delta. Delta River Patrol Group has met the enemy on every occasion with unyielding courage and intrepid valor, wresting from the Viet Cong control of the rivers of the region, and regaining for the Vietnamese civilian much of his traditional freedom of movement along the waterways. Ranging the Mekong Delta in the air, on the land, and on the rivers, the officers and men of the Delta River Patrol Group have contributed substantially to the counterinsurgency effort in the Republic of Vietnam. Their gallantry, professionalism, and total dedication to duty were in keeping with the highest traditions of the United States Naval Service.

LYNDON B. JOHNSON

266 Presidential Unit Citation Awarded the 602d Fighter Squadron, Pacific Air Forces. *May 22, 1968*

CITATION TO ACCOMPANY THE AWARD OF

THE PRESIDENTIAL UNIT CITATION

TO THE

602D FIGHTER SQUADRON

The 602d Fighter Squadron, Pacific Air Forces, distinguished itself by extraordinary heroism while engaged in military operations against an opposing armed force in Southeast Asia from 1 July 1965 to 30 June 1966. During this period, flying A–1E aircraft, personnel of the 602d Fighter Squadron accomplished close air support, armed reconnaissance, forward air control, and search and rescue missions under the most hazardous and demanding conditions. Their collective efforts have resulted in the recovery and rescue of 72 downed friendly pilots from hostile territory. Pitting slow, vulnerable, propeller driven aircraft against intense ground fire and tropical monsoon storms, members of this squadron contributed significantly to the interdiction of troops and supplies moving south and to the defeat of the Viet Cong Monsoon Offensive. Despite heavy losses of aircraft and pilots, the members of the 602d Fighter Squadron displayed extraordinary gallantry, professionalism, and combat effectiveness in performing one of the most varied and dangerous mission assign-

ments in Southeast Asia. The outstanding courage, esprit de corps, and dedication to mission accomplishment displayed by the members of the 602d Fighter Squadron exemplify the highest military traditions and standards of performance and their actions reflect great credit upon themselves and the United States Air Force.

LYNDON B. JOHNSON

267   Remarks Upon Presenting the Presidential Unit Citation to the 26th Marines (Reinforced), 3d Marine Division (Reinforced). *May 23, 1968*

Secretary Ignatius, General Watson, Congressman Brooks, General Chapman, Colonel Lownds, Sergeant Major Smith, ladies and gentlemen:

It was 23 years ago that the 26th Marines took part in a mission that some people believed to be impossible—the capture of Iwo Jima, the most heavily fortified island in the world.

That mission was accomplished, and the 26th—after being awarded a Presidential Unit Citation for its part in that battle—passed from the active rolls of the Marine Corps on into history.

In January of 1966, the 26th was reborn as the first regiment of the reactivated 5th Marine Division. Again, the colors of the 26th Marines were carried into our fight for freedom in Asia.

Again they were assigned a task believed by many to be impossible.

Reinforced with a battalion from a sister regiment—the 1st Battalion, 9th Marines—and joined by a battalion of valiant South Vietnamese Rangers, the 26th was given the job of defending the vital combat base at Khe Sanh.

The 6,000 allied troops faced more than

20,000 determined North Vietnamese. Some say there are no North Vietnamese in that area.

But in the face of this threat, after most mature deliberation here, we asked General Westmoreland for his judgment about whether we should hold the position or remove our forces.

He was told to give no thought to the psychological or political repercussions of withdrawal in the United States.

The judgment of this battlefield general differed considerably from that of some here at home who then predicted that Khe Sanh would be another Dienbienphu.

General Westmoreland's decision was that the base should and could and would be held. That decision was confirmed by the Joint Chiefs and other officials here.

His faith in the 26th Marines was more than justified. For more than 70 days and nights they held despite massive and merciless attacks by the enemy.

The North Vietnamese mounted an assault identical to that which ended in their victory at Dienbienphu 14 years ago. But they had not counted on the most overwhelming, intelligent, and effective use of air power in the history of warfare; nor had they counted on the courage and the endurance—and the artillery—of the Marines at Khe Sanh. So unable to conquer, the enemy withdrew.

Some have asked what the gallantry of these Marines and airmen accomplished. Why did we choose to pay the price to defend those dreary hills?

The fortress at Khe Sanh straddled critical supply and infiltration routes that the North Vietnamese were using. Route 9, which it commanded, was to be a major avenue for the enemy into populated areas and into the cities of South Vietnam.

By pinning down—and by decimating—two North Vietnamese divisions, the few thousand Marines and their gallant South Vietnamese allies prevented those divisions from entering other major battles such as those for Hué and Quang Tri.

I believe that our initiative toward talks with North Vietnam was greatly strengthened by what these men did at Khe Sanh—for they vividly demonstrated to the enemy the utter futility of his attempts to win a military victory in the South.

All of us in America hope that the road to peace will lead through the talks in Paris.

But it is still not clear that Hanoi is ready for an early or an honorable peace.

The flow of infiltrators and of equipment from North Vietnam has never been greater than it is now. There is still very bitter fighting in many areas of South Vietnam.

There has been no visible lessening of Hanoi's aggressive efforts. In fact, Hanoi is today telling its forces in the South that they must continue their offensive to support their negotiators in Paris.

For our part, we shall seriously and soberly pursue negotiations toward an honorable and peaceful settlement of this war. But this should also be clear: We shall not be defeated on the battlefield while the talks go on. We shall not permit the enemy's mortars and rockets to go unanswered and to permit him to achieve a victory that would make a mockery of the negotiations.

We have faith that an honorable peace can be achieved in Vietnam. But if there must be more fighting before it comes, then we shall not be found wanting.

Brave men such as the 26th Marines will carry on the fight for freedom in Vietnam. Soon, God willing, they will come home. We would like nothing more than to see that day. But until they do, we shall express—at moments such as these—on behalf of all our American people our great gratitude for the protection they have given us and our great appreciation for their selfless bravery.

The Secretary of the Navy will now read the citation.

[Secretary of the Navy Paul R. Ignatius read the citation, the text of which follows.]

The President of the United States takes pleasure in presenting the Presidential Unit Citation to the

TWENTY-SIXTH MARINES (REINFORCED)
THIRD MARINE DIVISION (REINFORCED)

for service as set forth in the following

CITATION:

For extraordinary heroism in action against North Vietnamese Army forces during the battle for Khe Sanh in the Republic of Vietnam from 20 January to 1 April 1968. Throughout this period, the 26th Marines (Reinforced) was assigned the mission of holding the vital Khe Sanh Combat Base and positions on Hills 881, 861-A, 558 and 950, which dominated strategic enemy approach routes into Northern I Corps. The 26th Marines was opposed by numerically superior forces—two North Vietnamese

Army divisions, strongly reinforced with artillery, tank, anti-aircraft artillery and rocket units. The enemy, deployed to take advantage of short lines of communications, rugged mountainous terrain, jungle, and adverse weather conditions, was determined to destroy the Khe Sanh Combat Base in conjunction with large scale offensive operations in the two northern provinces of the Republic of Vietnam. The 26th Marines, occupying a small but critical area, was daily subjected to hundreds of rounds of intensive artillery, mortar and rocket fire. In addition, fierce ground attacks were conducted by the enemy in an effort to penetrate the friendly positions. Despite overwhelming odds, the 26th Marines remained resolute and determined, maintaining the integrity of its positions and inflicting heavy losses on the enemy. When monsoon weather greatly reduced air support and compounded the problems of aerial resupply, the men of the 26th Marines stood defiantly firm, sustained by their own professional esprit and high sense of duty. Through their indomitable will, staunch endurance, and resolute courage, the 26th

Marines and supporting units held the Khe Sanh Combat Base. The actions of the 26th Marines contributed substantially to the failure of the Viet Cong and North Vietnamese Army winter/spring offensive. The enemy forces were denied the military and psychological victory they so desperately sought. By their gallant fighting spirit and their countless individual acts of heroism, the men of the 26th Marines (Reinforced) established a record of illustrious courage and determination in keeping with the highest traditions of the Marine Corps and the United States Naval Service.

LYNDON B. JOHNSON

NOTE: The President spoke at 11:38 a.m. in the Cabinet Room at the White House. In his opening words he referred to Secretary of the Navy Paul R. Ignatius, Postmaster General W. Marvin Watson, Representative Jack Brooks of Texas, Gen. Leonard F. Chapman, Jr., Commandant of the Marine Corps, Col. David E. Lownds, commander of the 26th Marines at Khe Sanh, and Sgt. Maj. Agrippa Warren Smith of the 1st Battalion, 9th Marines, which reinforced the 26th. During his remarks the President referred to Gen. William C. Westmoreland, Commander, United States Military Assistance Command, Vietnam.

268   Presidential Unit Citation Awarded the 14th Air Commando Wing, USAF.   *May 23, 1968*

CITATION TO ACCOMPANY THE AWARD OF

THE PRESIDENTIAL UNIT CITATION

TO THE

14TH AIR COMMANDO WING

The 14th Air Commando Wing, United States Air Force distinguished itself by extraordinary heroism, exceptional gallantry and outstanding performance of duty in action against hostile forces in Southeast Asia from 8 March 1966 to 7 March 1967. Flying thousands of widely diversified sorties, elements of the Wing caused many enemy casualties and destroyed or damaged more than 8,500 structures, 500 trucks and 60 fuel sites as well as numerous automatic weapon positions, radio stations, bridges and boats. Flying the venerable C–47 aircraft, one squadron of the Wing helped abort a large number of night hostile operations against friendly forts and hamlets through flare drops and minigun saturation fire. Despite the often heavy and accurate enemy antiaircraft fire, the search and rescue missions of the Wing recovered 91 skilled airmen during this period. In addition, the Wing's psychological warfare missions directly or indirectly influenced the surrender of thousands of enemy soldiers. Through their valorous acts and untiring devotion to mission accomplishment personnel of the Wing have equaled the highest standards of performance in the United States Air Force and their actions reflect credit upon themselves and the armed forces of their country.

LYNDON B. JOHNSON

269   Presidential Unit Citation Awarded the 36th Tactical Fighter Squadron, Pacific Air Forces.   *May 23, 1968*

CITATION TO ACCOMPANY THE AWARD OF
THE PRESIDENTIAL UNIT CITATION
TO THE
36TH TACTICAL FIGHTER SQUADRON

The 36th Tactical Fighter Squadron, Pacific Air Forces, distinguished itself by extraordinary gallantry in connection with military operations against an opposing armed force in Southeast Asia, from 26 August 1965 to 28 October 1965. During this period, the gallantry, professionalism, determination, and esprit de corps consistently demonstrated by the members of the 36th Tactical Fighter Squadron were instrumental factors in the successful completion of their assigned mission under extremely difficult and hazardous conditions. As a result of their missions, the enemy's support of his forces in South Vietnam, and his ability to carry out his aggressive tactics against friendly forces were made more difficult and costly. The pilots of the 36th Tactical Fighter Squadron were directly responsible for the destruction or heavy damage to major military targets, which included ammunition dumps, supply routes, and radar sites. The extraordinary heroism displayed by this unit in the pursuit of its mission is in keeping with the highest standards of performance and traditions of the United States. By their gallantry and untiring devotion to duty, the personnel of the 36th Tactical Fighter Squadron reflected great credit upon themselves and the United States Air Force.

LYNDON B. JOHNSON

270   Remarks in Atlantic City at the International Ladies' Garment Workers Union Convention.   *May 25, 1968*

Governor Hughes, President Stulberg, Dave Dubinsky, Luigi Antonini, ladies and gentlemen:

Mr. Stulberg, I had to come here today because through all of my trials and tribulations—and the problems and the burdens—that go with the office I hold, you and your union have stood by my side in day and night, in sunshine and in sorrow.

If you could stay with me during what we have gone through the last few months, you can stay with these folks all through the years until we win what we are after.

I told Dave Dubinsky, I said, "I am glad to be here today with all of my friends of the Old Left."

Some of us can remember the good old days when we were the New Left back there more than 30 years ago when I was first captured by some of your leaders and enlisted in a great cause. I was an up-and-coming young radical liberal from the South.

Three from my State followed the recommendations of the leadership of this union. They were such radical recommendations that two of those three were defeated. I survived.

Some of your leadership got Mr. Roosevelt, who was then President, to send a message to the Congress on May 24, 1937. That message arrived at the House of Representatives just about the time I arrived as a young Member.

Among the things the President said in that message are the following:

"Mr. Justice Brandeis, Mr. Justice Clarke, and Mr. Justice McKenna agreed" with Mr. Justice Holmes. "A majority of the Supreme Court, however, decided 5–4 against Mr. Justice Holmes and laid down a rule of constitutional law which has ever since driven into impractical distinctions and subterfuges all attempts to assert the fundamental power of the national government over interstate commerce.

"But although Mr. Justice Holmes spoke for a *minority* of the Supreme Court he spoke for a *majority* of the American people." [1]

Upon that message, the Congress enacted into law—I will just read a part of section 6—that radical provision of other years:

"Every employer shall pay to each of his employees who is engaged in commerce or in the production of goods for commerce wages at the following rates—

"(1) during the first year from the effective date of this section, not less than 25 cents an hour,

"(2) during the next six years from such date, not less than 30 cents an hour,

And "(3) after the expiration of seven"—

should I say long—"years from such date, not less than 40 cents an hour, or the rate (not less than 30 cents an hour) prescribed in the applicable order of the Administrator issued under section 8, whichever is lower. . . . This section shall take effect upon the expiration of one hundred and twenty days from the date of enactment of this Act.

"No employer shall, except as otherwise provided . . . employ any of his employees . . . in commerce or in the production of goods for commerce—for a workweek longer than forty-four hours" and so on and so forth.

You did not require that law to protect your people. Your thinking had been more advanced. But you required that law to protect all the working people of the United States. That is what has been so wonderful about your union. You haven't just tried to look after yourself—you have tried to help look after all of us.

But times have changed. Today, we hear something about new politics and "participatory democracy."

So I have come here to participate with you—the very model in my judgment of the Old and the New Democracy.

Whenever I hear talk about new alignments and the new liberalism, I think of my old friends in the ILGWU. You have always had your slogans, too. You were the prophets of liberalism. You preached and you practiced your faith.

Politics—politics, thank God—has long been a religion with you—but never on Saturday.

And I came here today, Mr. Stulberg, to tell you and the members of this great union that the old-time religion is good enough for me. And the old-time liberalism is good enough for me.

Being here in this great hall in Atlantic

---

[1] President Roosevelt was referring to the Supreme Court decision of June 3, 1918, in *Hammer* v. *Dagenhart* (United States Supreme Court Reports, Lawyers' Edition, Book 62, p. 1101).

City, Governor Hughes, brings back many fond memories for me. I guess you all know why this city means so much to me. I don't think there is a man, woman, or child in all of this country who doesn't get a lump in his throat watching the Miss America contest each September.

There is one difference between today and the night I was here in August of 1964 at the Democratic Convention. It is a difference that some of you former cutters, pressers, operators, and finishers may be especially interested in knowing about. You have a chance to look at the only man in the long history of the needles trade who used a speech rather than the scissors to cut off his own coattails.

I must admit that your reception puts me in somewhat of a sentimental mood today. There is something about this union—something about this convention—something about Louis Stulberg—something about David Dubinsky—something about Evelyn Dubrow—that makes me feel right at home. It is something about all of these three and all of you out there that makes me feel right at home.

It is not just that you are my friends and that you have demonstrated your loyalty time and time and time again at the ballot box and in your influence on good legislation. It is much more than that.

Somehow, the ILGWU seems to me to be a model in miniature of the great America that we all seek and we all dream of.

As I look out from this podium today, I see delegates, I see Americans of every race, of every color, of every creed. You work together in harmony because you share a common ideal which is more important than anything else. You are building, and you are running one of the greatest democratic trade unions in all of the world.

This, of course, is because you have always asked the right question when admitting people to your membership. You don't ask:

"Is he white?" or,
"Is he Jewish?" or,
"Is he Catholic?"

You simply say, "Is he—or much more often she—a garment worker?"

I have been involved in national politics now since 1931—almost 38 years—and as I am about ready to go back home, I think I would like to leave one message with my dear friends here. I would like to leave this message behind me. I would like to carve it in rock. "Ask the right question."

And I would add that in both your experience and mine, the right question is usually *how?*—not *what?*

Back in the first decade of this century, every social reformer knew what was necessary to eliminate the terrible sweatshops, the Triangle firetraps in which the garment workers were literally held in wage-slavery.

There were economic treatises.

There were politicians out with sonorous speeches.

There were catastrophe-mongers who wanted to destroy the whole system to eliminate its abuses.

There were alleged intellectuals who were talking about us.

But what do the intellectuals know about us?

There were innumerable answers to the question, "What should be done?"

The system we knew had to be changed.

But when it came to "How?", there was only one group that had an answer that made sense. They didn't say, "We will meet in Union Square daily and we will carry signs and we will make speeches and we will give our treatises and our lectures and our seminars until there is a change in the system."

If so, they would still be there.

They said, "We will build a union."

Of course, all the professional cynics—

they had them then, too—said it was impossible—you couldn't beat the system—the men and women, mostly immigrants, didn't have the staying power.

Then, in 1909, when I was 1 year old, out came the waistmakers in a strike that "couldn't last."

But it did, and those girls—there may be a few here today, no longer girls, but still committed unionists—put the world to shame and brought a wave of support from decent Americans throughout this land everywhere.

So, a great union was born. And it grew because a few dedicated Americans—often with strange accents—took the ideals of our society at face value and said, "How can we put them into practice?"

It has not been an easy half century. You had your extremists with a vested interest in catastrophe who argued that destruction was the road to construction.

But your leaders—men like David Dubinsky and Louis Stulberg—and to those of us that were on down the line—Evy—they knew that you cannot build a utopia on ashes. And, after a terrible struggle which almost broke your union, these false prophets were defeated.

Since then, we have had wages and hours from 25 cents an hour to $1.60 applied to all the working people in this land.

In this last half century, we have passed four comprehensive far-reaching civil rights bills from the right to vote to a right to equal housing—and on all four of those measures you and I have led the way.

We have junked and discarded our archaic immigration laws. And we stood with pen in hand in front of the Statue of Liberty in this administration and wrote a new immigration law that permits families to again be reunited and puts another humane statute on our books.

We have passed meat inspection, auto safety, truth in lending, and we have just begun with a long list of more than a dozen other consumer measures that will be written into the law of this land because of your help.

For almost 200 years, we shunned our responsibility of national leadership in educating our children. But in the last 4 years we have declared it our national policy that every boy and girl born in this country has a right to all the education that he or she can take.

And we are—I am here to tell you—practicing what we preach.

While others have written their learned treatises and flourished their rhetoric from coast to coast, we have put them from Head Start at 4 to adult education at 74. And the ILGWU has had among its most cardinal principles performance instead of promises.

And as we meet here today, those Head Start kids at 4 and those adult education grandmas at 74 are learning to read and write in the classrooms of this country.

We have inaugurated the greatest conservation programs since the days of Teddy and Franklin D. Roosevelt. And this year we are putting more land for recreation back in the public domain—for the first year in decades—than we have taken out with highways and freeways.

We are putting that land not out in Montana or Wyoming where you can't get to it unless you have got a jet. But we are putting it near the centers of population where you can get to it in your flivver in an hour and a half.

We talked about Medicare from the time Harry S. Truman—that great President—proposed it. We talked about it and thought about it and dreamed about it for more than 20 years.

But we wrote it into law. And you got your

Medicare payments. Twenty million of you have your Medicare cards. You don't have to go and consult your son-in-law before you go to the hospital when you need it.

And I am telling you something else. This may not have been done with charisma or style. But it has been done.

I will tell you something else. What this great union has done with Medicare I am charging you with the responsibility of doing with "kiddie care."

The blush of shame ought to come to the cheeks of every proud American who talks about the most powerful and richest nation in the world when it realizes that in infant mortality the United States ranks not one—but 15 down the list.

Just as we have tried to cope with the problem of our aged, we have got to cope with the problem of our babies. We have got to get to them before it is too late. We have got to correct the deficiencies of their eyes, or their teeth, or their ears, or their bodies due to lack of proper treatment to their mothers.

You have got to have her examinations at critical periods. They have got to have treatments of doctors when they need them.

We can no longer go on in the days ahead as we have gone on in the days past—and our next goal is on to "kiddie care" now that we have got Medicare.

Oh, I wish I could talk all day. But I can't. I have other things to do and so do you. But I just want to summarize by saying to those of you who abhor colonialism and to those of you who have fought and bled and died to reject totalitarianism that neither colonialism nor totalitarianism has made any advances in these 5 years. They have retreated instead.

And aggression—wherever it has reared its ugly head—has been stopped in its tracks.

And freedom has not retreated an inch.

Every foot of soil that freedom held in 1963, freedom holds in 1968.

But I did not come here to give you a history of your union or of the last 5 years. I just wanted to point out a few of the high spots.

There have been more than 200 major basic measures enacted to better humanity that will compare favorably with all the measures enacted in the previous years in the social field.

But I think you know this story maybe far better than I do since you helped build this organization and since this organization gave the leadership and answered "aye" on every rollcall that advanced these measures.

I have drawn upon your history this morning because I find when I study it and I look upon it that it is both valuable and comforting to me in a time of stress and anguish. To the officers of this great union, Louis Stulberg and your retiring president, David Dubinsky—men that will give loyalty to principles and give loyalty to me as they have during every day of this 5 years—will give loyalty to you.

There is a great deal of rhetoric in the air these days. And as is natural in an election year, there is a speaker on every stump—and some places where they can't find stumps.

As I conclude—and as one who will shortly be a private citizen—I want to give you some advice. When you listen to the speakers, draw upon your own experience—draw upon the collective wisdom that you have accumulated in the years that you have been building this great union.

When men—or women, or boys, or girls—come to you and give you their prescriptions for America, listen to what they think is the matter with America.

But before it is all over, you demand from them an answer to the crucial question,

"How, how are they going to do anything about it?" It is not "What?" It is "How?" It is not the promise. It is the performance.

For the essence of politics, like trade unionism, is the ability to put a cutting edge on abstractions, to find an administrative remedy for a rhetorical dilemma.

And power—power as my old friend, Eric Hoffer, puts it—just does **not** "come in cans." You can't go down to the corner drugstore or the supermarket and pick some of it up in a basket.

Power for the ideals that we cherish has to be created by little, by the small and the seemingly insignificant decisions of dedicated, courageous men and women—most of whom are invisible, most of whom never make speeches, most of whom never issue manifestos, and most of whom never get on the television or get their pictures in the papers.

It is these people—people of this caliber—who have made the ILGWU a model—a model—of democratic trade unionism in the world.

It is your kind of people who make it possible for anyone to be President of the United States.

I want to conclude with this little note. I want to thank every member of this union here and those that can't be here.

I particularly want to thank Louis Stulberg for his fidelity and his dedication, his loyalty and his leadership.

Sitting there on the banks of the Pedernales, I am going to see how—how—he does it in the years ahead because I know that he and you and I are going to do it.

I also need not tell you how much I owe to you or how long I have admired your union and your great leader and crusader, David Dubinsky.

In these days more than ever I can envy him. He has made me wish many, many times in the last few days that our Founding Fathers had established another union—the AURP—the American Union for Retired Presidents. If that had happened, then I could look forward to a retirement plan like David Dubinsky's.

How would you like the sound of "Honorary President, Lyndon Johnson?"

Talk about liberal, how about these fringe benefits:

—a weekend in Atlantic City or Chicago,
—invitations to a dinner at the White House,
—a warm place in the hearts of all of your people, and
—a sure place in the spotlight of every convention?

But a greater satisfaction and more fringe benefits than all of those can come to an honorary president, has come to your honorary president because the man who picked up the leadership where he left off is carrying forward, onward to new and greater and far-reaching heights and benefits that will better humanity.

If I could have one hope today, it would be this: that whoever may be President, wherever he may reside, whatever party he belongs to, he will look at the social record of the last 5 years and say, "We have just begun."

As your union is dedicated to carrying forward on the slogan, "We have just begun," I hope our next President will have just begun and will continue as you have to build, to heal, and to unite the greatest nation in all the world.

Destructive people, mischievous people, ambitious people, and folks who look to what we have, and want to take what we have got, and envy the liberty and freedom that is ours, can destroy this Nation. But they will not.

The reason they will not is out there in

front of me in the form of the constructive, dedicated members of this union, who are builders instead of wreckers.

If I don't get an invitation to your next convention, I am going to reach back in that closet of mine where we pack our souvenirs and I am going to pull out an old badge that says "Honorary President" and I am going to invite myself to come back here.

NOTE: The President spoke at 11:15 a.m. in Convention Hall at Atlantic City. In his opening words he referred to Richard J. Hughes, Governor of New Jersey, Louis Stulberg, president, David Dubinsky, past president (1932–1965), and Luigi Antonini, first vice president of the International Ladies' Garment Workers Union. During his remarks he referred to Evelyn Dubrow, legislative representative for the union.

271   Remarks of Welcome at the White House to Prime Minister John Gorton of Australia.   *May 27, 1968*

Mr. Prime Minister and Mrs. Gorton, Secretary and Mrs. Rusk, distinguished guests, ladies and gentlemen:

Mr. Prime Minister, it is a very great pleasure for Mrs. Johnson and me to welcome you and your most charming wife to our country.

We have very little to offer in the way of surprises. Mrs. Gorton is a native of New England. We have some New England weather for her this morning. But she already knows all of our secrets anyway. Even if she did not, you, yourself, Mr. Prime Minister, are the Prime Minister of Australia—and the Australians and the Americans have so much in common that we seem to understand each other almost on sight anyway.

Our peoples have been molded by the same forces. Both of our continents are vast. Both of our histories are young. Both of our governments are free. All of our people were drawn from many lands. We both enjoy an abundance which, for most of the world, is yet just a dream.

We share a common vision. We see a world where might does not make right. We strive for a world where nations can live together in peace and freedom under the rule of law.

We have been fighting for this dream for a long time now. Twenty-five years ago we fought side by side from the Middle East to the South Pacific. Today we are fighting side by side in the rice fields in Vietnam.

I do not know how close we may be to success in our common—and our historic—cause.

But I do know that you, Mr. Prime Minister, come here at a moment of very historic importance. Our American aim is now, as it has been from the beginning, to achieve peace with honor, a peace which will permit the people of Asia and the South Pacific to work out their own destiny in their own way. We have never sought anything else, and we will not accept anything else.

I believe that Australia shares that aim, and I look forward with a great deal of anticipation to our conversations about this— and about many other common concerns.

Mr. Prime Minister, you and your countrymen are always welcome in Washington. I think you will soon find that, although you are half a world away from Australia, you are still very much at home.

Thank you very much.

NOTE: The President spoke at 11:35 a.m. in the East Room at the White House. In his opening words he referred also to Secretary of State and Mrs. Dean

Rusk. A planned formal welcoming ceremony on the South Lawn was cancelled because of rain. Prime Minister Gorton responded as follows:

Mr. President, Mrs. Johnson, Secretary Rusk and Mrs. Rusk, distinguished guests:

Thank you, Mr. President, on behalf of all Australians, for the honor which, through me, you do my country.

We value this the more since it comes from a power which is not only great, but which, since the end of the last World War, has assumed all the burdens and responsibilities of being great.

You helped reconstruct Europe. In large measure, you financed the constructive work of the United Nations. You have without stint given blood and treasure to protect small nations from subjugation by force or by threat. And you seek to raise the living standards of people in every corner of the world.

For this your country has received scant thanks—yet at one time, through sole possession of atomic power, you could have imposed your will upon the world—and did not. You could have chosen to conquer, but chose to set free. You could have looked inward, but instead you chose to look out.

If the United Nations has not brought that end to war which its founders sought, if the world is still torn by strife as it is, that is the fault of others, not of yours.

You have assumed, sir, as I said, many burdens, and today one dominates our minds.

Even as we stand here, our men fight in Vietnam together, as they fought in other wars, to protect small nations from overthrow by force of governments elected by the people. Even as we stand here, diplomats in Paris seek to discover whether there is hope of ending that fighting and securing a peace—just, lasting, and honorable—giving to the people of South Vietnam a chance themselves to choose their future path without fear or threat.

You, Mr. President, bore the lonely weight of decision to continue to resist force with force. You, Mr. President, by your recent gesture, brought the North Vietnamese to talk. You, Mr. President, relinquished chance of further office to give those talks such chance of success as they may have. And for that we admire and salute you.

It is that struggle which engrosses us today, but when it is decided, that solution will be one step only in the solution of other problems to which men and nations are born, which have arisen in the past, which exist now, and which will arise in the future in a world in transition.

So the Revolutionary War decided whether America would or would not be independent. The War Between the States decided whether the Union would continue or fragment. The Second World War decided whether the world would be subject to Fascist tyranny.

Just as those decisions engrossed the hearts and consciences of those then living, and decided a particular matter but did not provide solutions for future conflict or for progress, so will the outcome of the war in Vietnam decide that matter—but not those questions for decision arising in the years ahead. As Australians see it, those problems, although worldwide, are likely to be most acute in Asia.

We see there an area which needs an economic and technical base such as Europe already has. We see there an area where development and progress are essential if the peoples of those divergent nations are to support and defend something dynamic and developing—not something stagnant.

We see there an area crying for technical skills, a more experienced administration, a more equitable sharing of an increasing income—and we see there an area subject, above all, to the threat of subversion, terrorism, and aggression.

In some way, sir, because of internal division, parts of Asia are reminiscent of the Balkans before World War I—and in some ways they may pose the same dangers, dangers aggravated by the eagerness of agitators to exploit divisions.

Perhaps, Mr. President, though I don't think so, we Australians see this out of perspective—because it is here that we, contiguous to Asia, part of the Southeast Asian region, live and breathe and have our present and our future. It is here that we feel that we can best contribute to stability and to progress and to preserving a political freedom which seeks economic freedom as its concomitant. It is here that we can play our part. But we cannot effectively play it alone.

As for ourselves—we are not a great power, though we are destined so to be.

In our nation are new frontiers and boundless opportunities for those who will risk in order to win; for those who will work in order to build; for those who will endure initial hardship to gain distant goals.

We shall grow in numbers and in industrial power, and further develop the use of our natural resources, and in growing, Mr. President, will grapple with existing problems and prepare for those which wait in the corridors of the future.

But for the present, we, who for two centuries were shielded by the British Navy, have as our major shield the ANZUS Pact, and behind that, and because of that, we can the sooner grow to that stature we shall reach. We can the sooner reach a position to repulse any attack the future may hold from any quarter, and by any means. We can the sooner grow in capacity to offer more economic and technical assistance to the governments and peoples of our region.

I don't mean that we do not now play our part in defense, as we do in aid, or in seeking to foster trade which may be more important than aid.

But I do mean that because of your assistance, because of the ANZUS Treaty and what it implies, we can divert to building a future strength, resources which would otherwise be now diverted to defense, to the future detriment of defense, and to the future diminution of our ability to render as much help in the region as we would wish.

This is to us the virtue of the ANZUS Pact. And allied to it is the sure knowledge that you—while providing that shield—recognize that behind it we, as we build our country, are free to make and will make our own foreign policy decisions subject only to our treaty obligations.

Sir, I have not been here before in my present office, yet I feel I come not as a stranger.

On too many fields of battle we have stood together fighting for the concept of freedom, fighting against aggression. On too many occasions we have cooperated in the economic plans to help the world's underprivileged advance their standards of living.

There is too much common heritage of a system under which governments are chosen by a majority, dismissed by a majority, protect minority rights, yet refuse to be coerced by organized minority demonstrations. There are too many bonds for any Australian Prime Minister ever to feel that here he is a stranger.

And so as in the past, so may it be in the future. Looking down the vista of the years, I hope that you in your greatness now, and we in our present strength and our greatness to come, will together give protection, stability, advancement, encouragement, will help to foster, along with and depending on the people who live in that region, a new world in Asia to redress the balance of the old.

If this can be done, if we can do this together successfully, then the price to be now paid will, in the future, be thought by humanity small.

Thank you, sir.

272   Remarks Upon Signing Bills Providing Salary Increases for Teachers, Police, and Firemen in the District of Columbia. *May 27, 1968*

Mayor Washington, Chairman Hechinger, Members of Congress, ladies and gentlemen:

Public order and public education—these are the crucial concerns of any society. They are at the heart of the laws that I sign today for the Nation's Capital.

This legislation does not set forth any new theories. It deals with a real-life problem. It deals with a bread-and-butter issue for most of our valued public servants. It provides higher pay for the teacher in the classroom, the policeman on the beat who guards the safety of our families and homes, and the fireman who is called upon to answer the midnight bell.

These are the men and women who serve and who sustain our community. They should not be forced to live on the margin.

Last March, Mayor Washington and I asked the Congress to raise their salaries. Now the Congress has responded. As a result, beginning July 1, the starting teachers in the District schools will earn $7,000 a year. This will move the District all the way from 15th place to 3d place among the Nation's larger cities.

Beginning July 1, the police rookie and the new fireman will earn $8,000 a year. This moves the District from 11th to 3d place in the Nation.

The needs of all the Nation's cities are highlighted and magnified here at the seat of the National Government. The agenda is heavy, but every hour of every day I try to work on it some—on the schools, on the jobs, on the homes, on the opportunities, on the safe streets for all the people.

The police of Washington have always shown the face of responsibility in an hour of danger and crisis. True, they are a small force. But they have responded magnificently.

The Mayor has recommended to me that their ranks be increased by 1,000, to a total of 4,100. I have asked the Mayor to submit to the Congress as rapidly as possible a proposal to carry this forward.

I have made no secret whatever of my hopes for this great and beautiful city. I want to see this community the pride of our democracy—in its schools, in its neighborhoods, in the lives of all of its people.

Washington, D.C., has been my home for all the years of my public life. I have been proud to work with the men of good will and vision—work with them in the community and in the Congress—to try to advance the city's future.

The good day will come when all our hopes will be achieved—of that I am certain. The work we do today is just another small step and just another part of that great effort that is so necessary for all of us to make in the days ahead.

Thank you very much.

NOTE: The President spoke at 1:09 p.m. in the Fish Room at the White House. In his opening words he referred to Walter E. Washington, Commissioner of the District of Columbia, and John W. Hechinger, Chairman of the District of Columbia Council.

As enacted, the District of Columbia Teachers' Salary Act Amendments of 1968 (H.R. 16409) is Public Law 90–319 (82 Stat. 132), and the District of Columbia Police and Firemen's Salary Amendments of 1968 (H.R. 15131) is Public Law 90–320 (82 Stat. 140).

273   Toasts of the President and Prime Minister Gorton of Australia.   *May 27, 1968*

Mr. Prime Minister and Mrs. Gorton, Secretary and Mrs. Katzenbach, Ambassador and Mrs. Waller, distinguished guests, ladies and gentlemen:

Mr. Prime Minister, I have a confession to make tonight: I have been talking quite privately to your wife.

I hope and I believe this was not a violation of protocol. But I needed advice. Two years ago your predecessor—our late and beloved friend, Harold Holt—made a promise to me. During our visit prior to the Manila Conference, in the cool of the evening over a mint julep, he generously said that if things ever went wrong here in the United States, I would always have a political future in Australia. Mr. Prime Minister, I have been somewhat curious to know whether this still might be true.

Bettina, as you know, Mr. Prime Minister, is a daughter of New England. She said, "Mr. President, you will always be welcome. But Australians are a lot like you Texans— you are never as bad as they say you are

when they're mad . . . and you are never as good as they say you are when they love you."

Mr. Prime Minister, let me assure you tonight that I do not intend—I may reassess that a little later—I do not intend to stand for office in Canberra. This is a considerable sacrifice, since I can truthfully say there is no place outside my own native land where I really feel more at home.

Mr. Prime Minister and Mrs. Gorton, I hope that you will feel equally at home here in America and I trust that you will be able to come to visit us often. Lady Bird and I are pleased and honored that we should have this opportunity to be the first to welcome you to our country as Prime Minister.

The friendship that joins our two countries is a vital force in the struggle to transform the world's hopes into tomorrow's realities. It is a partnership which grows stronger and deeper with the passage of time. It extends from trade and mutual defense to man's newest frontier—the exploration of outer space.

Right now that partnership is being tested—tested in the hardest way that the ties between nations can be tested, and that is by the commitment of our men to combat. Tonight we are in a decisive phase of the struggle for peace and order in Southeast Asia. Talks have begun, but the other side is forcing the pace of battle; it is pouring men and supplies into South Vietnam at an unprecedented rate.

Let me tell you this:

—In Paris we shall remain patient but firm in the quest for an honorable peace. Ambassador Vance will be here in the morning to report to me and the Security Council, and to report to you, Mr. Prime Minister, on the developments there.

—In Vietnam tonight your men and ours—and the gallant South Vietnamese, the South Koreans, and the Thais who have fought so long for the right of self-determination—and all of our allies—will turn back this offensive.

—In time—and I pray it may be soon—the other side will turn from fantasy to reality; from violence to genuine peacemaking.

I know there are some in Asia and elsewhere who are wondering tonight whether the United States will maintain its commitments in Asia; who are wondering tonight whether the strains of this struggle will lead us to withdraw and leave two-thirds of humanity to its fate without American assistance or American support.

As you so well know, Mr. Prime Minister, with your years in political life, I cannot speak for my successor, but I can speak for myself, and the answer is no; we will not withdraw until there is an honorable peace. I do not think that my country will permit us to do otherwise.

If you look back over the years since 1941, you will see how steady the performance of the American Nation has been. You must put aside the Senate speeches that have been made and the debates that have gone on and you will see from one administration to another—from Republican to Democrat—that the United States of America and all of its people have steadily understood its interests in Asia and have acted on them.

I deeply believe that this will be true in the future as it has in the past. All the energy and influence that I can command will be in that direction. I think, Mr. Prime Minister, it will be true for a very simple reason: Every year that passes brings us closer to Asia and brings us really closer to the other regions of the world, closer in terms of military technology, closer in terms of communications, closer in economic ties, and closer in terms of simple human friendships.

If I may depart, Mr. Prime Minister, I think you will be interested to know that this afternoon I saw a report that on the list of choices for R&R—rest and recreation—in Vietnam, Australia was the first choice of the American fighting man.

I think you will also be pleased to know that of the thousands who have gone there, who have been taken into your homes, and they have been entertained as if they were their own sons, that so far as we have been able to ascertain, there has not been one single misunderstanding or violation of your hospitality or your courtesy—and that is saying something for Vietnam fighting men who are on rest and recreation in Australia.

In the years ahead, we hope that the new Asia that is being born will be increasingly organized to shape its own destiny. It should be able to do more for itself and rely less on the United States. But I have no doubt that there will be no return here to isolation. I have no doubt that America will remain the partner of Australia, and I have no doubt that Australia will continue to give leadership to the new Asia and the Free Asia as far ahead as any of us can see.

One of the comforting and pleasing developments of the last few years has been to see the leadership that the Government of Australia has given to this huge population that makes up two-thirds of the world; that this little country, through its leaders, has gone out and met with them, visited with them, exchanged views with them, and let them know that we are one and that we are trying to build toward a better day where we can fight the enemies of hunger, disease, and poverty that are so rampant in all of that area.

Mr. Prime Minister, your presence tonight is proof that this partnership is still vital and still growing. We are so pleased that you could bring your Maine lady with you and join us on the boat last night and that we could find all the differences that we had and solve most of them before the dinner tonight.

We think this visit of yours, so soon after you have taken over the responsibilities of the Prime Ministership, will be of great help to us and will endear you to this country.

Mr. Prime Minister, we hope that your visit here—and you will be visiting other parts of our country—will give you an insight into the affection that the American people hold for the Australian people. In sunshine and in sorrow, we have stood side by side.

Although Ed and Ann Clark found it so pleasant out there that they dared not take more than 2 years of it, we are sending you some other Texans who we hope will be representative of this country and be concerned with the future of Australia.

The young Ambassador said to me, "Mr. President," when I talked to him about two or three countries, "Why are you so high on

Australia?" I said, "If I could be Ambassador—and I am not sure I can under the next administration—if I could be, the one country that I would want to be Ambassador to is Australia." That is when he made his choice. That is when he decided he wanted to go to Australia.

So, Mr. Prime Minister, we welcome you and your party. We know that our talks will be fruitful. We assure you of our continuing cooperation and friendship.

We now ask you to join us in a toast to the great lady who symbolizes our common heritage, Her Majesty, The Queen.

NOTE: The President proposed the toast at 10:17 p.m. in the State Dining Room at the White House. In his opening words he referred to Prime Minister and Mrs. John Grey Gorton, Under Secretary of State and Mrs. Nicholas deB. Katzenbach, and Australian Ambassador and Mrs. Keith Waller. During his remarks he referred to Ambassador Cyrus R. Vance, U.S. negotiator at the Paris peace talks with North Vietnam, Edward Clark, returning U.S. Ambassador to Australia, and his successor Ambassador William Crook of Texas. Prime Minister Gorton responded as follows:

Mr. President, Mrs. Johnson, members of the diplomatic corps, distinguished guests:

I must first of all thank you, sir, for extending such a warm welcome to myself and to my Maine lady—that is spelled with an "e".

You know, sir, you have spoken tonight of a number of matters which beset us today. But in doing so, you have mentioned other matters which beset us in the past and which you will remember because you came to Australia at the time when these things were threatening then.

You went on missions over Papua and New Guinea in the defense of Australia at the time these things were threatening. I flew at that stage in company with pilots of the United States Air Force who had come to see what was threatening then did not prevail—and it did not prevail.

These difficulties, these problems, are borne on me tonight more than they ever have been before, because I stand here in a historic residence and my mind goes back to the time when, for example, one former President sat here and mourned the loss of more Americans in conflict than have been lost in all the wars since, between 1860 and 1865, and exercised will and exercised judgment in order to see that a nation due to become great did become great, and did not become split.

I can imagine well—because you showed me today upstairs, the room in which this great man slept—what those 5 years or 6 years, however long it was that man sat there, beset not only by an enemy across the Potomac—and I am bound to say that I speak as a convinced Confederate; at least I would have been then—but not only by an enemy across the Potomac—but by the Copperheads inside the Union, by the riots taking place in New York so that regiments had to be brought back from the Army of the Potomac to put it down; by the vilification and attacks of Horace Greeley and the newspapers—and newspapers are now much the same as they were then—and through it all, because the end was an end that was good, he saw that whatever was required to be done was done, and it was.

If it had not so been done, then there would not now be a United States of America.

Things don't change that much. I know that at one subsequent stage, part of the house in which I stand apparently inadvertently caught fire. But that has, of course, nothing to do with Australia, sir. I dare say that people responsible for it eventually finished up in Botany Bay as transportees.

I don't think that I should, on this occasion—which is a happy and a festive occasion—for too long talk about matters that are too serious.

I tried this morning to set forth what Australians think about what you are doing in the United States. When you speak of leadership that we give, we give that leadership, if we do, and we try to, because we are protected and shielded by a greater power. We will give greater leadership in the future because we will have in the past been protected and shielded by a greater power.

The coat of arms of my own country, sir, is borne on one side by a kangaroo and on the other by an emu. Neither one of these creatures, so the "Botanists" tell me, is physically able to move backwards; they can only move forward. We will and we have.

There is little time for figures to be presented to a meeting such as this, but at least in the last decade one can say that the gross national product of my country has doubled, at an average rate of 5½ percent; that the expenditure on foreign aid has doubled; that the expenditure on defense has trebled; that our population has increased by one-third. But that is all in the past.

I remember, sir, if I may translate it a little later into idiom, something which struck my mind when I was young. All of the past is prelude, which means "You ain't seen nothing yet."

But still we, like you, do have to contribute more than we would wish to to the protection of other peoples against attack, to the building up of a region which you could have said, which was once said

by a British Prime Minister, was a faraway region of which we know nothing, but which, as far as we are concerned, is a close region of which we know much.

We have to contribute to that because unless it happens, unless the people living there have a greater chance to improve their living standards to be able to live a reasonable and decent life, then in the future there is little hope for a reduction in that money necessary, but in one sense wasted, for defense.

So, we have to do it, and you make it possible for us to do it. But if this is achieved, if it is possible to beat the swords into plowshares, if it is possible to translate the aircraft into factories, if it is possible to take people out of uniform to be productive, then we can see in that area of the world something growing, something growing not only for their own benefit, but for our own, because we will sell them things for your own, because you will sell them things for our own, because we will buy from them that which they peculiarly can produce.

And we may—who knows, because man is born to travel as the sparks fly upward—but we may achieve an era nearer to a time when men can live in peace, when men can live in peace throughout the world, when these great political schisms which, for so long as I can remember, have torn the world to pieces may become muted and instead of people saying, "I will run through fascism all the people of the world," or "I will run through communism all the people in the world," we may have instead a brotherhood of men.

Who knows? I don't, but I am sure that what you are doing and what we are trying to help you do in a minor way is the only method by which this shining goal might eventually be achieved.

So I do not, as I say, wish tonight to make too serious a speech, but I would like to repeat a tribute that I made this morning, and that is: that the power inside this country, utilized as it is being utilized by this country, is to me the only sure—not sure—the only hopeful beacon, not only for this country, or for mine, but for the peoples generally of the world.

Well, the "Maine lady" of whom you spoke, long ago said to me something which she said I was to remember on any occasion when I spoke to a gathering of people. It is a little quatrain. It says, "I love the finished speaker, I really truly do. I don't mean one who is polished, I just mean one who is through."

Mr. President, though I could for an hour go on expressing the same feelings that you have expressed, I think it is unnecessary because I think between friends short exchanges are understood and detailed explanations are not required.

Therefore, I am through.

274 Special Message to the Congress: "Greater Prosperity Through Expanded World Trade." *May 28, 1968*

To the Congress of the United States:

A nation's trade lines are its life lines. Open trade lines and active commerce lead to economic health and growth. Closed trade lines end in economic stagnation.

Franklin D. Roosevelt recognized these truths more than thirty years ago, when the nation and the world were in the grip of Depression.

On that March day in 1934 when he asked the Congress to pass the historic Reciprocal Trade Act, he pointed to America's declining world trade and what it meant to the nation: "idle hands, still machines, ships tied to their docks."

That Act set in motion three and a half decades of descending tariff barriers and rising world trade. Our producers and farmers found new markets abroad, and American exports multiplied twenty-fold.

This era of commercial progress was capped by the Kennedy Round Agreements reached at Geneva last year—the greatest success in all the history of international trade negotiations.

When I reported to the Congress last November on the Kennedy Round, I said it would mean new factories, more jobs, lower prices to families, and higher incomes for American workers and for our trading partners throughout the world.

Already, through these Agreements, tariff barriers everywhere are falling, bringing savings to consumers, and opening new overseas markets for competitive producers.

But the problems and the promises of world trade are always changing. We must have the tools not only to adjust to change, but to turn change to our advantage.

To prepare for the era of world trade unfolding before us now, I submit to the Congress today the Trade Expansion Act of 1968. This measure will:

—maintain our negotiating authority to settle—advantageously—trade problems and disputes.

—carry out the special Geneva agreement on chemicals and other products.

—improve the means through which American firms and workers can adjust to new competition from increased imports.

OUR INTERNATIONAL RESPONSIBILITIES

The Trade Expansion Act of 1968 will strengthen relations with our trading partners in three ways.

First, it will extend through June 30, 1970, the President's authority to conduct negotiations for tariff reductions. This authority was contained in provisions of the Trade Expansion Act of 1962 that have expired.

Most of this authority was used in negotiating the Kennedy Round. The unused portion of that authority will give the President the flexibility to adjust tariff rates as future developments might require.

For example, the United States might find it necessary to increase the duty on a particular article—as the result of an "escape clause" action or a statutory change in tariff classification. In such event, we would be obliged to give other nations compensatory tariff adjustments for their trade losses.

Without this authority, we would invite retaliation and endanger American markets abroad.

I recommend that the President's authority to make these tariff adjustments be extended through June 30, 1970.

Second, the Trade Expansion Act of 1968 will eliminate the American Selling Price system of customs valuation. This action is necessary to carry out the special agreement reached during the Kennedy Round.

The American Selling Price system has outlived its purpose. It should be ended.

The generally accepted method of valuing goods for tariff purposes—which we and all our trading partners employ—is to use the actual price of the item to the importer.

But many years ago, to protect a few of our fledgling industries, we imposed on competing foreign goods—in addition to a substantial tariff—the special requirement that their tariff value be determined by American prices. Today this unusual system often produces tariff protection of more than 100 percent of the import cost of the product.

Such excessive protection is both unfair and unnecessary.

This system is unfair because it:

—Gives to a few industries a special privilege available to no other American business.

—Rests on an arbitrary method of valuation which no other nation uses.

—Diverges from the provisions of the General Agreement on Tariffs and Trade.

—Imposes an unjustified burden on the U.S. consumer.

This system is unnecessary because the few industries which it covers no longer need special government protection.

It applies primarily to the chemical industry in the benzenoid field. Yet chemicals, and benzenoids in particular, are among our most efficient and rapidly expanding industries. They have done well at home. They have done well in the international market. They are in a strong position to face normal competition from imports.

A supplementary agreement was nego-

tiated at Geneva which will lower foreign tariffs on American chemicals and reduce certain non-tariff barriers—road taxes and tariff preferences—on American automobiles and tobacco. To receive these important concessions, the United States must eliminate the American Selling Price valuation system and thereby give foreign producers of chemicals and a few other products normal access to our markets. This bargain is clearly in our national interest—good for our industries, good for our workers, and good for our consumers.

I recommend that the Congress eliminate the American Selling Price system to remove inequities in our tariffs and enable us to take advantage of concessions negotiated in the Kennedy Round.

Third, the Trade Expansion Act of 1968 will provide for specific funding of our participation in the General Agreement on Tariffs and Trade.

This is the procedure we follow in meeting our financial responsibilities to all other international organizations.

The General Agreement on Tariffs and Trade has become the most important forum for the conduct of international trade relations. The Kennedy Round took place under its auspices. Yet since 1947, we have financed our annual contribution to this Agreement through general contingency funds rather than through a specific authorization.

I recommend that the Congress authorize specific appropriations for the American share of the expenses for the General Agreement on Tariffs and Trade.

OUR NEEDS AT HOME

When trade barriers fall, the American people and the American economy benefit. Open trade lines:

—Reduce prices of goods from abroad.

—Increase opportunities for American

businesses and farms to export their products. This means expanded production and more job opportunities.

—Help improve the efficiency and competitive strength of our industries. This means a higher rate of economic growth for our nation and higher incomes for our people.

Some firms, however, have difficulty in meeting foreign competition, and need time and help to make the adjustment.

Since international trade strengthens the nation as a whole, it is only fair that the government assist those businessmen and workers who face serious problems as a result of increased imports.

The Congress recognized this need—in the Trade Expansion Act of 1962—by establishing a program of trade adjustment assistance to businessmen and workers adversely affected by imports.

Unfortunately, this program has been ineffective. The test of eligibility has proved to be too rigid, too technical, and too complicated.

As part of a comprehensive trade expansion policy, I propose that we make our adjustment assistance program fair and workable.

I recommend that Congress broaden the eligibility for this assistance. The test should be simple and clear: relief should be available whenever increased imports are a substantial cause of injury.

I intend to pattern the administration of this program on the Automotive Products Trade Act of 1965. Determinations of eligibility will be made jointly by the Secretaries of Labor, Commerce and Treasury.

The adjustment assistance provisions of Automotive Products Trade Act of 1965 have been successful. They have well served American automobile firms and their workers as we have moved to create an integrated U.S.-Canadian auto market.

These provisions will expire on June 30.

I recommend that the Congress extend the adjustment assistance provisions of the Automotive Products Trade Act through June 30, 1971.

TRADE INITIATIVES FOR THE FUTURE

The measures I have recommended today will help us carry forward the great tradition of our reciprocal trade policy.

But even as we consolidate our past gains, we must look to the future.

First and foremost, we must ensure that the progress we have made is not lost through new trade restrictions.

One central fact is clear. A vicious cycle of trade restrictions arms most the nation which trades most. And America is that nation.

At the present time, proposals pending before the Congress would impose quotas or other trade restrictions on the imports of over twenty industries. These measures would cover about $7 billion of our imports—close to half of all imports subject to duty.

In a world of expanding trade, such restrictions would be self-defeating. Under international rules of trade, a nation restricts imports only at the risk of its own exports. Restriction begets restriction.

In reality, "protectionist" measures do not protect any of us:

—They do not protect the American working man. If world markets shrink, there will be fewer jobs.

—They do not protect the American businessman. In the long run, smaller markets will mean smaller profits.

—They do not protect the American consumer. He will pay more for the goods he buys.

The fact is that every American—directly or indirectly—has a stake in the growth and vitality of an open economic system.

Our policy of liberal trade has served this nation well. It will continue to advance our interests in the future.

But these are critical times for the nation's economy. We have launched a series of measures to reduce a serious balance of payments deficit. As part of this program, I have called for a major long-run effort to increase our trade surplus. This requires that we push ahead with actions to keep open the channels of trade.

Many of our trading partners have indicated a willingness to cooperate in this effort by accelerating some of their tariff reductions agreed to in the Kennedy Round, and by permitting the United States to defer a portion of our tariff reductions. Furthermore, a number of Western European countries are now taking more active steps to achieve a higher rate of economic growth. This promises to increase the demand for our exports and improve our trade position.

To take full advantage of the expanded trading opportunities that lie ahead, we must improve the competitive position of American goods. *Passage of the anti-inflation tax is the most critical action we could take now to strengthen our position at home and in world markets.* The tax measure I have recommended will help prevent destructive price increases—which can sap the vitality and strength of our economy. Continued rapid increases in our prices would mean fewer exports and higher imports.

Second, other nations must join with us to put an end to non-tariff barriers.

Trade is a two-way street. A successful trade policy must be built upon reciprocity. Our own trade initiatives will founder unless our trading partners join with us in these efforts.

The Kennedy Round was an outstanding example of international cooperation. But major non-tariff barriers continue to impede the free flow of international commerce. These barriers now block many U.S. products from competing for world markets.

Some non-tariff barriers violate provisions of the General Agreement on Tariffs and Trade. We will step up our efforts to secure the prompt removal of these illegal restrictions.

Other non-tariff barriers may not be illegal, but they clearly hamper and hinder trade. Such barriers are found in all countries; the American Selling Price system is an example of one of our non-tariff barriers.

We have initiated a major international study to assess the effect of non-tariff barriers on world trade.

We have already begun action in the General Agreement on Tariffs and Trade and other international organizations to deal with some of these non-tariff barriers.

Efforts such as these are an important element in our trade policy. All sides must be prepared to dismantle unjustified or unreasonable barriers to trade.

Reciprocity and fair play are the essential standards for international trade. America will insist on these conditions in all our negotiations to lower non-tariff barriers.

Third, we must develop a long-range policy to guide American trade expansion through the 1970's.

I have directed the President's Special Representative for Trade Negotiations to make an intensive study of our future trade requirements and needs.

I would hope that Members of the Congress and leaders of Labor, Business and Agriculture will work with the Executive Branch in this effort. To help develop the foundations of a far-reaching policy, I will issue an Executive Order that establishes a wide basis for consultation and assistance in this important work.

AN EXPANDING ERA IN WORLD TRADE

The proposals in this message have been shaped to one purpose—to develop the promise of an expanding era in world trade.

We started on this road three and a half decades ago. In the course of that journey, the American farmer, the businessman, the worker and the consumer have benefitted.

The road ahead can lead to new levels of prosperity and achievement for the American people. The Trade Expansion Act of 1968 will speed us on the way.

I urge the Congress to give this impor-tant measure its prompt and favorable consideration.

LYNDON B. JOHNSON

The White House

May 28, 1968

NOTE: The Revenue and Expenditure Control Act of 1968, which enacted the recommended tax increase, was approved by the President on June 28, 1968 (see Item 343).

The Trade Expansion Act of 1968 and the Automotive Products Trade Act extension were not enacted by the 90th Congress.

On August 30, 1968, the President signed Executive Order 11425 "Study of United States Foreign Trade Policy" (4 Weekly Comp. Pres. Docs., p. 1286; 33 F.R. 12363; 3 CFR, 1968 Comp., p. 133).

275 The President's News Conference of May 28, 1968

THE PRESIDENT'S OPENING STATEMENT

THE PRESIDENT. [1.] I don't want to de-tain you long. Some of you may be going to the Press Club, but George [1] was getting a good many inquiries and I had two or three things that I thought you would be inter-ested in.

I will try to have these mimeographed as quickly as possible.

AMBASSADOR VANCE'S REPORT ON THE PARIS TALKS

But on the Vance talks this morning, I talked with Ambassador Vance at some length before our breakfast briefing.

As you know, he is home on consultations from Paris. He and Mrs. Vance have spent the night at the White House.

He described the exchanges which have taken place in Paris and gave me his evalua-tion of them in some detail.

As you know, he and Ambassador Harri-man [2] are associate spokesmen for us in Paris. The other side has sought to use these talks for two purposes: First, to see if we could be pressured to stop the bombing com-pletely in the southern panhandle of North Vietnam, without any compensatory action on their part.

At the present time, they are pouring men and supplies through this area at an unprece-dented rate. The supplies go directly to the battle in South Vietnam. We are destroying something over 20 percent of what is coming through to the South.

Without our attacks, our men and our al-lies would be bearing a considerable extra burden. It would be translated into casual-ties—American, South Vietnamese, Austral-ian, Korean, Thai, and Filipino casualties.

Those casualties have been very heavy, particularly since the Paris talks began, and

---

[1] George E. Christian, Special Assistant to the President.

[2] Cyrus R. Vance and Ambassador at Large W. Averell Harriman, U.S. negotiators at the Paris peace talks with North Vietnam.

the stepped-up attacks that they have made.

Our negotiators, Ambassador Harriman and his associate, Mr. Vance, have made it clear that we have already taken a very major step, as I announced in my March 31 speech,[3] both personally and officially, in connection with the bombing of large segments of their population and territory.

We have withdrawn some 90 percent of the population from the area that we bombed and some 78 percent of the territory. Now we have stopped the bombing of most of the territory and population in North Vietnam.

We made it clear if North Vietnam responded, if they would show some similar restraint, we are prepared to make further decisions to try to reduce the violence.

That has been our position since the formula was presented on March 31, which brought about the Paris negotiations. That is our position today, and it will remain our position.

Second, the other side has been using the occasion of these talks for obviously very wide-ranging propaganda. They have been unwilling to enter into serious, quiet discussion of the conditions for ending the bombing or any other matters of substance.

On the other hand, Ambassador Harriman and Ambassador Vance have been putting forward a series of constructive proposals, including the reestablishment of an effective demilitarized zone and the implementation of the Laos accord of 1962.

They have also indicated the principles that we believe should govern a total settlement of the problem, including the withdrawal of forces from South Vietnam and a political settlement.

I discussed with Ambassador Vance, and a number of my other senior advisers, the positions that had been taken and that we should take in Paris in the future.

While our men deal with Communist forces in the field, we shall continue patiently to see whether the Paris talks can yield anything in the way of constructive results.

In our judgment, it is time to move from fantasy and propaganda to the realistic and constructive work of bringing peace to Southeast Asia.

In addition, at 6:00 this afternoon, Ambassador Vance will meet with me here at the White House, and I have invited to be my guests the bipartisan leadership. We expect Members from both parties—leadership in the Senate and House, to be present for that briefing.

I think that you have been told that the same briefing given to me was given to the Prime Minister from Australia this morning.

MESSAGE TO THE CONGRESS ON THE TRADE EXPANSION ACT

[2.] We are submitting a message on the Trade Expansion Act.[4] There will be some notes on what this proposal does.

It extends the provisions of the Trade Expansion Act of 1962. It allows the President to conduct negotiations for tariff reductions. It eliminates the American selling price system of customs valuation which is necessary to implement the last of the Kennedy Round agreements.

It authorizes specific appropriations to pay our share in the General Agreement on Tariffs and Trade. It produces a new adjustment assistance program. It also asks as a part of this bill an extension of the adjustment assistance provisions of the Automotive Products Trade Act. This act has allowed us to create an integrated U.S.-Canadian auto market and assist workers in firms who might be injured.

---

[3] See Item 170.

[4] See Item 274.

It comes out strongly against quota bills now pending in the Congress. It makes a strong statement on the need to join with other nations in eliminating nontariff barriers. It states that the President will shortly sign an Executive order to initiate a full-scale study of long-range American trade policy.[5]

There will be a detailed briefing for that if those of you interested in that subject want to get it when the message goes up.

I think that is all that I have.

I will be glad to take any questions that you may have. I don't want to run this unnecessarily long because any of you who can go to the Prime Minister's meeting, I want you to go there.

QUESTIONS

[3.] Q. Mr. President?
THE PRESIDENT. Yes, Mr. Lisagor?[6]

THE PARIS TALKS

Q. The two points that you gave us that the other side is making, were those Mr. Vance's report to you, or are they two points that you have concluded from his report?

THE PRESIDENT. Those are my statements. I didn't want to go into the specifics of Mr. Vance's report. I don't think we will. I am not sure that that would contribute anything to the negotiations.

Q. Mr. President, did Mr. Vance express his hope or confidence that in time North Vietnam will move away——

THE PRESIDENT. I don't want to go into

Mr. Vance's report or the details of his conversation. As I said to Mr. Lisagor, Mr. Young,[7] I don't think anything can come from this that would be helpful. I would not be drawing contrary conclusions though.

TAX INCREASE AND SPENDING CUTS

[4.] Q. Mr. President, in your Trade Expansion Act message, you mentioned the need for a tax increase again. Are you ready yet to say whether you would accept the $6 billion cut in Federal spending as part of the tax package?

THE PRESIDENT. I am ready to say that there is a compelling and overriding necessity for a tax bill as soon as possible;[8] that the President believes that expenditure reductions in a very tight budget that Congress is already increasing in votes in the Senate and the House is not in accordance with his best judgment.

For that reason, I sent a tight, lean budget to the Congress. And I have not advocated reductions in it. My press conference statement still stands on that.

I think that if the Congress insists that before they give us a tax bill that will produce $10 billion, that they are willing to reduce expenditures by $4 billion, the President would try to accept their judgment and live with that. That's what I said at the last press conference.

Mr. Burke of Massachusetts[9] is making a motion to that effect that will be voted on tomorrow morning. Now, the men who do the appropriating tell me—and they have been there for years, 30 years and up—that

[5] Executive Order 11425 "Study of United States Foreign Trade Policy" (4 Weekly Comp. Pres. Docs., p. 1286; 33 F.R. 12363; 3 CFR, 1968 Comp., p. 133).
[6] Peter Lisagor, Chicago Daily News.

[7] Robert C. Young, Chicago Tribune Press Service.
[8] The Revenue and Expenditure Control Act of 1968 was approved by the President on June 28, 1968 (see Item 343).
[9] Representative James A. Burke of Massachusetts.

they do not believe the Congress, when it votes on specific reductions, will vote and let stand very long more than $4 billion, if that much.

They predict less than half that much, actually. So in my press conference, I said I doubt that they will vote $4 billion actual specific reductions and allow them to stand. Anything they vote above that, I think, would be changed later. In effect, I think I referred to it as "phony" or something that would be unreal and unlasting over a long period of time.

Now if Congress is willing to vote the $4 billion by supporting the Burke motion, we would do our best to live with it. If they don't vote the $4 billion, we will have to look at the situation, and we will draw whatever conclusions we think are justified.

We feel that a tax bill is very essential. The President will do everything he can to meet the Congress more than halfway once the Congress can determine what it is willing and has the power to vote.

It would do no good if the President arbitrarily assumed the appropriation power and just impounded funds if Congress did not agree with it, because the Congress could restore it very quickly.

Any other questions?

THE POOR PEOPLE'S MARCH ON WASHINGTON

[5.] Q. Do you have any message for the poor people marchers who are camped near here?

THE PRESIDENT. I covered that rather fully in my last press conference.[10]

We have $78 billion in messages on social programs in the Congress. We are doing everything that we can to get those measures

---

[10] See Item 223 [9].

approved by both authorizations and appropriations, and we are making rather substantial progress in most of those fields.

FUNDS FOR ASIAN DEVELOPMENT BANK AND INTERNATIONAL DEVELOPMENT ASSOCIATION

[6.] Q. Mr. President, the Foreign Relations Committee voted down funds for the Asian Bank and deferred funds for IDA. How do you feel about that?

THE PRESIDENT. I think that all Americans should share my concern about the effect of this action. I think it goes to the fundamental American commitment to try to help Asia help itself.

I do not think it is wise to defer this action. The forces of change are at work in Asia, and they should not be put off. If we act now, change can be progress, and if we delay, I think it can be tragedy.

I would hope that in this close vote, the Members who have doubts could try to resolve those doubts by discussing the matter with Mr. Black,[11] who is a very eminent specialist in this field, and an American whom all of us respect.

If we are ever to get away from the aid-grant programs, we ought to try to encourage the regional development banks and encourage other nations to join with us in sharing part of this load.

I believe that Mr. Black has made a very convincing case. I would hope that Members of the Congress would keep an open mind and see if there could not be a meeting of minds that would permit favorable action before the session ends.

---

[11] Eugene R. Black, Adviser to the President on Southeast Asian Economic and Social Development and former President of the International Bank for Reconstruction and Development.

THE SUBMARINE "SCORPION"

[7.] Q. Mr. President, do you have any late reports on the submarine *Scorpion?* [12]
THE PRESIDENT. We are conducting an in-

tensive search. We are all quite distressed, and we have been since the middle of the afternoon yesterday. We are quite concerned about it. We have nothing that is encouraging to report.

Helen Thomas, United Press International: Thank you, Mr. President.

[12] The nuclear submarine U.S.S. *Scorpion* was reported missing on May 29, 1968, when she had been 2 days overdue at Norfolk, Va., following training exercises with the 6th Fleet in the Mediterranean. The ship, with 99 men aboard, was listed as "presumed lost" on June 5 after a fruitless search by the Navy.

NOTE: President Johnson's one hundred and twenty-sixth news conference was held in his office at the White House at 12:30 p.m. on Tuesday, May 28, 1968.

276   Remarks at the Swearing In of John Robson as Under Secretary and Stanford Ross as General Counsel, Department of Transportation.   *May 28, 1968*

Secretary Boyd, Members of the Congress, ladies and gentlemen:

I have been slightly delayed because of a transportation problem. I wanted to avoid calling on the experts if I could, but my problem is how to get General Westmoreland from Saigon to Johnson City and get the Prime Minister of Australia from Washington to Johnson City, and get both of them there at the same time for a briefing, with the present transportation facilities we have.

I know that down the road Secretary Boyd and his Department will have the answers to all these problems but I am confronted with it here today at lunch.

As we meet here to swear in these two young lawyers, we might begin with a quotation from the Bible:

". . . Woe unto you also, ye lawyers! For ye lade men with burdens grievous to be borne, and ye yourselves touch not the burdens with one of your fingers."

Now I have known lawyers like that, but the two young men with us today are not among them. Anyone who accepts a position of responsibility in the field of transportation policy can be said to have touched the bur-

dens with both hands.

Much of the history of America is written in the story of transportation. The clipper ship, Conestoga wagon, iron horse, and Model T symbolized growth and symbolized greatness in the past. The high-speed train, the giant cargo plane, the swifter ships will just as surely be part of our American future.

The quality of transportation has a vital and a daily effect on the quality of life in America. How quickly and how safely and how efficiently we move ourselves and our goods helps determine the health, safety, convenience, and prosperity of our people.

Transportation is our youngest Government department. It is an area where young Americans eager to influence America's destiny can find immense challenge and mighty satisfaction.

So the challenges of transportation are clear:

—When man can orbit the earth in only a little more time than a truck can cross Manhattan at rush hour.

—When railroads can move freight more speedily than they can move people.

—When congestion at airports means delay and inconvenience on the ground, and danger in the sky.

—When traffic chokes our cities and fouls the air above them, slowing commerce and imperiling health.

America is blessed when she has brilliant young men who are directing the destiny of the Department of Transportation, particularly young men like Secretary Boyd and these other young men who have agreed to come here and make a career of meeting these challenges.

John Robson and Stan Ross are two such men.

John Robson, the first General Counsel of the Department of Transportation, is being promoted to Under Secretary. Stan Ross replaces him as General Counsel.

They have much in common: They are young. They are dedicated. They have high achievement. They have—for all their youth—very deep experience in the ways of Government. They understand how to move a concept through the bureaucracy of Joe Califano's office into the physical reality of an act of Congress. Now we will see if they can take these acts and if they can move millions of their fellow Americans and tons of freight across this country. And we hope they can move the people as smoothly and efficiently as they can move the freight.

Under the leadership of this young, dynamic, wise Secretary, Alan Boyd, I believe they can and at least I am going to, along with these youngsters here, put my money on them.

NOTE: The President spoke at 12:56 p.m. in the Cabinet Room at the White House. His opening words referred to Alan S. Boyd, Secretary of Transportation, who administered the oath of office to Mr. Robson and Mr. Ross. Later he referred to Joseph A. Califano, Jr., Special Assistant to the President.

277   Joint Statement Following Discussions With the Prime Minister of Australia.   *May* 28, 1968

AT THE INVITATION of President Lyndon B. Johnson of the United States, the Rt. Hon. J. G. Gorton, Prime Minister of Australia, paid an official visit to Washington on May 27 and 28. This was Prime Minister Gorton's first visit to the United States since assuming office. It afforded the President and the Prime Minister an opportunity to exchange views on matters of mutual concern, including the situation in Southeast Asia.

Australia-U.S. Relations

The President and the Prime Minister reviewed the current state of Australia-U.S. relations. They expressed profound satisfaction that the historic partnership between their two countries was continuing to deepen and grow in significance for the security and progress of the Pacific region. They reaffirmed specifically the importance of the ANZUS Treaty as an expression of the United States' continuing strategic interest in the region and the continuing cooperation of the two Governments in the maintenance of stability and security in Asia and the Pacific.

The Prime Minister and the President expressed their gratification with the existing scientific cooperation between the two countries. Such cooperation has advanced the state of science not only to the benefit of both countries but to mankind generally. They agreed that the Special Assistant to the President for Science and Technology and a team of leading United States scientists would visit Australia soon to meet with the Australian Minister of Education and Science and his colleagues, to identify additional areas appropriate for cooperative activities and explore ways in which the close cooperation between the American and Australian scientific communities could be broadened and extended.

Stressing the importance of the soundness of the dollar to the maintenance of prosperous international economic conditions, the Prime Minister reiterated his full support for the President's program to reduce the United States balance of payments deficit. The President assured the Prime Minister that the United States would strive to avoid undesirable effects on Australia or other nations of measures taken under the program.

Vietnam

The President and the Prime Minister reviewed in detail the situation in South Vietnam, where Australian and American forces are fighting side by side to assure the right of the Vietnamese people to determine their own destiny free of outside interference. They agreed that the establishment of a just and viable peace called both for a strong military posture and for intensive diplomatic efforts.

The Prime Minister expressed his gratification that the President's initiative of March 31 had led to conversations with North Vietnamese representatives. The President reviewed in detail the progress of these talks to date. He reaffirmed that the United States Government would continue to consult fully with the Australian Government and other Allies as the talks proceed. They agreed that the Allied nations which have helped to defend the Republic of Vietnam should participate in any settlement of the conflict.

At the invitation of the President the Prime Minister joined him this morning at his meeting with Mr. Cyrus Vance, who returned from Paris last night. Mr. Vance reported to the President and the Prime Minister on the course of the discussions in Paris with the representatives from North Vietnam.

The President expressed particular appreciation for the warm hospitality which the Australian people have extended to American servicemen on leave from Vietnam.

Pacific Regional Cooperation

The President and the Prime Minister reviewed the favorable trends in regional cooperation in the Pacific area which had been noted at the ANZUS and SEATO Council meetings in April 1968. They expressed satisfaction that, despite Communist expansionism, many constructive forces are promoting social and economic development in the area. They reaffirmed a hope that the impressive growth of regional groupings in Asia would continue, and expressed willingness to assist in every appropriate and feasible way.

The President and Prime Minister recognized that the United Kingdom's decision to accelerate withdrawal of its military forces from Southeast Asia increased the need for regional consultation and cooperation. The President welcomed Australia's interest in the area, and assured the Prime Minister of his keen interest in the progress of the consultations and in the outcome of the forthcoming Five Power Conference in Kuala Lumpur.

278   Letter to Senator Sparkman Following Senate Passage of the Housing and Urban Development Bill.   *May 29, 1968*

Dear Mr. Chairman:

Yesterday was a time of triumph for the American people and the American city.

The United States Senate—under your leadership—passed the most massive housing authorization bill in the Nation's history ever recommended by a President.

And now—in this $5 billion measure—the promise of hope and home moves a little closer to reality for millions of poor American families.

Last February, in a special message, I called upon the Congress to enact a far-reaching program to stamp out degradation and misery in our great urban centers—to rebuild the cities and restore to them the values as old as the Republic itself: equality and justice, and the opportunity for self-respect in a true community of neighbors.

That call was answered in the Housing and Urban Development Act of 1968 passed by the Senate yesterday.

It was answered by approving our recommendations for:

—$1 billion for Model Cities, which can rebuild the entire core of decaying neighborhoods.

—$1.75 billion for urban renewal, revised and strengthened, as a humane instrument to restore slum areas.

—Continued life for rent supplements, through which homes for the poor are built by private enterprise.

—New public housing, expanded and recognizing the needs of families as more than mere shelters.

It was answered in approving our recommendations for new approaches and fresh solutions to the stubborn and lingering problems of the cities:

—In the new programs through which hundreds of thousands of poor families can achieve the dream of owning their own homes.

—In the vast expansion and redirection of assistance for private rental housing for low and moderate income families.

—In the National Housing Partnership which can focus the talents of private industry and labor on the job of high volume production of low-income homes.

—In the start of new communities on the city's rim.

—In new insurance protection for the home owner and the businessman in the inner city.

The Senate has made a major breakthrough. Now we must move to the follow-through.

I hope the House of Representatives will join with the Senate in making the Housing Act of 1968 the testament of freedom for the American city.

Time will not wait. We dare not lose this opportunity to act.

Sincerely,

LYNDON B. JOHNSON

[Honorable John J. Sparkman, Chairman, Banking and Currency Committee, United States Senate, Washington, D.C.]

NOTE: The Housing and Urban Development Act of 1968 was approved by the President on August 1, 1968 (see Item 426).

For the President's special message to Congress of February 22 on urban problems, see Item 87.

279   Memorial Day Message to the Men and Women of the Armed Forces.   *May 29, 1968*

FOR A CENTURY now, Americans have set aside one special day to remember those who have given their lives in the Nation's defense.

The battlefields on which they fell span the long generations of our history, from the slopes of Bunker Hill to the A Shau Valley.

The cost of their sacrifice is beyond reckoning. But the result of their sacrifice, and of the service of all their comrades-in-arms, is beyond price: We are a nation; we are united; we are free.

On Memorial Day 1968, we yearn for an end to war, for a time when the guns will be silenced forever and men can live as they wish.

That peace, when it comes, will be the lasting memorial of all who have fought to give it birth, and whose service and sacrifice we honor today.

280   Remarks Upon Signing the Consumer Credit Protection Act.   *May 29, 1968*

Mr. Vice President, Members of the Cabinet, Members of the Congress, my beloved friend Senator Douglas, distinguished guests, ladies and gentlemen:

I ask your indulgence for being late. We had a rather extended briefing on a subject that means more to all of us than any other subject, and that is how we can get peace in the world.

I have been talking to Mr. Vance since before 8 o'clock this morning, reviewing all the developments of the past 2 weeks. He is preparing to return to Paris. He has been briefing our Cabinet and evaluating for us the developments there.

I assume it is not inappropriate here to observe that back last August we searched our minds and our hearts and our principles and laid down a program which was subsequently announced in San Antonio that we were hopeful would lead to the peace table.

That program was rejected outright and we searched many other avenues and many other conferences.

On March 31st, I reached a decision that if we would take the unusual step of exercising great restraint on our own part by eliminating our offensive efforts over 90 percent of the population in North Vietnam and 78 percent of the territory, if we did that unilaterally, without expecting anything from them or asking anything from them, that might lead to the talk table where we could discuss this matter. If we could talk, that might lead to some agreement sometime.

It was an adventure. There were no guarantees involved about what it would do. But we thought it offered enough hope. I didn't feel that it was a matter that could be involved in partisan-year politics or personal ambition. So for that reason, I said that we will do this to try to get to the table; and to convince not only everyone abroad, but everyone at home that it is no election year gimmick, I made the additional decision not to seek reelection.

We have gone part of the way. We are at the table. It took us a month to get there. Some people were not helpful to us in getting there but we are there, thank goodness.

The next question is: "What do we do

there?" We hope we make progress. We don't know. We have not made much up to date. We can't see the future, but we are going to try. That is why we have been delayed. Thank you very much for your understanding.

Today is a day that most Americans have been waiting for for 8 long years. With this bill, the Consumer Credit Protection Act, we are entering a new era of honesty in the marketplace.

At long last the consumer will receive the treatment he deserves when he borrows money. The buyer will be allowed to know what the seller has always known—that is, how much interest he will have to pay on a credit purchase.

This bill, I think, is an example of government working at its best—government responding to the growing and the changing needs of the people. Good government does respond to change.

Here is just one example of how those needs have grown: In 1946, one year after the end of the war, consumer credit amounted to $8 billion.

This year the figure will be not $8 billion, but well over $100 billion.

Yet all during those 22 years of great growth, our laws did not grow. They have not changed at all to meet these new demands.

The old argument was that telling a man exactly how much interest he would be called upon to pay would confuse him.

Well, today we know better. We know that our consumers should be able to shop for credit as knowledgeably as they shop for groceries or merchandise.

When our parents have to borrow for their children's education or to pay medical bills, they should be told not just how much a month they will be paying, but the total debt that they are pledging themselves to

sign up for.

When a housewife opens a charge account at a department store, she will not have to compute how much 1½ percent a month comes to. She will be told that the annual rate is 18 percent, and exactly how much of her total bill goes to finance charges.

When a man takes out a personal loan to pay for a new car, the finance company won't be able to say simply "$5 down and $25 a month." The buyer must be told how many months he will be paying, how much of his money pays interest and other carrying charges.

If a man falls into debt, he will not be punished by unreasonable garnishment of his salary. He will not be deprived of food for his family or money for his rent. He will not be fired out of hand.

If a householder or a small businessman falls prey to loan sharks, his body and his property will be protected from extortionists by stiff Federal penalties.

As President, I know of no single piece of legislation which is of more pressing or more personal concern to more of our consumers than this bill. This bill is truly a triumph for truth.

We are establishing today a National Commission on Consumer Finance to continue to study these problems and to make sure we don't again let our actions fall behind our needs.

I don't think any of you know how pleased I am and how happy I am to see Senator Paul Douglas, our old friend, here with us in the East Room today. He is a battle-scarred warrior with many victories and many defeats under his belt. But this is one of his proudest victories. This is his bill. He has been championing it for 8 years.

This bill also belongs to many other people. It belongs to our good lady friend, that able Congresswoman from Missouri, Congresswoman Sullivan. She fought—and I say "fought"—for a strong and an effective bill when others would have settled for less. She was supported by her colleagues in the House, particularly her Chairman of the Banking and Currency Committee, Congressman Patman, whom I am glad to welcome here today.

It is Senator Proxmire's bill, too. He recognized the needs of this Nation and he saw to it that those needs were met.

But most of all, this bill belongs to all 200 million of us—alert, aware, and demanding consumers that we are.

I want to particularly thank every Member of Congress, House and Senate, for what you may have done to make this occasion possible.

I particularly want to single out one person in the executive department, one of our much overlooked individuals, the career public servant, Mr. Cedric W. Kroll of the Treasury Department. Mr. Kroll is the Government's actuary. He is a veteran of more than 25 years of Federal service.

He and his colleagues in the Treasury's Office of Public Debt Analysis had a tough job to do before we could even begin to get a truth-in-lending bill. The lenders had argued that any bill was unworkable because of the variety of credit transactions involved. They said the requirements were just too complicated to be calculated with accuracy.

Well, Mr. Kroll and his associates didn't buy those arguments. They put their heads together and came up with a set of interest rate tables and schedules that make disclosure of the many varieties of credit transactions relatively simple. They cracked this tough, impossible, big, technical problem that had stalled a truth-in-lending bill for years.

These few men, these quiet, effective men, whom the Government is filled with—men and women like them—are called bureaucrats

sometimes in the heat of debate in the Congress. I call them real patriots. They were working backstage and they proved that this bill could be made to work. These men, and thousands like them, are living proof of how our Government works for the people.

We owe this bill and other good bills to our career civil servants who are always working behind the scenes to better our lives and usually doing the things for which we take the credit.

I am proud today to speak for not only our consumers and for all of our people in recognizing our debt and paying our thanks to the public servants who go unheralded, unknown, and unsung, and who make our prosperity and our security better by their careers.

But I want to again pay my compliments and salute the selflessness of Miss Betty Furness, who came here to undertake consumer leadership and who has not only undertaken it, she has provided plenty of it.

Thank you very much.

This is unusual, and I don't want to take much more of your time, but we do have another man who has given 8 or 9 years of his life to Federal service in many capacities—in the legislative branch of the Government, in the military branch of the Government, in the diplomatic branch of the Government—and he is one of the great public servants of our time. I want him to take the next few minutes of your time on the thing that is most in your heart—peace in the world. Cy Vance.

AMBASSADOR VANCE. *Mr. President, ladies and gentlemen:*

As a result of the President's speech of March 31st, and the actions announced therein, we are now at the conference table in Paris.

It took us a month to get to the conference table. How long it will take us to achieve a just and honorable peace at the conference table, we do not know.

The road ahead, I believe, will probably be long and difficult. However, we will persevere in our search for a just and honorable peace so that peace and prosperity may be brought to Southeast Asia and to the world.

Thank you, Mr. President.

NOTE: The President spoke at 1:26 p.m. in the East Room at the White House. In his opening words he referred to Hubert H. Humphrey, Vice President of the United States, and Paul H. Douglas, Senator from Illinois 1949–1967. During his remarks he referred to, among others, Ambassador Cyrus R. Vance, U.S. negotiator at the Paris peace talks with North Vietnam, Leonor K. (Mrs. John B.) Sullivan, Representative from Missouri, Wright Patman, Representative from Texas, William Proxmire, Senator from Wisconsin, and Betty Furness, Special Assistant to the President for Consumer Affairs.

As enacted, the Consumer Credit Protection Act (S. 5) is Public Law 90–321 (82 Stat. 146).

On January 20, 1969, President Johnson announced his three appointments to the National Commission on Consumer Finance (5 Weekly Comp. Pres. Docs., p. 137).

281   Remarks at a Reception in Fort Worth Honoring Representative James C. Wright of Texas. *May 29, 1968*

Congressman and Mrs. Wright, Congressman Teague and other members of the delegation, Mr. and Mrs. Johnson, distinguished clergy, guests, ladies and gentlemen:

I am so happy to see so many familiar faces here this afternoon.

This is a great treat for me, to come back to Fort Worth.

When I saw my dear friend of many, many decades here at the head table—Raymond Buck—it reminded me of the good old days when I used to be in politics.

Looking around at all of you happy people, and all of you happy politicians, I can only think of one thing to say right now. That is, I'd rather be "Wright"—than President.

I especially wanted to be here this afternoon to lend my support to Jim Wright and "Tiger" Teague in their campaigns. They face a very tough race this year, as all of us do.

One of my staff, a young man from Harvard, somewhat unfamiliar with these parts, told me that Jim Wright and "Tiger" Teague are both running against the same opponent—a man with a very odd name:

"Un Opposed."

I called in one of my staff and asked him what he knew about this man. He laughed and said, "Mr. President, you have been gone much too long. That is unopposed."

Actually, I have something in common with both Jim and "Tiger": We are all three running unopposed. They are running for the Congress, and I am running for the ranch.

As you may know, I am going to be at TCU later tonight to receive a degree. I hope this will come in handy when I resume my teaching career.

But I could not pass up this party. I am going to be a resident of Texas again after January. As I told Senator Yarborough and Mrs. Yarborough coming down, and as every Texan already knows, it is mighty good to have some friends in Washington.

It is particularly good to have a friend who is a winner. The one and only time that Jim Wright ever had any competition in a primary he wound up with only 92 percent of the vote.

He carried every one of his 153 precincts and in two of them—I never could quite understand this—the opposition received no votes at all.

Now that is my idea of a winner. And Jim Wright is a winner for one reason: Because he is always on the people's side. No one knows this better than I do.

Jim and I have been on the same team in Washington for a good many years. We stood together for Texas and America on Capitol Hill.

During the past 5 years, when the showdowns for progress came in the Congress, there are none who have been of more help to me than the members of the Texas delegation.

With Senator Yarborough in the Senate—he wouldn't want to admit this publicly, maybe—there is no Senator who has a finer voting record in helping the Johnson administration do what they think is best for all the people of this country.

And "Tiger" Teague, Graham Purcell, "Chick" Kazen, Earle Cabell—and the many other Congressmen—I don't know how many of them came down here, though we had several on the plane—have all been very generous and very helpful to me.

I broke "Tiger" in before he came to Washington. He came to Austin before he came to Washington to talk to me about what he wanted to do in Washington.

He has been doing it ever since—a very good job for all the people.

Tonight, somewhere in this city, there is a boy from a poor family who has made it to college. He is just one of a million and a half young Americans who would not have had this chance 5 years ago, but who can now pursue a college education because the leaders of the Texas delegation, who sit at this table, and their colleagues in Congress, have seen to it that their Government is interested in that young man.

Tonight there is a man with a job—a man who was out of work 5 years ago. He is only one of 7 million new workers who have found employment since 1963.

And for the entire labor force, which is 75.5 million strong today, our paychecks are bigger, our retirement is more secure, our working conditions are better.

For employers and businessmen, the past 7 years—the last 87 months, in fact—have had no parallel in all of American history.

Seven straight, uninterrupted years of prosperity without a single dip, recession, depression, or whatnot.

Tonight, there is an old couple who can face their golden years with a new serenity and a new security. If they get sick, they are no longer a burden to their children or their son-in-law. They have earned the dignity of independence—because almost 20 million elderly families are tonight covered by Medicare, by a program which did not exist 5 years ago, but which these men helped us to pass.

Once these were all visions—just visions, just dreams. But to the boy in college, to the couple in retirement, to the worker on the job, to the businessman in his shop, they are actualities and realities today.

Other visions have been made reality, too. Other dreams have come true, too: The child of the slum, who can now get a head start and an equal chance in life; the 5.5 million Americans who no longer live in poverty.

In health, in elementary and secondary education, in equal justice, in conservation, in recreation, in farm and rural programs, in every area where government can help people, we are leveling old problems and we are building new hopes.

Before I left Washington this afternoon, I signed into law the Consumer Credit Protection Act. That brings truth to the lending market for every purchaser in America.

Jim Wright, "Tiger" Teague, Ralph Yarborough, Earle Cabell and "Chick" Kazen—all these Congressmen here at this table helped pass that measure which helps every American.

To Congressman Purcell and all the others I mentioned, I want to say we owe each of you a debt of thanks and gratitude.

Proud? Yes, we are proud. But satisfied? No. Never. This is a world of change, and we want to change. We want to improve with every change. We want to become better. We want to become richer. We want to become more powerful. We want to conquer our ancient enemies of disease, ignorance, and poverty.

We want the world where every man can be free, be equal, and not be burdened with these ancient enemies.

In 8 months, I will come back home to be a teacher and a private citizen again. But good men, like those in the Texas delegation at this table, will remain in Washington, working to give substance to your dreams—working to carry on the unfinished business of America.

I know there are many of you in this group who are here on rainchecks 4 years old. I was sorry to disappoint you then. But remember, 4 years ago my subject would have been promises.

Tonight I have been able to talk about performances.

There was a little lady from the Temperance Union who once called upon a great government leader, a Prime Minister of Great Britain, Winston Churchill, to make her complaint.

She said, "Mr. Prime Minister, I am told that during the war, you have drunk enough brandy, if it were poured out in this room, to come up to here [*indicating*] on all of us standing."

Mr. Churchill looked at her, listened very attentively, looked at the floor, looked at the ceiling, and he said, "My dear little lady, so much we have done; so much we have yet to do."

There is so much that we have done in this country. All of us live better than our fathers and our grandfathers, those who made it possible for us to enjoy our liberty and freedom.

But there is so much yet for all of us to do.

If we can only arrest our impatience, if we can only keep our eye on the ball, if we can only love instead of hate, if we can only unite instead of divide, if we can only apply all of our energies and our talents to constructive endeavors, there is a better world over yonder for all of us.

To the good, progressive, generous people of Fort Worth, I want to thank you for the quality of your Congressmen and your delegation.

More than that, I want to thank you for the strength and comfort that your friendship has given me through the years.

Thank you very much.

NOTE: The President spoke at 7:10 p.m. at the Will Rogers Memorial Center in Fort Worth, Texas. In his opening words he referred to Representative James C. Wright, Jr., of Texas, Mrs. Wright, Representative Olin E. Teague of Texas, J. Lee Johnson III, vice president of the Fort Worth Star Telegram and president of the Jim Wright Congressional Club, and Mrs. Johnson. During his remarks he referred to Raymond E. Buck, Fort Worth lawyer, and to Senator Ralph Yarborough and Representatives Graham Purcell, Abraham Kazen, Jr., and Earle Cabell, all of Texas.

282 Commencement Address at Texas Christian University. *May 29, 1968*

Dr. Moudy, and fellow students:

Any political speaker who comes to a college campus today does so at his own risk. I want to make it very clear at the beginning—I come here tonight not as a politician but as a student.

Just like you, I am here to get my degree. I am honored to appear here with seven others who will receive honorary degrees tonight. Perhaps my degree means more to me than it does to them. I am the only one who is a college dropout—from the electoral college, that is.

Dr. Moudy, I appreciate your doctor of laws degree for another reason, too. As someone who has spent the better part of his life doctoring laws, it is nice to finally have a license.

So I appreciate it and I am delighted to be welcomed into the fraternity of educated men.

I may even apply for a Fulbright Scholarship, although I am not very hopeful of my chances. No one can come to TCU without paying homage to its great quarterbacks like Sammy Baugh and Davy O'Brien. Fort Worth is known as the home of great quarterbacks. So is the National Capital, Washington. The only difference is that your quarterbacks play on Saturday and ours do their work on Monday mornings.

We meet here tonight at a time when the American university is at the center of rapid change and the center of heated controversy.

Perhaps this is a good time to reflect on the nature of change in America—on affirmations and discontent among our young people and on your opportunity to share in the on-going discovery of our country.

It is an unchanging habit of commencement orators to talk about change. The speakers who tell their audiences this year that times are changing, however, should not be accused of dealing in platitudes. For America and the world are altering themselves at a dizzying speed. The citizen, the student and the public servant may find it difficult to fathom the nature and the meaning of all of this change.

But all of us can feel it happening. All of us are stirred by it. All of us are sometimes elated—and sometimes quite disturbed by it.

A stranger to America might well wonder how a people so active and so successful can be so troubled.

Why do we take so little comfort in the undeniable triumphs of the past few years? Why do we scarcely seem to notice how far we have come—in such a short time—toward solving the problems that have plagued our democracy for generations?

In the past 3 years, a stranger might point out, America has brought the franchise to almost a million new citizens who had been systematically denied the right to vote in the past.

In this administration alone, the Nation's economy—and our common efforts to conquer want—have lifted more than 8 million people up from poverty; created more than 7 million new jobs; cut unemployment to the lowest level in 15 years; and increased the real income of the average American, after taxes, by more than 20 percent.

In a few years, the Congress has broken the deadlock of years and pioneered new programs in health, in education, in consumer protection, in conservation, in civil rights. Your own Senator Yarborough and Congressman Wright and Congressman Teague and others have supported the leadership in this field.

Yet for all this accomplishment, the American people are anything but satisfied. We are, as countless orators and observers remind us, a restless nation.

Why? Part of the answer lies, I believe, in the very progress we have made. For a nation—as for an individual—success brings its own problems and raises its own vexing questions.

More than a century ago, a shrewd French visitor to our shores made this observation: "The sufferings that are endured patiently, as being inevitable, become intolerable—at the moment it appears that there might be an escape. Reform, then, only serves to reveal more clearly what still remains oppressive, and now all the more unbearable. The suffering, it is true, has been reduced—but one's sensitivities have become much more acute."

Certainly our sensitivities have become more acute. We are today more keenly aware of lingering poverty amid our growing wealth—of public squalor amid private luxury. Our people, especially our younger people, are more impatient than ever with "what still remains oppressive"—with racial injustice, urban decay, outworn institutions, bitterness and war between nations.

By almost every measure, we have moved closer—yes, much closer—to solving these problems that vex us. But although some of the solutions are in sight, many of them remain frustratingly beyond our reach. With all our advances in computer technology, we are still unable to set a precise date for the arrival of equality, the advent of peace, the curing of old ills and the healing of old wounds.

As President Kennedy put it, we are destined—all of us—"to live out most, if not all, of our lives in uncertainty and challenge and peril."

Well, how should we face this uncer-

tainty? Will we master an uncertain age, or will we let it overwhelm us?

Do we have the strength, the tolerance, the vitality—and the faith—to weather the "burden and the heat of the day"?

Much will depend on the answer your generation gives us. And sometimes your answer is not encouraging.

Today, as in every time in our history, there are those who doubt the power of our democracy to make early and significant progress.

There are extremists whose aim is to rule—or to wreck. They speak only in slogans, and sometimes they are deaf—deaf to reasoned reply. They are chiefly united in the certainty with which they advance their views—and in the vehemence with which they mock the views of others.

Theirs is not the spirit of liberty—which Judge Learned Hand once defined as "the spirit which is not too sure that it is right."

Thomas Jefferson, the drafter of our Declaration of Independence, the great philosopher of individual liberty, and the defender of individual conscience, wrote a kinsman in 1808 that public men should from all student "disputants ... keep aloof, as you would from the infected subjects of yellow fever or pestilence. Consider yourself, when with them, as among the patients of Bedlam, needing medical more than moral counsel. Be a listener only, keep within yourself . . . the habit of silence, especially on politics. In the fevered state of our country, no good can ever result from any attempt to set one of these fiery zealots to rights, either in fact or principle. They are determined as to the facts they will believe, and the opinions on which they will act. Get by them, therefore, as you would by an angry bull; it is not for a man of sense to dispute the road with such an animal."

I might point out that Thomas Jefferson

wrote this during the last year of his Presidency.

It would be interesting to compare his views with those privately expressed by several modern presidents in recent weeks.

But my purpose, this evening, is to talk to you about change—and those who glorify violence as a form of political action are really the best friends the status quo ever had. They provoke a powerful conservative reaction among millions of people. They inspire, among many people, a blind allegiance to things as they are—even when those things ought to be changed.

But though they are great in volume, these young totalitarians of opinion are few in number among America's graduating classes this spring.

For almost 40 years—since I was graduated from a small college down in San Marcos—I have been observing the quality of each year's crop of university graduates. I must speak to you frankly, and without any attempt at flattery.

I believe that this generation of young college people is the best I have ever seen. Healthier—as you would expect—quicker of mind, and better trained.

But beyond those things—which could be, after all, only the results of affluence and evolution—there is a moral energy in this generation that exceeds any I have ever seen before.

Even that may stem in part from historical circumstances. Most of those who are graduating from college now have had a degree of leisure, in which to contemplate the society around them. Most have had a measure of confidence in their ability to secure a prosperous place in that society. And so they have been spared the pressure of meeting society's demands—of shaping themselves to be acceptable to a very restricted job market.

However it has come about, they have had an opportunity to look at their country—at its institutions, its people, its promise, and its performance.

You have had a chance to feel the force of change in modern life—even if you—like the rest of us—cannot sometimes entirely comprehend it. You have already experienced the impersonality of modern institutions—that affords you a degree of privacy, while it sometimes deprives you of a sense that you count.

You know that your chances for long and prosperous lives have never been better. Your life expectancy is far from what the graduate's was of yesteryear. But you wonder whether you will continue to live side by side with desperate want, ugliness, and with racial animosity.

You know that your country is the most powerful Nation on earth. But you wonder how its power, and its idealism, may help to bring peace to a tormented world.

These are not new concerns. What is new is the desire of the young college graduates today to ask the right questions—and the desire of your country to try to find the right answers.

Here are some of the questions that I hope you will ask—and then I hope you will take part in answering them:

—How can the quality of education be improved—not only in the ghetto classrooms, but throughout the Nation's entire educational system, from preschool to graduate school? From Head Start to adult education? How can education be improved?

—What are the best means of helping our poor to lead more secure and productive lives?

—How can good medical care be provided at reasonable cost to every citizen in our land?

—How can the transportation of people

668

be made safer, swifter, less frustrating, and more efficient?

—How can we take advantage of technological change, and the economy of massive enterprises, without submerging the individual?

—How can we best help the people of the underdeveloped world in their struggle against poverty?

—How can we help the world—and help ourselves—find rational solutions to conflict, and end the threat of a nuclear war?

These are formidable questions. You may feel somewhat ill-equipped to deal with them. I assure you that I do.

But they must be answered, if conditions in our country and the world are to change in a manner that will serve man, and not master him. And it is your generation that must answer them.

You must begin now—in industry, in government, in universities, in politics, in private life—to examine the alternatives, to seek the programs, the politicians, and the public support for progressive change.

I believe that leaders in your government can contribute to the education of this college generation. I should like to see outstanding leaders from the junior classes in the colleges all over America come to Washington each year, for direct discussions with their government leaders on these key issues of our times that we must find the answers to. I would like to see them spend, without losing credit, a month to 6 weeks in the National Capital each spring—deepening their understanding of the prospects and the problems that we face.

I have, as President, called upon the White House Fellows—young citizens who have served a year at the highest levels of our Government—to develop a plan for accomplishing this, and to submit their plan to me

early in the fall.

It is a time to widen the opportunities for excellence. It is a time to widen the opportunities for service in public affairs. I have tried to do this in a number of ways:

—through VISTA, Volunteers in Service to America, where young men and women help those who need it most;

—through the White House Fellows program;

—through the recognition of Presidential Scholars from every State in the Union;

—and, not least, through going out to college campuses and finding and using the best young talent that is available for service in our Government.

Now, I believe we should extend the range of young people's participation in public life. I believe we should move forward—now—to grant the vote to 18-year-olds.

Several States have already done so. A majority of the people and many in Congress approve the idea. The great majority of young people in America have demonstrated their maturity; their desire to participate; their zeal for service.

But we can do more than open the door to participation for a chosen few. I think there is a basic and fundamental need to open our political system to the participation of the many.

I strongly believe, therefore, that the time is already here for this Nation to recognize and to grant the right to vote to 18-year-olds. We have everything to gain by extending to these young people the most precious right and responsibility of citizenship—the right to vote.

So I leave you, this evening, a faith:

—faith in you,

—faith in our institutions,

—faith in our country,

—faith in your capacity to change our country for the better.

My faith is built on what young people have achieved, in these past few years, on their bravery and steadfastness in battle, on their idealism and perseverance in the cause of social justice.

It is built, as well, on the country itself: on its ability to move out of apathy and bigotry, and move toward dignity for all of its people; on its steady assumption of responsibility in the world.

I know the future will be often perilous and frustrating. The past, you know, has been that way, too. But what we have accomplished in these years—and what you are tonight—tells me that we have only begun

to achieve the greatness that is our destiny.

Good night, and God bless you all.

NOTE: The President spoke at 8:08 p.m. in the coliseum at Texas Christian University in Fort Worth. His opening words referred to Dr. James M. Moody, Chancellor of the University. During his remarks he referred to Senator Ralph Yarborough and Representatives James C. Wright, Jr. and Olin E. Teague, all of Texas.

The plan requested by the President for visits to Washington and discussions with Government leaders by college undergraduates is contained in a report presented to him by the White House Fellows Association on October 29, 1968. An announcement of the presentation ceremony is printed in the Weekly Compilation of Presidential Documents (vol. 4, p. 1553). For remarks by the President concerning the report, see Item 570.

---

283   The President's News Conference at the LBJ Ranch. May 30, 1968

OPENING STATEMENTS BY THE PRESIDENT

THE PRESIDENT. [1.] *Prime Minister and Mrs. Gorton, General Westmoreland, ladies and gentlemen:*

We are delighted to have you here with us today.

I have an announcement or two to make.

VICE CHIEF OF STAFF OF THE ARMY

First, I should like to announce the promotion of Lieutenant General Bruce Palmer, Jr., to the full rank of General.

General Palmer will be retiring from his current position as Deputy Commanding General, U.S. Army, Vietnam, to become Vice Chief of Staff of the United States Army with headquarters in Washington.

He will serve as the Vice Chief of Staff to

General Westmoreland,[1] who will be Chief of Staff.

General Palmer has a distinguished military career spanning 31 years of service. He has been in Vietnam since March 1967, serving as the Commanding General of the Second Field Forces and as the Deputy Commanding General.

COMMANDER IN CHIEF OF THE ARMY IN THE PACIFIC

[2.] In addition, I am announcing the reassignment of General Ralph E. Haines, Jr., as Commander in Chief of the U.S. Army in the Pacific.

He will replace General Dwight E. Beach,

---

[1] Gen. William C. Westmoreland, Commander, United States Military Assistance Command, Vietnam, became Army Chief of Staff in July 1968.

who is retiring.

General Haines presently serves as Vice Chief of Staff of the United States Army.

I am also announcing numerous other promotions which will be supplied to you by the Press Secretary.

TALKS WITH PRIME MINISTER GORTON

[3.] We are delighted to have with us today the distinguished Prime Minister, Mr. Gorton, and Mrs. Gorton, from Australia. Although Mr. Gorton and I had met before in Canberra, this was our first meeting since he became Prime Minister.

We took the occasion to spend a good deal of time together since his arrival last Monday.

As all of you know, the ties between Australia and the United States grow stronger each year. As part of this shared vision, and to honor our common interests and commitments, our men are now fighting side by side under General Westmoreland's leadership in Vietnam.

So we have reviewed together, with Ambassador Vance,[2] who returned from the Paris talks, the progress of the Paris talks.

This morning, with General Westmoreland, we reviewed the course of the battle on the ground.

As a result of our talks, I am confident that we have strengthened the bonds between our two countries as we face together the hard but the productive tasks which lie before us in the months ahead.

PRESIDENTIAL UNIT CITATION

[4.] It now gives me very special pride to award a Presidential Unit Citation to the D Company of the 6th Battalion of the Royal

Australian Regiment for extraordinary heroism while serving in Vietnam.

I have long had reason to know personally what we have learned as a nation over the past half century since the World War. That is, that in a fight, there is no better man to have by your side than an Australian.

Only yesterday morning I received a typical report of Australians in combat. A very small unit of the 3d Royal Australian Regiment was blocking an infiltration route toward Saigon 26 miles northeast of the capital. About 1,000 of the enemy, some fresh from North Vietnam, threw themselves against this Australian base.

Heavy fighting took place over 2 hours. The enemy withdrew, leaving 44 dead and 32 weapons on the battlefield. Seven prisoners were captured.

General Westmoreland sent a message of congratulations to Major General MacDonald who commands the Australian forces in Vietnam.

Now this is the kind of steady courage that we have come to expect from the Australians, and I think this is a very good moment to remind all of the American people of this fact.

The war is not being fought in Vietnam simply by Americans; it is being fought by the South Vietnamese, the Australians, the New Zealanders, the Koreans, the Thais, and the Filipinos.

Together, we shall bring a just and honorable peace to Southeast Asia, for that is our objective—and I want to repeat, that is our only objective.

From last summer to the end of March of this year, we have made a very special effort to move this war to the conference table and to peace talks.

On March 31, in a speech to the Nation,[3]

---

[2] Ambassador Cyrus R. Vance, U.S. negotiator at the Paris peace talks with North Vietnam.

[3] See Item 170.

I said that we would undertake a major unilateral act of de-escalation. We would lift the bombing from most of the territory and population of North Vietnam, including Hanoi and Haiphong, and we would free our hands so we could concentrate every resource at our command in the search for peace.

At that time I announced that I would not seek or accept the Presidential nomination.

I felt that these two steps might—just might—bring Hanoi to the conference table.

A month went by, but that has now happened, and these talks are being conducted in Paris.

I cannot report to the American people any substantive progress, nor can I even report that Hanoi has matched our restraint with theirs.

But if Hanoi will take responsive action, we are ready to go far and fast with them, and with others, to reduce the violence and to build a stable peace in Southeast Asia.

We have done everything that we know how to do to bring us to this point, and we shall continue to do everything that we know how to do to bring peace to the world.

Now it gives me great pleasure to present the Presidential Unit Citation to the distinguished Prime Minister.

We would be glad to have a word from him if he cares to.

REMARKS OF PRIME MINISTER GORTON

[5.] PRIME MINISTER GORTON. *Mr. President, Mrs. Johnson, General Westmoreland, ladies and gentlemen:*

I accept with a feeling of very great pride in my countrymen this Presidential Citation which has been awarded for their heroism in action. So I shall take it and hand it to the

Chief of Staff of the Australian Army. He and all Australians will feel the same pride that I do, that this has been presented for what they on that day did.

I would like, too, to thank you, sir, during this brief visit of mine to the United States, for I leave tomorrow, for all the time which you have put aside for discussions with me, and for all the time which your senior officials and secretaries of relevant departments have put aside for discussions with me. I feel that this has been of great advantage to me, and I believe that we know each other's minds as to the problems of the Southeast Asian area generally, and as to the future we both wish to see in the Southeast Asian area generally—a future where prosperity is able to be based upon peace and peace is able to be based on an absence from fear.

I thank you, sir.

REMARKS OF GENERAL WESTMORELAND

[6.] THE PRESIDENT. General Westmoreland arrived earlier this morning and briefed me, and together—I heard a somewhat detailed report with the Prime Minister of Australia of developments in South Vietnam. I should like to ask him to summarize for the American people and for those of you who have come here today, briefly, that report he has given to us.

General Westmoreland.

GENERAL WESTMORELAND. *Mr. President, Mr. Prime Minister, ladies and gentlemen:*

I am happy to summarize my discussion on the situation in Vietnam.

First, what are the current objectives of the enemy?

In my opinion, his primary objective is to destroy the Government of South Vietnam.

This has been his objective since 1958, but Hanoi is now emphasizing this objective more than ever before.

Secondly, he wants to develop an image of strength in the eyes of the people of the United States and the world in the hope that this will bring about an attitude of futility toward the success of our objective of a free and independent South Vietnam.

How is he attempting to accomplish these objectives?

First, by resorting to terrorizing the people, creating refugees, and attempting to coerce the people to demonstrate against the Government.

Second, by waging a massive worldwide propaganda campaign based on distorted information.

Third, by defeating Vietnamese troops and isolating them from the American and free world forces.

Fourth, by defeating the United States units for propaganda purposes.

Finally, by seizing territory and thereby strengthening his posture in the South.

The enemy is having to deploy ever-larger numbers of men from the North, and the war is destined to become increasingly more and more of a North Vietnamese invasion of the South.

The North Vietnamese are strangers to the people in the South and are unfamiliar with the area. In fact, now over 72 percent of the organized combat forces, excluding guerrillas, are North Vietnamese.

It is estimated that there are approximately 90,000 North Vietnamese soldiers in the South, with more arriving every day.

The façade that the enemy has carefully created, that this is a war of the people, has been destroyed with the influx of hordes of North Vietnamese.

But in spite of this total effort, his only victories of the last few years have been in the propaganda field.

In this connection, I am confident that the enemy is receiving false reports from his field commanders. This partially explains his alleged and exaggerated battlefield successes, which are distorted by a factor of from 3 to 12, and in some cases even more.

In summary, the enemy seems to be approaching a point of desperation; his forces are deteriorating in strength and quality.

I forecast that these trends will continue.

On the other hand, the South Vietnamese armed forces are becoming progressively stronger and more effective. Our troops and those of our free world allies continue to perform in magnificent fashion.

However, we must be prepared for continued heavy fighting ahead, especially in the northern area, the highlands, and around Saigon.

But time is on our side. Endurance on the battlefield and patience at home are required.

THE PRESIDENT. Thank you very much, General Westmoreland. It is very difficult to give, in a few minutes, the full report that you have made today.

I have asked the General to take the statement that he dictated and reviewed with the Prime Minister and me and to make it available to you.[4] You will have an opportunity to review the details of it much more at length than he has been able to go over with you now.

We are very happy General Westmoreland is returning to Washington to take the place formerly occupied by General "Black Jack" Pershing, George Marshall, and Dwight Eisenhower as Chief of Staff of the United States Army and the leader of the United States Army in this country.

His performance has been exceptional and brilliant. I look forward to working very

---

[4] The full text of General Westmoreland's statement is printed in the Weekly Compilation of Presidential Documents (vol. 4, p. 888).

closely with him in the days ahead.

If there are any questions that you care to ask, I will be glad to receive them.

QUESTIONS

THE BOMBING PAUSE

[7.] Q. Mr. President, in view of the step-up of the war on the enemy side, the unprecedented infiltration of men and supplies, do you have any plan to reconsider your partial bombing pause?

THE PRESIDENT. We have under consideration appropriate actions every day. They are constantly being considered. What is the proper course to bring peace in the world? What is the proper course to bring an end to the war in South Vietnam?

THE TAX BILL AND THE 6 BILLION DOLLAR SPENDING CUT

[8.] Q. Mr. President, this week the House took action that would indicate the sense of the Congress is to tie a $6 billion cut in Federal spending to any tax increase. Would you be prepared to sign a tax bill that has that big a Federal cut in it?

THE PRESIDENT. Yes. Yes, for nearly 2 years I have urged the Congress to pass a tax bill. That tax amounts to about 1 cent on the dollar.

With it, though, I think America could follow a sound fiscal course, and I have repeated those recommendations week after week and month after month.

Without it, the gates of economic chaos, I think, could open, and I think the country would face several serious problems.

First, an inflation tax of at least 4 cents on every dollar.

Second, interest rates could go up as high as 10 percent.

Third, a severe housing depression would be in the offing.

Fourth, the disappearance of our world trade surplus.

Fifth, the end of our unprecedented 87 months of prosperity in this country.

Now the Nation and the Congress are faced with a tax bill. But it has coupled with it a $6 billion requirement in a reduction of expenditures. I deeply regret that we are faced with such a choice, as I have said on several occasions.

The budget that I submitted in January blended fiscal responsibility with what we considered urgent national purpose. That tight budget was my best judgment in January, and that is my best judgment today.

Nevertheless, the President does not make laws alone. He only approves measures that the Congress has passed.

I have indicated that I would approve a tax increase with a $4 billion cutback in 1969 expenditures.

Yesterday, however, the House of Representatives defeated a motion to limit the expenditure cutback to $4 billion.

So the only choice remaining now is whether the need for a tax increase is so urgent that we must accept the $6 billion reduction.

I believe that the need for a tax increase is that urgent. I believe that the national interest requires the tax increase as soon as possible.

Therefore, if the Congress will vote for the conference report containing the tax increase and the $6 billion expenditure cut, I shall approve it.

I urge the Congress to adopt the conference report at as early a date as possible, and give me the opportunity to sign the measure.[5]

THE PARIS PEACE TALKS

[9.] Q. Mr. President, do you share the belief of Cyrus Vance that because North Vietnam is at the conference table in Paris, it eventually wants peace and that, therefore, these talks are going to, as Mr. Vance put it, move to the end and go into full-scale peace negotiations?

THE PRESIDENT. We feel that as a result of our statement back in March, as I repeated earlier, that we had two steps to take: One was to try to get Hanoi to the conference table. That has been done.

Now how far we are going to get in those conferences is pure speculation. We don't know. We hope that we can have a satisfactory conference that will produce results.

I don't care to speculate. I do not feel it has produced any substantive results to this date.

I think we must all continue to try to explore every possible avenue; get down to substantive discussions as soon as possible.

But as to what the outcome might be, I think I would rather let developments take care of that.

THE TAX BILL

[10.] Q. Mr. President, could you tell us where, if you get this bill now through Congress, you feel you would be forced to make most of these cuts in human terms, what the country is likely to lose from that kind of a spending cut?

THE PRESIDENT. We will have to make announcements on that. But I wouldn't want to make an announcement on a measure that I have not seen, and expenditure cuts that have not been made.

After the measure gets to me, and if it is in the amount that the conference report contains, I will sign it. Then we will ask the Budget Director to review with all the departments the cuts.

We generally feel that they will be divided in non-Vietnam defense expenditures and other budget expenditures. But I do not have the time or the information that would permit me to outline in specific detail how they would add up.

DEVELOPMENTS IN FRANCE

[11.] Q. Mr. President, today, in light of what has been happening in France, there is quite a run on the French franc. I wonder if you could give us your judgment on whether that will increase or decrease the pressures on the U.S. dollar.

THE PRESIDENT. We are very hopeful that the leadership of France and the people of France will find ways and means to bring stability in that country.

We realize that the developments there not only have a serious effect on France but on the entire world. We are watching the situation very closely.

The leadership of France is taking certain steps and putting in motion certain actions. I don't care to speculate on how successful those actions will be or what their outcome will be.

I do know that it is very important to the American people and the rest of the world

---

[5] The tax increase was enacted by the Revenue and Expenditure Control Act of 1968, approved June 28 (see Item 343).

that we have stability in France. We deeply regret the problems that face the French people.

THE ANTI-CRIME BILL

[12.] Q. Mr. President, is the administration determined to accept an anti-crime bill even if amendments remain which would authorize wiretapping and attempt to limit Supreme Court decisions?

THE PRESIDENT. The administration very strongly favors an anti-crime bill and has for several years, and has urged the Congress to take action on a crime bill. Both Houses have now acted. That measure is in conference.

When the conferees reconcile their views, we hope the measure will come to the President. Then I will review the details of it and take the action that I believe is in the best interest of the American people.

I hope the conferees can work out the differences between the two bodies and reconcile their different viewpoints.

I would, of course, express the hope that the measure that comes to me is as near the measure that I recommended as possible, although I know that that is too much to expect.[6]

VIETNAM CONFLICT

[13.] Q. Did General Westmoreland report that his position on the ground has been

weakened by the partial halt in bombing?

THE PRESIDENT. No.

LOWERING THE VOTING AGE TO 18

[14.] Q. Mr. President, last night you advocated that the right to vote be granted to 18-year-olds across the country. Since the States set this voting age, is there anything you can do or intend to do in the time you have left in the Presidency to bring this about?

THE PRESIDENT. Over the weekend, we will be working on a very special message to Congress. A constitutional amendment will be required. The President will send that message to Congress, I hope, next week, making his recommendation.[7]

TROOP STRENGTH IN VIETNAM

[15.] Q. Mr. President, in view of the reports of increased casualties, and General Westmoreland's report to you on battlefield conditions, does the administration foresee any need for a step-up or an increase in our troop strength in Vietnam beyond what you have already announced?

THE PRESIDENT. General Westmoreland has made no such recommendation.

Helen Thomas, United Press International: Thank you, Mr. President.

NOTE: President Johnson's one hundred and twenty-seventh news conference was held at the LBJ Ranch, Johnson City, Texas, at 12:32 p.m. on Thursday, May 30, 1968.

---

[6] The Omnibus Crime Control and Safe Streets Act of 1968 was approved June 19 (see Item 320).

[7] See Item 341.

---

284   Statement by the President Announcing Increased Interest Rates on U.S. Savings Bonds and Freedom Shares. *May 31, 1968*

I AM TODAY announcing an increase, to become effective June 1, 1968, on the interest rates for both United States savings bonds and Freedom Shares.

The new rate on both series E and H savings bonds will move from 4.15 to 4.25

percent—the maximum permitted by law. This higher rate will apply not only to newly purchased bonds but also proportionately to all outstanding E and H bonds for their remaining period to next maturity. Thus, present bond-owners will be rewarded for investing in America and will not have to cash in their present bonds to take advantage of the higher rates.

The rate on Freedom Shares will be increased from the present 4.74 percent to a full 5 percent when held to maturity of 4½ years. Since these are savings notes, rather than savings bonds, there is no provision in the law for applying this increase to Freedom Shares which are outstanding. I am assured, however, that because of the rising scale of Freedom Share interest accruals, most of these outstanding shares will earn a comparably high rate for their remaining period of maturity.

Limitations on the combination purchase of bonds and Freedom Shares will also be relaxed so that any American, at any time, may buy this attractive savings package over the counter at his bank rather than only through a "bond-a-month" plan.

Savings bonds and Freedom Shares now become a more attractive investment than ever before.

As a direct obligation of the United States they are the ultimate in safety—a solid and secure base on which any family's savings and investment program might well be founded. They pay a good, and absolutely guaranteed, return. They are ideally suited for any important long-range goal, such as education, homeownership, or retirement. But aside from these practical benefits, these securities offer much more. They offer an opportunity for the citizen to participate in America's goals and dreams—to become involved in the achievement of all the things to which we aspire as a free people.

The savings bonds program offers a partnership in which we should all be members. I extend my warmest invitation to every family to join.

NOTE: The statement was released at Austin, Texas.

285   Statement by the President on the Death of Helen Keller. *June 3, 1968*

OF THE MILLIONS who mourn Helen Keller today, there are countless numbers whose personal burdens will always be lightened by the memory of her magnificent faith, courage, and achievements. The gifts she has left behind—the gifts of character and conviction—are America's most precious heritage.

NOTE: Helen Keller died on June 1 at the age of 87 at her home in Easton, Conn.

The statement was released at Austin, Texas.

286   Message to the Congress Transmitting Annual Report on the United States-Japan Cooperative Medical Science Program. *June 3, 1968*

To the Congress of the United States:

We in America are fortunate that our lives are almost completely free of the scourges of cholera, leprosy, exotic viruses, and parasitic diseases. Some of our citizens are still struck by tuberculosis and malnutrition, but we are making significant progress against them.

Yet in Asia today, millions are killed or crippled by those six diseases. They also continue to pose a serious threat to our fighting men stationed in Southeast Asia.

The U.S. Japan Cooperative Medical Science Program was begun in 1965 to find ways, through medical research, to eliminate or control those diseases.

I am pleased to transmit to the Congress today the annual report on that program. In slightly more than a year since the research efforts began

—Fifteen separate conferences dealing with specific diseases have been held in the United States and Asia.

—Contracts and grants were awarded for

further intensive study of each disease.

—Additional steps were taken toward the development of a vaccine capable of conferring long-term immunity against cholera.

I believe you will find this report encouraging and enlightening, and I commend it to your attention.

LYNDON B. JOHNSON

The White House

June 3, 1968

NOTE: The report is entitled "Report to Congress Pursuant to Section 5(h) of Public Law 86–610 (The International Health Research Act of 1960); U.S.-Japan Cooperative Medical Science Program" (19 pp., processed).

The U.S.-Japan Cooperative Medical Science Program was authorized on October 2, 1965 (see 1965 volume, this series, Book II, Item 544).

287 Message to the Congress Transmitting Report of the National Commission on Architectural Barriers to Rehabilitation of the Handicapped. *June 3, 1968*

To the Congress of the United States:

To most Americans, a stairway poses no problem. A narrow doorway is little more than an inconvenience. But for more than 20 million of our citizens, these simple structures bar the living of a normal life.

One in every ten Americans suffers from some disability which keeps him from using buildings designed—not cruelly, but thoughtlessly—only for the physically fit. Problems in the design of our buildings pose the greatest single obstacle to employment of the handicapped.

If we are to give the millions of handicapped Americans the opportunity to live life to the fullest, we must not put unnecessary barriers in their path.

We want our schools, libraries, office buildings, theaters, museums, stadiums and transportation systems to be accessible to all.

In 1966, the Secretary of Health, Education, and Welfare appointed a National Commission on Architectural Barriers to Rehabilitation of the Handicapped. I am pleased now to transmit to the Congress the report of that Commission entitled "Design for all Americans."

The report shows increased awareness of the problems by State and local governments, architects, and the general public. In the past year, the General Services Administration has substantially modified its design standards to give more consideration to the handicapped.

But the report also shows that a substantial task lies ahead.

—In many cases, State laws are sadly inadequate. Some cover only State-owned buildings; others do not spell out the needed standards.

—No school of architecture gives special or continuing attention to the problem of accessibility.

In the next thirty years, more buildings will be constructed in this country than have been built in the past two hundred years. And as we go about this tremendous task, we must make sure that the needs of the handicapped are not overlooked.

I commend this Report to your attention.

LYNDON B. JOHNSON

The White House
June 3, 1968

NOTE: The report, entitled "Design for All Americans; A Report of the National Commission on Architectural Barriers to Rehabilitation of the Handicapped," was published by the Rehabilitation Services Administration, Social and Rehabilitation Service, Department of Health, Education, and Welfare (26 pp. plus appendices).

288   Commencement Address at Glassboro State College. *June 4, 1968*

Dr. Robinson, Governor Hughes, members of the faculty, members of the graduating class, student body, ladies and gentlemen:

I am glad to return to Glassboro. I shall always remember this town as a place of warm friendship and hospitable people. The world will remember Glassboro, I hope, as a place where understanding between nations was advanced by the United States and the Soviet Union.

It was last June—about a year ago—that Chairman Kosygin and I sat down in President Robinson's living room for 2 days of discussions. Our talks ranged over the whole globe, but we talked mainly about four urgent matters:

First, we discussed the steps toward peace in the Middle East.

Second, we discussed ways to move the conflict in Vietnam from the battlefield to the conference table.

Third, we tried to move forward a treaty banning the spread of nuclear weapons.

Fourth, we stressed the need for broad talks at high levels between our two countries to halt the arms race in strategic weapons.

The year since then has been eventful and uncertain—like the age that we live in. We have lived through a year of achievement—and frustration. Too often, the frustration seemed to obscure hope. Too often, angry recriminations seemed to dominate the public dialogue in America.

But hope and achievement are certainly there to see. Our relations with the Soviet Union offer an example. This has been a time of unusual strain and difficulty. But what period in our history has been more productive in promoting cooperation between our two countries?

Many feared that the war in Vietnam would prevent any progress. Many predictions were made to this effect. But despite the predictions and despite the difficulties, we have agreed upon a treaty outlawing armaments in outer space. We have negotiated a treaty banning the spread of nuclear weapons, and it has now been tabled. We have achieved a civil air agreement that permits Soviet Union planes to land in the United States and United States planes to land in the Soviet Union. And we are moving toward other agreements.

So I think my return visit to Glassboro is a good time to reflect upon that progress—although in this day and time to talk about progress sometimes is taboo. It is a good time,

I think, also to talk about some principles which underlie our search for peace—principles which I hope that each of you and that all Americans would do well to remember. They are principles which are underscored by the events of this tumultuous year since the Glassboro meeting.

The first one, often stated but often overlooked, is this: Making peace is a tough, difficult, slow business—often much tougher and often much slower than making war.

Certainly these months have taught us that peace cannot be bought by the cheap currency of wishful thinking, or by slogans. It cannot be won by withdrawal, or isolation, or indifference, or wishing that we could have peace or by desiring peace. Nor can it be achieved by the expensive currency of nuclear weaponry.

Peace must be earned, and that requires a continuous process of building—building brick by brick, agreement by agreement. That requires patience. That requires sturdiness. That requires judgment.

The cause of peace demands responsibility and demands restraint from all of us—from the young and from the old, from the political leaders and the candidates, and from the plain citizens, from the officeholders and from the officeseekers.

Today in two areas of danger and conflict—the Middle East and Vietnam—events drive home the difficulty of making peace.

In the Middle East, it has been almost a year since the Six Day War—a year in which millions have been denied peace and progress.

The people of that region deserve a peace that is based upon a true and a lasting settlement—a settlement which respects the integrity of every nation, which frees every nation from the threat of attack, a settlement which the nations of the region themselves should reach. So far, progress has not

been very satisfying. But we shall continue, and we must continue, to try.

The United States has been working every day, in world capitals and in the United Nations, trying to promote a fair and a stable peace.

Ambassador Jarring, acting with the authority of the United Nations Security Council, is in contact with the parties. The United States strongly supports the Security Council Resolution of November 22, 1967, and Ambassador Jarring's peacemaking efforts. And we are urging that neither side pass up any reasonable path to negotiations.

In Vietnam, the agonizing difficulties of building peace are made clear every day—just as they are in the Middle East.

Two months ago, with a major act of de-escalation, taken upon our initiative, we brought about the talks in Paris. We have moved at least a step closer, I hope, toward peace in Southeast Asia. But as yet, the other side has had nothing of substance to say to those of us who seek a just peace in Asia.

First, in response to our concrete proposals, the other side has offered only propaganda.

Second, their representatives in Paris continue to deny a fact which all the world knows to be true: the massive presence of their North Vietnamese troops in South Vietnam.

Finally, the North Vietnamese in Paris will say to us only, "Stop the rest of your bombing"—at a time when North Vietnamese supplies and materiel, more North Vietnamese supplies and materiel than ever before, are flooding into South Vietnam.

An honorable peace requires some gestures on the other side toward peace. Thus far, we have met with little more than bellicose statements and evasions.

So—until the men in Hanoi face the real problems of ending the war—we must stand firm and fast. We must stand patiently and hopefully, but with determination, too.

A second principle in the search for peace is this: The road there is far less rocky when the world's two greatest powers—the United States and the Soviet Union—are willing to travel part of the way together.

Our progress toward a nuclear nonproliferation treaty in the past year gives evidence of this.

The control of nuclear weapons is a matter which goes far beyond the interest of the United States and the Soviet Union. It touches the life of every nation—and every human being—on this earth.

One of my first acts, upon becoming President of the United States, was to immediately instruct our negotiators to seek actively a nonproliferation treaty. Now, after more than 4 long years of discussion, a treaty to prevent the spread of nuclear weapons has been laid before the United Nations General Assembly.

I do not want to anticipate the vote of the United Nations on this treaty. But I do hope—and I do believe—that an overwhelming majority of the nations will support it. If they do—and if we build upon this treaty in the years to come—then we can all remember the year 1968 as a year of victory in the world, a year in which mankind took its most creative step since the dawn of the atomic age.

But beyond the treaty, there is much more to be done. The nations which we are asking to forgo nuclear weapons are now, in turn, urging the two great powers, the United States and the Soviet Union, to scale down the nuclear arms race—and these nations deserve an answer from us. The answer can only be found in disarmament.

For our part, the United States is ready now to move immediately in the direction of disarmament—if our two nations can reach binding agreements which preserve the security of each nation. The United States is ready now to begin such agreements.

A third principle underscored in the last year is this: Peace will be achieved not only by resolving the bitter conflicts of today. Even after we end these conflicts, there remains another task: to build a pattern of cooperation in the world.

The Middle East, Vietnam, the nuclear arms race—these are all conflicts, and as we all know, conflicts are the stuff of headlines. Conflicts are the life-or-death issues of foreign policy. They are our daily fare—the breakfast, the lunch, the dinner—of those who are responsible for America's security today.

But during the past year, the work of peace has been going on in many ways that rarely make headlines—on some issues which are less than life-or-death matters. But as these issues touch on our relations with another great power, the Soviet Union, which you good people here at Glassboro, at the college and in the community did so much to try to help us promote, they are important nonetheless.

During the last year we completed work with the Soviet Union on a treaty forbidding weapons in outer space.

During the last year we completed work with the Soviet Union on an agreement to assist astronauts downed in either country.

We completed work during the last year on a new consular treaty.

We completed work during the last year on an agreement permitting the Soviet Union's planes to land in the United States, and the planes of the United States of America to land in the Soviet Union.

Only yesterday your Government began talks with the Soviet Union about a renewal of our cultural exchange agreement with the Soviet Union.

Now we believe genuinely that every one of those steps is a step toward peace.

The disagreements between the Soviet Union and the United States, of course, have not been removed—not by any means.

We believe that there should be a realistic enforcement of the 1962 Geneva Accords on Laos. We believe that agreements solemnly made should be solemnly honored.

We have been unable to cooperate on steps toward a successful peace in the Middle East.

We have yet to win an agreement which would avoid a costly anti-ballistic missile race between the United States and the Soviets. We are ready to make such an agreement; and we urge the Soviets to join us, as we urged them to set a date for such a meeting when we met here at your college campus.

But in the last year, we have made some progress. We have proved that we can agree, can agree in part, on some occasions at least on some issues. We have proved that our two countries can behave as responsible members of the family of nations. And that is a hopeful sign, indeed.

To those of you who helped us to that end, again I say, "Thank you."

There are many other fields in which we should begin to build new programs of cooperation. Today in response to the invitation of your great Governor—Governor Hughes—and your President—President Robinson—to come back to Glassboro, I want to make some additional suggestions in the form of proposals.

Scientists from this country and the Soviet Union—and from 50 other countries—have already begun an international biological program to enrich our understanding of man and his environment.

I propose that we make this effort a permanent concern of our nations. I propose that

the United States scientists join with the scientists of the Soviet Union and other nations to form an international council on the human environment.

Second, I propose that we step up our efforts to develop a global satellite communications system. The United States believes that better communications are essential to mutual understanding between nations. That is why we proposed such a system in 1963. Now, more than 60 nations, large and small, have joined. We look forward to the day when the Soviet Union and the nations of Eastern Europe will join the system.

Finally, I can suggest other opportunities for cooperation between the United States, the Soviet Union, and other nations—cooperation to extend our knowledge, cooperation to develop our resources which man has scarcely touched.

There is the problem of exploring the deep-ocean floor.

There is the American proposal for an international decade of undersea exploration.

There is the continuing exploration of the Arctic and the Antarctic. In the Antarctic, we are already working with the Soviet Union—and the area has been freed from military tension by our treaty of 1962.

Finally, there is the great task of turning to productive uses the great, rain-rich forests of the tropics.

While great conflicts persist, we tend to overlook these opportunites. But it is by small threads, too, that we will weave a strong fabric of peace in the world.

A great scientist was once asked what moved him to seek out the great principles of physics. He replied, "I hope that I leave this world a little more orderly than I found it."

It was with this aim that I came here last year to meet with Chairman Kosygin. And it is with this aim that I come here again today.

I hope that those of you in this year's graduating class will recognize the sacrifices, the investment, the hopes that have gone into bringing you to this day.

I hope that you will realize that we will now look to you to give back to society not only the great investment that society has made in you, but will produce for it, not only a return of that investment, but rich dividends that will flow from it.

I believe that the old antagonisms which we call the "cold war" must fade—and I believe they will fade under stable, under enlightened leadership.

I believe that all of the nations of the world will try to develop and provide that leadership, as I believe we have developed it and are providing it here at Glassboro this morning.

I believe that the nations of the world that are now haunted by the ancient hatreds, still fearful of new steps toward accommodation, will in time, someday, come to use their talents and their resources to enrich the whole human family. After all, that is our excuse and that is our justification for being here— to better humanity.

I believe that the two great powers who met here in your hospitable surroundings last year have begun—have begun however haltingly—to bridge the gulf that has separated them for a quarter of a century. And in this day when some are not too hopeful, I am optimistic and I believe that—with the leadership that you and the leaders of your nation and the leadership of people like you in other nations through their leaders—we can bridge the gulf that has separated us for more than a quarter of a century.

I believe that other nations that are now locked in bitterness and strife will someday come to understand their own responsibilities

for world peace and for world progress. And thus—the threat of disaster for us all will subside.

We must recognize that there is another world and that we are a part of that world. We must recognize that we cannot long exist as a lone fortress.

Now, the threats that I spoke of will not subside overnight. We will continue to face grave and serious difficulties. We will face reverses and setbacks. The right answers will often seem unclear.

There will be much frustration and abuse. But I hope that you—and all our fellow citizens—will try in the days ahead to display the fortitude, and display the forbearance, and display the understanding that has symbolized the Glassboro that I know—the Glassboro that extended the friendly hand last year, the Glassboro that said to two leaders, "Yes, we will be ready in an hour to provide an atmosphere and the accommodations necessary in the hope that something fruitful will eventually develop." This forbearance and this fortitude are going to be essential in this age.

Our calling, your calling, and my calling is to seek the answers, not the slogans—to strive to tip the balance in the right direction: from war to peace, from hostility to reconciliation, from stalemate to progress.

Our calling, yours and mine, in the words that I repeated only a moment ago, is to leave this world a little more orderly than we found it.

When we look at the headlines and we review the map of Asia or the map of Europe or the map of our own States, when we undertake the assignment of leaving this world a little more orderly than we found it, we have plenty of objectives. We have an agenda that is full.

But the town of Glassboro—and this wonderful college campus—will always be associated with the goal of leaving this world a little more orderly than we found it.

I want to thank the President and the faculty and every member of this college graduating class for giving me this pleasant assignment and giving me something to remember always.

Thank you.

NOTE: The President spoke at 9:30 a.m. at Glassboro State College in Glassboro, N.J., to more than 5,000 persons attending a commencement ceremony. In his opening words he referred to Dr. Thomas E.

Robinson, President of Glassboro State College, and Richard J. Hughes, Governor of New Jersey. During his remarks he referred to Gunnar Jarring, Swedish Ambassador to the Soviet Union and United Nations mediator in the Middle East dispute.

For remarks of the President following his meetings in June 1967 with Premier Aleksei N. Kosygin of the Soviet Union, see 1967 volume, this series, Book I, Items 280, 282, 283.

The United Nations Security Council Resolution of November 22, 1967, is printed in the Department of State Bulletin (vol. 57, p. 843). The Nuclear Nonproliferation Treaty was signed on July 1, 1968, by representatives of 56 nations (see Item 349).

289   Remarks of Welcome at the White House to President Trejos of Costa Rica. *June 4*, 1968

President Trejos and Mrs. Trejos, Secretary Rostow, distinguished guests, ladies and gentlemen:

President Trejos, Mrs. Johnson and I welcome you and Mrs. Trejos here to Washington as very old friends of the United States of America.

Twenty-one years ago you were a student here with us. Eleven years ago you were here as our guest at the Department of State. Today you come here as the guest of all of the people of the United States.

We Americans know, Mr. President, that your country is famous for many qualities, but three above all:

—the fragrance of your coffee,

—the beauty of your women,

—the vitality of your democracy.

Fortunately, it is the virtue of democracy that men are not compelled to choose between such blessings. At least that is true in Costa Rica.

Other nations, our own included, may well envy the advanced stage of your democracy—where men count it as their inalienable right to enjoy a good cup of coffee— and to always have it served by a very beautiful woman.

In this time of worldwide ideological turmoil, the concepts of freedom, self-determination, representative democracy all have been much distorted.

For a nation to label itself a democracy is not enough. One must really look behind the label to determine the genuineness of the real product.

Costa Rica is one place where I believe the label fits the product.

Your record of elections and peaceful transfers of power is very plain for all of the people of the world to see.

President Trejos, your country has more schools than barracks. Your country has more teachers than soldiers. You devote one-third of your entire national budget to education. The payoff is in your high level of literacy and your success in building a sound economy with real social justice.

A little over a year ago you will recall we were together at Punta del Este. We measured the advances under the Alliance for Progress. We measured the advances against the goals that we seek.

We all agreed that we still have a long way to go, but we all know that we are really moving.

In Costa Rica you are making the Alliance work. It is reflected in the high priority that is given to education, in your more than 6 percent increase in farm production last year, in your industrial growth which has averaged 11 percent per year during the past several years.

Mr. President, it is dramatically demonstrated in the 400 percent increase in regional trade achieved by Costa Rica and its partners of the Central American Common Market.

These figures tell a story of real progress. It is a record that cheers all of your friends, Mr. President, in the United States, and should cheer all friends of democracy throughout the world.

Mr. President, we are glad that you have come. We want you to feel at home in this city. This First House of the land is your house.

Bienvenidos.

NOTE: The President spoke at 12 noon on the South Lawn at the White House, where President José Joaquín Trejos Fernandez was given a formal welcome with full military honors. In his opening words he also referred to Eugene V. Rostow, Under Secretary of State for Political Affairs.

President Trejos responded as follows:

Mr. President, thank you. Thank you very much for your kind words so graceful and so inspired.

It is a great privilege and an honor for me to bring you the message of greetings, of friendship, and of affection on the part of the people and of the Government of Costa Rica.

It is a message that comes from a hard-working people that bases its means of education as its best hope for development and progress.

It is a fraternal greeting coming from a people that expresses sincere friendship to the people of the United States, not only because it believes that geography has marked a common destiny for all of the nations of the American Continent, but also because it shares with its people the same ideals of liberty, of justice, of respect for the great dignity of the human being, and of love for the democratic standard, according to which the people can freely choose the government that they wish to carry out their own aspirations.

This message comes also from a people that considers that these ideals are just as alive today as they were during the American Revolution. In the restless world of our time, it is up to us to give these ideals new vigor and adapt them to the circumstances of the era in order that they continue reaching the heart of the patriots of each nation as they have done in the western world—these humanist ideals throughout the centuries.

I also bring you, Mr. President, the affection of the people of Costa Rica, that not only supports these ideals which they share with the people of the United States, but live these ideals fully and effectively.

I am also a bearer of the aspirations of a country that is working for a larger amount of dignity in the life of each family.

So we are working for a larger degree of dignity in the life of each Costa Rican family and together with all of the people of Latin America, hope that we will give a new impetus to a greater degree of fairness in the economic relationships in the contemporary world.

President Johnson and Mrs. Johnson, may God preserve forever the best attributes of the people of the United States and give to you and to your distinguished family the greatest happiness.

290   Remarks Upon Signing Bill Authorizing an Increase in the Capital of the Inter-American Development Bank. *June 4, 1968*

President Trejos, members of the Diplomatic Corps, Secretary General Plaza, Dr. Herrera, Dr. Sanz, Members of Congress, distinguished Secretary of State and Secretary of the Treasury, my friends:

We are quite honored this morning to have with us a valued friend and partner from Costa Rica. By happy coincidence, we were able to greet President Trejos with new evidence of our commitment to the Alliance for Progress.

The Congress has now passed a bill that

authorizes us, the United States, to support a $1 billion increase in the capital of the Inter-American Development Bank. The subscription share of the United States in this increase is almost $412 million. With the new authority, the bank can now enter the private capital markets of the world for new investment in the development of this great hemisphere of ours.

So this morning I asked you to come here to the East Room so that I could take this opportunity to pay tribute to the Inter-American Bank, its distinguished President, Board of Directors, and staff for their achievement in building an institution that is so responsive to present needs and with such vision of future challenges and opportunities. President Trejos and I spent most of our time this morning talking about what good had resulted from this development.

The past 5 years have been years of unparalleled growth, as you can see in the charts that we have put here in the room this morning.

—The bank will have tripled its capital resources with this new authorization.
—Its loan portfolio has increased 175 percent, to almost $2½ billion.
—These loans, in turn, have generated an additional $4 billion of investment.

The Inter-American Bank was established in 1959 during the administration of President Dwight David Eisenhower, and was established with the bipartisan support of the United States Congress. It was my great privilege to be the Majority Leader of the Senate at that time, and to introduce the bill that authorized the United States participation in the bank.

When I became President, the bank had $1 billion 400 million to draw on, of which the United States had contributed almost $850 million of that $1 billion 400 million. I am very proud that during my Presidency the bank's resources have now climbed to $6 billion, from $1 billion 400 million, with the United States adding $2.7 billion of that as the United States share.

I am equally proud that in this period the Latin American members have greatly increased the ratio of their contribution for the bank's special operations. In 1964 it stood at 11 to 1; today it stands at 3 to 1. This vitality has won the respect and the support of countries outside our regional system. Six countries in Europe, Canada, Israel, and Japan are investing over $200 million in the development of the hemisphere through the Inter-American Bank.

I had the pleasure of discussing the possibility of Australia's interest in this only last week with the Prime Minister of that great country.

So we know from experience that capital investment, to be truly productive, must be joined by investment in the health and education and the well-being of the people. The bank's portfolio reflects this balance of investment between man and machine:

—Agricultural loans are bringing almost 6 million acres of farmland into production, and they are helping more than 500,000 farmers with individual credits.
—Industrial loans are at work in 49 large plants and 2,700 smaller businesses.
—Road loans have built or improved more than 2,000 miles of main highways and nearly 10,000 miles of farm-to-market roads.
—Water and sewage loans have built 3,000 city and rural water systems and 270 sewage systems benefiting almost 40 million people.
—Housing loans have built over 300,000 units for low-income families totaling 2 million people.
—Education loans have modernized 120 centers of higher learning.

While the bank wrestles with the needs of the present, its planners are now at work on the requirements of the future. With great vision, the bank has assumed leadership, together with the Inter-American Committee on the Alliance for Progress, in encouraging the physical integration of Latin America.

During 1961, 1962, and 1963, an average of $203 million per year was appropriated. If this session of the Congress appropriates the amount authorized as we have asked, we will have more than doubled the yearly United States appropriations during the last 5 years. Since 1963 we will have appropriated an average of $430 million per year.

Dr. Herrera, the bill I am about to sign carries the pledge of the United States support to the bank, to the Alliance for Progress and to the inter-American system.

If you want to see what we are accomplishing by this cooperation of the Inter-American Bank, the Alliance for Progress, the World Bank, and our other programs, you only have to look at the very fine record of the people of Costa Rica.

I observed a few minutes ago, in welcoming their great and distinguished President, the high priority that they gave to education in Costa Rica, the 6 percent increase in farm production last year, the large industrial growth of 11 percent, and a 400 percent increase in regional trade.

So there we have people who are concentrating on education, concentrating on farm production, concentrating on industrial growth, concentrating on regional trade. That is making better lives for all of the people of that country. That is setting an example that the rest of the hemisphere I think is very proud of, and can profit by.

I think what the Alliance for Progress and the inter-American system have done is a major contribution to social justice and

economic development and freedom in this hemisphere.

There are now before the Congress other items that are essential to the achievement of this goal, such as our second installment of the Inter-American Bank's Fund for Special Operations, the replenishment of the International Development Association. All of these are vital to maintaining the momentum of development that has been achieved during the past 5 years.

Some day I hope that I will be able to come and see what you have done with this bank and with the Alliance for Progress in this hemisphere, working together. I want to see first hand what this great institution, the Inter-American Bank, is doing to touch the lives of these millions of people that we have mentioned this morning.

I want to see what you are doing to unite the hemisphere with strong ties of industry and communication. I want to see what you are doing in cooperation with the Alliance for Progress and the other programs we are having to conquer these ancient enemies of all of us—the enemies of disease, ignorance, and poverty.

We want to pay special tribute to you, Dr. Herrera, today for your leadership and for the success that this bank has had. We particularly want to thank President Trejos for being here on this occasion so we could honor not only him, but his people who have helped us to make a success in all of these adventures.

Thank you very much.

NOTE: The President spoke at 1:10 p.m. in the East Room at the White House. In his opening words he referred to José Joaquín Trejos Fernandez, President of Costa Rica, Galo Plaza, Secretary General of the Organization of American States, Felipe Herrera, President of the Inter-American Development Bank, Carlos Sanz de Santamaría, Chairman of the Inter-American Committee on the Alliance for Progress, Dean Rusk, Secretary of State, and Henry H. Fowler, Secretary of the Treasury.

As enacted, the bill (H.R. 15364) is Public Law 90–325 (82 Stat. 168).

On the same day the White House Press Office also released background information on the Inter-American Development Bank bill (4 Weekly Comp. Pres. Docs., p. 911).

291 Toasts of the President and President Trejos of Costa Rica. *June 4, 1968*

President Trejos and Mrs. Trejos, distinguished guests, ladies and gentlemen:

Mr. President, we welcome you and your lady to this First House of the land as the democratic leader of a country with a long democratic tradition.

The President and I spent a very pleasant and productive day together. We had a third party attending most of our discussions. I am happy tonight to thank Mother Nature for bringing so much sunshine today to our meeting. The lovely weather today was a great relief to the people in the State Department.

You know, Mr. President, they are always so grateful over in Foggy Bottom, where our State Department is located, for even the very smallest ray of sunshine of any kind. But they also had a very special reason for being anxious about your visit.

The Secretary of State and the Chief of Protocol were just a little nervous. They thought they might have to negotiate with Mother Nature to arrange a very special reception for you, something that they thought would try to equal the spectacular show that you put on the last time an American President visited in your country.

I am told that when President Kennedy arrived in Costa Rica in 1963, a volcano erupted. If that had happened to me, Mr. President, I would have felt perfectly at home.

You have been in Washington now, Mr. President, for more than 10 hours. There are not many days when this political capital can go that long without some natural erup-

tion. But we may still be able to put on a proper show for you. Later tonight we might pick up some tremors from a disturbance out in California.

Since I got out of politics, I don't know whose side Mother Nature is on out there, but she is certainly being courted by all of the candidates. One of them is praying for an earthquake to bury his opponent; one of them is praying for an upheaval; and a third candidate is just praying from a safe distance.

I understand, Mr. President, that Costa Rica has solved one of the problems of election campaigns that still troubles and vexes us here in the United States.

In your country the Congress appropriates funds to cover the campaign expenses of the presidential candidates. I believe anyone who gets 10 percent of the votes in Costa Rica is reimbursed in proportion to the number of votes he receives.

When Lady Bird was reading over the background book the State Department sent over, she looked up at me in the wee hours this morning and said, "Lyndon, you ran in the wrong country in 1964."

But the way things are going here in 1968, Mr. President, I expect some candidates may also recall what Will Rogers once said: "Politics has got so expensive that it takes lots of money," in this country, "to even get beat with."

The revolutionary times in which we live teach three lessons about the quest for freedom that we all cherish so much. They are not new, but because of recent events they have been given new meaning.

The first is that tyranny cannot suppress the human longing for liberty. This ancient truth remains as valid in the world of technology in the 20th century as it did many centuries ago when our common creed of freedom developed on the shores of the Mediterranean.

The second is that the defense of liberty sometimes carries a very heavy price. The people of South Vietnam and their allies know very well that freedom does not come free. I pray that the aggressors will someday come to understand the full depth of our resolve, as President Kennedy once said, to "pay any price, bear any burden . . . to assure the survival and the success of liberty."

The third is that democracy does not come in a single model. Each people knows how best to adapt the mechanics of representative government to the special needs of its people. We do not seek to impose a particular system. But we will defend the right of a people to determine their own destiny, free from coercion, and we are not fooled by false models.

Mr. President, your country, Costa Rica, and the United States differ in size. But they are equal in what really counts most—their love of liberty and freedom. That is the most cherished bond that unites the United States and Costa Rica.

The United States will never forget how quickly Costa Rica joined our cause after Pearl Harbor when we were attacked. We remember the prompt offer of ports and airfields during the terrible Cuban missile crisis. We remember that Costa Rican guardsmen stood shoulder to shoulder with our soldiers and those of the other American Republics to guard the peace in the Dominican Republic and to safeguard and to preserve the right of self-determination for the Dominican people.

I am particularly grateful to you, personally, Mr. President, for your always strong support, your strong moral support, in the defense of freedom in Asia.

Ladies and gentlemen, those of you who have come here from across the Nation to pay honor to this distinguished leader of our neighboring country, I should like to ask you to rise to toast the cause of liberty throughout the world and to toast one of its greatest champions, President José Trejos—teacher, scholar, statesman, citizen, and President of the sister Republic of Costa Rica.

NOTE: The President proposed the toast at 10:15 p.m. in the State Dining Room at the White House. During his remarks he referred to Dean Rusk, Secretary of State, and Angier Biddle Duke, Chief of Protocol.

President José Joaquín Trejos Fernandez responded as follows:

Mr. President, Mrs. Johnson, ladies and gentlemen:

I wish I had this fine humor, the fine spirit of President Johnson, to express my feelings more freely and not in the rather formal way that I have to take to read in Spanish. I would make up some other minor things, but that grace and that fine spirit, unfortunately, I do not have at all.

We are pleased, Mr. President, by the great interest in the Costa Rican nation and the constant increase in the centers of teaching which we have carried to even the most remote and smallest of our towns and villages, trying to make them every day better and more complete.

We are stimulated by the constant clamor of our rural and urban communities to have better services of public health and hygiene.

It is a source of great satisfaction to us to see the constant demands of our simple farmers to have better ways of communication, roads and highways that go deeper, and the opening up of new areas.

But most of all, we are proud of the passion of the Costa Rican people in the defense of the liberties of man and of his dignity as a human being, and for the respect of the results of the ballot box.

You, Mr. President, who began your life as a public servant by teaching young people as a grammar school teacher, and I who left my place as a professor to accept the public office which I now hold, agree in the high esteem that we give to the educational activity of the government to this high concept that we have of the school and of the educator as shapers of the future of our countries and of the high place that we grant them as key pieces in a strategy for the development of people.

We have been fortunate in Costa Rica. The imagination of our leaders for independence was captured in the early days by the ideals of Jefferson, of Paine, of Adams, and of Hamilton, who, together with other great men, were building this grand experiment of a democratic system of government.

Later on in the century, the apostle of the poorest man and his disciples for a broader dissemination of primary schools as an indispensable base of effective democracy found a favorable response in our governments which, since that time, set forth as slogans of action to build more roads and to open more schools.

We still share this and hold this aspiration, but not as just a total program of the government which exhausts thus the lists of the duties of the government, because to those postulates which I have mentioned, we have added during this century the ideals in insuring better health for the people, a larger degree of social justice for the workers.

Since by good fortune we have been able to do without military expenditures that other nations have to take, practically all of our total public income is devoted to expenses in the field of education, health, social welfare, and public roads.

You have been kind enough to praise my country because of its vocation for peace and for democratic life.

On my part, I must tell you, interpreting the sentiments of the Costa Rican people, we admire you for the struggle that this powerful nation is waging on 1,000 fronts in favor of the survival of democracy and the fighting abroad against totalitarianism and in your internal fighting against incomprehension and the inertia that serve as a brake to social progress.

We know of your efforts to achieve the elimination of social inequalities and to ease the life of the groups that are more weak economically and of your efforts to give the Alliance for Progress the dimensions that are required in order that we may make of our America the continent of hope.

On behalf of my people, on behalf of Costa Rica, I tell you, thank you very much, President Johnson.

I know that I faithfully interpret the sentiments of the Costa Rican people in expressing our gratitude to you as I have just done. But I would like to give the Costa Rican people, whom you have praised so highly, an opportunity for you to know how great

their appreciation for your country and for you is.

I take pleasure in extending to you the warmest invitation for you to visit Costa Rica together with Mrs. Johnson as our most distinguished guests at a time which you consider opportune.

I still have the hope that your duties will not be an obstacle for you to accept this invitation.

Until I can speak in my own country these words, let me express now my most fervent hope for the United States of America, for you, its distinguished President, and for your gracious First Lady, Mrs. Johnson.

President Johnson, Mrs. Johnson, ladies and gentlemen, nothing that I could have brought with me in writing could really express in any sense the deep sentiment and emotion that I feel at this time and that the members of the party accompanying me feel in being here on this occasion because I feel this is a feeling of, perhaps, one that has never been achieved before that inter-American friendship is a reality.

I say this because in looking around me I see the faces of friendship that surround us and even more than faces of friendship, perhaps I see the expressions of brotherhood on the faces of each and every one of the persons who are with us here.

The feeling that I am talking about is this atmosphere, this spirit that flows around us and binds us, perhaps above anything else that we might think of because this is the spirit that we feel that we must all exert every possible effort to do everything that we can to raise the dignity of man throughout the world, to do this to each family of each man throughout all the countries of the world.

Because to raise the dignity of man, to elevate the dignity of man means to provide him with an atmosphere in which he can live with freedom in its fullest dimension.

We cannot conceive that he can begin to do this if any man is subject to a dictatorship, no matter what its nature or orientation might be.

So, we find and we feel that human dignity and democracy are united as one. I see that here. What gives me this emotion, and that is a very natural one and a historical one, and for a thousand reasons I feel this is an event that we will always treasure for the rest of our lives because it represents the spirit that we share which is in turn a representation of the noblest humanist ideals of man.

May God bless our continent, Latin America, and the United States in our own united goal that we be united in the future and may God bless this great family of President and Mrs. Johnson.

292   Statement by the President Following the Shooting of Senator Robert F. Kennedy. *June 5, 1968*

THERE ARE no words equal to the horror of this tragedy. Our thoughts and our prayers are with Senator Kennedy, his family, and the other victims.

All America prays for his recovery. We also pray that divisiveness and violence be driven from the hearts of men everywhere.

NOTE: The President's statement was made available by George E. Christian, Special Assistant to the President, at 6:45 a.m. He also issued the following announcement on the President's activities after he was informed of the shooting of Senator Robert F. Kennedy of New York, in the Ambassador Hotel, Los Angeles, Calif.

The President was notified of Senator Kennedy having been shot at 3:31 e.d.t., by Special Assistant Walt Rostow who had been called immediately by the White House Situation Room as first reports were received.

The President has been up since then, talking three times with the Attorney General, twice with Secret Service Director Jim Rowley, with Secretary of Defense Clark Clifford, and with FBI Director J. Edgar Hoover.

The President has asked that a protective U.S. Secret Service detail be placed with each presidential candidate and with their family. There is not authorizing legislation for this action, but the President has asked that this be done.

The President has directed the FBI to assist with supplying manpower if necessary to supplement the Secret Service details.

The President also talked this morning with Senator Monroney, Senator Dirksen, Senator Mansfield, and Congressman Tom Steed of Oklahoma. The President advised these Members of Congress of the actions he had taken in placing Secret Service details with each of the presidential candidates and discussed the need for authorizing legislation to follow up this action.

See also Items 293–295.

293   Address to the Nation Following the Attack on Senator Kennedy. *June 5, 1968*

My fellow citizens:

I speak to you this evening not only as your President, but as a fellow American who is shocked and dismayed, as you are, by the attempt on Senator Kennedy's life, deeply disturbed, as I know you are, by lawlessness and violence in our country, of which this tragedy is the latest spectacular example.

We do not know the reasons that inspired the attack on Senator Kennedy. We know only that a brilliant career of public service has been brutally interrupted; that a young leader of uncommon energy and dedication, who has served his country tirelessly and well, and whose voice and example have touched millions throughout the entire world, has been senselessly and horribly stricken.

At this moment, the outcome is still in the balance. We pray to God that He will spare Robert Kennedy and will restore him to full health and vigor. We pray this for the Nation's sake, for the sake of his wife and his children, his father and his mother, and in memory of his brother, our beloved late President.

The Kennedy family has endured sorrow enough, and we pray that this family may be spared more anguish.

Tonight this Nation faces once again the consequences of lawlessness, hatred, and unreason in its midst. It would be wrong, it would be self-deceptive, to ignore the connection between that lawlessness and hatred and this act of violence. It would be just as wrong, and just as self-deceptive, to conclude from this act that our country itself is sick, that it has lost its balance, that it has lost its sense of direction, even its common decency.

Two hundred million Americans did not strike down Robert Kennedy last night any more than they struck down President John F. Kennedy in 1963 or Dr. Martin Luther King in April of this year.

But those awful events give us ample warning that in a climate of extremism, of disrespect for law, of contempt for the rights of others, violence may bring down the very best among us. A Nation that tolerates violence in any form cannot expect to be able to confine it to just minor outbursts.

My fellow citizens, we cannot, we just must not, tolerate the sway of violent men among us. We must not permit men who are filled with hatred, and careless of innocent lives, to dominate our streets and fill our homes with fear.

We cannot sanction the appeal to violence, no matter what its cause, no matter what the grievance from which it springs.

There is never—and I say never—any justification for the violence that tears at the fabric of our national life; that inspires such fear in peaceful citizens that they arm themselves with deadly weapons; that sets citizen against citizen or group against group.

A great nation can guarantee freedom for its people and the hope of progressive change only under the rule of law. So let us, for God's sake, resolve to live under the law.

Let us put an end to violence and to the preaching of violence.

Let the Congress pass laws to bring the insane traffic in guns to a halt, as I have appealed to them time and time again to do. That will not, in itself, end the violence, but reason and experience tell us that it will slow it down; that it will spare many innocent lives.

Let us purge the hostility from our hearts and let us practice moderation with our tongues.

Let us begin in the aftermath of this great tragedy to find a way to reverence life, to protect it, to extend its promise to all of our people.

This Nation and its people have suffered grievously from violence and assassination. For this reason, I am appointing, with the recommendation of the leadership of the Congress—with whom I have talked this evening—a commission of most distinguished Americans to immediately examine this tragic phenomenon. They are: Dr. Milton Eisenhower, the former distinguished President of Johns Hopkins University, Archbishop Terence Cooke of New York, Albert E. Jenner, Jr., of Illinois, Ambassador Patricia Harris, Mr. Eric Hoffer, Senator Philip A. Hart, Senator Roman Hruska, Congressman Hale Boggs, Congressman William McCulloch, and Judge Leon Higginbotham.

The commission will look into the causes, the occurrence, and the control of physical violence across this Nation, from assassination that is motivated by prejudice and by ideology, and by politics and by insanity, to violence in our cities' streets and even in our homes.

What in the nature of our people and the environment of our society makes possible such murder and such violence?

How does it happen? What can be done to prevent assassination? What can be done to further protect public figures? What can be done to eliminate the basic causes of these aberrations?

Supported by the suggestions and recommendations of criminologists, sociologists, and psychologists, all of our Nation's medical and social sciences, we hope to learn why we inflict such suffering on ourselves. I hope and pray that we can learn how to stop it.

This is a sober time for our great democracy, but we are a strong and we are a resilient people who can, I hope, learn from our misfortunes, who can heal our wounds, who can build and find progress in public order.

We can. We must.

So I appeal to every American citizen tonight: Let us begin tonight.

NOTE: The President spoke at 10:07 p.m. in the Fish Room at the White House for broadcast by radio and television.

See also Items 292, 294, 295.

294   Statement by the President on the Death of Senator Kennedy. *June 6, 1968*

THIS IS a time of tragedy and loss. Senator Robert Kennedy is dead.

Robert Kennedy affirmed this country—affirmed the essential decency of its people, their longing for peace, their desire to improve conditions of life for all.

During his life, he knew far more than his share of personal tragedy.

Yet he never abandoned his faith in America. He never lost his confidence in the spiritual strength of ordinary men and women. He believed in the capacity of the young for excellence—and in the right of the old and poor to a life of dignity.

Our public life is diminished by his loss.

Mrs. Johnson and I extend our deepest sympathy to Mrs. Kennedy and his family. I have issued a proclamation calling upon our Nation to observe a day of mourning for Robert Kennedy.

NOTE: The President read the statement and portions of the proclamation for broadcast by radio and television. For the text of the proclamation, see Item 295.

See also Items 292, 293.

295   Proclamation 3853, Death of Robert F. Kennedy. *June 6, 1968*

By the President of the United States of America, a Proclamation

To the People of the United States:

A noble and compassionate leader, a good and faithful servant of the people, in the full vigor of his promise, lies dead from an assassin's bullet.

The tragedy and the senseless violence of Robert F. Kennedy's death casts a deep shadow of grief across America and across the world.

This is a moment for all Americans to join hands and walk together through this dark night of common anguish into a new dawn of healing unity.

Now, THEREFORE, I, LYNDON B. JOHNSON,

President of the United States, do call upon all Americans to observe Sunday next, the ninth day of June, as a day of national mourning in his memory throughout the United States. In our churches, in our homes, and in our hearts let us resolve before God and before each other that the purpose of progress and justice for which Robert F. Kennedy lived shall endure.

I direct that until interment the flag of the United States shall be flown at half-staff on all buildings, grounds and naval vessels of the Federal Government in the District of Columbia and throughout the United States and its Territories and possessions.

I also direct that the flag shall be flown at

half-staff for the same length of time at all United States embassies, legations, consular offices, and other facilities abroad, including all military facilities and naval vessels and stations.

IN WITNESS WHEREOF, I have hereunto set my hand this sixth day of June, in the year of our Lord nineteen hundred and sixty-eight and of the Independence of the United States of America the one hundred and ninety-second.

LYNDON B. JOHNSON

The White House
June 6, 1968

NOTE: See also Items 292–294.

296 Letter to the President of the Senate and to the Speaker of the House Urging Passage of an Effective Gun Control Law. *June 6, 1968*

Dear Mr. President: (Dear Mr. Speaker:)

Today the Nation cries out to the conscience of the Congress.

Criminal violence from the muzzle of a gun has once again brought heartbreak to America.

Surely this must be clear beyond question: the hour has come for the Congress to enact a strong and effective Gun Control Law, governing the full range of lethal weapons.

I have sought—and fought for—such a law through all the days of my Presidency.

On occasions before, I have spoken of the terrible toll inflicted on our people by firearms:

—750,000 Americans dead since the turn of the century. This is far more than have died at the hands of our enemies in all the wars we have fought.

—sorrow and suffering that cannot be counted, and fear that cannot be measured.

Each year, in this country, guns are involved in more than 6,500 murders. This compares with 30 in England, 99 in Canada, 68 in West Germany, and 37 in Japan. 44,000 aggravated assaults are committed with guns in America each year. 50,000 robberies are committed with guns in America each year.

I have told the Congress and the Nation of the brutal loopholes in our laws. Two million guns were sold in the United States last year. Far too many were bought by the demented, the deranged, the hardened criminal and the convict, the addict, and the alcoholic. We cannot expect these irresponsible people to be prudent in their protection of us, but we can expect the Congress to protect us from them.

Weapons of destruction can be purchased by mail as easily as baskets of fruit or cartons of cigarettes. We must eliminate the dangers of mail-order murder.

The Congress has finally begun to take action. The Senate has passed a watered-down version of the Gun Control Law I recommended. The House has taken action on the Senate Bill.

But this half-way measure is not enough.

It covers adequately only transactions involving hand guns. It leaves the deadly commerce in lethal shotguns and rifles without effective control—fifty-five long months after the mail-order murder of President John F. Kennedy.

So today, I call upon the Congress in the name of sanity, in the name of safety—and in the name of an aroused nation—to give America the Gun Control Law it needs.

I urge the Congress to make it unlawful to sell rifles and shotguns—as well as hand guns—by mail order.

I urge the Congress to make it unlawful to sell rifles and shotguns—as well as hand guns—to persons who are too young to bear the terrible responsibility that is placed in the hands of a gun owner.

I urge the Congress to make it unlawful to sell rifles and shotguns—as well as hand guns—in one State to residents of another.

This will not prevent legitimate hunters or sportsmen from purchasing firearms but with this reinforced law we can give the States the proper incentive to shape their own gun control legislation, and the country can at long last have a network of systematic safeguards for all our citizens.

I am asking the Governors of the fifty States immediately and comprehensively to review their gun laws and to amend them where necessary to fully protect citizens of their States from deadly weapons in dangerous hands.

The voices of the few must no longer prevail over the interests of the many.

When I last appealed to the Congress on this subject again only a month ago, I asked this question: "What in the name of conscience will it take to pass a truly effective gun control law?"

In this new hour of tragedy, that question should at last be answered. Let us now spell out our grief in constructive action.

Sincerely,

LYNDON B. JOHNSON

NOTE: This is the text of identical letters addressed to the Honorable Hubert H. Humphrey, President of the Senate, and to the Honorable John W. McCormack, Speaker of the House of Representatives. The President also read the letter for radio and television broadcast.

The Omnibus Crime Control and Safe Streets Act of 1968 which contains gun control provisions, was approved by the President on June 19, 1968 (see Item 320). The Gun Control Act of 1968 was approved by the President on October 22, 1968 (see Item 553).

On June 7, 1968, the White House released a telegram from Price Daniel, Assistant to the President for Federal-State Relations, to all Governors urging them to revise State gun laws for "the purpose of initiating any amendments that may be necessary to provide additional safeguards and protection against deadly weapons in dangerous hands." (4 Weekly Comp. Pres. Docs., p. 919)

---

297 Memorandum Directing the Development of Contingency Plans for Oil Spill Emergencies. *June 7*, 1968

Memorandum for Honorable Clark M. Clifford, Secretary of Defense; Honorable Stewart L. Udall, Secretary of the Interior; Honorable Alan S. Boyd, Secretary of Transportation; Honorable Donald F. Hornig, Director, Office of Science and Technology:

SUBJECT: Federal Plans for Oil Spill Emergencies

The Nation's readiness for responding promptly and effectively to an oil spill along our coasts and waterways is of increasing importance. On the recommendation of the National Council on Marine Resources and Engineering Development, I am asking you to assume special responsibilities in order to strengthen our preparedness to act in the event of such an emergency.

Federal Government responsibilities and capabilities for dealing with oil spills, to the extent now available, are divided among several departments. The Department of the Interior has legislative responsibility in the Oil Pollution Act of 1924, and recent Administration proposals for legislation would expand that authority if passed by the Congress. The Department has expertise in water pollution and protection of natural resources in general. The Department of Transportation, through the Coast Guard, has general responsibility for safety of life and property along the coast and has men and equipment available for water-borne operations in most of the coastal areas. The Army Corps of Engineers has similar capabilities in certain local areas. The Administration's legislative proposals concerning assignment of responsibilities with respect to oil pollution are pending before the Congress.

Early development of contingency plans for dealing with spills—identifying emergency actions and responsible officials—is urgent. Notwithstanding substantial Federal effort to date, more rapid progress in the development of multi-agency contingency plans is needed.

Accordingly, I am asking the Secretary of the Interior immediately to assume primary responsibility for completing at the earliest possible date multi-agency contingency plans for responding to oil spill emergencies, with the understanding that he will work closely with the Secretaries of Transportation and Defense in this effort. I shall depend on the Secretary of the Interior to draft contingency plans for each coastal region and other relevant bodies of water of the United States to me by July 31, 1968.

The Office of Science and Technology has special capabilities applicable to the oil spill problem, as well as responsibilities related to our water resources. Therefore, I am asking the Director of the Office of Science and Technology to establish an ad hoc Committee to include appropriate officials of the Executive Office of the President to cooperate with the departments and review the plans as they are being developed.

Until the completion of these plans, I am asking the Secretary of the Interior to assume primary responsibility, with due regard for the authorities and capabilities of participating agencies, for coordinating the use of appropriate Government resources for dealing with the pollution aspects of oil spills in or threatening the coastal zone or other relevant waters with the understanding that: (a) The Secretary of the Interior will immediately request the Secretary of Transportation (or the Secretary of Defense in particular local areas where more appropriate) to assume interim responsibility for on-scene operational coordination and interim control in emergencies of multi-agency actions for dealing with such incidents; and (b) The Secretary of the Interior will provide to the Secretary of Transportation (or Secretary of Defense) expert advice to the local operational commander with respect to water quality and conservation goals, protection of natural resources, the use of chemicals in clean-up activities, and the like. Non-Federal interests will be assisted in preparing for emergency actions by timely public announcement of the on-scene command official in each area.

The Departments of Defense and Transportation have important resources and capabilities for dealing with oil spill problems and protecting our natural resources from their consequences. I am consequently asking both the Secretary of Defense and the Secretary of Transportation to participate fully in the development of contingency plans. Further, their readiness to assume emergency responsibilities in the interim period, as requested by the Secretary of the Interior, will be an important contribution to protecting the Nation's resources.

I personally look forward to expeditious

completion of well considered plans for appropriate protection from the hazards of pollution from oil spills.

Lyndon B. Johnson

NOTE: On November 13, 1968, the President announced approval of a national contingency plan for combating oil spills (see Item 586).

298   Remarks and Statement Upon Signing Order Establishing the National Commission on the Causes and Prevention of Violence. *June* 10, 1968

Dr. Eisenhower, Mr. Attorney General, ladies and gentlemen of the Commission:

As I reviewed with you in the Fish Room earlier, I shall shortly, in your presence here, sign the Executive order creating the Commission and will ask the Congress for authority for subpoena power of the Commission.

It is anticipated that there will be, as the order outlines, additional appointees to the Commission, perhaps two, maybe more. The request to the Congress for additional authority will go up this afternoon.

Following the signing of the order, I will make a statement of some 10 or 15 minutes that will give you my views, as well as a background, I think, that will be appropriate for you to review in the light of the responsibilities which you are undertaking.

I want to, before I go into the formal statement, again express to Dr. Eisenhower, as I do to each member of this Commission, my deep and lasting gratitude on not only my part but, I think, on the part of the American people for their willingness to assume this responsibility. I am grateful to each of you.

[At this point the President signed the Executive order. He then resumed speaking.]

This troubled world will long remember the scar of the past week's violence, but when the week is remembered, let this be remembered, too: that out of anguish came a national resolve to search for the causes and to find the cures for the outbursts of violence which have brought so much heartbreak to our Nation.

Violence has erupted in many parts of the globe, from the streets of newly emerging nations to the old cobblestones of Paris. But it is the episodes of violence in our own country which must command our attention now.

Our inquiry into that violence brings all of us together here this afternoon in the Cabinet Room at the White House. You members of this Commission come here from the church, the university, the Senate and the House, the judiciary, the ranks of the workingman on the waterfront, and the professions.

My charge to you is simple and direct: I ask you to undertake a penetrating search for the causes and prevention of violence— a search into our national life, our past as well as our present, our traditions as well as our institutions, our culture, our customs, and our laws.

I hope your search will yield:

First, an understanding and an insight into the kinds of violent aberrations which have struck down public figures and private citizens alike.

One out of every five Presidents since 1865 has been assassinated—Abraham Lincoln in April 1865, Garfield in July 1881, McKinley in September 1901, and John Fitzgerald

Kennedy in November 1963.

In this same period, there have been attempts on the lives of one out of every three of our Presidents, including President Theodore Roosevelt while campaigning in October 1912, President-elect Franklin D. Roosevelt in February 1933, and Harry S. Truman in November 1950. In the attempt on Roosevelt's life, Mayor Anton Cermak of Chicago was killed. In the attack on President Harry Truman, a White House policeman lost his life.

The list of assassinations during the last 5 years is also long and shocking. Here are just some of them:

In 1963: Medgar Evers, ambushed by a sniper; four Negro girls killed in a church bombing; President John F. Kennedy assassinated. 8,500 Americans were murdered that year, also, in America.

In 1964: three civil rights workers murdered as part of a Ku Klux Klan conspiracy; Lieutenant Colonel Lemuel Penn shot down on a highway. 9,250 Americans were murdered that year in America, also.

In 1965: Mrs. Viola Liuzzo. 9,850 Americans were murdered that year in America, too.

In 1966: Malcolm X. 10,920 Americans were murdered that year.

In 1967: George Lincoln Rockwell. 12,230 Americans were murdered that year.

In 1968: Martin Luther King, Jr., and Senator Robert F. Kennedy.

Just yesterday, the morning paper records that a Jordanian grocer living on Chicago's South Side was shot to death and police speculate that the killing may have been in revenge for the assassination of Senator Kennedy.

Second, I hope your search will uncover the causes of disrespect for law and order—disrespect for proper authority in the home

and disrespect for public officials—and of violent disruptions of public order by individuals and groups.

Third, I hope your search will lead to sensible and practical actions to control or prevent these outbreaks of violence.

Here are some of the questions I hope you will consider:

Is there something in the environment of American society or the structure of our American institutions that causes disrespect for the law, that causes contempt for the rights of others, and incidents of violence? If there is, how can we correct it?

Has permissiveness toward extreme behavior in our society encouraged an increase of violence?

Why do some individuals and groups reject the peaceful political and institutional processes of change in favor of violent means?

Are the seeds of violence nurtured through the public's airwaves, the screens of neighborhood theaters, the news media, and other forms of communication from our leaders that reach the family and reach our young? I am asking the heads of the radio and television networks and the Chairman and the members of the Federal Communications Commission to cooperate wholeheartedly with this Commission.

Is violence a contagious phenomenon? To the extent that it is, are there ways we can reduce the contagion?

What is the relationship between mass disruption of public order and the individual acts of violence?

What is the relationship between mental derangement and violence—remembering that half of our hospital beds in America are now occupied by the mentally ill?

Does the democratic process which stresses exchanges of ideas permit less physical contact with masses of people—as a matter of security against the deranged individual and obsessed fanatic?

To the extent that we can identify the basic causes of violence and disrespect for the law, what practical steps then can we and should we take to eliminate them?

Can our society any longer tolerate the widespread possession of deadly firearms by private citizens?

What—beyond firm and effective Federal and State gun control laws which are so desperately needed—can be done to give further protection to public leaders and to private citizens?

How can the government at all levels, the churches, the schools, and the parents help to dispel the forces that lead to violence?

These are some of the questions that are on the minds of Americans today. But I will and I must leave to you the task of defining precisely the scope and boundaries of this inquiry. For you will be venturing into uncharted ground.

Some of the questions I have asked and the matters you look into may be beyond the frontiers of man's knowledge. Nevertheless, I urge you to go as far as man's knowledge takes you.

Even where basic causes are beyond the knowledge and control of man, you may still be able to propose actions and laws and institutions which can limit the opportunities for violence by individuals and groups, for as I said to the Nation only last Friday:

"Two million guns were sold in the United States last year. Far too many were bought by the demented, the deranged, the hardened criminal and the convict, the addict, and the alcoholic. We cannot expect these irresponsible people to be prudent in their protection of us, but we can expect the Congress to protect us from them. . . .

"I have spoken of the terrible toll inflicted on our people by firearms: 750,000 Americans dead since the turn of the century. This is far more than have died at the hands of our enemies in all the wars we have fought. . . .

"Each year, in this country, guns are involved in more than 6,500 murders. This compares with 30 in England, 99 in Canada, 68 in West Germany, and 37 in Japan. 44,000 aggravated assaults are committed with guns in America each year. 50,000 robberies are committed with guns in America each year."

The truths you seek will yield stubbornly to search. But I do want to be sure that that search is made, and that search must be started now.

Your work should help us all move toward that day when hatred and violence will have no sway in the affairs of men. Since violence is an international phenomenon, your work will be a service not only to your countrymen, but, I hope, to the world.

The agony of these past days lies heavy on the hearts of all the American people.

But let us all now have the will and have the purpose to forge our sorrow into a constructive force for public order and progress, for justice and compassion. This is the spirit that has sustained the Nation, and sustained it in all the years of our history.

This is the spirit, I believe, that can see us emerge from this hour of sorrow—and emerge as a stronger and a more unified people.

NOTE: The President spoke at 2:24 p.m. in the Cabinet Room at the White House upon signing Executive Order 11412 "Establishing a National Commission on the Causes and Prevention of Violence" (4 Weekly Comp. Pres. Docs., p. 938; 33 F.R. 8583; 3 CFR, 1968 Comp., p. 114). In his opening words he referred to Dr. Milton S. Eisenhower, Chairman of the Commission, and Attorney General Ramsey Clark, member of the Commission.

Before the ceremony the President announced the appointment of Lloyd N. Cutler as Executive Director of the Commission.

299 Remarks for the Press Following the President's Meeting With Governor Nelson Rockefeller. *June 10, 1968*

Gentlemen:

I have reviewed with Governor Rockefeller, at his request, the summary of the discussions in Paris, the Vietnam situation as we see it, the tax bill and the economic situation, together with many of our domestic problems, the problems of the cities, the $78 billion worth of programs we have pending in the Congress now.

We have covered that in the few minutes we have been together.

Secretary Rusk will review and brief the Governor fully on the political and diplomatic fronts.

General Wheeler will review the military situation in Vietnam and around the world.

This meeting is the result of my statement that we would be glad to brief the candidates at any time. Governor Rockefeller found it convenient and I arranged for Secretary Rusk and General Wheeler to come here and meet with him.

This is the statement on our part. If Governor Rockefeller has anything to say to you after the briefing, I am sure you will be available out in the press lobby.

NOTE: The President spoke at 3:20 p.m. in the Cabinet Room at the White House following his meeting with Governor Nelson A. Rockefeller of New York, contender for the 1968 Republican presidential nomination. During his remarks the President referred to Dean Rusk, Secretary of State, and Gen. Earle G. Wheeler, Chairman of the Joint Chiefs of Staff, both of whom met with the Governor during a preconvention briefing on domestic and foreign issues.

The remarks of the Governor following the meeting with the President are printed in the Weekly Compilation of Presidential Documents (vol. 4, p. 939).

As printed above, this item follows the text released by the White House Press Office.

300 Remarks at a Reception for the Presidential Scholars of 1968. *June 10, 1968*

Mrs. Johnson, members of the Cabinet, parents, distinguished young scholars:

I hope that you feel as special about this award and this event—at least as special—as we feel about those who have been selected for this great honor.

"Of those to whom much is given," it is said, "much will be required." Those words apply both to you, with your great gifts, as well as to the country that we all love, with the country's great wealth and its great resources.

Certainly, we all recognize that we are living in a time which requires a great deal from all of us. This time demands that we sacrifice for our country in many ways: ways that are difficult, in causes that all of us don't always understand.

The times demand that all of us solve problems which at times appear to some of us to be unsolvable, problems that we inherited, problems that are thrust upon us by years of injustice and years of neglect.

Finally, this time in America has required us to endure events which seem unbelievable—and almost, at times, unbearable—tragedies of violence and unreason.

You and I must face the difficulty of being citizens and we must face it in a difficult time.

Really, there never has been an easy age in America.

No one ever promised that this democracy of ours would be easy. No one ever promised that this Nation's great experiment could be carried without great pain.

Every time for our country has been a difficult time.

But every time has also been a time of hope, too.

The greatest question facing this country today, as we meet here this afternoon in the East Room of the first house of the land, is not whether we can rebuild our cities; of course we can do that. It is not whether we can improve our schools; of course we can and we must do that.

It is not whether we can create and build more housing or create more jobs. Those are all, I think, questions of will—not questions of capacity.

The critical question that we face is whether we can, as one people, hold fast to our faith—in each other and in this Nation's purpose.

If we answer that question in the affirmative,

—we will overcome injustice;

—we will erase the stain of violence;

—we will heal and help this country.

I hope that every one of the Presidential Scholars, of whom we are all so proud, with your considerable talents, will be active participants in that effort.

Ask yourself not what you can say or do that will create doubt or will plant fear, but ask yourself what you can do that will heal, build, and be constructive.

The honor that your Nation pays you today is not just a reward for past achievement. It is a way of recognizing your special talents and expressing the confidence of the country in you.

We want, in return, for you to express confidence in your country and try to provide ability to lead and to return your great gifts to the country that has given you so much.

In effect, we want you and your ability to make your difficult time, which we all realize is difficult, to be also a time of hope.

In all the periods of doubt and uncertainty and trouble that have faced this Nation—and there have been many critical moments in our history—there has always been hope that led us out of it, and always young people and their faith that I think have made us the greatest land in all the world.

I have not the slightest doubt about the future as long as a country can develop young men and women with faith like you, with hope like you, with the leadership that I hope you will give all of us.

Thank you very much.

NOTE: The President spoke at 5:06 p.m. in the East Room at the White House.

The 121 Presidential Scholars of 1968, announced by the President on May 27, were chosen for their superior intellectual attainment and potential from among the Nation's outstanding secondary school graduates. The Presidential Scholars were selected by a commission appointed by the President and headed by Dr. J. E. Wallace Sterling, president of Stanford University. The group, composed of 64 boys and 57 girls, included at least one boy and one girl from each State, the District of Columbia, and Puerto Rico. Two were selected from Americans living abroad.

The Presidential Scholars program was established in 1964 "to recognize the most precious resource of the United States—the brain power of its young people—and to encourage the pursuit of intellectual attainment among all our youth."

The names of the 1968 Presidential Scholars and the members of the commission which selected them are printed in the Weekly Compilation of Presidential Documents (vol. 4, p. 855).

301 Remarks at the Graduation Exercises of the Capitol Page School. *June 11, 1968*

Dr. DeKeyser, Members of Congress, distinguished guests, pages, and members of the pages' families:

I am sorry that I have had to delay you, but I have been out to the hospital to visit with General Eisenhower and Justice Douglas, Senator Russell, and dozens of our fighting men who have contributed themselves, their bodies, their arms and their legs, to preserving our independence and giving us this glorious free land of ours where we have more liberty than any people in all the world and where we have more prosperity and more of the good things of life than any other people anywhere because of:

—men like General Eisenhower, who served in uniform for many years;

—men like Justice Douglas and Senator Russell, who has been Chairman of the Armed Services Committee throughout all that period;

—boys from all the States of the Union, with smiles on their faces, with their chins up and their chests out, most of them wounded severely. Some of them lost an arm, some a leg, but all of them are proud of their service and welcoming the opportunity, and some of them, I am sad to say, were even saying they hoped that they could go back, because they do so much want to contribute their part to whatever their obligations as citizens happen to be.

So you young men who are here graduating this morning have completed your work at a very unique institution of learning. Next January, so shall I.

I never had the privilege of being a page in the Congress. I was a temporary page in the State legislature when I was a little boy. I was a doorkeeper in the Congress more than 35 years ago. But after 37 years in public service, next January I am going to graduate and, I hope, go back to the classroom.

I hope that most of you young men will choose some kind of a public career, too.

All my life I have said that I wanted to be a teacher or a preacher or a public servant. A little part of my life I have spent teaching; a good part of my life I have spent in the public service.

I hope that you will choose a career of public service. It is a vocation that I highly recommend for those who seek deep, personal satisfaction and who seek self-fulfillment.

You young fellows have had an insider's view of the best legislative body in all the world. Congress, I think, offers a classic example of how different kinds of people, from different sections of the country, with different colors and different educations and different backgrounds, under different, conflicting pressures, can get together and work together for the common good of all.

As we meet here in the East Room of the White House this morning, a very critical time in our Nation's history, we Americans are facing exceedingly difficult questions about our country, about order, about lawlessness, about violence, and about progress. I think it is important and I think it is crucial that we make some vital distinctions and that we try to answer some of these questions that are being raised.

For instance, we must distinguish between the twisted logic of a political assassin and the inherent decency of the vast majority of the people. We must distinguish between those who reject outright our entire social and political system and hate it, and who want to destroy it, and those who are trying to use positive forces to improve, to change, and to reshape our society.

We must distinguish between compassionate understanding of our fellow citizens' problems and blind permissiveness, between the sometimes heedless impatience of youth and the need to readjust, and we do need to readjust some outworn values and change some of our traditional beliefs.

Now, this is a very difficult period. But with understanding and with perspective, we are going to see it through. There are no short cuts. There are no overnight miracles.

I think most of our people understand this. We have gone through many sad moments since that terrible day in November 1963, but our Nation pulled itself together. We united for a period. We were strong. We faced the problems that came. We had a period where we provided more solutions than any time in our history.

Now the time has come again where I hope most of our people understand. I hope they have the endurance. I hope they have the wisdom to work with—not against—those who want to progress and to move forward.

So I hope you young men will devote your energies in the years ahead to fulfillment of our promise as a great nation.

Mr. Rayburn, who was quite a hero among the pages and among the Congress for more than half a century, used to say that "any mule can kick a barn down; it takes a good carpenter to build one."

The easiest thing in the world you can do is find what's wrong with this room—the rug is not the right color, the lights are too bright, the windows are too many, the shades are too long. You can kick it down, but I hope that before you do that, you will ask yourself the question:

"Is what I say and what I do going to build my country, going to make it stronger and going to make it more united; or is it going to divide it?"

Is it going to create suspicions? Is it going to produce hate? What is going to be the effect? What are the consequences of your act?

You have been a very fortunate lot. This is a great country. The problems that we have are problems that they have in Germany, in the streets of Paris, in Italy, in Latin America, in Canada, and all over the world. The quesiton is—not the problem—but the question: How do we deal with those problems? What do we do about it?

If we sit and do nothing, we can expect no rewards. But you young men are not going to be satisfied with the status quo. You are not going to be satisfied to stand still. You must not be.

There has never been a period in our national history when the need was greater for new ideas and new solutions to old problems—problems we have neglected for a century. We are faced with that.

In the Congress at this moment you have $78 billion worth of requests to deal with social problems—problems that the Commission on Civil Disorders recognized, problems that the Crime Commission pointed out, problems we outlined yesterday to the Eisenhower Commission on Violence, problems we reviewed with the leadership this morning.

We have a lot of sick people in this country, but the country is not sick. The country was never stronger, was never richer, never more powerful, never had as many boys and girls in school or young men and women in college, never had more resources being applied to education and health and poverty.

But that doesn't mean that we have answers to those problems. Just as we need good doctors when we have a shortage of doctors, just as we must have good pilots when we have a shortage of helicopter pilots, we have a shortage of outstanding young men and women who are needed in the city halls and the courthouses, the Congresses and the statehouses, the Presidency, and the Cabinet itself.

I am going back home and I am going to try to help produce some of those. I may even produce some Republican public servants. It is not important, really, what party they belong to. What is important is what they stand for, what they do about it, and whether they put on the uniform like the men who protect our independence.

The Fourth of July is coming up pretty soon. We are going to have many Fourth of July speeches about how great our land is and how much we appreciate our freedom, our liberty, and our independence that was won for us.

Well, let's show them how much we appreciate it. Let's do something about it. Let's build a stronger nation. Let's try to heal the wounds, instead of deepening the divisions.

Men in public life sometimes see the divisiveness and can't do anything about it. On March 31st I thought this country was divided. I didn't know how much I contributed to that divisiveness. I hoped I didn't contribute anything. I never tried to say any mean things or hateful things.

But I felt in the atmosphere that perhaps if I did not indicate that I had any personal ambition whatever, that it might somehow contribute to improving the political atmosphere and the divisions among us. This might make me better able to unite the Nation, to lead them, and ask them to stand up and rally around us instead of going off

in all different directions, and it might say to the world that we were genuinely interested more in peace than in anything else.

It took a few days, but we did, finally, as a result of that proposal, go to a conference table. Ambassador Harriman, Ambassador Vance, and Secretary Rusk are, every day in every way, trying to find an answer.

You have to have more than a desire—you have to have strength. You have to have more than a hope—you have to have judgment. We are trying every way we know how to bring peace in the world. We need all the help we can get—in private life, if that is where you need to go.

I hope those of you who have this training will go into public service. There can be no more worthy, no more honorable calling. You can have no better experience for that than the experience you have had.

I congratulate you for listening to this speech which I assume will be your final speech at least as students. You have listened to a lot of speeches. If you were in the Senate you have heard some longer ones than the one I have made. If you were in the House maybe they have been under the 5-minute rule.

In any event, I congratulate you and I salute you. I express the hope that some day some of you will be standing where I am, trying to heal and to build and to lead a nation that is worthy of the very best we can produce.

Thank you very much.

NOTE: The President spoke at 12:21 p.m. in the East Room at the White House before presenting diplomas to graduates of the Capitol Page School. In his opening words he referred to Dr. Henry L. DeKeyser, principal of the Capitol Page School.

Later he referred to former President Dwight D. Eisenhower, who was recuperating at Walter Reed Army Hospital from a heart attack suffered on April 29, William O. Douglas, Associate Justice of the Supreme Court, Senator Richard Russell of Georgia, Sam Rayburn, Representative from Texas

1913–1961, who served as Speaker of the House of Representatives 1940–1947, 1949–1953, 1955–1961, Ambassador at Large W. Averell Harriman and Cyrus R. Vance, U.S. negotiators at the Paris peace talks with North Vietnam, and Dean Rusk, Secretary of State.

During his remarks the President referred to the assassination of President John F. Kennedy on November 22, 1963, in Dallas, Texas.

302 Statement by the President on the Tie Vote on a Gun Control Bill in the House Judiciary Committee. *June 11, 1968*

THE DEADLOCK in the House Judiciary Committee, which resulted in the defeat of the strict gun control legislation I recommended yesterday, is a bitter disappointment to all Americans and to the President. There is no excuse whatsoever for failure to act to prohibit the interstate mail-order sale of rifles. Of the 2 million guns added each year to the arsenal already in the hands of millions of Americans, 1 million are sold by mail-order houses in interstate commerce. And 30 percent of the murders by firearms committed each year in this country are by rifle and shotgun fire.

I hope that the House Judiciary Committee will promptly reconsider this shocking blow to the safety of every citizen in this country.

NOTE: The Gun Control Act of 1968 was approved by the President on October 22, 1968 (see Item 553). The Omnibus Crime Control and Safe Streets Act of 1968, containing gun control provisions, was approved by the President on June 19, 1968 (see Item 320).

303 Message to the Congress Transmitting Annual Report on Federal Statutory Salary Systems. *June 11, 1968*

To the Congress of the United States:

I forward herewith the annual comparison of Federal salaries with the salaries paid in private enterprise, as provided by section 5302 of title 5, United States Code.

The report, prepared by the Director of the Bureau of the Budget and the Chairman of the Civil Service Commission, compares the present Federal statutory salary rates with average salary rates paid for the same levels of work in private enterprise as reported in the Bureau of Labor Statistics Bulletin No. 1585, *National Survey of Professional, Administrative, Technical, and Clerical Pay, June 1967.*

In addition, the report develops July 1968 adjustments in statutory salary schedules which the President is directed to make under section 212 of P.L. 90–206, the Federal Salary Act of 1967.

Also transmitted is a copy of an Executive order promulgating the adjustments of statutory salary rates to become effective on the first day of the first pay period beginning on or after July 1, 1968.

Public Law 90–206 provides that comparable adjustments shall be made by administrative action of appropriate officers, in the salary rates of employees of the judicial and legislative branches and those of Agricultural Stabilization and Conservation County Committee employees.

LYNDON B. JOHNSON

The White House

June 11, 1968

NOTE: The report is printed in House Document 327 (90th Cong., 2d sess.).

In the message the President referred to Executive Order 11413 "Adjusting Rates of Pay for Certain Statutory Schedules" (4 Weekly Comp. Pres. Docs., p. 944; 33 F.R. 8641; 3 CFR, 1968 Comp., p. 116) signed on June 11, 1968. On the same day the President also signed Executive Order 11414 "Adjusting the Rates of Monthly Basic Pay for Members of the Uniformed Services" (4 Weekly Comp. Pres. Docs., p. 946; 33 F.R. 8645; 3 CFR, 1968 Comp., p. 119).

304 Toasts of the President and the Shah of Iran. June 11, 1968

Your Imperial Majesty, our beloved Chief Justice, distinguished guests, ladies and gentlemen:

Your Majesty's visit tonight reminds me of how often we have gathered here in this room to welcome distinguished visitors from abroad. Personally, I find that one of the real pleasures of the Presidency—I might even say, one of the few pleasures.

I am told that this administration has actually set some kind of a record. We have welcomed almost 200 heads of state and chiefs of government to this house in the 5 years of the Presidency, and that has made everybody happy, including, of course, my economic advisers. They are so grateful for every little bit of help on the balance of payments problem that we can get.

I guess all of you know that I am not overly impressed by records or tallies such as head counts or rollcalls or polls. I don't know where I could have acquired such a reputation. I guess maybe I just read it somewhere.

But just the same, when I looked over the number of foreign visitors in my administration—almost 200 in less than 5 years—I just happened to notice, Your Majesty, a striking statistic. That comes out to an average of four-fifths of a potentate a week.

But, Your Majesty, we do not parcel out your welcome in fractions. We are so happy, Mrs. Johnson and I, to greet you tonight with the full measure of all of our respect as well as our deep affection.

We greet you as an old friend, not just an old friend of ours, but of the United States.

We regret only that His Majesty's lovely Empress is not with him this evening.

A poet once said that the best mirror is an old friend. Each time I talk with His Majesty I see the reflection of common values and a common desire to use the resources that God has given both of our countries and to use those resources for the benefit of both of our peoples.

Years ago, His Imperial Majesty determined to break the grip of poverty and disease and ignorance in his own ancient land. Now, in less than a decade, smallpox has been destroyed as a threat to the health of Iran. Ninety-five percent of the total population has been immunized. Malaria, which used to infect almost three of every four Iranian families, now infects fewer than one in 20.

Government expenditures for education have more than doubled in this decade. There are 400 new schools for nomad children alone, and seven of every 10 males of school age are literate. More than 2½ million tenant farmers have achieved the dignity of freeholders who own and who till their own land.

These great revolutionary reforms do not stand alone. They are great inspiration to others. They are part of a green revolution, a revolution of seed and fertilizer and agricultural credit and land reform and water which is taking place all over the world and which is a lasting and living tribute to such statesmen as our honored guest tonight.

In passing, I should like to pay tribute to another statesman who has helped both of us in this field and who helps us all around the world—Mr. David Lilienthal—who honors me by being at our table.

I knew that all of this would come about when I visited Iran in 1962 with Mrs. Johnson and we saw so clearly the deep commitment of this genuine, dedicated, sincere leader.

We here in America know that it is this kind of revolution which will ultimately really decide the fate of this world. We are so proud to have had a very little part in Iran's story through Mr. Lilienthal and through some of the people in our Government who have counseled with His Majesty.

But this story has been largely written, as such stories always are written, by great people with a courageous leader and with, most of all, the will—the will to help themselves.

It is such a pleasure to have all of you representing the farms, the labors, the industries, the church, and the educational institutions of this country, and the business world, the newspapers, to come here and join us in honoring this most distinguished citizen of the world.

I ask you, ladies and gentlemen, to join me in a toast to my friend and America's friend, His Imperial Majesty, the Shah of Iran.

NOTE: The President proposed the toast at 10:11 p.m. in the State Dining Room at the White House. In his opening words he referred to Mohammad Reza Pahlavi, Shah of Iran, and Earl Warren, Chief Justice of the United States. During his remarks he referred to David Lilienthal, chairman of the Development and Resources Corporation, an organization engaged in providing planning, managerial, and technical services throughout the world.

His Imperial Majesty responded as follows:

Mr. President, Mrs. Johnson, Your Excellencies, ladies and gentlemen:

I am happy indeed to have been able to be the guest of your great President tonight in less than 1 year's time. The President inferred that they have had so many guests—200 in 5 years' time—I hope I have not overdone my visits to your country.

I am very grateful to you, Mr. President, for the very kind words that you have had towards my country and what we are trying to do.

But before the first time you had visited our country we had read about you. We knew that you dedicated your life for the betterment of the condition of your people, especially the needy people of your country, and you had a very long record on that subject.

When my wife and I had the pleasure of knowing you and Mrs. Johnson personally, we immediately noticed that your past actions, your behavior, was not the behavior of someone who wants to create an image, but that was a behavior coming from your soul and your heart. That was the real person who was working and not a person who was acting.

May I say, Mr. President, that more than ever you have shown this disposition of yours during your Presidency. Every action that you have undertaken, every decision that you have made was according to your conscience and to the high responsibility of this high office that you are holding so valiantly and with such courage, dignity, and honor.

This is a sort of inspiration. I wish and I hope that many more people would do the same and be true to themselves, to their country, to their people, and do what they think is best for them.

So it is a moment of joy to see you and Mrs. Johnson again. I wish these meetings could be repeated many more times, and especially you know how welcome you and your family would be to come and see us, because we shall never forget your comprehension of our problems, the interest that you have shown as the great leader of a great country. We shall never forget the true friendship that your country has always extended to us since the day we started to have diplomatic relationships together. You have never failed us so far, and I am sure that you will never fail us, as you have never failed anybody, any people, any country.

I am glad and proud, Mr. President, that you count us among your friends and the friends of your country. We shall continue to be so because we believe in the same ideals as you do. We try to be worthy of ourselves, of our history, which is mainly based on the respect of the individual and of the human being. In wishing you, Mr. President and Mrs. Johnson, all the best, the fulfillment of your wishes, of your ideals, I would like to ask this distinguished audience to join me in a toast to the health of the President of the United States of America, and of Mrs. Johnson.

305   Remarks to Student Winners of a Contest Sponsored by the National Rural Electric Cooperative Association. *June 12, 1968*

Mr. Chairman, ladies and gentlemen, boys and girls:

I am happy that I can meet with you this morning here on the White House lawn. The White House is the symbol of what is good in the leadership of our country. I hope that every young man and woman will always feel thrilled to stand on the soil of the White House lawn in the shadow of this, the first house of the land.

I am particularly happy to welcome this group because of my years of association with the REA.

When I was your age, our job, our crusade, our revolution, was against the kerosene lamp and the lantern, and to light up the countryside and to bring power to rural America.

We have largely done that. In the 33 years since REA was formed by an Executive order of a daring President with great vision, you have done that job. Our rural people have made great progress—more progress than any other people anywhere in the world, more than your fathers made and more than your grandfathers made.

But just as you have come far, there is still a long way to go. If we are not to stand still, if we are not to be content with the status quo, if we are to dream dreams and make them come true, then you young people are going to have to get with it and stay with it and do something about it; call them as you see them and take an active part in making those dreams come true.

What should we dream?

First of all, I thought many years ago that it was important to reach down to the soil of America—back to the rural home, back to the countryside, back to the land—and give the young people who grow up there—without a polluted atmosphere or polluted water, where they can keep their cool without the roar of the streetcar or the bumpers hitting each other, where they could make judgments—give them an opportunity to provide leadership in government.

So I asked the REA to take on that task—not just to light up America, but to light up some young people and get them interested, bring them to Washington, let them serve as interns and work in Congressmen's offices and in Senators' offices and in executive department offices.

I went to Chicago to one of the REA conventions. And I proposed that program. It was adopted and a good many young men and women have come here and have made good. They have provided leadership. They have learned. They have taught.

They were poor people. They came from the rural countryside. They were not millionaires, but they had what it took. They have given a good accounting of themselves.

Thirty-three years ago I was working for a poverty program, a poor program, with rural people in Texas. It was called the National Youth Administration. We dealt with people your age. Those people worked for $10 and $12 a month. Just think of it. That is unbelievable, but that is what we paid them.

A year or so ago I went back to the place where I went to school when I was your age. We opened up a Job Corps camp to take care of some of the fine, young people of our country. We had a platform there that day and a lot of people sitting on it, as you have here today. We had the mayor, who was the presiding officer—they usually are, you know. He introduced the rest of us.

Then we had the Congressmen; then we had the chairman of the board of regents for all the State schools and colleges; then we had the Circuit Judge of the Fifth Circuit; then we had the Governor of the State; then we had the director of the poverty program, Sargent Shriver; then we had the President.

I looked back 35 years, and all of those individuals—the mayor, the Congressmen, the Federal Circuit Judge, the Governor of the State, the chairman of the college board of regents, Sargent Shriver, and the President of the United States—all worked for NYA and came out of that organization.

I would like to look back 30 years from now and see some Presidents, some Governors, some mayors, some Congressmen, and some Federal judges come out of the REA organization—these young people that they send to Washington.

You have your obligation to your parents, to your teachers, to your principals. But you also have a very strong, compelling obligation to your country.

If we are going to survive as a free nation; if we are going to have the liberty, independence, and freedom that we want; if we are going to have the opportunity, the prosperity, the jobs, the housing, and the beautification—all the things that we like and want—we are going to have to have, first, qualified leaders.

You can't find better talent to work on than you young people who come from rural America. Now, a good many of you are out in Vietnam. I went to the hospital yesterday where I saw boys from Kentucky, West Virginia, Oklahoma, Arizona, New York, and California who had left an arm or a leg in Vietnam so you would be free to come here this morning and examine what the President had to say and accept it or reject it; so you would be free to go into your classroom and listen to what they had to say and accept it or reject it; so you would have some independence. They had been there fighting for you.

Now, I don't know what you have been doing here for them. They have not asked you to parade much. They have not asked you to sing for them. Not many of them have asked you to even buy bonds to support them.

But you have an obligation to them and, most of all, to this country, the same as they do. You don't have to be in a uniform. You don't have to be drafted by your local draft board.

Every person born in this world not only has an obligation to their country; they have an obligation to themselves, and that is to justify their being here. We pay taxes every month in order that we can pay your teachers, in order that we can buy your books, in order that we can get you to and from school, in order that you can go to college.

As you receive much, you also must give much. You have to ask yourself this morning, "What am I giving to my country?"

I think you ought to give a part of your time, your talent, and your training, and learn how to be a public leader in a democracy. I think every person in this land ought to have some governmental responsibility sometime in his lifetime.

So I want to thank the REA for sponsoring a program that would interest young people in coming to their Capital where they can look out and see the Lincoln Memorial and review the critical period that Lincoln went through; where they can see the Washington Monument and remember what he sacrificed in order that you could be here; where they can look at that house and see all that has come and gone since the British burned it; and where, most of all, they can look at themselves and engage in a little introspection and go back home and say, "I do have an obligation to better humanity. I do have an obligation to make things better in this world, not to dream dreams that can never come true, but to dream dreams and then make them come true."

Young people have the energy. They have the vim, vigor, and vitality. They can if they will. The trouble is that some of you have just been too busy, interested in yourselves and looking after things at home, without really asking yourselves what obligations you have to your fellow man, what obligations you have to your country.

Well, I think that you are, in a way, meeting those obligations both to your fellow man and your country by coming here on this trip and learning something about your Government and learning something about public service.

And I hope when you go back that you will have a little more interest in government. When the election comes around—first of all, you ought to tell everybody you see that you think they ought to have a vote for 18-year-olds.

I have a daughter over there in the house who is a young mother. She hasn't been able to vote yet. But she has been a better qualified voter for 4 or 5 years than I was when I first

voted, because she learned more, she had better teachers, better training, and better opportunity. The young people of today do, too. They are capable, and if they have the responsibility, they will prepare themselves to vote.

I hope you will see who is running for mayor, who is running for Congress, who is running for Governor, who is running for the Senate, and who is running for President, and you will get active on whatever side your conscience tells you you ought to be on and do something about it.

Education is the guardian genius of democracy. If we are going to preserve this Government, and not allow it to decay, not allow it to be said of us some day—what they remind us of now, the glory that was Greece and the grandeur that was Rome—not have it said that America does not occupy the position a century from now that she occupies today, it is going to be because of what you do.

So I hope you do it. I hope you ask yourselves, while I am talking and when you leave here, what you can do to be a better citizen, what you can do to better humanity, what you can do to satisfy and discharge the obligation you owe your country.

You won't have to give it an arm or a leg, we hope. You won't have to go away in a foxhole and stay many months. You can do a lot of it right there at the general merchandise store, the gin, or by the cultivator, the baler, the dairy barn, or wherever you live, by taking an interest in what is happening in your own community, your own county, your own State, and your own Nation.

I expect every person here—and I think I can say this without violating the Hatch

Act; I am not a candidate for anything—
but I expect every person here who accepted
my invitation to come to the White House
this morning to do something about who
lives in that White House next year.

You say, "Okay, what do you expect me
to do?" I expect you to look at any and
all whom you think are qualified. Then use
your head and your heart. Select the person
who you think will best serve this wonderful land of ours, because we have so much
to preserve and so much to protect. There
is so much good about it and you just hear
about the bad things.

I want to do something about the bad

things instead of just talking about the bad
things. I want you to help me—won't you?

Thank you very much.

NOTE: The President spoke at 11:17 a.m. on the
South Lawn at the White House. His opening
words "Mr. Chairman" referred to Robert D.
Partridge, general manager of the National Rural
Electric Cooperative Association. During his remarks he referred to his daughter Mrs. Patrick J.
(Luci) Nugent, and R. Sargent Shriver, Director of
the Office of Economic Opportunity. The President
also referred to Executive Order 7037 "Establishment of the Rural Electrification Administration,"
signed by President Franklin D. Roosevelt on May 11,
1935.

The group was composed of about 800 high
school students, winners of an annual essay contest
sponsored by the association.

306   Special Message to the Congress Transmitting Report on New Urban Transportation Systems. *June 12, 1968*

To the Congress of the United States:

I am transmitting today a report on the
study of new systems for urban transportation, entitled *Tomorrow's Transportation.*

Undertaken by the Secretary of the Department of Housing and Urban Development in accordance with the Urban Mass
Transportation Amendments of 1966, the
study has involved research and analytic
effort by 17 contractors over a period of 18
months. It has explored areas of transportation research and development to ease the
problems of Americans who live in or com-
mute to work in cities.

The report identifies research and development which offers promising prospects for
transportation improvements in our cities
in the near future. It suggests a longer term
program of research and development, concentrated in areas of greatest promise and
benefit.

I commend the report for study by the

Congress and the concerned Federal, State
and local agencies. It provides a good foundation for decisions upon the program of research and development required to develop
the needed new systems of transportation for
our crowded metropolitan areas.

LYNDON B. JOHNSON

The White House
June 12, 1968

NOTE: The report is entitled "Tomorrow's Transportation: New Systems for the Urban Future"
(Government Printing Office, 100 pp.).

A White House press release issued on June 12
stated that the report discussed new transportation
systems for meeting the needs of the urban traveler
and improved methods of urban transit management.
The release also listed possible transportation systems
of the future as well as areas of transportation research and development to be studied. The full text
of the release is printed in the Weekly Compilation
of Presidential Documents (vol. 4, p. 952).

The Urban Mass Transportation Amendments of
1966 was approved by the President on September 8,
1966 (Public Law 89–562, 80 Stat. 715).

307   Joint Statement Following Discussions With the Shah of Iran. *June 12, 1968*

THE SHAHANSHAH and the President met on June 12 and discussed topics of mutual interest to their two countries. Their talks were conducted in the spirit of close friendship and cooperation that marks Iranian-US relations and the personal associations of His Majesty and the President. The President congratulated the Shahanshah on the continuing impressive pace of Iran's economic and social development.

The President informed His Majesty of the course of talks now occurring in Paris, and both leaders expressed hope that these discussions would lead to an early and durable peace in Southeast Asia.

They discussed the situation in the Middle East and agreed that the peaceful development of the area could be accomplished only through respect for the sovereignty of Middle Eastern states and cooperation among the states of the region for their security and independence. Both leaders expressed their intention of continuing to support efforts made through the United Nations to reduce tensions in the area, reaffirming their support for a just and lasting peace based on the resolution adopted by the Security Council of the United Nations on November 22, 1967.

The Shahanshah reaffirmed Iran's determination to sustain an adequate modern defense force to ensure Iran's national security, and the President expressed the desire of the United States to continue cooperating with Iran to this end.

Of special interest to the Shahanshah and the President was a recent exchange of letters between the two governments in which it was agreed to initiate a program of scientific cooperation in areas of mutual interest. This program is expected to increase the exchange of personnel between the two countries, facilitate the transfer of scientific and technical information and stimulate collaborative research projects between Iranian and American scientists. It was decided that in Iran the Executive agency for implementation of this agreement will be the Ministry of Science and Higher Education, and for the United States the Smithsonian Institution.

His Majesty expressed to the President his profound sorrow over the death of Senator Robert F. Kennedy.

The Shahanshah in taking leave of the President expressed his appreciation for the warm and friendly reception accorded him. Both the Shahanshah and the President agreed that the considerations which have motivated Iranian and American cooperation are today more pertinent than ever.

308   Remarks Before the U.N. General Assembly Following Its Endorsement of the Nuclear Nonproliferation Treaty. *June 12, 1968*

Mr. President, Mr. Secretary General, Your Excellencies, delegates to the General Assembly:

I have asked for the privilege of address-

ing you this afternoon

—to acknowledge this momentous event in the history of nations; and

—to pledge, on behalf of the United States,

our determination to make this but a first step toward ending the peril of nuclear war.

Four and a half years ago, shortly after the awesome responsibility of leadership was thrust into my hands, I instructed our negotiators at Geneva to seek a treaty to prevent the spread of nuclear weapons.

I recalled the modest and mutual reductions in arms spending that had been achieved by the United States and the Soviet Union. And I said then, "Let us pray that the tide has turned—that further and far-reaching agreements lie ahead—and that future generations will mark 1964 as the year the world turned for all time away from the horrors of war and constructed new bulwarks for peace."

Four and a half years of patient and painstaking negotiations in Geneva—and of further debate and refinement here in the United Nations—were to follow. Now, at last, the work of many governments has become one instrument of international peace and sanity. The hands of many peoples have written a testament to reason—and to the will of mankind to endure.

The resolution that you have just approved commends to the governments of the world for their speedy ratification the treaty for the nonproliferation of nuclear weapons.

It is the most important international agreement in the field of disarmament since the nuclear age began.

It goes far to prevent the spread of nuclear weapons.

It commits the nuclear powers to redouble their efforts to end the nuclear arms race and to achieve nuclear disarmament.

It will insure the equitable sharing of the peaceful uses of nuclear energy—under effective safeguards—for the benefit of all nations.

On behalf of the Government and the people of the United States, let me congratulate all who have contributed to this historic event.

But we should not linger long in mutual congratulations. The quest—and the need—for disarmament is too urgent for that.

Many further steps are needed if this treaty is to fulfill its great purposes, and if we are to move beyond it toward the ultimate goal that we all seek—peace in the world.

As regards the treaty itself, no time should be lost in bringing it into force. I pledge you this afternoon that we of the United States will move rapidly

—to open the treaty for signature,
—to sign it on behalf of our own Government, and
—to seek its prompt ratification in accordance with our Constitution.

We shall urge other nations to complete their ratification speedily so that the treaty can enter into force at the earliest possible date.

I further pledge that, as soon as the treaty has entered into force, we of the United States will carry out our responsibilities under it—in full measure.

First, we shall fully and scrupulously discharge our obligations as a nuclear-weapon party:

—not to transfer nuclear weapons, or control over them, to any recipient whatsoever; and
—not to help any nonnuclear state acquire such weapons.

Second, we shall cooperate fully in bringing the treaty's safeguards into being—safeguards that will prevent the diversion of nuclear energy from peaceful uses to weapons.

Third, we shall, as the treaty requires, facilitate the fullest possible exchange of equipment, materials, scientific and technical information for the peaceful uses of nuclear energy. We shall give particular attention to the needs of the developing nations.

We shall share our technical knowledge and experience in peaceful nuclear research fully, and we shall share it without reservation. This will include very important new developments in electrical power generation, agriculture, medicine, industry, and in the desalting of sea water.

Fourth, we shall continue our research and development into the use of nuclear explosions for peaceful purposes. We shall make available to the nonnuclear treaty partners—without delay, and under the treaty's provisions—the benefits of such explosions.

Finally—in keeping with our obligations under the treaty—we shall, as a major nuclear-weapon power, promptly and vigorously pursue negotiations on effective measures to halt the nuclear arms race and to reduce existing nuclear arsenals.

It is right that we should be so obligated. The nonnuclear states—who undertake with this treaty to forgo nuclear weapons—are entitled to the assurance that powers possessing them, particularly the United States and the Soviet Union, will lose no time in finding the way to scale down the nuclear arms race.

We desire—yes, we urgently desire—to begin early discussions on the limitation of strategic offensive and defensive nuclear weapons systems.

We shall search for an agreement that will not only avoid another costly and futile escalation of the arms race, but will de-escalate it.

I believe that this treaty can lead to further measures that will inhibit the senseless continuation of the arms race. I believe that it can give the world time—very precious time—to protect itself against Armageddon.

If my faith is well founded, as I believe that it is, then this treaty will truly deserve to be recorded as the most important step toward peace since the founding of the United Nations.

Further, the nonproliferation treaty will serve not only as a deterrent to the spread of nuclear weapons, but also as a powerful stimulus for the peaceful use of the atom.

When this treaty comes into force, the growing number of nuclear-power reactors around the world—with their inevitable by-product of plutonium—need no longer cause anxiety as potential sources of nuclear weapons material. Under the safeguards of the treaty, those reactors will be pledged and will be guaranteed as peaceful sources of energy—as vital instruments of growth and development.

My fellow citizens of the world, what we have achieved here today few men would have dared to even hope for a decade ago.

Nations that were long beset by differences have—in this great treaty—found common ground in their need to use the incredible force of the atom for peace, and not for war.

From this ground that we have won here together, then let us press forward

—to halt and to reverse the buildup of nuclear arsenals;

—to find new ways to eliminate the threat of conventional conflicts that might grow into nuclear disaster.

In the name of our common humanity, let us insure our survival—so that we may achieve our high destiny on earth. Let us work for the ultimate self-interest of mankind: for that peace in which future generations may build a world without fear, and without want—a world that is fit for the sons of man.

In closing, Mr. President, permit me to pay my cordial respects to you. In your conduct of the affairs of this Assembly, Mr.

President, you have won new honors for your country and for yourself.

Mr. Secretary General, we of the United States are very grateful for your contributions to the United Nations and to its universal goals of peace.

To all of the delegates here assembled, to all of you who have labored hard and fruitfully throughout this historic session, we extend our sincere good wishes; and to those who are about to leave our shores, we bid each of you Godspeed and a safe and pleasant journey home.

Thank you.

NOTE: The President spoke at 5:09 p.m. at the United Nations General Assembly in New York City shortly after the General Assembly voted 95 to 4, with 21 abstentions, in support of the Nuclear Nonproliferation Treaty. In his opening words the President referred to the President of the General Assembly, Corneliu Manescu of Romania, and Secretary General U Thant.

The Nuclear Nonproliferation Treaty was signed on July 1, 1968, by representatives of 56 nations (see Item 349).

309 Remarks at the Ratification Ceremony for the Consular Convention Between the United States and the Soviet Union. *June 13, 1968*

Mr. Ambassador, Secretary Rusk, Members of Congress, distinguished guests:

The treaty we proclaim today is historic. It is the first bilateral treaty between the Soviet Union and the United States. When we entered into diplomatic relations 35 years ago, we agreed on the need for such a treaty. Now we have succeeded in concluding it.

The intervening years have been filled with momentous events. Both of our nations, I think, have made very great progress. During these years, we have been joined together in war, and we have been separated in uneasy and partial peace.

There are still many problems that we have not solved—for which our two countries bear a very heavy responsibility. Some of them remain dangerous.

Nevertheless—if there is the will on both sides—I am convinced that we can move forward to overcome these animosities and suspicions, and the difficulties which have clouded our relations during the past quarter of a century—and which, unfortunately, still cloud them.

The consular convention between the United States and the Soviet Union provides for the performance of consular functions in both countries to facilitate commerce between these two countries. The convention provides also for the protection of the citizens of each country when they are present in the territory of the other. This treaty will promote and encourage normal contacts between the two countries and their citizens.

As reference has already been made yesterday, I was very proud to participate in the overwhelming approval of the nonproliferation treaty by the United Nations. There our two countries have been able to work together and, with the other nations of the world, achieve a new kind of victory—for mankind, for peace, and for the control of arms.

We shall soon act on still another front. Within the next few days, I plan to send the astronaut assistance and return agreement to the Senate for their consideration. This agreement and the outer space treaty represent the first two steps in man's effort to bring the rule of law and the pledge of cooperation to the cosmos. We are grateful to all the nations which have contributed so much to these agreements.

Let us be clear. We still have deep and dangerous differences on certain issues with the Soviet Union. But the peace of the world is too important to let these differences prevent us from exploring every avenue to a more peaceful relationship and to a more cooperative world.

The United States and the Soviet Union have enormous power—and, therefore, they have very great responsibility.

—We must come to grips constructively with these issues which still divide us.

—We must move in parallel where our vital interests permit it.

—We must work together wherever and whenever we can.

We can hope that this treaty between the Soviet Union and the United States will be a sign for the future. It could help to establish a pattern of progress—in disarmament, in space, in science, in the arts, and—I hope—ultimately in a broadening area of politics.

At the end of that road is the welfare and the prosperity of 450 million Russians and Americans—and more than 3½ billion citizens of the community that we call the world.

NOTE: The President spoke at 11:50 a.m. in the East Room at the White House. In his opening words he referred to Anatoly F. Dobrynin, Soviet Ambassador to the United States, and Dean Rusk, Secretary of State, both of whom signed for their respective countries.

The treaty was favorably considered by the Senate on March 16, 1967, was proclaimed by the President on June 13, 1968, and entered into force on July 13, 1968. The text of the treaty is printed in the Department of State Bulletin (vol. 50, p. 979) and in Treaties and Other International Acts Series (TIAS 6503).

310 Remarks Upon Accepting the "Swords Into Plowshares" Award. *June 13, 1968*

Mr. Roboff, Dr. Seaborg, distinguished guests:

It gives me great pleasure to receive this award today, as it gave me great pleasure yesterday to appear at the United Nations and make the statement that it was possible to make.

It had been almost 5 years since the nonproliferation treaty was little more than a dream, when I first asked our people to try to begin work that finally resulted in the action that the General Assembly of the United Nations took.

In my judgment, a century from now those who write of today will conclude that this is one of the most, if not the most important agreement and understanding that the nations reached with each other during this period of our history.

I am very grateful for the time, thought, and purpose that went into your effort here today.

I shall treasure this award and try to keep it on display with some of the other mementos that I have collected in the Presidency, so that future generations may be inspired by the good cause which it serves.

I am convinced that all of the 3½ billion people of the world want peace more than they want anything else. I believe that while it still appears to us to be quite elusive, each day we are making progress in that direction.

Thanks to all of you who contribute so much of your talent and dedication to that end.

NOTE: The President spoke at 1:20 p.m. in the Cabinet Room at the White House upon receiving the "Swords into Plowshares" Award. In his opening words he referred to Stanley B. Roboff, President and Chairman of Nuclear Week in New York, Inc., and Glenn T. Seaborg, Chairman of the Atomic Energy Commission.

Mr. Roboff presented the award in recognition of the President's leadership in sponsoring the Nuclear

Nonproliferation Treaty which was signed on July 1, 1968, by representatives of 56 nations (see Item 349).

According to a White House press release issued on June 13, the award consisted of a 22-inch statue of the Biblical prophet Isaiah, holding aloft a broken sword (4 Weekly Comp. Pres. Docs., p. 958).

311   Message to the Congress Transmitting Annual Report on the National Wilderness Preservation System. *June 14, 1968*

To the Congress of the United States:

I am pleased to transmit the fourth annual report on the status of the National Wilderness Preservation System, covering the year 1967.

The Federal Government continues to carry on programs to preserve the natural beauty of our land and make outdoor recreation facilities available to all our citizens. We must also preserve, for use by this and future generations, some of the America that tempered and formed our national character.

—An America with undisturbed mountains and plains, forests, and valleys.

—An America with placid lakes and lonely shores which will not be dominated by man and his technology.

—An America where a man can be alone with all the glories of nature, and can renew his spirit in solitary communion with the land.

This was the reason for the Wilderness Act.

And this is the reason why we shall not be

content until we have a National Wilderness Preservation System adequately symbolic of our great national heritage.

To pursue this goal, I recently transmitted to the Congress 26 recommended additions to the National Wilderness Preservation System. I urge that the Congress take early and favorable action on them.

Each generation has its own rendezvous with the land. May ours be one that understands the heritage of America, that passes it on for the welfare and enjoyment of future generations.

LYNDON B. JOHNSON

The White House
June 14, 1968

NOTE: The 21-page report is entitled "Fourth Joint Annual Report of the Secretaries of Agriculture and Interior Concerning the Status of the National Wilderness Preservation System, Prepared in Accordance With Section 7 of the Wilderness Act, P.L. 88–577, dated September 3, 1964."

For the President's recommendation to Congress of 26 additions to the National Wilderness Preservation System, see Item 168.

312   Message to the Congress Transmitting Annual Report of the National Advisory Council on Extension and Continuing Education. *June 17, 1968*

To the Congress of the United States:

I am pleased to transmit the Second Annual Report of the National Advisory Council on Extension and Continuing Education.

In the second year of community service and continuing education programs under the Higher Education Act of 1965, 314 colleges and universities conducted more than 600 programs in 53 states and territories. Seminars, workshops, conferences, special courses, counseling, and consultative services were sponsored throughout the country to help in meeting the complex task of improving the quality of life in our communities. The programs were designed to find new answers and to bring new skills and energies to bear on the broad spectrum of community problems—in government, education, health, manpower, housing and other areas.

Nearly half of the 425,000 participants in continuing education and community service programs were employees of state and local governments and other public bodies. The others represented a wide variety of occupations and professions, ranging from workers in private social welfare agencies to owners of small businesses. Each of these participants has gained increased knowledge of the dimensions of the community problems and acquired new skills to cope with them.

Last year, after consultation with the Council, the Administration developed and submitted legislation to the Congress to improve our Continuing Education programs

under the Higher Education Act by:
—Extending the program for another five years.
—Enabling smaller colleges and universities to continue to participate.
—Providing additional funds for experimental projects.

This year, the Administration has added to the still-pending legislation a number of the suggestions made by the Council in this report, including the vital recommendation that appropriations be provided in advance of the academic year during which they will be used.

I commend this report to your attention and urge prompt action on the pending legislation to improve the important program.

LYNDON B. JOHNSON

The White House
June 17, 1968

NOTE: The Council was established by Title I of the Higher Education Act of 1965 (Public Law 89–329, 79 Stat. 1219).

Its report is entitled "Second Annual Report of the National Advisory Council on Extension and Continuing Education Presented to the President of the United States and the Secretary of Health, Education, and Welfare, March 31, 1968" (42 pp., processed).

313 Message to Chancellor Kiesinger on the Situation in Berlin. June 17, 1968

My dear Mr. Chancellor:

It is a matter of great regret to me that while the Federal Republic and we are pursuing objectives that I believe all mankind shares, namely to live in peace with our neighbors, Berlin is once again threatened.

Our government and yours, along with the British and French, are consulting on this latest totally unprovoked and unjustified aggravation of the situation. I want to ex-

press to you on this "Day of German Unity" that our support of free Berlin and the goal of a German people united in peace remains as firm as ever.

Sincerely,

LYNDON B. JOHNSON

[The Honorable Kurt Georg Kiesinger, Chancellor of the Federal Republic of Germany]

NOTE: On June 11, 1968, as reported in the press, new travel regulations were imposed by East Germany on routes to West Berlin, including a visa and passport requirement, a higher transport fee for use of the autobahn, and a surtax on freight carried through East Germany by West German carriers.

The message was released at Austin, Texas.

314 Statement by the President on Signing Bills Amending the Federal Voting Assistance Act of 1955. *June 18, 1968*

TODAY I am signing two bills designed to extend the voting franchise for overseas American citizens.

Both of these bills—S. 1581 and S. 2884—are amendments to the Federal Voting Assistance Act of 1955. That act is a purely hortatory statute that encourages the States to provide absentee ballot facilities for the following four categories of voters and their spouses and dependents:

—members of the Armed Forces,

—members of the Merchant Marine,

—overseas civilian employees of the Government,

—members of religious or welfare groups assisting servicemen.

The provisions of the Voting Assistance Act apply to all elections—Federal, State, or local. Under it, the States are encouraged to provide a simplified system of absentee registration and voting, including uniform procedures for ballot applications and adequate time for ballots to be transmitted. To expedite the ballot applications, the act provides for a standard Federal postcard application form, with free airmail handling. To prevent fraud, the application requires a sworn statement giving the identity and domestic address of the applicant, as well as a sworn statement that the applicant is not voting elsewhere.

The first bill that I am signing today—S. 1581—amends the Voting Assistance Act to encourage the States to allow members of the Armed Forces and their dependents residing on military reservations to register

and vote in the State where the reservation is located. At the present time, all but three of the States refuse to allow such military personnel to vote as residents of the State.

In addition, S. 1581 urges the States to authorize certain overseas Federal officials to administer oaths in connection with the absentee registration and voting requirements of State law. At the present time, only a narrow category of Federal officials is authorized to administer such oaths under the Voting Assistance Act. As a result, an official authorized to administer the oath is frequently inaccessible to overseas employees of the Government, especially employees who are assigned in relatively small groups to isolated areas. For example, Mr. Vaughn, the Director of the Peace Corps, has informed me that a major obstacle to voting by Peace Corps trainees and volunteers is their inability to obtain access to an officer authorized to administer oaths for their ballot applications.

The second bill that I am signing today—S. 2884—extends the benefits of the Voting Assistance Act to all citizens of the United States temporarily residing outside the country. The benefits of the Act are, of course, already available to overseas employees of the Government. S. 2884 would make these benefits available to all overseas Americans, whether or not employed by the Government. The amendment is thus a modest step toward enfranchising thousands of Americans engaged in business, teaching, and other activities abroad.

As is true of the existing provisions of the Voting Assistance Act, the amendments made by the two bills that I am signing today are merely recommendations to the States, and the States are under no obligation to accept them.

Although I welcome the opportunity to sign these measures into law, I regret that the Congress has not yet seen fit to act on the Residency Voting Act, which I submitted to the Congress more than a year ago on behalf of the administration. I proposed the Residency Voting Act in order to eliminate the arbitrary disfranchisements imposed on American citizens residing within the United States itself. In every presidential election year in the United States, millions of Americans are unable to vote for their President because of the arbitrary and unreasonable residence requirements operating in the 50 States. Since the provisions of the Residency Voting Act would apply only in the case of presidential elections, the bill would not infringe any legitimate interest of any State.

An analysis of the 1960 presidential election, the most recent election year for which reliable figures are available, indicates that between 5 and 8 million Americans were disfranchised because they moved their residence from one State to another, or even, in many cases, simply from one county to another. The only fault of these citizens is the exercise of their constitutionally protected right to travel freely within the United States—to pull up stakes and seek a new life.

The bills that I sign today, although significant in terms of overseas American voters, do not reach the plight of our disfranchised voters here at home. I urge the Congress to recognize the grave injustice in depriving these citizens of the precious right to vote— the right that is preservative of all other rights in our society. I urge the Congress to act in this session on the Residency Voting Act.

NOTE: As enacted, S. 1581 is Public Law 90–344 (82 Stat. 181) and S. 2884 is Public Law 90–343 (82 Stat. 180).

315 Message to the Congress Transmitting First Report of the National Advisory Council on Economic Opportunity. *June 18, 1968*

To the Congress of the United States:

America's War on Poverty is fought on many fronts, with many weapons. Dozens of programs span the entire spectrum of human need. They range from increased social security benefits to financial aid for slum schools; from medical care for the poor and aged to a higher minimum wage for the Nation's workers.

In their varying ways, all these programs have helped to improve the conditions of life for millions of Americans in the past five years.

With the Economic Opportunity Act of 1964, the Nation mapped a concentrated poverty-fighting strategy around two basic concepts.

The first was that assistance to the poor would be most meaningful in the form of expanded opportunities—in jobs, education and training. Consequently, the programs of the Office of Economic Opportunity are designed to help a man increase his skill and earning power, and broaden his opportunity to participate in the mainstream of the country's economic and social life.

The second concept was that poverty can ultimately be defeated only by action at the local level—in the cities and towns and rural areas where it holds a paralyzing grip on people's lives. Programs and guidelines can be drawn up and administered in Washington and in regional and State headquarters. But their effectiveness depends on how they turn to action in the neighborhoods where the poor live.

This is the concept of Community Action. In principle, it means that the citizens of a community—government officials, welfare and other agency representatives, and members of the poor themselves plan and carry out comprehensive attacks on the causes and conditions of poverty in their area, tailoring a wide variety of special programs to the particular needs of that community.

The National Advisory Council on Economic Opportunity which the Congress established to review the operation of programs under the Economic Opportunity Act, focused its attention in its first year primarily on Community Action as an instrument to combat poverty. In its first report, which I am transmitting to the Congress today, the Council documents the effect of Community Action in practice.

The report tells what the anti-poverty program has meant to a Mexican American migrant worker who lived with his wife and eight children in a shack in Visalia, California. When he could find work, he earned less than $2,200 a year. When he could not, his family existed on welfare.

He had never gone beyond grade school. But when an adult education course was made available—through a Community Action Program—he enrolled, and earned the equivalent of a high school diploma.

He then signed up for another program and received on-the-job training as a butcher. Through still other programs he was able to get a low-interest loan for a decent home—and learn enough construction skills to help build the house himself and thus provide his equity with his own labor.

Locally organized counselling services gave him his first guidance in how to budget his newly earned income, pay his debts, and start a savings account.

The effect on that man's life is nothing less than a shattering of the pattern of poverty and failure in which he and his children were born.

Not all the stories of success through these programs are as complete. For the great work we have undertaken to banish poverty from America must proceed against stubborn problems of long entrenchment.

But the great story of our day is that we *are* moving. The heartening success which has transformed the life of a migrant worker in Visalia is quietly reflected—at least in part—in the lives of millions of men and women and youngsters across this land.

Today there are about 1,000 Community Action Agencies operating in every part of the United States.

City and county government officials, school officers, health and welfare councils, and federally financed agencies are working with the poor for the first time to attack the roots of poverty. Neighborhood centers are being established and strengthened to provide greater access to social, health, welfare and other public services for those who need them most.

However difficult these accomplishments are to measure statistically, they have had great impact in terms of new hope, an increased sense of citizenship, and better days in the minds and the lives of many poor citizens.

I think it is vitally important that the American public understand what these programs have done and can yet do to break the cycle of poverty.

This report will contribute to that understanding. I am pleased to commend it to the attention of the Congress.

LYNDON B. JOHNSON

The White House
June 18, 1968

NOTE: The report is entitled "Focus on Community Action: Report of the National Advisory Council on Economic Opportunity, March 1968" (Government Printing Office, 57 pp.).

The National Advisory Council on Economic Opportunity was established on November 8, 1966, by Title VI of the Economic Opportunity Amendments of 1966 (Public Law 89–794, 80 Stat. 1451).

316 Statement by the President Following Senate Subcommittee Approval of the Gun Control Bill. *June 18, 1968*

I AM delighted at the action of the Juvenile Delinquency Subcommittee of the Senate Judiciary Committee in reporting out the gun control bill I recommended to the Congress last week. I urge the full committee promptly to approve the action of its subcommittee and send the bill to the Senate floor for immediate consideration. Americans should not have to wait any longer for a strict gun control law. The time for action is now. We must give our people the protection they deserve from lethal rifles and shotguns as soon as possible.

NOTE: The Gun Control Act of 1968 was approved by the President on October 22, 1968 (see Item 553).

317 Remarks Upon Signing the Special Drawing Rights Act. *June 19, 1968*

Secretary Fowler, Chairman Martin, Members of Congress, ladies and gentlemen:

Seven weeks ago I asked the Congress to approve an amendment to the International Monetary Fund Agreement which provided for the creation of a new form of international reserves—the Special Drawing Rights.

Today we meet here to sign this historic bill into law. I think it is quite fitting that the United States should be among the first nations to approve this measure, and thereby cast its vote for a stronger world economy.

For the first time in the world's financial history, nations will be able to create international reserves by deliberate and joint decision—and in amounts needed to support sound growth in world trade and payments.

Pessimists doubted that a meaningful international agreement could be reached in this complicated and sensitive area. But they were wrong.

The creation of these new reserve assets will take place within the framework of the International Monetary Fund. This remarkably successful institution has been at the center of the international monetary system since the end of World War II. Its importance to the world economy has been demonstrated over the years.

The new Special Drawing Rights will be a logical extension of the Bretton Woods agreements that fathered the International

Monetary Fund and our present international financial machinery. By working together, the member nations of the Fund have demonstrated that they can adapt this machinery to current needs.

We and the other member nations of the Fund have chosen the evolutionary approach—building on existing foundations to meet present and future needs. This is not an emergency action—but it will help prevent future emergencies.

Our experience shows that sustained growth in the world economy requires orderly growth in international reserves. Special Drawing Rights, we believe, will meet this need.

I am very proud that this administration played a major role in the long negotiations that led to this agreement. Farsighted congressional leaders of both parties backed our efforts and developed guidelines for our negotiations. Key figures in the banking, financial, and academic world, under the leadership of the distinguished former Secretary of the Treasury, Honorable Douglas Dillon,[1] gave their support and their wise counsel.

For Secretary Fowler, Chairman Martin, Under Secretary Deming, and Governor Daane—as well as for those of you who worked closely with them—this has been a very long and a very difficult journey. You have returned not with a pot of gold, but with something better.

We can all take great satisfaction in this accomplishment. We are proving here again—as we must prove, and continue to prove in the future—that by all of us working together, nations can deal with a common problem in the common interest.

I notice Chairman Patman and Mr. Widnall in the back of the room. If you would come over and join us, we would appreciate it very much.

In concluding, I would just like to pay a very special recognition to the most indefatigable, determined, conscientious, genuine public servant that I have been associated with in all of my years here—in the most complicated business, whether it is drawing rights, whether it is fiscal problems, whether it is international agreements, whether it is monetary policies, whether it is tax bills, whether it is economic issues.

There has been no person that I know of who has contributed more or deserved more credit than the brilliant, prudent, wise Secretary of the Treasury, Henry Fowler.

He never asks for credit. He never seeks the limelight. But he always delivers the goods. I want to personally recognize him and thank him for his service not only to this administration, but every administration since I have been in Washington. He has always put the Nation's interest above his own personal affairs.

NOTE: The President spoke at 11:55 a.m. in the Fish Room at the White House. In his opening words he referred to Henry H. Fowler, Secretary of the Treasury, and William McC. Martin, Jr., Chairman of the Board of Governors of the Federal Reserve System. During his remarks he referred to among others, Frederick L. Deming, Under Secretary of the Treasury for Monetary Affairs, J. Dewey Daane, member of the Board of Governors of the Federal Reserve System, Representative Wright Patman of Texas, Chairman of the House Banking and Currency Committee, and Representative William B. Widnall of New Jersey, member of the House Banking and Currency Committee.

As enacted, the bill (H.R. 16911) is Public Law 90-349 (82 Stat. 188).

[1] 1961-1965.

318 Presidential Unit Citation Awarded the 11th Tactical Reconnaissance Squadron, Pacific Air Forces. *June 19, 1968*

CITATION TO ACCOMPANY THE AWARD OF
THE PRESIDENTIAL UNIT CITATION
TO THE
11TH TACTICAL RECONNAISSANCE SQUADRON

The 11th Tactical Reconnaissance Squadron, Pacific Air Forces, distinguished itself by extraordinary gallantry in connection with military operations against an opposing armed force in Southeast Asia, from 26 July 1966 to 31 March 1967. During this period, the 11th Tactical Reconnaissance Squadron was responsible for providing the major portion of all daylight tactical reconnaissance and all night tactical reconnaissance over North Vietnam. Although operating under extremely difficult and dangerous conditions of an enemy air defense system that was expanding daily and becoming more complex and deadly, aircrews of the 11th Tactical Reconnaissance Squadron accomplished their arduous missions in an outstanding manner. Their exemplary performance contributed significantly to the success of the United States Air Force's tactical reconnaissance program in North Vietnam. The extraordinary heroism and outstanding combat professionalism consistently displayed by the Unit's aircrews were matched by similarly superb efforts from the Squadron's maintenance and support personnel. By their gallantry, professionalism and untiring devotion to duty, personnel of the 11th Tactical Reconnaissance Squadron upheld the highest standards of performance and traditions of the military service and reflected great credit upon themselves and the United States Air Force.

LYNDON B. JOHNSON

319 Statement by the President Following House Committee Action on the Housing Bill. *June 19, 1968*

I APPLAUD the action of the House Committee on Banking and Currency today in reporting out the most far-reaching and comprehensive housing bill in the Nation's history.

This measure is a triumph for all the American people.

I hope this measure will be scheduled for full House debate at the earliest possible date.

For with the enactment of the legislation I recommended in February, this Nation can begin a massive program to build 6 million housing units for low and middle income families. This bill alone authorizes the expenditure of more than $5 billion. It authorizes a rate of housing production more than 10 times greater than any other housing bill in our history.

NOTE: The Housing and Urban Development Act of 1968 was approved by the President on August 1, 1968 (see Item 426).

320   Statement by the President Upon Signing the Omnibus Crime Control and Safe Streets Act of 1968. *June* 19, 1968

THE Safe Streets and Crime Control Act of 1968 has had a long journey.

The work behind the principal title of the act began in July 1965 when I appointed the national crime commission. The work of the Congress started more than 16 months ago, in February 1967, when I called upon it to strike a sure and swift blow against crime in America.

Now, almost 500 days later, the legislative process has run its full course. The measure before me carries out many of the objectives I sought. But it also contains several other provisions which are unwise and which will not aid effective law enforcement.

Over the past 10 days, I have given full consideration to this intricate, 110-page bill. I have carefully weighed the good features against the undesirable, the questions of law and policy it raises against the remedial actions I might take to resolve those questions, the immediate crisis of local law enforcement against the bill's response.

My decision has been made only after consulting with the wisest counselors available to the President. I have asked 11 Government departments and agency heads, including those most affected, such as the Attorney General, the Director of the Federal Bureau of Investigation, the Secretary of the Treasury, the Chairman of the Federal Communications Commission, and the Mayor of the District of Columbia, for their views. No department has recommended veto. On the basis of their advice and my own searching examination, I have decided that this measure contains more good than bad and that I should sign it into law.

I sign the bill because it responds to one of the most urgent problems in America today—the problem of fighting crime in the local neighborhood and on the city street.

The program I recommended 16 months ago—the Safe Streets Act—is the heart of this measure.

My program was based on the most exhaustive study of crime ever undertaken in America—the work of the President's national crime commission. The commission—composed of the Nation's leading criminologists, police chiefs, educators, and urban experts—spotlighted the weaknesses in our present system of law enforcement. It concluded that the States and local communities need large-scale Federal financial assistance to help them plan, organize, and mount a concerted and effective attack on crime.

The bill I sign today provides much of that urgently needed assistance. It will give help to the ill-equipped and poorly-trained policeman on the beat, to the overburdened courtroom, to the antiquated correctional institution. The legislation honors the deeply rooted principle that the Federal Government should supplement—but never supplant—local efforts and local responsibility to prevent and control crime.

This measure moves in new directions to fight crime by:

—Authorizing $400 million in Federal grants over a 2-year period for planning and launching action programs to strengthen the sinews of local law enforcement—from police to prisons to parole.

—Creating a National Institute of Law Enforcement and Criminal Justice to begin a modern research and development venture which will put science and the laboratory to work in the detection of criminals and the prevention of crime.

—Establishing a pioneering aid-to-education program of forgivable college loans and tuition grants to attract better law enforcement officers and give them better education and preparation.

—Providing greatly expanded training for State and local police officers at the National Academy of the Federal Bureau of Investigation.

—Permitting Federal funds to be used to supplement police salaries and to encourage the specialized training of community service officers whose mission will be to ease tensions in ghetto neighborhoods.

These are among the prime advantages of this bill I sign today.

The measure also ends three decades of inaction on the problem of gun controls. Interstate traffic in handguns and their sales to minors will now be prohibited by law. The majority of all the murders by firearms in this Nation are committed by these small but deadly weapons.

But as I have told the Nation and the Congress repeatedly, this is only a halfway step toward the protection of our families and homes. We must go further and stop mail-order murder by rifle and shotgun. We must close a glaring loophole in the law by controlling the sale of these lethal weapons, as well as the sale of ammunition for all guns.

A week ago I submitted my proposal for more stringent safeguards. I asked, as I had before, "What in the name of conscience will it take to pass a truly effective gun control law?"

In the next few days, the Congress has the opportunity to answer that question. The call for action is compelling. We dare delay no longer. I urge the Congress to act on this bill immediately. I am asking the Attorney General to explore what further steps should be taken in the gun control area so that I may recommend them when the Congress has acted on the legislation I submitted last week.

Title III of this legislation deals with wiretapping and eavesdropping.

My views on this subject are clear. In a special message to Congress in 1967 and again this year, I called—in the Right of Privacy Act—for an end to the bugging and snooping that invade the privacy of citizens.

I urge that the Congress outlaw "all wiretapping and electronic eavesdropping, public and private, wherever and whenever it occurs." The only exceptions would be those instances where "the security of the Nation itself was at stake—and then only under the strictest safeguards."

In the bill I sign today, Congress has moved part of the way by

—banning all wiretapping and eavesdropping by private parties;

—prohibiting the sale and distribution of "listening-in" devices in interstate commerce.

But the Congress, in my judgment, has taken an unwise and potentially dangerous step by sanctioning eavesdropping and wiretapping by Federal, State, and local law officials in an almost unlimited variety of situations.

If we are not very careful and cautious in our planning, these legislative provisions could result in producing a nation of snoopers bending through the keyholes of the homes and offices in America, spying on our neighbors. No conversation in the sanctity of the bedroom or relayed over a copper telephone wire would be free of eavesdropping by those who say they want to ferret out crime.

Thus, I believe this action goes far beyond the effective and legitimate needs of law enforcement. The right of privacy is a valued right. But in a technologically advanced society, it is a vulnerable right. That is why we must strive to protect it all the more against erosion.

I call upon the Congress immediately to reconsider the unwise provisions of Title III and take steps to repeal them. I am directing the Attorney General to confer as soon as possible with the appropriate committee chairmen and warn them of the pitfalls that lie ahead, in the hope that the Congress will move to repeal the dangerous provisions of this title.

Until that can be accomplished we shall pursue—within the Federal Government—carefully designed safeguards to limit wiretapping and eavesdropping. The policy of this administration has been to confine wiretapping and eavesdropping to national security cases only—and then only with the approval of the Attorney General.

This policy, now in its 3d year, will continue in force. I have today directed the Attorney General to assure that this policy of privacy prevails and is followed by all Federal law enforcement officers.

Many States have protected the citizen against the invasion of privacy by making wiretapping illegal. I call upon the State and local authorities in the other States to apply the utmost restraint and caution if they exercise the broad powers of Title III. We need not surrender our privacy to win the war on crime.

Title II of the legislation deals with certain rules of evidence only in Federal criminal trials—which account for only 7 percent of the criminal felony prosecutions in this country. The provisions of Title II, vague and ambiguous as they are, can, I am advised by the Attorney General, be interpreted in harmony with the Constitution, and Federal practices in this field will continue to conform to the Constitution.

Under long-standing policies, for example, the Federal Bureau of Investigation and other Federal law enforcement agencies have consistently given suspects full and fair warning of their constitutional rights. I have asked the Attorney General and the Director of the Federal Bureau of Investigation to assure that these policies will continue.

My overriding concern today, as it has been since the first day I became President, is for safe streets in America. I believe this measure, despite its shortcomings, will help to lift the stain of crime and the shadow of fear from the streets of our communities.

That promise, contained largely in Title I and in the reinforced gun control law I have asked for, must not be deterred.

I believe it is in America's interest that I sign this law today.

Crime will never yield to demagogic lament—only to action. With this measure, we are beginning to act. The Federal Government is taking a long overdue step.

But at a time when crime is on the tip of every American's tongue, we must remember that our protection rests essentially with local and State police officers. For of the 40,000 law enforcement agencies in this Nation, more than 39,750 are local, while some 200 are State and only the remaining 40-plus are Federal. Of the 371,000 full-time law enforcement officers in the Nation, 308,000 are local, while 40,000 are State and only 23,000 are Federal. The essential duties these 23,000 Federal officers are authorized by law to perform are to protect the President, ferret out crime in interstate commerce, investigate crime in interstate commerce, guard our borders, and enforce the tax and customs laws.

Today the Federal Government is acting.

But action must now also come from the cities and counties and States across America.

The cities must increase the size of their police forces.

The cities must pay their law enforcement officials more.

The local communities must train them better.

The cities and the States must streamline their courts and correctional institutions.

Both the cities and States must plan with care and imagination to use the new Federal funds we will make available under the act I sign today.

Today, I ask every Governor, every mayor, and every county and city commissioner and councilman to examine the adequacy of their State and local law enforcement systems and to move promptly to support the policemen, the law enforcement officers, and the men who wage the war on crime day after day in all the streets and roads and alleys in America.

Most important of all, I call upon every

citizen in this Nation to support their local police officials with respect and with the resources necessary to enable them to do their job for justice in America.

I call upon our church leaders and every parent to provide the spiritual and moral leadership necessary to make this a law-abiding Nation, with respect for the rights of others, respect for their system of government, and support for those charged with the responsibility of protecting our lives, our homes, and our liberties.

NOTE: As enacted, the bill (H.R. 5037) is Public Law 90–351 (82 Stat. 197).

In a letter to the President of the Senate on June 26, 1968, the President requested a fiscal 1969 budget amendment to provide appropriations for the Omnibus Crime Control and Safe Streets Act of 1968 (4 Weekly Comp. Pres. Docs., p. 1017).

The Gun Control Act of 1968 was approved by the President on October 22, 1968 (see Item 553).

For a statement by the President of July 26, 1965, on establishing the President's Commission on Law Enforcement and Administration of Justice and for his message to Congress of February 6, 1967, on crime in America, see 1965 and 1967 volumes, this series, Items 382 and 35, respectively.

321 Statement by the President Upon Signing Bill Permitting Photographic Reproductions of Postage Stamps. June 20, 1968

TO BE EFFECTIVE, laws must be in step with the needs of our people. An effective government of laws must not be burdened by the dead weight of past problems and obsolete provisions.

Today I am pleased to sign an amendment removing such a provision from our statute books.

In the past, it was illegal to reproduce United States postage stamps in color. Such reproduction, it was felt, might facilitate the work of counterfeiting.

Since stamp counterfeiting is today virtually nonexistent, this restriction is no longer necessary. There is no reason now why the full meaning and beauty of our postage stamps cannot be communicated to all the world in color reproduction.

On July 4th, for example, we will issue a beautiful series of 10 stamps depicting the history of our national flag. It is a magnificent history which the stamps portray colorfully and fittingly.

Because of this bill, introduced by Congressman Thaddeus Dulski, Chairman of the House Committee on Post Office and Civil Service, we can share the story and significance of our flag with the peoples and nations of our earth.

There is no longer any reason, in law or logic, to deny such valued contributions to man's experience by restricting color re-production of postage stamps. I am pleased that Congressman Dulski's initiative has given me this opportunity to strike an obsolete provision from our lawbooks. In doing so, we make government an even more effective instrument of the people's needs and will.

NOTE: As enacted, the bill (H.R. 15972) is Public Law 90–353 (82 Stat. 240).

322 Letter to the Speaker of the House Urging Passage of the Tax Bill. *June* 20, 1968

[Released June 20, 1968. Dated June 19, 1968]

Dear Mr. Speaker:

The House of Representatives will vote tomorrow on a measure of overriding importance to the health and strength of the national economy—the anti-inflation tax bill.

I have urged the Congress for nearly two years to enact this essential legislation. Now the hour is here and the time has come to help America sustain the unparalleled record of unbroken prosperity of the past eighty-eight months.

We dare not lose this opportunity to act. I call upon the House to meet its responsibilities and to pass this crucial measure.

The tax bill has been coupled with a $6 billion expenditure reduction. The need for the tax increase is so imperative and so essential to the national interest that I have previously stated that I would accept this package. I reaffirm that position.

Passage of the tax bill will not only strengthen the economy, it will help the poor children of America. Last year the Congress placed a ceiling on the number of poor children who could receive Federal welfare payments. The tax measure before the Congress contains a provision to defer this welfare "freeze". It will permit almost a half million poor children and their parents to receive the money they need to live with human dignity and hope. If the tax bill is not enacted, the freeze will continue, and tens of thousands of children will be denied the assistance they need for the basic essentials of life—food, clothing, and shelter. This will be a cruel and bitter disappointment to the poor children who so desperately need help.

I ask every Member concerned with bettering humanity to take this into consideration when they vote tomorrow. We must not strip from the arms of the poor children of America the life-line of sustenance they so urgently require.

So I urge the House to put delay behind it and to vote this measure into law.

Sincerely,

LYNDON B. JOHNSON

[Honorable John W. McCormack, Speaker of the House of Representatives, Washington, D.C.]

NOTE: The Revenue and Expenditure Control Act of 1968 was approved by the President on June 28, 1968 (see Item 343).

323 Presidential Unit Citation Awarded the 1st Platoon, Company B, 1st Battalion, 69th Armor, USA. *June 20, 1968*

BY VIRTUE of the authority vested in me as President of the United States and as Commander-in-Chief of the Armed Forces of the United States I have today awarded

THE PRESIDENTIAL UNIT CITATION (ARMY)

FOR EXTRAORDINARY HEROISM

TO

1ST PLATOON, COMPANY B, 1ST BATTALION,

69TH ARMOR UNITED STATES ARMY

The 1st Platoon distinguished itself by extraordinary heroism and outstanding professionalism while serving under the operational control of the 9th Company, 1st Cavalry Regiment, Republic of Korea Army during the defense of Landing Zone Twenty-Seven Victor, Pleiku Province, Republic of Vietnam during the night of 9–10 August 1966. About one hour before midnight the sounds of digging outside the defensive perimeter were reported to one of the tank commanders by a Korean officer. The tank commander illuminated the suspicious area with the tank searchlight and reconnoitered it with machine gun fire. This action triggered the first of a series of violent attacks made against the position by a North Viet-

namese Army battalion and reinforced by heavy fire from recoilless rifles, mortars, and rockets. During the next six hours, the foe made repeated assaults from different directions, only to be beaten back by the coordinated fire of the stalwart defenders. Battlefield illumination was augmented by the two available tank searchlights until the latter were destroyed by enemy fire. Despite one fourth of its members being wounded, the 1st Platoon greatly assisted the 9th Company in holding the position under the intense ground attacks. The tenacious defense and subsequent mop-up of the battlefield virtually eliminated the enemy battalion as an effective fighting unit. The heavy losses inflicted upon the numerically superior enemy force attest to the physical courage, determination, and skill of the defenders. The close coordination and mutual cooperation between the Republic of Korea and the United States forces resulted in a fighting team undaunted by the enemy onslaught. This action of the 1st Platoon, Company B, 1st Battalion, 69th Armor is in keeping with the highest traditions of the United States Army.

LYNDON B. JOHNSON

324 Statement by the President Following House Committee Approval of the Gun Control Bill. *June 20, 1968*

I APPLAUD the action of the House Judiciary Committee in its overwhelming endorsement of my request of last week to enact stringent controls over the interstate sales of shotguns, rifles, and ammunition.

The American people have had enough

of murder at muzzle point by shotgun and rifle. The action by the House Committee today is a major step forward in the protection of our homes and our families, and the security of every citizen.

Each day brings tragic new evidence of

the toll of death and destruction at gunpoint. I have just received from the Federal Bureau of Investigation the following report.

In 1967, there were:

—7,700 murders with guns, compared with 6,500 in 1966;

—55,000 aggravated assaults with guns, compared with 43,000 in 1966;

—over 71,000 robberies with guns, compared with 60,000 in 1966.

I repeat again what I told the American people June 5. What in the name of conscience will it take to pass a truly effective gun control law?

I urge the leaders in both the House and the Senate to schedule this bill for floor action before they take their next recess over the July 4th weekend.

NOTE: The Gun Control Act of 1968 was approved by the President on October 22, 1968 (see Item 553).

For the President's address to the Nation on June 5, 1968, see Item 293.

The President requested approval of the gun control bill by the House Judiciary Committee in a statement of June 11, 1968 (see Item 302).

325   Letter to the Governors on the Need for Improving State Law Enforcement Systems and Gun Control Legislation. *June 20, 1968*

Dear Governor——:

I write to you today because as Chief Executives we share a common concern and a powerful purpose—to wipe the stain of crime from States and cities and neighborhoods of America.

Last night I signed the Safe Streets and Crime Control Act of 1968. The heart of this new law is Title I. It gives you the unparalleled opportunity—and confronts you with the urgent obligation—to strengthen law enforcement and criminal justice throughout your State.

For the first time in our Nation's history, the Federal Government will be able to devote substantial resources—$400 million over the next two years—to supplement the efforts of States and cities to:

—Better train, equip and pay policemen, the blue line of defense against the robber and the racketeer, the murderer and the mugger.

—Streamline and improve their over-burdened and over-taxed court systems and their outmoded correctional institutions.

—Apply the most advanced scientific techniques to prevent crime and to ferret out the criminal.

We have achieved the breakthrough. Now you must act to follow through.

The law places primary responsibility on your shoulders.

I hope that you will develop imaginative and comprehensive anti-crime blueprints and action programs with the cities and counties in your State to use wisely and efficiently and promptly the new Federal funds this act now makes available.

I urge you to examine carefully and to improve your law enforcement systems and to support the brave men who wage the hourly and daily battle against crime on the front lines of the city street, the alleys, and the local neighborhoods.

I urge you again to review your gun control laws and to speed work on the development of stringent legislation to assure that deadly weapons are kept out of the hands of the criminal, the demented, the alcoholic, and those too young to bear the terrible responsibility of owning weapons of destruction. We are moving to develop an airtight system of interstate protection. The Congress has already enacted legislation which I signed last night to control the interstate sale of hand guns which account for a majority of the firearm murders in this country. Last week I urged Congress to cover shotguns and rifles. We will appreciate any support you may feel you want to give us. We will consider further legislative gun measures once the Congress acts on this one. But we must now act to perfect this network within your State to shield our homes and families from the horrors of murder at muzzle point.

For your information, I am enclosing a copy of my statement when I signed the Safe Streets and Crime Control Act of 1968. I pledge to you the full support of all the agencies of the Federal Government in this new crime-fighting partnership which this new law makes possible. I have asked the Attorney General and my Assistant for Federal-State Relations, Governor Price Daniel, to cooperate in every way with you.

The hour is late but there is still time—if we take full advantage of the golden opportunity which the Safe Streets Program presents to State and local officials throughout this Nation.

I ask you to enlist now in this vital effort as we seek to control crime and enlarge public safety.

Sincerely,

LYNDON B. JOHNSON

NOTE: This is the text of identical letters addressed to all 50 Governors following the approval of the Omnibus Crime Control and Safe Streets Act of 1968 (see Item 320). The Gun Control Act of 1968 was approved by the President on October 22, 1968 (see Item 553).

326 Statement by the President Following House Approval of the Tax Bill. *June* 20, 1968

THE House of Representatives today declared itself for a responsible fiscal policy. Its voice will be heard around the world. Our democracy has passed a critical test. This is a landmark decision:

—to help safeguard the pockets and pocketbooks of all Americans from the pilferage of inflation;

—to help insure a healthy flow of credit through our economic system;

—to help defend the value of the dollar at home and abroad;

—to sustain our remarkable 88-month record of economic advance.

I have been pleading for this action for many long months, and I hail this decision as a victory for the entire Nation. The tax bill is essential insurance against economic chaos. Surely it is not a full and final solution for our economic problems, but it is a passport toward further economic progress.

I am very hopeful and confident that the Senate will promptly complete the legislative action on this measure.

NOTE: The Revenue and Expenditure Control Act of 1968 was approved by the President on June 28, 1968 (see Item 343).

327 Remarks at a Reception for Members of the Foreign Policy Conference for Education Leaders. *June* 20, 1968

Mr. Vice President, Secretary Rusk, distinguished educators, my friends:

Several times in the past years I have come over here to the State Department, fresh from a discussion of some serious international or domestic crisis, to address a group of educators. Each time I had the feeling that I was coming from a world of strife and tension to a world of serene tranquillity—from those who deal with a world of shouts and turmoil, to those who live in an atmosphere of order and tolerance.

How times do change.

I suppose I really ought to ask some of you for a battlefield report this evening.

I would be interested to know how the pacification program is really coming along—or how much progress you are making in reform—or how things are going in the outlying buildings, and whether you really still hold the central administration offices.

What is clear, even without a report, is that both American education and the country itself are undergoing a rapid process of change.

And change is almost never comfortable. Old values are challenged; new beliefs are pressed with a passionate certainty. Some grow impatient with the pace of change, and violently reject the system that it seeks to transform. Others just hold on tenaciously to the things as they are.

But in between, there is a vast legion of people who want a better America and who pray for a safer world and a more just society here at home, and peace between the nations.

They know that there must be sacrifices if these things are to be accomplished. They know that America has real obligations to its poor, and it must keep those obligations

—to its allies abroad, which it must honor;
—to human freedom itself, whose mightiest guardian we are.

For 20 years now this legion of thoughtful Americans has supported a great and a costly effort of responsibility in our world affairs. There have always been other choices available to us: isolationism, under various sophisticated names; at the other extreme, the quest for an end to all of our problems through a massive military "victory."

But for 20 years, they have rejected those extremes. They have sought to give the world a measure of stability, in which men and nations might seek prosperity and might seek understanding. They have given of their own treasure and skills to help their fellow man—in Europe first, and then in Asia, Latin America, Africa, and the Middle East.

What they have done did not stop the violence in the world. But in an age of great nuclear danger, it did seem to help to give mankind two decades of relative peace—certainly relative to what it might have been.

When the struggle in Vietnam is over, this legion of thoughtful men and women will have to decide, anew, what America's role in the world should be.

I hope that you—all of you—will take an active part in making that decision—in helping to lay out the alternatives, the costs and the benefits of each course. I hope that you will review and examine the path that we have taken and judge, as best you can, what would have happened if we had taken another path.

In my judgment, from my viewpoint, from where I stand, we can be proud, very proud, of what we have done in this time of tumultuous change. I hope that you will make it possible for another President to say that, with the same conviction, two decades from tonight.

Thank you.

NOTE: The President spoke at 7:13 p.m. in the Benjamin Franklin Room at the Department of State. In his opening words he referred to Vice President Hubert H. Humphrey and Secretary of State Dean Rusk.

328 Telegram on the Performance of the National Alliance of Businessmen in Aid of the Hard-Core Unemployed and Needy Youth. *June* 21, 1968

[Released June 21, 1968. Dated June 20, 1968]

WARMEST congratulations to you and your National Alliance of Businessmen associates on your remarkable performance in surpassing the job pledge goal for the hard-core unemployed. You have the Nation's deep thanks for the intensive drive, long hours and hard work that you put into your campaign for these critical job commitments in the private sector.

Having attained the first milestone in your historic mission, I now urge you to redouble your efforts to secure the 200,000 jobs for needy youth in our cities this summer. When you succeed, you will have made it possible for us to achieve a 50% increase over last year in the number of summer jobs for disadvantaged youth—taking us far toward our goal of providing opportunities for all youth who want to learn and earn during the summer.

I am extremely pleased to note that your city—Detroit—and nine other cities nationally have demonstrated that the youth quota can be met. You and your associates throughout the Nation must spare no effort to match Detroit's splendid example.

I call on you to rally your forces for an all-out drive to meet your youth quota. Only you can answer the question whether this summer will be a time of hope and opportunity—or a time of frustration and despair—for the youth in our cities.

You have my best wishes for the same outstanding success in your youth drive as you have had in your hard-core campaign.

LYNDON B. JOHNSON

[Mr. Henry Ford II, Chairman, Ford Motor Company, The American Road, Dearborn, Michigan 48121]

329 Remarks at the Swearing In of Frederick DelliQuadri as Chief of the Children's Bureau. *June* 21, 1968

Secretary Cohen, Mr. Justice White, Mr. DelliQuadri, Members of Congress, ladies and gentlemen:

Fred DelliQuadri is a man of broad humanitarian vision.

All of his experience and his compassion will be required in his new job, because today:

—10 percent of all American children are referred to juvenile court for delinquency before their 18th birthday.

—Nearly a million young people drop out of school each year.

—Half a million children have cerebral palsy; half a million more have epilepsy.

—And almost 12 million children under 18 live in families that are too poor to feed or to house them adequately or to provide them with satisfactory medical care.

Our Nation does not have the best record of the nations of the world in infant mortality. There are at least 14 nations doing better than the United States. It is a truism to say that today's children are tomorrow's leaders. They are also tomorrow's suffering adults. They are also tomorrow's criminals. They are also tomorrow's failures.

What we do now in our families, in our churches, schools, and homes, and through agencies such as this wonderful agency—the Children's Bureau—to strengthen, to guide, and to care for our children, will determine how many of our children wind up in each of the categories I have mentioned.

I believe that, through the leadership of men like Wilbur Cohen and Mr. Delli-Quadri, we can mightily increase the number of tomorrow's leaders and mightily decrease those who wind up at the bottom of the heap.

We are delighted to welcome you to this new position, Mr. DelliQuadri. Justice White, I guess, breaks another record this morning of swearing in a cane holder.

NOTE: The President spoke at 11:44 a.m. in the Cabinet Room at the White House. In his opening words he also referred to Wilbur J. Cohen, Secretary of Health, Education, and Welfare, and Byron R. White, Associate Justice of the United States Supreme Court, who administered the oath of office.

330   Remarks at a Ceremony Opening by Remote Control the Flathead Tunnel in Montana. *June 21, 1968*

Senator Mansfield, Congressman Olsen, Engineer Cole, ladies and gentlemen:

Forty years ago, from the White House, President Calvin Coolidge sent a signal that fired the final blast linking both ends of the New Cascade Tunnel on the Great Northern Railway.

Here today we begin the era of Flathead Tunnel. And it is now my turn to send the signal that will join together a new tunnel and a great new era of progress for the wonderful State of Montana.

Flathead Tunnel provides an important link on one of America's great rail lines. It also represents a step forward toward the completion of Libby Dam.

Libby, one of the biggest hydroelectric power projects in the entire Northwest, will mean new sources of inexpensive power, better flood control, and new recreational opportunities in the years ahead. For Montana and the Northwest are on the move.

This has been a dream of Senator Mansfield and the Montana delegation for many, many years. You people in Montana are not only blessed with natural beauty, with vast resources, with great leadership, particularly in the Congress, but you are blessed with the wisdom to harness nature's abundance for the greatest good for all of us.

We have not in this country always had the good sense to preserve our natural wealth. And we have often paid a high price for our wastefulness.

But today we show what foresight and planning can accomplish for our people.

And as I send the signal which opens Flathead Tunnel, I have no doubt that it will be a forerunner of new progress for the people of your great State who are so ably represented here at the White House this morning by your distinguished Senator and your distinguished Congressman.

Thank you.

NOTE: The President spoke at 1:06 p.m. in the Fish Room at the White House. In his opening words he referred to Senator Mike Mansfield of Montana, Representative Arnold Olsen of Montana, and Phillip L. Cole, resident engineer for the U.S. Army Corps of Engineers at Libby Dam, Montana. During the ceremony Mr. Cole remained in communication with the President from the Flathead Tunnel site in Montana.

After his remarks the President set off the final charge of explosives completing the 7-mile tunnel, part of the railroad relocation at the Libby Dam, a project under construction by the U.S. Army Corps of Engineers and one of the key structures for controlling the water resources of the Columbia River Basin in Canada and the United States.

331 Message to the Congress Transmitting Annual Report of the Railroad Retirement Board. *June 24, 1968*

To the Congress of the United States:

It is with special satisfaction that I transmit the Annual Report of the Railroad Retirement Board for fiscal year 1967.

During the year, more than one million individuals received $1.3 billion in retirement and survivor benefits, an increase of $65 million over the preceding year.

In the same period, unemployment and sickness benefits were only $71 million. This represented the lowest total paid under the railroad unemployment and sickness insurance system in 15 years, with the decrease reflecting in large part the continued high level of economic activity in the Nation.

Even greater protection for railroad beneficiaries will soon be available, thanks to the recent legislation enacted by the Congress. These amendments to the basic laws administered by the Railroad Retirement Board were jointly recommended by railroad management and railroad labor. They are to be commended for their continued cooperation in improving these laws.

As a result of these amendments, every one of the million retirement and survivor beneficiaries will receive added benefits. In addition, the benefit rates under the unemployment-sickness system will rise by almost 25 percent, and protection will be extended to those with prolonged illnesses.

The latest amendments continue the record of steady improvement in our system of protection for railroad workers and their families against the economic hazards accompanying old age, unemployment, illness and death.

This report shows the fruits of our common and continued efforts to lift the elderly citizens of our country out of the ranks of poverty, and thereby to give more meaning to their years of retirement.

I commend the report to your attention.

LYNDON B. JOHNSON

The White House

June 24, 1968

NOTE: The report is entitled "Railroad Retirement Board: 1967 Annual Report for the Fiscal Year Ended June 30" (Government Printing Office, 186 pp.).

332   Remarks at a Luncheon of the YMCA Youth Governors Conference. *June 24, 1968*

Mr. Rogers, Mr. Alexander, ladies and gentlemen:

I was told when we called over here this morning to make arrangements for this luncheon that you had a Mr. Johnson scheduled to speak to you but that Mr. Johnson had let you down and canceled.

When I inquired I found out it was Mr. Tom Johnson, my Deputy Press Secretary. And I asked where you were having this meeting. They told me the Roger Smith Hotel.

I asked the hotel management where the hotel had gotten this name because I realized as you do that Roger Smith is a name that is very rich in history and in meaning. And I was told by the management that the Roger Smith Hotel is a combination of the maiden names of the wives of the owners—Miss Roger and Miss Smith.

I welcome this chance to come here and talk to you this afternoon about what I believe is good news and will have a good effect on young America.

Within the week—in the next 2 or 3 days—I will have completed my recommendations and suggestions to submit to the Congress on what I believe will be very historic legislation that will affect young America.

I will ask the Congress for an amendment to our Constitution to lower the voting age to 18 years of age.

As you know, the ballot box is the great anvil of democracy. There the will of the people shapes our government, and it is there that the real voice of our democracy speaks out.

We all know that the right to vote is one of the basic rights of free men and women.

It is the right upon which all other rights ultimately rest.

Throughout our long national history, we have wisely and carefully extended that right to more and more people as we went along.

With each extension—each step of the way—I believe that the record will show that our Nation has gained new strength and new vitality from those steps.

First, our Founding Fathers cast aside the tests of religion and poverty and just after the Civil War the 15th amendment ended all tests of race and color.

In 1965, in the Voting Rights Act that we passed, we reinforced that right for all time.

In 1920, the 19th amendment gave women the right to vote and gave them a truly equal place in our democracy.

In 1961, the 23d amendment gave the citizens of the Nation's Capital the right to vote for the President and Vice President.

Four years ago the 24th amendment struck down the false and artificial test of the poll tax as a requirement for voting.

Today, we will take another giant stride in this march of democracy. Today, 10 million young men and women between the ages of 18 and 21 are adults in every sense of the word—they shoulder family responsibilities, they shoulder civic responsibilities as you have demonstrated, they are already a part of our labor force, they share civic duties with their elders, they risk their lives for our Nation in the Armed Forces of our Nation around the world, they serve in VISTA and the Peace Corps here and in most of the nations of the world—a thousand other community ventures they are involved in.

They bring new meaning to the concept of service. But today the young people of America are asking again for the opportunity to give their talents, their abilities, their energies, and their enthusiasms in the greater tasks.

We live in a world that is young. And the world is growing younger each year.

Of all nations none has more generously invested in preparing young people for constructive citizenship and none has been more faithfully served by its young than America.

So now I believe that America must extend to the young the most fundamental right of all—the right to participate in the basic process of democracy—the right to vote.

This is a national affirmation of faith in our youth, for a nation without faith in its sons and without faith in its daughters is a nation that is without faith in itself.

The generation gap that we hear about is not to be measured in years alone. It is a difference between those who carry responsibility and those who are allowed to stand only on the sideline.

So I believe that this amendment, as much as any other action that we in America can take today, will help to close that gap.

I believe that this amendment will help to unite us all and for the first time it will join us all—every adult in America—in the great work of governing all America.

In the hours ahead we will continue to prepare this message. When it is ready it will be delivered to the Congress.

I ask you as a young group that provides leadership for America to each review this message, if you will. Look at the arguments that we present, the reasons that we give, and the justification that is there. If you can accept it as I believe you will, then I hope that you will rally support in each of the States of this Union for this great opportunity for the young people of America.

If Mr. Rogers or someone can give me the name and address of each of you, I will ask Mr. Larry Levinson of my staff to personally send to each of you this message that I would like to deliver to you today. But it will come out of the typewriter in the next day or so.

I will be looking for you at the White House and would be delighted to see you.

We hope your visit in Washington is a very profitable and exciting one.

NOTE: The President spoke at 12:58 p.m. in the Roger Smith Hotel in Washington. In his opening words he referred to Alfred C. Rogers and Jesse N. Alexander, Jr., general executive and assistant general executive of the YMCA of Metropolitan Washington. Mr. Alexander also served as director of the National YMCA Youth Governors Conference. During his remarks the President referred to Lawrence E. Levinson, Deputy Special Counsel to the President.

The sixth annual YMCA Youth Governors Conference was attended by 36 young people from throughout the United States, chosen by members of the YMCA youth and government program in local-level elections. The Conference was sponsored by the Reader's Digest Foundation of Pleasantville, N.Y.

For the President's message to Congress proposing a constitutional amendment to lower the voting age to 18, see Item 341.

333 Statement by the President on His Gun Control Proposals. *June 24, 1968*

WITHIN the hour, in some city in America, a gunshot will ring out and someone will fall dead or wounded.

The latest report of the Federal Bureau of

Investigation documents a shocking increase in crimes where deadly weapons are the tools of violence.

In 1967, there were 7,700 murders with

guns—1,200 more murders than the year before.

In 1967, there were 55,000 aggravated assaults with guns—12,000 more aggravated assaults than the year before.

In 1967, there were over 71,000 robberies with guns—again, almost 12,000 more robberies than in 1966.

We are finally moving, after 200 years of inaction, to do something about this shocking slaughter in our midst.

With the Safe Streets Act that I signed only last week, we took the first major step to control mail-order murder. That measure outlaws interstate traffic in pistols, and prohibits the sale of these lethal weapons to children.

Now we are in sight of a second major step—the control of interstate traffic in shotguns, in rifles, and in ammunition.

I asked the Congress on June 6th to enact these safeguards. That legislation must be brought to a vote without delay. And now I propose that Congress go further to give Americans the elementary protection that the people of every other civilized nation have long enjoyed.

I propose first the national registration of every gun in America.

Second, I propose that every individual in this country be required to obtain a license before he is entrusted with a gun.

Registration and licensing have long been an accepted part of daily life in America. Autos, boats, and even dogs and bicycles are commonly registered. Our citizens must get licenses to keep dogs and other pets, to fish, to drive a car.

Certainly no less should be required for the possession of lethal weapons that have caused so much heartbreak and horror in this country in this century.

Surely, the slight inconvenience for the few is minimal when measured against the protection for all.

The course I propose is sane and sensible. It will lead to a safer and a better America.

I talked to the distinguished mayor of San Francisco today about the plea that he made to the citizens of San Francisco, urging them to voluntarily turn in their old, unwanted, and unnecessary guns. Mayor Alioto made a special plea to the parents of San Francisco and he assured the citizens of San Francisco that there would be no questions asked if they would turn in their guns to their local police stations, fire stations, and churches.

I hope that every mayor in every city in our Nation will carefully examine the proposal that the mayor of San Francisco made to his people and will, if they can, follow the lead of this distinguished mayor and establish in all the cities of America a voluntary program, as he has established in San Francisco, so that all Americans can turn in their guns if they do not need or do not want those guns.

Thank you very much.

NOTE: The President made the statement at 4:37 p.m. in the Fish Room at the White House.

The Gun Control Act of 1968 which was approved on October 22, 1968 (see Item 553), did not contain the national registration and licensing provisions requested by the President.

For the President's letter of June 6, 1968, to the President of the Senate and the Speaker of the House urging passage of an effective gun control bill, see Item 296.

See also Item 334.

334 Special Message to the Congress: "The People's Right to Protection." *June 24, 1968*

To the Congress of the United States:

Within the hour, in some city in America, a gun shot will ring out. And someone will fall dead or wounded.

Unless we act purposefully to prevent it, reckless and wild gunfire will be heard again—tomorrow, the day after, and all the days to follow

—as it was last Tuesday, in Denver, when a 71-year-old gas station attendant was shot to death in the course of a $75 armed robbery;

—as it was last Wednesday, in Graceville, Florida, when a mental patient shot a three-year-old boy through the back of the head;

—as it was last Thursday, in Chicago, when a young man was killed and three others injured by shotgun blasts fired by a band of roving teenagers.

These tragedies are imbedded in the grim statistics of death and destruction at gun point. The terrible toll is rising.

The latest report of the Federal Bureau of Investigation documents a shocking increase in crimes where deadly weapons are the instruments of violence.

In 1967, there were:

—7,700 murders with guns. In 1966 there were 6,500.

—55,000 aggravated assaults with guns. In 1966 there were 43,000.

—Over 71,000 robberies with guns. In 1966 there were 60,000.

It took this country nearly two centuries to respond to the danger of guns in criminal and incompetent hands. The first Federal action came in the early 1930's, when the Congress enacted safeguards controlling the use of sawed-off shotguns and submachine guns to answer the public indignation and fear arising out of organized gang wars in the cities.

But very little was done in the next three decades, while the velocity of speeding bullets exacted their deadly toll across America. Alone among the modern nations of the world, we remained without the gun control laws that other countries accept as an elementary need and condition of life. We can see the difference in the last reported comparisons of homicides by gunfire. Out of 15 countries reporting, the U.S. ranked worst—with a rate of 2.7 gun murders per 100,000 population. Here are some of the statistics:

—2.7 for the U.S.—.03 in the Netherlands, and .04 in Japan,

—2.7 for the U.S.—.05 in England and Wales,

—2.7 for the U.S.—.12 in West Germany and .70 in Italy,

—2.7 for the U.S.—.52 in Canada and .26 in Belgium.

Since I first became President, I have fought for strong gun control laws.

Now—at long last—we have begun to move.

When I signed the Safe Streets Act last week, America took the first major step to control deadly firearms. That measure outlawed the interstate traffic in handguns and prohibited the sale of these small and lethal weapons to minors.

We are now within sight of the second major step—the control of interstate traffic in shotguns, rifles and ammunition, as I requested of the Congress on June 6. I hope the Congress will move with the greatest speed to complete its action on this proposal for protection.

But even before that step is finally completed, we must look to the next advance for the safety of the American people.

With the enactment of these measures, we will have constructed the Nation's first foundation upon which the States can build and develop their own gun control laws. Without this bulwark of interstate protection, even the best State laws would be exercises in futility.

To assure the protection of our people, Federal law needs two additional reinforcements:

—A national registration of all firearms, both those already in private hands and those acquired in the future.

—Federal licensing of all possessors of firearms in those States whose laws fail to meet minimum Federal standards.

Registration and licensing have long been an accepted part of daily life in America. Automobiles, boats—even dogs and bicycles in many communities—are commonly registered. Our citizens must get licenses to fish, to hunt, and to drive. Certainly no less should be required for the possession of lethal weapons that have caused so much horror and heartbreak in this country. Surely the slight inconvenience for the few is minimal, when measured against protection for all.

I propose, first, the national registration of every gun in America.

There are now more firearms than families in America. The estimates range between 50 and 100 million guns in this country. Last year more than 3 million guns were added to private stocks, building a massive arsenal which arms the murderer and the robber.

Registration will tell us how many guns there are, where they are, and in whose hands they are held.

Car registration has been the major factor in solving hit-and-run auto deaths. The new National Crime Information Center, operated by the Federal Bureau of Investigation has already begun to compile and computerize data on stolen automobiles, stolen guns, fugitives from justice, and other criminal activities.

Now, for the first time, computer technology has made the national registration of guns practical and workable. The registration of guns can be fed into a computer bank at the National Crime Information Center. Through this system, the owner of a gun anywhere in the country can be identified in a matter of seconds.

Second, I propose that every individual in this country be required to obtain a license before he is entrusted with a gun.

Every murder by gunfire is a criminal confrontation in which—by design or through a conspiracy of events—the criminal faces his victim through the telescope cross-hairs of a rifle or over the barrel of a pistol. An inflamed moment seizes the criminal's mind, and his finger presses the trigger.

We may never be able to keep that criminal mind from erupting into violence, but we can stay the finger that squeezes the trigger—by keeping the gun out of the murderer's hand.

The surest route to accomplish this is to require every person who wants a gun to be licensed, first proving that he meets the qualifications.

The initiative for licensing should, of course, rest with the States for there licensing can most effectively be carried out. Some States have already enacted comprehensive licensing laws which prevent the vicious, the irresponsible and the insane from acquiring firearms. In New Jersey, for example, which has had a licensing law for only a short period of time, over 1,500 disqualified persons have been denied access to lethal weapons. And States which have licensing requirements have lower homicide rates.

741

The States are now working on model gun control laws through a special committee of the National Association of Attorneys General, the National Council of State Governments, and the National Governors Conference. I have urged that their work be expeditiously pursued.

To assure uniformity and adequate protection, the law I propose would establish minimum Federal licensing standards. These would prevent firearms from being sold to or possessed by criminals, dope addicts, alcoholics, the mentally ill, and any others whose possession of guns would be harmful to the public health, safety or welfare.

The Federal licensing law would go into effect only in those States without at least comparable standards, and only after the States have been given an opportunity to act first.

I call upon every Governor and State legislature to move as rapidly as they can to enact forceful laws for the protection of their people.

Nothing in these proposals will impair the legitimate ownership or use of guns in this country. In other countries which have sensible laws, the hunter and the sportsman thrive. These measures will entail no more inconvenience for the gun owner than dog tags or automobile license plates pose for any citizen. Nor are they threats to the mystique of manhood, or to the heritage of our people. Only the potential murderer's chance to kill and only the potential robber's chance to terrorize are threatened. The only heritage that is harmed is the record of violent death and destruction that shames our history.

The proposals in this message are no more and no less than commonsense safeguards which any civilized nation must apply for the safety of its people.

The American people have been too long without them. The cost of inaction through the decades affronts our conscience.

Homes and city streets across the Nation which might have rung with gunfire will be spared the tragedy of senseless slaughter. We will never be able to measure this violence that does not erupt. But our history tells us America will be a safer country if we move now—once and forever—to complete the protection so long denied our people.

I urge the Congress, as I have throughout all the days of my Presidency, to act immediately to control interstate sales of shotguns, rifles and ammunition. Hearings on this legislation have long since been completed. The legislation has been reported favorably by the House Judiciary Committee and the Juvenile Delinquency Subcommittee of the Senate Judiciary Committee. That legislation—providing basic protection against interstate slaughter by firearms—should be brought to a vote without delay.

Once that foundation of interstate protection has been established, the registration and licensing proposals made in this message should be enacted. But these proposals afford no justification for delay in enacting strong and effective controls over interstate traffic of deadly weapons. Indeed, they build upon the foundation of interstate control which is so essential to their effectiveness.

Let us delay no longer in enacting that basic foundation of interstate protection and then let us go on to build—through registration and licensing—the kind of protection so long denied the American citizen.

LYNDON B. JOHNSON

The White House
June 24, 1968

NOTE: The Gun Control Act of 1968 was approved by the President on October 22, 1968 (see Item 553). However, the national registration and licensing provisions requested by the President were not enacted during the 2d session of the 90th Congress.

For the President's letter of June 6, 1968, to the President of the Senate and the Speaker of the House urging passage of an effective gun control bill, see Item 296.

See also Item 333.

335　Remarks at the Swearing In of George Ball as U.S. Representative to the United Nations. *June* 24, 1968

Mr. Vice President, Chief Justice Warren, Ambassador and Mrs. Goldberg, Ambassador and Mrs. Ball, members of the Cabinet, ladies and gentlemen:

Ambassador George Ball is one of those "gifted amateurs" who has given his country brilliant professional service in roles of very great public responsibility.

He has held important official positions, including that of Under Secretary of State, and he has served the President unofficially in many other ways. His counsel has been unfailingly judicious; his grasp of world affairs is broad and deep; his powers as an advocate are justly famous. Beyond all of these qualifications is that of loyalty—to the United States of America, to democratic values, and to the President for whom he works.

Now once again this afternoon, he puts his talents to the service of international diplomacy. He assumes America's embassy to the world in the United Nations.

Extraordinary men have preceded Ambassador Ball in that post during this administration—Adlai Stevenson, who was George Ball's closest friend, and Arthur Goldberg.

It has been 3 years since Arthur Goldberg left the Supreme Court, and reentered the heat of the negotiating kitchen. For 3 eventful years of crisis and achievement, Ambassador Goldberg has served his country and has served all mankind.

The treaty on outer space; the nonproliferation agreement; the United Nations action during the India-Pakistan, Middle East, and Cyprus fighting; all of these bear the mark of Arthur Goldberg's outstanding skill as a mediator for peace.

So this afternoon, I thank Ambassador Goldberg—on behalf of the Presidents and the Nation that he has served so well.

The central task of the United Nations demands men such as these. Put simply, the task is to reflect the diversity, the growing independence of nations, and at the same time to convert that independence into constructive action for peace and development in the world.

No other institution can perform that task. That is why—despite the disappointments that have sometimes accompanied its real achievements—millions of people in this country and abroad look to the United Nations with hope and with continuing expectation.

They believe—as I believe—that what the United Nations has achieved is only prologue. It will without question play a major role in economic and social development during the next decade. It can help the world move from adversary relations to reconciliation, from violence as a habit of history to its rejection as a means of change.

I am very proud that George Ball will be our Representative to the United Nations during part of its historic period of development. And this afternoon on behalf of the American people, whom he has brilliantly served in the past, I welcome him once again into America's official family.

Thank you.

743

NOTE: The President spoke at 5:40 p.m. in the East Room at the White House. In his opening words he referred to Vice President Hubert H. Humphrey, Chief Justice of the United States Earl Warren, who administered the oath of office, Arthur J. Goldberg, outgoing U.S. Representative to the United Nations, Mrs. Goldberg, George W. Ball, former Under Secretary of State, and Mrs. Ball. During his re-marks the President referred to Adlai E. Stevenson, U.S. Representative to the United Nations 1961–1965.

Following the administration of the oath of office, Mr. Ball spoke briefly. The text of his remarks is printed in the Weekly Compilation of Presidential Documents (vol. 4, p. 1009).

336 Statement by the President on the 30th Anniversary of the Food, Drug, and Cosmetic Act. *June 25, 1968*

THIRTY YEARS AGO, on June 25, 1938, President Franklin D. Roosevelt signed into law a great landmark in this Nation's history of consumer protection: the Federal Food, Drug, and Cosmetic Act.

That legislation was an initial effort to meet a whole new set of problems as the American marketplace moved from the corner grocery into the age of the supermarket.

It set forth this Government's basic principles for maintaining the quality and integrity of the market in the 20th century, and it directed the agencies of this Government to ensure that these principles would prevail.

These principles have been buttressed over the past 30 years by a series of amendments that have benefited both buyer and merchant—both the American consumer and American business. They have provided:

—for the certification of insulin, penicillin, and other lifesaving antibiotics;

—for setting limits on the usage of pesticides;

—for establishing the safe use of food additives and color additives;

—for assuring that all drugs are safe as well as effective, and for the control of stimulant, depressant, and hallucinogenic drugs.

Meanwhile, there have been long strides in other areas of consumer protection. In the last 3 years, the Congress has enacted major legislation to provide for highway safety, fair packaging, wholesome meat, protection against flammable fabrics, home appliance safety, safe toys, adequate clinical laboratory standards, fire research and safety, truth-in-lending, and the establishment of a National Commission on Product Safety.

We have new Federal guardians of the marketplace: the first Special Assistant to the President for Consumer Affairs, the first Consumer Counsel in the Department of Justice, the first Presidential Committee on Consumer Interests, and, within the last 2 weeks, the new Consumer Protection and Environmental Health Service in the Department of Health, Education, and Welfare.

With all that, however, the Food, Drug, and Cosmetic Act continues to provide an important basis for expanding the protection that American consumers need to remain the sovereign of the marketplace.

During this week, while we are paying tribute to the historical significance of the Food, Drug, and Cosmetic Act, I hope that each of us will pause to consider the genius of the American marketplace, which is the envy of the world. But let us also resolve that our great ability to raise, manufacture, distribute, and sell products to meet every human need be used to enhance the quality of American life for every man, woman, and child—for every American consumer.

337 Presidential Unit Citation Awarded the 8th Tactical Fighter Wing, Pacific Air Forces. *June 25*, 1968

CITATION TO ACCOMPANY THE AWARD OF
THE PRESIDENTIAL UNIT CITATION
TO THE
8TH TACTICAL FIGHTER WING

The 8th Tactical Fighter Wing, Pacific Air Forces, distinguished itself by extraordinary heroism, outstanding professionalism, and exceptional dedication to mission accomplishment in action against enemy forces in Southeast Asia from 16 December 1966 to 2 January 1967. Given the task to prepare for and to conduct a maximum attack on enemy aircraft while continuing its normal combat missions, personnel of the Wing met the task with comprehensive planning, careful preparation, extra effort and aggressive execution. The gallantry, determination, and esprit de corps shown by the men of the Wing led to a highly successful fighter sweep on 2 January 1967. Displaying superb airmanship and outstanding combat professionalism, aircrews of the 8th Tactical Fighter Wing destroyed seven MIG–21 high performance aircraft within a 15 minute period without loss or damage to friendly aircraft. This outstanding aerial achievement, carried out under extremely difficult and hazardous conditions, significantly reduced the hostile forces' fighter defenses thereby making an important contribution to the Free World forces' ability to maintain air superiority over enemy territory. The outstanding success of the mission testifies to the singular valor and the unselfish devotion to duty displayed by the personnel of the 8th Tactical Fighter Wing, and reflects great credit upon themselves and the United States Air Force.

LYNDON B. JOHNSON

338 Statement by the President Urging House Action on the Natural Gas Pipeline Safety Bill. *June* 26, 1968

TODAY the House of Representatives has an opportunity to prevent tragedy before it strikes and to protect every American family against the threat of danger and destruction.

That protection can be provided in the form of a strong natural gas pipeline safety bill, which I recommended in a special consumer message 16 months ago. The Senate has already enacted a measure encompassing my recommendations.

More than 800,000 miles of pipeline criss-cross the continent reaching into virtually every city and town in the Nation. Many lines run under our homes and crowded city streets. Many other lines will rest under communities of the future as our population grows and shifts.

Lives and property have already been lost in terrible explosions, ignited by gas pipeline failures, such as those in Natchitoches, La., and in Jamaica, N.Y. And we know that the potential for even greater tragedy lurks in pipelines lowered into place almost half a century ago.

I urge the House, as it meets today, to enact a measure conforming to the Senate bill, and to make these points clear:

—that existing as well as new pipelines will be covered by the law,

—that Federal minimum safety standards and enforcement regulations will go into effect within 2 years—and interim standards at once—unless the States can show that their procedures are at least equal to Federal procedures,

—that Federal grants to develop modern and workable safety standards will be made available to the States without delay.

This 90th Congress has served the American consumer well. It has provided landmark protection in the truth-in-lending, wholesome meat, flammable fabrics, product safety, and fire safety laws. Now the House has the opportunity—and the obligation—to extend and enlarge that record by writing into law a strong and effective natural gas pipeline safety bill.

NOTE: The Natural Gas Pipeline Safety Act of 1968 was approved by the President on August 12, 1968 (see Item 441).

For the President's special consumer message of February 16, 1967, see 1967 volume, this series, Book I, Item 57.

339 The President's News Conference of *June 26, 1968*

RESIGNATION OF CHIEF JUSTICE
EARL WARREN

THE PRESIDENT. [1.] On June 13th I received letters from the Chief Justice of the Supreme Court which read as follows:

"Pursuant to the provisions of 28 U.S.C., section 371(b), I hereby advise you of my intention to retire as Chief Justice of the United States effective at your pleasure.

"Respectfully yours,

"EARL WARREN."

"My dear Mr. President:

"In connection with my retirement letter of today, I desire to state my reason for doing so at this time.

"I want you to know that it is not because of reasons of health or on account of any personal or associational problems, but solely because of age. I have been advised that I am in as good physical condition as a person of my age has any right to expect. My as-

sociations on the Court have been cordial and satisfying in every respect, and I have enjoyed each day of the fifteen years I have been here.

"The problem of age, however, is one that no man can combat and, therefore, eventually must bow to it. I have been continuously in the public service for more than fifty years. When I entered the public service, 150 million of our 200 million people were not yet born. I, therefore, conceive it to be my duty to give way to someone who will have more years ahead of him to cope with the problems which will come to the Court.

"I believe there are few people who have enjoyed serving the public or who are more grateful for the opportunity to have done so than I. I take leave of the Court with the warmest of feelings for every member on it and for the institution which we have jointly served in the years I have been privileged to be part of it.

"With my very best wishes for your continued good health and happiness, I am

"Sincerely,

"EARL WARREN"

I responded to that letter today, June 26th, as follows:

"My dear Mr. Chief Justice:

"It is with the deepest regret that I learn of your desire to retire, knowing how much the Nation has benefited from your service as Chief Justice. However, in deference to your wishes, I will seek a replacement to fill the vacancy in the office of Chief Justice that will be occasioned when you depart. With your agreement, I will accept your decision to retire effective at such time as a successor is qualified.

"You have won for yourself the esteem of your fellow citizens. You have served your Nation with exceptional distinction and deserve the Nation's gratitude.

"Under your leadership, the Supreme Court of the United States has once again demonstrated the vitality of this Nation's institutions and their capacity to meet with vigor and strength the challenge of changing times. The Court has acted to achieve justice, fairness, and equality before the law for all people.

"Your wisdom and strength will inspire generations of Americans for many decades to come.

"Fortunately, retirement does not mean that you will withdraw from service to your Nation and to the institutions of the law. I am sure that you will continue, although retired from active service as Chief Justice, to respond to the calls which will be made upon you to furnish continued inspiration and guidance to the development of the rule of law both internationally and in our own Nation. Nothing is more important than this work which you undertook so willingly and have so well advanced.

"Sincerely,

"LYNDON B. JOHNSON"

NOMINATION OF NEW CHIEF JUSTICE AND ASSOCIATE JUSTICE

[2.] I have the nomination for the Chief Justice. The nomination will go to the Senate shortly. It is Justice Abe Fortas of the State of Tennessee. His background will be available to you as prepared by the Justice Department.

To the Associate Justice of the Supreme Court, when Mr. Fortas is elevated, I am nominating Judge Thornberry, presently on the fifth circuit. Also he is a former Federal district judge, and his home is in Austin, Texas. I think most of you know him.

I will sign those nominations momentarily. They will be at the Senate when the Senate opens today.

QUESTIONS

SUPREME COURT APPOINTMENTS

Q. Judge Thornberry's first name?

THE PRESIDENT. Homer.

Q. Sir, have you decided whom you are going to name to take Mr. Thornberry's place on the fifth circuit?

THE PRESIDENT. No.

Q. Mr. President, do you anticipate any trouble in having the Senate ratify these?

THE PRESIDENT. I would suspect that they would review their records very carefully. I believe when they do, that they will meet with the approval of the Senate.

Q. Did you discuss this with Senator

Eastland [1] or anybody else on the Judiciary Committee?

THE PRESIDENT. Yes. I have discussed it with the leadership, with several Members of the Senate, the Democratic leadership and the Republican leadership, and the leadership of the committee.

GUN CONTROL

[3.] Q. Mr. President, do you judge the temper of Congress now to be such that you might expect to get any, if not all, or most of the restrictions that you have proposed in the gun legislation yesterday?

THE PRESIDENT. I would hope that we could. I am not able to predict. This is the first day they are taking testimony in the Senate. I haven't followed that this morning. I understand that the Attorney General, Mr. Glenn, and others were appearing, along with Mayor Lindsay.[2] But I don't have an up-to-date report on that testimony or what action they will take.

Q. Mr. President, Monday I think you recommended that other mayors follow the example of Mayor Alioto [3] on a set of programs to try to encourage people to turn in guns. I know that you happen to have some guns down at the ranch. I was wondering by any chance if you are thinking of turning in some of your guns?

THE PRESIDENT. If we have any that would meet that qualification, we would be glad to do it.

---

[1] Senator James O. Eastland of Mississippi, Chairman of the Senate Judiciary Committee.

[2] Attorney General Ramsey Clark, Col. John H. Glenn, Jr., former astronaut and leader of a nationwide write-in campaign organized by the Emergency Committee for Gun Control, and Mayor John V. Lindsay of New York City.

[3] Mayor Joseph Alioto of San Francisco.

NORTH VIETNAMESE ACTION

[4.] Q. Mr. President, there are reports that the North Vietnamese are infiltrating at a larger rate into the South. Would you comment on that and comment on the ground situation, as well as reports that some offensive on their part is expected?

THE PRESIDENT. No, I don't think I would want to comment on that now.

AMBASSADOR HARRIMAN'S REVIEW OF THE PARIS TALKS

[5.] Q. Mr. President, can you tell us anything about your talks with Ambassador Harriman? [4]

THE PRESIDENT. The Ambassador reviewed with me the situation as he saw it. He brought me up to date on the exchanges and gave me his evaluations. I don't think there is a great deal that he said to me that he hasn't said in meeting the press following these various meetings. We discussed some of the thoughts he had in mind and certain ideas that he had, and reviewed them. We exchanged views.

COMMUNIST PRESSURE ON WEST BERLIN

[6.] Q. Mr. President, what do you think are the reasons for the intensified Communist pressure on West Berlin at this time?

THE PRESIDENT. I am not able to evaluate the reasons for the Communist action.

POOR PEOPLE'S CAMPAIGN

[7.] Q. Mr. President, the Resurrection City encampment has now been ended and

---

[4] W. Averell Harriman, Ambassador at Large and U.S. Representative to the Paris peace talks with North Vietnam.

some of its leaders are embarking on the strategy of civil disobedience and the rest are wanting to be arrested. Do you think any good purpose can be served by this kind of behavior?

THE PRESIDENT. I made a rather lengthy statement at my press conference before the march.[5] There is not much I can add to that. I think that everyone in Washington in a position to serve the people of this country is going to do everything he can to aid the poor.

I have pending between $70 billion and $80 billion worth of programs that are regarded as social programs.

We are doing everything we can to get those programs funded by the Appropriations Committee. I would hope that anyone who is concerned with the poor would make appropriate representations and certainly express their viewpoints, but not do it in such a way that finds them conflicting with the law of the land.

UNITED STATES-SOVIET RELATIONS

[8.]   Q. Mr. President, you directed yourself to relations with the Soviet Union three times recently—Glassboro and twice subsequently. Is there anything you would like to add to that; possibly evaluate the relationship?

THE PRESIDENT. No.

ANTIPOVERTY FUNDS

[9.]   Q. Mr. President, in connection with the poor, would you like to see the House restore the funds cut by the Appropriations Committee for education in the antipoverty program?

THE PRESIDENT. Yes. We have made our recommendations to the committee during

the consideration of the bill. And we have done so since they have acted.

SENATOR MC CARTHY AND THE PARIS TALKS

[10.]   Q. Mr. President, Senator McCarthy[6] has said he may go over to Paris to find out more about the peace talks and perhaps talk to the representatives of Hanoi.

Do you have any comment on that?
THE PRESIDENT. No.

PRIME MINISTER TRUDEAU

[11.]   Q. Mr. President, do you have any plans to meet Prime Minister Trudeau?[7]
THE PRESIDENT. I have no plans, no.

SIGNING OF THE TAX BILL

[12.]   Q. Mr. President, can you give us any indication when you might sign the tax bill?[8]

THE PRESIDENT. I would think shortly, in the next day or two. I think that all of you are familiar with the problems we have with these bills. Under the Constitution, the President has 10 days to act.

When these bills are messaged down, they go to a central point in the executive branch of the Government. They don't come to the President's desk. He, in turn, circulates the measures for examination to all the other departments concerned.

Depending on how much new material is in it and how familiar they are with the various sections, the groups meet and analyze and evaluate and make their recommenda-

[5] See Item 223 [9].

[6] Senator Eugene J. McCarthy of Minnesota, candidate for the 1968 Democratic presidential nomination.
[7] Prime Minister Pierre Elliott Trudeau of Canada.
[8] See Item 343.

tions. That is true on every piece of general legislation.

Some of them can make evaluations quicker than others. It is easier if the bill that you submit is passed as you submitted it, because you have already considered it. But if they change it as they do in most bills, you have to go back and have all that reviewed and see how it affects the expenditures and the policies of the Government.

I am not sure just when this examination process will be completed. As soon as it is, and I can read their comments, I will be prepared to act.

MEETING WITH PRESIDENT THIEU

[13.] Q. Mr. President, do you expect to meet soon with President Thieu of South Vietnam?

THE PRESIDENT. I am not sure just when that meeting will take place. I don't have a date on it now.

POSSIBILITY OF SUMMIT MEETING OR TRIP TO SOVIET UNION

[14.] Q. Mr. President, we keep getting these reports or rumors from abroad that a summit meeting between yourself and Mr. Kosygin [9] may be forthcoming soon, or before January 20 of next year.

---

[9] Premier Aleksei N. Kosygin of the Soviet Union.

Is there anything in the works for a summit meeting or a trip to the Soviet Union by yourself?

THE PRESIDENT. I know of no basis for those rumors. I have no plans for it.

POSSIBILITY OF LATIN AMERICAN TRIP

[15.] Q. As long as we are on the subject of possible travel, Mr. President, there are also recurring rumors or reports that you might go to Latin America at about the time you go down to the HemisFair celebration.

Can you pin those down for us one way or the other?

THE PRESIDENT. When I can, I will.

I wouldn't deal in rumors very much though, if I were you. George [10] will always make this available to you just the first moment he can.

As a matter of fact, before I could sign these nominations that came over from the Justice Department, we called you in.

I am going to proceed to sign them so we can get them up there before 12 o'clock.

Douglas Cornell, Associated Press: Thank you, Mr. President.

NOTE: President Johnson's one hundred and twenty-eighth news conference was held in his office at the White House at 11:38 a.m. on Wednesday, June 26, 1968.

[10] George E. Christian, Special Assistant to the President.

---

340   Message to the Bonin Islanders on the Return of the Islands to Japanese Administration. *June 26, 1968*

THIS IS an historic occasion for the United States and Japan, and in particular for you, the people of the Bonin Islands.

In November of 1967, Prime Minister Sato and I reviewed the status of the Bonin

Islands and agreed that the mutual security interests of Japan and the United States could be accommodated within arrangements for the return of administration of these islands to Japan. I take pleasure in the fact that these consultations have now been successfully concluded. I fully share Prime Minister Sato's view as stated in our joint communiqué of November 15, 1967, that the return of administrative rights over the Bonin Islands will contribute to solidifying the ties of friendship between Japan and the United States.

As you begin your new lives today once again under Japanese administration, I extend to you my best wishes for the future.

NOTE: For the President's joint statement with Prime Minister Eisaku Sato of Japan on November 15, 1967, see 1967 volume, this series, Book II, Item 491.

The message was made available by the White House Press Office. It was not made public in the form of a White House press release.

341 Special Message to the Congress: "To Vote at Eighteen— Democracy Fulfilled and Enriched." *June 27,* 1968

To the Congress of the United States:

The ballot box is the great anvil of democracy, where government is shaped by the will of the people. It is through the ballot that democracy draws its strength, renews its processes, and assures its survival.

Throughout the life of our Republic, no single, enduring question has so engaged generation after generation of Americans as this: Who among our citizens shall be eligible to participate as voters in determining the course of our public affairs?

On four occasions we have amended our Constitution to enlarge or to protect that participation. In recent years, Congress itself has been attentive to sheltering and assuring the free exercise of the right to vote.

Such a concern is altogether fitting. Under a government of, by and for the people, the right to vote is the most basic right of all. It is the right on which all others finally stand.

Such a right is not to be idly conferred or blindly withheld. But the stability of our Republic from the beginning has been served—well and faithfully—by the willingness of Americans to lay aside the constraints of custom and tradition and heed the appeals of reason and reality to welcome into the American electorate those of our citizens fitted by the precepts of our society's values to participate in the exercise of the

ultimate right of citizenship.

At the inception of the Republic, the promise of the new Nation was strengthened because our forefathers cast aside tests of religion and property.

At midpassage, America's moral strength was fortified when the test of color was removed by the Fifteenth Amendment. The Voting Rights Act of 1965 has reinforced this principle for all time.

At the beginning of the modern era in this twentieth century, reason and reality wisely prevailed when the women of America— through the Nineteenth Amendment to the Constitution—were granted the equality of citizenship so long denied them.

In 1961, the Twenty-Third Amendment to the Constitution gave citizens of the Nation's capital the right to vote for President and Vice President.

Four years ago, the Twenty-Fourth Amendment struck down the tests of the poll tax which had for almost a century disenfranchised thousands of Americans.

ENLARGING THE AMERICAN FRANCHISE

In all these instances time has affirmed the wisdom and the right of these decisions to enlarge participation in the Nation's affairs. Time, too, has already affirmed the wisdom

751

and justice of our continuing efforts in the last decade to perfect, protect and shelter the right of all citizens to vote and to put an end to the unconscionable techniques of studied discrimination.

Today, I believe it is time once more for Americans to measure the constraints of custom and tradition against the compelling force of reason and reality in regard to the test of age. The hour has come to take the next great step in the march of democracy. We should now extend the right to vote to more than ten million citizens unjustly denied that right. They are the young men and women of America between the ages of 18 and 21.

The practice of admitting young Americans to the electorate at the age of twenty-one has its roots in the dim and distant mists of medieval England—but it is a practice and limitation without roots in the American experience.

Throughout our history as a young Nation, young people have been called upon by the age of eighteen to shoulder family responsibilities and civic duties identical with their elders.

At the age of eighteen, young Americans are called upon to bear arms.

At the age of eighteen, young Americans are treated as adults before many courts of law and are held responsible for their acts.

The age of eighteen, far more than the age of twenty-one, has been and is the age of maturity in America—and never more than now.

Reason does not permit us to ignore any longer the reality that eighteen year old young Americans are prepared—by education, by experience, by exposure to public affairs of their own land and all the world—to assume and exercise the privilege of voting.

The essential stability of our system is not served, the moral integrity of our cause is not strengthened, the value we place on the worth of the individual is not honored by denying to more than ten million citizens—solely because of their age—the right to full participation in determining our country's course.

This denial of the right to vote limits our democracy. It diminishes every modern concept of citizenship.

The young people of America in this decade are far more ready, far better qualified, far more able to discharge the highest duty of citizenship than any generations of the past.

We know—and the young men and women know also—that this is so.

They are better educated than their counterparts of a generation ago. They graduate from high school and enter college in greater proportions. Already this group—although many have not yet completed their schooling—have a higher education level than the general electorate.

Mass communication and greater opportunities for travel expose them earlier and more frequently to the issues of the day than the young men and women of the 1940's, or even the 1950's.

The young men of today serve their Nation in uniform with the same devotion as their fathers and brothers of earlier days showed. But duties unknown a decade ago have summoned the devotion of young men and women alike, by the tens of thousands. Their participation in the Peace Corps, in VISTA, and in other community ventures has elevated our national life and brought new meaning to the concept of service.

For myself, I deeply believe that America can only prosper from the infusion of youthful energy, initiative, vigor and intelligence into our political processes.

We live in a world that is young and growing younger each year. Of all nations, none has more generously invested in preparing its young people for constructive citizenship and none has been more faithfully served by its young than has America.

Today, the young people of America are asking the opportunity to give of their talents and abilities, their energies and enthusiasms, to the greater tasks of their times. I believe their proper request can and must be properly answered by a national affirmation of our faith in them. For a nation without faith in its sons and daughters is a nation without faith in itself.

What I Propose

I accordingly propose that the Congress of the United States approve and submit for ratification of the legislatures of three-fourths of the States an amendment to the Constitution of the United States to provide, as follows:

"The right of any citizen of the United States to vote shall not be denied or abridged by the United States or by any State on account of age if a citizen is eighteen years of age or older."

In proposing submission of such an amendment I am mindful that:

—The State of Georgia since 1943, and the State of Kentucky, since 1955, have permitted eighteen year old residents to vote.

—The two new States of Alaska and Hawaii have permitted nineteen and twenty year old residents, respectively, to vote.

—The first proposal for such an amendment was advanced in 1942 by Senator Arthur Vandenberg.

—President Dwight D. Eisenhower, in his 1954 State of the Union Address, urged an Amendment to lower the voting age to eighteen.

—In the 90th Congress, more than fifty proposed Constitutional Amendments to extend voting rights to eighteen year old citizens have been introduced, and many of these measures have broad bi-partisan support.

The concept has been tried and tested. Its merit has been established. Its rightness is now beyond dispute.

Full Participation in Our American Democracy

The time has come to grant our youth what we ask of them but still deny to them— full and responsible participation in our American democracy.

In this year of national decision, as Americans in every State prepare to choose their leadership for the decisive and fateful years before us, the Congress has a rare opportunity through the submission of this amendment to signify to our young people that they are respected, that they are trusted, that their commitment to America is honored and that the day is soon to come when they are to be participants, not spectators, in the adventure of self-government.

Every time before, when America has extended the vote to citizens whose hour has come, new vitality has been infused into the lifestream of the Nation, and America has emerged the richer.

Now the hour has come again to take another step in Democracy's great journey.

LYNDON B. JOHNSON

The White House
    June 27, 1968

342 Statement by the President Upon Signing the Uniform Holiday Bill. *June 28, 1968*

THE BILL that we sign today will help Americans to enjoy more fully the country that is their magnificent heritage. It will also aid the work of Government and bring new efficiency to our economy.

This bill provides that three of our national holidays will be celebrated on Monday:

—Washington's Birthday on the third Monday in February,

—Memorial Day on the last Monday in May,

—Veterans Day on the fourth Monday in October.

The bill will take effect on January 1, 1971. State legislatures will thus have time to act for observances in local government offices and in private employment.

This will mean a great deal to our families and our children. It will enable families who live some distance apart to spend more time together. Americans will be able to travel farther and see more of this beautiful land of ours. They will be able to participate in a wider range of recreational and cultural activities.

The bill also establishes Columbus Day as a Federal holiday—to be celebrated on the second Monday in October. Thirty-four of our States have already established a day honoring Christopher Columbus. It is fitting now that we give national expression to our faith in the spirit of discovery embodied by this great adventurer. This new holiday will henceforth honor one of our finest and most cherished national characteristics—our ability to live and work together, men and women of all national origins, as one united and progressive nation.

The provisions of this bill insure a minimum of five regularly recurring 3-day weekends each year for Federal employees. The costs will be offset to an important degree by avoiding disruptions of Government business through Monday observance of holidays.

The private employer will enjoy similar gains in efficiency. The Monday holiday will stimulate greater industrial and commercial production, sparing business and labor the penalty of midweek shutdowns.

NOTE: As enacted, the bill (H.R. 15951) is Public Law 90–363 (82 Stat. 250).

343 Statement by the President Upon Signing the Tax Bill. *June 28, 1968*

FOUR AND A HALF years ago—just a few months after becoming President—I signed the biggest tax cut in the Nation's history. Then, the economy was dragging. Five and a half percent of the labor force was out of work. We were underachievers—falling almost $30 billion short of our productive capacity.

We had to put our foot on the accelerator then. The income tax reduction and the later excise tax cuts brought new vigor and health to America's economy. They helped us to roll up an unparalleled and impressive record: 88 months of sustained prosperity.

This has meant higher paychecks to the worker and higher profits to the businessman. The unemployment rate has dropped all the way down to 3.5 percent, the lowest in 15 years. Never before have so many of our citizens shared in so much of the Nation's prosperity.

The same principles of good fiscal management summon us here today for a tax increase. The special costs of supporting our fighting men in Vietnam and the costs of launching and supporting comprehensive education, health, city, job, and conservation programs in our society have added many billions to our budget. The Nation's economy is moving too fast because of an unacceptable budgetary deficit. We must now apply the fiscal brakes.

With the measure I sign today, we will cut $20 billion from the deficit in fiscal year 1969. This marks the largest shift of the budget toward restraint in the past two decades.

Now we can attack decisively—at the roots—the threats to our prosperity: accelerating inflation, soaring interest rates, deteriorating world trade performance.

Now we can mobilize the defense of our dollar at home and abroad and fulfill our obligations to world monetary stability.

Now we are assured that we can continue to rely on free markets, unfettered by damaging Government controls.

This temporary surcharge will return to the Treasury about half the tax cuts I signed into law in 1964 and 1965. For the average taxpayer it will mean an additional penny on the dollar of income in the coming year. It honors the democratic principle that taxes should be based on ability to pay.

Here is how the surcharge will affect the American family:

—For a family of 4 with a yearly income of up to $5,000 it will not increase taxes at all.

—For a $10,000 income family, it will amount to slightly over $2 a week. This leaves them nearly $3 a week ahead of the tax rates prevailing when I became President.

—For an affluent family with $30,000 a

year, it will amount to 2 cents on the dollar.

For every American family—rich or poor—the tax bill is the very best insurance policy we can buy to protect our prosperity.

A modest and equitable temporary income tax is far better than the cruel and haphazard tax of rising prices and spiraling interest rates, which would continue to squeeze millions of Americans—salaried workers, homebuyers, the elderly couple living on a pension, and all the others who are defenseless against inflation—just as it has unnecessarily squeezed them over the past 2 years.

The tax bill gives us—not a guarantee—but an opportunity for further economic progress. We must fully grasp that opportunity. This will take a concerted effort on many fronts:

—by the Government in continuing to meet its obligations for sound fiscal and monetary management and improvement in our balance of payments,

—by business and labor in exercising the utmost restraint in price and wage decisions,

—by American industry in working energetically to strengthen our world trade position.

This bill deals with expenditures as well as taxes. It requires the President to reduce Federal expenditures by $6 billion from the January budget for the fiscal 1969.

The January budget was lean and tight. It blended fiscal responsibility with our very urgent national purposes—to pursue the work we must do for the cities, for the farmers, for the poor, and for the common defense. But the Congress—as a condition of its approval for the tax bill—has imposed a deep reduction in that budget.

I have accepted this decision of the Congress because the tax bill is so imperative to the economic health of the Nation.

It is my belief that in the course of the normal appropriations process Congress will reduce the budget by considerably less than $6 billion. In that event, under the law I sign today, Congress will shift to the President the responsibility for making reductions in programs which the Congress itself is unwilling to do.

This departure from the traditional appropriations process is most unwise. I believe the Congress also acted unwisely in the requirement that Federal employment be rolled back to the level of 2 years ago. This conflicts with the needs of a growing Nation for increased and efficient public services.

In carrying out these congressional mandates, I will do my best to fulfill our most urgent priorities and to continue the essential operations of Government. We must not falter in our efforts to root out injustice and unrest from the land.

With the enactment of the tax bill, our democracy passed a critical test. Raising taxes is never a pleasant task, least of all in a national election year. But in finally acting Congress has fulfilled an important responsibility.

I believe that the decision should have come sooner and should never have been in doubt. This is not the last time that we will have to act in applying flexible and rational fiscal policies to keep our economy flourishing. We must study the lessons of the past 2 years and ask these questions:

—How can we avoid in the future the costly inaction and the threat of fiscal stalemate we have just experienced?

—How can we develop procedures to assure the timely adjustment of fiscal policy and the closest cooperation between the executive and legislative branches in this area?

But as we review that experience let us also remember that action did come and that the processes of American Government rose to meet the challenge of fiscal responsibility.

NOTE: As enacted, the Revenue and Expenditure Control Act of 1968 (H.R. 15414) is Public Law 90–364 (82 Stat. 251).

344   Memorandum on the Need for Reduced Spending by Federal Agencies Following Enactment of the Tax Bill. *June 29, 1968*

[Released June 29, 1968.   Dated June 28, 1968]

Memorandum for the Heads of Departments and Agencies:

I have today signed Public Law 90–364. Its provisions will require significant readjustments, and I shall expect you to achieve these promptly and in a manner consistent with the Nation's interests.

We must reduce spending and lending by at least $6 billion below my original estimates for fiscal 1969. It will also be necessary to restrict hiring until Federal civilian employment is reduced to the June 1966 level.

I regard this situation as a challenge to management ingenuity. Make every dollar available to you go a little further; make sure every person in your agency is being used in the most effective way possible. This must not be a mechanical, across-the-board exercise. That's the easy way.

I will expect each of you to concern yourself personally with management decisions that will best allocate your diminished resources in money and manpower. All decisions should be made in the light of agency-wide priorities.

The necessary procedures on hiring restrictions and budget reductions are being sent to you by the Budget Director. However, the precise dollar limitations for each agency must await completion by Congress of the 1969 appropriations. In the interim, I shall expect you to proceed with caution in obligating funds so that you can be sure that your

agency will be able to make the necessary adjustments under the new law in an orderly manner.

LYNDON B. JOHNSON

NOTE: On August 20, 1968, Charles J. Zwick, Director, Bureau of the Budget, notified the President on procedures being adopted to limit hiring by Federal agencies in order to conform with provisions of the Revenue and Expenditure Control Act of 1968 (4 Weekly Comp. Pres. Docs., p. 1260).

345 Remarks at the Dedication of the J. Percy Priest Project, Nashville, Tennessee. *June 29, 1968*

Governor Ellington, Senator Gore, Congressman Fulton, Congressman Anderson, Congressman Blanton, Mayor Briley, my dear friend Mrs. Priest, her daughter, ladies and gentlemen:

To my old and dear friend, Governor Ellington, may I say that you have been one of the most able, loyal, and dedicated public servants that I have ever known.

On the platform is my longtime colleague in the United States Senate, Albert Gore. We have been through a great deal together, and he has always represented his State, his Nation, and served his country with a great ability, honor, and distinction.

Mayor Briley, the first mayor of the Greater Nashville Metropolitan Government, is nationally recognized amongst the city governments throughout this land.

Congressman Richard Fulton has so well represented this district since 1963, and has been a wonderful and fine successor to the congressional seat once held by beloved Percy Priest.

In Washington, we have some arm twisters, and Dick Fulton did a little arm twisting of his own to get us down here today.

He said, "Mr. President, I know that you have a heavy schedule, but I want you to see for yourself a living example of the new con-

servation that we have been working so hard for in the Nation. I want you to come to Tennessee to see it."

Congressman Bill Anderson is with us today. He has served his country as warrior and statesman in the fine tradition of Tennessee.

In Congressman Blanton, Tennessee has sent to the 90th Congress a young man who has rapidly gained the respect and admiration of his colleagues. We know he has a fine future before him.

To Mrs. Priest, I want to say how much the country has missed the solid wisdom of her late and her great husband.

I wanted to be here today because this dam was named for him. I served with him for many years, and I had great respect and affection for Percy Priest.

I want also to pay tribute to three outstanding former Governors of Tennessee who honor us with their presence.

TVA could not have become a reality without the dedicated efforts of Governor Browning, Governor Cooper, and Governor Clement.

Also here on the platform is my dear, old friend Hub Walters, with whom I served in the United States Senate when he represented Tennessee.

Though this is not a political affair, I trust no one will demand equal time if I happen to mention that Hub is presently doing a fine job as a Democratic National Committeeman from Tennessee.

Though our friend Joe Evins could not be here today—we are so sorry he is ill—he has sent his lovely daughter Mary to represent him.

His State and his country are proud of Congressman Evins' service as Chairman of the House Select Committee on Small Business.

Finally, I would like to introduce another Tennessean. All of you should be very proud of him. All Tennessee should be proud of him. I brought him with me from Washington today. He doesn't know what I am about to say.

I am right now naming a native son of Tennessee, Marine Lieutenant Colonel Haywood Smith, of Memphis, as the Armed Forces Aide to the President of the United States.

Colonel Smith will succeed Colonel James U. Cross, recently promoted to general and assigned to a fighter squadron.

Colonel Smith has been a Marine Aide since 1964. He has served with the United States Marines since 1953, and he has distinguished himself as a fighter pilot and as a most able administrator during his military career.

He is a graduate of Memphis State University.

His President and his country are very proud of him.

The project we are dedicating has many purposes. It will protect your homes and your families against the ravages of flood. It will provide the additional electric power that the growing, historic city of Nashville needs in order to prosper and to attract new industries. It will store water for periods of drought.

But most important—to me, at least—it will create a beautiful new recreation area within 10 miles of the very center of this historic city of Nashville. It is a perfect example of the new conservation: 18,000 acres of unspoiled nature, within easy driving distance of a half-a-million people, for boating, camping, hiking, and swimming.

Natural beauty is a priceless asset—and it has become harder and more costly to preserve with each passing year.

The great conservationists of another generation did preserve for us some of the scenic wonders of the American West. President Theodore Roosevelt and Gifford Pinchot fought with all of their strength to save just a small portion of those open spaces and those untouched forests.

But today, most Americans do not live near those great western parks out yonder. Not everyone can afford to travel across half a continent to visit Wyoming, Montana, and other Western States.

The new conservation, therefore, must concern itself with all the people of all America. We can no longer go in search of far horizons while we neglect the land that is under our feet.

We can no longer accept the unsightly and destructive scars of modern civilization.

This is not a question of coming to terms with civilization. It is a question of controlling and directing its spread, so that ultimate values are not lost in satisfying immediate needs for land.

We can have a new conservation in our land—a conservation which preserves the pleasures but avoids the pitfalls and pollutions of modern society.

Our new conservation must build on a new principle: bringing nature closer to the people.

That has been my goal since I became President. Along with peace in the world and progress at home, there is no legacy that I would rather leave than a permanent program of real conservation for this Nation.

That is not just my dream. It is happening. It is happening right here today in Tennessee. It is coming true all over this Nation. In my time as President, we have had three of the most conservation-minded Congresses of any time in our history.

The Tennessee delegation, led by your senior Senator, Albert Gore, has been in the forefront of all conservation legislation.

We have already passed 138 bills to restore and preserve the beauty of America. That is an average of more than 2½ conservation bills for every month of my Presidency. And we have 42 more conservation bills awaiting action in the Congress right now.

We need to pass all of these 42 bills. Six of them are in the balance. The Congress is today considering six major legislative measures that can bring new beauty and new pleasure to our people—as well as bring new riches to our Nation.

The Congress should pass these six bills now, without delay:

—the Redwood National Park bill,
—the Scenic Rivers bill,
—the Lower Colorado River Basin bill,
—the amendments to the Land and Water Conservation Fund Act,
—the Northern Cascades National Park bill, and, finally,
—the bill to establish a real National Water Commission.

The Congress has already recognized the importance and urgency of these bills. Each of them is in a stage of final action now.

So I ask the Congress today—in the name of you, and in the name of our people—to proceed to final passage of this legislation without delay.

When I took office, we were losing hundreds of thousands of acres every year to the bulldozers.

Today, we are actually reclaiming more land than we are losing.

—1.1 million acres were reclaimed in 1965.
—1.2 million acres in 1966.
—1.7 million acres in 1967.

That is a little over 4 million acres. That is more than the combined areas of Yellowstone, Yosemite, and Glacier National Parks.

Those 4 million acres will all be within an easy day's drive of tens of millions of our people.

But providing seashores, lakeshores, and parks is not enough. The land that we use for living and working is in danger, too.

—Rivers that were once carriers of commerce are now carriers of disease.
—Lakes that have served every generation of Americans are now being destroyed in a lifetime.
—The air that gives life to us all now threatens our health and it chokes our cities with pollution.
—Our search for minerals continues to scar and ravage the surface of the earth.

These are the sordid byproducts of civilization that we must correct.

You know the problem better than most people know it, here in Tennessee. Flying down here this morning I saw the ravages of progress—in the midst of the most beautiful scenery that any nation could ever boast. I saw the strip mines—the slag and the rusted cars in the streams—the naked and the ugly hillsides.

But I have seen something else that gives me great hope. I have seen what the people of Tennessee have done, what they are doing, and what they can do in the future.

It was just 4 years ago last month that I first came to Tennessee at the suggestion of your great Governor—Buford Ellington—as President of the United States. I saw for myself the plight of a proud and a productive people.

In 1964, Eastern Tennessee—an area just a stone's throw from here—was the symbol of the Appalachian problem. Today, it is the symbol of Appalachian progress.

Since I signed the Appalachian Act in 1965, employment in Eastern Tennessee has gone up nearly 7 percent—6.8 percent. Compare that to the national rate. In the national rate as a whole, employment has gone up not 7 percent, but up about 5 percent—5.1. You have gone up 7 percent and the rest of the Nation has gone up only 5 percent.

But the important part of this story is not told by statistics or by laws passed in Washington. It is measured by the energy and the hope of the people who live here.

So I appeal to all of you today to help us save what is best and most beautiful in our lives—our own country. I ask you to set an example for the entire Nation. And I have faith that you will do this because you understand so well that, as President Theodore Roosevelt once said, "It is not what we have that will make us a great nation, but the way in which we use what we have."

Years of stubborn, dedicated effort lie behind our great achievements in conservation. This is the case, for example, in education, in health, in housing, in race relations.

The same is true of foreign policy. The nonproliferation treaty,[1] which will be signed in the White House on Monday and

sent to the Senate, is such an achievement. We have been working towards that treaty for more than 4 years. Along with the test ban treaty, it stands as a monument to the proposition that men are determined to control the dangers of the nuclear age—instead of being destroyed by them.

But more is required. We must now turn to a task at least equally complex and difficult: to bring under control in this world the nuclear arms race—offensive and defensive weapons—in ways which do not endanger the security of the United States, our allies, or others.

It would be easy for the United States and the Soviet Union to continue on the present course of piling weapon system on weapon system, diverting billions upon billions of dollars, while adding nothing to the security of either country.

But the time is now at hand to find security in a more rational way.

I hope to have you join me when I say more to the Nation and to the world on this important subject Monday morning next.

You and I, my friends, live in a time of peril as well as a time of hope. But that has always been true of this land—this land which was really conceived in hope and peril.

We have never been satisfied and we have never rested.

More than a century ago, Emerson said of our young land: "This time, like every other time, is a good one if we but know how to use it."

So, my friends, of Tennessee, I would close by saying let us use our time—use it to build a nation; use it to heal the wounds; use it to help establish a world of peace, beauty, pleasure, order, and opportunity for every boy and girl in the world.

Thank you.

NOTE: The President spoke at 11:21 a.m. at the dedication of the J. Percy Priest Dam in Nashville,

---

[1] See Item 349.

Tenn. The dam, named in honor of the man who served as Representative from the Fifth District of Tennessee 1941–1956, is part of a coordinated plan for the development of water resources in the Cumberland River Basin in Tennessee and Kentucky.

In his opening words the President referred to Governor Buford Ellington, Senator Albert Gore, and Representatives Richard H. Fulton, William R. Anderson, and Ray Blanton, all of Tennessee, Mayor

C. Beverly Briley of Nashville, Mrs. J. Percy Priest, widow of the former Representative, and her daughter Harriet Frances Priest.

During his remarks the President referred, among others, to former Governors Gordon Browning, Prentice Cooper, and Frank G. Clement, Herbert S. Walters, Democratic National Committeeman, Representative Joe L. Evins, and his daughter Mary Evins, all of Tennessee.

346 Statement by the President on the Second Anniversary of the Medicare Program. *June* 29, 1968

TOMORROW America celebrates the second anniversary of Medicare—a program of healing a quarter of a century in the making.

It was Harry S. Truman who planted the compassionate seeds of this program a generation ago, and now all America is reaping its rich harvest. As Medicare enters its third year, it is fitting to reflect on just what this program has meant to the Nation and its millions of elderly citizens.

A man from Morrisonville, Ill., who had endured six major operations, with medical bills soaring to almost $5,000, wrote to me recently, "I don't know what we would have done without Medicare—without it we would have lost everything."

His testimony is not unique. It is reflected in the experiences of new hope and renewed health that light up thousands of lives in every community of this land.

These are the facts of Medicare—and they speak eloquently of its success and achievement:

—Twenty million Americans, 65 and over, 10 percent of the Nation's population are protected by the program.

—$8.4 billion has paid the expenses incurred in 10.6 million hospital stays and 45 million medical bills.

—Well over a million of our elderly have received the post-hospital care they need in nursing homes and in their own bedrooms. They have been attended by visiting nurses, physical therapists, and other health specialists.

—Almost 1.5 million senior citizens have benefited from hospital out-patient diagnostic services.

For the generation of the Nation's grandparents, Medicare has brought dignity and security.

For the generation of America's young families, concerned for their mothers and fathers, it has brought assurance that their parents will never be neglected in the golden years.

Two years after the dream became reality we can say this of Medicare: By honoring the fundamental humanity which is the spirit of democracy, it is a triumph of rightness in America.

NOTE: On June 29, 1968, the White House Press Office announced that Secretary of Health, Education, and Welfare Wilbur J. Cohen had appointed a 12-member Advisory Council on Health Insurance for the Disabled to study coverage of the disabled under Medicare. The Council, composed of outstanding leaders in the fields of medicine, business, and labor, was chaired by Dr. Henry H. Kessler, director of the Kessler Institute for Rehabilitation in Newark, N.J. The names of the other 11 members are printed in the Weekly Compilation of Presidential Documents (vol. 4, p. 1042).

INDEX

[Main references are to items except as otherwise indicated]

Index

Index

[Main references are to items except as otherwise indicated]

[Main references are to items except as otherwise indicated]

[Main references are to items except as otherwise indicated]

[Main references are to items except as otherwise indicated]

Index

Index

[Main references are to items except as otherwise indicated]

Index

[Main references are to items except as otherwise indicated]

Index

Index

Index

[Main references are to items except as otherwise indicated]

[Main references are to items except as otherwise indicated]

Index

[Main references are to items except as otherwise indicated]

[Main references are to items except as otherwise indicated]

Index

[Main references are to items except as otherwise indicated]

Index

[Main references are to items except as otherwise indicated]

[Main references are to items except as otherwise indicated]

[Main references are to items except as otherwise indicated]

Index

Index

[Main references are to items except as otherwise indicated]

[Main references are to items except as otherwise indicated]

Index

Index

Index

Gold—Continued
  Sales, 2, 47 (p. 133), 146, 500
Goldberg, Arthur J., 335, 696 [6]
  See also United Nations
Goldberg, Mrs. Arthur J., 335
Goldstein, E. Ernest, 1 [1], 388 n.
Goldwater, Barry, 228 ftn. (p. 573), 690
Gonzalez, Repr. Henry B., 7
Goodell, Sen. Charles E., 540
Goodpaster, Lt. Gen. Andrew J., 191 [6]
Gordon, Elinor L., 42
Gordon, Kermit, 38, 215, 350, 677
Gore, Sen. Albert, 345, 691
Gorham, William, 215
Gorton, John (Prime Minister of Australia),
  223 [7], 271, 273, 275 [1, 2], 276, 277,
  283 [1, 3–6], 290, 513 n.
Gorton, Mrs. John, 271, 273, 283 [1]
Gossett, William T., 694
Government, Commission on organization
  of the Executive Branch of the, 59, 60,
  227
Government contracts, 26, 587, 678, (p.
  1280)
Government cooperation with business,
  labor, and education
  Anti-inflation measures, 14 (pp. 32, 33)
  Arts and humanities, support of, 686
  Balance of payments, 2, 136
  Economic, 684 (pp. 1312, 1316, 1321)
  Employment, 47 (p. 142), 50, 91, 141,
    678 (p. 1294)
  Housing, 47 (p. 140), 278, 470, 471, 506,
    678 (p. 1289)
  Insurance in riot-affected areas, 36
  Job training, 14 (p. 28), 24, 25, 37, 105,
    164, 220, 227, 328, 498
  Marine and water resources development,
    593, 692
  Personnel interchange, 490, 498
  Price stability, 47 (pp. 127, 140), 76, 89,
    241, 350, 404, 427, 469, 492, 612
  Scientific research, 687
  Strike prevention, 47 (p. 135)
  Trade, international, 274
  Transportation, 118
  Urban renewal, 115

Government employees, 84, 280, 498, 526,
  570, 630, 667
  Associations of Federal officials, 464
  Education and training, 39 (p. 110), 84,
    312, 526, 539, 667, 673
  Equal opportunity, 84
  Executives Assignment System, 84, 667
  Foreign Service officers, 454
  Handicapped, 548
  Hiring restrictions, 344, 678 (pp. 1282,
    1284, 1285)
  Holidays, 342
  Interchange with private sector, 490, 498
  Minority groups, 667
  Negroes, 631
  Overseas, 2, 11, 15, 47 (p. 135), 63, 146,
    169 [1]
    Absentee voting, 314
  Pay, 14 (p. 32), 39 (pp. 88, 91, 92, 97,
    98), 303, 667, 678 (pp. 1280, 1282,
    1305)
  Recruiting, 84
  Red Cross support, 55
  Reduction, 63, 403
  Retirement, 678 (p. 1298)
  Safety, 489
  Savings bond purchases, 174
  Spanish speaking, 437
  State and local, 84, 100, 312, 539
  Veterans, 40, 67, 667
  Women, 138
  Youth, 305, 570, 667, 673
Government management, 39 (p. 109)
Government Special Task Force on Travel,
  Industry, 1 ftn. (p. 1), 2 n.
Government spending. *See* Spending,
  Government
Governors
  Conferences, 100, 102, 334, 406, 483
  Law enforcement and gun control, let-
    ter to, 325
Governors' Committees on Employment of
  the Handicapped, 548 n.
Graduate Public Health Training Amend-
  ments of 1964, 111
Grady, Henry, 575
Graf, David E., 219

Index

Index

[Main references are to items except as otherwise indicated]

Index

Index

Index

[Main references are to items except as otherwise indicated]

Index

[Main references are to items except as otherwise indicated]

Index

Index

[Main references are to items except as otherwise indicated]

[Main references are to items except as otherwise indicated]

[Main references are to items except as otherwise indicated]

Index

Index

Index

[Main references are to items except as otherwise indicated]

Index

Index

Index

Index

[Main references are to items except as otherwise indicated]

Index

[Main references are to items except as otherwise indicated]

[Main references are to items except as otherwise indicated]

Index

Index

Index

[Main references are to items except as otherwise indicated]

[Main references are to items except as otherwise indicated]

Index

Index

Index

[Main references are to items except as otherwise indicated]

Index

[Main references are to items except as otherwise indicated]

Index

Index

Index

Index

Index

[Main references are to items except as otherwise indicated]

[Main references are to items except as otherwise indicated]

[Main references are to items except as otherwise indicated]

Index

DATE DUE